THE MINSTER FRENCH DICTIONARY

THE MINSTER FRENCH *DICTIONARY*

MINSTER BOOKS

First published in 1976 by
The Hamlyn Publishing Group Limited
Published in 1983 by Newnes Books.
Michelin House, 81 Fulham Road,
London SW3 6RB

This 1992 edition reprinted exclusively for MINSTER BOOKS

ISBN 0 600 36563 8

Printed at Thomson Press (India) Ltd,
Faridabad (Haryana)

Foreword

This dictionary aims to give concise and accurate definitions of 24,000 of the most important words in use in the English and French languages today.

A pronunciation system based on the International Phonetic Alphabet is used (see *Key to symbols used in pronunciation*). Pronunciation is given for all headwords in both sections of the dictionary, and also for selected subentries in the French-English section.

Modern technical, commercial, and informal usage is given particular attention, in preference to outmoded terms or other expressions not in common contemporary use. Definitions are numbered in order to distinguish senses, and abbreviations are used to indicate use in specific technical, scientific, or commercial fields (see *Abbreviations used in the Dictionary*). An additional feature is the inclusion of idiomatic expressions and phrases, so necessary for the understanding and use of the foreign language.

This dictionary, with its emphasis on modernity, together with its compact form and clear typeface, should prove indispensable in the home, at school, in the office, and abroad.

Abbreviations used in the Dictionary

adj	adjective	*indef art*	indefinite article	*poss*	possessive
adv	adverb	*inf*	informal	*pref*	prefix
anat	anatomy	*infin*	infinitive	*prep*	preposition
arch	architecture	*interj*	interjection	*pron*	pronoun
aux	auxiliary	*invar*	invariable	*rel*	religion
aviat	aviation	*lit*	literature	*s*	singular
bot	botany	*m*	masculine	*sci*	science
cap	capital	*math*	mathematics	*sl*	slang
comm	commerce	*med*	medical	*suff*	suffix
conj	conjunction	*mil*	military	*tab*	taboo
cul	culinary	*min*	minerals	*Tdmk*	trademark
def art	definite article	*mod*	modal	*tech*	technical
derog	derogatory	*mot*	motoring	*Th*	theatre
dom	domestic	*mus*	music	*US*	United States
educ	education	*n*	noun	*v*	verb
fam	familiar	*naut*	nautical	*vi*	intransitive verb
fml	formal	*neg*	negative	*v imp*	impersonal verb
game	cards, chess, etc.	*pers*	person	*vr*	reflexive verb
gram	grammar	*phot*	photography	*vt*	transitive verb
geog	geography	*pol*	politics	*zool*	zoology

Notes on the use of the Dictionary

Irregular plural forms of French nouns and adjectives are shown in the headword list of the French-English section and in the text of the English-French section: for example, *journal, -aux; jeu, jeux; ail, aulx*. A plural is considered to be irregular if it is not formed by adding *-s* to the singular. Exceptions are nouns and adjectives ending in *-x*, such as *vieux*, which do not vary in the plural.
The abbreviation *invar* means that a noun or adjective does not vary in the plural.

Irregular feminine forms are shown in the same way: for example, *lion, lionne; sec, sèche; relatif, -ive*. A feminine is considered to be irregular if it is not formed by adding *-e* to the masculine. Exceptions are nouns and adjectives ending in *-e*, such as *brave*, which do not vary in the feminine.

Variant masculine forms of adjectives used before an initial vowel sound are shown in the French-English section: for example, *vieux, vieil, vieille* (as in *un vieil homme*); *beau, bel, belle, beaux, belles* (as in *un bel arbre*).

Irregular verbs are marked with an asterisk in the headword lists of both sections of the dictionary. The principal parts of these verbs are shown in the verb tables. For compounds, see the base form in the table; for example, for *comprendre*, see *prendre*. Verbs ending in *-e + consonant + er*, such as *appeler* and *mener*, which either double the consonant or take a grave accent before mute endings, are not considered to be irregular.

Adverbs derived from adjectives are not shown in either section of the dictionary unless a separate translation is required, or unless the formation is not regular. French adverbs are considered regular if they add the suffix *-ment* to the feminine singular of the adjective, English adverbs are considered regular if they add *-ly* to the adjective.

When the same word may be both an adjective and a noun, the gender of the noun is given only when it is fixed. Thus, **coopératif, -ive** . . . *adj,nf* . . . (cooperative) indicates that the word may be an adjective or a feminine noun (*la coopérative*); **métis, -isse** . . . *adj,n* . . . (half-breed) indicates that the word may be an adjective and a masculine or feminine noun (*le métis, la métisse*).

A swung dash (~) before a change of part of speech indicates that the part of speech refers to the headword, not the preceding subentry in heavy type.

Key to symbols used in pronunciation

English

Vowels

i:	meet	u	*put*	ai	*fly*
i	b*i*t	u:	shoot	au	*how*
e	g*e*t	ʌ	c*u*t	ɔi	*boy*
æ	h*a*t	ə	*a*go	iə	*here*
ɑ:	heart	ə:	*sir*	ɛə	*air*
ɔ	hot	ei	*late*	uə	*poor*
ɔ:	*ought*	ou	*go*		

Consonants

θ	*thin*
ð	*then*
ŋ	*sing*
j	*yes*
ʃ	*ship*
ʒ	*measure*
tʃ	*chin*
dʒ	*gin*

' indicates that the following syllable is stressed, as in *ago* (ə'gou).

ˌ placed under an *n* or *l* indicates that the *n* or *l* is pronounced as a syllable, as in *button* ('bʌtn̩) and *flannel* ('flænl̩).

French

Vowels

i:	*il*	u:	*ou*	ɑ̃	blan*c*
e:	*été*	y	*tu*	ɥ	*lui*
ɛ	*elle*	œ	*sœur*	i:j	*fille*
a	patte	ə	*le*	ɛj	sol*eil*
ɑ	*âge*	ɛ̃	*vin*	aj	trav*ail*
ɔ	mort	œ̃	*un*	œj	*feuille*
o	*rôle*	ɔ̃	*bon*		

Consonants

j	*hier*
ʃ	*chat*
ʒ	*je*
ɲ	*agneau*

' indicates that the following syllable is stressed, as in *été* (e:'te:).

English irregular verbs

Infinitive	Past Tense	Past Participle
abide	abode *or* abided	abode *or* abided
arise	arose	arisen
awake	awoke *or* awaked	awoke *or* awaked
be	was	been
bear[1]	bore	borne *or* born
beat	beat	beaten
become	became	become
begin	began	begun
bend	bent	bent
bet	bet	bet
beware[2]		
bid	bid	bidden *or* bid
bind	bound	bound
bite	bit	bitten *or* bit
bleed	bled	bled
blow	blew	blown
break	broke	broken
breed	bred	bred
bring	brought	brought
build	built	built
burn	burnt *or* burned	burnt *or* burned
burst	burst	burst
buy	bought	bought
can	could	
cast	cast	cast
catch	caught	caught
choose	chose	chosen
cling	clung	clung
come	came	come
cost	cost	cost
creep	crept	crept
crow	crowed *or* crew	crowed
cut	cut	cut
deal	dealt	dealt
dig	dug *or* digged	dug *or* digged
do	did	done

Infinitive	Past Tense	Past Participle
draw	drew	drawn
dream	dreamed *or* dreamt	dreamed *or* dreamt
drink	drank	drunk
drive	drove	driven
dwell	dwelt	dwelt
eat	ate	eaten
fall	fell	fallen
feed	fed	fed
feel	felt	felt
fight	fought	fought
find	found	found
flee	fled	fled
fling	flung	flung
fly	flew	flown
forbid	forbade *or* forbad	forbidden *or* forbid
forget	forgot	forgotten *or* forgot
forgive	forgave	forgiven
forsake	forsook	forsaken
freeze	froze	frozen
get	got	got
give	gave	given
go	went	gone
grind	ground	ground
grow	grew	grown
hang[3]	hung *or* hanged	hung *or* hanged
have	had	had
hear	heard	heard
hide	hid	hidden *or* hid
hit	hit	hit
hold	held	held
hurt	hurt	hurt
keep	kept	kept
kneel	knelt	knelt
knit	knitted *or* knit	knitted *or* knit
know	knew	known

English irregular verbs

Infinitive	Past Tense	Past Participle
lay	laid	laid
lead	led	led
lean	leant *or* leaned	leant *or* leaned
leap	leapt *or* leaped	leapt *or* leaped
learn	learnt *or* learned	learnt *or* learned
leave	left	left
lend	lent	lent
let	let	let
lie	lay	lain
light	lit *or* lighted	lit *or* lighted
lose	lost	lost
make	made	made
may	might	
mean	meant	meant
meet	met	met
mow	mowed	mown
must		
ought		
panic	panicked	panicked
pay	paid	paid
picnic	picnicked	picnicked
put	put	put
quit	quitted *or* quit	quitted *or* quit
read	read	read
rid	rid *or* ridded	rid *or* ridded
ride	rode	ridden
ring	rang	rung
rise	rose	risen
run	ran	run
saw	sawed	sawn *or* sawed
say	said	said
see	saw	seen
seek	sought	sought
sell	sold	sold
send	sent	sent
set	set	set
sew	sewed	sewn *or* sewed
shake	shook	shaken
shall	should	
shear	sheared	sheared *or* shorn
shed	shed	shed
shine	shone	shone
shoe	shod	shod
shoot	shot	shot
show	showed	shown
shrink	shrank *or* shrunk	shrunk *or* shrunken
shut	shut	shut
sing	sang	sung
sink	sank	sunk
sit	sat	sat
sleep	slept	slept
slide	slid	slid
sling	slung	slung
slink	slunk	slunk
slit	slit	slit
smell	smelt *or* smelled	smelt *or* smelled
sow	sowed	sown *or* sowed
speak	spoke	spoken
speed	sped *or* speeded	sped *or* speeded
spell	spelt *or* spelled	spelt *or* spelled
spend	spent	spent
spill	spilt *or* spilled	spilt *or* spilled
spin	spun	spun
spit	spat *or* spit	spat *or* spit
split	split	split
spread	spread	spread
spring	sprang	sprung
stand	stood	stood
steal	stole	stolen
stick	stuck	stuck
sting	stung	stung
stink	stank *or* stunk	stunk
stride	strode	stridden
strike	struck	struck

Infinitive	Past Tense	Past Participle
string	strung	strung
strive	strove	striven
swear	swore	sworn
sweep	swept	swept
swell	swelled	swollen *or* swelled
swim	swam	swum
swing	swung	swung
take	took	taken
teach	taught	taught
tear	tore	torn
tell	told	told
think	thought	thought
throw	threw	thrown
thrust	thrust	thrust
traffic	trafficked	trafficked
tread	trod	trodden *or* trod
wake	woke	woken
wear	wore	worn
weave	wove	woven *or* wove
weep	wept	wept
will	would	
win	won	won
wind	wound	wound
wring	wrung	wrung
write	wrote	written

[1] when *bear* means *give birth to,* the past participle is always *born*.

[2] used only in the infinitive or as an imperative.

[3] the preferred form of the past tense and past participle when referring to death by hanging is *hanged*.

French irregular verbs

Infinitive	Present Indicative	Present Participle	Imperfect	Past Participle	Future
absoudre	absous	absolvant	absolvais	absous	absoudrai
acquérir	acquiers	acquérant	acquérais	acquis	acquerrai
aller	vais	allant	allais	allé	irai
apercevoir[1]	aperçois	apercevant	apercevais	aperçu	apercevrai
assaillir	assaille	assaillant	assaillais	assailli	assaillirai
asseoir	assieds *or* assois	asseyant	asseyais *or* assoyais	assis	assiérai *or* assoirai
atteindre[2]	atteins	atteignant	atteignais	atteint	atteindrai
avoir	ai	ayant	avais	eu	aurai
battre	bats	battant	battais	battu	battrai
boire	bois	buvant	buvais	bu	boirai
bouillir	bous	bouillant	bouillais	bouilli	bouillirai
circoncire	circoncis	circoncisant	circoncisais	circoncis	circoncirai
clore	clos	closant		clos	clorai
conclure	conclus	concluant	concluais	conclu	conclurai
conduire[3]	conduis	conduisant	conduisais	conduit	conduirai
confire	confis	confisant	confisais	confit	confirai
conquérir	conquiers	conquérant	conquérais	conquis	conquerrai
contraindre	contrains	contraignant	contraignais	contraint	contraindrai
coudre	couds	cousant	cousais	cousu	coudrai
courir	cours	courant	courais	couru	courrai
couvrir	couvre	couvrant	couvrais	couvert	couvrirai
craindre	crains	craignant	craignais	craint	craindrai
croire	crois	croyant	croyais	cru	croirai
croître	crois	croissant	croissais	crû	croîtrai
cueillir	cueille	cueillant	cueillais	cueilli	cueillerai
cuire	cuis	cuisant	cuisais	cuit	cuirai
devoir	dois	devant	devais	dû	devrai
dire	dis	disant	disais	dit	dirai
dissoudre	dissous	dissolvant	dissolvais	dissous	dissoudrai
dormir	dors	dormant	dormais	dormi	dormirai
échoir	il échoit *or* échet	échéant		échu	il échoira *or* écherra
écrire[4]	écris	écrivant	écrivais	écrit	écrirai
envoyer	envoie	envoyant	envoyais	envoyé	enverrai
être	suis	étant	étais	été	serai
exclure	exclus	excluant	excluais	exclu	exclurai
faillir		faillant		failli	faillirai
faire	fais	faisant	faisais	fait	ferai
falloir	il faut		il fallait	fallu	il faudra
férir				féru	
frire	fris			frit	frirai

Infinitive	Present Indicative	Present Participle	Imperfect	Past Participle	Future
fuir	fuis	fuyant	fuyais	fui	fuirai
gésir	gis	gisant	gisais		
haïr	hais	haïssant	haïssais	haï	haïrai
importer	il importe	important		importé	
inclure	inclus	incluant	incluais	inclus	inclurai
joindre	joins	joignant	joignais	joint	joindrai
lire	lis	lisant	lisais	lu	lirai
luire	luis	luisant	luisais	lui	luirai
maudire	maudis	maudissant	maudissais	maudit	maudirai
mentir	mens	mentant	mentais	menti	mentirai
messeoir	il messied	messéant	il messeyait		il messiéra
mettre	mets	mettant	mettais	mis	mettrai
moudre	mouds	moulant	moulais	moulu	moudrai
mourir	meurs	mourant	mourais	mort	mourrai
mouvoir	meus	mouvant	mouvais	mû	mouvrai
naître	nais	naissant	naissais	né	naîtrai
nuire	nuis	nuisant	nuisais	nui	nuirai
offrir	offre	offrant	offrais	offert	offrirai
ouïr		oyant		ouï	ouïrai
ouvrir	ouvre	ouvrant	ouvrais	ouvert	ouvrirai
paître	pais	paissant	paissais		paîtrai
paraître[5]	parais	paraissant	paraissais	paru	paraîtrai
partir	pars	partant	partais	parti	partirai
plaindre	plains	plaignant	plaignais	plaint	plaindrai
plaire	plais	plaisant	plaisais	plu	plairai
pleuvoir	il pleut	pleuvant	il pleuvait	plu	il pleuvra
pourvoir	pourvois	pourvoyant	pourvoyais	pourvu	pourvoirai
pouvoir	peux *or* puis	pouvant	pouvais	pu	pourrai
prendre	prends	prenant	prenais	pris	prendrai
repaître	repais	repaissant	repaissais	repu	repaîtrai
se repentir	me repens	se repentant	me repentais	repenti	me repentirai
requérir	requiers	requérant	requérais	requis	requerrai
résoudre	résous	résolvant	résolvais	résolu	résoudrai
rire	ris	riant	riais	ri	rirai
saillir	il saillit *or* saille	saillissant *or* saillant	il saillissait *or* saillait	sailli	il saillira *or* saillera
savoir	sais	sachant	savais	su	saurai
sentir	sens	sentant	sentais	senti	sentirai
seoir	il sied	séant *ou* seyant	il seyait	sis	il siéra
servir	sers	servant	servais	servi	servirai
sortir	sors	sortant	sortais	sorti	sortirai

French irregular verbs

Infinitive	Present Indicative	Present Participle	Imperfect	Past Participle	Future
souffrir	souffre	souffrant	souffrais	souffert	souffrirai
suffire	suffis	suffisant	suffisais	suffi	suffirai
suivre	suis	suivant	suivais	suivi	suivrai
surseoir	sursois	sursoyant	sursoyais	sursis	surseoirai
taire	tais	taisant	taisais	tu	tairai
tenir	tiens	tenant	tenais	tenu	tiendrai
traire	trais	trayant	trayais	trait	trairai
tressaillir	tressaille	tressaillant	tressaillais	tressailli	tressaillirai
vaincre	vaincs	vainquant	vainquais	vaincu	vaincrai
valoir	vaux	valant	valais	valu	vaudrai
venir	viens	venant	venais	venu	viendrai
vêtir	vêts	vêtant	vêtais	vêtu	vêtirai
vivre	vis	vivant	vivais	vécu	vivrai
voir	vois	voyant	voyais	vu	verrai
vouloir	veux	voulant	voulais	voulu	voudrai

[1] All other verbs ending in *-cevoir* are conjugated like *apercevoir*.
[2] All other verbs ending in *-eindre* are conjugated like *atteindre*.
[3] All other verbs ending in *-uire* are conjugated like *conduire*.
[4] All other verbs ending in *-crire* are conjugated like *écrire*.
[5] All other verbs ending in *-aître* are conjugated like *paraître*.

A

a (a) *v* see **avoir.**

à (a) *prep* **1** to. **2** at. **3** in. **4** by. **5** from. **6** for. **7** according to.

abaisser (abɛ'se:) *vt* **1** lower, let down. **2** reduce. **s'abaisser** *vr* **1** humble oneself. **2** decrease. **abaissement** *nm* **1** humiliation, degradation. **2** lowering.

abandon (abɑ̃'dɔ̃) *nm* **1** desertion. **2** surrender. **3** neglect. **à l'abandon** uncared for.

abandonner (abɑ̃dɔ'ne:) *vt* **1** abandon, desert. **2** give up, surrender. **3** let go. **s'abandonner à** *vr* **1** give way to. **2** indulge in.

abasourdir (abasu:r'di:r) *vt* **1** astound, dumbfound. **2** bewilder.

abats (a'ba) *nm pl* offal.

abattoir (aba'twar) *nm* abattoir, slaughterhouse.

abattre* (a'batr) *vt* **1** knock or pull down. **2** slaughter. **3** lay. **4** shoot down. **s'abattre** *vr* **1** fall, collapse. **2** abate. **3** become depressed. **abat-jour** *nm invar* lampshade. **abattu** *adj* depressed, disheartened.

abbaye (abɛ'ji:) *nf* abbey, monastery.

abbé (a'be:) *nm* **1** abbot. **2** priest. **abbesse** (a'bɛs) *nf* abbess.

abcès (ap'sɛ) *nm* abscess.

abdiquer (abdi:'ke:) *vt* **1** abdicate. **2** renounce.

abdomen (abdɔ'mɛn) *nm* abdomen.

abeille (a'bɛj) *nf* bee.

abhorrer (abɔ're:) *vt* abhor, loathe.

abîmer (abi:'me:) *vt* **1** spoil, damage. **2** injure. **s'abîmer** *vr* **1** be engulfed. **2** get damaged. **abîme** *nm* abyss.

abnégation (abnɛga'sjɔ̃) *nf* self-sacrifice.

aboi (a'bwa) *nm* bark. **aux abois** in a desperate situation. **aboiement** *nm* **1** barking. **2** bark.

abolir (abɔ'li:r) *vt* abolish. **abolition** *nf* **1** abolition. **2** repeal.

abominable (abɔmi:'nabl) *adj* abominable.

abonder (abɔ̃'de:) *vi* abound, be plentiful. **abondamment** *adv* abundantly. **abondance** *nf* **1** abundance. **2** wealth. **abondant** *adj* abundant, plentiful.

s'abonner (sabɔ'ne:) *vr* subscribe. **abonnement** *nm* **1** subscription. **2** season ticket.

abord (a'bɔr) *nm* access, approach. **d'abord** *adv* at first.

aborder (abɔr'de:) *vi* land. *vt* **1** approach, accost. **2** collide with. **3** deal with. **abordable** *adj* **1** approachable. **2** accessible. **3** reasonable.

aborigène (abɔri:'ʒɛn) *adj* **1** Aboriginal. **2** native. *nm,f* Aborigine.

abortif, -ive (abɔr'ti:f, -'ti:v) *adj* abortive.

aboutir (abu:'ti:r) *vi* **1** end. **2** lead, result. **3** succeed.

aboyer (abwa'je:) *vi* bark.

abrasif, -ive (abra'zi:f, -'zi:v) *adj,nm* abrasive.

abréger (abre:'ʒe:) *vt* **1** abbreviate. **2** abridge, cut down. **abrégé** *nm* precis, summary.

abreuver (abrœ've:) *vt* **1** water (animals). **2** soak. **s'abreuver** *vr* quench one's thirst.

abréviation (abre:vja'sjɔ̃) *nf* abbreviation.

abri (a'bri:) *nm* shelter. **à l'abri** **1** sheltered, under cover. **2** safe.

abriter (abri:'te:) *vt* shelter, protect. **s'abriter** *vr* take cover or shelter.

abricot (abri:'ko) *nm* apricot. **abricotier** *nm* apricot tree.

abrutissant (abryti:'sɑ̃) *adj* **1** stunning. **2** extremely tedious.

absence (ap'sɑ̃s) *nf* absence. **absent** *adj* absent, missing.

abside (ap'si:d) *nf* apse.

absinthe (ap'sɛ̃t) *nf* absinthe.

absolu (apsɔ'ly) *adj* absolute, complete, utter. **absolument** *adv* absolutely.

absolvant (apsɔl'vɑ̃) *v* see **absoudre.**

absorber (apsɔr'be:) *vt* **1** absorb. **2** engross, occupy.

absoudre* (ap'su:dr) *vt* absolve, forgive.

absous (ap'su:) *v* see **absoudre.**

s'abstenir (sapstə'ni:r) *vr* **s'abstenir de** abstain or refrain from. **abstention** *nf* abstention. **abstinence** *nf* abstinence.

abstrait (ap'strɛ) *adj* abstract.

absurde (ap'syrd) *adj* absurd, ridiculous.

abus (a'by) *nm* **1** abuse, misuse. **2** error.

Abyssinie (abi:si:'ni:) *nf* Abyssinia. **abyssinien, -ienne** (abi:si:'njɛ̃, -'njɛn) *adj,n* Abyssinian.

académie (akade:'mi:) *nf* **1** academy. **2** college, school. **académique** *adj* academic.

acajou (aka'ʒu:) *nm* mahogany.

accabler (akɑ'ble:) *vt* **1** overwhelm. **2** overload. **accablé** *adj* **1** overwhelmed, overcome. **2** tired out.

accaparer (akapa're:) *vt* **1** monopolize, take possession of. **2** hoard.

accéder (akse:'de:) *vi* **accéder à 1** agree to, comply with. **2** have access to.

accélérer (akse:le:'re:) *vt* accelerate, quicken. **accélérateur** (akse:lɛra'tœr) *nm* accelerator.

accent (ak'sɑ̃) *nm* **1** accent. **2** stress. **3** pronunciation. **4** expression.

accentuer (aksɑ̃'tɥe:) *vt* stress, accentuate, emphasize.

accepter (aksɛp'te:) *vt* accept. *vi* agree. **acceptable** *adj* **1** acceptable, reasonable. **2** welcome.

accès (ak'sɛ) *nm* **1** access. **2** fit, attack.

accessoire (aksɛ'swar) *adj,nm* accessory.

accident (aksi:'dɑ̃) *nm* accident, mishap. **accidenté** *adj* **1** uneven. **2** eventful. **accidentel, -elle** *adj* accidental.

acclamer (akla'me:) *vt* acclaim, applaud, cheer. **acclamation** *nf* **1** acclamation. **2** *pl* cheers.

acclimater (akli:ma'te:) *vt* acclimatize. **s'acclimater** *vr* get acclimatized.

accommoder (akɔmɔ'de:) *vt* **1** suit. **2** cook. **3** adapt. **s'accommoder à** *vr* **1** adapt oneself to. **2** come to an agreement with. **s'accommoder de** *vr* put up with. **accommodant** *adj* easygoing.

accompagner (akɔ̃pa'ɲe:) *vt* accompany. **accompagnement** *nm* **1** accompaniment. **2** *pl* trimmings.

accomplir (akɔ̃'pli:r) *vt* **1** complete. **2** accomplish, achieve. **3** fulfil. **accompli** *adj* **1** accomplished, perfect. **2** finished.

accord (a'kɔr) *nm* **1** agreement. **2** *mus* chord. **d'accord!** agreed! **être d'accord** agree.

accorder (akɔr'de:) *vt* grant. **s'accorder** *vr* **1** agree. **2** correspond, tally.

accordéon (akɔrde:'ɔ̃) *nm* accordion.

accoucher (aku'ʃe:) *vi* give birth.

accoutumer (aku:ty'me:) *vt* accustom. **s'accoutumer à** *vr* get used to.

accrocher (akrɔ'ʃe:) *vt* **1** hook, catch. **2** hang up. **3** collide with. **s'accrocher** *vr* cling or hang on. **accrocheur, -euse** (akrɔ'ʃœr, -'ʃœz) *adj* **1** tenacious. **2** eye-catching.

accroître* (a'krwatr) *vt* **1** increase. **2** add to.

s'accroupir (sakru:'pi:r) *vr* crouch, squat.

accueil (a'kœj) *nm* **1** reception. **2** welcome.

accueillir* (akœ'ji:r) *vt* **1** receive. **2** welcome. **3** greet.

accumuler (akymy'le:) *vt* **1** accumulate, amass. **2** hoard.

accuser (aky'ze:) *vt* **1** accuse. **2** accentuate. **3** indicate. **accuser réception de** acknowledge receipt of. **accusation** *nf* accusation, charge. **accusé** *adj* prominent. *nm* accused (person).

acerbe (a'sɛrb) *adj* **1** harsh. **2** bitter.

s'acharner (saʃar'ne:) *vr* persist. **s'acharner à** keep at. **acharné** *adj* **1** eager, keen. **2** desperate. **acharnement** (aʃarnə'mɑ̃) *nm* **1** eagerness. **2** relentlessness.

achat (a'ʃa) *nm* purchase. **faire des achats** go shopping.

acheminer (aʃəmi:'ne:) *vt* dispatch, forward. **s'acheminer** *vr* make one's way.

acheter (aʃ'te:) *vt* buy.

achever (aʃ've:) *vt* complete, finish. **achevé** *adj* accomplished. **achèvement** (aʃɛv'mɑ̃) *nm* completion.

acide (a'si:d) *adj* **1** acid. **2** sour, sharp. *nm* acid.

acier (a'sje:) *nm* steel.

acné (ak'ne:) *nf* acne.

acompte (a'kɔ̃t) *nm* instalment.

acoustique (aku:'sti:k) *adj* acoustic. *nf* acoustics.

acquérir* (ake:'ri:r) *vt* **1** acquire. **2** secure, get.

acquiers (aki'ɛr) *v see* **acquérir.**

acquiescer (akjɛ'se:) *vt* acquiesce, agree.

acquis (a'ki:) *v see* **acquérir.**

acquit (a'ki:) *nm comm* receipt.

acquitter (aki:'te:) *vt* **1** acquit. **2** pay off. **3** receipt. **s'acquitter de** *vr* fulfil, carry out.

âcre (ɑkr) *adj* **1** bitter, sharp. **2** pungent.

acrilique (akri:'li:k) *adj* acrylic.

acrimonie (akri:mɔ'ni:) *nf* acrimony, bitterness.

acrobate (akrɔ'bat) *nm,f* acrobat. **acrobatique** *adj* acrobatic.

acte[1] (akt) *nm* **1** act, action, deed. **2** record. **acte de décès/mariage/naissance** death/marriage/birth certificate.

acte[2] (akt) *nm Th* act.

acteur, -trice (ak'tœr, -'tri:s) *nm,f* actor, actress.

actif, -ive (ak'ti:f, -'ti:v) *adj* **1** active, busy. **2** brisk. *nm comm* credit.

action (ak'sjɔ̃) *nf* **1** action, act. **2** effect. **3** *comm* share.

activer (akti:'ve:) *vt* **1** stir up, activate. **2** quicken. **activiste** *nm* activist. **activité** *nf* activity, industry.

actuaire (ak'tɥɛr) *nm* actuary.

actualité (aktɥali:'te:) *nf* **1** reality. **2** topical event or question. **3** *pl* news, current events.

actuel, -elle (ak'tɥɛl) *adj* **1** current, present, topical. **2** real. **à l'heure actuelle** at the present time.

acuponcture (akypɔ̃k'tyr) *nf* acupuncture.

adapter (adap'te:) *vt* **1** adjust, fit. **2** adapt.

addenda (adɛ̃'da) *nm invar* addendum.

addition (adi:'sjɔ̃) *nf* **1** addition. **2** bill.

additionner (adi:sjɔ̃'ne:) *vt* add up.

adénoïde (ade:nɔ'i:d) *adj* adenoidal. **végétations adénoïdes** *nf pl* adenoids.

adhérer (ade:'re:) *vi* adhere, stick. **adhérer à** join (a party). **adhérent** *adj* adherent, sticky.

adhésion (ade:'zjɔ̃) *nf* **1** adhesion. **2** membership. **adhésif, -ive** (ade:'zi:f, -'zi:v) *adj* adhesive.

adieu, -eux (a'djœ) *interj* goodbye! farewell! *nm* farewell. **faire ses adieux à** say goodbye to, take one's leave of.

adjacent (adʒa'sɑ̃) *adj* adjacent.

adjectif, -ive (adʒɛk'ti:f, -'ti:v) *nm* adjective. *adj* adjectival.

adjoint (a'dʒwɛ̃) *nm* assistant, deputy.

adjudication (adʒydi:ka'sjɔ̃) *nf* adjudication, award. **mettre en adjudication** put up for auction.

adjuger (adʒy'ʒe:) *vt* **1** award. **2** allocate. **une fois! deux fois! trois fois! adjugé!** going! going! gone!

admettre* (ad'mɛtr) *vt* **1** admit. **2** allow. **3** suppose. **4** acknowledge.

administrer (admi:ni:'stre:) *vt* administer, manage. **administrateur** *nm* administrator, manager. **administratif, -ive** (admi:ni:stra'ti:f, -'ti:v) *adj* administrative. **administration** *nf* **1** administration, management. **2** civil service.

admirer (admi:'re:) *vt* **1** admire. **2** wonder at. **admirable** *adj* admirable, wonderful. **admiration** *nf* admiration.

admission (admi:'sjɔ̃) *nf* admission. **admissible** (admi:'si:bl) *adj* **1** allowable. **2** eligible.

adolescence (adɔlɛs'sɑ̃s) *nf* adolescence. **adolescent** *adj* teenage, adolescent. *nm* teenager, adolescent.

s'adonner (sadɔ'ne:) *vr* **s'adonner à 1** devote oneself to, go in for. **2** become addicted to.

adopter (adɔp'te:) *vt* **1** adopt. **2** take up. **3** *pol* pass, carry. **adopté** *nm* adopted child.

adorer (adɔ're:) *vt* **1** adore. **2** worship.

adoucir (adu:'si:r) *vt* **1** soften. **2** alleviate. **3** pacify, calm.

adrénaline (adrɛna'li:n) *nf* adrenaline.

adresser (adrɛ'se:) *vt* address, direct. **s'adresser à** *vr* **1** apply to. **2** speak to. **adresse** *nf* **1** address. **2** skill.

adriatique (adri:a'ti:k) *adj* Adriatic. **(Mer) Adriatique** *nf* Adriatic (Sea).

adroit (a'drwa) *adj* **1** skilful, dexterous, adroit. **2** shrewd.

adulation (adyla'sjɔ̃) *nf* adulation, flattery.

adulte (a'dylt) *adj,n* adult.

adultère (adyl'tɛr) *nm* adultery.

adultérer (adylte:'re:) *vt* adulterate.

advenir* (advə'ni:r) *v imp* **1** occur to. **2** happen to.

adverbe (ad'vɛrb) *nm* adverb. **adverbial, -aux** (advɛr'bjal, -'bjo) *adj* adverbial.

adverse (ad'vɛrs) *adj* **1** adverse. **2** opposite. **adversaire** *nm* **1** opponent. **2** enemy.

aérer (ae:'re:) *vt* ventilate, air. **aérien, -ienne** (ae:'rjɛ̃, -'rjɛn) *adj* aerial, air.

aérodynamique (ae:rɔdi:na'mi:k) *adj* aerodynamic. *nf* aerodynamics.

aéroglisseur (ae:rɔgli:'sœr) *nm* hovercraft.

aéronautique (ae:rɔno'ti:k) *adj* aeronautical. *nf* aeronautics.

aéroport (ae:rɔ'pɔr) *nm* airport.

aéroporté (ae:rɔpɔr'te:) *adj* airborne.

aérosol (e:rɔ'sɔl) *nm* aerosol.

affable (a'fabl) *adj* affable.

affaiblir (afɛ'bli:r) *vt* **1** weaken. **2** impair. **3** reduce. **s'affaiblir** *vr* become weak, flag.

affaire (a'fɛr) *nf* **1** business. **2** matter. **3** trouble. **4** *pl* belongings, things. **avoir affaire à** have to do with. **faire l'affaire de** suit. **affairé** *adj* busy.

s'affaisser (safɛ'se:) *vr* **1** subside. **2** collapse.

affamer (afa'me:) *vt* starve. **affamé** *adj* hungry, ravenous.

affecter[1] (afɛk'te:) *vt* **1** feign, affect. **2** be partial to. **3** assume.

affecter[2] (afɛk'te:) *vt* allocate.

affecter[3] (afɛk'te:) *vt* move, touch, affect.

affecter[4] (afɛk'te:) *vt* concern.

affection (afɛk'sjɔ̃) *nf* **1** affection, liking. **2**

ailment. **affectueux, -euse** (afɛk'tɥœ, -'tɥœz) *adj* loving, affectionate.
affiche (a'fi:ʃ) *nf* **1** placard. **2** poster, bill.
affilier (afi:'lje:) *vt* affiliate. **s'affilier à** *vr* affiliate oneself to, join.
affinité (afi:ni:'te:) *nf* **1** affinity. **2** resemblance.
affirmer (afi:r'me:) *vt* **1** affirm. **2** assert. **affirmatif, -ive** (afi:rma'ti:f, -'ti:v) *adj* **1** affirmative. **2** positive. **affirmation** *nf* affirmation, assurance.
affliction (afli:k'sjɔ̃) *nf* affliction, grief.
affliger (afli:'ʒe:) *vt* **1** afflict. **2** distress. **s'affliger** *vr* grieve.
affluence (afly'ɑ̃s) *nf* **1** abundance, plenty. **2** crowd.
affoler (afɔ'le:) *vt* **1** distract. **2** drive crazy. **s'affoler** *vr* **1** panic. **2** be infatuated. **affolé** *adj* crazy, frantic.
affranchir (afrɑ̃'ʃi:r) *vt* **1** (set) free. **2** stamp.
affréter (afre:'te:) *vt* charter (a ship).
affreux, -euse (a'frœ, -'frœz) *adj* **1** horrible, dreadful. **2** atrocious.
affront (a'frɔ̃) *nm* affront, insult.
Afghanistan (afgani:'stɑ̃) *nm* Afghanistan. **afghan** *adj,n* Afghan.
afin (a'fɛ̃) **afin de** *prep* to, in order to. **afin que** *conj* so that, in order that.
Afrique (a'fri:k) *nf* Africa. **Afrique du Sud** South Africa. **africain** *adj,n* African.
agacer (aga'se:) *vt* **1** annoy. **2** jar, set on edge. **agaçant** *adj* annoying.
âge (ɑʒ) *nm* **1** age. **2** period. **d'un certain âge** middle-aged. **quel âge avez-vous?** how old are you? **âgé** *adj* aged, elderly.
agence (a'ʒɑ̃s) *nf* agency. **agence de voyages** travel agency. **agent** *nm* agent. **agent de change** stockbroker. **agent de police** policeman. **agent immobilier** estate agent.
s'agenouiller (saʒnu'je:) *vr* kneel down.
agglomération (aglɔmɛra'sjɔ̃) *nf* **1** built-up area. **2** mass.
aggraver (agra've:) *vt* **1** aggravate. **2** worsen. **3** increase.
agile (a'ʒi:l) *adj* **1** agile, nimble. **2** quick.
agir (a'ʒi:r) *vi* **1** act, do. **2** behave. **3** influence. **s'agir de** *v imp* concern, be a question of. **de quoi s'agit-il?** what's it all about?
agiter (aʒi:'te:) *vt* **1** wave, shake. **2** agitate. **3** discuss. **s'agiter** *vr* fidget.
agneau, -aux (a'ɲo) *nm* lamb.
agnostique (agnɔ'sti:k) *adj,n* agnostic.
agonie (agɔ'ni:) *nf* death agony. **à l'agonie** dying.
agrafe (a'graf) *nf* **1** hook, clasp. **2** clamp **3** staple.
agraire (a'grɛr) *adj* agrarian.
agrandir (agrɑ̃'di:r) *vt* **1** enlarge. **2** increase, magnify.
agréer (agre:'e:) *vt* **1** accept. **2** approve. **3** please. **agréable** *adj* **1** agreeable, pleasant. **2** comfortable. **agrément** *nm* **1** pleasure. **2** consent, approval. **3** amenities.
agression (agrɛ'sjɔ̃) *nf* agression. **agressif, -ive** (agrɛ'si:f, -'si:v) *adj* aggressive.
agricole (agri:'kɔl) *adj* agricultural.
agriculture (agri:kyl'tyr) *nf* agriculture. **agriculteur** *nm* farmer.
agrumes (a'grym) *nm pl* citrus fruits.
aguets (a'gɛ) *nm pl* **aux aguets** watchful.
ahurir (ay'ri:r) *vt* **1** astound, flabbergast. **2** bewilder.
ai (ɛ) *v* see **avoir.**
aider (ɛ'de:) *vt* help, assist, aid. **aide** *nf* **1** help, aid. **2** assistant. **3** relief. **à l'aide!** help! **venir en aide à** come to the help of.
aïeul (a'jœl) *nm* **1** *pl* **aïeuls** grandfather. **2** *pl* **aïeux** forefather.
aigle (ɛgl) *nm* **1** eagle. **2** genius. **3** lectern.
aiglefin (ɛglə'fɛ̃) *nm* haddock.
aigrir (ɛ'gri:r) *vt* **1** sour. **2** embitter. *vi* turn sour. **aigre** *adj* **1** sour, tart. **2** shrill. **aigreur** *nf* **1** sourness. **2** bitterness.
aigu, -uë (e:'gy) *adj* **1** sharp, pointed. **2** acute. **3** shrill.
aiguille (e:'gɥi:j) *nf* **1** needle. **2** hand (of a clock). **aiguille à tricoter** knitting needle.
aiguillon (e:gɥi:'jɔ̃) *nm* **1** incentive. **2** sting.
aiguiser (e:gɥi:'ze:) *vt* **1** sharpen, point. **2** stimulate.
ail (aj) *nm, pl* **aulx** garlic.
aile (ɛl) *nf* **1** wing (of bird, building, car, or aircraft). **2** aisle. **ailé** *adj* winged. **aileron** (ɛl'rɔ̃) *nm* fin.
ailleurs (a'jœr) *adv* elsewhere. **d'ailleurs** besides.
aimant (ɛ'mɑ̃) *nm* magnet.
aimer (ɛ'me:) *vt* **1** like, care for. **2** love. **aimer mieux** prefer. **aimable** *adj* amiable, kind.
aine (ɛn) *nf* groin.
aîné (ɛ'ne:) *adj* **1** elder. **2** eldest. **3** senior.
ainsi (ɛ̃'si:) *adv* thus, in this way. **et ainsi de suite** and so on. **pour ainsi dire** so to speak. ~*conj* so. **ainsi que 1** just as. **2** as well as.
air[1] (ɛr) *nm* **1** air, atmosphere. **2** wind.
air[2] (ɛr) *nm* **1** look, appearance. **2** way. **avoir l'air** look, seem.

air[3] (ɛr) *nm* tune, melody.
airain (ɛ'rɛ̃) *nm* brass.
aire (ɛr) *nf* area.
aise (ɛz) *nf* ease, comfort. **être à l'aise** 1 be comfortable. 2 be well off. ~*adj* glad, pleased. **aisé** *adj* easy.
aisselle (ɛ'sɛl) *nf* armpit.
ajonc (a'ʒɔ̃) *nm* gorse.
ajourner (aʒu:r'ne:) *vt* 1 adjourn. 2 postpone.
ajouter (aʒu:'te:) *vt* 1 add. 2 add up.
ajuster (aʒy'ste:) *vt* 1 adjust, fit. 2 put in order.
alarme (a'larm) *nf* 1 alarm. 2 fear.
Albanie (alba'ni:) *nf* Albania. **albanais** *adj,n* Albanian.
albatros (alba'trɔs) *nm* albatross.
album (al'bɔm) *nm* album.
alcali (alka'li:) *nm* alkali.
alchimie (alʃi:'mi:) *nf* alchemy.
alcool (al'kɔl) *nm* 1 alcohol. 2 spirits. **alcoolique** *adj,n* alcoholic.
aléatoire (ale:a'twar) *adj* 1 contingent. 2 risky.
alentour (alɑ̃'tu:r) *adv* around, about. **alentours** *nm pl* 1 neighbourhood. 2 surroundings.
alerte (a'lɛrt) *adj* alert, agile. *nf* alarm, warning. **fin d'alerte** *nf* all clear.
algèbre (al'ʒɛbr) *nf* algebra.
Algérie (alʒe:'ri:) *nf* Algeria. **algérien, -ienne** (alʒe:'rjɛ̃, -'rjɛn) *adj,n* Algerian.
algue (alg) *nf* seaweed.
alibi (ali:'bi:) *nm* alibi.
aliéner (alje:'ne:) *vt* alienate. **aliénable** *adj* transferable. **aliéné** *adj* mad, mentally ill.
aligner (ali:'ɲe:) *vt* align, put in a row.
aliment (ali:'mɑ̃) *nm* food. **alimentaire** *adj* alimentary. **alimentation** *nf* 1 nourishment, feeding. 2 foodstuffs.
alinéa (ali:ne:'a) *nm* paragraph.
aliter (ali:'te:) *vt* confine to bed.
allée (a'le:) *nf* garden path.
alléger (ale:'ʒe:) *vt* 1 relieve, alleviate. 2 lighten.
allégorie (alle:gɔ'ri:) *nf* allegory.
allègre (al'lɛgr) *adj* 1 lively. 2 cheerful, lighthearted. 3 brisk.
alléguer (ale:'ge:) *vt* 1 allege. 2 plead, urge.
alléluia (ale:ly'ja) *nm* hallelujah.
Allemagne (al'maɲ) *nf* Germany. **allemand** (al'mɑ̃) *adj,n* German. *nm* German (language).
aller* (a'le:) *vi (aux être)* 1 go. 2 suit, fit. **aller chercher** fetch. **ça va!** OK! **comment allez-vous?** how are you? **vas-y! allez-y!** go on! **y aller de** stake, be at stake. **s'en aller** *vr* go away, depart. ~*nm* 1 single ticket. 2 outward journey. **au pis aller** if the worst comes to the worst.
allergie (alɛr'ʒi:) *nf* allergy. **allergique** *adj* allergic.
allier (a'lje:) *vt* 1 unite. 2 mix, blend. **alliage** *nm* alloy. **alliance** *nf* 1 alliance. 2 marriage. 3 wedding ring. **allié** *adj* 1 allied. 2 related by marriage. *nm* ally.
alligator (ali:ga'tɔr) *nm* alligator.
allitération (alli:tɛra'sjɔ̃) *nf* alliteration.
allô (a'lo) *interj* (on the telephone) hello!
allocation (allɔka'sjɔ̃) *nf* 1 allocation. 2 allowance.
allocution (allɔky'sjɔ̃) *nf* address, short speech.
allonger (alɔ̃'ʒe:) *vt* 1 lengthen. 2 thin (a sauce). 3 stretch out. **allonger une gifle à** slap.
allouer (a'lwe:) *vt* 1 grant. 2 allocate.
allumer (aly'me:) *vt* 1 light. 2 excite. **s'allumer** *vr* catch fire. **allumé** *adj* alight. **allume-feu** *nm invar* firelighter. **allumette** *nf* match.
allure (a'lyr) *nf* 1 pace, speed. 2 gait. 3 behaviour. 4 look. **à toute allure** at top speed.
allusion (ally'zjɔ̃) *nf* allusion. **faire allusion à** refer to.
almanach (alma'na) *nm* almanac.
aloi (a'lwa) *nm* quality. **de bon aloi** genuine.
alors (a'lɔr) *adv* 1 then, at that time. 2 so, in that case. **alors même que** even when. **alors que** when.
alouette (a'lwɛt) *nf* lark.
alourdir (alu:r'di:r) *vt* 1 make heavy. 2 make stupid.
aloyau, -aux (alwa'jo) *nm* sirloin.
Alpes (alp) *nf pl* Alps. **alpestre** *adj* alpine. **alpin** *adj* alpine. **alpiniste** *nm* mountaineer.
alphabet (alfa'bɛ) *nm* alphabet. **alphabétique** (alfabe:'ti:k) *adj* alphabetical.
altercation (altɛrka'sjɔ̃) *nf* dispute, squabble.
altérer (alte:'re:) *vt* 1 alter. 2 adulterate, corrupt. 3 make thirsty.
alterner (altɛr'ne:) *vi* alternate, take turns. *vt* alternate. **alternatif, -ive** (altɛrna'ti:f, -'ti:v) alternative, alternate. *nf* alternative.
Altesse (al'tɛs) *nf* Highness.
altier, -ière (al'tje:, -'tjɛr) *adj* haughty, arrogant.
altitude (alti:'tyd) *nf* altitude.
alto (al'to) *nm* 1 alto. 2 viola.
aluminium (alymi'njɔm) *nm* aluminium.
amadouer (ama'dwe:) *vt* coax.
amaigrir (amɛ'gri:r) *vt* make thin, emaciate.

amalgamer (amalga'me:) *vt* amalgamate, blend.
amande (a'mãd) *nf* almond.
amant (a'mã) *nm* lover.
amarrer (ama're:) *vt* **1** moor. **2** tie up.
amas (a'ma) *nm* pile, heap, mass. **amasser** (ama'se:) *vt* **1** pile up. **2** amass.
amateur, -trice (ama'tœr, -'tri:s) *nm,f* **1** enthusiast. **2** patron. **3** amateur.
ambassade (ãba'sad) *nf* embassy. **ambassadeur** *nm* ambassador.
ambiance (ã'bjãs) *nf* **1** surroundings. **2** atmosphere.
ambidextre (ãbi:'dɛkstr) *adj* ambidextrous.
ambigu, -uë (ãbi:'gy) *adj* ambiguous. **ambiguïté** *nf* ambiguity.
ambition (ãbi:'sjɔ̃) *nf* ambition. **ambitieux, -euse** (ãbi:'sjœ, -'sjœz) *adj* ambitious.
ambivalent (ãbi:va'lã) *adj* ambivalent.
ambre (ãbr) *nm* amber.
ambulance (ãby'lãs) *nf* ambulance.
ambulant (ãby'lã) *adj* **1** wandering. **2** travelling.
âme (am) *nf* **1** soul. **2** spirit. **3** mind. **4** feeling. **5** person. **6** core. **7** bore (of a gun).
améliorer (ame:ljɔ're:) *vt* improve. **amélioration** *nf* improvement.
aménager (amɛna'ʒe:) *vt* arrange, lay out. **aménagement** *nm* **1** fittings. **2** development.
amender (amã'de:) *vt* **1** improve. **2** amend. **amende** *nf* fine.
amener (am'ne:) *vt* **1** bring. **2** lead. **3** induce.
amer, -ère (a'mɛr) *adj* bitter. **amertume** *nf* bitterness.
Amérique (ame:'ri:k) *nf* America. **Amérique du Nord/Sud** North/South America. **américain** *adj,n* American.
améthyste (ame:'ti:st) *nf* amethyst.
ameublement (amœblə'mã) *nm* **1** furnishing. **2** furniture.
ami (a'mi:) *nm* **1** friend. **2** boyfriend. *adj* friendly. **amiable** *adj* amicable, friendly. **amical, -aux** (ami:'kal, -'ko) *adj* friendly. **amitié** *nf* **1** friendship. **2** kindness, favour.
amiante (a'mjãt) *nm* asbestos.
amibe (a'mi:b) *nf* amoeba.
amidon (ami:'dɔ̃) *nm* starch.
amiral, -aux (ami:'ral, -'ro) *nm* admiral. **amirauté** *nf* admiralty.
ammoniaque (amɔ'njak) *nf* ammonia.
amnistie (amni:'sti:) *nf* amnesty.
amoindrir (amwɛ̃'dri:r) *vt* reduce, diminish.
amollir (amɔ'li:r) *vt* **1** soften. **2** weaken.
amonceler (amɔ̃'sle:) *vt* heap up. **s'amonceler** *vr* gather. **amoncellement** *nm* **1** heap. **2** accumulation.
amont (a'mɔ̃) **en amont** *adv* upstream. **en amont de** above.
amoral, -aux (amɔ'ral, -'ro) *adj* amoral.
amorcer (amɔr'se:) *vt* **1** bait. **2** begin. **amorce** *nf* **1** bait. **2** beginning.
amorphe (a'mɔrf) *adj* amorphous.
amortir (amɔr'ti:r) *vt* **1** deaden, soften. **2** pay off. **amortissement** *nm* **1** deadening. **2** redemption. **amortisseur** *nm* shock absorber.
amour (a'mu:r) *nm* love, affection. **amoureux, -euse** (amu'rœ, -'rœ:z) *adj* loving. **être amoureux de** be in love with. **amour-propre** *nm* **1** self-respect. **2** vanity.
ampère (ã'pɛr) *nm* ampere.
amphétamine (ãfe:ta'mi:n) *nf* amphetamine.
amphibie (ãfi:'bi:) *adj* amphibious. *nm* amphibian.
ample (ãpl) *adj* **1** ample. **2** full. **3** spacious **ampleur** *nf* fullness.
amplifier (ãpli:'fje:) *vt* **1** amplify. **2** magnify. **amplificateur** (ãpli:fi:ka'tœr) *nm* amplifier.
ampoule (ã'pu:l) *nf* **1** bulb. **2** blister.
amputer (ãpy'te:) *vt* **1** amputate. **2** cut, reduce.
amuser (amy'ze:) *vt* amuse, entertain. **s'amuser** *vr* enjoy oneself. **amusement** *nm* **1** pastime. **2** recreation.
amygdale (ami:'dal) *nf* tonsil. **amygdalite** *nf* tonsillitis.
an (ã) *nm* year. **avoir six ans** be six years old. **tous les ans** every year.
anachronisme (anakrɔ'ni:sm) *nm* anachronism.
anal, -aux (a'nal, -'no) *adj* anal.
analogie (analɔ'ʒi:) *nf* analogy.
analphabète (analfa'bɛt) *adj* illiterate.
analyser (anali:'ze:) *vt* analyse. **analyse** *nf* analysis.
ananas (ana'na) *nm* pineapple.
anarchie (anar'ʃi:) *nf* anarchy. **anarchiste** *adj,n* anarchist.
anatomie (anatɔ'mi:) *nf* anatomy.
ancêtre (ã'sɛtr) *nm,f* **1** ancestor. **2** forefather.
anchois (ã'ʃwa) *nm* anchovy.
ancien, -ienne (ã'sjɛ̃, -'sjɛn) *adj* **1** ancient. **2** old, past. **3** former. **4** senior. **ancienneté** *nf* **1** antiquity. **2** seniority.
ancre (ãkr) *nf* anchor.
Andorre (ã'dɔr) *nm* Andorra. **andorran** *adj,n* Andorran.
âne (an) *nm* **1** donkey, ass. **2** fool.
anéantir (ane:ã'ti:r) *vt* annihilate, destroy.

s'anéantir *vr* **1** come to nothing. **2** humble oneself. **anéanti** *adj* **1** exhausted. **2** prostrate.
anecdote (anɛk'dɔt) *nf* anecdote.
anémie (ane:'mi:) *nf* anaemia. **anémique** *adj* anaemic.
anémone (ane:'mɔn) *nf* anemone.
anesthésier (anɛste:'zje:) *vt* anaesthetize. **anesthésique** *adj,nm* anaesthetic.
anfractueux, -euse (ɑ̃frak'tɥœ, -'tɥœz) *adj* **1** winding. **2** irregular, rugged.
ange (ɑ̃ʒ) *nm* angel.
angélique[1] (ɑ̃ʒe:'li:k) *adj* angelic.
angélique[2] (ɑ̃ʒe:'li:k) *nf* angelica.
angine (ɑ̃'ʒi:n) *nf* sore throat, tonsillitis.
angle (ɑ̃gl) *nm* **1** angle. **2** corner. **3** point of view. **angle droit** right angle.
Angleterre (ɑ̃glə'tɛr) *nf* England. **anglais** (ɑ̃'glɛ) *adj* English. *nm* **1** Englishman. **2** English (language).
anglican (ɑ̃gli:'kɑ̃) *adj,n* Anglican.
angoisse (ɑ̃'gwas) *nf* **1** anguish. **2** distress. **angoissant** (ɑ̃gwa'sɑ̃) *adj* **1** distressing. **2** alarming.
anguille (ɑ̃'gi:j) *nf* eel.
anguleux, -euse (ɑ̃gy'lœ, -'lœz) *adj* **1** angular. **2** bony.
anhydride (ani:'dri:d) *nm* **anhydride carbonique** carbon dioxide.
animal, -aux[1] (ani:'mal, -'mo) *nm* animal.
animal, -aux[2] (ani:'mal, -'mo) *adj* **1** animal. **2** brutal. **3** sensual.
animer (ani:'me:) *vt* **1** animate. **2** prompt. **3** brighten. **s'animer** *vr* **1** come to life. **2** become excited. **animé** *adj* **1** lively. **2** bright.
animosité (ani:mɔzi:'te:) *nf* spite.
anis (a'ni:) *nm* aniseed.
annales (an'nal) *nf pl* annals.
anneau, -aux (a'no) *nm* **1** ring. **2** link. **3** ringlet.
année (a'ne:) *nf* year. **bonne année!** Happy New Year!
annexer (anɛk'se:) *vt* **1** annex. **2** attack. **annexe** *nf* annexe.
annihiler (ani:i:'le:) *vt* annihilate, destroy.
anniversaire (ani:vɛr'sɛr) *adj* anniversary. *nm* **1** birthday. **2** anniversary.
annoncer (anɔ̃'se:) *vt* **1** announce. **2** advertise. **3** indicate. **s'annoncer bien** *vr* look promising. **annonce** *nf* **1** announcement. **2** advertisement. **petites annonces** *nf pl* classified advertisements.
annoter (anɔ'te:) *vt* annotate.
annuaire (a'nɥɛr) *nm* **1** almanac. **2** annual. **3** telephone directory.
annuel, -elle (a'nɥɛl) *adj* annual.
annuler (any'le:) *vt* annul, cancel.
anode (a'nɔd) *nf* anode.
anomalie (anɔma'li:) *nf* anomaly.
anonyme (anɔ'ni:m) *adj* anonymous. *nm* anonymity.
anormal, -aux (anɔr'mal, -'mo) *adj* **1** abnormal. **2** irregular.
anse (ɑ̃s) *nf* **1** handle. **2** cove.
antagonisme (ɑ̃tagɔ'ni:sm) *nm* antagonism. **antagoniste** *adj* antagonistic. *nm* opponent.
antarctique (ɑ̃tar'ti:k) *adj* antarctic. *nm cap* Antarctic.
antenne (ɑ̃'tɛn) *nf* **1** aerial. **2** antenna. **3** horn.
antérieur (ɑ̃te:'rjœr) *adj* **1** former, previous, prior. **2** fore.
anthologie (ɑ̃tɔlɔ'ʒi:) *nf* anthology.
anthropologie (ɑ̃trɔpɔlɔ'ʒi:) *nf* anthropology.
anti-aérien, -ienne (ɑ̃ti:ae:'rjɛ̃, -'rjɛn) *adj* anti-aircraft.
antialcoolique (ɑ̃ti:alkɔ'li:k) *adj* teetotal. *nm,f* teetotaller.
antibiotique (ɑ̃ti:bjɔ'ti:k) *adj, nm* antibiotic.
anticiper (ɑ̃ti:si:'pe:) *vt,vi* anticipate. **anticipation** *nf* anticipation.
anticonceptionnel, -elle (ɑ̃ti:kɔ̃sɛpsjɔ'nɛl) *adj* contraceptive.
anticorps (ɑ̃ti:'kɔr) *nm* antibody.
anticyclone (ɑ̃ti:si:'klɔn) *nm* anticyclone.
antidater (ɑ̃ti:da'te:) *vt* backdate.
antidote (ɑ̃ti:'dɔt) *nm* antidote.
anti-gel (ɑ̃ti:'ʒɛl) *nm invar* antifreeze.
Antilles (ɑ̃'ti:j) *nf pl* West Indies. **antillais** *adj,n* West Indian.
antilope (ɑ̃ti:'lɔp) *nf* antelope.
antique (ɑ̃'ti:k) *adj* **1** ancient. **2** antique. *nf* antique. **antiquaire** *nm* antique dealer. **antiquité** *nf* **1** antiquity. **2** *pl* antiques.
antisémitique (ɑ̃ti:se:mi:'ti:k) *adj* anti-Semitic.
antiseptique (ɑ̃ti:sɛp'ti:k) *adj,nm* antiseptic.
antisocial, -aux (ɑ̃ti:sɔ'sjal, -'sjo) *adj* antisocial.
antithèse (ɑ̃ti:'tɛz) *nf* antithesis.
antonyme (ɑ̃tɔ'ni:m) *nm* antonym.
antre (ɑ̃tr) *nm* **1** cave. **2** den.
anus (a'nys) *nm* anus.
anxiété (ɑ̃ksje:'te:) *nf* anxiety, worry. **anxieux, -euse** (ɑ̃k'sjœ, -'sjœz) *adj* anxious, concerned.
août (u:) *nm* August.
apaiser (apɛ'ze:) *vt* **1** calm, appease. **2** alleviate. **3** quench. **s'apaiser** *vr* **1** calm down. **2** abate.
apathie (apa'ti:) *nf* apathy. **apathique** *adj* apathetic.
apercevoir* (apɛrsə'vwar) *vt* **1** perceive. **2** catch

sight of. **s'apercevoir** *vr* 1 notice. 2 realize. **aperçu** *nm* 1 glimpse. 2 outline.

apéritif (ape:ri'ti:f) *nm* aperitive.

aphis (a'fi:s) *nm* greenfly.

aplanir (apla'ni:r) *vt* 1 smooth, plane. 2 level.

aplatir (apla'ti:r) *vt* flatten. **s'aplatir** *vr* 1 go flat. 2 grovel.

aplomb (a'plɔ̃) *nm* 1 equilibrium. 2 uprightness. 3 self-assurance. **d'aplomb** upright, vertical.

apogée (apɔ'ʒe:) *nm* apex, climax.

apologie (apɔlɔ'ʒi:) *nf* 1 defence. 2 justification.

apostrophe (apɔ'strɔf) *nf* apostrophe.

apôtre (a'potr) *nm* apostle.

apparaître* (apa'rɛtr) *vi* (*aux* être) appear, become visible.

apparat (apa'ra) *nm* pomp, show. **d'apparat** formal.

appareil (apa'rɛj) *nm* 1 display. 2 apparatus. 3 machine, appliance. 4 *inf* phone. **appareil photo** camera.

apparence (apa'rɑ̃s) *nf* appearance, look. **en apparence** apparently. **apparent** *adj* 1 visible. 2 obvious. 3 apparent.

apparenter (aparɑ̃'te:) *vt* connect (by marriage).

appartement (apartə'mɑ̃) *nm* flat.

appartenir* (apartə'ni:r) *vi* **appartenir à** belong to. *v imp* concern.

appas (a'pa) *nm pl* charm, attraction.

appât (a'pɑ) *nm* bait.

appel (a'pɛl) *nm* 1 appeal. 2 call. **appel d'incendie** fire alarm.

appeler (ap'le:) *vt* 1 call. 2 summon. 3 appeal. 4 ring, telephone. **faire appeler** send for. **s'appeler** *vr* be called.

appendice (apɛ̃'di:s) *nm* appendix. **appendicite** *nf* appendicitis.

appentis (apɑ̃'ti:) *nm* 1 penthouse. 2 shed, outhouse.

appétit (ape:'ti:) *nm* 1 appetite. 2 desire. **bon appétit!** enjoy your meal!

applaudir (aplo'di:r) *vt* 1 applaud. 2 commend. 3 praise. **applaudissement** *nm* applause.

appliquer (apli:'ke:) *vt* 1 apply. 2 enforce. **application** *nf* 1 application. 2 diligence. **applicable** *adj* 1 applicable. 2 appropriate. **appliqué** *adj* 1 applied. 2 studious.

appointements (apwɛ̃t'mɑ̃) *nm pl* salary.

apporter (apɔr'te:) *vt* 1 bring. 2 provide.

apposer (apo'ze:) *vt* affix.

apprécier (apre:'sje:) *vt* 1 appreciate. 2 appraise, value. **appréciable** *adj* appreciable. **appréciation** *nf* 1 estimate. 2 appreciation.

appréhender (apre:ɑ̃'de:) *vt* 1 seize. 2 apprehend, fear. **apprehensif, -ive** (apre:ɑ̃si:f, -'si:v) *adj* apprehensive, timid.

apprendre* (a'prɑ̃dr) *vt* 1 learn. 2 teach. 3 inform.

apprenti (aprɑ̃'ti:) *nm* apprentice.

apprivoiser (apri:vwa'ze:) *vt* 1 tame. 2 domesticate. **s'apprivoiser** *vr* grow tame.

approbation (aprɔba'sjɔ̃) *nf* consent, approval.

approcher (aprɔ'ʃe:) *vt* approach, bring near. *vi* approach, draw near. **s'approcher de** *vr* approach, come near to. **approche** *nf* approach.

approfondir (aprɔfɔ̃'di:r) *vt* 1 make deeper. 2 examine thoroughly. **approfondi** *adj* 1 deep. 2 thorough.

approprier (aprɔpri:'e:) *vt* 1 appropriate. 2 fit. **s'approprier à** *vr* adapt oneself to.

approuver (apru:'ve:) *vt* 1 approve. 2 agree to.

approximatif, -ive (aprɔksi:ma'ti:f, -'ti:v) *adj* approximate, rough.

appui (a'pɥi:) *nm* prop, support.

appuyer (apɥi:'je:) *vt* 1 support. 2 rest. 3 hold. **appuyer sur** 1 lean or press on. 2 emphasize. **s'appuyer sur** *vr* 1 lean on. 2 rely on.

âpre (ɑpr) *adj* 1 rough, harsh. 2 sharp. 3 keen. 4 greedy.

après (a'prɛ) *prep* after. **d'après** according to. ~*adv* afterwards, later. **après que** after, when. **et après?** what then? **après-demain** *adv* the day after tomorrow. **après-midi** *nm invar* afternoon.

à-propos (aprɔ'po) *nm* aptness.

apte (apt) *adj* 1 suited. 2 capable. **aptitude** *nf* 1 aptitude. 2 capacity.

aquarelle (akwa'rɛl) *nf* watercolour.

aquarium (akwa'rjɔm) *nm* aquarium.

aquatique (akwa'ti:k) *adj* aquatic.

aqueux, -euse (a'kœ, -'kœz) *adj* watery.

Arabie (ara'bi:) *nf* Arabia. **Arabie Séoudite** Saudi Arabia. **arabe** *adj* 1 Arab. 2 Arabic. *nm* 1 Arab. 2 Arabic (language).

arable (a'rabl) *adj* arable.

arachide (ara'ʃi:d) *nf* peanut.

araignée (arɛ'ɲe:) *nf* spider.

arbitre[1] (ar'bi:tr) *nm* umpire, referee.

arbitre[2] (ar'bi:tr) *nm* **libre arbitre** free will.

arbitrer (arbi:'tre:) *vt* 1 arbitrate. 2 umpire. **arbitraire** (arbi:'trɛr) *adj* arbitrary.

arbre (arbr) *nm* 1 tree. 2 shaft, axle. **arbre de Noël** Christmas tree. **arbre vert** evergreen.

arbuste (ar'byst) *nm* 1 bush. 2 shrub.

arc (ark) *nm* **1** bow. **2** arc. **3** arch. **arc-en-ciel** *nm, pl* **arcs-en-ciel** rainbow.

arcade (ar'kad) *nf* **1** archway. **2** arcade.

archaïque (arka'i:k) *adj* archaic.

arche[1] (arʃ) *nf* ark.

arche[2] (arʃ) *nf* **1** arch. **2** hoop.

archéologie (arke:ɔlɔ'ʒi:) *nf* archaeology. **archéologique** *adj* archaeological. **archéologue** *nm,f* archaeologist.

archet (ar'ʃɛ) *nm mus* bow.

archevêque (arʃə'vɛk) *nm* archbishop.

archi- (arʃi:) *pref* **1** arch. **2** utterly. **archibondé** (arʃi:bɔ̃'de:) *adj* crammed full. **archifou** (arʃi:'fu:) *adj* stark mad. **archiplein** (arʃi:'plɛ̃) *adj* packed.

archiduc (arʃi:'dyk) *nm* archduke.

archipel (arʃi:'pɛl) *nm* archipelago.

architecte (arʃi:'tɛkt) *nm,f* architect. **architecture** *nf* architecture.

archives (ar'ʃi:v) *nf pl* **1** archives. **2** public records.

arctique (ark'ti:k) *adj* arctic. *nm cap* Arctic.

ardent (ar'dɑ̃) *adj* **1** burning. **2** ardent, keen. **ardemment** (arda'mɑ̃) *adv* ardently, eagerly.

ardeur (ar'dœr) *nf* **1** heat. **2** ardour, eagerness.

ardoise (ar'dwaz) *nf* slate.

ardu (ar'dy) *adj* **1** steep. **2** difficult, arduous.

are (ar) *nm* unit of measure, equal to 100 square metres.

arène (a'rɛn) *nf* arena, ring.

arête (a'rɛt) *nf* **1** fish bone. **2** edge. **3** ridge.

argent (ar'ʒɑ̃) *nm* **1** silver. **2** money. **argent comptant** cash. **argent liquide** ready money. **argenté** *adj* silvered. **argenterie** *nf* plate.

Argentine (arʒɑ̃'ti:n) *nf* Argentina. **argentin** *adj* Argentine, Argentinian. *nm* Argentinian.

argile (ar'ʒi:l) *nf* clay.

argot (ar'go) *nm* slang.

argument (argy'mɑ̃) *nm* **1** argument. **2** synopsis.

aride (a'ri:d) *adj* **1** arid, dry. **2** barren.

aristocratie (ari:stɔkra'si:) *nf* aristocracy. **aristocrate** *nm,f* aristocrat. **aristocratique** *adj* aristocratic.

arithmétique (ari:tme:'ti:k) *nf* arithmetic.

armer (ar'me:) *vt* **1** arm. **2** strengthen. **3** equip. **4** load (a gun). **arme** *nf* **1** arm, weapon. **2** *pl* coat of arms. **armée** *nf* army. **armée de l'air** air force. **armure** *nf* armour.

armoire (ar'mwar) *nf* **1** wardrobe. **2** cupboard.

arome (a'rom) *nm* aroma.

arpenter (arpɑ̃'te:) *vt* **1** measure. **2** pace up and down.

arquer (ar'ke:) *vt* arch, bend. *vi* become bent, sag. **arqué** *adj* bent, curved.

arracher (ara'ʃe:) *vt* **1** tear away. **2** snatch, seize. **d'arrache-pied** *adv* steadily.

arranger (arɑ̃'ʒe:) *vt* **1** arrange. **2** settle. **3** accommodate. **s'arranger** *vr* **1** manage. **2** come to an agreement. **arrangement** *nm* **1** arrangement. **2** agreement.

arrérages (arɛ'raʒ) *nm pl* arrears.

arrestation (arɛsta'sjɔ̃) *nf* arrest.

arrêt (a'rɛ) *nm* **1** stop. **2** decree.

arrêter (arɛ'te:) *vt* **1** stop. **2** restrain. **3** arrest. **4** fix. *vi* stop. **s'arrêter** *vr* stop, halt. **s'arrêter sur** dwell on. **arrêté** *adj* fixed. *nm* **1** decision. **2** decree.

arrhes (ar) *nf pl* deposit (of money).

arrière (a'rjɛr) *nm invar* **1** back, back part of. **2** *sport* back. **en arrière** **1** behind. **2** arrears. **3** backwards. ~*adj invar* back, rear. **arriéré** *adj* **1** backward. **2** old-fashioned. **arrière-garde** *nf, pl* **arrière-gardes** rearguard. **arrière-plan** *nm, pl* **arrière-plans** background.

arriver (ari:'ve:) *vi* (*aux* être) **1** arrive. **2** come. **3** succeed. **4** happen. **arrivée** *nf* arrival. **arriviste** *nm,f* social climber.

arrogance (arɔ'gɑ̃s) *nf* arrogance. **arrogant** *adj* arrogant, haughty.

arrondissement (arɔ̃di:s'mɑ̃) *nm* **1** district of a town. **2** division of a French department.

arroser (aro'ze:) *vt* **1** water. **2** sprinkle. **arrosoir** *nm* watering-can.

arsenic (arsə'ni:k) *nm* arsenic.

art (ar) *nm* **1** art. **2** skill.

artère (ar'tɛr) *nf* **1** artery. **2** thoroughfare. **tension artérielle** *nf* blood pressure.

arthrite (ar'tri:t) *nf* arthritis.

artichaut (arti:'ʃo) *nm* globe artichoke.

article (ar'ti:kl) *nm* **1** article. **2** item, commodity. **article-réclame** *nm, pl* **articles-réclame** special offer. **articles de Paris** fancy goods.

articuler (arti:ky'le:) *vt* articulate. **articulation** *nf* **1** *anat* joint. **2** link. **3** articulation. **articulation du doigt** knuckle. **articulé** *adj* articulate, distinct.

artifice (arti:'fi:s) *nm* **1** guile. **2** deceit.

artificiel, -elle (arti:fi:'sjɛl) *adj* **1** artificial. **2** imitation.

artillerie (arti:j'ri:) *nf* artillery.

artisan (arti'zɑ̃) *nm* craftsman.

artiste (ar'ti:st) *nm,f* **1** artist. **2** performer. **3** actor. **artistique** *adj* artistic.

as[1] (ɑs) *nm* **1** ace. **2** expert, first-rate performer.

as[2] (a) *v see* **avoir.**

asbeste (az'bɛst) *nm* asbestos.
ascendance (asɑ̃'dɑ̃s) *nf* **1** ascent. **2** ancestry. **ascendant** *adj* upward.
ascenseur (asɑ̃'sœr) *nm* lift.
Asie (a'zi:) *nf* Asia. **asiatique** *adj* Asiatic, Asian. *nm* Asian.
asile (a'zi:l) *nm* **1** refuge. **2** asylum. **sans asile** homeless.
aspect (a'spɛ) *nm* **1** sight. **2** appearance. **3** point of view. **4** aspect.
asperge (a'spɛrʒ) *nf* asparagus.
asphalte (as'falt) *nm* asphalt.
aspirer (aspi:'re:) *vt* **1** aspire. **2** inhale. **aspirant** *nm* candidate. **aspirateur** *nm* vacuum cleaner.
aspirine (aspi:'ri:n) *nf* aspirin.
assaillir (asa'ji:r) *vt* attack.
assainir (asɛ'ni:r) *vt* **1** make healthier. **2** cleanse.
assaisonner (asɛzɔ'ne:) *vt* season.
assassin (asa'sɛ̃) *nm* murderer, assassin. **assassinat** *nm* assassination, murder.
assassiner (asasi:'ne:) *vt* assassinate, murder.
assaut (a'so) *nm* attack, assault.
assembler (asɑ̃'ble:) *vt* **1** assemble. **2** gather, collect. **3** put together. **assemblage** *nm* assembling. **assemblée** *nf* assembly. **Assemblée Nationale** Lower Chamber of French Parliament.
assentiment (asɑ̃ti:'mɑ̃) *nm* assent.
asseoir* (a'swar) *vt* **1** seat, set. **2** establish. **s'asseoir** *vr* sit down.
assez (a'se:) *adv* **1** enough, sufficient. **2** fairly, rather. **j'en ai assez!** I'm fed up with it!
asseyant (asɛ'jɑ̃) *v* see **asseoir.**
assidu (asi:'dy) *adj* **1** industrious, diligent. **2** regular. **assidûment** *adv* **1** diligently. **2** constantly.
assieds (a'sjɛ) *v* see **asseoir.**
assiéger (asje:'ʒe:) *vt* **1** besiege. **2** surround.
assiette (a'sjɛt) *nf* **1** plate. **2** seat, position. **3** situation. **4** base. **assiette creuse** soup plate. **assiette plate** dinner plate.
assigner (asi:'ɲe:) *vt* **1** assign. **2** appoint. **3** summon. **assignation** *nf* **1** assignment. **2** summons.
assimiler (asi:mi:'le:) *vt* assimilate, digest.
assis (a'si:) *v* see **asseoir.** *adj* seated. **assises** *nf pl* assizes.
assister (asi:'ste:) *vt* help, assist. **assister à** attend, be present. **assistance** *nf* **1** audience. **2** congregation. **3** assistance. **assistant** *nm* **1** onlooker. **2** assistant.
associer (asɔ'sje:) *vt* associate, connect. **s'associer à** *vr* **1** join in. **2** go into partnership with. **association** *nf* **1** association. **2** society, company. **3** partnership. **associé** *nm* **1** partner. **2** associate member.
assommer (asɔ'me:) *vt* **1** knock senseless, overpower. **2** *inf* bore. **assommant** *adj* **1** overwhelming. **2** boring.
assortir (asɔr'ti:r) *vt* **1** assort. **2** match. **3** stock. **assorti** *adj* **1** assorted. **2** matched. **assortiment** *nm* **1** assortment. **2** set.
assoupir (asu:'pi:r) *vt* **1** make sleepy. **2** allay. **s'assoupir** *vr* doze off.
assourdir (asu:r'di:r) *vt* **1** make deaf. **2** deaden. **3** muffle.
assujettir (asyʒe:'ti:r) *vt* **1** subdue. **2** subject. **3** fasten.
assurer (asy're:) *vt* **1** assure. **2** make secure. **3** affirm. **4** insure. **assurance** *nf* **1** assurance. **2** insurance. **assuré** *adj* **1** sure. **2** safe. **3** certain. **4** confident. **5** insured.
astérisque (aste:'ri:sk) *nm* asterisk.
asthme (asm) *nm* asthma.
astre (astr) *nm* star.
astreindre* (a'strɛ̃dr) *vt* **1** force. **2** subject. **s'astreindre à** *vr* keep to.
astrologie (astrɔlɔ'ʒi:) *nf* astrology. **astrologique** *adj* astrological.
astronomie (astrɔnɔ'mi:) *nf* astronomy. **astronomique** *adj* astronomical.
astronaute (astrɔ'not) *nm* astronaut.
astucieux, -euse (asty'sjœ, -'sjœz) *adj* **1** astute. **2** artful.
atelier (atə'lje:) *nm* **1** workshop. **2** studio.
athée (a'te:) *nm* atheist. **athéisme** *nm* atheism.
Athènes (a'tɛn) *nf* Athens.
athlète (at'lɛt) *nm* athlete. **athlétique** *adj* athletic. **athlétisme** *nm* athletics.
atlantique (atlɑ̃'ti:k) *adj* Atlantic. **(Océan) Atlantique** *nm* Atlantic (Ocean).
atlas (at'lɑs) *nm* atlas.
atmosphère (atmɔ'sfɛr) *nf* atmosphere. **atmosphérique** *adj* atmospheric.
atome (a'tom) *nm* atom. **atomique** (atɔ'mi:k) *adj* atomic.
atout (a'tu:) *nm* trump.
âtre (ɑtr) *nm* hearth.
atroce (a'trɔs) *adj* **1** atrocious. **2** terrible. **atrocité** *nf* atrocity.
s'attabler (sata'ble:) *vr* sit down to table.
attacher (ata'ʃe:) *vt* **1** attach. **2** fasten. **s'attacher** *vr* **1** cling. **2** apply oneself. **attache** *nf* **1** fastening. **2** tie. **3** leash. **attaché** *adj* attached. *nm pol* attaché.

attaquer (ata'ke:) *vt* **1** attack. **2** assault. **3** begin. **s'attaquer à** *vr* **1** attack, tackle. **2** grapple with. **attaque** *nf* **1** attack. **2** bout, fit. **3** stroke.

attarder (atar'de:) *vt* keep late. **s'attarder** *vr* linger, delay.

atteignant (atɛ'ɲɑ̃) *v* see **atteindre.**

atteindre* (a'tɛ̃dr) *vt* **1** reach. **2** touch, hit. **3** attain.

atteint (a'tɛ̃) *v* see **atteindre. atteinte** (a'tɛ̃t) *nf* **1** reach. **2** blow, hit, attack. **hors d'atteinte** out of reach.

attenant (at'nɑ̃) *adj* adjacent, next.

attendre (a'tɑ̃dr) *vt* **1** wait for. **2** expect. **en attendant** in the meantime. **faire attendre** keep waiting. **s'attendre** *vr* expect. **attendu** *adj* expected. *prep* considering. **attendu que** seeing that.

attendrir (atɑ̃'dri:r) *vt* **1** make tender, soften. **2** move. **s'attendrir** *vr* **1** become tender. **2** be moved. **attendrissement** *nm* **1** emotion. **2** pity.

attentat (atɑ̃'ta) *nm* **1** criminal attempt. **2** outrage.

attente (a'tɑ̃t) *nf* **1** waiting. **2** expectation.

attention (atɑ̃'sjɔ̃) *nf* **1** attention. **2** care. **faire attention à** pay attention to. *interj* look out! **attentif, -ive** (atɑ̃'ti:f, -'ti:v) *adj* **1** attentive. **2** careful.

atténuer (ate'nɥe:) *vt* **1** weaken, lessen. **2** make allowance for.

atterrer (atɛ're:) *vt* overwhelm.

atterrir (atɛ'ri:r) *vi* land. **atterrissage** *nm* landing.

attester (atɛ'ste:) *vt* testify.

attirail (ati'raj) *nm* **1** apparatus, outfit. **2** show. **3** *inf* stuff, rubbish.

attirer (ati:'re:) *vt* **1** attract. **2** bring on. **3** lure. **attirant** *adj* **1** attractive. **2** engaging.

attitré (ati:'tre:) *adj* **1** appointed. **2** regular.

attitude (ati:'tyd) *nf* **1** attitude. **2** posture.

attraction (atrak'sjɔ̃) *nf* attraction. **attractif, -ive** (atrak'ti:f, -'ti:v) *adj* attractive.

attrait (a'trɛ) *nm* **1** attraction. **2** charm.

attraper (atra'pe:) *vt* **1** catch. **2** trap. **3** trick. **4** seize. **attrape** *nm* **1** trap. **2** trick. **attrape-nigaud** *nm, pl* **attrape-nigauds** practical joke.

attrayant (atrɛ'jɑ̃) *adj* attractive.

attribuer (atri'bɥe:) *vt* **1** assign. **2** attribute. **s'attribuer** *vr* **1** assume. **2** claim. **attribut** (atri'by) *nm* attribute.

au, aux (o) contraction of **à le, à les**

aubaine (o'bɛn) *nf* windfall, piece of good luck.

aube[1] (ob) *nf* dawn.

aube[2] (ob) *nf* paddle.

aubépine (obe:'pi:n) *nf* hawthorn.

auberge (o'bɛrʒ) *nf* inn. **auberge de la jeunesse** youth hostel.

aubergine (obɛr'ʒi:n) *nf* aubergine, eggplant.

aucun (o'kœ̃) *pron,adj* any. **ne...aucun** **1** none, no. **2** no-one. **aucunement** *adv* in no way, not at all.

audace (o'das) *nf* **1** audacity. **2** impudence. **audacieux, -euse** (oda'sjœ, -'sjœz) *adj* **1** audacious, bold. **2** impudent.

au-delà (o'dla) *adv* beyond. *nm* next world. **au-delà de** beyond, on the other side of.

au-dessous (od'su:) *adv* below, underneath. **au-dessous de** below, under.

au-dessus (od'sy) *adv* above, over. **au-dessus de** above, over, beyond.

au-devant (od'vɑ̃) *adv* **aller au-devant** go to meet.

audible (o'di:bl) *adj* audible.

audience (o'djɑ̃s) *nf* **1** audience, hearing. **2** session.

auditeur (odi:'tœr) *nm* listener.

audition (odi:'sjɔ̃) *nf* **1** audition. **2** hearing.

auditoire (odi:'twar) *nm* **1** auditorium. **2** audience.

auge (oʒ) *nf* trough.

augmenter (ɔgmɑ̃'te:) *vt,vi* **1**, increase. **2** raise. **augmentation** *nf* **1** increase. **2** rise.

aujourd'hui (oʒu:r'dɥi) *adv* **1** today. **2** nowadays. **d'aujourd'hui en huit** today week.

aumône (o'mon) *nf* alms. **aumônier** *nm* chaplain.

auparavant (opara'vɑ̃) *adv* **1** before, first. **2** previously.

auprès (o'prɛ) *adv* close by, near. **auprès de** **1** close to, near. **2** beside. **3** in comparison with.

auquel, auxquels (o'kɛl) contraction of **à lequel, à lesquels.**

aurai (ɔ'rɛ) *v* see **avoir.**

aurais (ɔ'rɛ) *v* see **avoir.**

auréole (ɔre:'ɔl) *nf* **1** halo. **2** glory.

aurore (ɔ'rɔr) *nf* dawn, daybreak.

aussi (o'si:) *adv* **1** as, so. **2** also, too. *conj* therefore, consequently. **aussi bien que** as well as. **aussitôt** (osi:'to) *adv* immediately, at once. **aussitôt que** as soon as.

austère (ɔ'stɛr) *adj* **1** austere, severe. **2** stern.

Australie (ɔstra'li:) *nf* Australia. **australien, -ienne** (ɔstra'ljɛ̃, -'ljɛn) *adj,n* Australian.

autant (o'tɑ̃) *adv* **1** as much. **2** as many. **autant**

que 1 as much as. 2 as far as. **d'autant plus/moins** the more/less. **d'autant que** more especially as.
autel (o'tɛl) *nm* altar.
auteur (o'tœr) *nm* 1 author. 2 inventor, maker.
authentique (otɑ̃'ti:k) *adj* authentic, genuine.
autistique (oti:'sti:k) *adj also* **autiste**. autistic.
auto (ɔ'to) *nf* car. **auto-école** *nf, pl* **auto-écoles** driving school. **faire de l'auto-stop** hitchhike.
autobiographie (otɔbjɔgra'fi:) *nf* autobiography. **autobiographique** *adj* autobiographical.
autobus (otɔ'bys) *nm* bus. **autobus à impériale** double-decker bus.
autographe (otɔ'graf) *nm* autograph.
automatique (otɔma'ti:k) *adj* automatic.
automatisation (ɔtɔmati:za'sjɔ̃) *nf* automation.
automne (o'tɔn) *nm* autumn.
automobile (otɔmɔ'bi:l) *nf* motor car. **automobiliste** *nm* motorist.
autonome (otɔ'nɔm) *adj* autonomous.
autopsie (otɔp'si:) *nf* post-mortem.
autoriser (otɔri:'ze:) *vt* authorize.
autorité (otɔri:'te:) *nf* authority. **autoritaire** *adj* domineering.
autoroute (ɔtɔ'ru:t) *nf* motorway.
autour (o'tu:r) *adv* round, about. **autour de** around, about.
autre (otr) *adj* 1 other. 2 different. *pron* other. **autre chose** something else. **autre part** elsewhere. **d'autre part** on the other hand. **d'un moment à l'autre** from one moment to the next. **l'un et l'autre** both. **quelqu'un d'autre** someone else. **tout autre** quite different. **autrement** (otrə'mɑ̃) *adv* otherwise.
autrefois (otrə'fwa) *adv* formerly, in the past.
Autriche (o'tri:ʃ) *nf* Austria. **autrichien, -ienne** (otri'ʃjɛ̃, -ʃjɛn) *adj,n* Austrian.
autruche (o'tryʃ) *nf* ostrich.
autrui (o'trɥi:) *pron invar* others, other people.
aux (o) see **au**.
auxiliaire (ɔksi:'ljɛr) *adj* auxiliary. *nm* 1 auxiliary. 2 assistant.
avais (a'vɛ) *v* see **avoir**.
aval (a'val) *nm* lower part. **en aval** downstream.
avalanche (ava'lɑ̃ʃ) *nf* avalanche.
avaler (ava'le:) *vt* swallow.
avancer (avɑ̃'se:) *vt* advance, put forward. *vi* advance. **s'avancer** *vr* 1 move forward. 2 progress. **avance** *nf* 1 advance. 2 loan. **à l'avance** or **d'avance** beforehand. **être en avance** 1 be early. 2 be fast. **avancement** *nm* 1 promotion. 2 progress.
avant[1] (a'vɑ̃) *prep* before. *adv* 1 before. 2 far, deep. **en avant** forward, in front.
avant[2] (a'vɑ̃) *nm* 1 *naut* bow. 2 *sport* forward. *adj invar* fore. *In the following compounds* **avant** *is invar; the noun or adjective takes the plural.* **avant-bras** *nm* forearm. **avant-centre** *nm sport* centre-forward. **avant-cour** *nf* forecourt. **avant-coureur** *nm* forerunner. **avant-dernier, -ière** *adj* last but one. **avant-goût** *nm* foretaste. **avant-hier** *adv* day before yesterday. **avant-main** *nm sport* forehand. **avant-propos** *nm* preface.
avantage (avɑ̃'taʒ) *nm* advantage. **avantageux, -euse** (avɑ̃ta'ʒœ, -'ʒœz) *adj* advantageous.
avare (a'var) *adj* miserly. *nm,f* miser.
avarie (ava'ri:) *nf* damage.
avec (a'vɛk) *prep* with. *adv* with it.
avènement (avɛn'mɑ̃) *nm* 1 coming. 2 accession.
avenir (av'ni:r) *nm* future. **à l'avenir** in future, henceforth.
Avent (a'vɑ̃) *nm* Advent.
aventure (avɑ̃'tyr) *nf* 1 adventure. 2 chance. **à l'aventure** at random. **dire la bonne aventure** tell fortunes. **aventureux, -euse** (avɑ̃ty'rœ, -'rœz) *adj* 1 adventurous. 2 risky.
avenue (av'ny) *nf* avenue.
averse (a'vɛrs) *nf* downpour.
aversion (avɛr'zjɔ̃) *nf* aversion, dislike.
avertir (avɛr'ti:r) *vt* 1 warn. 2 notify. **avertissement** *nm* 1 warning. 2 notice.
aveu, aveux (a'vœ) *nm* confession.
aveugler (avœ'gle:) *vt* 1 blind. 2 dazzle. **s'aveugler sur** *vr* shut one's eyes to. **aveugle** (a'vœgl) *adj* blind. *nm,f* blind person.
avez (a'vɛ) *v* see **avoir**.
aviateur (avja'tœr) *nm* airman. **aviation** *nf* aviation.
avide (a'vi:d) *adj* 1 greedy, avid. 2 grasping.
avilir (avi:'li:r) *vt* 1 degrade. 2 depreciate. **s'avilir** *vr* disgrace oneself.
avion (a'vjɔ̃) *nm* 1 aircraft. 2 plane. **par avion** by airmail.
aviron (avi:'rɔ̃) *nm* 1 oar. 2 rowing. **faire de l'aviron** row.
avis ('avi:) *nm* 1 opinion. 2 advice. 3 notice. **changer d'avis** change one's mind.
aviser (avi:'ze:) *vt* 1 perceive, catch a glimpse of. 2 *comm* advise, inform. **aviser à** see

about. **s'aviser de** *vr* take it into one's head to. **avisé** *adj* **1** prudent. **2** shrewd.
avocat[1] (avɔ'ka) *nm* barrister.
avocat[2] (avɔ'ka) *nm* avocado.
avoine (a'vwan) *nf* oats.
avoir*[1] (a'vwar) *vt* **1** have, possess. **2** get. *v aux* have. **en avoir à** or **contre** bear a grudge against. **il y a 1** there is, are. **2** ago. **il n'y a pas de quoi** don't mention it. **qu'est ce-qu'il y a?** what's the matter?
avoir[2] (a'vwar) *nm* **1** possession. **2** property.
avoisiner (avwazi:'ne:) *vt* be near, border on.
avons (a'vɔ̃) *v* see **avoir.**
avorter (avɔr'te:) *vi* **1** miscarry. **2** fail. **avortement** *nm* abortion.
avouer (a'vwe:) *vt* **1** admit. **2** acknowledge. **avoué** *nm* solicitor.
avril (a'vri:l) *nm* April.
axe (aks) *nm* **1** axis. **2** axle.
ayant (ɛ'jɑ̃) *v* see **avoir.**
ayez (a'je:) *v* see **avoir.**
ayons (ɛ'jɔ̃) *v* see **avoir.**
azalée (aza'le:) *nf* azalea.
azote (a'zɔt) *nm* nitrogen.

B

babiller (babi:'je:) *vi* **1** chatter, prattle. **2** babble. **babillage** *nm* chatter, prattle. **babillard** *adj* talkative.
bâbord (ba'bɔr) *nm naut* port (side).
babouin (ba'bwɛ̃) *nm* baboon.
bac (bak) *nm* **1** ferry. **2** ferryboat.
baccalauréat (bakalɔre:'a) *nm* school leaving examination.
bâche (bɑʃ) *nf* **1** canvas cover. **2** tank, cistern.
bachelier, -ière (baʃə'lje:, -'ljɛr) *nm,f* one who has passed the school leaving examination.
bâcler (bɑ'kle:) *vt* **1** bar, bolt. **2** do in a slapdash way.
bactérie (bakte:'ri:) *nf* bacteria.
badigeonner (badi:ʒɔ'ne:) *vt* **1** whitewash. **2** paint.
badiner (badi:'ne:) *vi* trifle, joke. **badinage** *nm* **1** jest. **2** play. **badine** *nf* cane.
bafouiller (bafu:'je:) *vi,vt* **1** stammer. **2** splutter.
bagage (ba'gaʒ) *nm* **1** baggage. **2** *pl* luggage. **bagages à main** *nm pl* hand luggage. **bagages non accompagnés** *nm pl* luggage in advance.
bagarre (ba'gar) *nf* brawl, scuffle.
bagatelle (baga'tɛl) *nf* trifle.
bagne (baɲ) *nm* prison.
bagnole (ba'ɲɔl) *nf inf* old car.
bague (bag) *nf* (jewellery) ring.
baguette (ba'gɛt) *nf* **1** rod, stick. **2** wand. **3** long thin loaf of French bread.
bahut (ba'y) *nm* **1** cupboard. **2** *sl* school.
bai (bɛ) *adj* bay.
baie[1] (bɛ) *nf geog* bay.
baie[2] (bɛ) *nf arch* bay. **fenêtre en baie** *nf* bay window.
baie[3] (bɛ) *nf* berry.
baigner (bɛ'ɲe:) *vt* **1** bathe. **2** wash. *vi* soak, steep. **se baigner** *vr* **1** have a bath. **2** bathe. **baigneur, -euse** (bɛ'ɲœr, -'ɲœz) *nm,f* bather. **baignoire.** *nf* bath.
bail (baj) *nm, pl* **baux** lease.
bâiller (bɑ'je:) *vi* **1** yawn. **2** be ajar. **bâillement** *nm* yawn.
bâillon (bɑ'jɔ̃) *nm* gag.
bâillonner (bɑjɔ'ne:) *vt* gag.
bain (bɛ̃) *nm* **1** bath. **2** bathe. **prendre un bain** have a bath.
baïonnette (bajɔ'nɛt) *nf* bayonet.
baiser (bɛ'ze:) *vt* kiss. *nm* kiss.
baisser (bɛ'se:) *vt* **1** lower. **2** bend. *vi* go down, decline. **se baisser** *vr* bend down. **baisse** *nf* **1** fall. **2** decline. **3** ebb.
bal (bal) *nm* ball, dance. **bal travesti** fancy-dress ball.
balader (bala'de:) *vi* saunter. **se balader** *vr* stroll. **se balader en auto** go for a drive.
balafrer (bala'fre:) *vt* gash. **balafre** *nf* **1** gash. **2** scar. **balafré** *adj* scarred.
balai (ba'lɛ) *nm* broom, brush.
balancer (balɑ̃'se:) *vt* **1** balance. **2** swing, rock. *vi* **1** swing. **2** hesitate. **se balancer** *vr* sway, swing. **balance** *nf* **1** balance. **2** pair of scales. **3** *cap* Libra. **4** hesitation. **être en balance** be in suspense. **balancier** *nm* **1** pendulum. **2** beam. **balançoire.** *nf* **1** swing. **2** seesaw.
balayer (balɛ'je:) *vt* sweep.
balbutier (balby'sje:) *vi,vt* stammer, mumble.
balcon (bal'kɔ̃) *nm* **1** balcony. **2** *Th* dress circle.
baldaquin (balda'kɛ̃) *nm* canopy.
baleine (ba'lɛn) *nf* whale.
balise (ba'li:z) *nf* **balise flottante** buoy.
balistique (bali:'sti:k) *adj* ballistic.
baliverne (bali:'vɛrn) *nf* **1** idle story. **2** nonsense.
ballade (ba'lad) *nf* ballad.
balle (bal) *nf* **1** ball. **2** bullet. **3** bale. **à l'épreuve des balles** bullet-proof. **balle de golf** golfball.

ballet (ba'lɛ) *nm* ballet.
ballon (ba'lɔ̃) *nm* **1** balloon. **2** football.
ballotter (balɔ'te:) *vt* toss about, shake. *vi* **1** rattle. **2** toss.
balnéaire (balne:'ɛr) *adj* bathing. **station balnéaire** *nf* seaside resort.
Baltique (bal'ti:k) *adj* Baltic. **(Mer) Baltique** *nf* Baltic (Sea).
balustrade (baly'strad) *nf* handrail.
balustre (ba'lystr) *nm* banister.
bambou (bɑ̃'bu:) *nm* bamboo.
ban (bɑ̃) *nm* **1** ban. **2** proclamation. **3** *pl* banns. **4** banishment.
banal, -aux (ba'nal, -'no) *adj* **1** common, banal. **2** commonplace, trite.
banane (ba'nan) *nm* banana. **bananier** *nm* banana tree.
banc (bɑ̃) *nm* **1** bench. **2** pew. **3** bed. **4** bank. **banc des prévenus** *law* dock. **bancal** *adj* **1** bandy-legged. **2** wobbly.
bandage (bɑ̃'daʒ) *nm* **1** bandage. **2** tyre.
bande[1] (bɑ̃d) *nf* band, strip. **bande magnétique** recording tape. **bande sonore** soundtrack.
bande[2] (bɑ̃d) *nf* party, gang, group.
bander (bɑ̃'de:) *vt* **1** bandage, bind. **2** tighten. **bander les yeux à** blindfold. **bandé** *adj* **1** bandaged. **2** taut.
bandit (bɑ̃'di:) *nm* **1** bandit. **2** ruffian.
banlieue (bɑ̃'ljœ) *nf* **1** suburb. **2** outskirts.
banne (ban) *nf* **1** hamper. **2** awning.
bannière (ba'njɛr) *nf* banner.
bannir (ba'ni:r) *vt* **1** banish, exile. **banni** *adj* banished, outlawed. *nm* exile, outlaw.
banque (bɑ̃k) *nf* **1** bank. **2** banking. **banquier, -ière** (bɑ̃'kje:, -'kjɛr) *adj* banking. *nm* banker.
banqueroute (bɑ̃k'ru:t) *nf* bankruptcy. **faire banqueroute** go bankrupt.
banquet (bɑ̃'kɛ) *nm* banquet, feast.
banquette (bɑ̃'kɛt) *nf* **1** seat. **2** bench.
baptême (ba'tɛm) *nm* baptism, christening.
baptiser (bati:'ze:) *vt* baptize, christen.
bar (bar) *nm* **1** public bar. **2** pub.
baragouiner (baragwi:'ne:) *vi,vt* gabble.
baraque (ba'rak) *nf* **1** hut, shanty. **2** stall, booth.
baratte (ba'rat) *nf* churn.
barbare (bar'bar) *adj* **1** barbaric. **2** barbarous, cruel. *nm,f* barbarian. **barbarie** *nf* barbarity.
barbe (barb) *nf* **1** beard. **2** whiskers (of an animal). **quelle barbe!** what a nuisance! **se faire la barbe** shave. **barbu** *adj* bearded.
barbecue (barbə'kju:) *nm* barbecue.
barbier (bar'bje:) *nm* barber.
barbiturate (barbity'rat) *nm* barbiturate.
barboter (barbɔ'te:) *vi* **1** paddle. **2** bubble. **3** *inf* get confused. *vt sl* steal.
barbouiller (barbu:'je:) *vt* **1** smear. **2** blot. **3** scribble.
barème (ba'rɛm) *nm* scale, schedule.
bariolé (barjɔ'le:) *adj* gaudy.
baromètre (barɔ'mɛtr) *nm* barometer.
baron (ba'rɔ̃) *nm* baron.
baronnet (barɔ'nɛ) *nm* baronet.
baroque (ba'rɔk) *adj* odd, quaint.
barque (bark) *nf* boat.
barrage (ba'raʒ) *nm* **1** obstruction. **2** dam.
barrer (bɑ're:) *vt* **1** fasten with bars. **2** bar, obstruct. **3** *naut* steer. **4** cross. **5** cross out. **barre** *nf* **1** bar, rod. **2** tiller, helm. **3** stroke. **barreau, -aux 1** small wooden or metal bar. **2** prison bar. **3** *law* bar. **barrière** *nf* **1** barrier. **2** tollgate.
barricade (bari:'kad) *nf* barricade.
baryton (bari:'tɔ̃) *adj,nm* baritone.
bas, basse (bɑ, bɑs) *adj* **1** low. **2** deep. **3** mean, base. **bas** *adv* **1** low. **2** quietly. *nm* **1** bottom, lower part. **2** stocking. **à bas** down. **en bas 1** below. **2** downstairs. **en bas de** at the foot of. **mettre bas** lay down. **basse** *nf mus* bass. **basse-cour** *nf* farmyard.
basculer (basky'le:) *vi,vt* **1** rock. **2** tip. **bascule** *nf* seesaw.
base-ball (bas'bal) *nm* baseball.
baser (bɑ'ze:) *vt* **1** base. **2** ground. **se baser** *vr* **1** be founded. **2** rely. **base** *nf* **1** base. **2** basis.
basilic (bazi:'li:k) *nm* basil.
basket-ball (baskɛt'bal) *nm also* **basket** basketball.
bassin (ba'sɛ̃) *nm* **1** basin. **2** dock. **3** ornamental pond. **4** *anat* pelvis.
basson (bɑ'sɔ̃) *nm* bassoon.
bastille (ba'sti:j) *nf* small fortress.
bataclan (bata'klɑ̃) *nm inf* belongings.
bataille (ba'tɑj) *nf* battle. **bataillon** *nm* battalion.
bâtard (bɑ'tar) *adj,n* bastard.
bateau, -aux (ba'to) *nm* boat. **bateau à vapeur** steamship. **bateau à voiles** sailing boat. **bateau de sauvetage** lifeboat.
bâtir[1] (bɑ'ti:r) *vt* build, construct. **bâti** *nm* frame. **bien bâti** well-built. **bâtiment** *nm* **1** building, construction. **2** building trade. **3** ship. **bâtisse** *nf* ramshackle building.
bâtir[2] (bɑ'ti:r) *vt* (sewing) tack.

bâton (bɑ'tɔ̃) *nm* stick. **à bâtons rompus** by fits and starts.

batterie (ba'tri:) *nf* **1** fight. **2** *mil* battery. **3** set. **4** drums.

battre* (batr) *vt* **1** beat, thrash. **2** shuffle. *vi* beat. **se battre** *vr* fight. **battant** *adj* **1** beating. **2** pelting. **à dix heures battant** on the stroke of ten. **tout battant neuf** brand-new. ~*nm* **1** leaf (of a table). **2** clapper (of a bell). **battement** *nm* **1** banging. **2** throbbing. **3** interval. **battement de paupières** blink.

battu (ba'ty) *v* see **battre.**

bavard (ba'var) *adj* talkative.

bavarder (bavar'de:) *vi* **1** chatter. **2** gossip. **bavardage** *nm* chatter.

baver (ba've:) *vi* dribble. **bave** *nf* dribble. **bavette** *nf* bib.

béant (be:'ɑ̃) *adj* open, gaping.

béat (be:'a) *adj* complacent, smug.

beau, bel, belle, beaux, belles (bo, bɛl, bɛl, bo, bɛl) *adj* **1** beautiful, handsome, good-looking. **2** fine. **au beau milieu** right in the middle. **bel et bien** well and truly. **beauté** *nf* beauty.

beaucoup (bo'ku:) *adv* **1** much. **2** many. **3** a great deal, a lot. **de beaucoup** by far.

beau-fils *nm, pl* **beaux-fils** **1** son-in-law. **2** stepson.

beau-frère *nm, pl* **beaux-frères** brother-in-law.

beau-père *nm, pl* **beaux-pères** **1** father-in-law. **2** stepfather.

beaux-arts *nm pl* fine arts.

bébé (be:'be:) *nm* baby.

bec (bɛk) *nm* **1** beak. **2** spout. **3** mouthpiece. **bec de plume** pen nib. **prise de bec** *nf* argument, row.

bécane (bɛ'kan) *nf inf* bicycle.

bécasse (bɛ'kas) *nf* woodcock. **bécassine** *nf* snipe.

bêcher (bɛ'ʃe:) *vt* dig. **bêche** *nf* spade.

becqueter (bɛk'te:) *vt* **1** peck at. **2** *inf* kiss.

bedaine (bə'dɛn) *nf* paunch.

bée (be:) *adj* **bouche bée** open-mouthed.

beffroi (bɛ'frwa) *nm* belfry.

bégayer (be:gɛ'je:) *vi* stutter, stammer.

bégueule (be:'gœl) *nf* prude.

béguin (be:'gɛ̃) *nm* hood. **avoir un béguin pour** have a fancy for.

beige (bɛʒ) *adj* **1** beige. **2** natural coloured. *nf* beige.

beignet (bɛ'ɲɛ) *nm* **1** fritter. **2** doughnut.

bel (bɛl) *adj* see **beau.**

bêler (bɛ'le:) *vi* bleat.

belette (bə'lɛt) *nf* weasel.

Belgique (bɛl'ʒi:k) *nf* Belgium. **belge** *adj,n* Belgian.

bélier (be:'lje:) *nm* **1** ram. **2** *cap* Aries.

belle (bɛl) *adj* see **beau.**

belle-fille *nf, pl* **belles-filles** **1** daugher-in-law. **2** stepdaughter.

belle-mère *nf, pl* **belles-mères** **1** mother-in-law. **2** stepmother.

belle-sœur *nf, pl* **belles-sœurs** sister-in-law.

bémol (be:'mɔl) *nm mus* flat.

bénédicité (be:ne:di:si:'te:) *nm* grace (before meals). **bénédiction** *nf* blessing.

bénéficier (be:ne:fi:'sje:) *vi* **1** benefit. **2** make a profit. **bénéfice** *nm* **1** profit. **2** benefit.

bénévole (be:ne:'vɔl) *adj* **1** benevolent, kind. **2** voluntary.

benin, -igne (be'nɛ̃, -'ni:ɲ) *adj* **1** kindly. **2** mild, gentle.

bénir (be:'ni:r) *vt* **1** bless. **2** consecrate. **bénit** *adj* consecrated, holy.

béquille (be:'ki:j) *nf* crutch.

bercer (bɛr'se:) *vt* **1** rock. **2** lull. **se bercer** *vr* delude oneself. **berceau, -aux** *nm* cradle. **berceuse** *nf* lullaby.

berger, -ère (bɛr'ʒe:, -'ʒɛr) *n* shepherd, shepherdess.

besogne (bə'zɔɲ) *nf* **1** work. **2** task. **besogneux, -euse** (bəzɔ'ɲœ, -'ɲœz) *adj* needy, poor.

besoin (bə'zwɛ̃) *nm* **1** want, need. **2** necessity. **au besoin** if necessary. **avoir besoin de** need.

bétail (be:'taj) *nm, pl* **bestiaux** (bɛ'stjo) **1** cattle. **2** livestock.

bête (bɛt) *nf* **1** beast, animal. **2** fool. *adj* stupid. **bête à bon Dieu** ladybird. **bête noire** pet aversion. **bêtise** (be:'ti:z) *nf* **1** stupidity. **2** stupid remark. **3** trifle. **4** blunder. **5** *pl* nonsense.

béton (be:'tɔ̃) *nm* concrete.

betterave (bɛ'trav) *nf* beet. **betterave rouge** beetroot. **betterave sucré** sugarbeet.

beugler (bœ'gle:) *vi* **1** low. **2** bellow. *vt* bellow.

beurre (bœr) *nm* butter.

bévue (be:'vy) *nf* blunder.

biais (bjɛ) *adj* **1** sloping. **2** askew. **3** oblique. *nm* **1** slant. **2** bias. **3** expedient. **de biais** sideways. **en biais.** on the slant.

bibelot (bi:'blo) *nm* knick-knack.

biberon (bi:'brɔ̃) *nm* feeding bottle.

Bible (bi:bl) *nf* Bible. **biblique** *adj* biblical.

bibliographie (bi:bli:ɔgra'fi:) *nf* bibliography. **bibliographique** *adj* bibliographical.
bibliothécaire (bi:bli:ɔte:'kɛr) *nm,f* librarian.
bibliothèque (bi:bli:ɔ'tɛk) *nf* **1** library. **2** bookcase.
biceps (bi:'sɛps) *adj,nm* biceps.
biche (bi:ʃ) *nf* **1** *zool* hind. **2** *inf* darling.
bicyclette (bi:si:'klɛt) *nf* bicycle.
bidon (bi:'dɔ̃) *nm* can, drum.
bien (bjɛ̃) *adv* **1** well. **2** properly. **3** good. **4** very. **5** many. **6** quite. **eh bien!** well then! **bien que** although. ~*nm* **1** good. **2** property. **3** *pl* belongings.
bien-aimé *adj* or *n, pl* **bien-aimés** darling.
bien-être *nm* well-being.
bienfaisant (bjɛ̃fɛ'zɑ̃) *adj* charitable, kind.
bienheureux, -euse (bjɛ̃nœ'rœ, -'rœz) *adj* **1** happy. **2** fortunate.
biennal, -aux (bi:ɛ'nal, -'no) *adj* biennial.
bienséance (bjɛ̃se:'ɑ̃s) *nf* propriety. **bienséant** *adj* proper, seemly.
bientôt (bjɛ̃'to) *adv* soon, before long. **à bientôt!** so long!
bienveillance (bjɛ̃vɛ'jɑ̃s) *nf* goodwill. **bienveillant** *adj* kind, benevolent.
bienvenu (bjɛ̃və'ny) *adj* welcome. **bienvenue** *nf* welcome.
bière[1] (bjɛr) *nf* beer. **bière à la pression** draught beer. **bière blonde 1** pale ale. **2** lager.
bière[2] (bjɛr) *nf* coffin.
biffer (bi:'fe:) *vt* delete.
bifteck (bi:f'tɛk) *nm* steak.
bifurcation (bi:fyrka'sjɔ̃) *nf* fork (in a road).
bigamie (bi:ga'mi:) *nf* bigamy.
bigorneau, -aux (bi:gɔr'no) *nm* winkle.
bigot (bi:'go) *adj* **1** devout. **2** bigoted.
bijou, -oux (bi:'ʒu:) *nm* **1** jewel. **2** *inf* darling. **bijouterie** *nf* **1** jewellery. **2** jeweller's shop. **bijoutier** *nm* jeweller.
bikini (bi:ki:'ni:) *nm* bikini.
bilan (bi:'læ) *nm comm* balance sheet.
bile (bi:l) *nf* **1** bile. **2** anger. **se faire de la bile** fret.
bilingue (bi'lɛ̃g) *adj* bilingual.
billard (bi:'jar) *nm* billiards.
bille (bi:j) *nf* **1** marble. **2** billiard ball.
billet (bi'jɛ) *nm* **1** note. **2** ticket. **billet d'aller et retour** return ticket. **billet de banque** banknote. **billet de faveur** free ticket. **billet simple** single ticket.
billot (bi:'jo) *nm* block (of wood).
binaire (bi:'nɛr) *adj* binary.
biner (bi:'ne:) *vt* hoe. **binette** *nf* hoe.
biographie (bi:ɔgra'fi:) *nf* biography. **biographique** *adj* biographical.
biologie (bi:ɔlɔ'ʒi:) *nf* biology. **biologique** *adj* biological.
bis (bi:s) *adv* **1** twice. **2** repeat. *interj* encore!
bisannuel, -elle (bi:za'nɥɛl) *adj* biennial.
biscornu (bi:skɔr'ny) *adj* **1** irregular. **2** *inf* odd, queer.
biscotte (bi:'skɔt) *nf* French toast, rusk.
biscuit (bi:'skɥi:) *nm* biscuit.
bise[1] (bi:z) *nf* north wind.
bise[2] (bi:z) *nf inf* kiss.
bisque (bi:sk) *nf* shellfish soup.
bissextile (bi:sɛk'sti:l) **année bissextile** *nf* leap year.
bistro (bi:'stro) *nm also* **bistrot 1** French cafe. **2** pub.
bizarre (bi:'zar) *adj* **1** peculiar. **2** strange.
blafard (bla'far) *adj* **1** dim. **2** pale.
blaguer (bla'ge:) *vi* **1** tell lies. **2** tease. **blague** *nf* **1** hoax. **2** joke. **sans blaque?** really?
blaireau, -aux (blɛ'ro) *nm* **1** badger. **2** shaving brush.
blâmer (blɑ'me:) *vt* blame. **blâme** *nm* blame.
blanc, blanche (blɑ̃, blɑ̃ʃ) *adj* **1** white. **2** clean. **3** pale. **4** blank. *nm* white. *nf mus* minim. **blancheur** *nf* whiteness.
blanchir (blɑ̃'ʃi:r) *vt* **1** whiten. **2** bleach. **3** wash. **4** whitewash. *vi* turn white. **blanchissage** *nm* washing. **blanchisserie** *nf* laundry.
blanquette (blɑ̃'kɛt) *nf* veal stew.
blaser (blɑ'ze:) *vt* **1** blunt. **2** surfeit. **se blaser** *vr* become indifferent.
blason (blɑ'zɔ̃) *nm* **1** coat of arms. **2** heraldry.
blasphémer (blasfe:'me:) *vi,vt* blaspheme.
blatte (blat) *nf* cockroach.
blé (ble:) *nm* **1** corn. **2** wheat.
blêmir (ble:'mi:r) *vi* turn pale. **blême** (blɛm) *adj* very pale.
blesser (blɛ'se:) *vt* **1** wound. **2** injure. **3** hurt. **blessé** *adj* wounded. *nm* casualty. **blessure** *nf* **1** wound. **2** injury.
blet, blette (blɛ, blɛt) *adj* (of fruit) soft, over-ripe.
bleu (blœ) *adj* blue. *nm* **1** blue. **2** bruise. **3** novice. **bleu clair/foncé** light/dark blue. **bleuet** *nm also* **bluet** cornflower.
blindé (blɛ̃'de:) *adj* armour-plated.
bloc (blɔk) *nm* **1** block. **2** lump. **3** *pol* coalition. **à bloc** thoroughly. **en bloc** in one piece.
blocus (blɔ'kys) *nm* blockade.
blond (blɔ̃) *adj* **1** fair, blond. **2** light.

blondir (blɔ̃'di:r) *vi* turn yellow. *vt* bleach.

bloquer (blɔ'ke:) *vt* **1** block up. **2** obstruct. **3** jam.

se blottir (blɔ'ti:r) *vr* **1** squat, crouch. **2** nestle.

blouse (blu:z) *nf* **1** blouse. **2** overall.

bluff (blœf, blyf) *nm* bluff.

bobine (bɔ'bi:n) *nf* **1** reel, spool. **2** coil.

bocage (bɔ'kaʒ) *nm* grove.

bock (bɔk) *nm* glass of beer.

bœuf (bœf) *nm* **1** bullock. **2** beef.

bohème (bɔ'ɛm) *adj* unconventional, bohemian. *nf* group of artists.

boire* (bwar) *vt* **1** drink. **2** absorb. **boire à petits coups** sip.

bois (bwɑ) *nm* **1** wood, woodland. **2** timber, wood. **3** *pl* antlers. **4** woodwind instruments. **bois contre-plaqué** plywood. **de** or **en bois** wooden. **boiserie** (bwɑz'ri:) *nf* woodwork.

boisson (bwa'sɔ̃) *nf* drink, beverage.

boîte (bwat) *nf* **1** box. **2** tin. **3** *inf* nightclub, discotheque. **boîte aux lettres** letter-box. **boîte d'allumettes** matchbox. **boîte de vitesses** gearbox.

boiter (bwa'te:) *vi* **1** limp. **2** be lame. **boiteux, -euse** (bwa'tœ, -'tœz) *adj* lame. *nm,f* cripple.

bol (bɔl) *nm* bowl, basin.

bombarder (bɔ̃bar'de:) *vt* **1** bombard. **2** bomb. **bombardier** *nm aviat* bomber.

bombe (bɔ̃b) *nf* bomb. **bombe atomique** atom bomb.

bomber (bɔ̃'be:) *vt* **1** stick out. **2** arch. *vi* bulge. **bombé** *adj* bulging.

bon, bonne (bɔ̃, bɔn) *adj* **1** good. **2** kind. **3** right. **4** nice. *nm* **1** good. **2** voucher. **3** *comm* bond. **à quoi bon?** what's the use? **pour de bon** for good. ~*interj* right!

bonasse (bɔ'nas) *adj* **1** simple. **2** silly.

bonbon (bɔ̃'bɔ̃) *nm* sweet.

bond (bɔ̃) *nm* **1** leap, jump. **2** bounce.

bondé (bɔ̃'de:) *adj* packed, crowded.

bondir (bɔ̃'di:r) *vi* **1** jump, leap. **2** bounce.

bonheur (bɔ'nœr) *nm* **1** happiness. **2** good fortune. **au petit bonheur** in a haphazard way. **par bonheur** fortunately.

bonhomie (bɔnɔ'mi:) *nf* good nature.

bonhomme (bɔ'nɔm) *nm* **1** good-humoured man. **2** old man.

boni (bɔ'ni:) *nm* **1** surplus. **2** profit.

bonjour (bɔ̃'ʒu:r) *interj, nm* good morning, good afternoon.

bonne (bɔn) *nf* housemaid.

bonne-maman *nf, pl* **bonnes-mamans** granny.

bonnet (bɔ'nɛ) *nm* **1** cap. **2** bonnet. **c'est bonnet blanc et blanc bonnet** it's six of one and half a dozen of the other. **gros bonnet** *inf* bigwig. **bonneterie** *nf* hosiery. **bonnetier** *nm* hosier.

bon-papa *nm, pl* **bons-papas** grandad.

bonsoir (bɔ̃'swar) *interj, nm* good evening.

bonté (bɔ̃'te:) *nf* **1** kindness. **2** goodness.

bord (bɔr) *nm* **1** edge. **2** rim. **3** hem. **4** bank. **5** side. **à bord** on board, aboard. **au bord de la mer** at the seaside. **bordure** *nf* **1** border. **2** edging. **3** kerb.

bordeaux (bɔr'do) *nm* **1** Bordeaux wine. **2** *cap* Bordeaux. **bordeaux rouge** *nm* claret.

bordel (bɔr'dɛl) *nm* brothel.

border (bɔr'de:) *vt* **1** line. **2** edge, skirt.

bordereau, -aux (bɔrdə'ro) *nm* **1** memorandum. **2** account, statement.

borgne (bɔrɲ) *adj* **1** blind in one eye **2** (of a cafe, hotel, etc.) disreputable.

borner (bɔr'ne:) *vt* **1** mark out the boundary. **2** limit. **borne** *nf* boundary, limit. **borne milliaire** milestone. **borné** *adj* **1** limited. **2** narrow-minded.

bosquet (bɔ'skɛ) *nm* grove.

bosse (bɔs) *nf* **1** bump. **2** hump. **avoir la bosse de** have a gift for.

bosseler (bɔs'le:) *vt* **1** emboss. **2** dent. **bosselure** *nf* dent.

bossu (bɔ'sy) *adj* hunchbacked. *nm* hunchback.

bot (bo) **pied bot** *nm* **1** club foot. **2** club-footed person.

botanique (bɔta'ni:k) *nf* botany. *adj* botanical.

botte[1] (bɔt) *nf* bunch.

botte[2] (bɔt) *nf* high boot. **bottier** *nm* shoemaker.

botte[3] (bɔt) *nf* (fencing) thrust.

botteler (bɔt'le:) *vt* put in bunches.

botter (bɔ'te:) *vt* **1** put boots on. **2** kick.

Bottin (bɔ'tɛ̃) *nm Tdmk* French street and trade directory.

bouc (bu:k) *nm* billy-goat. **bouc émissaire** scapegoat.

boucaner (bu:ka'ne:) *vt cul* cure.

bouche (bu:ʃ) *nf* **1** mouth. **2** opening. **bouchée** *nf* mouthful.

boucher[1] (bu:'ʃe:) *vt* **1** stop or fill up. **2** cork.

boucher[2] (bu:'ʃe:) *nm* butcher. **boucherie** *nf* butcher's shop.

bouchon (bu:'ʃɔ̃) *nm* **1** cork, stopper. **2** wisp (of straw).

boucler (bu:'kle:) *vt* **1** buckle, fasten. **2** curl. *vi* be curly. **boucle** *nf* **1** buckle **2** loop. **3** ring. **4**

curl. **boucle d'oreille** earring. **bouclier** *nm* shield.

bouddhisme (bu:'di:sm) *nm* Buddhism. **bouddhiste** *adj,n* Buddhist.

bouder (bu:'de:) *vi* sulk. **boudeur, -euse** (bu:'dœr, -'dœz) *adj* sulky.

boudin (bu:'dɛ̃) *nm* black pudding.

boue (bu:) *nf* **1** mud. **2** filth, dirt. **boueur** *nm* **1** dustman. **2** roadsweeper. **boueux, -euse** (bu:'œ, -'œz) *adj* muddy.

bouée (bu:'e:) *nf* buoy. **bouée de sauvetage** lifebuoy.

bouffer (bu:'fe:) *vi,vt* **1** puff out. **2** eat greedily. **bouffant** *adj* **1** puffed. **2** baggy. **bouffée** *nf* **1** puff. **2** gust. **3** whiff.

bouffir (bu:'fi:r) *vi,vt* swell. **bouffissure** *nf* swelling.

bouffon, -onne (bu:'fɔ̃, -'fɔn) *adj* comical. *nm,f* clown, fool.

bouger (bu:'ʒe:) *vi* move, stir. *vt* move.

bougie (bu:'ʒi:) *nf* candle. **bougeoir** *nm* candlestick.

bouillabaisse (bu:ja'bɛs) *nf* Provençal fish stew.

bouillir* (bu:'ji:r) *vi* boil. **bouillant** *adj* **1** boiling. **2** hot-tempered. **bouilloire** *nf* kettle.

bouillon *nm* **1** bubble. **2** soup. **3** stock.

bouillonner (bu:jɔ'ne:) *vi* **1** bubble. **2** seethe.

bouillotte (bu:'jɔt) *nf* hot-water bottle.

boulangerie (bu:lɑ̃ʒ'ri:) *nf* **1** bakery. **2** baking. **boulanger** *nm* baker.

boule (bu:l) *nf* **1** ball. **2** bulb. **3** *sl* face. **partie de boules** *nf* game of bowls.

bouleau, -aux (bu:'lo) *nm* birch tree.

bouledogue (bu:l'dɔg) *nm* bulldog.

boulevard (bu:l'var) *nm* avenue.

bouleverser (bu:lvɛr'se:) *vt* **1** overturn. **2** upset. **3** astound. **bouleversement** *nm* **1** overturning. **2** confusion, upheaval.

boulon (bu:'lɔ̃) *nm* bolt.

boulot[1]**, -otte** (bu:'lo, -'lot) *adj* chubby, plump. *nm inf* food.

boulot[2] (bu:'lo) *nm inf* job, work.

boulotter (bu:lɔ'te:) *vi* jog along. *vt inf* eat.

bouquet (bu:'kɛ) *nm* **1** bunch. **2** clump. **3** aroma.

bouquin (bu:'kɛ̃) *nm* **1** old book. **2** *inf* book. **bouquiniste** *nm* second-hand bookseller.

bourbe (bu:rb) *nf* mud.

bourdon (bu:r'dɔ̃) *nm* **1** *mus* drone. **2** bumble bee.

bourdonner (bu:rdɔ'ne:) *vi* **1** buzz. **2** hum. **bourdonnement** *nm* buzz.

bourg (bu:r) *nm* **1** market town. **2** borough.

bourgeois (bu:r'ʒwa) *adj* **1** middle-class. **2** plain. **3** common. *nm* citizen. **bourgeoisie** *nf* middle class.

bourgeon (bu:r'ʒɔ̃) *nm* bud.

bourgeonner (bu:rʒɔ'ne:) *vi* come into bud.

Bourgogne (bu:r'gɔɲ) *nf* Burgundy. **(vin de) Bourgogne** *nm* Burgundy wine.

bourrade (bu:'rad) *nf* blow, thump.

bourrage (bu:'raʒ) *nm* padding, stuffing.

bourrasque (bu:'rask) *nf* gust of wind.

bourreau, -aux (bu:'ro) *nm* **1** executioner. **2** torturer.

bourrelet (bu:r'lɛ) *nm* **1** pad. **2** fold, swelling.

bourrer (bu:'re:) *vt* **1** stuff. **2** cram.

bourriche (bu:'ri:ʃ) *nf* hamper.

bourru (bu:'ry) *adj* **1** surly. **2** gruff.

bourse (bu:rs) *nf* **1** purse. **2** scholarship. **3** *cap* Stock Exchange.

boursoufler (bu:rsu:'fle:) *vt* **1** swell. **2** blister. **boursouflure** *nf* swelling.

bousculer (bu:sky'le:) *vt* **1** jostle. **2** upset, knock over. **bousculade** *nf* scuffle.

bousiller (bu:zi:'je:) *vt* **1** hurry through. **2** *inf* smash.

boussole (bu:'sɔl) *nf* compass.

bout (bu:) *nm* **1** end. **2** tip. **3** bit. **à bout de forces** exhausted. **à bout portant** pointblank. **au bout de 1** at the end of. **2** after. **au bout du compte** after all. **de bout en bout** through and through. **venir à bout 1** manage. **2** overcome. **boutade** *nf* **1** whim. **2** outburst. **3** flash of wit.

bouteille (bu:'tɛj) *nf* bottle. **bouteille Thermos** *Tdmk* Thermos flask.

boutique (bu:'ti:k) *nf* shop. **boutiquier, -ière** (bu:ti:'kje:, -'kjɛr) *n* shopkeeper.

bouton (bu:'tɔ̃) *nm* **1** button. **2** bud. **3** handle. **4** spot, pimple. **bouton à pression** press-stud. **bouton de col** stud. **bouton d'or** buttercup. **boutons de manchettes** cufflinks. **boutonnière** *nf* buttonhole.

boutonner (bu:tɔ'ne:) *vt* button.

bouvier (bu:'vje:) *nm* cowhand.

boxer (bɔk'se:) *vi,vt sport* box. **boxe** *nf* boxing.

boyau, -aux (bwa'jo) *nm* **1** bowel, guts. **2** passage, trench.

boycotter (bɔjkɔ'te:) *vt* boycott.

bracelet (bra'slɛ) *nm* **1** bracelet, bangle. **2** (watch) strap.

braconner (brakɔ'ne:) *vi,vt* poach. **braconnier** *nm* poacher.

braguette (bra'gɛt) *nf* fly (of trousers).

braille (braj) *nm* braille.
brailler (bra'je:) *vi* bawl, shout.
braire (brɛr) *vi* bray.
braise (brɛz) *nf* embers.
braiser (brɛ'ze:) *vt* braise.
brancard (brɑ̃'kar) *nm* **1** stretcher. **2** shaft.
brancher (brɑ̃'ʃe:) *vi* perch. *vt tech* connect, plug in. **branche** *nf* **1** branch. **2** division.
brandir (brɑ̃'di:r) *vt* flourish, wave.
branler (brɑ̃'le:) *vi,vt* **1** shake. **2** move. **branle** *nm* motion.
braquer (bra'ke:) *vt* aim, point.
bras (bra) *nm* **1** arm. **2** handle. **3** *pl* labour. **bras dessus bras dessous** arm in arm.
brasier (bra'zje:) *nm* fire, blaze.
brasse (bras) *nf* **1** *naut* fathom. **2** stroke. **3** breaststroke.
brassée (bra'se:) *nf* armful.
brasser (bra'se:) *vt* **1** brew, mash. **2** stir. *nf* **1** brewery. **2** restaurant, café.
braver (bra've:) *vt* brave, face. **brave** *adj* **1** brave. **2** honest. **3** good. **bravoure** *nf* bravery, courage.
brebis (brə'bi:) *nf* **1** ewe. **2** sheep.
brèche (brɛʃ) *nf* **1** breach. **2** gap.
bredouiller (brədu:'je:) *vt,vi* mumble, stammer.
bref, brève (brɛf, brɛv) *adj* brief, short. **bref** *adv* briefly. **en bref** in short.
breloque (brə'lɔk) *nf* charm, trinket.
Bretagne (brə'taɲ) *nf* Brittany. **breton, -onne** (brə'tɔ, -'tɔn) *adj,n* Breton.
bretelle (brə'tɛl) *nf* **1** strap. **2** *pl* braces.
breuvage (brœ'vaʒ) *nm* drink, beverage.
brevet (brə'vɛ) *nm* **1** patent. **2** certificate.
breveter (brəv'te:) *vt* **1** grant a patent to. **2** patent.
bribes (bri:b) *nf pl* scraps, fragments.
bricoler (bri:kɔ'le:) *vi* do odd jobs, tinker about. *vt* arrange.
brider (bri:'de:) *vt* **1** bridle. **2** check. **3** fasten. **bride** *nf* **1** bridle. **2** rein. **3** strap. **à bride abattue** at full speed.
bridge (bri:dʒ) *nm game* bridge.
brièvement (brjɛv'mɑ̃) *adv* briefly.
brigade (bri:'gad) *nf* **1** brigade. **2** gang.
brigand (bri:'gɑ̃) *nm* **1** robber. **2** rascal.
brigue (bri:g) *nf* intrigue.
briller (bri:'je:) *vi* shine, sparkle. **brillamment** *adv* brilliantly. **brillant** *adj* **1** brilliant. **2** shining. *nm* **1** brilliance. **2** shine.
brin (brɛ̃) *nm* **1** blade. **2** sprig. **3** strand. **brindille** *nf* **1** twig. **2** sprig.
brioche (bri:'ɔʃ) *nf cul* bun.
brique (bri:k) *nf* brick. **briquet** *nm* cigarette lighter.
brise (bri:z) *nf* breeze.
briser (bri:'ze:) *vt* break, smash.
britannique (bri:ta'ni:k) *adj* British.
broc (brɔ) *nm* jug.
brocanter (brɔkɑ̃'te:) *vi* deal in second-hand goods. *vi* **1** barter. **2** sell. **brocanteur** *nm* second-hand dealer.
broche (brɔʃ) *nf* **1** *cul* spit. **2** peg. **3** brooch.
broché (brɔ'ʃe:) *adj* stitched. **livre broché** *nm* hardback book.
brochet (brɔ'ʃɛ) *nm zool* pike.
brochette (brɔ'ʃɛt) *nf* **1** skewer. **2** kebab.
brochure (brɔ'ʃyr) *nf* brochure, leaflet.
brocoli (brɔkɔ'li:) *nm* broccoli.
broder (brɔ'de:) *vt* **1** embroider. **2** embellish. **broderie** *nf* **1** embroidery. **2** embellishment.
broncher (brɔ̃'ʃe:) *vt* **1** stumble. **2** shy. **3** falter.
bronchite (brɔ̃'ʃi:t) *nf* bronchitis.
bronzer (brɔ̃'ze:) *vt* **1** bronze. **2** tan. **bronze** *nm* bronze.
brosser (brɔ'se:) *vt* brush. **brosse** *nf* brush. **brosse à cheveux/dents/habits** hairbrush/toothbrush/clothes brush. **brosse dure** *nf* scrubbing brush.
brouette (bru:'ɛt) *nf* wheelbarrow.
brouhaha (bru:a'a) *nm* uproar, din.
brouillard (bru:'jar) *nm* fog, mist.
brouiller (bru:'je:) *vt* **1** mix up. **2** confuse. **se brouiller** *vr* **1** get confused. **2** quarrel, fall out. **brouille** *nf* quarrel.
brouillon (bru:'jɔ̃) *nm* rough copy.
broussaille (bru:'saj) *nf* undergrowth.
brouter (bru:'te:) *vt* graze.
broyer (brwa'je:) *vt* **1** pound. **2** pulverize.
bru (bry) *nf* daughter-in-law.
bruiner (brɥi:'ne:) *v imp* drizzle.
bruire (brɥi:r) *vi* rustle.
bruit (brɥi:) *nm* **1** noise, din. **2** rumour. **3** fuss.
brûler (bry'le:) *vi* **1** be on fire, burn. **2** be eager. *vt* **1** burn. **2** scorch. **brûlure** *nf* **1** burn. **2** scald.
brume (brym) *nf* mist, fog. **brumeux, -euse** (bry'mœ, -'mœz) *adj* foggy.
brun (brœ) *adj* **1** brown. **2** dark. *nm* brown. **brune** *nf* dusk.
brunir (bry'ni:r) *vi* become dark. *vt* brown, darken, tan.
brusque (brysk) *adj* **1** abrupt, brusque. **2** sudden. **3** sharp.
brut (bryt) *adj* **1** raw. **2** rough. **3** *comm* gross. **brute** *nf* brute, beast.

brutal, -aux (bry'tal, -'to) *adj* 1 brutal. 2 coarse. 3 rough. 4 blunt. **brutalité** *nf* brutality.
brutaliser (brytali:'ze:) *vt* 1 ill-treat. 2 bully.
Bruxelles (bry'sɛl) *nf* Brussels.
bruyant (bry'jɑ̃) *adj* noisy.
bruyère (bry'jɛr) *nf* 1 heather. 2 heath.
bu (by) *v* see **boire.**
bucarde (by'kard) *nf* cockle.
buccin (byk'sɛ̃) *nm* whelk.
bûche (byʃ) *nf* 1 log. 2 idiot.
bûcher[1] (by'ʃe:) *nm* 1 woodshed. 2 stake. **bûcheron** *nm* lumberjack.
bûcher[2] (by'ʃe:) *vi,vt inf* work hard, swot.
budget (by'dʒɛ) *nm* budget.
buée (bɥe:) *nf* steam, vapour.
buffet (by'fɛ) *nm* 1 sideboard. 2 refreshment room. **buffet de cuisine** dresser.
buffle (byfl) *nm* buffalo.
buisson (bɥi:'sɔ̃) *nm* 1 bush. 2 thicket. **faire l'école buissonnière** play truant.
bulbe (bylb) *nf bot* bulb.
Bulgarie (bylga'ri:) *nf* Bulgaria. **bulgare** *adj,n* Bulgarian.
bulle (byl) *nf* bubble.
bulletin (byl'tɛ̃) *nm* 1 bulletin. 2 report. 3 ticket. **bulletin de vote** voting paper. **bulletin météorologique** weather forecast.
bungalow (bɛ̃ga'lo) *nm* bungalow.
bureau, -aux (by'ro) *nm* 1 desk. 2 office. 3 board, committee. **bureau de poste** post office.
bureaucratie (byrokra'si:) *nf* 1 bureaucracy. 2 *inf* red tape. **bureaucrate** (byro'krat) *nm* bureaucrat.
buriner (byri:'ne:) *vt* engrave.
burlesque (byr'lɛsk) *adj* comical, ludicrous.
buste (byst) *nm* bust.
but (byt) *nm* 1 aim. 2 purpose. 3 target. 4 goal.
buter (by'te:) *vi* 1 knock. 2 strike. 3 stumble. **se buter** *vr* 1 prop oneself up. 2 be set on.
butin (by'tɛ̃) *nm* plunder, loot.
butoir (by'twar) *nm* buffer.
butte (byt) *nf* mound. **être en butte à** be exposed to.
buvant (by'vɑ̃) *v* see **boire.**
buvard (by'var) *adj* **papier buvard** *nm* blotting paper.
buvette (by'vɛt) *nf* refreshment bar.
buveur (by'vœr) *nm* drinker.
byzantin (bi:zɑ̃'tɛ̃) *adj* Byzantine.

C

c' *pron* see **ce**[1].
ça (sa) *pron inf* contraction of **cela.**
çà (sa) *adv* here. **çà et là** here and there.
cabale (ka'bal) *nf* intrigue, plot.
cabane (ka'ban) *nf* hut.
cabaret (kaba'rɛ) *nm* 1 public house. 2 restaurant. 3 cabaret.
cabillaud (kabi:'jo) *nm* fresh cod.
cabine (ka'bi:n) *nf* 1 cabin. 2 callbox. 3 cab (of a lorry). **cabine d'essayage** cubicle, fitting room. **cabinet** *nm* 1 closet. 2 office. 3 collection. 4 *pol* cabinet. 5 lavatory. **cabinet de toilette** dressing-room. **cabinet de travail** study.
câbler (kɑ'ble:) *vt* 1 cable. 2 wire up. **câble** *nm* cable, rope. **câblogramme** *nm* cable.
cabosser (kabɔ'se:) *vt* 1 bump. 2 dent.
se cabrer (kɑ'bre:) *vr* 1 rear. 2 revolt against.
cabriole (kabri:'ɔl) *nf* 1 leap. 2 somersault.
cacahouette (kaka'wɛt) *nf also* **cacahuète** peanut.
cacao (kaka'o) *nm* cocoa.
cachemire (kaʃ'mi:r) *nm* cashmere.
cacher (ka'ʃe:) *vt* hide, conceal. **se cacher de** *vr* hide from. **cache-cache** *nm* hide-and-seek. **cache-nez** *nm invar* scarf.
cachet (ka'ʃɛ) *nm* 1 seal. 2 stamp. 3 mark. 4 style.
cacheter (kaʃ'te:) *vt* seal.
cachette (ka'ʃɛt) *nf* hiding place. **en cachette** on the quiet.
cachot (ka'ʃo) *nm* dungeon.
cactus (kak'tys) *nm* cactus.
cadavre (ka'dɑvr) *nm* 1 corpse. 2 carcass.
cadeau, -aux (ka'do) *nm* present, gift.
cadenas (kad'nɑ) *nm* padlock.
cadence (ka'dɑ̃s) *nf* 1 cadence. 2 rhythm. **cadencé** *adj* rhythmical.
cadet, -ette (ka'dɛ, -'dɛt) *adj* 1 younger. 2 junior. *nm* cadet.
cadran (ka'drɑ̃) *nm* dial. **cadran solaire** sundial.
cadrer (kɑ'dre:) *vi* agree, tally. **cadre** *nm* 1 frame. 2 framework. 3 executive. 4 limits. 5 plan.
caduc, -uque (ka'dyk) *adj* 1 decayed. 2 infirm.
cafard (ka'far) *adj* hypocritical. *nm* 1 cockroach. 2 *inf* sneak, telltale. **avoir le cafard** be fed up.

café (ka'fe:) *nm* **1** coffee. **2** cafe. **café crème** or **au lait** white coffee. **café nature** or **noir** black coffee.
caféine (kafe:'i:n) *nf* caffeine.
cafetier, -ière (kaf'tje:, -'tjɛr) *nm,f* owner of a cafe. *nf* coffee pot.
cage (kaʒ) *nf* **1** cage. **2** casing. **cage à poules** coop.
cagnotte (ka'ɲɔt) *nf game* kitty.
cagoule (ka'gu:l) *nf* hood.
cahier (ka'je:) *nm* exercise book.
cahin-caha (kaɛ̃ka'a) *adv* so-so.
cahot (ka'o) *nm* **1** jolt. **2** bump.
cahoter (kaɔ'te:) *vi,vt* **1** jolt. **2** bump.
caille (kaj) *nf* quail.
cailler (ka'je:) *vt* **1** clot. **2** curdle. **3** congeal. **caillot** *nm* clot.
caillou, -oux (ka'ju:) *nm* pebble, stone.
caisse (kɛs) *nf* **1** case. **2** box. **3** tub. **4** till, cash desk. **5** *mus* drum. **caisse d'épargne** savings bank. **caissier, -ière** (kɛ'sje:, -'sjɛr) *nm,f* cashier.
cajoler (kaʒɔ'le:) *vt* coax.
calamité (kalami:'te:) *nf* disaster.
calcaire (kal'kɛr) *adj* chalky. *nm* limestone.
calcium (kal'sjɔm) *nm* calcium.
calcul (kal'kyl) *nm* **1** calculation. **2** arithmetic.
calculer (kalky'le:) *vt* **1** calculate. **2** reckon. **calculé** *adj* **1** premeditated. **2** deliberate.
cale (kal) *nf* **1** *naut* hold. **2** chock, wedge.
caleçon (kal'sɔ̃) *nm* men's pants. **caleçon de bain** bathing trunks.
calembour (kalɑ̃'bu:r) *nm* pun.
calendrier (kalɑ̃dri:'je:) *nm* **1** calendar. **2** diary.
calepin (kal'pɛ̃) *nm* notebook.
caler (ka'le:) *vt* **1** wedge. **2** stall. **3** adjust. *vi* stall.
calfeutrer (kalfœ'tre:) *vt* block up.
calibre (ka'li:br) *nm* **1** calibre. **2** bore (of a gun). **3** size.
califourchon (kali:fu:r'ʃɔ̃) **à califourchon** *adv* astride.
câlin (kɑ'lɛ̃) *adj* **1** caressing. **2** winning.
câliner (kɑli:'ne:) *vt* caress, fondle.
calleux, -euse (ka'lœ, -'lœz) *adj* horny, callous.
calmar (kal'mar) *nm* squid.
calmer (kal'me:) *vt* **1** calm. **2** quiet. **3** soothe. **se calmer** *vr* calm down. **calmant** *nm* sedative. **calme** *adj* **1** calm. **2** still. *nm* **1** calm. **2** peace.
calomnier (kalɔm'nje:) *vt* slander. **calomnie** *nf* libel, slander.
calorie (kalɔ'ri:) *nf* calorie.
calorifère (kalɔri:'fɛr) *nm* **1** central heating apparatus. **2** stove.
calorifuger (kalɔri:fy'ʒe:) *vt* insulate.
calquer (kal'ke:) *vt* trace.
calvitie (kalvi:'si:) *nf* baldness.
camarade (kama'rad) *nm,f* comrade, mate, friend.
Cambodge (kɑ̃'bɔdʒ) *nm* Cambodia. **cambodgien, -ienne** (kɑ̃bɔ'dʒjɛ̃, -'dʒjɛn) *adj,n* Cambodian.
cambrer (kɑ̃'bre:) *vt* **1** bend. **2** arch. **se cambrer** *vr* brace oneself.
cambrioler (kɑ̃bri:ɔ'le:) *vt* burgle. **cambriolage** *nm* burglary. **cambrioleur, -euse** (kɑ̃bri:ɔ'lœr, -'lœz) *nm,f* burglar.
caméléon (kame:le:'ɔ̃) *nm* chameleon.
camelote (kam'lɔt) *nf* rubbish, junk.
camembert (kamɑ̃'bɛr) *nm* a French cheese.
caméra (kame:'ra) *nf* cinecamera.
camion (ka'mjɔ̃) *nm* lorry. **camionnette** *nf* van.
camoufler (kamu:'fle:) *vt* disguise, camouflage. **camouflage** *nm* camouflage.
camp (kɑ̃) *nm* **1** camp. **2** side.
campagne (kɑ̃'paɲ) *nf* **1** country, countryside. **2** campaign. **en rase campagne** in the heart of the country. **campagnard** *adj* **1** rustic. **2** country.
camper (kɑ̃'pe:) *vi* camp. **camping** *nm* **1** camping. **2** camping ground.
campus (kɑ̃'pys) *nm* campus.
Canada (kana'da) *nm* Canada. **canadien, -ienne** (kana'djɛ̃, -'djɛn) *adj,n* Canadian.
canaille (ka'naj) *nf inf* **1** rabble. **2** scoundrel. *adj* vulgar, coarse.
canal, -aux (ka'nal, -'no) *nm* **1** canal. **2** channel. **3** pipe.
canapé (kana'pe:) *nm* couch, sofa.
canard (ka'nar) *nm* **1** duck. **2** drake. **3** false report.
canari (kana'ri:) *nm* canary.
Canaries (kana'ri:) **îles Canaries** *nf pl* Canary Islands.
cancan (kɑ̃'kɑ̃) *nm* **1** gossip. **2** *pl* scandal.
cancer (kɑ̃'sɛr) *nm* **1** cancer. **2** *cap* Cancer.
cancre (kɑ̃kr) *nm* **1** crab. **2** dunce.
candeur (kɑ̃'dœr) *nf* **1** frankness. **2** artlessness.
candidat (kɑ̃di:'da) *nm* **1** candidate. **2** applicant.
candide (kɑ̃'di:d) *adj* **1** frank. **2** open.
cane (kan) *nf* duck. **caneton** *nm* duckling.
canevas (kan'vɑ) *nm* **1** canvas. **2** outline.
caniche (ka'ni:ʃ) *nm,f* poodle.
canif (ka'ni:f) *nm* penknife.

canin (ka'nɛ̃) *adj* canine.
caniveau, -aux (kani:'vo) *nm* gutter.
canne (kan) *nf* **1** cane. **2** walking stick. **canne à pêche** fishing rod. **canne à sucre** sugar cane.
canneler (kan'le:) *vt* **1** groove. **2** flute. **cannelure** *nf* groove, channel.
cannelle (ka'nɛl) *nm* cinnamon.
canon[1] (ka'nɔ̃) *nm mil* **1** cannon. **2** barrel.
canon[2] (ka'nɔ̃) *nm* canon.
cañon (ka'ɲɔ̃) *nm* canyon.
canoniser (kanɔni:'ze:) *vt* canonize.
canot (ka'no) *nm* **1** canoe. **2** boat. **canot de sauvetage** lifeboat. **canot glisseur** speedboat. **canotage** *nm* boating. **faire du canotage** row. **canotier** *nm* **1** oarsman. **2** straw hat.
cantatrice (kɑ̃ta'tri:s) *nf* singer.
cantine (kɑ̃'ti:n) *nf* canteen.
canton (kɑ̃'tɔ̃) *nm* district, canton. **cantonade** *nf Th* wings.
cantonnier (kɑ̃tɔ'nje:) *nm* road mender.
caoutchouc (kau:'tʃu:) *nm* **1** rubber. **2** mackintosh.
cap (kap) *nm geog* cape.
capable (ka'pabl) *adj* able, fit, capable.
capacité (kapasi:'te:) *nf* **1** capacity. **2** ability.
cape (kap) *nf* cape, cloak.
capitaine (kapi:'tɛn) *nm* captain.
capital, -aux (kapi:'tal, -'to) *adj* **1** capital. **2** principal. *nm comm* capital. *nf* capital (city). **capitalisme** *nm* capitalism.
capitaliser (kapi:tali:'ze:) *vt* **1** capitalize. **2** save.
capiteux, -euse (kapi:'tœ, -'tœz) *adj* **1** (of wine) strong. **2** sensuous.
capitonner (kapi:tɔ'ne:) *vt* pad. **capitonnage** *nm* upholstery.
caporal, -aux (kapɔ'ral, -'ro) *nm* corporal.
capot (ka'po) *nm* **1** cover. **2** bonnet.
capote (ka'pɔt) *nf* **1** overcoat. **2** *mot* hood.
câpre (kɑpr) *nf* caper.
caprice (ka'pri:s) *nm* whim. **capricieux, -euse** (kapri:'sjœ, -'sjœz) *adj* **1** capricious. **2** temperamental. **3** wayward.
Capricorne (kapri:'kɔrn) *nm* Capricorn.
capsule (kap'syl) *nf* capsule.
capter (kap'te:) *vt* **1** obtain by fraud. **2** win over. **3** tune in. **captieux, -euse** (kap'sjœ, -'sjœz) *adj* **1** cunning. **2** insidious.
captif, -ive (kap'ti:f, -'ti:v) *adj,n* captive. **captivité** *nf* captivity.
captiver (kapti:'ve:) *vt* captivate, charm.
capuchon (kapy'ʃɔ̃) *nm* **1** hood. **2** cap.
capucine (kapy'si:n) *nf* nasturtium.
caquet (ka'kɛ) *nm* cackle.
caqueter (kak'te:) *vi* **1** cackle. **2** *inf* chatter.
car[1] (kar) *conj* because, for, as.
car[2] (kar) *nm* bus.
carabine (kara'bi:n) *nf* rifle.
caractère (karak'tɛr) *nm* **1** character. **2** nature. **3** type. **4** letter. **d'un caractère facile** good-humoured. **caractéristique** *adj* **1** characteristic. **2** typical. *nm* characteristic.
carafe (ka'raf) *nf* decanter.
caramel (kara'mɛl) *nm* caramel. **caramel au beurre** butterscotch.
carapace (kara'pas) *nf* shell.
carat (ka'ra) *nm* carat.
caravane (kara'van) *nf* caravan.
carbone (kar'bɔn) *nm* carbon.
carboniser (karbɔni:'ze:) *vt* **1** char. **2** carbonize.
carburant (karby'rɑ̃) *nm* motor fuel.
carburateur (karbyra'tœr) *nm* carburettor.
carcasse (kar'kas) *nf* **1** carcass. **2** framework.
cardiaque (kar'djak) *adj* cardiac.
cardinal, -aux (kardi:'nal, -'no) *adj* cardinal. *nm rel* cardinal.
carême (ka'rɛm) *nm* Lent.
carène (ka'rɛn) *nf naut* hull.
caresser (karɛ'se:) *vt* **1** caress. **2** cherish. **caresse** *nf* caress.
cargaison (kargɛ'zɔ̃) *nf* **1** cargo. **2** freight.
caricaturer (kari:katy're:) *vt* caricature. **caricature** *nf* caricature.
carier (ka'rje:) *vt* rot. **carie** *nf* decay.
carillon (kari:'jɔ̃) *nm* **1** chime. **2** peal of bells.
carillonner (kari:jɔ'ne:) *vi* **1** chime. **2** peal. **carillonneur** *nm* bellringer.
carnage (kar'naʒ) *nm* slaughter.
carnassier, -ière (karna'sje:, -'sjɛr) *adj* carnivorous.
carnaval (karna'val) *nm* carnival.
carnet (kar'nɛ) *nm* notebook. **carnet de chèques** chequebook.
carnivore (karni:'vɔr) *adj* carnivorous.
carotte (ka'rɔt) *nf* **1** carrot. **2** *inf* trick.
carpette (kar'pɛt) *nf* rug.
carquois (kar'kwa) *nm sport* quiver.
carreau, -aux (ka'ro) *nm* **1** small square. **2** tile **3** pane. **4** *game* diamonds.
carrefour (kar'fu:r) *nm* **1** crossroads. **2** square.
carreler (kɑr'le:) *vt* **1** pave. **2** tile. **3** draw squares. **carrelage** *nm* tiling. **carrelé** *adj* checked.
carrelet (kɑr'lɛ) *nm* plaice.
carrer (kɑ're:) *vt* square. **se carrer** *vr* swagger.

carré *adj* **1** square. **2** plain. *nm* **1** square. **2** landing. **carrément** *adv* **1** squarely. **2** bluntly, straightforwardly.

carrière[1] (kɑ'rjɛr) *nf* quarry.

carrière[2] (kɑ'rjɛr) *nf* career.

carrosse (kɑ'rɔs) *nm* coach. **carrosserie** *nf mot* body.

carrousel (karu:'zɛl) *nm* **1** tournament. **2** merry-go-round.

carrure (kɑ'ryr) *nf* **1** breadth (across shoulders). **2** stature.

cartable (kar'tabl) *nm* satchel.

carte (kart) *nf* **1** map. **2** card. **3** playing card. **4** list. **5** menu. **carte à jouer** playing card. **carte d'abonnement** season ticket. **carte de crédit** credit card. **carte d'identité** identity card. **carte postale** postcard. **donner carte blanche à** give a free hand to.

cartilage (karti:'laʒ) *nm* **1** cartilage. **2** gristle.

carton (kar'tɔ̃) *nm* **1** cardboard. **2** cardboard box. **3** cartoon. **carton-pâte** *nm invar* papier-mâché.

cartouche (kar'tu:ʃ) *nf* **1** cartridge. **2** carton. **3** refill.

carvi (kar'vi:) *nm* caraway.

cas (kɑ) *nm* **1** case. **2** matter. **3** circumstance. **cas urgent** emergency. **faire cas de** value. **le cas échéant** should the occasion arise.

cascade (ka'skad) *nf* **1** cascade. **2** waterfall.

caser (kɑ'ze:) *vt* **1** put away. **2** *inf* find a place for. **se caser** *vr* settle down. **case** *nf* **1** hut. **2** compartment.

caserne (ka'zɛrn) *nf* barracks.

casino (kazi:'no) *nm* casino.

casque (kask) *nm* helmet. **casque protecteur** crash-helmet. **casque téléphonique** headphones. **casquette** *nf* cap.

casse (kɑs) *nf* breakage, damage.

casser (kɑ'se:) *vt* **1** break. **2** cashier. **3** quash. **se casser la tête** rack one's brains. **cassant** *adj* **1** brittle. **2** crisp. **3** abrupt. **cassé** *adj* **1** broken. **2** worn out. **casse-cou** *nm invar* **1** reckless fellow. **2** danger spot. **casse-croûte** *nm invar* snack. **casse-noisette** *nm invar* nutcrackers. **cassure** *nf* **1** break. **2** fracture.

casserole (ka'srɔl) *nf* **1** saucepan. **2** stew.

cassette (ka'sɛt) *nf* **1** case. **2** moneybox.

cassis (kɑ'si:s) *nm* **1** blackcurrant. **2** blackcurrant bush.

cassonade (kasɔ'nad) *nf* brown sugar.

castagnettes (kasta'ɲɛt) *nf pl* castanets.

caste (kast) *nf* caste.

castor (ka'stɔr) *nm* beaver.

casuel, -elle (kɑ'zɥɛl) *adj* **1** accidental. **2** casual.

cataloguer, (katalɔ'ge:) *vt* catalogue, list. **catalogue** *nm* **1** catalogue. **2** list.

catamaran (katama'rɑ̃) *nm* catamaran.

Cataphote (kata'fɔt) *nm Tdmk mot* cat's eye.

cataplasme (kata'plasm) *nm* poultice.

cataracte (kata'rakt) *nf* cataract.

catarrhe (ka'tar) *nm* catarrh.

catastrophe (kata'strɔf) *nf* catastrophe, disaster.

catéchisme (kate:'ʃism) *nm* catechism.

catégoriser (kate:gɔri:'ze:) *vt* categorize. **catégorie** *nf* category. **catégorique** *adj* **1** categorical. **2** explicit.

cathédrale (kate:'dral) *nf* cathedral.

cathode (ka'tɔd) *nf* cathode.

catholique (katɔ'li:k) *adj* **1** catholic. **2** orthodox. *adj,n* Roman Catholic.

cauchemar (kɔ'ʃmar) *nm* nightmare.

causer[1] (ko'ze:) *vt* cause, bring about. **cause** *nf* **1** cause. **2** *law* brief, suit. **à cause de** on account of. **et pour cause** for a very good reason.

causer[2] (ko'ze:) *vi* chat, talk. **causerie** *nf* chat.

caustique (ko'sti:k) *adj* **1** caustic. **2** cutting. *nm* caustic.

cauteleux, -euse (kot'lœ, -'lœz) *adj* cunning, sly.

caution (ko'sjɔ̃) *nf* **1** security. **2** guarantee.

cautionnement (kosjɔn'mɑ̃) *nm* **1** *comm* guarantee. **2** deposit. **cautionnement judiciaire** bail.

cavalerie (kaval'ri:) *nf* cavalry. **cavalier, -ière** (kava'lje:, -'ljɛr) *adj* offhand. *nm* **1** horseman. **2** partner. **3** *game* knight.

cave[1] (kav) *adj* hollow.

cave[2] (kav) *nf* cellar. **caveau, -aux** (ka'vo) *nm* **1** small cellar. **2** vault. **caverne** *nf* **1** cave. **2** den.

caviar (ka'vjar) *nm* caviar.

cavité (kavi:'te:) *nf* cavity, hollow.

cayenne (ka'jɛn) *nf* cayenne.

ce[1] (sə) *pron* he, she, it. **ce que** what, which. **pour ce qui est de** as regards. **sur ce** thereupon.

ce[2], **cet, cette** (sə, sɛt, sɛt) *adj* this, that. **ce dernier** the latter. **ceci** *pron* this.

cécité (se:si:'te:) *nf* blindness.

céder (se:'de:) *vt* **1** give up, surrender. **2** make over. *vi* yield. **le céder à** be inferior to.

cédille (se:'di:j) *nf* cedilla.

cèdre (sɛdr) *nm* cedar.

ceindre* (sɛ̃dr) *vt* **1** encircle. **2** put on.

ceinture (sɛ̃'tyr) *nf* **1** belt. **2** girdle. **3** sash. **4** waist. **ceinture de securité** safety belt.
cela (sə'la, sla) *pron also inf* **ça** **1** that. **2** it. **3** so. **c'est ça** that's right. **comme ci comme ça** so-so. **où ça?** where?
célèbre (se:'lɛbr) *adj* famous. **célébrité** *nf* celebrity.
célébrer (se:le:'bre:) *vt* **1** celebrate. **2** observe.
celer (sə'le:) *vt* conceal.
céleri (se:l'ri:) *nm* celery.
céleste (se:'lɛst) *adj* celestial, heavenly.
célibataire (se:li:ba'tɛr) *adj* celibate, single. *nm* bachelor.
celle (sɛl) *pron* see **celui.**
Cellophane (sɛlɔ'fan) *nf Tdmk* Cellophane.
cellule (sɛ'lyl) *nf* cell.
celte (sɛlt) *nm,f* Celt.
celui, celle (sə'lɥi:, sɛl) *pron* **1** he, she. **2** the one. **celui-ci, celle-ci** **1** this one. **2** the latter. **celui-là, celle-là** **1** that one. **2** the former.
cendre (sɑ̃dr) *nf* **1** ash. **2** cinder. **cendrier** *nm* ashtray.
cène (sɛn) *nf* Last Supper.
censé (sɑ̃'se:) *adj* supposed.
censeur (sɑ̃'sœr) *nm* **1** critic. **2** censor.
censurer (sɑ̃sy're:) *vt* **1** censure. **2** censor. **censure** *nf* censure, blame.
cent (sɑ̃) *adj* one hundred. *nm* **1** hundred. **2** cent. **faire les cent pas** walk up and down. **centaine** *nf* about a hundred. **centième** *adj* hundredth.
centenaire (sɑ̃t'nɛr) *nm* centenary.
centigrade (sɑ̃ti:'grad) *adj* centigrade.
centime (sɑ̃'ti:m) *nm* centime.
centimètre (sɑ̃ti:'mɛtr) *nm* **1** centimetre. **2** *inf* tape measure.
central, -aux (sɑ̃'tral, -'tro) *adj* **1** central, middle. **2** principal.
centraliser (sɑ̃trali:'ze:) *vt* centralize.
centre (sɑ̃tr) *nm* centre, middle.
cep (sɛp) **cep de vigne** *nm* vine plant.
cependant (səpɑ̃'dɑ̃) *adv* meanwhile. *conj* however, still, yet.
céramique (sɛra'mi:k) *adj* ceramic. *nf* ceramics.
cerceau, -aux (sɛr'so) *nm* hoop.
cercle (sɛrkl) *nm* **1** circle. **2** club.
cercueil (sɛr'kœj) *nm* coffin.
céréale (se:re:'al) *adj* cereal. **céréales** *nf pl* cereals, corn.
cérébral, -aux (se:rɛ'bral, -'bro) *adj* of the brain.
cérémonie (se:re:mɔ'ni:) *nf* ceremony. **sans cérémonie** informally. **cérémonieux, -euse** (se:re:mo'njœ, -'njœz) ceremonious, formal.
cerf (sɛr) *nm* stag. **cerf-volant** *nm, pl* **cerfs-volants** kite.
cerise (sə'ri:z) *nf* cherry. **cerisier** *nm* cherry tree.
cerner (sɛr'ne:) *vt* encircle, surround. **avoir les yeux cernés** have bags under one's eyes.
certain (sɛr'tɛ̃) *adj* **1** certain, sure. **2** fixed. *pron pl* some, certain.
certes (sɛrt) *adv* indeed, most certainly.
certifier (sɛrti:'fje:) *vt* **1** certify. **2** witness. **certificat** *nm* certificate.
certitude (sɛrti:'tyd) *nf* certainty.
cerveau, -aux (sɛr'vo) *nm* **1** brain. **2** mind. **3** intellect.
cervelle (sɛr'vɛl) *nf anat* brain. **avoir une cervelle de lièvre** have a brain like a sieve.
Cervin (sɛr'vɛ̃) **Mont Cervin** *nm* Matterhorn.
ces (se:, sɛ) *adj pl* these, those.
cesser (sɛ'se:) *vi,vt* cease, stop. **faire cesser** put a stop to. **cesse** *nf* cease, respite.
cet (sɛt) *adj* see **ce**[2].
cette (sɛt) *adj* see **ce**[2].
ceux (sœ) *pron pl* those. **ceux-ci** **1** these. **2** the latter. **ceux-là** **1** those. **2** the former.
Ceylan (se:'lɑ̃) *nm* Ceylon.
chacal (ʃa'kal) *nm* jackal.
chacun (ʃa'kœ̃) *pron* **1** each. **2** everybody, everyone.
chagrin[1] (ʃa'grɛ̃) *adj* **1** sad, downcast. **2** peevish.
chagrin[2] (ʃa'grɛ̃) *nm* **1** grief, sorrow. **2** worry.
chagriner (ʃagri:'ne:) *vt* **1** grieve. **2** vex.
chahut (ʃa'y) *nm* row, uproar.
chaîne (ʃɛn) *nf* **1** chain. **2** cable. **3** channel (television). **4** *pl* fetters. **chaîne de montage** assembly line.
chair (ʃɛr) *nf* **1** flesh. **2** meat. **3** pulp. **4** skin (of a person).
chaire (ʃɛr) *nf* **1** pulpit. **2** *educ* chair.
chaise (ʃɛz) *nf* chair, seat. **chaise à bascule** rocking chair. **chaise-longue** *nf* couch.
chaland (ʃa'lɑ̃) *nm* barge.
châle (ʃɑl) *nm* shawl.
chalet (ʃa'lɛ) *nm* chalet, cottage.
chaleur (ʃa'lœr) *nf* **1** heat, warmth. **2** ardour. **chaleureux, -euse** (ʃalœ'rœ, -'rœz) *adj* **1** warm. **2** cordial.
chaloupe (ʃa'lu:p) *nf* launch.
chalumeau, -aux (ʃaly'mo) *nm* **1** straw. **2** *mus* pipe.

chaluter (ʃaly'te:) *vi* trawl. **chalutier** *nm* trawler.
se chamailler (ʃamɑ'je:) *vr* squabble.
chambellan (ʃɑ̃bɛ'lɑ̃) *nm* chamberlain.
chambranle (ʃɑ̃'brɑ̃l) *nm* **1** frame. **2** mantelpiece.
chambre (ʃɑ̃br) *nf* **1** room, bedroom. **2** chamber. **chambre d'ami** spare room. **chambre d'enfants** nursery. **Chambre des Communes/Lords** House of Commons/Lords. **Chambre des Députés** French equivalent of the House of Commons.
chameau, -aux (ʃa'mo) *nm* **1** camel. **2** *sl* scoundrel.
chamois (ʃa'mwa) *nm* chamois.
champ (ʃɑ̃) *nm* field. **sur le champ** immediately. **champ d'aviation** airfield. **champ de courses/foire** racecourse/fairground. **champêtre** *adj* rustic, rural.
champagne (ʃɑ̃'paɲ) *nf* champagne.
champignon (ʃɑ̃pi:'ɲɔ̃) *nm* mushroom.
champion, -ionne (ʃɑ̃'pjɔ̃, -'pjɔn) *nm,f* champion. **championnat** *nm* championship.
chance (ʃɑ̃s) *nf* **1** luck. **2** chance. **pas de chance!** bad luck! **chanceux, -euse** (ʃɑ̃'sœ, -'sœz) *adj* **1** hazardous. **2** fortunate.
chanceler (ʃɑ̃s'le:) *vi* **1** stagger. **2** totter. **chancelant** *adj* **1** staggering, unsteady. **2** delicate.
chancelier (ʃɑ̃sə'lje:) *nm* chancellor.
chandail (ʃɑ̃'daj) *nm* sweater.
chandelle (ʃɑ̃'dɛl) *nf* **1** candle. **2** prop, support. **3** *sport* lob. **chandelier** *nm* candlestick.
changer (ʃɑ̃'ʒe:) *vt* **1** change, exchange. **2** alter. *vi* change. **change** *nm* exchange. **changeant** *adj* changing, fickle. **changement** *nm* change, alteration.
chanoine (ʃan'wan) *nm rel* canon.
chanson (ʃɑ̃'sɔ̃) *nf* **1** song. **2** *pl* nonsense. **chanson d'enfants** nursery rhyme. **chanson populaire** folksong.
chant (ʃɑ̃) *nm* **1** singing. **2** song. **3** chant. **chant de Noël** carol.
chanter (ʃɑ̃'te:) *vt* **1** sing. **2** chirp. **faire chanter** blackmail. **chantage** *nm* blackmail. **chanteur, -euse** (ʃɑ̃'tœr, -'tœz) *nm,f* singer.
chantier (ʃɑ̃'tje:) *nm* yard. **chantier naval** shipyard.
chantonner (ʃɑ̃tɔ'ne:) *vi,vt* hum.
chanvre (ʃɑ̃vr) *nm* hemp.
chaos (ka'o) *nm* chaos. **chaotique** *adj* chaotic.
chape (ʃap) *nf* **1** *rel* cope. **2** covering.
chapeau, -aux (ʃa'po) *nm* **1** hat. **2** cover.
chapelain (ʃa'plɛ̃) *nm* chaplain.
chapelet (ʃa'plɛ) *nm* rosary, beads.
chapelle (ʃa'pɛl) *nf* chapel.
chapelure (ʃa'plyr) *nf* breadcrumbs.
chapitre (ʃa'pi:tr) *nm* **1** chapter. **2** subject.
chaque (ʃak) *adj* each, every.
char (ʃar) *nm* **1** chariot. **2** wagon. **char de combat** *mil* tank. **char funèbre** hearse.
charabia (ʃara'bja) *nm* gibberish, double dutch.
charbon (ʃar'bɔ̃) *nm* **1** coal. **2** carbon. **charbon de bois** charcoal.
charcuterie (ʃarky'tri:) *nf* **1** pork butcher's shop. **2** delicatessen.
chardon (ʃar'dɔ̃) *nm* thistle.
chardonneret (ʃardɔn'rɛ) *nm* goldfinch.
charger (ʃar'ʒe:) *vt* **1** load. **2** charge. **3** instruct. **se charger de** *vr* undertake. **charge** *nf* **1** load. **2** burden. **3** responsibility. **4** office. **5** expense. **6** charge. **à charge de** on condition that. **chargement** *nm* **1** loading. **2** cargo.
chariot (ʃa'rjo) *nm* **1** wagon. **2** trolley.
charisme (ʃa'ri:sm) *nm* charisma.
charité (ʃari:'te:) *nf* charity, alms.
charivari (ʃari:va'ri:) *nm inf* din, racket.
charlatan (ʃarla'tɑ̃) *nm* quack.
charmer (ʃar'me:) *vt* **1** charm. **2** delight. **charme** *nm* **1** charm. **2** spell. **3** attraction.
charnel, -elle (ʃar'nɛl) *adj* carnal, sensual.
charnière (ʃar'njɛr) *nf* hinge.
charnu (ʃar'ny) *adj* fleshy, plump.
charpente (ʃar'pɑ̃t) *nf* framework.
charrette (ʃa'rɛt) *nf* cart. **charrette à bras** barrow.
charrue (ʃa'ry) *nf* plough.
charte (ʃart) *nf* charter.
châsse (ʃɑs) *nf* shrine.
chasser (ʃa'se:) *vt* **1** chase. **2** hunt. **3** shoot. **4** drive out. **5** dismiss. *vi* hunt. **chasse** *nf* **1** hunting. **2** shooting. **3** hunt. **4** shoot. **5** chase. **chasse d'eau** flush. **chasse-neige** *nm invar* snowplough. **chasseur** *nm* huntsman.
châssis (ʃɑ'si:) *nm* **1** frame. **2** chassis.
chaste (ʃast) *adj* pure, chaste.
chat, chatte (ʃa, ʃat) *nm,f* cat. **chaton** *nm* kitten. *nm* catkin.
châtaigne (ʃɑ'tɛɲ) *nf* chestnut. **châtaignier** *nm* sweet-chestnut tree.
châtain (ʃɑ'tɛ̃) *adj invar* auburn, chestnut-brown.
château, -aux (ʃɑ'to) *nm* **1** castle. **2** mansion.
châteaubriant (ʃɑtobri:'ɑ̃) *nm* grilled steak.
châtier (ʃɑ'tje:) *vt* **1** punish, chastise. **2** correct. **châtiment** *nm* punishment, chastisement.

chatouiller (ʃatu:ˈje:) *vt* tickle. **chatouilleux, -euse** (ʃatu:ˈjœ, -ˈjœz) *adj* **1** ticklish. **2** sensitive.

chatoyer (ʃatwaˈje:) *vi* **1** shimmer. **2** sparkle. **chatoiement** *nm* **1** shimmer. **2** glistening.

châtrer (ʃaˈtre:) *vt* castrate.

chaud (ʃo) *adj* hot, warm. *nm* warm. **avoir chaud** (of a person) be hot. **tenir au chaud** keep in a warm place. **chaudière** *nf* boiler.

chauffer (ʃoˈfe:) *vt* **1** heat, warm. **2** stoke. **3** swot. *vi* get hot. **chauffage** *nm* heating. **chauffage central** central heating. **chauffe-assiette** *nm, pl* **chauffe-assiettes** hotplate. **chauffeur** *nm* **1** stoker. **2** chauffeur.

chaume (ʃom) *nm* **1** thatch. **2** stubble. **chaumière** *nf* thatched cottage.

chaussée (ʃoˈse:) *nf* **1** causeway. **2** road.

chausser (ʃoˈse:) *vt* **1** put on (shoes). **2** supply with shoes. **se chausser** *vr* put on one's shoes. **chaussette** *nf* sock. **chausson** *nm* slipper. **chaussure** *nf* **1** footwear. **2** shoe, boot.

chauve (ʃov) *adj* bald. **chauve-souris** *nf, pl* **chauves-souris** *zool* bat.

chauvinisme (ʃovi:ˈni:sm) *nm* chauvinism.

chaux (ʃo) *nf* lime. **blanchir à la chaux** whitewash. **lait** or **blanc de chaux** *nm* whitewash.

chavirer (ʃavi:ˈre:) *vi* capsize. *vt* turn upside down, upset.

chef (ʃɛf) *nm* **1** head. **2** chief. **3** leader. **chef de bande** ringleader. **chef de cuisine** chef. **chef d'équipe** *sport* captain. **chef de gare** stationmaster. **chef d'orchestre** conductor.

chef-d'œuvre (ʃɛˈdœvr) *nm, pl* **chefs-d'œuvre** masterpiece.

chef-lieu (ʃɛfˈljœ) *nm, pl* **chefs-lieux** chief town.

cheik (ʃɛk) *nm* sheikh.

chelem (ʃlɛm) *nm* (in bridge, etc.) slam.

chemin (ʃmɛ̃) *nm* **1** way. **2** road, path. **à moitié chemin** halfway. **chemin de fer** railway. **chemin faisant** on the way. **grand chemin** highway. **se mettre en chemin** set off.

chemineau, -aux (ʃmi:ˈno) *nm* tramp.

cheminée (ʃmi:ˈne:) *nf* **1** fireplace. **2** mantelpiece. **3** chimney. **4** funnel.

cheminer (ʃmi:ˈne:) *vi* tramp, walk.

chemise (ʃmi:z) *nf* **1** shirt. **2** folder, jacket. **chemise de nuit** nightdress, nightgown.

chêne (ʃɛn) *nm* oak.

chenille (ʃəˈni:j) *nf* caterpillar.

chèque (ʃɛk) *nm* cheque. **chèque de voyage** traveller's cheque.

cher, chère (ʃɛr) *adj* **1** dear. **2** expensive. *adv* at a high price, dearly.

chercher (ʃɛrˈʃe:) *vt* look for, seek. **chercher à** attempt to.

chérir (ʃe:ˈri:r) *vt* cherish. **chéri** *adj,n* dear, darling.

chérubin (ʃe:ryˈbɛ̃) *nm* cherub.

chétif, -ive (ʃe:ˈti:f, -ˈti:v) *adj* **1** weak, sickly. **2** miserable, poor.

cheval, -aux (ʃəˈval, -ˈvo) *nm* horse. **à cheval** on horseback. **cheval à bascule** rocking horse. **cheval de course** racehorse. **cheval pur sang** thoroughbred. **chevaux de bois** *nm pl* merry-go-round.

chevalet (ʃəvaˈlɛ) *nm* **1** support. **2** trestle. **chevalet de peintre** easel.

chevalier (ʃəvaˈlje:) *nm* **1** knight. **2** horseman. **chevalerie** *nf* chivalry. **cheval-vapeur** *nm, pl* **chevaux-vapeur** horsepower.

chevaucher (ʃəvoˈʃe:) *vi,vt* ride. *vt* overlap.

chevelu (ʃəˈvly) *adj* hairy. **chevelure** *nf* hair, head of hair.

chevet (ʃəˈvɛ) *nm* bedside.

cheveu, -eux (ʃəˈvœ) *nm* **1** hair. **2** *pl* (head of) hair.

cheville (ʃəˈvi:j) *nf* **1** peg, pin. **2** bolt. **3** ankle.

chèvre (ʃɛvr) *nf* goat. **chevreau, -aux** (ʃəˈvro) *nm zool* kid.

chèvrefeuille (ʃɛvrəˈfœj) *nm* honeysuckle.

chevron (ʃəˈvrɔ̃) *nm* **1** rafter. **2** stripe.

chez (ʃe:) *prep* **1** at. **2** care of. **3** with. **4** among. **5** in. **6** at the house of. **chez soi** at home.

chic (ʃi:k) *nm* **1** skill. **2** style. *adj invar* **1** smart, elegant. **2** first-rate.

chicaner (ʃi:kaˈne:) *vi* quibble. *vt* wrangle with.

chiche (ʃi:ʃ) *adj* **1** poor. **2** mean.

chicorée (ʃi:kɔˈre:) *nf* **chicorée sauvage** chicory. **chicorée frisée** endive.

chien, chienne (ʃjɛ̃, ʃjɛn) *nm,f* dog, bitch. **chien de berger/garde** sheepdog/watchdog. **entre chien et loup** in the twilight.

chiffe (ʃi:f) *nf* rag.

chiffon (ʃi:ˈfɔ̃) *nm* **1** rag. **2** scrap. **3** duster. **4** chiffon.

chiffonner (ʃi:fɔˈne:) *vt* **1** crumple. **2** annoy.

chiffrer (ʃi:ˈfre:) *vi* calculate. *vt* **1** number. **2** code. **3** work out. **chiffre** *nm* **1** figure, number. **2** code. **chiffre d'affaires** *comm* turnover.

chignon (ʃiˈɲɔ̃) *nm* bun, coil of hair.

Chili (ʃi:'li:) *nm* Chile. **chilien, -ienne** (ʃi:'ljɛ̃, -'ljɛn) *adj,n* Chilean.

chimère (ʃi:'mɛr) *nf* illusion. **chimérique** *adj* fanciful.

chimie (ʃi:'mi:) *nf* chemistry. **chimique** *adj* chemical. **chimiste** *nm,f sci* chemist.

chimpanzé (ʃɛ̃pɑ̃'ze:) *nm* chimpanzee.

Chine (ʃi:n) *nf* China. **chinois** *adj,n* Chinese. *nm* Chinese (language).

chiot (ʃjo) *nm* puppy.

chiper (ʃi:'pe:) *vt inf* **1** pinch. **2** scrounge.

chipoter (ʃi:pɔ'te:) *vi* waste time. *vt* nibble.

chiquenaude (ʃi:k'nod) *nf* flick (of fingers).

chiromancie (ki:rɔmɑ̃'si:) *nf* palmistry.

chiropracteur (ki:rɔprak'tœr) *nm* osteopath.

chirurgie (ʃi:ryr'ʒi:) *nf* surgery. **chirurgie plastique** plastic surgery. **chirurgien, -ienne** (ʃi:ryr'ʒjɛ̃, -'ʒjɛn) *nm,f* surgeon. **chirurgique** *adj* surgical.

chlore (klɔr) *nm* chlorine.

chlorophylle (klɔrɔ'fi:l) *nf* chlorophyll.

choc (ʃɔk) *nm* **1** shock. **2** impact. **3** clash.

chocolat (ʃɔkɔ'la) *nm* chocolate. *adj invar* chocolate-coloured.

chœur (kœr) *nm* **1** chorus. **2** choir.

choir* (ʃwar) *vi* fall.

choisir (ʃwa'zi:r) *vt* choose, select. **choisi** *adj* **1** selected. **2** choice.

choix (ʃwa) *nm* **1** choice. **2** selection. **de tout premier choix** first-class, best quality.

choléra (kɔlɛ'ra) *nm* cholera.

chômer (ʃo'me:) *vi* **1** be unemployed. **2** take a holiday. **chômage** *nm* unemployment. **chômeur** *nm* unemployed person.

chope (ʃɔp) *nf* tankard.

chopine (ʃɔ'pi:n) *nf* half-pint.

choquer (ʃɔ'ke:) *vt* **1** shock. **2** offend. **3** strike. **se choquer** *vr* **1** be shocked. **2** collide. **se choquer de** take offence at.

choral (kɔ'ral) *adj* choral.

chorégraphie (kɔre:gra'fi:) *nf* choreography. **chorégraphe** *nm* choreographer.

chose (ʃoz) *nf* **1** thing. **2** matter. **être tout chose** feel queer.

chou, choux (ʃu:) *nm* **1** cabbage. **2** rosette. **chou de Bruxelles** Brussels sprout. **chou-fleur** *nm, pl* **choux-fleurs** cauliflower. **mon petit chou** my dear.

choucas (ʃu:'kɑ) *nm* jackdaw.

choucroute (ʃu:'kru:t) *nf* sauerkraut.

chouette (ʃwɛt) *nf* owl. *adj,interj* fine, excellent.

choyer (ʃwa'je:) *vt* **1** pet. **2** cherish.

chrétien, -ienne (kre:'tjɛ̃, -'tjɛn) *adj,n* Christian.

Christ (kri:st) *nm* Christ.

christianisme (kri:stja'ni:sm) *nm* Christianity.

chrome (krom) *nm* **1** chromium. **2** chrome. **chromatique** *adj* chromatic. **chromé** *adj* chrome.

chromo (krɔ'mo) *nm inf* colour photo.

chromosome (kromo'zom) *nm* chromosome.

chronique[1] (krɔ'ni:k) *nf* **1** history. **2** report.

chronique[2] (krɔ'ni:k) *adj* chronic.

chronologique (krɔnɔlɔ'ʒi:k) *adj* chronological.

chronométrer (krɔnɔme:'tre:) *vt* time, keep the time. **chronomètre** *nm* stopwatch.

chrysalide (kri:za'li:d) *nf* chrysalis.

chrysanthème (kri:zɑ̃'tɛm) *nm* chrysanthemum.

chuchoter (ʃyʃɔ'te:) *vi,vt* whisper.

chuinter (ʃɥɛ̃'te:) *vi* (of an owl) hoot.

chut (ʃyt) *interj* hush!

chute (ʃyt) *nf* **1** fall. **2** downfall. **chute d'eau** waterfall.

Chypre (ʃi:pr) *nf* Cyprus. **chypriot** *adj,n* Cypriot.

ci[1] (si:) *adv* here.

ci[2] (si:) *pron invar* this. **ci-après** *adv* further on. **ci-contre** *adv* opposite, on the other side. **ci-dessous** *adv* below. **ci-dessus** *adv* above. **ci-devant** *adv* formerly, previously. **ci-inclus** *adj* enclosed. **ci-joint** *adj* attached.

cible (si:bl) *nf* target.

ciboule (si:'bu:l) *nf* spring onion. **ciboulette** *nf* chives.

cicatrice (si:ka'tri:s) *nf* scar.

cidre (si:dr) *nm* cider.

ciel (sjɛl) *nm, pl* **ciels** or **cieux** **1** sky. **2** heaven. **3** climate.

cierge (sjɛrʒ) *nm rel* candle.

cigale (si:'gal) *nf* cicada.

cigare (si:'gar) *nm* cigar. **cigarette** *nf* cigarette.

cigogne (si:'gɔɲ) *nf* stork.

cil (si:l) *nm* eyelash.

cime (si:m) *nf* summit, top.

ciment (si:'mɑ̃) *nm* cement.

cimenter (si:mɑ̃'te:) *vt* cement.

cimetière (sim'tjɛr) *nf* churchyard, graveyard, cemetery.

cinéaste (si:ne:'ast) *nm* film producer.

cinéma (si:nɛ'mɑ) *nm* cinema. **cinématographique** *adj* film.

cinétique (si:ne:'ti:k) *adj* kinetic.

cingalais (sɛ̃ga'lɛ) *adj,n* Ceylonese.

cingler (sɛ̃'gle:) *vt* whip, lash. **cinglant** *adj* biting, cutting, scathing.

cinq (sɛ̃k) *adj,nm* five. **cinquième** *adj* fifth.

cinquante (sɛ̃'kɑ̃t) *adj,nm* fifty. **cinquantième** *adj* fiftieth.
cintrer (sɛ̃'tre:) *vt* **1** arch. **2** bend. **cintre** *nm* **1** curve. **2** arch. **3** coat-hanger.
circoncire* (si:rkɔ̃'si:r) *vt* circumcise. **circoncision** *nf* circumcision.
circonférence (si:rkɔ̃fɛ'rɑ̃s) *nf* circumference, perimeter.
circonflexe (si:rkɔ̃'flɛks) *adj* circumflex.
circonscrire* (si:rkɔ̃'skri:r) *vt* **1** circumscribe. **2** encircle. **3** limit. **circonscription** *nf pol* division, district. **circonscription électorale** constituency.
circonstance (si:rkɔ̃'stɑ̃s) *nf* **1** circumstance. **2** event.
circuit (si:r'kɥi:) *nm* circuit. **circuit touristique** organized tour.
circuler (si:rky'le:) *vi* circulate. **circulaire** *adj,nf* circular. **circulation** *nf* **1** circulation. **2** traffic.
cirer (si:'re:) *vt* **1** wax. **2** polish. **cire** *nf* wax. **ciré** *adj* **1** waxed. **2** polished. *nm* oilskin.
cirque (si:rk) *nm* circus.
cisaille (si:'zɑj) *nf* shears.
ciseau, -aux (si:'zo) *nm* **1** chisel. **2** *pl* scissors.
ciseler (si:'zle:) *vt* **1** engrave. **2** chisel.
cité (si:'te:) *nf* city. **cité universitaire** student's hall of residence.
citer (si:'te:) *vt* quote, cite. **citation** *nf* quotation.
citerne (si:'tɛrn) *nf* cistern, tank.
cithare (si:'tar) *nf* zither.
citoyen, -enne (si:twa'jɛ̃, -'jɛn) *nm,f* citizen.
citron (si:'trɔ̃) *nm* **1** *bot* lemon. **2** citrus. **3** lemon (colour). **citron pressé** lemon juice. **citronnier** *nm* lemon tree.
citrouille (si:'tru:j) *nf* pumpkin.
civette (si:'vɛt) *nf* chives.
civière (si:'vjɛr) *nf* stretcher.
civil (si:'vi:l) *adj* **1** civil. **2** civilian. **3** polite. *nm* civilian. **en civil** in plain clothes.
civiliser (si:vi:li:'ze:) *vt* civilize. **civilisation** *nf* civilization.
civique (si:'vi:k) *adj* civic.
clair (klɛr) *adj* **1** clear. **2** obvious, plain. **3** bright. **4** pale. *adv* clearly, plainly. *nm* light. **clair de lune** moonlight.
clairon (klɛ'rɔ̃) *nm* bugle.
clairsemé (klɛrsə'me:) *adj* **1** scattered. **2** thinly sown.
clairvoyant (klɛrvwa'jɑ̃) *adj* shrewd.
clameur (kla'mœr) *nf* clamour, outcry.
clan (klɑ̃) *nm* **1** clan. **2** set.

clandestin (klɑ̃dɛ'stɛ̃) *adj* secret, clandestine, underground.
claquer (kla'ke:) *vi* **1** clap. **2** bang. **3** snap. **4** *sl* die. *vt* smack. **claque** *nf* smack, slap.
clarifier (klari:'fje:) *vi* clarify.
clarinette (klari:'nɛt) *nf* clarinet.
clarté (klar'te:) *nf* **1** clarity. **2** light, brightness.
classer (klɑ'se:) *vt* **1** class. **2** sort out. **3** file. **classe** *nf* **1** class. **2** form. **aller en classe** go to school. **de première classe** first-class. **faire la classe** teach. **classeur** *nm* **1** rack. **2** filing cabinet.
classifier (klasi:'fje:) *vt* classify.
classique (kla'si:k) *adj* **1** classic. **2** classical. **3** academic. *nm pl* classics.
claustrophobie (klɔstrɔfɔ'bi:) *nf* claustrophobia.
clavecin (klav'sɛ̃) *nm* harpsichord.
clavicule (klavi:'kyl) *nf* collarbone.
clavier (kla'vje:) *nm* keyboard.
claxon (klak'sɔ̃) *nm* hooter.
claxonner (klaksɔ'ne:) *vi* hoot.
clef (kle:) *nf also* **clé** **1** key. **2** clue. **3** *mus* clef. **sous clef** under lock and key.
clémence (klɛ'mɑ̃s) *nf* mercy. **clément** *adj* **1** lenient, merciful. **2** mild.
cleptomanie (klɛptoma'ni:) *nf* kleptomania. **cleptomane** *nm,f* kleptomaniac.
clerc (klɛr) *nm* **1** clerk. **2** scholar. **faire un pas de clerc** make a blunder.
clergé (klɛr'ʒe:) *nm* clergy, priesthood.
clérical, -aux (kle:ri:'kal, -'ko) *adj rel* clerical.
cliché (kli:'ʃe:) *nm* **1** *phot* negative. **2** stock phrase.
client (kli:'ɑ̃) *nm* client, patient, customer. **clientèle** *nf* **1** customers. **2** *med* practice.
cligner (kli:'ɲe:) *vi,vt* blink, screw up one's eyes. **clignement** *nm* **1** blink. **2** flicker.
clignoter (kli:ɲɔ'te:) *vi* **1** blink. **2** twitch. **3** twinkle. **clignotant** *nm* indicator.
climat (kli:'ma) *nm* climate. **climatisation** *nf* air-conditioning.
clin d'œil (klɛ̃) *nm* wink.
clinique (kli:'ni:k) *adj* clinical. *nf* nursing home.
clinquant (klɛ̃'kɑ̃) *nm* **1** tinsel. **2** glitter. *adj* flashy.
cliqueter (kli:k'te:) *vi* rattle, clank.
cliquette (kli:'kɛt) *nf* pair of castanets.
clitoris (kli:tɔ'ri:s) *nm* clitoris.
clochard (klɔ'ʃar) *nm* tramp.
cloche (klɔʃ) *nf* **1** bell. **2** cover.
clocher[1] (klɔ'ʃe:) *nm* **1** belfry. **2** steeple.
clocher[2] (klɔ'ʃe:) *vi* limp, hobble.

cloison (klwa'zɔ̃) *nf* partition.
cloître (klwɑtr) *nm* **1** cloister. **2** monastery. **3** close.
clopin-clopant (klɔpɛ̃klɔ'pɑ̃) *adv* **aller clopin-clopant** limp along.
clore* (klɔr) *vt* **1** close. **2** end. **clos** *adj* **1** closed. **2** finished. *nm* enclosure.
clôture (klo'tyr) *nf* **1** fence. **2** closing.
clou (klu:) *nm* **1** nail. **2** boil. **3** *Th* main attraction. **4** old car. **clou de girofle** *cul* clove.
clouer (klu:'e:) *vt* **1** nail. **2** hold fast. **être cloué au lit** be bedridden.
clouter (klu:'te:) *vt* stud.
clovisse (klɔ'vi:s) *nf* clam.
clown (klu:n) *nm* clown.
club (klɔb) *nm* **1** club. **2** golf club.
coaguler (koagy'le:) *vt* congeal.
coalition (koali:'sjɔ̃) *nf* coalition, union.
coasser (koa'se:) *vi* croak.
cobaye (kɔ'baj) *nm* guineapig.
cobra (kɔ'bra) *nm* cobra.
cocarde (kɔ'kard) *nf* rosette.
cocasse (kɔ'kas) *adj* funny, humorous.
coccinelle (kɔksi:'nɛl) *nf* ladybird.
cocher[1] (kɔ'ʃe:) *nm* coachman, driver.
cocher[2] (kɔ'ʃe:) *vt* mark off. **coche** *nf* notch.
cochon, -onne (kɔ'ʃɔ̃, -'ʃɔn) *adj* **1** *inf* indecent. **2** dirty. *nm* **1** pig. **2** swine. **cochon d'Inde** guineapig. **cochonnerie** *nf inf* **1** filthiness. **2** rubbish. **3** dirty trick.
cocktail (kɔk'tɛl) *nm* **1** cocktail. **2** cocktail party.
coco (kɔ'ko) **noix de coco** *nm* coconut. **cocotier** *nm* coconut palm.
cocon (kɔ'kɔ̃) *nm* cocoon.
cocotte[1] (kɔ'kɔt) *nf* **1** child's word for chicken. **2** *sl* tart.
cocotte[2] (kɔ'kɔt) *nf* stewpan.
code (kɔd) *nm* **1** law. **2** code. **code de la route** highway code.
codéine (kɔde:'i:n) *nf* codeine.
coéducation (koe:dyka'sjɔ̃) *nf* co-education.
cœur (kœr) *nm* **1** heart. **2** mind. **3** courage. **4** middle. **5** *game* hearts. **au cœur léger** light-hearted. **de bon/mauvais cœur** willingly/reluctantly.
coexister (koe:gzi:'ste:) *vi* coexist.
coffre (kɔfr) *nm* **1** chest, box. **2** *mot* boot. **coffre-fort** *nm, pl* **coffres-forts** safe.
cognac (kɔ'ɲak) *nm* brandy.
cogner (kɔ'ɲe:) *vt* hammer, hit. *vi,vt* **1** knock. **2** bump. **cognée** *nf* hatchet, axe.
cohabiter (koabi:'te:) *vi* cohabit, live together.
cohérent (kɔɛ'rɑ̃) *adj* coherent.
cohue (kɔ'y) *nf* crowd, mob.
coiffer (kwa'fe:) *vt* **1** cover. **2** put on (a hat). **se coiffer** *vr* **1** put on one's hat. **2** do one's hair. **coiffeur, -euse** (kwa'fœr, -'føz) *nm,f* hairdresser. *nf* dressing table. **coiffure** *nf* **1** hairdressing. **2** hairstyle.
coin (kwɛ̃) *nm* **1** corner. **2** spot. **3** wedge.
coincer (kwɛ̃'se:) *vt* wedge. *vi* jam, stick.
coïncider (kɔɛ̃si:'de:) *vi* coincide. **coïncidence** *nf* coincidence.
coing (kwɛ̃) *nm* quince.
col (kɔl) *nm* **1** neck. **2** collar. **3** pass (of a mountain).
coléoptère (kɔle:ɔp'tɛr) *nm* beetle.
colère (kɔ'lɛr) *nf* anger. **coléreux, -euse** (kɔle:'rœ, -'rœz) *adj* quick-tempered.
colimaçon (kɔli:ma'sɔ̃) *nm* snail. **en colimaçon** spiral.
colique (kɔ'li:k) *nf* stomach ache.
colis (kɔ'li:) *nm* **1** parcel, package. **2** piece of luggage. **par colis postal** by parcel post.
collaborer (kɔlabɔ're:) *vi* collaborate. **collaborateur** *nm* **1** collaborator. **2** contributor.
collant (kɔ'lɑ̃) *adj* **1** sticky. **2** close-fitting. *nm* tights.
colle (kɔl) *nf* paste, glue.
collectif, -ive (kɔlɛk'ti:f, -'ti:v) *adj* collective. **collectivité** *nf* **1** group. **2** community.
collection (kɔlɛk'sjɔ̃) *nf* collection.
collectionner (kɔlɛksjɔ'ne:) *vt* collect.
collège (kɔ'lɛʒ) *nm* **1** college. **2** school. **collège d'enseignement général** secondary modern school. **collège privé** public school. **collégien, -ienne** (kɔle:'ʒjɛ̃, -'ʒjɛn) *nm,f* schoolboy, schoolgirl.
collègue (kɔl'lɛg) *nm,f* colleague.
coller (kɔ'le:) *vt* paste, glue. *vi* stick, cling. **se coller** *vr* stick or cling close. **colle** *nf* glue, paste.
collet (kɔ'lɛ) *nm* collar. **collet monté** *adj invar* prim, prudish.
collier (kɔ'lje:) *nm* **1** necklace. **2** collar.
colline (kɔ'li:n) *nf* hill.
collision (kɔli:'zjɔ̃) *nf* **1** collision. **2** clash.
colombe (kɔ'lɔ̃b) *nf* pigeon, dove. **colombier** *nm* dovecote.
Colombie (kɔlɔ̃'bi:) *nf* Columbia. **colombien, -ienne** *adj,n* Columbian.
colonel (kɔlɔ'nɛl) *nm* colonel.
colonie (kɔlɔ'ni:) *nf* colony. **colonie de vacances** children's holiday camp. **colonial, -aux** (kɔlɔ'njal, -'njo) *adj,n* colonial.

colonne (kɔ'lɔn) *nf* **1** column. **2** pillar. **colonne vertébrale** backbone.
colorer (kɔlɔ're:) *vt* **1** colour. **2** stain.
coloris (kɔlɔ'ri:) *nm* colouring.
colossal, -aux (kɔlɔ'sal, -'so) *adj* colossal, huge.
colporter (kɔlpɔr'te:) *vt* **1** peddle. **2** spread (news). **colporteur** *nm* pedlar.
coma (kɔ'ma) *nm* coma.
combat (kɔ̃'ba) *nm* **1** combat, fight. **2** conflict. **hors de combat** disabled.
combattre (kɔ̃'batr) *vt* fight, combat. *vi* fight, struggle.
combien (kɔ̃'bjɛ̃) *adv* how much, how many. **le combien sommes-nous?** what day of the month is it?
combiner (kɔ̃bi:'ne:) *vt* **1** combine. **2** contrive. **combinaison** *nf* **1** combination. **2** plan.
comble[1] (kɔ̃bl) *nm* **1** heap. **2** top, summit. **3** roof. **ça, c'est le comble!** that's the limit!
comble[2] (kɔ̃bl) *adj* **1** heaped. **2** full, crowded.
combler (kɔ̃'ble:) *vt* **1** fill, fill to overflowing. **2** make good.
combustion (kɔ̃by'stjɔ̃) *nf* combustion. **combustible** *adj* combustible. *nm* fuel.
comédie (kɔme:'di:) *nf* **1** comedy. **2** play. **jouer la comédie** act a part. **comédien, -ienne** (kɔme:'djɛ̃, -'djɛn) *nm,f* **1** comedian. **2** actor, actress.
comestible (kɔmɛ'sti:bl) *adj* edible. *nm* **1** article of food. **2** *pl* provisions.
comète (kɔ'mɛt) *nf* comet.
comique (kɔ'mi:k) *adj* **1** comic. **2** comical. *nm* **1** comedy. **2** comedian.
comité (kɔmi:'te:) *nm* committee, board.
commander (kɔmɑ̃'de:) *vt* **1** order, command. **2** govern. **3** control. **commandant** *nm mil* officer in command, major. **commande** *nf* order. **de commande** forced. **fait sur commande** made to order. **commandement** *nm* **1** command. **2** commandment.
commanditer (kɔmɑ̃di:'te:) *vt* finance.
comme (kɔm) *adv* **1** as, like. **2** in the way of. **3** how. *conj* as.
commémorer (kɔmme:mɔ're:) *vt* commemorate.
commencer (kɔmɑ̃'se:) *vi,vt* begin, commence. **commençant** *nm* beginner. **commencement** *nm* beginning.
comment (kɔ'mɑ̃) *adv* **1** how. **2** what. **3** *interj* what! why!
commenter (kɔmɑ̃'te:) *vi,vt* **1** comment. **2** annotate. **commentaire** *nm* **1** commentary. **2** comment. **commentateur, -trice** (kɔmɑ̃ta'tœr, -'tri:s) *nm,f* commentator.
commérage (kɔmɛ'raʒ) *nm* gossip.
commerce (kɔ'mɛrs) *nm* commerce, trade. **commerçant** *adj* business, mercantile. *nm* tradesman. **commercial, -aux** (kɔmɛr'sjal, -'sjo) *adj* commercial. **commerciale** *nf* estate car.
commettre* (kɔ'mɛtr) *vt* **1** commit. **2** entrust.
commis (kɔ'mi:) *nm* **1** clerk. **2** assistant.
commissaire (kɔmi:'sɛr) *nm* commissioner. **commissaire de police** police superintendent. **commissaire-priseur** *nm, pl* **commissaires-priseurs** auctioneer.
commissariat (kɔmi:sa'rja) *nm* police station.
commission (kɔmi:'sjɔ̃) *nf* **1** commission. **2** message, errand. **3** board, committee.
commissionnaire (kɔmi:sjɔ'nɛr) *nm* messenger.
commode (kɔ'mɔd) *adj* **1** convenient. **2** comfortable. **3** accommodating. *nf* chest of drawers. **commodité** *nf* **1** convenience. **2** comfort.
commotion (kɔmo'sjɔ̃) *nf* **1** commotion. **2** concussion.
commun (kɔ'mœ̃) *adj* **1** common. **2** general. **3** usual. **4** vulgar. **peu commun** unusual.
commune (kɔ'myn) *nf* **1** commune. **2** parish. **communal, -aux** (kɔmy'nal, -'no) *adj* **1** common. **2** communal. **communauté** *nf* community.
communiant (kɔmy'njɑ̃) *nm* communicant.
communication (kɔmyni:ka'sjɔ̃) *nf* **1** communication. **2** connection. **3** telephone call. **4** message.
communion (kɔmy'njɔ̃) *nf* communion.
communiquer (kɔmyni:'ke:) *vt* **1** communicate. **2** convey. *vi* communicate. **se communiquer** *vr* **1** be communicative. **2** spread.
communisme (kɔmy'ni:sm) *nm* communism. **communiste** *nm,f* communist.
compact (kɔ̃'pakt) *adj* **1** compact. **2** close.
compagnie (kɔ̃pa'ɲi:) *nf* **1** company. **2** party, group. **compagnon, compagne** *nm,f* companion.
comparer (kɔ̃pa're:) *vt* compare. **comparable** *adj* comparable. **comparaison** *nf* comparison. **comparatif, -ive** (kɔ̃para'ti:f, -'ti:v) *adj* comparative. **comparé** *adj* comparative.
compartiment (kɔ̃parti:'mɑ̃) *nm* compartment.
compas (kɔ̃'pɑ) *nm* **1** pair of compasses. **2** scale.
compassion (kɔ̃pa'sjɔ̃) *nf* compassion, pity. **avoir compassion de** take pity on.
compatible (kɔ̃pa'ti:bl) *adj* compatible.
compatir (kɔ̃pɑ'ti:r) *vi* **compatir à 1** sympathize

with. **2** be indulgent with. **compatissant** *adj* **1** soft-hearted. **2** indulgent.

compenser (kɔ̃pɑ̃'se:) *vt* compensate.

compère (kɔ̃'pɛr) *nm* **1** accomplice. **2** comrade.

compétent (kɔ̃pɛ'tɑ̃) *adj* competent. **avec compétence** *adv* competently.

compétition (kɔ̃pe:ti:'sjɔ̃) *nf* **1** competition. **2** race.

compiler (kɔ̃pi'le:) *vt* compile.

complaisance (kɔ̃plɛ'zɑ̃s) *nf* **1** kindness. **2** self-satisfaction. **complaisant** *adj* **1** obliging. **2** self-satisfied, complacent.

complément (kɔ̃ple:'mɑ̃) *nm* complement.

complet, -ète (kɔ̃'plɛ, -'plɛt) *adj* **1** complete, entire. **2** full. *nm* suit.

compléter (kɔ̃ple:'te:) *vt* complete.

complexe (kɔ̃'plɛks) *adj* **1** complex. **2** intricate. *nm* complex. **complexité** *nf* complexity.

complice (kɔ̃'pli:s) *adj* **1** accessory. **2** accomplice. *nm,f* accomplice.

compliment (kɔ̃pli:'mɑ̃) *nm* **1** compliment. **2** *pl* compliments. **3** *pl* congratulations.

complimenter (kɔ̃pli:mɑ̃'te:) *vt* **1** compliment. **2** congratulate.

compliquer (kɔ̃pli:'ke:) *vt* complicate.

complot (kɔ̃'plo) *nm* plot, conspiracy.

comploter (kɔ̃plɔ'te:) *vt* plot, scheme.

comporter (kɔ̃pɔr'te:) *vt* **1** allow. **2** require. **3** comprise. **4** involve. **se comporter** *vr* behave.

composer (kɔ̃po'ze:) *vt* **1** compose. **2** arrange. **composer avec** come to terms with. **se composer de** *vr* consist of. **composé** *adj* **1** compound. **2** composed. *nm* compound. **compositeur, -trice** (kɔ̃pɔzi:'tœr, -'tri:s) *nm,f* composer. **composition** *nf* **1** composition. **2** arrangement.

compote (kɔ̃'pɔt) *nf* stewed fruit.

compréhensif, -ive (kɔ̃pre:ɑ̃'si:f, -'si:v) *adj* **1** comprehensive. **2** intelligent.

comprendre* (kɔ̃'prɑ̃dr) *vt* **1** include, comprise. **2** understand, comprehend. **se faire comprendre** make oneself understood. **y compris** including.

comprimer (kɔ̃pri:'me:) *vt* **1** compress. **2** restrain. **comprimé** *adj* compressed. *nm* tablet.

compromettre* (kɔ̃prɔ'mɛtr) *vi,vt* compromise. **compromis** *nm* compromise.

comptable (kɔ̃'tabl) *adj* **1** of bookkeeping. **2** responsible. *nm,f* accountant. **comptabilité** *nf* bookkeeping.

compter (kɔ̃'te:) *vt* **1** count, reckon. **2** charge. **3** expect. *vi* rely. **comptant** *nm* cash. **compte** *nm* **1** account. **2** calculation. **compte à rebours** countdown. **compte rendu** **1** report. **2** review. **en fin de compte** all things considered.

compteur (kɔ̃'tœr) *nm* **1** counter. **2** meter. **compteur de stationnement** parking meter.

comptoir (kɔ̃t'war) *nm* counter.

comte (kɔ̃t) *nm* (title) count. **comtesse** *nf* countess.

comté (kɔ̃'te:) *nm* county.

concave (kɔ̃'kav) *adj* concave.

concéder (kɔ̃se:'de:) *vt* **1** concede. **2** grant. **3** admit.

concentrer (kɔ̃sɑ̃'tre:) *vt* **1** concentrate. **2** focus. **3** repress. **concentration** *nf* concentration. **concentré** *adj* **1** concentrated. **2** reserved. *nm* extract, concentrate.

concentrique *adj* concentric.

concept (kɔ̃'sɛpt) *nm* concept.

conception (kɔ̃sɛp'sjɔ̃) *nf* **1** conception. **2** idea. **conception dirigée** birth control.

concerner (kɔ̃sɛr'ne:) *vt* concern, affect.

concert (kɔ̃'sɛr) *nm* **1** concert. **2** harmony.

concerto (kɔ̃sɛr'to) *nm* concerto.

concession (kɔsɛ'sjɔ̃) *nf* concession.

concevoir* (kɔ̃sə'vwar) *vt* **1** conceive. **2** imagine. **3** understand.

concierge (kɔ̃'sjɛrʒ) *nm,f* **1** caretaker. **2** porter.

concilier (kɔ̃si:'lje:) *vt* **1** settle. **2** reconcile.

concis (kɔ̃'si:) *adj* concise.

conclure* (kɔ̃'klyr) *vt* **1** conclude. **2** finish. **conclusion** *nf* **1** conclusion, decision. **2** end.

concombre (kɔ̃'kɔ̃br) *nm* cucumber.

concourir* (kɔ̃ku:'ri:r) *vi* **1** converge. **2** unite. **3** compete.

concours (kɔ̃'ku:r) *nm* **1** gathering. **2** assistance. **3** competition. **4** show.

concret, -ète (kɔ̃'krɛ, -'krɛt) *adj* **1** concrete. **2** solid.

concurrence (kɔ̃ky'rɑ̃s) *nf* competition. **concurrent** *adj* **1** competitive. **2** rival. *nm* **1** competitor. **2** candidate. **3** contestant.

condamner (kɔ̃dɑ'ne:) *vt* **1** condemn. **2** sentence. **3** reprove. **4** block up. **condamnation** *nf* **1** condemnation. **2** *law* sentence.

condenser (kɔ̃dɑ̃'se:) *vt* condense. **condensation** *nf* condensation.

condescendre (kɔ̃dɛ'sɑ̃dr) *vi* condescend.

condition (kɔ̃di:'sjɔ̃) *nf* **1** condition, proviso. **2** position. **3** *pl* terms. **à condition** on approval. **à condition de** provided that. **conditionnel, -elle** *adj* conditional.

conditionner (kɔ̃di:sjɔ'ne:) *vt* **1** condition. **2** *comm* package.

condoléance (kɔ̃dɔle:'ɑ̃s) *nf* condolence.
conducteur, -trice (kɔ̃dyk'tœr, -'tri:s) *nm,f* **1** driver. **2** leader. *adj* conducting.
conduire* (kɔ̃'dɥi:r) *vt* **1** conduct. **2** lead. **3** drive. **4** manage. **se conduire** *vr* behave. **conduit** *nm* **1** passage. **2** pipe. **conduite** *nf* **1** behaviour. **2** management. **3** driving. **4** leading. **conduite intérieure** saloon car.
cône (kon) *nm* cone.
confectionner (kɔ̃fɛksjɔ'ne:) *vt* **1** make up. **2** manufacture. **confectionné** *adj* ready-made.
confédérer (kɔ̃fe:de:'re:) *vt* confederate. **confédération** *nf* confederation.
conférer (kɔ̃fe:'re:) *vt* **1** compare. **2** award. *vi* confer. **conférence** *nf* **1** conference. **2** lecture. **conférencier, -ière** (kɔ̃fe:rɑ̃'sje:, -'sjɛr) *nm,f* lecturer.
confesser (kɔ̃fɛ'se:) *vt* confess.
confetti (kɔ̃fɛt'ti:) *nm pl* confetti.
confidentiel, -ielle (kɔ̃fi:dɑ̃'sjɛl) *adj* confidential.
confier (kɔ̃'fje:) *vt* **1** trust. **2** confide. **se confier à** *vr* put one's trust in. **confiance** *nf* confidence, trust. **digne de confiance** reliable, trustworthy. **confiant** *adj* **1** confiding. **2** confident, assured.
confire* (kɔ̃'fi:r) *vt cul* preserve (food).
confirmer (kɔ̃fi:r'me:) *vt* confirm. **confirmation** *nf* confirmation.
confiserie (kɔ̃fi:'zri:) *nf* **1** confectioner's shop. **2** confectionery. **confiseur** *nm* confectioner.
confisquer (kɔ̃fi:'ske:) *vt* confiscate, seize.
confiture (kɔ̃fi:'tyr) *nf* jam. **confiture d'oranges** marmalade.
conflagration (kɔ̃flagra'sjɔ̃) *nf* blaze, fire.
conflit (kɔ̃'fli:) *nm* **1** conflict. **2** clash.
confluer (kɔ̃fly'e:) *vi* join, meet.
confondre (kɔ̃'fɔ̃dr) *vt* **1** confound, baffle. **2** confuse, mistake. **se confondre** *vr* blend. **confondu** *adj* **1** overwhelmed. **2** confused.
conforme (kɔ̃'fɔrm) *adj* **conforme à 1** according to. **2** consistent with. **conformément** *adv* accordingly.
conformer (kɔ̃fɔr'me:) *vt* **1** shape. **2** conform. **se conformer à** *vr* comply with.
confort (kɔ̃'fɔr) *nm* comfort. **confortable** *adj* comfortable, cosy.
confrère (kɔ̃'frɛr) *nm* **1** colleague. **2** *rel* brother.
confus (kɔ̃'fy) *adj* **1** confused. **2** vague. **3** obscure. **confusion** *nf* confusion, muddle.
congé (kɔ̃'ʒe:) *nm* **1** leave, holiday. **2** notice.
congédier (kɔ̃ʒe:'dje:) *vt* **1** dismiss. **2** discharge.
congeler (kɔ̃'ʒle:) *vt* **1** freeze. **2** congeal. **congélateur** *nm* deep-freeze. **congélation** *nf* freezing.
congestion (kɔ̃ʒɛs'tjɔ̃) *nf* congestion. **congestion cérébrale** *med* stroke. **congestion pulmonaire** pneumonia. **congestionné** *adj* flushed, red in the face.
congrès (kɔ̃'grɛ) *nm* congress.
conifère (kɔni:'fɛr) *nm* conifer.
conique (kɔ'ni:k) *adj* conical.
conjoint (kɔ̃'ʒwɛ̃) *adj* **1** joined. **2** married. **conjoints** *nm pl* husband and wife.
conjonction (kɔ̃ʒɔ̃k'sjɔ̃) *nf* **1** union. **2** conjunction.
conjugal, -aux (kɔ̃ʒy'gal, -'go) *adj* conjugal.
conjuguer (kɔ̃ʒy'ge:) *vt* conjugate. **conjugaison** *nf* conjugation.
connaissance (kɔnɛ'sɑ̃s) *nf* **1** knowledge. **2** acquaintance. **3** consciousness. **4** *pl* learning. **sans connaissance** unconscious. **connaisseur** *nm* connoisseur, expert. *adj* expert.
connaître* (kɔ'nɛtr) *vt* **1** know. **2** be acquainted with. **3** have a thorough knowledge of. **4** distinguish. **se connaître en** *vr* know all about.
connu (kɔ'ny) *v* see **connaître.**
conquérir* (kɔ̃ke:'ri:r) *vt* **1** conquer. **2** win over.
conquête (kɔ̃'kɛt) *nf* conquest.
conquis (kɔ̃'ki:) *v* see **conquérir.**
consacrer (kɔ̃sa'kre:) *vt* **1** consecrate. **2** devote. **consacré** *adj* sacred.
consanguin (kɔ̃sɑ̃'gɛ̃) **frère consanguin** *nm* half-brother. **sœur consanguine** *nf* half-sister.
conscience (kɔ̃'sjɑ̃s) *nf* **1** conscience. **2** consciousness. **avoir conscience de** be aware of. **consciencieux, -euse** (kɔ̃sjɑ̃'sjœ, -'sjœz) *adj* conscientious. **conscient de** *adj* conscious of.
conscription (kɔ̃skri:p'sjɔ̃) *nf* conscription.
conscrit (kɔ̃'skri:) *nm* conscript.
consécutif, -ive (kɔ̃se:ky'ti:f, -'ti:v) *adj* consecutive.
conseil (kɔ̃'sɛj) *nm* **1** advice. **2** counsel. **3** council. **conseil d'administration** board of directors. **conseil de guerre** court-martial. **conseil des ministres** *pol* cabinet. **conseil général** county council.
conseiller (kɔ̃sɛ'je:) *vt* advise, counsel.
consentir (kɔ̃sɑ̃'ti:r) *vi* consent, agree. **consentement** *nm* consent.
conséquence (kɔsɛ'kɑ̃s) *nf* **1** consequence. **2** importance. **conséquent** *adj* **1** consistent. **2** following. **par conséquent** consequently.

conservatoire (kɔ̃sɛrva'twar) *nm* school, academy (of music).

conserver (kɔ̃sɛr've:) *vt* **1** preserve. **2** keep. **conservateur, -trice** (kɔ̃sɛrva'tœr, -'tri:s) *nm,f* **1** curator, warden. **2** *pol* conservative.

considérer (kɔ̃si:de:'re:) *vt* **1** consider. **2** contemplate. **3** regard. **considérable** *adj* **1** considerable. **2** large. **3** eminent, important. **considération** *nf* **1** consideration. **2** reason. **3** respect.

consigner (kɔ̃si:'ɲe:) *vt* **1** deposit. **2** consign. **3** record. **4** confine to barracks. **non consigné** non-returnable. **consignation** *nf* **1** deposit. **2** consignment. **consigne** *nf* **1** order. **2** cloakroom.

consister (kɔ̃si:'ste:) *vi* consist. **consistance** *nf* consistency. **consistant** *adj* firm, solid.

consoler (kɔ̃sɔ'le:) *vt* console, comfort.

consolider (kɔ̃sɔli:'de:) *vt* consolidate. **se consolider** *vr* **1** become firm. **2** heal.

consommer (kɔ̃sɔ'me:) *vt* **1** consume. **2** accomplish. **consommateur, -trice** (kɔ̃sɔma'tœr, -'tri:s) *nm,f* **1** consumer. **2** customer (in restaurant). **consommation** *nf* **1** consumption. **2** accomplishment. **3** drink. **consommé** *nm* clear soup.

consonne (kɔ̃'sɔn) *nf* consonant.

conspirer (kɔ̃spi:'re:) *vi,vt* conspire, plot. **conspiration** *nf* plot.

conspuer (kɔ̃'spɥe:) *vt* to shout down.

constant (kɔ̃'stɑ̃) *adj* **1** constant, steadfast. **2** firm. **constamment** *adv* constantly.

constater (kɔ̃sta'te:) *vt* **1** ascertain. **2** state. **3** certify.

constellation (kɔ̃stɛlla'sjɔ̃) *nf* constellation.

consterner (kɔ̃stɛr'ne:) *vt* dismay.

constipation (kɔ̃sti:pa'sjɔ̃) *nf* constipation.

constituer (kɔ̃sti'tɥe:) *vt* **1** constitute. **2** form. **3** assign. **4** *comm* incorporate. **constituant** *adj* constituent. *nm* **1** component. **2** constituent. **constitution** *nf* **1** constitution. **2** composition.

construction (kɔ̃stryk'sjɔ̃) *nf* **1** construction. **2** building. **construction mécanique** mechanical engineering.

construire* (kɔ̃'strɥi:r) *vt* **1** construct. **2** build.

consul (kɔ̃'syl) *nm* consul.

consulat (kɔ̃sy'la) *nm* consulate.

consulter (kɔ̃syl'te:) *vt* consult. **se consulter** *vr* consider. **consultation** *nf* **1** consultation. **2** advice, opinion.

consumer (kɔ̃sy'me:) *vt* **1** consume. **2** destroy. **3** use up. **se consumer** *vr* burn up.

contact (kɔ̃'takt) *nm* contact, touch.

contagieux, -euse (kɔ̃ta'ʒjœ, -'ʒjœz) *adj* contagious, catching.

contaminer (kɔ̃tami:'ne:) *vt* **1** contaminate. **2** infect.

conte (kɔ̃t) *nm* story, tale. **conte de fées** fairytale.

contempler (kɔ̃tɑ̃'ple:) *vt* **1** contemplate. **2** meditate. **3** gaze at.

comtemporain (kɔ̃tɑ̃pɔ'rɛ̃) *adj,n* contemporary.

contenance (kɔ̃t'nɑ̃s) *nf* **1** look. **2** content. **faire bonne contenance** put on a brave face.

contenir* (kɔ̃t'ni:r) *vt* **1** contain. **2** restrain. **contenu** *adj* **1** restrained. **2** reserved. *nm* **1** contents. **2** subject.

content (kɔ̃'tɑ̃) *adj* **1** content, satisfied. **2** pleased.

contenter (kɔ̃tɑ̃'te:) *vt* **1** content, satisfy. **2** gratify. **contentement** *nm* contentment, satisfaction.

conter (kɔ̃'te:) *vt* tell, relate. **conteur** *nm* narrator.

contester (kɔ̃tɛs'te:) *vi,vt* contest, dispute. **contestable** *adj* debatable. **contestation** *nf* debate.

contexte (kɔ̃'tɛkst) *nm* context.

contigu, -ë (kɔ̃ti'gy) *adj* adjoining, adjacent.

continent (kɔ̃ti:'nɑ̃) *nm* continent. **continental, -aux** (kɔ̃ti:nɑ̃'tal, -'to) *adj* continental.

contingent (kɔ̃tɛ̃'ʒɑ̃) *nm* quota, allowance.

continuer (kɔ̃ti:'nɥe:) *vi,vt* continue. **continu** *adj* continuous. **continuel, -elle** (kɔ̃ti:'nɥɛl) *adj* continual. **continuité** *nf* continuity.

contour (kɔ̃'tu:r) *nm* **1** outline. **2** contour.

contourner (kɔ̃tu:r'ne:) *vt* **1** shape. **2** skirt. **3** twist. **route de contournement** *nf* bypass.

contraception (kɔ̃trasɛp'sjɔ̃) *nf* contraception.

contracter[1] (kɔ̃trak'te:) *vt* **1** contract, incur. **2** catch.

contracter[2] (kɔ̃trak'te:) *vt* contract, draw together.

contractuel, -elle (kɔ̃trak'tɥɛl) *nm,f* traffic warden.

contradiction (kɔ̃tradi:k'sjɔ̃) *nf* **1** contradiction. **2** discrepancy. **contradictoire** *adj* contradictory, conflicting.

contraindre* (kɔ̃'trɛ̃dr) *vt* **1** compel. **2** restrain. **contrainte** *nf* **1** constraint. **2** compulsion.

contraire (kɔ̃'trɛr) *adj* **1** contrary, opposite. **2** adverse. *nm* contrary, reverse.

contrarier (kɔ̃tra'rje:) *vt* **1** oppose. **2** annoy.

contraster (kɔ̃tras'te:) *vi,vt* contrast. **contraste** *nm* contrast.

contrat (kɔ̃'tra) *nm* contract, agreement.

contravention (kɔ̃travɑ̃'sjɔ̃) *nf* **1** infringement, minor offence. **2** fine.
contre (kɔ̃tr) *prep* **1** against. **2** for. **3** from. **4** to. **5** by. *adv* **1** against. **2** close to. **le pour et le contre** the pros and cons.
contre-amiral, -aux *nm* rear admiral.
contre-attaque *nf* counterattack.
contre-avion *adj* anti-aircraft.
contrebande (kɔ̃trə'bɑ̃d) *nf* **1** contraband. **2** smuggling. **faire la contrebande** smuggle. **contrebandier** *nm* smuggler.
contrebasse (kɔ̃trə'bɑs) *nf* double bass.
contre-boutant *nm* buttress.
contrecarrer (kɔ̃trəka're:) *vt* thwart, cross.
contre-cœur (kɔ̃trə'kœr) **à contre-cœur** *adv* reluctantly.
contre-coup *nm* **1** repercussion. **2** reaction.
contredire* (kɔ̃trə'di:r) *vt* contradict.
contrée (kɔ̃'tre:) *nf* region.
contrefaçon (kɔ̃trəfa'sɔ̃) *nf* counterfeit, forgery.
contrefaire* (kɔ̃trə'fɛr) *vt* **1** forge, counterfeit. **2** feign. **3** imitate.
contre-interroger *vt* cross-question, cross-examine.
contremaître (kɔ̃trə'mɛtr) *nm* foreman.
contremander (kɔ̃trəmɑ̃'de:) *vt* **1** cancel. **2** call off.
contre-pied *nm* opposite view. **à contre-pied** contrary to.
contre-plaqué *nm* plywood.
contre-poil *adv* **à contre-poil** the wrong way.
contre-poison *nm* antidote.
contre-sens *nm* **1** misunderstanding. **2** wrong way. **à contre-sens** in the wrong direction.
contretemps (kɔ̃trə'tɑ̃) *nm* **1** mishap. **2** hitch.
contre-torpilleur *nm naut* destroyer.
contrevenir (kɔ̃trə'vni:r) *vt (aux* avoir) contravene.
contrevent (kɔ̃trə'vɑ̃) *nm* shutter.
contre-voie *adv* **à contre-voie** **1** in the wrong direction. **2** on the wrong side.
contribuer (kɔ̃tri:'bɥe:) *vi* **contribuer à** contribute to. **contribuable** *nm,f* taxpayer. **contribution** *nf* **1** contribution. **2** tax.
contrôler (kɔ̃tro'le:) *vt* **1** inspect. **2** check. **3** control. **4** hallmark. **contrôle** *nm* **1** inspection, checking. **2** control. **3** list. **contrôleur** *nm* **1** inspector. **2** ticket collector.
controverse (kɔ̃trɔ'vɛrs) *nf* controversy.
contusionner (kɔ̃tyzjɔ'ne:) *vt* bruise.
convaincre* (kɔ̃'vɛ̃kr) *vt* **1** convince. **2** convict.
convalescence (kɔ̃valɛs'sɑ̃s) *nf* convalescence. **convalescent** *adj,n* convalescent.
convenir* (kɔ̃'vni:r) *vi (aux* avoir) **1** suit. **2** agree. **3** admit. **convenable** *adj* **1** suitable, appropriate. **2** proper. **convenance** *nf* **1** agreement. **2** suitability. **3** convenience. **4** propriety. **5** *pl* convention. **convenu** *adj* **1** agreed. **2** appointed.
convention (kɔ̃vɑ̃'sjɔ̃) *nf* **1** convention. **2** agreement. **3** condition. **conventionnel, -elle** (kɔ̃vɑ̃sjɔ'nɛl) *adj* conventional.
converger (kɔ̃vɛr'ʒe:) *vi* converge.
convers (kɔ̃'vɛr) *adj* **1** *rel* lay. **2** converse.
conversation (kɔ̃vɛrsa'sjɔ̃) *nf* conversation, talk.
conversion (kɔ̃vɛr'zjɔ̃) *nf* conversion.
convertir (kɔ̃vɛr'ti:r) *vt* convert. **converti** *nm* convert.
convexe (kɔ̃'vɛks) *adj* convex.
conviction (kɔ̃vi:k'sjɔ̃) *nf* conviction.
convier (kɔ̃'vje:) *vt* **1** invite. **2** urge.
convive (kɔ̃'vi:v) *nm,f* guest.
convocation (kɔ̃vɔka'sjɔ̃) *nf* summons.
convoi (kɔ̃'vwa) *nm* convoy, train.
convoiter (kɔvwa'te:) *vt* desire.
convoquer (kɔ̃vɔ'ke:) *vt* summon, call together.
coopérer (koɔpe:'re:) *vi* cooperate. **coopératif, -ive** (koɔpe:ra'ti:f, -'ti:v) *adj,nf* cooperative. **coopération** *nf* cooperation.
coordonner (koɔrdɔ'ne:) *vt* coordinate.
copain (kɔ'pɛ̃) *nm inf* friend, pal.
Copenhague (kɔpɛ'nag) *nf* Copenhagen.
copier (kɔ'pje:) *vt* **1** copy. **2** imitate. **copie** *nf* **1** copy. **2** reproduction.
copine (kɔ'pi:n) *nf inf* friend.
coq (kɔk) *nm* **1** cock. **2** weathercock. **coq-à-l'âne** *nm invar* cock-and-bull story.
coque (kɔk) *nf* **1** shell (of an egg). **2** *naut* hull. **3** cockle. **coquetier** *nm* eggcup.
coquelicot (kɔkli:'ko) *nm* poppy.
coqueluche (kɔ'klyʃ) *nf* whooping cough.
coquet, -ette (kɔ'kɛ, -'kɛt) *adj* **1** coy. **2** smart. **3** trim. *nf* flirt.
coquille (kɔ'ki:j) *nf* **1** shell. **2** misprint. **coquille d'œuf** *nf* eggshell. **coquillage** *nm* **1** shellfish. **2** shell.
coquin (kɔ'kɛ̃) *adj* naughty. *nm* rascal.
cor (kɔr) *nm* **1** *mus* horn. **2** *med* corn.
corail, -aux (kɔ'raj, -'ro) *nm* coral.
corbeau, -aux (kɔr'bo) *nm* crow.
corbeille (kɔr'bɛj) *nf* **1** basket. **2** flowerbed. **corbeille à papier** wastepaper basket.
corbillard (kɔrbi:'jar) *nm* hearse.
corder (kɔr'de:) *vt* **1** twist. **2** rope. **3** string. **cordage** *nm naut* **1** rope. **2** rigging. **corde** *nf* **1** rope, cord. **2** *mus* chord. **3** string. **4** note.

corde à linge clothes line. **corde de remorque** towrope. **corde tendue** tightrope. **cordée** *nf sport* line, group.

cordial, -aux (kɔr'djal, -'djo) *adj* cordial, hearty. *nm* cordial.

cordon (kɔr'dɔ̃) *nm* **1** strand. **2** cord, rope. **3** ribbon. **4** row, cordon. **cordonnier** *nm* cobbler.

coriace (kɔ'rjas) *adj* **1** tough. **2** (of a person) hard.

corne (kɔrn) *nf* horn. **cornet** *nm* **1** small horn. **2** cornet.

corneille (kɔr'nɛj) *nf* crow.

cornemuse (kɔrnə'myz) *nf* bagpipes.

cornichon (kɔrni:'ʃɔ̃) *nm* gherkin.

cornu (kɔr'ny) *adj* horned.

corporation (kɔrpɔra'sjɔ̃) *nf* **1** corporation. **2** guild.

corporel, -elle (kɔrpɔ'rɛl) *adj* corporal.

corps (kɔr) *nm* **1** body. **2** corpse. **3** main part. **4** corps. **corps à corps** hand to hand.

corpulent (kɔrpy'lɑ̃) *adj* stout, fat.

correct (kɔ'rɛkt) *adj* **1** correct. **2** proper. **correction** *nf* **1** correction. **2** accuracy. **3** punishment.

correspondre (kɔrɛ'spɔ̃dr) *vi* **1** agree, tally. **2** correspond, match. **correspondance** *nf* **1** correspondence. **2** connection (train, etc.). **correspondant** *adj* corresponding. *nm* **1** correspondent. **2** penfriend.

corrida (kɔri:'da) *nf* bullfight.

corridor (kɔri:'dɔr) *nm* corridor, passage.

corriger (kɔri:'ʒe:) *vt* **1** correct. **2** punish.

corroder (kɔrrɔ'de:) *vt* corrode.

corrompre (kɔ'rɔ̃pr) *vt* **1** corrupt. **2** bribe. **3** taint. **corrompu** *adj* **1** corrupt. **2** tainted.

corsage (kɔr'saʒ) *nm* bodice.

Corse (kɔrs) *nf* Corsica. **corse** *adj,n* Corsican.

corset (kɔr'sɛ) *nm* corset.

cortège (kɔr'tɛʒ) *nm* **1** procession. **2** train.

corvée (kɔr've:) *nf* drudgery, unpleasant task.

cosmétique (kɔsme:'ti:k) *adj,nm* cosmetic.

cosmique (kɔs'mi:k) *adj* cosmic.

cosmopolite (kɔsmɔpɔ'li:t) *adj,n* cosmopolitan.

cosmos ('kɔsmɔs) *nm* cosmos.

cosse (kɔs) *nf* pod, husk, hull.

cossu (kɔ'sy) *adj* well-off, rich.

costaud (kɔ'sto) *adj* **1** strong. **2** well-built.

costume (kɔ'stym) *nf* **1** costume. **2** dress. **3** suit (of clothes).

cote (kɔt) *nf* **1** share. **2** number. **3** *comm* quotation.

côte (kot) *nf* **1** rib. **2** coast. **3** hill. **côte à côte** side by side. **côtier, -ière** (ko'tje:, -'tjɛr) *adj* coastal.

côté (ko'te:) *nm* **1** side. **2** way. **3** direction. **à côté de** beside. **à côté l'un de l'autre** or **côte à côte** side by side. **de côté** sideways. **de l'autre côté** on the other side or hand.

coteau, -aux (kɔ'to) *nm* hillside.

côtelette (kot'lɛt) *nf* cutlet, chop.

coter (kɔ'te:) *vt* **1** assess. **2** classify. **3** *comm* quote.

se cotiser (kɔti:'ze:) *vr* **1** subscribe. **2** club together. **cotisation** *nf* **1** subscription. **2** contribution, share.

coton (kɔ'tɔ̃) *nm* **1** cotton. **2** cottonwool.

côtoyer (kotwa'je:) *vt* coast along.

cou (ku:) *nm* neck. **cou-de-pied** *nm, pl* **cous-de-pied** instep.

coucher (ku:'ʃe:) *vt* **1** put to bed. **2** lay down. *vi* sleep. **se coucher** *vr* **1** go to bed. **2** lie down. **coucher** *nm* setting. **coucher du soleil** sunset. **couchant** *adj* setting. *nm* **1** west. **2** decline. **couche** *nf* **1** couch. **2** *pl med* labour. **3** nappy. **4** layer. **couché sociale** social class. **fausse couche** miscarriage. **couché** *adj* **1** lying. **2** in bed. **couchette** *nf* **1** cot. **2** berth.

coucou (ku:'ku:) *nm* cuckoo.

coude (ku:d) *nm* **1** elbow. **2** bend.

coudre* (ku:dr) *vt* sew, stitch.

coudrier (ku:'drje:) *nm* hazel tree.

couenne (kwen) *nf* rind.

couic (kwi:k) *nm* **1** chirp. **2** squeak.

couin-couin (kwɛ̃'kwɛ̃) *nm* quack.

couler (ku:'le:) *vt* **1** pour. **2** strain. **3** sink. **4** cast. *vi* **1** flow, run. **2** leak. **3** sink. **se couler** *vr* slip, glide. **coulant** *adj* running, flowing. **coulé** *adj* (of metal) cast. *nm mus* slur.

couleur (ku:'lœr) *nf* **1** colour. **2** paint. **3** *game* suit.

couleuvre (ku:'lœvr) *nf* grass snake.

coulisse (ku:'li:s) *nf* **1** slot. **2** *pl Th* wings. **à coulisse** sliding.

couloir (ku:l'war) *nm* **1** corridor, passage. **2** *pol* lobby.

coup (ku:) *nm* **1** blow. **2** knock. **3** stroke. **4** attempt. **coup de bec** peck. **coup de coude** nudge. **coup de feu** shot. **coup de froid** chill. **coup d'envoi** kick-off. **coup de pied** kick. **coup de soleil** sunstroke. **coup d'œil** glance. **coup illicite** *sport* foul. **du coup** now at last. **du premier coup** at the first attempt. **tout à coup** suddenly.

coupable (ku:'pabl) *adj* guilty. *nm* culprit.

coupe[1] (ku:p) *nf* cup.
coupe[2] (ku:p) *nf* cutting, cut.
couper (ku:'pe:) *vt* **1** cut. **2** cross. **3** interrupt, stop. **4** dilute. **se couper** *vr* **1** cut oneself. **2** intersect. **3** contradict oneself. **coupant** *adj* cutting, sharp. **coupure** *nf* **1** cut, gash. **2** cutting.
couperose (ku:p'roz) *nf* acne.
coupler (ku:'ple:) *vt* **1** couple. **2** connect. **couple** *nm* pair, couple. *nf* couple, brace.
couplet (ku:'plɛ) *nm* verse.
coupon (ku:'pɔ̃) *nm* **1** coupon, warrant. **2** piece cut off or detached. **3** *pl* remnants.
cour (ku:r) *nf* **1** court. **2** courtyard. **3** courtship. **4** playground. **cour de ferme** farmyard.
courage (ku:'raʒ) *nm* courage, pluck. **courageux, -euse** (ku:ra'ʒœ, -'ʒœz) *adj* brave.
couramment (ku:ra'mɑ̃) *adv* **1** fluently, easily. **2** generally, currently.
courant (ku:'rɑ̃) *v* see **courir.** *adj* **1** running. **2** current, present. *nm* **1** current. **2** stream. **3** course. **courant d'air** draught. **être au courant de** know all about. **mettre au courant** inform.
courbature (ku:rba'tyr) *nf* **1** stiffness. **2** tiredness. **courbaturé** *adj* **1** stiff. **2** aching.
courber (ku:r'be:) *vt* bend, curve. *vi* sag. **se courber** *vr* stoop. **courbe** *nf* curve, bend. **courbé** *adj* curved.
courge (ku:rʒ) *nf* gourd. **courge à la moelle** marrow. **courgette** *nf* courgette.
courir* (ku:'ri:r) *vi* **1** run. **2** race. **3** be current. *vt* **1** run. **2** hunt. **3** roam. **coureur, -euse** (ku:'rœr, -'rœz) *nm,f* **1** runner. **2** wanderer.
couronner (ku:rɔ'ne:) *vt* **1** crown. **2** cap. **3** award. **couronne** *nf* **1** crown. **2** wreath. **couronnement** *nm* **1** coronation. **2** crowning.
courrier (ku:'rje:) *nm* **1** mail, letters. **2** post. **3** messenger. **4** courier.
courroie (ku:r'wa) *nf* strap.
courroux (ku:'ru:) *nm* anger.
cours (ku:r) *nm* **1** course. **2** path. **3** circulation. **4** quotation. **5** lesson. **cours de change** rate of exchange. **en cours** in progress, current.
course (ku:rs) *nf* **1** run. **2** race. **3** journey. **4** errand. **5** path. **faire des courses 1** go shopping. **2** run errands.
court[1] (ku:r) *adj* short, brief. *adv* short. **à court de** short of. **tout court** simply, merely.
court[2] (ku:r) *nm* tennis court.
courtier (ku:r'tje:) *nm* broker.
courtisan (ku:rti:'zɑ̃) *nm* courtier.
courtois (ku:r'twa) *adj* courteous, polite. **courtoisie** *nf* courtesy.
cousant (ku:sɑ̃) *v* see **coudre.**
cousin[1] (ku:'zɛ̃) *nm* cousin. **cousin germain** first cousin.
cousin[2] (ku:'zɛ̃) *nm* gnat.
coussin (ku:'sɛ̃) *nm* cushion. **coussinet** *nm* pad.
cousu (ku:'zy) *v* see **coudre.**
coût (ku:) *nm* cost.
couteau, -aux (ku:'to) *nm* knife. **couteau à découper** carving-knife.
coutellerie (ku:tɛl'ri:) *nf* cutlery.
coûter (ku:'te:) *vi* cost. **coûter cher/peu** be expensive/cheap. **coûteux, -euse** (ku:'tœ, -'tœz) *adj* expensive, dear.
coutume (ku:'tym) *nf* custom, habit.
couture (ku:'tyr) *nf* **1** needlework. **2** seam. **couturier, -ière** (ku:ty'rje:, -'rjɛr) *nm,f* dressmaker.
couvent (ku:'vɑ̃) *nm* convent.
couver (ku:'ve:) *vt* **1** sit on. **2** hatch. **3** brood. *vi* **1** smoulder. **2** brew, be imminent **couvée** *nf* clutch, brood. **couveuse artificielle** *nf* incubator.
couvercle (ku:'vɛrkl) *nm* **1** lid. **2** cover.
couvrir* (ku:'vri:r) *vt* **1** cover. **2** conceal. **se couvrir** *vr* **1** put on one's hat. **2** become overcast. **couvert** *adj* **1** covered. **2** overcast. *nm* **1** shelter. **2** place at table. **mettre/ôter le couvert** lay/clear the table. **couverture** *nf* **1** cover. **2** rug. **3** blanket. **4** *pl* bedclothes. **couverture de lit** bedspread. **couvre-feu** *nm invar* curfew. **couvre-lit** *nm, pl* **couvre-lits** bedspread.
crabe (krab) *nm* crab.
crac (krak) *interj,nm* **1** crack. **2** snap.
cracher (kra'ʃe:) *vi* spit. *vt* **1** spit out. **2** *sl* cough up. **crachat** *nm* spit.
crachiner (kraʃi:'ne:) *vi* drizzle.
craie (krɛ) *nf* chalk.
craignant (kre'ɲɑ̃) *v* see **craindre.**
craindre* (krɛ̃dr) *vt* **1** fear, dread. **2** be afraid of.
craint (krɛ̃) *v* see **craindre.**
crainte (krɛ̃t) *nf* fear, dread. **craintif, -ive** (krɛ̃'ti:f, -'ti:v) *adj* **1** timid. **2** afraid.
cramoisi (kramwa'zi:) *adj,nm* crimson.
crampe (krɑ̃p) *nf* cramp.
crampon (krɑ̃'pɔ̃) *nm* **1** clamp. **2** stud (for a boot).
cramponner (krɑ̃pɔ'ne:) *vt* **1** clamp. **2** *inf* buttonhole. **se cramponner à** *vr* hang on to.
cran (krɑ̃) *nm* **1** notch. **2** catch. **3** *inf* pluck.

crâner (kra'ne:) *vi* swagger, swank. **crâne** *nf* skull. *adj* **1** swaggering. **2** plucky.

crapaud (kra'po) *nm* toad.

crapuleux, -euse (krapy'lœ, -'lœz) *adj* **1** lewd. **2** filthy.

craquer (kra'ke:) *vi* **1** crack. **2** crackle. **craquelure** *nf* crack.

crasse (kras) *adj f* gross. *nf* **1** dirt. **2** meanness. **crasseux, -euse** (kra'sœ, -'sœz) *adj* **1** filthy. **2** squalid.

cratère (kra'tɛr) *nm* crater.

cravate (kra'vat) *nf* scarf, necktie.

crayon (krɛ'jɔ̃) *nm* **1** pencil. **2** stick. **3** sketch.

crayonner *vt* **1** make a pencil sketch. **2** note.

créance (kre:'ɑ̃s) *nf* **1** belief. **2** trust. **3** credit.

créateur, -trice (kre:a'tœr, -'tri:s) *adj* creative. *nm,f* **1** creator. **2** inventor.

création (kre:a'sjɔ̃) *nf* creation.

créature (kre:a'tyr) *nf* creature.

crèche (krɛʃ) *nf* **1** crib, manger. **2** day nursery.

crédence (krɛ'dɑ̃s) *nf* sideboard.

crédit (kre:'di:) *nm* **1** credit. **2** trust. **3** influence. **créditeur, -trice** (kre:di:'tœr, -'tri:s) *nm,f* creditor. *adj* credit.

créer (kre:'e:) *vt* **1** create. **2** found.

crémaillère (krɛma'jɛr) *nf* **pendre la crémaillère** have a house warming.

crématoire (krɛma'twar) **four crématoire** *nm* crematorium.

crème (krɛm) *nf* **1** cream. **2** custard. **3** best.

crémer (kre:'me:) *vi* cream. **crémerie** *nf* dairy.

crénelé (krɛn'le:) *adj* **1** notched. **2** toothed.

crêpe (krɛp) *nf* pancake.

crêper (krɛ'pe:) *vt* fizz. **crépu** *adj* **1** crisp. **2** crinkled.

crépiter (kre:pi:'te:) *vi* crackle.

crépuscule (kre:py'skyl) *nm* dusk, twilight.

cresson (krə'sɔ̃) *nm* cress.

crête (krɛt) *nf* **1** *zool* crest. **2** ridge.

creuser (krœ'ze:) *vt* **1** hollow out. **2** excavate. **3** go deeply into.

creux, creuse (krœ, krœz) *adj* **1** hollow. **2** empty. **3** slack. **4** sunken. *nm* **1** hollow. **2** pit.

crevaison (krəvɛ'zɔ̃) *nf* puncture.

crevasser (krəva'se:) *vt* **1** crack. **2** chap. **crevasse** *nf* **1** crack. **2** crevice.

crever (krə've:) *vi* **1** burst. **2** split. **3** *sl* die. *vt* burst, puncture.

crevette (krə'vɛt) *nf* **1** shrimp. **2** prawn.

cri (kri:) *nm* **1** cry. **2** shout. **3** shriek. **le dernier cri** the latest fashion.

criailler (kri:a'je:) *vi* **1** bawl. **2** whine.

cribler (kri:'ble:) *vt* **1** riddle. **2** sift. **crible** *nm* **1** sieve. **2** riddle.

cric (kri:k) *nm* jack.

cricri (kri:'kri:) *nm zool* cricket.

cricket (kri:'kɛ) *nm sport* cricket.

criée (kri:'e:) *nf* auction.

crier (kri:'e:) *vi* **1** cry. **2** shout. **3** scream. *vt* shout. **criant** *adj* flagrant, gross. **criard** *adj* **1** crying. **2** shrill. **3** loud, flashy.

crime (kri:m) *nm* crime. **criminel, -elle** (kri:mi:'nɛl) *adj* **1** guilty. **2** criminal. *nm,f* criminal. **incendie criminel** *nm* arson.

crin (krɛ̃) *nm* horsehair. **crinière** *nf* mane.

crique (kri:k) *nf* cove.

criquet (kri:'kɛ) *nm* **1** locust. **2** *zool* cricket.

crise (kri:z) *nf* **1** crisis. **2** attack, fit. **3** shortage. **crise cardiaque** heart attack.

crisper (kri'spe:) *vt* **1** contract. **2** clench. **se crisper** *vr* **1** contract. **2** shrivel up. **crispé** *adj* on edge.

crisser (kri:'se:) *vi,vt* **1** grate. **2** grind.

cristal, -aux (kri:'stal, -'sto) *nm* crystal. **cristal taillé** cut glass.

cristalliser (kri:stali:'ze:) *vi,vt* crystallize.

critère (kri:'tɛr) *nm also* **critérium** criterion.

critiquer (kri:ti:'ke:) *vt* **1** criticize. **2** censure. **critique** *adj* **1** critical. **2** crucial. *nf* **1** criticism. **2** censure. *nm* critic.

croasser (krɔa'se:) *vi* croak.

croc (kro) *nm* **1** hook. **2** fang. **3** tusk. **faire** or **donner un croc en jambe à** trip.

croche (krɔʃ) *nf mus* quaver.

crochet (krɔ'ʃɛ) *nm* **1** hook. **2** crochet. **3** swerve. **4** *pl* square brackets. **faire du crochet** crochet.

crochu (krɔ'ʃy) *adj* **1** hooked. **2** crooked.

crocodile (krɔkɔ'di:l) *nm* crocodile.

crocus (krɔ'kys) *nm* crocus.

croire* (krwar) *vt* **1** believe. **2** think. **croire à** or **en** believe in.

croisade (krwa'zad) *nf* crusade.

croiser (krwa'ze:) *vt* **1** cross. **2** pass. *vi* **1** fold over. **2** cruise. **croisée** *nf* crossing. **croisement** *nm* **1** crossing. **2** intersection. **croisière** *nf* cruise.

croissance (krwa'sɑ̃s) *nf* growth.

croissant (krwa'sɑ̃) *v see* **croître.** *adj* **1** growing. **2** increasing. **3** rising. *nm* **1** crescent. **2** bread roll in a crescent shape.

croître* (krwatr) *vi* **1** grow. **2** increase. **3** rise.

croix (krwa) *nf* cross. **croix gammée** swastika.

croquer (krɔ'ke:) *vt* **1** crunch. **2** munch. **3**

sketch. **croquant** *adj* crisp. *nm* **1** gristle. **2** crackling.
croquet (krɔ'kɛ) *nm* croquet.
croquis (krɔ'ki:) *nm* sketch.
crosse (krɔs) *nf* **1** crook. **2** *sport* stick, club. **3** butt (of a rifle). **crosse de golf** golf club.
crotter (krɔ'te:) *vt* dirty, soil. **crotte** *nf* **1** dirt. **2** mud. **3** dung. **une crotte de chocolat** a chocolate.
crouler (kru:'le:) *vi* **1** collapse. **2** totter. **3** crumble. **croulement** *nm* collapse.
croupe (kru:p) *nf* **1** rump. **2** ridge. **3** *pl zool* buttocks.
croupir (kru:'pi:r) *vi* **1** wallow. **2** stagnate.
croustiller (kru:sti:'je:) *vi* crunch. **croustillant** *adj* **1** crisp. **2** spicy.
croûte (kru:t) *nf* **1** crust. **2** rind. **3** scab. **casser une croûte** have a snack. **croûton** *nm* piece of crust.
croyance (krwa'jɑ̃s) *nf* belief. **croyable** *adj* **1** credible. **2** trustworthy.
croyant (krwa'jɑ̃) *v* see **croire.** *adj* believing. *nm* believer.
cru[1] (kry) *adj* **1** raw. **2** coarse. **3** crude.
cru[2] (kry) *nm* **1** wine-growing district. **2** vintage.
cru[3] (kry) *v* see **croire.**
crû (kry) *v* see **croire.**
cruauté (kryo'te:) *nf* cruelty.
crucifier (krysi:'fje:) *vt* crucify.
crucifix (krysi:'fi:) *nm* crucifix.
crudité (krydi:'te:) *nf* **1** rawness. **2** crudeness. **3** coarseness.
crue (kry) *nf* **1** rising. **2** flood.
cruel, -elle (kry'ɛl) *adj* cruel.
crûment (kry'mɑ̃) *adv* **1** crudely. **2** roughly.
crustacés (krysta'se:) *nm pl* shellfish.
crypte (kri:pt) *nf* crypt.
cube (kyb) *nm* cube. **cubique** *adj* cubic.
cueillir* (kœ'ji:r) *vt* **1** gather. **2** pick.
cuiller (kyi:'je:) *nf also* **cuillère** spoon. **cuiller à bouche/dessert/pot/thé** tablespoon/dessertspoon/ladle/teaspoon. **cuillerée** *nf* spoonful.
cuir (kɥi:r) *nm* **1** leather. **2** hide. **3** skin. **cuir chevelu** scalp. **cuir verni** patent leather.
cuirasse (kɥi:'ras) *nf* armour. **cuirassé** *adj* armoured, armour-plated. *nm* battleship.
cuire* (kɥi:r) *vt* **1** cook. **2** fire, bake. *vi* **1** cook. **2** smart. **cuire au four** roast, bake. **cuit à point** done to a turn. **cuisant** *adj* **1** burning. **2** smarting. **3** bitter.
cuisine (kɥi:'zi:n) *nf* **1** kitchen. **2** cookery. **3** cooking. **faire la cuisine** cook. **cuisinier, -ière** (kɥi:zi:'nje:, -'njɛr) *nm,f* cook. *nf* cooker.
cuisse (kɥi:s) *nf* thigh. **cuisses de grenouille** *nf pl* frogs' legs.
cuivre (kɥi:vr) *nm* copper. **cuivre jaune** brass.
cul (kyl) *nm* **1** bottom. **2** behind. **3** rump. **cul-de-sac** *nm, pl* **culs-de-sac** dead end, blind alley.
culbuter (kylby'te:) *vi* somersault. *vt* **1** overthrow. **2** tip. **culbute** *nf* **1** somersault. **2** tumble.
culinaire (kyli:'nɛr) *adj* culinary.
culminant (kylmi:'nɑ̃) *adj* highest.
culot (ky'lo) *nm* **1** bottom, base. **2** *sl* cheek.
culotte (ky'lɔt) *nf* **1** shorts. **2** pants.
culpabilité (kylpabi:li:'te:) *nf* guilt.
culte (kylt) *nm* **1** worship. **2** cult.
cultiver (kylti:'ve:) *vt* **1** farm. **2** cultivate. **cultivateur** *nm* farmer. **cultivé** *adj* **1** cultivated. **2** cultured.
culture (kyl'tyr) *nf* **1** culture. **2** cultivation. **culturel, -elle** (kylty'rɛl) *adj* cultural.
cupide (ky'pi:d) *adj* greedy. **cupidité** *nf* greed.
cure (kyr) *nf* **1** care. **2** cure.
curé (ky're:) *nm* parish priest.
curer (ky're:) *vt* **1** pick. **2** clean out. **cure-dents** *nm invar* toothpick.
curieux, -euse (ky'rjœ, -'rjœz) *adj* **1** curious. **2** interested. **3** inquisitive. **4** odd.
curiosité (kyrjɔzi:'te:) *nf* **1** curiosity. **2** peculiarity.
cuver (ky've:) *vi,vt* ferment. **cuve** *nf* **1** vat. **2** tub. **cuve à lessive** copper. **cuvette** *nf* **1** washbasin. **2** basin.
cycle[1] (si:kl) *nm* cycle.
cycle[2] (si:kl) *nm* bicycle. **cycliste** *nm,f* cyclist.
cyclomoteur (si:klomɔ'tœr) *nm* moped.
cyclone (si:'klon) *nm* cyclone.
cygne (si:ɲ) *nm* swan.
cylindre (si:'lɛ̃dr) *nm* cylinder. **cylindre compresseur** steamroller.
cymbale (sɛ̃'bal) *nf* cymbal.
cynique (si:'ni:k) *adj* **1** cynical. **2** brazen. *nm* cynic.
cyprès (si:'prɛ) *nm* cypress.
cypriote (si:pri:'ɔt) *adj,n* Cypriot.

D

dactylographier (dakti:lɔgra'fje:) *vt* type. **dactylographe** *nm,f* typist.
dague (dag) *nf* dagger.

daigner (dɛ'ɲe) *vt* condescend.
daim (dɛ̃) *nm* **1** deer. **2** buck. **3** suede.
dais (dɛ) *nm* canopy.
daller (da'le:) *vt* pave, flag. **dalle** *nf* tile.
daltonien, -ienne (daltɔ'njɛ̃, -'njɛn) *adj* colour-blind. **daltonisme** *nm* colour-blindness.
damas (da'mɑ) *nm* damson.
dame[1] (dam) *interj* **1** indeed! **2** rather!
dame[2] (dam) *nf* **1** lady. **2** *game* queen. **3** *pl* draughts.
damier (da'mje:) *nm* chessboard.
damner (dɑ'ne:) *vt* damn. **damnable** *adj* **1** damnable. **2** frightful.
dandiner (dɑ̃di:'ne:) *vi* strut. **se dandiner** *vr* waddle.
Danemark (dan'mark) *nm* Denmark. **danois** *adj* Danish. *nm* **1** Dane. **2** Danish (language).
danger (dɑ̃'ʒe:) *nm* **1** danger, peril. **2** risk. **dangereux, -euse** (dɑ̃ʒ'rœ, -'rœz) *adj* dangerous.
dans (dɑ̃) *prep* **1** in. **2** within. **3** into. **4** during.
danser (dɑ̃'se:) *vi,vt* dance. **danse** *nf* **1** dance. **2** dancing. **danseur, -euse** (dɑ̃'sœr, -'sœz) *nm,f* dancer.
dard (dar) *nm* **1** dart. **2** sting.
darder (dar'de:) *vt* **1** hurl. **2** dart. **3** shoot out.
dater (da'te:) *vi,vt* date. **date** *nf* date.
datte (dat) *nf bot* date. **dattier** *nm* date palm.
daube (dob) *nf* stew.
dauphin (do'fɛ̃) *nm* **1** dolphin. **2** eldest son of the French king.
davantage (davɑ̃'taʒ) *adv* more, any more.
de (də) *prep* **1** from. **2** of. **3** by. **4** with. **5** in. **6** made of. **7** some.
dé (de:) *nm* **1** dice. **2** tee. **dé (à coudre)** thimble.
débâcle (de:'bɑkl) *nf* **1** collapse, downfall. **2** breaking up.
déballer (de:ba'le:) *vt* unpack.
débander[1] (de:bɑ̃'de:) *vt* **1** relax. **2** unbend.
débander[2] (de:bɑ̃'de:) *vt* disband. **se débander** *vr* disperse. **débandade** *nf* stampede.
débarbouiller (de:barbu:'je:) *vt* wash, clean. **se débarbouiller** *vr* wash one's face.
débarcadère (de:barka'dɛr) *nm* wharf, landing stage.
débardeur (de:bar'dœr) *nm* docker.
débarquer (de:bar'ke:) *vi,vt* **1** land. **2** disembark. *vt* unload. **débarquement** *nm* **1** landing. **2** arrival.
débarras (de:ba'rɑ) *nm* riddance.
débarrasser (de:bara'se:) *vt* **1** rid. **2** free. **3** clear. **se débarrasser de** *vr* get rid of.
débat (de:'ba) *nm* **1** debate. **2** discussion. **3** dispute.
débattre* (de:'batr) *vt* **1** debate. **2** discuss. **se débattre** *vr* struggle.
débaucher (de:bo'ʃe:) *vt* **1** lead astray. **2** discharge. **se débaucher** *vr* go astray, misbehave.
débile (de:'bi:l) *adj* weak, feeble.
débit[1] (de:'bi:) *nm* **1** sale. **2** retail shop. **3** cutting up. **4** delivery. **5** output. **débit de boissons** public house.
débit[2] (de:'bi) *nm* debit.
débiter[1] (de:bi:'te:) *vt* **1** retail. **2** cut up. **3** supply. **4** recite.
débiter[2] (de:bi:'te:) *vt* debit.
déblai (de:'blɛ) *nm* **1** clearing. **2** excavation. **3** rubbish.
déblayer (de:blɛ'je:) *vt* **1** clear. **2** remove.
déboîter (de:bwa'te:) *vt* **1** dislocate. **2** disconnect.
débonnaire (de:bɔ'nɛr) *adj* easygoing.
déborder (de:bɔr'de:) *vi,vt* overflow. *vt* project, protrude. **débordé** *adj* **1** overflowing. **2** busy.
déboucher[1] (de:bu:'ʃe:) *vt* **1** clear. **2** open.
déboucher[2] (de:bu:'ʃe:) *vi* **1** emerge. **2** come from. **débouché** *nm* **1** outlet. **2** opening
débourser (de:bu:r'se:) *vt* spend.
debout (də'bu:) *adj* **1** upright. **2** standing.
déboutonner (de:bu:tɔ'ne:) *vt* unbutton.
débraillé (de:brɑ'je:) *adj* **1** untidy. **2** slovenly. **3** improper.
débrayer (de:brɛ'je:) *vt* disconnect. *vi* declutch. **débrayage** *nm* **1** disconnecting. **2** *mot* clutch.
débris (de:'bri:) *nm pl* **1** remains. **2** rubbish.
débrouiller (de:bru:'je:) *vt* **1** sort out. **2** extricate. **se débrouiller** *vr* manage.
débuter (de:by'te:) *vi* begin, start. **début** *nm* **1** beginning. **2** first appearance. **débutant** *nm* beginner.
deçà (də'sa) *adv* on this side. **deçà delà** here and there.
décade (dɛ'kad) *nf* decade.
décadent (de:ka'dɑ̃) *adj* **1** decadent. **2** in decay. **décadence** *nf* **1** decline. **2** decay.
décaler (de:ka'le:) *vt* shift, displace. **décalé** *adj* off balance.
décamper (de:kɑ̃'pe:) *vi* **1** *inf* clear off. **2** bolt.
décanter (de:kɑ̃te:) *vt* decant.
décéder (de:se:'de:) *vi* decease, die.
déceler (de:s'le:) *vt* **1** disclose. **2** reveal.
décembre (de:'sɑ̃br) *nm* December.
décent (de:'sɑ̃) *adj* **1** decent. **2** proper.

déception (de:sɛp'sjɔ̃) *nf* **1** deception. **2** disappointment.
décerner (de:sɛr'ne:) *vt* **1** award. **2** confer.
décès (de:'sɛ) *nm* decease, death.
décevoir* (de:sə'vwar) *vt* **1** deceive. **2** disappoint.
déchaîner (de:ʃɛ'ne:) *vt* let loose, loose. **se déchaîner** *vr* break out, rage.
décharger (de:ʃar'ʒe:) *vt* **1** unload. **2** discharge, let off. **décharge** *nf* **1** unloading. **2** discharge. **3** rebate.
décharné (de:ʃar'ne:) *adj* emaciated, skinny.
se déchausser (de:sho'se:) *vr* take off one's shoes.
déchéance (de:ʃe:'ɑ̃s) *nf* **1** fall. **2** downfall. **3** loss.
déchet (de:'ʃɛ) *nm* **1** loss. **2** *pl* waste, scraps.
déchiffrer (de:ʃi:'fre:) *vt* **1** decipher. **2** sight-read.
déchiqueter (de:ʃi:k'te:) *vt* **1** slash. **2** tear. **3** cut.
déchirer (de:ʃi:'re:) *vt* tear. **déchirure** *nf* tear, slit.
déchoir* (de:'ʃwar) *vi* (*aux* être) fall.
décibel (de:si:'bɛl) *nm* decibel.
décider (de:si:'de:) *vt* **1** decide. **2** settle. **3** persuade. **se décider à** *vr* make up one's mind to.
décimale (de:si:'mal) *nf* decimal. **decimal, -aux** (de:si:'mal, -'mo) *adj* decimal.
décisif, -ive (de:si:'si:f, -'si:v) *adj* **1** decisive. **2** critical.
décision (de:si:'zjɔ̃) *nf* **1** decision. **2** determination.
déclarer (de:kla're:) *vt* **1** declare. **2** make known. **déclaration** *nf* declaration.
déclencher (de:klɑ̃'ʃe:) *vt* **1** release. **2** launch.
déclin (de:'klɛ̃) *nm* **1** decline. **2** close. **3** end.
décliner (de:kli:'ne:) *vi,vt* decline. *vt* refuse. **déclinaison** *nf* declension.
décoiffé (de:kwa'fe:) *adj* dishevelled.
décoller (de:kɔ'le:) *vt* loosen. *vi* take off. **se décoller** *vr* work loose. **décollage** *nm* take-off. **décolleté** *adj* low-necked. *nm* neckline.
décolorer (de:kɔlɔ're:) *vt* **1** fade. **2** bleach.
décombres (de:'kɔ̃br) *nm pl* **1** rubbish. **2** ruins.
décommander (de:kɔmɑ̃'de:) *vt* cancel.
décomposer (de:kɔ̃po'ze:) *vt* **1** rot. **2** distort.
décompte (de:'kɔ̃t) *nm* **1** deduction. **2** disappointment.
déconcerter (de:kɔ̃sɛr'te:) *vt* **1** confound. **2** baffle.
décongeler (de:kɔ̃ʒ'le:) *vt* thaw.
déconseiller (de:kɔ̃sɛ'je:) *vt* dissuade.
décontracter (de:kɔ̃trak'te:) *vt* relax.
déconvenue (de:kɔ̃və'ny) *nf* disappointment.
décor (de:'kɔr) *nm* **1** decoration. **2** arrangement. **3** *pl Th* scenery.
décorer (de:kɔ're:) *vt* decorate. **décoration** *nf* **1** medal. **2** decoration.
découper (de:ku:'pe) *vt* **1** cut up. **2** carve. **3** cut out.
décourager (de:ku:ra'ʒe:) *vt* **1** discourage. **2** deter.
décousu (de:ku:'zy) *adj* **1** undone. **2** disconnected. **3** disjointed.
découverte (de:ku:'vɛrt) *nf* discovery.
découvrir (de:ku:'vri:r) *vt* **1** discover. **2** uncover.
décrasser (de:kra'se:) *vt* **1** clean. **2** scour.
décret (de:'krɛ) *nm* decree.
décrire* (de:'kri:r) *vt* describe.
décrocher (de:krɔ'ʃe:) *vt* **1** take down. **2** disconnect.
décroître* (de:'krwatr) *vi* **1** decrease. **2** diminish. **décroissance** *nf* **1** decrease. **2** decline.
dédaigner (de:dɛ'ɲe:) *vt* scorn. **dédaigneux, -euse** (de:dɛ'ɲœ, -'ɲœz) *adj* scornful.
dédain (de:'dɛ̃) *nm* **1** scorn. **2** contempt.
dédale (de:'dal) *nm* maze, labyrinth.
dedans (də'dɑ̃) *adv* inside, within. *nm* **1** inside. **2** interior.
dédier (de:'dje:) *vt* dedicate. **dédicace** *nf* dedication.
dédit (de:'di:) *nm* **1** forfeit. **2** retraction.
dédommager (de:dɔma'ʒe:) *vt* compensate.
déduction (de:dyk'sjɔ̃) *nf* deduction.
déduire* (de:'dɥi:r) *vt* **1** deduce. **2** deduct. **3** infer.
déesse (de:'ɛs) *nf* goddess.
défaillir* (de:fa'ji:r) *vi* **1** grow weak. **2** fail. **3** faint. **défaillance** *nf* **1** lapse. **2** weakness. **3** faint.
défaire* (de:'fɛr) *vt* **1** undo. **2** untie. **3** defeat. **défaite** *nf* defeat.
défalquer (de:fal'ke:) *vt* deduct.
défaut (de:'fo) *nm* **1** defect. **2** fault. **3** lack.
défection (de:fɛk'sjɔ̃) *nf* defection. **defectueux, -euse** (de:fɛk'tɥœ, -'tɥœz) *adj* **1** defective. **2** deficient.
défendre (de:'fɑ̃dr) *vt* **1** defend. **2** protect. **3** forbid.
défense (de:'fɑ̃s) *nf* **1** defence. **2** tusk. **défense de fumer** no smoking.

déférer (de:fɛ're:) *vt* **1** refer. **2** hand over. **3** confer. *vi* defer. **déférent** *adj* deferential.
défi (de:'fi:) *nm* **1** challenge. **2** defiance.
déficeler (de:fi:'sle:) *vt* untie.
déficit (de:fi:'si:) *nm* **1** deficit. **2** shortage.
défier (de:'fje:) *vt* **1** challenge. **2** defy. **se défier** *vr* mistrust. **défiance** *nf* **1** mistrust, distrust. **2** suspicion. **défiant** *adj* **1** wary. **2** suspicious.
défigurer (de:fi:gy're:) *vt* **1** disfigure. **2** distort. **3** deface.
défilé (de:fi:'le:) *nm* **1** pass. **2** procession.
définir (de:fi:'ni:r) *vt* define. **défini** *adj* definite. **définitif, -ive** (de:fi:ni:'ti:f, -'ti:v) *adj* **1** final. **2** permanent. **définition** *nf* **1** definition. **2** clue.
défoncer (de:fɔ̃'se:) *vt* break up. **se défoncer** *vr* collapse.
déformer (de:fɔr'me:) *vt* **1** deform. **2** distort.
défraîchi (de:frɛ'ʃi:) *adj* **1** faded. **2** soiled.
défricher (de:fri:'ʃe:) *vt* **1** clear. **2** reclaim (land).
défunt (de:'fœ̃) *adj* **1** deceased. **2** defunct.
dégager (de:ga'ʒe:) *vt* **1** redeem. **2** clear. **3** release. **dégagé** *adj* **1** free. **2** easy. **3** offhand.
dégarnir (de:gar'ni:r) *vt* strip off.
dégât (de:'ga) *nm* damage.
dégel (de:'ʒɛl) *nm* thaw.
dégeler (de:'ʒle:) *vi,vt* thaw.
dégénérer (de:ʒe:ne:'re:) *vi* degenerate. **dégénéré** *adj* degenerate.
dégivrer (de:ʒi:'vre:) *vt* defrost.
dégonfler (de:gɔ̃'fle:) *vt* **1** deflate. **2** reduce. **se dégonfler** *vr* **1** collapse. **2** subside. **3** *inf* back down.
dégorger (de:gɔr'ʒe:) *vt* free, clear. *vi* overflow.
dégourdir (de:gu:r'di:r) *vt* **1** revive. **2** remove stiffness. **dégourdi** *adj* sharp, astute.
dégoûter (de:gu:'te:) *vt* **1** disgust. **2** sicken.
dégrader (de:gra'de:) *vt* **1** degrade. **2** deface. **se dégrader** *vr* lower oneself.
dégrafer (de:gra'fe:) *vt* undo.
dégraisser (de:grɛ'se:) *vt* **1** clean. **2** skim the fat off.
degré (də'gre:) *nm* **1** degree. **2** step.
dégringoler (de:grɛ̃gɔ'le:) *vi,vt* tumble down. **dégringolade** *nf* **1** tumble. **2** collapse.
dégriser (de:gri:'ze:) *vt* sober.
déguenillé (de:gni:'je:) *adj* ragged, in rags.
déguerpir (de:gɛr'pi:r) *vi* **1** move out. **2** clear out or off.
déguiser (de:gi:'ze:) *vt* disguise. **déguisement** *nm* **1** disguise. **2** fancy dress.
déguster (de:gy'ste:) *vt* taste, sample.
dehors (də'ɔr) *adv* out, outside, outdoors. *nm* outside, exterior.
déité (de:i:'te:) *nf* deity.
déjà (dɛ'ʒa) *adv* **1** already. **2** before. **3** yet.
déjeuner (de:ʒœ'ne:) *vi* **1** have lunch. **2** breakfast. *nm* lunch. **petit déjeuner** breakfast.
delà (də'la) *prep* beyond. **par delà** beyond. **au delà de** beyond. **par delà** on the other side. **en delà** further away.
délabré (de:la'bre:) *adj* **1** dilapidated. **2** in ruins.
délai (de:'lɛ) *nm* **1** delay. **2** notice.
délaisser (de:lɛ'se:) *vt* **1** forsake, desert. **2** relinquish.
délasser (de:la'se:) *vt* **1** rest. **2** refresh. **délassement** *nm* relaxation.
délateur (dɛla'tœr) *nm* informer.
délavé (de:la've:) *adj* faded, washed out.
délayer (de:lɛ'je:) *vt* **1** mix with water. **2** dilute. **3** spin out.
déléguer (de:le:'ge:) *vt* **1** delegate. **2** assign. **délégation** *nf* delegation. **délégué** *nm* **1** delegate. **2** deputy.
délibérer (de:li:be:'re:) *vi* deliberate, ponder. *vt* discuss. **délibération** *nf* **1** discussion. **2** reflection.
délicat (de:li:'ka) *adj* **1** delicate. **2** dainty. **3** sensitive. **4** tricky. **délicatesse** *nf* delicacy.
délice (de:'li:s) *nm* delight. **délicieux, -euse** (de:li:'sjœ, -'sjœz) *adj* delicious.
délier (de:'lje:) *vt* **1** untie. **2** release. **se délier** *vr* come undone. **délié** *adj* **1** slender. **2** thin.
délinquance (de:lɛ̃'kɑ̃s) *nf* delinquency.
délit (de:'li:) *nm* offence.
délivrer (de:li:'vre:) *vt* **1** deliver. **2** rescue. **délivrance** *nf* rescue.
déloyal, -aux (de:lwa'jal, -'jo) *adj* **1** unfaithful, disloyal. **2** false. **3** unfair.
delta (dɛl'ta) *nm* delta.
déluge (de:'lyʒ) *nm* **1** flood. **2** downpour.
déluré (de:ly're:) *adj* astute, sharp.
se démailler (de:ma'je:) *vr* (of a stocking) ladder.
demain (də'mɛ̃) *adv,nm* tomorrow. **à demain!** see you tomorrow! **demain en huit** tomorrow week.
demander (dəmɑ̃'de:) *vt* **1** ask. **2** ask for. **3** enquire. **4** want. **5** require. **se demander** *vr* wonder. **demande** *nf* **1** request. **2** question. **3** application. **4** *comm* demand.
démanger (de:mɑ̃'ʒe:) *vi* itch.
démaquiller (de:maki:'je:) *vt* remove make-up.
démarche (de:'marʃ) *nf* **1** gait, walk. **2** step. **3** proceedings.

démarrer (de:ma're:) *vt* start (a car). *vi* drive off.
démêler (de:me:'le:) *vt* unravel.
démembrer (de:mɑ̃'bre:) *vt* cut up.
déménager (de:mɛna'ʒe:) *vi* move house. **déménagement** *nm* removal.
démence (dɛ'mɑ̃s) *nf* lunacy.
se démener (de:m'ne:) *vr* struggle.
démentir* (de:mɑ̃'ti:r) *vt* **1** contradict. **2** deny. **démenti** *nm* **1** denial. **2** contradiction.
démesuré (de:mzy're:) *adj* **1** huge. **2** excessive.
démettre* (de:'mɛtr) *vt* **1** dislocate. **2** dismiss. **se démettre** *vr* resign.
demeurer (dəmœ're:) *vi (aux* être) **1** live. **2** remain, stay. **au demeurant** *adv* after all. **demeure** *nf* **1** abode. **2** delay. **à demeure** permanent.
demi (də'mi:) *adj,n* half. **à demi** half.
demi-arrière *nm* half-back.
demi-cercle *nm* semicircle.
demi-douzaine *nf* half-a-dozen.
demi-finale *nf* semifinal.
demi-frère *nm* **1** half-brother. **2** stepbrother.
demi-heure *nf* half-hour.
demi-sœur *nf* **1** half-sister. **2** stepsister.
démission (de:mi:'sjɔ̃) *nf* resignation. **donner sa démission** resign.
demi-teinte *nf* halftone.
demi-tour *nm* **1** half-turn. **2** U-turn.
démocratie (de:mɔkra'si:) *nf* democracy. **démocratique** *adj* democratic.
démodé (de:mɔ'de:) *adj* old-fashioned.
demoiselle (dəmwa'zɛl) *nf* **1** young lady. **2** spinster.
démolir (de:mɔ'li:r) *vt* **1** demolish. **2** pull down.
démon (de:'mɔ̃) *nm* demon, fiend.
démonter (de:mɔ̃'te:) *vi* **1** dismantle. **2** upset. **se démonter** *vr* **1** come apart. **2** *inf* get upset.
démontrer (de:mɔ̃'tre:) *vt* **1** demonstrate. **2** prove.
démoraliser (de:mɔrali:'ze:) *vt* **1** demoralize. **2** dishearten.
démordre (de:'mɔrdr) *vi* **1** let go. **2** give up.
démuni (de:my'ni:) *adj*. **démuni de** short, out of.
dénaturé (de:naty're:) *adj* unnatural.
dénégation (de:nega'sjɔ̃) *nf* denial.
dénicher (de:ni:'ʃe:) *vt* find, discover.
denier (də'nje:) *nm* small coin, penny.
dénigrer (de:ni:'gre:) *vt* disparage.
dénombrement (de:nɔ̃brə'mɑ̃) *nm* **1** census. **2** count.
dénominateur (de:nɔmi:na'tœr) *nm* denominator.
dénomination (de:nɔmi:na'sjɔ̃) *nf* denomination.
dénommer (de:nɔ'me:) *vt* name.
dénoncer (de:nɔ̃'se:) *vt* **1** denounce. **2** declare. **3** betray.
dénoter (de:nɔ'te:) *vt* denote.
dénouer (de:'nwe:) *vt* **1** undo, untie. **2** untangle. **se dénouer** *vr* **1** come undone. **2** end. **dénouement** *nm* **1** end. **2** outcome.
denrée (dɑ̃'re:) *nf* commodity.
densité (dɑ̃si:'te:) *nf* density.
dent (dɑ̃) *nf* **1** tooth. **2** prong. **3** cog. **avoir une dent contre** bear a grudge against. **dentaire** *adj* dental. **dental, -aux** (dɑ̃'tal, -'to) *adj* dental.
denteler (dɑ̃t'le:) *vt* **1** notch. **2** indent.
dentelle *nf* lace.
dentier (dɑ̃'tje:) *nm* denture.
dentifrice (dɑ̃ti:'fri:s) *nm* toothpaste.
dentiste (dɑ̃'ti:st) *nm,f* dentist.
dénuder (de:ny'de:) *vt* **1** strip. **2** lay bare.
dénuer (de:'nɥe:) *vt* strip. **se dénuer de** *vr* part with. **dénué** *adj* **1** devoid. **2** destitute.
dépanner (de:pa'ne:) *vt* **1** repair. **2** help out.
dépaqueter (de:pak'te:) *vt* unpack.
dépareillé (de:parɛ'je:) *adj* **1** odd. **2** ill-assorted.
départ (de:'par) *nm* **1** departure. **2** start.
département (de:partə'mɑ̃) *nm* department.
départir (de:par'ti:r) *vt* **1** divide. **2** allot. **se départir de** *vr* **1** deviate from. **2** part with.
dépasser (de:pɑ'se:) *vt* **1** pass beyond. **2** exceed. **3** overtake.
dépaysé (de:pe:i:'ze:) *adj* **1** lost. **2** bewildered.
dépêcher (de:pe:'ʃe:) *vt* dispatch. **se dépêcher** *vr* hurry, make haste. **dépêche** *nf* **1** dispatch. **2** telegram.
dépeindre* (de:'pɛ̃dr) *vt* **1** depict. **2** describe.
dépendre[1] (de:'pɑ̃dr) *vi* **dépendre de** **1** depend on. **2** be subject to. **3** belong to.
dépendre[2] (de:'pɑ̃dr) *vt* take down.
dépens (de:'pɑ̃) *nm pl law* costs.
dépenser (de:pɑ̃'se:) *vt* spend. **dépense** *nf* **1** expense. **2** expenditure. **dépensier, -ière** (de:pɑ̃'sje', -'sjɛr) *adj* extravagant. *nm,f* spendthrift.
dépérir (de:pe:'ri:r) *vi* **1** waste away. **2** decay.
dépêtrer (de:pe:'tre:) *vt* extricate.
dépister (de:pi:'ste:) *vt* **1** track down. **2** outwit.
dépit (de:'pi:) *nm* **1** spite. **2** resentment.
déplacer (de:pla'se:) *vt* **1** displace. **2** take the

place of. **se déplacer** *vr* **1** move. **2** travel. ~*nm* **1** displacement. **2** transfer. **3** travelling.
déplaire* (de:'plɛr) *vt* **1** displease. **2** offend. **se déplaire à** *vr* dislike.
déplantoir (de:plan'twar) *nm* trowel.
déplier (de:pli:'e:) *vt* unfold.
déplorer (de:'plɔre:) *vt* **1** deplore. **2** regret. **3** mourn.
déployer (de:plwa'je:) *vt* **1** spread out. **2** display.
déplumer (de:ply'me:) *vt* pluck. **se déplumer** *vr* moult.
déporter (de:pɔr'te:) *vt* deport.
déposer[1] (de:po'ze:) *vt* **1** lay down. **2** deposit.
déposer[2] (de:po'ze:) *vt* depose.
dépositaire (de:pɔzi:'tɛr) *nm* trustee. **dépositaire de journaux** newsagent.
dépot (de:'po) *nm* **1** deposit. **2** trust. **3** store, depot. **4** sediment.
dépouiller (de:pu:'je:) *vt* **1** skin, strip. **2** deprive. **se dépouiller** *vr* cast off, shed. **dépouille** *nf* **1** skin, hide. **2** remains.
dépourvu (de:pu:r'vy) *adj* **1** destitute. **2** devoid. **au dépourvu** unawares.
dépraver (de:pra've:) *vt* deprave.
déprécier (de:pre:'sje:) *vt* **1** depreciate. **2** underrate. **3** disparage.
dépression (de:prɛ'sjɔ̃) *nf* **1** depression. **2** fall. **3** hollow. **4** gloom. **dépression nerveuse** nervous breakdown.
déprimer (de:pri:'me:) *vt* depress.
depuis (də'pɥi:) *prep* **1** since. **2** for. **3** from. **depuis lors** ever since. **depuis que** since.
députation (de:pyta'sjɔ̃) *nf* deputation.
député (de:py'te:) *nm* **1** deputy. **2** member of parliament.
déraciner (de:rasi:'ne:) *vt* uproot.
dérailler (de:ra'je:) *vi* become derailed.
déraisonnable (de:rɛzɔ'nabl) *adj* **1** unreasonable. **2** irrational.
déranger (de:rɑ̃ʒe:) *vt* **1** disturb. **2** trouble. **3** upset. **se déranger** *vr* **1** make way. **2** put oneself out.
déraper (de:ra'pe:) *vi* skid.
derechef (dəre:'ʃɛf) *adv* a second time, once more.
dérégler (de:re:'gle:) *vt* **1** upset. **2** put out of order. **déréglé** *adj* **1** out of order. **2** irregular. **3** immoral.
dérision (de:ri:'zjɔ̃) *nf* ridicule, mockery. **dérisoire** *adj* ridiculous.
dériver[1] (de:ri:'ve:) *vt* **1** divert. **2** derive. *vi* be diverted.
deriver[2] (de:ri:'ve:) *vi* drift. **dérive** *nf* drift.
dernier, -ière (dɛr'nje:, -'njɛr) *adj* **1** last, latest. **2** latter. **3** utmost. **4** extreme.
dérober (de:rɔ'be:) *vt* **1** steal. **2** hide. **se dérober** *vr* **1** escape. **2** evade. **3** give way. **dérobé** *adj* **1** secret. **2** hidden.
dérogatoire (de:rɔga'twar) *adj* derogatory.
dérouiller (de:ru:'je:) *vt* rub the rust off. **se dérouiller** *vr* brush up.
dérouler (de:ru:'le:) *vt* **1** unwind. **2** unfold. **se dérouler** *vr* **1** unfold. **2** happen.
dérouter (de:ru:'te:) *vt* **1** lead astray. **2** baffle. **3** divert. **déroute** *nf* rout, defeat.
derrière (dɛr'jɛr) *prep* behind. *adv* behind, at the back. *nm* **1** rear. **2** *inf* behind.
des (de:) contraction of **de les.**
dès (dɛ) *prep* **1** from. **2** since. **dès lors** ever since. **dès que 1** as soon as. **2** when.
désabuser (de:zaby'ze:) *vt* disillusion.
désaccord (de:za'kɔr) *nm* **1** disagreement. **2** clash **3** *mus* discord.
désagréable (de:zagre:'abl) *adj* **1** disagreeable. **2** unpleasant. **3** offensive.
désagréger (de:zagre:'ʒe:) *vt* disintegrate.
désagrément (de:zagre:'mɑ̃) *nm* trouble.
se désaltérer (de:zalte:'re:) *vr* quench one's thirst.
désappointer (de:zapwɛ̃'te:) *vt* disappoint.
désapprobation (de:zaprɔba'sjɔ̃) *nf* disapproval.
désapprouver (de:zapru:'ve:) *vt* disapprove of.
désarmer (de:zar'me:) *vt* disarm.
désarroi (de:za'rwa) *nm* disorder, confusion.
désassocier (de:zasɔ'sje:) *vt* dissociate.
désassorti (de:zasɔr'ti:) *adj* made up of odd pieces.
désastre (de:'zastr) *nm* disaster.
désavantage (de:zavɑ̃'taʒ) *nm* disadvantage, drawback.
désaveu, -eux (de:za'vœ) *nm* denial.
désavouer (de:za'vwe:) *vt* **1** repudiate. **2** disown.
désaxé (de:zak'se:) *adj* eccentric.
descendre (dɛ'sɑ̃dr) *vi* (*aux* être) **1** descend. **2** come or go down. **3** alight. *vt* **1** go down. **2** take or bring down. **descendant** *adj* descending, downward. *nm* descendant.
descente (dɛ'sɑ̃t) *nf* **1** descent. **2** slope. **3** raid. **descente de lit** bedside rug.
description (de:skrip'sjɔ̃) *nf* description.
désembarquer (de:zɑ̃bar'ke:) *vi,vt* disembark.
désemparer (de:zɑ̃pa're:) *vt* **1** disable. **2** undo.

sans désemparer without stopping. **désemparé** *adj* 1 in distress. 2 crippled.
désencombrer (de:zɑ̃kɔ̃'bre:) *vt* 1 clear. 2 free.
désenfler (de:zɑ̃'fle:) *vt* deflate. *vi* go down.
désengager (de:zɑ̃ga'ʒe:) *vt* release, free.
désert (de:'zɛr) *adj* 1 deserted. 2 lonely. *nm* 1 desert. 2 wilderness.
déserter (de:zɛr'te:) *vt* desert.
désespérer (de:zɛspe:'re:) *vi* despair. *vt* drive to despair. **désespéré** *adj* 1 desperate. 2 hopeless.
désespoir (de:zɛ'spwar) *nm* despair.
déshabiller (de:zabi:'je:) *vt* undress.
déshériter (de:ze:ri:'te:) *vt* disinherit.
déshonnête (de:zɔ'nɛt) *adj* indecent, improper.
déshonneur (de:zɔ'nœr) *nm* 1 disgrace. 2 dishonour.
déshonorer (de:zɔnɔ're:) *vt* 1 dishonour, disgrace. 2 disfigure.
déshydrater (de:zi:dra'te:) *vt* dehydrate.
désigner (de:zi'ɲe:) *vt* 1 designate, show. 2 appoint. **désignation** *nf* 1 designation. 2 description. 3 appointment.
désinfecter (de:zɛ̃fɛk'te:) *vt* disinfect. **désinfectant** *adj,nm* disinfectant.
désintégrer (de:zɛ̃te'gre:) *vt* disintegrate.
désinvolte (de:zɛ̃'vɔlt) *adj* 1 easy. 2 casual. 2 cheeky.
désir (de:'zi:r) *nm* desire, wish. **désireux, -euse** (de:zi:'rœ, -'rœz) *adj* eager, anxious.
désirer (de:zi:'re:) *vt* desire, wish.
désobéir (de:zɔbe:'i:r) *vt* disobey. **désobéissant** *adj* disobedient.
désodorisant (de:zɔdɔri:'zɑ̃) *nm* deodorant.
désœuvré (dezœ'vre:) *adj* idle.
désoler (de:zɔ'le:) *vt* 1 distress, grieve. 2 desolate. 3 devastate. **se désoler** *vr* grieve. **désolé** *adj* 1 desolate, dreary. 2 grieved, sad, sorry.
désordonné (de:zɔrdɔ'ne:) *adj* 1 untidy. 2 wild, extravagant.
désordre (de:'zɔrdr) *nm* 1 disorder. 2 *pl* riots.
désorganisé (de:zɔrgani:'ze:) *adj* disorganized.
désorienter (de:zɔrjɑ̃'te:) *vt* bewilder. **se désorienter** *vr* 1 lose one's bearings. 2 get confused.
désormais (de:zɔr'mɛ) *adv* from now on.
désosser (de:zo'se:) *vt* bone.
dessécher (de:se:'ʃe:) *vt* 1 dry. 2 wither. **se déssecher** *vr* wither; dry up.
dessein (dɛ'sɛ̃) *nm* 1 plan, scheme. 2 intention.
desserrer (de:sɛ're:) *vt* 1 loosen. 2 unscrew.
dessert (de:'sɛr) *nm* dessert.
desservir (de:sɛr'vi:r) *vt* 1 clear (the table). 2 do a bad turn. 3 serve, connect.
dessin (de:'sɛ̃) *nm* 1 drawing. 2 design. **dessin animé** (cinema) cartoon. **dessinateur** *nm* 1 designer. 2 draughtsman.
dessiner (de:si:'ne:) *vt* 1 draw, sketch. 2 design. 3 outline. **se dessiner** *vr* stand out.
dessous (də'su:) *prep,adv* below, beneath, underneath. *nm* 1 underneath. 2 lower part. **avoir le dessous** get the worst of it. **dessous de plat** tablemat.
dessus (də'sy) *prep,adv* 1 above, over. 2 on. **de dessus** from, off. **en dessus** on top. ~*nm* top. **avoir le dessus** have the upper hand. **dessus de cheminée** mantelpiece.
destin (dɛ'stɛ̃) *nm* destiny, fate.
destiner (dɛsti:'ne:) *vt* 1 destine. 2 intend. **destination** *nf* destination. **destinée** *nf* destiny.
destituer (dɛsti:'tɥe:) *vt* dismiss.
destruction (dɛstryk'sjɛ̃) *nf* destruction.
désuet, -ète (de:'sɥɛ, -'sɥɛt) *adj* obsolete.
désunir (de:zy'ni:r) *vt* 1 divide. 2 detach.
détacher[1] (de:ta'ʃe:) *vt* 1 detach. 2 untie, undo. **se détacher** *vr* come undone. **se détacher de** *vr* break away from.
détacher[2] (de:ta'ʃe:) *vt* remove stains from.
détail (de:'taj) *nm* 1 detail. 2 retail.
détailler (de:ta'je:) *vt* 1 cut up. 2 retail. 3 relate in detail.
détective (de:tɛk'ti:v) *nm* detective.
déteindre* (de:'tɛ̃dr) *vi* lose colour, run.
détendre (de:'tɑ̃dr) *vt* slacken, relax. **se détendre** *vr* 1 relax. 2 spring out.
détenir (de:t'ni:r) *vt* 1 hold. 2 detain. 3 withhold. **détenu** *nm* prisoner.
détente (de:'tɑ̃t) *nf* 1 relaxation. 2 easing (of a political situation). 3 trigger.
détergent (de:tɛr'ʒɑ̃) *nm* detergent.
détériorer (de:te:rjɔ're:) *vt* damage, spoil. **se détériorer** *vr* deteriorate.
déterminer (de:tɛrmi:'ne:) *vt* 1 determine. 2 fix. 3 bring about. **déterminer de** decide to. **se déterminer** *vr* make up one's mind. **détermination** *nf* determination. **déterminé** *adj* 1 resolute. 2 specific.
déterrer (de:tɛ're:) *vt* 1 dig up. 2 discover.
détester (de:tɛ'ste:) *vt* detest.
détoner (de:tɔ'ne:) *vi* detonate. **détonant** *adj,nm* explosive.
détonner (de:tɔ'ne:) *vi* 1 be out of tune. 2 clash.
détour (de:'tu:r) *nm* 1 detour. 2 curve.

détourner (de:tu:rˈne:) *vt* **1** divert. **2** turn away. **3** embezzle. **4** hijack. **détournement** *nm* diversion.
détraqué (de:traˈke:) *adj* **1** out of order. **2** crazy.
détremper (de:trɑ̃ˈpe:) *vt* **1** moisten. **2** soak.
détresse (de:ˈtrɛs) *nf* distress.
détritus (de:tri:ˈtys) *nm* refuse.
détruire* (de:ˈtrɥi:r) *vt* **1** demolish. **2** destroy. **3** overthrow.
dette (dɛt) *nf* debt.
deuil (dœj) *nm* mourning.
deux (dœ) *adj,nm* two. **tous les deux** both. **tous les deux jours** every other day. **deux-points** *nm* colon. **deuxième** *adj* second.
dévaler (de:vaˈle:) *vi,vt* rush down. *vi* descend.
dévaliser (de:vali:ˈze:) *vt* rob, burgle.
dévaluer (de:vaˈlɥe:) *vt* devalue.
devancer (dəvɑ̃ˈse:) *vt* precede. **2** leave behind. **3** forestall. **devancier, -ière** (dəvɑ̃ˈsje:, -ˈsjɛr) *nm,f* predecessor.
devant (dəˈvɑ̃) *prep* before, in front of. *adv* in front, ahead. *nm* front. **devanture** *nf* **1** front. **2** window.
dévaster (de:vaˈste:) *vt* devastate.
développer (de:viɔˈpe:) *vt* **1** develop. **2** spread out. **3** explain.
devenir* (dəvˈni:r) *vi* (*aux* être) become, grow, get.
dévers (de:ˈvɛr) *nm* **1** slope. **2** warp.
déverser (de:vɛrˈse:) *vt* **1** pour. **2** dump.
dévêtir (de:ve:ˈti:r) *vt* strip, undress.
dévier (de:ˈvje:) *vi* **1** deviate. **2** swerve. **déviation** *nf* **1** deviation. **2** diversion. **3** bypass.
deviner (dəvi:ˈne:) *vt* guess. **devinette** *nf* riddle.
devis (dəˈvi:) *nm* estimate.
dévisager (de:vi:zaˈʒe:) *vt* stare at.
devise (dəˈvi:z) *nf* **1** motto. **2** slogan. **3** currency.
dévisser (de:vi:ˈse:) *vt* unscrew.
dévoiler (de:vwaˈle:) *vt* reveal.
devoir* (dəˈvwar) *vt* **1** have to, must. **2** owe. *nm* **1** duty. **2** task. **3** exercise. **4** *pl* homework.
dévorer (de:vɔˈre:) *vt* devour.
dévot (de:ˈvo) *adj* devout, religious. *nm* religious person. **faux dévot** hypocrite.
dévouer (de:ˈvwe:) *vt* **1** dedicate. **2** devote. **dévouement** *nm* devotion.
dextérité (dɛkste:ri:ˈte:) *nf* skill.
diabète (djaˈbɛt) *nm* diabetes.
diable (djabl) *nm* devil. **diablerie** *nf* mischief, fun.
diagonal, -aux (djagɔˈnal, -ˈno) *adj* diagonal. **diagonale** *nf* diagonal.
dialecte (djaˈlɛkt) *nm* dialect.
dialogue (djaˈlɔg) *nm* dialogue.
diamant (djaˈmɑ̃) *nm* diamond.
diamètre (djaˈmɛtr) *nm* diameter.
diaphragme (djaˈfragm) *nm* diaphragm.
diapositive (diapɔzi:ˈti:v) *nf phot* slide.
diaprer (djaˈpre:) *vt* mottle.
diarrhée (djaˈre:) *nf* diarrhoea.
dictateur (di:ktaˈtœr) *nm* dictator. **dictature** *nf* dictatorship.
dicter (di:kˈte:) *vt* dictate. **dictée** *nf* dictation.
dictionnaire (di:ksjɔˈnɛr) *nm* dictionary.
dicton (di:kˈtɔ̃) *nm* maxim, saying.
dièse (djɛz) *nm mus* sharp.
diète (djɛt) *nm pol* diet.
dieu, dieux (djœ) *nm* god.
diffamer (di:ffaˈme:) *vt* **1** slander. **2** libel.
différence (di:fe:ˈrɑ̃s) *nf* difference. **à la différence de** contrary to. **différent** *adj* different.
différencier (di:fɛrɑ̃ˈsje:) *vt* differentiate.
différend (di:fe:ˈrɑ̃) *nm* difference, dispute.
différentiel, -elle (di:fe:rɑ̃ˈsjɛl) *adj,nf* differential.
différer (di:fe:ˈre:) *vt* **1** defer. **2** put off. *vi* differ.
difficile (di:fi:ˈsi:l) *adj* difficult. **difficulté** *nf* difficulty.
difforme (di:ˈfɔrm) *adj* deformed.
diffuser (di:fyˈze:) *vt* **1** spread. **2** broadcast.
digérer (di:ʒe:ˈre:) *vt* **1** digest. **2** assimilate.
digestion (di:ʒɛsˈtjɔ̃) *nf* digestion.
digitale (di:ʒi:ˈtal) **digitale pourprée** *nf* foxglove.
digne (di:ɲ) *adj* **1** worthy. **2** dignified. **digne d'éloges** praiseworthy. **digne de remarque** noteworthy.
dignité (di:ɲi:ˈte:) *nf* dignity.
digue (di:g) *nf* **1** embankment. **2** dam. **3** jetty. **4** obstacle.
dilapider (di:lapi:ˈde:) *vt* squander.
dilater (di:laˈte:) *vt* expand.
dilemme (di:ˈlɛm) *nm* dilemma.
diligent (di:li:ˈʒɑ̃) *adj* **1** diligent. **2** industrious. **3** busy.
diluer (di:ˈlɥe:) *vt* dilute.
dimanche (di:ˈmɑ̃ʃ) *nm* Sunday. **dimanche des rameaux** Palm Sunday.
dimension (dimɑ̃ˈsjɔ̃) *nf* **1** dimension, size. **2** *pl* measurements.
diminuer (di:mi:ˈnɥe:) *vt* **1** diminish. **2** reduce.

vi **1** decrease. **2** abate. **diminutif, -ive** (di:mi:ny'ti:f, -'ti:v) *adj,nm* diminutive. **diminution** *nf* decrease.
dindon (dɛ̃'dɔ̃) *nm* turkey.
dîner (di:'ne:) *vi* dine, have dinner. *nm* dinner.
dingue (dɛ̃g) *adj inf* daft, mad.
dinosaure (di:nɔ'sɔr) *nm* dinosaur.
diocèse (djɔ'sɛz) *nm* diocese.
diphtongue (di:f'tɔ̃g) *nf* diphthong.
diplomatie (di:plɔma'si:) *nf* diplomacy. **diplomate** *nm* diplomat. **diplomatique** *adj* diplomatic.
diplôme (di:'plom) *nm* diploma. **diplômé** *nm* graduate.
dire* (di:r) *vt* **1** say. **2** tell. **c'est à dire** that is to say.
direct (di:rɛkt) *adj* **1** direct. **2** straight.
directeur (di:rɛk'tœr) *nm* **1** director. **2** manager. **3** headmaster. **4** governor.
direction (di:rɛk'sjɔ̃) *nf* **1** direction. **2** management. **3** steering.
diriger (di:ri:'ʒe:) *vt* **1** manage. **2** direct. **3** aim. **se diriger vers** *vr* go towards.
discerner (di:sɛr'ne:) *vt* discern, distinguish.
disciple (di:'si:pl) *nm* disciple.
discipline (di:si'pli:n) *nf* discipline, order.
discontinuer (di:skɔ̃ti:'nɥe:) *vi,vt* discontinue.
discorde (di:s'kɔrd) *nf* discord.
discothèque (diskɔ'tɛk) *nf* **1** discotheque. **2** record library.
discours (di:'sku:r) *nm* **1** talk. **2** speech.
discret, -ète (di'skrɛ, -skrɛt) *adj* **1** discreet. **2** quiet. **discrétion** *nf* discretion.
discriminer (di:skrimi:'ne:) *vt* discriminate.
discussion (di:sky'sjɔ̃) *nf* **1** discussion. **2** debate.
discuter (di:sky'te:) *vt* **1** discuss. **2** question.
disette (di:'zɛt) *nf* scarcity. **disette d'eau** drought.
disgrâce (di:z'grɑs) *nf* disgrace.
disgracieux, -euse (di:zgra'sjœ, -'sjœz) *adj* **1** awkward. **2** uncouth. **3** unsightly.
disloquer (di:slɔ'ke:) *vt* dislocate. **se disloquer** *vr* break up.
disparaître* (di:spa'rɛtr) *vi* (*aux* être or avoir) **1** disappear. **2** vanish. **disparu** *adj* **1** missing. **2** extinct.
disparate (di:spa'rat) *adj* dissimilar.
dispendieux, -euse (di:spɑ̃'djœ, -'djœz) *adj* expensive.
dispenser (di:spɑ̃'se:) *vt* **1** exempt. **2** dispense. **se dispenser de** *vr* get out of, excuse oneself. **dispensaire** *nm* dispensary.
disperser (di:spɛr'se:) *vt* scatter, disperse.
disponible (di:spɔ'ni:bl) *adj* **1** available. **2** free. **3** vacant.
dispos (di:'spo) *adj* fit, active.
disposer (di:spo'ze:) *vt* **1** dispose. **2** arrange. **disposer de** have at one's disposal. **se disposer à** *vr* be ready to. **disposition** *nf* **1** disposition. **2** arrangement. **3** disposal. **4** tendency. **5** *pl* provisions.
dispositif (di:spozi:'ti:f) *nm* apparatus, device.
disputer (di:spy'te:) *vt* **1** discuss. **2** dispute, argue. *vi* quarrel. **se disputer** *vr* argue, quarrel. **dispute** *nf* dispute, quarrel.
disqualifier (di:skali:'fje:) *vt* disqualify.
disque (di:sk) *nf* **1** disc. **2** record.
dissemblable (di:sɑ̃'blabl) *adj* dissimilar, different.
disséminer (di:se:mi:'ne:) *vt* scatter, spread.
dissentiment (di:sɑ̃ti:'mɑ̃) *nm* dissent.
disséquer (di:se:'ke:) *vt* dissect.
dissimuler (di:si:my'le:) *vt* **1** conceal. **2** disguise. **se dissimuler** *vr* hide. **dissimulation** *nf* deceit.
dissiper (di:si:'pe:) *vt* **1** waste. **2** dispel.
dissoudre* (di:'su:dr) *vt* dissolve. **se dissoudre** *vr* **1** melt. **2** break up.
dissuader (di:sɥa'de:) *vt* dissuade. **forces de dissuasion** *nf pl mil* deterrent.
distance (di:'stɑ̂s) *nf* distance. **distant** *adj* **1** distant. **2** aloof.
distiller (di:sti:'le:) *vt* distil.
distinct (di:'stɛ̃) *adj* **1** distinct, clear. **2** separate. **distinctif, -ive** (di:stɛ̃k'ti:f, -'ti:v) *adj* distinctive. **distinction** *nf* **1** distinction. **2** honour. **3** rank.
distinguer (di:stɛ̃'ge:) *vt* **1** distinguish. **2** discern. **3** honour. **distingué** *adj* **1** eminent. **2** refined.
distraire* (di'strɛr) *vt* **1** divert, take out. **2** distract. **3** entertain. **se distraire** *vr* amuse oneself. **distrait** *adj* absent-minded.
distribuer (di:stri:'bɥe:) *vt* **1** distribute. **2** give out. **3** deliver. **distribution** *nf* **1** distribution. **2** delivery.
divaguer (di:va'ge:) *vi* **1** wander. **2** ramble.
divan (di:'vɑ̃) *nm* **1** divan. **2** couch.
diverger (di:vɛr'ʒe:) *vi* diverge.
divers (di:'vɛr) *adj* **1** changing. **2** diverse, sundry. **3** varied.
divertir (di:vɛr'ti:r) *vt* entertain. **divertissement** *nm* entertainment, recreation.
dividende (di:vi:'dɑ̃d) *nm* dividend.
divin (di:'vɛ̃) *adj* divine, holy.

diviser (di:vi: ze:) *vt* divide. **divisible** *adj* divisible. **division** *nf* **1** division. **2** department. **3** discord.

divorcer (di:vɔr'se:) *vi* divorce. **divorce** *nm* divorce.

divulguer (di:vyl'ge:) *vt* divulge, disclose.

dix (di:s, di:) *adj,nm* ten. **dixième** *adj* tenth.

dix-huit *adj,nm* eighteen. **dix-huitième** *adj* eighteenth.

dix-neuf *adj,nm* nineteen. **dix-neuvième** *adj* nineteenth.

dix-sept *adj,nm* seventeen. **dix-septième** *adj* seventeenth.

dizaine (di:'zɛn) *nf* about ten.

docile (dɔ'si:l) *adj* docile, manageable.

docte (dɔkt) *adj* learned.

docteur (dɔk'tœr) *nm* doctor.

doctrine (dɔk'tri:n) *nf* doctrine.

document (dɔky'mɑ̃) *nm* document. **documentaire** *adj,nm* documentary.

documenter (dɔkymɑ̃'te:) *vt* document.

dodo (dɔ'do) *nm inf* sleep. **faire dodo** go to sleep.

dodu (dɔ'dy) *adj* plump.

dogmatique (dɔgma'ti:k) *adj* dogmatic.

dogme (dɔgm) *nm* dogma.

doigt (dwa) *nm* **1** finger. **2** digit. **doigt de pied** toe. **doigté** *nm* **1** *inf* tact. **2** *mus* fingering.

dois (dwa) *v* see **devoir.**

doit (dwa) *nm* debit.

dol (dɔl) *nm* fraud.

doléances (dɔle:'ɑ̃s) *nf pl* complaints.

dollar (dɔ'lar) *nm* dollar.

Dolomites (dɔlɔ'mi:t) *nf pl* Dolomites.

domaine (dɔ'mɛn) *nm* **1** domain, estate. **2** scope, field.

dôme (dom) *nm* dome.

domestiquer (dɔmɛsti:'ke:) *vt* domesticate. **domestique** *adj* domestic. *nm,f* servant.

domicile (dɔmi:'si:l) *nm* residence, abode.

dominer (dɔmi:'ne:) *vi* rule. *vt* **1** dominate. **2** master. **3** overlook. **dominant** *adj* **1** ruling. **2** dominant. **domination** *nf* rule.

dominion (dɔmi:'njɔ̃) *nm* dominion.

dommage (dɔ'maʒ) *nm* damage, harm. **quel dommage!** what a pity! **dommages-intérêts** *nm pl* damages.

dompter (dɔ̃'te:) *vt* **1** tame. **2** subdue.

don (dɔ̃) *nm* **1** gift, present. **2** talent.

donc (dɔ̃k) *conj* therefore, so. *adv* **1** well. **2** just.

donner (dɔ'ne:) *vt* **1** give. **2** donate. **3** *game* deal. **4** provide. **donner contre** run into. **donner dans** fall into. **donner sur** look out onto. **s'en donner** *vr* enjoy oneself. **donne** *nf game* deal. **donnée** *nf* **1** fundamental idea. **2** *pl* data.

dont (dɔ̃) *pron* **1** of whom or which. **2** by, with, from whom or which. **3** whose.

dorénavant (dɔre:na'vɑ̃) *adv* from now on.

dorer (dɔ're:) *vt* **1** gild. **2** brown.

dorloter (dɔrlɔ'te:) *vt* **1** fondle, cuddle. **2** pamper.

dormir* (dɔr'mi:r) *vi* sleep, be asleep. **dormant** *adj* **1** sleeping. **2** dormant. **3** stagnant.

dors (dɔr) *v* see **dormir.**

dortoir (dɔr'twar) *nm* dormitory.

dorure (dɔ'ryr) *nf* gilt, gilding.

dos (do) *nm* back.

dose (doz) *nf* dose. **dosage** *nm* dosage.

dossier (do'sje:) *nm* **1** file. **2** record. **3** back (of a chair).

dot (dɔt) *nf* dowry.

doter (dɔ'te:) *vt* endow.

douane (dwan) *nf* customs.

doubler (du:'ble:) *vt* **1** double. **2** line. **3** overtake. **4** quicken. **5** understudy. **double** *adj,nm* double, duplicate. **doublure** *nf* **1** lining. **2** understudy.

douceur (du:'sœr) *nf* **1** sweetness. **2** softness. **3** comfort. **4** gentleness.

douche (du:ʃ) *nf* shower (bath).

douer (dwe:) *vt* endow. **doué** *adj* gifted.

douille (du:j) *nf* **1** socket. **2** case, casing. **3** sleeve.

douillet, -ette (du:'jɛ, -'jɛt) *adj* **1** soft. **2** delicate.

douleur (du:'lœr) *nf* **1** pain. **2** sorrow. **douloureux, -euse** (du:lu:'rœ, -'rœz) *adj* **1** sore, painful. **2** sad, distressing.

douter (du:'te:) *vi* doubt. **se douter de** *vr* suspect. **doute** *nm* **1** doubt. **2** misgiving. **mettre en doute** question. **douteux, -euse** (du:'tœ, -'tœz) *adj* **1** uncertain. **2** dubious.

douve (du:v) *nf* **1** ditch. **2** moat.

Douvres (du:vr) *nf* Dover.

doux, douce (du:, du:s) *adj* **1** sweet. **2** soft. **3** gentle. **4** pleasant. **5** mild.

douze (du:z) *adj,nm* twelve. **douzaine** *nf* dozen. **douzième** *adj* twelfth.

doyen, -enne (dwa'jɛ̃, -'jɛn) *nm,f* **1** dean. **2** senior.

drachme (drakm) *nf* drachma.

dragée (dra'ʒe:) *nf* **1** sugared almond. **2** lozenge.

dragon (dra'gɔ̃) *nm* dragon.

draguer (dra'ge:) *vt* dredge, drag.

dramatiser (dramati:'ze:) *vt* dramatize. **dramatique** *adj* dramatic.
dramaturge (drama'tyrʒ) *nm,f* dramatist.
drame (dram) *nm* **1** drama. **2** play.
drap (dra) *nm* **1** cloth. **2** sheet. **drapeau, -aux** (dra'po) *nm* **1** flag. **2** *mil* colours.
draper (dra'pe:) *vt* **1** drape. **2** hang. **draperie** *nf* drapery. **drapier, -ière** (dra'pje:, -'pjɛr) *nm,f* draper.
drelin (drə'lɛ̃) *nm* tinkle.
dresser (drɛ'se:) *vt* **1** raise. **2** set, lay. **3** draw up. **4** train. **dresser les oreilles** prick one's ears. **se dresser** *vr* stand up, rise. **dressage** *nm* breaking in, training. **dressoir** *nm* dresser.
drogue (drɔg) *nf* **1** drug. **2** chemical.
droit[1] (drwa) *adj* **1** straight. **2** upright. **3** right (side, etc.). **4** honest. *adv* **1** straight. **2** directly. **tout droit** straight on.
droit[2] (drwa) *nm* **1** right. **2** charge, tax. **3** law. **droit d'auteur** copyright. **droits d'auteur** *nm pl* royalties. **droit de passage** right of way. **exempt de droit** duty-free.
droite (drwat) *nf* right, right-hand side.
drôle (drol) *adj* **1** funny, comic. **2** odd. *nm* rascal.
dromadaire (drɔma'dɛr) *nm* dromedary.
dru (dry) *adj* **1** thick. **2** strong. **3** dense. *adv* **1** thickly. **2** heavily.
du (dy) contraction of **de le.**
dû, due (dy) *v* see **devoir.** *adj* **1** due. **2** owing. **3** proper. *nm* due.
duc (dyk) *nm* duke. **duchesse** (dy'ʃɛs) *nf* duchess.
duel (dɥɛl) *nm* duel.
dûment (dy'mɑ̃) *adv* duly.
dune (dyn) *nf* dune.
Dunkerque (dœ̃'kɛrk) *nf* Dunkirk.
duo (dyo) *nm mus* duet.
duper (dy'pe:) *vt* trick, take in.
dur (dyr) *adj* **1** hard. **2** tough. **3** difficult. **4** harsh. *adv* hard. **durcir** (dyr'si:r) *vi,vt* harden.
durer (dy're:) *vi* **1** last. **2** endure. **durant** *prep* during. **durée** *nf* **1** duration. **2** life, wear.
duvet (dy'vɛ) *nm* **1** down, fluff. **2** quilt.
dynamique (di:na'mi:k) *adj* dynamic.
dynamite (di:na'mi:t) *nf* dynamite.
dynastie (di:na'sti:) *nf* dynasty.
dysenterie (di:sɑ̃'tri:) *nf* dysentery.

E

eau, eaux (o) *nf* water. **eau douce 1** soft water. **2** freshwater. **eau-de-vie** *nf, pl* **eaux-de-vie 1** spirits. **2** brandy. **eau minérale** mineral water. **eaux d'égout** *nf pl* sewage. **faire eau** leak.
ébahir (e:ba'i:r) *vt* astound, flabbergast. **s'ébahir de** *vr* be amazed at. **ébahissement** *nm* astonishment.
ébats (e:'ba) *nm pl* sport, frolics.
ébaucher (e:bo'ʃe:) *vt* **1** sketch. **2** outline. **ébauche** *nf* **1** rough sketch. **2** outline.
ébène (e:'bɛn) *nf* ebony. **ébéniste** *nm* cabinet-maker.
éberlué (e:bɛr'lɥe:) *adj* flabbergasted.
éblouir (e:blu:'ir) *vt* dazzle. **éblouissement** *nm* **1** dazzle. **2** fit of dizziness.
éboulement (e:bu:l'mɑ̃) *nm* landslide.
ébouriffer (e:bu:ri:'fe:) *vt* **1** ruffle. **2** amaze.
ébranler (e:brɑ̃'le:) *vt* **1** shake. **2** loosen. **3** disturb. **s'ébranler** *vr* **1** totter. **2** move off. **ébranlement** *nm* **1** shaking. **2** shock. **3** commotion.
ébrécher (e:bre:'ʃe:) *vt* **1** notch. **2** chip.
ébrouer (e:bru:'e:) *vi* snort. **ébrouement** *nm* snort.
ébullition (e:byli:'sjɔ̃) *nf* **1** boiling. **2** turmoil.
écailler (e:kɑ'je:) *vt* scale. **s'écailler** *vr* flake off. **écaille** *nf* **1** scale. **2** shell. **3** flake.
écaler (e:ka'le:) *vt* shell, husk. **écale** *nf* shell, pod.
écarlate (e:kar'lat) *adj,nf* scarlet.
écarquiller (e:karki:'je:) *vt* open wide.
écart (e:'kar) *nm* **1** distance apart. **2** deviation, swerve. **3** remote place. **à l'écart** aside, on one side. **faire le grand écart** do the splits. **faire un écart** shy.
écarter (e:kar'te:) *vt* **1** separate. **2** keep off. **3** divert. **s'écarter** *vr* **1** move aside. **2** diverge. **s'écarter de** stray from. **écarté** *adj* **1** isolated, remote. **2** apart.
ecclésiastique (ɛkle:zja'sti:k) *adj* ecclesiastical. *nm* clergyman.
écervelé (e:sɛrvə'le:) *adj* **1** thoughtless. **2** crazy. **3** light-headed.
échafaud (e:ʃa'fo) *nm* scaffold. **échafaudage** *nm* scaffolding.
échalote (e:ʃa'lɔt) *nf* shallot.
échancrer (e:ʃɑ̃'kre:) *vt* **1** cut out. **2** indent.
échanger (e:ʃɑ̃'ʒe:) *vt* exchange.

échantillon (e:ʃɑ̃ti:ˈjɔ̃) *nm* **1** sample, specimen. **2** pattern.

échapper (e:ʃaˈpe:) *vi* (*aux* être or avoir) escape. **s'échapper** *vr* **1** break free. **2** escape. **3** leak. **échappatoire** *nf* loophole, way out. **échappement** *nm* **1** escape. **2** leakage. **3** exhaust.

écharde (e:ˈʃard) *nf* splinter.

écharpe (e:ˈʃarp) *nf* **1** scarf. **2** sash. **3** sling.

échasse (e:ˈʃɑs) *nf* stilt.

échauder (e:ʃoˈde:) *vt* scald.

échauffer (e:ʃoˈfe:) *vt* **1** overheat. **2** heat. **3** rouse. **s'échauffer** *vr* **1** get overheated. **2** warm up. **échauffé** *adj* **1** overheated. **2** excited.

échéance (e:ʃe:ˈɑ̃s) *nf* **1** date (of payment). **2** maturity. **3** expiration. **échéant** *adj* payable, falling due.

échec (e:ˈʃɛk) *nm* **1** check. **2** failure, setback. **3** *pl* chess. **échec et mat** checkmate.

échelle (e:ˈʃɛl) *nf* **1** ladder. **2** scale.

échelon (e:ʃˈlɔ̃) *nm* **1** rung. **2** step. **3** level.

échelonner (e:ʃlɔˈne:) *vt* space out.

échevelé (e:ʃɛvˈle:) *adj* **1** dishevelled. **2** wild.

échine (e:ˈʃi:n) *nf* spine, backbone.

échiquier (e:ʃi:ˈkje:) *nm* chessboard.

écho (e:ˈko) *nm* echo.

échoir* (e:ˈʃwar) **1** fall. **2** mature. **3** expire.

échoppe (e:ˈʃɔp) *nf* booth, stall.

échouer (e:ˈʃwe:) *vi,vt* ground. *vi* **1** be stranded. **2** fail.

éclabousser (e:klabu:ˈse:) *vt* splash.

éclair (e:ˈklɛr) *nm* **1** flash. **2** *pl* lightning. **3** eclair.

éclaircir (e:klɛrˈsi:r) *vt* **1** clear up. **2** lighten. **3** explain. **s'éclaircir** *vr* **1** clear up. **2** thin out. **éclaircie** *nf* **1** break, opening. **2** clearing.

éclairer (e:klɛˈre:) *vt* **1** light. **2** enlighten. **s'éclairer** *vr* **1** light up. **2** clear. **éclairage** *nm* **1** lighting. **2** illumination. **éclaireur** *nm* scout.

éclat (e:ˈkla) *nm* **1** splinter. **2** chip. **3** burst. **4** flash. **5** brightness.

éclater (e:klaˈte:) *vi,vt* **1** burst. **2** splinter. *vi* **1** explode. **2** break out. **éclater de rire** burst out laughing. **éclatant** *adj* **1** bright. **2** brilliant. **3** loud.

éclipser (e:kli:pˈse:) *vt* **1** eclipse. **2** obscure. **éclipse** *nf* eclipse.

éclisse (e:ˈkli:s) *nf* **1** wedge. **2** *med* splint.

éclopé (e:klɔˈpe:) *adj* lame. *nm* cripple.

éclore* (e:ˈklɔr) *vi* (*aux* être) **1** hatch. **2** open, blossom.

écluse (e:ˈklyz) *nf* **1** sluice. **2** lock.

écœurer (e:kœˈre:) *vt* **1** disgust. **2** nauseate.

école (e:ˈkɔl) *nf* school. **école maternelle/primaire** nursery/primary school.

écologie (e:kɔlɔˈʒi:) *nf* ecology.

éconduire* (e:kɔ̃ˈdɥi:r) *vt* **1** show out. **2** reject.

économe (e:kɔˈnɔm) *adj* economical. **économie** *nf* **1** economy. **2** *pl* savings. **faire des économies** save. **économique** *adj* economic.

économiser (e:kɔnɔmi:ˈze:) *vt* economize, save.

écoper (e:kɔˈpe:) *vt naut* bail out.

écorcer (e:kɔrˈse:) *vt* skin, peel. **écorce** *nf* **1** rind, peel. **2** bark.

écorcher (e:kɔrˈʃe:) *vt* **1** skin. **2** graze. **3** fleece. **écorchure** *nf* **1** graze. **2** scratch.

écornifler (e:kɔrni:ˈfle:) *vt* scrounge, sponge.

Ecosse (e:ˈkɔs) *nf* Scotland. **écossais** *adj* Scottish, Scotch, Scots. *nm* Scot.

écot (eˈko) *nm* share, quota.

écouler (e:ku:ˈle:) *vt* get rid of. **s'écouler** *vr* **1** flow out. **2** pass, elapse. **écoulement** *nm* **1** flow. **2** discharge. **3** sale.

écouter (e:ku:ˈte:) *vt* **1** listen to. **2** pay attention to. **écouter à la porte** eavesdrop. **écouteur** *nm* **1** listener. **2** receiver. **3** headphone.

écran (e:ˈkrɑ̃) *nm* screen.

écraser (e:krɑˈze:) *vt* **1** crush. **2** overcome. **3** flatten. **4** run over. **se faire écraser** get run over. **s'écraser** *vr* **1** collapse. **2** crash. **écrasant** *adj* **1** crushing. **2** overwhelming.

écrémer (e:kre:ˈme:) *vt* skim.

écrevisse (e:krəˈvi:s) *nf* crayfish.

s'écrier (se:ˈkrje:) *vr* **1** exclaim. **2** cry out.

écrin (e:ˈkrɛ̃) *nm* (jewel) case.

écrire* (e:ˈkri:r) *vt* **1** write. **2** note down. **s'écrire** *vr* be written. **écrit** *adj* written. *nm* **1** writing. **2** written examination. **écriteau, -aux** (e:kri:ˈto) *nm* placard. **écriture** *nf* writing.

écrit (e:ˈkri:) *v see* **écrire.**

écrivain (e:kri:ˈvɛ̃) *nm* author, writer.

écrivant (e:kri:ˈvɑ̃) *v see* **écrire.**

écrivasser (e:kri:vaˈse:) *vt* scribble.

écrou (e:ˈkru:) *nm tech* nut.

s'écrouler (se:kru:ˈle:) *vr* collapse, fall in. **écroulement** *nm* **1** collapse. **2** ruin.

écru (e:ˈkry) *adj* **1** natural. **2** raw.

écu (e:ˈky) *nm* **1** shield. **2** crown (money).

écueil (e:ˈkœj) *nm* **1** reef, rock. **2** snag.

écuelle (e:ˈkɥɛl) *nf* bowl.

écumer (e:kyˈme:) *vi* foam, froth. *vt* skim. **écume** *nf* **1** foam, froth. **2** scum.

écureuil (e:kyˈrœj) *nm* squirrel.

écurie (e:kyˈri:) *nf* stable.

écuyer (e:kɥi:ˈje:) *nm* **1** squire. **2** horseman.
édenté (e:dɑ̃ˈte:) *adj* toothless.
édifier (e:di:ˈfje:) *vt* **1** build, erect. **2** enlighten. **édifice** *nm* **1** building. **2** structure.
Edimbourg (edɛ̃ˈbu:r) *nm* Edinburgh.
édit (e:ˈdi:) *nm* decree.
éditer (e:di:ˈte:) *vt* **1** edit. **2** publish. **éditeur** *nm* **1** editor. **2** publisher. **édition** *nf* edition, issue. **éditorial, -aux** (e:di:tɔˈrjal, -ˈrjo) *adj* editorial. *nm* newspaper leader.
édredon (e:drəˈdɔ̃) *nm* eiderdown.
éducation (e:dykaˈsjɔ̃) *nf* **1** education. **2** upbringing. **3** breeding.
éduquer (e:dyˈke:) *vt* **1** bring up. **2** train.
effacer (ɛfaˈse:) *vt* erase, rub out. **s'effacer** *vr* **1** wear away. **2** fade. **3** stand aside.
effarer (ɛfaˈre:) *vt* **1** scare. **2** bewilder.
effaroucher (ɛfaru:ˈʃe:) *vt* **1** scare away. **2** startle. **s'effaroucher** *vr* be startled.
effectif, -ive (e:fɛkˈti:f, -ˈti:v) *adj* **1** effective. **2** actual.
effectuer (e:fɛkˈtɥe:) *vt* effect, carry out.
efféminé (e:fe:mi:ˈne:) *adj* effeminate.
effervescence (e:fɛrvɛˈsɑ̃s) *nf* effervescence.
effet (eˈfɛ) *nm* **1** effect, result. **2** impression. **3** *pl* bills. **4** *pl* belongings. **en effet** indeed.
s'effeuiller (e:fœˈje:) *vr* shed its leaves or petals.
efficace (e:fi:ˈkas) *adj* **1** effective. **2** efficient.
effigie (e:fi:ˈʒi:) *nf* effigy.
effiler (e:fi:ˈle:) *vt* **1** unravel. **2** taper.
effleurer (e:flœˈre:) *vt* **1** skim, touch lightly. **2** touch on.
effondrer (e:fɔ̃ˈdre:) *vt* break in. **s'effondrer** *vr* **1** cave in. **2** collapse. **3** slump. **effondrement** *nm* **1** collapse. **2** subsidence.
s'efforcer (se:fɔrˈse:) *vr* **s'efforcer de** strive to.
effort (e:ˈfɔr) *nm* **1** effort. **2** strain.
effrayer (e:frɛˈje:) *vt* frighten, scare.
effréné (e:fre:ˈne:) *adj* frantic.
effroi (e:ˈfrwa) *nm* fear, dread. **effroyable** *adj* **1** dreadful. **2** awful.
effronté (e:frɔ̃ˈte:) *adj* **1** bold. **2** impudent, cheeky. **effronterie** *nf* impudence, cheek.
égal, -aux (e:ˈgal, -ˈgo) *adj* **1** equal. **2** level. **3** even. **4** regular. **cela m'est égal** it's all the same to me. **également** *adv* **1** equally. **2** likewise. **3** also. **égalité** *nf* **1** equality. **2** regularity.
égaler (e:gaˈle:) *vt* **1** equal. **2** match.
égaliser (e:gali:ˈze:) *vi,vt* equalize. *vt* smooth.
égard (e:ˈgar) *nm* **1** respect. **2** regard. **3** consideration.
égarer (e:gaˈre:) *vt* **1** lead astray. **2** mislay. **3** bewilder. **s'égarer** *vr* lose one's way. **égaré** *adj* **1** stray. **2** distracted.
égayer (e:gɛˈje:) *vt* **1** cheer up. **2** amuse.
égée (e:ˈʒe:) *adj* Aegean. **(Mer) Egée** *nf* Aegean (Sea).
église (e:ˈgli:z) *nf* church.
ego (ˈe:go) *nm* ego. **égocentrique** (e:gɔsɑ̃ˈtri:k) *adj* self-centred, egocentric. **égoïste** (e:gɔˈi:st) *adj* selfish. **égoïsme** *nm* selfishness, egoism.
égorger (e:gɔrˈʒe:) *vt* **1** cut the throat of. **2** massacre. **3** ruin.
égout (e:ˈgu:) *nm* **1** drain. **2** sewer. **3** gutter.
égoutter (e:gu:ˈte:) *vt* **1** drain. **2** drip.
égratigner (e:grati:ˈɲe:) *vt* scratch. **égratignure** *nf* scratch.
égrener (e:grəˈne:) *vt* **1** shell. **2** pick.
Egypte (ˈe:ʒi:pt) *nf* Egypt. **égyptien, -ienne** (e:ʒi:pˈsjɛ̃, -ˈsjɛn) *adj,n* Egyptian.
éjaculer (e:ʒakyˈle:) *vt* ejaculate.
éjecter (e:ʒɛkˈte:) *vt* eject.
élaborer (e:laboˈre:) *vt* **1** elaborate. **2** work out.
élaguer (e:laˈge:) *vt* **1** prune. **2** cut down.
élan (e:ˈlɑ̃) *nm* **1** spring, bound. **2** dash. **3** impetus. **4** burst.
s'élancer (se:lɑ̃ˈse:) *vr* **1** spring. **2** rush. **élancé** *adj* slender. **élancement** *nm* **1** throb. **2** twinge.
élargir (e:larˈʒi:r) *vt* **1** widen. **2** enlarge. **3** extend. **4** release.
élastique (e:laˈsti:k) *adj* elastic. *nm* **1** elastic. **2** rubber band.
élection (e:lɛkˈsjɔ̃) *nf* **1** election. **2** choice.
électoral, -aux (e:lɛktɔˈral, -ˈro) *adj* electoral. **électorat** *nm* electorate.
électricité (e:lɛktri:si:ˈte:) *nf* electricity.
électrifier (e:lɛktri:ˈfje:) *vt* electrify.
électrique (e:lɛkˈtri:k) *adj* electric.
électriser (e:lɛktri:ˈze:) *vt* **1** electrify. **2** excite.
électrocuter (e:lɛktrɔkyˈte:) *vt* electrocute.
électrode (e:lɛkˈtrɔd) *nf* electrode.
électron (e:lɛkˈtrɔ̃) *nm* electron.
électronique (e:lɛktrɔni:k) *adj* electronic. *nf* electronics.
élégant (e:le:ˈgɑ̃) *adj* **1** elegant. **2** smart.
élément (e:le:ˈmɑ̃) *nm* **1** element. **2** unit. **3** *pl* rudiments. **élémentaire** *adj* **1** elementary. **2** elemental.
éléphant (e:le:ˈfɑ̃) *nm* elephant.
élevage (ɛlˈvaʒ) *nm* stockbreeding.
élévation (e:le:vaˈsjɔ̃) *nf* **1** elevation. **2** rise. **3** raising. **4** height. **élévateur** *nm* elevator.

élève (e:'lɛv) *nm,f* pupil. **élevé** *adj* **1** high. **2** raised. **bien/mal élevé** well/ill-bred.
élever (e:l've:) *vt* **1** raise. **2** elevate. **3** erect. **4** bring up. **s'élever** *vr* rise up.
elfe (ɛlf) *nm* elf.
éligible (e:li:'ʒi:bl) *adj* eligible.
éliminer (e:li:mi:'ne:) *vt* **1** eliminate. **2** get rid of.
élire* (e:'li:r) *vt* **1** elect. **2** choose.
élite (e:'li:t) *nf* **1** elite. **2** cream. **d'élite** crack.
elle (ɛl) *pron 3rd pers fs* **1** she. **2** her. **3** it. **elle-même** *pron 3rd pers fs* **1** herself. **2** itself.
elles (ɛl) *pron 3rd pers f pl* **1** they. **2** them. **elles-mêmes** *pron 3rd pers f pl* themselves.
ellipse (ɛl'li:ps) *nf* ellipse.
élocution (e:lɔky'sjɔ̃) *nf* elocution.
éloge (e:'lɔʒ) *nm* praise.
éloigner (e:lwa'ɲe:) *vt* **1** remove. **2** send away. **3** postpone. **s'éloigner** *vr* **1** go away. **2** stand back. **éloigné** *adj* **1** distant. **2** remote. **éloignement** *nm* **1** removal. **2** distance. **3** absence. **4** aversion.
éloquent (e:lɔ'kã) *adj* eloquent.
élu (e:'ly) *adj* **1** chosen. **2** successful.
élucider (e:lysi:'de:) *vt* elucidate.
éluder (e:ly'de:) *vt* elude, evade.
émail, -aux (e:'maj, -'mo) *nm* **1** enamel. **2** glaze.
émailler (e:ma'je:) *vt* **1** enamel. **2** glaze. **3** dot.
émanciper (e:mãsi:'pe:) *vt* emancipate.
émaner (e:ma'ne:) *vi* **émaner de** emanate or come from.
emballer (ãba'le:) *vt* **1** pack. **2** wrap up. **3** excite. **s'emballer** *vr* **1** bolt, run away. **2** get carried away. **emballage** *nm* wrapping, packing.
embarcadère (ãbarka'dɛr) *nm* **1** quay, wharf. **2** platform.
embargo (ãbar'go) *nm* embargo.
embarquer (ãbar'ke:) *vi,vt* embark. *vt* **1** ship. **2** *inf* arrest. **s'embarquer** *vr* embark.
embarras (ãba'ra) *nm* **1** obstacle. **2** embarrassment, confusion. **3** difficulty. **4** *pl* fuss.
embarrasser (ãbara'se:) *vt* **1** embarrass. **2** encumber. **3** obstruct. **4** perplex. **5** confuse. **s'embarrasser** *vr* burden oneself.
embaucher (ãbo'ʃe:) *vt* engage, take on.
embaumer (ãbo'me:) *vt* **1** embalm. **2** perfume.
embellir (ãbɛ'li:r) *vt* **1** embellish. **2** improve in looks.
embêter (ãbɛ'te:) *vt inf* **1** annoy. **2** bother.
emblée (ã'ble:) **d'emblée** *adv* straightaway.
emblème (ã'blɛm) *nm* emblem.
emboîter (ãbwa'te:) *vt* **1** pack in boxes. **2** fit together.
embouchure (ãbu:'ʃyr) *nf* **1** mouthpiece. **2** *geog* mouth.
embouteiller (ãbu:tɛ'je:) *vt* **1** bottle. **2** block up. **embouteillage** *nm* **1** bottling. **2** traffic jam.
emboutir (ãbu:'ti:r) *vt* collide with.
embrancher (ãbrã'ʃe:) *vt* join up. **embranchement** *nm* **1** branch, fork. **2** junction.
embraser (ãbra'ze:) *vt* set on fire. **s'embraser** *vr* catch fire.
embrasser (ãbra'se:) *vt* **1** embrace. **2** hug. **3** kiss. **4** include. **embrassement** *nm* embrace.
embrayer (ãbrɛ'je:) *vt* **1** connect. **2** let in the clutch. **embrayage** *nm* **1** connecting. **2** *mot* clutch.
embrouiller (ãbru:'je:) *vt* **1** tangle. **2** confuse, muddle.
embryon (ã'brjɔ̃) *nm* embryo.
embuscade (ãby'skad) *nf* ambush.
éméché (e:me:'ʃe:) *adj* tipsy.
émeraude (ɛm'rod) *adj,nf* emerald.
émerger (e:mɛr'ʒe:) *vi* emerge.
émerveiller (e:mɛrvɛ'je:) *vt* amaze. **s'émerveiller de** *vr* marvel at.
émettre* (e:'mɛtr) *vt* **1** emit. **2** utter. **3** broadcast. **4** issue. **émetteur** *nm* transmitter.
émeu (e:'mœ) *nm* emu.
émeute (e:mœt) *nf* riot.
émietter (e:mjɛ'te:) *vt* crumble.
émigrer (e:mi:'gre:) *vi* **1** emigrate. **2** migrate. **émigrant** *nm* emigrant. **émigré** *nm* refugee.
éminent (e:mi:'nã) *adj* eminent.
émission (e:mi:'sjɔ̃) *nf* **1** emission. **2** broadcast. **3** issue.
emmagasiner (ãmagazi:'ne:) *vt* **1** store. **2** store up.
emmancher (ãmã'ʃe:) *vt* **1** put a handle on. **2** fit together. **3** begin.
emmanchure (ãmã'ʃyr) *nf* armhole.
emmêler (ãmɛ'le:) *vt* entangle, mix up.
emménager (ãmɛna'ʒe:) *vi* move into a new house.
emmener (ãm'ne:) *vt* take or lead away.
emmitoufler (ãmi:tu'fle:) *vt* muffle up.
émoi (e:mwa) *nm* **1** emotion. **2** agitation.
émonder (e:mɔ̃'de:) *vt* prune.
émotion (e:mo'sjɔ̃) *nf* **1** emotion. **2** excitement.
émousser (e:mu:'se:) *vt* **1** blunt. **2** deaden.
émouvoir* (e:mu:'vwar) *vt* **1** move, touch. **2** rouse. **émouvant** *adj* **1** moving. **2** stirring.

empailler (ãpa'je:) *vt* **1** pack in straw. **2** stuff.
empaqueter (ãpak'te:) *vt* pack up.
s'emparer (sãpa're:) *vr* **s'emparer de** **1** seize. **2** take possession of.
empâter (ãpɑ'te:) *vt* **1** paste. **2** make sticky. **3** fatten.
empêcher (ãpe:'ʃe:) *vt* **1** prevent. **2** hinder. **n'empêche que** nevertheless. **s'empêcher de** *vr* refrain from.
empereur (ãp'rœr) *nm* emperor.
empeser (ãpɔ'ze:) *vt* starch.
empester (ãpɛ'ste:) *vt* **1** stink. **2** infect.
empêtrer (ãpɛ'tre:) *vt* entangle.
empiéter (ãpje:'te:) *vi* **1** encroach. **2** infringe.
empiffrer (ãpi:'fre:) *vt inf* stuff.
empiler (ãpi:'le:) *vt* stack.
empire (ã'pi:r) *nm* **1** empire. **2** dominion.
empirer (ãpi:'re:) *vi* worsen. *vt* make worse, aggravate.
empirique (ãpi:'ri:k) *adj* empirical.
emplacement (ãplas'mã) *nm* **1** site. **2** place.
emplâtre (ã'plɑtr) *nm* plaster.
emplette (ã'plɛt) *nf* purchase.
emplir (ã'pli:r) *vt* fill, fill up.
emploi (ã'plwa) *nm* **1** use. **2** employment.
employer (ãplwa'je:) *vt* **1** use. **2** employ. **s'employer** *vr* occupy oneself. **employé** *nm* clerk, employee. **employeur** *nm* employer.
empoigner (ãpwa'ɲe:) *vt* **1** grasp. **2** arrest. **3** grip.
empoisonner (ãpwazɔ'ne:) *vt* **1** poison. **2** infect. **3** corrupt. **4** bore.
emporter (ãpɔr'te:) *vt* carry, take away. **l'emporter sur** get the better of. **s'emporter** *vr* lose one's temper, get very annoyed. **emporté** *adj* quick-tempered, hot-tempered.
empourpré (ãpu:r'pre:) *adj* crimson.
empreindre* (ã'prɛ̃dr) *vt* imprint, stamp.
empreinte (ã'prɛ̃t) *nf* impression, mark. **empreinte de pas** footprint. **empreinte digitale** fingerprint.
s'empresser (sãprɛ'se:) *vr* hurry. **s'empresser à** be eager to. **empressé** *adj* eager, fervent.
emprisonner (ãpri:zɔ'ne:) *vt* put in prison.
emprunt (ã'prœ̃) *nm* loan.
emprunter (ãprœ̃'te:) *vt* **1** borrow. **2** assume.
ému (e:'my) *adj* moved, touched.
émulsion (e:myl'sjɔ̃) *nf* emulsion.
en[1] (ã) *prep* **1** in. **2** into. **3** to. **4** as. **5** while. **6** by. **en-tête** *nm, pl* **en-têtes** **1** heading. **2** headline.
en[2] (ã) *adv* **1** from there. **2** because of that. *pron invar* **1** of it or them. **2** about it or them. **3** some, any. **4** for that.
encadrer (ãka'dre:) *vt* frame. **encadrement** *nm* **1** frame. **2** framework.
encaisser (ãkɛ'se:) *vt* **1** pack in boxes. **2** collect. **3** cash. **encaisse** *nf* cash in hand.
enceinte[1] (ã'sɛ̃t) *nf* **1** surrounding wall. **2** *sport* ring.
enceinte[2] (ã'sɛ̃t) *adj* pregnant.
encens (ã'sã) *nm* incense.
encercler (ãsɛr'kle:) *vt* encircle.
enchaîner (ãʃɛ'ne:) *vt* **1** chain up. **2** curb. **3** connect.
enchanter (ãʃã'te:) *vt* **1** enchant. **2** delight. **enchantement** *nm* **1** magic. **2** charm. **3** delight.
enchère (ã'ʃɛr) *nf* **1** bid. **2** auction.
enchérir (ãʃe:'ri:r) *vi* **1** go up in price. **2** make a higher bid. **enchérissement** *nm* increase, rise.
enchevêtrer (ãʃvɛ'tre:) *vt* **1** mix up, confuse. **2** entangle.
enclin (ã'klɛ̃) *adj* **enclin à** inclined or prone to.
enclore* (ã'klɔr) *vt* enclose, fence in. **enclos** *nm* **1** enclosure. **2** paddock.
enclume (ã'klym) *nf* anvil.
encoche (ã'kɔʃ) *nf* notch.
encoignure (ãkɔ'ɲyr) *nf* corner.
encolure (ãkɔ'lyr) *nf* **1** neck. **2** neck size.
encombrer (ãkɔ̃'bre:) *vt* **1** encumber. **2** crowd. **3** litter. **encombrant** *adj* **1** cumbersome. **2** clumsy. **sans encombre** *adv* without a hitch. **encombrement** *nm* **1** obstruction. **2** litter.
encontre (ã'kɔ̃tr) **à l'encontre** *adv* to the contrary. **à l'encontre de** **1** against. **2** contrary to.
encore (ã'kɔr) *adv* **1** still. **2** yet. **3** again. **4** more.
encorner (ãkɔr'ne:) *vt* gore.
encourager (ãku:ra'ʒe:) *vt* encourage. **encouragement** *nm* encouragement.
encourir* (ãku:'ri:r) *vt* **1** incur. **2** bring upon onself.
encrasser (ãkra'se:) *vt* **1** dirty, soil. **2** clog.
encre (ãkr) *nf* ink.
encroûter (ãkru:'te:) *vt* cake.
encyclopédie (ãsi:klɔpe:'di:) *nf* encyclopedia.
endémique (ãde:'mi:k) *adj* endemic.
s'endetter (sãdɛ'te:) *vr* get into debt.
endiablé (ãdja'ble:) *adj* **1** reckless. **2** wild.
s'endimancher (ãdi:mã'ʃe:) *vr* dress in one's Sunday best.
endive (ã'di:v) *nf* endive.

endolori (ɑ̃dɔlɔ'ri:) *adj* **1** sore. **2** tender.
endommager (ɑ̃dɔma'ʒe:) *vt* damage.
endormir* (ɑ̃dɔr'mi:r) *vt* **1** send to sleep. **2** deaden. **s'endormir** *vr* fall asleep. **endormi** *adj* asleep.
endosser (ɑ̃do'se:) *vt* **1** put on. **2** endorse.
endroit (ɑ̃'drwa) *nm* **1** place. **2** spot. **3** part. **4** right side.
enduire* (ɑ̃'dɥi:r) *vt* coat, smear. **enduit** *nm* layer, coat.
endurcir (ɑ̃dyr'si:r) *vt* harden.
endurer (ɑ̃dy're:) *vt* endure, bear.
énergie (enɛr'ʒi:) *nf* **1** energy, drive. **2** force. **énergie atomique** atomic energy.
énerver (enɛr've:) *vt* get on someone's nerves. **s'énerver** *vr* get irritable or excited.
enfance (ɑ̃'fɑ̃s) *nf* **1** childhood. **2** infancy. **3** children. **enfant** *nm,f* **1** child. **2** infant. **d'enfant** *adj* childish. **enfant de chœur** choirboy. **enfantin** *adj* **1** childlike. **2** childish.
enfanter (ɑ̃fɑ̃'te:) *vt* give birth to.
enfer (ɑ̃'fɛr) *nm* hell.
enfermer (ɑ̃fɛr'me:) *vt* **1** shut up. **2** shut in. **3** surround.
enfiler (ɑ̃fi:'le:) *vt* **1** thread. **2** string. **3** go along. **4** slip on. **enfilade** *nf* succession.
enfin (ɑ̃'fɛ̃) *adv* **1** finally. **2** in fact. **3** at last.
enflammer (ɑ̃fla'me:) *vt* **1** inflame. **2** ignite. **s'enflammer** *vr* **1** catch fire. **2** become inflamed.
enfler (ɑ̃'fle:) *vi,vt* swell. *vt* puff out.
enfoncer (ɑ̃fɔ̃'se:) *vt* **1** drive in. **2** break in. *vi* sink. **s'enfoncer** *vr* plunge, go deep.
enfouir (ɑ̃'fwi:r) *vt* **1** bury. **2** hide under the ground.
enfreindre* (ɑ̃'frɛ̃dr) *vt* infringe.
s'enfuir* (sɑ̃'fɥi:r) *vr* **1** flee. **2** run away. **3** elope. **4** leak.
engager (ɑ̃ga'ʒe:) *vt* **1** pledge. **2** engage. **3** begin. **4** urge. **s'engager** *vr* **1** undertake. **2** enlist. **engagement** *nm* engagement, commitment.
engelure (ɑ̃ʒ'lyr) *nf* chilblain.
engendrer (ɑ̃ʒɑ̃'dre:) *vt* **1** breed. **2** produce.
engin (ɑ̃'ʒɛ̃) *nm* **1** engine. **2** device. **3** missile. **4** *pl* tackle, equipment.
englober (ɑ̃glɔ'be:) *vt* **1** include. **2** unite.
engloutir (ɑ̃glu:'ti:r) *vt* **1** gulp down. **2** engulf.
engorger (ɑ̃gɔr'ʒe:) *vt* block up.
engouffrer (ɑ̃gu:'fre:) *vt* **1** engulf. **2** swallow up.
engourdir (ɑ̃gu:r'di:r) *vt* **1** numb. **2** dull.
engrais (ɑ̃'grɛ) *nm* **1** manure. **2** fertilizer.
engraisser (ɑ̃grɛ'se:) *vt* **1** fatten. **2** manure.
engrenage (ɑ̃grɛ'naʒ) *nm* **1** gearing. **2** intricacy.
engueuler (ɑ̃gœ'le:) *vt sl* **1** blow up, shout at. **2** abuse.
enhardir (ɑ̃ar'di:r) *vt* encourage. **s'enhardir** *vr* pluck up courage.
énigme (e:'ni:gm) *nf* **1** enigma. **2** riddle.
enivrer (ɑ̃ni:'vre:) *vt* intoxicate. **s'enivrer** *vr* get drunk.
enjamber (ɑ̃ʒɑ̃'be:) *vt* step over.
enjeu, -eux (ɑ̃'ʒœ) *nm game* stake.
enjôler (ɑ̃ʒo'le:) *vt* coax.
enjoué (ɑ̃'ʒwe:) *adj* **1** lively. **2** cheerful.
enlaidir (ɑ̃le:'di:r) *vt* disfigure. *vi* grow ugly.
enlever (ɑ̃l've:) *vt* **1** remove. **2** carry or take off. **3** abduct. **4** kidnap. **s'enlever** *vr* **1** come off. **2** rise. **enlèvement** (ɑ̃lɛv'mɑ̃) *nm* **1** removal. **2** kidnapping.
enliser (ɑ̃li:'ze:) *vt* suck in. **s'enliser** *vr* get bogged down.
ennemi (ɛn'mi:) *nm* enemy, foe. *adj* hostile.
ennui (ɑ̃'nɥi:) *nm* **1** worry, anxiety. **2** boredom.
ennuyer (ɑ̃nɥi:'je:) *vt* **1** worry. **2** annoy. **3** bore. **s'ennuyer** *vr* be bored. **ennuyant** *adj* annoying. **ennuyeux, -euse** (ɑ̃nɥi:'jœ, -'jœz) *adj* tedious, boring.
énoncer (e:nɔ̃'se:) *vt* **1** state. **2** enunciate.
s'enorgueillir (sɑ̃nɔrgœ'ji:r) *vr* become proud.
énorme (e:'nɔrm) *adj* enormous, huge. **énormément** *adj* enormously, tremendously.
s'enquérir (sɑ̃ke:'ri:r) *vr* inquire.
enquête (ɑ̃'kɛt) *nf* **1** inquiry. **2** investigation. **3** inquest.
enraciné (ɑ̃rasi:'ne:) *adj* deep-seated.
enrager (ɑ̃ra'ʒe:) *vt* **1** enrage. **2** excite. **enragé** *adj* **1** mad. **2** keen. *nm* fan.
enrayer (ɑ̃rɛ'je:) *vt* **1** lock. **2** jam. **3** check.
enregistrer (ɑ̃rəʒi:'stre:) *vt* **1** register. **2** record.
s'enrhumer (ɑ̃ry'me:) *vr* catch a cold.
enrichir (ɑ̃ri:'ʃi:r) *vt* enrich.
enrôler (ɑ̃ro'le:) *vt* **1** enrol. **2** enlist.
enroué (ɑ̃'rwe:) *adj* **1** hoarse. **2** husky.
enseigne[1] (ɑ̃'seɲ) *nf* sign, mark.
enseigne[2] (ɑ̃'seɲ) *nf mil* ensign.
enseigner (ɑ̃sɛ'ɲe:) *vt* teach. **enseignement** *nm* **1** teaching. **2** education.
ensemble (ɑ̃'sɑ̃bl) *adv* together. *nm* **1** whole. **2** general effect. **3** set. **dans l'ensemble** on the whole.
ensemencer (ɑ̃smɑ̃'se:) *vt* sow.
ensevelir (ɑ̃sə'vli:r) *vt* **1** bury. **2** shroud. **ensevelissement** *nm* burial.

ensoleillé (ɑ̃sɔlɛ'je:) *adj* sunny.
ensorceler (ɑ̃sɔrsə'le:) *vt* **1** put a spell on. **2** captivate.
ensuite (ɑ̃'sɥi:t) *adv* **1** then. **2** afterwards. **3** next.
s'ensuivre* (sɑ̃'sɥi:vr) *vr* follow.
entaille (ɑ̃'taj) *nf* **1** notch. **2** slash.
entamer (ɑ̃ta'me:) *vt* **1** cut into. **2** start.
entasser (ɑ̃ta'se:) *vt* **1** accumulate. **2** heap up. **3** pack.
entendre (ɑ̃'tɑ̃dr) *vt* **1** hear. **2** understand. **3** mean. **entendre parler de** hear of. **s'entendre** *vr* **1** agree. **2** understand one another. **entendu** *adj* **1** capable. **2** sensible. **3** agreed. **bien entendu** certainly, of course.
entente (ɑ̃'tɑ̃t) *nf* **1** understanding. **2** agreement.
enterrer (ɑ̃tɛ're:) *vt* bury. **enterrement** *nm* **1** burial. **2** funeral.
entêté (ɑ̃tɛ'te:) *adj* **1** obstinate. **2** headstrong.
enthousiasme (ɑ̃tu:'zjasm) *nm* enthusiasm. **enthousiaste** *nm,f* enthusiast. *adj* enthusiastic.
s'enticher (sɑ̃ti:'ʃe:) *vr* **s'enticher de** become infatuated with.
entier, -ière (ɑ̃'tje:, -'tjɛr) *adj* entire, whole. **en entier** in full.
entité (ɑ̃ti:'te:) *nf* entity.
entonnoir (ɑ̃tɔ'nwar) *nm* funnel.
entorse (ɑ̃'tɔrs) *nf* **1** sprain. **2** twist.
entortiller (ɑ̃tɔrti:'je:) *vt* **1** twist. **2** wind. **3** get round. **s'entortiller** *vr* coil, twine.
entourer (ɑ̃tu:'re:) *vt* surround, encircle. **entourage** *nm* **1** setting. **2** circle of friends.
entracte (ɑ̃'trakt) *nm* **1** *Th* interval. **2** interlude.
entrailles (ɑ̃'traj) *nf pl* entrails.
entrain (ɑ̃'trɛ̃) *nm* spirit, vigour, zest.
entraîner (ɑ̃trɛ'ne:) *vt* **1** drag away. **2** involve. **3** lead astray. **4** bring about. **5** train.
entraver (ɑ̃tra've:) *vt* **1** fetter. **2** hinder. **entrave** *nf* **1** fetter. **2** obstacle.
entre (ɑ̃tr) *prep* **1** between. **2** among. **entretemps** *adv* in the meantime. *nm* interval.
entrebâillé (ɑ̃trəba'je:) *adj* ajar.
s'entrechoquer (sɑ̃trəʃɔ'ke:) *vr* collide.
entrecôte (ɑ̃trə'kot) *nf* rib steak.
entrecouper (ɑ̃trəku:'pe:) *vt* **1** intersect. **2** interrupt.
s'entrecroiser (sɑ̃trəkrwa'ze:) *vr* **1** cross each other. **2** intersect.
entrefaite (ɑ̃trə'fɛt) *nf* interval. **sur ces entrefaites** **1** at this moment. **2** meanwhile.
entrefilet (ɑ̃trəfi:'lɛ) *nm* paragraph.
entregent (ɑ̃trə'ʒɑ̃) *nm* tact.
entremets (ɑ̃trə'mɛ) *nm* dessert, sweet.
s'entremettre* (sɑ̃trə'mɛtr) *vr* intervene.
entrepôt (ɑ̃trə'po) *nm* **1** warehouse. **2** store.
entreprendre* (ɑ̃trə'prɑ̃dr) *vt* **1** undertake. **2** attempt. **3** contract for.
entrepreneur (ɑ̃trəprə'nœr) *nm* contractor. **entrepreneur de pompes funèbres** undertaker.
entreprise (ɑ̃trə'pri:z) *nf* **1** enterprise. **2** venture. **3** firm.
entrer (ɑ̃'tre:) *vi* (*aux* être) **1** enter. **2** begin. **faire entrer** show in. **entrée** *nf* **1** entrance. **2** entry. **3** admission. **4** beginning. **5** first course.
entretenir* (ɑ̃trət'ni:r) *vt* **1** maintain, keep up. **2** support. **s'entretenir** *vr* converse. **entretien** *nm* **1** upkeep. **2** conversation. **3** interview.
entrevoir* (ɑ̃trə'vwar) *vt* catch a glimpse of.
entrevue (ɑ̃trə'vy) *nf* interview.
entrouvert (ɑ̃tru:'vɛr) *adj* ajar.
envahir (ɑ̃va'i:r) *vt* **1** invade. **2** overrun.
envelopper (ɑ̃vlɔ'pe:) *vt* **1** envelop. **2** wrap up. **3** cover. **4** shroud. **enveloppe** *nf* **1** cover. **2** envelope.
envenimer (ɑ̃vni:'me:) *vt* **1** poison. **2** embitter. **s'envenimer** *vr* fester.
envergure (ɑ̃vɛr'gyr) *nf* span, spread.
envers[1] (ɑ̃'vɛr) *prep* **1** towards. **2** to.
envers[2] (ɑ̃'vɛr) *nm* **1** wrong side. **2** reverse. **à l'envers** **1** inside out. **2** upside down.
envier (ɑ̃'vje:) *vt* **1** envy. **2** begrudge. **envie** *nf* **1** desire. **2** envy. **3** birthmark. **avoir envie de** feel like, fancy.
environ (ɑ̃vi:'rɔ̃) *adv* about. **environs** *nm pl* **1** outskirts. **2** neighbourhood.
environnement (ɑ̃vi:rɔn'mɑ̃) *nm* environment.
envisager (ɑ̃viza'ʒe:) *vt* **1** envisage. **2** consider. **3** anticipate.
envoi (ɑ̃'vwa) *nm* **1** dispatch, sending. **2** parcel.
s'envoler (sɑ̃vɔ'le:) *vr* **1** fly away. **2** take off.
envoyer* (ɑ̃vwa'je:) *vt* **1** send. **2** dispatch. **envoyer chercher** send for. **envoyer en chandelle** lob. **envoyé** *nm* **1** messenger. **2** envoy. **envoyé spécial** correspondent.
enzyme (ɑ̃'zi:m) *nf* enzyme.
épagneul (e:pa'ɲœl) *nm* spaniel.
épais, -aisse (e:'pɛ, -'pɛs) *adj* **1** thick. **2** dense. **épaisseur** *nf* **1** thickness. **2** density.
épaissir (e:pɛ'si:r) *vt* thicken.
épancher (e:pɑ̃'ʃe:) *vt* pour out.
épandre (e:'pɑ̃dr) *vt* spread.
s'épanouir (e:pa'nwi:r) *vr* **1** open out. **2** bloom. **3** beam. **épanoui** *adj* in full bloom.

épargner (e:par'ɲe:) *vt* **1** save. **2** economize. **3** spare. **épargne** *nf* **1** saving. **2** economy.

éparpiller (e:parpi:'je:) *vt* **1** scatter. **2** disperse.

épars (e:'par) *adj* **1** scattered. **2** stray.

épater (e:pa'te:) *vt* stagger, amaze.

épaule (e:'pol) *nf* shoulder. **épaulette** *nf* epaulet.

épave (e:'pav) *nf* **1** wreck. **2** waif. **3** debris.

épée (e:'pe:) *nf* sword.

épeler (e:'ple:) *vt* spell.

éperdu (e:pɛr'dy) *adj* **1** distracted, distraught. **2** wild, mad. **3** desperate.

éperon (e:'prɔ̃) *nm* spur.

éphémère (e:fe:'mɛr) *adj* ephemeral.

épi (e:'pi:) *nm* **1** ear (of corn). **2** cluster.

épice (e:'pi:s) *nf* spice. **épicerie** *nf* grocer's shop. **épicier** *nm* grocer.

épicrâne (e:pi:'krɑn) *nm* scalp.

épidémie (e:pi:de:'mi:) *nf* epidemic.

épier (e:'pje:) *vt* **1** spy. **2** watch for.

épilepsie (e:pi:lɛp'si:) *nf* epilepsy. **épileptique** *adj* epileptic.

épilogue (e:pi:'lɔg) *nm* epilogue.

épiloir (e:pi:'lwar) *nm* tweezers.

épinards (e:pi:'nar) *nm pl* spinach.

épine (e:'pi:n) *nf* thorn. **épine dorsale** spine.

épingler (e:pɛ̃'gle:) *vt* pin. **épingle** *nf* pin. **épingle à cheveux** hairgrip. **épingle de nourrice** or **sûreté** safety pin.

Epiphanie (e:pi:fa'ni:) *nf* Epiphany.

épique (e:'pi:k) *adj* epic.

épiscopal, -aux (e:pi:skɔ'pal, -'po) *adj* episcopal.

épisode (e:pi:'zɔd) *nm* episode.

épitaphe (e:pi:'taf) *nf* epitaph.

épitomé (e:pi:tɔ'me:) *nm* epitome.

éploré (e:plɔ're:) *adj* in tears, weeping.

éplucher (e:ply'ʃe:) *vt* **1** clean. **2** peel. **3** examine.

éponger (e:pɔ̃'ʒe:) *vt* **1** sponge. **2** mop. **éponge** *nf* sponge.

épopée (e:pɔ'pe:) *nf* epic.

époque (e:'pɔk) *nf* **1** epoch, age. **2** time, period.

épouser (e:pu:'ze:) *vt* marry. **épousée** *nf* bride.

épousseter (e:pu:'ste:) *vt* dust, clean.

épouvanter (e:pu:vɑ̃'te:) *vt* terrify. **épouvantable** *adj* dreadful, frightful. **épouvantail** *nm* scarecrow. **épouvante** *nf* terror, dread.

époux, -ouse (e:'pu:, -'pu:z) *nm,f* husband, wife.

s'éprendre (se:'prɑ̃dr) *vr* **s'éprendre de** fall in love with.

épreuve (e:'prœv) *nf* **1** test. **2** trial. **3** proof. **4** print.

éprouver (e:pru:'ve:) *vt* **1** try, test. **2** experience, suffer. **éprouvette** *nf* test tube.

épuiser (e:pɥi:'ze:) *vt* **1** exhaust. **2** empty. **3** use up. **épuisé** *adj* **1** exhausted. **2** worn out.

épurer (e:py're:) *vt* **1** purify. **2** refine.

équateur (e:kwa'tœr) *nm* **1** equator. **2** *cap* Ecuador. **équatorial, -aux** (e:kwatɔ'rjal, -'rjo) *adj* equatorial.

équation (e:kwa'sjɔ̃) *nf* equation.

équerre (e:'kɛr) *nf* **1** square. **2** right angle.

équestre (e:'kɛstr) *adj* equestrian.

équilatéral, -aux (e:kɥi:late:'ral, -'ro) *adj* equilateral.

équilibrer (e:ki:li:'bre:) *vt* balance. **équilibre** *nm* **1** balance. **2** equilibrium.

équinoxe (e:ki:'nɔks) *nm* equinox.

équiper (e:ki:'pe:) *vt* **1** equip. **2** fit out. **équipage** *nm* **1** crew. **2** equipment. **équipe** *nf* **1** gang. **2** *sport* team, side.

équitable (e:ki:'tabl) *adj* fair, just.

équitation (e:ki:ta'sjɔ̃) *nf* riding.

équité (e:ki:'te:) *nf* equity.

équivaloir* (e:ki:va'lwar) *vi* be equivalent or equal. **équivalent** *adj,nm* equivalent.

équivoque (e:ki:'vɔk) *adj* **1** ambiguous. **2** dubious.

érable (ɛ'rabl) *nm* maple tree.

érafler (e:rɑ'fle:) *vt* **1** graze. **2** scratch. **éraflure** *nf* graze.

eraillé (e:'raj) *adj* **1** frayed. **2** scratched. **3** raucous.

ère (ɛr) *nf* **1** era. **2** epoch.

éreinter (e:rɛ̃'te:) *vt inf* **1** exhaust. **2** smash. **3** *inf* slate, severely criticize. **s'éreinter** *vr* tire oneself out. **s'éreinter à** slave at.

ériger (e:ri:'ʒe:) *vt* **1** erect. **2** set up.

ermite (ɛr'mi:t) *nm* hermit.

éroder (e:rɔ'de:) *vt* **1** erode. **2** eat away.

érotique (e:rɔ'ti:k) *adj* erotic.

errer (ɛ're:) *vi* **1** wander, roam. **2** stray. **3** err. **erreur** *nf* **1** error. **2** mistake. **3** fallacy.

éruption (e:ryp'sjɔ̃) *nf* **1** eruption. **2** *med* rash.

es (ɛ) *v* see **être.**

ès (ɛs) *prep* contraction of **en les. licencié ès lettres/sciences** Bachelor of Arts/Science.

escabeau, -aux (ɛska'bo) *nm* **1** stool. **2** stepladder.

escadre (ɛs'kadr) *nf naut* squadron. **escadrille** *nf aviat* squadron. **escadron** *nm mil* troop.

escale (ɛs'kal) *nf* **1** port of call. **2** stop.

escalier (ɛska'lje:) *nm* **1** staircase. **2** stairs.

escalier roulant escalator. **escalier tournant** spiral staircase.
escalope (ɛska'lɔp) *nf* escalope.
escamoter (ɛskamɔ'te:) *vt* **1** make disappear. **2** *inf* swipe. **escamoteur** *nm* conjuror.
escarbilles (ɛskar'bi:j) *nf pl* ashes, cinders.
escargot (ɛskar'go) *nm* snail.
escarmouche (ɛskar'mu:ʃ) *nf* skirmish.
escarpé (ɛskar'pe:) *adj* steep, sheer.
escarpolette (ɛskarpɔ'lɛt) *nf* swing.
escient (ɛ'sjɑ̃) *nm* knowledge. **à bon escient** deliberately.
esclandre (ɛs'klɑ̃dr) *nm* scandal.
esclave (ɛ'sklav) *nm,f* slave.
escompter (ɛskɔ̃'te:) *vt* **1** discount. **2** *inf* anticipate. **escompte** *nm* **1** discount. **2** rebate.
escorte (ɛ'skɔrt) *nf* **1** escort. **2** *naut* convoy.
escrime (ɛ'skri:m) *nf* fencing. **faire de l'escrime** fence.
escroc (ɛ'skro) *nm* crook, swindler.
escroquer (ɛskrɔ'ke:) *vt* **1** cheat. **2** swindle. **escroquerie** *nf* swindle.
espace (ɛ'spas) *nm* space.
espadon (ɛspa'dɔ̃) *nm* swordfish.
Espagne (ɛ'spaɲ) *nf* Spain. **espagnol** *adj* Spanish. *nm* **1** Spaniard. **2** Spanish (language).
espèce (ɛ'spɛs) *nf* **1** kind, sort. **2** species.
espérer (ɛspe:'re:) *vt* **1** hope. **2** trust. **espérance** *nf* **1** hope. **2** expectation.
espiègle (ɛ'spjɛgl) *adj* mischievous.
espion, -onne (ɛ'spjɔ̃, -'spjɔn) *nm,f* spy.
espionner (ɛspjɔ'ne:) *vt* spy on. **espionnage** *nm* espionage.
esplanade (ɛspla'nad) *nf* esplanade, promenade.
espoir (ɛ'spwar) *nm* hope.
esprit (ɛ'spri:) *nm* **1** spirit. **2** ghost. **3** soul. **4** mind. **5** wit. **à l'esprit étroit/large** narrow/broad-minded. **faible d'esprit** weak-minded.
esquimau, -aude, -aux (ɛski:'mo, -'mod, -'mo) *adj,n* Eskimo.
esquisser (ɛski:'se:) *vt* **1** sketch. **2** outline. **esquisse** *nf* **1** sketch. **2** outline. **3** draft.
esquiver (ɛski:'ve:) *vt* dodge, evade. **s'esquiver** *vr* slip off.
essai (e:'sɛ) *nm* **1** trial, test. **2** attempt. **3** essay. **4** *sport* try. **à l'essai** on approval or trial.
essaim (ɛ'sɛ̃) *nm* swarm.
essaimer (e:sɛ'me:) *vi* swarm.
essayer (e:sɛ'je:) *vt* **1** try, test. **2** try on.
essence (ɛ'sɑ̃s) *nf* **1** essence. **2** petrol. **3** extract.
essentiel, -elle (ɛsɑ̃'sjɛl) *adj* essential. *nm* main point.
essieu, -ieux (e:'sjœ) *nm* axle.
essor (ɛ'sɔr) *nm* **1** flight. **2** scope. **3** rise.
essorer (e:sɔ're:) *vt* wring out. **essoreuse** *nf* **1** spin-dryer. **2** mangle.
essoufflé (e:su:'fle:) *adj* out of breath.
essuyer (e:sɥi:'je:) *vt* **1** wipe. **2** dry. **3** suffer. **essuie-glace** *nm, pl* **essuie-glaces** windscreen wiper. **essuie-main** *nm invar also* **essuie-mains** towel. **essuie-pieds** *nm invar* doormat.
est[1] (ɛst) *nm* east. *adj invar* east, eastern. **à l'est** in the east. **d'est** easterly. **vers l'est** eastward, eastwards.
est[2] (ɛ) *v see* **être.**
estaminet (ɛstami:'nɛ) *nm* public house.
estamper (ɛstɑ̃'pe:) *vt* **1** print, engrave. **2** stamp.
estampille (ɛstɑ̃'pi:j) *nf* **1** official stamp. **2** trademark.
esthétique (ɛste:'ti:k) *adj* aesthetic. *nf* aesthetics.
estimer (ɛsti:'me:) *vt* **1** estimate. **2** consider. **3** esteem. **estime** *nf* esteem.
estivant (ɛsti:'vɑ̃) *nm* holiday-maker.
estomac (ɛstɔ'ma) *nm* stomach.
estomper (ɛstɔ̃'pe:) *vt* blur.
estrade (ɛ'strad) *nf* platform, stage.
estragon (ɛstra'gɔ̃) *nm* tarragon.
estropier (ɛstrɔ'pje:) *vt* **1** cripple. **2** maim. **3** ruin.
estuaire (ɛs'tɥɛr) *nm* estuary.
esturgeon (ɛstyr'ʒɔ̃) *nm* sturgeon.
et (e:) *conj* and. **et...et** both...and.
établir (e:ta'bli:r) *vt* **1** establish. **2** set up. **3** draw up. **4** lay down. **s'établir** *vr* establish oneself, settle. **établissement** *nm* **1** establishment. **2** institution.
étage (e:'taʒ) *nm* floor, storey. **étagère** *nf* **1** shelf. **2** set of shelves.
étai (e:'tɛ) *nm* stay, prop.
étain (e:'tɛ̃) *nm* **1** tin. **2** pewter.
étais (e:'tɛ) *v see* **être.**
étaler (e:ta'le:) *vt* **1** display. **2** set out. **3** spread out. **4** *inf* show off. **s'étaler** *vr* stretch oneself out. **étalage** *nm* **1** display. **2** window-dressing. **faire étalage de** show off.
étalon[1] (e:ta'lɔ̃) *nm* stallion.
étalon[2] (e:ta'lɔ̃) *nm* standard.
étancher (e:tɑ̃'ʃe:) *vt* **1** stop, staunch. **2** quench. **3** make watertight or airtight. **étanche** *adj* **1** watertight. **2** airtight.

étang (e:'tã) *nm* pond.
étant (e:'tã) *v* see **être.**
étape (e:'tap) *nf* **1** stage. **2** halt.
état (e:'ta) *nm* **1** state. **2** condition. **3** statement. **4** profession. **faire état de 1** take into account. **2** depend on. **étatisme** *nm* state control. **état-major** *nm, pl* **états-major 1** *mil* staff. **2** management.
Etats-Unis *nm pl* United States of America.
étayer (e:tɛ'je:) *vt* **1** prop up. **2** support.
été[1] (e:'te:) *nm* summer.
été[2] (e:'te:) *v* see **être.**
éteindre* (e:'tɛ̃dr) *vi* **1** extinguish, put out. **2** turn off. **3** soften. **s'éteindre** *vr* die out. **éteint** *adj* **1** extinguished. **2** extinct. **3** dim.
étendard (e:tã'dar) *nm* standard, flag.
étendre (e:'tãdr) *vt* **1** stretch. **2** spread. **3** extend, enlarge. **s'étendre** *vr* **1** stretch oneself out. **2** spread. **étendu** *adj* **1** extensive. **2** wide. **3** far-reaching. **étendue** *nf* **1** extent. **2** expanse.
éternel, -elle (e:tɛr'nɛl) *adj* **1** eternal. **2** everlasting.
éternité (e:tɛrni:'te:) *nf* eternity.
éternuer (e:tɛr'nɥe:) *vi* sneeze. **éternuement** *nm* **1** sneeze. **2** sneezing.
êtes (ɛt) *v* see **être.**
éther (e:'tɛr) *nm* ether. **éthéré** *adj* ethereal.
Ethiopie (e:tjɔ'pi:) *nf* Ethiopia. **éthiopien, -ienne** (e:tjɔ'pjɛ̃, -'pjɛn) *adj,n* Ethiopian.
éthique (e:'ti:k) *adj* ethical. *nf* ethics.
ethnique (ɛt'ni:k) *adj* ethnic.
étinceler (e:tɛ̃'sle:) *vi* **1** sparkle. **2** glitter. **étincelle** *nf* spark.
étiquette (e:ti:'kɛt) *nf* **1** label. **2** tag. **3** etiquette. **4** ceremony.
étirer (e:ti:'re:) *vt* **1** stretch. **2** draw out.
étoffe (e:'tɔf) *nf* **1** material, fabric. **2** stuff, potential.
étoile (e:'twal) *nf* **1** star. **2** decoration. **3** fate. **étoile polaire** Pole Star.
étole (e:'tɔl) *nf* stole.
étonner (e:tɔ'ne:) *vt* astonish, amaze. **s'étonner** *vr* **1** be astonished. **2** wonder.
étouffer (e:tu:'fe:) *vi,vt* **1** suffocate. **2** choke. *vt* **1** stifle. **2** smother. **3** hush up. **étouffant** *adj* **1** stifling. **2** stuffy. **3** sultry. **cuire à l'étouffée** braise.
étourdir (e:tu:r'di:r) *vt* **1** stun. **2** daze. **3** make dizzy. **4** deafen. **étourderie** *nf* **1** thoughtlessness. **2** blunder. **étourdi** *adj* **1** giddy. **2** thoughtless. **3** light-headed. **à l'étourdie** thoughtlessly.
étourneau, -aux (e:tu:r'no) *nm* starling.
étrange (e:'trãʒ) *adj* **1** strange. **2** odd. **3** peculiar. **4** weird. **étranger, -ère** (e:trã'ʒe:, -'ʒɛr) *adj* **1** foreign. **2** unfamiliar. **3** irrelevant. *nm,f* **1** stranger. **2** foreigner. **à l'étranger** abroad.
étrangler (e:trãgle:) *vt* **1** strangle. **2** throttle. **3** choke. **étranglé** *adj* **1** choked. **2** narrow.
étrave (e:'trav) *nf naut* bow.
être* (ɛtr) *vi* **1** be. **2** exist. *v aux* be. **être à 1** belong to. **2** be in or at. ~*nm* **1** existence. **2** being. **3** individual. **être humain** human being.
étreindre* (e:'trɛ̃dr) *vt* **1** embrace. **2** grasp. **3** clasp. **4** wring. **étreinte** *nf* **1** grasp. **2** hug.
étrenne (e:'trɛn) *nf* New Year's present.
étrier (e:tri:'e:) *nm* stirrup.
étriqué (e:tri:'ke:) *adj* tight.
étroit (e:'trwa) *adj* **1** narrow. **2** tight. **3** confined. **4** strict. **étroitesse** *nf* **1** narrowness. **2** tightness.
étude (e:'tyd) *nf* **1** study. **2** research. **3** chambers.
étudier (e:ty'dje:) *vt* **1** study. **2** investigate. **s'étudier à** *vr* endeavour to. **étudiant** *nm* **1** student. **2** undergraduate.
étui (e:'tɥi:) *nm* case, box.
étuver (e:ty've:) *vt* **1** dry. **2** heat. **3** steam.
étymologie (e:ti:mɔlɔ'ʒi:) *nf* etymology.
eu (y) *v* see **avoir.**
eucalyptus (œkali:p'tys) *nm* eucalyptus.
eucharistie (œkari:'sti:) *nf* Eucharist.
eunuque (œ'nyk) *nm* eunuch.
euphémisme (œfe:'mi:sm) *nm* euphemism.
euphorie (œfɔ'ri:) *nf* euphoria.
Europe (œ'rɔp) *nf* Europe. **européen, -enne** (œrɔpe:'ɛ̃, -'ɛn) *adj,n* European.
eus (y) *v* see **avoir.**
euthanasie (œtana'zi:) *nf* euthanasia.
eux (œ) *pron 3rd pers m pl* **1** they. **2** them. **eux-mêmes** *pron 3rd pers m pl* themselves.
évacuer (e:va'kɥe:) *vt* **1** evacuate. **2** empty. **3** vacate.
s'évader (se:va'de:) *vr* escape.
évaluer (e:va'lɥe:) *vt* **1** value. **2** assess. **3** estimate.
évangélique (e:vãʒe:'li:k) *adj* **1** Evangelical. **2** Protestant. **évangéliste** *nm* Evangelist.
évangile (e:vã'ʒi:l) *nm* gospel.
s'évanouir (se:va'nwi:r) *vr* **1** vanish. **2** faint. **évanouissement** *nm* **1** disappearance. **2** faint.
évaporer (e:vapɔ're:) *vt* evaporate.
évasion (e:va'zjɔ̃) *nf* escape.

éveil (e:ˈvɛj) *nm* 1 awakening. 2 alert. 3 alarm.
éveiller (e:vɛˈje:) *vt* 1 wake up, waken. 2 arouse. **s'éveiller** *vr* awake, wake up.
événement (e:vɛnˈmɑ̃) *nm* 1 event. 2 incident. 3 outcome.
éventail (e:vɑ̃ˈtaj) *nm* fan.
éventer (e:vɑ̃ˈte:) *vt* 1 air. 2 fan. 3 get wind of. **s'éventer** *vr* 1 spoil. 2 go flat or stale. **éventé** *adj* stale, flat.
éventrer (e:vɑ̃ˈtre:) *vt* 1 gut. 2 rip open.
éventuel, -elle (e:vɑ̃ˈtɥɛl) *adj* 1 possible. 2 eventual. **éventualité** *nf* contingency.
évêque (e:ˈvɛk) *nm* bishop.
s'évertuer (se:vɛrˈtɥe:) *vr* do one's utmost.
évidence (e:vi:ˈdɑ̃s) *nf* 1 obviousness. 2 evidence. **évidemment** (e:vi:daˈmɑ̃) *adv* evidently. **évident** *adj* evident, clear.
évider (e:vi:ˈde:) *vt* hollow out.
évier (e:ˈvje:) *nm* sink.
évincer (e:vɛ̃ˈse:) *vt* evict.
éviter (e:vi:ˈte:) *vt* 1 avoid. 2 shun.
évoluer (e:vɔˈlɥe:) *vi* 1 manoeuvre. 2 evolve.
évoquer (e:vɔˈke:) *vt* 1 evoke. 2 conjure up.
exact (ɛgˈzakt) *adj* 1 exact. 2 accurate. 3 true. 4 punctual. 5 strict.
exagérer (ɛgzaʒe:ˈre:) *vt* exaggerate. **exagération** *nf* exaggeration.
exalter (ɛgzalˈte:) *vt* 1 exalt. 2 excite.
examen (ɛgzaˈmɛ̃) *nm* 1 examination. 2 inspection.
examiner (ɛgzami:ˈne:) *vt* 1 examine. 2 inspect.
exaspérer (ɛgzaspe:ˈre:) *vt* 1 aggravate. 2 exasperate.
exaucer (ɛgzoˈse:) *vt* 1 grant. 2 hear. 3 fulfil.
excaver (ɛkskaˈve:) *vt* excavate.
excédant (ɛkse:ˈdɑ̃) *adj* surplus, excess.
excellent (ɛksɛˈlɑ̃) *adj* excellent. **excellence** *nf* 1 excellence. 2 *cap* Excellency.
exceller (ɛksɛˈle:) *vi* excel.
excentrique (ɛksɑ̃ˈtri:k) *adj* eccentric.
excepter (e:ksɛpˈte:) *vt* exclude. **excepté** *prep* except, save, but. **exception** *nf* exception. **exceptionnel, -elle** (e:ksɛpsjɔˈnɛl) *adj* exceptional.
excès (e:kˈsɛ) *nm* excess. **excessif, -ive** (e:ksɛˈsi:f, -ˈsi:v) *adj* excessive.
exciter (e:ksi:ˈte:) *vt* 1 excite. 2 arouse. 3 animate. 4 inflame. **s'exciter** *vr* get excited.
s'exclamer (sɛksklaˈme:) *vr* exclaim. **exclamation** *nf* exclamation.
exclure* (ɛksˈklyr) *vt* exclude. **exclusif, -ive** (ɛksklyˈsi:f, -ˈsi:v) *adj* 1 exclusive. 2 sole.
excommunier (ɛkskɔmyˈnje:) *vt* excommunicate.
excursion (ɛkskyrˈzjɔ̃) *nf* 1 excursion. 2 tour. 3 trip.
excuser (ɛkskyˈze:) *vt* 1 excuse. 2 pardon. **s'excuser** *vr* apologize. **excuse** *nf* 1 excuse. 2 *pl* apology.
exécrer (e:gze:ˈkre:) *vt* loathe. **exécrable** (e:gzɛˈkrabl) *adj* abominable.
exécuter (e:gze:kyˈte:) *vt* 1 execute. 2 carry out. 3 perform. **exécutif, -ive** (e:gze:kyˈti:f, -ˈti:v) *adj* executive.
exemple (e:gˈzɑ̃pl) *nm* 1 example. 2 lesson. 3 precedent. **par exemple** 1 for instance. 2 indeed. **exemplaire** *nm* 1 copy. 2 sample.
exempt (e:gˈzɑ̃) *adj* exempt, free.
exempter (e:gzɑ̃ˈte:) *vt* exempt.
exercer (e:gzɛrˈse:) *vt* 1 exercise. 2 train. 3 exert. 4 practise, pursue.
exercice (e:gzɛrˈsi:s) *nm* 1 exercise. 2 *mil* drill. 3 use. 4 practice.
exhaler (ɛgzaˈle:) *vt* 1 exhale. 2 emit. 3 vent.
exhiber (e:gzi:ˈbe:) *vt* 1 show. 2 exhibit. **exhibition** *nf* exhibition, display.
exiger (egzi:ˈʒe:) *vt* 1 exact. 2 demand. 3 require.
exigu, -uë (e:gzi:ˈgy) *adj* 1 tiny. 2 slender.
exil (e:gˈzi:l) *nm* exile.
exiler (e:gzi:ˈle:) *vt* 1 exile. 2 banish.
existentialisme (e:gzi:stɑ̃sjaˈli:sm) *nm* existentialism.
exister (e:gzi:ˈste:) *vi* 1 exist. 2 live.
exorbitant (ɛgzɔrbi:ˈtɑ̃) *adj* 1 exorbitant. 2 outrageous.
exorciser (ɛgzɔrsi:ˈze:) *vt* exorcize.
exotique (ɛgzɔˈti:k) *adj* exotic.
expatrier (ɛkspatri:ˈe:) *vt* expatriate. **expatrié** *adj,n* expatriate.
expédier (ɛkspeˈdje:) *vt* 1 dispatch. 2 hurry through. 3 send off. **expédient** *adj,nm* expedient. **expéditeur** *nm* sender. **expédition** *nf* 1 expedition. 2 copy. 3 forwarding. 4 consignment.
expérience (ɛkspe:ˈrjɑ̃s) *nf* 1 experience. 2 experiment. 3 test.
expérimenter (ɛkspe:ri:mɑ̃ˈte:) *vt* 1 test. 2 try. *vi* experiment. **expérimenté** *adj* 1 experienced. 2 skilled.
expert (ɛkˈspɛr) *adj* 1 skilled. 2 expert. *nm* expert.
expier (ɛkˈspje:) *vt* atone for.
expirer (ɛkspi:ˈre:) *vt* breathe out. *vi* 1 die. 2 expire.

explétif, -ive (ɛksple:'ti:f, -'ti:v) *adj,nm* expletive.
explication (ɛkspli:ka'sjɔ̃) *nf* explanation.
explicite (ɛkspli'si:t) *adj* **1** explicit. **2** clear.
expliquer (ɛkspli'ke:) *vt* **1** explain. **2** account for.
exploit (ɛk'splwa) *nm* **1** exploit. **2** feat. **3** writ.
exploiter (ɛksplwa'te:) *vt* **1** exploit. **2** cultivate. **3** take advantage of.
explorer (ɛksplɔ're:) *vt* explore. **explorateur** *nm* explorer.
exploser (ɛksplo'ze:) *vi* explode. **explosif, -ive** (ɛksplo'si:f, -'si:v) *adj,nm* explosive.
exporter (ɛkspɔr'te:) *vt* export. **exportation** *nf* export.
exposer (ɛkspo'ze:) *vt* **1** show. **2** exhibit. **3** explain. **4** expose. **exposé** *nm* **1** account. **2** short talk. **exposition** *nf* **1** exhibition. **2** exposure.
exprès, -esse (ɛk'sprɛ, -'sprɛs) *adj* **1** express. **2** explicit. **exprès** *adv* on purpose.
express (ɛk'sprɛs) *nm* express train.
expression (ɛksprɛ'sjɔ̃) *nf* expression.
exprimer (ɛkspri:'me:) *vt* **1** express. **2** squeeze out.
expulser (ɛkspyl'se:) *vt* **1** expel. **2** turn out.
exquis (ɛk'ski) *adj* exquisite.
extase (ɛk'stɑz) *nf* ecstasy.
extension (ɛkstɑ̃'sjɔ̃) *nf* **1** extension. **2** spread. **3** extent.
exténuer (ɛkste:'nɥe:) *vt* exhaust.
extérieur (ɛkste:'rjœr) *adj* **1** exterior. **2** outer. **3** foreign. *nm* **1** exterior. **2** outside. **à l'extérieur** **1** outside. **2** abroad.
exterminer (ɛkstɛrmi:'ne:) *vt* exterminate.
externe (ɛk'stɛrn) *adj* external. *nm* **1** day pupil. **2** outpatient. **externat** *nm* day school.
extirper (ɛksti:r'pe:) *vt* **1** uproot. **2** eradicate.
extra (ɛk'stra) *nm invar* extra. *adj invar inf* first-class, excellent.
extraire* (ɛk'strɛr) *vt* **1** extract. **2** pull out. **extrait** *nm* **1** extract. **2** excerpt. **3** certificate.
extraordinaire (ɛkstrɔrdi:'nɛr) *adj* **1** extraordinary. **2** unusual.
extravagant (ɛkstrava'gɑ̃) *adj* **1** extravagant. **2** foolish. **3** exorbitant.
extraverti (ɛkstravɛr'ti:) *adj,n* extrovert.
extrême (ɛk'strɛm) *adj* **1** extreme. **2** farthest. **3** utmost. **4** intense. *nm* extreme limit. **extrémité** *nf* **1** extremity. **2** end. **3** tip. **4** limit.
Extrême-Orient *nm* Far East.
exubérant (egzybɛ'rɑ̃) *adj* exuberant.

F

fable (fabl) *nf* **1** fable. **2** story.
fabricant (fabri:'kɑ̃) *nm* manufacturer.
fabriquer (fabri:'ke:) *vt* **1** manufacture. **2** make. **fabriquer en série** mass-produce. **fabrique** *nf* **1** manufacture. **2** factory.
fabuleux, -euse (faby'lœ, -'lœz) *adj* fabulous.
façade (fa'sad) *nf* **1** facade. **2** front.
face (fas) *nf* **1** face. **2** front. **3** aspect. **en face** opposite. **face à** facing.
facétie (fase:'si:) *nf* joke. **facétieux, -euse** (fase:'sjœ, -'sjœz) *adj* facetious.
fâcher (fɑ'ʃe:) *vt* make angry. **se fâcher** *vr* get angry. **fâché** *adj* **1** angry, cross. **2** sorry. **fâcheux, -euse** (fɑ'ʃœ, -'ʃœz) *adj* **1** annoying. **2** unfortunate.
facile (fa'si:l) *adj* **1** easy. **2** facile, ready. **3** weak.
faciliter (fasi:li:'te:) *vt* facilitate. **facilité** *nf* **1** easiness. **2** gift, talent. **3** facility.
façon (fa'sɔ̃) *nf* **1** manner. **2** way. **3** making. **4** make. **5** *pl* fuss. **à façon** made to measure. **de façon à** so as to. **de toute façon** anyway, in any case.
façonner (fasɔ'ne:) *vt* **1** shape. **2** fashion. **3** mould.
fac-similé (faksi:mi:'le:) *nm, pl* **fac-similés** facsimile.
facteur (fak'tœr) *nm* **1** postman. **2** factor. **3** agent.
factice (fak'ti:s) *adj* **1** artificial. **2** imitation. **3** dummy.
faction (fak'sjɔ̃) *nf* **1** faction. **2** guard.
facture (fak'tyr) *nf* invoice.
facultatif, -ive (fakylta'ti:f, -'ti:v) *adj* optional.
faculté (fakyl'te:) *nf* **1** option. **2** right. **3** ability. **4** faculty. **5** *pl* resources.
fadaise (fa'dɛz) *nf* **1** silly remark. **2** *pl* nonsense.
fade (fad) *adj* **1** dull. **2** tasteless.
fagot (fa'go) *nm* bundle.
fagoter (fagɔ'te:) *vt* dress without taste.
faiblir (fɛ'bli:r) *vi* **1** grow weaker. **2** fail. **faible** (fɛbl) *adj* **1** weak. **2** feeble. *nm* failing. **faiblesse** *nf* **1** weakness. **2** failing.
faïence (fa'jɑ̃s) *nf* **1** crockery. **2** earthenware.
faillible (fa'ji:bl) *adj* fallible.
faillir* (fa'ji:r) *vi* fail. **faillir tomber** nearly fall. **failli** *adj,n* bankrupt. **faillite** *nf* bankruptcy. **faire faillite** go bankrupt.
faim (fɛ̃) *nf* hunger. **avoir faim** be hungry.

fainéant (fɛne:ˈɑ̃) *adj* idle, lazy.
faire* (fɛr) *vt* **1** make. **2** do. **3** matter. **4** be. **5** arrange. **6** cause. **7** *sport* go in for. **ça ne fait rien** that doesn't matter. **faire faire** have made or done. **faire voir** show. **faites attention!** be careful! **il n'y a rien à faire** nothing can be done about it. **que faire?** what is to be done? **se faire** *vr* **1** develop. **2** become. **3** accustom oneself. **4** be. **se faire fort de** undertake to. **faire-part** *nm invar* announcement.
faisable (fəˈzabl) *adj* feasible.
faisan (fɛˈzɑ̃) *nm* pheasant.
faisant (fɛˈzɑ̃) *v* see **faire.**
faisceau, -aux (fɛˈso) *nm* bundle.
fait[1] (fɛ) *v* see **faire.** *adj* **1** done. **2** made. **3** fully grown. **4** ripe.
fait[2] (fɛ) *nm* **1** act. **2** deed. **3** fact. **4** exploit. **5** incident. **au fait** after all. **de** or **en fait** actually, in actual fact. **de son fait** of one's own accord. **fait-divers** *nm* news item.
faîte (fɛt) *nm* **1** top, summit. **2** ridge.
faix (fɛ) *nm* **1** burden. **2** load.
falaise (faˈlɛz) *nf* cliff.
falloir* (faˈlwar) *v imp* **1** need. **2** be necessary. **3** must. **comme il faut 1** proper. **2** properly. **s'en falloir** *vr* **1** be lacking. **2** be far from.
falsifier (falsi:ˈfje:) *vt* **1** falsify. **2** forge.
famé (faˈme:) *adj* **bien/mal famé** of good/evil repute.
fameux, -euse (faˈmœ, -ˈmœz) *adj* **1** famous. **2** *inf* great, excellent.
familial, -aux (fami:ˈljal, -ˈljo) *adj* family.
familier, -ière (fami:ˈlje:, -ˈljɛr) *adj* **1** domestic. **2** of the family. **3** familiar.
famille (faˈmi:j) *nf* **1** family. **2** household. **3** relations. **en famille** informally.
famine (faˈmi:n) *nf* famine.
fanal, -aux (faˈnal, -ˈno) *nm* lantern.
fanatique (fanaˈti:k) *adj* fanatical. *nm,f* fanatic.
faner (faˈne:) *vt* **1** make hay. **2** cause to fade. **se faner** *vr* **1** droop. **2** wilt. **3** fade.
fanfare (fɑ̃ˈfar) *nf* **1** *mus* flourish. **2** brass band.
fange (fɑ̃ʒ) *nf* **1** mud. **2** filth.
fantaisie (fɑ̃tɛˈzi:) *nf* **1** imagination. **2** fantasy. **3** fancy. **4** whim.
fantasmagorique (fɑ̃tasmagɔˈri:k) *adj* **1** weird. **2** fantastic.
fantastique (fɑ̃taˈsti:k) *adj* **1** fantastic. **2** *inf* incredible.
fantoche (fɑ̃ˈtɔʃ) *nm* puppet.
fantôme (fɑ̃ˈtom) *nm* **1** ghost. **2** phantom.
faon (fɑ̃) *nm zool* fawn.

farce (fars) *nf* **1** farce. **2** prank.
farcir (farˈsi:r) *vt cul* stuff.
fard (far) *nm* **1** make-up. **2** rouge. **3** disguise.
fardeau, -aux (farˈdo) *nm* burden.
farder (farˈde:) *vt* **1** make up. **2** disguise.
farfouiller (farfu:ˈje:) *vi* rummage.
farine (faˈri:n) *nf* **1** flour. **2** meal. **farine d'avoine** oatmeal. **farine de maïs** cornflour.
farouche (faˈru:ʃ) *adj* **1** wild. **2** savage. **3** sullen. **4** shy. **5** cruel.
fart (far) *nm* wax.
fasciner (fassi:ˈne:) *vt* fascinate.
fascisme (faˈsi:sm) *nm* fascism. **fasciste** *adj,n* fascist.
faste (fast) *nm* **1** pomp. **2** display.
fastidieux, -euse (fasti:ˈdjœ, -ˈdjœz) *adj* **1** tedious. **2** boring.
fastueux, -euse (faˈstɥœ, -ˈstɥœz) *adj* **1** ostentatious. **2** pompous.
fatal (faˈtal) *adj* **1** fatal. **2** inevitable. **fatalité** *nf* **1** fatality. **2** fate.
fatiguer (fati:ˈge:) *vt* **1** tire. **2** overwork. **3** bore. *vi mot* labour. **se fatiguer** *vr* get tired. **fatigue** *nf* fatigue, tiredness.
fatras (faˈtrɑ) *nm* **1** jumble. **2** rubbish.
faubourg (foˈbu:r) *nm* suburb.
faucher (foˈʃe:) *vt* **1** reap, cut. **2** *inf* pinch, steal. **fauché** *adj* **1** cut. **2** *inf* broke.
faucon (foˈkɔ̃) *nm* **1** falcon. **2** hawk.
faudra (fo:ˈdra) *v* see **falloir.**
faufiler (fofi:ˈle:) *vt* **1** (sewing) tack. **2** baste. **3** insert. **se faufiler** *vr* creep.
faune (fon) *nf* fauna.
fausser (foˈse:) *vt* **1** falsify. **2** *mus* put out of tune. **3** pervert. **4** bend.
faut (fo:) *v* see **falloir.**
faute (fot) *nf* **1** fault. **2** error. **3** lack. **faute de** for want of. **sans faute** without fail.
fauteuil (foˈtœj) *nm* **1** armchair. **2** *educ* chair.
fauve (fov) *adj* fawn. *nm* **1** fawn (colour). **2** *pl* wild beasts.
faux[1], **fausse** (fo, fos) *adj* **1** false. **2** untrue. **3** wrong. **4** counterfeit. *nm* **1** falsehood. **2** forgery. **à faux** wrongly. **faux-filet** *nm, pl* **faux-filets** sirloin.
faux[2] (fo) *nf* scythe.
faveur (faˈvœr) *nf* favour. **en faveur de** on behalf of. **favorable** *adj* favourable.
favori, -ite (favɔˈri:, -ˈri:t) *adj,n* favourite.
favoriser (favɔri:ˈze:) *vt* **1** favour. **2** assist. **3** patronize. **4** promote.
fébrile (fe:ˈbri:l) *adj* feverish.
fécond (fe:ˈkɔ̃) *adj* **1** fertile. **2** prolific.

fédérer (fe:de:ˈre:) *vt* federate. **fédéral, -aux** (fe:de:ˈral, -ˈro) *adj* federal.
fée (fe:) *nf* fairy.
feindre* (fɛ̃dr) *vt* feign. **feindre de** pretend to. **feinte** *nf* feint, pretence.
fêler (fɛˈle:) *vt* crack. **fêlure** *nf* crack.
féliciter (fe:li:siˈte:) *vt* congratulate. **félicitations** *nf pl* congratulations.
félin (fe:ˈlɛ̃) *adj* feline.
femelle (fəˈmɛl) *adj,nf* female, she.
féminin (fe:mi:ˈnɛ̃) *adj* **1** feminine. **2** female.
femme (fam) *nf* **1** woman. **2** wife. **femme de chambre 1** chambermaid. **2** housemaid. **femme de charge/ménage** housekeeper/charwoman.
fémur (fe:ˈmyr) *nm* thighbone.
fendre (fɑ̃dr) *vt* split.
fenêtre (fəˈnɛtr) *nf* window.
fenouil (fəˈnu:j) *nm* fennel.
fente (fɑ̃t) *nf* **1** crack. **2** crevice. **3** split. **4** slit. **5** slot.
féodal, -aux (fe:ɔˈdal, -ˈdo) *adj* feudal.
fer (fɛr) *nm* **1** iron. **2** sword. **3** *pl* chains. **fer à cheval** horseshoe. **fer à repasser** *dom* iron. **fer blanc** tin. **fer forgé** wrought iron.
ferai (fəˈre) *v* see **faire.**
férié (fe:ˈrje:) **jour férié** *nm* **1** holiday **2** bank holiday.
férir* (fe:ˈri:r) *vt* strike.
ferme[1] (fɛrm) *adj* **1** firm. **2** steady. **3** steadfast. *adv* **1** firmly. **2** hard. **fermeté** *nf* firmness.
ferme[2] (fɛrm) *nf* **1** farm. **2** farmhouse. **fermier** (fɛrˈmje:) *nm* farmer.
fermenter (fɛrmɑ̃ˈte:) *vi* **1** ferment. **2** rise.
fermer (fɛrˈme:) *vi,vt* **1** close. **2** shut. *vt* **1** turn or switch off. **2** fasten. **fermer à clef** lock. **fermeture** *nf* **1** closing. **2** shutting. **Fermeture Eclair** *nf Tdmk* zip.
féroce (fe:rɔs) *adj* **1** wild. **2** ferocious.
ferraille (fɛˈraj) *nf* scrap iron.
ferré (fɛˈre:) *adj* **1** fitted with iron **2** hobnailed.
ferroviaire (fɛrrɔˈvjɛr) *adj* railway.
fertile (fɛrˈti:l) *adj* **1** fertile. **2** fruitful.
fertiliser (fɛrti:li:ˈze:) *vt* fertilize.
fervent (fɛrˈvɑ̃) *adj* **1** fervent. **2** ardent. *nm* enthusiast.
ferveur (fɛrˈvœr) *nf* fervour.
fesser (fɛˈse:) *vt* spank. **fesse** *nf* **1** buttock. **2** *pl inf* bottom. **fessée** *nf* spanking.
festin (fɛˈstɛ̃) *nm* **1** banquet. **2** feast.
feston (fɛˈstɔ̃) *nm* **1** festoon. **2** scallop.
festonner (fɛstɔˈne:) *vt* **1** festoon. **2** scallop.
fêter (fɛˈte:) *vt* **1** celebrate. **2** keep as a holiday
fête *nf* **1** feast. **2** festival. **3** holiday. **4** entertainment. **5** festivity.
fétiche (fe:ˈti:ʃ) *nm* **1** fetish. **2** mascot.
fétide (fe:ˈti:d) *adj* fetid.
feu[1], **feux** (fœ) *nm* **1** fire. **2** heat. **3** passion. **4** light. **feu d'artifice** fireworks, firework display. **feu de joie** bonfire. **feu de position** sidelight. **feux de circulation** *n pl* traffic lights.
feu[2] (fœ) *adj* late, deceased.
feuille (fœj) *nf* **1** leaf. **2** sheet (of paper). **feuillage** *nm* foliage. **feuillet** *nm* leaf (of a book). **feuilleton** *nm* serial story.
feuilleter (fœjˈte:) *vt* flip through (a book).
feutre (fœtr) *nm* felt.
fève (fɛv) *nf* bean. **grosse fève** broad bean.
février (fe:vri:ˈe:) *nm* February.
fiacre (fjakr) *nm* cab.
se fiancer (fjɑ̃ˈse:) *vr* get engaged. **fiançailles** (fjɑ̃ˈsaj) *nf pl* engagement. **fiancé** *nm* fiancé.
fiasco (fjaˈsko) *nm invar* fiasco, wash-out.
fibre (fi:br) *nf* **1** fibre. **2** grain.
ficeler (fi:ˈsle:) *vt* tie up. **ficelle** *nf* string.
ficher (fi:ˈʃe:) *vt* **1** drive in. **2** *sl* stick. **3** give **4** do: **fiche-moi la paix!** clear off! **se ficher de** *vr* make fun of. **je m'en fiche!** I don't care. **fiche** *nf* **1** peg. **2** plug. **3** slip of paper. **4** voucher **5** form. **fichu** *adj sl* **1** awful. **2** done for.
fiction (fi:kˈsjɔ̃) *nf* fiction. **fictif, -ive** (fi:kˈti:f, -ˈti:v) *adj* fictitious.
fidèle (fi:ˈdɛl) *adj* **1** faithful **2** loyal **fidélité** *nf* **1** loyalty. **2** fidelity.
fiel (fjɛl) *nm* gall, bile.
fiente (fjɑ̃t) *nf* droppings.
fier[1], **fière** (fjɛr) *adj* **1** proud **2** haughty. **fierté** *nf* pride.
se fier[2] (fje:) *vr* trust.
fièvre (fjɛvr) *nf* **1** fever, temperature. **2** excitement.
figer (fi:ˈʒ:e) *vt* **1** congeal, clot. **2** fix.
figue (fi:g) *nf* fig **figuier** *nm* fig tree.
figurer (fi:gyˈre:) *vt* **1** represent. **2** appear. **se figurer** *vr* imagine. **figure** *nf* **1** shape **2** figure. **3** face. **figuré** *adj* **1** figured **2** figurative
fil (fi:l) *nm* **1** thread. **2** yarn. **3** edge. **4** grain **5** current. **fil de fer** wire
filament (fi·laˈmɑ̃) *nm* **1** filament **2** fibre.
filer (fi:ˈle:) *vt* **1** spin **2** prolong **3** shadow *vi* **1** flow smoothly. **2** slip by. **3** ladder **4** slip off. **filer à l'anglaise** take French leave **file** *nf* **1** line. **2** row **filé** *nm* thread.

filet[1] (fi:ˈlɛ) *nm* **1** thin thread. **2** streak. **3** trickle.
filet[2] (fi:ˈlɛ) *nm* fillet.
filet[3] (fi:ˈlɛ) *nm* net.
filial, -aux (fi:ˈljal, -ˈljo) *adj* filial. **filiale** *nf* **1** subsidiary company. **2** *comm* branch.
fille (fi:j) *nf* **1** daughter. **2** girl. **jeune fille** young woman or girl. **vieille fille** spinster. **fillette** *nf* little girl.
filleul (fi:ˈljœl) *nm* **1** godchild. **2** godson. **filleule** *nf* goddaughter.
film (fi:lm) *nm* film.
filou (fi:ˈlu:) *nm* **1** pickpocket. **2** cheat.
filouter (fi:lu:ˈte:) *vt* **1** rob. **2** swindle.
fils (fi:s) *nm* **1** son. **2** boy.
filtrer (fi:lˈtre:) *vi,vt* **1** filter. **2** strain. *vi* percolate. **filtre** *nm* filter.
fin[1] (fɛ̃) *nf* **1** end. **2** close. **3** aim. **4** purpose. **en fin de compte** finally.
fin[2] (fɛ̃) *adj* **1** fine. **2** choice. **3** delicate. **4** shrewd. **5** expert. **6** slender. **7** semiprecious.
final (fi:ˈnal) *adj* **1** final. **2** last. **3** ultimate. **finale** *nf sport* final.
finance (fi:ˈnɑ̃s) *nf* **1** finance. **2** *pl* resources. **financier, -ière** (fi:nɑ̃ˈsje:, -ˈsjɛr) *adj* financial. *nm* financier.
finaud (fi:ˈno) *adj* cunning, sly.
finesse (fi:ˈnɛs) *nf* **1** delicacy. **2** shrewdness.
finir (fi:ˈni:r) *vt* **1** finish. **2** end. **3** complete. *vi* come to an end. **fini** *adj* **1** finished. **2** accomplished. **3** finite.
Finlande (fɛ̃ˈlɑ̃d) *nf* Finland. **finlandais** *adj* Finnish. **finnois** (fi:ˈnwa) *adj* Finnish. *nm* **1** Finn. **2** Finnish (language).
fisc (fi:sk) *nm* **1** treasury. **2** exchequer. **3** Inland Revenue. **fiscal, -aux** (fi:ˈskal, -ˈsko) *adj* fiscal.
fission (fi:ˈsjɔ̃) *nf* fission.
fissure (fi:ˈsyr) *nf* fissure, crack.
fixer (fi:kˈse:) *vt* **1** fix. **2** determine. **3** settle. **fixe** *adj* **1** fixed, immovable. **2** firm. **3** regular. **4** settled.
fjord (fjɔr) *nm also* **fiord** fiord.
flacon (flaˈkɔ̃) *nm* bottle.
flageller (flaʒɛlˈle:) *vt* flog.
flagrant (flaˈgrɑ̃) *adj* **1** flagrant. **2** obvious.
flair (flɛr) *nm* **1** scent. **2** gift, flair.
flairer (flɛˈre:) *vt* **1** scent, smell out. **2** sniff.
flamand (flaˈmɑ̃) *adj* Flemish. *nm* **1** Fleming. **2** Flemish (language).
flamant (flaˈmɑ̃) *nm* flamingo.
flamber (flɑ̃ˈbe:) *vi* **1** blaze. **2** burn. *vt* singe. **flambeau, -aux** (flɑ̃ˈbo) *nm* **1** torch. **2** light. **3** candlestick.
flamboyant (flɑ̃bwaˈjɑ̃) *adj* **1** blazing. **2** gaudy.
flamme (flɑm) *nf* **1** flame. **2** blaze. **3** passion. **flammèche** (flaˈmɛʃ) *nf* spark.
flan (flɑ̃) *nm* custard tart.
flanc (flɑ̃) *nm* **1** flank. **2** side.
flanelle (flaˈnɛl) *nf* flannel.
flâner (flɑˈne:) *vi* **1** stroll. **2** dawdle.
flanquer (flɑ̃ˈke:) *vt* **1** flank. **2** chuck, throw.
flaque (flak) *nf* puddle, pool.
flasque (flask) *adj* **1** flabby. **2** limp. **3** weak.
flatter (flaˈte:) *vt* **1** stroke, pat. **2** delude. **3** flatter.
fléau, -aux (fle:ˈo) *nm* **1** scourge. **2** pest.
flèche (flɛʃ) *nf* **1** arrow. **2** spire.
fléchir (fle:ˈʃi:r) *vt* **1** bend. **2** move to pity. *vi* **1** give way. **2** sag.
flegme (flɛgm) *nm* calmness.
flet (flɛ) *nm zool* flounder.
flétan (fle:ˈtɑ̃) *nm* halibut.
flétrir[1] (fle:ˈtri:r) *vt* **1** wither. **2** fade. **3** spoil.
flétrir[2] (fle:ˈtri:r) *vt* **1** brand. **2** disgrace.
fleur (flœr) *nf* **1** flower. **2** bloom. **3** blossom. **4** prime. **fleuriste** *nm,f* florist.
fleurir (flœˈri:r) *vi* **1** flower, bloom. **2** prosper. *vt* decorate with flowers. **fleuri** *adj* **1** in bloom or flower. **2** flowery.
fleuve (flœv) *nm* river.
flexible (flɛkˈsibl) *adj* flexible.
flibustier (fli:byˈstje:) *nm* **1** pirate. **2** rogue.
flic (fli:k) *nm inf* copper, policeman.
flirter (flœrˈte:) *vi* flirt.
flocon (flɔˈkɔ̃) *nm* **1** flake. **2** tuft.
flore (flɔr) *nf* flora.
florissant (flɔri:ˈsɑ̃) *adj* prosperous.
flot (flo) *nm* **1** wave. **2** flood. **3** surge. **à flot** afloat. **à flots** in torrents.
flotter (flɔˈte:) *vi,vt* float. *vi* **1** waft. **2** waver. **3** wander. **flotte** *nf* **1** fleet. **2** float.
flou (flu:) *adj* **1** blurred. **2** woolly.
fluctuer (flykˈtɥe:) *vi* fluctuate.
fluet, -ette (flyˈɛ, -ˈɛt) *adj* thin, slender.
fluide (flyˈi:d) *adj,nm* fluid.
flûte (flyt) *nf* **1** flute. **2** long thin loaf of bread. **3** tall champagne glass.
flux (fly) *nm* **1** flow. **2** flux.
focal, -aux (fɔˈkal, -ˈko) *adj* focal.
fœtus (fe:ˈtys) *nm* foetus.
foi (fwa) *nf* **1** faith. **2** trust. **3** belief.
foie (fwa) *nm* liver.
foin (fwɛ̃) *nm* hay.
foire (fwar) *nf* fair.
fois (fwa) *nf* **1** time. **2** occasion. **à la fois** at the same time. **une fois** once.

foison (fwa'zɔ̃) *nf* plenty.
foisonner (fwazɔ'ne:) *vi* **1** abound. **2** increase.
fol (fɔl) *adj* see **fou.**
folâtre (fɔ'lɑtr) *adj* **1** playful. **2** lively.
folie (fɔ'li:) *nf* **1** madness. **2** folly.
folle (fɔl) *adj* see **fou.**
follet, -ette (fɔ'lɛ, -'lɛt) *adj* merry.
follicule (fɔli:'kyl) *nm* follicle.
foncer (fɔ̃'se:) *vi* **1** rush. **2** charge. *vt* sink. **se foncer** *vr* get darker. **foncé** *adj* dark.
foncier, -ière (fɔ̃'sje:, -'sjɛr) *adj* **1** of the land. **2** fundamental.
fonction (fɔ̃k'sjɔ̃) *nf* **1** function. **2** office. **fonctionnaire** *nm* **1** official. **2** civil servant.
fonctionner (fɔ̃ksjɔ'ne:) *vi* **1** function. **2** work. **3** run.
fond (fɔ̃) *nm* **1** bottom. **2** depth. **3** back. **4** background. **5** foundation. **à fond** thoroughly. **de fond** basic, fundamental.
fondamental, -aux (fɔ̃damɑ̃'tal, -'to) *adj* basic, fundamental.
fonder (fɔ̃'de:) *vt* **1** found. **2** establish. **3** base. **se fonder sur** *vr* **1** be based on. **2** rely on.
fondre (fɔ̃dr) *vi,vt* **1** melt. **2** dissolve. *vt* **1** cast. **2** blend. *vi* bounce.
fondrière (fɔ̃dri:'ɛr) *nf* **1** bog. **2** hollow.
fonds (fɔ̃) *nm* **1** land. **2** business. **3** fund. **4** funds. **5** *pl* cash.
font (fɔ̃) *v* see **faire.**
fontaine (fɔ̃'tɛn) *nf* **1** spring. **2** fountain. **3** cistern.
fonts (fɔ̃) *nm pl* font.
football (fu:t'bal) *nm* football.
for (fɔr) **for intérieur** *nm* conscience.
forain (fɔ'rɛ̃) *adj* travelling.
forçat (fɔr'sa) *nm* convict.
forcené (fɔrsə'ne:) *adj* **1** furious. **2** frantic.
forcer (fɔr'se:) *vt* **1** force. **2** break open. **3** compel. **force** *nf* **1** strength. **2** force. **3** power. *adj invar* a lot of. **à force de** by means of. **forcé** *adj* **1** forced. **2** compulsory. **forcément** *adv* **1** necessarily. **2** forcibly.
forer (fɔ're:) *vt* **1** drill. **2** bore.
forêt (fɔ'rɛ) *nf* forest.
forfait[1] (fɔr'fɛ) *nm* serious crime.
forfait[2] (fɔr'fɛ) *nm* contract.
forfait[3] (fɔr'fɛ) *nm* forfeit.
forficule (fɔrfi:'kyl) *nf* earwig.
forger (fɔr'ʒe:) *vt* **1** forge. **2** counterfeit. **3** fabricate. **forge** *nf* forge.
formaliser (fɔrmali:'ze:) *vt* offend. **se formaliser** *vr* take offence.
former (fɔr'me:) *vt* **1** form. **2** create. **3** train. **4** develop. **5** constitute. **se former** *vr* take shape. **formalité** *nf* **1** formality. **2** ceremony. **formation** *nf* **1** formation. **2** structure. **3** education, training. **4** development, growth. **forme** *nf* **1** form. **2** figure. **3** method. **4** *pl* manners. **être en forme** be fit. **formel, -elle** (fɔr'mɛl) *adj* **1** formal. **2** explicit. **3** definite.
formidable (fɔrmi:'dabl) *adj* **1** formidable. **2** *inf* tremendous, terrific.
formuler (fɔrmy'le:) *vt* **1** formulate. **2** state. **3** express. **formule** *nf* **1** formula. **2** prescription. **3** form.
fors (fɔr) *prep* except, but.
fort[1] (fɔr) *adj* **1** strong. **2** large, stout. **3** loud. **4** clever. **5** thick. **6** violent. *nm* **1** strong part. **2** height. **3** fort.
fort[2] (fɔr) *adv* **1** hard. **2** much. **3** very.
forteresse (fɔrtə'rɛs) *nf* fortress.
fortifier (fɔrti:'fje:) *vt* **1** strengthen. **2** fortify.
fortuit (fɔr'tɥi) *adj* **1** chance. **2** accidental. **3** casual.
fortune (fɔr'tyn) *nf* **1** chance. **2** luck. **3** fortune. **4** wealth. **fortuné** *adj* **1** fortunate. **2** happy. **3** rich.
fosse (fos) *nf* **1** hole. **2** pit. **3** grave. **fossé** *nm* **1** ditch. **2** moat. **fossette** *nf* dimple.
fossile (fɔ'si:l) *adj,nm* fossil.
fou, fol, folle (fu:, fɔl, fɔl) *adj* **1** mad. **2** foolish, silly. **3** insane. *nm,f* **1** lunatic. **2** fool.
foudre (fu:dr) *nm* lightning. **coup de foudre** *nm* **1** flash of lightning. **2** love at first sight.
foudroyer (fu:drwa'je:) *vt* **1** strike by lightning. **2** overwhelm. **foudroyant** *adj* **1** terrifying. **2** overwhelming. **3** terrific.
fouet (fwɛ) *nm* **1** whip. **2** lash.
fouetter (fwɛ'te:) *vt* **1** whip. **2** flog. **3** beat. **4** whisk.
fougère (fu:'ʒɛr) *nf* fern.
fougue (fu:g) *nf* **1** ardour. **2** spirit. **fougueux, -euse** (fu:'gœ, -'gœz) *adj* **1** ardent. **2** fiery. **3** impetuous.
fouiller (fu:'je:) *vt* **1** excavate. **2** dig. **3** search. *vi* rummage. **fouille** *nf* **1** excavation. **2** search.
fouillis (fu:'ji:) *nm* muddle, jumble.
fouir (fwi:r) *vt* burrow, dig.
foulard (fu:'lar) *nm* **1** silk handkerchief. **2** scarf.
fouler (fu:'le:) *vt* **1** crush. **2** trample. **3** sprain. **foule** *nf* crowd, mob. **foulure** *nf* sprain.
four (fu:r) *nm* **1** oven. **2** kiln. **3** furnace.
fourbe (fu:rb) *adj* crafty. *nm* **1** cheat. **2** rogue. **fourberie** (fu:rbə'ri:) *nf* **1** swindle. **2** deceit.

fourche (fu:rʃ) *nf* fork, pitchfork. **fourchette** *nf cul* fork.
fourgon[1] (fu:r'gɔ̃) *nm* poker.
fourgon[2] (fu:r'gɔ̃) *nm* 1 van. 2 wagon.
fourmi (fu:r'mi:) *nf* ant. **avoir des fourmis** have pins and needles.
fourmiller (fu:rmi:'je:) *vi* 1 swarm. 2 tingle.
fourneau, -aux (fu:r'no) *nm* 1 furnace. 2 stove.
fournir (fu:r'ni:r) *vt* 1 supply. 2 provide. **fourni** *adj* 1 thick. 2 bushy. **fournisseur** (fu:rni:'sœr) *nm* tradesman. **fourniture** *nf pl* materials.
fourrer (fu:'re:) *vt* 1 stuff, cram. 2 shove. 3 line with fur. **fourreau, -aux** (fu:'ro) *nm* 1 sheath. 2 case, cover. **fourre-tout** *nm invar* holdall. **fourreur** *nm* furrier. **fourrure** *nf* 1 fur, skin. 2 lining.
foutre* (fu:tr) *vt* 1 *tab* have sexual intercourse with. 2 *sl* do. **je m'en fous** I don't give a damn.
foyer (fwa'je:) *nm* 1 hearth, fireplace 2 centre 3 home. 4 focus. 5 *Th* entrance hall.
fracas (fra'ka) *nm* 1 uproar. 2 din.
fracasser (fraka'se:) *vt* 1 smash. 2 shatter
fraction (frak'sjɔ̃) *nf* fraction.
fracturer (frakty're:) *vt* 1 break. 2 fracture **fracture** *nf* fracture.
fragile (fra'ʒi:l) *adj* 1 fragile. 2 delicate.
fragment (frag'mɑ̃) *nm* 1 fragment 2 scrap
frai (frɛ) *nm* spawn
frais[1], **fraiche** (frɛ, frɛʃ) *adj* 1 fresh 2 cool 3 new. **fraicheur** *nf* 1 coolness 2 freshness
frais[2] (frɛ) *nm pl* 1 expenses 2 cost
fraise[1] (frɛz) *nf* strawberry.
fraise[2] (frɛz) *nf* ruff.
framboise (frɑ̃'bwaz) *nf* raspberry.
franc[1] (frɑ̃) *nm* franc.
franc[2], **franche** (frɑ̃, frɑ̃ʃ) *adj* 1 free 2 frank, candid, honest 3 aboveboard.
France (frɑ̃s) *nf* France. **français** *adj* French *nm* 1 Frenchman 2 French (language)
franchir (frɑ̃'ʃi:r) *vt* 1 jump over 2 cross
franchise (frɑ̃'ʃi:z) *nf* 1 franchise 2 freedom 3 exemption 4 frankness
franco (frɑ̃'ko) *adv* free of charge
frange (frɑ̃ʒ) *nf* fringe
frapper (fra'pe:) *vt* 1 hit. 2 mint 3 knock **frappe** *nf* 1 striking 2 stamp, mark
fraternel, -elle (fratɛr'nɛl) *adj* fraternal **fraternité** *nf* 1 fraternity 2 brotherhood
fraterniser (fratɛrni'ze:) *vi* fraternize
fraude (frod) *nf* 1 fraud 2 deceit 3 false pretences. **passer en fraude** smuggle through.
frayer (frɛ'je:) *vt* 1 rub, scrape. 2 clear or open up. *vi* 1 spawn. 2 associate.
fredaine (frə'dɛn) *nf* prank.
fredonner (frədɔ'ne:) *vt* hum.
frein (frɛ̃) *nm* 1 brake. 2 curb. 3 horse's bit.
freiner (frɛ'ne:) *vi* brake. *vt* check.
frêle (frɛl) *adj* 1 frail. 2 delicate.
frelon (frə'lɔ̃) *nm* hornet.
frémir (fre:'mi:r) *vi* 1 quiver. 2 rustle. 3 tremble. 4 shudder.
frêne (frɛn) *nm* ash tree.
frénésie (fre:ne:'zi:) *nf* frenzy. **frénétique** *adj* frantic.
fréquence (frɛ'kɑ̃s) *nf* 1 frequence 2 frequency. **fréquent** *adj* frequent.
fréquenter (frɛkɑ̃'te:) *vt* 1 visit. 2 associate
frère (frɛr) *nm* brother.
fresque (frɛsk) *nf* fresco.
fret (frɛ) *nm* freight.
fréter (fre:'te:) *vt* 1 freight 2 charter.
frétiller (fre:ti:'je:) *vi* 1 wriggle. 2 wag
freux (frœ) *nm invar* rook.
friand (fri:'ɑ̃) *adj* 1 fond of delicacies 2 fond.
fricoter (fri:kɔ'te:) *vi,vt inf* cook.
friction (fri:k'sjɔ̃) *nf* friction.
frictionner (fri:ksjɔ'ne:) *vt* rub.
Frigidaire (fri:ʒi:'dɛr) *nm Tdmk* refrigerator **frigo** (fri:'go) *nm* fridge.
frigide (fri:'ʒi:d) *adj* frigid.
frileux, -euse (fri'lœ, -'lœz) *adj* chilly, sensitive to cold.
frimas (fri:'ma) *nm* frost
friper (fri:'pe:) *vt* 1 crumple 2 crush
fripon, -onne (fri'pɔ̃, -'pɔn) *nm,f* rogue, rascal
frire* (fri:r) *vi,vt* fry.
frise (fri:z) *nf* frieze.
friser (fri:'ze:) *vi,vt* curl *vt* skim
frisson (fri'sɔ̃) *nm* shiver
frissonner (frisɔ'ne:) *vi* 1 shiver 2 shudder
frit (fri:) *v see* **frire.**
frivole (fri'vɔl) *adj* 1 frivolous 2 empty
froid (frwa) *adj* 1 cold 2 cool 3 indifferent **avoir froid** feel cold ~*nm* cold, coldness **froideur** *nf* coldness
froisser (frwa'se:) *vt* 1 crumple 2 crease 3 hurt. **se froisser** *vr* take offence
frôler (fro'le:) *vt* touch lightly, brush
fromage (frɔ'maʒ) *nm* cheese
froment (frɔ'mɑ̃) *nm* wheat
froncer (frɔ̃'se:) *vt* wrinkle **froncer les sourcils** frown **fronce** *nf* crease

fronde (frɔ̃d) *nf* sling.
front (frɔ̃) *nm* **1** forehead. **2** front. **3** brow. **frontal, -aux** (frɔ̃'tal, -'to) *adj* front, frontal. **frontière** *nf* frontier.
frotter (frɔ'te:) *vt* **1** rub. **2** strike. **3** scrub. **frottoir** *nm* **1** polisher. **2** scrubbing brush.
fructueux, -euse (fryk'tɥœ, -'tɥœz) *adj* fruitful.
frugal, -aux (fry'gal, -'go) *adj* frugal.
fruit (frɥi:) *nm* fruit.
fruste (fryst) *adj* **1** worn. **2** defaced. **3** rough.
frustrer (fry'stre:) *vt* **1** frustrate. **2** disappoint. **frustration** *nf* frustration.
fuir* (fɥi:r) *vi* **1** flee. **2** recede. **3** leak. *vt* **1** avoid. **2** shun. **fuite** *nf* **1** flight. **2** leak.
fumer (fy'me:) *vi,vt* smoke. *vi* steam. **fumée** *nf* smoke.
fumier (fy'mje:) *nm* manure, dung.
funèbre (fy'nɛbr) *adj* **1** funereal. **2** dismal.
funérailles (fynɛ'rɑj) *nf pl* funeral.
funeste (fy'nɛst) *adj* fatal, deadly.
fur (fyr) **au fur et à mesure** *adv* **1** as. **2** gradually.
furet (fy'rɛ) *nm* ferret.
fureter (fyr'te:) *vi* **1** ferret, rummage. **2** pry.
fureur (fy'rœr) *nf* **1** fury, rage. **2** mania. **furibond** *adj* furious. **furie** *nf* fury, rage. **furieux, -euse** (fy'rjœ, -'rjœz) *adj* furious.
furoncle (fy'rɔ̃kl) *nm* boil.
furtif, -ive (fyr'ti:f, -'ti:v) *adj* furtive.
fusée (fy'ze:) *nf* **1** rocket. **2** fuse.
fusil (fy'zi:) *nm* gun. **fusil rayé** rifle.
fusiller (fyzi:'je:) *vt* shoot, execute.
fusion (fy'zjɔ̃) *nf* **1** fusion. **2** melting.
fusionner (fyzjɔ'ne:) *vi,vt* **1** blend. **2** unite.
fustiger (fysti:'ʒe:) *vt* thrash, flog.
fût (fy) *nm* **1** shaft. **2** handle. **3** barrel.
futaie (fy'tɛ) *nf* forest.
futaille (fy'tɑj) *nf* barrel.
futile (fy'ti:l) *adj* **1** futile. **2** trivial.
futur (fy'tyr) *adj,nm* future.
fuyant (fy'jɑ̃) *v see* **fuir**.

G

gâche (gɑʃ) *nf tech* staple.
gâcher (gɑ'ʃe:) *vt* **1** spoil. **2** bungle. **3** waste. **gâchis** *nm* **1** mud, slush. **2** mess.
gâchette (gɑ'ʃɛt) *nf* trigger.
gaffe (gaf) *nf* **1** boathook. **2** blunder.
gager (ga'ʒe:) *vt* **1** bet. **2** hire. **gage** *nm* **1** pledge. **2** token. **3** forfeit. **4** *pl* wages.
gagner (ga'ɲe:) *vt* **1** earn. **2** gain. **3** win. **4** reach. **gagne-pain** *nm invar* breadwinner.
gai (ge:) *adj* **1** gay. **2** merry. **3** bright. **gaieté** *nf* gaiety, mirth.
gaillard[1] (ga'jar) *adj* **1** strong. **2** healthy. **3** merry. **4** free. *nm* chap, fellow.
gaillard[2] (ga'jar) **gaillard arrière** *nm* quarter-deck.
gain (gɛ̃) *nm* **1** gain. **2** profit.
gaine (gɛn) *nf* **1** sheath. **2** cover. **3** case.
galant (ga'lɑ̃) *adj* **1** gallant. **2** courteous, polite. **galamment** *adv* gallantly.
galaxie (galak'si:) *nf* galaxy.
galbe (galb) *nm* **1** contour. **2** outline. **3** figure.
gale (gal) *nf* mange.
galère (ga'lɛr) *nf* galley.
galerie (gal'ri:) *nf* gallery.
galet (ga'lɛ) *nm* pebble. **gros galet** boulder.
Galles (gal) **pays de Galles** Wales. **gallois** (gal'wa) *adj* Welsh. *nm* **1** Welshman. **2** Welsh (language).
gallon (ga'lɔ̃) *nm* gallon.
galon (ga'lɔ̃) *nm* **1** braid. **2** stripe.
galop (ga'lo) *nm* gallop. **petit galop** canter.
galoper (galɔ'pe:) *vi* gallop.
galvaniser (galvani'ze:) *vt* galvanise.
gambade (gɑ̃'bad) *nf* leap, gambol.
gamin (ga'mɛ̃) *n* **1** *inf* rascal. **2** youngster.
gamme (gam) *nf* **1** *mus* scale. **2** range.
gangster (gɑ̃g'stɛr) *nm* gangster.
gant (gɑ̃) *nm* glove. **gant de toilette** facecloth.
garage (ga'raʒ) *nm* **1** garage. **2** shed. **3** storage.
garant (ga'rɑ̃) *nm* **1** guarantor. **2** bail.
garantir (garɑ̃'ti:r) *vt* **1** guarantee. **2** vouch for. **3** protect. **4** insure. **garantie** *nf* guarantee.
garce (gars) *nf inf* bitch.
garçon (gar'sɔ̃) *nm* **1** boy. **2** lad. **3** bachelor. **4** waiter. **garçon d'honneur** best man.
garde-boue (gardə'bu:) *nm invar* mudguard.
garde-chasse (gardə'ʃas) *nm, pl* **gardes-chasse(s)** gamekeeper.
garde-côte (gardə'kot) *nm, pl* **gardes-côte(s)** coastguard.
garde-feu (gardə'fœ) *nm invar* fireguard.
garde-malade (gardma'lad) *nm or f,pl* **gardes-malades** nurse.
garde-manger (gardmɑ̃'ʒe:) *nm invar* larder, pantry.
garder (gar'de:) *vt* **1** guard. **2** take care of. **3** watch. **4** keep. **garder les bébés** baby-sit. **se garder** *vr* protect oneself. **se garder de** beware of. **garde** *nf* **1** care. **2** custody. **3** guard. **prendre garde à/de** take care to/not

to. ~*nm* **1** keeper. **2** warder. **garde du corps** bodyguard. **guardien, -ienne** (gar'djɛ̃, -'djɛn) *nm,f* guardian. **guardien de but** goalkeeper.
garde-robe (gardə'rɔb) *nf, pl* **gardes-robes** wardrobe.
gare[1] (gar) *nf* railway station.
gare[2] (gar) *interj* look out!
garenne (ga'rɛn) *nf* warren.
garer (ga're:) *vt* **1** dock. **2** park. **3** shunt. **se garer** *vr* get out of the way.
se gargariser (gargari:'ze:) *vr* gargle.
gargouiller (gargu:'je:) *vi* **1** gurgle. **2** rumble. **gargouille** *nf* **1** gargoyle. **2** spout.
garnir (gar'ni:r) *vt* **1** strengthen. **2** provide. **3** decorate. **4** garnish. **garnison** *nf* garrison. **garniture** *nf* **1** fittings. **2** *cul* trimmings.
gars (gɑ) *nm inf* lad.
gaspiller (gaspi:'je:) *vt* **1** waste. **2** squander. **gaspillage** *nm* **1** waste. **2** wastefulness.
gastrique (ga'stri:k) *adj* gastric.
gastronomique (gastrɔnɔ'mi:k) *adj* gastronomic.
gâteau, -aux (gɑ'to) *nm* cake.
gâter (gɑ'te:) *vt* **1** spoil. **2** harm. **gâte-tout** *nm invar* spoilsport.
gauche (goʃ) *adj* **1** left. **2** clumsy, gauche. *nf* left. **gaucher, -ère** (go'ʃe:, -'ʃɛr) *adj* left-handed.
gaufre (gofr) *nf* waffle. **gaufrette** (go'frɛt) *nf* wafer.
gaz (gɑz) *nm* gas.
gaze (gɑz) *nf* gauze.
gazéifier (gɑze:i:'fje:) *vt* aerate.
gazelle (ga'zɛl) *nf* gazelle.
gazon (gɑ'zɔ̃) *nm* **1** lawn. **2** turf.
gazouiller (gazu:'je:) *vi* **1** twitter. **2** babble.
géant (ʒe:'ɑ̃) *nm* giant. *adj* gigantic.
geindre* (ʒɛ̃dr) *vi* **1** whine. **2** whimper.
gel (ʒɛl) *nm* **1** frost. **2** freezing.
gélatine (ʒɛla'ti:n) *nf* gelatine.
geler (ʒə'le:) *vt* freeze. *vi* become frozen. *v imp* freeze. **gelé** *adj* frozen. **gelée** *nf* **1** frost. **2** jelly.
gélignite (ʒe:li:g'ni:t) *nf* gelignite.
Gémeaux (ʒe:'mo) *nm pl* Gemini.
gémir (ʒe:'mi:r) *vi* **1** groan. **2** moan. **3** wail. **gémissement** *nm* **1** groan. **2** moan.
gemme (ʒɛm) *nf* gem.
gencive (ʒɑ̃'si:v) *nf anat* gum.
gendarme (ʒɑ̃'darm) *nm* policeman.
gendre (ʒɑ̃dr) *nm* son-in-law.
gène (ʒɛn) *nm* gene.
généalogie (ʒe:ne:alɔ'ʒi:) *nf* genealogy. **généalogique** *adj* genealogical.
gêner (ʒe:'ne:) *vt* **1** hinder, obstruct. **2** embarrass, inconvenience. **se gêner** *vr* put oneself out. **gênant** (ʒɛ'nɑ̃) *adj* **1** awkward. **2** embarrassing. **gêne** (ʒɛn) *nf* **1** difficulty. **2** embarrassment. **3** need.
général, -aux (ʒe:nɛ'ral, -'ro) *adj,nm* general. **général de brigade/division** brigadier/ major general.
généraliser (ʒe:nɛrali:'ze:) *vt* generalize.
génération (ʒe:nɛra'sjɔ̃) *nf* generation.
généreux, -euse (ʒe:ne:'rœ, -'rœz) *adj* generous. **générosité** *nf* generosity.
générique (ʒe:ne:'ri:k) *adj* generic.
génétique (ʒe:ne:'ti:k) *adj* genetic. *nf* genetics.
Genève (ʒə'nɛv) *nf* Geneva.
génie (ʒe:'ni:) *nm* **1** spirit. **2** genius. **génial, -aux** (ʒe:'njal, -'njo) *adj* inspired, brilliant.
genièvre (ʒə'njɛvr) *nf* **1** juniper berry. **2** gin.
génital, -aux (ʒe:ni:'tal, -'to) *adj* genital.
genou, -oux (ʒə'nu:) *nm* knee.
genre (ʒɑ̃r) *nm* **1** kind, sort, type. **2** genus, family. **3** gender. **4** style. **genre humain** mankind.
gens (ʒɑ̃) *nm,f pl* people, folk.
gentiane (ʒɑ̃'sjan) *nf* gentian.
gentil[1], **-ille** (ʒɑ̃'ti:, -'ti:j) *adj* **1** nice. **2** kind. **3** pretty. **4** good. **gentilhomme** *nm* **1** nobleman. **2** gentleman. **gentillesse** *nf* **1** kindness. **2** prettiness. **gentiment** *adv* **1** nicely. **2** kindly. **3** prettily.
gentil[2] (ʒɑ̃'ti:) *nm* Gentile.
génuflexion (ʒe:nyflɛk'sjɔ̃) *nf* genuflection.
géographie (ʒe:ɔgra'fi:) *nf* geography. **géographique** *adj* geographic.
geôle (ʒol) *nf* jail, prison.
géométrie (ʒe:ɔme:'tri:) *nf* geometry. **géométrique** *adj* geometric.
géranium (ʒɛra'njɔm) *nm* geranium.
gerbe (ʒɛrb) *nf* **1** sheaf. **2** bunch.
gercer (ʒɛr'se:) *vt* **1** crack. **2** chap. **gerçure** *nf* **1** crack. **2** fissure.
gérer (ʒe:'re:) *vt* manage, run. **gérance** (ʒɛ'rɑ̃s) *nf* management. **gérant** (ʒɛ'rɑ̃) *nm* **1** manager. **2** director.
germanique (ʒɛrma'ni:k) *adj* Germanic.
germer (ʒɛr'me:) *vi* **1** germinate. **2** sprout, shoot. **germe** *nm* **1** germ. **2** sprout.
gérondif (ʒe:rɔ̃'di:f) *nm* gerund.
gésir* (ʒe:'zi:r) *vi* lie. **ci-gît** here lies.
geste (ʒɛst) *nm* **1** gesture. **2** movement. **3** sign.
gesticuler (ʒɛsti:ky'le:) *vi* gesticulate.

gestion (ʒɛ'stjɔ̃) *nf* **1** management. **2** administration.
geyser (ʒi:'zɛr) *nm* geyser.
ghetto (gɛ'to) *nm* ghetto.
gibet (ʒi:'bɛ) *nm* gallows.
gibier (ʒi:'bje:) *nm* (hunting) game.
giboulée (ʒi:bu:'le:) *nf* shower (of rain).
gicler (ʒi:'kle:) *vi* squirt out. **giclée** *nf* squirt.
gifler (ʒi:'fle:) *vt* **1** slap. **2** smack. **gifle** *nf* slap.
gigantesque (ʒi:gɑ̃'tɛsk) *adj* gigantic, huge.
gigot (ʒi:'go) *nm* leg of mutton.
gigue (ʒi:g) *nf* jig.
gilet (ʒi:'lɛ) *nm* **1** waistcoat. **2** cardigan. **gilet de sauvetage** lifejacket.
gin (dʒi:n) *nm* gin.
gingembre (ʒɛ̃'ʒɑ̃br) *nm* ginger.
girafe (ʒi:'raf) *nf* giraffe.
girofle (ʒi:'rɔfl) *nm bot* clove. **giroflée jaune** *nf* wallflower.
giron (ʒi:'rɔ̃) *nm* lap.
gisement (ʒi:z'mɑ̃) *nm* layer, bed. **gisement petrolifère** oilfield.
gît (ʒi:) *v* see **gésir.**
gitan (ʒi:'tɑ̃) *nm* Gipsy.
gîte (ʒi:t) *nm* **1** shelter, refuge. **2** home.
givre (ʒi:vr) *nm* hoarfrost.
glabre (glabr) *adj* smooth.
glacer (gla'se:) *vt* **1** freeze. **2** chill. **3** ice. **4** glaze. **glace** *nf* **1** ice. **2** ice-cream. **3** glass. **4** mirror. **glacé** *adj* **1** frozen. **2** icy. **glaçon** *nm* icicle.
glacier (gla'sje:) *nm* glacier.
glaise (glɛz) *nf* clay.
gland (glɑ̃) *nm* **1** acorn. **2** tassel.
glande (glɑ̃d) *nf* gland.
glaner (gla'ne:) *vt* glean.
glapir (gla'pi:r) *vi* yelp, yap.
glisser (gli:'se:) *vi* **1** slide. **2** skid. **3** glide. *vt* slip. **se glisser** *vr* creep. **glissade** *nf* **1** slip. **2** slide. **glissière** *nf* **1** groove. **2** chute.
globe (glɔb) *nm* **1** globe. **2** sphere. **globe de l'œil** eyeball. **global, -aux** (glɔ'bal, -'bo) *adj* **1** total. **2** inclusive.
gloire (glwar) *nf* **1** glory. **2** pride. **3** honour. **4** halo. **glorieux, -euse** (glɔ'rjœ, -'rjœz) *adj* glorious.
glorifier (glɔri:'fje:) *vt* **1** glorify. **2** praise. **se glorifier** *vr* boast.
gloser (glo'ze:) *vt* **1** gloss. **2** criticize. **glose** *nf* **1** gloss. **2** comment.
glossaire (glɔs'sɛr) *nm* glossary.
glouglou (glu:'glu:) *nm* gurgle.
glouglouter (glu:glu:'te:) *vi* gurgle.
glouton, -onne (glu:'tɔ̃, -'tɔn) *adj* greedy. *nm,f* glutton.
gluant (gly'ɑ̃) *adj* sticky.
glucose (gly'koz) *nm* glucose.
glycine (gli:'si:n) *nf* wisteria.
gnome (gnom) *nm* gnome.
go (go) **tout de go** *adv inf* **1** all of a sudden. **2** without a hitch.
gobelet (gɔ'blɛ) *nm* tumbler, mug.
gobelin (gɔ'blɛ̃) *nm* goblin.
gober (gɔ'be:) *vt* **1** swallow, gulp down. **2** *sl* believe. **se gober** *vr* fancy oneself.
godasse (gɔ'das) *nf sl* shoe.
godet (gɔ'dɛ) *nm* **1** mug. **2** bowl.
godiche (gɔ'di:ʃ) *adj inf* **1** awkward. **2** simple.
goéland (gɔɛ'lɑ̃) *nm* seagull.
goélette (gɔɛ'lɛt) *nf* schooner.
goémon (gɔɛ'mɔ̃) *nm* seaweed.
gogo (gɔ'go) **à gogo** *adv inf* galore.
golf (gɔlf) *nm* golf.
golfe (gɔlf) *nm* gulf, bay.
gommer (gɔ'me:) *vt* **1** gum. **2** rub out. **gomme** *nf* **1** gum. **2** eraser.
gond (gɔ̃) *nm* hinge.
gondole (gɔ̃'dɔl) *nf* gondola. **gondolier** *nm* gondolier.
gonfler (gɔ̃'fle:) *vt* **1** inflate, blow up. **2** swell.
gong (gɔ̃) *nm* gong.
gorge (gɔrʒ) *nf* **1** throat. **2** breast. **3** gorge. **4** (mountain) pass. **5** groove. **gorgée** *nf* mouthful. **petite gorgée** sip.
gorille (gɔ'ri:j) *nm* gorilla.
gosier (go'zje:) *nm* **1** gullet. **2** throat.
gosse (gɔs) *nm,f inf* kid, youngster.
gothique (gɔ'ti:k) *adj* Gothic.
goudron (gu:'drɔ̃) *nm* tar.
gouffre (gu:fr) *nm* gulf, abyss.
goulot (gu:'lo:) *nm* neck (of a bottle).
goulu (gu:'ly) *adj* greedy. *nm* glutton.
gourde (gu:rd) *nf* **1** gourd. **2** flask. **3** *inf* fool.
gourmand (gu:r'mɑ̃) *adj* greedy. *nm* glutton.
gousse (gu:s) *nf* pod, shell, husk. **gousse d'ail** clove of garlic.
goût (gu:) *nm* **1** taste. **2** flavour. **3** liking. **4** style.
goûter (gu:'te:) *vt* **1** taste. **2** enjoy. **goûter à** taste, try. ~*nm* afternoon tea.
goutte (gu:t) *nf* **1** drop. **2** spot. **gouttière** *nf* **1** gutter. **2** spout.
gouvernail (gu:vɛr'naj) *nm* **1** rudder. **2** helm.
gouverner (gu:vɛr'ne:) *vt* **1** govern, rule. **2** control. **3** steer. **gouvernante** *nf* governess.

gouvernement (gu:vɛrnə'mɑ̃) *nm* government. **gouverneur** *nm* governor.
grâce (grɑs) *nf* **1** grace. **2** charm. **3** favour. **4** pardon. **de bonne grâce** willingly. **grâce à** thanks to. **gracieux, -euse** (gra'sjœ, -'sjœz) *adj* **1** gracious. **2** kind. **3** free.
gracile (gra'si:l) *adj* **1** slender. **2** slim.
grade (grad) *nm* **1** grade. **2** rank. **3** degree. **gradient** *nm* gradient.
gradin (gra'dɛ̃) *nm* **1** tier. **2** step.
graduer (gra'dɥe:) *vt* **1** graduate. **2** grade. **graduel, -elle** (gra'dɥɛl) *adj* gradual.
graffitti (graffi:'ti:) *nm pl* graffiti.
grain (grɛ̃) *nm* **1** grain. **2** corn. **3** bean. **4** particle. **5** bead. **grain de café** coffee bean. **grain de poivre** peppercorn. **grain de raisin** grape.
graine (grɛn) *nf* seed. **graine de lin** linseed.
graisser (grɛ'se:) *vt* **1** grease. **2** oil. **graisse** *nf* **1** grease. **2** fat. **graisse de porc/rognon** lard/suet.
grammaire (gram'mɛr) *nf* grammar. **grammatical, -aux** (gramati:'kal, -'ko) *adj* grammatical.
gramme (gram) *nm* gram.
grand (grɑ̃) *adj* **1** big. **2** tall. **3** chief, main. **4** great. **5** grand. **grandeur** *nf* **1** size. **2** height. **3** importance. **4** grandeur. **5** *cap* (title) Grace.
grand-chose *nm invar* much.
Grande-Bretagne *nf* Great Britain.
grandiose (grɑ̃'djoz) *adj* grand, imposing.
grandir (grɑ̃'di:r) *vi* **1** grow, grow up. **2** increase. *vt* **1** exaggerate. **2** enlarge.
grand-maman *nf, pl* **grands-mamans** granny.
grand-mère *nf, pl* **grands-mères** grandmother.
grand-parent *nm, pl* **grands-parents** grandparent.
grand-père *nm, pl* **grands-pères** grandfather.
grand-route *nf, pl* **grands-routes** highroad.
grand-voile *nf, pl* **grands-voiles** mainsail.
grange (grɑ̃ʒ) *nf* barn.
granit (gra'ni:) *nm* granite.
graphique (gra'fi:k) *adj* graphic. *nm* **1** graph. **2** diagram.
grappe (grap) *nf* **1** bunch. **2** cluster.
gras, grasse (grɑ, grɑs) *adj* **1** fat. **2** rich. **3** thick. *nm* fat. **grassouillet, -ette** (grɑsu:'jɛ, -'jɛt) *adj* plump, chubby.
gratifier (grati:'fje:) *vt* **1** confer. **2** give.
gratin (gra'tɛ̃) *nm* burnt part. **au gratin** cooked with breadcrumbs and grated cheese.
gratitude (grati:'tyd) *nf* gratitude.
gratter (gra'te:) *vt* **1** scratch. **2** scrape. **gratte-ciel** *nm invar* skyscraper.
gratuit (gra'tɥi:) *adj* free.
grave (grav) *adj* **1** grave, serious. **2** severe. **3** important. **4** *mus* low. **gravité** *nf* gravity.
graver (gra've:) *vt* **1** engrave. **2** carve. **gravure** *nf* **1** engraving. **2** etching.
gravier (gra'vje:) *nm* gravel.
gravir (gra'vi:r) *vt* climb.
gré (gre:) *nm* **1** will. **2** liking.
Grèce (grɛs) *nf* Greece. **grec, grecque** *adj* Greek, Grecian. *nm* **1** Greek. **2** Greek (language).
gredin (grə'dɛ̃) *nm* scoundrel.
gréer (gre:'e:) *vt naut* rig.
greffer (grɛ'fe:) *vt* graft. **greffe** *nf* graft.
greffier (grɛ'fje:) *nm* registrar.
grégaire (gre:'gɛr) *adj* gregarious.
grêle[1] (grɛl) *nf* hail. **grêlon** *nm* hailstone.
grêle[2] (grɛl) *adj* slender, thin.
grêler (grɛ'le:) *v imp* hail.
grelotter (grəlɔ'te:) *vi* **1** tremble, shiver. **2** jingle.
grenade[1] (grə'nad) *nf* **1** pomegranate. **grenadier** *nm* pomegranate tree. **grenadine** *nf* syrup made of pomegranate juice.
grenade[2] (grə'nad) *nf* grenade. **grenade à main** hand grenade.
grenier (grə'nje:) *nm* **1** granary. **2** loft.
grenouille (grə'nu:j) *nf* frog.
grès (grɛ) *nm* grit, sandstone.
grésil (gre:'zi:) *nm* sleet.
grésiller[1] (gre:zi:'je:) *v imp* sleet.
grésiller[2] (gre:zi:'je:) *vi* **1** crackle. **2** sizzle.
grève[1] (grɛv) *nf* bank, shore.
grève[2] (grɛv) *nf* strike. **grève de la faim** hunger-strike. **grève de zèle** work to rule. **se mettre en grève** go on strike.
grever (grə've:) *vt* **1** mortgage. **2** encumber.
grief (gri:'ɛf) *nm* grievance.
griffer (gri:'fe:) *vt* scratch. **griffe** *nf* **1** claw. **2** signature. **griffe à papiers** paperclip.
griffonner (gri:fɔ'ne:) *vt* scrawl, scribble. **griffonnage** *nm* scrawl, scribble.
grignoter (gri:ɲɔ'te:) *vt* nibble (at).
gril (gri:) *nm* grill.
grille (gri:j) *nf* **1** grille. **2** gate.
griller (gri:'je:) *vt* **1** grill. **2** toast. **3** burn. **grille-pain** *nm invar* toaster.
grillon (gri:'jɔ̃) *nm zool* cricket.
grimacer (gri:ma'se:) *vi* **1** grimace. **2** grin. **grimace** *nf* **1** grimace. **2** grin.
grimer (gri:'me:) *vt Th* make up.
grimper (grɛ̃'pe:) *vi* climb up. *vt* climb.
grincer (grɛ̃'se:) *vi* **1** grate. **2** gnash. **3** creak.

grincheux, -euse (grɛ̃'ʃœ, -'ʃœz) *adj* **1** bad-tempered. **2** grumpy.
grippe (gri:p) *nf* influenza.
gris (gri:) *adj* **1** grey. **2** tipsy. *nm* grey.
grive (gri:v) *nf* thrush.
Groenland (grɔɛn'lɑ̃d) *nm* Greenland. **groenlandais** *adj* of Greenland. *nm* Greenlander.
grogner (grɔ'ɲe:) *vi* **1** grunt. **2** growl. **3** grumble. **4** groan.
groin (grwɛ̃) *nm* snout (of a pig).
grommeler (grɔm'le:) *vi* grumble. *vt* mutter.
gronder (grɔ̃'de:) *vt* scold. *vi* **1** growl. **2** rumble.
gros, grosse (gro, gros) *adj* **1** big. **2** stout. **3** thick. **4** coarse. **5** gross. **6** pregnant. **gros** *adv* much. *nm* **1** bulk. **2** wholesale. **en gros 1** wholesale. **2** on the whole. **grosse** *nf* gross. **grossesse** *nf* pregnancy. **grosseur** *nf* **1** size. **2** thickness. **grossier, -ière** (gro'sje:, -'sjɛr) *adj* **1** coarse, rough. **2** vulgar, rude.
groseille (gro'zɛj) *nf* currant. **groseille à maquereau** gooseberry. **groseille rouge** redcurrant. **groseillier** *nm* currant bush.
grossir (gro'si:r) *vi* **1** increase. **2** grow bigger. *vt* **1** enlarge. **2** magnify. **grossissant** *adj* **1** growing. **2** magnifying.
grotesque (grɔ'tɛsk) *adj* **1** grotesque. **2** absurd ludicrous. *nm* grotesque.
grotte (grɔt) *nf* grotto.
grouiller (gru:'je:) *vi* crawl.
grouper (gru:'pe:) *vt* group, arrange. **groupe** *nf* **1** group, party. **2** clump.
grue (gry) *nf zool,tech* crane.
grumeau, -aux (gry'mo) *nm* clot, lump.
se grumeler (grym'le:) *vr* clot.
gué (ge:) *nm* ford.
guenille (gə'ni:j) *nf* rag.
guépard (gɛ'par) *nm* cheetah.
guêpe (gɛp) *nf* wasp.
guère (gɛr) *adv* **1** hardly, scarcely. **2** not much or many.
guérilla (ge:ri:l'la) *nf* band of guerillas.
guérillero (ge:ri:llɛ'ro) *nm* guerilla.
guérir (ge:'ri:r) *vt* **1** cure. **2** heal. *vi* recover. **guérison** *nf* **1** cure. **2** recovery.
Guernesey (gɛrnə'zɛ) *nm* Guernsey.
guerre (gɛr) *nf* **1** war. **2** warfare. **guerrier** *nm* warrior.
guerroyer (gɛrwa'je:) *vi* war, wage war.
guet (gɛ) *nm* watch, guard. **guet-apens** *nm invar* **1** ambush. **2** trap.
guetter (gɛ'te:) *vt* **1** lie in wait for. **2** watch for.
gueuler (gœ'le:) *vi* bawl, yell. **gueule** *nf* **1** mouth (of animals). **2** jaws. **3** *sl* mouth (of humans). **4** large opening. **avoir la gueule de bois** have a hangover. **ta gueule!** shut up!
gueux, -euse (gœ, gœz) *nm,f* beggar. *adj* poor.
gui (gi:) *nm* mistletoe.
guichet (gi:'ʃɛ) *nm* **1** barrier. **2** box office. **3** counter. **4** grille.
guide[1] (gi:d) *nm* **1** guide. **2** guidebook.
guide[2] (gi:d) *nf* rein.
guider (gi:'de:) *vt* **1** guide. **2** direct. **3** lead.
guidon (gi:'dɔ̃) *nm* handlebar.
guigne (gi:ɲ) *nf* bad luck.
guillemets (gi:j'mɛ) *nm pl* quotation marks. **entre guillemets** in inverted commas.
guilleret, -ette (gi:j'rɛ, -'rɛt) *adj* lively, gay.
guillotine (gi:jɔ'ti:n) *nf* guillotine.
guimauve (gi:'mo:v) *nf* marshmallow.
guindé (gɛ̃'de:) *adj* stiff, formal.
guindeau, -aux (gɛ̃'do) *nm* windlass.
guinée (gi:'ne:) *nf* guinea.
guingan (gɛ̃'gɑ̃) *nm* gingham.
guingois (gɛ̃'gwa) **de guingois** *adv* askew, lopsided.
guirlande (gi:r'lɑ̃d) *nf* **1** garland. **2** wreath.
guise (gi:z) *nf* manner, way.
guitare (gi:'tar) *nf* guitar.
gymnase (ʒi:m'nɑz) *nm* gymnasium. **gymnaste** *nm,f* gymnast. **gymnastique** *adj* gymnastic.
gynécologie (ʒi:ne:kɔlɔ'ʒi:) *nf* gynaecology. **gynécologiste** *nm,f also* **gynécologue** gynaecologist.

H

(The asterisk denotes that the initial h is aspirate and that there is therefore no liaison or elision.)

habile (a'bi:l) *adj* **1** clever. **2** able. **3** cunning. **habileté** *nf* **1** ability, skill. **2** cleverness.
habiller (abi:'je:) *vt* **1** dress. **2** clothe. **3** prepare. **s'habiller** *vr* dress. **habillement** *nm* **1** clothing. **2** clothes.
habit (a'bi:) *nm* **1** dress. **2** coat. **3** evening dress. **4** *pl* clothes.
habiter (abi:'te:) *vi* live, reside. *vt* dwell or live in. **habitable** *adj* habitable. **habitant** *nm* **1** inhabitant. **2** resident. **habitation** *nf* **1** dwelling. **2** abode.
habituer (abi:'tɥe:) *vt* accustom. **s'habituer à** *vr* get used to. **habitude** *nf* **1** habit. **2** custom. **3** knack. **4** practice. **comme d'habitude**

as usual. **d'habitude** usually. **habitué** *nm* regular customer. **habituel, -elle** (abi:'tɥɛl) *adj* 1 usual. 2 habitual.

***hâbler** (ɑ'ble:) *vi* boast, brag.

***hacher** (a'ʃe:) *vt* 1 chop. 2 hack. 3 mince. ***hache** *nf* axe. ***hachette** *nf* hatchet. ***hachis** *nm* mince. ***hachoir** *nm* chopper.

***hagard** (a'gar) *adj* haggard, drawn.

***haie** (ɛ) *nf* 1 hedge. 2 hurdle. 3 line.

***haillon** (a'jɔ̃) *nm* rag.

haïr (a'i:r) *vt* hate, detest. ***haine** *nf* 1 hatred, hate. 2 spite.

***halage** (ɑ'laʒ) *nm* towing.

***hâle** (ɑl) *nm* 1 sunburn. 2 tan.

haleine (a'lɛn) *nf* breath.

***haler** (ɑ'le:) *vt* 1 tow. 2 haul.

***haleter** (al'te:) *vi* 1 pant. 2 gasp (for breath).

***hall** (al) *nm* 1 hall. 2 hotel lounge.

***halle** (al) *nf* covered market. **Les Halles** *nf pl* old site of markets in Paris.

hallucination (alysi:na'sjɔ̃) *nf* hallucination.

***halte** (alt) *nm* stop, halt. **faire halte** halt.

haltérophilie (alte:rɔfi:'li:) *nf* weight-lifting.

***hamac** (a'mak) *nm* hammock.

***hameau, -aux** (a'mo) *nm* hamlet.

hameçon (am'sɔ̃) *nm* 1 (fish) hook. 2 bait.

***hampe** (ɑ̃p) *nf* 1 shaft. 2 handle. 3 pole.

***hamster** (am'stɛr) *nm* hamster.

***hanche** (ɑ̃ʃ) *nf* 1 hip. 2 haunch.

***handicap** (ɑ̃di:'kap) *nm sport* handicap.

***handicaper** (ɑ̃di:ka'pe:) *vt sport* handicap.

***hangar** (ɑ̃'gar) *nm* 1 shed. 2 outhouse.

***hanter** (ɑ̃'te:) *vt* haunt. ***hantise** *nf* obsession.

***happer** (a'pe:) *vt* seize, snatch, snap up. ***happe** *nf* staple.

***haras** (a'rɑ) *nm zool* stud.

***harasser** (ara'se:) *vt* 1 tire out. 2 harass.

***harceler** (arsə'le:) *vt* 1 harass. 2 worry. 3 pester.

***harde** (ard) *nf* herd, flock.

***hardes** (ard) *nf pl inf* clothes.

***hardi** (ar'di:) *adj* 1 bold. 2 daring. 3 rash. 4 impudent. *interj* courage! ***hardiesse** *nf* 1 daring. 2 pluck.

***hareng** (a'rɑ̃) *nm* herring. **hareng salé et fumé** kipper. **hareng saur** red herring.

***hargneux, -euse** (ar'ɲœ, -'ɲœz) *adj* 1 peevish. 2 cross. 3 surly.

***haricot** (ari:'ko) *nm* kidney bean. **haricot vert** French bean.

harmonica (armɔni:'ka) *nm* harmonica.

harmoniser (armɔni:'ze:) *vt* 1 *mus* harmonize. 2 match. **s'harmoniser avec** *vr* 1 be in keeping with. 2 tone in with. **harmonie** *nf* 1 harmony. 2 agreement. **harmonieux, -euse** (armɔ'njœ, -'njœz) *adj* harmonious. **harmonique** *adj,nm mus* harmonic.

***harnais** (ar'nɛ) *nm* harness.

***harpe** (arp) *nf* harp.

***harpon** (ar'pɔ̃) *nm* harpoon.

***hasard** (a'zar) *nm* 1 chance. 2 luck. 3 accident. 4 risk. 5 hazard.

***hasarder** (azar'de:) *vt* 1 risk. 2 venture.

***haschich** (a'ʃi:ʃ) *nm* hashish.

***hâter** (ɑ'te:) *vt* hasten, quicken. ***hâte** *nf* haste, hurry.

***hausser** (o'se:) *vt* 1 raise. 2 lift. *vi* rise. **hausser les épaules** shrug one's shoulders. ***hausse** *nf* rise.

***haut** (o) *adj* 1 high. 2 tall. 3 lofty. 4 loud. 5 upper. *nm* 1 height. 2 top. 3 head. **de haut en bas** 1 downwards. 2 from top to bottom. **en haut** 1 upstairs. 2 above.

***haut-de-forme** *nm, pl* **hauts-de-forme** top-hat.

***haut-parleur** *nm, pl* **haut-parleurs** loud-speaker.

***hautain** (o'tɛ̃) *adj* haughty.

***hautbois** (o'bwɑ) *nm* oboe.

***hâve** (ɑv) *adj* 1 haggard. 2 hollow. 3 sunken.

***hâvre** (ɑvr) *nm* 1 harbour. 2 haven.

***havresac** (ɑvrə'sak) *nm* haversack.

***Haye, La** (ɛ) *nf* The Hague.

hebdomadaire (ɛbdɔma'dɛr) *adj* weekly.

héberger (e:bɛr'ʒe:) *vt* 1 lodge. 2 shelter.

hébéter (e:be:'te:) *vt* 1 dull. 2 daze.

hébraïque (e:bra'i:k) *adj* Hebrew.

hébreu, -eux (e:'brœ) *adj* Hebrew. *nm* 1 Hebrew. 2 Hebrew (language).

hectare (ɛk'tar) *nm* French measurement equivalent to 2.47 acres.

hélas (e:'lɑs) *interj* alas!

***héler** (e:'le:) *vt* hail, call.

hélice (ɛ'li:s) *nf* screw, propeller.

hélicoptère (e:li:kɔp'tɛr) *nm* helicopter.

helvétique (ɛlve:'ti:k) *adj* Swiss.

hémisphère (e:mi:'sfɛr) *nm* hemisphere.

hémorragie (e:mɔra'ʒi:) *nf* haemorrhage.

hémorroïde (e:mɔrɔ'i:d) *nf med* pile.

***henné** (ɛn'ne:) *nm* henna.

***hennir** (ɛ'ni:r) *vi* neigh.

***héraut** (e:'ro) *nm* herald.

herbe (ɛrb) *nf* 1 grass. 2 herb. 3 plant. **fines herbes** *nf pl* herbs used for seasoning. **mauvaise herbe** weed. **herbicide** *nm* weedkiller.

hérédité (e:re:di:ˈte:) *nf* heredity. **héréditaire** *adj* hereditary.

hérésie (e:re:ˈzi:) *nf* heresy.

***hérisser** (e:ri:ˈse:) *vt* **1** bristle up. **2** ruffle. **se hérisser** *vr* **1** bristle. **2** (of hair) stand on end. ***hérisson** *nm* hedgehog.

hériter (e:ri:ˈte:) *vt* inherit. **héritage** *nm* **1** inheritance, heritage. **2** legacy. **héritier, -ière** (e:ri:ˈtje:, -ˈtjɛr) *nm,f* heir, heiress.

hermétique (ɛrme:ˈti:k) *adj* **1** airtight. **2** watertight.

hermine (ɛrˈmi:n) *nf* **1** stoat. **2** ermine.

héroïne[1] (e:rɔˈi:n) *nf* heroine.

héroïne[2] (e:rɔˈi:n) *nf* heroin.

***héron** (e:ˈrɔ̃) *nm* heron.

***héros** (e:ˈro) *nm* hero. **héroïque** *adj* heroic. **héroïsme** *nm* heroism.

hésiter (e:zi:ˈte) *vi* **1** hesitate. **2** falter. **3** waver.

hétéroclite (e:te:rɔˈkli:t) *adj* **1** irregular. **2** strange, odd.

***hêtre** (ɛtr) *nm* beech tree. **hêtre rouge** copper beech tree.

heure (œr) *nf* **1** hour. **2** time. **3** o'clock. **à tout à l'heure** see you later. **de bonne heure** early. **dernière heure** latest news. **être à l'heure** be punctual. **heures d'affluence** ou **de pointes** *nf pl* rush hour. **heures supplémentaires** *nf pl* overtime. **tout à l'heure** just now.

heureux, -euse (œˈrœ, -ˈrœz) *adj* **1** happy. **2** lucky, fortunate. **3** successful.

***heurt** (œr) *nm* **1** shock. **2** bump. **sans heurt** smoothly.

***heurter** (œrˈte:) *vi,vt* **1** knock (against). **2** run (into). *vt* **1** shock. **2** offend. **se heurter** *vr* collide. **heurtoir** *nm* doorknocker.

hexagone (ɛgzaˈgɔn) *nm* hexagon. *adj* hexagonal.

hiberner (i:bɛrˈne:) *vi* hibernate.

***hibou, -oux** (i:ˈbu:) *nm* owl.

***hideux, -euse** (i:ˈdœ, -ˈdœz) *adj* hideous.

hier (i:ˈɛr) *adv,nm* yesterday.

***hiérarchie** (jɛrarˈʃi:) *nf* hierarchy.

hippique (i:pˈpi:k) *adj* of horses.

hippodrome (i:pɔˈdrɔm) *nm* racecourse.

hippopotame (i:pɔpɔˈtam) *nm* hippopotamus.

hirondelle (i:rɔ̃ˈdɛl) *nf* swallow.

***hisser** (i:ˈse:) *vt* hoist. **se hisser** *vr* pull oneself up.

histoire (i:ˈstwar) *nf* **1** history. **2** story, tale. **faire des histoires** make a fuss. **historien, -ienne** (i:stɔˈrjɛ̃, -ˈrjɛn) *nm,f* historian.

hiver (i:ˈvɛr) *nm* winter.

hiverner (i:vɛrˈne:) *vi* hibernate.

***hocher** (ɔˈʃe:) *vt* **1** shake. **2** toss. **3** nod.

***hockey** (ɔˈkɛ) *nm* hockey. **hockey sur glace** ice hockey.

***Hollande** (ɔˈlɑ̃d) *nf* Holland. ***hollandais** *adj* Dutch. *nm* **1** Dutchman. **2** Dutch (language).

***homard** (ɔˈmar) *nm* lobster.

hommage (ɔˈmaʒ) *nm* **1** homage. **2** token. **3** *pl* respects.

homme (ɔm) *nm* **1** man. **2** mankind. **homme de loi** lawyer. **homme d'état** statesman. **homme politique** politician.

homonyme (ɔmɔˈni:m) *nm* **1** homonym. **2** namesake.

homosexuel, -elle (ɔmɔsɛkˈsɥɛl) *adj,n* homosexual.

***Hongrie** (ɔ̃ˈgri:) *nf* Hungary. ***hongrois** *adj,n* Hungarian. *nm* Hungarian (language).

honnête (ɔˈnɛt) *adj* **1** honest, upright. **2** honourable. **3** decent. **4** well-bred. **5** reasonable. **honnêteté** *nf* **1** honesty. **2** fairness.

honneur (ɔˈnœr) *nm* **1** honour. **2** credit.

honoraire (ɔnɔˈrɛr) *adj* honorary.

honorer (ɔnɔˈre:) *vt* **1** honour. **2** respect. **honorable** *adj* **1** honourable. **2** respectable.

***honte** (ɔ̃t) *nf* **1** shame. **2** disgrace. **avoir honte** be ashamed. **faire honte à** put to shame. ***honteux, -euse** (ɔˈtœ, -ˈtœz) *adj* **1** ashamed. **2** shamefaced. **3** shameful.

hôpital, -aux (ɔpi:ˈtal, -ˈto) *nm* hospital.

***hoquet** (ɔˈkɛ) *nm* **1** hiccup. **2** gasp.

horaire (ɔˈrɛr) *nm* timetable.

***horde** (ɔrd) *nf* horde.

horizon (ɔri:ˈzɔ̃) *nm* horizon.

horizontal, -aux (ɔri:zɔ̃ˈtal, -ˈto) *adj* horizontal.

horloge (ɔrˈlɔʒ) *nf* clock.

***hormis** (ɔrˈmi:) *prep* except, but, save.

hormone (ɔrˈmɔn) *nf* hormone.

horoscope (ɔrɔˈskɔp) *nm* horoscope.

horreur (ɔrˈrœr) *nf* **1** horror. **2** disgust. **3** *pl* atrocities. **avoir en horreur** **1** hate. **2** have a horror of.

horrible (ɔrˈri:bl) *adj* **1** horrible. **2** awful.

horrifier (ɔrri:ˈfje:) *vt* horrify.

***hors** (ɔr) *prep* **1** outside. **2** out of. **3** beyond. **4** except. **hors de** outside, out of. **être hors de soi** be beside oneself. ***hors-bord** *nm invar* speedboat. **hors de combat** out of action, disabled. ***hors-d'œuvre** *nm invar* a dish served as the first course of a meal. ***hors-jeu** *adj invar* offside. ***hors-la-loi** *nm invar* outlaw.

horticulture (ɔrti:kyl'tyr) *nf* horticulture. **horticulteur** *nm* horticulturist.
hospice (ɔ'spi:s) *nm* **1** home, institution. **2** asylum.
hospitalier, -ière (ɔspi:ta'lje:, -'ljɛr) *adj* hospitable. **hospitalité** *nf* hospitality.
hostile (ɔ'sti:l) *adj* **1** hostile. **2** adverse.
hôte, hôtesse (ot, o'tɛs) *nm,f* **1** host, hostess. **2** landlord, landlady. **3** guest. **hôtesse de l'air** air-hostess.
hôtel (o'tɛl) *nm* **1** hotel. **2** mansion. **hôtel de ville** town hall. **hôtel des Postes** General Post Office.
***houblon** (u:'blɔ̃) *nm bot* hop.
***houer** (u:'e:) *vt* hoe. ***houe** *nf* hoe.
***houille** (u:j) *nf* coal. ***houille blanche** hydroelectric power. ***houillère** *nf* coalmine. ***houilleur** *nm* coal-miner.
***houle** (u:l) *nf* swell (of the sea). **houleux, -euse** (u:'lœ, -'lœz) *adj* rough.
***houppe** (u:p) *nf* **1** tuft. **2** bunch. **3** crest.
***hourra** (u:'rɑ) *interj,nm* hurrah.
***houspiller** (u:spi:'je:) *vt* **1** hustle. **2** jostle. **3** abuse. **4** reprimand.
***houx** (u:) *nm* holly.
***hublot** (hy'blo) *nm* porthole.
***huer** (y'e:) *vi* **1** shout, boo. **2** (of an owl) hoot.
huiler (ɥi:'le:) *vt* oil, grease. **huile** (ɥi:l) *nf* oil.
huis (ɥi:) **à huis clos** *adv* behind closed doors, in camera.
huissier (ɥi:'sje:) *nm* bailiff.
***huit** (ɥi:t) *adj,nm* eight. ***huitaine** *nf* **1** about eight. **2** week. ***huitième** *adj* eighth.
huître (ɥi:tr) *nf* oyster.
humain (y'mɛ̃) *adj* **1** human. **2** humane. **humanisme** *nm* humanism. **humanitaire** *adj* **1** humanitarian. **2** humane. **humanité** *nf* **1** humanity. **2** mankind. **3** kindness.
humble (œbl) *adj* **1** humble. **2** lowly.
humecter (ymɛk'te:) *vt* dampen, moisten.
humer (y'me:) *vt* breathe in, sniff.
humeur (y'mœr) *nf* humour, mood. **avoir l'humeur vive** be quick-tempered. **de mauvaise humeur** bad-tempered. **d'humeur égale** even-tempered.
humide (y'mi:d) *adj* **1** humid. **2** damp. **3** watery. **humidité** *nf* **1** moisture. **2** dampness. **3** humidity.
humilier (ymi:'lje:) *vt* humiliate. **humilité** *nf* humility.
humour (y'mu:r) *nm* humour. **humoriste** *adj* humorous. *nm* humorist. **humoristique** *adj* humorous.
***huppe** (yp) *nf zool* crest.
***hurler** (yr'le:) *vi* **1** yell. **2** howl. ***hurlement** (yrlə'mɑ̃) *nm* **1** yell. **2** howl.
***hussard** (y'sar) *nm* hussar.
***hutte** (yt) *nf* hut, shed.
hybride (i:'bri:d) *adj,nm* hybrid.
hydrate (i:'drat) **hydrate de carbone** *nm* carbohydrate.
hydraulique (i:dro'li:k) *adj* hydraulic. *nf* hydraulics.
hydro-électrique (i:drɔe:lɛk'tri:k) *adj* hydroelectric.
hydrofuge (i:drɔ'fyʒ) *adj* waterproof.
hydrogène (i:drɔ'ʒɛn) *nm* hydrogen.
hydrophile (i:drɔ'fi:l) *adj* absorbent.
hyène (jɛn) *nf* hyena.
hygiène (i:'ʒjɛn) *nf* hygiene. **hygiénique** *adj* **1** hygienic. **2** healthy. **3** sanitary.
hymne (i:m) *nm* **1** song, anthem. **hymne national** national anthem. ~*nf* hymn. **hymnaire** *nm* hymnbook.
hypnose (i:p'noz) *nf* hypnosis. **hypnotisme** *nm* hypnotism.
hypocondrie (i:pɔkɔ̃'dri:) *nf* hypochondria. **hypocondriaque** *adj,n* hypochondriac.
hypocrisie (i:pɔkri:'zi:) *nf* hypocrisy. **hypocrite** *adj* hypocritical. *nm,f* hypocrite.
hypodermique (i:pɔdɛr'mi:k) *adj* hypodermic.
hypothéquer (i:pɔte:'ke:) *vt* mortgage. **hypothèque** *nf* mortgage.
hypothèse (i:pɔ'tɛz) *nf* hypothesis. **hypothétique** *adj* hypothetical.
hystérectomie (i:ste:rɛktɔ'mi:) *nf* hysterectomy.
hystérie (i:ste:'ri:) *nf* hysteria. **hystérique** *adj* hysterical.

I

Ibérie (i:be:'ri:) *nf* Iberia. **ibère** *adj,n* Iberian.
iceberg (i:s'bɛrk) *nm* iceberg.
ici (i:'si:) *adv* **1** there. **2** now. **d'ici là** between now and then. **d'ici peu** before long. **ici et là** here and there.
icône (i:'kon) *nf* icon.
idéal, -als or **-aux** (i:de:'al, -'al, -'o) *adj,nm* ideal. **idéaliste** *adj* idealistic. *nm,f* idealist.
idéaliser (i:de:ali:'ze:) *vt* idealize.
idée (i:'de:) *nf* **1** idea. **2** thought, notion. **3** opinion. **4** mind. **idée fixe/lumineuse** obsession/brainwave.

identifier (i:dɑ̃ti:'fje:) *vt* identify. **identique** *adj* identical. **identité** *nf* identity.
idéologie (i:de:ɔlɔ'ʒi:) *nf* ideology. **idéologique** *adj* ideological.
idiome (i:'djom) *nm* **1** idiom. **2** dialect.
idiosyncrasie (i:djɔsɛ̃kra'zi:) *nf* idiosyncrasy.
idiot (i:'djo) *adj* **1** idiotic. **2** absurd. *nm* idiot.
idiotisme (i:djɔ'ti:sm) *nm* idiom.
idolâtrer (i:dɔlɑ'tre:) *vt* idolize. **idolâtrie** *nf* idolatry.
idole (i:'dɔl) *nf* idol.
idyllique (i:di:'li:k) *adj* idyllic.
if (i:f) *nm* yew.
igloo (i:'glu:) *nm* igloo.
ignorer (i:ɲɔ're:) *vt* not to know, be unaware of.
il (i:l) *pron 3rd pers ms* **1** he. **2** it. **3** there. **il y a** there is or are.
île (i:l) *nf* island, isle. **îles Anglo-Normandes** *nf pl* Channel Islands.
illégal, -aux (i:llɛ'gal, -'go) *adj* illegal, unlawful.
illégitime (i:lle:ʒi:'ti:m) *adj* illegitimate.
illettré (i:llɛ'tre:) *adj* illiterate.
illicite (i:lli:'si:t) *adj* illicit, unlawful.
illimité (i:lli:mi:'te:) *adj* **1** boundless. **2** indefinite.
illisible (i:lli:'zi:bl) *adj* illegible.
illuminer (i:lymi:'ne:) *vt* **1** illuminate. **2** enlighten. **illumination** *nf* illumination, lighting.
illusion (i:lly'zjɔ̃) *nf* illusion.
illustrer (i:lly'stre:) *vt* illustrate. **illustration** *nf* illustration. **illustre** *adj* famous.
ils (i:l) *pron 3rd pers m pl* they.
image (i:maʒ) *nf* **1** image. **2** picture. **3** likeness. **4** reflection. **5** simile, metaphor. **imagé** (i:ma'ʒe:) *adj* vivid. **imagerie** *nf* imagery.
imaginer (i:maʒi:'ne:) *vt* **1** imagine. **2** conceive. **3** invent. **4** suppose. **s'imaginer** *vr* think, fancy. **imaginaire** *adj* imaginary. **imaginatif, -ive** (i:maʒi:na'ti:f, -'ti:v) *adj* imaginative. **imagination** *nf* **1** imagination. **2** fancy.
imbécile (ɛ̃be:'si:l) *adj* silly. *nm,f* idiot, halfwit.
imbiber (ɛ̃bi:'be:) *vt* **1** soak. **2** steep. **3** absorb. **s'imbiber** *vr* **1** absorb. **2** become saturated.
imbrisable (ɛ̃bri:'sabl) *adj* unbreakable.
imiter (i:mi:'te:) *vt* **1** imitate. **2** mimic. **3** copy. **4** forge.
immaculé (i:mmaky'le:) *adj* immaculate.
immanquable (ɛ̃mɑ̃'kabl) *adj* **1** inevitable. **2** infallible.
immatriculer (i:mmatri:ky'le:) *vt* register.
immaturité (i:mmatyri:'te:) *nf* immaturity.
immédiat (i:mme:'djat) *adj* **1** immediate. **2** near. **3** urgent.
immense (i:m'mɑ̃s) *adj* huge, vast, immense.
immerger (i:mmɛr'ʒe:) *vt* **1** immerse. **2** plunge.
immeuble (i:m'mœbl) *adj law* real, fixed. *nm* block of flats.
immigrer (i:mmi:'gre:) *vi* immigrate. **immigrant** *nm* immigrant. **immigration** *nf* immigration.
imminent (i:mmi:'nɑ̃) *adj* imminent.
immiscer (i:mmi:'se:) *vt* involve. **s'immiscer dans** *vr* interfere with.
immobile (i:mmɔ'bi:l) *adj* immobile, still. **immobilier, -ière** (i:mmɔbi:'lje:, -'ljɛr) *adj* of land, property.
immobiliser (i:mmɔbi:li:'ze:) *vt* immobilize.
immonde (i:m'mɔ̃d) *adj* **1** filthy. **2** foul.
immortel, -elle (i:mmɔr'tɛl) *adj* immortal, everlasting. **immortalité** *nf* immortality.
immuniser (i:mmyni:'ze:) *vt* immunize.
impair (ɛ̃'pɛr) *adj* odd, uneven.
imparfait (ɛ̃par'fɛ) *adj* imperfect. *nm* imperfect tense.
impartial, -aux (ɛ̃par'sjal, -'sjo) *adj* impartial.
impasse (ɛ̃'pɑs) *nf* **1** deadlock. **2** dead end.
impassible (ɛ̃pa'si:bl) *adj* **1** unmoved. **2** callous.
impatience (ɛ̃pa'sjɑ̃s) *nf* impatience. **impatient** *adj* **1** impatient. **2** eager.
impatienter (ɛ̃pasjɑ̃'te:) *vt* annoy. **s'impatienter** *vr* lose one's patience.
impeccable (ɛ̃pɛ'kabl) *adj* faultless, impeccable.
imper (ɛ̃'pɛr) *nm inf* mac.
impératif, -ive (ɛ̃pɛra'ti:f, -'ti:v) *adj,nm* imperative.
impératrice (ɛ̃pɛra'tri:s) *nf* empress.
impérial, -aux (ɛ̃pɛ'rjal, -'ro) *adj* imperial. **impériale** *nf* top deck (of a bus).
imperméable (ɛ̃pɛrme:'abl) *adj* waterproof. *nm* mackintosh.
impersonnel, -elle (ɛ̃pɛrsɔ'nɛl) *adj* impersonal.
impétueux, -euse (ɛ̃pe:'tɥœ, -'tɥœz) *adj* impetuous.
impitoyable (ɛ̃pi:twa'jabl) *adj* **1** ruthless. **2** cruel.
implicite (ɛ̃pli:'si:t) *adj* **1** implicit. **2** absolute.
impliquer (ɛ̃pli:'ke:) *vt* **1** involve. **2** imply.
impopulaire (ɛ̃pɔpy'lɛr) *adj* unpopular.
implorer (ɛ̃plɔ're:) *vt* implore, entreat.
importer[1] (ɛ̃pɔr'te:) *vt* import.
importer*[2] (ɛ̃pɔr'te:) *vi* matter, be important. **n'importe** never mind. **n'importe comment/quand/qui/quoi** anyhow/anytime/anyone/

anything. **importance** *nf* importance. **important** *adj* 1 important. 2 large. 3 considerable.
importuner (ɛ̃pɔrty'ne:) *vt* 1 pester. 2 trouble, inconvenience.
imposer (ɛ̃po'ze:) *vt* 1 impose. 2 inflict. 3 tax. **imposant** *adj* imposing, grand.
impossible (ɛ̃pɔ'si:bl) *adj* impossible.
imposteur (ɛ̃pɔ'stœr) *nm* imposter.
impôt (ɛ̃'po) *nm* tax, duty.
impotent (ɛ̃pɔ'tɑ̃) *adj* 1 helpless. 2 infirm. *nm* cripple.
imprécis (ɛ̃pre:'si:) *adj* 1 vague, indefinite. 2 inaccurate.
impression (ɛ̃prɛ'sjɔ̃) *nf* 1 impression. 2 printing. 3 print.
impressionner (ɛ̃prɛsjɔ'ne:) *vt* 1 impress. 2 move. **impressionnant** *adj* 1 impressive. 2 sensational.
imprévu (ɛ̃pre:'vy) *adj* unexpected.
imprimer (ɛ̃pri:'me:) *vt* 1 print. 2 imprint. 3 publish. 4 stamp. **imprimé** *nm* 1 printed matter. 2 form. **imprimeur** *nm* printer.
improbable (ɛ̃prɔ'babl) *adj* improbable, unlikely.
impromptu (ɛ̃prɔ̃'ty) *adj,adv* without preparation, impromptu.
improviser (ɛ̃prɔvi:'ze:) *vt* 1 improvise. 2 adlib. **à l'improviste** *adv* unexpectedly, without warning.
imprudent (ɛ̃pry'dɑ̃) *adj* imprudent, rash.
impudent (ɛ̃py'dɑ̃) *adj* cheeky, impudent.
impuissant (ɛ̃pɥi:'sɑ̃) *adj* 1 impotent. 2 helpless. 3 incapable.
impulsion (ɛ̃pyl'sjɔ̃) *nf* 1 impulse. 2 impetus. **impulsif, -ive** (ɛ̃pyl'si:f, -'si:v) *adj* impulsive.
impur (ɛ̃'pyr) *adj* 1 impure. 2 indecent, lewd.
imputer (ɛ̃py'te:) *vt* 1 attribute. 2 charge.
inadapté (i:nadap'te:) *nm* (social) misfit.
inadéquat (i:nade:'kwa) *adj* inadequate.
inadvertance (i:nadvɛr'tɑ̃s) *nf* oversight.
inalliable (i:na'ljabl) *adj* incompatible.
inappréciable (i:napre:'sjabl) *adj* 1 not perceptible. 2 invaluable.
inapte (i:'napt) *adj* unfit, not suited.
inarticulé (i:narti:ky'le:) *adj* inarticulate.
inaugurer (i:nogy're:) *vt* inaugurate, open. **inaugural, -aux** (i:nogy'ral, -'ro) *adj* 1 opening. 2 maiden.
incapable (ɛ̃ka'pabl) *adj* 1 incapable, unable. 2 unfit.
incapacité (ɛ̃kapasi:'te:) *nf* inability.
incendier (ɛ̃sɑ̃'dje:) *vt* set fire to. **incendiaire** *adj* incendiary. **incendie** *nm* fire. **incendie volontaire** arson.
incertain (ɛ̃sɛr'tɛ̃) *adj* 1 uncertain, unsettled. 2 doubtful. **incertitude** *nf* uncertainty, doubt.
incessant (ɛ̃sɛ'sɑ̃) *adj* ceaseless, incessant. **incessamment** *adv* immediately.
inceste (ɛ̃'sɛst) *nm* incest.
incident (ɛ̃si:'dɑ̃) *nm* 1 incident. 2 hitch, difficulty. *adj* incidental. **incidemment** (ɛ̃si:da'mɑ̃) *adv* incidentally. **incidentel, -elle** (ɛ̃si:dɑ̃'tɛl) *adj* incidental.
incinérer (ɛ̃si:ne:'re:) *vt* cremate. **incinération** (ɛ̃si:nɛra'sjɔ̃) *nf* cremation.
inciter (ɛ̃si:'te:) *vt* incite, urge.
incliner (ɛ̃kli:'ne:) *vt* 1 slope, slant. 2 tilt. 3 bend. **incliner à** be inclined to. **s'incliner** *vr* bow. **inclinaison** *nf* 1 slope. 2 nod.
inclure* (ɛ̃'klyr) *vt* include. **inclusif, -ive** (ɛ̃kly'zi:f, -'zi:v) *adj* inclusive.
incohérent (ɛ̃kɔɛ'rɑ̃) *adj* incoherent.
incolore (ɛ̃kɔ'lɔr) *adj* colourless.
incommoder (ɛ̃kɔmɔ'de:) *vt* 1 inconvenience. 2 annoy. 3 upset. **incommode** *adj* 1 inconvenient. 2 uncomfortable. **incommodité** *nf* inconvenience.
incompatible (ɛ̃kɔ̃pa'ti:bl) *adj* incompatible, inconsistent.
incompétent (ɛ̃kɔ̃pɛ'tɑ̃) *adj* incompetent.
inconnu (ɛ̃kɔ'ny) *adj* unknown. *nm* stranger.
inconscience (ɛ̃kɔ̃'sjɑ̃s) *nf* unconsciousness. **inconscient** *adj,nm* unconscious.
inconséquent (ɛ̃kɔ̃sɛ'kɑ̃) *adj* 1 inconsistent. 2 irresponsible.
inconstant (ɛ̃kɔ̃'stɑ̃) *adj* 1 fickle. 2 erratic.
incontestable (ɛ̃kɔ̃tɛ'stabl) *adj* undeniable.
inconvenant (ɛ̃kɔ̃v'nɑ̃) *adj* improper, indecent.
inconvénient (ɛ̃kɔ̃ve:'njɑ̃) *nm* drawback, disadvantage.
incorporer (ɛ̃kɔrpɔ're:) *vt* incorporate.
incriminer (ɛ̃kri:mi:'ne:) *vt* 1 incriminate. 2 accuse.
incroyable (ɛ̃krwa'jabl) *adj* incredible, unbelievable.
incuber (ɛ̃ky'be:) *vt* 1 incubate. 2 hatch. **incubateur** *nm* incubator.
inculper (ɛ̃kyl'pe:) *vt law* charge.
inculte (ɛ̃'kylt) *adj* 1 wild. 2 untidy.
Inde (ɛ̃d) *nf* India. **indien, -ienne** (ɛ̃'djɛ̃, -'djɛn) *adj,n* Indian.
indéchiffrable (ɛ̃de:ʃi:'frabl) *adj* illegible.
indécis (ɛ̃de:'si:) *adj* 1 undecided. 2 vague. 3 uncertain.
indéfini (ɛ̃de:fi:'ni:) *adj* indefinite.

indemne (ɛ̃'dɛmn) *adj* unhurt. **indemnité** *nf* **1** compensation. **2** allowance.

indemniser (ɛ̃dɛmni:'ze:) *vt* compensate.

indépendant (ɛ̃de:pɑ̃'dɑ̃) *adj* **1** independent. **2** free. **3** self-contained. **indépendance** *nf* independence.

index (ɛ̃'dɛks) *nm* **1** forefinger, index finger. **2** index.

indication (ɛ̃di:ka'sjɔ̃) *nf* **1** indication. **2** information. **3** sign. **4** *pl* instructions. **indicateur, -trice** (ɛ̃di:ka'tœr, -'tri:s) *adj* indicating. *nm* **1** indicator. **2** timetable. **3** gauge. **indicatif, -ive** (ɛ̃di:ka'ti:f, -'ti:v) *adj* indicative. *nm* indicative mood.

indice (ɛ̃'di:s) *nm* **1** sign. **2** indication. **3** index.

indifférent (ɛ̃di:fɛ'rɑ̃) *adj* indifferent.

indigence (ɛ̃di:'ʒɑ̃s) *nf* poverty. **indigent** *adj* poor, needy.

indigène (ɛ̃di:'ʒɛn) *adj,n* native.

indigestion (ɛ̃di:ʒɛ'stjɔ̃) *nf* indigestion.

indigner (ɛ̃di:'ɲe) *vt* make indignant. **s'indigner** *vr* become indignant. **indigné** *adj* indignant.

indiquer (ɛ̃di:'ke:) *vt* **1** indicate. **2** point out. **3** show.

indiscipliné (ɛ̃di:si:pli:'ne:) *adj* unruly.

indispensable (ɛ̃di:spɑ̃'sabl) *adj* essential.

indisposé (ɛ̃di:spo'ze:) *adj* unwell.

individu (ɛ̃di:vi:'dy) *nm* **1** individual. **2** *inf* fellow. **individuel, -elle** (ɛ̃di:vi:'dɥɛl) *adj* **1** individual. **2** personal, private.

indolent (ɛ̃dɔ'lɑ̃) *adj* indolent, lazy.

indolore (ɛ̃dɔ'lɔr) *adj* painless.

induire* (ɛ̃'dɥi:r) *vt* **1** induce. **2** infer.

indulgence (ɛ̃dyl'ʒɑ̃s) *nf* indulgence. **indulgent** *adj* **1** indulgent. **2** lenient.

industrie (ɛ̃dy'stri:) *nf* **1** industry. **2** trade. **3** activity. **industriel, -elle** (ɛ̃dystri:'ɛl) *adj* industrial. **industrieux, -euse** (ɛ̃dy'strɥœ, -'strɥœz) *adj* industrious.

inébranlable (i:ne:brɑ̃'labl) *adj* **1** firm, solid. **2** resolute, steadfast.

inégal, -aux (i:ne:'gal, -'go) *adj* **1** unequal. **2** uneven. **3** irregular. **inégalité** *nf* inequality.

inéluctable (i:ne:lyk'tabl) *adj* inevitable.

inepte (i:'nɛpt) *adj* inane, idiotic.

inestimable (i:nɛsti:'mabl) *adj* invaluable.

inévitable (i:ne:vi:'tabl) *adj* unavoidable, inevitable.

inexact (i:nɛg'zakt) *adj* **1** incorrect. **2** inaccurate. **3** unreliable.

infaillible (ɛ̃fa'ji:bl) *adj* **1** infallible. **2** sure.

infâme (ɛ̃'fɑm) *adj* **1** infamous. **2** vile, foul.

infanterie (ɛ̃fɑ̃'tri:) *nf* infantry.

infatuer (ɛ̃fa'tɥe:) *vt* infatuate. **s'infatuer** *vr* become infatuated.

infécond (ɛ̃fe:'kɔ̃) *adj* barren, sterile.

infect (ɛ̃'fɛkt) *adj* foul, putrid.

infecter (ɛ̃fɛk'te:) *vt* **1** infect. **2** pollute. **s'infecter** *vr* turn septic. **infectieux, -euse** (ɛ̃fɛk'sjœ, -'sjœz) *adj* infectious. **infection** *nf* **1** infection. **2** stink.

inférieur (ɛ̃fe:'rjœr) *adj* **1** inferior. **2** lower. **3** poor. *nm* inferior.

infester (ɛ̃fɛ'ste:) *vt* **1** infest. **2** overrun.

infidèle (ɛ̃fi:'dɛl) *adj* **1** unfaithful, disloyal. **2** false. **3** faithless. **infidélité** *nf* infidelity.

s'infiltrer (ɛ̃fi:l'tre:) *vr* **1** infiltrate, seep. **2** filter in.

infime (ɛ̃fi:m) *adj* minute.

infini (ɛ̃fi:'ni:) *adj* infinite. **infinité** *nf* infinity. **infinitif, -ive** (ɛ̃fi:ni:'ti:f, -'ti:v) *adj,nm* infinitive.

infirme (ɛ̃'fi:rm) *adj* **1** disabled. **2** crippled. **3** infirm. **infirmier, -ière** (ɛ̃fi:r'mje:, -'mjɛr) *nm,f* nurse. **infirmité** *nf* disability.

inflammable (ɛ̃fla'mabl) *adj* inflammable.

inflation (ɛ̃fla'sjɔ̃) *nf* inflation.

inflexion (ɛ̃flɛk'sjɔ̃) *nf* inflection.

infliger (ɛ̃fli:'ʒe:) *vt* inflict.

influencer (ɛ̃flyɑ̃'se:) *vt* influence. **influence** *nf* influence.

influenza (ɛ̃flyɑ̃'za) *nf* influenza.

influer (ɛ̃fly'e:) *vi* **influer sur** influence, have an effect upon.

informer (ɛ̃fɔr'me:) *vt* inform. **s'informer** *vr* make enquiries. **information** *nf* **1** information. **2** inquiry. **3** *pl* news.

infortune (ɛ̃fɔr'tyn) *nf* misfortune. **infortuné** *adj* unfortunate.

infraction (ɛ̃frak'sjɔ̃) *nf* **1** infringement. **2** breach.

infroissable (ɛ̃frwa'sabl) *adj* crease-resistant.

ingénieur (ɛ̃ʒe:'njœr) *nm* engineer.

ingénieux, -euse (ɛ̃ʒe:'njœ, -'njœz) *adj* ingenious.

ingénu (ɛ̃ʒe:'ny) *adj* **1** simple, naive. **2** candid.

s'ingérer (sɛ̃ʒe:'re:) *vr* **1** interfere. **2** meddle.

ingrat (ɛ̃'gra) *adj* **1** ungrateful. **2** thankless. **3** unpleasant.

ingrédient (ɛ̃gre:'djɑ̃) *nm* ingredient.

inhabile (i:na'bi:l) *adj* **1** clumsy. **2** unfit. **3** incompetent.

inhaler (i:na'le:) *vt* inhale.

inhérent (i:nɛ'rɑ̃) *adj* inherent.

inhiber (i:ni:'be:) *vt* inhibit. **inhibition** *nf* inhibition.
inhumain (i:ny'mɛ̃) *adj* inhuman.
initial, -aux (i:ni:'sjal, -'sjo) *adj* initial, starting. *nf* initial.
initier (i:ni:'sje:) *vt* initiate. **initiative** *nf* initiative.
injecter (ɛ̃ʒɛk'te:) *vt* inject. **injection** *nf* injection.
injurier (ɛ̃ʒy'rje:) *vt* insult, abuse. **injure** *nf* **1** insult. **2** *pl* abuse. **3** wrong. **injurieux, -euse** (ɛ̃ʒy'rjœ, -'rjœz) *adj* **1** abusive. **2** offensive.
injuste (ɛ̃'ʒyst) *adj* unfair. **injustice** *nf* **1** injustice. **2** wrong.
inné (i:n'ne:) *adj* innate.
innocent (i:nɔ'sɑ̃) *adj* **1** innocent, pure. **2** simple. **3** harmless. *nm* idiot. **innocence** *nf* innocence.
innovation (i:nnɔva'sjɔ̃) *nf* innovation.
inoccupé (i:nɔky'pe:) *adj* **1** idle. **2** vacant.
inoculer (i:nɔky'le:) *vt* **1** inoculate. **2** inject.
inonder (i:nɔ̃'de:) *vt* **1** flood. **2** inundate. **inondation** *nf* flood.
inopiné (i:nɔpi:'ne:) *adj* **1** sudden. **2** unexpected.
inouï (i:'nwi:) *adj* **1** extraordinary, incredible. **2** outrageous.
inquiet, -iète (ɛ̃'kjɛ, -'kjɛt) *adj* anxious, worried.
inquiéter (ɛ̃kje:'te:) *vt* **1** alarm. **2** disturb, trouble. **s'inquiéter** *vr* worry. **inquiétude** *nf* **1** anxiety. **2** concern.
inquisition (ɛ̃ki:zi:'sjɔ̃) *nf* inquisition, inquiry.
insciemment (ɛ̃sja'mɑ̃) *adv* unconsciously.
inscription (ɛ̃skri:'psjɔ̃) *nf* **1** registration. **2** inscription.
inscrire* (ɛ̃'skri:r) *vt* **1** inscribe, write down. **2** enrol. **3** register. **4** inscribe. **s'inscrire** *vr* **1** enrol. **2** register.
insecte (ɛ̃'sɛkt) *nm* insect. **insecticide** *nm* insecticide.
inséminer (ɛ̃se:mi:'ne:) *vt* inseminate.
insensé (ɛ̃sɑ̃'se:) *adj* **1** mad, insane. **2** wild. **3** ridiculous.
insensible (ɛ̃sɑ̃'si:bl) *adj* **1** insensitive. **2** indifferent. **3** callous.
insérer (ɛ̃se:'re:) *vt* insert.
insidieux, -euse (ɛ̃si:'djœ, -'djœz) *adj* insidious.
insigne (ɛ̃'si:ɲ) *adj* **1** remarkable. **2** notorious. *nm* **1** badge. **2** emblem. **3** medal.
insinuer (ɛ̃si:'nɥe:) *vt* **1** insinuate. **2** hint at, suggest. **s'insinuer** *vr* **1** creep in. **2** slip in.
insister (ɛ̃si:'ste:) *vi* insist. **insister sur** lay stress on.
insolation (ɛ̃sɔla'sjɔ̃) *nf* sunstroke.
insolent (ɛ̃sɔ'lɑ̃) *adj* insolent, cheeky.
insomnie (ɛ̃sɔm'ni:) *nf* insomnia.
insonore (ɛ̃sɔ'nɔr) *adj* soundproof.
insouciant (ɛ̃su:'sjɑ̃) *adj* carefree. **insoucieux, -euse** (ɛ̃su:'sjœ, -'sjœz) *adj* heedless.
inspecter (ɛ̃spɛk'te:) *vt* inspect, examine. **inspecteur, -trice** (ɛ̃spɛk'tœr, -'tri:s) *nm,f* inspector.
inspirer (ɛ̃spi:'re:) *vt* **1** inspire. **2** breathe in. **inspiration** *nf* **1** inspiration. **2** suggestion.
instabilité (ɛ̃stabi:li:'te:) *nf* instability.
installer (ɛ̃sta'le:) *vt* **1** install. **2** equip. **s'installer** *vr* **1** settle down. **2** move in. **installation** *nf* **1** installation. **2** fittings. **3** *tech* plant.
instant (ɛ̃'stɑ̃) *adj* **1** urgent. **2** imminent. *nm* moment, instant. **à l'instant 1** a moment ago. **2** at once. **par instants** on and off. **instantané** *adj* instantaneous. *nm* snapshot.
instar (ɛ̃'star) **à l'instar de** *prep* like, after the fashion of.
instiller (ɛ̃sti:'le:) *vt* instil.
instinct (ɛ̃'stɛ̃) *nm* instinct. **instinctif, -ive** (ɛ̃stɛ̃k'ti:f, -'ti:v) *adj* instinctive.
instituer (ɛ̃sti:'tɥe:) *vt* **1** set up, institute. **2** appoint. **institut** *nm* **1** institute. **2** institution. **instituteur, -trice** (ɛ̃sti:ty'tœr, -'tri:s) *nm,f* **1** primary school teacher. **2** founder. **institution** *nf* **1** establishment, institution. **2** boarding school.
instruire* (ɛ̃'strɥi:r) *vt* **1** inform. **2** teach, instruct. **3** train. **instruction** *nf* **1** instruction. **2** education. **3** *pl* directions.
instrument (ɛ̃stry'mɑ̃) *nm* **1** instrument. **2** tool, implement. **instrumental, -aux** (ɛ̃strymɑ̃'tal, -'to) *adj* instrumental.
insu (ɛ̃'sy) **à l'insu de** *prep* unknown to.
insubordonné (ɛ̃sybɔrdɔ'ne:) *adj* insubordinate.
insuccès (ɛ̃syk'sɛ) *nm* failure.
insuffisant (ɛ̃syfi:'zɑ̃) *adj* **1** inadequate. **2** incompetent.
insulaire (ɛ̃sy'lɛr) *adj* insular.
insuline (ɛ̃sy'li:n) *nf* insulin.
insulter (ɛ̃syl'te:) *vt* insult. **insulte** *nf* insult.
insupportable (ɛ̃sypɔr'tabl) *adj* unbearable.
s'insurger (sɛ̃syr'ʒe:) *vr* **1** rebel. **2** revolt. **insurgé** *nm* rebel.
intact (ɛ̃'takt) *adj* whole, intact.
intégrer (ɛ̃te:'gre:) *vt* integrate. **intégral, -aux** (ɛ̃tɛ'gral, -'gro) *adj* entire, whole, integral **intégrant** (ɛ̃tɛ'grɑ̃) *adj* integral. **intègre** *adj* honest, upright. **intégrité** *nf* **1** integrity, honesty. **2** entirety.

intellect (ɛ̃tɛl'lɛkt) *nm* intellect. **intellectuel, -elle** (ɛ̃tɛlɛk'tɥɛl) *adj,n* intellectual.

intelligence (ɛ̃tɛli:'ʒɑ̃s) *nf* **1** intelligence, intellect. **2** understanding. **intelligent** *adj* clever, intelligent. **intelligible** *adj* intelligible, clear.

intendant (ɛ̃tɑ̃'dɑ̃) *nm* **1** steward. **2** administrator.

intensifier (ɛ̃tɑ̃si:'fje:) *vt* intensify. **intense** *adj* intense, severe. **intensif, -ive** (ɛ̃tɑ̃'si:f, -'si:v) *adj* intensive. **intensité** *nf* intensity, strength.

intention (ɛ̃tɑ̃'sjɔ̃) *nf* intention, purpose. **à l'intention de** for, in honour of. **avoir l'intention de** intend to.

intercepter (ɛ̃tɛrsɛp'te:) *vt* intercept.

interdire* (ɛ̃tɛr'di:r) *vt* **1** forbid, prohibit. **2** bewilder

intéresser (ɛ̃te:rɛ'se:) *vt* **1** interest. **2** concern. **s'intéresser à** *vr* be interested in.

intérêt (ɛ̃te:'rɛ) *nm* **1** interest. **2** advantage. **3** profit. **4** share. **avoir intérêt à** be in one's interest to.

intérieur (ɛ̃te:'rjœr) *adj* **1** interior. **2** inner. **3** internal. **4** domestic. *nm* interior, inside. **à l'intérieur** inside.

intérim (ɛ̃te:'ri:m) *nm* interim.

interjection (ɛ̃tɛrʒɛk'sjɔ̃) *nf* interjection.

interloquer (ɛ̃tɛrlɔke:) *vt* disconcert.

intermède (ɛ̃tɛr'mɛd) *nm* interlude. **intermédiaire** *adj* intermediate. *nm* intermediary.

intermission (ɛ̃tɛrmi:'sjɔ̃) *nf* intermission.

intermittent (ɛ̃tɛrmi:t'tɑ̃) *adj* irregular, intermittent.

international, -aux (ɛ̃tɛrnasjɔ'nal, -'no) *adj* international.

interner (ɛ̃tɛr'ne:) *vt* intern, confine. **internat** *nm* boarding school. **interne** *adj* **1** internal. **2** interior. *nm* **1** boarder. **2** medical student.

interpeller (ɛ̃tɛrpɛ'le:) *vt* **1** challenge. **2** heckle. **interpellation** *nf* **1** question. **2** challenge.

interposer (ɛ̃tɛrpo'ze:) *vt* interpose. **s'interposer** *vr* intervene.

interpréter (ɛ̃tɛrpre:'te:) *vt* interpret. **interprétation** (ɛ̃tɛrpreta'sjɔ̃) *nf* interpretation. **interprète** *nm,f* interpreter.

interroger (ɛ̃tɛrɔ'ʒe:) *vt* question, examine, interrogate. **interrogatif, -ive** (ɛ̃tɛrɔga'ti:f, -'ti:v) *adj* interrogative. **interrogation** *nf* **1** interrogation, questioning. **2** question.

interrompre (ɛ̃tɛ'rɔ̃pr) *vt* **1** interrupt. **2** stop. **3** break, cut short.

interruption (ɛ̃tɛryp'sjɔ̃) *nf* interruption. **interrupteur** *nm* switch.

intervalle (ɛ̃tɛr'val) *nm* **1** interval. **2** gap. **3** period. **dans l'intervalle** in the meantime.

intervenir* (ɛ̃tɛrvə'ni:r) *vi* (*aux* être) **1** intervene. **2** interfere. **3** happen.

intervertir (ɛ̃tɛrvɛr'ti:r) *vt* invert.

interview (ɛ̃tɛr'vju:) *nm,f* interview.

intestin (ɛ̃tɛ'stɛ̃) *adj* internal. *nm* **1** intestine. **2** gut. **3** *pl* bowels.

intime (ɛ̃'ti:m) *adj* **1** intimate, close. **2** private. **3** interior.

intimider (ɛ̃ti:mi:'de:) *vt* intimidate, frighten.

intituler (ɛ̃ti:ty'le:) *vt* **1** entitle, give a title to. **intitulé** *nm* title.

intolérable (ɛ̃tɔlɛ'rabl) *adj* intolerable, unbearable.

intonation (ɛ̃tɔna'sjɔ̃) *nf* intonation.

intoxiquer (ɛ̃tɔksi:'ke:) *vt* poison.

intransitif, -ive (ɛ̃trɑ̃zi:'ti:f, -'ti:v) *adj* intransitive.

intrépide (ɛ̃tre:'pi:d) *adj* bold, daring.

intriguer (ɛ̃tri:'ge:) *vt* **1** puzzle. **2** intrigue. *vi* plot. **intrigue** *nf* plot, scheme.

intrinsèque (ɛ̃trɛ̃'sɛk) *adj* intrinsic.

introduire* (ɛ̃trɔ'dɥi:r) *vt* **1** introduce. **2** insert. **3** show in. **s'introduire** *vr* get in, enter. **introduction** *nf* **1** introduction. **2** admission. **3** preface

introverti (ɛ̃trɔvɛr'ti:) *nm* introvert.

intrusion (ɛ̃try'zjɔ̃) *nf* intrusion. **faire intrusion** intrude.

intuition (ɛ̃tɥi:'sjɔ̃) *nf* intuition. **intuitif, -ive** (ɛ̃tɥi:'ti:f, -'ti:v) *adj* intuitive.

inutile (i:ny'ti:l) *adj* **1** useless. **2** unnecessary. **3** vain.

invaincu (ɛ̃vɛ̃'ky) *adj* unbeaten.

invalide (ɛ̃va'li:d) *adj* **1** infirm, invalid. **2** *law* invalid, null. *nm,f med* invalid.

invariable (ɛ̃va'rjabl) *adj* invariable.

invasion (ɛ̃va'zjɔ̃) *nf* invasion.

inventer (ɛ̃vɑ̃'te:) *vt* **1** invent. **2** discover. **inventaire** *nm* **1** inventory. **2** stocktaking. **invention** *nf* **1** invention. **2** device.

inverser (ɛ̃vɛr'se:) *vt* reverse. **inverse** *adj* **1** opposite. **2** reverse. **3** inverted. *nm* opposite, reverse.

invertébré (ɛ̃vɛrte:'bre:) *adj* invertebrate.

invertir (ɛ̃vɛr'ti:r) *vt* invert, reverse.

investir (ɛ̃vɛ'sti:r) *vt* invest. **investissement** *nm* investment.

invisible (ɛ̃vi:'zi:bl) *adj* invisible.

inviter (ɛ̃vi:'te:) *vt* **1** invite. **2** ask, request. **invitation** *nf* invitation. **invité** *nm* guest.

invoquer (ɛ̃vɔ'ke:) *vt* **1** plead, call upon. **2** bring forward.
invraisemblable (ɛ̃vrɛsɑ̃'blabl) *adj* **1** unlikely, improbable. **2** unbelievable.
iode (i:'ɔd) *nm* iodine.
ion (i:'ɔ̃) *nm* ion.
iouler (ju:'le:) *vi* yodel.
irai (i:'rɛ) *v see* **aller.**
Irak (i:'rak) *nm* Iraq. **irakien, -ienne** (i:ra'kjɛ̃, -'kjɛn) *adj,n* Iraqi.
Iran (i:'rɑ̃) *nm* Iran. **iranien, -ienne** (i:ra'njɛ̃, -'njɛn) *adj,n* Iranian.
iris (i:'ri:s) *nm anat,bot* iris.
Irlande (i:r'lɑ̃d) *nf* Ireland. **irlandais** *adj* Irish. *nm* Irishman.
ironie (i:rɔ'ni:) *nf* irony. **ironique** *adj* ironic.
irrationnel, -elle (irrasjɔ'nɛl) *adj* irrational.
irréfléchi (irre:fle:'ʃi:) *adj* **1** thoughtless. **2** rash.
irrégulier, -ière (i:rre:gy'lje:, -'ljɛr) *adj* irregular.
irrésistible (i:rre:zi:'stabl) *adj* irresistible.
irrespect (i:rrɛ'spɛ) *nm* disrespect. **irrespectueux, -euse** (i:rrɛspɛk'tɥœ, -'tɥœz) *adj* disrespectful.
irresponsable (i:rrɛspɔ̃'sabl) *adj* irresponsible.
irrévocable (i:rre:vɔ'kabl) *adj* irrevocable.
irriguer (i:rri:'ge:) *vt* irrigate. **irrigation** *nf* irrigation.
irriter (i:rri:'te:) *vt* **1** annoy, provoke. **2** irritate. **s'irriter** *vr* **1** get angry. **2** become inflamed.
irruption (i:rryp'sjɔ̃) *nf* **1** raid, attack. **2** flood. **faire irruption dans** burst or rush into.
Islam (i:'slam) *nm* Islam. **islamique** *adj* Islamic.
Islande (i:'slɑ̃d) *nf* Iceland. **islandais** *adj* Icelandic. *nm* **1** Icelander. **2** Icelandic (language).
isoler (i:zɔ'le:) *vt* **1** isolate. **2** insulate. **isolé** *adj* **1** isolated, remote. **2** lonely. **3** detached.
isorel (i:zɔ'rɛl) *nm Tdmk* hardboard.
Israël (i:zra'ɛl) *nm* Israel. **israélien, -ienne** (i:zrae:'ljɛ̃, -'ljɛn) *adj,n* Israeli.
issu (i:'sy) **issu de** *adj* descended from.
issue (i:'sy) *nf* **1** exit. **2** escape. **3** end, result.
Italie (i:ta'li:) *nf* Italy. **italien, -ienne** (i:ta'ljɛ̃, -'ljɛn) *adj,n* Italian. *nm* Italian (language).
italique (i:ta'li:k) *adj* italic. *nm* italics.
itinéraire (i:ti:ne:'rɛr) *nm* **1** route, itinerary. **2** guidebook.
ivoire (i:'vwar) *nm* ivory.
ivre (i:vr) *adj* drunk, drunken. **ivrogne** *nm* drunkard.

J

jabot (ʒa'bo) *nm* **1** *zool* crop. **2** frill.
jacasser (ʒaka'se:) *vt* chatter. **jacasse** *nf inf* **1** magpie. **2** chatterbox.
jachère (ʒa'ʃɛr) *nf* fallow.
jacinthe (ʒa'sɛ̃t) *nf* hyacinth. **jacinthe des bois** or **près** *nf* bluebell.
jade (ʒad) *nm* jade.
jadis (ʒa'di:s) *adv* **1** formerly. **2** once.
jaguar (ʒa'gwar) *nm* jaguar.
jaillir (ʒa'ji:r) *vi* **1** squirt, gush out. **2** run, spread. **3** flash. **4** spring up.
jais (ʒɛ) *nm min* jet.
jalonner (ʒalɔ'ne:) *vt* **1** mark out. **2** set out.
jaloux, -ouse (ʒa'lu:, -'lu:z) *adj* **1** jealous. **2** anxious, keen. **jalousie** *nf* jealousy.
Jamaïque (ʒama'i:k) *nf* Jamaica. **jamaïquain** *adj,n* Jamaican.
jamais (ʒa'mɛ) *adv* ever. **à tout jamais** for ever and ever. **ne...jamais** never.
jambe (ʒɑ̃b) *nf* **1** leg. **2** prop, stay.
jambon (ʒɑ̃'bɔ̃) *nm* ham.
janséniste (ʒɑ̃se:'ni:st) *adj,n* Jansenist.
jante (ʒɑ̃t) *nf* rim (of a wheel).
janvier (ʒɑ̃'vje:) *nm* January.
Japon (ʒa'pɔ̃) *nm* Japan. **japonais** *adj,n* Japanese. *nm* Japanese (language).
japper (ʒa'pe:) *vi* yap, yelp.
jaquette (ʒa'kɛt) *nf* **1** (lady's) jacket. **2** morning coat.
jardin (ʒar'dɛ̃) *nm* garden. **jardin d'enfants** kindergarten. **jardin maraîcher** market garden.
jardiner (ʒardi:'ne:) *vi* garden. **jardinage** *nm* gardening. **jardinier, -ière** (ʒardi:'nje:, -'njɛr) *adj* garden. *nm,f* gardener. *nf* window box. **jardiniste** *nm* landscape gardener.
jargon (ʒar'gɔ̃) *nm* **1** jargon. **2** slang.
jarret (ʒa'rɛ) *nm* **1** bend of the knee. **2** *zool* hock. **3** *cul* knuckle, shin.
jars (ʒar) *nm* gander.
jaser (ʒa'ze:) *vi* **1** chatter. **2** gossip.
jasmin (ʒa'smɛ̃) *nm* jasmine.
jatte (ʒat) *nf* bowl, basin.
jauger (ʒo'ʒe:) *vt* **1** gauge. **2** measure. **jauge** *nf* gauge.
jaune (ʒon) *adj* yellow. *nm* **1** yellow. **2** yolk (of an egg). **3** blackleg. **jaunir** *vt* make or turn yellow. *vi* turn yellow. **jaunisse** *nf* jaundice.
javelot (ʒa'vlo) *nm* javelin.

jazz (ʒaz) *nm* jazz.
je, j' (ʒə) *pron 1st pers m,f s* I.
jeep (dʒi:p) *nf* jeep.
jersey (ʒɛr'zɛ) *nm* jersey, jumper.
Jersey (ʒɛr'zɛ) *nm* Jersey.
Jérusalem (ʒɛryza'lɛm) *nf* Jerusalem.
jésuite (ʒe:'zɥi:t) *nm* Jesuit. **jésuitique** *adj* **1** Jesuit. **2** hypocritical.
Jésus (ʒe:'zy) *nm* Jesus.
jet (ʒɛ) *nm* **1** throw. **2** cast. **3** jet, stream, ray, spurt.
jeter (ʒə'te:) *vt* throw, fling. **jetée** *nf* jetty. **jeton** *nm* **1** counter. **2** token.
jeu, jeux (ʒœ) *nm* **1** game. **2** play. **3** set. **4** gambling. **jeu de cartes** pack of cards. **jeu de mots** pun. **prendre du jeu** work loose.
jeudi (ʒœ'di:) *nm* Thursday. **jeudi saint** Maundy Thursday.
jeun (ʒœ̃) **à jeun** *adv* fasting.
jeune (ʒœn) *adj* **1** young. **2** juvenile. **3** junior, younger. **jeunesse** *nf* **1** youth. **2** childhood, boyhood, girlhood. **3** young people.
jeûner (ʒœ'ne:) *vi* fast. **jeûne** *nm* fast.
joaillier, -ière (ʒwa'je:, -'jɛr) *nm,f* jeweller. **joaillerie** *nf* **1** jewellery. **2** jeweller's shop.
jockey (ʒɔ'kɛ) *nm* jockey.
joie (ʒwa) *nf* joy, delight.
joindre* (ʒwɛ̃dr) *vt* **1** join. **2** combine. **3** add. **4** clasp. *vi* fit. **se joindre** *vr* join, unite. **joint** *adj* joined, united. *nm* join, joint. **jointure** *nf* joint. **jointure du doigt** knuckle.
joli (ʒɔ'li:) *adj* **1** pretty. **2** good-looking. **3** pleasant, nice. **joliment** *adv* **1** prettily. **2** nicely. **3** *inf* very, awfully.
jonc (ʒɔ̃) *nm bot* rush. **jonc à balais** reed.
joncher (ʒɔ̃'ʃe:) *vt* scatter, litter.
jonction (ʒɔ̃k'sjɔ̃) *nf* junction.
jongler (ʒɔ̃'gle:) *vi* juggle. **jongleur** *nm* juggler.
jonquille (ʒɔ̃'ki:j) *nm* daffodil.
Jordanie (ʒɔrda'ni:) *nf* Jordan. **jordanien, -ienne** (ʒɔrda'njɛ̃, -'njɛn) *adj,n* Jordanian.
joue (ʒu:) *nf anat* cheek.
jouer (ʒwe:) *vi* **1** play. **2** gamble. **3** be loose. *vt* **1** stake. **2** play. **3** perform. **4** trick. **se jouer de** *vr* make fun of. **jouet** *nm* toy. **joueur, -euse** (ʒwœr, ʒwœz) *nm,f* **1** player. **2** gambler. **joujou, -oux** (ʒu:'ʒu:) *nm inf* toy.
joufflu (ʒu:'fly) *adj* chubby.
joug (ʒu:g) *nm* yoke.
jouir (ʒwi:r) *vi* **jouir de** enjoy. **jouissance** *nf* **1** enjoyment. **2** possession.
jour (ʒu:r) *nm* **1** day. **2** daylight. **3** light. **4** hole, gap. **au jour le jour 1** from day to day. **2** from hand to mouth. **de nos jours** nowadays. **jour de semaine** weekday. **journée** *nf* **1** day. **2** day's work. **toute la journée** all day long.
journal, -aux (ʒu:r'nal, -'no) *nm* **1** newspaper. **2** diary. **3** journal. **journalier, -ière** (ʒu:rna'lje:, -'ljɛr) *adj* daily. **journalisme** *nm* journalism. **journaliste** *nm,f* journalist.
jovial, -aux (ʒɔ'vjal, -'vjo) *adj* jolly, jovial.
joyau, -aux (ʒwa'jo) *nm* jewel.
joyeux, -euse (ʒwa'jœ, -'jœz) *adj* **1** merry. **2** glad.
jubilé (ʒybi:'le:) *nm* jubilee.
jucher (ʒy'ʃe:) *vi* **1** perch. **2** roost.
judaïsme (ʒyda'i:sm) *nm* Judaism.
judiciaire (ʒydi:'sjɛr) *adj* **1** judicial. **2** legal.
judicieux, -euse (ʒydi:'sjœ, -'sjœz) *adj* judicious.
juger (ʒy'ʒe:) *vt* **1** judge. **2** *law* try. **3** adjudicate. **4** consider, think. **au jugé** *adv* **1** by guesswork. **2** at random. **juge** *nm* **1** judge. **2** umpire. **jugement** *nm* **1** judgment. **2** *law* trial.
juif, juive (ʒɥi:f, ʒɥi:v) *nm,f* Jew. *adj* Jewish.
juillet (ʒɥi:'jɛ) *nm* July.
juin (ʒɥɛ̃) *nm* June.
jumeler (ʒym'le:) *vt* pair, arrange in pairs. **jumeau, -elle, -aux, -elles** (ʒy'mo:, -'mɛl, -'mo, -'mɛl) *adj,n* twin. **jumelles** *nf pl* binoculars.
jument (zy'mɑ̃) *nf* mare.
jungle (ʒɔ̃gl) *nf* jungle.
junte (ʒɔ̃t) *nf* junta.
jupe (ʒyp) *nf* skirt. **jupon** *nm* petticoat.
Jupiter (ʒypi:'tɛr) *nm* Jupiter.
jurer (ʒy're:) *vt* swear, vow. *vi* **1** curse, use bad language. **2** clash. **juré** *adj* sworn. *nm* **1** juror. **2** *pl* jury. **juron** *nm* **1** oath. **2** swearword. **jury** *nm* jury.
juridique (ʒyri:'di:k) *adj* **1** judicial. **2** legal.
jus (ʒy) *nm* **1** juice. **2** gravy.
jusant (ʒy'zɑ̃) *nm* ebb.
jusque (ʒysk) *prep* **1** as far as. **2** up to. **3** till, until. **4** even. **jusqu'à ce que** until. **jusqu'ici** so far, up to now. **jusqu'où?** how far?
juste (ʒyst) *adj* **1** just, fair. **2** right, exact. **3** upright. **4** tight. *adv* **1** just. **2** exactly. **3** barely. **justesse** *nf* **1** accuracy. **2** correctness.
justice (ʒy'sti:s) *nf* **1** justice. **2** law.
justifier (ʒysti:'fje:) *vt* **1** justify. **2** clear.
jute (ʒyt) *nm* jute.
juteux, -euse (ʒy'tœ, -'tœz) *adj* juicy.
juvénile (ʒyve:'ni:l) *adj* juvenile.

juxtaposer (ʒykstapo'ze:) *vt* juxtapose, put side by side.

K

kaki (ka'ki:) *adj invar,nm* khaki.
kaléidoscope (kale:i:dɔ'skɔp) *nm* kaleidoscope.
kangourou (kãgu:'ru:) *nm* kangaroo.
karaté (kara'te:) *nm* karate.
képi (ke:'pi:) *nm mil* cap.
kermesse (kɛr'mɛs) *nf* village fair.
kérosène (ke:rɔ'zɛn) *nm* paraffin oil.
kibboutz (ki:'bu:ts) *nm* kibbutz.
kilo (ki:'lo) *nm inf* kilo.
kilogramme (ki:lɔ'gram) *nm* kilogram.
kilomètre (ki:lɔ'mɛtr) *nm* kilometre. **kilométrique** *adj* kilometric.
kilowatt (ki:lɔ'wat) *nm* kilowatt.
kimono (ki:mɔ'no) *nm* kimono.
kiosque (kjɔsk) *nm* **1** kiosk. **2** newspaper stall. **3** summerhouse.
kiwi (ki:'wi:) *nm* kiwi.
klaxon (klak'sɔ̃) *nm* hooter, horn.
klaxonner (klaksɔ'ne:) *vi* blow one's horn, hoot.
kleptomanie (klɛptɔma'ni:) *nf* kle omania. **kleptomane** *adj,n* kleptomaniac.

L

l' *def art* see **le** and **la.**
la, l' (la) *def art f* **1** the. **2** a. *pron 3rd pers fs* **1** her. **2** it.
là (la) *adv* **1** there. **2** then. **3** that. **là-bas** *adv* **1** over there, yonder. **2** down there. **là-dedans** *adv* **1** in there. **2** within, in it or them. **là-dessous** *adv* **1** under there. **2** under it, that, or them. **3** underneath. **là-dessus** *adv* **1** on that. **2** thereupon. **là-haut** *adv* up there.
laboratoire (labɔra'twar) *nm* laboratory.
labourer (labu:'re:) *vt* till, plough. **laborieux, -euse** (labɔ'rjœ, -'rjœz) *adj* **1** hard-working. **2** arduous. **labourable** *adj* arable.
labyrinthe (labi:'rɛ̃t) *nm* labyrinth, maze.
lac (lak) *nm* lake, loch.
lacer (la'se:) *vt* lace (up). **lacet** *nm* **1** lace, shoelace. **2** noose. **en lacet** winding.
lacérer (lasɛ're:) *vt* **1** slash. **2** tear.
lâcher (lɑ'ʃe:) *vt* **1** let go, release. **2** drop. **3** slacken. **4** divulge. **lâcher pied** give way. **lâche** *adj* **1** cowardly, faint-hearted. **2** loose, slack. *nm* coward. **lâcheté** *nf* cowardice.
lacrymogène (lakri:mɔ'ʒɛn) **gaz lacrymogène** *nm* tear-gas.
lacté (lak'te:) *adj* milky.
lacune (la'kyn) *nf* **1** gap. **2** break. **3** blank.
ladre (lɑdr) *adj* mean. *nm* miser.
laid (lɛ) *adj* **1** ugly, plain. **2** unsightly. **laideur** *nf* ugliness.
laine (lɛn) *nf* wool. **de laine** **1** woollen. **2** woolly. **laine filée** yarn. **laineux, -euse** (lɛ'nœ, -'nœz) *adj* woolly.
laïque (la'i:k) *adj* lay, secular. *nm* **1** layman. **2** *pl* laity.
laisser (lɛ'se:) *vt* **1** let, allow. **2** leave. **laisse** *nf* lead, leash. **laisser-aller** *nm invar* **1** carefreeness. **2** neglect. **laisser-passer** *nm invar* pass, permit.
lait (lɛ) *nm* milk. **laiterie** *nf* dairy. **laitier, -ière** (lɛ'tje:, -'tjɛr) *adj* dairy. *nm* milkman.
laiton (lɛ'tɔ̃) *nm* brass.
laitue (lɛ'ty) *nf* lettuce.
lama (la'ma) *nm* llama.
lambeau, -aux (lã'bo) *nm* **1** scrap. **2** shred.
lambrequin (lãbrə'kɛ̃) *nm* pelmet.
lame (lam) *nf* **1** blade. **2** strip, sheet. **3** *naut* wave.
se lamenter (lamã'te:) *vr* wail, lament, bewail. **lamentation** *nf* lament.
lampe (lãp) *nf* lamp.
lamper (lã'pe:) *vt inf* swig. **lampée** *nf* swig, gulp.
lancer (lã'se:) *vt* **1** throw, fling, hurl. **2** start, set going. **3** launch. **se lancer** *vr* rush, dash. **lance** (lãs) *nf* spear. **lance-pierre** *nm invar* catapult.
lanciner (lãsi:'ne:) *vi* throb.
landau (lã'do) *nm* pram.
lande (lãd) *nf* heath.
landier (lã'dje:) *nm* gorse.
langage (lã'gaʒ) *nm* **1** language. **2** speech. **3** talk.
langouste (lã'gu:st) *nf* crayfish. **langoustines** *nf pl* scampi.
langue (lãg) *nf* **1** *anat* tongue. **2** language. **langue maternelle** mother tongue.
languir (lã'gi:r) *vi* pine, yearn. **languissant** *adj* **1** listless. **2** dull.
lanterne (lã'tɛrn) *nf* lantern.
laper (la'pe:) *vt* lap.
lapin (la'pɛ̃) *nm* rabbit.
Laponie (lapɔ'ni:) *nf* Lapland. **lapon** *adj,n* Lapp.
laque (lak) *nm* lacquer. **laquer** *vt* lacquer.
larcin (lar'sɛ̃) *nm* larceny.

lard (lar) *nm* bacon.
larder (larˈde:) *vt* **1** lard. **2** cover.
large (larʒ) *adj* **1** broad. **2** wide. **3** ample. **4** generous. **5** big. *nm* **1** width. **2** room, space. **3** sea. *adv* **1** largely. **2** broadly. **3** loosely. **largeur** *nf* breadth, width.
larme (larm) *nf* tear, teardrop.
larmoyer (larmwaˈje:) *vi* **1** weep. **2** snivel. **larmoyant** *adj* tearful.
larron (laˈrɔ̃) *nm* thief.
larve (larv) *nf* larva, grub.
laryngite (larɛ̃ˈʒi:t) *nf* laryngitis.
larynx (laˈrɛ̃ks) *nm* larynx.
las, lasse (lɑ, lɑs) *adj* tired, weary.
lascif, -ive (laˈsi:f, -ˈsi:v) *adj* lewd.
lasser (lɑˈse:) *vt* **1** tire. **2** exhaust. **se lasser** *vr* grow, get tired.
lasso (laˈso) *nm* lasso. **prendre au lasso** lasso.
latent (laˈtɑ̃) *adj* latent, hidden.
latin (laˈtɛ̃) *adj,nm* Latin.
latitude (lati:ˈtyd) *nf* **1** latitude. **2** scope.
laurier (lɔˈrje:) *nm* laurel.
lavabo (lavaˈbo) *nm* **1** washbasin. **2** lavatory.
lavande (laˈvɑ̃d) *nf* lavender.
lave (lav) *nf* lava.
laver (laˈve:) *vt* **1** wash. **2** bathe. **se laver** *vr* wash oneself, have a wash. **laverie** *nf* laundry. **lavette** *nf* dishcloth.
laxatif, -ive (laksaˈti:f, -ˈti:v) *adj,nm* laxative.
le, l' (lə) *def art m* **1** the. **2** a. *pron 3rd pers ms* **1** him. **2** it. *pron* so.
lécher (le:ˈʃe:) *vt* **1** lick. **2** polish, refine. **lèche-vitrines** *nm* windowshopping. **faire du lèche-vitrines** windowshop.
leçon (ləˈsɔ̃) *nf* lesson.
lecteur, -trice (lɛkˈtœr, -ˈtri:s) *nm,f* **1** reader. **2** foreign language assistant (in a university). **lecture** *nf* reading.
ledit, ladite (ləˈdi:, laˈdi:t) *adj, pl* **lesdits, lesdites** aforesaid.
légal, -aux (leˈgal, -ˈgo) *adj* **1** legal, lawful. **2** statutory.
légaliser (le:gali:ˈze:) *vt* **1** legalize. **2** certify
légataire (lɛgaˈtɛr) *nm,f* heir.
légende (lɛˈʒɑ̃d) *nf* legend, myth, fable. **légendaire** *adj* legendary.
léger, -ère (le:ˈʒe:, -ˈʒɛr) *adj* **1** light. **2** slight. **3** agile. **4** loose, fast. **5** mild. **6** weak. **à la légère** lightly. **légèreté** *nf* lightness.
légiférer (le:ʒi:fe:ˈre:) *vi* legislate.
légion (le:ˈʒjɔ̃) *nf* **1** legion. **2** crowd, host.
légitime (le:ʒi:ˈti:m) *adj* legitimate, lawful.
legs (lɛ) *nm* legacy.
léguer (le:ˈge:) *vt* leave, bequeath.
légume (le:ˈgym) *nm* vegetable.
lendemain (lɑ̃dˈmɛ̃) *nm* next day, day after.
lent (lɑ̃) *adj* slow. **lenteur** *nf* slowness.
lentille (lɑ̃ˈti:j) *nf* **1** lentil. **2** lens. **3** freckle. **lentilles de contact** *nf pl* contact lenses.
léopard (le:ɔˈpar) *nm* leopard.
lèpre (lɛpr) *nf* leprosy. **lépreux, -euse** (le:ˈprœ, -ˈprœz) *nm,f* leper.
lequel, laquelle (ləˈkɛl, laˈkɛl) *pron, pl* **lesquels, lesquelles** **1** who, whom. **2** which.
les (lɛ) *def art m,f pl* the. *pron 3rd pers m,f pl* them.
lesbien (lɛsˈbjɛ̃) *adj* lesbian. **lesbienne** (lɛsˈbjɛn) *nf* lesbian.
léser (le:ˈze:) *vt* **1** wrong, wound. **2** injure.
lésiner (le:zi:ˈne:) *vi* **1** be mean. **2** haggle.
lessive (lɛˈsi:v) *nf* **1** washing. **2** detergent.
lest (lɛst) *nm* ballast.
leste (lɛst) *adj* **1** lively, nimble, agile. **2** sharp, smart. **3** free, brazen.
léthargie (lɛtarˈʒi:) *nf* **1** lethargy. **2** apathy. **léthargique** *adj* lethargic.
lettre (lɛtr) *nf* **1** letter (of the alphabet). **2** letter, note. **3** *pl* literature, letters. **4** *pl* arts. **lettré** *adj* **1** literate. **2** learned. *nm* scholar.
leu (lœ) **à la queue leu leu** *adv* in single file.
leucémie (lœse:ˈmi:) *nf* leukaemia.
leur (lœr) *poss adj 3rd pers pl* their. *poss pron 3rd pers m,f pl* **le** or **la leur** **1** theirs. **2** their own. **3** to them.
leurrer (lœˈre:) *vt* **1** lure. **2** bait. **3** entice. **se leurrer** *vr* delude oneself. **leurre** *nm* **1** lure. **2** bait. **3** decoy.
lever (ləˈve:) *vt* **1** lift, raise. **2** collect. **3** levy. **4** adjourn. **se lever** *vr* **1** rise. **2** get up. **3** stand up. ~*nm* rising. **lever du soleil** *nm* sunrise. **levant** *adj* rising. *nm* east. **levé** *adj* raised. *nm* survey. **levée** *nf* **1** lifting. **2** levy. **3** collection. **4** embankment. **5** *game* trick. **levier** *nm* lever.
lèvre (lɛvr) *nf* lip.
lévrier (le:vri:ˈe:) *nm* greyhound.
levure (ləˈvyr) *nf* yeast.
lézard (lɛˈzar) *nm* lizard.
lézarder (lɛzarˈde:) *vt* crack, split. *vi inf* **1** bask in the sun. **2** lounge. **lézarde** *nf* **1** crack. **2** crevice.
liaison (ljɛˈzɔ̃) *nf* **1** joining, liaison. **2** connection. **3** relationship. **4** *mus* slur.
liasse (ljas) *nf* **1** bundle, wad. **2** file.
Liban (li:ˈbɑ̃) *nm* Lebanon. **libanais** *adj,n* Lebanese.

libelle (li:ˈbɛl) *nf* libel.
libellule (li:bɛlˈlyl) *nf* dragonfly.
libérer (li:be:ˈre:) *vt* **1** free, liberate. **2** release. **3** discharge. **libéral, -aux** (li:bɛˈral, -ˈro) *adj* **1** broad, wide. **2** free. **3** generous. **4** *pol* liberal. **liberté** *nf* liberty, freedom.
librairie (li:brɛˈri:) *nf* **1** bookshop. **2** publishing house. **libraire** *nm,f* bookseller.
libre (li:br) *adj* **1** free. **2** clear, open. **3** independent. **4** exempt. **5** vacant. **libre-service** *nm, pl* **libres-services** self-service (shop or restaurant, etc.).
Libye (li:ˈbi:) *nf* Libya. **libyen, -enne** (li:ˈbjɛ̃, -ˈbjɛn) *adj,n* Libyan.
licence (li:ˈsɑ̃s) *nf* **1** licence. **2** leave, permission. **3** *educ* degree. **4** excessive liberty. **licencié** *nm* **1** graduate. **2** licensee.
licorne (li:ˈkɔrn) *nf* unicorn.
licou (li:ˈku:) *nm* halter.
lie (li:) *nf* dregs.
liège (ljɛʒ) *nm* cork.
lier (lje:) *vt* **1** fasten, bind. **2** link, connect. **3** *cul* thicken. **lien** *nm* **1** tie, bond. **2** link. **3** fetter. **4** strap.
lierre (ljɛr) *nm* ivy.
lieu, -eux (ljœ) *nm* **1** place. **2** spot. **3** reason. **4** *pl* premises. **au lieu de** instead of. **au lieu que** whereas. **avoir lieu** take place. **donner lieu à** give rise to. **lieux d'aisances** *nm pl* lavatory.
lieutenant (ljœtˈnɑ̃) *nm* lieutenant. **lieutenant-colonel** *nm, pl* **lieutenants-colonels** **1** lieutenant colonel. **2** wing commander.
lièvre (ljɛvr) *nm* hare.
ligne (liɲ) *nf* **1** line. **2** row. **3** cord. **4** formation. **à la ligne** new paragraph. **hors ligne** outstanding. **soigner sa ligne** watch one's figure.
ligoter (li:gɔˈte:) *vt* bind, tie.
ligue (li:g) *nf* league, alliance.
lilas (li:ˈlɑ) *nm* lilac. *adj invar* lilac.
limace (li:ˈmas) *nf* slug. **limaçon** (li:maˈsɔ̃) *nm* snail.
limaille (li:ˈmaj) *nf* filings.
limer (li:ˈme:) *vt* file. **lime** *nf* file. **lime à ongles** nailfile.
limiter (li:mi:ˈte:) *vt* **1** limit, restrict. **2** mark the bounds of. **limite** (li:ˈmi:t) *nf* **1** boundary. **2** limit. **3** *pl* bounds.
limon[1] (li:ˈmɔ̃) *nm* silt, mud.
limon[2] (li:ˈmɔ̃) *nm* lime.
limonade (li:mɔˈnad) *nf* lemonade.
lin (lɛ̃) *nm* **1** flax. **2** linen.
linceul (lɛ̃ˈsœj) *nm* shroud.
linéaire (li:ne:ˈɛr) *adj* linear.
linge (lɛ̃ʒ) *nm* **1** linen. **2** household linen. **linge de corps** underwear. **lingerie** *nf* lingerie, underwear.
linguiste (lɛ̃ˈgɥi:st) *nm,f* linguist. **linguistique** *adj* linguistic. *nf* linguistics.
lino (li:ˈno) *nm inf* lino.
linoléum (li:nɔle:ˈɔm) *nm* linoleum.
lion (ljɔ̃) *nm* **1** lion. **2** *cap* Leo.
liqueur (li:ˈkœr) *nf* **1** liquor. **2** liqueur. **3** drink.
liquider (li:ki:ˈde:) *vt* **1** liquidate. **2** settle. **3** realize. **liquide** *adj,nm* liquid.
lire* [1] (li:r) *vt* read. **lire à vue** sightread. **lisible** *adj* legible.
lire[2] (li:r) *nf* lira.
lis[1] (li:) *v see* **lire**[1].
lis[2] (li:s) *nm* lily.
lisière (li:ˈzjɛr) *nf* edge, border.
lisser (li:ˈse:) *vt* **1** smooth, gloss. **2** polish.
liste (li:st) *nf* **1** list. **2** register. **liste des abonnés** mailing list.
lit (li:) *nm* **1** bed. **2** layer. **3** bottom. **lit d'enfant** cot, crib. **lit de camp** or **de sangle** camp bed.
litanies (li:taˈni:) *nf pl* litany.
litée (li:ˈte:) *nf* litter.
litre (li:tr) *nm* litre.
littéraire (li:te:ˈrɛr) *adj* literary.
littéral, -aux (li:tɛˈral, -ˈro) *adj* literal.
littérature (li:tɛraˈtyr) *nf* literature.
littoral, -aux (li:tɔˈral, -ˈro) *adj* coastal. *nm* coastline.
livide (li:ˈvi:d) *adj* **1** livid. **2** ghastly, pale.
livre[1] (li:vr) *nm* book. **livre à succès** or **à fort tirage** bestseller. **livre de poche** paperback. **livret** *nm* **1** booklet. **2** handbook.
livre[2] (li:vr) *nf* **1** pound (weight). **2** pound (money). **livre sterling** pound sterling.
livrer (li:ˈvre:) *vt* **1** surrender, give up. **2** deliver. **3** confide. **se livrer** *vr* give oneself up. **se livrer à** give way to, indulge in. **livraison** *nf* **1** delivery. **2** instalment.
lobe (lɔb) *nm* lobe.
local, -aux (lɔˈkal, -ˈko) *adj* local. *nm* **1** building. **2** premises. **localité** *nf* **1** place. **2** area.
localiser (lɔkali:ˈze:) *vt* **1** localize. **2** locate.
locataire (lɔkaˈtɛr) *nm,f* tenant.
location (lɔkaˈsjɔ̃) *nf* **1** hiring. **2** renting. **3** booking. **en location** on hire.
locomotive (lɔkɔmɔˈti:v) *nf* locomotive, engine.
locuste (lɔˈkyst) *nf* locust.
locution (lɔkyˈsjɔ̃) *nf* expression, saying.

logarithme (lɔga'ri:tm) *nm* logarithm.

loger (lɔ'ʒe:) *vi* **1** lodge, stay. **2** live. *vt* **1** accommodate, house. **2** put, plant. **loge** *nf* **1** hut. **2** lodge. **3** cabin. **4** *Th* box. **5** dressing-room. **logement** *nm* **1** accommodation, housing. **2** lodgings. **logeur, -euse** (lɔ'ʒœr, -'ʒœz) *nm,f* landlord, landlady. **logis** *nm* dwelling.

logique (lɔ'ʒi:k) *nf* logic. *adj* logical.

loi (lwa) *nf* **1** law. **2** authority. **3** *pol* act.

loin (lwɛ̃) *adv* **1** far. **2** distant. **au loin** in the distance. **de loin 1** by far. **2** from afar. **plus loin** further. **lointain** *adj* distant, remote. *nm* **1** distance. **2** background.

loir (lwar) *nm* dormouse.

loisir (lwa'zi:r) *nm* leisure.

lombric (lɔ̃'bri:k) *nm* earthworm.

Londres (lɔ̃dr) *nm* London.

long, longue (lɔ̃, lɔ̃g) *adj* **1** long. **2** lengthy. **3** slow. **longue-vue** *nf, pl* **longues-vues** telescope. ~*nm* length. **de long en large** up and down, to and fro. **le long de** along, alongside. **tout au long de** throughout. **tout le long du jour** all day long. **longueur** *nf* length. **longueur d'onde** wavelength.

longer (lɔ̃'ʒe:) *vt* **1** walk along. **2** skirt round.

longévité (lɔ̃ʒe:vi:'te:) *nf* longevity.

longitude (lɔ̃ʒi:'ty:d) *nf* longitude.

longtemps (lɔ̃'tɑ̃) *adv* long, a long time.

loque (lɔk) *nf* rag.

loquet (lɔ'kɛ) *nm* latch.

lorgner (lɔr'ɲe:) *vt* **1** make eyes at. **2** leer at.

lors (lɔr) *adv* **1** even. **2** at the time, when.

lorsque (lɔrsk) *conj* when.

lot (lo) *nm* **1** share, portion. **2** batch, lot. **3** prize.

loterie (lɔ'tri:) *nf* **1** lottery. **2** raffle.

lotion (lɔ'sjɔ̃) *nf* lotion.

lotus (lɔ'tys) *nm* lotus.

louche[1] (lu:ʃ) *adj* **1** cross-eyed. **2** suspicious.

louche[2] (lu:ʃ) *nf* ladle.

loucher (lu:'ʃe:) *vi* squint.

louer[1] (lwe:) *vt* praise, commend. **louable** *adj* praiseworthy. **louange** *nf* praise.

louer[2] (lwe:) *vt* **1** let. **2** rent, hire. **3** reserve.

loufoque (lu:'fɔk) *adj* mad, eccentric.

loup (lu:) *nm* wolf. **loup-cervier** *nm, pl* **loups-cerviers** lynx.

loupe (lu:p) *nf* magnifying glass.

louper (lu:'pe:) *vt inf* **1** bungle, fluff. **2** fail. **3** miss.

lourd (lu:r) *adj* **1** heavy. **2** clumsy. **3** stupid, dull. **4** close, sultry. **lourdeur** *nf* **1** heaviness. **2** clumsiness. **3** dullness.

loutre (lu:tr) *nm* **1** otter. **2** sealskin.

loyal, -aux (lwa'jal, -'jo) *adj* **1** loyal, faithful. **2** honest. **3** fair. **loyauté** *nf* **1** loyalty. **2** honesty.

loyer (lwa'je:) *nm* rent.

lu (ly) *v* see **lire**[1].

lubie (ly'bi:) *nf* whim.

lucarne (ly'karn) *nf* attic window.

lucide (ly'si:d) *adj* lucid, clear.

lucratif, -ive (lykra'ti:f, -'ti:v) *adj* lucrative.

lueur (lɥœr) *nf* **1** glimmer. **2** flash.

luge (lyʒ) *nf* toboggan.

lugubre (ly'gybr) *adj* dismal, gloomy.

lui (lɥi:) *pron 3rd pers ms* **1** he. **2** it. **3** him. **4** to him, her, or it. **lui-même** *pron 3rd pers ms* himself.

luire* (lɥi:r) *vi* **1** shine. **2** glimmer, glitter. **luisant** *adj* **1** shining, bright. **2** glossy. *nm* **1** shine. **2** gloss.

lumière (ly'mjɛr) *nf* **1** light. **2** *pl* knowledge. **lumineux, -euse** (lymi:'nœ, -'nœz) *adj* **1** luminous. **2** lucid.

lundi (lœ̃'di:) *nm* Monday.

lune (lyn) *nf* moon. **lune de miel** honeymoon. **lunaire** *adj* lunar.

lunette (ly'nɛt) *nf* **1** telescope. **2** *pl* spectacles. **[illegible]** *nf pl* goggles. **lunettes de soleil** *nf pl* sunglasses.

luron (ly'rɔ̃) *nm inf* jolly fellow.

lustrer (ly'stre:) *vt* **1** polish. **2** gloss. **lustre** *nm* **1** lustre, polish. **2** chandelier.

luth (lyt) *nm* lute.

lutin (ly'tɛ̃) *nm* **1** imp. **2** *inf* mischievous child. *adj* mischievous.

lutrin (ly'trɛ̃) *nm* lectern.

lutter (ly'te:) *vi* **1** struggle, fight. **2** compete. **3** wrestle. **lutte** *nf* **1** struggle, fight. **2** contest. **3** wrestling.

luxe (lyks) *nm* luxury. **luxueux, -euse** (lyk'sɥœ, -'sɥœz) *adj* luxurious.

Luxembourg (lyksɑ̃'bu:r) *nm* Luxembourg.

lycée (li:'se:) *nm* grammar school.

lyncher (lɛ̃'ʃe:) *vt* lynch.

lynx (lɛ̃ks) *nm* lynx.

Lyon (ljɔ̃) *nm* Lyons.

lyre (li:r) *nf* lyre.

lyrique (li:'ri:k) *adj* lyrical.

M

ma (ma) *poss adj* see **mon.**

macabre (ma'kɑbr) *adj* gruesome, macabre.

macédoine (mase:'dwan) *nf* **1** salad. **2** miscellany.
mâcher (ma'ʃe:) *vt* **1** chew. **2** munch. **mâchoire** (ma'ʃwar) *nf* jaw.
machin (ma'ʃɛ̃) *nm inf* gadget, thing.
machine (ma'ʃi:n) *nf* **1** machine. **2** engine. **3** device, apparatus. **4** *pl* machinery. **machine á calculer** calculator. **machine à coudre** sewing machine. **machine à écrire** typewriter. **machine à sous** fruit machine. **machinal, -aux** (maʃi:'nal, -'no) *adj* mechanical, unconscious.
macis (ma'si:) *nm cul* mace.
maçon (ma'sɔ̃) *nm* mason.
maçonner (masɔ'ne:) *vt* build. **maçonnerie** *nf* masonry.
maculer (maky'le:) *vt* stain, spot. **macule** *nf* **1** stain, spot. **2** blemish.
madame (ma'dam) *nf, pl* **mesdames** **1** madam. **2** *cap* Mrs.
mademoiselle (madmwa'zɛl) *nf, pl* **mesdemoiselles** **1** miss. **2** young lady. **3** *cap* Miss.
madone (ma'dɔn) *nf* madonna.
madrier (madri:'e) *nm* **1** beam. **2** joist.
magasin (maga'zɛ̃) *nm* **1** shop. **2** warehouse. **3** stock. **grand magasin** store. **magasin à succursales multiples** chain-store.
magazine (maga'zi:n) *nm* magazine.
magie (ma'ʒi:) *nf* magic. **magicien** *nm* magician, wizard. **magique** *adj* magic.
magistrat (maʒi:'stra) *nm* magistrate. **magistral, -aux** (maʒi:'stral, -'stro) *adj* **1** authoritative, magisterial. **2** brilliant.
magnat (mag'na) *nm* magnate, tycoon.
magnétiser (maɲe:ti:'ze:) *vt* **1** magnetize. **2** mesmerize. **magnétique** *adj* magnetic. **magnétisme** (maɲe:'ti:sm) *nm* **1** magnetism. **2** mesmerism. **3** attraction.
Magnétophone (maɲe:tɔ'fɔn) *nm Tdmk* tape-recorder.
magnifique (maɲi:'fi:k) *adj* magnificent, splendid.
magnitude (magni:'tyd) *nf* magnitude.
mai (mɛ) *nm* **1** May. **2** Maypole. **le premier mai** May Day.
maigrir (mɛ'gri:r) *vi* slim, lose weight. **maigre** *adj* **1** thin, skinny. **2** lean. **3** meagre. **4** frugal. **maigreur** *nf* thinness.
maille (maj) *nf* **1** mesh. **2** (knitting) stitch. **3** link.
maillet (ma'jɛ) *nm* mallet.
maillot (ma'jo) *nm* **1** *sport* vest. **2** tights. **maillot de bain** swimming costume.
main (mɛ̃) *nf* **1** hand. **2** handwriting. **3** *game* deal. **à main** by hand. **main-d'œuvre** *nf* manpower, labour. **sous la main** to or at hand.
maint (mɛ̃) *adj* many a.
maintenant (mɛ̃t'nɑ̃) *adv* now.
maintenir* (mɛ̃t'ni:r) *vt* **1** uphold. **2** support. **3** maintain, hold. **se maintenir** *vr* **1** hold one's own. **2** continue. **maintien** *nm* **1** maintenance. **2** deportment.
maire (mɛr) *nm* mayor. **mairie** *nf* town hall.
mais (mɛ) *conj* **1** but. **2** why.
maïs (ma'i:s) *nm* maize.
maison (mɛ'zɔ̃) *nf* **1** house. **2** home. **3** household. **maison de commerce** firm. **maison de santé** nursing home.
maître, -esse (mɛtr, mɛ'trɛs) *nm,f* master, mistress. **maître de chapelle** choirmaster. **maître d'hôtel** **1** butler. **2** head waiter. **~** *adj* chief, principal.
maîtriser (mɛtri:'ze:) *vt* **1** master. **2** control. **maîtrise** *nf* command, control.
majesté (maʒɛ'ste:) *nf* **1** majesty. **2** dignity. **3** grandeur. **majestueux, -euse** (maʒɛ'stɥœ, -'stɥœz) *adj* majestic.
majeur (ma'ʒœr) *adj* **1** major, greater. **2** chief, main. **3** *law* of age.
majorer (maʒɔ're:) *vt* raise or increase the price of. **majorité** *nf* **1** majority. **2** coming of age.
majuscule (maʒy'skyl) *adj* large, capital. *nf* capital letter.
mal[1]**, maux** (mal, mo) *nm* **1** evil. **2** wrong, ill. **3** harm. **4** pain, ache. **5** difficulty. **avoir le mal de mer** be seasick. **avoir le mal du pays** be homesick. **avoir mal à l'oreille** have earache. **mal de dents** toothache. **mal de tête** headache. **se donner du mal à** take pains to.
mal[2] (mal) *adv* **1** badly. **2** ill. **3** amiss. **4** uncomfortably. **pas mal de** a good many, a lot of.
malade (ma'lad) *adj* ill, unwell, sick. *nm* invalid. **maladie** *nf* **1** illness. **2** disease. **3** ailment.
maladresse (mala'drɛs) *nf* **1** awkwardness. **2** blunder.
maladroit (mala'drwa) *adj* **1** clumsy, awkward. **2** tactless.
malaise (ma'lɛz) *nm* **1** uneasiness. **2** indisposition.
Malaisie (malɛ'zi:) *nf* **1** Malaya. **2** Malaysia. **malais** (ma'lɛ) *adj,n* Malay. *nm* Malay (language).

malappris (mala'pri:) *adj* **1** ill-bred. **2** uncouth.

malavisé (malavi:'ze:) *adj* rash, unwise.

malchance (mal'ʃɑ̃s) *nf* bad luck. **malchanceux, -euse** (malʃɑ̃'sœ, -'sœz) *adj* unfortunate, unlucky.

malcommode (malkɔ'mɔd) *adj* inconvenient.

mâle (mɑl) *nm* male. *adj* **1** male, cock, dog. **2** virile.

malédiction (male:di:k'sjɔ̃) *nf* curse.

malentendu (malɑ̃tɑ̃'dy) *nm* misunderstanding.

malfaisant (malfə'zɑ̃) *adj* **1** harmful. **2** evil.

malgré (mal'gre:) *prep* in spite of.

malheur (ma'lœr) *nm* **1** misfortune. **2** accident. **malheureux, -euse** (malœ'rœ, -'rœz) *adj* **1** unfortunate. **2** unhappy, wretched. **3** poor.

malhonnête (malɔ'nɛt) *adj* **1** dishonest. **2** rude. **3** improper.

malice (ma'li:s) *nf* **1** mischievousness. **2** prank. **3** spite, malice.

malin, -igne (ma'lɛ̃, -'li:ɲ) *adj* **1** mischievous. **2** shrewd, sly. **3** malignant.

malingre (ma'lɛ̃gr) *adj* sickly.

malle (mal) *nf* **1** (luggage) trunk. **2** *mot* boot.

malmener (malmɔ'ne:) *vt* maltreat, manhandle.

malotru (malɔ'try) *adj* **1** vulgar. **2** uncouth.

malpropre (mal'prɔpr) *adj* **1** grubby, dirty. **2** immoral. **3** dishonest.

malsain (mal'sɛ̃) *adj* unhealthy.

malséant (malse:'ɑ̃) *adj* improper.

malt (malt) *nm* malt.

Malte (malt) *nf* Malta. **maltais** *adj,n* Maltese. *nm* Maltese (language).

maltraiter (maltrɛ'te:) *vt* **1** ill-treat. **2** misuse.

maman (ma'mɑ̃) *nf inf* mummy.

mamelle (ma'mɛl) *nf* **1** breast. **2** udder. **mamelon** *nm* **1** nipple. **2** teat.

mammifère (mammi:'fɛr) *nm* mammal.

mammouth (mam'mu:t) *nm* mammoth.

manche[1] (mɑ̃ʃ) *nf* **1** sleeve. **2** *cap* English Channel. **manchette** *nf* **1** cuff. **2** headline. **manchon** *nm* muff.

manche[2] (mɑ̃ʃ) *nm* handle.

manchot (mɑ̃'ʃo) *adj* one-armed. *nm* penguin.

mandarine (mɑ̃da'ri:n) *nf* mandarin, tangerine.

mander (mɑ̃'de:) *vt* **1** order. **2** summon. **3** report. **mandat** *nm* **1** mandate. **2** warrant. **mandat-poste** *nm, pl* **mandats-postes** postal or money order.

mandoline (mɑ̃dɔ'li:n) *nf* mandolin.

manège (ma'nɛʒ) *nm* **1** horsemanship. **2** *inf* trick. **3** behaviour. **manège (de chevaux de bois)** roundabout, merry-go-round.

manette (ma'nɛt) *nf* handle.

manger (mɑ̃'ʒe:) *vt* **1** eat. **2** squander. *nm* food. **mangeable** *adj* edible.

mangue (mɑ̃g) *nf* mango. **manguier** *nm* mango tree.

manie (ma'ni:) *nf* **1** mania. **2** craze.

manier (ma'nje:) *vt* **1** feel. **2** handle. **3** control.

manière (ma'njɛr) *nf* **1** manner, way. **2** style. **3** kind, sort. **4** *pl* manners. **d'une manière ou d'une autre** somehow or other. **maniéré** *adj* affected. **maniérisme** *nm* mannerism.

manifeste[1] (mani:'fɛst) *adj* evident, obvious, manifest.

manifeste[2] (mani:'fɛst) *nm* manifesto.

manifester (mani:fɛ'ste:) *vt* **1** reveal, manifest. **2** demonstrate. **manifestation** *nf* **1** demonstration. **2** manifestation.

manipuler (mani:py'le:) *vt* **1** manipulate. **2** handle. **3** operate.

manivelle (mani'vɛl) *nf* crank, handle.

manne (man) *nf* hamper, basket.

manœuvrer (manœ'vre:) *vt* operate, work. *vi* **1** manoeuvre. **2** *inf* scheme. **manœuvre** *nf* **1** working. **2** *mil* drill. **3** manoeuvre. *nm* labourer.

manoir (ma'nwar) *nm* manor.

manquer (mɑ̃'ke:) *vi* **1** lack. **2** fail. **3** be missing. *vt* miss. **elle a manqué (de) tomber** she nearly fell. **ne pas manquer de** be sure to. **manque** (mɑ̃k) *nm* lack, want.

mansarde (mɑ̃'sard) *nf* attic.

manteau, -aux (mɑ̃'to) *nm* **1** coat. **2** cloak.

manuel, -elle (ma'nyɛl) *adj* manual. *nm* manual, handbook.

manuscrit (many'skri:) *nm* manuscript.

manutention (manytɑ̃'sjɔ̃) *nf* **1** administration. **2** handling.

manxois (mɑ̃k'swa) *adj* Manx.

maori (maɔ'ri:) *adj,n* Maori.

maquereau, -aux[1] (ma'kro) *nm* mackerel.

maquereau, -aux[2] (ma'kro) *nm* pimp.

maquette (ma'kɛt) *nf Art* model.

maquiller (maki:'je:) *vt* **1** make up (the face). **2** fake. **maquillage** *nm* make-up.

maquis (ma'ki:) *nm* scrub, bush.

maraîcher (marɛ'ʃe:) *nm* market gardener.

marais (ma'rɛ) *nm* marsh, bog.

marathon (mara'tɔ̃) *nm* marathon.

marâtre (ma'rɑtr) *nf* stepmother.

marbre (marbr) *nm* marble.

marchand (mar'ʃɑ̃) *nm* **1** shopkeeper. **2** dealer. **3** merchant. **4** tradesman. **marchand de poisson** fishmonger. **marchand en détail**

retailer. **marchand en gros** wholesaler. ~*adj* commercial, market.

marchander (marʃɑ̃'de:) *vt* haggle, bargain. **marchandise** *nf* merchandise, goods.

marché (mar'ʃe:) *nm* **1** market. **2** deal, contract. **bon marché** cheap. **marché commun** Common Market.

marcher (mar'ʃe:) *vi* **1** walk. **2** tread. **3** go, move. **4** work, run. **5** march. **marche** *nf* **1** step, stair. **2** walk. **3** march. **4** progress, development. **marche arrière** *mot* reverse. **mettre en marche** start, set going. **marchepied** *nm* **1** step. **2** step-ladder.

mardi (mar'di:) *nm* Tuesday. **mardi gras** Shrove Tuesday.

mare (mar) *nf* **1** pool. **2** pond.

marécage (marɛ'kaʒ) *nm* **1** bog, swamp. **2** marsh.

maréchal, -aux (marɛ'ʃal, -'ʃo) *nm* **1** marshal. **2** field marshal. **maréchal-ferrant** *nm, pl* **maréchaux-ferrants** blacksmith.

marée (ma're:) *nf* tide.

margarine (marga'ri:n) *nf* margarine.

marge (marʒ) *nf* **1** margin. **2** edge, border.

marguerite (margə'ri:t) *nf* daisy.

mari (ma'ri:) *nm* husband.

marier (mar'je:) *vt* **1** marry. **2** blend. **se marier** *vr* marry, get married. **mariage** (mar'jaʒ) *nm* **1** marriage. **2** wedding. **nouveau marié** *nm* bridegroom. **nouvelle mariée** *nf* bride.

marihuana (mariwa'na) *nf* marijuana.

marin (ma'rɛ̃) *adj* **1** marine. **2** nautical. *nm* sailor, seaman.

marine (ma'ri:n) *nf* seamanship. **marine de guerre** navy. **marine marchande** merchant navy.

mariner (mari:'ne:) *vt* pickle. *vi* marinate. **marinade** *nf* **1** pickle. **2** marinade.

marionnette (marjɔ'nɛt) *nf* puppet.

marital, -aux (mari:'tal, -'to) *adj* marital.

maritime (mari:'ti:m) *adj* maritime.

marjolaine (marʒɔ'lɛn) *nf* marjoram.

mark (mark) *nm comm* mark.

marmite (mar'mi:t) *nf* saucepan, pot.

marmonner (marmɔ'ne:) *vt* mumble.

marmot (mar'mo) *nm inf* child, brat.

marmotter (marmɔ'te:) *vt* mumble, mutter.

Maroc (ma'rɔk) *nm* Morocco. **marocain** (marɔ'kɛ̃) *adj,n* Moroccan.

marotte (ma'rɔt) *nf* hobby.

marquer (mar'ke:) *vt* **1** mark. **2** note down. **3** score. **4** indicate. *vi* stand out. **marque** *nf* **1** mark. **2** brand, make. **3** score. **4** token. **marque de fabrique** trademark. **marque de standing** status symbol.

marquis (mar'ki) *nm* marquess.

marquise (mar'ki:z) *nf* **1** marchioness. **2** marquee. **3** porch.

marraine (ma'rɛn) *nf* godmother.

marrant (ma'rɑ̃) *adj inf* **1** funny. **2** strange, odd.

marron (mɑ'rɔ̃) *nm* chestnut. **marron d'Inde** horse chestnut. ~*adj* maroon. **marronnier** *nm* chestnut tree. **maronnier d'Inde** horse chestnut tree.

mars (mars) *nm* **1** March. **2** *cap* Mars.

Marseille (mar'sɛj) *nf* Marseilles. **marseillaise** *nf* French national anthem.

marsouin (mar'swɛ̃) *nm* porpoise.

marsupial, -aux (marsy'pjal, -'pjo) *adj,nm* marsupial.

marteau, -aux (mar'to) *nm* **1** hammer. **2** door-knocker. **marteau pneumatique** pneumatic drill.

marteler (martɔ'le:) *vt* hammer.

martial, -aux (mar'sjal, -'sjo) *adj* martial.

martinet (marti:'nɛ) *nm* swift.

martin-pêcheur (martɛ̃pɛ'ʃœr) *nm, pl* **martins-pêcheurs** kingfisher.

martre (martr) *nf* **martre du Canada** mink. **martre zibeline** sable.

martyr (mar'ti:r) *nm* martyr. **martyre** *nm* martyrdom.

marxisme (mark'si:sm) *nm* Marxism. **marxiste** *adj,n* Marxist.

mascara (maska'ra) *nm* mascara.

mascarade (maska'rad) *nf* masquerade.

mascotte (ma'skɔt) *nf* mascot.

masculin (masky'lɛ̃) *adj* masculine, male. *nm* masculine gender.

masochisme (mazɔ'ʃi:sm) *nm* masochism. **masochiste** *nm,f* masochist.

masquer (mas'ke:) *vt* **1** mask. **2** hide. **3** disguise. **masque** *nm* **1** mask. **2** expression. **3** pretence. **masque anti-rides** *nm* face-pack.

massacrer (masa'kre:) *vt* **1** massacre. **2** spoil. **massacre** *nm* massacre.

masse[1] (mas) *nf* **1** mass. **2** bulk.

masse[2] (mas) *nf* **1** sledge-hammer. **2** mace.

massepain (mas'pɛ̃) *nm* marzipan.

masser[1] (ma'se:) *vt* mass. **se masser** *vr* mass together.

masser[2] (ma'se:) *vt* massage. **massage** *nm* massage.

massif, -ive (ma'si:f, -'si:v) *adj* **1** massive. **2** solid. **3** heavy. *nm* **1** clump, bed (of flowers). **2** mountain range.

massue (ma'sy) *nf* club.
mastic (ma'sti:k) *nm* putty.
mastiquer[1] (masti:'ke:) *vt* chew, masticate.
mastiquer[2] (masti:'ke:) *vt* fill with cement.
se masturber (mastyr'be:) *vr* masturbate.
mat[1] (mat) *adj invar* checkmated. *nm* checkmate.
mat[2] (mat) *adj* **1** dull, matt. **2** heavy.
mât (mɑ) *nm* **1** mast. **2** pole.
matelas (mat'lɑ) *nm* mattress.
matelot (mat'lo) *nm* sailor, seaman.
matérialiser (mate:rjali:'ze:) *vt* materialize. **matérialiste** *nm,f* materialist. *adj* materialistic.
matériaux (mate:'rjo) *nm pl tech* materials.
matériel, -elle (mate:'rjɛl) *adj* **1** material. **2** physical. *nm* **1** *tech* plant. **2** equipment.
maternel, -elle (matɛr'nɛl) *adj* maternal. **maternité** *nf* maternity, motherhood.
mathématique (mate:ma'ti:k) *adj* mathematical. *nf* mathematics.
matière (ma'tjɛr) *nf* **1** matter, substance. **2** material. **3** subject. **matières grasses** *nf pl* fats. **matières premières** *nf pl* raw materials.
matin (ma'tɛ̃) *nm* morning. **de bon matin** early in the morning. **le matin** in the morning. **matinal, -aux** (mati:'nal, -'no) *adj* **1** morning. **2** early. **matinée** *nf* **1** morning. **2** *Th* afternoon performance.
matois (ma'twa) *adj* sly, crafty.
matriarcal, -aux (matri:ar'kal, -'ko) *adj* matriarchal.
matrice (ma'tri:s) *nf* **1** matrix. **2** womb.
matriculer (matri:ky'le:) *vt* register.
matrimonial, -aux (matri:mɔ'njal, -'njo) *adj* matrimonial.
maturité (matyri:'te:) *nf* maturity.
maudire* (mo'di:r) *vt* curse.
maure (mɔr) *nm,f* Moor. *adj* Moorish.
Maurice (mɔ'ri:s) **île Maurice** *nm* Mauritius.
mausolée (mozɔ'le:) *nm* mausoleum.
maussade (mo'sad) *adj* **1** sullen. **2** surly. **3** dismal.
mauvais (mɔ'vɛ) *adj* **1** evil, wicked. **2** bad. **3** poor. **4** unpleasant. *adv* bad.
mauve (mov) *adj, nm* mauve.
maxime (mak'si:m) *nf* maxim.
maximum (maksi:'mɔm) *adj,nm* maximum.
mayonnaise (majɔ'nɛz) *nf* mayonnaise.
mazout (ma'zu) *nm* fuel oil.
me, m' (mə) *pron 1st pers m,f s* **1** me. **2** to me. **3** myself. **4** to myself.
méandre (me:'ɑ̃dr) *nm* meander, bend.
mec (mɛk) *nm sl* bloke, fellow.
mécaniser (mɛkani:'ze:) *vt* mechanize. **mécanicien** *nm* **1** mechanic. **2** engineer. **mécanique** *adj* mechanical. *nf* mechanics.
mécanisme (mɛka'ni:sm) *nm* **1** mechanism. **2** machinery.
méchant (mɛ'ʃɑ̃) *adj* **1** wicked, evil. **2** naughty. **3** spiteful. **4** vicious. **5** miserable. **méchanceté** *nf* **1** wickedness. **2** spite, malice.
mèche (mɛʃ) *nf* **1** lock (of hair). **2** wisp. **être de mèche avec** be in league with.
mécompte (me:'kɔ̃t) *nm* **1** error. **2** disappointment.
mécontent (me:kɔ̃'tɑ̃) *adj* dissatisfied.
mécontenter (me:kɔ̃tɑ̃'te:) *vt* displease.
médaille (mɛ'daj) *nf* medal.
médecin (mɛt'sɛ̃) *nm* doctor, physician. **médecin chirurgien** surgeon. **médecin de médecine générale** general practitioner. **médecine** *nf* medicine.
médial, -aux (me:'djal, -'djo) *adj* medial.
médian (me:'djɑ̃) *adj* median.
médical, -aux (me:di:'kal, -'ko) *adj* medical.
médicament (me:di:ka'mɑ̃) *nm* medicine.
médication (me:di:ka'sjɔ̃) *nf* medication.
médiéval, -aux (me:dje:'val, -'vo) *adj* medieval.
médiocre (me:'djɔkr) *adj* **1** moderate, mediocre. **2** second-rate, indifferent.
médire* (me:'di:r) *vi* slander.
méditer (me:di:'te:) *vt* contemplate, have in mind. *vi* **1** meditate. **2** muse.
méditerrané (me:di:tɛra'ne:) **(Mer) Méditerranée** *nf* Mediterranean (Sea). **méditerranéen, -enne** (me:di:tɛrane:'ɛ̃, -'ɛn) *adj* Mediterranean.
méduse (me:dyz) *nf* jellyfish.
méfait (me:'fɛ) *nm* **1** misdeed. **2** *pl* damage.
se méfier (me:'fje:) *vr* **se méfier de** **1** distrust, mistrust. **2** beware of. **méfiance** *nf* distrust, mistrust. **méfiant** *adj* **1** suspicious. **2** timid.
mégaphone (mɛga'fɔn) *nm* megaphone.
mégarde (me'gard) **par mégarde** *adv* inadvertently.
mégère (me:'ʒɛr) *nf* shrew.
mégot (me:'go) *nm sl* fag-end, stub (of a cigarette).
meilleur (mɛ'jœr) *adj* better. **le meilleur** best. ~*adv* better.
mélancolie (mɛlɑ̃kɔ'li:) *nf* melancholy, gloom.
mélanger (mɛlɑ̃'ʒe:) *vt* mix, mingle, blend. **mélange** *nm* **1** mixture, blend. **2** jumble. **3** miscellany.
mélasse (mɛ'las) *nf* treacle.

mêler (me:'le:) *vt* **1** mix. **2** tangle. **3** involve. **4** shuffle. **mêlée** *nf* fray, scuffle.

mélèze (me:'lɛz) *nm* larch.

mélodie (me:lɔ'di:) *nf* melody, tune.

mélodrame (me:lɔ'dram) *nm* melodrama. **mélodramatique** *adj* melodramatic.

melon (mə'lɔ̃) *nm* **1** melon. **2** bowler hat.

membrane (mɑ̃'bran) *nf* **1** membrane. **2** web.

membre (mɑ̃br) *nm* **1** member. **2** limb.

même (mɛm) *adj* **1** same. **2** very. **3** self. *pron* same thing. *adv* even. **de même** in the same way. **tout de même** all the same.

mémento (me:mɛ̃'to) *nm* **1** note, memento. **2** notebook.

mémoire[1] (me:'mwar) *nf* **1** memory. **2** recollection.

mémoire[2] (me:'mwar) *nm* **1** statement. **2** bill, account. **3** thesis. **4** *pl* memoirs.

mémorable (me:mɔ'rabl) *adj* **1** memorable. **2** eventful.

mémorandum (me:mɔrɑ̃'dɔm) *nm* **1** memorandum. **2** notebook.

menacer (məna'se:) *vt* threaten. **menace** *nf* threat, menace.

ménager (me:na'ʒe:) *vt* **1** save. **2** be sparing. **3** manage. **4** arrange. **ménage** *nm* **1** housekeeping. **2** household. **3** married couple. **faire le ménage** do the housework. **ménagement** *nm* **1** consideration. **2** tact. **3** care. **ménager, -ère** (mena'ʒe:, -'ʒɛr) *adj* **1** domestic. **2** thrifty. *nf* housewife.

mendier (mɑ̃dje:) *vi* beg. *vt* beg for. **mendiant** *nm* beggar.

mener (mə'ne:) *vt* **1** lead. **2** conduct. **3** drive. **4** manage. **menée** *nf* intrigue, plot. **meneur** *nm* **1** leader. **2** ringleader.

ménestrel (me:nɛ'strɛl) *nm* minstrel.

ménopause (me:nɔ'poz) *nf* menopause.

menottes (mə'nɔt) *nf pl* handcuffs.

mensonge (mɑ̃'sɔ̃ʒ) *nm* lie, falsehood. **petit mensonge** fib.

menstruel, -elle (mɑ̃stry'ɛl) *adj* menstrual.

mensuel, -elle (mɑ̃'syɛl) *adj* monthly.

mensurer (mɑ̃sy're:) *vt* measure. **mensuration** (mɑ̃syra'sjɔ̃) *nf* measurement.

mental, -aux (mɑ̃'tal, -'to) *adj* mental. **mentalité** *nf* mentality.

menthe (mɑ̃t) *nf* mint. **menthe anglaise** or **poivrée** peppermint.

menthol (mɛ̃'tɔl) *nm* menthol.

mention (mɑ̃'sjɔ̃) *nf* **1** mention. **2** (on a letter) reference. **faire mention de** refer to.

mentionner (mɑ̃sjɔ'ne:) *vt* mention.

mentir* (mɑ̃'ti:r) *vi* lie, tell lies. **menteur, -euse** (mɑ̃'tœr, -'tœz) *nm,f* liar. *adj* **1** false. **2** deceptive.

menton (mɑ̃'tɔ̃) *nm* chin.

menu (mə'ny) *adj* **1** small, fine. **2** slender, slight. **3** petty. *adv* small, finely. *nm cul* menu.

menuisier (mənɥi:'zje:) *nm* carpenter, joiner. **menuiserie** *nf* woodwork, carpentry.

se méprendre (me:'prɑ̃dr) *vr* make a mistake.

mépris (me:'pri:) *nm* scorn, contempt.

méprise (me:'pri:z) *nf* mistake, error.

mépriser (me:pri:'ze:) *vt* despise, scorn.

mer (mɛr) *nf* sea. **en/sur mer** at sea/afloat.

mercantile (mɛrkɑ̃'ti:l) *adj* commercial.

mercenaire (mɛrsə'nɛr) *adj* mercenary. *nm* mercenary.

merci (mɛr'si:) *nf* mercy. *nm* thanks. *adv* **1** thank you. **2** no thank you. **merci bien** thank you very much.

mercier, -ière (mɛr'sje:, -'sjɛr) *nm,f* haberdasher. **mercerie** *nf* haberdashery.

mercredi (mɛrkrə'di:) *nm* Wednesday. **mercredi des cendres** Ash Wednesday.

mercure (mɛr'kyr) *nm* mercury.

mère (mɛr) *nf* **1** mother. **2** *zool* dam. **3** source. **mère nourricière** fostermother. **mère supérieure** mother superior.

méridien (me:ri:'djɛ̃) *nm* meridian. **méridienne** *nf* **1** meridian line. **2** *inf* siesta.

méridional, -aux (me:ri:djɔ'nal, -'no) *adj* southern.

meringue (mə'rɛ̃g) *nf* meringue.

mériter (me:ri:'te:) *vt* **1** deserve, merit. **2** earn, gain. **mérite** *nm* **1** merit, credit. **2** worth. **3** talent.

merlan (mɛr'lɑ̃) *nm* whiting.

merle (mɛrl) *nm* blackbird.

merveille (mɛr'vɛj) *nf* marvel, wonder. **à merveille** excellently. **merveilleux, -euse** (mɛrvɛ'jœ, -'jœz) *adj* marvellous, wonderful.

mes (mɛ) *poss adj* see **mon.**

mésaventure (me:zavɑ̃'tyr) *nf* mishap.

mesquin (mɛ'skɛ̃) *adj* **1** shabby. **2** petty. **3** mean.

message (mɛ'saʒ) *nm* message. **messager, -ère** (mɛsa'ʒe:, -'ʒɛr) *nm, f* messenger. **messagerie** (mɛsaʒ'ri:) *nf* **1** parcels office. **2** goods department.

messe (mɛs) *nf rel* mass.

messeoir* (me:'swar) *vi* be unbecoming.

mesurer (məzy're:) *vt* **1** measure. **2** calculate. **3** distribute. **mesure** *nf* **1** measure. **2** measurement. **3** gauge. **4** limit. **5** size. **6** *mus* time. **à**

mesure que (in proportion) as. **dépasser la mesure** overstep the mark. **fait sur mesure** made to measure. **mesuré** *adj* **1** measured. **2** moderate, restrained.

mésuser (me:zy'ze:) *vt* **mésuser de 1** misuse. **2** abuse. **mésusage** *nm* misuse.

métabolisme (mɛtabɔ'li:sm) *nm* metabolism.

métal, -aux (me:'tal, -'to) *nm* metal.

métallurgie (me:tallyr'ʒi:) *nf* metallurgy.

métamorphose (mɛtamɔr'foz) *nf* metamorphosis.

métaphore (mɛta'fɔr) *nf* metaphor. **métaphorique** *adj* metaphorical.

métaphysique (mɛtafi:'zi:k) *adj* metaphysical. *nf* metaphysics.

météore (me:te:'ɔr) *nm* meteor.

météorologie (me:te:ɔrɔlɔ'ʒi:) *nf* meteorology. **météorologique** *adj* meteorological. **météorologiste** *nm* meteorologist.

méthane (mɛ'tan) *nm* methane.

méthode (me:'tɔd) *nf* **1** method, system. **2** way. **méthodique** *adj* methodical, systematic. **méthodologie** *nf* methodology.

méthodiste (me:tɔ'di:st) *adj,n* Methodist.

méticuleux, -euse (me:ti:ky'lœ, -'lœz) *adj* meticulous, particular.

métier (me:'tje:) *nm* trade, profession, craft. **métier à tisser** loom

métis, -isse (me:'ti:, -'ti:s) *adj,n* half-breed, hybrid, mongrel.

métrage (mɛ'traʒ) *nm* **1** measure. **2** length.

mètre (mɛtr) *nm* **1** metre. **2** rule. **mètre à ruban** tape-measure. **métrique** *adj* metric.

métro (me:'tro) *nm* underground, tube.

métropole (me:trɔ'pɔl) *nf* **1** metropolis. **2** capital. **métropolitain** (me:trɔpɔli:'tɛ̃) *adj* metropolitan.

mets (mɛ) *nm* **1** dish (of food). **2** food.

mettre* (mɛtr) *vt* **1** put, set, place. **2** wear. **3** contribute. **mettre les pieds dans le plat** put one's foot in it. **se mettre** *vr* **1** go. **2** dress. **se mettre à** begin, set about. **metteur en scène** *nm* **1** *Th* producer. **2** director (of films).

meubler (mœ'ble:) *vt* **1** furnish. **2** stock. **meuble** *adj* movable. *nm* **1** piece of furniture. **2** *pl* furniture.

meugler (mœ'gle:) *vi* low, moo. **meuglement** *nm* lowing.

meule (mœl) *nf* **1** millstone. **2** stack, pile. **meule de foin** haystack.

meurs (mœr) *v* see **mourir.**

meurtre (mœrtr) *nm* murder. **meurtrier, -ière** (mœrtri:'e:, -'ɛr) *nm, f* murderer, murderess. *adj* deadly, murderous.

meurtrir (mœr'tri:r) *vt* bruise. **meurtrissure** *nf* bruise.

meute (mœt) *nf* **1** *zool* pack. **2** *inf* mob.

Mexique (mɛk'si:k) *nm* Mexico. **mexicain** *adj,n* Mexican.

mi (mi:) *pref* **1** half. **2** mid. **3** semi. **à mi-chemin** *adv* halfway. **à mi-corps** *adv* to the waist. **à mi-côte** *adv* halfway up or down. **mi-matin** *nf* midmorning. **mi-temps** *nf* half-time, interval. **à mi-temps** part-time.

miaou (mjau) *nm* miaow.

miauler (mjo'le:) *vi* miaow.

miche (mi:ʃ) *nf* round loaf.

micro (mi:'kro) *nm inf* microphone, mike.

microbe (mi:'krɔb) *nm* **1** microbe. **2** germ.

microphone (mi:krɔ'fɔn) *nm* microphone.

microscope (mi:krɔ'skɔp) *nm* microscope. **microscopique** *adj* microscopic.

microsillon (mi:krosi:'jɔ̃) *nm* long-playing record.

midi (mi:'di:) *nm* **1** midday, noon. **2** south. **3** *cap* South of France.

mie (mi:) *nf* crumb.

miel (mjɛl) *nm* honey

mien, mienne (mjɛ̃, mjɛn) *poss pron 1st pers s* **le mien, la mienne 1** mine. **2** my own.

miette (mjɛt) *nf* soft part of bread.

mieux (mjœ) *adj,adv* better. **le mieux** best.

mièvre (mjɛvr) *adj* **1** affected. **2** delicate.

mignard (mi:'ɲar) *adj* affected, mincing.

mignon, -onne (mi:'ɲɔ̃, -'ɲɔn) *adj* **1** dainty, delicate. **2** sweet. *nm,f* darling.

migraine (mi:'grɛn) *nf* migraine.

mijoter (mi:ʒɔ'te:) *vi,vt* **1** stew. **2** simmer. *vt* plot.

mil (mi:l) *adj* thousand.

milieu, -eux (mi:'ljœ) *nm* **1** middle, midst. **2** environment. **3** class, circle. **4** mean. **au (beau) milieu de** (right) in the middle of. **juste milieu** happy medium.

militaire (mi:li:'tɛr) *adj* military. *nm* soldier. **militant** *adj* militant.

mille[1] (mi:l) *adj,nm* thousand. **millénium** *nm* millennium. **millième** *adj* thousandth. **millier** *nm* about a thousand.

mille[2] (mi:l) *nm* mile. **mille-feuille** *nf* pastry filled with cream and jam. **mille-pattes** *nm invar* centipede.

milligramme (mi:lli:'gram) *nm* milligram.

millilitre (mi:lli:'li:tr) *nm* millilitre.

millimètre (mi:lli:'mɛtr) *nm* millimetre.

million (mi:'ljɔ̃) *nm* million. **milliard** *nm* **1** one thousand million. **2** *US* billion. **millionième** *adj* millionth.

mimer (mi:'me:) *vt* **1** mimic. **2** imitate. **mime** *nm* **1** mime. **2** mimic.

minable (mi:'nabl) *adj* **1** shabby. **2** miserable, wretched.

minauder (mi:no'de:) *vi* smirk.

mince (mɛ̃s) *adj* **1** thin. **2** slim. **3** scanty. *interj* blast! **minceur** *nf* thinness.

mine[1] (mi:n) *nf* **1** appearance, look. **2** expression. **avoir bonne/mauvaise mine** look well/ill.

mine[2] (mi:n) *nf* **1** mine, pit. **2** *mil* mine. **3** lead (of a pencil). **mine de houille** coalmine. **mine d'or** goldmine.

minérai (mi:n'rɛ) *nm* ore.

minéral, -aux (mi:ne:'ral, -'ro) *adj,nm* mineral.

mineur[1] (mi:'nœr) *adj* **1** minor. **2** under age. *nm law* minor, infant.

mineur[2] (mi:'nœr) *nm* miner.

miniature (mi:nja'tyr) *nf* miniature.

minimiser (mi:ni:mi'ze:) *vt* minimize. **minime** *adj* **1** very small. **2** trivial. **minimum** *adj,nm* minimum.

ministère (mi:ni:'stɛr) *nm* **1** ministry. **2** agency. **3** government office, department. **ministre** *nm* **1** *pol* minister, secretary. **2** clergyman. **premier ministre** prime minister.

minorité (mi:nɔri:'te:) *nf* minority.

Minorque (mi:'nɔrk) *nf* Minorca. **minorquin** *adj,n* Minorcan.

minuit (mi:'nɥi:) *nm* midnight.

minuscule (mi:ni:'skyl) *adj* **1** minute, tiny. **2** small.

minute (mi:'nyt) *nf* **1** minute. **2** moment. **3** record, draft.

minutieux, -euse (mi:ny'sjœ, -'sjœz) *adj* **1** scrupulous, extremely careful. **2** thorough, detailed.

mioche (mjɔʃ) *nm,f inf* brat, small child.

miracle (mi:'rakl) *nm* miracle. **miraculeux, -euse** (mi:raky'lœ, -'lœz) *adj* miraculous, marvellous.

mirage (mi:'raʒ) *nm* mirage.

mirer (mi:'re:) *vt* aim at. **se mirer** *vr* look at oneself.

miroir (mi:r'war) *nm* mirror.

miroiter (mi:rwa'te:) *vi* **1** gleam, shimmer. **2** flash.

mis (mi:) *v* see **mettre.**

miscellanées (mi:sɛlla'ne:) *nf pl* miscellany.

mise (mi:z) *nf* **1** placing. **2** dress, appearance. **3** *game* stake. **4** bid. **être de mise** be the done thing. **mise en scène** *Th* production.

miser (mi:'ze:) *vt* **1** *game* stake. **2** bid.

misérable (mi:zɛ'rabl) *adj* **1** miserable, unhappy. **2** wretched, destitute. *nm* wretch, rogue.

misère (mi:'zɛr) *nf* **1** misery, distress. **2** poverty. **3** *inf* trifle. **crier misère** plead poverty. **dans la misère** poverty-stricken. **faire des misères à 1** tease. **2** worry.

miséricorde (mi:ze:ri:'kɔrd) *nf* mercy.

mission (mi:'sjɔ̃) *nf* mission. **missionnaire** *nm* missionary.

mistral (mi:'stral) *nm* cold north wind.

mitaine (mi:'tɛn) *nf* mitten.

mite (mi:t) *nf* moth. **mité** *adj* moth-eaten. **miteux, -euse** (mi:'tœ, -'tœz) *adj* shabby.

mitoyen, -enne (mi:twa'jɛ̃, -'jɛn) *adj* intermediate, middle, dividing.

mitrailleuse (mi:tra'jœz) *nf* machine-gun. **mitraillette** *nf* submachine gun.

mitre (mi:tr) *nf* **1** mitre. **2** chimneypot.

mixte (mi:kst) *adj* mixed.

mobile (mɔ'bi:l) *adj* **1** mobile, movable. **2** changeable. **3** detachable. *nm* **1** motive. **2** mobile. **mobilier, -ière** (mɔbi:'lje:, -'ljɛr) *adj* **1** personal. **2** movable. *nm* furniture.

mobiliser (mɔbi:li:'ze:) *vt* mobilize.

moche (mɔʃ) *adj sl* **1** ugly. **2** rotten, lousy.

mode[1] (mɔd) *nf* **1** fashion. **2** manner. **à la mode** in fashion.

mode[2] (mɔd) *nm* **1** *gram* mood. **2** method, mode. **mode d'emploi** directions for use.

modeler (mɔd'le:) *vt* model, mould. **modèle** *nm* **1** model. **2** pattern.

modérer (mɔde:'re:) *vt* moderate, restrain. **se modérer** *vr* control oneself. **modéré** *adj* **1** moderate. **2** temperate.

moderne (mɔ'dɛrn) *adj* modern.

moderniser (mɔdɛrni:'ze:) *vt* modernize.

modeste (mɔ'dɛst) *adj* unassuming, humble.

modifier (mɔdi:'fje:) *vt* **1** modify. **2** alter.

modique (mɔ'di:k) *adj* **1** modest, slender. **2** moderate, reasonable.

module (mɔ'dyl) *nm* **1** module. **2** unit.

moduler (mɔdy'le:) *vt* modulate.

moelle (mwal) *nf* **1** *anat* marrow. **2** pith. **moelleux, -euse** (mwa'lœ, -'lœz) *adj* **1** mellow. **2** soft.

mœurs (mœrs) *nf pl* **1** customs. **2** manners. **3** morals.

mohair (mɔ'ɛr) *nm* mohair.

moi (mwa) *pron 1st pers m,f s* **1** I. **2** me. *nm*

ego, self. **moi-même** *pron 1st pers m,f s* myself.

moindre (mwɛ̃dr) *adj* **1** less, minor. **2** least.

moine (mwan) *nm* monk, friar.

moineau, -aux (mwa'no) *nm* sparrow.

moins (mwɛ̃) *adv* **1** less. **2** under. **3** least. **à moins de** unless, barring. **à moins que** unless. **au moins** at least, not less than. **de moins en moins** less and less. **du moins** at least. **moins de** less than. ~*prep* minus.

mois (mwa) *nm* month.

moisir (mwa'zi:r) *vi* go mouldy. **moisissure** *nf* mildew, mould.

moisson (mwa'sɔ̃) *nf* **1** harvest. **2** crop.

moissonner (mwasɔ'ne:) *vt* harvest, reap. **moissonneuse-batteuse** *nf, pl* **moissonneuses-batteuses** combine harvester.

moite (mwat) *adj* moist, clammy.

moitié (mwa'tje:) *nf* half. **à moitié** half. **moitié moitié** half-and-half.

molécule (mɔle:'kyl) *nf* molecule.

molester (mɔlɛ'ste:) *vt* molest.

mollasse (mɔ'las) *adj* **1** flabby. **2** apathetic, lazy.

mollesse (mɔ'lɛs) *nf* **1** softness. **2** slackness. **3** apathy.

mollet, -ette (mɔ'lɛ, -'lɛt) *adj* soft. *nm anat* calf.

mollir (mɔ'li:r) *vt* slacken. *vi* **1** soften. **2** abate. **3** slacken.

mollusque (mɔ'lysk) *nm* mollusc.

môme (mom) *nm,f sl* kid.

moment (mɔ'mɑ̃) *nm* **1** moment. **2** time, instant. **3** occasion.

momie (mɔ'mi:) *nf* mummy (dead body).

mon, ma, mes (mɔ̃, ma, mɛ) *poss adj 1st pers s* my.

monarque (mɔ'nark) *nm* monarch.

monastère (mɔna'stɛr) *nm* monastery. **monastique** *adj* monastic.

monceau, -aux (mɔ̃'so) *nm* pile, heap.

monde (mɔ̃d) *nm* **1** world. **2** people. **3** society. **tout le monde** everybody, everyone. **mondain** *adj* **1** worldly. **2** mundane. **mondial, -aux** (mɔ̃'djal, -'djo) *adj* worldwide.

monétaire (mɔne:'tɛr) *adj* monetary.

moniteur, -trice (mɔni:'tœr, -'tri:s) *nm,f* **1** monitor. **2** instructor. **3** *sport* coach.

monnayer (mɔnɛ'je:) *vt* **1** coin, mint. **2** *inf* cash in on. **monnaie** *nf* **1** money. **2** currency. **3** change. **petite monnaie** small change.

monogamie (mɔnɔga'mi:) *nf* monogamy.

monologue (mɔnɔ'lɔg) *nm* monologue.

monopole (mɔnɔ'pɔl) *nm* monopoly.

monopoliser (mɔnɔpɔli:'ze:) *vt* monopolize.

monosyllabe (mɔnɔsi:l'lab) *adj* monosyllabic. *nm* monosyllable.

monotone (mɔnɔ'tɔn) *adj* monotonous.

monseigneur (mɔ̃sɛ'ɲœr) *nm* **1** *pl* **nosseigneurs** His or Your Royal Highness, His Grace. **2** *pl* **messeigneurs** Your Grace, His or Your Lordship.

monsieur (mə'sjœ) *nm, pl* **messieurs** **1** sir. **2** master. **3** gentleman. **4** *cap* Mr.

monstre (mɔ̃str) *nm* monster. *adj* huge, enormous. **monstrueux, -euse** (mɔ̃stry'œ, -'œz) *adj* **1** monstrous. **2** huge. **3** scandalous.

mont (mɔ̃) *nm* mount, mountain.

montagne (mɔ̃'taɲ) *nf* mountain. **montagnard** *adj* mountain, highland. *nm* highlander, person living in the mountains. **montagneux, -euse** (mɔ̃ta'ɲœ, -'ɲœz) *adj* mountainous.

monter (mɔ̃'te:) *vi (aux usu* être) **1** climb. **2** go up. **3** ride. **4** mount. **5** rise. *vt* **1** climb, ascend. **2** carry or take up. **3** erect. **4** *Th* produce. **monter à cheval** ride. **montant** *adj* **1** rising. **2** uphill. *nm* **1** upright. **2** rise. **3** (total) amount. **monté** *adj* **1** mounted. **2** equipped. **montée** *nf* **1** rise. **2** step. **monture** *nf* **1** mount (a horse, etc.). **2** setting. **3** frame. **4** handle.

montrer (mɔ̃'tre:) *vt* **1** show. **2** display. **3** point out. **4** teach. **se montrer** *vr* appear. **montre** *nf* **1** watch. **2** show, display. **montre-bracelet** *nf, pl* **montres-bracelets** wristwatch.

monument (mɔny'mɑ̃) *nm* monument.

se moquer (mɔ'ke:) *vr* **se moquer de** mock, make fun of. **moquerie** *nf* mockery, ridicule.

moral, -aux (mɔ'ral, -'ro) *adj* **1** moral. **2** ethical. **3** mental. **morale** *nf* **1** morals. **2** ethics. **3** moral. **moralité** *nf* **1** morality. **2** moral.

moraliser (mɔrali:'ze:) *vi* moralize. *vt* lecture.

morbide (mɔr'bi:d) *adj* morbid.

morceau, -aux (mɔr'so) *nm* **1** piece. **2** bit, scrap.

mordre (mɔrdr) *vt* **1** bite. **2** nip. **mordant** *adj* **1** biting, caustic. **2** sarcastic. **mordu** *adj sl* mad, keen.

morgue (mɔrg) *nf* **1** mortuary. **2** pride.

moribond (mɔri:'bɔ̃) *adj* dying.

morne (mɔrn) *adj* **1** gloomy. **2** dreary, dull.

morose (mɔ'roz) *adj* morose, sullen.

morphine (mɔr'fi:n) *nf* morphine.

mors (mɔr) *nm* bit (of a bridle).

morse[1] (mɔrs) *nm* walrus.

morse[2] (mɔrs) *nm* morse code.

morsure (mɔr'syr) *nf* bite.

mort[1] (mɔr) *v* see **mourir.** *adj* **1** dead. **2** stagnant. **3** neutral. **mort-né** *adj, pl* **mort-nés** stillborn. **morte-saison** *nf, pl* **mortes-saisons** off-season.
mort[2] (mɔr) *nf* death.
mortalité (mɔrtali:'te:) *nf* **1** mortality. **2** death rate.
mortel, -elle (mɔr'tɛl) *adj* **1** mortal. **2** fatal. **3** deadly.
mortier (mɔr'tje:) *nm* mortar.
mortifier (mɔrti:'fje:) *vt* **1** mortify, hurt. **2** *cul* hang.
mortuaire (mɔr'tɥɛr) *adj* mortuary.
morue (mɔ'ry) *nf* cod.
morveux, -euse (mɔr'vœ, -'vœz) *nm,f* brat, child.
mosaïque (mɔza'i:k) *adj,nf* mosaic.
mosquée (mɔ'ske:) *nf* mosque.
mot (mo) *nm* **1** word. **2** saying. **3** hint. **gros mot** swearword. **mots croisés** crossword.
motel (mɔ'tɛl) *nm* motel.
moteur, -trice (mɔ'tœr, -'tri:s) *adj* motive, driving. *nm* motor, engine. **moteur-fusée** *nm, pl* **moteurs-fusées** rocket.
motif (mɔ'ti:f) *nm* **1** motive, reason. **2** pattern. **3** *mus* theme.
motion (mɔ'sjɔ̃) *nf* motion, proposal.
motiver (mɔti:'ve:) *vt* **1** give the reason for. **2** warrant.
motocyclette (mɔtɔsi:'klɛt) *nf* motorcycle.
motte (mɔt) *nf* **1** mound. **2** lump. **3** *cul* pat, roll.
mou, mol, molle (mu:, mɔl, mɔl) *adj* **1** soft. **2** weak. **3** slack. **4** limp. *nm* **1** slack. **2** *zool* lungs.
mouche (mu:ʃ) *nf* **1** fly. **2** spot, stain.
moucher (mu:'ʃe:) *vt* **1** wipe (the nose of). **2** snuff. **se moucher** *vr* blow one's nose.
moucheter (mu:ʃ'te:) *vt* speckle, spot. **moucheture** *nf* speckle, fleck, spot.
mouchoir (mu:'ʃwar) *nm* handkerchief.
moudre* (mu:dr) *vt* grind.
moue (mu:) *nf* pout. **faire la moue** pout, sulk.
mouette (mwɛt) *nf* gull.
moufette (mu:'fɛt) *nf* skunk.
moufle (mu:fl) *nf* mitten.
mouiller (mu:'je:) *vt* **1** dampen, moisten. **2** anchor. **se mouiller** *vr* get wet.
moule[1] (mu:l) *nm* mould.
moule[2] (mu:l) *nf* mussel.
mouler (mu:'le:) *vt* **1** cast. **2** mould.
moulin (mu:'lɛ̃) *nm* mill. **moulin à eau** watermill. **moulin à poivre** peppermill. **moulin à vent** windmill. **moulinet** *nm sport* reel.
moulu (mu:'ly) *v* see **moudre.** *adj* ground.
mourir* (mu:'ri:r) *vi (aux* être) die. **se mourir** *vr* **1** be dying. **2** die out.
mousse[1] (mu:s) *nf* **1** moss. **2** foam, froth. **3** lather. **4** mousse.
mousse[2] (mu:s) *nm* cabin boy.
mousseline (mu:s'li:n) *nf* muslin.
mousser (mu:'se:) *vi* **1** froth, foam. **2** lather. **3** sparkle.
mousson (mu:'sɔ̃) *nf* monsoon.
moustache (mu:'staʃ) *nf* **1** moustache. **2** *zool* whiskers.
moustique (mu:'sti:k) *nm* mosquito.
moutarde (mu:'tard) *nf* mustard.
mouton (mu:'tɔ̃) *nm* **1** sheep. **2** mutton.
mouvoir* (mu:'vwar) *vt* **1** move. **2** drive. **3** prompt, activate. **se mouvoir** *vr* move. **mouvant** *adj* **1** moving. **2** mobile. **3** fickle. **mouvement** *nm* **1** movement. **2** change. **3** impulse. **4** emotion. **mouvementé** *adj* **1** lively. **2** thrilling.
moyen[1], **-enne** (mwa'jɛ̃, -'jɛn) *adj* **1** middle. **2** average. **3** medium. **moyen âge** Middle Ages. ~*nf* average.
moyen[2] (mwa'jɛ̃) *nm* **1** means. **2** way. **3** *pl* ability.
moyennant (mwajɛ'nɑ̃) *prep* for, at (a price). **moyennant que** on condition that.
Moyen Orient *nm* Middle East.
moyeu, -eux (mwa'jœ) *nm* hub.
muer (mɥe:) *vi* **1** moult. **2** (of the voice) break.
muet, -ette (mɥɛ, mɥɛt) *adj* **1** dumb, mute. **2** silent.
mufle (myfl) *nm* **1** muzzle. **2** *sl* mug, face. **3** *sl* swine.
muge (myʒ) *nm* mullet.
mugir (my'ʒi:r) *vi* **1** moo. **2** bellow. **3** roar.
muguet (my'gɛ) *nm* lily-of-the-valley.
mule[1] (myl) *nf* mule.
mule[2] (myl) *nf* slipper.
multiplier (mylti:pli:'e:) *vi,vt* multiply. **multiple** *adj* multiple, manifold. *nm* multiple.
multitude (mylti:'tyd) *nf* multitude, crowd.
municipal, -aux (myni:si:'pal; -'po) *adj* municipal. **municipalité** *nf* **1** municipality. **2** town hall. **3** town council.
munir (my'ni:r) *vt* **munir de 1** provide, supply. **2** equip. **munitions** *nf pl* **1** ammunition. **2** supplies.
mur (myr) *nm* wall.
mûr (myr) *adj* **1** ripe. **2** mature. **3** mellow.
mural, -aux (my'ral, -'ro) *adj* mural.

mûre (myr) *nf* mulberry. **mûre sauvage** blackberry. **mûrier** *nm* mulberry tree or bush.
mûrir (my'ri:r) *vi,vt* **1** ripen. **2** mature.
murmurer (myrmy're:) *vi* **1** murmur. **2** grumble. *vt* whisper. **murmure** *nm* murmur.
musc (mysk) *nm* musk.
muscade (my'skad) *nf* nutmeg.
muscle (myskl) *nm* muscle. **musclé** *adj* muscular.
museau, -aux (my'zo) *nm* muzzle, snout.
musée (my'ze:) *nm* museum. **musée de peinture** or **beaux arts** art gallery.
museler (my'zle:) *vt* muzzle. **muselière** *nf* muzzle.
muser (my'ze:) *vi* dawdle, loiter.
muséum (myze:'ɔm) *nm* natural history museum.
musique (my'zi:k) *nf* **1** music. **2** *mil* band. **musique de chambre** chamber music. **musical, -aux** (myzi'kal, -'ko) *adj* musical. **musicien, -ienne** (myzi:'sjɛ̃, -'sjɛn) *nm,f* musician. *adj* musical.
musulman (myzyl'mɑ̃) *adj,n* Muslim.
mutiler (myti:'le:) *vt* **1** maim. **2** mutilate, deface. **mutilé** *adj* maimed, disabled.
mutin (my'tɛ̃) *adj* insubordinate, disobedient.
se mutiner (myti:'ne:) *vr* mutiny, revolt. **mutinerie** *nf* mutiny, rebellion.
mutisme (my'ti:sm) *nm* dumbness.
mutuel, -elle (my'tɥɛl) *adj* mutual.
myope (mjɔp) *adj* short-sighted. **myopie** *nf* short-sightedness.
myrrhe (myr) *nf* myrrh.
myrte (mi:rt) *nm* myrtle.
myrtille (mi:r'ti:j) *nf* bilberry.
mystère (mi:'stɛr) *nm* mystery. **mystérieux, -euse** (mi:ste:'rjœ, -'rjœz) *adj* mysterious.
mystifier (mi:sti:'fje:) *vt* **1** hoax, fool. **2** mystify.
mystique (mi:'sti:k) *adj,n* mystic. *nf* mystique.
mythe (mi:t) *nm* myth, legend.
mythologie (mi:tɔlɔ'ʒi:) *nf* mythology. **mythologique** *adj* mythological.

N

nabot (na'bo) *nm* dwarf, midget.
nacré (na'kre:) *adj* pearly.
nager (na'ʒe:) *vi* **1** swim. **2** float. **3** row. **nager debout** tread water. **nage** *nf* **1** rowing. **2** swimming. **3** stroke. **nageoire** *nf* fin.
naguère (na'gɛr) *adv* not long ago.
naïf, -ïve (na'i:f, -'i:v) *adj* **1** naive, simple. **2** innocent.
nain (nɛ̃) *adj,n* dwarf.
naissance (nɛ'sɑ̃s) *nf* **1** birth. **2** descent. **3** source.
naître* (nɛtr) *vi (aux* être) **1** be born. **2** originate, rise. **faire naître** provoke, arouse.
nappe (nap) *nf* **1** tablecloth. **2** cloth. **3** cover. **4** sheet.
naquis (na'ki:) *v* see **naître.**
narcotique (narkɔ'ti:k) *adj,nm* narcotic.
narine (na'ri:n) *nf* nostril.
narquois (nar'kwa) *adj* sneering, mocking.
narrer (na're:) *vt* narrate, relate. **narratif, -ive** (narra'ti:f, -'ti:v) *adj* narrative. **narration** *nf* **1** narration. **2** narrative.
nasal, -aux (na'zal, -'zo) *adj* nasal. **naseau, -aux** (na'zo) *nm zool* nostril.
natal (na'tal) *adj* native (country, town, etc.). **natalité** *nf* birthrate.
natation (nata'sjɔ̃) *nf* swimming.
natif, -ive (na'ti:f, -'ti:v) *adj* **1** native. **2** natural.
nation (na'sjɔ̃) *nf* nation. **national, -aux** (nasjɔ'nal, -'no) *adj* national. **nationalité** *nf* nationality.
nationaliser (nasjɔnali:'ze:) *vt* nationalize.
nativité (nati:vi:'te:) *nf* nativity.
natter (na'te:) *vt* plait. **natte** *nf* **1** mat. **2** plait.
naturaliser (natyrali:'ze:) *vt* naturalize.
nature (na'tyr) *nf* **1** nature. **2** character. **3** temperament. **4** kind. **nature morte** still life. ~*adj invar* plain, natural. **naturaliste** *nm,f* naturalist.
naturel, -elle (naty'rɛl) *adj* **1** natural. **2** unaffected. **3** illegitimate. *nm* disposition.
naufrage (no'fraʒ) *nm* shipwreck.
nauséabond (noze:a'bɔ̃) *adj* **1** nauseating. **2** foul. **nausée** *nf* nausea.
nautique (no'ti:k) *adj* nautical.
naval (na'val) *adj* naval, nautical.
navet (na'vɛ) *nm* **1** turnip. **2** *inf* rubbish.
naviguer (navi:'ge:) *vi* **1** sail. **2** navigate. **navigateur** *nm* navigator.
navire (na'vi:r) *nm* ship, vessel.
navrer (na'vre:) *vt* grieve. **navré** *adj* sad, distressed, sorry.
ne, n' (nə) *adv* not.
né (ne:) *v* see **naître.** *adj* born.
néanmoins (ne:ɑ̃'mwɛ̃) *adv* nevertheless, yet.
néant (ne:'ɑ̃) *nm* nought, nothing.
nébuleux, -euse (ne:by'lœ, -'lœz) *adj* **1** nebulous. **2** cloudy. **3** vague, obscure.
nécessité (ne:sɛsi:'te:) *nf* **1** necessity. **2** need,

want. **nécessaire** *adj* 1 necessary. 2 essential.

nécrologie (ne:krɔlɔ'ʒi) *nf* obituary notice, deaths column.

néerlandais (ne:ɛrlɑ̃'dɛ) *adj* Dutch. *nm* Dutchman.

nef (nɛf) *nf* nave. **nef latérale** aisle.

néfaste (ne:'fast) *adj* 1 baneful. 2 evil.

nèfle (nɛfl) *nf* medlar. **néflier** *nm* medlar tree.

négatif, -ive (ne:ga'ti:f, -'ti:v) *adj* negative. *nm phot* negative. *nf* negative, refusal.

négliger (ne:gli:'ʒe:) *vt* 1 neglect. 2 disregard. **négligé** *adj* 1 neglected. 2 careless. **négligence** *nf* 1 carelessness. 2 neglect. **négligent** *adj* negligent, careless.

négocier (ne:gɔ'sje:) *vt* negotiate. **négoce** *nm* trade. **négociant** *nm* merchant. **négociateur** *nm* negotiator. **négotiation** *nf* 1 negotiation. 2 transaction.

nègre, négresse (nɛgr, ne:'grɛs) *nm,f* Negro, Negress. **parler petit nègre** speak pidgin French. ~*adj* Negro.

neiger (ne:'ʒe:) *v imp* snow. **neige** (nɛʒ) *nf* snow.

nénuphar (ne:ny'far) *nm* waterlily.

néon (ne:'ɔ̃) *nm* neon.

néo-Zélandais (ne:oze:lɑ̃'dɛ) *adj* New Zealand. *nm* New Zealander.

nerf (nɛrf) *nm* 1 nerve. 2 energy. 3 sinew. **nerveux, -euse** (nɛr'vœ, -'vœz) *adj* 1 *med* nervous. 2 vigorous. 3 excitable, hysterical. **nervosité** (nɛrvozi:'te:) *nf* nerves, irritability.

net, nette (nɛt) *adj* 1 clean. 2 clear. 3 distinct. 4 net. *adv* 1 plainly. 2 clearly. 3 outright. **netteté** *nf* 1 cleanness. 2 clearness.

nettoyer (nɛtwa'je:) *vt* 1 clean. 2 scour. 3 wipe. 4 clear out. **nettoyer à fond** spring-clean. **nettoyer à sec** dry-clean. **nettoiement** *nm also* **nettoyage** 1 cleaning. 2 clearing.

neuf[1] (nœf) *adj,nm* nine. **neuvième** *adj* ninth.

neuf[2], **neuve** (nœf, nœv) *adj* new. **à neuf** again.

neutraliser (nœtrali:'ze:) *vt* neutralize.

neutralité (nœtrali:'te:) *nf* neutrality.

neutre (nœtr) *adj* 1 neutral. 2 neuter. *nm* neuter.

neveu, -eux (nə'vœ) *nm* nephew.

névrose (ne:'vroz) *nf* neurosis. **névrosé** *adj,n* neurotic.

nez (ne:) *nm* 1 nose. 2 scent.

ni (ni:) *conj* nor, or. **ni...ni** neither...nor.

niais (ni:'ɛ) *adj* 1 simple, foolish. 2 inane. *nm* fool.

nicher (ni:'ʃe:) *vi* 1 nest. 2 lodge. **se nicher** *vr* nestle. **niche** *nf* 1 recess. 2 kennel.

nickel (ni:'kɛl) *nm* nickel.

nicotine (ni:kɔ'ti:n) *nf* nicotine.

nid (ni:) *nm* nest.

nièce (njɛs) *nf* niece.

nier (ni:'e:) *vt* deny.

nigaud (ni:'go) *adj* simple, stupid. *nm* idiot.

Nigeria (ni:ʒɛ'rja) *nf* Nigeria. **nigérien, -ienne** (ni:ʒɛ'rjɛ̃, -'rjɛn) *adj,n* Nigerian.

Nil (ni:l) *nm* Nile.

nimbe (nɛ̃b) *nm* halo.

nitouche (ni:'tu:ʃ) **sainte nitouche** *nf inf* little hypocrite.

niveau, -aux (ni:'vo) *nm* 1 level. 2 standard.

niveler (ni:v'le:) *vt* level.

noble (nɔbl) *adj* 1 noble. 2 lofty. *nm* nobleman. **noblesse** *nf* nobility.

noce (nɔs) *nf* wedding.

nocif, -ive (nɔ'si:f, -'si:v) *adj* harmful.

nocturne (nɔk'tyrn) *adj* nocturnal.

Noël (nɔ'ɛl) *nm* Christmas.

nœud (nœ) *nm* 1 knot. 2 bow. 3 bond. **nœud coulant** noose.

noir (nwar) *adj* 1 black. 2 dark. 3 gloomy. 4 dirty. 5 base. *nm* 1 black. 2 *cap* Black. *nf mus* crotchet. **noirceur** *nf* 1 blackness. 2 darkness. 3 baseness. **noircir** *vi* turn black, darken. *vt* blacken.

noisette (nwa'zɛt) *nf* hazelnut. *adj invar* hazel. **noisetier** *nm* hazel tree.

noix (nwa) *nf* 1 nut. 2 walnut. **noix de coco** coconut.

nom (nɔ̃) *nm* 1 name. 2 noun. **nom de famille** surname. **nom de jeune fille** maiden name.

nomade (nɔ'mad) *adj* nomadic. *nm* nomad.

nombre (nɔ̃br) *nm* number. **nombreux, -euse** (nɔ̃'brœ, -'brœz) *adj* 1 numerous. 2 many.

nombril (nɔ̃'bri:) *nm* navel.

nominal, -aux (nɔmi:'nal, -'no) *adj* nominal.

nommer (nɔ'me:) *vt* 1 call, name. 2 mention by name. 3 appoint.

non (nɔ̃) *adv* 1 no. 2 non-. *nm invar* no. **non-être** *nm* nonentity.

nonne (nɔn) *nf* nun.

nonobstant (nɔnɔp'stɑ̃) *prep* notwithstanding. *adv* nevertheless.

nord (nɔr) *nm* north. *adj invar* north, northern. **au nord** in the north. **du nord** 1 northern. 2 northerly. **vers le nord** northward, northwards. **nord-est** *nm* north-east. *adj invar* north-east. **du nord-est** 1 north-eastern. 2 north-easterly. **nord-ouest** *nm* north-west. *adj*

invar north-west. **du nord-ouest 1** north-western. **2** north-westerly.
normal, -aux (nɔr'mal, -'mo) *adj* **1** normal. **2** standard. **école normale** *nf* teacher-training college.
Normandie (nɔrmã'di:) *nf* Normandy. **normand** *adj, n* Norman.
norme (nɔrm) *nf* norm, standard.
Norvège (nɔr'vɛʒ) *nf* Norway. **norvégien, -ienne** (nɔrve:'ʒjɛ̃, -'ʒjɛn) *adj,n* Norwegian. *nm* Norwegian (language).
nos (no) *poss adj* see **notre.**
nostalgie (nɔstal'ʒi:) *nf* nostalgia, homesickness. **nostalgique** (nɔstal'ʒi:k) *adj* homesick.
notable (nɔ'tabl) *adj* **1** notable, considerable. **2** eminent.
notaire (nɔ'tɛr) *nm* lawyer.
notamment (nɔta'mã) *adv* in particular.
notation (nɔta'sjɔ̃) *nf* notation.
noter (nɔ'te:) *vt* **1** note, observe. **2** make a note of. **note** *nf* **1** note. **2** notice. **3** *educ* mark. **4** bill. **5** *mus* note.
notice (nɔ'ti:s) *nf* **1** account. **2** *lit* review. **3** directions (for use).
notifier (nɔti:'fje:) *vt* notify, inform.
notion (nɔ'sjɔ̃) *nf* notion, idea.
notoire (nɔ'twar) *adj* **1** well-known. **2** evident. **notoriété** *nf* **1** notoriety. **2** repute. **notoriété publique** common knowledge.
notre, nos (nɔtr, no) *poss adj 1st pers pl* our.
nôtre (notr) *poss pron 1st pers pl* **le** *or* **la nôtre 1** ours. **2** our own.
nouer (nu:'e:) *vt* **1** tie. **2** knot. **3** establish. **noueux, -euse** (nu:'œ, -'œz) *adj* **1** knotted. **2** gnarled.
nouilles (nu:j) *nf pl* noodles.
nounou (nu:'nu:) *nf inf* nanny.
nounours (nu:'nu:rs) *nm inf* teddy.
nourrice (nu:'ri:s) *nf* nurse. **nourricier, -ière** (nu:ri:'sje:, -'sjɛr) *adj* **1** nutritious. **2** foster.
nourrir (nu:'ri:r) *vt* **1** nourish, feed. **2** rear. **3** foster, harbour. **nourrisson, -onne** (nu:ri:'sɔ̃, -'sɔn) *nm,f* fosterchild. **nourriture** *nf* **1** food. **2** board, keep.
nous (nu) *pron 1st pers m,f pl* **1** we. **2** us. **3** to us. **4** ourselves. **5** each other. **nous-mêmes** *pron 1st pers m,f pl* ourselves.
nouveau, -el, -elle, -aux (nu:'vo, -'vɛl, -'vɛl, -'vo) *adj* **1** new. **2** recent. **3** fresh. **4** another. **à/de nouveau** afresh/again. **nouvel an** *nm* New Year. **nouveauté** *nf* **1** novelty. **2** change.
nouvelle[1] (nu:'vɛl) *adj* see **nouveau.**
nouvelle[2] (nu:'vɛl) *nf* **1** piece of news. **2** news. **3** short story.
Nouvelle-Zélande (ze:'lãd) *nf* New Zealand.
novateur, -trice (nɔva'tœr, -'tri:s) *nm,f* innovator. *adj* innovating.
novembre (nɔ'vãbr) *nm* November.
novice (nɔ'vi:s) *nm,f* novice.
noyau, -aux (nwa'jo) *nm* **1** stone (of fruit). **2** kernel. **3** nucleus.
noyer[1] (nwa'je:) *vt* **1** drown. **2** swamp. **3** flood. **noyade** *nf* drowning.
noyer[2] (nwa'je:) *nm* walnut tree.
nu (ny) *adj* **1** naked, nude. **2** bare. **3** plain. *nm* nude. **à nu** bare, exposed.
nuage (nɥaʒ) *nm* **1** cloud. **2** haze. **nuageux, -euse** (nɥa'ʒœ, -ʒœz) *adj* cloudy.
nuancer (nɥã'se:) *vt* **1** blend. **2** vary. **nuance** *nf* **1** shade. **2** nuance.
nucléaire (nykle:'ɛr) *adj* nuclear.
nuée (nɥe:) *nf* **1** cloud. **2** swarm. **3** host, crowd.
nuire* (nɥi:r) *vt* **nuire à 1** harm. **2** prejudice. **nuisible** *adj* harmful.
nuit (nɥi:) *nf* **1** night. **2** darkness. **bonne nuit!** good night! **cette nuit 1** tonight. **2** last night.
nul, nulle (nyl) *adj* **1** no, not one. **2** worthless. **nul et non avenu** null and void. **nulle part** nowhere.
numéral, -aux (nymɛ'ral, -'ro) *adj, nm* numeral.
numéro (nyme:'ro) *nm* **1** number. **2** *lit* issue.
numéroter (nyme:rɔ'te:) *vt* number.
nuptial, -aux (nyp'sjal, -'sjo) *adj* bridal.
nutrition (nytri:'sjɔ̃) *nf* nutrition.
nylon (ni:'lɔ̃) *nm* nylon.
nymphe (nɛ̃f) *nf* nymph.

O

oasis (oa'zi:s) *nf* oasis.
obéir (ɔbe:'i:r) *vi* **obéir à 1** obey. **2** yield. **obéissance** *nf* **1** obedience. **2** submission. **obéissant** *adj* **1** obedient. **2** docile. **3** dutiful.
obèse (ɔ'bɛz) *adj* obese, fat.
obituaire (ɔbi:'tɥɛr) *nm* obituary.
objecter (ɔbʒɛk'te:) *vt* object.
objectif (ɔbʒɛk'ti:f) *adj* objective. *nm* **1** aim, objective. **2** target. **3** lens.
objection (ɔbʒɛk'sjɔ̃) *nf* objection.
objet (ɔb'ʒɛ) *nm* **1** object, thing. **2** aim, purpose. **3** *gram* object. **objet d'art** work of art. **objets trouvés** *pl* lost property.
obliger (ɔbli:'ʒe:) *vt* **1** oblige, compel. **2** help. **obligation** *nf* **1** obligation, duty. **2** *law*

agreement. **3** *comm* bond. **obligatoire** *adj* obligatory.

oblique (ɔ'bli:k) *adj* **1** oblique. **2** underhand.

oblitérer (ɔbli:te:'re:) *vt* **1** obliterate. **2** cancel.

oblong, -ongue (ɔb'lɔ̃, -'lɔ̃g) *adj* oblong.

obscène (ɔp'sɛn) *adj* obscene.

obscur (ɔp'skyr) *adj* **1** dark, gloomy. **2** obscure. **3** humble. **obscurité** *nf* obscurity.

obscurcir (ɔpskyr'si:r) *vt* **1** darken. **2** dim. **3** obscure.

obséder (ɔpse:'de:) *vt* **1** haunt. **2** obsess. **3** worry.

obsèques (ɔp'sɛk) *nf pl* funeral.

observer (ɔpsɛr've:) *vt* **1** observe, comply with. **2** watch. **3** note. **s'observer** *vr* be careful. **observance** *nf* observance. **observateur, -trice** (ɔpsɛrva'tœr, -'tri:s) *nm,f* observer. *adj* observant. **observatoire** *nm* observatory.

obsession (ɔpsɛ'sjɔ̃) *nf* obsession.

obstacle (ɔp'stakl) *nm* obstacle, hindrance.

s'obstiner (sɔpsti:'ne:) *vr* **s'obstiner à** persist in. **obstination** *nf* obstinacy. **obstiné** *adj* obstinate, stubborn.

obstruer (ɔpstry'e:) *vt* obstruct, block.

obtenir* (ɔptə'ni:r) *vt* **1** obtain, get. **2** achieve.

obtus (ɔp'ty) *adj* **1** obtuse. **2** blunt. **3** dull.

obus (ɔ'bys) *nm mil* shell.

occasion (ɔka'zjɔ̃) *nf* **1** opportunity. **2** bargain. **3** cause. **d'occasion** second-hand. **occasionnel, -elle** (ɔkazjɔ'nɛl) *adj* occasional.

occident (ɔksi:'dɑ̃) *nm* **1** west. **2** Occident. **occidental, -aux** (ɔksi:dɑ̃'tal, -'to) *adj* western.

occulte (ɔ'kylt) *adj* **1** occult. **2** hidden.

occuper (ɔky'pe:) *vt* **1** occupy. **2** live in. **3** take up. **s'occuper de** *vr* attend to. **occupant** *nm* occupant. **occupation** *nf* **1** occupation. **2** employment. **3** profession. **occupé** *adj* **1** busy. **2** engaged, taken.

océan (ɔse:'ɑ̃) *nm* ocean.

ocre (ɔkr) *nf* ochre.

octane (ɔk'tan) *nm* octane.

octave (ɔk'tav) *nf* octave.

octobre (ɔk'tɔbr) *nm* October.

octogone (ɔktɔ'gɔn) *nm* octagon. **octogonal, -aux** (ɔktɔgɔ'nal, -'no) *adj* octagonal.

octroi (ɔk'trwa) *nm* concession.

octroyer (ɔktrwa'je:) *vt* grant, concede.

oculiste (ɔky'li:st) *nm* oculist. **oculaire** *adj* ocular. **témoin oculaire** *nm* eyewitness.

ode (ɔd) *nf* ode.

odeur (o'dœr) *nf* **1** smell, odour. **2** scent.

odorant *adj* fragrant. **odorat** *nm* sense of smell.

odieux, -euse (ɔ'djœ, -'djœz) *adj* **1** odious. **2** hateful.

œil (œj) *nm, pl* **yeux 1** eye. **2** sight. **3** look. **œil poché** black eye. **œillade** *nf* **1** glance. **2** leer. **œillet** *nm* **1** eyelet. **2** *bot* pink, carnation.

œstre (ɛstr) *nm* oestrus.

œuf (œf) *nm* **1** egg. **2** *pl* roe, spawn. **œuf à la coque** boiled egg. **œuf dur/poché** hard-boiled/poached egg. **œufs brouillés** scrambled eggs. **œuf sur le plat** fried egg.

œuvre (œvr) *nf* **1** work. **2** act. *nm* works (of an artist, etc.).

offenser (ɔfɑ̃'se:) *vt* **1** offend. **2** shock. **offensant** *adj* offensive. **offense** *nf* **1** offence. **2** sin. **offensif, -ive** (ɔfɑ̃'si:f, -'si:v) *adj* offensive. *nf mil* offensive.

offert (ɔ'fɛr) *v* see **offrir.**

office (ɔ'fi:s) *nm* **1** office, duty. **2** help. **3** *rel* service. **4** office. *nf* pantry. **officiel, -elle** (ɔfi:'sjɛl) *adj* **1** official. **2** formal. *nm* official. **officier** *nm* officer.

officieux, -euse (ɔfi:'sjœ, -'sjœz) *adj* **1** officious. **2** unofficial.

officine (ɔfi:'si:n) *nf* dispensary.

offrir* (ɔ'fri:r) *vt* **1** offer. **2** give. **3** bid. **4** afford, present. **offrande** *nf* **1** offering. **2** present. **offre** *nf* **1** offer. **2** proposal. **3** tender. **4** bid.

offusquer (ɔfy'ske:) *vt* **1** veil, obscure. **2** shock.

ogre, ogresse (ɔgr, ɔ'grɛs) *nm,f* ogre, ogress.

oie (wa) *nf* goose.

oignon (ɔ'ɲɔ̃) *nm* **1** onion. **2** *bot* bulb.

oindre* (wɛ̃dr) *vt* **1** oil. **2** anoint.

oiseau, -aux (wa'zo) *nm* bird.

oisif, -ive (wa'zi:f, -'zi:v) *adj* **1** idle. **2** lazy.

oison (wa'zɔ̃) *nm* gosling.

olive (ɔ'li:v) *nf* olive. **olivier** *nm* olive tree.

ombrage (ɔ̃'braʒ) *nm* **1** shade. **2** offence.

ombre (ɔ̃br) *nf* **1** shadow. **2** shade. **3** darkness.

omettre* (ɔ'mɛtr) *vt* **1** omit, fail. **2** leave out. **omission** *nf* omission.

omnibus (ɔmni:'bys) *nm* **1** omnibus. **2** slow train. *adj invar* general, blanket.

omnipotent (ɔmni:pɔ'tɑ̃) *adj* omnipotent, almighty.

omoplate (ɔmɔ'plat) *nf* shoulder-blade.

on (ɔ̃) *indef pron s* one, people, they, we, you. **on demande** wanted. **on dit** it is said. **on y va?** shall we go?

once (ɔ̃s) *nf* ounce.

oncle (ɔ̃kl) *nm* uncle.

onde (ɔ̃d) *nf* wave. **grande onde** long wave. **onde courte** short wave. **ondée** *nf* heavy shower.

on-dit *nm invar* rumour.

ondoyer (ɔ̃dwa'je:) *vi* wave, ripple.

onduler (ɔ̃dy'le:) *vi* ripple. *vt* wave, curl.

ongle (ɔ̃gl) *nm* **1** fingernail. **2** claw. **3** talon.

onguent (ɔ̃'gɑ̃) *nm* ointment.

ont (ɔ̃) *v* see **avoir.**

onze (ɔ̃z) *adj,nm* eleven. **onzième** *adj* eleventh.

opale (ɔ'pal) *nf* opal.

opaque (ɔ'pak) *adj* opaque.

opéra (ɔpɛ'ra) *nm* **1** opera. **2** opera house.

opérer (ɔpe:re:) *vt* **1** operate. **2** work. **3** effect. **se faire opérer** undergo an operation. **opération** *nf* **1** operation. **2** process. **3** transaction.

s'opiniâtrer (sɔpi:njɑ'tre:) *vr* be stubborn, obstinate. **opiniâtre** *adj* **1** stubborn, obstinate. **2** headstrong. **3** persistent.

opinion (ɔpi:'njɔ̃) *nf* opinion, view.

opportun (ɔpɔr'tœ̃) *adj* **1** opportune, favourable. **2** expedient. **opportunité** *nf* **1** timeliness. **2** favourable occasion. **3** expediency.

opposer (ɔpo'ze:) *vt* **1** oppose. **2** place opposite. **opposer à** compare with. **s'opposer à** *vr* oppose, be opposed to. **opposé** *adj* **1** opposed. **2** opposite. **3** contrary. **opposite** *nm* opposite, contrary. **opposition** *nf* **1** opposition. **2** contrast.

opprimer (ɔpri:'me:) *vt* oppress.

opprobre (ɔ'prɔbr) *nm* shame, disgrace.

opter (ɔp'te:) *vi* opt, choose. **option** *nf* option, choice.

opticien (ɔpti:'sjɛ̃) *nm* optician.

optimisme (ɔpti:'mi:sm) *nm* optimism. **optimiste** *adj* optimistic. *nm,f* optimist.

optique (ɔp'ti:k) *adj* **1** optical. **2** optic. *nf* optics.

opulent (ɔpy'lɑ̃) *adj* **1** opulent. **2** abundant.

or[1] (ɔr) *nm* gold. **d'or** *adj* golden.

or[2] (ɔr) *conj* **1** now. **2** well. **3** but.

orage (ɔ'raʒ) *nm* thunderstorm. **orageux, -euse** (ɔra'ʒœ, -'ʒœz) *adj* stormy.

oraison (ɔrɛ'zɔ̃) *nf* **1** oration. **2** prayer.

oral, -aux (ɔ'ral, -'ro) *adj* **1** oral. **2** verbal. *nm* oral examination.

orange (ɔ'rɑ̃ʒ) *nf* **1** *bot* orange. **2** orange (colour). *adj invar* orange. **oranger** *nm* orange tree.

orateur (ɔra'tœr) *nm* orator.

orbite (ɔr'bi:t) *nf* orbit.

Orcades (ɔr'kad) *nf pl* Orkneys.

orchestrer (ɔrkɛ'stre:) *vt* orchestrate. **orchestre** *nm* orchestra.

orchidée (ɔrki:'de:) *nf* orchid.

ordinaire (ɔrdi:'nɛr) *adj* **1** ordinary. **2** usual. **3** common. *nm* habit.

ordinal, -aux (ɔrdi:'nal, -'no) *adj* ordinal.

ordinateur (ɔrdi:na'tœr) *nm* computer.

ordonner (ɔrdɔ'ne:) *vt* **1** arrange. **2** order. **3** ordain. **ordonnance** *nf* **1** arrangement. **2** order. **3** prescription. **ordonné** *adj* **1** orderly. **2** tidy.

ordre (ɔrdr) *nm* **1** order. **2** discipline. **3** sequence. **4** class, category. **5** *pl* holy orders. **ordre du jour** agenda.

ordure (ɔr'dyr) *nf* **1** filth, dirt. **2** filthiness. **3** *pl* refuse.

oreille (ɔ'rɛj) *nf* ear. **oreiller** *nm* pillow. **oreillons** *nm pl* mumps.

ores (ɔr) *adv* **d'ores et déjà** here and now.

orfèvre (ɔr'fɛvr) *nm* goldsmith.

organe (ɔr'gan) *nm* **1** organ. **2** voice. **3** agency, means. **4** mouthpiece.

organique (ɔrga'ni:k) *adj* organic.

organiser (ɔrgani:'ze:) *vt* **1** organize. **2** arrange. **3** set up. **organisation** *nf* **1** organization. **2** structure. **3** system. **organisé** *adj* **1** organic. **2** organized. **organisme** *nm* organism.

orge (ɔrʒ) *nf* barley.

orgie (ɔr'zi:) *nf* orgy.

orgue (ɔrg) *nm mus* organ.

orgueil (ɔr'gœj) *nm* pride. **orgueilleux, -euse** (ɔrgœ'jœ, -'jœz) *adj* **1** proud. **2** arrogant.

orient (ɔ'rjɑ̃) *nm* **1** Orient. **2** east. **oriental, -aux** (ɔrjɑ̃'tal, -'to) *adj* **1** eastern. **2** oriental.

orienter (ɔrjɑ̃'te:) *vt* **1** orientate. **2** direct.

origan (ɔri:'gɑ̃) *nm* oregano.

originaire (ɔri:ʒi:'nɛr) *adj* **1** native. **2** original.

origine (ɔri:'ʒi:n) *nf* **1** origin. **2** beginning. **3** source. **4** descent. **à l'origine** originally. **original, -aux** (ɔri:zi:'nal, -'no) *adj* **1** original. **2** novel. **3** eccentric. **originalité** *nf* **1** originality. **2** eccentricty.

orme (ɔrm) *nm* elm tree.

ornement (ɔrnə'mɑ̃) *nm* ornament. **ornemental, -aux** (ɔrnəmɑ̃tal, -'to) *adj* ornamental.

orner (ɔr'ne:) *vt* **1** decorate. **2** adorn.

ornière (ɔr'njɛr) *nf* **1** rut. **2** groove.

ornithologie (ɔrni:tɔlɔ'ʒi:) *nf* ornithology.

orphelin (ɔrfə'lɛ̃) *nm* orphan. **orphelinat** *nm* ophanage.

orteil (ɔr'tɛj) *nm* toe.

orthodoxe (ɔrtɔ'dɔks) *adj* orthodox, conventional.

orthographe (ɔrtɔ'graf) *nf* orthography, spelling.

orthopédique (ɔrtɔpe:ˈdi:k) *adj* orthopaedic.
ortie (ɔrˈti:) *nf* nettle.
os (ɔs) *nm* bone. **os à moelle** marrowbone.
osciller (ɔsi:ˈje:) *vi* **1** sway. **2** waver. **3** fluctuate.
oser (oˈze:) *vt* dare. **osé** *adj* bold.
ossature (ɔssaˈtyr) *nf* **1** skeleton. **2** framework.
ostentation (ɔstɑ̃taˈsjɔ̃) *nf* ostentation, show.
ostraciser (ɔstrasi:ˈze:) *vt* ostracize.
otage (ɔˈtaʒ) *nm* hostage.
ôter (oˈte:) *vt* **1** remove. **2** take away.
ou (u:) *conj* **1** or. **2** either. **3** else. **ou bien** or else. **ou...ou** either...or.
où (u:) *adv* **1** where. **2** when.
ouater (waˈte:) *vt* pad, wad. **ouate** *nf* **1** cotton-wool. **2** wadding.
oubli (u:ˈbli:) *nm* **1** forgetfulness. **2** oblivion. **3** oversight. **oublie** *nf* wafer.
oublier (u:bli:ˈe:) *vt* **1** forget. **2** overlook. **oublieux, -euse** (u:bli:ˈœ, -ˈœz) *adj* **1** forgetful. **2** oblivious.
ouest (wɛst) *nm* west. *adj invar* west, western. **à l'ouest** westward. **de l'ouest** westerly. **vers l'ouest** westward, westwards.
oui (wi:) *adv,nm invar* yes.
ouïr* (wi:r) *vt* hear. **ouï-dire** *nm invar* hearsay. **ouïe** *nf* **1** sense of hearing. **2** *pl zool* gill.
ouragan (u:raˈgɑ̃) *nm* hurricane.
ourler (u:rˈle:) *vt* hem. **ourlet** *nm* hem.
ours (u:rs) *nm* bear. **ours blanc** polar bear.
outil (u:ˈti:) *nm* **1** tool. **2** implement. **outillage** *nm* **1** set of tools. **2** equipment. **3** *tech* plant.
outiller (u:ti:ˈje:) *vt* equip with tools.
outrager (u:traˈʒe:) *vt* **1** insult. **2** outrage. **outrage** *nm* **1** outrage. **2** insult, affront.
outrance (u:ˈtrɑ̃s) *nf* excess.
outre (u:tr) *prep* **1** beyond. **2** in addition to. *adv* further. **en outre** **1** besides. **2** moreover. **outre-mer** *adv* abroad, overseas.
outrer (u:ˈtre:) *vt* **1** carry to excess, overdo. **2** exaggerate. **3** exasperate.
ouvert (u:ˈvɛr) *v* see **ouvrir.** *adj* **1** open. **2** frank. **3** exposed. **ouverture** *nf* **1** opening. **2** hole. **3** overture.
ouvrable (u:ˈvrabl) **jour ouvrable** *nm* weekday.
ouvrage (u:ˈvraʒ) *nm* **1** work. **2** piece of work. **3** workmanship.
ouvrier, -ière (u:vri:ˈe:, -ˈɛr) *adj* **1** working. **2** labour, industrial. *nm* **1** worker. **2** workman.
ouvrir* (u:ˈvri:r) *vt* **1** open. **2** turn on. **3** cut through. **4** begin, start. *vi* open. **ouvre-boîte** *nm invar* tin-opener. **ouvre-bouteille** *nm, pl* **ouvre-bouteilles** bottle-opener.
ovaire (ɔˈvɛr) *nm* ovary.
ovale (ɔˈval) *adj,nm* oval.
ovation (ɔvaˈsjɔ̃) *nf* ovation.
oxygène (oksi:ˈʒɛn) *nm* oxygen.

P

pacage (paˈkaʒ) *nm* **1** pasture. **2** grazing.
pacifier (pasi:ˈfje:) *vt* **1** pacify. **2** appease. **se pacifier** *vr* calm down. **pacifisme** *nm* pacifism.
pacifique (pasi:ˈfi:k) *adj* peaceful. **(Océan) Pacifique** *nm* Pacific (Ocean).
pacte (pakt) *nm* pact, agreement.
pagaie (paˈgɛ) *nf* paddle (for a canoe).
pagaïe (paˈgaj) *nf* disorder, confusion, chaos.
pagayer (pagɛˈje:) *vi,vt* paddle (a boat).
page[1] (paʒ) *nf* page.
page[2] (paʒ) *nm* page (boy).
pagode (paˈgɔd) *nf* **1** pagoda. **2** temple.
paie (pɛ) *nf* **1** pay. **2** wages. **paiement** *nm* payment.
païen, -ïenne (paˈjɛ̃, -jɛn) *adj,n* pagan.
paillasson (pajaˈsɔ̃) *nm* **1** mat. **2** doormat.
paille (pɑj) *nf* **1** straw. **2** flaw. **paillette** *nf* **1** grain. **2** flake. **3** flaw.
pain (pɛ̃) *nm* **1** bread. **2** loaf. **pain d'épice** gingerbread. **pain de savon** cake of soap. **pain grillé** toast. **petit pain** roll.
pair[1] (pɛr) *adj* **1** equal. **2** even.
pair[2] (pɛr) *nm* peer. **pairesse** *nf* peeress.
paire (pɛr) *nf* pair, brace.
paisible (pɛˈzi:bl) *adj* **1** peaceful, calm. **2** quiet.
paître* (pɛtr) *vt* **1** graze (cattle). **2** feed upon. *vi* **1** graze. **2** feed.
paix (pɛ) *nf* **1** peace. **2** quiet.
Pakistan (paki:ˈstɑ̃) *nm* Pakistan. **pakistanais** *adj,n* Pakistani.
palace (paˈlas) *nm* luxury hotel.
palais[1] (paˈlɛ) *nm* palace. **palais de justice** law courts.
palais[2] (paˈlɛ) *nm* **1** palate. **2** sense of taste.
pâle (pɑl) *adj* **1** pale. **2** faint. **pâleur** *nf* paleness.
palefrenier (palfrəˈnje:) *nm* groom.
Palestine (palɛˈsti:n) *nf* Palestine. **palestinien, -ienne** *adj,n* Palestinian.
palette (paˈlɛt) *nf* **1** bat. **2** blade (of an oar). **3** palette.
palier (palˈje:) *nm* (of stairs) landing.
pâlir (pɑˈli:r) *vi* **1** turn or grow pale. **2** grow dim. **3** fade. *vt* make pale.

palissader (pali:sa'de:) *vt* enclose, fence in. **palissade** *nf* fence.

palmarès (palma'rɛs) *nm* prize list.

palme (palm) *nf* **1** palm (branch). **2** victory. **palmier** *nm* palm tree.

palombe (pa'lɔ̃b) *nf* woodpigeon.

palourde (pa'lu:rd) *nf* clam.

palper (pal'pe:) *vt* **1** feel. **2** finger.

palpiter (palpi:'te:) *vi* **1** quiver. **2** throb.

paludisme (paly'di:sm) *nm* malaria.

pâmer (pɑ'me:) *vi* faint. **se pâmer de** *vr* be overcome with.

pamphlet (pɑ̃'flɛ) *nm* pamphlet.

pamplemousse (pɑ̃plə'mu:s) *nm* grapefruit.

pan (pɑ̃) *nm* **1** flap (of a garment). **2** section. **3** side.

panache (pa'naʃ) *nm* **1** plume. **2** tuft. **avoir du panache** have style or dash. **panaché** *adj* **1** mixed. **2** plumed. *nm* shandy.

panais (pa'nɛ) *nm* parsnip.

pancarte (pɑ̃'kart) *nf* **1** placard. **2** poster, bill.

pancréas (pɑ̃kre:'ɑs) *nm* pancreas.

panda (pɑ̃'da) *nm* panda.

panier (pa'nje:) *nm* basket. **gros panier** hamper.

panique (pa'ni:k) *adj,nf* panic.

panne (pan) *nf* **1** breakdown. **2** failure.

panneau, -aux (pa'no) *nm* **1** snare. **2** trap. **3** panel. **4** board. **panneau-réclame** *nm, pl* **panneaux-réclames** hoarding.

panorama (panɔra'ma) *nm* panorama. **panoramique** *adj* panoramic.

panse (pɑ̃s) *nf* **1** *inf* belly. **2** paunch.

panser (pɑ̃'se:) *vt* **1** *med* dress. **2** groom (a horse). **pansement** *nm med* dressing.

pantalon (pɑ̃ta'lɔ̃) *nm* trousers.

panteler (pɑ̃t'le:) *vi* **1** pant. **2** gasp.

panthère (pɑ̃'tɛr) *nf* panther.

pantomime (pɑ̃tɔ'mi:m) *nf* **1** pantomime. **2** mime.

pantoufle (pɑ̃'tu:fl) *nf* slipper.

paon (pɑ̃) *nm* peacock.

papa (pa'pa) *nm inf* dad.

pape (pap) *nm* pope. **papal, -aux** (pa'pal, -'po) *adj* papal. **papauté** *nf* papacy.

papeterie (pap'tri:) *nf* **1** stationer's shop. **2** stationery. **papetier** *nm* stationer.

papier (pa'pje:) *nm* **1** paper. **2** document. **papier à écrire** notepaper. **papier buvard** blotting paper. **papier de verre** sandpaper. **papier ministre** foolscap. **papier teint** wallpaper.

papillon (papi:'jɔ̃) *nm* **1** butterfly. **2** moth. **3** leaflet. **4** ticket.

paquebot (pak'bo) *nm* **1** liner. **2** steamer.

pâquerette (pɑk'rɛt) *nf* daisy.

Pâques (pak) *nf pl* Easter. **pâque** *nf* Passover.

paquet (pa'kɛ) *nm* **1** parcel. **2** packet. **3** bundle.

paqueter (pak'te:) *vt* parcel up.

par (par) *prep* **1** by. **2** through. **3** in. **4** out of, for the sake of. **par-ci par-là** here and there. **par-dessous** *prep,adv* under, underneath. **par-dessus** *prep,adv* over. **par ici/là** this/that way.

parabole (para'bɔl) *nf* parable.

parachuter (paraʃy'te:) *vt* parachute. **parachute** *nm* parachute. **parachutiste** *nm* **1** parachutist. **2** paratrooper.

parade (pa'rad) *nf* **1** parade. **2** show, display.

paradigme (para'di:gm) *nm* paradigm.

paradis (para'di:) *nm* **1** paradise. **2** *inf Th* gallery.

paradoxe (para'dɔks) *nm* paradox. **paradoxal, -aux** (paradɔk'sal, -'so) *adj* paradoxical.

paraffine (para'fi:n) *nf* paraffin.

parages (pa'raʒ) *nm pl* district, area.

paragraphe (para'graf) *nm* paragraph.

paraître (pa'rɛtr) *vi* **1** appear. **2** show, be visible. **3** seem. **4** be published. *v imp* seem. **faire paraître** publish.

parallèle (paral'lɛl) *adj* parallel.

paralyser (parali:'ze:) *vt* paralyse. **paralysie** *nf* paralysis.

paraphraser (parafrɑ'ze:) *vt* paraphrase. **paraphrase** *nf* paraphrase.

parapluie (para'plɥi:) *nm* umbrella.

parasite (para'zi:t) *nm* **1** parasite. **2** *pl tech* interference. *adj* parasitic.

parc (park) *nm* **1** park. **2** pen. **parc de stationnement** car park.

parcelle (par'sɛl) *nf* **1** particle. **2** plot, patch.

parce que (pars kə) *conj* because.

parchemin (parʃə'mɛ̃) *nm* parchment.

parcomètre (parkɔ'mɛtr) *nm* parking meter.

parcourir* (parku:'ri:r) *vt* **1** travel through. **2** wander. **3** glance through.

parcours (par'ku:r) *nm* **1** distance. **2** route. **3** course.

pardessus (pardə'sy) *nm* overcoat.

pardon (par'dɔ̃) *nm* **1** forgiveness. **2** pardon. **pardonner** (pardɔ'ne:) *vt* **1** pardon. **2** forgive. **3** excuse.

pareil, -eille (pa'rɛj) *adj* **1** like, similar. **2** same. **3** such.

parement (par'mã) *nm* **1** ornament. **2** facing. **3** cuff (of a coat, etc.).
parent (pa'rã) *nm* **1** parent. **2** relative.
parenthèse (parã'tɛzʃ *nf* **1** parenthesis. **2** bracket.
parer[1] (pa're:) *vt* **1** decorate. **2** adorn. **3** prepare. **se parer de** *vr* dress oneself in.
parer[2] (pa're:) *vt* **1** ward off. **2** avoid. **pare-boue** *nm invar* mudguard. **pare-brise** *nm invar* windscreen. **pare-choc** *nm invar* bumper.
paresseux, -euse (parɛ'sœ, -'sœz) *adj* lazy.
parfait (par'fɛ) *adj* **1** perfect. **2** complete.
parfois (par'fwa) *adv* sometimes, occasionally.
parfum (par'fœ̃) *nm* **1** perfume. **2** scent. **3** flavour.
parfumer (parfy'me:) *vt* **1** scent, perfume. **2** flavour.
pari (pa'ri:) *nm* bet. **parier** *vt* bet.
Paris (pa'ri:) *nm* Paris. **parisien, -ienne** (pari:-'zjɛ̃, -'zjɛn) *adj,n* Parisian.
parité (pari:'te:) *nf* parity, equality.
parjure (par'ʒyr) *nm* perjury.
parking (par'ki:ɲ) *nm* car park.
parlement (parlə'mã) *nm* parliament.
parler (par'le:) *vi* **1** speak. **2** talk. **tu parles!** you can say that again! ~*nm* speech. **parleur, -euse** ((par'lœr,-'lœz) *nm,f* speaker. **parloir** *nm* parlour.
parmi (par'mi:) *prep* among, amid.
parodie (parɔ'di:) *nf* parody.
paroi (par'wa) *nf* **1** partition. **2** wall. **3** lining.
paroisse (par'was) *nf* parish.
parole (pa'rɔl) *nf* **1** word. **2** remark. **3** parole. **4** speech.
parquet (par'kɛ) *nm* **1** floor. **2** *cap* magistrate.
parrain (pa'rɛ̃) *nm* **1** godfather. **2** patron.
parrainer (parɛ'ne:) *vt* sponsor.
pars (par) *v* see **partir.**
parsemer (parsə'me:) *vt* sprinkle, scatter.
part (par) *nf* **1** share, portion. **2** participation. **3** part. **à part** apart. **autre/nulle/quelque part** elsewhere/nowhere/somewhere. **d'autre part** moreover.
partager (parta'ʒe:) *vt* **1** divide. **2** share. **partage** *nm* **1** division. **2** sharing. **3** share.
partance (par'tãs) *nf* departure. **en partance pour** bound for.
partenaire (partə'nɛr) *nm,f* partner.
parterre (par'tɛr) *nm* **1** flowerbed. **2** *Th* stalls.
parti (par'ti:) *nm* **1** party. **2** side, part. **3** decision. **4** advantage. **parti pris** bias.
partial, -aux (par'sjal, -'sjo) *adj* partial, biased. **partialité** *nf* partiality, bias.
participe (parti:'si:p) *nm* participle. **participe passé** past participle.
participer (parti:si:'pe:) *vi* **participer à 1** participate in. **2** take part in. **participer de** partake of. **participant** *nm* participant. **participation** *nf* **1** participation. **2** interest, share.
particulariser (parti:kylari:'ze:) *vt* specify.
particule (parti:'kyl) *nf* particle.
particulier, -ière (parti:ky'lje:, -'ljɛr) *adj* **1** particular. **2** special. **3** characteristic. **4** private. *nm* private individual.
partie (par'ti:) *nf* **1** part. **2** party. **3** game. **4** client. **partie carrée** foursome. **partie nulle** *sport* draw. **partiel, -elle** (par'sjɛl) *adj* partial, part.
partir* (par'ti:r) *vi* (*aux* être) **1** depart. **2** leave. **3** set off. **4** start. **à partir de** as from.
partisan (parti:'zã) *nm* partisan, supporter.
partout (par'tu:) *adv* everywhere. **partout où** wherever. **un peu partout** all over the place.
paru (pa'ry) *v* see **paraître.**
parure (pa'ryr) *nf* **1** ornament. **2** dress. **3** set (of clothing, etc.).
parvenir* (parvə'ni:r) *vi* (*aux* être) **parvenir à 1** reach. **2** succeed. **parvenu** *nm* self-made man.
pas[1] (pɑ) *nm* **1** pace, stride. **2** step. **3** footstep. **4** doorstep. **5** pass. **à pas de loup** slyly.
pas[2] (pɑ) *adv* not. **ne...pas** not. **pas du tout** not at all.
passage (pɑ'saʒ) *nm* **1** passage. **2** crossing. **3** way. **passage à niveau** level crossing. **passage clouté** pedestrian crossing. **passage interdit** no thoroughfare. **passage souterrain** subway. **passager, -ère** (pɑsa'ʒe:, -'ʒɛr) *adj* **1** migratory. **2** momentary. **3** busy. *nm,f* passenger. **passager clandestin** stowaway.
passer (pɑ'se:) *vi* (*aux* avoir or être) **1** go by or through. **2** pass. **3** call. **4** cease. **5** become. *vt* **1** cross. **2** pass. **3** show. **4** spend. **5** surpass. **6** filter, strain. **en passant** by the way. **passer un examen** sit an exam. **se passer** *vr* **1** happen. **2** decay. **se passer de** do without. **passe** *nf* **1** passing. **2** permit. **3** pass. **passé** *adj,nm* past. *prep* after, beyond.
passeport (pɑs'pɔr) *nm* passport.
passerelle (pɑs'rɛl) *nf* footbridge. **passerelle de service** *naut* gangway.
passe-temps *nm invar* pastime.
passif, -ive (pa'si:f, -'si:v) *adj* passive.
passion (pɑ'sjɔ̃) *nf* passion.

passionner (pɑsjɔ'ne:) *vt* **1** interest greatly. **2** thrill, exite. **se passionner pour** *vr* become very fond of. **passionnant** (pɑsjɔ'nɑ̃) *adj* thrilling. **passionné** *adj* **1** passionate. **2** ardent. *nm* enthusiast.

pastel (pa'stɛl) *nm* **1** crayon. **2** pastel.

pastèque (pa'stɛk) *nf* watermelon.

pasteuriser (pastœri:'ze:) *vt* pasteurize.

pastille (pa'sti:j) *nf* pastille.

pastis (pa'sti:s) *nm* **1** aniseed aperitif. **2** *inf* muddle.

pat (pat) *nm invar* stalemate.

pataud (pa'to) *adj* clumsy.

patauger (pato'ʒe:) *vi* **1** paddle. **2** flounder.

pâte (pɑt) *nf* **1** paste. **2** dough. **3** *pl* pasta. **pâte à modeler** Plasticine *Tdmk*. **pâte dentifrice** toothpaste. **pâte lisse** batter.

pâté (pɑ'te:) *nm* **1** meat paste. **2** blot. **3** block (of houses). **pâté en croûte** pie.

patelin (pat'lɛ̃) *adj* **1** glib. **2** wheedling. *nm inf* place, locality.

patelle (pa'tɛl) *nf* limpet.

patenôtre (pat'notr) *nf* Lord's Prayer.

patent (pa'tɑ̃) *adj* **1** patent. **2** obvious.

patenter (patɑ̃'te:) *vt* license. **patente** *nf* **1** licence. **2** tax.

patère (pa'tɛr) *nf* peg (for coats, etc.).

paterne (pa'tɛrn) *adj* benevolent, kind.

paternel, -elle (patɛr'nɛl) *adj* paternal.

pâteux, -euse (pɑ'tœ, -'tœz) *adj* **1** pasty. **2** thick. **3** dull.

pathétique (pate:'ti:k) *adj* **1** pathetic. **2** touching. *nm* pathos.

pathologie (patɔlɔ'ʒi:) *nf* pathology. **pathologique** *adj* pathological. **pathologiste** *nm,f* pathologist.

patience (pa'sjɑ̃s) *nf* patience. **patiemment** *adv* patiently. **patient** *adj* **1** patient. **2** long-suffering. *nm med* patient.

patin (pa'tɛ̃) *nm* skate. **patin à roulette** roller-skate.

patiner (pati:'ne:) *vi* **1** skate. **2** skid. **patinage** *nm* skating. **patinoire** *nf* skating rink.

pâtir (pɑ'ti:r) *vi* suffer.

pâtisserie (pɑti:s'ri:) *nf* **1** pastry. **2** cake. **3** cake shop.

patois (pa'twa) *nm* **1** dialect. **2** jargon.

patouiller (patu:'je:) *vi* splash, flounder. *vt* **1** finger. **2** meddle with.

patrie (pa'tri:) *nf* fatherland, native country.

patrimoine (patri:'mwan) *nm* heritage.

patriote (patri:'ɔt) *nm,f* patriot. *adj* patriotic.

patriotique *adj* patriotic. **patriotisme** *nm* patriotism.

patron (pa'trɔ̃) *nm* **1** patron. **2** proprietor. **3** patron saint. **4** employer. **5** skipper. **6** *inf* boss. **7** pattern (for a dress). **patronage** *nm* **1** patronage. **2** club. **patronat** *nm* **1** body of employers. **2** management.

patrouiller (patru:'je:) *vi* patrol. **patrouille** *nf* patrol.

patte (pat) *nf* **1** *zool* paw, foot, leg. **2** flap. **patte de derrière** hindleg. **patte de devant** foreleg. **patte de mouche** scrawl.

pâture (pɑ'tyr) *nf* **1** pasture. **2** food.

paume (pom) *nf anat* palm.

paupière (po'pjɛr) *nf* eyelid.

pause (poz) *nf* **1** pause. **2** rest. **pause café** tea-break.

pauvre (povr) *adj* **1** poor. **2** unfortunate. **3** wretched. **pauvreté** *nf* poverty.

se pavaner (pava'ne:) *vr* strut about.

paver (pa've:) *vt* pave. **pavé** *nm* **1** pavement. **2** highway. **3** slab,flagstone.

pavillon (pavi:'jɔ̃) *nm* **1** pavilion. **2** tent. **3** flag.

pavot (pa'vo) *nm* poppy.

payer (pɑ'je:) *vt* pay.

pays (pe:'i:) *nm* **1** land, country. **2** district. **3** nation. **4** home. **pays chauds** *nm pl* tropics. **paysage** *nm* **1** landscape. **2** scenery. **paysan, -anne** (pe:i:'zɑ̃, -'zan) *adj,n* **1** peasant. **2** rustic.

Pays-Bas *nm pl* Netherlands.

péage (pe:'aʒ) *nm* toll.

peau, peaux (po) *nf* **1** *anat* skin. **2** *zool* fur, hide, pelt. **3** peel. **peau de mouton** sheepskin. **peau-rouge** *nm, pl* **peaux-rouges** Red Indian.

pêche[1] (pɛʃ) *nf* peach.

pêche[2] (pɛʃ) *nf* **1** fishing. **2** catch (of fish). **aller à la pêche** go fishing.

pécher (pe:'ʃe:) *vi* sin. **péché** *nm* sin. **pécheur, -eresse** (pe:'ʃœr, pɛʃ'rɛs) *nm,f* **1** sinner. **2** offender. *adj* sinful.

pêcher[1] (pe:'ʃe:) *nm* peach tree.

pêcher[2] (pe:'ʃe:) *vt* fish for. **pêcher à la ligne** angle. **pêcheur** *nm* fisherman.

pédaler (pɛda'le:) *vi* **1** pedal. **2** *inf* cycle. **pédale** *nf* pedal.

pédéraste (pe:dɛ'rast) *nm* homosexual.

pédicure (pe:di:'kyr) *nm,f* chiropodist.

peignant (pɛ'ɲɑ̃) *v* see **peindre.**

peigner (pɛ'ɲe:) *vt* comb. **peigne** *nm* **1** comb. **2** *zool* scallop. **bien/mal peigné** trim/slovenly. **peignoir** *nm* dressing-gown.

peindre* (pɛ̃dr) *vt* **1** paint. **2** depict. **3** describe.

peine (pɛn) *nf* **1** punishment. **2** sorrow. **3** trouble. **4** difficulty. **à peine** hardly, scarcely.
peiner (pɛ'ne:) *vt* **1** grieve. **2** tire. *vi* toil.
peint (pɛ̃) *v* see **peindre.**
peintre (pɛ̃tr) *nm* **1** painter. **2** decorator. **peinture** *nf* **1** painting. **2** picture. **3** paint.
péjoratif, -ive (pe:ʒɔra'ti:f, -'ti:v) *adj* pejorative, disparaging.
pelage (pə'laʒ) *nm* coat, fur (of an animal).
pêle-mêle (pɛl'mɛl) *adv* pell-mell. *nm invar* jumble.
peler (pə'le:) *vi,vt* peel. *vt* skin.
pèlerin (pɛl'rɛ̃) *nm* pilgrim. **pèlerinage** *nm* pilgrimage. **pèlerine** *nf* cloak.
pélican (pe:li:'kɑ̃) *nm* pelican.
pelle (pɛl) *nf* **1** shovel. **2** scoop. **pelle à poussière** dustpan.
pelleter (pɛl'te:) *vt* shovel.
pelletier (pɛl'tje:) *nm* furrier.
pellicule (pɛlli:'kyl) *nf* **1** film, layer. **2** *phot* film. **3** *pl* dandruff.
pelote (plɔt) *nf* **1** ball (of wool). **2** wad. **pelote à épingles** pincushion.
peloton (plɔ'tɔ̃) *nm* **1** ball (of wool). **2** group. **3** squad.
pelotonner (plɔtɔ'ne:) *vt* wind into a ball. **se pelotonner** *vr* **1** curl up. **2** crowd together.
pelouse (plu:z) *nf* lawn.
pelu (pə'ly) *adj* hairy.
pelure (plyr) *nf* **1** peel. **2** rind.
pénal, -aux (pe:'nal, -'no) *adj* penal.
pénaliser (pe:nali:'ze:) *vt* penalize. **pénalité** *nf* penalty.
penaud (pə'no) *adj* shamefaced.
pencher (pɑ̃'ʃe:) *vi* **1** lean. **2** slope. **3** incline. *vt* tilt. **se pencher** *vr* **1** bend. **2** lean. **penchant** *adj* sloping. *nm* **1** slope. **2** tendency. **3** taste.
pendant[1] (pɑ̃'dɑ̃) *adj* **1** hanging. **2** flabby. *nm* **1** pendant. **2** pair, match.
pendant[2] (pɑ̃'dɑ̃) *prep,adv* during. **pendant que** *conj* whilst.
pendiller (pɑ̃di:'je:) *vi* dangle.
pendre (pɑ̃dr) *vt* hang (up). *vi* **1** hang. **2** sag. **se pendre à** *vr* cling to. **pendule** *nm* pendulum.
pêne (pɛn) *nm* bolt, latch.
pénétrer (pe:ne:'tre:) *vi* **1** enter. **2** break into. *vt* **1** penetrate. **2** fathom. **pénétrant** *adj* **1** penetrating. **2** sharp. **3** keen.
pénible (pe:'ni:bl) *adj* **1** hard. **2** laborious. **3** painful. **4** *inf* annoying.
péniche (pe:'ni:ʃ) *nf* barge.
pénicilline (pe:ni:si:'li:n) *nf* penicillin.
péninsule (pe:nɛ̃'syl) *nf* peninsula.
pénis (pe:'ni:s) *nm* penis.
pénitent (pe:ni:'tɑ̃) *adj,n* penitent. **pénitence** *nf* **1** repentance. **2** penance.
penser (pɑ̃'se:) *vi,vt* think. *vt* **1** imagine. **2** believe. **penser à** think about. **penser de** think of, have an opinion of. **penser faire** expect to do. ~*nm* thought. **pensée** *nf* **1** thought. **2** *bot* pansy.
pension (pɑ̃'sjɔ̃) *nf* **1** pension. **2** board and lodging. **3** boarding school. **pension de famille** boarding house. **pensionnat** *nm* boarding school.
pentagone (pɛ̃ta'gɔn) *nm* pentagon. *adj* pentagonal.
pente (pɑ̃t) *nf* **1** slope. **2** gradient.
Pentecôte (pɑ̃t'kot) *nf* **1** Whitsun. **2** Pentecost.
pénurie (pe:ny'ri:) *nf* **1** scarcity. **2** lack. **3** poverty.
pépier (pe:'pje:) *vi* chirp.
pépin (pe:'pɛ̃) *nm* **1** pip. **2** *bot* stone. **3** *inf* hitch. **pepinière** *nf bot* nursery.
pépite (pe:'pi:t) *nf* nugget.
perception (pɛrsɛp'sjɔ̃) *nf* **1** collection. **2** tax-office. **3** perception. **percepteur, -trice** (pɛrsɛp'tœr, -'tri:s) *adj* discerning. *nm* tax-collector. **perceptible (à l'oreille)** *adj* audible. **perceptif, -ive** (pɛrsɛp'ti:f, -'ti:v) *adj* perceptive.
percer (pɛr'se:) *vt* **1** pierce. **2** break through. **3** penetrate. *vi* come through. **perçant** *adj* **1** piercing. **2** sharp. **3** shrill. **perce-neige** *nm invar* snowdrop. **perce-oreille** *nm, pl* **perce-oreilles** earwig.
percevoir* (pɛrsə'vwar) *vt* **1** perceive. **2** collect.
perche[1] (pɛrʃ) *nf zool* perch.
perche[2] (pɛrʃ) *nf* pole.
percher (pɛr'ʃe:) *vi* **1** perch. **2** roost. **perchoir** *nm* **1** perch. **2** roost.
perclus (pɛr'kly) *adj* **1** crippled. **2** stiff.
percussion (pɛrky'sjɔ̃) *nf* **1** impact. **2** *mus* percussion.
perdre (pɛrdr) *vt* **1** lose. **2** ruin. **3** waste. **4** leak. *vi* **1** deteriorate. **2** leak. **se perdre** *vr* **1** get lost. **2** disappear.
perdrix (pɛr'dri:) *nf* partridge.
père (pɛr) *nm* father.
perfection (pɛrfɛk'sjɔ̃) *nf* perfection.
perfide (pɛr'fi:d) *adj* treacherous.
perforer (pɛrfɔ're:) *vt* **1** perforate. **2** punch. **3** drill. **4** puncture. **perforation** *nf* **1** perforation. **2** hole.
péril (pe:'ri:l) *nm* peril, danger.

périmé (pe:ri:'me:) *adj* out-of-date.
périmètre (pe:ri:'mɛtr) *nm* **1** perimeter. **2** area.
période (pe:'rjɔd) *nf* **1** period. **2** era. **périodique** *adj* periodical. *nm* periodical (magazine).
périphérie (pe:ri:fe:'ri:) *nf* **1** periphery. **2** outskirts. **boulevard périphérique** *nm* ring-road.
périr (pe:'ri:r) *vi* **1** perish. **2** be destroyed. **3** die. **périssable** *adj* perishable.
périscope (pe:ri:'skɔp) *nm* periscope.
périssoire (pe:ri:'swar) *nf* canoe.
perle (pɛrl) *nf* **1** pearl. **2** bead.
permanent (pɛrma'nɑ̃) *adj* **1** permanent. **2** continuous. **permanence** *nf* permanence.
perméable (pɛrme:'abl) *adj* porous.
permettre* (pɛr'mɛtr) *vt* **1** permit. **2** allow. **3** enable.
permis (pɛr'mi:) *adj* **1** allowed. **2** permissible. *nm* **1** permit. **2** licence. **permis de conduire** *nm* driving licence.
permission (pɛrmi:'sjɔ̃) *nf* **1** permission. **2** *mil* leave.
permutation (pɛrmyta'sjɔ̃) *nf* **1** exchange. **2** permutation.
pernicieux, -euse (pɛrni:'sjœ, -'sjœz) *adj* **1** injurious. **2** harmful.
peroxyde (pɛrɔk'si:d) *nm* peroxide.
perpendiculaire (pɛrpɑ̃di:ky'lɛr) *adj,nf* perpendicular.
perpétuer (pɛrpe:'tɥe:) *vt* perpetuate. **se perpétuer** *vr* **1** endure. **2** survive. **perpétuel, -elle** (pɛrpe:'tɥɛl) *adj* **1** perpetual. **2** constant. **perpétuité** *nf* endlessness. **à perpétuité** for ever, for life.
perplexe (pɛr'plɛks) *adj* perplexed, puzzled.
perquisition (pɛrki:zi:'sjɔ̃) *nf* house search.
perron (pɛ'rɔ̃) *nm* flight of steps.
perroquet (pɛrɔ'kɛ) *nm* parrot.
perruque (pɛ'ryk) *nf* wig.
persécuter (pɛrse:ky'te:) *vt* **1** persecute. **2** harass. **persécution** *nf* persecution.
persévérer (pɛrse:ve:'re:) *vi* **1** persevere. **2** persist. **persévérance** (pɛrse:vɛ'rɑ̃s) *nf* perseverance. **persévérant** (pɛrse:vɛ'rɑ̃) *adj* **1** persevering. **2** steadfast.
persienne (pɛr'sjɛn) *nf* shutter.
persifler (pɛrsi:'fle:) *vt* mock.
persil (pɛr'si:l) *nm* parsley.
persister (pɛrsi:'ste:) *vi* **persister à** persist in. **persistance** *nf* persistance. **persistant** *adj* **1** persistent. **2** lasting.
personne (pɛr'sɔn) *nf* **1** person. **2** individual. *pron* anyone, anybody. **ne...personne** no one, nobody. **personnage** *nm* **1** person. **2** *lit* character. **personnalité** *nf* **1** personality. **2** important person. **3** personal remark. **personnel, -elle** (pɛrsɔ'nɛl) *adj* personal. *nm* personnel, staff.
personnifier (pɛrsɔni:'fje:) *vt* **1** personify. **2** impersonate.
perspective (pɛrspɛk'ti:v) *nf* **1** outlook. **2** prospect. **3** perspective.
perspicace (pɛrspi:'kas) *adj* shrewd. **perspicacité** *nf* **1** insight. **2** shrewdness.
persuader (pɛrsɥa'de:) *vt* **1** persuade. **2** convince. **3** induce. **persuasif, -ive** (pɛrsɥa'zi:f, -'zi:v) *adj* **1** persuasive. **2** convincing. **persuasion** *nf* **1** persuasion. **2** belief.
perte (pɛrt) *nf* **1** loss. **2** waste. **3** ruin. **4** death. **à perte de vue** as far as the eye can see.
pertinent (pɛrti:'nɑ̃) *adj* pertinent, relevant. **pertinemment** (pɛrti:na'mɑ̃) *adv* pertinently. **pertinence** *nf* relevance.
perturbateur, -trice (pɛrtyrba'tœr, -'tri:s) *adj* disturbing. *nm,f* agitator. **perturbation** *nf* disturbance.
pervers (pɛr'vɛr) *adj* **1** perverse. **2** depraved.
pervertir (pɛrvɛr'ti:r) *vt* **1** pervert. **2** corrupt. **perverti** *nm* pervert.
peser (pə'ze:) *vt* weigh. *vi* be heavy. **pesage** *nm* **1** weighing. **2** *sport* paddock. **pesant** *adj* **1** heavy. **2** clumsy. *nm* weight. **pesanteur** *nf* **1** weight. **2** *sci* gravity. **3** heaviness. **4** dullness.
pessimisme (pɛsi:'mi:sm) *nm* pessimism. **pessimiste** *adj* pessimistic. *nm,f* pessimist.
peste (pɛst) *nf* **1** plague. **2** *inf* pest.
pet (pɛ) *nm sl* fart.
pétale (pɛ'tal) *nm* petal.
pétanque (pe:'tɑ̃ʀ) *nf* game of bowls.
pétarader (pe:tara'de:) *vi* backfire.
pétard (pɛ'tar) *nm* **1** blast. **2** firework, banger. **3** *inf* row, noise.
pet-de-nonne (pɛdə'nɔn) *nm, pl* **pets-de-nonne** *cul* fritter.
pétiller (pe:ti:'je:) *vi* **1** crackle. **2** sparkle.
petit (pə'ti:) *adj* **1** small, little. **2** petty, insignificant. **en petit** in miniature. **petit-enfant** *nm, pl* **petits-enfants** grandchild. **petite-fille** *nf, pl* **petites-filles** granddaughter. **petit-fils** *nm, pl* **petits-fils** grandson. **petitesse** *nf* **1** smallness. **2** pettiness.
pétition (pe:ti:'sjɔ̃) *nf* petition.
pétrifier (pe:tri:'fje:) *vt* petrify.
pétrir (pe:'tri:r) *vt* **1** knead. **2** mould.

pétrole (pe:'trɔl) *nm* petroleum. **pétrole brut** crude oil. **pétrolier, -ière** (pe:trɔ'lje:, -'ljɛr) *adj* oil. *nm* tanker. **pétrolifère** *adj* oil-producing.

pétulant (pe:ty'lɑ̃) *adj* lively.

peu (pœ) *adv* **1** little. **2** few. **3** not very. *nm* little, bit. **à peu près** almost, more or less.

peupler (pœ'ple:) *vt* people, populate. **peuple** *nm* **1** people. **2** nation. **3** masses.

peuplier (pœpli:'e:) *nm* poplar tree.

peur (pœr) *nf* **1** fear. **2** fright. **3** dread. **peureux, -euse** (pœ'rœ, -'rœz) *adj* **1** timid. **2** shy. **3** nervous.

peut (pœ) *v* see **pouvoir.**

peut-être (pœ'tɛtr) *adv* **1** perhaps. **2** maybe. **3** possibly.

peux (pœ) *v* see **pouvoir.**

phallus (fal'lys) *nm* phallus.

phare (far) *nm* **1** lighthouse. **2** headlamp.

pharmacie (farma'si:) *nf* **1** pharmacy. **2** chemist's shop. **pharmacien, -ienne** (farma'sjɛ̃, -'sjɛn) *nm,f* **1** chemist. **2** pharmacist.

pharynx (fa'rɛ̃ks) *nm* pharynx.

phase (fɑz) *nf* **1** phase. **2** stage.

phénix (fe:'ni:ks) *nm* **1** phoenix. **2** paragon.

phénomène (fe:nɔ'mɛn) *nm* **1** phenomenon. **2** *inf* freak. **phénoménal, -aux** (fe:nɔmɛ'nal, -'no) *adj* **1** phenomenal. **2** extraordinary.

philanthropie (fi:lɑ̃trɔ'pi:) *nf* philanthropy. **philanthrope** *nm,f* philanthropist.

philatélie (fi:late:'li:) *nf* philately. **philatéliste** *nm,f* philatelist.

philistin (fi:li:'stɛ̃) *adj,nm* Philistine.

philosophie (fi:lɔzɔ'fi:) *nf* philosophy. **philosophe** *nm,f* philosopher. *adj* philosophical. **philosophique** *adj* philosophical.

phobie (fɔ'bi:) *nf* phobia.

phonétique (fɔne:'ti:k) *adj* phonetic. *nf* phonetics.

phonographe (fɔnɔ'graf) *nm* gramophone.

phoque (fɔk) *nm* seal.

phosphate (fɔs'fat) *nm* phosphate.

phosphore (fɔs'fɔr) *nm* phosphorus.

photo (fɔ'to) *nf* photo.

photocopier (fɔtɔkɔ'pje:) *vt* photocopy. **photocopie** *nf* photocopy.

photographier (fɔtɔgra'fje:) *vt* photograph. **photographe** *nm,f* photographer. **photographie** *nf* **1** photography. **2** photograph. **photographique** *adj* photographic.

phrase (frɑz) *nf* **1** sentence. **2** phrase.

physiologie (fi:zjɔlɔ'ʒi:) *nf* physiology. **physiologique** *adj* physiological. **physiologiste** *nm,f* physiologist.

physiothérapie (fi:zjɔte:ra'pi:) *nf* physiotherapy. **physiothérapiste** *nm,f* physiotherapist.

physique[1] (fi:'zi:k) *adj* physical. *nm* physique.

physique[2] (fi:'zi:k) *nf* physics. **physicien, -ienne** (fi:zi:'sjɛ̃, -'sjɛn) *nm,f* physicist.

piaffer (pja'fe:) *vi* **1** prance. **2** paw the ground.

piailler (pjɑ'je:) *vi* **1** chirp. **2** squeal.

piano (pja'no) *nm* piano. **piano à queue** grand piano. **pianiste** *nm,f* pianist.

piauler (pjo'le:) *vi* whine.

pic[1] (pi:k) *nm* woodpecker.

pic[2] (pi:k) *nm* pick.

pic[3] (pi:k) *nm* peak. **à pic** sheer. **tomber à pic** **1** fall sheer. **2** happen just in time.

picoter (pi:kɔ'te:) *vt* **1** peck (at). **2** prick. **3** sting. *vi* **1** smart. **2** tingle.

pie (pi:) *nf* magpie.

pièce (pjɛs) *nf* **1** piece. **2** part. **3** room (in a house). **4** fragment. **5** chessman. **à la pièce** separately. **pièce de monnaie** coin. **pièce de théâtre** play.

pied (pje:) *nm* **1** foot. **2** leg (of a chair, etc.). **3** stem. **à pied** on foot. **en pied** full-length. **mettre sur pied** establish, start. **pied bot** club foot. **pied-noir** *nm, pl* **pieds-noirs** Algerian of French origin. **pied plat** flat-footed.

piédestal, -aux (pje:dɛ'stal, -'sto) *nm* pedestal.

piéger (pje:'ʒe:) *vt* trap. **piège** *nm* trap.

pierre (pjɛr) *nf* stone. **pierre à briquet** flint. **pierre à chaux** limestone. **pierre précieuse** gem. **pierres de gué** *nf pl* stepping stones.

piété (pje:'te:) *nf* **1** piety. **2** devotion.

piétiner (pje:ti:'ne:) *vt* **1** trample. **2** tread under foot. **3** stamp.

piéton (pje:'tɔ̃) *nm* pedestrian.

pieu, pieux (pjœ) *nm* stake, pole.

pieuvre (pjœvr) *nf* octopus.

pieux, pieuse (pjœ, pjœz) *adj* pious, devout.

pigeon (pi:'ʒɔ̃) *nm* pigeon.

pigment (pi:g'mɑ̃) *nm* pigment.

pignon (pi:'ɲɔ̃) *nm* **1** gable. **2** pinion.

pile[1] (pi:l) *nf* **1** pile, heap. **2** battery.

pile[2] (pi:l) *nf* reverse (of a coin). **pile ou face** heads or tails.

piler (pi:'le:) *vt* **1** pound. **2** crush. **3** grind.

pilier (pi:l'je:) *nm* **1** pillar. **2** column.

piller (pi:'je:) *vt* plunder, pillage. **pillage** *nm* pillage, looting.

piloter (pi:lɔ'te:) *vt* **1** pilot. **2** fly. **pilote** *nm* pilot.

pilule (pi:'lyl) *nf* **1** pill. **2** contraceptive pill.

piment (pi:'mɑ̃) *nm* **1** pimento. **2** capsicum.

pimenter (pi:mɑ̃'te:) *vt* season with spices.

pimpant (pɛ̃'pɑ̃) *adj* smart.

pin (pɛ̃) *nm* pine.

pinacle (pi:'nakl) *nm* pinnacle.

pinceau, -aux (pɛ̃'so) *nm* paintbrush.

pincer (pɛ̃'se:) *vt* **1** pinch. **2** nip. **3** *mus* pluck. **4** catch (a thief). **pince** *nf* **1** grip. **2** pincers. **3** forceps. **4** clip. **5** claw. **6** dart (in clothes). **pince à épiler** tweezers. **pince à linge** clothes peg. **pincé** *adj* **1** affected. **2** prim. **pincée** *nf* pinch.

pingouin (pɛ̃'gwɛ̃) *nm* penguin.

Ping-pong (pi:ɲ'pɔɲ) *nm invar Tdmk* table-tennis.

pinson (pɛ̃'sɔ̃) *nm* chaffinch.

piocher (pjɔ'ʃe:) *vt* **1** dig (with a pick). **2** *sl* swot. **3** *game* pick up (a card, etc.). **pioche** *nf* pick.

pion (pjɔ̃) *nm* **1** *educ* junior master. **2** *game* pawn.

pionnier (pjɔ'nje:) *nm* pioneer.

pipe (pi:p) *nf* **1** pipe. **2** tube.

pipette (pi:'pɛt) *nf* pipette.

piquant (pi:'kɑ̃) *adj* **1** stinging. **2** cutting. **3** tart. **4** piquant. *nm* **1** point, pith. **2** sting. **3** quill.

pique[1] (pi:k) *nf mil* pike. *nm game* spade.

pique[2] (pi:k) *nf* pique, spite.

piquer (pi:'ke:) *vt* **1** prick. **2** sting. **3** offend. **4** excite. **5** stitch. **piqué** *adj* **1** quilted. **2** padded. **3** spotted. **4** vertical. **piqûre** *nf* **1** sting, bite. **2** prick. **3** small hole. **4** injection. **pique-nique** *nm, pl* **pique-niques** picnic.

piquet (pi:'kɛ) *nm* **1** peg. **2** stake. **3** picket.

pirate (pi:'rat) *nm* pirate.

pire (pi:r) *adj* worse. **le pire** worst.

pis[1] (pi:) *nm* udder.

pis[2] (pi:) *adv* worse. **de pis en pis** worse and worse. **le pis** worst. **tant pis!** too bad! it can't be helped! **pis-aller** *nm invar* makeshift.

piscine (pi:s'si:n) *nf* swimming pool.

pissenlit (pi:sɑ̃'li:) *nm* dandelion.

pistache (pi:'staʃ) *nf* pistachio.

piste (pi:st) *nf* **1** track. **2** trail. **3** scent. **piste cavalière** bridlepath. **piste d'envol** runway.

pistolet (pi:stɔ'lɛ) *nm* pistol.

piston (pi:'stɔ̃) *nm* **1** piston. **2** influence.

pitié (pi:'tje:) *nf* **1** pity. **2** compassion. **piteux, -euse** (pi:'tœ, -'tœz) *adj* pitiful, sorry. **pitoyable** *adj* **1** wretched. **2** pitiful. **3** contemptible.

pitre (pi:tr) *nm* clown.

pittoresque (pi:ttɔ'rɛsk) *adj* picturesque.

pivot (pi:'vo) *nm* **1** pivot. **2** axis. **3** centre.

pivoter (pi:vɔ'te:) *vi* **1** pivot. **2** revolve. **3** swivel. **pivoter sur** hinge on.

plaçage (pla'saʒ) *nm* veneer.

placard (pla'kar) *nm* **1** poster. **2** placard. **3** wall cupboard.

placer (pla'se:) *vt* **1** place. **2** invest. **3** sell. **4** find a job for. **se placer** *vr* **1** take one's place. **2** sit. **3** find a job. **place** *nf* **1** place. **2** seat. **3** room. **4** job. **5** spot. **6** square. **rester sur place** stay put.

placide (pla'si:d) *adj* placid, calm.

plafond (pla'fɔ̃) *nm* ceiling.

plage (plaʒ) *nf* **1** beach. **2** shore. **3** seaside resort.

plagier (pla'ʒje:) *vt* plagiarize. **plagiaire** *nm,f* plagiarist. **plagiat** *nm* plagiarism.

plaider (plɛ'de:) *vi,vt* plead.

plaie (plɛ) *nf* **1** wound. **2** sore. **3** evil, misfortune.

plaignant (plɛ'ɲɑ̃) *v* see **plaindre.**

plaindre* (plɛ̃dr) *vt* pity. **se plaindre de** *vr* complain about.

plaine (plɛn) *nf geog* plain.

plain-pied (plɛ'pje:) **de plain-pied** *adv* **1** on a level. **2** easily.

plaint (plɛ̃) *v* see **plaindre.**

plainte (plɛ̃t) *nf* **1** complaint. **2** groan.

plaire* (plɛr) *vt* **plaire à** **1** please. **2** suit. **s'il vous plaît** please. **se plaire** *vr* be happy. **se plaire à** enjoy.

plaisance (plɛ'zɑ̃s) *nf* pleasure. **plaisancier** *nm* **1** yacht. **2** yachtsman.

plaisant (plɛ'zɑ̃) *adj* **1** attractive. **2** agreeable. **3** amusing.

plaisanter (plɛzɑ̃'te:) *vi* joke, jest. *vt* tease. **plaisanterie** *nf* joke, jest.

plaisir (plɛ'zi:r) *nm* **1** pleasure. **2** delight. **3** amusement.

plan[1] (plɑ̃) *adj* **1** flat. **2** level. **3** even. *nm* **1** plane. **2** sphere. **premier plan** *nm* foreground.

plan[2] (plɑ̃) *nm* **1** plan. **2** project. **3** draft. **4** model.

planche (plɑ̃ʃ) *nf* **1** board. **2** plank. **3** shelf. **faire la planche** float on one's back.

plancher (plɑ̃'ʃe:) *nm* floor.

plancton (plɑ̃k'tɔ̃) *nm* plankton.

planer[1] (pla'ne:) *vt* plane, smooth.

planer[2] (pla'ne:) *vi* **1** soar. **2** hover. **3** *aviat* glide. **planeur** *nm* glider.

planète (pla'nɛt) *nf* planet.
plant (plɑ̃) *nm* **1** plantation. **2** sapling. **jeune plant** *nm* seedling.
plantation (plɑ̃ta'sjɔ̃) *nf* **1** plantation. **2** planting.
plante[1] (plɑ̃t) *nf anat* sole.
plante[2] (plɑ̃t) *nf* plant. **plante verte** evergreen.
planter (plɑ̃'te:) *vt* **1** plant. **2** set, place. **planter là** jilt. **se planter** *vr* stand.
planton (plɑ̃'tɔ̃) *nm* **1** *mil* orderly. **2** usher.
plaque (plak) *nf* **1** sheet (of metal). **2** slab. **3** plaque. **4** badge. **plaque chauffante** hotplate. **plaque tournante** turntable.
plaquer (pla'ke:) *vt* **1** veneer. **2** plate. **3** plaster. **4** *sport* tackle. **5** *inf* abandon. **se plaquer** *vr* lie flat.
plastique (pla'sti:k) *adj,nm* plastic.
plat (pla) *adj* **1** flat. **2** level. **3** dull. *nm* **1** flat (of the hand). **2** dish. **3** course. **à plat 1** flat. **2** *inf* exhausted. **plate-bande** *nf, pl* **plates-bandes** flowerbed. **plate-forme** *nf, pl* **plates-formes** platform.
plateau, -aux (pla'to) *nm* **1** tray. **2** plateau. **3** platform. **4** stage. **plateau à thé** teatray.
platine (pla'ti:n) *nm* platinum.
platonique (platɔ'ni:k) *adj* **1** platonic. **2** futile.
plâtrer (plɑ'tre:) *vt* **1** plaster. **2** patch up. **plâtre** *nm* **1** plaster. **2** plaster cast. **plâtre de moulage** plaster of Paris. **plâtrier** *nm* plasterer.
plausible (plo'zi:bl) *adj* likely, probable.
plectre (plɛktr) *nm* plectrum.
plein (plɛ̃) *adj* **1** full. **2** complete. **3** solid. **4** (of animals) with young. *adv* full. **en plein air/jour** in the open air/in broad daylight. **faire le plein** fill up.
pleurer (plœ're:) *vi* **1** cry, weep. **2** water. **3** drip. *vt* mourn for. **pleurard** *adj* tearful.
pleurnicher (plœrni:'ʃe:) *vi* **1** whine. **2** snivel.
pleuvoir* (plœ'vwar) *v imp* rain.
pli (pli:) *nm* **1** fold. **2** pleat. **3** crease. **4** bend. **5** envelope. **6** note. **petit pli** tuck.
plie (pli:) *nf* plaice.
plier (pli:'e:) *vt* **1** fold. **2** bend. *vi* **1** bend. **2** submit. **pliant** *adj* **1** flexible. **2** collapsible. *nm* folding chair.
plisser (pli:'se:) *vt* **1** crease. **2** pleat.
plomb (plɔ̃) *nm* lead. **à plomb** vertically. **plombier** *nm* plumber.
plomber (plɔ̃'be:) *vt* **1** cover with lead. **2** stop, fill (a tooth). **3** seal.
plonger (plɔ̃'ʒe:) *vi* **1** dive. **2** plunge. *vt* **1** immerse. **2** thrust. **plonge** *nf* washing-up. **plongée** *nf* **1** dive. **2** plunge. **3** slope. **plongée autonome** skin diving. **plongeoir** *nm* diving board. **plongeur, -euse** (plɔ̃'ʒœr, -'ʒœz) *nm,f* **1** diver. **2** washer-up.
ployer (plwa'je:) *vt* bend. *vi* bow, give way.
plu[1] (ply) *v see* **plaire.**
plu[2] (ply) *v see* **pleuvoir.**
pluie (plɥi:) *nf* rain. **pluie battante** downpour.
plumer (ply'me:) *vt* **1** pluck. **2** *sl* fleece. **plume** *nf* **1** feather. **2** pen. **3** nib.
plupart (ply'par) *nf* **1** most. **2** the greater part. **pour la plupart** mostly.
pluriel, -elle (ply'rjɛl) *adj,nm* plural.
plus (ply) *adv* **1** more. **2** most. **3** plus, in addition. *nm* **1** more. **2** most. **de plus 1** more. **2** besides. **en plus** in addition. **(tout) au plus** at most or best. **plus-que-parfait** *nm* pluperfect.
plusieurs (ply'zjœr) *adj,pron pl* several.
Pluton (ply'tɔ̃) *nm* Pluto.
plutôt (ply'to) *adv* **1** rather. **2** on the whole.
pluvieux, -euse (ply'vjœ, -'vjœz) *adj* rainy, wet.
pneu (pnœ) *nm* tyre.
pneumatique (pnœma'ti:k) *adj* pneumatic. *nm* **1** tyre. **2** express letter (in Paris).
pneumonie (pnœmɔ'ni:) *nf* pneumonia.
pochard (pɔ'ʃar) *nm* drunkard.
poche (pɔʃ) *nf* **1** pocket. **2** bag. **pochette** *nf* **1** small pocket. **2** handbag. **3** fancy handkerchief.
pocher (pɔ'ʃe:) *vt* **1** *cul* poach. **2** sketch. **pochade** *nf* sketch.
poêle[1] (pwɑl) *nm* stove, cooker.
poêle[2] (pwɑl) *nf* frying pan.
poème (pɔ'ɛm) *nm* poem. **poésie** *nf* **1** poetry. **2** poem. **poète** *nm* poet. **poétique** *adj* poetic.
poids (pwɑ) *nm* **1** weight. **2** importance. **3** burden. **poids léger** lightweight. **poids lourd 1** heavyweight. **2** heavy goods vehicle.
poignant (pwa'ɲɑ̃) *adj* poignant, gripping.
poignard (pwa'ɲar) *nm* dagger.
poignarder (pwaɲar'de:) *vt* stab.
poigne (pwaɲ) *nf* **1** grip. **2** energy. **3** will. **poignée** *nf* **1** handful. **2** handle. **poignée de main** handshake. **poignet** *nm* **1** wrist. **2** cuff (of a garment).
poil (pwal) *nm* **1** hair, fur (of animals). **2** hair (of humans). **3** nap (of material). **4** *inf* mood. **à poil 1** hairy. **2** *inf* naked. **poilu** *adj* hairy.
poinçon (pwɛ̃'sɔ̃) *nm* **1** *tech* punch. **2** stamp, mark. **3** hallmark.
poinçonner (pwɛ̃sɔ'ne:) *vt* **1** stamp. **2** hallmark. **3** punch, clip.

poindre* (pwɛ̃dr) *vi* **1** dawn. **2** sprout.
poing (pwɛ̃) *nm* fist.
point[1] (pwɛ̃) *nm* **1** point. **2** stitch. **3** dot. **4** extent. **5** full stop. **6** score, mark. **à point** perfect, to a turn. **mettre au point 1** focus. **2** perfect. **deux points** colon. **point d'exclamation** exclamation mark. **point d'interrogation** question mark. **point du jour** daybreak. **point-virgule** *nm* semicolon.
point[2] (pwɛ̃) *adv* **1** not. **2** no. **3** not at all. **ne...point** not any.
pointe (pwɛ̃t) *nf* **1** point. **2** tip. **3** touch, hint. **4** peak.
pointer[1] (pwɛ̃'te:) *vt* **1** check. **2** tick off. **3** aim, train.
pointer[2] (pwɛ̃'te:) *vt* **1** prick. **2** stab. **3** point. *vi* **1** appear. **2** sprout. **3** rise. **4** soar. **pointu** *adj* pointed.
pointiller[1] (pwɛ̃ti:'je:) *vt* dot. **pointillé** *adj* dotted. *nm* dotted line.
pointiller[2] (pwɛ̃ti:'je:) *vi* bicker.
pointilleux, -euse (pwɛ̃ti:'jœ, -'jœz) *adj* **1** touchy. **2** fastidious.
pointure (pwɛ̃'tyr) *nf* size (in clothes).
poire (pwar) *nf* **1** pear. **2** *sl* mug, face. **3** *sl* fool, dupe. **poirier** *nm* pear tree.
poireau, -aux (pwa'ro) *nm* leek.
pois (pwa) *nm* **1** pea. **2** spot. **petits pois** *nm pl* green peas. **pois de senteur** sweet pea.
poison (pwa'zɔ̃) *nm* poison.
poisson (pwa'sɔ̃) *nm* **1** fish. **2** *cap pl* Pisces. **poisson d'avril** April fool. **poisson rouge** goldfish. **poissonnerie** *nf* fish shop. **poissonnier, -ière** (pwasɔn'je:, -'jɛr) *nm,f* fishmonger.
poitrine (pwa'tri:n) *nf* **1** chest. **2** breast, bosom.
poivrer (pwa'vre:) *vt* season with pepper. **poivre** *nm* pepper. **poivre de Cayenne** Cayenne pepper. **poivré** *adj* **1** peppery. **2** spicy. **poivron** *nm* sweet pepper.
poix (pwa) *nf* pitch. **poix liquide** tar.
polaire (pɔ'lɛr) *adj* polar.
polariser (pɔlari:'ze:) *vt* polarize.
pôle (po:l) *nm* pole. **pôle nord** North Pole. **pôle sud** South Pole.
polémique (pɔle:'mi:k) *adj,nf* polemic.
poli[1] (pɔ'li:) *adj* **1** polite. **2** courteous. **poliment** *adv* politely.
poli[2] (pɔ'li:) *adj* **1** polished. **2** glossy. *nm* **1** polish. **2** gloss.
police[1] (pɔ'li:s) *nf* police. **faire la police** keep order. **policier, -ière** (pɔli:'sje:, -'sjɛr) *adj* **1** police. **2** detective. *nm* policeman.
police[2] (pɔ'li:s) *nf comm* policy.
polir (pɔ'li:r) *vt* **1** polish. **2** perfect.
polisson, -onne (pɔli:'sɔ̃, -'sɔn) *adj* **1** naughty. **2** depraved. *nm,f* rascal, rogue. **polissonnerie** *nf* **1** mischievousness. **2** depravity.
politesse (pɔli:'tɛs) *nf* **1** politeness. **2** courtesy.
politique (pɔli:'ti:k) *adj* **1** political. **2** diplomatic. *nf* **1** politics. **2** policy. **politicien, -ienne** (pɔli:ti:'sjɛ̃, -'sjɛn) *nm,f* politician.
pollen (pɔl'lɛn) *nm* pollen.
polliniser (pɔli:ni:'ze:) *vt* pollinate.
polluer (pɔl'lɥe:) *vt* pollute. **pollution** *nf* pollution.
Pologne (pɔ'lɔɲ) *nf* Poland. **polonais** *adj* Polish. *nm* **1** Pole. **2** Polish (language).
poltron, -onne (pɔl'trɔ̃, -'trɔn) *adj* **1** timid. **2** cowardly. **poltronnerie** *nf* cowardice.
polygamie (pɔli:ga'mi:) *nf* polygamy. **polygame** *adj* polygamous. *nm,f* polygamist.
polygone (pɔli:'gɔn) *nm* polygon. **polygonal, -aux** (pɔl:gɔn'al, -'no) *adj* polygonal.
polytechnique (pɔli:tɛk'ni:k) *adj* polytechnic.
polythène (pɔli:'tɛn) *nm* polythene.
pommade (pɔ'mad) *nf* ointment.
pomme (pɔm) *nf* apple. **pomme d'Adam** Adam's apple. **pomme de pin** pine cone. **pomme de terre** potato. **pommé** *adj* **1** rounded. **2** *inf* utter, complete. **pommelé** *adj* mottled. **pommier** *nm* apple tree.
pommeau, -aux (pɔ'mo) *nm* pommel.
pommette (pɔ'mɛt) *nf* cheekbone.
pompe[1] (pɔ̃p) *nf* pomp, ceremony. **pompeux, -euse** (pɔ̃'pœ, -'pœz) *adj* **1** pompous. **2** stately.
pompe[2] (pɔ̃p) *nf* pump. **pompe à incendie** fire-engine. **pompier** *nm* fireman.
pomper (pɔ̃'pe:) *vt* **1** pump. **2** suck up.
ponce (pɔ̃s) *nf* pumice stone.
ponctuel, -elle (pɔ̃k'tɥɛl) *adj* punctual. **ponctualité** *nf* punctuality.
ponctuer (pɔ̃k'tɥe:) *vt* **1** punctuate. **2** emphasize. **ponctuation** *nf* punctuation.
pondéré (pɔ̃de:'re:) *adj* **1** level-headed. **2** calm.
pondre (pɔ̃dr) *vt* **1** lay (eggs). **2** produce. **pondaison** *nf* laying (of eggs).
poney (pɔ'ni:) *nm* pony.
pont (pɔ̃) *nm* **1** bridge. **2** *naut* deck. **3** axle. **4** public holiday. **pont à bascule** weighbridge. **pont aérien** airlift. **pont-levis** *nm, pl* **ponts-levis** drawbridge. **pont suspendu** suspension bridge.
populace (pɔpy'las) *nf* rabble.
populaire (pɔpy'lɛr) *adj* **1** popular. **2** *pol* peo-

ple's. **popularité** *nf* popularity. **populeux, -euse** (pɔpy'lœ, -'lœz) *adj* densely populated.
population (pɔpyla'sjɔ̃) *nf* population.
porc (pɔr) *nm* **1** pig. **2** pork. **3** *sl* swine. **porc-épic** *nm, pl* **porcs-épics** porcupine.
porcelaine (pɔrsə'lɛn) *nf* **1** porcelain. **2** china.
porche (pɔrʃ) *nm* porch.
porcherie (pɔrʃə'ri:) *nf* pigsty.
pore (pɔr) *nm* pore. **poreux, -euse** (pɔ'rœ, -'rœz) *adj* porous.
pornographie (pɔrnɔgra'fi:) *nf* pornography. **pornographique** *adj* pornographic.
port[1] (pɔr) *nm* **1** port. **2** harbour.
port[2] (pɔr) *nm* **1** carriage. **2** transport. **3** bearing.
porte (pɔrt) *nf* **1** door. **2** doorway. **3** entrance. **4** gate. **5** *pl geog* pass.
porte-affiches *nm invar* notice board.
porte-bagages *nm invar* luggage rack.
porte-bébé *nm invar* carrycot.
porte-bonheur *nm invar* **1** mascot. **2** charm.
porte-clefs *nm invar* keyring.
porte-fenêtre *nf, pl* **portes-fenêtres** French window.
portefeuille (pɔrtə'fœj) *nm* **1** portfolio. **2** wallet.
porte-monnaie *nm invar* purse.
porte-parole *nm invar* spokesman.
porter (pɔr'te:) *vt* **1** carry. **2** wear. **3** bear. **4** enter. **5** induce. *vi* **1** rest. **2** hit, strike home. **se porter** *vr* proceed. **se porter bien/mal** be in good/bad health. **portable** *adj* wearable. **portatif, -ive** (pɔrta'ti:f, -'ti:v) *adj* portable. **porté** *adj* inclined, prone. **portée** *nf* **1** span. **2** litter. **3** reach, range. **4** significance. **5** *mus* scale. **porteur, -euse** (pɔr'tœr, -'tœz) *nm, f* porter, carrier, bearer.
porte-vêtements *nm invar* coat-hanger.
porte-voix *nm invar* megaphone.
portière (pɔr'tjɛr) *nf* door (of a car, train, etc.).
portion (pɔr'sjɔ̃) *nf* **1** portion, helping. **2** part.
portique (pɔr'ti:k) *nm* porch.
porto (pɔr'to) *nm* port (wine).
portrait (pɔr'trɛ) *nm* **1** portrait. **2** likeness.
Portugal (pɔrty'gal) *nm* Portugal. **portugais** *adj,n* Portuguese. *nm* Portuguese (language).
poser (po'ze:) *vt* **1** set, put. **2** place. **3** fix up. **4** suppose. *vi* **1** rest, lie. **2** pose. **se poser** *vr* alight. **se poser en** set oneself up as. **pose** *nf* **1** pose. **2** attitude. **3** affectation. **4** laying. **posé** *adj* **1** sedate. **2** steady. **3** staid.
positif, -ive (pɔzi:'ti:f, -'ti:v) *adj* **1** positive. **2** certain. **3** actual. **4** practical.
position (pɔzi:'sjɔ̃) *nf* **1** position. **2** posture. **3** status. **4** job.
posséder (pɔse:'de:) *vt* possess, own. **possédé** *adj* possessed. *nm* madman.
possessif, -ive (pɔsɛ'si:f, -'si:v) *adj* possessive. **possession** *nf* possession.
possible (pɔ'si:bl) *adj* possible. **possibilité** *nf* possibility.
poste[1] (pɔst) *nf* **1** post. **2** post office. **mettre à la poste** post (a letter). **postal, -aux** (pɔ'stal, -'sto) *adj* postal.
poste[2] (pɔst) *nm* **1** post, station. **2** position. **3** *inf* television set. **4** (telephone) extension. **poste de police** local police station. **poste d'incendie** fire station.
poster (pɔ'ste:) *vt* post, station.
postérieur (pɔste:'rjœr) *adj* **1** subsequent. **2** hind. *nm inf* bottom, posterior. **postérité** *nf* posterity.
posthume (pɔ'stym) *adj* posthumous.
postiche (pɔ'sti:ʃ) *adj* **1** false. **2** imitation. *nm* wig.
postscolaire (pɔstskɔ'lɛr) *adj* after-school.
post-scriptum (pɔstskri:p'tɔm) *nm invar* postscript.
postuler (pɔsty'le:) *vt* **1** apply for. **2** postulate. **postulant** *nm* applicant.
posture (pɔ'styr) *nf* **1** posture. **2** position.
pot (po) *nm* **1** pot. **2** jug. **3** can. **pot-au-feu** *nm invar* beef and vegetable stew. **pot-de-vin** *nm, pl* **pots-de-vin** *inf* bribe. **pot en étain** tankard. **prendre un pot** *inf* have a drink.
potable (pɔ'tabl) *adj* drinkable.
potage (pɔ'taʒ) *nm* soup.
potager, -ère (pɔta'ʒe:, -'ʒɛr) *adj* for cooking. *nm* kitchen garden.
poteau, -aux (pɔ'to) *nm* stake, post.
potelé (pɔt'le:) *adj* **1** plump. **2** chubby.
potence (pɔ'tɑ̃s) *nf* **1** gallows. **2** support.
potentiel, -elle (pɔtɑ̃'sjɛl) *adj,nm* potential.
poterie (pɔ'tri:) *nf* pottery. **potier, -ière** (pɔ'tje:, -'tjɛr) *nm,f* potter.
potin (pɔ'tɛ̃) *nm* **1** *pl* gossip. **2** row, noise.
potiner (pɔti:'ne:) *vi* gossip.
potion (pɔ'sjɔ̃) *nf med* potion, mixture.
potiron (pɔti:'rɔ̃) *nm* pumpkin.
pou, poux (pu:) *nm* louse.
poubelle (pu:'bɛl) *nf* dustbin.
pouce (pu:s) *nm* **1** thumb. **2** big toe. **3** inch. **manger sur le pouce** have a snack.
poudrer (pu:'dre:) *vt* powder. **poudre** *nf* **1** powder. **2** explosive. **poudre à canon** gun-

powder. **poudreux, -euse** (pu:'drœ, -'drœz) *adj* dusty.

pouffer (pu:'fe:) *vi* burst out laughing.

poulain (pu:'lɛ̃) *nm* **1** foal. **2** colt.

poule (pu:l) *nf* **1** hen. **2** fowl. **3** *sl* tart. **poulet** *nm* **1** chicken. **2** *inf* cop, policeman.

pouliche (pu:'li:ʃ) *nf* filly.

poulie (pu:'li:) *nf* pulley.

poulpe (pu:lp) *nm* octopus.

pouls (pu) *nm* pulse.

poumon (pu:'mɔ̃) *nm* lung.

poupe (pu:p) *nf naut* stern.

poupée (pu:'pe:) *nf* **1** doll. **2** puppet.

pour (pu:r) *prep* **1** for. **2** instead of. **3** for the sake of. **4** as to. **5** to. **pour que** in order that.

pourboire (pu:r'bwar) *nm* tip, gratuity.

pourceau, -aux (pu:r'so) *nm* swine, pig.

pour-cent *nm invar* per cent. **pourcentage** *nm* percentage.

pourchasser (pu:rʃa'se:) *vt* pursue.

pourpre (pu:rpr) *nf* purple. *adj,nm* crimson.

pourquoi (pu:r'kwa) *adv,conj* why. **pourquoi faire?** what for?

pourrai (pu:'rɛ) *v* see **pouvoir.**

pourrir (pu:'ri:r) *vi,vt* rot. *vi* **1** decay. **2** go bad. **pourriture** *nf* **1** rot. **2** decay.

poursuivre (pu:r'sɥi:vr) *vt* **1** pursue, chase. **2** *law* prosecute. **3** continue. **poursuite** *nf* **1** pursuit. **2** chase. **3** *pl law* proceedings.

pourtant (pu:r'tɑ̃) *adv* **1** however. **2** yet. **3** still.

pourtour (pu:r'tu:r) *nm* **1** circumference. **2** precincts.

pourvoir* (pu:r'vwar) *vt* **1** supply. **2** equip. **pourvoir à** provide.

pourvu (pu:r'vy) *v* see **pourvoir.**

pourvu que (pu:r'vy) *conj* provided that.

pousser (pu:'se:) *vt* **1** push. **2** thrust. **3** urge. **4** utter. **5** shoot out. *vi* **1** grow. **2** push forward or on. **pousser du coude** nudge. **pousse** *nf* **1** growth. **2** *bot* shoot. **poussé** *adj* **1** elaborate. **2** thorough. **poussée** *nf* **1** push, shove. **2** thrust. **3** growth. **poussette** *nf* pushchair.

poussière (pu:'sjɛr) *nf* **1** dust. **2** powder. **3** spray. **poussiéreux, -euse** (pu:sje:'rœ, -'rœz) *adj* dusty.

poussin (pu:'sɛ̃) *nm* chick.

poutre (pu:tr) *nf* **1** beam. **2** girder.

pouvoir* (pu:'vwar) *vt* **1** be able. **2** be allowed. *v imp* be possible. **n'en plus pouvoir** be tired out. **on n'y peut rien** nothing can be done about it. ~*nm* **1** power. **2** command.

pragmatique (pragma'ti:k) *adj* pragmatic.

prairie (prɛ'ri:) *nf* **1** meadow. **2** prairie.

praticable (prati:'kabl) *adj* **1** practicable. **2** feasible. **3** passable.

pratique[1] (pra'ti:k) *nf* **1** practice. **2** application. **3** custom. **4** habit.

pratique[2] (pra'ti:k) *adj* **1** practical. **2** useful.

pratiquer (prati:'ke:) *vt* **1** practise. **2** employ. **3** do.

pré (pre:) *nm* meadow.

préalable (pre:a'labl) *adj* **1** previous. **2** preliminary. **au préalable** to begin with.

préavis (pre:a'vi:) *nm* (previous) notice.

précaire (pre:'kɛr) *adj* **1** precarious. **2** uncertain. **3** delicate. **précarité** *nf* precariousness.

précaution (pre:ko'sjɔ̃) *nf* **1** precaution. **2** care.

précéder (pre:se:'de:) *vt* precede. **précédement** *adv* previously, already. **précédence** *nf* precedence, priority. **précédent** *adj* **1** preceding, previous. **2** former. *nm* precedent.

précepteur, -trice (pre:sɛp'tœr, -'tri:s) *nm,f* tutor, governess.

prêcher (pre:'ʃe:) *vt* preach. **prêche** (prɛʃ) *nm* sermon.

précieux, -euse (pre:'sjœ, -'sjœz) *adj* **1** precious. **2** valuable. **3** affected.

précipiter (pre:si:pi:'te:) *vt* **1** precipitate. **2** rush. **3** throw down. **précipitamment** *adv* **1** headlong. **2** in a hurry. **précipité** *adj* **1** precipitate. **2** hasty. **3** headlong.

précis (pre:'si:) *adj* **1** precise. **2** accurate. **3** clear. *nm* summary, precis.

préciser (pre:si:'ze:) *vt* **1** state precisely. **2** specify. **se préciser** *vr* become clear. **précisément** *adv* precisely, just. **précision** *nf* **1** precision. **2** accuracy. **3** *pl* full details.

précoce (pre:'kɔs) *adj* **1** precocious. **2** early. **3** advanced, forward.

préconcevoir* (pre:kɔ̃sə'vwar) *vt* preconceive.

préconiser (pre:kɔni:'ze:) *vt* **1** recommend. **2** praise.

prédateur, -trice (pre:da'tœr, -'tri:s) *adj* predatory. *nm* beast of prey.

prédécesseur (pre:de:sɛ'sœr) *nm* predecessor.

prédestiner (pre:dɛsti:'ne:) *vt* predestine.

prédicat (pre:di:'ka) *nm* predicate.

prédicateur (pre:di:ka'tœr) *nm* preacher.

prédire* (pre:'di:r) *vt* predict, foretell.

prédominer (pre:dɔmi:'ne:) *vi* predominate, prevail. **prédominance** *nf* predominance. **prédominant** *adj* **1** predominant. **2** prevalent.

prééminent (pre:e:mi:'nɑ̃) *adj* pre-eminent.

préfabriquer (pre:fabri:'ke:) *vt* prefabricate.

préface (prɛ'fas) *nf* preface.

préfecture (pre:fɛk'tyr) *nf* headquarters of the prefect of a French department. **préfecture de police** headquarters of the Paris police.
préférer (pre:fe:'re:) *vt* prefer. **préféré** *adj,n* favourite. **préférence** *nf* preference. **préférentiel, -elle** (pre:fɛrɑ̃'sjɛl) *adj* preferential.
préfet (pre:'fɛ) *nm* prefect. **préfet de police** chief commissioner of Paris police.
préfixe (pre:'fi:ks) *nm* prefix.
préhistorique (pre:i:stɔ'ri:k) *adj* prehistoric.
préjudice (pre:ʒy'di:s) *nm* **1** wrong. **2** detriment. **3** prejudice.
préjugé (pre:ʒy'ʒe:) *nm* prejudice, bias.
prélever (pre:l've:) *vt* levy. **prélèvement** *nm* levy, tax.
préliminaire (pre:li:mi:'nɛr) *adj* preliminary.
prélude (pre:'lyd) *nm* prelude.
prématuré (pre:maty're:) *adj* premature.
préméditer (pre:me:di:'te:) *vt* premeditate. **préméditation** *nf* premeditation. **prémédité** *adj* deliberate.
premier, -ière (prə'mje:, -'mjɛr) *adj* **1** first. **2** original. **3** foremost. **4** maiden (voyage, speech, etc.). *nf* first class.
prémisse (pre:'mi:s) *nf* premise.
prenant (prə'nɑ̃) *v see* **prendre.**
prénatal (pre:na'tal) *adj* antenatal.
prendre* (prɑ̃dr) *vt* **1** take. **2** seize. **3** assume. *vi* **1** set, congeal. **2** take, catch on. **se prendre** *vr* catch, get caught. **s'en prendre à** blame. **se prendre à 1** cling to. **2** begin. **s'y prendre** set about.
prénom (pre:'nɔ̃) *nm* Christian name.
prénuptial, -aux (pre:nyp'sjal) *adj* premarital.
préoccupé (pre:ɔky'pe:) *adj* **1** preoccupied. **2** engrossed. **3** anxious. **préoccupation** *nf* **1** preoccupation. **2** anxiety. **3** obsession.
préparer (prɛpa're:) *vt* **1** prepare. **2** get ready. **se préparer à** *vr* get ready for. **préparatifs** *nm pl* preparations. **préparation** *nf* preparation. **préparatoire** *adj* preparatory.
préposition (pre:pɔzi:'sjɔ̃) *nf* preposition.
prérogative (pre:rɔga'ti:v) *nf* prerogative.
près (prɛ) *adv* near. **à cela près** with that exception. **à peu près 1** approximately. **2** nearly. **de près** closely, near to. **près de** *prep* near to.
présager (prɛza'ʒe:) *vt* **1** predict. **2** foresee. **3** signify. **présage** *nm* omen.
presbyte (prɛz'bi:t) *adj* long-sighted.
presbytère (prɛzbi:'tɛr) *nm* vicarage.
prescrire* (prɛ'skri:r) *vt* **1** prescribe. **2** order. **3** demand. **prescription** *nf* **1** prescription. **2** instruction. **3** *med* directions for use.
préséance (pre:se:'ɑ̃s) *nf* **1** precedence. **2** priority.
présence (pre:'zɑ̃s) *nf* presence.
présent[1] (pre:'zɑ̃) *adj* present. *nm* present (time or tense). **à présent** now. **jusqu'à présent** as yet, up to now.
présent[2] (pre:'zɑ̃) *nm* present, gift.
présenter (pre:zɑ̃'te:) *vt* **1** present. **2** offer. **3** introduce. **se présenter** *vr* **1** present oneself. **2** occur. **présentateur, -trice** (pre:zɑ̃ta'tœr, -'tri:s) *nm,f* **1** presenter. **2** disc jockey. **présentation** (pre:zɑ̃ta'sjɔ̃) *nf* **1** presentation. **2** introduction.
préserver (pre:zɛr've:) *vt* **1** preserve. **2** protect. **préservateur, -trice** (pre:zɛrva'tœr, -'tri:s) *adj* preserving. **préservatif, -ive** (pre:zɛrva'ti:f, -'ti:v) *adj* **1** preservative. **2** protective. *nm* contraceptive sheath.
présider (pre:zi:'de:) *vt* preside over. *vi* be in the chair. **président** *nm* **1** president. **2** chairman. **présidentiel, -elle** (pre:zi:dɑ̃'sjɛl) *adj* presidential.
presque (prɛsk) *adv* **1** almost, nearly. **2** hardly.
presqu'île (prɛ'ski:l) *nf* peninsula.
presser (prɛ'se:) *vt* **1** press. **2** squeeze. **3** hurry. **se presser** *vr* **1** hurry. **2** crowd. **pressant** *adj* urgent. **presse** *nf* **1** press. **2** press, newspapers. **3** pressure. **4** crowd. **pressé** *adj* **1** crowded. **2** hurried. **3** urgent. **pression** *nf* pressure.
preste (prɛst) *adj* **1** quick. **2** nimble. **3** alert.
prestidigitateur (prɛsti:di:ʒi:ta'tœr) *nm* conjurer. **prestidigitation** *nf* conjuring.
prestige (prɛ'sti:ʒ) *nm* **1** prestige. **2** attraction. **prestigieux, -euse** (prɛsti:'ʒjœ, -'ʒjœz) *adj* marvellous.
présumer (pre:zy'me:) *vt* presume, assume.
prêt[1] (prɛ) *adj* **1** ready. **2** prepared. **prêt à porter** ready-made (clothes).
prêt[2] (prɛ) *nm* loan.
prétendre (prɛ'tɑ̃dr) *vt* **1** claim. **2** require. **3** maintain. **prétendant** (prɛtɑ̃'dɑ̃) *nm* **1** applicant. **2** candidate. **prétendu** (prɛtɑ̃'dy) *adj* **1** alleged. **2** so-called.
prétention (prɛtɑ̃'sjɔ̃) *nf* **1** pretension. **2** claim. **prétentieux, -euse** (prɛtɑ̃'sjœ, -'sjœz) *adj* **1** pretentious. **2** conceited.
prêter (prɛ'te:) *vt* **1** lend. **2** attribute. *vi* stretch. **prête-nom** *nm, pl* **prête-noms** figurehead. **prêter attention** pay attention. **prêteur,**

-euse (prɛ'tœr, -'tœz) *nm,f* lender. **prêteur sur gages** *nm* pawnbroker.
prétexte (pre:'tɛkst) *nm* pretext, excuse.
prêtre (prɛtr) *nm* priest. **prêtrise** *nf* priesthood.
preuve (prœv) *nf* **1** proof. **2** evidence.
prévaloir* (prɛval'war) *vi* prevail. **se prévaloir de** *vr* take advantage of.
prévenir* (pre:v'ni:r) *vt* **1** warn. **2** forestall. **3** prevent. **4** prejudice. **prévenance** *nf* **1** attention. **2** kindness. **prévenant** *adj* **1** attentive. **2** considerate. **3** pleasing.
préventif, -ive (pre:vɑ̃'ti:f, -'ti:v) *adj* preventive. **prévention** *nf* **1** prejudice. **2** imprisonment. **3** prevention.
prévenu (pre:v'ny) *adj* prejudiced. *nm law* accused.
prévision (pre:vi:'zjɔ̃) *nf* **1** forecast. **2** expectation.
prévoir* (pre:'vwar) *vt* **1** foresee. **2** provide for. **prévoyance** *nf* **1** foresight. **2** precaution.
prévu (pre:'vy) *v* see **prévoir.**
prier (pri:'e:) *vt* **1** pray. **2** ask. **3** invite. **je vous en prie** don't mention it. **prière** *nf* **1** prayer. **2** request.
prieuré (pri:œ're:) *nm* priory.
primaire (pri:'mɛr) *adj* primary.
prime[1] (pri:m) *adj* first. **de prime abord** at first.
prime[2] (pri:m) *nf* **1** premium. **2** bonus.
primer[1] (pri:'me:) *vt* excel.
primer[2] (pri:'me:) *vt* award a prize to. **primé** *adj* **1** prized. **2** subsidized.
primerose (pri:m'roz) *nf* hollyhock.
primesautier, -ière (pri:mso'tje:, -'tjɛr) *adj* **1** impulsive. **2** spontaneous.
primeur (pri:'mœr) *nf* **1** newness. **2** freshness. **3** *pl* early vegetables.
primevère (pri:m'vɛr) *nf* primrose.
primitif, -ive (pri:mi:'ti:f, -'ti:v) *adj* **1** primitive. **2** original.
primordial, -aux (pri:mɔr'djal, -'djo) *adj* **1** prime. **2** primeval.
prince (prɛ̃s) *nm* prince.
princesse (prɛ̃'sɛs) *nf* princess.
principal, -aux (prɛ̃si:'pal, -'po) *adj* principal, chief, main. *nm* **1** chief. **2** headmaster. **3** main thing. **principauté** *nf* principality.
principe (prɛ̃'si:p) *nm* principle.
printanier, -ière (prɛ̃ta'nje:, -'njɛr) *adj* spring.
printemps (prɛ̃'tɑ̃) *nm* spring, springtime.
priorité (pri:ɔri:'te:) *nf* priority.
pris (pri:) *v* see **prendre.** *adj* **1** engaged, occupied. **2** busy.
prise (pri:z) *nf* **1** hold. **2** grip. **3** solidification. **4** capture. **5** pinch. **en prise** in gear. **lâcher prise** let go. **prise de courant 1** (electric) socket. **2** plug.
priser (pri:'ze:) *vt* **1** value. **2** prize.
prisme (pri:sm) *nm* prism.
prison (pri:'zɔ̃) *nf* **1** prison, jail. **2** imprisonment. **prisonnier, -ière** (pri:zɔ'nje:, -'njɛr) *nm,f* prisoner.
privé (pri:'ve:) *adj* **1** private. **2** privy.
priver (pri:'ve:) *vt* deprive. **se priver** *vr* deny oneself. **privation** *nf* deprivation.
privilège (pri:vi:'lɛʒ) *nm* **1** privilege. **2** licence. **privilégié** *adj* **1** privileged. **2** licensed.
prix (pri:) *nm* **1** price. **2** cost. **3** worth. **4** prize. **à tout prix** at all costs.
prix-courant *nm, pl* **prix-courants** price-list.
probable (prɔ'babl) *adj* probable, likely. **probabilité** *nf* probability, likelihood.
probe (prɔb) *adj* honest. **probité** *nf* integrity.
problème (prɔ'blɛm) *nm* problem.
procéder (prɔse:'de:) *vi* **1** proceed. **2** originate. **procédé** *nm* **1** dealing. **2** process. **3** behaviour. **procédure** *nf law* procedure.
procès (prɔ'sɛ) *nm law* **1** case. **2** trial. **procès-verbal** *nm, pl* **procès-verbaux 1** official report. **2** minutes. **3** *law* particulars.
procession (prɔsɛ'sjɔ̃) *nf* procession.
processus (prɔsɛs'sys) *nm* **1** process. **2** method.
prochain (prɔ'ʃɛ̃) *adj* **1** next. **2** nearest. **3** immediate. *nm* neighbour. **prochainement** *adv* soon.
proche (prɔʃ) *adv* near. *adj* near, close.
Proche Orient *nm* Near East.
proclamer (prɔkla'me:) *vt* **1** proclaim. **2** announce. **3** declare. **proclamation** *nf* proclamation.
procréer (prɔkre:'e:) *vt* procreate.
procurer (prɔky're:) *vt* **1** procure, get. **2** obtain. **procuration** (prɔkyra'sjɔ̃) *nf* power of attorney. **procureur** *nm* attorney. **procureur général** Attorney General.
prodige (prɔ'di:ʒ) *nm* prodigy, marvel.
produire* (prɔ'dɥi:r) *vt* **1** produce. **2** bring about. **3** yield. **productif, -ive** (prɔdyk'ti:f, -'ti:v) *adj* productive. **production** *nf* **1** production. **2** product. **produit** *nm* product.
proéminence (prɔe:mi:'nɑ̃s) *nf* prominence. **proéminent** *adj* protruding.
profane (prɔ'fan) *adj* **1** profane. **2** secular. *nm* layman.
professer (prɔfɛ'se:) *vt* **1** profess. **2** teach.

professeur *nm* **1** professor. **2** teacher. **3** instructor.

profession (prɔfɛ'sjɔ̃) *nf* profession, trade. **professionnel, -elle** (prɔfɛsjɔ'nɛl) *adj* **1** professional. **2** vocational. *nm,f* professional.

profil (prɔ'fi:l) *nm* profile.

profit (prɔ'fi:) *nm* **1** profit, gain. **2** advantage.

profiter (prɔfi:'te:) *vi* **1** profit. **2** make a profit. **profiter de** take advantage of.

profond (prɔ'fɔ̃) *adj* **1** deep. **2** profound. **3** deep-seated. **profondeur** *nf* depth.

profus (prɔ'fy) *adj* profuse, abundant.

programme (prɔ'gram) *nm* **1** programme. **2** syllabus. **3** plan.

progrès (prɔ'grɛ) *nm* **1** progress. **2** improvement.

progressif, -ive (prɔgrɛ'si:f, -'si:v) *adj* **1** progressive. **2** gradual.

prohiber (prɔi:'be:) *vt* prohibit, forbid.

proie (prwa) *nf* prey.

projecteur (prɔʒɛk'tœr) *nm* **1** projector. **2** searchlight. **3** floodlight. **projectile** *nm* **1** missile. **2** projectile. **projection** *nf* **1** projection. **2** slide, film.

projet (prɔ'ʒɛ) *nm* **1** project, scheme. **2** (rough) plan. **projet de loi** *pol* bill.

prolétariat (prɔlɛta'rja) *nm* proletariat.

prolifique (prɔli:'fi:k) *adj* prolific.

prolonger (prɔlɔ̃'ʒe:) *vt* prolong, extend.

promener (prɔm'ne:) *vt* take for a walk. **se promener** *vr* **1** go for a walk. **2** wander. **promenade** *nf* **1** walk. **2** walking. **3** outing. **4** promenade.

promesse (prɔ'mɛs) *nf* promise.

promettre* (prɔ'mɛtr) *vt* **1** promise. **2** make a promise.

promouvoir* (prɔmu:'vwar) *vt* promote. **promotion** *nf* promotion.

prompt (prɔ̃) *adj* **1** quick, prompt. **2** hasty.

prône (pron) *nm* sermon.

pronom (prɔ'nɔ̃) *nm* pronoun.

prononcer (prɔnɔ̃'se:) *vt* **1** pronounce. **2** deliver (a speech). **se prononcer** *vr* express one's opinion. **prononciation** *nf* pronunciation.

propagande (prɔpa'gɑ̃d) *nf* **1** propaganda. **2** publicity. **faire de la propagande** advertise.

propager (prɔpa'ʒe:) *vt* **1** propagate. **2** spread.

prophète, prophétesse (prɔ'fɛt, prɔfe:'tɛs) *nm,f* prophet, prophetess. **prophétie** (prɔfe:'si:) *nf* prophecy. **prophétique** *adj* prophetic.

prophétiser (prɔfe:ti:'ze:) *vt* prophesy.

propice (prɔ'pi:s) *adj* favourable.

proportion (prɔpɔr'sjɔ̃) *nf* **1** proportion. **2** ratio. **3** *pl* size. **proportionnel, -elle** (prɔpɔrsjɔ'nɛl) *adj* proportional.

propos (prɔ'po) *nm* **1** purpose. **2** subject. **3** remark. **4** *pl* gossip. **à propos 1** by the way. **2** at the right moment. **à propos de** with regard to, concerning.

proposer (prɔpo'ze:) *vt* propose. **se proposer** *vr* **1** offer oneself. **2** intend. **proposition** *nf* **1** proposal. **2** proposition.

propre (prɔpr) *adj* **1** proper. **2** own. **3** appropriate. **4** clean. **propre à 1** suitable to. **2** peculiar to. **propreté** *nf* **1** cleanness. **2** tidiness.

propriétaire (prɔpri:e:'tɛr) *nm,f* **1** proprietor, proprietress. **2** landlord, landlady. **propriété** *nf* **1** property. **2** ownership. **3** propriety.

propulser (prɔpyl'se:) *vt* propel. **propulseur** *nm* propeller. **propulsion** *nf* propulsion, drive.

proscrire* (prɔ'skri:r) *vt* banish. **proscrit** *nm* outlaw.

prose (proz) *nf* prose.

prospectif, -ive (prɔspɛk'ti:f, -'ti:v) *adj* prospective.

prospérer (prɔspe:'re:) *vi* prosper, do well. **prospère** *adj* **1** prosperous. **2** thriving. **prospérité** *nf* prosperity.

se prosterner (prɔstɛr'ne:) *vr* **1** bow down. **2** *inf* grovel. **prosterné** *adj* prostrate.

prostituée (prɔsti:ty'e:) *nf* prostitute. **prostitution** *nf* prostitution.

protagoniste (prɔtagɔ'ni:st) *nm* protagonist.

protecteur, -trice (prɔtɛk'tœr, -'tri:s) *nm,f* **1** protector. **2** patron, patroness. *adj* protective. **protection** *nf* **1** protection. **2** patronage.

protéger (prɔte:'ʒe:) *vt* **1** protect. **2** shelter. **3** patronize. **protégé** *nm* dependant.

protéine (prɔte:'i:n) *nf* protein.

protester (prɔtɛ'ste:) *vt* declare. *vi* protest. **protestant** *adj,n* Protestant. **protestation** *nf* protest.

protocole (prɔtɔ'kɔl) *nm* protocol.

proton (prɔ'tɔ̃) *nm* proton.

proue (pru:) *nf naut* bow, prow.

prouesse (pru:'ɛs) *nf* prowess, bravery.

prouver (pru:'ve:) *vt* prove.

provençal, -aux (prɔvɑ̃'sal, -'so) *adj,nm* Provençal.

provenir* (prɔv'ni:r) *vi* **provenir de 1** arise from. **2** originate in or from. **provenance** *nf* **1** source. **2** origin. **en provenance de** coming from.

proverbe (prɔ'vɛrb) *nm* proverb. **proverbial, -aux** (prɔvɛr'bjal, -'bjo) *adj* proverbial.
province (prɔ'vɛ̃s) *nf* province. **provincial, -aux** (prɔvɛ̃'sjal, -'sjo) *adj* provincial.
proviseur (prɔvi:'zœr) *nm* headmaster.
provision (prɔvi:'zjɔ̃) *nf* **1** provision. **2** stock. **3** funds.
provisoire (prɔvi:'zwar) *adj* **1** provisional. **2** temporary. **à titre provisoire** provisionally.
provoquer (prɔvɔ'ke:) *vt* **1** provoke. **2** challenge. **3** arouse. **4** cause. **provocant** *adj* **1** provocative. **2** aggressive. **provocateur, -trice** (prɔvɔka'tœr, -'tri:s) *adj* provocative. **provocation** *nf* provocation.
proximité (prɔksi:mi:'te:) *nf* proximity.
prude (pryd) *nf* prude. *adj* prudish.
prudent (pry'dɑ̃) *adj* **1** prudent, wise. **2** discreet. **prudemment** (pryda'mɑ̃) *adv* prudently. **prudence** *nf* prudence, carefulness.
prune (pryn) *nf* plum. **prune de damas** damson. **pruneau, -aux** (pry'no) *nm* prune. **prunelle** *nf* **1** *anat* pupil. **2** sloe. **prunier** *nm* plum tree.
psaume (psom) *nm* psalm.
pseudonyme (psœdɔ'ni:m) *nm* pseudonym.
psychanalyse (psi:kana'li:z) *nf* psychoanalysis
psychédélique (psi:ke:de:'li:k) *adj* psychedelic.
psychiatrie (psi:kja'tri:) *nf* psychiatry. **psychiatre** *nm,f* psychiatrist. **psychiatrique** *adj* psychiatric.
psychique (psi:'ʃi:k) *adj* psychic.
psychologie (psi:kɔlɔ'ʒi:) *nf* psychology. **psychologique** *adj* psychological. **psychologue** *nm,f* psychologist.
psychopathique (psi:kɔpa'ti:k) *adj* psychopathic.
psychosomatique (psi:kosɔma'ti:k) *adj* psychosomatic.
pu (py) *v* see **pouvoir.**
puanteur (pɥɑ̃'tœr) *nf* stink.
puberté (pybɛr'te:) *nf* puberty.
public, -ique (py'bli:k) *adj* **1** public. **2** common. *nm* public. **grand public** general public.
publicité (pybli:si:'te:) *nf* **1** publicity. **2** advertising. **publicitaire** *adj* advertising.
publier (pybli:'e:) *vt* **1** publish. **2** proclaim. **publication** *nf* **1** publication. **2** publishing.
puce (pys) *nf* flea. **puceron** *nm* greenfly.
pudeur (py'dœr) *nf* modesty, decency.
pudique (py'di:k) *adj* **1** modest. **2** chaste.
puer (pɥe:) *vi* stink.
puéril (pɥe:'ri:l) *adj* childish.
pugilat (pyʒi:'la) *nm* boxing. **pugiliste** *nm* boxer.
puîné (pɥi:'ne:) *adj* younger.
puis[1] (pɥi:) *adv* **1** then. **2** afterwards. **3** besides.
puis[2] (pɥi:) *v* see **pouvoir.**
puiser (pɥi:'ze:) *vt* **1** draw (water). **2** derive.
puisque (pɥi:sk) *conj* since, as.
puissance (pɥi:'sɑ̃s) *nf* **1** power. **2** authority. **puissant** *adj* **1** powerful. **2** strong. **3** potent.
puits (pɥi:) *nm* **1** well. **2** shaft.
pull-over (pu:lo'vɛr) *nm* pullover.
pulluler (pylly'le:) *vi* swarm.
pulpe (pylp) *nf* pulp.
pulsation (pylsa'sjɔ̃) *nf* throb. **pulsation du cœur** heartbeat.
pulvériser (pylve:ri:'ze:) *vt* **1** pulverize. **2** grind.
punaise (py'nɛz) *nf* **1** bug. **2** drawing pin.
punch[1] (pɔ̃ʃ) *nm* (drink) punch.
punch[2] (pœnʃ) *nm sport* punch.
punir (py'ni:r) *vt* punish. **punition** *nf* **1** punishment. **2** forfeit.
pupille[1] (py'pi:l) *nm,f law* ward.
pupille[2] (py'pi:l) *nf anat* pupil.
pupitre (py'pi:tr) *nm* desk.
pur (pyr) *adj* **1** pure. **2** genuine. **3** clear. **4** innocent. **pur sang** *nm invar* thoroughbred. **pureté** *nf* purity.
purée (py're:) *nf* **1** mash. **2** thick soup.
purgatoire (pyrga'twar) *nm* purgatory.
purger (pyr'ʒe:) *vt* **1** purge. **2** cleanse. **3** clear. **purge** *nf* **1** purge. **2** cleaning.
purifier (pyri:'fje:) *vt* **1** purify. **2** refine.
puritain (pyri:'tɛ̃) *nm* Puritan.
pus (py) *nm med* pus.
pusillanime (pyzi:lla'ni:m) *adj* faint-hearted.
pustule (py'styl) *nf* pimple.
putain (py'tɛ̃) *nf sl* prostitute.
putride (py'tri:d) *adj* putrid.
puzzle (pyzl) *nm* jigsaw.
pygmée (pi:g'me:) *adj,n* pygmy.
pyjama (pi:ʒa'ma) *nm* pyjamas.
pyramide (pi:ra'mi:d) *nf* pyramid.
Pyrénées (pi:re:'ne:) *nf pl* Pyrenees.

Q

quadrant (ka'drɑ̃) *nm* quadrant.
quadrilatéral, -aux (kwadri:latɛ'ral, -'ro) *adj* quadrilateral.
quadrilatère (kwadri:la'tɛr) *nm* **1** quadrilateral. **2** quadrangle.
quadrillé (kadri:'je:) *adj* squared, checked.

quadrupède (kwadry'pɛd) *nm* quadruped.

quadrupler (kwadry'ple:) *vi,vt* quadruple. **quadruplés** *nm pl* quadruplets.

quai (ke:) *nm* 1 quay, wharf. 2 platform. 3 embankment. **Quai d'Orsay** French Foreign Office.

quaker, -eresse (kwa'kɛr, -'krɛs) *nm,f* Quaker.

qualifier (kali:'fje:) *vt* 1 call, term. 2 qualify. **qualification** *nf* 1 qualification. 2 title.

qualité (kali:'te:) *nf* 1 quality. 2 excellence. 3 property. 4 qualification. 5 title. 6 rank. **en qualité de** as, in the capacity of.

quand (kɑ̃) *conj, adv* when. **quand même** 1 all the same. 2 even if.

quant (kɑ̃t) *prep* **quant à** with regard to.

quantifier (kɑ̃ti:'fje:) *vt* quantify.

quantité (kɑ̃ti:'te:) *nf* quantity, amount.

quarante (ka'rɑ̃t) *adj,nm* forty. **quarantaine** *nf* 1 about forty. 2 quarantine. **faire quarantaine** be in quarantine. **quarantième** *adj* fortieth.

quart (kar) *nm* quarter, fourth part. **quart de finale** quarterfinal. **quart d'heure** quarter of an hour. **trois quarts** *nm pl* threequarters.

quartier (kar'tje:) *nm* 1 quarter. 2 piece. 3 district. **bas quartier** slum. **quartier général** *mil* headquarters.

quartz (kwarts) *nm* quartz.

quasi (ka'zi:) *adv* almost.

quatorze (ka'tɔrz) *adj,nm* fourteen. **quatorzième** *adj* fourteenth.

quatre (katr) *adj,nm* four. **à quatre pattes** on all fours. **quatrième** *adj* fourth.

quatre-vingt-dix *adj,nm* ninety. **quatre-vingt-dixième** *adj* ninetieth.

quatre-vingts *adj,nm* eighty. **quatre-vingtième** *adj* eightieth.

quatuor (kwa'tɥɔr) *nm* quartet.

que[1] (kə) *conj* 1 that. 2 lest, in case. 3 but. 4 as. 5 than. **à ce que** or **de ce que** that. **ne...que** only. **que...ou non** whether...or not. **que...que** whether...or.

que[2] (kə) *adv* 1 how. 2 how much or many.

que[3] (kə) *pron* 1 that. 2 whom. 3 which. 4 what. **qu'est-ce que** or **qui?** what?

quel, quelle (kɛl) *adj,pron* 1 what. 2 which. **quel que** 1 whatever. 2 whoever. **quelconque** *adj* 1 any (whatever). 2 some kind of. 3 ordinary, commonplace. **quelque** *adj* 1 some. 2 *pl* some, a few. *adv* 1 about. 2 some. **quelque chose** *pron m invar* something, anything. **quelquefois** *adv* sometimes. **quelque part** *adv* somewhere. **quelque...que** or **qui** 1 whatever, whatsoever. 2 however. **quelqu'un, quelqu'une** (kɛl'kœ̃, kɛl'kyn) *pron, pl* **quelques-uns, quelques-unes** one.

quémander (ke:mɑ̃'de:) *vi* beg. *vt* beg for.

quenelle (kə'nɛl) *nf* fish or mincemeat ball.

quereller (kərɛ'le:) *vt* quarrel with. **se quereller** *vr* quarrel. **querelle** *nf* quarrel. **querelleur, -euse** (kərɛ'lœr, -'løz) *adj* quarrelsome.

quérir (ke:'ri:r) *vt* 1 fetch. 2 send for.

question (kɛ'stjɔ̃) *nf* 1 question, query. 2 matter, issue. **question pour la forme** rhetorical question. **questionnaire** *nm* questionnaire.

questionner (kɛstjɔ'ne:) *vt* 1 question. 2 ask questions.

quêter (kɛte:) *vt* 1 collect (money, etc.). 2 look for. **quête** (kɛt) *nf* 1 search, quest. 2 *rel* collection.

queue (kœ) *nf* 1 tail. 2 end. 3 queue. 4 *sport* cue. **faire la queue** queue up.

qui (ki:) *pron* 1 who. 2 whom. 3 which. 4 that. **qui est-ce qui/que?** who/whom? **qui...que** whoever. **quiconque** *pron* 1 whoever. 2 anyone.

quiche (ki:ʃ) *nf* flan filled with cheese, eggs, cream, and bacon, etc.

quignon (ki:'ɲɔ̃) *nm* hunk (of bread, etc.).

quille[1] (ki:j) *nf* 1 skittle. 2 *pl sl* pins, legs.

quille[2] (ki:j) *nf* keel.

quincaillerie (kɛ̃kaj'ri:) *nf* 1 ironmongery. 2 hardware shop. **quincaillier** *nm* ironmonger.

quintal, -aux (kɛ̃'tal, -'to) *nm* (approx.) hundredweight.

quinte (kɛ̃t) *nf* 1 fit, bout. 2 *mus* fifth.

quintessence (kɛ̃tɛs'sɑ̃s) *nf* quintessence.

quintette (kɛ̃'tɛt) *nm* quintet.

quinze (kɛ̃z) *adj,nm* fifteen. **quinze jours** *nm pl* fortnight. **quinzaine** *nf* 1 fortnight. 2 about fifteen. **quinzième** *adj* fifteenth.

quiproquo (ki:prɔ'ko) *nm* 1 mistake. 2 misunderstanding.

quittance (ki:'tɑ̃s) *nf* receipt.

quitter (ki:'te:) *vt* leave, quit. **quitte** *adj* 1 quit. 2 free, rid. **quitte à quitte** quits.

quoi (kwa) *pron* 1 what. 2 which. **à quoi bon?** what's the use? **avoir de quoi** be well-off. **quoi que** or **qui** whatever. **sans quoi** otherwise. **quoique** *conj* although, though.

quote-part (kot'par) *nf* quota.

quotidien, -ienne (kɔti:'djɛ̃, -'djɛn) *adj* 1 daily. 2 everyday. *nm* daily newspaper.

R

rabâcher (rabɑ'ʃe:) *vi* keep repeating the same thing.

rabais (ra'bɛ) *nm* **1** reduction. **2** discount.

rabaisser (rabɛ'se:) *vt* **1** lower. **2** disparage.

rabattre* (ra'batr) *vt* **1** fold back. **2** lower, bring down. **3** reduce. **4** *sport* beat. *vi* turn off. **rabat-joie** *nm,f invar* spoil-sport.

rabbin (ra'bɛ̃) *nm* rabbi.

rabot (ra'bo) *nm tech* plane.

raboter (rabɔ'te:) *vt* **1** plane. **2** file down. **raboteux, -euse** (rabɔ'tœ, -'tœz) *adj* **1** uneven, rough. **2** rugged.

rabougrir (rabu:'gri:r) *vt* stunt.

racaille (ra'kɑj) *nf* rabble.

raccommoder (rakɔmɔ'de:) *vt* **1** mend, repair. **2** darn. **3** reconcile. **raccommodage** *nm* **1** mending. **2** mend.

raccorder (rakɔr'de:) *vt* join, connect.

raccourcir (raku:r'si:r) *vt* **1** shorten. **2** abridge. *vi* grow shorter, shorten. **raccourci** *nm* **1** abridgment. **2** short cut.

raccrocher (rakrɔ'ʃe:) *vt* **1** hang up again. **2** ring off. **3** get hold of again. **se raccrocher à** *vr* clutch, cling to.

race (ras) *nf* **1** race. **2** breed. **3** descent. **racial, -aux** (ra'sjal, -'sjo) *adj* racial. **racisme** *nm* racialism.

rachat (ra'ʃa) *nm* **1** repurchase. **2** atonement. **3** ransom.

racheter (raʃ'te:) *vt* **1** buy back. **2** atone for. **3** redeem. **4** ransom.

racine (ra'si:n) *nf* root.

racler (rɑ'kle:) *vt* scrape. **se racler la gorge** clear one's throat. **raclée** *nf inf* thrashing, hiding. **raclure** *nf* scrapings.

racoler (rakɔ'le:) *vt* recruit.

raconter (rakɔ̃'te:) *vt* tell, relate. **racontar** *nm inf* gossip. **raconteur, -euse** (rakɔ̃'tœr, -'tœz) *nm,f* narrator, storyteller.

radar (ra'dar) *nm* radar.

radeau, -aux (ra'do) *nm* raft.

radial, -aux (ra'djal, -'djo) *adj* radial.

radiateur (radja'tœr) *nm* radiator.

radiation[1] (radja'sjɔ̃) *nf* **1** crossing out. **2** cancellation.

radiation[2] (radja'sjɔ̃) *nf* radiation.

radical, -aux (radi:'kal, -'ko) *adj* radical.

radier (ra'dje:) *vt* **1** erase. **2** cross out.

radieux, -euse (ra'djœ, -'djœz) *adj* **1** radiant. **2** brilliant.

radin (ra'dɛ̃) *adj inf* mean, miserly.

radio (ra'djo) *nf* **1** radio. **2** X-ray. **passer à radio** X-ray. **radioactif, -ive** (radjoak'ti:f, -'ti:v) *adj* radioactive. **radioactivité** *nf* radioactivity.

radiodiffuser (radjodi:ffy'ze:) *vt* broadcast.

radis (ra'di:) *nm* radish.

radium (ra'djɔm) *nm* radium.

radoter (radɔ'te:) *vi* talk nonsense, ramble. **radotage** *nm* nonsense.

radoucir (radu:'si:r) *vt* **1** calm down. **2** soften. **se radoucir** *vr* grow softer or milder.

rafale (ra'fal) *nf* gust, blast (of wind).

raffermir (rafɛr'mi:r) *vt* **1** harden. **2** strengthen. **3** restore. **se raffermir** *vr* **1** improve. **2** recover.

raffiner (rafi:'ne:) *vt* refine. **raffinage** *nm* refining. **raffiné** *adj* **1** refined. **2** subtle. **3** delicate.

raffoler (rafɔ'le:) *vi* **raffoler de** rave about, love madly.

raffut (ra'fy) *nm inf* din, uproar.

rafistoler (rafi:stɔ'le:) *vt inf* patch up, mend

rafle (rafl) *nf* raid (by police).

rafraîchir (rafrɛ'ʃi:r) *vt* **1** cool. **2** refresh. **3** revive. **rafraîchissement** *nm* **1** cooling. **2** refreshing, brushing up. **3** *pl* refreshments.

rager (ra'ʒe:) *vi* be in a rage. **rage** (raʒ) *nf* **1** rage, fury. **2** mania. **3** rabies. **rageur, -euse** (ra'ʒœr, -'ʒœz) *adj* **1** passionate. **2** hot-tempered.

ragot (ra'go) *nm* gossip, scandal.

ragoût (ra'gu:) *nm* stew.

raidir (rɛ'di:r) *vt* **1** stiffen. **2** tighten. **se raidir** *vr* **1** stiffen. **2** brace oneself. **raide** *adj* **1** stiff, rigid. **2** taut. **3** steep. **4** *inf* hard. *adv* hard. **raideur** *nf* **1** stiffness. **2** steepness.

raie[1] (rɛ) *nf* **1** line. **2** streak, stripe. **3** parting (of hair).

raie[2] (rɛ) *nf zool* skate.

raifort (rɛ'fɔr) *nm* horseradish.

rail (rɑj) *nm* rail (of a railway track).

railler (rɑ'je:) *vt* **1** jeer at. **2** tease. **raillerie** (rɑj'ri:) *nf* jest, joke.

rainure (rɛ'nyr) *nf* groove, channel.

raisin (rɛ'zɛ̃) *nm* grape. **raisin de Corinthe/Smyrne** currant/sultana. **raisin sec** raisin.

raison (rɛ'zɔ̃) *nf* **1** reason. **2** reasoning. **3** satisfaction. **4** ratio. **avoir raison** be right. **raisonnable** *adj* **1** reasonable. **2** rational.

raisonner (rɛzɔ'ne:) *vi* **1** reason. **2** argue. *vt* **1**

consider. 2 reason with. **raisonnement** *nm* 1 reasoning. 2 argument.
rajeunir (raʒœ'ni:r) *vt* 1 rejuvenate. 2 renovate. *vi* get younger.
rajuster (raʒy'ste:) *vt* 1 readjust. 2 put straight.
ralentir (ralɑ̃'ti:r) *vt,vi* slow down, slacken. **ralenti** *adj* slow.
rallier (ral'je:) *vt* 1 rally, assemble. 2 win over.
rallonger (ralɔ̃'ʒe:) *vt* lengthen, let down. *vi* draw out. **rallonge** *nf* extension.
ramas (ra'mɑ) *nm* 1 heap. 2 collection
ramasser (ramɑ'se:) *vt* 1 gather together. 2 collect. 3 pick up. **se ramasser** *vr* pick oneself up. **ramassé** *adj* 1 thickset. 2 squat. 3 concise. **ramasse-poussière** *nm invar* dust-pan.
rame[1] (ram) *nf* oar.
rame[2] (ram) *nf* stick, prop. **rameau, -aux** (ra'mo) *nm* branch.
rame[3] (ram) *nf* train.
ramener (ram'ne:) *vt* 1 bring back or round. 2 restore.
ramer (ra'me:) *vi* row. **rameur** *nm* oarsman.
ramier (ra'mje:) *nm* woodpigeon.
se ramifier (rami:'fje:) *vr* branch out.
ramollir (ramɔ'li:r) *vt* 1 soften. 2 weaken.
ramoner (ramɔ'ne:) *vt* sweep (a chimney). **ramoneur** *nm* chimneysweep.
ramper (rɑ̃'pe:) *vi* 1 creep. 2 trail. 3 grovel. **rampe** *nf* 1 slope. 2 banister, handrail. 3 *Th* footlights.
rancart (rɑ̃'kar) *nm* **mettre au rancart** cast aside.
rance (rɑ̃s) *adj* 1 rancid. 2 rank.
rançon (rɑ̃'sɔ̃) *nf* ransom.
rançonner (rɑ̃sɔ'ne:) *vt* ransom, hold to ransom.
rancune (rɑ̃'kyn) *nf* 1 spite. 2 malice. 3 grudge.
rang (rɑ̃) *nm* 1 row, line. 2 rank. 3 status. **de premier rang** first-rate.
ranger (rɑ̃ʒe:) *vt* 1 arrange. 2 put away. 3 tidy. **se ranger** *vr* 1 draw up. 2 settle down. **rangé** *adj* 1 tidy, orderly. 2 staid. **rangée** *nf* row, line.
ranimer (rani:'me:) *vt* 1 revive. 2 stir up.
rapace (ra'pas) *adj* 1 rapacious. 2 predatory.
rapatrier (rapatri:'e:) *vt* repatriate. **rapatrié** *nm* repatriate.
râper (rɑ'pe:) *vt* 1 *cul* grate. 2 grind. 3 wear out. **râpé** *adj* 1 shabby. 2 grated.
rapetisser (rapti:'se:) *vt* 1 make smaller. 2 shrink. *vi* 1 shorten. 2 become smaller.
raphia (ra'fja) *nm* raffia.
rapide (ra'pi:d) *adj* rapid, swift. *nm* express train. **rapidité** *nf* rapidity.
rapiécer (rapje:'se:) *vt* patch (a garment).
rapin (ra'pɛ̃) *nm inf* art student.
rappel (ra'pɛl) *nm* 1 recall. 2 repeal. 3 reminder.
rappeler (ra'ple:) *vt* 1 recall. 2 remind. 3 repeal. **se rappeler** *vr* remember.
rapport (ra'pɔr) *nm* 1 return, yield. 2 report. 3 connection. 4 relations, relationship. **par rapport à** 1 with regard to. 2 in comparison with.
rapporter (rapɔr'te:) *vt* 1 bring back. 2 yield. 3 report. 4 *inf* tell tales. **se rapporter** *vr* 1 tally. 2 refer. **s'en rapporter à** rely on. **rapporteur, -euse** (rapɔr'tœr, -'tœz) *nm,f* sneak. *nm* 1 reporter. 2 chairman.
rapprocher (raprɔ'ʃe:) *vt* 1 bring nearer. 2 bring together. 3 compare. **se rapprocher de** *vr* 1 draw nearer to. 2 reconcile with. **rapprochement** *nm* 1 nearness. 2 comparison. 3 reconciliation.
raquette (ra'kɛt) *nf sport* racket.
rare (rɑr) *adj* 1 rare. 2 unusual. 3 exceptional. 4 sparse.
ras (rɑ) *adj* 1 short, cropped. 2 smooth, level. 3 bare. **au ras de** on a level with. **avoir ras le bol de** be sick of. **faire table rase** make a clean sweep.
raser (rɑ'ze:) *vt* 1 shave. 2 brush, skim. 3 *sl* bore. **rasoir** *nm* 1 razor. 2 *inf* bore.
rassasier (rasa'zje:) *vt* satisfy (hunger). **se rassasier** *vr* eat one's fill.
rassembler (rasɑ̃'ble:) *vt* assemble.
se rasséréner (rase:re:'ne:) *vr* 1 (of weather) clear up. 2 brighten up.
rassir (ra'si:r) *vi* get stale. **rassis** *adj* 1 stale. 2 staid. 3 sedate.
rassurer (rasy're:) *vt* 1 reassure. 2 strengthen.
rat (ra) *nm* rat.
ratatiner (ratati:'ɲe:) *vt* 1 shrivel up. 2 shrink.
râteau, -aux (rɑ'to) *nm* rake.
râteler (rɑt'le:) *vt* rake up. **râtelier** *nm* 1 rack. 2 denture.
rater (ra'te:) *vi* 1 misfire. 2 fail. *vt* miss.
ration (ra'sjɔ̃) *nf* ration, allowance.
rationaliser (rasjɔnali:'ze:) *vt* rationalize. **rationnel, -elle** (rasjɔ'nɛl) *adj* rational.
rationner (rasjɔ'ne:) *vt* ration.
ratisser (rati:'se:) *vt* 1 rake. 2 *inf* raid. **ratissoire** *nm* hoe.
rattacher (rata'ʃe:) *vt* 1 fasten. 2 bind. 3 link. **se rattacher à** *vr* 1 be fastened to. 2 be connected with.

rattraper (ratra'pe:) *vt* **1** catch again. **2** catch up. **3** recover. **se rattraper** *vr* save oneself.
rauque (rok) *adj* raucous, hoarse.
ravager (rava'ʒe:) *vt* **1** devastate. **2** ruin. **3** ravage. **ravages** *nm pl* havoc.
ravauder (ravo'de:) *vt* mend, patch.
ravir (ra'vi:r) *vt* **1** ravish, delight. **2** carry off. **ravi de** *adj* **1** overjoyed at. **2** delighted to. **ravissant** *adj* lovely. **ravisseur** *nm* kidnapper.
se raviser (ravi:'ze:) *vr* change one's mind.
rayer (rɛ'je:) *vt* **1** rule. **2** stripe. **3** scratch. **4** delete.
rayon[1] (rɛ'jɔ̃) *nm* **1** ray. **2** beam. **3** radius. **4** spoke (of a wheel). **rayon X** X-ray.
rayon[2] (rɛ'jɔ̃) *nm* **1** shelf. **2** department (in a shop). **3** counter (of a shop). **rayon de miel** honeycomb.
rayon[3] (rɛ'jɔ̃) *nm* **1** drill (for seed). **2** row.
rayonne (rɛ'jɔn) *nf* rayon.
rayonner (rɛjɔ'ne:) *vi* **1** radiate. **2** beam. **rayonnant** *adj* **1** radiant. **2** beaming. **rayonnement** *nm* **1** radiation. **2** radiance. **3** influence.
rayure (rɛ'jyr) *nf* **1** stripe, streak. **2** scratch. **3** deletion.
razzia (rad'zja) *nf* raid.
réaction (re:ak'sjɔ̃) *nf* reaction. **réacteur** *nm* reactor. **réactionnaire** *adj* reactionary.
réagir (re:a'ʒi:r) *vi* react.
réaliser (re:ali:'ze:) *vt* **1** realize. **2** carry out. **3** sell out.
réalité (re:ali:'te:) *nf* reality. **en réalité** really. **réalisme** *nm* realism. **réaliste** *adj* realistic. *nm,f* realist.
rébarbatif, -ive (re:barba'ti:f, -'ti:v) *adj* **1** grim. **2** surly.
rebattu (rəba'ty) *adj* hackneyed, trite.
rebelle (rə'bɛl) *adj* **1** rebellious. **2** stubborn. **3** opposed. *nm,f* rebel. **rébellion** *nf* rebellion, revolt.
rebondir (rəbɔ̃'di:r) *vi* **1** rebound. **2** bounce.
rebord (rə'bɔr) *nm* **1** edge. **2** rim. **3** hem.
rebours (rə'bu:r) *nm* **1** wrong way. **2** reverse. **à rebours** **1** the wrong way. **2** against the grain.
rebrousser (rəbru:'se:) *vt* brush up (hair or nap). *vi* turn back. **rebrousser chemin** retrace one's steps. **à rebrousse-poil** *adv* the wrong way. **à rebrousse-poil** *adv* the wrong way.
rebuffade (rəby'fad) *nf* snub.
rebut (rə'by) *nm* **1** waste. **2** scrap. **3** *pl* rejects.
rebutant (rəby'tɑ̃) *adj* **1** tedious. **2** repulsive.
recéler (rase:'le:) *vt* **1** receive. **2** contain.
récemment (re:sa'mɑ̃) *adv* recently.
recensement (rəsɑ̃s'mɑ̃) *nm* census.
récent (re:'sɑ̃) *adj* recent, fresh.
récepteur, -trice (re:sɛp'tœr, -'tri:s) *adj* receiving. *nm* receiver. **réception** *nf* **1** receipt. **2** welcome. **3** reception.
récession (re:sɛ'sjɔ̃) *nf* recession, slump.
recette (rə'sɛt) *nf* **1** takings. **2** receipt. **3** recipe.
recevable (rəsə'vabl) *adj* allowable.
receveur, -euse (rəsə'vœr, -'vœz) *nm,f* **1** receiver. **2** collector. **3** (bus) conductor.
recevoir* (rəsə'vwar) *vt* **1** receive. **2** entertain. **3** accept. **être reçu à un examen** pass an exam.
rechange (rə'ʃɑ̃ʒ) *nm* replacement, refill, spare. **de rechange** *adj* spare.
réchapper (re:ʃa'pe:) *vi* (*aux* être or avoir) **réchapper de** **1** escape from. **2** recover from.
recharge (rə'ʃarʒ) *nf* refill.
réchaud (re:'ʃo) *nm* **1** portable stove. **2** hotplate.
réchauffer (re:ʃo'fe:) *vt* **1** reheat. **2** warm up.
rêche (rɛʃ) *adj* **1** harsh. **2** rough.
rechercher (rəʃɛr'ʃe:) *vt* **1** search for. **2** inquire into. **recherche** *nf* **1** search. **2** research. **3** affectation. **recherché** *adj* **1** in demand. **2** choice. **3** affected.
rechute (rə'ʃyt) *nf* relapse.
récif (re:'si:f) *nm* reef.
récipient (re:si:'pjɑ̃) *nm* container, receptacle.
réciproque (re:si:'prɔk) *adj* reciprocal, mutual.
récit (re:'si:) *nm* **1** narrative, story. **2** account.
réciter (re:si:'te:) *vt* recite. **récital** *nm mus* recital. **récitant** *adj,n mus* solo.
réclame (re:'klam) *nf* **1** publicity, advertising. **2** advertisement. **3** sign. **en réclame** on offer. **faire de la réclame** advertise. **réclamation** *nf* complaint.
recoin (rə'kwɛ̃) *nm* recess.
reçois (rə'swa) *v* see **recevoir.**
récolter (re:kɔl'te:) *vt* **1** harvest. **2** gather **récolte** *nf* **1** crop. **2** harvest. **3** harvesting.
recommander (rəkɔmɑ̃'de:) *vt* **1** recommend. **2** advise. **3** register (mail).
recommencer (rəkɔmɑ̃'se:) *vt,vi* begin again.
récompenser (re:kɔ̃pɑ̃'se:) *vt* recompense, reward. **récompense** *nf* reward.
réconcilier (re:kɔ̃si:'lje:) *vt* reconcile.
reconduire (rəkɔ̃'dɥi:r) *vt* **1** accompany back. **2** escort home. **3** see out.
réconforter (re:kɔ̃fɔr'te:) *vt* **1** cheer up. **2** fortify.
reconnaissant (rəkɔnɛ'sɑ̃) *adj* **1** grateful. **2**

thankful. **reconnaissance** *nf* 1 recognition. 2 acknowledgment. 3 gratitude. 4 thankfulness.
reconnaître* (rəkɔ'nɛtr) *vt* 1 recognize. 2 acknowledge, admit. 3 explore.
reconstituer (rəkɔ̃sti:'tɥe:) *vt* restore.
record (rə'kɔr) *nm* record.
recours (rə'ku:r) *nm* recourse, resort.
récréation (re:kre:a'sjɔ̃) *nf* 1 recreation, amusement. 2 *educ* break.
recrue (rə'kry) *nf* recruit.
recruter (rəkry'te:) *vt* 1 recruit. 2 enlist.
rectangle (rɛk'tɑ̃g) *adj* right-angled. *nm* rectangle. **rectangulaire** *adj* rectangular.
recteur (rɛk'tœr) *nm* 1 *educ* vice-chancellor. 2 rector.
rectifier (rɛkti:'fje:) *vt* 1 straighten. 2 rectify. 3 correct. 4 adjust.
rectitude (rɛkti:'tyd) *nf* 1 straightness. 2 correctness. 3 integrity.
reçu (rə'sy) *v* see **recevoir.** *adj* 1 received. 2 recognized. *nm* 1 receipt. 2 voucher.
recueil (rə'kœj) *nm* 1 collection. 2 selection. **recueil d'expressions** phrasebook.
recueillir* (rəkœ'ji:r) *vt* 1 gather. 2 pick up, obtain. 3 take in. **se recueillir** *vr* collect one's thoughts. **recueillement** *nm* 1 meditation. 2 composure. **recueilli** *adj* meditative.
recul (rə'kyl) *nm* 1 retreat. 2 setback.
reculer (rəky'le:) *vi* 1 move back. 2 draw back. *vt* 1 move back. 2 postpone. **reculé** *adj* remote. **à reculons** *adv* backwards.
récupérer (re:kype:'re:) *vt* 1 recover. 2 retrieve. 3 make up. 4 *inf* scrounge.
récurer (re:ky're:) *vt* scour, clean.
récurrent (re:kyr'rɑ̃) *adj* recurrent.
rédacteur, -trice (re:dak'tœr, -'tri:s) *nm,f* 1 writer. 2 editor. **rédacteur en chef** editor (of a newspaper, etc.). **rédaction** *nf* 1 writing. 2 editing. 3 editorial staff.
rédiger (re:di:'ʒe:) *vt* 1 draft. 2 write. 3 edit.
redire* (rə'di:r) *vt* repeat. **trouver à redire à** find fault with.
redondant (rədɔ̃'dɑ̃) *adj* superfluous. **redondance** *nf* superfluity.
redouter (rədu:'te:) *vt* fear, dread. **redoutable** *adj* 1 formidable. 2 dangerous.
redresser (rədrɛ'se:) *vt* 1 set upright again. 2 straighten. 3 rectify.
réduire* (re:'dɥi:r) *vt* reduce. **se réduire à** *vr* 1 amount to. 2 confine oneself to. **réduction** *nf* reduction, cut. **réduit** *nm* 1 retreat. 2 nook.
réel, réelle (re:ɛl) *adj* 1 real. 2 actual. 3 true. *nm* reality.
refaire* (rə'fɛr) *vt* 1 do or make again. 2 repair. **se refaire** *vr* recover.
réfectoire (re:fɛk'twar) *nm* refectory.
référendum (re:fe:rɛ̃'dɔm) *nm* referendum.
référer (re:fe:'re:) *vt* 1 refer. 2 ascribe. **se référer à** *vr* refer to. **référence** *nf* reference.
réfléchir (re:fle:'ʃi:r) *vt* reflect. *vi* think, ponder. **réfléchir à** consider. **réfléchi** *adj* 1 thoughtful. 2 deliberate. 3 reflexive.
réflecteur (re:flɛk'tœr) *nm* reflector.
reflet (rə'flɛ) *nm* reflection.
refléter (rəfle:'te:) *vt* reflect.
réflexe (re:'flɛks) *adj,nm* reflex.
réflexion (re:flɛk'sjɔ̃) *nf* 1 reflection. 2 thought.
reflux (rə'fly) *nm* ebb (tide).
réformer (re:fɔr'me:) *vt* 1 reform. 2 discharge. **réformation** *nf* reformation. **réforme** *nf* 1 reform. 2 discharge.
refouler (rəfu:'le:) *vt* 1 drive back. 2 repress.
refrain (rə'frɛ̃) *nm* 1 refrain. 2 chorus.
réfrigérer (re:fri:ʒe:'re:) *vt* refrigerate. **réfrigérateur** *nm* refrigerator.
refroidir (rəfrwa'di:r) *vt* cool, chill. *vi* cool down. **refroidissement** *nm* 1 cooling. 2 *med* chill.
refuge (rə'fyʒ) *nm* refuge, shelter.
se réfugier (re:fy'ʒje:) *vr* take refuge. **réfugié** *nm* refugee.
refus (rə'fy) *nm* refusal.
refuser (rəfy'ze:) *vt* 1 refuse. 2 decline. 3 deny. 4 reject. **être refusé** fail.
réfuter (re:fy'te:) *vt* refute, disprove.
regagner (rəgɑ'ɲe:) *vt* 1 recover, regain. 2 catch up. 3 return to.
regain (rə'gɛ̃) *nm* 1 aftermath. 2 renewal.
régal (re:'gal) *nm* 1 feast. 2 treat.
régaler (re:ga'le:) *vt* 1 entertain. 2 treat.
regard (rə'gar) *nm* 1 look. 2 gaze. 3 glance. 4 manhole. **regard fixe** stare.
regarder (rəgar'de:) *vt* 1 look at. 2 consider. 3 concern. **regarder fixement** stare at.
régent (re:'ʒɑ̃) *nm* regent. **régence** (re:'ʒɑ̃s) *nf* regency.
régie (re:'ʒi:) *nf* administration.
régime (re:'ʒi:m) *nm* 1 regime. 2 system. 3 diet.
régiment (re:ʒi:'mɑ̃) *nm* regiment. **régimentaire** *adj* regimental.
région (re:'ʒjɔ̃) *nf* 1 region. 2 territory. **régional, -aux** (re:ʒjɔ'nal, -'no) *adj* 1 regional. 2 local.
régir (re:'ʒi:r) *vt* 1 govern. 2 manage. **régisseur** *nm* 1 manager. 2 agent. 3 stage manager.
registre (rə'ʒi:str) *nm* register.

régler (re:'gle:) *vt* **1** rule (paper, etc.). **2** regulate. **3** adjust. **4** settle. **règle** *nf* **1** rule. **2** ruler. **3** *pl med* period. **en règle** in order. **règle à calcul** *nf* slide rule. **réglé** *adj* **1** ruled. **2** regular. **3** methodical. **règlement** *nm* **1** regulation. **2** settlement. **réglementaire** (rɛglәmɑ̃'tɛr) *adj* **1** regulation. **2** compulsory, statutory.

réglisse (re:'gli:s) *nf* liquorice.

régner (rɛ'ɲe:) *vi* reign. **règne** *nm* **1** reign. **2** kingdom.

regret (rә'grɛ) *nm* regret.

regretter (rәgrɛ'te:) *vt* regret, be sorry.

régulier, -ière (re:gy'lje:, -'ljɛr) *adj* **1** regular. **2** steady. **3** even. **régularité** *nf* regularity.

réhabiliter (re:abi:li:'te:) *vt* rehabilitate.

rehausser (re:o'ze:) *vt* **1** raise. **2** accentuate. **3** enhance.

rein (rɛ̃) *nm* **1** kidney. **2** *pl* back.

réincarnation (re:ɛ̃karna'sjɔ̃) *nf* reincarnation.

reine (rɛn) *nf* queen. **reine-claude** *nf, pl* **reines-claude** greengage.

réintégrer (re:ɛ̃te:'gre:) *vt* **1** reinstate. **2** resume.

rejeter (rәʒә'te:) *vt* **1** throw back. **2** cast aside. **3** reject. **se rejeter sur** *vr* fall back on.

rejoindre* (rә'ʒwɛ̃dr) *vt* **1** rejoin. **2** connect. **3** catch up. **se rejoindre** *vr* meet.

réjouir (re:'ʒwi:r) *vt* **1** amuse. **2** please. **se réjouir** *vr* **1** be delighted. **2** rejoice.

relâcher (rәla'ʃe:) *vt* **1** slacken. **2** relax. **3** release. **se relâcher** *vr* **1** become slack. **2** abate. **relâche** *nm* **1** relaxation. **2** respite. *nf* port of call.

relais (rә'lɛ) *nm* **1** relay. **2** shift (in a factory, etc.). **relais d'essence** filling station.

relatif, -ive (rәla'ti:f, -'ti:v) *adj* relative.

relation (rәla'sjɔ̃) *nf* **1** relation. **2** communication, contact. **3** statement.

relativité (rәlati:vi:'te:) *nf* relativity.

relayer (rәlɛ'je:) *vt* **1** relay. **2** relieve.

relever (rәl've:) *vt* **1** raise. **2** pick up. **3** point out. **4** relieve. **relever de** be dependent on. **relève** *nf* **1** relief. **2** changing of the guard. **relevé** *adj* **1** raised. **2** high. *nm* **1** abstract. **2** summary. **relevé de compte** bank statement.

relief (rә'ljɛf) *nm Art* relief.

religion (rәli:'ʒjɔ̃) *nf* religion. **religieux, -euse** (rәli:'ʒjœ, -'ʒjœz) *adj* **1** religious. **2** sacred. *nm* monk. *nf* nun.

relique (rә'li:k) *nf* relic.

relire* (rә'li:r) *vt* re-read.

reluire (rә'lɥi:r) *vi* **1** shine. **2** glitter.

remanier (rәma'nje:) *vt* adapt, alter.

remarquer (rәmar'ke:) *vt* notice. **faire remarquer** point out. **se faire remarquer** attract attention. **remarque** *nf* remark.

remblai (rɑ̃'blɛ) *nm* embankment.

rembourrer (rɑ̃bu:'re:) *vt* stuff, pad.

rembourser (rɑ̃bu:r'se:) *vt* reimburse, refund. (rɑ̃bu:rsә'mɑ̃) *nm* repayment.

remédier (rәme:'dje:) *vi* **remédier à** remedy. **remède** *nm* remedy, cure.

remercier (rәmɛr'sje:) *vt* **1** thank. **2** dismiss. **remerciement** *nm* thanks.

remettre* (rә'mɛtr) *vt* **1** put back. **2** hand over. **3** recollect. **4** postpone.

remise (rә'mi:z) *nf* **1** delivery. **2** remittance. **3** discount. **4** garage.

rémission (re:mi:'sjɔ̃) *nf* remission.

remonter (rәmɔ̃'te:) *vi* (*aux* être) **1** go up again. **2** go back. *vt* **1** climb up again. **2** carry or pull up, raise. **3** wind up. **remontant** *nm* tonic. **remontée** *nf* climb. **remontée du visage** facelift.

remords (rә'mɔr) *nm* remorse.

remorquer (rәmɔr'ke:) *vt* tow. **remorque** *nf* **1** towing. **2** towrope. **3** trailer.

remous (rә'mu:) *nm* [illegible] swirl, wash.

rempart (rɑ̃'par) *nm* rampart.

remplacer (rɑ̃pla'se:) *vt* **1** replace. **2** substitute. **3** succeed. **remplaçant** *nm* substitute.

rempli (rɑ̃'pli:) *nm* tuck (in a dress).

remplir (rɑ̃'pli:r) *vt* **1** refill. **2** fill up or in. **3** fulfil.

remporter (rɑ̃pɔr'te:) *vt* **1** take away. **2** carry off. **3** win.

remuer (rә'mɥe:) *vt* **1** move. **2** stir. *vi* fidget.

rémunérer (re:myne:'re:) *vt* **1** remunerate. **2** reward. **rémunérateur, -trice** (re:myne:ra'tœr, -'tri:s) *adj* remunerative.

renâcler (rәna'kle:) *vi* snort.

renaissance (rәnɛ'sɑ̃s) *nf* renaissance.

renard (rә'nar) *nm* fox.

renchérir (rɑ̃ʃe:'ri:r) *vi* increase in price.

rencontrer (rɑ̃kɔ̃'tre:) *vt* **1** meet. **2** encounter. **se rencontrer** *vr* **1** meet. **2** collide. **3** agree. **rencontre** *nf* **1** meeting. **2** encounter. **3** occasion.

se rendormir (rɑ̃dɔr'mi:r) *vr* go back to sleep.

rendre (rɑ̃dr) *vt* **1** give back. **2** render. **3** restore. **4** yield. **5** deliver. **6** surrender. **7** make. **se rendre** *vr* **1** go. **2** surrender. **rendez-vous** *nm invar* **1** appointment. **2** meeting place.

rêne (rɛn) *nf* rein.

renfermer (rɑ̃fɛr'me:) *vt* **1** shut up. **2** contain, comprise. **renfermé** *adj* uncommunicative, reserved.

renforcer (rɑ̃fɔr'se:) *vt* **1** reinforce. **2** strengthen. **3** intensify. *vi* grow stronger.

renfort (rɑ̃'fɔr) *nm* reinforcement(s).

se renfrogner (rɑ̃frɔ'ɲe:) *vr* **1** scowl. **2** frown. **renfrogné** *adj* sullen.

rengaine (rɑ̃'gɛn) *nf* hackneyed story.

renier (rə'nje:) *vt* **1** disown. **2** repudiate, deny. **reniement** *nm* **1** repudiation, denial.

renifler (rəni:'fle:) *vi,vt* sniff.

renne (rɛn) *nm* reindeer.

renommée (rənɔ'me:) *nf* renown, fame. **renommé** *adj* famous.

renoncer (rənɔ̃'se:) *vt* **1** renounce. **2** give up.

renoncule (rənɔ̃'kyl) *nf* buttercup.

renouer (rə'nwe:) *vt* **1** tie up again. **2** resume.

renouveler (rənu:'vle:) *vt* renew. **se renouveler** *vr* recur.

rénover (re:nɔ've:) *vt* **1** renovate. **2** restore.

renseigner (rɑ̃sɛ'ɲe:) *vt* inform. **se renseigner sur** *vr* make enquiries about. **renseignement** *nm* information.

rente (rɑ̃t) *nf* **1** private income. **2** pension. **3** rent.

rentrer (rɑ̃'tre:) *vi* (*aux* être) **1** return. **2** come in again. **3** go home. *vt* take or bring in. **rentrée** *nf* **1** return. **2** reopening. **3** beginning of school term.

renverser (rɑ̃vɛr'se:) *vt* **1** turn upside down. **2** knock over. **3** invert. **4** *inf* amaze. **se renverser** *vr* overturn. **renverse** *nf* **1** turn. **2** change. **renversement** *nm* **1** reversal, inversion. **2** overthrow.

renvoi (rɑ̃'vwa) *nm* **1** return. **2** dismissal. **3** postponement.

renvoyer* (rɑ̃vwa'je:) *vt* **1** send back. **2** dismiss. **3** postpone. **4** refer.

réorganiser (re:ɔrgani:'ze:) *vt* reorganize.

repaire (rə'pɛr) *nm* **1** den. **2** refuge.

répandre (re:'pɑ̃dr) *vt* **1** spill. **2** spread. **3** scatter. **se répandre** *vr* be spread. **répandu** *adj* **1** widespread. **2** well-known.

reparaître* (rəpa'rɛtr) *vi* reappear.

réparer (re:pa're:) *vt* **1** repair. **2** make amends. **réparation** *nf* **1** repair. **2** amends.

repartie (rəpar'ti:) *nf* **1** repartee. **2** retort.

répartir (re:par'ti:r) *vt* **1** distribute. **2** divide. **3** allocate. **répartition** *nf* **1** distribution. **2** allocation.

repas (rə'pa) *nm* meal.

repasser (rəpɑ'se:) *vi* (*aux* être) pass again. *vt* **1** pass over. **2** go over. **3** sharpen. **4** iron. **repassage** *nm* **1** sharpening. **2** ironing.

se repentir* (rəpɑ̃'ti:r) *vr* repent, be sorry. **repenti** *adj* repentant. **repentir** *nm* repentance.

répercussion (re:pɛrky'sjɔ̃) *nf* repercussion.

répercuter (re:pɛrky'te:) *vt* **1** reverberate. **2** reflect.

repérer (rəpe:'re:) *vt* spot, locate. **repère** *nm* reference. **point de repère** *nm* landmark.

répertoire (re:pɛr'twar) *nm* **1** index, catalogue. **2** repertoire. **3** repertory.

répéter (re:pe:'te:) *vt* **1** repeat. **2** rehearse. **répétiteur, -trice** (re:pe:ti:'tœr, -'tri:s) *nm,f* tutor. **répétition** *nf* **1** repetition. **2** rehearsal. **répétition générale** dress rehearsal.

répit (re:'pi:) *nm* respite.

replacer (rəpla'se:) *vt* **1** put back. **2** reassign.

repli (rə'pli:) *nm* **1** fold, crease. **2** coil.

replier (rəpli:'e:) *vt* **1** fold up. **2** turn back.

répliquer (re:pli:'ke:) *vi* retort. **réplique** *nf* **1** retort. **2** *Th* cue. **3** *Art* replica.

répondre (re:'pɔ̃dr) *vt* **1** reply, answer. **2** respond. **répondre de** answer for.

réponse (re:'pɔ̃s) *nf* **1** answer, reply. **2** response.

reporter[1] (rəpɔr'te:) *vt* **1** carry back. **2** defer. **se reporter** *vr* refer.

reporter[2] (rəpɔr'te:) *nm* reporter. **reportage** *nm* **1** report. **2** reporting.

repos (rə'po) *nm* **1** rest. **2** peace.

reposer[1] (rəpo'ze:) *vt* put back, replace.

reposer[2] (rəpo'ze:) *vt* rest. *vi* **1** lie. **2** be based. **se reposer** *vr* **1** rest. **2** settle. **3** rely.

repousser (rəpu:'se:) *vt* **1** push back. **2** repulse. **3** reject.

reprendre* (rə'prɛ̃dr) *vt* **1** take back. **2** resume. **3** reply. **4** reprimand. *vi* recommence. **se reprendre** *vr* **1** pull oneself together. **2** correct oneself.

représailles (rəprɛ'zaj) *nf pl* retaliation, reprisal. **user de représailles** retaliate.

représenter (rəpre:zɑ̃'te:) *vt* **1** represent. **2** depict. **3** act for. **4** *Th* perform. **représentant** *adj,n* representative. **représentation** *nf* **1** representation. **2** agency. **3** *Th* performance.

répressif, -ive (re:prɛ'si:f, -'si:v) *adj* repressive. **répression** *nf* repression.

réprimander (re:pri:mɑ̃'de:) *vt* reprimand, censure. **réprimande** *nf* reprimand.

réprimer (re:'pri:'me:) *vt* **1** repress. **2** quell.

reprise (rə'pri:z) *nf* **1** renewal. **2** revival. **3**

repetition. **4** darning. **5** *sport* round. **à plusieurs reprises** again and again.
reprocher (rəprɔ'ʃe:) *vt* **1** reproach. **2** grudge. **reproche** *nm* reproach.
reproduction (rəprɔdyk'sjɔ̃) *nf* reproduction.
reproduire (rəprɔ'dɥi:r) *vt* reproduce. **se reproduire** *vr* recur.
reptile (rɛp'ti:l) *adj,nm* reptile.
répu (re:'py) *adj* well fed, sated.
républicain (re:pybli:'kɛ̃) *adj,n* republican.
république (re:py'bli:k) *nf* republic.
répudier (re:py'dje:) *vt* repudiate.
répulsif, -ive (re:pyl'si:f, -'si:v) *adj* repulsive. **répulsion** *nf* repulsion.
réputation (re:pyta'sjɔ̃) *nf* reputation, repute. **réputé** *adj* famous, well-known.
requérir* (rəke:'ri:r) *vt* **1** ask, request. **2** demand.
requête (rə'kɛt) *nf* **1** request. **2** petition.
requiem (re:kɥi:'ɛm) *nm invar* requiem.
requin (rə'kɛ̃) *nm* shark.
requis (rə'ki:) *adj* necessary.
rescapé (rɛska'pe:) *nm* survivor.
réseau, -aux (re:'zo) *nm* network, system.
réserver (re:zɛr've:) *vt* reserve. **réserve** *nf* **1** reservation. **2** reserve. **3** caution. **4** store. **réservé** *adj* **1** reserved. **2** cautious. **3** secretive. **réservoir** *nm* **1** reservoir. **2** tank.
résider (re:zi:'de:) *vi* **1** reside, live. **2** consist. **résidence** *nf* residence. **résident** *nm* resident. **résidentiel, -elle** (re:zi:dɑ̃'sjɛl) *adj* residential.
résidu (re:si:'dy) *nm* residue.
se résigner (re:zi:'ɲe:) *vr* resign oneself.
résilier (re:zi:l'je:) *vt* cancel, annul.
résille (re:'zi:j) *nf* hairnet.
résine (re:'zi:n) *nf* resin.
résister (re:zi:'ste:) *vi* (of colours) be fast. **résister à 1** resist. **2** withstand. **3** oppose. **résistance** *nf* **1** resistance. **2** strength.
résolu (re:zɔ'ly) *v* see **résoudre.** *adj* determined, resolute. **résolution** *nf* **1** solution (of a problem). **2** resolution. **3** resolve.
résolvant (re:zɔl'vɑ̃) *v* see **résoudre.**
résonner (re:zɔ'ne:) *vi* resound, reverberate.
résoudre* (re:'zu:dr) *vt* **1** dissolve. **2** solve, settle. **3** resolve.
respect (rɛ'spɛ) *nm* respect. **respect de soi** self-respect.
respecter (rɛspɛk'te:) *vt* **1** respect. **2** abide by. **respectable** *adj* respectable. **respectueux, -euse** (rɛspɛk'tɥœ, -'tɥœz) *adj* respectful. **respectueux des lois** law-abiding.
respectif, -ive (rɛspɛk'ti:f, -'ti:v) *adj* respective.
respirer (rɛspi:'re:) *vi,vt* breathe. **respiration** *nf* breathing. **respiration artificielle** artifical respiration.
resplendir (rɛsplɑ̃'di:r) *vi* **1** glitter. **2** glow.
responsable (rɛspɔ̃'sabl) *adj* responsible. **responsabilité** *nf* responsibility.
resquiller (rɛski:'je:) *vi* gatecrash. *vt inf* wangle.
ressaisir (rəsɛ'zi:r) *vt* seize again. **se ressaisir** *vr* pull oneself together.
ressembler (rəsɑ̃'ble:) *vt* resemble. **se ressembler** *vr* be alike. **ressemblance** *nf* resemblance.
ressentir* (rəsɑ̃'ti:r) *vt* feel. **ressentiment** *nm* resentment.
ressort[1] (rə'sɔr) *nm* **1** spring. **2** energy. **3** elasticity.
ressort[2] (rə'sɔr) *nm* scope, province.
ressortir* (rəsɔr'ti:r) *vi* (*aux* être) **1** come or go out again. **2** stand out. *vt* bring out again. **ressortir de** follow from.
ressource (rə'su:rs) *nf* **1** resource. **2** expedient. **3** *pl* means.
ressusciter (re:sysi:'te:) *vt* restore to life. *vt,vi* revive.
restaurer (rɛstɔ're:) *vt* **1** restore. **2** refresh. **restauration** *nf* restoration.
rester (rɛ'ste:) *vi* (*aux* être) **1** remain, stay. **2** be left. **restant** *adj* remaining. *nm* remainder. **reste** *nm* **1** remainder. **2** *pl* remains. **du reste** moreover.
restituer (rɛsti:'tɥe:) *vt* **1** restore. **2** return.
restreindre* (rɛ'strɛ̃dr) *vt* restrict, limit.
restriction (rɛstri:k'sjɔ̃) *nf* restriction.
résulter (re:zyl'te:) *vi* (*aux* être) result, follow. **résultat** *nm* **1** result. **2** outcome.
résumer (re:zy'me:) *vt* summarize. **résumé** *nm* summary, résumé.
résurrection (re:zyrɛk'sjɔ̃) *nf* resurrection.
rétablir (re:ta'bli:r) *vt* **1** re-establish. **2** restore. **3** reinstate. **rétablissement** *nm* **1** restoration. **2** recovery.
retard (rə'tar) *nm* delay. **en retard 1** late, behindhand. **2** backward.
retarder (rətar'de:) *vt* retard, delay. *vi* be late. **retardataire** *adj* **1** late. **2** backward.
retenir* (rət'ni:r) *vt* **1** hold back. **2** detain. **3** secure. **4** retain. **5** book, reserve. **se retenir** *vr* **1** restrain oneself. **2** cling.
retentir (rətɑ̃'ti:r) *vi* **1** resound. **2** reverberate. **3** echo. **retentissement** *nm* **1** repercussion. **2** reverberation.

retenue (rəˈny) *nf* 1 discretion. 2 withholding. 3 detention. **retenu** *adj* prudent.
réticent (re:ti:ˈsɑ̃) *adj* reticent, reserved.
rétif, -ive (re:ˈti:f, -ˈti:v) *adj* obstinate.
rétine (re:ˈti:n) *nf* retina.
retirer (rəti:ˈre:) *vt* 1 withdraw. 2 pull out. 3 remove. **se retirer** *vr* retire, withdraw.
retomber (rətɔ̃ˈbe:) *vi* (*aux* être) 1 fall back. 2 hang down.
retors (rəˈtɔr) *adj* 1 twisted. 2 cunning.
retoucher (rətu:ˈʃe:) *vt* touch up, improve. **retouche** *nf* small alteration.
retour (rəˈtu:r) *nm* return. **être de retour** be back.
retourner (rətu:rˈne:) *vt* 1 turn (inside out). 2 turn round or back. 3 return. *vi* (*aux* être) go back. **se retourner** *vr* turn round or back.
rétracter[1] (re:trakˈte:) *vt* retract, withdraw.
rétracter[2] (re:trakˈte:) *vt* retract, draw in.
retraite (rəˈtrɛt) *nf* 1 retreat. 2 *mil* tattoo. 3 retirement. 4 refuge. **prendre sa retraite** retire. **retraité** *nm* pensioner.
retrancher (rətrɑ̃ˈʃe:) *vt* 1 cut off or down. 2 entrench.
rétrécir (re:tre:ˈsi:r) *vi,vt* 1 narrow. 2 contract, shrink. **rétrécissement** *nm* shrinkage.
rétribuer (re:tri:ˈbɥe:) *vt* remunerate, pay.
rétroaction (re:troakˈsjɔ̃) *nf* feedback.
rétrograder (re:trɔgraˈde:) *vi* retrogress, go backwards. **rétrograde** *adj* retrograde, backward.
rétrospectif, -ive (re:trɔspɛkˈti:f, -ˈti:v) *adj* retrospective.
retrousser (rətru:ˈse:) *vt* 1 turn up. 2 tuck up. 3 roll up.
retrouver (rətru:ˈve:) *vt* 1 find again. 2 regain.
rétroviseur (re:trɔvi:ˈzœr) *nm* driving mirror.
réunir (re:yˈni:r) *vt* reunite. **se réunir** *vr* gather together. **réunion** *nf* reunion, meeting.
réussir (re:yˈsi:r) *vi* succeed. **réussi** *adj* successful. **réussite** *nf* 1 success. 2 *pl game* patience.
revanche (rəˈvɑ̃ʃ) *nf* 1 revenge. 2 return match. **en revanche** 1 in return. 2 on the other hand.
rêvasser (rɛvaˈse:) *vi* daydream.
rêve (rɛv) *nm* dream.
revêche (rəˈvɛʃ) *adj* 1 perverse, difficult. 2 harsh, churlish.
réveiller (re:vɛˈje:) *vt* wake, awaken. **se réveiller** *vr* awake, wake up. **réveille-matin** *nm invar* alarm clock.
révéler (re:ve:ˈle:) *vt* 1 reveal, disclose. 2 show. **révélateur, -trice** (re:ve:laˈtœr, -ˈtri:s) *adj* revealing, telltale.
revendiquer (rəvɑ̃di:ˈke:) *vt* 1 claim, demand. 2 assume. **revendication** *nf* demand.
revenir* (rəvˈni:r) *vi* (*aux* être) 1 return, come back. 2 go back on. 3 cost. 4 amount. **revenir de** recover. **en revenir** get over it. **revenant** *adj* pleasing. *nm* ghost. **revenu** *nm* revenue, income.
rêver (rɛˈve:) *vi* 1 dream. 2 muse.
réverbérer (re:vɛrbe:ˈre:) *vt* reflect. *vi* reverberate. **réverbère** *nm* 1 streetlamp. 2 reflector.
révérence (re:vɛˈrɑ̃s) *nf* 1 reverence. 2 bow, curtsy.
revers (rəˈvɛr) *nm* 1 reverse. 2 wrong side. 3 lapel.
revêtir* (rəvɛˈti:r) *vt* 1 clothe, dress. 2 coat, case.
revirement (rəvi:rˈmɑ̃) *nm* sudden change.
reviser (rəvi:ˈze:) *vt* revise, modify. **revision** *nf* 1 revision. 2 inspection.
revivre* (rəˈvi:vr) *vi* relive. **faire revivre** revive.
revoir* (rəˈvwar) *vt* 1 see again. 2 revise. **au revoir!** *interj* goodbye!
révolter (re:vɔlˈte:) *vt* 1 rouse, stir up. 2 disgust. **révolte** *nf* revolt. **révolté** *nm* rebel.
révolution (re:vɔlyˈsjɔ̃) *nf* revolution. **révolutionnaire** *adj* revolutionary.
revolver (re:vɔlˈvɛr) *nm* revolver.
révoquer (re:vɔˈke:) *vt* 1 revoke. 2 dismiss.
revue (rəˈvy) *nf* 1 inspection. 2 review. 3 revue.
rez-de-chaussé (re:dʃoˈse:) *nm invar* ground floor.
rhétorique (re:tɔˈri:k) *nf* rhetoric.
Rhin (rɛ̃) *nm* Rhine.
rhinocéros (rinɔse:ˈrɔs) *nm* rhinoceros.
Rhodésie (rɔde:ˈzi:) *nf* Rhodesia. **rhodésien, -ienne** (rɔde:ˈzjɛ̃, -ˈzjɛn) *adj,n* Rhodesian.
Rhône (ron) *nm* Rhone.
rhubarbe (ryˈbarb) *nf* rhubarb.
rhum (rɔm) *nm* rum.
rhumatisme (rymaˈti:sm) *nm* rheumatism.
rhume (rym) *nm med* cold. **rhume des foins** hayfever.
ri (ri:) *v* see **rire.**
riant (ri:ˈɑ̃) *v* see **rire.**
ricaner (ri:kaˈne:) *vi* sneer.
riche (ri:ʃ) *adj* 1 rich, wealthy. 2 valuable. 3 fertile. **richesse** *nf* 1 wealth. 2 richness.
rider (ri:ˈde:) *vt* 1 wrinkle. 2 shrivel. **se rider** *vr* 1 wrinkle. 2 shrivel. 3 ripple. **ride** *nf* 1

wrinkle. **2** ripple. **ridé** *adj* **1** wrinkled. **2** corrugated.
rideau, -aux (ri:'do) *nm* **1** curtain. **2** screen. **Rideau de Fer** Iron Curtain.
ridectomie (ri:dɛktɔ'mi:) *nf* facelift.
ridicule (ri:di:'kyl) *adj* ridiculous. *nm* **1** absurdity. **2** ridicule.
rien (rjɛ̃) *pron* anything. **ne...rien** nothing. **cela ne fait rien** that doesn't matter. **il n'y a rien à faire** it can't be helped. ~*nm* trifle, trivial thing or affair.
rigide (ri:'ʒi:d) *adj* **1** rigid. **2** stiff. **3** tense. **rigidité** *nf* rigidity.
rigole (ri:'gɔl) *nf* drain, gutter.
rigoler (ri:gɔ'le:) *vi inf* **1** laugh. **2** enjoy oneself. **3** joke. **rigolo, -ote** *adj* funny, comical.
rigoureux, -euse (ri:gu:'rœ, -'rœz) *adj* **1** rigorous. **2** harsh. **3** strict.
rigueur (ri:'gœr) *nf* **1** rigour, strictness. **2** severity. **3** hardship. **à la rigueur** **1** strictly. **2** if need be. **de rigueur** compulsory.
rimer (ri:'me:) *vi* rhyme. **rime** *nf* rhyme.
rincer (rɛ̃'se:) *vt* rinse.
riposter (ri:pɔ'ste:) *vi* retort. **riposte** *nf* retort.
rire* (ri:r) *vi* **1** laugh. **2** joke. **rire nerveusement** giggle. **rire tout bas** chuckle. **se rire de** *vr* laugh at. ~*nm* **1** laughter. **2** laugh. **petit rire nerveux** giggle. **rire étouffé** chuckle.
ris (ri:) **ris de veau** *nm* sweetbread.
risquer (ri:'ske:) *vt* risk. **se risquer** *vr* take a risk. **risque** *nm* risk.
ristourne (ri:'stu:rn) *nf* **1** refund, rebate. **2** discount.
rite (ri:t) *nm* rite. **rituel, -elle** (ri:'tɥɛl) *adj,nm* ritual.
rival, -aux (ri:'val, -'vo) *adj,n* rival.
rivaliser (ri:vali:'ze:) *vi* **1** rival. **2** compete. **rivalité** *nf* rivalry.
rive (ri:v) *nf* **1** bank (of a river). **2** shore. **3** riverside. **4** edge. **rivage** *nm* **1** bank (of a river). **2** shore.
river (ri:'ve:) *vt* rivet. **rivet** *nm* rivet.
rivière (ri:'vjɛr) *nf* **1** river. **2** stream.
rixe (ri:ks) *nf* brawl, scuffle.
riz (ri:) *nm* rice.
robe (rɔb) *nf* **1** dress. **2** gown. **3** robe. **4** skin (of an onion, etc.). **robe de chambre** dressing-gown. **robe du soir** evening dress.
robinet (rɔbi:'nɛ) *nm* tap.
robot (ro'bo) *nm* robot.
robuste (rɔ'byst) *adj* **1** robust. **2** sturdy. **3** hardy.
roche (rɔʃ) *nf* rock, boulder. **rocher** *nm* rock.
rôder (ro'de:) *vi* prowl.
rogner (rɔ'ɲe:) *vt* clip, trim.
rognon (rɔ'ɲɔ̃) *nm cul* kidney.
rogue (rɔg) *adj* arrogant.
roi (rwa) *nm* king.
roitelet (rwat'lɛ) *nm* wren.
rôle (rol) *nm* **1** roll. **2** part, role.
romain (rɔ'mɛ̃) *adj,n* Roman.
roman[1] (rɔ'mɑ̃) *nm* **1** novel. **2** *pl* fiction. **roman policier** detective novel. **romancier, -ière** (rɔmɑ̃'sje:, -'sjɛr) *nm,f* novelist.
roman[2] (rɔ'mɑ̃) *adj* **1** romance. **2** Romanesque.
romanesque (rɔma'nɛsk) *adj* romantic.
romantique (rɔmɑ̃'ti:k) *adj* romantic.
romarin (rɔma'rɛ̃) *nm* rosemary.
Rome (rɔm) *nf* Rome.
rompre (rɔ̃pr) *vt* **1** break. **2** snap. **3** break off or up. *vi* break. **rompu** *adj* broken.
ronce (rɔ̃s) *nf* **1** blackberry bush. **2** *pl* thorns.
rond (rɔ̃) *adj* **1** round. **2** plump. **3** *sl* drunk. *nm* **1** ring, circle. **2** washer. **3** disc. **rond-de-cuir** *nm, pl* **ronds-de-cuir** *inf* **1** clerk. **2** bureaucrat. **rond-point** *nm, pl* **ronds-points** roundabout. **ronde** *nf* **1** round, inspection. **2** semibreve.
ronfler (rɔ̃'fle:) *vi* **1** snore. **2** (of a fire) roar. **3** hum. **ronflement** *nm* **1** snore. **2** snoring. **3** buzzing.
ronger (rɔ̃'ʒe:) *vt* **1** gnaw. **2** corrode. **3** erode. **rongeur, -euse** (rɔ̃'ʒœr, -'ʒœz) *adj* gnawing. *nm* rodent.
ronron (rɔ̃'rɔ̃) *nm* purr.
ronronner (rɔ̃rɔ'ne:) *vi* purr.
roquet (rɔ'kɛ) *nm* mongrel.
roquette (rɔ'kɛt) *nf* rocket.
rosaire (ro'zɛr) *nm* rosary.
rosbif (rɔs'bi:f) *nm* roast beef.
rose (roz) *nf* rose. **rose trémière** hollyhock. *adj* pink, rosy. *nm* pink. **rosé** *adj* pink. *nm* rosé wine. **rosier** *nm* rose bush or tree.
roseau, -aux (ro'zo) *nm* reed.
rosée (ro'ze:) *nf* dew.
roselet (ro'zlɛ) *nm* ermine.
rosette (ro'zɛt) *nf* **1** bow (of ribbon). **2** rosette.
rosser (rɔ'se:) *vt* give a beating. **rossée** *nf inf* thrashing.
rossignol (rɔsi:'ɲɔl) *nm* **1** nightingale. **2** *inf* piece of junk.
rotatif, -ive (rɔta'ti:f, -'ti:v) *adj* rotary. **rotation** *nf* rotation.
rôtir (ro'ti:r) *vt,vi* **1** roast. **2** toast. **3** scorch. **rôti** *nm* roast (meat). **rôtisserie** *nf* grillroom.
rotor (rɔ'tɔr) *nm* rotor.

rotule (rɔ'tyl) *nf* kneecap.
rouage (rwaʒ) *nm* **1** works, machinery. **2** wheel.
roublard (ru:'blar) *adj inf* sly, artful.
rouble (ru:bl) *nm* rouble.
roue (ru:) *nf* wheel. **faire la roue 1** strut. **2** do a cartwheel.
roué (rwe:) *adj* cunning.
rouelle (rwɛl) *nf* round slice, round.
rougeole (ru:'ʒɔl) *nf* measles.
rougir (ru:'ʒi:r) *vt* redden. *vi* **1** turn red. **2** blush. **rouge** *adj* red. **rouge-gorge** *nm, pl* **rouges-gorges** robin. *nm* **1** red. **2** rouge. **rougeur** *nf* **1** redness. **2** blush, flush.
rouiller (ru:'je:) *vi* **1** rust. **2** mildew. **rouille** *nf* **1** rust. **2** mildew.
rouler (ru:'le:) *vt* **1** roll. **2** *inf* take in, swindle. **3** turn over. *vi* **1** roll (over or down). **2** rumble. **3** roam. **4** turn. **se rouler** *vr* roll. **roulage** *nm* carriage, haulage. **roulant** *adj* **1** sliding, moving. **2** smooth. **3** *sl* hilarious. **rouleau, -aux** (ru:'lo) *nm* **1** roller. **2** roll. **3** spool. **4** rolling pin. **rouleau compresseur** steam-roller. **rouleau de papier hygiénique** toilet roll. **roulette** *nf* **1** castor, small wheel. **2** roulette.
roulotte (ru:'lɔt) *nf* (gipsy) caravan.
roupiller (ru:pi:'je:) *vi inf* sleep, snooze. **roupillon** *nm* snooze.
rouquin (ru:'kɛ̃) *adj inf* red-haired, ginger.
rouspéter (ru:spe:'te:) *vi* **1** protest. **2** grumble.
roussir (ru:'si:r) *vi,vt* turn brown. *vi* singe, get scorched. **rousseur** *nf* redness (of hair).
route (ru:t) *nf* **1** road, track. **2** route. **route nationale** main road, trunk road.
routine (ru:'ti:n) *nf* routine.
roux, rousse (ru:, ru:s) *adj* **1** red-haired. **2** reddish.
royal, -aux (rwa'jal, -'jo) *adj* royal, regal.
royaume (rwa'jom) *nm* **1** kingdom. **2** realm. **royauté** (rwajo'te:) *nf* royalty.
Royaume-Uni *nm* United Kingdom.
ruban (ry'bɑ̃) *nm* **1** ribbon. **2** band.
rubéole (rybe:'ɔl) *nf* German measles.
rubis (ry'bi:) *nm* ruby.
rubrique (ry'bri:k) *nf* heading, title.
ruche (ryʃ) *nf* beehive.
rude (ryd) *adj* **1** hard. **2** rough. **3** harsh. **4** uncouth. **5** gruff. **rudement** *adv inf* very. **rudesse** *nf* **1** harshness. **2** severity. **3** roughness.
rudiment (rydi:'mɑ̃) *nm* rudiment.
rudoyer (rydwa'je:) *vt* **1** treat roughly. **2** bully.
rue (ry) *nf* street, thoroughfare. **rue à sens unique** one-way street. **ruelle** *nf* alley, lane.
ruer (rɥe:) *vi* (of a horse, etc.) kick (out). **se ruer** *vr* **1** fling oneself. **2** rush. **ruée** *nf* rush.
rugir (ry'ʒi:r) *vi* **1** roar. **2** howl. **rugissement** *nm* **1** roar. **2** roaring.
rugueux, -euse (ry'gœ, -'gœz) *adj* **1** rough. **2** rugged. **3** wrinkled.
ruiner (rɥi:'ne:) *vt* ruin. **se ruiner** *vr* **1** go to ruin. **2** ruin oneself. **ruine** *nf* **1** ruin. **2** downfall. **3** destruction.
ruisseau, -aux (rɥi:'so) *nm* **1** gutter. **2** brook. **3** stream.
ruisseler (rɥi:'sle:) *vi* **1** trickle, drip. **2** stream, flow.
rumeur (ry'mœr) *nf* **1** murmur, distant noise. **2** din. **3** rumour.
rupture (ryp'tyr) *nf* **1** breaking. **2** rupture.
rural, -aux (ry'ral, -'ro) *adj* rural.
ruse (ryz) *nf* trick, stratagem. **rusé** *adj* sly.
Russie (ry'si:) *nf* Russia. **russe** *adj,n* Russian. *nm* Russian (language).
rustique (ry'sti:k) *adj* **1** rustic. **2** rural.
rutabaga (rytaba'ga) *nm* swede.
rythme (ri:tm) *nm* **1** rhythm. **2** *mus* beat. **rythmique** *adj* rhythmical.

S

sa (sa) *poss adj* see **son.**
sabbat (sa'ba) *nm* Sabbath.
sable[1] (sɑbl) *nm* sand. **sables mouvants** *nm pl* quicksand. **sableux, -euse** (sa'blœ, -'blœz) *adj* sandy. **sablière** (sɑbli:'ɛr) *nf* sandpit.
sable[2] (sɑbl) *nm* sable.
sabot (sa'bo) *nm* **1** clog. **2** hoof.
sabotage (sabɔ'taʒ) *nm* sabotage.
sabre (sabr) *nm* **1** sabre. **2** swordfish.
sac (sak) *nm* **1** sack. **2** bag. **sac à dos** rucksack. **sac à main** handbag. **sac de couchage** sleeping-bag.
saccade (sa'kad) *nf* jolt, jerk. **par saccades** by fits and starts.
saccager (saka'ʒe:) *vt* **1** pillage. **2** ransack, cause havoc.
saccharine (sakka'ri:n) *nf* saccharin.
sacerdoce (sasɛr'dɔs) *nm* priesthood.
sachant (sə'ʃɑ̃) *v* see **savoir.**
sachet (sa'ʃɛ) *nm* **1** small bag. **2** sachet.
sacoche (sa'kɔʃ) *nf* **1** saddlebag. **2** satchel.
sacrement (sakrə'mɑ̃) *nm* sacrament.
sacrer (sa'kre:) *vt* anoint, crown. *vi* swear.

sacre *nm* **1** coronation. **2** consecration. **sacré** *adj* **1** holy, sacred. **2** *sl* damned, cursed.

sacrifier (sakri:'fje:) *vt* **1** sacrifice. **2** give up. **sacrifice** *nm* sacrifice.

sacrilège (sakri:'lɛʒ) *nm* sacrilege. *adj* sacrilegious.

sacristie (sakri:'sti:) *nf* vestry.

sadisme (sa'di:sm) *nm* sadism. **sadique** *adj* sadistic. *nm,f* sadist.

safran (sa'frɑ̃) *nm* **1** saffron. **2** crocus.

sagace (sa'gas) *adj* shrewd.

sage (saʒ) *adj* **1** wise. **2** discreet. **3** well-behaved. **4** chaste. **sois sage!** be good! **sage-femme** *nf, pl* **sages-femmes** midwife. **sagesse** *nf* **1** wisdom. **2** prudence.

Sagittaire (saʒi:t'tɛr) *nm* Sagittarius.

sagou (sa'gu:) *nm* sago.

saigner (sɛ'ɲe:) *vi,vt* bleed. **saignant** *adj* **1** bleeding. **2** *cul* underdone, rare.

saillir* (sa'ji:r) *vi* **1** gush out. **2** protrude. **3** stand out. **saillant** *adj* **1** prominent, protruding. **2** outstanding. **saillie** *nf* **1** spurt. **2** bound. **3** flash of wit. **4** ledge.

sain (sɛ̃) *adj* **1** healthy. **2** sound. **3** wholesome. **sain et sauf** safe and sound.

saindoux (sɛ̃'du:) *nm* lard

saint (sɛ̃) *adj* **1** holy. **2** saintly. **3** hallowed. *nm* saint. **sainteté** *nf* holiness.

Saint-Esprit *nf* Holy Ghost.

sais (sɛ) *v* see **savoir.**

saisir (sɛ'zi:r) *vt* **1** seize, grab. **2** understand. **se saisir de** *vr* **1** seize upon. **2** lay hands on. **saisie** *nf* seizure. **saisissant** *adj* **1** striking. **2** piercing. **3** thrilling. **saisissement** *nm* **1** shock. **2** shiver.

saison (sɛ'zɔ̃) *nf* season. **de saison** in season. **saisonnier, -ière** (sɛzɔ'nje:, -'njɛr) *adj* seasonal.

salade (sa'lad) *nf* **1** salad. **2** lettuce. **3** *sl* mess.

salaire (sa'lɛr) *nm* **1** wages, salary. **2** reward.

salamandre (sala'mɑ̃dr) *nf* salamander. **salamandre aquatique** newt.

sale (sal) *adj* **1** dirty, filthy. **2** offensive, obscene. **saleté** *nf* **1** dirt. **2** trash. **3** obscenity. **4** dirty trick.

saler (sa'le:) *vt* **1** salt. **2** *cul* cure. **3** *inf* overcharge. **salaison** *nf cul* curing. **salé** *adj* **1** salted. **2** *inf* spicy. **3** *sl* exorbitant. **salière** *nf* salt-cellar.

salir (sa'li:r) *vt* **1** dirty, soil. **2** sully.

saliver (sali:'ve:) *vi* salivate. **salive** *nf* saliva.

salle (sal) *nf* **1** room. **2** *Th* house. **3** *pol* lobby. **salle à manger** dining room. **salle d'attente** waiting room. **salle de bain** bathroom. **salle de bal** ballroom. **salle de classe** classroom. **salle de séjour** living room. **salle de spectacle** theatre. **salle d'hôpital** *med* ward. **salle d'opérations** *med* theatre.

salon (sa'lɔ̃) *nm* **1** drawing room. **2** saloon. **3** salon.

saloperie (salɔ'pri:) *nf* **1** filthiness. **2** *inf* rubbish. **3** dirty trick.

salopette (salɔ'pɛt) *nf* **1** overalls. **2** dungarees.

saltimbanque (saltɛ̃'bɑ̃k) *nm* **1** showman. **2** charlatan.

salubre (sa'lybr) *adj* **1** healthy. **2** wholesome.

saluer (sal'ɥe:) *vt* **1** greet. **2** salute. **3** bow.

salut (sa'ly) *nm* **1** safety. **2** salvation. **3** bow. **4** greeting. **5** salute. *interj* hello! **salutation** *nf* **1** greeting. **2** bow.

salutaire (saly'tɛr) *adj* **1** beneficial. **2** healthy.

samedi (sam'di:) *nm* Saturday.

sanctifier (sɑ̃kti:'fje:) *vt* hallow.

sanction (sɑ̃k'sjɔ̃) *nf* **1** sanction, approval. **2** *law* penalty.

sanctionner (sɑ̃ksjɔ'ne:) *vt* **1** sanction, approve. **2** penalize.

sanctuaire (sɑ̃k'tɥɛr) *nm* sanctuary.

sandale (sɑ̃'dal) *nf* sandal.

sandwich (sɑ̃'dwi:tʃ) *nm* sandwich.

sang (sɑ̃) *nm* **1** blood. **2** relationship. **à sang chaud/froid** warm/cold-blooded. **sang-froid** *nm* composure, coolness. **sang-mêlé** *nm invar* half-caste.

sanglant (sɑ̃'glɑ̃) *adj* **1** covered in blood. **2** scathing.

sangler (sɑ̃'gle:) *vt* **1** strap, tie up. **2** thrash. **sangle** *nf* **1** strap. **2** girth.

sanglier (sɑ̃gli:'e:) *nm* wild boar.

sanglot (sɑ̃'glo) *nm* sob. **sangloter** *vi* sob.

sangsue (sɑ̃'sy) *nf* leech.

sanguin (sɑ̃'gɛ̃) *adj* blood. **sanguinaire** *adj* bloodthirsty.

sanitaire (sani:'tɛr) *adj* sanitary.

sans (sɑ̃) *prep* **1** without. **2** but for. **sans que** without. **sans-abri** *nm invar* homeless person. **sans-façon** *adj* homely. *nm* straightforwardness. **sans-gêne** *adj* offhand, blunt. *nm inf* cheek. **sans-souci** *adj invar* carefree, easygoing.

sansonnet (sɑ̃sɔ'nɛ) *nm* starling.

santé (sɑ̃'te:) *nf* health. **à votre santé!** cheers!

saper (sa'pe:) *vt* undermine.

sapeur (sa'pœr) *nm mil* pioneer, scout. **sapeur-**

pompier *nm, pl* **sapeurs-pompiers 1** fireman. **2** *pl* fire brigade.
saphir (sa'fi:r) *nm* sapphire.
sapin (sa'pɛ̃) *nm* fir.
sarcasme (sar'kasm) *nm* sarcasm. **sarcastique** *adj* sarcastic.
sarcler (sar'kle:) *vt* **1** weed. **2** hoe.
Sardaigne (sar'dɛɲ) *nf* Sardinia. **sarde** *adj,n* Sardinian.
sardine (sar'di:n) *nf* **1** pilchard. **2** sardine.
sardonique (sardɔ'ni:k) *adj* sardonic.
Satan (sa'tɑ̃) *nm* Satan.
satin (sa'tɛ̃) *nm* satin.
satire (sa'ti:r) *nf* satire. **satirique** *adj* satirical.
satisfaction (sati:sfak'sjɔ̃) *nf* satisfaction.
satisfaire* (sati:s'fɛr) *vt* **1** satisfy, content. **2** meet, fulfil. **satisfaisant** *adj* satisfactory.
saturer (saty're:) *vt* saturate.
Saturne (sa'tyrn) *nm* Saturn.
sauce (sos) *nf* **1** sauce. **2** gravy.
saucée (so'se:) *nf sl* **1** downpour. **2** telling-off
saucisse (so'si:s) *nf* sausage. **saucisson** *nm* large dry sausage.
sauf, sauve (sof, sov) *adj* safe, intact. **sauf** *prep* save, except, but.
sauge (soʒ) *nf bot* sage.
saugrenu (sogrə'ny) *adj* absurd, ridiculous.
saule (sol) *nm* willow.
saumon (so'mɔ̃) *nm* salmon.
saumure (so'myr) *nf* pickle.
sauna (so'na) *nm* sauna.
saupoudrer (sopu:'dre:) *vt* sprinkle, dust.
saurai (so:'rɛ) *v see* **savoir.**
saut (so) *nm* leap, jump. **saut-de-lit** *nm, pl* **sauts-de-lit** bedside rug. **saut-de-mouton** *nm, pl* **sauts-de-mouton** *mot* flyover. **saute-mouton** *nm* leapfrog. **saut périlleux** somersault.
sauter (so'te:) *vi* **1** jump, leap. **2** skip. **3** explode. **4** (of a fuse) blow. *vt* jump over. **sauterelle** *nf* grasshopper. **sauterie** *nf* **1** jumping. **2** private party.
sautiller (soti:'je:) *vt* **1** hop. **2** skip.
sauvage (so'vaʒ) *adj* **1** savage, wild. **2** primitive. **3** shy. *nm,f* savage. **sauvagerie** *nf* **1** brutality. **2** unsociability.
sauvegarder (sovgar'de:) *vt* safeguard, protect. **sauvegarde** *nf* **1** safeguard, protection. **2** bodyguard.
sauver (so've:) *vt* **1** save, rescue. **2** protect. **se sauver** *vr* **1** escape. **2** run away. **sauve-qui-peut** *nm invar* stampede, panic. **sauvetage** *nm* **1** rescue. **2** salvage. **sauveur** *nm* **1** saviour. **2** rescuer.
savant (sa'vɑ̃) *adj* **1** learned, scholarly. **2** able. **3** skilful. *nm* **1** scientist. **2** scholar. **savamment** *adv* **1** knowingly. **2** skilfully.
savate (sa'vat) *nf* **1** old shoe. **2** French boxing. **savetier** *nm* cobbler.
saveur (sa'vœr) *nf* **1** taste, flavour. **2** piquancy.
savoir* (sa'vwar) *vt* **1** know. **2** be aware of. **3** be able. **c'est à savoir** that remains to be seen. **faire savoir à** inform. **savoir-faire** *nm invar* **1** ability. **2** tact. **savoir-vivre** *nm invar* breeding, good manners. ~*nm* knowledge.
savon (sa'vɔ̃) *nm* soap. **savon en poudre** soap powder.
savonner (savɔ'ne:) *vt* soap, lather.
savourer (savu:'re:) *vt* **1** relish. **2** enjoy. **savoureux, -euse** (savu:'rœ, -'rœz) *adj* **1** tasty. **2** *inf* juicy.
scabreux, -euse (skɑ'brœ, -'brœz) *adj* **1** difficult, ticklish. **2** indecent.
scandale (skɑ̃'dal) *nm* **1** scandal. **2** disgrace.
scandaliser (skɑ̃dali:'ze:) *vt* shock, offend.
Scandinavie (skɑ̃di:na'vi:) *nf* Scandinavia. **scandinave** *adj,n* Scandinavian.
scaphandrier (skafɑ̃'dri:'e:) *nm* diver.
sceau, sceaux (so) *nm* **1** seal. **2** stamp, mark.
scélérat (ske:lɛ'ra) *adj* wicked, criminal. *nm* **1** scoundrel. **2** villain.
sceller (sɛ'le:) *vt* **1** seal. **2** confirm. **scellé** *nm* seal.
scène (sɛn) *nf* **1** stage. **2** scene. **3** *inf* quarrel, scene.
sceptique (sɛp'ti:k) *nm,f* sceptic. *adj* sceptical. **scepticisme** *nm* scepticism.
schéma (skɛ'ma) *nm* diagram.
schizophrénie (ski:zɔfre:'ni:) *nf* schizophrenia. **schizophrène** *adj* schizophrenic.
scie (si:) *nf* **1** saw. **2** *inf* bore.
sciemment (sja'mɑ̃) *adv* knowingly.
science (sjɑ̃s) *nf* **1** knowledge, learning. **2** science. **sciences naturelles** *nf pl* natural science.
scientifique (sjɑ̃ti:'fi:k) *adj* scientific. *nm,f* scientist.
scier (sje:) *vt* **1** saw (off). **2** *inf* bore. **scierie** *nf* sawmill. **sciure de bois** *nf* sawdust.
scintiller (sɛ̃ti:'je:) *vi* **1** sparkle. **2** twinkle. **3** flicker.
scolaire (skɔ'lɛr) *adj* scholastic.
scooter (sku:'tɛr) *nm* scooter.
scorpion (skɔr'pjɔ̃) *nm* **1** scorpion. **2** *cap* Scorpio.

scrupuleux, -euse (skrypy'lœ, -'lœz) *adj* scrupulous.
scruter (skry'te:) *vt* scrutinize.
scrutin (skry'tɛ̃) *nm* **1** poll. **2** ballot. **3** voting.
sculpter (skyl'te:) *vt* **1** sculpt. **2** carve. **sculpteur** *nm* sculptor. **sculpture** *nf* sculpture.
se, s' (sə) *pron 3rd pers m,f s,pl* **1** oneself, himself, herself, itself, themselves. **2** each other, one another.
séance (se:'ɑ̃s) *nf* **1** meeting. **2** *pol* session. **3** sitting. **4** *Th* performance.
séant (se:'ɑ̃) *adj* fitting, seemly. *nm inf* bottom.
seau, sceaux (so) *nm* bucket.
sec, sèche (sɛk, sɛʃ) *adj* **1** dry. **2** dried. **3** curt. **4** harsh. *nf sl* fag, cigarette.
sécher (se:'ʃe:) *vt,vi* dry. **sécheresse** (se:ʃ'rɛs) *nf* **1** dryness. **2** drought. **3** harshness.
second (sə'gɔ̃) *adj* second. *nm* second in command. **en second** in second place. **seconde** *nf* **1** second, moment. **2** second class. **secondaire** *adj* secondary, subordinate.
secouer (sə'kwe:) *vt* **1** shake. **2** jolt. **3** shake off.
secourir* (səku:'ri:r) *vt* help. **secours** *nm* help, assistance. **au secours!** help! **premiers secours** *nm pl* first aid.
secousse (sə'ku:s) *nf* **1** jolt, jerk. **2** shock.
secret[1]**, -ète** (sə'krɛ, -'krɛt) *adj* **1** secret, confidential. **2** hidden.
secret[2] (sə'krɛ) *nm* **1** secret. **2** secrecy.
secrétaire (səkre:'tɛr) *nm,f* **1** secretary. **2** clerk. *nm* bureau, desk.
sécréter (se:kre:'te:) *vt* secrete.
secte (sɛkt) *nf* sect, group. **sectaire** *adj,n* sectarian.
secteur (sɛk'tœr) *nm* **1** sector. **2** area, district.
section (sɛk'sjɔ̃) *nf* **1** section. **2** branch, division. **3** stage (on a bus route).
séculaire (se:ky'lɛr) *adj* **1** occurring once in a century. **2** venerated.
séculier, -ière (se:ky'lje:, -'ljɛr) *adj* secular. *nm* layman.
sécurité (se:kyri:'te:) *nf* **1** security. **2** safety.
sédatif, -ive (sɛda'ti:f, 'ti:v) *adj,nm* sedative.
sédiment (se:di:'mɑ̃) *nm* sediment.
séduire* (se:'dɥi:r) *vt* **1** seduce. **2** lead astray. **3** charm. **séduisant** *adj* **1** seductive. **2** attractive.
segment (sɛg'mɑ̃) *nm* segment.
ségrégation (se:grɛga'sjɔ̃) *nf* segregation.
seigle (sɛgl) *nm* rye.
seigneur (sɛ'ɲœr) *nm* lord.
sein (sɛ̃) *nm* breast, bosom.
séisme (se:'i:sm) *nm* earthquake.
seize (sɛz) *adj,nm* sixteen. **seizième** *adj* sixteenth.
séjour (se:'ʒu:r) *nm* **1** stay. **2** residence.
séjourner (se:ʒu:r'ne:) *vi* **1** stay. **2** reside.
sel (sɛl) *nm* **1** salt. **2** wit.
sélection (se:lɛk'sjɔ̃) *nf* selection, choice. **sélectif, -ive** (se:lɛk'ti:f, -'ti:v) *adj* selective.
sélectionner (se:lɛksjɔ'ne:) *vt* select, choose.
selle (sɛl) *nf* **1** saddle. **2** stool. **sellier** *nm* saddler.
selon (sə'lɔ̃) *prep* according to.
Seltz (sɛls) **eau de Seltz** *nm Tdmk* soda-water.
semaine (sə'mɛn) *nf* week.
sémantique (se:mɑ̃'ti:k) *adj* semantic. *nf* semantics.
sémaphore (sɛma'fɔr) *nm* semaphore.
sembler (sɑ̃'ble:) *vi* seem, appear. **semblable** *adj* **1** similar, alike. **2** such. **semblant** *nm* appearance, show. **faire semblant de** pretend.
semelle (sə'mɛl) *nf* sole (of a shoe).
semence (sə'mɑ̃s) *nf* seed.
semer (sə'me:) *vt* **1** sow. **2** scatter.
semestre (sə'mɛstr) *nm* **1** term. **2** half-year.
séminaire (se:mi:'nɛr) *nm* **1** seminary. **2** seminar.
semi-voyelle (səmi:vwa'jɛl) *nf* semivowel.
semoule (sə'mu:l) *nf* semolina.
sénat (sɛ'na) *nm* senate. **sénateur** *nm* senator.
sénile (se:'ni:l) *adj* senile.
sens (sɑ̃s) *nm* **1** sense. **2** judgment. **3** meaning. **4** direction. **bon sens** commonsense. **dans le sens des aiguilles d'une montre** clockwise. **sens dessus dessous** upside down. **sens interdit** no entry.
sensation (sɑ̃sa'sjɔ̃) *nf* **1** sensation. **2** feeling. **sensationnel, -elle** (sɑ̃sasjɔ'nɛl) *adj* **1** sensational. **2** *inf* superb.
sensé (sɑ̃'se:) *adj* sensible.
sensible (sɑ̃'si:bl) *adj* **1** sensitive. **2** susceptible. **3** sympathetic. **4** tender. **5** apparent. **sensibilité** *nf* **1** sensibility. **2** sensitivity. **3** feeling. **4** tenderness.
sensuel, -elle (sɑ̃'sɥɛl) *adj* sensual, sensuous.
sentence (sɑ̃'tɑ̃s) *nf* **1** *law* sentence. **2** maxim.
sentier (sɑ̃'tje:) *nm* path, footpath.
sentiment (sɑ̃ti:'mɑ̃) *nm* **1** feeling. **2** sensation. **3** opinion. **4** sentiment. **sentimental, -aux** *adj* sentimental.
sentinelle (sɑ̃ti:'nɛl) *nf* sentry.
sentir* (sɑ̃'ti:r) *vt* **1** feel. **2** be conscious of. **3** smell. *vi* **1** smell of. **2** taste of. **sentir mauvais** stink.

seoir* (swar) *vi* suit, become.
séparer (sɛpa're:) *vt* **1** separate. **2** divide. **séparation** *nf* separation. **séparé** *adj* **1** separate. **2** apart.
sept (sɛt) *adj,nm* seven. **septième** (sɛ'tjɛm) *adj* seventh.
septembre (sɛp'tɑ̃br) *nm* September.
septentrional, -aux (sɛptɑ̃ri:ɔ'nal, -'no) *adj* north, northern.
septique (sɛp'ti:k) *adj* septic.
séquence (sɛ'kɑ̃s) *nf* sequence.
sequin (sə'kɛ̃) *nm* sequin.
serai (sə'rɛ) *v* see **être.**
serais (sə'rɛ) *v* see **être.**
serein (sə'rɛ̃) *adj* serene, calm.
sérénade (se:rɛ'nad) *nf* serenade.
serf, serve (sɛrf, sɛrv) *nm,f* serf.
sergent (sɛr'ʒɑ̃) *nm* sergeant.
série (se:'ri:) *nf* **1** series, succession. **2** range. **3** set. **hors série 1** specially made. **2** outsize.
sérieux, -euse (se:'rjœ, -'rjœz) *adj* **1** serious. **2** grave. **3** earnest. **4** important. *nm* gravity.
serin (sə'rɛ̃) *nm* canary.
seringue (sə'rɛ̃g) *nf* syringe.
serment (sɛr'mɑ̃) *nm* oath.
sermon (sɛr'mɔ̃) *nm* sermon.
serpent (sɛr'pɑ̃) *nm* snake, serpent.
serpenter (sɛrpɑ̃'te:) *vi* meander, wind.
serrer (sɛ're:) *vt* **1** squeeze, clench. **2** put away. **3** tighten. **4** close (up). **serrer la main à** shake hands with. **se serrer** *vr* group together. **serre** *nf* **1** greenhouse, conservatory. **2** claw. **3** grip. **serre chaude** hothouse. **serré** *adj* **1** close. **2** tight. **3** concise. **4** *inf* mean. **serre-tête** *nm invar* crash-helmet.
serrure (sɛ'ryr) *nf* lock.
sers (sɛr) *v* see **servir.**
servante (sɛr'vɑ̃t) *nf* maid.
serveur, -euse (sɛr'vœr, -'vœz) *nm,f* **1** barman, barmaid. **2** waiter, waitress.
service (sɛr'vi:s) *nm* **1** service. **2** attendance. **3** department. **4** duty. **5** set.
serviette (sɛrv'jɛt) *nf* **1** napkin. **2** towel. **3** briefcase. **serviette hygiénique** sanitary towel.
servir* (sɛr'vi:r) *vt* **1** serve. **2** attend to. **3** help. *vi* be useful. **servir de** be used as. **se servir de** *vr* use. **serviteur** *nm* servant.
ses (se:) *poss adj* see **son.**
session (sɛ'sjɔ̃) *nf* session, sitting.
seuil (sœj) *nm* **1** threshold. **2** doorstep.
seul (sœl) *adj* **1** only. **2** single, sole. **3** alone. **seulement** *adv* only.
sève (sɛv) *nf* sap.
sévère (se:'vɛr) *adj* **1** harsh, hard. **2** strict. **3** severe. **sévérité** *nf* **1** severity. **2** strictness.
sévir (se:'vi:r) *vi* **1** punish severely. **2** rage.
sexe (sɛks) *nm* sex. **sexualité** *nf* sexuality. **sexuel, -elle** (sɛk'sɥɛl) *adj* sexual.
sextuor (sɛk'stɥɔr) *nm* sextet.
shampooing (ʃɑ̃pu:'i:ɲ) *nm* shampoo.
shérif (ʃɛ'ri:f) *nm* sheriff.
si[1] (si:) *conj* **1** if. **2** whether.
si[2] (si:) *adv* **1** so, so much. **2** such. **3** as. **4** yes. **si...que** however.
Sicile (si:'si:l) *nf* Sicily. **sicilien, -ienne** (si:si:'ljɛ̃, -'ljɛn) *adj,n* Sicilian.
siècle (sjɛkl) *nm* **1** century. **2** age, time.
siéger (sjɛ'ʒe:) *vi* **1** *pol* sit. **2** be centred. **siège** *nm* **1** seat. **2** chair. **3** siege. **4** see. **siège central** *comm* head office.
sien, sienne (sjɛ̃, sjɛn) *poss pron 3rd pers s* **le sien, la sienne 1** his, hers, one's. **2** his, hers, one's or its own.
sieste (sjɛst) *nf* **1** siesta. **2** *inf* nap.
siffler (si:'fle:) *vi,vt* whistle, hiss. **sifflet** *nm* whistle.
signal, -aux (si:'ɲal, -'ɲo) *nm* signal.
signaler (si:ɲa'le:) *vt* **1** point out. **2** signal. **3** report. **4** give a description of. **se signaler** *vr* distinguish oneself. **signalement** *nm* description, particulars. **signalisateur anti-vol** *nm* burglar alarm.
signature (si:ɲa'tyr) *nf* **1** signature. **2** signing.
signe (si:ɲ) *nm* **1** sign. **2** mark. **3** gesture. **faire signe à** beckon. **signet** *nm* bookmark.
signer (si:'ɲe) *vt* sign.
signifier (si:ɲi:'fje:) *vt* signify, mean. **significatif, -ive** (si:ɲi:fi:ka'ti:f, -'ti:v) *adj* significant. **signification** *nf* meaning.
silence (si:'lɑ̃s) *nm* silence. **silencieux, -euse** (si:lɑ̃'sjœ, -'sjœz) *adj* silent.
silex (si:'lɛks) *nm* flint.
silhouette (si:l'wɛt) *nf* silhouette, outline.
sillon (si:'jɔ̃) *nm* **1** furrow. **2** trail. **3** groove.
sillonner (si:jɔ'ne:) *vt* **1** furrow. **2** streak. **3** wrinkle.
simagrée (si:ma'gre:) *nf* **1** pretence. **2** *pl* grimaces. **3** *pl* affectation.
simple (sɛ̃pl) *adj* **1** simple. **2** single. **3** ordinary. **4** plain. **simplicité** *nf* simplicity.
simplifier (sɛ̃pli:'fje:) *vt* simplify.
simulacre (si:my'lakr) *nm* **1** pretence, show. **2** image.
simuler (si:my'le:) *vt* feign, counterfeit.

simultané (si:mylta'ne:) *adj* simultaneous. **simultanément** *adv* simultaneously.

sincère (sɛ̃'sɛr) *adj* **1** sincere. **2** genuine. **3** true. **sincérité** *nf* **1** sincerity. **2** honesty. **3** candour.

singe (sɛ̃ʒ) *nm* monkey, ape.

singer (sɛ̃'ʒe:) *vt* ape, mimic. **singerie** *nf* grimace.

singulier, -ière (sɛ̃gy'lje:, -'ljɛr) *adj* **1** singular. **2** peculiar. **3** strange. *nm* singular. **singularité** *nf* **1** singularity. **2** peculiarity. **3** eccentricity.

sinistre (si:'ni:str) *adj* **1** sinister, ominous. **2** dangerous. **3** gloomy. *nm* disaster.

sinon (si:'nɔ̃) *conj* **1** otherwise, or else. **2** except.

sinueux, -euse (si:'nɥœ, -'nɥœz) *adj* winding.

sionisme (sjɔ'ni:sm) *nm* Zionism. **sioniste** *adj,n* Zionist.

siphon (si:'fɔ̃) *nm* siphon.

sirène (si:'rɛn) *nf* **1** siren, hooter. **2** mermaid.

sirop (si:'ro) *nm* syrup.

siroter (si:rɔ'te:) *vt inf* sip.

site (si:t) *nm* **1** beauty spot. **2** site.

sitôt (si:'to) *adv* as soon. **sitôt que** as soon as.

situer (si:'tɥe:) *vt* situate, place. **situation** *nf* **1** situation. **2** position. **3** condition. **4** appointment, job. **situation difficile** predicament.

six (si:s) *adj,nm* six. **sixième** *adj* sixth.

ski (ski:) *nm* **1** ski. **2** skiing. **faire du ski** ski. **ski-nautique** *nm* water-skiing.

slip (sli:p) *nm* underpants, briefs.

slogan (slɔ'gɑ̃) *nm* slogan.

smoking (smɔ'ki:ɲ) *nm* dinner jacket.

snob (snɔb) *adj invar* **1** *inf* smart. **2** snobbish. *nm* snob.

sobre (sɔbr) *adj* **1** temperate. **2** sober. **3** economical. **sobriété** *nf* **1** sobriety. **2** moderation.

sobriquet (sɔbri:'kɛ) *nm* nickname.

sociable (sɔ'sjabl) *adj* sociable.

social, -aux (sɔ'sjal, -'sjo) *adj* social. **socialisme** *nm* socialism. **socialiste** *adj,n* socialist.

société (sɔsje:'te:) *nf* **1** society. **2** community. **3** club. **4** company. **5** companionship. **sociétaire** *nm,f* **1** member. **2** shareholder.

sociologie (sɔsjɔlɔ'ʒi:) *nf* sociology. **sociologique** *adj* sociological. **sociologue** *nm,f* sociologist.

socle (sɔkl) *nm* **1** pedestal. **2** base.

socquette (sɔ'kɛt) *nf* ankle-sock.

sœur (sœr) *nf* **1** sister. **2** nun.

soi (swa) *pron 3rd pers m,f s* oneself, himself, herself, itself. **soi-disant** *adj invar* so-called. *adv* supposedly. **soi-même** *pron 3rd pers m,f s* oneself.

soie (swɑ) *nf* **1** silk. **2** bristle (of a badger, etc.). **soie artificielle** rayon.

soif (swaf) *nf* thirst. **avoir soif** be thirsty.

soigner (swa'ɲe) *vt* **1** look after. **2** nurse. **3** do carefully. **se soigner** *vr* look after oneself. **soigné** (swa'ɲe:) *adj* **1** neat, tidy. **2** carefully done. **soigneux, -euse** (swa'ɲœ, -'ɲœz) *adj* **1** careful. **2** painstaking. **3** tidy.

soin (swɛ̃) *nm* care.

soir (swar) *nm* **1** evening. **2** night. **ce soir** tonight. **hier soir** last night. **soirée** *nf* **1** evening. **2** party.

sois (swa) *v see* **être.**

soit (swa) *interj* agreed!. *conj* whether. **soit... soit** either...or.

soixante (swa'sɑ̃t) *adj,nm* sixty. **soixantième** *adj* sixtieth.

soixante-dix *adj,nm* seventy. **soixante-dixième** *adj* seventieth.

soja (sɔʒa) *nm* soya bean.

sol (sɔl) *nm* **1** ground, earth. **2** soil.

solaire (sɔ'lɛr) *adj* **1** solar. **2** sun.

soldat (sɔl'da) *nm* soldier.

solde[1] (sɔld) *nf mil* pay.

solde[2] (sɔld) *nm* **1** *comm* balance. **2** surplus stock. **3** (clearance) sale.

sole (sɔl) *nf cul* sole.

soleil (sɔ'lɛj) *nm* **1** sun. **2** sunshine.

solennel, -elle (sɔla'nɛl) *adj* **1** solemn. **2** state, official.

solidarité (sɔli:dari:'te:) *nf* **1** solidarity. **2** fellowship.

solide (sɔ'li:d) *adj* **1** solid. **2** strong. **3** sound.

solidifier (sɔli:di:'fje:) *vt* solidify.

soliste (sɔ'li:st) *nm,f* soloist.

solitaire (sɔli:'tɛr) *adj* solitary, lonely. *nm* hermit.

solitude (sɔli:'tyd) *nf* solitude.

solive (sɔ'li:v) *nf* **1** joist. **2** beam.

solliciter (sɔlli:si:'te:) *vt* **1** request. **2** incite.

solo (sɔ'lo) *adj invar,nm* solo.

soluble (sɔ'lybl) *adj* soluble.

solution (sɔly'sjɔ̃) *nf* **1** solution. **2** answer, explanation.

solvable (sɔl'vabl) *adj* solvent.

sombre (sɔ̃br) *adj* **1** sombre, gloomy. **2** dark. **3** dejected.

sombrer (sɔ̃'bre:) *vi* sink.

sommaire (sɔm'mɛr) *adj* **1** concise. **2** elementary. **3** rapid. *nm* summary.

sommation (sɔma'sjɔ̃) *nf law* summons.

somme[1] (sɔm) *nm* nap, snooze.
somme[2] (sɔm) *nf* sum, amount. **en somme** 1 on the whole. 2 in short.
somme[3] (sɔm) **bête de somme** *nf* beast of burden.
sommeil (sɔ'mɛj) *nm* 1 sleep. 2 sleepiness. **avoir sommeil** be sleepy.
sommeiller (sɔmɛ'je:) *vi* doze, sleep lightly.
sommelier (sɔmə'lje:) *nm* wine waiter.
sommer (sɔ'me:) *vt law* summon.
sommes (sɔm) *v* see **être**.
sommet (sɔ'mɛ) *nm* summit, top.
somnambule (sɔmnɑ̃'byl) *nm,f* sleepwalker. **somnambulisme** *nm* sleepwalking. **somnifère** *nm* sleeping-pill.
somnoler (sɔmnɔ'le:) *vi* doze, drowse. **somnolent** *adj* sleepy.
son[1], **sa, ses** (sɔ̃, sa, se:) *poss adj 3rd pers s* his, her, its, one's.
son[2] (sɔ̃) *nm* sound.
son[3] (sɔ̃) *nm* bran.
sonate (sɔ'nat) *nf* sonata.
sonder (sɔ̃'de:) *vt* 1 sound. 2 probe, examine. 3 fathom. **sondage** *nm* 1 sounding. 2 *min* boring. 3 opinion poll.
songer (sɔ̃'ʒe:) *vi* 1 dream. 2 imagine. 3 muse. **songer à** think about. **songe** *nm* dream. **songerie** *nf* dreaming. **songeur, -euse** (sɔ̃'ʒœr, -'ʒœz) *nm,f* dreamer. *adj* pensive.
sonique (sɔ'ni:k) *adj* sonic.
sonner (sɔ'ne:) *vi,vt* 1 ring. 2 toll. *vi* 1 sound. 2 strike. **sonnerie** *nf* 1 ringing. 2 chimes. 3 bell. 4 trumpet call. **sonnette** *nf* 1 small bell. 2 doorbell.
sonnet (sɔ'nɛ) *nm* sonnet.
sonore (sɔ'nɔr) *adj* 1 resonant. 2 loud.
sont (sɔ̃) *v* see **être**.
soprano (sɔpra'no) *nm,f* soprano.
sorcier, -ière (sɔr'sje:, -'sjɛr) *nm,f* wizard, witch. **sorcellerie** *nf* witchcraft.
sordide (sɔr'di:d) *adj* 1 sordid, squalid. 2 base.
sors (sɔr) *v* see **sortir**.
sort (sɔr) *nm* 1 fate. 2 lot. 3 spell.
sorte (sɔrt) *nf* 1 sort, kind. 2 manner. **de sorte que** so that.
sortir* (sɔr'ti:r) *vi* 1 go out. 2 come up. 3 leave. *vt* take or bring out. **sortie** *nf* 1 way out, exit. 2 leaving. 3 outing. 4 *inf* outburst. **sortie de secours** emergency exit.
sot, sotte (so, sɔt) *adj* 1 stupid. 2 ridiculous. 3 sheepish. *nm,f* fool, idiot. **sottise** (sɔ'ti:z) *nf* 1 stupidity. 2 silly remark or action.
sou (su:) *nm* penny. **sans le sou** penniless.
soubresaut (su:brə'so) *nm* sudden start, jerk.
souche (su:ʃ) *nf* 1 stump. 2 stub. 3 counterfoil.
souci[1] (su:'si:) *nm* 1 worry. 2 anxiety. 3 care. **sans souci** carefree.
souci[2] (su:'si:) *nm* marigold.
se soucier (su:'sje:) *vr* 1 care, concern oneself. 2 be anxious. **soucieux, -euse** (su:'sjœ, -'sjœz) *adj* 1 anxious. 2 thoughtful. 3 preoccupied.
soucoupe (su:'ku:p) *nf* saucer.
soudain (su:'dɛ̃) *adj* 1 sudden. 2 unexpected. *adv* suddenly.
soude (su:d) *nf* soda.
souder (su:'de:) *vt* 1 solder. 2 weld. **se souder** *vr* 1 weld. 2 join together.
soudoyer (su:dwa'je:) *vt* 1 hire. 2 bribe.
souffler (su:'fle:) *vi* 1 blow. 2 pant. 3 breathe. *vt* 1 blow out or up. 2 utter. 3 *inf* trick. **souffler son rôle à** prompt. **souffle** *nm* 1 breath. 2 puff. 3 blast. 4 inspiration. **soufflet** *nm* 1 bellows. 2 box (the ears). 3 *inf* insult.
souffleter (su:flə'te:) *vt* 1 slap. 2 insult.
souffrir* (su:'fri:r) *vt* 1 endure. 2 permit. *vi* suffer, be in pain. **souffrance** *nf* 1 suspense. 2 pain. **souffrant** *adj* 1 suffering. 2 unwell. **souffre-douleur** *nm invar* 1 drudge. 2 butt (of jokes, etc.).
soufre (su:fr) *nm* sulphur.
souhait (swɛ) *nm* wish. **souhaiter** *vt* wish, desire.
souiller (su:'je:) *vt* 1 soil. 2 pollute. 3 tarnish. **souillure** *nf* 1 spot, stain. 2 blemish.
soûl (su:) *adj inf* 1 drunk. 2 full.
soulager (su:la'ʒe:) *vt* 1 relieve, ease. 2 soothe. **soulagement** *nm* 1 relief. 2 comfort.
se soûler (su:'le:) *vr* 1 get drunk. 2 gorge oneself. **soûlard** *nm sl* drunkard.
soulever (su:l've:) *vt* 1 lift. 2 raise. 3 rouse. 4 provoke. **soulèvement** *nm* 1 raising. 2 revolt. 3 protest.
soulier (su:'lje:) *nm* shoe.
souligner (su:li:'ɲe) *vt* 1 underline. 2 emphasize.
soumettre* (su:'mɛtr) *vt* 1 subdue. 2 subject. 3 submit, refer. **se soumettre** *vr* submit, yield **soumis** *adj* obedient.
soumission (su:mi:'sjɔ̃) *nf* 1 submission. 2 obedience. 3 *comm* tender.
soupape (su:'pap) *nf* 1 valve. 2 plug.
soupçon (su:p'sɔ̃) *nm* 1 suspicion. 2 slight flavour, dash.
soupçonner (su:psɔ'ne:) *vt* 1 suspect. 2 guess.

soupçonneux, -euse (su:psɔˈnœ, -ˈnœz) *adj* suspicious.
soupe (su:p) *nf* soup.
soupente (su:ˈpɑ̃t) *nf* loft.
souper (su:ˈpe:) *vi* have supper. *nm* supper.
soupir (su:ˈpi:r) *nm* sigh. **soupirer** *vi* sigh.
soupirail, -aux (su:pi:ˈraj, -ˈro) *nm* ventilator.
souple (su:pl) *adj* **1** supple. **2** flexible. **3** adaptable. **souplesse** *nf* **1** suppleness. **2** flexibility.
source (su:rs) *nf* **1** source. **2** spring, well. **3** origin.
sourcil (su:rˈsi:) *nm* eyebrow.
sourd (su:r) *adj* **1** deaf. **2** dull, muffled. **3** hollow. **4** secret. *nm* deaf person. **sourd-muet, sourde-muette** *adj,pl* **sourds-muets, sourdes-muettes** deaf-and-dumb. *nm,f* deaf-mute.
souricière (su:ri:ˈsjɛr) *nf* **1** mousetrap. **2** trap.
sourire* (su:ˈri:r) *vi* smile. **sourire à belles dents** grin. ~*nm* smile. **large sourire** grin. **sourire affecté** smirk.
souris (su:ˈri:) *nf* mouse.
sournois (su:rˈnwa) *adj* **1** sly. **2** cunning. **3** underhand. *nm* sneak.
sous (su:) *prep* **1** under. **2** below. **3** within (time). **sous la pluie** in the rain. **sous terre** underground.
sous-alimentation *nf* malnutrition.
souscrire* (su:ˈskri:r) *vt* **1** subscribe. **2** sign. **souscription** *nf* **1** subscription. **2** signature. **3** contribution.
sous-développé *adj* underdeveloped.
sous-entendre *vt* **1** imply. **2** understand. **sous-entendu** *nm* implication.
sous-estimer *vt* underestimate.
sous-marin *adj* underwater.
sous-sol *nm* basement.
sous-titrer *vt* subtitle. **sous-titre** *nm* subtitle.
soustraire* (su:ˈstrɛr) *vt* **1** take away. **2** withdraw. **3** subtract. **4** protect. **se soustraire** *vr* escape. **soustraction** *nf* **1** removal. **2** subtraction.
sous-traiter *vt* subcontract.
soutane (su:ˈtan) *nf* cassock.
soutenir* (su:tˈni:r) *vt* **1** support. **2** prop up. **3** maintain. **4** encourage. **5** withstand. **6** sustain. **se soutenir** *vr* **1** support oneself. **2** continue. **soutenu** *adj* **1** sustained. **2** elevated. **3** constant.
souterrain (su:tɛˈrɛ̃) *adj* underground. *nm* **1** underground passage. **2** vault.
soutien (su:ˈtjɛ̃) *nm* **1** support, prop. **2** supporter. **soutien-gorge** *nm invar* brassiere, bra.
souvenir* (su:vˈni:r) *v imp* come to mind. **se souvenir de** *vr* remember, recall. ~*nm* **1** memory. **2** remembrance, recollection. **3** memento. **4** souvenir.
souvent (su:ˈvɑ̃) *adv* often. **peu souvent** seldom.
souverain (su:vˈrɛ̃) *adj* **1** sovereign. **2** supreme. *nm* sovereign. **souveraineté** *nf* sovereignty.
soyez (swaˈje:) *v see* **être.**
soyons (swaˈjɔ̃) *v see* **être.**
spacieux, -euse (spaˈsjœ, -ˈsjœz) *adj* spacious.
spasme (spasm) *nm* spasm. **spasmodique** *adj* spasmodic.
spatial, -aux (spaˈsjal, -ˈsjo) *adj* spatial.
spatule (spaˈtyl) *nf* spatula.
spécial, -aux (spe:ˈsjal, -ˈsjo) *adj* **1** special. **2** especial. **3** particular.
spécialiser (spe:sjali:ˈze:) *vt* specialize. **se spécialiser dans** *vr* specialize in. **spécialiste** *nm,f* **1** expert. **2** *med* specialist. **spécialité** *nf* speciality.
spécieux, -euse (spe:ˈsjœ, -ˈsjœz) *adj* plausible.
spécifier (spe:si:ˈfje:) *vt* specify. **spécifique** *adj* specific.
spécimen (spe:si:ˈmen) *nm* specimen.
spectacle (spɛkˈtakl) *nm* **1** sight, spectacle. **2** *Th* play. **3** show. **spectaculaire** *adj* spectacular.
spectateur, -trice (spɛktaˈtœr, -ˈtri:s) *nm,f* **1** onlooker, spectator. **2** *pl* audience.
spectre (spɛktr) *nm* **1** ghost, apparition. **2** spectrum.
spéculer (spe:kyˈle:) *vi* speculate. **spéculateur, -trice** (spe:kylaˈtœr, -ˈtri:s) *nm,f* speculator. **spéculation** *nf* speculation.
spéléologie (spe:le:ɔlɔˈʒi:) *nf* potholing. **spéléologue** *nm* potholer.
sperme (spɛrm) *nm* sperm.
sphère (sfɛr) *nf* **1** sphere. **2** globe. **3** field, area.
spiral, -aux (spi:ˈral, -ˈro) *adj* spiral. **spirale** *nf* spiral.
spirituel, -elle (spi:ri:ˈtɥɛl) *adj* **1** spiritual. **2** witty.
splendeur (splɑ̃ˈdœr) *nf* **1** splendour. **2** magnificence. **3** pomp. **splendide** *adj* **1** splendid, magnificent. **2** superb.
spolier (spɔˈlje:) *vt* rob, plunder.
spontané (spɔ̃taˈne:) *adj* spontaneous.
sport (spɔr) *nm* sport, games. **sportif, -ive** (spɔrˈti:f, -ˈti:v) *adj* sporting.

square (skwar) *nm* small square with a (public) garden.
squelette (skə'lɛt) *nm* **1** skeleton. **2** framework.
stabiliser (stabi:li:'ze:) *vt* stabilize, steady.
stable (stabl) *adj* stable, steady, firm.
stade (stad) *nm* **1** stadium. **2** stage, phase.
stage (staʒ) *nm* **1** probationary period. **2** training course.
stagnant (stag'nɑ̃) *adj* stagnant.
stalle (stal) *nf* stall, seat.
standard (stɑ̃'dar) *nm* **1** switchboard. **2** standard.
station (sta'sjɔ̃) *nf* **1** stop. **2** (tube) station. **3** standing. **station-service** *nf, pl* **stations-service** service station.
stationner (stasjɔ'ne:) *vi* **1** stop. **2** park. **stationnaire** *adj* stationary. **stationnement** *nm* parking.
statique (sta'ti:k) *adj* static.
statistique (stati:'sti:k) *nf* statistics. *adj* statistical.
statue (sta'ty) *nf* statue.
statuer (sta'tɥe:) *vi* decide. *vt* decree.
stature (sta'tyr) *nf* stature.
statut (sta'ty) *nm* **1** statute, rule. **2** status.
sténodactylographe (ste:nɔdakti:lɔ'graf) *nm,f* shorthand typist.
sténographie (ste:nɔgra'fi:) *nf* shorthand.
stéréophonique (ste:re:ɔfɔ'ni:k) *adj* stereophonic.
stéréotype (ste:re:ɔ'ti:p) *adj* stereotype.
stérile (ste:'ri:l) *adj* **1** sterile. **2** barren. **3** fruitless. **stérilité** *nf* sterility.
stériliser (ste:ri:li:'ze:) *vt* sterilize.
sterling (stɛr'lɛ̃) *adj invar* sterling.
stéthoscope (ste:tɔ'skɔp) *nm* stethoscope.
stigmate (sti:g'mat) *nm* **1** stigma. **2** scar. **3** brand, mark. **4** stain.
stimuler (sti:my'le:) *vt* **1** stimulate. **2** incite. **stimulant** *adj* stimulating. *nm* **1** stimulus. **2** tonic.
stipuler (sti:py'le:) *vt* stipulate.
stock (stɔk) *nm* stock (of goods, etc.).
stocker (stɔ'ke:) *vt* **1** stock. **2** stockpile.
stoïque (stɔ'i:k) *adj* stoical.
stop (stɔp) *nm* **faire du stop** hitch-hike.
store (stɔr) *nm* blind.
strabisme (stra'bi:sm) *nm* squint.
strapontin (strapɔ̃'tɛ̃) *nm* folding seat.
stratégie (strate:'ʒi:) *nf* strategy. **stratégique** *adj* strategic.
strict (stri:kt) *adj* **1** strict, severe. **2** exact.
strident (stri:'dɑ̃) *adj* **1** shrill. **2** piercing.
strié (stri:'e:) *adj* **1** streaked. **2** scratched.
strophe (strɔf) *nf* verse.
structure (stryk'tyr) *nf* structure.
studieux, -euse (sty'djœ, -'djœz) *adj* studious.
studio (sty'djo) *nm* **1** studio. **2** small or one-room flat.
stupéfier (stype:'fje:) *vt* astound, dumbfound. **stupéfaction** (stypɛfak'sjɔ̃) *nf* amazement. **stupéfait** *adj* astounded. **stupéfiant** *adj* amazing. *nm* narcotic, drug.
stupide (sty'pi:d) *adj* stupid, silly. **stupidité** *nf* stupidity.
style (sti:l) *nm* style.
stylo (sti:'lo) *nm* fountain pen. **stylo à bille** ball-point pen.
su (sy) *v* see **savoir.**
suaire (sɥɛr) *nm* shroud.
suant (sɥɑ̃) *adj* sweating, sweaty.
suave (sɥav) *adj* **1** sweet, mellow. **2** soft, delicate.
subconscient (sybkɔ̃'sjɑ̃) *adj,nm* subconscious.
subir (sy'bi:r) *vt* **1** undergo. **2** endure. **3** suffer.
subit (sy'bi:) *adj* sudden. **subitement** *adv also inf* **subito** suddenly.
subjectif, -ive (sybʒɛk'ti:f, -'ti:v) *adj* subjective.
subjonctif, -ive (sybʒɔ̃k'ti:f, -'ti:v) *adj,nm* subjunctive.
subjuguer (sybʒy'ge:) *vt* **1** subdue. **2** captivate.
sublime (sy'bli:m) *adj* sublime, exalted.
submerger (sybmɛr'ʒe:) *vt* **1** submerge. **2** immerse. **3** swamp.
subordonner (sybɔrdɔ'ne:) *vt* subordinate. **subordonné** *adj,n* subordinate.
subséquent (sybsɛ'kɑ̃) *adj* subsequent. **subséquemment** (sybsɛka'mɑ̃) *adv* subsequently.
subsister (sybsi:'ste:) *vi* remain, subsist.
substance (syb'stɑ̃s) *nf* **1** substance. **2** matter. **3** stuff. **substantiel, -elle** (sybstɑ̃'sjɛl) *adj* substantial. **substantif** *nm* substantive.
substituer (sybsti:'tɥe:) *vt* substitute. **substitut** *nm* substitute.
subtil (syp'ti:l) *adj* **1** subtle. **2** sharp, penetrating. **3** fine. **subtilité** *nf* subtlety.
suburbain (sybyr'bɛ̃) *adj* suburban.
subvenir* (sybvə'ni:r) *vt* provide, supply.
subvention (sybvɑ̃'sjɔ̃) *nv* subsidy, grant.
subventionner (sybvɑ̃sjɔ'ne:) *vt* subsidize.
suc (syk) *nm* **1** juice. **2** quintessence.
succédané (syksɛda'ne:) *nm* substitute.
succéder (sykse:'de:) *vt* **1** succeed, inherit. **2** follow. **succès** (syk'sɛ) *nm* **1** success. **2** result, issue. **succession** (syksɛ'sjɔ̃) *nf* suc-

cession. **successeur** *nm* successor. **successif, -ive** (syksɛ'si:f, -'si:v) *adj* successive.

succomber (sykɔ̃'be:) *vi* 1 succumb. 2 die.

succulent (syky'lɑ̃) *adj* succulent, tasty.

succursale (sykyr'sal) *nf comm* branch.

sucer (sy'se:) *vt* suck. **sucette** *nf* lollipop.

sucrer (sy'kre:) *vt* sugar, sweeten. **sucre** *nm* sugar. **sucre d'orge** 1 barley-sugar. 2 lollipop.

sud (syd) *nm* south. *adj invar* south, southerly, southern. **au sud** in the south. **du sud** southern, southerly. **vers le sud** southward, southwards. **sud-est** *nm,adj invar* south-east. **du sud-est** 1 south-eastern. 2 south-easterly. **sud-ouest** *nm,adj invar* south-west. **du sud-ouest** south-western, south-westerly.

Suède (sɥɛd) *nf* Sweden. **suède** *nf* suede. **suédois** *adj,n* Swedish. *nm* Swedish (language).

suer (sɥe:) *vi* sweat, perspire. **sueur** *nf* sweat, perspiration.

suffire* (sy'fi:r) *vi* be sufficient. **suffisant** *adj* 1 sufficient, adequate. 2 conceited.

suffixe (syf'fi:ks) *nm* suffix.

suffoquer (syfɔ'ke:) *vt* suffocate, stifle. *vi* choke.

suffrage (sy'fraʒ) *nm* 1 franchise. 2 vote.

suggérer (sygʒe:'re:) *vt* suggest. **suggestion** *nf* suggestion.

se suicider (sɥi:si:'de:) *vr* commit suicide. **suicide** *nm* suicide.

suie (sɥi:) *nf* soot.

suinter (sɥɛ̃'te:) *vi* 1 ooze, seep. 2 leak.

suis[1] (sɥi:) *v* see **être.**

suis[2] (sɥi:) *v* see **suivre.**

Suisse (sɥi:s) *nf* Switzerland. **suisse** *adj,n* Swiss.

suite (sɥi:t) *nf* 1 continuation. 2 sequel. 3 consistency. 4 sequence. 5 suite, train. **de suite** in succession. **par la suite** 1 later on. 2 consequently. **tout de suite** immediately.

suivre* (sɥi:vr) *vt* 1 follow. 2 attend. 3 accompany. *v imp* result. **faire suivre** forward (a letter). **suivant** *adj* next, following. *prep* according to. **suivi** *adj* 1 consistent. 2 steady. 3 coherent.

sujet, -ette (sy'ʒɛ, -'ʒɛt) *adj* 1 subject. 2 dependent. 3 exposed. 4 liable. *nm,f* subject (person). *nm* 1 subject. 2 cause. 3 theme.

sultan (syl'tɑ̃) *nm* sultan.

superbe (sy'pɛrb) *adj* 1 superb, splendid. 2 stately. 3 arrogant.

supercherie (sypɛrʃə'ri:) *nf* 1 deceit. 2 fraud. 3 hoax.

superficie (sypɛrfi:'si:) *nf* 1 surface. 2 *math* area.

superficiel, -elle (sypɛrfi:'sjɛl) *adj* superficial.

superflu (sypɛr'fly) *adj* 1 superfluous. 2 useless.

supérieur (sype:'rjœr) *adj* 1 upper. 2 superior. 3 higher. *nm* superior. **supériorité** *nf* superiority.

superlatif, -ive (sypɛrla'ti:f, -'ti:v) *adj,nm* superlative.

supermarché (sypɛrmar'ʃe:) *nm* supermarket.

supersonique (sypɛrsɔ'ni:k) *adj* supersonic.

superstition (sypɛrsti:'sjɔ̃) *nf* superstition. **superstitieux, -euse** (sypɛrsti:'sjœ, -'sjœz) *adj* superstitious.

suppléer (syple:'e:) *vt* 1 make up or good. 2 deputize. **suppléer à** 1 make up for. 2 fill. **suppléant** *adj* temporary. *nm* 1 substitute. 2 deputy. **supplément** *nm* 1 supplement. 2 addition. 3 extra charge. **supplémentaire** *adj* 1 supplementary. 2 additional.

supplice (sy'pli:s) *nm* 1 corporal punishment. 2 torture. 3 torment. **dernier supplice** death penalty.

supplier (sypli:'e:) *vt* implore, entreat.

support (sy'pɔr) *nm* 1 support, prop. 2 stand, rest.

supporter (sypɔr'te:) *vt* 1 support, prop up. 2 endure. 3 tolerate.

supposer (sypo'ze:) *vt* 1 suppose, imagine. 2 imply.

supprimer (sypri:'me:) *vt* 1 suppress. 2 abolish. 3 omit. 4 *inf* kill.

suprême (sy'prɛm) *adj* 1 supreme, highest. 2 last. **suprématie** (syprɛma'si:) *nf* supremacy.

sur (syr) *prep* 1 on. 2 upon. 3 after. 4 about. 5 out of. 6 by. **sur ce** whereupon. **sur-le-champ** *adv* immediately.

sûr (syr) *adj* 1 sure. 2 trustworthy. 3 certain. **à coup sûr** for certain. **bien sûr!** of course!

surabondance (syrabɔ̃'dɑ̃s) *nf* surfeit.

suranné (syra'ne:) *adj* 1 out of date. 2 old-fashioned.

surcharger (syrʃar'ʒe:) *vt* 1 overload. 2 overwork. **surcharge** *nf* 1 overload. 2 surcharge.

surchauffer (syrʃo'fe:) *vt* overheat.

surcroît (syr'krwa) *nm* increase. **par surcroît** in addition.

surdité (syrdi:'te:) *nf* deafness.

sureau, -aux (sy'ro) *nm* elder tree.

surélever (syre:l've:) *vt* 1 heighten. 2 raise.

surenchère (syrɑ̃ˈʃɛr) *nf* higher bid.
surestimer (syrɛsti:ˈme:) *vt* overestimate.
sûreté (syrˈte:) *nf* **1** safety, protection. **2** sureness. **3** guarantee.
surface (syrˈfas) *nf* **1** surface. **2** outside.
surfaire* (syrˈfɛr) *vt* **1** overcharge. **2** overestimate.
surgeler (syrʒəˈle:) *vt* deep-freeze.
surgir (syrˈʒi:r) *vt* **1** rise. **2** loom, crop up.
surhumain (syryˈmɛ̃) *adj* superhuman.
surimposer (syrɛ̃poˈze:) *vt* **1** superimpose. **2** increase the tax on.
surlendemain (syrlɑ̃dˈmɛ̃) *nm* next day but one, two days later.
surmener (syrməˈne:) *vt* overwork. **surmenage** *nm* overworking.
surmonter (syrmɔ̃ˈte) *vt* **1** surmount. **2** dominate, overcome.
surnaturel, -elle (syrnatyˈrɛl) *adj* supernatural.
surnom (syrˈnɔ̃) *nm* nickname.
surnombre (syrˈnɔ̃br) *nm* excess.
surpasser (syrpɑˈse:) *vt* surpass, transcend.
surplomb (syrˈplɔ̃) *nm* overhang.
surplomber (syrplɔ̃ˈbe:) *vi,vt* overhang.
surplus (syrˈply) *nm* surplus, excess. **au surplus** besides.
surprendre* (syrˈprɑ̃dr) *vt* **1** surprise, astonish. **2** catch in the act. **surprise** *nf* surprise.
surréalisme (syre:aˈli:sm) *nm* surrealism. **surréaliste** *adj,n* surrealist.
sursaut (syrˈso) *nm* start, jump.
surseoir* (syrˈswar) *vt* suspend, put off. **sursis** *nm* **1** delay. **2** reprieve.
surtout (syrˈtu:) *adv* **1** above all. **2** especially, particularly. **surtout que** especially as.
surveiller (syrvɛˈje:) *vt* **1** supervise. **2** inspect. **3** observe, watch. **4** look after. **surveillance** *nf* supervision. **surveillant** *nm* **1** supervisor. **2** superintendent. **3** master on duty.
survenir* (syrvəˈni:r) *vi* **1** happen, occur. **2** crop up.
survêtement (syrvɛtˈmɑ̃) *nm* tracksuit.
survivre* (syrˈvi:vr) *vi* **survivre à** outlive. **survivance** *nf* survival. **survivant** *nm* survivor.
sus (sys) **en sus** *adv* in addition.
susceptible (sysɛpˈti:bl) *adj* **1** susceptible. **2** capable. **3** sensitive. **4** thin-skinned. **peu susceptible** thick-skinned.
susciter (syssi:ˈte:) *vt* **1** rouse. **2** create.
susdit (syzˈdi:) *adj* aforesaid.
suspect (sysˈpɛ) *adj* suspicious, dubious. *nm* suspect.
suspendre (sysˈpɑ̃dr) *vt* **1** suspend. **2** hang up. **suspension** *nf* suspension.
suspens (sysˈpɑ̃) **en suspens** *adv* **1** in suspense. **2** undecided.
susurrer (sysyˈre:) *vi* murmur, rustle.
suture (syˈtyr) *nf* join. **point de suture** *nm med* stitch.
svastika (svasti:ˈka) *nm* swastika.
svelte (svɛlt) *adj* slim, slender.
sycomore (sikɔˈmɔr) *nm* sycamore.
syllabe (si:lˈlab) *nf* syllable.
sylvestre (si:lˈvɛstr) *adj* woodland.
symbole (sɛ̃ˈbɔl) *nm* symbol. **symbolique** *adj* symbolic.
symboliser (sɛ̃bɔli:ˈze:) *vt* symbolize. **symbolisme** *nm* symbolism.
symétrie (si:me:ˈtri:) *nf* symmetry. **symétrique** *adj* symmetrical.
sympathie (sɛ̃paˈti:) *nf* **1** liking, attraction. **2** sympathy. **sympathique** *adj* likeable, attractive.
symphonie (sɛ̃fɔˈni:) *nf* symphony.
symposium (sɛ̃pɔˈzjɔm) *nm* symposium.
symptôme (sɛ̃pˈtom) *nm* **1** symptom. **2** sign.
synagogue (si:naˈgɔg) *nf* synagogue.
synchroniser (sɛ̃krɔni:ˈze:) *vt* synchronize.
syndicat (sɛ̃di:ˈka) *nm* **1** syndicate. **2** association. **3** trade union. **syndicat d'initiative** tourist information bureau. **syndical, -aux** (sɛ̃di:ˈkal, -ˈko) *adj* trade-union. **syndicaliste** *nm,f* trade unionist. **syndiqué** *nm* trade-union member.
syndrome (sɛ̃ˈdrom) *nm* syndrome.
synonyme (si:nɔˈni:m) *adj* synonymous. *nm* synonym.
syntaxe (sɛ̃ˈtaks) *nf* syntax.
synthèse (sɛ̃ˈtɛz) *nf* synthesis.
synthétique (sɛ̃te:ˈti:k) *adj* synthetic.
syphilis (si:fi:ˈli:s) *nf* syphilis.
Syrie (si:ˈri:) *nf* Syria. **syrien, -ienne** (si:ˈrjɛ̃, -ˈrjɛn) *adj,n* Syrian.
système (si:ˈstɛm) *nm* **1** system. **2** network. **3** device. **systématique** *adj* systematic.

T

ta (ta) *poss adj* see **ton.**
tabac (taˈba) *nm* tobacco. **tabac à priser** snuff.
table (tabl) *nf* **1** table. **2** tablet, slab. **3** list. **table roulante** trolley. **tableau, -aux** (taˈblo) *nm* **1** picture. **2** board. **3** list. **tableau d'annonces** notice board. **tableau noir** black-

board. **tablette** *nf* 1 shelf. 2 slab. **tablier** *nm* apron.
tabou (ta'bu:) *adj,nm* taboo.
tabouret (tabu:'rɛ) *nm* stool.
tacher (ta'ʃe:) *vt* 1 stain, spot. 2 impair. **tache** *nf* 1 stain, spot. 2 blot. **tache de rousseur** freckle.
tâcher (tɑ'ʃe:) *vi* try, strive. **tâche** *nf* task, job.
tacheté (taʃ'te:) *adj* flecked, mottled.
tact (takt) *nm* 1 sense of touch. 2 tact. **avoir du tact** be tactful.
tactique (tak'ti:k) *adj* tactical. *nf* tactics.
taffetas (taf'tɑ) *nm* taffeta.
taie (tɛ) *nf* **taie d'oreiller** pillowcase.
tailler (ta'je:) *vt* 1 cut. 2 prune. 3 trim. 4 sharpen. **taillade** *nf* 1 slash. 2 gash. **taille** *nf* 1 cutting. 2 cut. 3 stature. 4 waist. **taille-crayon** *nm invar* pencil-sharpener. **taille de cheveux** haircut. **tailleur** *nm* 1 tailor. 2 cutter. 3 (woman's) suit.
tain (tɛ̃) *nm* tinfoil.
taire* (tɛr) *vt* conceal, hide. **faire taire** silence. **se taire** *vr* be quiet, hold one's tongue.
talc (talk) *nm* talcum powder.
talent (ta'lɑ̃) *nm* 1 talent, gift. 2 ability.
talon (ta'lɔ̃) *nm* 1 heel. 2 stock. 3 remainder. 4 voucher.
talonner (talɔ'ne:) *vt* 1 follow closely. 2 spur on.
tambour (tɑ̃'bu:r) *nm* 1 drum. 2 barrel. **tambour de basque** tambourine.
tamis (ta'mi:) *nm* sieve.
tamiser (tami:'ze:) *vt* 1 sieve. 2 strain, filter.
tampon (tɑ̃'pɔ̃) *nm* 1 plug. 2 *med* wad. 3 stamp, mark. 4 buffer.
tamponner (tɑ̃pɔ'ne:) *vt* 1 plug. 2 dab. 3 collide with. **tamponnement** *nm* 1 plugging. 2 collision.
tancer (tɑ̃'se:) *vt inf* scold.
tandis que (tɑ̃'di: kə) *conj* 1 whereas. 2 whilst.
tangent (tɑ̃'ʒɑ̃) *nf* tangent.
Tanger (tɑ̃'ʒe:) *nm* Tangier.
tanguer (tɑ̃'ge:) *vi naut* pitch.
tanière (ta'njɛr) *nf* den, earth, hole.
tan-sad (tɑ̃'sad) *nm mot* pillion.
tant (tɑ̃) *adv* 1 so much. 2 so many. 3 as much. 4 as many. 5 so. **en tant que** in so far as. **tant mieux/pis!** so much the better/too bad! **tant s'en faut** far from it.
tante (tɑ̃t) *nf* aunt.
tantôt (tɑ̃'to) *adv* 1 soon. 2 a little while ago. **tantôt...tantôt** sometimes....sometimes.
taon (tɑ̃) *nm* horsefly.
tapage (ta'paʒ) *nm* din, racket. **tapageur, -euse** (tapa'ʒœr, -'ʒœz) *adj* 1 rowdy, noisy. 2 showy.
taper (ta'pe:) *vt* 1 tap. 2 hit. 3 beat. 4 *inf* borrow. **ça tape** it's hot. **taper à la machine** type. **taper sur les nerfs** get on one's nerves. **tape** *nf* tap, pat.
se tapir (ta'pi:r) *vr* crouch.
tapis (ta'pi:) *nm* 1 carpet. 2 rug. 3 cover. **tapis de sol** groundsheet.
tapisser (tapi:'se:) *vt* paper (a room). **tapisserie** *nf* 1 tapestry. 2 wallpaper. **tapissier** *nm* upholsterer.
tapoter (tapɔ'te:) *vt inf* 1 pat. 2 strum.
taquin (ta'kɛ̃) *adj* teasing. **taquiner** *vt* tease. **taquinerie** *nf* teasing.
tard (tar) *adv* late.
tarder (tar'de:) *vi* delay. **tardif, -ive** (tar'di:f, -'di:v) *adj* 1 late. 2 backward.
tarif (ta'ri:f) *nm* 1 price-list. 2 tariff. 3 fare.
tarir (ta'ri:r) *vt,vi* dry up.
tarte (tart) *nf* 1 tart. 2 flan. **tartine** *nf* slice of bread and butter.
tas (tɑ) *nm* 1 pile. 2 *inf* group, crew. 3 *inf* lot.
tasse (tɑs) *nf* cup. **tasse à thé** teacup. **tassée** *nf* cupful.
tasser (ta'se:) *vt* 1 cram together. 2 press down. **se tasser** *vr* 1 settle. 2 huddle together.
tâter (tɑ'te:) *vt* 1 feel, handle. 2 sound. 3 try.
tâtonner (tɑtɔ'ne:) *vi* 1 grope. 2 feel one's way.
tâtons (tɑ'tɔ̃) **à tâtons** *adv* warily.
tatouer (ta'twe:) *vt* tattoo.
taudis (to'di:) *nm* slum.
taupe (top) *nf zool* mole.
taureau, -aux (tɔ'ro) *nm* 1 bull. 2 *cap* Taurus.
taux (to) *nm* rate, scale.
taverne (ta'vɛrn) *nf* 1 tavern. 2 restaurant.
taxer (tak'se:) *vt* 1 tax. 2 regulate the price. 3 accuse. **taxe** *nf* 1 fixed price. 2 charge. 3 tax.
taxi (tak'si:) *nm* taxi.
Tchécoslovaquie (tʃekɔslɔva'ki:) *nf* Czechoslovakia. **tchèque** (tʃɛk) *adj,n* Czech. *nm* Czech (language).
te, t' (tə) *pron 2nd pers m,f s fam* 1 you. 2 to you.
technique (tɛk'ni:k) *adj* technical. *nf* technique. **technicien** *nm* technician. **technologie** *nf* technology. **technologique** *adj* technological.
teck (tɛk) *nm also* **tek** teak.
teindre* (tɛ̃dr) *vt* 1 dye. 2 tinge. 3 colour.
teint (tɛ̃) *nm* 1 dye. 2 complexion.
teinter (tɛ̃'te:) *vt* tint. **teinte** *nf* 1 tint. 2 tinge. **teinture** *nf* 1 dyeing. 2 colour. 3 dye.

tel, telle (tɛl) *adj* **1** such. **2** as. **3** like. **tel que** such as. *pron* **1** such a one. **2** many a.
télégramme (te:le:ˈgram) *nm* telegram.
télégraphier (te:le:graˈfje:) *vt* telegraph. **télégraphe** *nm* telegraph.
téléphérique (te:le:fe:ˈri:k) *nm* cable car.
téléphoner (te:le:fɔˈne:) *vt,vi* telephone. **téléphone** *nm* telephone. **téléphoniste** *nm,f* operator.
télésiège (te:le:ˈsjɛʒ) *nm* chair-lift.
téléski (te:le:ˈski:) *nm* ski-lift.
téléviser (te:le:vi:ˈze:) *vt* televise. **télévision** *nf* television.
tellement (tɛlˈmɑ̃) *adv* **1** so. **2** in such a way.
téméraire (te:me:ˈrɛr) *adj* **1** rash. **2** reckless.
témoigner (te:mwaˈɲe:) *vi* give evidence. *vt* **1** testify. **2** show. **3** prove. **témoignage** *nm* **1** evidence. **2** *law* statement. **3** token, mark. **témoin** *nm* **1** witness. **2** *sport* baton.
tempe (tɑ̃p) *nf anat* temple.
tempérament (tɑ̃pɛraˈmɑ̃) *nm* **1** temperament. **2** *med* constitution. **3** *comm* instalment.
tempérant (tɑ̃pɛˈrɑ̃) *adj* temperate.
température (tɑ̃pɛraˈtyr) *nf* temperature.
tempérer (tɑ̃pe:ˈre:) *vt* moderate.
tempête (tɑ̃ˈpɛt) *nf* storm. **tempétueux, -euse** (tɑ̃pe:ˈtɥœ, -ˈtɥœz) *adj* stormy, tempestuous.
temple (tɑ̃pl) *nm* **1** *rel* temple. **2** church.
tempo (tɛ̃ˈpo) *nm* tempo.
temporaire (tɑ̃pɔˈrɛr) *adj* **1** temporary. **2** provisional.
temporel, -elle (tɑ̃pɔˈrɛl) *adj* temporal.
temps (tɑ̃) *nm* **1** time. **2** age, period. **3** weather. **4** tense. **5** *mus* beat. **à temps** on time. **de temps en temps** now and again. **quel temps fait-il?** what's the weather like?
tenace (təˈnas) *adj* **1** tenacious. **2** tough. **3** stubborn. **ténacité** *nf* tenacity.
tenailles (təˈnaj) *nf pl* pincers.
tendance (tɑ̃ˈdɑ̃s) *nf* tendency, trend.
tendon (tɑ̃ˈdɔ̃) *nm* **1** tendon. **2** sinew.
tendre[1] (tɑ̃dr) *adj* **1** tender. **2** affectionate. **3** delicate. **tendresse** *nf* **1** affection. **2** tenderness. **3** *pl* caress. **tendreté** *nf cul* tenderness.
tendre[2] (tɑ̃dr) *vt* **1** stretch. **2** strain. **3** tighten. **4** hold out. **5** set. **tendre à 1** tend to. **2** aim at. **se tendre** *vr* become taut or strained. **tendu** *adj* **1** taut. **2** strained. **3** tense.
ténèbres (te:ˈnɛbr) *nf pl* darkness, gloom. **ténébreux, -euse** (te:ne:ˈbrœ, -ˈbrœz) *adj* **1** dark, gloomy. **2** sinister. **3** mysterious.
tenir* (təˈni:r) *vt* **1** hold. **2** keep. **3** run. **4** restrain. **5** occupy. *vi* **1** hold. **2** stick. **3** remain. **4** last. **tenir à 1** value. **2** result from. **tenir bon** hold out. **tenir compte de** take into consideration. **tenir de** take after. **se tenir** *vr* **1** keep. **2** remain. **3** contain oneself. **se tenir à 1** hold on to. **2** abide by. **se tenir bien** behave.
tennis (tɛˈni:s) *nm* **1** tennis. **2** tennis court.
ténor (te:ˈnɔr) *nm* tenor.
tension (tɑ̃ˈsjɔ̃) *nf* **1** tension. **2** pressure. **3** voltage. **tension artérielle** blood pressure.
tente (tɑ̃t) *nf* **1** tent. **2** awning.
tenter (tɑ̃ˈte:) *vt* **1** tempt. **2** try. **3** attempt. **tentant** *adj* tempting. **tentation** *nf* temptation. **tentative** *nf* attempt.
tenture (tɑ̃ˈtyr) *nf* **1** tapestry. **2** wallpaper.
tenu (təˈny) *v* see **tenir.** *adj* **bien tenu** neat, tidy. **être tenu à** be bound to. **mal tenu 1** neglected. **2** untidy. **tenue** *nf* **1** holding. **2** bearing. **3** behaviour. **4** dress. **tenue de soirée** evening dress. **tenue des livres** bookkeeping.
ténu (te:ˈny) *adj* **1** fine. **2** thin. **3** tenuous. **4** subtle.
tenure (təˈnyr) **tenure à bail** *nf* leasehold.
térébenthine (te:re:bɑ̃ˈti:n) *nf* turpentine.
tergiverser (tɛrʒi:vɛrˈse:) *vi* **1** beat about the bush. **2** hesitate.
terme (tɛrm) *nm* **1** limit. **2** term, expression. **3** quarter's rent. **avant terme** prematurely. **mettre terme à** put an end to.
terminer (tɛrmi:ˈne:) *vt* end, terminate. **terminaison** *nf* ending.
terminologie (tɛrmi:nɔlɔˈʒi:) *nf* terminology.
terminus (tɛrmi:ˈnys) *nm* terminus, terminal.
ternir (tɛrˈni:r) *vt* **1** tarnish. **2** dull. **terne** *adj* **1** dull. **2** lifeless.
terrain (tɛˈrɛ̃) *nm* **1** ground. **2** plot of land. **terrain de jeux** playing field.
terrasse (tɛˈras) *nf* **1** terrace. **2** bank.
terre (tɛr) *nf* **1** earth. **2** world. **3** land, soil. **4** estate. **descendre à terre** go ashore. **par terre** on the ground. **basses terres** *nf pl* lowlands. **hautes terres** *nf pl* highlands.
terrestre (tɛˈrɛstr) *adj* **1** terrestrial. **2** worldly.
terreur (tɛˈrœr) *nf* terror, fear.
terrible (tɛˈri:bl) *adj* **1** terrible, awful. **2** *inf* terrific.
terrier (tɛˈrje:) *nm* hole, burrow.
terrifier (tɛri:ˈfje:) *vt* terrify.
terrine (tɛˈri:n) *nf* **1** earthenware dish. **2** potted meat.
territoire (tɛri:ˈtwar) *nm* territory. **territorial, -aux** (tɛri:tɔˈrjal, -ˈrjo) *adj* territorial.

terroir (tɛr'war) *nm* soil.

terroriser (tɛrɔri:'ze:) *vt* terrorize. **terrorisme** *nm* terrorism. **terroriste** *nm,f* terrorist.

Térylène (te:ri:'lɛn) *nm Tdmk* Terylene.

tes (te:) *poss adj* see **ton.**

tesson (tɛ'sɔ̃) *nm* broken fragment (of glass, etc.).

testament (tɛsta'mɑ̃) *nm* **1** *law* will. **2** testament. **ancien Testament** Old Testament. **nouveau Testament** New Testament.

testicule (tɛsti:'kyl) *nm* testicle.

têtard (tɛ'tar) *nm* tadpole.

tête (tɛt) *nf* **1** head. **2** brains. **3** front. **4** top. **en tête** in front, ahead. **forte tête** strong-minded. **tenir tête à** resist. **tête-à-tête** *nm invar* private interview. **têtu** *adj* stubborn.

tétin (te:'tɛ̃) *nm* nipple, teat.

tétras (te:'trɑ) *nm zool* grouse.

texte (tɛkst) *nm* **1** text. **2** passage. **3** subject.

textile (tɛk'sti:l) *adj,nm* textile.

texture (tɛk'styr) *nf* texture.

thé (te:) *nm* tea. **théière** *nf* teapot.

théâtre (te:'ɑtr) *nm* **1** theatre. **2** stage. **3** drama. **théâtral, -aux** (te:ɑ'tral, -'tro) *adj* theatrical.

thème (tɛm) *nm* **1** theme, subject. **2** *educ* prose.

théologie (te:ɔlɔ'ʒi:) *nf* theology. **théologien** *nm* theologian. **théologique** *adj* theological.

théorème (te:ɔ'rɛm) *nm* theorem.

théorie (te:ɔ'ri:) *nf* theory. **théorique** *adj* theoretical.

théoriser (te:ɔri:'ze:) *vi* theorize.

thérapeutique (tɛrapœ'ti:k) *adj* therapeutic.

thérapie (te:ra'pi:) *nf* therapy.

thermal, -aux (tɛr'mal, -'mo) *adj* thermal.

thermodynamique (tɛrmɔdi:na'mi:k) *nf* thermodynamics.

thermomètre (tɛrmɔ'mɛtr) *nm* thermometer.

thermonucléaire (tɛrmɔnykle:'ɛr) *adj* thermonuclear.

thermoplongeur (termɔplɔ̃'ʒœr) *nm* immersion heater.

Thermos (tɛr'mɔs) *nm Tdmk* Thermos flask.

thermostat (tɛrmɔ'sta) *nm* thermostat.

thésauriser (te:zɔri:'ze:) *vt,vi* hoard.

thèse (tɛz) *nf* **1** proposition. **2** theory. **3** thesis.

thon (tɔ̃) *nm* tunny, tuna fish.

thym (tɛ̃) *nm* thyme.

tiare (tjar) *nf* tiara.

tic (ti:k) *nm* **1** *med* twitch. **2** mannerism.

ticket (ti:'kɛ) *nm* **1** ticket. **2** slip.

tiède (tjɛd) *adj* tepid, lukewarm.

tien, tienne (tjɛ̃, tjɛn) **le tien, la tienne** *poss pron 2nd pers s fam* **1** yours. **2** your own.

tiens[1] (tjɛ̃) *v* see **tenir.**

tiens[2] (tjɛ̃) *interj* **1** hello! **2** look!

tiers, tierce (tjɛr, tjɛrs) *adj* third. *nm* **1** third. **2** third person or party.

tige (ti:ʒ) *nf* **1** stem, stalk. **2** *bot* trunk. **3** rod.

tigre (ti:gr) *nm* tiger. **tigré** *adj* **1** spotted. **2** striped.

tilleul (ti:'jœl) *nm* linden or lime tree.

timbale (tɛ̃'bal) *nf* **1** kettledrum. **2** *pl* timpani. **3** metal mug.

timbrer (tɛ̃'bre:) *vt* **1** stamp. **2** postmark. **timbre** *nm* **1** stamp. **2** bell.

timide (ti:'mi:d) *adj* **1** timid. **2** shy.

tintamarre (tɛ̃ta'mar) *nm* din, racket.

tinter (tɛ̃'te:) *vt* ring, toll (a bell). *vi* **1** tinkle. **2** jingle. **3** clink.

tir (ti:r) *nm* **1** shooting. **2** firing. **tir à l'arc** archery.

tirelire (ti:r'li:r) *nf* moneybox.

tirer (ti:'re:) *vt* **1** pull. **2** draw (out). **3** drag. **4** take out. **5** shoot. *vi* **1** pull. **2** incline. **se tirer** *vr* extricate oneself. **tirage** *nm* **1** pulling. **2** draw (of a lottery). **3** *comm* circulation. **tire** *nf* pull. **tire-bouchon** *nm, pl* **tire-bouchons** corkscrew.

tiret (ti:'rɛ) *nm* **1** hyphen. **2** dash.

tiroir (ti'rwar) *nm, pl* drawer. **tiroir-caisse** *nm, pl* **tiroirs-caisses** till.

tisane (ti:'zan) *nf* infusion.

tisonner (ti:zɔ'ne:) *vt* poke, stir. **tisonnier** *nm* poker.

tisser (ti:'se:) *vt* weave. **tissu** *nm* **1** material. **2** fabric. **3** *zool* tissue.

titre (ti:tr) *nm* **1** title. **2** diploma. **3** claim. **4** *comm* bond. **à titre de** by virtue of.

tituber (ti:'ty'be:) *vi* stagger, lurch.

toast (tɔst) *nm* toast (drink).

toi (twa) *pron 2nd pers m,f s fam* you. **toi-même** *pron 2nd pers m,f s fam* yourself.

toile (twal) *nf* **1** linen. **2** canvas. **3** oil painting. **4** *Th* curtain. **toile cirée** oilskin. **toile d'araignée** cobweb.

toilette (twa'lɛt) *nf* **1** washing, toilet. **2** dressing-table. **3** lavatory. **4** dress.

toise (twaz) *nf* fathom.

toison (twa'zɔ̃) *nf* fleece.

toit (twa) *nm* **1** roof. **2** *inf* home.

tôle (to:l) *nf* metal sheet.

tolérer (tɔle:'re:) *vt* tolerate. **tolérance** *nf* tolerance. **tolérant** *adj* tolerant.

tomate (tɔ'mat) *nf* tomato.

tombe (tɔ̃b) *nf* **1** tomb. **2** tombstone. **tombeau, -aux** (tɔ̃'bo) *nm* **1** tomb. **2** monument (over a grave).

tomber (tɔ̃'be:) *vi* (*aux* être) **1** fall. **2** hang. **3** subside. **laisser tomber** drop. **tomber juste** **1** happen at the right moment. **2** guess right. **tombée** *nf* fall.

tome (tɔm) *nm* volume (of a book).

ton[1], **ta, tes** (tɔ̃, ta, te:) *poss adj 2nd pers s fam* your.

ton[2] (tɔ̃) *nm* **1** tone. **2** colour. **3** *mus* pitch. **4** *mus* key.

tondre (tɔ̃dr) *vt* shear, clip, mow. **tondeuse** *nf* **1** shears. **2** lawn-mower.

tonifier (tɔni:'fje:) *vt* invigorate, brace.

tonique (tɔ'ni:k) *nm* tonic.

tonne (tɔn) *nf* ton.

tonneau, -aux (tɔ'no) *nm* barrel.

tonner (tɔ'ne:) *vi* thunder. **tonnerre** *nm* thunder.

topaze (tɔ'paz) *nf* topaz.

toper (tɔ'pe:) *vi inf* agree. **tope!** *interj* done!

torche (tɔrʃ) *nf* torch.

torchon (tɔr'ʃɔ̃) *nm* **1** duster. **2** dishcloth.

tordre (tɔrdr) *vt* **1** twist. **2** wring. **3** distort. **se tordre** *vr* writhe.

tornade (tɔr'nad) *nf* tornado.

torpille (tɔr'pi:j) *nf* torpedo.

torréfier (tɔrre:'fje:) *vt* **1** roast. **2** scorch.

torrent (tɔ'rɑ̃) *nm* torrent. **torrentiel, -elle** (tɔrɑ̃'sjɛl) *adj* torrential.

tors (tɔr) *adj* **1** twisted. **2** crooked.

torse (tɔrs) *nm* torso.

tort (tɔr) *nm* **1** wrong. **2** fault. **3** harm. **avoir tort** be wrong.

torticolis (tɔrti:kɔ'li:) *nm* stiff neck.

tortiller (tɔrti:'je:) *vt* **1** twist. **2** twiddle. *vi* **1** wriggle. **2** quibble. **se tortiller** *vr* **1** writhe. **2** squirm.

tortu (tɔr'ty) *adj* crooked.

tortue (tɔr'ty) *nf* tortoise. **tortue de mer** turtle.

tortueux, -euse (tɔr'tɥœ, -'tɥœz) *adj* **1** winding. **2** underhand.

torturer (tɔrty're:) *vt* torture. **torture** *nf* torture.

Tory (tɔ'ri:) *adj or nm, pl* **Tories** Tory.

tôt (to) *adv* **1** soon. **2** early. **tôt ou tard** sooner or later.

total, -aux (tɔ'tal, -'to) *adj* **1** total, whole. **2** complete, absolute. *nm* total. **au total** on the whole. **totalitaire** *adj* totalitarian. **totalité** *nf* whole.

toucher (tu:'ʃe:) *vt* **1** touch. **2** hit. **3** cash. **4** receive. **5** move. **6** concern. **toucher à** **1** be near to. **2** affect. **3** meddle with. **se toucher** *vr* adjoin. ~*nm* touch, feel. **touche** *nf* **1** touch. **2** *mus* key.

touffu (tu:'fy) *adj* **1** bushy. **2** thick. **3** complicated.

toujours (tu:'ʒu:r) *adv* **1** always, ever, forever. **2** still. **3** all the same.

toupet (tu:'pɛ) *nm* **1** tuft (of hair). **2** forelock. **3** *sl* cheek, nerve.

toupie (tu:'pi:) *nf* top (toy).

tour[1] (tu:r) *nf* tower.

tour[2] (tu:r) *nm* **1** turn. **2** revolution. **3** circumference. **4** lathe. **5** stroll. **6** trick. **à tour de rôle** in turn. **tour de main** knack.

tourbe (tu:rb) *nf* peat, turf.

tourbillon (tu:rbi:'jɔ̃) *nm* whirlwind.

tourelle (tu:'rɛl) *nf* turret.

tourisme (tu:'ri:sm) *nm* tourism. **touriste** *nm,f* tourist.

tourment (tu:r'mɑ̃) *nm* **1** torment. **2** anguish. **tourmenter** *vt* **1** torture. **2** harass. **3** pester.

tourmente (tu:r'mɑ̃) *nf* **1** storm. **2** upheaval.

tournedos (tu:rnə'do) *nm* fillet steak.

tourner (tu:r'ne:) *vt* **1** turn. **2** rotate. **3** dodge. **4** wind. *vi* **1** revolve. **2** result. **3** curdle. **tourner un film** shoot a film. **tournant** *adj* **1** turning. **2** winding. *nm* **1** bend, turning. **2** turning point. **tourne-disques** *nm invar* record-player. **tournée** *nf* **1** round, circuit. **2** tour. **tournevis** *nm* screwdriver.

tournesol (tu:rnə'sɔl) *nm* sunflower.

tourniquet (tu:rni:'kɛ) *nm* **1** turnstile. **2** tourniquet.

tournoi (tu:r'nwa) *nm* tournament.

tournoyer (tu:rnwa'je:) *vi* whirl.

tournure (tu:r'nyr) *nf* **1** shape, appearance. **2** form, figure.

tourte (tu:rt) *nf* **1** pie. **2** *inf* idiot.

tourterelle (tu:rtə'rɛl) *nf* turtle dove.

Toussaint (tu:'sɛ̃) *nf* All Saints' Day.

tousser (tu:'se:) *vi* cough.

tout (tu:) *adj, pl* **tous, toutes** **1** all. **2** every. **3** any. **de toute importance** of utmost importance. **tous les deux** both. **toutes les fois que** whenever. ~*pron* **1** all. **2** anything. **3** everything. *nm* **1** whole. **2** total. *adv* **1** quite, completely. **2** while. **3** though. **tout à fait** completely. **tout au plus** at the very most. **tout fait** ready-made. **tout neuf** brand new. **toutefois** *adv* however, yet. **tout-puissant** *adj* omnipotent.

toux (tu:) *nf* cough.

toxique (tɔk'si:k) *adj* **1** toxic. **2** poisonous. *nm* poison.
trac (trak) *nm sl* fright.
tracas (tra'ka) *nm* **1** worry. **2** bother.
tracasser (traka'sje:) *vt* **1** worry. **2** plague. **3** annoy.
tracer (tra'se:) *vt* **1** trace. **2** outline. **3** mark out. **4** plot. **trace** *nf* trace, trail, track.
tract (trakt) *nm pol* leaflet.
tracteur (trak'tœr) *nm* tractor.
tradition (tradi:'sjɔ̃) *nf* **1** tradition. **2** legend. **tradition populaire** folklore. **traditionnel, -elle** (tradi:sjɔ'nɛl) *adj* traditional.
traduire* (tra'dɥi:r) *vt* **1** translate. **2** interpret. **traducteur, -trice** (tradyk'tœr, -'tri:s) *nm,f* translator. **traduction** *nf* translation.
trafiquer (trafi:'ke:) *vi* **trafiquer en** traffic or deal in.
tragédie (traʒe:'di:) *nf* tragedy. **tragique** *adj* tragic.
trahir (tra'i:r) *vt* **1** betray. **2** reveal. **trahison** *nf* **1** betrayal. **2** treachery.
train (trɛ̃) *nm* **1** train. **2** line. **3** movement. **4** pace. **5** mood. **être en train de** be in the middle of. **mettre en train** start, set going. **train de marchandises** goods train. **train-train** *nm inf* routine.
traîner (trɛ'ne:) *vt* **1** drag. **2** trail. **3** drawl. **4** drag on or out. *vi* **1** trail. **2** linger. **3** languish. **se traîner** *vr* crawl. **traînant** *adj* **1** dragging. **2** listless. **traîneau, -aux** (trɛ'no) *nm* sledge. **traînée** *nf* **1** train. **2** trail.
traire* (trɛr) *vt* milk.
trait (trɛ) *nm* **1** gulp. **2** dart. **3** flash. **4** line. **5** stroke. **6** *anat* feature. **d'un trait** at a stretch. **trait d'union** hyphen.
traiter (trɛ'te:) *vt* **1** treat. **2** call. **3** discuss. **4** handle. *vi* negotiate. **traité** *nm* **1** treatise. **2** treaty. **traitement** *nm* **1** treatment. **2** salary.
traître, traîtresse (trɛtr, trɛ'trɛs) *adj* treacherous. *nm* traitor.
trajet (tra'ʒɛ) *nm* **1** journey. **2** passage.
trame (tram) *nf* **1** thread. **2** conspiracy.
tramway (tram'wɛ) *nm* tram.
trancher (trɑ̃'ʃe:) *vt* **1** cut. **2** break off. **3** solve. *vi* contrast. **tranche** *nf* **1** slice, portion. **2** slab. **3** edge. **tranchée** *nf* trench.
tranquille (trɑ̃'ki:l) *adj* **1** tranquil. **2** calm. **3** peaceful. **tranquillisant** *nm* tranquillizer. **tranquillité** *nf* **1** quiet. **2** calm. **3** stillness.
transaction (trɑ̃zak'sjɔ̃) *nf* **1** transaction. **2** compromise.
transatlantique (trɑ̃zatlɑ̃'ti:k) *adj* transatlantic. *nm* **1** liner. **2** deckchair.
transcrire* (trɑ̃'skri:r) *vt* transcribe.
transe (trɑ̃s) *nf* **1** trance. **2** fear.
transférer (trɑ̃sfe:'re:) *vt* **1** transfer. **2** remove. **3** convey. **transfert** *nm* transfer.
transformer (trɑ̃sfɔr'me:) *vt* **1** transform. **2** convert. **transformateur** *nm* transformer.
transfuge (trɑ̃s'fyʒ) *nm* deserter.
transfuser (trɑ̃sfy'ze:) *vt* transfuse. **transfusion** *nf* transfusion.
transiger (trɑ̃zi:'ʒe:) *vi* come to a compromise.
transir (trɑ̃'si:r) *vt* **1** chill. **2** seize (with fear).
transistor (trɑ̃zi:'stɔr) *nm* transistor.
transition (trɑ̃zi:'sjɔ̃) *nf* transition.
transmettre* (trɑ̃s'mɛtr) *vt* **1** transmit. **2** *law* transfer. **3** hand down.
transparent (trɑ̃spa'rɑ̃) *adj* transparent.
transpirer (trɑ̃spi:'re:) *vi* perspire. **transpiration** *nf* perspiration.
transplanter (trɑ̃splɑ̃'te:) *vt* transplant.
transport (trɑ̃'spɔr) *nm* **1** transport, carriage. **2** outburst.
transporter (trɑ̃spɔr'te:) *vt* **1** transport, convey. **2** carry away, delight.
transposer (trɑ̃spo'ze:) *vt* transpose.
transvaser (trɑ̃sva'ze:) *vt* decant.
trapèze (tra'pɛz) *nm* trapeze.
trappe (trap) *nf* **1** pitfall. **2** trapdoor.
trapu (tra'py) *adj* **1** stocky. **2** squat.
traquer (tra'ke:) *vt* **1** surround. **2** track down. **traquenard** *nm* trap.
trauma (tro'ma) *nm* trauma. **traumatique** *adj* traumatic.
travail, -aux (tra'vaj, -'vo) *nm* work. **travail à l'aiguille** needlework.
travailler (trava'je:) *vt* **1** work. **2** work on. *vi* **1** work, toil. **2** ferment. **travaillé** *adj* **1** elaborate. **2** wrought. **travailleur, -euse** (trava'jœr, -'jœz) *nm* workman. *adj* industrious. **travailliste** *nm,f* member of the Labour Party. *adj pol* Labour.
travers (tra'vɛr) *nm* **1** breadth. **2** fault, defect. **à travers** across. **au travers de** across. **de travers** amiss, the wrong way.
traverser (travɛr'se:) *vt* **1** cross. **2** go through. **traverse** *nf* **1** short cut. **2** *tech* sleeper. **3** hitch. **traversée** *nf* passage, crossing.
traversin (travɛr'sɛ̃) *nm* bolster.
travestir (travɛ'sti:r) *vt* disguise, dress up. **travesti** *adj* disguised. *nm* fancy dress.
trébucher (tre:by'ʃe:) *vi* **1** stumble. **2** trip. **faire trebucher** trip up.

trèfle (trɛfl) *nm* **1** clover. **2** *game* club.
treillis (trɛ'ji:) *nm* trellis, lattice.
treize (trɛz) *adj,nm* thirteen. **treizième** *adj* thirteenth.
trembler (trɑ̃'ble:) *vi* **1** tremble. **2** flicker. **3** shake. **4** quake. **tremblement** *nm* **1** trembling. **2** tremor. **tremblement de terre** earthquake.
trémière (tre:'mjɛr) **rose trémière** *nf* hollyhock.
se trémousser (tre:mu:'se:) *vr* **1** fidget. **2** flutter.
tremper (trɑ̃'pe:) *vt,vi* soak, steep. *vt* **1** drench. **2** dip. **3** mix.
tremplin (trɑ̃'plɛ̃) *nm* **1** springboard. **2** diving board.
trente (trɑ̃t) *adj,nm* thirty. **trentième** *adj* thirtieth.
trépas (tre:'pɑ) *nm* death.
trépider (tre:pi:'de:) *vi* vibrate.
trépied (tre:'pje:) *nm* tripod.
trépigner (tre:pi:'ɲe:) *vi* stamp, prance.
très (trɛ) *adv* **1** very. **2** most. **3** very much.
trésor (tre:'zɔr) *nm* **1** treasure. **2** *pl* riches. **3** treasury. **trésorerie** (tre:zɔr'ri:) *nf* treasury. **trésorier, -ière** (tre:zɔ'rje:, -'rjɛr) *nm,f* treasurer.
tressaillir* (trɛsa'ji:r) *vi* **1** start, jump. **2** quiver. **3** shudder. **tressaillir de douleur** wince. **tressaillement** *nm* **1** start, jump. **2** shudder. **3** wince.
tresser (trɛ'se:) *vt* **1** plait. **2** weave. **tresse** *nf* plait.
tréteau, -aux (tre:'to) *nm* **1** trestle. **2** support. **3** stage.
treuil (trœj) *nm* **1** winch. **2** windlass.
trêve (trɛv) *nf* truce.
tri (tri:) *nm* sorting. **triage** *nm* sorting.
triangle (tri:'ɑ̃gl) *nm* triangle. **triangulaire** *adj* triangular.
tribord (tri:'bɔr) *nm* starboard.
tribu (tri:'by) *nf* tribe.
tribunal, -aux (tri:by'nal, -'no) *nm* **1** tribunal. **2** *law* court. **tribune** *nf* **1** platform. **2** grandstand. **3** forum.
tribut (tri:'by) *nm* tribute.
tributaire (tri:by'tɛr) *adj,nm* tributary.
tricher (tri:'ʃe:) *vt,vi* **1** cheat. **2** trick.
tricolore (tri:kɔ'lɔr) *nm inf* French national flag, tricolour.
tricot (tri:'ko) *nm* **1** knitting. **2** jersey, jumper.
tricoter (tri:kɔ'te:) *vi* knit.
tricycle (tri:'si:kl) *nm* tricycle.
trier (tri:'e:) *vt* sort. **trier à la main** hand-pick.
trille (tri:j) *nm mus* trill.
trimestre (tri:'mɛstr) *nm* **1** *educ* term. **2** quarter, three months. **trimestriel, -elle** (tri:mɛstri:'ɛl) *adj* quarterly.
tringle (trɛ̃gl) *nf* rod, bar.
trinquer (trɛ̃'ke:) *vi* clink glasses.
trio (tri:'o) *nm* trio.
triompher (tri:ɔ̃'fe:) *vi* **1** triumph. **2** overcome. **triomphant** *adj* triumphant. **triomphe** *nm* triumph.
tripaille (tri:'pɑj) *nf inf* offal.
tripe (tri:p) *nf* **1** tripe. **2** *sl* guts.
tripler (tri:'ple:) *vt,vi* triple, treble. **triple** *adj* triple, treble. **triplés** *nm* triplets.
tripoter (tri:pɔ'te:) *vt inf* **1** meddle with. **2** deal dishonestly with. *vi* **1** mess about. **2** tamper with.
triste (tri:st) *adj* **1** sad. **2** melancholy. **3** dismal. **4** unfortunate. **tristesse** *nf* **1** sadness. **2** gloom. **3** bleakness.
triton (tri:'tɔ̃) *nm* newt.
trivial (tri:'vjal) *adj* **1** trite. **2** trivial. **3** vulgar. **4** obscene. **trivialité** *nf* **1** obscenity. **2** triviality.
troc (trɔk) *nm* **1** swop. **2** barter.
trognon (trɔ'ɲɔ̃) *nm* **1** core (of an apple, etc.). **2** stump.
trois (trwɑ) *adj,nm* three. **troisième** *adj* third. **trois-quarts** *nm invar* three-quarters.
trombe (trɔ̃b) *nf* **1** waterspout. **2** whirlwind.
trombone (trɔ̃'bɔn) *nm* **1** trombone. **2** paper-clip.
tromper (trɔ̃'pe:) *vt* **1** deceive. **2** cheat. **3** mislead. **4** baffle. **se tromper** *vr* be mistaken, make a mistake. **tromperie** *nf* deceit.
trompette (trɔ̃'pɛt) *nf* trumpet.
tronc (trɔ̃) *nm bot* trunk.
tronçon (trɔ̃'sɔ̃) *nm* **1** fragment. **2** stump, stub.
trône (tron) *nm* throne.
tronquer (trɔ̃'ke:) *vt* cut up, mutilate.
trop (tro) *adv* **1** too. **2** too much. *nm* too much or many. **de trop** too much or many. **trop-plein** *nm, pl* **trop-pleins** overflow.
trophée (trɔ'fe:) *nm* trophy.
tropique (trɔ'pi:k) *nm* tropic. *adj* tropical. **tropical, -aux** (trɔpi:'kal, -'ko) *adj* tropical.
troquer (trɔ'ke:) *vt* **1** swop. **2** barter.
trot (tro) *nm* trot.
trotter (trɔ'te:) *vi* trot.
trottoir (trɔ'twar) *nm* pavement.
trou (tru:) *nm* **1** hole. **2** *inf* pothole. **trou de serrure** keyhole. **trou d'homme** manhole.
trouble[1] (tru:bl) *adj* **1** cloudy. **2** confused.
trouble[2] (tru:bl) *nm* **1** disorder. **2** agitation.

troubler (tru:'ble:) *vt* **1** disturb. **2** confuse. **3** agitate. **4** make muddy. **se troubler** *vr* **1** become cloudy or overcast. **2** get confused.

trouer (tru:'e:) *vt* make a hole in, pierce. **trouée** *nf* **1** gap. **2** *mil* breakthrough.

troupe (tru:p) *nf* **1** troop, gang. **2** troupe. **3** herd. **4** *pl* troops. **troupeau, -aux** *nm* herd, flock.

trousser (tru:'se:) *vt* **1** turn up. **2** *inf* get through. **3** *inf* turn out. **trousse** *nf* **1** bundle. **2** kit. **trousseau, -aux** *nm* **1** bunch. **2** bride's outfit.

trouver (tru:'ve:) *vt* **1** find. **2** discover. **3** think. **se trouver** *vr* **1** be. **2** feel. **3** happen. **trouvaille** *nf* **1** find. **2** discovery. **3** windfall.

truc (tryk) *nm inf* **1** thing, gadget. **2** knack.

truelle (try'ɛl) *nf* trowel.

truffe (tryf) *nf* truffle.

truie (trɥi:) *nf* sow.

truite (trɥi:t) *nf* trout.

trumeau, -aux (try'mo) *nm arch* pier.

truquer (try'ke:) *vt* fake.

tsar (tsar) *nm* tsar.

tu[1] (tu) *pron 2nd pers m,f s fam* you.

tu[2] (ty) *v* see **taire.**

tuba (ty'ba) *nm* tuba.

tube (tyb) *nm* **1** tube. **2** pipe.

tuberculose (tybɛrky'loz) *nf* tuberculosis.

tuer (tɥe:) *vt* **1** kill. **2** slaughter. **à tue-tête** at the top of one's voice. **tuerie** *nf* slaughter.

tuile (tɥi:l) *nf* **1** tile. **2** *inf* bother, trouble.

tulipe (ty'li:p) *nf* tulip.

tumeur (ty'mœr) *nf* tumour, growth.

tumulte (ty'mylt) *nm* tumult, uproar. **tumultueux, -euse** (tymyl'tɥœ, -'tɥœz) *adj* noisy, riotous.

tunique (ty'ni:k) *nf* tunic.

Tunisie (tyni:'zi:) *nf* Tunisia. **tunisien, -ienne** (tyni:'zjɛ̃, -'zjɛn) *adj,n* Tunisian.

tunnel (ty'nɛl) *nm* tunnel.

turbulent (tyrby'lɑ̃) *adj* **1** turbulent, restless. **2** unruly.

turf (tyrf) *nm* **1** racecourse. **2** racing.

Turquie (tyr'ki:) *nf* Turkey. **turc, turque** (tyrk) *adj* Turkish. *nm,f* Turk. *nm* Turkish (language).

turquoise (tyr'kwaz) *nf* turquoise. *nm* turquoise (colour). *adj invar* turquoise.

tutelle (ty'tɛl) *nf* **1** guardianship. **2** protection.

tuteur, -trice (ty'tœr, -'tri:s) *nm,f* guardian. *nm* prop.

tutoyer (tytwa'je:) *vt* address as **tu,** be on familiar terms with.

tuyau, -aux (tɥi:'jo) *nm* **1** pipe, hose. **2** *inf* tip, hint.

tympan (tɛ̃'pɑ̃) *nm* eardrum.

type (ti:p) *nm* **1** type, pattern. **2** *inf* chap, bloke.

typhoïde (ti:fɔ'i:d) *adj,nf* typhoid.

typhon (ti:'fɔ̃) *nm* typhoon.

typique (ti:'pi:k) *adj* typical.

tyran (ti:'rɑ̃) *nm* tyrant. **tyrannie** *nf* tyranny. **tyrannique** *adj* tyrannical.

U

ulcérer (ylse:'re:) *vt* **1** ulcerate. **2** wound, embitter. **ulcère** *nm* ulcer.

ultérieur (ylte:'rjœr) *adj* **1** ulterior. **2** subsequent.

ultimatum (yltima'tɔm) *nm* ultimatum.

ultime (yl'ti:m) *adj* ultimate, final.

ultrasonique (yltrasɔ'ni:k) *adj* supersonic.

ultra-violet, -ette (yltravjɔle, -'lɛt) *adj, pl* **ultra-violets, -ettes** ultraviolet.

un, une (œ̃, yn) *indef art* a, an. *indef pron* one. *nm,f* one. **les uns...les autres** some...others. ~*adj* **1** one. **2** first. **unième** *adj* first.

unanime (yna'ni:m) *adj* unanimous.

uni (y'ni:) *adj* **1** united. **2** smooth. **3** plain.

unifier (yni:'fje:) *vt* **1** unify. **2** amalgamate. **3** standardize.

uniforme (yni:'fɔrm) *adj* uniform, unvarying. *nm* uniform. **uniformité** *nf* uniformity.

union (y'njɔ̃) *nf* **1** union. **2** society, association. **3** harmony, agreement.

unique (y'ni:k) *adj* **1** sole, only. **2** unique.

unir (y'ni:r) *vt* unite, join. **unité** *nf* **1** unity. **2** unit.

unisson (yni:'sɔ̃) *nf* unison.

univers (yni:'vɛr) *nm* universe. **universel, -elle** (yni:vɛr'sɛl) *adj* universal, worldwide.

université (yni:vɛrsi:'te:) *nf* university.

urbain (yr'bɛ̃) *adj* urban, town. **urbanisme** *nm* town-planning.

urgent (yr'ʒɑ̃) *adj* urgent, pressing. **urgence** *nf* **1** urgency. **2** emergency.

uriner (yri:'ne:) *vi* urinate. **urine** *nf* urine. **urinoir** *nm* urinal.

urne (yrn) *nf* **1** urn. **2** ballot-box.

user (y'ze:) *vt* **1** use, consume. **2** wear out. **user de** make use of. **s'user** *vr* wear away. **usage** *nm* **1** use. **2** custom. **3** practice. **4** wear. **5** breeding, manners. **usagé** *adj* second-hand. **usé** *adj* **1** worn. **2** threadbare. **3** hackneyed. **usité** *adj* current, in use.

usine (y'zi:n) *nf* factory, works.
ustensile (ytɑ̃'si:l) *nm* utensil, implement.
usuel, -elle (y'zɥɛl) *adj* **1** usual, customary. **2** current.
usurper (yzyr'pe:) *vt* usurp. **usurpateur, -trice** (yzyrpa'tœr, -'tri:s) *n* usurper.
utérus (yte:'rys) *nm* uterus.
utiliser (yti:li:'ze:) *vt* use, make use of. **utile** *adj* **1** useful, handy. **2** effective. **3** necessary. **utilité** *nf* use, utility.

V

va (va) *v* see **aller.**
vacance (va'kɑ̃s) *nf* **1** vacancy. **2** *pl* holidays. **vacant** *adj* vacant, empty.
vacarme (va'karm) *nm* din, racket.
vaccin (vak'sɛ̃) *nm* vaccine.
vacciner (vaksi:'ne:) *vt* vaccinate, inoculate. **vaccination** *nf* vaccination.
vache (vaʃ) *nf* **1** cow. **2** *sl* bitch. **vachement** *adv sl* terribly, very.
vaciller (vasi:'je:) *vi* **1** waver. **2** flicker. **3** wobble. **vacillant** *adj* **1** wobbly. **2** undecided.
va-et-vient *nm invar* **1** coming and going. **2** shuttle.
vagabond (vaga'bɔ̃) *adj* wandering. *nm* tramp, vagrant.
vagabonder (vagabɔ̃'de:) *vi* **1** roam. **2** wander.
vagin (va'ʒɛ̃) *nm* vagina.
vague[1] (vag) *nf* **1** wave. **2** generation, age-group. **vague de chaleur** heatwave.
vague[2] (vag) *adj* vague, hazy. *nm* vagueness.
vague[3] (vag) *adj* vacant, empty. *nm* empty space.
vaillant (va'jɑ̃) *adj* valiant, brave.
vain (vɛ̃) *adj* **1** vain, conceited. **2** empty, futile.
vaincre* (vɛ̃kr) *vt* **1** conquer. **2** beat, defeat. **vainqueur** *nm* **1** conqueror. **2** winner. *adj* victorious.
vaincu (vɛ̃'ky) *v* see **vaincre.**
vainquant (vɛ̃'kɑ̃) *v* see **vaincre.**
vais (vɛ) *v* see **aller.**
vaisseau, -aux (vɛ'so) *nm* **1** ship. **2** container.
vaisselle (vɛ'sɛl) *nf* crockery, plates and dishes. **faire la vaisselle** do the washing up.
val (val) *nm* valley.
valable (va'labl) *adj* valid.
valet (va'lɛ) *nm* **1** valet, servant. **2** *game* jack.
valeur (va'lœr) *nf* **1** value, worth. **2** courage. **3** *comm* assets.
valide (va'li:d) *adj* valid.
valise (va'li:z) *nf* suitcase.
vallée (va'le:) *nf* valley.
valoir* (val'war) *vt,vi* **1** be worth. **2** deserve. **3** yield. **faire valoir 1** make the most of. **2** put forward. **il vaut mieux** it is better.
valse (vals) *nf* waltz.
vandale (vɑ̃'dal) *nm* vandal. **vandalisme** *nm* vandalism.
vanille (va'ni:j) *nf* vanilla.
vanité (vani:'te:) *nf* **1** vanity, pride. **2** conceit. **vaniteux, -euse** (vani:'tœ, -'tœz) *adj* **1** vain. **2** conceited.
vantail, -aux (vɑ̃taj, -'to) *nm* leaf (of a table, etc.).
vanter (vɑ̃'te:) *vt* praise. **se vanter** *vr* boast. **se vanter de** pride oneself on.
vanterie (vɑ̃'tri:) *nf* **1** boasting. **2** boast.
vapeur (va'pœr) *nf* **1** vapour. **2** steam. *nm* steamer.
varicelle (vari:'sɛl) *nf* chickenpox.
varier (va'rje:) *vt,vi* vary. **variation** *nf* variation. **varié** *adj* **1** varied. **2** miscellaneous. **variété** *nf* variety.
variole (va'rjɔl) *nf* smallpox.
vase[1] (vɑz) *nm* **1** vase. **2** vessel.
vase[2] (vɑz) *nf* mud, slime.
vaste (vast) *adj* **1** vast, huge. **2** wide, spacious.
vau (vo) **à vau l'eau** *adv* **1** downstream. **2** to rack and ruin.
vaudou (vo'du:) *nm* voodoo.
vaudra (vo:'drɑ) *v* see **valoir.**
vaurien, -ienne (vo'rjɛ̃, -'rjɛn) *nm,f inf* scoundrel.
vautour (vo'tu:r) *nm* vulture.
vaux (vo:) *v* see **valoir.**
veau, veaux (vo) *nm* **1** *zool* calf. **2** veal. **3** calfskin.
vécu (ve:'ky) *v* see **vivre.**
vedette (və'dɛt) *nf* **1** motor boat. **2** *Th* star. **vedette de l'écran** filmstar.
végétal, -aux (ve:ʒɛ'tal, -'to) *adj* plant, vegetable. *nm* plant.
végétarien, -enne (ve:ʒɛta'rjɛ̃, -'rjɛn) *adj,n* vegetarian.
végétation (ve:zɛta'sjɔ̃) *nf* **1** vegetation. **2** *pl inf* adenoids.
véhément (ve:ɛ'mɑ̃) *adj* vehement, passionate, eager.
véhicule (ve:i:'kyl) *nm* vehicle.
veiller (vɛ'je:) *vi* **1** stay up. **2** watch. *vt* look after. **veiller à** see to. **veille** *nf* **1** wakefulness. **2** watch. **3** eve, day before. **veillée** *nf* **1** vigil. **2** party.

veine (vɛn) *nf* **1** vein. **2** *inf* luck.
vélo (ve:ˈlo:) *nm inf* bike.
vélocité (ve:lɔsi:ˈte:) *nf* speed, velocity.
velours (vəˈlu:r) *nm* **1** velvet. **2** corduroy.
velu (vəˈly) *adj* hairy.
venaison (vənɛˈzɔ̃) *nf* venison.
vendange (vɑ̃ˈdɑ̃ʒ) *nf* **1** grape harvest. **2** vintage.
vendre (vɑ̃dr) *vt* **1** sell. **2** betray. **vendeur, -euse** (vɑ̃ˈdœr, -ˈdœz) *nm,f* **1** seller. **2** shop assistant.
vendredi (vɑ̃drəˈdi:) *nm* Friday. **vendredi saint** Good Friday.
vénéneux, -euse (ve:ne:ˈnœ, -ˈnœz) *adj* poisonous.
vénérer (ve:ne:ˈre:) *vt* **1** venerate. **2** worship.
vénérien, -ienne (ve:ne:ˈrjɛ̃, -ˈrjɛn) *adj* venereal.
venger (vɑ̃ˈʒe:) *vt* avenge. **se venger** *vr* have one's revenge. **vengeance** *nf* revenge.
venin (vəˈnɛ̃) *nm* **1** poison. **2** spite. **venimeux, -euse** (vəni:ˈmœ, -ˈmœz) *adj* poisonous.
venir* (vəˈni:r) *vi* (*aux* être) **1** come. **2** result. **3** occur. **4** grow. **venir de** have just.
vent (vɑ̃) *nm* **1** wind, breeze. **2** scent. **Il fait du vent** it is windy.
vente (vɑ̃t) *nf* sale.
ventiler (vɑ̃ti:ˈle:) *vt* ventilate, air. **ventilateur** *nm* **1** ventilator. **2** fan.
ventre (vɑ̃tr) *nm* **1** abdomen. **2** stomach, belly. **3** paunch.
ventriloque (vɑ̃tri:ˈlɔk) *nm* ventriloquist.
venu (vəˈny) *v see* **venir.**
venue (vəˈny) *nf* **1** coming, arrival. **2** advent. **3** growth.
Vénus (ve:ˈnys) *nf* Venus.
ver (vɛr) *nm* **1** worm. **2** maggot. **ver à soie** silkworm.
véranda (verɑ̃ˈda) *nf* veranda.
verbe (vɛrb) *nm* verb. **verbal, -aux** (vɛrˈbal, -ˈbo) *adj* verbal.
verdir (vɛrˈdi:r) *vi* turn green. *vt* make green. **verdeur** *nf* **1** greenness. **2** tartness, sourness. **3** heartiness. **verdure** *nf* **1** greenness. **2** greenery.
verge (vɛrʒ) *nf* **1** rod, cane. **2** penis.
verger (vɛrˈʒe:) *nm* orchard.
verglas (vɛrˈglɑ) *nm* black ice.
vergogne (vɛrˈgɔɲ) *nf* shame.
véridique (ve:ri:ˈdi:k) *adj* truthful.
vérifier (ve:ri:ˈfje) *vt* **1** verify, check. **2** overhaul. **3** audit.
vérité (ve:ri:ˈte:) *nf* truth. **véritable** *adj* **1** true. **2** real, genuine.
vermeil, -eille (vɛrˈmɛj) *adj* bright red, rosy.
vermine (vɛrˈmi:n) *nf* vermin.
vermout (vɛrˈmu:t) *nm* vermouth.
vernir (vɛrˈni:r) *vt* **1** varnish. **2** polish. **vernis** *nm* **1** varnish. **2** polish. **3** glaze.
vérole (ve:ˈrɔl) *nf* **petite vérole** smallpox.
verrai (vɛre) *v see* **voir.**
verre (vɛr) *nm* glass. **verre (de lunettes)** lens.
verrou, -oux (vɛˈru:) *nm* bolt, bar.
verrouiller (vɛru:ˈje:) *vt* bolt, fasten.
verrue (vɛˈru:) *nf* wart.
vers[1] (vɛr) *nm* **1** line. **2** *pl* poetry, verse.
vers[2] (vɛr) *prep* **1** towards, to. **2** about.
versant (vɛrˈsɑ̃) *nm* **1** slope. **2** side, bank.
Verseau (vɛrˈso) *nm* Aquarius.
verser (vɛrˈse:) *vt* **1** pour. **2** shed. **3** pay in. **4** overturn. **à verse** in torrents. **versé** *adj* experienced. **versement** *nm* **1** payment. **2** *comm* instalment.
version (vɛrˈsjɔ̃) *nf* **1** version, account. **2** *educ* translation, unseen.
verso (vɛrˈso) *nm* back, reverse side.
vert (vɛr) *adj* **1** green. **2** unripe. **3** sharp, stern. **4** *inf* spicy. *nm* green (colour).
vertébré (vɛrte:ˈbre:) *adj,nm* vertebrate.
vertical, -aux (vɛrti:ˈkal, -ˈko) *adj* vertical, upright.
vertige (vɛrˈti:ʒ) *nm* dizziness. **avoir le vertige** feel dizzy. **vertigineux, -euse** (vɛrti:ʒi:ˈnœ, -ˈnœz) *adj* dizzy, giddy.
vertu (vɛrˈty) *nf* **1** virtue. **2** chastity. **3** quality, property. **vertueux, -euse** (vɛrˈtɥœ, -ˈtɥœz) *adj* virtuous.
verve (vɛrv) *nf* zest, vigour, go.
vessie (vɛˈsi:) *nf* bladder.
veste (vɛst) *nf* jacket. **veston** *nm* jacket.
vestiaire (vɛˈstjɛr) *nm* **1** cloakroom. **2** changing room.
vestibule (vɛsti:ˈbyl) *nm* **1** hall. **2** lobby.
vestige (vɛˈsti:ʒ) *nm* **1** mark, trace. **2** remnant, remains.
vêtement (vɛtˈmɑ̃) *nm* **1** garment. **2** *pl* clothing. **3** *pl* clothes.
vétéran (ve:tɛˈrɑ̃) *nm* veteran.
vétérinaire (ve:te:ri:ˈnɛr) *nm* veterinary surgeon. *adj* veterinary.
vêtir* (vɛˈti:r) *vt* **1** clothe. **2** dress.
veto (ve:ˈto) *nm* veto. **mettre son veto à** veto.
vêtu (vɛˈty) *v see* **vêtir.**
vétusté (ve:tyˈste:) *nf* decay.
veuf, veuve (vœf, vœv) *nm,f* widower, widow. *adj* widowed.
veule (vœl) *adj* **1** weak, soft. **2** flabby. **3** drab.

veulent (vœl) *v* see **vouloir.**
veux (vœ) *v* see **vouloir.**
vexer (vɛk'se:) *vt* **1** vex, annoy. **2** harass.
viable[1] (vjabl) *adj* strong enough to live.
viable[2] (vjabl) *adj* fit for traffic.
viaduc (vja'dyk) *nm* viaduct.
viager, -ère (vja'ʒe:, -'ʒɛr) *adj* for life.
viande (vjɑ̃d) *nf* meat.
vibrer (vi:'bre:) *vi* vibrate. **vibrant** *adj* **1** vibrating. **2** resonant. **vibration** *nf* **1** vibration. **2** resonance.
vicaire (vi:'kɛr) *nm* curate.
vice (vi:s) *nm* **1** vice, corruption. **2** fault, flaw. **vice-président** *nm, pl* **vice-présidents 1** vice-president. **2** vice-chairman.
vicié (vi:'sje:) *adj* corrupt.
vicieux, -euse (vi:'sjœ, -'sjœz) *adj* **1** vicious. **2** faulty. **3** perverted.
vicomte, -esse (vi:'kɔ̃t, -kɔ̃'tɛs) *nm,f* viscount, viscountess.
victime (vi:k'ti:m) *nf* victim.
victoire (vi:k'twar) *nf* victory. **victorieux, -euse** (vi:ktɔ'rjœ, -'rjœz) *adj* victorious.
vidange (vi:'dɑ̃ʒ) *nf* **1** emptying. **2** draining. **3** *mot* oil change.
vider (vi:'de:) *vt* **1** empty. **2** clear out. **3** drain. **4** settle (an argument). **vide** *adj* **1** empty. **2** vacant. *nm* **1** gap. **2** vacuum.
vie (vi:) *nf* **1** life. **2** existence. **3** living, livelihood.
vieillir (vjɛ'ji:r) *vi* grow old, age. **vieillard** *nm* old man. **vieillesse** *nf* old age.
viens (vjɛ̃) *v* see **venir.**
vierge (vjɛrʒ) *nf* **1** virgin. **2** *cap* Virgo. *adj* **1** virgin. **2** pure. **3** blank.
Viet-nam (vjɛt'nam) *nm* Vietnam. **vietnamien, -ienne** (vjɛtna'mjɛ̃, -'mjɛn) *adj,n* Vietnamese.
vieux, vieil, vieille (vjœ, vjɛj, vjɛj) *adj* old. **vieux** *nm* old man. **vieille** *nf* old woman.
vif, vive (vi:f, vi:v) *adj* **1** alive. **2** lively, vivacious. **3** brisk. **4** sharp, keen. **5** quick-tempered. **6** vivid. **7** bright. *nm* quick, core.
vigile (vi:'ʒi:l) *nf* vigil.
vigne (viɲ) *nf* **1** vine. **2** vineyard. **vigneron** *nm* vine-grower. **vignoble** *nm* vineyard.
vignette (vi:ɲɛt) *nf* **1** car tax label. **2** cigarette card.
vigoureux, -euse (vi:gu:'rœ, -'rœz) *adj* vigorous, strong.
vigueur (vi:'gœr) *nf* **1** vigour, strength. **2** effect, force.
vil (vi:l) *adj* **1** base, low, vile. **2** cheap.
vilain (vi:'lɛ̃) *adj* **1** unpleasant, nasty. **2** mean. **3** ugly. *nm* villain.
villa (vi:'la) *nf* villa, house.
village (vi:'laʒ) *nm* village.
ville (vi:l) *nf* town. **grande ville** city. **ville d'eau** spa.
villégiateur (vi:le:ʒja'tœr) *nm* holiday-maker.
vin (vɛ̃) *nm* wine. **vin du Rhin** hock. **vin ordinaire** table wine.
vinaigre (vi:'nɛgr) *nm* vinegar. **vinaigrette** *nf* French dressing.
vindicatif, -ive (vɛ̃di:ka'ti:f, -'ti:v) *adj* spiteful.
vingt (vɛ̃) *adj,nm* twenty. **vingtaine** *nf* about twenty, a score. **vingtième** *adj* twentieth.
viol (vjɔl) *nm* rape.
violence (vjɔ'lɑ̃s) *nf* violence, force. **violent** *adj* **1** violent. **2** intense. **3** strong.
violer (vjœ'le:) *vt* **1** violate, break. **2** rape.
violet, -ette (vjɔ'lɛ, -'lɛt) *adj,nm* violet (colour). *nf bot* violet.
violon (vjɔ'lɔ̃) *nm* **1** violin. **2** *sl* (prison) cell. **violoncelle** *nm* cello.
vipère (vi:'pɛr) *nf* adder, viper.
virage (vi:'raʒ) *nm* **1** turning. **2** sharp turn, bend.
virer (vi:'re:) *vi* turn. *vt comm* transfer.
virgule (vi:r'gyl) *nf* comma.
viril (vi:'ri:l) *adj* virile, manly. **virilité** *nf* **1** manliness. **2** manhood.
virtuel, -elle (vi:r'tɥɛl) *adj* virtual.
virus (vi:'rys) *nm* virus.
vis[1] (vi:) *v* see **vivre.**
vis[2] (vi:s) *nf* screw.
visa (vi:'za) *nm* **1** visa. **2** signature.
visage (vi:'zaʒ) *nm* **1** face. **2** countenance.
vis-à-vis (vi:za'vi:) *adv* opposite. **vis-à-vis de 1** opposite. **2** with regard to.
viser (vi:'ze:) *vt* **1** aim. **2** relate to. **3** allude to. **visée** *nf* **1** aim. **2** design, plan.
visible (vi:'zi:bl) *adj* **1** visible. **2** obvious, evident. **visibilité** *nf* visibility.
visière (vi:'zjɛr) *nf* **1** visor. **2** peak (of a cap).
vision (vi:'zjɔ̃) *nf* **1** vision, sight. **2** eyesight. **3** apparition, phantom.
visiter (vi:zi:'te:) *vt* **1** visit. **2** examine. **3** search. **visite** *nf* **1** visit. **2** inspection. **3** search. **rendre visite à** call on. **visiteur, -euse** (vi:zi:'tœr, -'tœz) *nm,f* visitor.
vison (vi:'zɔ) *nm* mink.
visser (vi:'se:) *vt* screw in or up.
visuel, -elle (vi:'zɥɛl) *adj* visual.
vital, -aux (vi:'tal, -'to) *adj* vital. **vitalité** *nf* vitality.

vitamine (vi:ta'mi:n) *nf* vitamin.

vite (vi:t) *adj* quick, rapid, fast. *adv* **1** quickly, fast. **2** soon. **au plus vite** as quickly as possible. **vitesse** *nf* **1** speed. **2** quickness.

vitrer (vi:'tre:) *vt* glaze (a window, etc.). **vitrail, -aux** (vi:'traj, -'tro) *nm* stained-glass window. **vitre** *nf* pane of glass. **vitrine** *nf* **1** shopwindow. **2** showcase. **3** glass case.

vivace (vi:'vas) *adj* **1** hardy. **2** perennial. **vivacité** *nf* **1** vivacity. **2** outburst of temper.

vivier (vi:'vje:) *nm* fishpond.

vivifier (vi:vi:'fje:) *vt* enliven, invigorate.

vivre* (vi:vr) *vi* **1** live. **2** be alive. *nm* **1** food. **2** *pl* provisions. **vivant** *adj* **1** living, alive. **2** lively.

vocabulaire (vɔkaby'lɛr) *nm* vocabulary.

vocal, -aux (vɔ'kal, -'ko) *adj* vocal.

vocation (vɔka'sjɔ̃) *nf* **1** vocation. **2** bent, inclination.

vœu, vœux (vœ) *nm* **1** wish. **2** vow.

voguer (vɔ'ge:) *vi* sail. **vogue** *nf* vogue, fashion.

voici (vwa'si:) *prep* here is or are.

voie (vwa) *nf* way, road, track. **voie d'eau 1** *naut* leak. **2** canal. **voie ferrée** railway line. **voie publique** public highway.

voilà (vwa'la) *prep* there is or are.

voile[1] (vwal) *nf* sail. **voilier** *nm* sailing vessel.

voile[2] (vwal) *nm* veil.

voiler (vwa'le:) *vt* **1** veil. **2** obscure, dim. **3** muffle. **se voiler** *vr* cloud over.

voir* (vwar) *vt* **1** see. **2** visit. **3** understand. **4** notice. **faire voir** show. **n'avoir rien à voir avec** have nothing to do with.

voire (vwar) *adv* indeed. **voire même** and even.

voirie (vwa'ri:) *nf* **1** highways. **2** refuse dump.

voisin (vwa'zɛ̃) *adj* neighbouring, near. *nm* neighbour. **voisinage** *nm* **1** neighbourhood, district. **2** proximity.

voiture (vwa'tyr) *nf* **1** car. **2** van. **voiture d'enfant** pram.

voix (vwa) *nf* **1** voice. **2** vote. **à haute voix** aloud. **voix publique** public opinion.

vol[1] (vɔl) *nm* **1** flight. **2** flying. **3** flock, swarm. **vol à voile** *aviat* gliding.

vol[2] (vɔl) *nm* theft. **vol à l'étalage** shoplifting. **vol avec effraction** burglary.

volaille (vɔ'laj) *nf* poultry.

volatil (vɔla'ti:l) *adj* volatile.

volcan (vɔl'kɑ̃) *nm* volcano. **volcanique** *adj* volcanic.

voler[1] (vɔ'le:) *vi* fly. **volant** *nm* **1** steering wheel. **2** shuttlecock. **volée** *nf* **1** flight. **2** volley.

voler[2] (vɔ'le:) *vt* **1** steal. **2** rob. **voleur, -euse** (vɔ'lœr, -'lœz) *nm,f* thief, robber. **voleur à tire** *nm* pickpocket. ~*adj* thieving.

volet (vɔ'lɛ) *nm* shutter.

volière (vɔ'ljɛr) *nf* aviary.

volontaire (vɔlɔ̃'tɛr) *adj* **1** voluntary. **2** deliberate. **3** headstrong. *nm* volunteer.

volonté (vɔlɔ̃'te:) *nf* **1** will. **2** *pl* whims. **bonne volonté** goodwill. **volontiers** *adv* willingly, with pleasure.

volt (vɔlt) *nm* volt. **voltage** *nm* voltage.

volte-face *nf invar* about turn.

voltiger (vɔlti:'ʒe:) *vi* flit.

volume (vɔ'lym) *nm* **1** volume. **2** bulk, mass. **3** capacity.

volupté (vɔlyp'te:) *nf* sensual pleasure.

vomir (vɔ'mi:r) *vt* vomit.

vont (vɔ̃) *v* see **aller.**

vorace (vɔ'ras) *adj* ravenous.

vos (vo) *poss adj* see **votre.**

voter (vɔ'te:) *vi* vote. *vt* **1** pass. **2** vote (money). **vote** *nm* vote.

votre, vos (vɔtr, vo) *poss adj 2nd pers s,pl* your.

vôtre (votr) *poss pron 2nd pers s,pl* **le** or **la vôtre 1** yours. **2** your own.

voudrai (vu:'drɛ) *v* see **vouloir.**

vouer (vwe:) *vt* devote, consecrate.

vouloir* (vu:'lwar) *vt* **1** be willing. **2** want. **3** mean. **4** consent. **5** need. **6** try. **en vouloir à** have a grudge against. ~*nm* will.

vous (vu:) *pron 2nd pers m,f* **1** *s fml* you. **2** *pl* you. **vous-même** *pron 2nd pers m,f s fml* yourself. **vous-mêmes** *pron 2nd pers m,f pl* yourselves.

voûter (vu:'te:) *vt* arch. **voûte** *nf* arch, vault.

vouvoyer (vu:vwa'je:) *vt* address as **vous.**

voyager (vwaja'ʒe:) *vi* travel. **voyage** *nm* journey, trip, tour. **voyageur, -euse** (vwaja'ʒœr, -'ʒœz) *nm,f* **1** traveller. **2** passenger. *adj* travelling.

voyant (vwa'jɑ̃) *adj* **1** gaudy. **2** conspicuous.

voyelle (vwa'jɛl) *nf* vowel.

voyou, -oux (vwa'ju:) *nm inf* hooligan.

vrai (vrɛ) *adj* **1** true. **2** real, genuine. **3** downright. *adv* really, truly. **à vrai dire** as a matter of fact. ~*nm* truth. **vraiment** *adv* **1** really. **2** indeed.

vraisemblable (vrɛsɑ̃'blabl) *adj* **1** probable. **2** credible. **vraisemblance** *nf* **1** probability, likelihood. **2** credibility.

vrille (vri:j) *nf* tendril.
vrombir (vrɔ̃'bi:r) *vi* hum, throb. **vrombissement** *nm* **1** humming. **2** drone
vu (vy) *v* see **voir.** *adj* **1** seen. **2** considered. *prep* considering, in view of. **vu que** *conj* seeing that. ~*nm* sight. **vue** *nf* **1** sight. **2** view. **3** intention, design.
vulgaire (vyl'gɛr) *adj* **1** vulgar **2** common.
vulnérable (vylnɛ'rabl) *adj* vulnerable.

W

wagon (va'gɔ̃) *nm* **1** (railway) carriage or coach. **2** waggon, truck. **wagon-lit** *nm, pl* **wagons-lits** sleeping-car.
watt (wat) *nm* watt. **wattage** *nm* wattage.
week-end (wi:k'ɛnd) *nm* weekend.
whist (wi:st) *nm* whist.

X

xénophobie (kse:nɔfɔ'bi:) *nf* xenophobia.
xérès (gze:'rɛs) *nm* sherry.

Y

y (i:) *adv* **1** there. **2** here. **ça y est!** that's it! **j'y suis** I've got it, I understand. **n'y être pour rien** have nothing to do with it. ~*pron invar* **1** at, by, or in it. **2** of them.
yacht (jɔt) *nm* yacht.
yaourt (ja'u:rt) *nm* yoghurt.
yeux (jœ) *nm pl* eyes.
yiddish (ji:'di:ʃ) *nm* Yiddish.
yoga (jɔ'ga) *nm* yoga.
Yougoslavie (ju:gɔ'sla'vi:) *nf* Yugoslavia. **yougoslave** *adj,n* Yugoslav.
youyou (ju:'ju:) *nm* dinghy.

Z

zèbre (zɛbr) *nm* zebra. **zébré** *adj* striped.
zèle (zɛl) *nm* zeal, ardour. **zélé** *adj* zealous.
zéro (ze:'ro) *nm* zero, nought.
zeste (zɛst) *nm cul* zest, outer skin.
zézayer (ze:zɛ'je:) *vi,vt* lisp. **zézaiement** *nm* **1** lisp. **2** lisping.
zigzag (zi:g'zag) *nm* zigzag. **zigzaguer** *vi* zigzag.
zinc (zɛ̃g) *nm* **1** zinc. **2** *sl* bar, counter (in a pub).
zodiaque (zɔ'djak) *nm* zodiac.
zone (zon) *nm* zone, area.
zoo (zo) *nm* zoo. **zoologie** (zɔɔlɔ'ʒi:) *nf* zoology. **zoologique** (zɔɔlɔ'ʒi:k) *adj* zoological. **zoologiste** (zɔɔlɔ'ʒi:st) *nm* zoologist.

A

a, an (ə, ən; *stressed* ei, æn) *indef art* un *m*. une *f*.

aback (ə'bæk) *adv* en arrière. **be taken aback** être déconcerté.

abandon (ə'bændən) *vt* **1** abandonner. **2** délaisser. **3** renoncer à. **abandoned** *adj* **1** abandonné. **2** dévergondé, dépravé. **abandonment** *n* **1** abandon *m*. **2** délaissement *m*.

abash (ə'bæʃ) *vt* confondre, déconcerter.

abate (ə'beit) *vt* diminuer, affaiblir. *vi* **1** s'affaiblir. **2** se calmer.

abattoir ('æbətwɑ:) *n* abattoir *m*.

abbess ('æbis) *n* abbesse *f*.

abbey ('æbi) *n* abbaye *f*.

abbot ('æbət) *n* abbé *m*.

abbreviate (ə'bri:vieit) *vt* abréger, raccourcir. **abbreviation** *n* abréviation *f*.

abdicate ('æbdikeit) *vt,vi* abdiquer. *vt* renoncer à. **abdication** *n* abdication *f*.

abdomen ('æbdəmən) *n* abdomen *m*.

abduct (æb'dʌkt) *vt* enlever. **abduction** *n* enlèvement *m*. **abductor** *n* ravisseur *m*.

abet (ə'bet) *vt* encourager. **abettor** *n* complice *m,f*.

abhor (əb'hɔ:) *vt* abhorrer, avoir horreur de. **abhorrent** *adj* **1** répugnant. **2** contraire.

abide* (ə'baid) *vi* **1** demeurer. **2** *inf* supporter. **abide by** **1** rester fidèle à. **2** se conformer à.

ability (ə'biliti) *n* **1** capacité *f*. **2** pouvoir *m*. intelligence *f*. **to the best of one's ability** de son mieux.

abject ('æbdʒekt) *adj* **1** abject, misérable. **2** vil. **abjection** *n* **1** abjection *f*. **2** misère *f*.

ablaze (ə'bleiz) *adv,adj* en flammes. *adj* enflammé.

able ('eibəl) *adj* capable, compétent, habile. **be able** **1** pouvoir. **2** savoir. **able-bodied** *adj* fort, robuste.

abnormal (æb'nɔ:məl) *adj* anormal, -aux. **abnormality** *n* **1** anomalie *f*. **2** malformation *f*.

aboard (ə'bɔ:d) *adv* à bord. **all aboard!** embarquez! **go aboard** s'embarquer. ~*prep* à bord de.

abode (ə'boud) *n* **1** demeure, habitation *f*. **2** *law* domicile *m*.

abolish (ə'bɔliʃ) *vt* abolir, supprimer. **abolition** *n* abolition *f*.

abominable (ə'bɔminəbəl) *adj* **1** abominable, odieux, -euse. **2** exécrable.

Aborigine (æbə'ridʒini) *n* aborigène, indigène *m*. **aboriginal** *adj* **1** aborigène, indigène. **2** primitif, -ive.

abort (ə'bɔ:t) *vi* avorter. **abortion** *n* **1** avortement *m*. **2** avorton *m*.

abound (ə'baund) *vi* abonder.

about (ə'baut) *adv, prep* **1** autour (de). **2** de ci de là. **3** environ. **4** au sujet de. **be about to** être sur le point de. **what is it about?** de quoi s'agit-il?

above (ə'bʌv) *prep* **1** au-dessus (de). **2** plus de. **above all** surtout. ~*adv* **1** en haut. **2** ci-dessus. **3** au-dessus. **aboveboard** *adj* loyal, -aux.

abrasion (ə'breiʒən) *n* **1** frottement *m*. **2** *med* écorchure *f*. **abrasive** *adj,n* abrasif, -ive *m*.

abreast (ə'brest) *adv* de front, sur la même ligne.

abridge (ə'bridʒ) *vt* **1** abréger. **2** restreindre.

abroad (ə'brɔ:d) *adv* **1** à l'étranger. **2** au loin.

abrupt (ə'brʌpt) *adj* **1** abrupt. **2** brusque. **abruptly** *adv* **1** à pic. **2** brusquement.

abscess ('æbses) *n* abcès *m*.

abscond (əb'skɔnd) *vi* **1** s'évader. **2** *law* se soustraire à.

absent (*adj* 'æbsənt; *v* ab'sent) *adj* **1** absent. **2** manquant. **absent-minded** *adj* distrait. **absent-mindedness** *n* distraction *f*. ~*v* **absent oneself** s'absenter. **absence** *n* **1** absence *f*. **2** manque *m*. **absentee** *n* absent *m*.

absolute ('æbsəlu:t) *adj* **1** absolu. **2** parfait. **3** catégorique. **absolutely** *adv* **1** absolument. **2** complètement.

absolve (əb'zɔlv) *vt* **1** absoudre. **2** *law* acquitter.

absorb (əb'zɔ:b) *vt* absorber. **absorbent** *adj* absorbant. **absorption** *n* **1** absorption *f.* **2** concentration *f.*

abstain (əb'stein) *vi* s'abstenir. **abstention** *n* abstention *f.* **abstinence** *n* abstinence *f.*

abstract (*adj,n* 'æbstrækt; *v* əb'strækt) *adj,n* abstrait *m.* *n* résumé *m.* *vt* **1** soustraire. **2** extraire. **abstraction** *n* abstraction *f.*

absurd (əb'sə:d) *adj* absurde.

abundance (ə'bʌndəns) *n* abondance *f.* **abundant** *adj* abondant, copieux, -euse. **abundantly** *adv* abondamment.

abuse (*v* ə'bju:z; *n* ə'bju:s) *vt* **1** abuser de. **2** médire. **3** injurier. *n* **1** abus *m.* **2** insultes *f pl.* **abusive** *adj* **1** abusif, -ive. **2** injurieux, -euse.

abyss (ə'bis) *n* abîme *m.* **abysmal** *adj* **1** sans fond. **2** profond.

academy (ə'kædəmi) *n* académie *f.* **academic** *adj* **1** académique. **2** universitaire. **3** théorique.

accelerate (ək'seləreit) *vt* accélérer. *vi* s'accélérer. **acceleration** *n* accélération *f.* **accelerator** *n* accélérateur *m.*

accent ('æksənt) *n* **1** accent *m.* **2** ton *m.* **accentuate** *vt* accentuer.

accept (ək'sept) *vt* **1** accepter. **2** admettre. **acceptance** *n* **1** acceptation *f.* **2** réception *f.*

access ('ækses) *n* **1** accès *m.* **2** entrée *f.* **accessible** *adj* accessible, abordable. **accession** *n* **1** accès *m.* **2** accession *f.* **3** accroissement *m.*

accessory (ək'sesəri) *adj* accessoire, subsidiaire. *n* **1** accessoire *m.* **2** *pl* équipement *m.* **3** *law* complice *m,f.*

accident ('æksidnt) *n* accident *m.* **by accident** par hasard. **accidental** *adj* **1** accidentel, -elle. **2** accessoire.

acclaim (ə'kleim) *vt* acclamer.

acclimatize (ə'klaimətaiz) *vt* acclimater. **get acclimatized** s'acclimater, s'habituer.

accommodate (ə'kɔmədeit) *vt* **1** accommoder. **2** rendre service à. **3** loger. **accomodating** *adj* complaisant. **accommodation** *n* **1** adaptation *f.* **2** arrangement *m.* **3** logement *m.*

accompany (ə'kʌmpəni) *vt* accompagner. **accompaniment** *n* accompagnement *m.* **accompanist** *n mus* accompagnateur, -trice.

accomplice (ə'kʌmplis) *n* complice *m,f.*

accomplish (ə'kʌmpliʃ) *vt* **1** accomplir, aboutir. **2** achever. **accomplishment** *n* **1** accomplissement, achèvement *m.* **2** talent *m.* **3** *pl* arts d'agrément *m pl.*

accord (ə'kɔ:d) *n* accord *m.* **of one's own accord** de son plein gré. ~*vt* accorder. *vi* s'accorder. **accordance** *n* conformité *f.* **according to** suivant, d'après.

accordion (ə'kɔ:diən) *n* accordéon *m.*

accost (ə'kɔst) *vt* accoster, aborder.

account (ə'kaunt) *n* **1** compte *m.* **2** valeur *f.* profit *m.* **3** récit *m.* description *f.* **take into account** tenir compte de. ~*v* **account for** expliquer. **accountant** *n* comptable *m.* **chartered accountant** expert comptable *m.*

accumulate (ə'kju:mjuleit) *vt* accumuler. *vi* s'accumuler. **accumulation** *n* accumulation *f.*

accurate ('ækjurət) *adj* **1** exact, juste. **2** fidèle. **accuracy** *n* exactitude, précision *f.*

accuse (ə'kju:z) *vt* accuser. **accusation** *n* accusation *f.*

accustom (ə'kʌstəm) *vt* accoutumer, habituer.

ace (eis) *n* **1** *game* as *m.* **2** atout *m.*

ache (eik) *n* mal *m.* douleur *f.* *vi* faire mal.

achieve (ə'tʃi:v) *vt* **1** accomplir. **2** acquérir. **3** atteindre. **achievement** *n* **1** accomplissement *m.* **2** exploit *m.*

acid ('æsid) *adj* **1** acide. **2** aigre. *n* acide *m.*

acknowledge (ək'nɔlidʒ) *vt* reconnaître. **acknowledgement** *n* **1** reconnaissance *f.* **2** aveu, -eux *m.*

acne ('ækni) *n* acné *f.*

acorn ('eikɔ:n) *n* gland *m.*

acoustic (ə'ku:stik) *adj* acoustique. **acoustics** *n* acoustique *f.*

acquaint (ə'kweint) *vt* informer, faire savoir. **be acquainted with** connaître. **acquaintance** *n* connaissance *f.*

acquiesce (ækwi'es) *vi* acquiescer.

acquire (ə'kwaiə) *vt* acquérir. **acquisition** *n* acquisition *f.* **acquisitive** *adj* âpre au gain.

acquit (ə'kwit) *vt* acquitter. **acquittal** *n* **1** acquittement *m.* **2** exécution *f.*

acre ('eikə) *n* arpent *m.*

acrimony ('ækriməni) *n* acrimonie *f.* **acrimonious** *adj* acrimonieux, -euse.

acrobat ('ækrəbæt) *n* acrobate *m,f.* **acrobatic** *adj* acrobatique. **acrobatics** *n pl* acrobatie *f.*

across (ə'krɔs) *adv,prep* à *or* en travers. *adv* de l'autre côté.

acrylic (ə'krilik) *adj* acrylique.

act (ækt) *n* **1** acte *m.* action *f.* **2** décret *m.* **3** *Th* acte *m.* *vt* jouer. *vi* agir.

action ('ækʃən) *n* action *f.*

active ('æktiv) *adj,n* actif, -ive *m.* **activate** *vt* activer. **activity** *n* **1** activité *f.* **2** *pl* occupations *f pl.*

actor ('æktə) *n* **1** acteur *m.* **2** comédien *m.*

actress (ˈæktris) *n* **1** actrice *f.* **2** comédienne *f.*
actual (ˈæktʃuəl) *adj* **1** réel, -elle. **2** actuel, -elle. **in actual fact** en fait. **actually** *adv* **1** réellement. **2** à l'heure actuelle, maintenant.
actuary (ˈæktʃuəri) *n* actuaire *m.*
acupuncture (ˈækjupʌŋktʃə) *n* acuponcture *f.*
acute (əˈkju:t) *adj* **1** aigu, -uë. **2** perspicace.
adamant (ˈædəmənt) *adj* insensible.
Adam's apple (ˈædəmz) *n* pomme d'Adam *f.*
adapt (əˈdæpt) *vt* adapter.
add (æd) *vt* **1** ajouter. **2** additionner. **add up 1** totaliser. **2** *inf* s'accorder. **addition** *n* addition *f.* **in addition** en outre. **additional** *adj* additionel, -elle, supplémentaire.
addendum (əˈdendəm) *n, pl* **addenda** addendum *m invar.* supplément *m.*
adder (ˈædə) *n* vipère *f.*
addict (*n* ˈædikt; *v* əˈdikt) *n* **drug addict** toxicomane *m,f.* *v* **be addicted to** s'adonner à.
address (əˈdres) *n* **1** adresse *f.* **2** discours *m.* *vt* **1** adresser. **2** aborder.
adenoids (ˈædinɔidz) *n pl* adénoïdes *f pl.*
adept (ˈædept) *adj* habile, expert. *n* **1** adepte *m.* **2** expert *m.*
adequate (ˈædikwət) *adj* **1** adéquat, suffisant. **2** proportionné.
adhere (ədˈhiə) *vi* adhérer. **adherent** *adj,n* adhérent *m.* **adhesion** *n* **1** adhésion *f.* **2** approbation *f.* **adhesive** *adj,n* adhésif, -ive *m.*
adjacent (əˈdʒeisənt) *adj* adjacent, contigu, -uë.
adjective (ˈædʒiktiv) *n* adjectif *m.*
adjoin (əˈdʒɔin) *vt* être contigu à, avoisiner.
adjourn (əˈdʒə:n) *vt* ajourner, différer. *vi* **1** s'ajourner. **2** lever la séance.
adjudicate (əˈdʒu:dikeit) *vt,vi* juger. **adjudication** *n* jugement *m.* **adjudicator** *n* arbitre *m.*
adjust (əˈdʒʌst) *vt* **1** concilier. **2** ajuster.
ad-lib (ædˈlib) *adv* à volonté. *vt inf* improviser.
administer (ədˈministə) *vt* **1** administrer. **2** rendre. **administration** *n* administration *f.* **administrative** *adj* administratif, -ive. **administrator** *n* administrateur, gestionnaire *m.*
admiral (ˈædmərəl) *n* amiral, -aux, *m.* **admiralty** *n* **1** amirauté *f.* **2** ministère de la marine *m.*
admire (ədˈmaiə) *vt* admirer. **admiration** *n* admiration *f.* **admirer** *n* soupirant *m.* **admiring** *adj* admiratif, -ive.
admission (ədˈmiʃən) *n* **1** admission *f.* **2** entrée *f.* **3** aveu, -eux *m.*
admit (ədˈmit) *vt* **1** admettre. **2** laisser entrer. **3** avouer. **admittance** *n* admission *f.* **no admittance** entrée interdite.
adolescence (ædəˈlesəns) *n* adolescence *f.* **adolescent** *adj,n* adolescent *m.*
adopt (əˈdɔpt) *vt* adopter. **adopted child** *n* enfant adoptif *m.* **adoption** *n* adoption *f.*
adore (əˈdɔ:) *vt* adorer. **adoration** *n* adoration *f.*
adorn (əˈdɔ:n) *vt* orner.
adrenaline (əˈdrenəlin) *n* adrénaline *f.*
Adriatic (eidriˈætik) *adj* adriatique. **Adriatic (Sea)** *n* (Mer) Adriatique *f.*
adrift (əˈdrift) *adv* à la dérive.
adroit (əˈdrɔit) *adj* adroit, habile.
adulation (ædjuˈleiʃən) *n* flatterie *f.*
adult (ˈædʌlt) *adj,n* adulte.
adulterate (əˈdʌltəreit) *vt* adultérer, falsifier. **adulteration** *n* adultération, falsification *f.*
adultery (əˈdʌltəri) *n* adultère *m.* **adulterer** *n* adultère *m,f.*
advance (ədˈvɑ:ns) *vt* **1** avancer. **2** faire progresser. **3** augmenter. *vi* (s')avancer. *n* **1** avance *f.* **2** progrès *m.* **3** hausse *f.*
advantage (ədˈvɑ:ntidʒ) *n* avantage *m.* **take advantage of** profiter de.
advent (ˈædvent) *n* **1** venue *f.* **2** *cap rel* Avent *m.*
adventure (ədˈventʃə) *n* aventure *f.* **adventurer** *n* aventurier *m.* **adventurous** *adj* **1** aventureux, -euse. **2** entreprenant.
adverb (ˈædvə:b) *n* adverbe *m.*
adverse (ˈædvə:s) *adj* **1** adverse, opposé. **2** hostile. **3** défavorable. **adversary** *n* adversaire *m,f.* **adversity** *n* adversité *f.*
advertise (ˈædvətaiz) *vi* **1** faire de la publicité. **2** insérer une annonce. *vt* annoncer. **advertisement** *n* **1** publicité *f.* **2** annonce *f.* **advertising** *n* publicité *f.*
advise (ədˈvaiz) *vt* **1** conseiller. **2** avertir. **advise with** (se) consulter avec. **advice** *n* avis, conseil *m.* **advisable** *adj* **1** recommendable, judicieux, -euse. **2** convenable.
advocate (*n* ˈædvəkət; *v* ˈædvəkeit) *n* **1** avocat *m.* **2** défenseur *m.* *vt* **1** préconiser. **2** défendre.
Aegean (iˈdʒi:ən) *adj* égée. **Aegean (Sea)** (Mer) Egée *f.*
aerate (ˈɛəreit) *vt* **1** aérer. **2** gazéifier. **aerated** *adj* **1** aéré. **2** gazeux, -euse.
aerial (ˈɛəriəl) *adj* aérien, -ienne. *n* antenne *f.*
aerodynamics (ɛəroudaiˈnæmiks) *n* aérodynamique *f.*
aeronautics (ɛərəˈnɔ:tiks) *n* aéronautique *f.*
aeroplane (ˈɛərəplein) *n* avion *m.*

aerosol ('ɛərəsɔl) *n* aérosol *m*.
aesthetic (is'θetik) *adj* esthétique. **aesthetics** *n* esthétique *f*.
afar (ə'fɑ:) *adv* **from afar** de loin.
affable ('æfəbəl) *adj* affable.
affair (ə'fɛə) *n* affaire *f*.
affect[1] (ə'fekt) *vt* **1** atteindre, affecter. **2** influer sur. **3** émouvoir. **affection** *n* affection *f*. **affectionate** *adj* affectueux, -euse.
affect[2] (ə'fekt) *vt* affecter, feindre. **affected** *adj* **1** affecté, maniéré. **2** simulé.
affiliate (ə'filieit) *vt* affilier. **affiliated firm** *n* filiale *f*. **affiliation** *n* affiliation *f*.
affinity (ə'finiti) *n* affinité *f*.
affirm (ə'fə:m) *vt* affirmer. **affirmative** *adj* affirmatif, -ive.
affix (*v* ə'fiks; *n* 'æfiks) *vt* apposer. *n* **1** addition *f*. **2** *gram* affixe *m*.
afflict (ə'flikt) *vt* affliger. **affliction** *n* **1** affliction *f*. **2** infirmité *f*.
affluent ('æfluənt) *adj* **1** abondant. **2** riche. **affluence** *n* richesse *f*.
afford (ə'fɔ:d) *vt* **1** avoir les moyens. **2** pouvoir. **3** fournir.
affront (ə'frʌnt) *n* affront *m*. *vt* **1** insulter. **2** faire honte à.
Afghanistan (æf'gænistɑ:n, -stæn) *n* Afghanistan *m*. **Afghan** *adj,n* afghan.
afield (ə'fi:ld) *adv* **far afield** très loin.
afloat (ə'flout) *adv* à flot.
afoot (ə'fut) *adv* à pied. **there's something afoot** il se prépare quelque chose.
aforesaid (ə'fɔ:sed) *adj* susdit.
afraid (ə'freid) *adj* **be afraid 1** avoir peur. **2** ne pas oser.
afresh (ə'freʃ) *adv* de *or* à nouveau.
Africa ('æfrikə) *n* Afrique *f*. **African** *adj,n* africain.
aft (ɑ:ft) *adv* à *or* sur l'arrière.
after ('ɑ:ftə) *adv* après, ensuite, d'après. *prep* **1** après. **2** suivant, selon. **after all** après tout. ~*conj* après que. **after-care** *n* surveillance *f*. **after-effects** *n pl* **1** suites *f pl*. **2** *med* reliquat *m*. **aftermath** *n* regain *m*. **afternoon** *n* après-midi *m*. **afterthought** *n* réflexion après coup, arrière-pensée *f*. **afterwards** *adv* ensuite, après.
again (ə'gen) *adv* de nouveau, encore. **again and again** à plusieurs reprises.
against (ə'genst) *prep* **1** contre. **2** vis-à-vis. **3** à l'encontre de.
age (eidʒ) *n* **1** âge *m*. **2** époque *f*. **age-group** *n* classe *f*. **be of age** être majeur. ~*vt,vi* vieillir. **aged** *adj* vieux, vieille, âgé.
agency ('eidʒənsi) *n* **1** *comm* agence *f*, bureau, -aux *m*. **2** action *f*.
agenda (ə'dʒendə) *n* ordre du jour *m*.
agent ('eidʒənt) *n* agent, représentant *m*.
aggravate ('ægrəveit) *vt* **1** aggraver. **2** *inf* exaspérer, agacer.
aggregate (*adj,n* 'ægrigit; *v* 'ægrigeit) *n* ensemble, total, -aux *m*. *adj* global, -aux, collectif, -ive. *vt* rassembler.
aggression (ə'greʃən) *n* agression *f*. **aggressive** *adj* agressif, -ive.
aghast (ə'gɑ:st) *adj* épouvanté, ébahi.
agile ('ædʒail) *adj* agile, leste. **agility** *n* agilité *f*.
agitate ('ædʒiteit) *vt* **1** agiter. **2** troubler. **agitated** *adj* ému, troublé. **agitation** *n* agitation *f*. **agitator** *n* agitateur, -trice.
agnostic (æg'nɔstik) *adj,n* agnostique.
ago (ə'gou) *adj,adv* il y a. **long ago** il y a longtemps.
agog (ə'gɔg) *adj* impatient. **be all agog** brûler d'envie.
agony ('ægəni) *n* **1** angoisse *f*. **2** *med* agonie *f*.
agrarian (ə'grɛəriən) *adj* agraire.
agree (ə'gri:) *vi* **1** consentir. **2** s'accorder. **3** être d'accord. **4** convenir. **agreeable** *adj* **1** plaisant, agréable. **2** consentant. **agreement** *n* **1** accord *m*. **2** contrat *m*.
agriculture ('ægrikʌltʃə) *n* agriculture *f*. **agricultural** *adj* agricole.
ahead (ə'hed) *adv* en avant, devant.
aid (eid) *vt* aider, assister. **aid and abet** être le complice de. ~*n* **1** aide *f*. **2** secours *m*. assistance *f*.
ailment ('eilmənt) *n* mal *m*. indisposition *f*.
aim (eim) *vt,vi* viser. *n* **1** but *m*. **2** objet *m*. **aimless** *adj* sans but.
air (ɛə) *n* **1** air *m*. **2** brise *f*. **3** apparence *f*. *vt* aérer.
airborne ('ɛəbɔ:n) *adj* aéroporté.
air-conditioning *n* climatisation *f*. **air-conditioned** *adj* climatisé.
aircraft ('ɛəkrɑ:ft) *n* avion *m*. **aircraft carrier** *n* porte-avions *m invar*.
airfield ('ɛəfi:ld) *n* terrain d'aviation *m*.
airforce ('ɛəfɔ:s) *n* armée de l'air *f*.
airhostess ('ɛəhoustis) *n* hôtesse de l'air *f*.
air lift *n* pont aérien *m*.
airline ('ɛəlain) *n* ligne aérienne *f*.
airmail ('ɛəmeil) *n* poste aérienne *f*. **by airmail** par avion.

airman (ˈɛəmən) *n* aviateur *m*.
airport (ˈɛəpɔ:t) *n* aéroport *m*.
air-raid *n* raid aérien *m*.
airtight (ˈɛətait) *adj* hermétique.
airy (ˈɛəri) *adj* **1** aéré. **2** léger, -ère. **3** sans consistance.
aisle (ail) *n* **1** *rel* nef latérale *f*. bas-côté *m*. **2** passage *m*.
ajar (əˈdʒɑ:) *adj,adv* entrouvert.
alabaster (ˈæləbɑ:stə) *n* albâtre *m*.
alarm (əˈlɑ:m) *n* alarme, alerte *f*. **alarm clock** *n* réveille-matin *m invar*. ~*vt* **1** alarmer. **2** effrayer.
alas (əˈlæs) *interj* hélas!
albatross (ˈælbətrɔs) *n* albatros *m*.
albeit (ɔ:lˈbi:it) *conj* quoique, bien que.
album (ˈælbəm) *n* album *m*.
alchemy (ˈælkəmi) *n* alchimie *f*.
alcohol (ˈælkəhɔl) *n* alcool *m*. **alcoholic** *adj,n* alcoolique. **alcoholism** *n* alcoolisme *m*.
alcove (ˈælkouv) *n* **1** alcôve *f*. **2** niche *f*.
alderman (ˈɔ:ldəmən) *n* conseiller municipal *m*.
ale (eil) *n* bière *f*.
alert (əˈlə:t) *adj,n* alerte *f*.
algebra (ˈældʒibrə) *n* algèbre *f*.
Algeria (ælˈdʒiəriə) *n* Algérie *f*. **Algerian** *adj,n* algérien, -ienne.
alias (ˈeiliəs) *adv* autrement dit.
alibi (ˈælibai) *n* alibi *m*.
alien (ˈeiliən) *adj,n* étranger, -ère. **alienate** *vt* aliéner. **alienation** *n* aliénation *f*.
alight[1] (əˈlait) *adj* en feu, allumé.
alight[2] (əˈlait) *vi* **1** descendre. **2** se poser.
align (əˈlain) *vt* aligner. *vi* s'aligner.
alike (əˈlaik) *adj* semblable. *adv* pareillement, également.
alimentary (æliˈmentəri) *adj* alimentaire.
alimony (ˈæliməni) *n* pension alimentaire *f*.
alive (əˈlaiv) *adj* **1** vivant. **2** éveillé. **be alive with** grouiller de.
alkali (ˈælkəlai) *n* alcali *m*.
all (ɔ:l) *pron,adj* tout, tous. **all of us** nous tous. ~*adv* tout, entièrement. **all but** presque. **all right** ça va. ~*n* totalité *f*. tout *m*.
allay (əˈlei) *vt* soulager, apaiser.
allege (əˈledʒ) *vt* alléguer. **allegation** *n* allégation *f*.
allegiance (əˈli:dʒəns) *n* fidélité *f*.
allegory (ˈæligəri) *n* allégorie *f*. **allegorical** *adj* allégorique.
allergy (ˈælədʒi) *n* allergie *f*. **allergic** *adj* allergique.
alleviate (əˈli:vieit) *vt* soulager.
alley (ˈæli) *n* **1** allée *f*. **2** passage *m*.
alliance (əˈlaiəns) *n* alliance *f*. **allied** *adj* **1** allié. **2** apparenté.
alligator (ˈæligeitə) *n* alligator *m*.
alliteration (əlitəˈreiʃən) *n* allitération *f*.
allocate (ˈæləkeit) *vt* allouer. **allocation** *n* allocation *f*.
allot (əˈlɔt) *vt* **1** attribuer. **2** distribuer. **allotment** *n* **1** répartition *f*. **2** jardin ouvrier *m*.
allow (əˈlau) *vt* **1** permettre. **2** admettre. **3** accorder. **allow for** tenir compte de. **allowance** *n* **1** allocation *f*. **2** pension *f*. **3** indemnité *f*. **4** *comm* remise *f*. **5** ration *f*.
alloy (ˈælɔi) *n* alliage *m*. *vt* allier.
All Saints' Day *n* Toussaint *f*.
allude (əˈlu:d) *vi* faire allusion. **allusion** *n* allusion *f*.
allure (əˈluə) *vt* attirer, séduire. **alluring** *adj* attrayant.
ally (*n* ˈælai; *v* əˈlai) *n* allié *m*. *vt* allier. *vi* s'allier.
almanac (ˈɔ:lmənæk) *n* almanach *m*.
almighty (ɔ:lˈmaiti) *adj* tout-puissant.
almond (ˈɑ:mənd) *n* amande *f*.
almost (ˈɔ:lmoust) *adv* presque, à peu près.
alms (ɑ:mz) *n pl* aumône *f*.
aloft (əˈlɔft) *adv* en haut.
alone (əˈloun) *adj* seul, solitaire. **leave alone** laisser tranquille.
along (əˈlɔŋ) *prep* le long de. **all along** tout le temps. **alongside** *adv* bord à bord.
aloof (əˈlu:f) *adv* à l'écart. *adj* **1** éloigné. **2** distant.
aloud (əˈlaud) *adv* à haute voix, haut.
alphabet (ˈælfəbet) *n* alphabet *m*. **alphabetical** *adj* alphabétique.
alpine (ˈælpain) *adj* alpin, alpestre.
Alps (ælps) *n pl* Alpes *f pl*.
already (ɔ:lˈredi) *adv* déjà.
Alsatian (ælˈseiʃən) *n* chien-loup *m*.
also (ˈɔ:lsou) *adv* aussi.
altar (ˈɔ:ltə) *n* autel *m*.
alter (ˈɔ:ltə) *vt,vi* changer. **alteration** *n* **1** changement *m*. **2** modification *f*.
alternate (*v* ˈɔ:ltəneit; *adj* ɔ:lˈtə:nit) *vt,vi* alterner. *adj* alternatif, -ive. **alternative** *n* alternative *f*. choix *m*.
although (ˈɔ:lðou) *conj* quoique, bien que.
altitude (ˈæltitju:d) *n* altitude *f*.
alto (ˈæltou) *n* alto *m*.
altogether (ɔ:ltəˈgeðə) *adv* **1** entièrement, tout à fait. **2** tout compris.
aluminium (æljuˈminiəm) *n* aluminium *m*.

always ('ɔ:lweiz) *adv* toujours.
am (əm; *stressed* æm) *v* see **be.**
amalgamate (ə'mælgəmeit) *vt* amalgamer, fusionner. *vi* s'amalgamer. **amalgamation** *n* 1 amalgamation *f.* 2 fusion *f.*
amass (ə'mæs) *vt* amasser.
amateur ('æmətə) *n* amateur *m.*
amaze (ə'meiz) *vt* stupéfier, étonner. **amazement** *n* stupéfaction *f.* étonnement *m.*
ambassador (æm'bæsədə) *n* ambassadeur *m.*
amber ('æmbə) *n* ambre *m.*
ambidextrous (æmbi'dekstrəs) *adj* ambidextre.
ambiguous (æm'bigjuəs) *adj* ambigu, -uë, équivoque. **ambiguity** *n* ambiguïté *f.*
ambition (æm'biʃən) *n* ambition *f.* **ambitious** *adj* ambitieux, -euse.
ambivalent (æm'bivələnt) *adj* ambivalent.
amble ('æmbəl) *vi* 1 aller l'ambie. 2 flâner. *n* 1 (of horse) amble *m.* 2 pas tranquille *m.*
ambulance ('æmbjuləns) *n* ambulance *f.*
ambush ('æmbuʃ) *n* embuscade *f.* *vt* attirer dans un piège.
amenable (ə'mi:nəbəl) *adj* 1 responsable. 2 soumis.
amend (ə'mend) *vt* amender, corriger. *vi* s'amender. **amendment** *n* 1 modification *f.* 2 *pol* amendement *m.*
amenity (ə'mi:niti) *n* 1 aménité *f.* agrément *m.* 2 *pl* commodités *f pl.*
America (ə'merikə) *n* Amérique *f.* **American** *adj,n* américain.
amethyst ('æmiθist) *n* améthyste *f.*
amiable ('eimiəbəl) *adj* aimable.
amicable ('æmikəbəl) *adj* 1 amical, -aux. 2 *law* à l'amiable.
amid (ə'mid) *prep also* **amidst** parmi, au milieu de.
amiss (ə'mis) *adv* 1 mal, de travers. 2 mal à propos. *adj* de travers, qui cloche.
ammonia (ə'mouniə) *n* ammoniaque *f.*
ammunition (æmju'niʃən) *n* munitions *f pl.*
amnesty ('æmnəsti) *n* amnistie *f.*
amoeba (ə'mi:bə) *n, pl* **-bae** *or* **-bes** amibe *f.*
among (ə'mʌŋ) *prep also* **amongst** parmi, entre.
amoral (ei'mɔrəl) *adj* amoral, -aux.
amorous ('æmərəs) *adj* amoureux, -euse.
amorphous (ə'mɔ:fəs) *adj* amorphe.
amount (ə'maunt) *n* 1 montant *m.* 2 quantité *f.* *vi* 1 s'élever. 2 revenir.
ampere ('æmpɛə) *n* ampère *m.*
amphetamine (æm'fetəmi:n) *n* amphétamine *f.*
amphibian (æm'fibiən) *n* amphibie *m.* **amphibious** *adj* amphibie.
amphitheatre ('æmfiθiətə) *n* amphithéâtre *m.*
ample ('æmpəl) *adj* 1 ample, vaste. 2 abondant.
amplify ('æmplifai) *vt* amplifier. **amplifier** *n* amplificateur *m.*
amputate ('æmpjuteit) *vt* amputer. **amputation** *n* amputation *f.*
amuse (ə'mju:z) *vt* amuser, divertir. **amusement** *n* divertissement *m.*
an (ən; *stressed* æn) *indef art* see **a.**
anachronism (ə'nækrənizəm) *n* anachronisme *m.*
anaemia (ə'ni:miə) *n* anémie *f.* **anaemic** *adj* anémique.
anaesthetic (ænis'θetik) *adj,n* anesthésique *m.* **anaesthetist** *n* anesthésiste *m,f.* **anaesthetize** *vt* anesthésier.
anagram ('ænəgræm) *n* anagramme *f.*
anal ('einl) *adj* anal, -aux.
analogy (ə'nælədʒi) *n* analogie *f.*
analysis (ə'nælisis) *n, pl* **analyses** analyse *f.* **analyse** *vt* analyser.
anarchy ('ænəki) *n* anarchie *f.* **anarchism** *n* anarchisme *m.* **anarchist** *n* anarchiste *m,f.*
anatomy (ə'nætəmi) *n* anatomie *f.*
ancestor ('ænsəstə) *n* ancêtre, aïeul, -eux *m.* **ancestral** *adj* héréditaire, de famille.
anchor ('æŋkə) *n* ancre. *f.* *vt* ancrer. *vi* jeter l'ancre.
anchovy ('æntʃəvi) *n* anchois *m.*
ancient ('einʃənt) *adj* ancien, -ienne, antique.
ancillary (æn'siləri) *adj* 1 subordonné. 2 auxiliaire.
and (ən, ənd; *stressed* ænd) *conj* et. **and so on** et ainsi de suite.
Andorra (æn'dɔ:rə) *n* Andorre *f.*
anemone (ə'neməni) *n* anémone *f.*
anew (ə'nju:) *adv* de nouveau.
angel ('eindʒəl) *n* ange *m.* **angelic** *adj* angélique.
angelica (æn'dʒelikə) *n* angélique *f.*
anger ('æŋgə) *n* colère *f.* *vt* irriter, mettre en colère. **angry** *adj* fâché, en colère.
angle[1] ('æŋgəl) *n* angle *m.*
angle[2] ('æŋgəl) *vi* pêcher à la ligne. **angler** *n* pêcheur à la ligne *m.*
Anglican ('æŋglikən) *adj,n* anglican.
anguish ('æŋgwiʃ) *n* angoisse *f.*
angular ('æŋgjulə) *adj* 1 angulaire. 2 anguleux, -euse. 3 maigre.
animal ('æniməl) *adj,n* animal, -aux *m.*
animate (*adj* 'ænimət; *v* 'ænimeit) *adj* animé. *vt* animer. **animation** *n* animation, vivacité *f.*
aniseed ('ænisi:d) *n* graine d'anis *f.*

ankle ('æŋkəl) *n* cheville *f*.
annals ('ænlz) *n pl* annales *f pl*.
annex (ə'neks) *vt* annexer. **annexe** *n* annexe *f*.
annihilate (ə'naiəleit) *vt* anéantir. **annihilation** *n* anéantissement *m*.
anniversary (æni'və:səri) *n* anniversaire *m*.
annotate ('ænəteit) *vt* annoter.
announce (ə'nauns) *vt* annoncer. **announcement** *n* annonce *f*. avis *m*. **announcer** *n* **1** annonceur *m*. **2** speaker *m*.
annoy (ə'nɔi) *vt* **1** gêner, ennuyer. **2** contrarier. **annoyance** *n* désagrément, ennui *m*.
annual ('ænjuəl) *adj* annuel, -elle. *n* **1** annuaire *m*. **2** *bot* plante annuelle *f*.
annul (ə'nʌl) *vt* annuler.
anode ('ænoud) *n* anode *f*.
anoint (ə'nɔint) *vt* oindre.
anomaly (ə'nɔməli) *n* anomalie *f*. **anomalous** *adj* anormal, -aux, irregulier, -ière.
anonymous (ə'nɔniməs) *adj* anonyme.
another (ə'nʌðə) *pron,adj* **1** encore un. **2** un autre. **one another** l'un l'autre, les uns les autres.
answer ('ɑ:nsə) *n* **1** réponse *f*. **2** solution *f*. *vt,vi* répondre. **answerable** *adj* responsable.
ant (ænt) *n* fourmi *f*.
antagonize (æn'tægənaiz) *vt* contrarier. **antagonism** *n* antagonisme *m*. **antagonist** *n* antagoniste, adversaire *m,f*.
Antarctic (æn'tɑ:ktik) *adj,n* antarctique *m*.
antelope ('æntiloup) *n* antilope *f*.
antenatal (ænti'neitl) *adj* prénatal, -aux.
antenna (æn'tenə) *n, pl* **antennae** antenne *f*.
anthem ('ænθəm) *n* hymne *m*.
anthology (æn'θɔlədʒi) *n* anthologie *f*.
anthropology (ænθrə'pɔlədʒi) *n* anthropologie *f*. **anthropologist** *n* anthropologiste *m,f*.
anti-aircraft *adj* antiaérien, -ienne.
antibiotic (æntibai'ɔtik) *n* antibiotique *m*.
antibody ('æntibɔdi) *n* anticorps *m*.
antic ('æntik) *n* singerie *f*.
anticipate (æn'tisipeit) *vt* **1** anticiper. **2** prévoir. **anticipation** *n* **1** anticipation *f*. **2** prévision *f*. **3** attente *f*.
anticlimax (ænti'klaimæks) *n* anticlimax *m*. chute, culbute *f*.
anticlockwise (ænti'klɔkwaiz) *adj* en sens inverse des aiguilles d'une montre.
anticyclone (ænti'saikloun) *n* anticyclone *m*.
antidote ('æntidout) *n* antidote *m*.
antifreeze ('æntifri:z) *n* antigel *m invar*.
antique (æn'ti:k) *adj* antique. *n* objet antique *m*. antiquité *f*. **antique dealer** *n* antiquaire *m*. **antique shop** *n* magasin d'antiquités *m*. **antiquated** *adj* **1** vieilli. **2** démodé. **antiquity** *n* antiquité *f*.
anti-Semitic *adj* antisémitique.
antiseptic (ænti'septik) *adj,n* antiseptique *m*.
antisocial (ænti'souʃəl) *adj* antisocial, -aux.
antithesis (æn'tiθəsis) *n, pl* **antitheses** antithèse *f*.
antler ('æntlə) *n* **1** andouiller *m*. **2** *pl* bois *m pl*.
antonym ('æntənim) *n* antonyme *m*.
anus ('einəs) *n* anus *m*.
anvil ('ænvil) *n* enclume *f*.
anxious ('æŋkʃəs) *adj* **1** soucieux, -euse. **2** désireux, -euse. **anxiety** *n* anxiété, angoisse *f*.
any ('eni) *adj,pron* **1** du, de la. **2** en. **3** aucun. **4** n'importe (le)quel. **5** tout. **any further** plus loin. **any more** encore. **anybody** *pron also* **anyone** n'importe qui, quelqu'un. **not anybody** personne. **anyhow** *conj also* **anyway** de toute façon. *adv* n'importe comment. **anything** *pron* **1** quelque chose. **2** n'importe quoi. **not anything** rien. **anywhere** *adv* n'importe où. **not anywhere** nulle part.
apart (ə'pɑ:t) *adv* de côté. **apart from** en dehors de. **apart from the fact that** hormis que.
apartheid (ə'pɑ:tait) *n* ségrégation *f*.
apartment (ə'pɑ:tmənt) *n* **1** pièce *f*. **2** appartement *m*. **3** *pl* logement *m*.
apathy ('æpəθi) *n* apathie *f*. **apathetic** *adj* apathique.
ape (eip) *n* singe *m*. *vt* singer.
aperitive (ə'peritiv) *n* apéritif *m*.
aperture ('æpətʃə) *n* ouverture *f*.
apex ('eipeks) *n* sommet *m*. apogée *f*.
apiece (ə'pi:s) *adv* chacun.
apology (ə'pɔlədʒi) *n* **1** excuses *f pl*. **2** apologie *f*. **apologetic** *adj* **1** d'excuse. **2** apologétique. **apologize** *vi* s'excuser, demander pardon.
apostle (ə'pɔsəl) *n* apôtre *m*.
apostrophe (ə'pɔstrəfi) *n* apostrophe *f*.
appal (ə'pɔ:l) *vt* épouvanter. **appalling** *adj* effroyable.
apparatus (æpə'reitəs) *n, pl* **-tus** *or* **-tuses** appareil *m*.
apparent (ə'pærənt) *adj* apparent, manifeste. **apparently** *adv* apparemment. **apparition** *n* apparition *f*.
appeal (ə'pi:l) *n* appel *m*. *vi* faire appel. **appeal to** **1** plaire à. **2** s'adresser à.
appear (ə'piə) *vi* **1** paraître, sembler. **2** apparaître. **appearance** *n* **1** apparition *f*. **2** apparence *f*.

appease (ə'pi:z) *vt* apaiser.
appendix (ə'pendiks) *n, pl* **appendices** appendice *m.* **appendicitis** *n* appendicite *f.*
appetite ('æpətait) *n* **1** appétit *m.* **2** désir *m.* **appetizer** *n* apéritif *m.* **appetizing** *adj* appétissant.
applaud (ə'plɔ:d) *vt,vi* applaudir. **applause** *n* applaudissements *m pl.*
apple ('æpəl) *n* pomme *f.*
apply (ə'plai) *vt* appliquer. *vi* s'adresser. **appliance** *n* **1** dispositif *m.* **2** *pl* accessoires *m pl.* **applicable** *adj* applicable. **applicant** *n* candidat *m.* **application** *n* **1** application *f.* **2** demande *f.*
appoint (ə'pɔint) *vt* **1** nommer. **2** fixer. **3** équiper. **appointment** *n* **1** rendez-vous *m.* **2** désignation *f.*
appraise (ə'preiz) *vt* estimer, apprécier. **appraisal** *n* évaluation *f.*
appreciate (ə'pri:ʃieit) *vt* apprécier. *vi* augmenter de valeur. **appreciation** *n* **1** appréciation *f.* **2** hausse de valeur *f.*
apprehend (æpri'hend) *vt* **1** appréhender. **2** comprendre. **apprehension** *n* **1** appréhension *f.* **2** crainte *f.* **3** arrestation *f.* **apprehensive** *adj* anxieux, -euse.
apprentice (ə'prentis) *n* apprenti *m.* *vt* mettre en apprentissage. **apprenticeship** *n* apprentissage *m.*
approach (ə'proutʃ) *vi* (s')approcher. *vt* (s')approcher de. *n* **1** approche *f.* **2** accès *m.*
appropriate (*adj* ə'proupriət; *v* ə'proupriei t) *adj* approprié, convenable. *vt* (s')approprier.
approve (ə'pru:v) *vt* approuver. **approval** *n* approbation *f.*
approximate (*adj* ə'prɔksimət; *v* ə'prɔksimeit) *adj* approximatif, -ive. *vt* rapprocher.
apricot ('eiprikɔt) *n* abricot *m.* **apricot tree** *n* abricotier *m.*
April ('eiprəl) *n* avril *m.* **April Fools' Day** *n* premier avril *m.*
apron ('eiprən) *n* tablier *m.*
apse (æps) *n* abside *f.*
apt (æpt) *adj* **1** porté à. **2** juste. **3** doué. **aptly** *adv* à propos.
aptitude ('æptitju:d) *n* **1** tendance *f.* **2** aptitude, disposition *f.*
aquarium (ə'kwɛəriəm) *n* aquarium *m.*
Aquarius (ə'kwɛəriəs) *n* Verseau *m.*
aquatic (ə'kwætik) *adj* aquatique. **acquatics** *n pl* sports nautiques *m pl.*
Arabia (ə'reibiə) *n* Arabie *f.* **Arab** *adj,n* arabe. **Arabian** *adj* arabe. **Arabic** *adj* arabique, arabe. **Arabic** (language) *n* arabe *m.*
arable ('ærəbəl) *adj* arable.
arbitrary ('ɑ:bitrəri) *adj* arbitraire.
arbitrate ('ɑ:bitreit) *vt,vi* arbitrer. **arbitration** *n* arbitrage *m.*
arc (ɑ:k) *n* arc *m.*
arcade (ɑ:'keid) *n* **1** arcade *f.* **2** passage *m.*
arch (ɑ:tʃ) *n* **1** arche *f.* **2** arc *m.* **3** voûte *f.* *vt* arquer. *vi* former voûte.
archaeology (ɑ:ki'ɔlədʒi) *n* archéologie *f.* **archaeological** *adj* archéologique. **archaeologist** *n* archéologue *m,f.*
archaic (ɑ:'keiik) *adj* archaïque.
archbishop (ɑ:tʃ'biʃəp) *n* archevêque *m.*
archduke (ɑ:tʃ'dju:k) *n* archiduc *m.* **archduchess** *n* archiduchesse *f.*
archery ('ɑ:tʃəri) *n* tir à l'arc *m.*
archetype ('ɑ:kitaip) *n* archétype *m.*
archipelago (ɑ:ki'peləgou) *n* archipel *m.*
architect ('ɑ:kitekt) *n* architecte *m.* **architecture** *n* architecture *f.*
archives ('ɑ:kaivz) *n pl* archives *f pl.*
Arctic ('ɑ:ktik) *adj* arctique. **Arctic (Ocean)** *n* (Océan) Arctique *m.*
ardent ('ɑ:dnt) *adj* ardent.
ardour ('ɑ:də) *n* ardeur *f.*
arduous ('ɑ:djuəs) *adj* **1** ardu. **2** acharné.
are (ə; *stressed* ɑ:) *v* see **be.**
area ('ɛəriə) *n* **1** aire, surface *f.* **2** territoire *m.* région *f.*
arena (ə'ri:nə) *n* arène *f.*
argue ('ɑ:gju:) *vi* **1** discuter. **2** se disputer. *vt* **1** prouver. **2** soutenir. **argument** *n* **1** argument *m.* **2** discussion *f.* **argumentative** *adj* raisonneur, -euse.
arid ('ærid) *adj* aride.
Aries ('ɛəri:z) *n* Bélier *m.*
arise* (ə'raiz) *vi* **1** s'élever. **2** se lever. **3** provenir.
aristocracy (æri'stɔkrəsi) *n* aristocratie *f.* **aristocrat** *n* aristocrate *m,f.* **aristocratic** *adj* aristocratique.
arithmetic (ə'riθmətik) *n* arithmétique *f.*
arm[1] (ɑ:m) *n anat* bras *m.* **at arm's length** à distance. **armchair** *n* fauteuil *m.* **armhole** *n* emmanchure *f.* **armpit** *n* aisselle *f.* **armful** *n* brassée *f.*
arm[2] (ɑ:m) *n* **1** *mil* arme *f.* **2** *pl* armoiries *f pl.* **be up in arms** se gendarmer. ~*vt* armer. *vi* s'armer. **armament** *n* armement *m.*
armour ('ɑ:mə) *n* **1** armure *f.* **2** blindage *f.* *vt*

cuirasser, blinder. **armour-plated** *adj* cuirassé, blindé. **armoury** *n* arsenal, -aux *m*.
army ('ɑ:mi) *n* armée *f*.
aroma (ə'roumə) *n* arome *m*. **aromatic** *adj* aromatique.
arose (ə'rouz) *v see* **arise**.
around (ə'raund) *prep* autour de. *adv* autour, à l'entour.
arouse (ə'rauz) *vt* **1** réveiller. **2** provoquer.
arrange (ə'reindʒ) *vt* **1** arranger, organiser. **2** ranger. *vi* s'arranger. **arrangement** *n* disposition *f*. arrangement *m*.
array (ə'rei) *vt* **1** ranger. **2** orner. *n* **1** ordre *m*. **2** atours *m pl*.
arrears (ə'riəz) *n pl* arrérages *m pl*. **in arrears** en retard.
arrest (ə'rest) *vt* arrêter. *n* **1** arrestation *f*. **2** arrêt *m*.
arrive (ə'raiv) *vi* arriver. **arrival** *n* arrivée *f*.
arrogance ('ærəgəns) *n* arrogance *f*. **arrogant** *adj* arrogant.
arrow ('ærou) *n* flèche *f*.
arsenic ('ɑ:snik) *n* arsenic *m*.
arson ('ɑ:sən) *n* crime d'incendie *m*.
art (ɑ:t) *n* **1** art *m*. **2** habileté *f*. **3** artifice *m*. **art gallery** *n* musée d'art *m*. **art school** *n* école de beaux arts *f*. **artful** *adj* **1** astucieux, -euse, rusé. **2** adroit.
artery ('ɑ:təri) *n* artère *f*. **arterial** *adj* artériel, -elle.
arthritis (ɑ:'θraitis) *n* arthrite *f*.
artichoke ('ɑ:titʃouk) *n* artichaut *m*.
article ('ɑ:tikəl) *n* **1** article *m*. **2** *pl law* contrat *m*. *vt* engager par contrat.
articulate (*v* ɑ:'tikjuleit; *adj* ɑ:'tikjulət) *vt* articuler, énoncer. *vi* s'articuler. *adj* **1** articulé. **2** distinct. **articulation** *n* articulation *f*.
artificial (ɑ:ti'fiʃəl) *adj* artificiel, -elle.
artillery (ɑ:'tiləri) *n* artillerie *f*.
artist ('ɑ:tist) *n* artiste *m,f*. **artistic** *adj* artistique.
as (əz; *stressed* æz) *adv* **1** aussi, si. **2** comme, en. *conj* **1** comme. **2** puisque. **3** au moment où. **4** à mesure que. **5** que. **as for** quant à. **as if** comme si. **as well** aussi.
asbestos (æs'bestəs) *n* amiante *m*.
ascend (ə'send) *vt,vi* monter. *vi* remonter. **ascension** *n* ascension *f*. **ascent** *n* montée *f*.
ascertain (æsə'tein) *vt* **1** constater. **2** vérifier.
ash[1] (æʃ) *n* cendre *f*. **ashtray** *n* cendrier *m*.
ash[2] (æʃ) *n bot* frêne *m*.
ashamed (ə'ʃeimd) *adj* honteux, -euse. **be ashamed of** avoir honte de.
ashore (ə'ʃɔ:) *adv* à terre. **go ashore** débarquer.
Asia ('eiʃə) *n* Asie *f*. **Asian** *adj,n also* **Asiatic** asiatique.
aside (ə'said) *adv* **1** de côté. **2** à l'écart. *n* aparté *m*.
ask (ɑ:sk) *vt* **1** demander, prier. **2** inviter. **ask about** se renseigner sur. **ask a question** poser une question. **ask for** demander.
askew (ə'skju:) *adv* de côté.
asleep (ə'sli:p) *adv* endormi. **be asleep** dormir. **fall asleep** s'endormir.
asparagus (ə'spærəgəs) *n* asperge *f*.
aspect ('æspekt) *n* aspect *m*. point de vue *f*.
asphalt ('æsfælt) *n* asphalte *m*. *vt* asphalter.
aspire (ə'spaiə) *vi* aspirer. **aspiring** *adj* ambitieux, -euse.
aspirin ('æsprin) *n* aspirine *f*.
ass (æs) *n* **1** âne, ânesse. **2** sot, sotte.
assassin (ə'sæsin) *n* assassin *m*. **assassinate** *vt* assassiner. **assassination** *n* assassinat *m*.
assault (ə'sɔ:lt) *n* attaque *f*. assaut *m*. *vt* attaquer.
assemble (ə'sembəl) *vt* assembler. *vi* s'assembler. **assembly** *n* **1** assemblée *f*. **2** montage *m*. **assembly line** *n* chaîne de montage *f*.
assent (ə'sent) *n* assentiment *m*. *vi* consentir.
assert (ə'sə:t) *vt* **1** affirmer. **2** revendiquer. **assertion** *n* **1** assertion *f*. **2** revendication *f*.
assess (ə'ses) *vt* **1** estimer. **2** imposer. **assessment** *n* **1** estimation *f*. **2** impôt *m*.
asset ('æset) *n* **1** avantage *m*. **2** *pl comm* actif *m*. **3** *pl* biens *m pl*.
assign (ə'sain) *vt* assigner. **assignment** *n* assignation *f*. **2** *law* transfert *m*.
assimilate (ə'simileit) *vt* assimiler.
assist (ə'sist) *vt,vi* assister. **assistance** *n* aide *f*. **assistant** *adj* auxiliaire. *n* **1** assistant *m,f*. adjoint *m*. **2** *comm* commis *m*.
assizes (ə'saiziz) *n pl* assises *f pl*.
associate (ə'souʃieit) *adj,n* associé. *n* collègue *m*. *vt* associer. *vi* s'associer. **association** *n* association *f*.
assort (ə'sɔ:t) *vt* assortir. *vi* s'associer. **assortment** *n* assortiment *m*.
assume (ə'sju:m) *vt* **1** supposer. **2** assumer. **3** affecter. **assumption** *n* supposition, présomption *f*.
assure (ə'ʃuə) *vt* assurer. **assurance** *n* assurance *f*.
asterisk ('æstərisk) *n* astérisque *m*.

asthma (ˈæsmə) *n* asthme *m*. **asthmatic** *adj,n* asthmatique.
astonish (əˈstɔniʃ) *vt* étonner. **astonishment** *n* étonnement *m*.
astound (əˈstaund) *vt* ébahir.
astray (əˈstrei) *adv* égaré.
astride (əˈstraid) *adv* à califourchon.
astrology (əˈstrɔlədʒi) *n* astrologie *f*. **astrologer** *n* astrologue *m*. **astrological** *adj* astrologique.
astronaut (ˈæstrənɔ:t) *n* astronaute *m*. **astronautics** *n* astronautique *f*.
astronomy (əˈstrɔnəmi) *n* astronomie *f*. **astronomer** *n* astronome *m*. **astronomical** *adj* astronomique.
astute (əˈstju:t) *adj* astucieux, -euse, avisé.
asunder (əˈsʌndə) *adv* en deux, à part.
asylum (əˈsailəm) *n* **1** asile *m*. **2** *med* hospice *m*.
at (ət; *stressed* æt) *prep* **1** à. **2** chez. **at first** d'abord. **at hand** sous la main. **at last** enfin. **at least** du moins. **at once** tout de suite.
ate (eit, et) *v* see **eat.**
atheism (ˈeiθiizəm) *n* athéisme *m*. **atheist** *n* athée *m,f*. **atheistic** *adj* athée.
Athens (ˈæθinz) *n* Athènes *f*.
athlete (ˈæθli:t) *n* athlète *m*. **athletic** *adj* athlétique. **athletics** *n* athlétisme *m*.
Atlantic (ətˈlæntik) *adj* atlantique. **Atlantic (Ocean)** *n* (Océan) Atlantique *m*.
atlas (ˈætləs) *n* atlas *m*.
atmosphere (ˈætməsfiə) *n* atmosphère *f*. **atmospheric** *adj* atmosphérique. **atmospherics** *n pl* parasites *m pl*.
atom (ˈætəm) *n* atome *m*. **atom bomb** *n* bombe atomique *f*. **atomic** *adj* atomique.
atone (əˈtoun) *vi* expier. **atonement** *n* expiation *f*.
atrocious (əˈtrouʃəs) *adj* atroce. **atrocity** *n* atrocité *f*.
attach (əˈtætʃ) *vt* attacher, lier. *vi* s'attacher. **attachment** *n* **1** attache *f*. **2** attachement *m*.
attaché (əˈtæʃei) *n* attaché *m*.
attack (əˈtæk) *vt* attaquer. *n* **1** attaque *f*. **2** *med* crise *f*. accès *m*.
attain (əˈtein) *vt,vi* atteindre, parvenir à.
attempt (əˈtempt) *n* **1** tentative *f*. **2** *law* attentat *m*. *vt* tenter, tâcher.
attend (əˈtend) *vt* **1** assister à. **2** servir, accompagner. **3** s'occuper de. *vi* faire attention. **attend to** s'occuper de. **attendance** *n* **1** assistance *f*. **2** fréquentation *f*. **3** service *m*. **attendant** *n* **1** serviteur *m*. **2** employé *m*. **attention** *n* attention *f*. **attentive** *adj* **1** attentif, -ive. **2** prévenant.
attic (ˈætik) *n* mansarde *f*. grenier *m*.
attire (əˈtaiə) *vt* vêtir. *n* vêtements *m pl*.
attitude (ˈætitju:d) *n* attitude *f*.
attorney (əˈtə:ni) *n* **1** avoué *m*. **2** mandataire *m*. **attorney general** *n* procureur général *m*.
attract (əˈtrækt) *vt* attirer. **attraction** *n* **1** attraction *f*. **2** *pl* attraits *m pl*. **attractive** *adj* attrayant, séduisant.
attribute (*v* əˈtribju:t; *n* ˈætribju:t) *vt* attribuer, imputer. *n* attribut *m*.
aubergine (ˈoubəʒi:n) *n* aubergine *f*.
auburn (ˈɔ:bən) *adj* châtain, roux, rousse.
auction (ˈɔ:kʃən) *n* vente aux enchères *f*. **auctioneer** *n* commissaire-priseur *m*.
audacious (ɔ:ˈdeiʃəs) *adj* audacieux, -euse. **audacity** *n* audace *f*.
audible (ˈɔ:dibəl) *adj* **1** audible. **2** intelligible. **audibly** *adv* distinctement.
audience (ˈɔ:diəns) *n* **1** audience *f*. **2** public *m*. spectateurs *m pl*.
audiovisual (ɔ:diouˈviʒuəl) *adj* audio-visuel, -elle.
audit (ˈɔ:dit) *n* vérification *f*. *vt* vérifier. **auditor** *n* expert comptable *m*.
audition (ɔ:ˈdiʃən) *n* audition *f*.
auditorium (ɔdiˈtɔ:riəm) *n, pl* **auditoria** *or* **auditoriums** auditorium *m*.
August (ˈɔ:gəst) *n* août *m*.
aunt (ɑ:nt) *n* tante *f*.
au pair (ou ˈpɛə) *n* (jeune fille) au pair *f*.
aura (ˈɔ:rə) *n* aura *f*.
austere (ɔ:ˈstiə) *adj* austère. **austerity** *n* austérité *f*.
Australia (ɔˈstreiliə) *n* Australie *f*. **Australian** *adj,n* australien, -ienne.
Austria (ˈɔ:striə) *n* Autriche *f*. **Austrian** *adj,n* autrichien, -ienne.
authentic (ɔ:ˈθentik) *adj* authentique. **authenticity** authenticité *f*.
author (ˈɔ:θə) *n* auteur *m*. **authoress** *n* femme auteur *f*.
authority (ɔ:ˈθɔriti) *n* autorité *f*. **authoritarian** *adj* autoritaire. **authoritative** *adj* **1** autoritaire. **2** impérieux, -ieuse. **3** autorisé.
authorize (ˈɔ:θəraiz) *vt* autoriser. **authorization** *n* autorisation *f*.
autistic (ɔ:ˈtistik) *adj* autistique.
autobiography (ɔ:təbaiˈɔgrəfi) *n* autobiographie *f*. **autobiographical** *adj* autobiographique.
autograph (ˈɔ:təgrɑ:f) *n* autographe *m*. *vt* signer, dédicacer.

automatic (ɔ:tə'mætik) *adj* automatique.
automation (ɔ:tə'meiʃən) *n* automatisation *f.*
autonomous (ɔ:'tɔnəməs) *adj* autonome. **autonomy** *n* autonomie *f.*
autumn ('ɔ:təm) *n* automne *m.*
auxiliary (ɔ:g'ziliəri) *adj,n* auxiliaire *m.*
available (ə'veiləbəl) *adj* **1** disponible. **2** valable.
avalanche ('ævəlɑ:nʃ) *n* avalanche *f.*
avenge (ə'vendʒ) *vt* venger.
avenue ('ævənju:) *n* avenue *f.*
average ('ævridʒ) *n* moyenne *f. adj* moyen, -enne. *vt* prendre la moyenne de. *vi* donner une moyenne.
aversion (ə'və:ʃən) *n* aversion *f.* **pet aversion** bête noire *f.*
aviary ('eiviəri) *n* volière *f.*
aviation (eivi'eiʃən) *n* aviation *f.*
avid ('ævid) *adj* avide. **avidity** *n* avidité *f.*
avocado (ævə'kɑ:dou) *n* avocat *m.*
avoid (ə'vɔid) *vt* éviter.
await (ə'weit) *vt* attendre.
awake* (ə'weik) *vt* **1** éveiller. **2** réveiller. *vi* s'éveiller, se réveiller. **awaken** *vt* **1** éveiller. **2** réveiller.
award (ə'wɔ:d) *n* **1** récompense *f.* **2** adjudication *f. vt* **1** décerner. **2** accorder.
aware (ə'wɛə) *adj* **1** conscient. **2** avisé. **be aware** savoir. **not be aware of** ignorer. **awareness** *n* conscience *f.*
away (ə'wei) *adv* **1** au loin, loin. **2** absent. **right away** tout de suite.
awe (ɔ:) *n* crainte *f.* **awe-inspiring** *adj* impressionnant. **awe-struck** *adj* trés impressionné.
awful ('ɔ:fəl) *adj* **1** redoutable. **2** imposant. **3** épouvantable.
awkward ('ɔ:kwəd) *adj* **1** maladroit. **2** gêné. **3** embarrassant. **4** incommode. **awkwardness** *n* **1** maladresse *f.* **2** embarras *m.* **3** inconvénient *m.*
awoke (ə'wouk) *v see* **awake.**
axe (æks) *n* hache *f.*
axis ('æksis) *n, pl* **axes** axe *m.*
axle ('æksəl) *n* essieu, -eux *m.*
azalea (ə'zeiliə) *n* azaleé *f.*

B

babble ('bæbəl) *vi* babiller. *n* babil, bavardage *m.*
baboon (bə'bu:n) *n* babouin *m.*
baby ('beibi) *n* bébé *m. adj* puéril. **baby-sit** *vi* garder des enfants. **baby-sitter** *n* garde d'enfants *m.,f.*
baccarat ('bækərɑ:) *n* baccara *m.*
bachelor ('bætʃələ) *n* célibataire *m.* **bachelor of Arts/Science** licencié ès lettres/sciences *m.* **bachelorhood** *n* célibat *m.*
back (bæk) *n* **1** dos *m.* reins *m pl.* **2** arrière, derrière *m.* **3** verso *m.* **4** fond *m.* **5** dossier *m. adj* arrière. *adv* en arrière. **be back** être de retour. **come back** revenir.
backache ('bækeik) *n* maux de reins *m pl.* courbature *f.*
backbone ('bækboun) *n* épine dorsale *f.*
backdate ('bækdeit) *vt* antidater.
backfire ('bækfaiə) *n* retour de flamme *m. vi* **1** *mot* pétarader. **2** *sl* eċhouer.
backgammon ('bækgæmən) *n* jacquet *m.*
background ('bækgraund) *n* arrière-plan, fond *m.*
backhand ('bækhænd) *n sport* revers *m.* **backhanded** *adj* injuste, équivoque. **backhander** *n sl* pot-de-vin *m.*
backlash ('bæklæʃ) *n* **1** battement *m.* **2** contrecoup *m.*
backlog ('bæklɔg) *n* arriéré *m.*
backstage (bæk'steidʒ) *adv* dans les coulisses
backstroke ('bækstrouk) *n* brasse sur le dos *f.*
backward ('bækwəd) *adj* arriéré, rétrograde, lent. **backwardness** *n* **1** retard *m.* **2** arriération mentale *f.* **backwards** *adv* en arrière, à reculons, à rebours.
backwater ('bækwɔtə) *n* eau stagnante *f.*
bacon ('beikən) *n* lard, bacon *m.*
bacteria (bæk'tiəriə) *n pl* bactéries *f pl.* **bacterial** *adj* bactérien, -ienne.
bad (bæd) *adj* **1** mauvais, mal. **2** méchant. **bad-tempered** *adj* acariâtre, de mauvaise humeur. **badly** *adv* **1** mal. **2** grièvement.
bade (bæd) *v see* **bid.**
badge (bædʒ) *n* **1** insigne *m.* **2** symbole *m.*
badger ('bædʒə) *n* blaireau, -aux *m. vt* harceler.
badminton ('bædmintən) *n* badminton, volant *m.*
baffle ('bæfəl) *vt* **1** déconcerter. **2** déjouer.
bag (bæg) *n* sac, sachet *m. vt* **1** mettre en sac. **2** *sl* chiper. **baggage** *n* bagages *m pl.* **baggy** *adj* bouffant. **bagpipes** *n pl* cornemuse *f.*
bail (beil) *n* **1** caution *f.* **2** répondant *m. vt* porter garant de.
bailiff ('beilif) *n* **1** huissier *m.* **2** régisseur *m.* **3** bailli *m.*
bait (beit) *n* **1** amorce *f.* **2** appât, leurre *m. vt* **1** amorcer. **2** *inf* harceler.

bake (beik) *vt,vi* cuire au four. **baker** *n* boulanger *m*. **bakery** *n* boulangerie *f*.
balance ('bæləns) *n* **1** balance *f*. **2** équilibre *m*. **3** solde *m*. *vt* **1** balancer, équilibrer. **2** solder. *vi* **1** se balancer, s'équilibrer. **2** se solder. **balance sheet** *n* bilan *m*.
balcony ('bælkəni) *n* balcon *m*.
bald (bɔ:ld) *adj* **1** chauve. **2** sec, sèche, plat.
bale[1] (beil) *vt* **bale out** écoper.
bale[2] (beil) *vt* empaqueter.
baleful ('beilfəl) *adj* sinistre, funeste.
ball[1] (bɔ:l) *n* **1** boule *f*. **2** balle *f*. ballon *m*. **3** boulet *m*. **4** pelote *f*. **5** *cul* boulette *f*. **ball-bearing** *n* roulement à bille *m*.
ball[2] (bɔ:l) *n* bal *m*. **ballroom** *n* salle de bal *or* de danse *f*.
ballad ('bæləd) *n* **1** *mus* romance *f*. **2** *lit* ballade *f*.
ballast ('bæləst) *n* **1** *naut* lest *m*. **2** ballast *m*. *vt* **1** lester. **2** empierrer, ballaster.
ballet ('bælei) *n* **1** ballet *m*. **2** corps de ballet *m*.
ballistic (bə'listik) *adj* balistique.
balloon (bə'lu:n) *n* **1** ballon à air *m*. **2** *aviat* ballon, aérostat *m*. *vi* se gonfler.
ballot ('bælət) *n* scrutin, vote *m*. *vi* voter au scrutin. **ballot-box** *n* urne électorale *f*.
Baltic ('bɔ:ltik) *adj* balte. **Baltic (Sea)** *n* (Mer) Baltique *f*.
bamboo (bæm'bu:) *n* bambou *m*.
ban (bæn) *n* **1** ban *m*. proscription *f*. **2** *rel* interdit *m*. *vt* interdire.
banal (bə'nɑ:l) *adj* banal, -aux.
banana (bə'nɑ:nə) *n* banane *f*.
band[1] (bænd) *n* **1** bande, troupe *f*. **2** orchestre *m*. *vt* liguer. *vi* se liguer.
band[2] (bænd) *n* **1** lien *m*. **2** bande *f*. **bandage** *n* bandage, pansement *m*. *vt* bander, panser.
bandit ('bændit) *n* bandit, brigand *m*.
bandy ('bændi) *vt* échanger. *adj* arqué. **bandy-legged** *adj* bancal.
bang (bæŋ) *n* **1** coup *m*. **2** détonation *f*. *interj* pan! *vi,vt* frapper. **bang the door** claquer la porte.
bangle ('bæŋgəl) *n* bracelet *m*.
banish ('bæniʃ) *vt* bannir, exiler. **banishment** *n* bannissement, exil *m*.
banister ('bænistə) *n* rampe *f*.
banjo ('bændʒou) *n* banjo *m*.
bank[1] (bæŋk) *n* **1** talus, remblai *m*. **2** *geog* berge, rive *f*. *vt* endiguer. **bank up** remblayer.
bank[2] (bæŋk) *n* *comm* banque *f*. **bank account** *n* compte en banque *m*. **bankbook** *n* carnet de banque *m*. **bank holiday** *n* jour férié légal *m*. **banknote** *n* billet de banque *m*. ~*vt* déposer en banque. **bank on** compter sur.
bankrupt ('bæŋkrʌpt) *n* banqueroutier *m*. *adj* en faillite, ruiné. **go bankrupt** faire faillite. ~*vt* mettre en faillite.
banner ('bænə) *n* bannière *f*.
banquet ('bæŋkwit) *n* banquet, festin *m*.
baptize (bæp'taiz) *vt* baptiser, surnommer. **baptism** *n* baptême *m*.
bar (bɑ:) *n* **1** bar *m*. **2** barre *f*. **3** *law* barreau, -aux *m*. **4** obstacle *m*. **5** *mus* mesure *f*. **6** tablette *f*. *vt* **1** barrer. **2** interdire. **barmaid** *n* serveuse *f*.
barbarian (bɑ:'bɛəriən) *adj,n* barbare. **barbaric** *adj* barbare, primitif, -ive. **barbarity** *n* barbarie, cruauté *f*. **barbarous** *adj* barbare.
barbecue ('bɑ:bikju:) *n* gril *m*. *vt* rôtir à la broche.
barbed wire (bɑ:bd) *n* fil de fer barbelé *m*.
barber ('bɑ:bə) *n* coiffeur *m*.
barbiturate (bɑ:'bitjurət) *n* barbiturique *m*.
bare (bɛə) *adj* **1** nu, dégarni. **2** sec, sèche, simple. *vt* mettre à nu, révéler. **barefoot** *adv* nu-pieds. **barely** *adv* à peine, tout juste.
bargain ('bɑ:gin) *n* affaire, occasion *f*.
barge (bɑ:dʒ) *n* péniche *f*. chaland *m*. *v* **barge into** bousculer, entrer en coup de vent.
baritone ('bæritoun) *n* baryton *m*.
bark[1] (bɑ:k) *n* aboiement *m*. *vi* aboyer.
bark[2] (bɑ:k) *n* *bot* écorce *f*.
barley ('bɑ:li) *n* orge *f*. **barley-sugar** *n* sucre d'orge *m*. **barley-water** *n* orgeat *m*.
barn (bɑ:n) *n* grange *f*.
barometer (bə'rɔmitə) *n* baromètre *m*.
baron ('bærən) *n* baron *m*. **baroness** *n* baronne *f*. **baronet** *n* baronnet *m*.
barracks ('bærəks) *n pl* caserne *f*.
barrel ('bærəl) *n* **1** tonneau, -aux *m*. **2** caque *f*. **3** cylindre *m*. **4** (of a gun) canon *m*.
barren ('bærən) *adj* stérile, aride.
barricade ('bærikeid) *n* barricade *f*. *vt* barricader.
barrier ('bæriə) *n* **1** barrière *f*. **2** obstacle *m*.
barrister ('bæristə) *n* avocat *m*.
barrow ('bærou) *n* brouette *f*.
barter ('bɑ:tə) *n* troc *m*. *vt* troquer.
base[1] (beis) *n* base *f*. fondement *m*. *vt* fonder. **baseball** *n* base-ball *m*. **basement** *n* **1** sous-sol *m*. **2** soubassement *m*.
base[2] (beis) *adj* vil, bas, basse.
bash (bæʃ) *n* coup *m*. *vt inf* taper sur, cogner.
bashful ('bæʃfəl) *adj* timide.

basic (ˈbeisik) *adj* **1** fondamental, -aux. **2** basique.

basil (ˈbæzəl) *n* basilic *m*.

basin (ˈbeisən) *n* **1** cuvette *f*. **2** *cul* bol *m*. **3** *geog* bassin *m*.

basis (ˈbeisis) *n, pl* **bases** base *f*. fondement *m*.

bask (bɑ:sk) *vi* se chauffer.

basket (ˈbɑ:skit) *n* panier *m*. corbeille *f*. **basketball** *n* basket-ball *m*.

bass[1] (beis) *n mus* basse *f*.

bass[2] (bæs) *n zool* perche *f*.

bassoon (bəˈsu:n) *n* basson *m*.

bastard (ˈbɑ:stəd) *n* bâtard *m*. *adj* bâtard, faux, fausse.

baste (ˈbeist) *vt* **1** arroser. **2** faufiler, bâtir.

bat[1] (bæt) *n* batte *f*. battoir *m*. **batsman** *n* batteur *m*.

bat[2] (bæt) *n zool* chauve-souris *f*.

batch (bætʃ) *n* **1** fournée *f*. **2** tas *m*.

bath (bɑ:θ) *n* **1** bain *m*. **2** baignoire *f*. *vt* baigner. *vi* prendre un bain. **bathrobe** *n* peignoir de bain *m*. **bathroom** *n* salle de bain *f*.

bathe (beið) *vt* baigner. *vi* se baigner. **bathing costume** *n* maillot de bain *m*. **bathing trunks** *n* caleçon de bain *m*.

baton (ˈbætɔn) *n* **1** bâton *m*. **2** matraque *f*.

battalion (bəˈtæliən) *n* bataillon *m*.

batter[1] (ˈbætə) *vt* **1** battre, rouer de coups. **2** démolir. **battered** *adj* délabré.

batter[2] (ˈbætə) *n* pâte lisse *f*.

battery (ˈbætəri) *n* **1** pile *f*. **2** *mil* batterie *f*.

battle (ˈbætl̩) *n* bataille *f*. combat *m*. *vi* se battre, lutter. **battlefield** *n* champ de bataille *m*. **battleship** *n* cuirassé *m*.

bawl (bɔ:l) *vi,vt* brailler.

bay[1] (bei) *n geog* baie *f*.

bay[2] (bei) *n arch* travée *f*. **bay window** *n* fenêtre en saillie *f*.

bay[3] (bei) *n* abois *m pl*. **keep at bay** tenir en échec. ~*vi* aboyer.

bay[4] (bei) *n bot* laurier *m*.

bayonet (ˈbeiənit) *n* baïonnette *f*.

be* (bi:) *vi* **1** être. **2** se trouver. **3** exister. *v aux* être. **there is** *or* **are** il y a.

beach (bi:tʃ) *n* plage *f*.

beacon (ˈbi:kən) *n* **1** feu, feux *m*. **2** balise *f*.

bead (bi:d) *n* **1** perle *f*. **2** grain *m*. **3** *pl* chapelet *m*.

beak (bi:k) *n* bec *m*.

beaker (ˈbi:kə) *n* gobelet *m*.

beam (bi:m) *n* **1** poutre *f*. **2** rayon, faisceau, -aux *m*. *vi* rayonner. **beaming** *adj* radieux, -euse.

bean (bi:n) *n* **1** grain *m*. **2** haricot *m*.

bear*[1] (bɛə) *vt* **1** porter, supporter. **2** produire. **3** donner naissance à. *vi* **1** souffrir. **2** peser. **3** avoir rapport. **bearable** *adj* supportable. **bearing** *n* **1** port, maintien *m*. conduite *f*. **2** rapport *m*. **lose one's bearings** perdre le nord.

bear[2] (bɛə) *n* ours *m*.

beard (biəd) *n* barbe *f*.

beast (bi:st) *n* **1** bête *f*. **2** animal, -aux *m*. brute *f*.

beat* (bi:t) *vt* **1** battre. **2** frapper. *n* **1** battement *m*. **2** ronde *f*. **3** *mus* mesure *f*. **beating** *n* **1** battement *m*. **2** *inf* rossée *f*.

beauty (ˈbju:ti) *n* beauté *f*. **beautiful** *adj* **1** beau, belle, beaux, magnifique. **2** admirable. **beauty queen** *n* reine de beauté *f*.

beaver (ˈbi:və) *n* castor *m*.

became (biˈkeim) *v* see **become.**

because (biˈkɔ:z) *conj* parce que, car. **because of** à cause de.

beckon (ˈbekən) *vt* faire signe à. *vi* faire signe.

become* (biˈkʌm) *vi* devenir, se faire. *vt* convenir. **becoming** *adj* **1** convenable. **2** seyant.

bed (bed) *n* **1** lit *m*. **2** parterre *m*. **3** couche *f*. **go to bed** se coucher. **bedclothes** *n pl* couvertures et draps de lit. **bedding** *n* literie *f*. **bedridden** *adj* alité, cloué au lit. **bedroom** *n* chambre (à coucher) *f*. **bedside** *n* chevet *m*. **bed-sitter** *n* chambre-studio *f*. **bedspread** *n* dessus de lit *m*.

bedraggled (biˈdrægəld) *adj* dépenaillé.

bee (bi:) *n* abeille *f*. **beehive** *n* ruche *f*. **beekeeper** *n* apiculteur *m*. **beeline** *n* ligne droite *f*.

beech (bi:tʃ) *n* hêtre *m*.

beef (bi:f) *n* bœuf *m*. **roast beef** rosbif *m*.

been (bi:n) *v* see **be.**

beer (biə) *n* bière *f*.

beet (bi:t) *n* betterave *f*. **beetroot** *n* betterave *f*.

beetle (ˈbi:tl̩) *n* scarabée, coléoptère *m*.

befall* (biˈfɔ:l) *vt* survenir, arriver.

before (biˈfɔ:) *adv* **1** avant, auparavant. **2** devant. *prep* **1** devant. **2** avant. *conj* avant que. **beforehand** *adv* au préalable.

befriend (biˈfrend) *vt* venir en aide à.

beg (beg) *vt* demander, prier. *vt,vi* mendier. **I beg your pardon 1** plaît-il? **2** *inf* comment? **beggar** *n* mendiant *m*. **poor beggar!** pauvre type!

begin* (biˈgin) *vt* commencer, entamer. **begin**

to se mettre à. **beginner** *n* débutant, novice *m.* **beginning** *n* commencement, début *m.*
begrudge (biˈgrʌdʒ) *vt* envier. **begrudge doing something** faire quelque chose à contre-cœur.
behalf (biˈhɑ:f) *n* **1** sujet *m.* **2** faveur *f.* **on behalf of** au nom de, pour le compte de.
behave (biˈheiv) *vi* se comporter. **behave yourself!** *inf* tiens-toi bien! **badly-behaved** mal élevé. **well-behaved** sage. **behaviour** *n* **1** conduite *f.* **2** tenue *f.* **3** manières *f pl.*
behind (biˈhaind) *adv* derrière, en arrière. *prep* derrière, en arrière de. *n* **1** derrière *m.* **2** *inf* cul *m.* **behindhand** *adj,adv* en retard, en arrière.
behold* (biˈhould) *vt* contempler, regarder.
beige (beiʒ) *adj,n* beige *m.*
being (ˈbi:iŋ) *n* **1** être *m.* **2** existence *f.* **for the time being** pour le moment.
belfry (ˈbelfri) *n* beffroi *m.*
Belgium (ˈbeldʒəm) *n* Belgique *f.* **Belgian** *adj,n* belge.
believe (biˈli:v) *vt,vi* croire. **I believe so** je crois que oui. **make believe** faire semblant. **belief** *n* **1** croyance *f.* **2** confiance *f.* **believable** *adj* croyable. **believer** *n* croyant *m.*
bell (bel) *n* **1** cloche *f.* **2** sonnette *f.* **bellringer** *n* sonneur, carillonneur *m.*
bellow (ˈbelou) *vt,vi* **1** beugler, mugir. **2** vociférer. *n* **1** mugissement *m.* **2** hurlement *m.*
bellows (ˈbelouz) *n pl* soufflet *m.*
belly (ˈbeli) *n* **1** ventre *m.* **2** panse *f.*
belong (biˈlɔŋ) *vi* **1** appartenir. **2** être propre. **belongings** *n pl* effets *m pl.* affaires *f pl.*
below (biˈlou) *adv* **1** en bas, (au-)dessous, ci-dessous. *prep* au-dessous de, sous.
belt (belt) *n* **1** ceinture *f.* **2** *tech* courroie *f.* **3** zone *m.*
bench (bentʃ) *n* **1** banc *m.* **2** établi *m.* **3** *law* tribunal, -aux *m.*
bend* (bend) *vt* plier, courber, fléchir. *vi* **1** se pencher. **2** se soumettre à. *n* **1** virage, tournant *m.* **2** coude *m.* courbe *f.*
beneath (biˈni:θ) *adv* au-dessous, en bas. *prep* sous, au-dessous de.
benefit (ˈbenifit) *n* **1** profit, avantage *m.* **2** bienfait *m.* **3** allocation *f.* *vt* profiter à, faire du bien à. **benefit by** profiter de. **beneficial** *adj* profitable, avantageux, -euse.
benevolent (biˈnevələnt) *adj* **1** bienveillant. **2** charitable.
bent (bent) *v* see **bend.** *adj* **1** courbé. **2** déterminé.

bequeath (biˈkwi:ð) *vt* léguer.
bereave* (biˈri:v) *vt* priver. **bereavement** *n* deuil *m.* perte *f.*
berry (ˈberi) n baie *f.*
berth (bə:θ) *n* **1** couchette *f.* **2** *naut* emplacement *m.* *vt* amarrer. *vi* mouiller.
beside (biˈsaid) *prep* **1** à côté de. **2** hors de. **besides** *adv* en outre, de plus.
besiege (biˈsi:dʒ) *vt* assiéger.
best (best) *adj,pron* le meilleur *m.* *adv,n* le mieux *m.* **best man** *n* garçon d'honneur *m.* **best-seller** *n* livre à succès *m.* **do one's best** faire de son mieux. **make the best of** tirer le meilleur parti de.
bestow (biˈstou) *vt* accorder.
bet* (bet) *vt* parier. *n* pari *m.* **betting shop** *n* bureau de pari *m.*
betray (biˈtrei) *vt* **1** trahir. **2** révéler. **betrayal** *n* trahison *f.*
better (ˈbetə) *adj* meilleur. *adv* mieux. **be better 1** aller mieux. **2** valoir mieux. **get better 1** s'améliorer. **2** guérir. **so much the better!** tant mieux! **think better of** se raviser.
between (biˈtwi:n) *prep* entre.
beverage (ˈbevridʒ) *n* boisson *f.*
beware* (biˈwɛə) *vi* prendre garde. **beware of** se méfier de.
bewilder (biˈwildə) *vt* désorienter. **bewildered** *adj* **1** ahuri. **2** abasourdi.
beyond (biˈjɔnd) *adv* au-delà, plus loin. *prep* au-delà de, par-delà, outre. **that is beyond me** cela me dépasse.
bias (ˈbaiəs) *n* **1** parti pris *m.* **2** penchant *m.* **3** biais *m.* *vt* prédisposer. **biased** *adj* partial, -aux.
bib (bib) *n* bavette *f.*
Bible (ˈbaibəl) *n* Bible *f.* **biblical** *adj* biblique.
bibliography (bibliˈɔgrəfi) *n* bibliographie *f.* **bibliographer** *n* bibliographe *m.* **bibliographical** *adj* bibliographique.
biceps (ˈbaiseps) *n* biceps *m.*
bicker (ˈbikə) *vi* se chamailler, se quereller. **bickering** *n* prise de bec *f.* querelles *f pl.*
bicycle (ˈbaisikəl) *n* **1** bicyclette *f.* **2** *inf* vélo *m.*
bid* (bid) *n* **1** offre, soumission *f.* **2** enchère *f.* *vt* **1** ordonner. **2** inviter à. **3** souhaiter. *vi* faire une offre.
biennial (baiˈeniəl) *adj* biennal, -aux.
big (big) *adj* grand, gros, grosse.
bigamy (ˈbigəmi) *n* bigamie *f.*
bigot (bigət) *n* fanatique *m,f.* **bigoted** *adj* à l'esprit étroit.

bikini (bi'ki:ni) *n* bikini *m*.
bilingual (bai'liŋgwəl) *adj* bilingue.
bilious ('biliəs) *adj* **1** bilieux, -euse. **2** colérique.
bill[1] (bil) *n* **1** facture, note, addition *f*. **2** effet *m*. **3** affiche *f*. **4** *pol* projet de loi *m*. **bill-board** *n* panneau d'affichage *m*.
bill[2] (bil) *n zool* bec *m*.
billiards ('biliədz) *n pl* billard *m*.
billion ('biliən) *n* **1** billion *m*. **2** *US* milliard *m*.
bin (bin) *n* coffre *m*. poubelle *f*.
binary ('bainəri) *adj* binaire.
bind* (baind) *vt* **1** lier. **2** attacher. **3** relier. **binding** *n* **1** reliure *f*. **2** ligature *f*. **3** fixation *f*. *adj* obligatoire.
binoculars (bi'nɔkjuləz) *n pl* jumelles *f pl*.
biography (bai'ɔgrəfi) *n* biographie *f*. **biographer** *n* biographe *m*. **biographical** *adj* biographique.
biology (bai'ɔlədʒi) *n* biologie *f*. **biological** *adj* biologique. **biologist** *n* biologiste *m*.
birch (bə:tʃ) *n* bouleau, -aux *m*.
bird (bə:d) *n* **1** oiseau, -aux *m*. **2** *inf* fille *f*. **birdcage** *n* volière, cage d'oiseau *f*. **bird's-eye view** vue à vol d'oiseau *f*.
birth (bə:θ) *n* **1** naissance *f*. **2** *zool* mise bas *f*. **3** origine *f*. **birth certificate** *n* acte de naissance *m*. **birth control** *n* limitation des naissances *f*. **birthday** *n* anniversaire *m*. **birthmark** *n* tache de naissance *f*. **birth rate** *n* natalité *f*.
biscuit ('biskit) *n* biscuit *m*.
bishop ('biʃəp) *n* **1** évêque *m*. **2** *game* fou *m*.
bit[1] (bit) *n* **1** (of a bridle) mors *m*. **2** mèche *f*.
bit[2] (bit) *n* morceau, -aux, bout *m*. *adv* un peu. **bit by bit** petit à petit.
bitch (bitʃ) *n* **1** chienne *f*. **2** femelle *f*. **3** *sl* garce *f*.
bite* (bait) *n* **1** morsure, piqûre *f*. **2** bouchée *f*. *vt* mordre, piquer. **biting** *adj* **1** mordant. **2** perçant.
bitter ('bitə) *adj* amer, -ère, aigre. *n* bière amère *f*. **bitterness** *n* **1** amertume *f*. **2** rancune, rancœur *f*.
bizarre (bi'zɑ:) *adj* bizarre.
black (blæk) *adj,n* noir *m*. *n cap* Noir *m*. **blacken** *vt* noircir *vi* se noircir. **blackness** *n* **1** noirceur *f*. **2** obscurité *f*.
blackberry ('blækbəri) *n* mûre *f*. **blackberry bush** *n* ronce *f*. mûrier *m*.
blackbird ('blækbə:d) *n* merle *m*.
blackboard ('blækbɔ:d) *n* tableau noir *m*.
blackcurrant (blæk'kʌrənt) *n* cassis *m*.
black eye *n* œil poché *m*.
blackleg ('blækleg) *n* jaune *m*.
blackmail ('blækmeil) *n* chantage *m*. *vt* faire chanter.
black market *n* marché noir *m*.
blackout ('blækaut) *n* **1** blackout *m*. **2** panne d'électricité *f*. **3** *med* évanouissement *m*. *vt* obscurcir. *vi* s'évanouir.
black pudding *n* boudin noir *m*.
blacksmith ('blæksmiθ) *n* forgeron, maréchal ferrant *m*.
bladder ('blædə) *n* vessie *f*. **gall-bladder** *n* vésicule biliaire *f*.
blade (bleid) *n* **1** brin *m*. **2** lame *f*. **3** pale *f*.
blame (bleim) *n* **1** reproches *m pl*. **2** faute *f*. *vt* blâmer.
blancmange (blə'mɔnʒ) *n* blanc-manger *m*.
blank (blæŋk) *adj* **1** blanc, -che, vierge. **2** vide. *n* vide *m*. lacune *f*.
blanket ('blæŋkit) *n* couverture *f*. **wet blanket** trouble-fête *m invar*.
blare (blɛə) *vi* sonner. *n* **1** sonnerie *f*. **2** fracas *m*.
blaspheme (blæs'fi:m) *vi,vt* blasphémer. **blasphemy** *n* blasphème *m*.
blast (bla:st) *n* **1** bouffée *f*. coup de vent *m*. **2** explosion *f*. **3** coup *m*. *vt* **1** faire sauter. **2** détruire.
blatant ('bleitn̩t) *adj* **1** criard. **2** criant, flagrant.
blaze (bleiz) *n* **1** feu *m*. flamme *f*. **2** éclat *m*. *vi* **1** flamber. **2** étinceler.
bleach (bli:tʃ) *vt,vi* blanchir. *n* eau de javel *f*.
bleak (bli:k) *adj* **1** désolé, nu. **2** triste, morne.
bleat (bli:t) *vi* bêler. *n* bêlement *m*.
bleed* (bli:d) *vi,vt* saigner. **bleeding** *n* **1** écoulement de sang *m*. **2** *med* saignée *f*.
blemish ('blemiʃ) *n* **1** imperfection *f*. **2** souillure, tache *f*. *vt* **1** tacher. **2** abîmer.
blend (blend) *n* mélange *m*. *vt* mélanger, mêler. *vi* **1** se fondre. **2** aller bien ensemble.
bless (bles) *vt* bénir, consacrer. **blessed** *adj* bienheureux, -euse, saint. **blessing** *n* **1** *rel* bénédiction *f*. **2** bienfait *m*.
blew (blu:) *v see* **blow**[2].
blind (blaind) *adj* **1** aveugle. **2** sans issue. *n* store *m*. abat-jour *m invar*. *vt* aveugler, éblouir. **blindfold** *adj,adv* les yeux bandés. *vt* bander les yeux à. **blindness** *n* cécité *f*.
blink (bliŋk) *vi* clignoter. *n* battement de paupières *m*. **blinker** *n* œillère *f*.
bliss (blis) *n* félicité *f*. **blissful** *adj* heureux, -euse, serein.
blister ('blistə) *n* **1** *med* ampoule *f*. vésicatoire

m. 2 cloque f. vi 1 se couvrir d'ampoules. 2 se cloquer.

blizzard ('blizəd) n tempête de neige f.

blob (blɔb) n tache f. pâté m.

bloc (blɔk) n bloc m.

block (blɔk) n 1 bloc m. 2 billot m. 3 obstacle m. **block of flats** immeuble m. ~vt obstruer, bloquer. **block up** boucher.

blockade (blɔ'keid) n blocus m. vt bloquer.

bloke (blouk) n inf type, mec m.

blond (blɔnd) adj blond. **blonde** adj,n blonde f.

blood (blʌd) n sang m. **bloodcurdling** adj à vous figer le sang. **blood pressure** n tension artérielle f. **bloodshot** adj injecté de sang. **bloodstream** n sang, flot sanguin m. **bloodthirsty** adj sanguinaire, avide de sang. **bloody** adj 1 ensanglanté. 2 sl sacré.

bloom (blu:m) n fleur, floraison f. vi 1 fleurir. 2 resplendir. **blooming** adj 1 en fleur. 2 florissant.

blossom ('blɔsəm) n fleur f. vi fleurir.

blot (blɔt) n 1 tache f. 2 pâté m. vt 1 tacher. 2 sécher. **blotting paper** n papier buvard m.

blouse (blauz) n blouse f. chemisier m.

blow[1] (blou) n coup m.

blow*[2] (blou) vt,vi souffler. vt sonner. **blow away** emporter. **blow one's nose** se moucher. **blow up** 1 éclater. 2 faire sauter. 3 gonfler.

blubber ('blʌbə) n graisse de baleine f.

blue (blu:) adj 1 bleu. 2 triste. 3 grivois. n bleu m. **bluebell** n jacinthe des prés f.

bluff (blʌf) n bluff m. vt bluffer.

blunder ('blʌndə) n bévue f. vi gaffer, faire une gaffe.

blunt (blʌnt) adj 1 émoussé. 2 épointé. 3 obtus. 4 brusque. vt émousser.

blur (blə:) vt 1 brouiller. 2 obscurcir. n 1 tache f. 2 brouillard m. **blurred** adj flou, confus.

blush (blʌʃ) n rougeur f. vi rougir.

boar (bɔ:) n verrat m. **wild boar** n sanglier m.

board (bɔ:d) n 1 planche f. 2 tableau, -aux m. 3 table, pension f. 4 naut bord m. 5 conseil m. 6 carton m. vi être en pension. vt monter dans, aborder. **boarder** n pensionnaire m,f. **boarding house** n pension de famille f. **boarding school** n pensionnat m.

boast (boust) vi se vanter. n vanterie f.

boat (bout) n bateau, -aux m. barque f. navire m.

bob (bɔb) vt 1 écourter. 2 secouer. vi s'agiter.

bodice ('bɔdis) n corsage m.

body ('bɔdi) n 1 corps m. 2 carrosserie f. 3 organisme m. 4 consistance f. **bodyguard** n gorille, garde du corps m.

bog (bɔg) n marais m. fondrière f. **boggy** adj marécageux, -euse.

bohemian (bə'hi:miən) adj,n 1 bohémien, -ienne. 2 bohème.

boil[1] (bɔil) vi bouillir. vt 1 faire bouillir. 2 cuire à l'eau. **boil down** se réduire. **boil over** déborder. **boiler** n chaudière f. **boiling** adj bouillant, en ébullition.

boil[2] (bɔil) n med furoncle m.

boisterous ('bɔistərəs) adj 1 turbulent. 2 tumultueux, -euse.

bold (bould) adj 1 hardi, audacieux, -euse. 2 effronté. **boldness** n 1 hardiesse, audace f. 2 impudence f.

bolster ('boulstə) n traversin m. vt 1 rembourrer. 2 soutenir, étayer.

bolt (boult) n 1 verrou, -oux m. 2 boulon m. vt 1 verrouiller. 2 avaler. vi décamper.

bomb (bɔm) n bombe f. vt bombarder. **bombshell** n 1 obus m. 2 grande surprise f. **bombard** vt 1 bombarder. 2 assaillir.

bond (bɔnd) n 1 lien m. attache f. 2 obligation f. bon m. 3 dépôt, entrepôt douanier m. **bondage** n servitude f.

bone (boun) n 1 os m. 2 (of fish) arête f. 3 pl ossements m pl. vt désosser. **bone-dry** adj archisec, archisèche. **bony** adj 1 osseux, -euse. 2 plein d'os.

bonfire ('bɔnfaiə) n feu de joie m.

bonnet ('bɔnit) n 1 bonnet, béret m. 2 capot m.

bonus ('bounəs) n gratification, prime, indemnité f.

booby trap ('bu:bi) n attrape-nigaud f.

book (buk) n 1 livre m. 2 inf bouquin m. 3 registre m. 4 (of tickets) carnet m. vt 1 inscrire. 2 retenir. 3 sl law dresser procès-verbal. **bookcase** n bibliothèque f. **bookkeeping** comptabilité f. **bookmaker** n bookmaker m. **bookseller** n libraire m. **bookshop** n librairie f. **bookstall** n 1 étalage de librairie m. 2 kiosque à livres m. **booking** n 1 réservation f. 2 enregistrement m. **booking office** n 1 guichet m. 2 bureau de location m. **booklet** n livret, fascicule m.

boom (bu:m) n 1 grondement m. 2 comm essor m. hausse f. vi 1 gronder. 2 comm être en hausse.

boost (bu:st) vt 1 faire de la réclame. 2 augmenter. 3 survolter. n poussée f. coup de pouce m.

boot (bu:t) *n* **1** botte *f.* **2** bottine, chaussure *f.* **3** *mot* coffre *m.*

booth (bu:θ) *n* **1** loge *f.* **2** cabine *f.*

booze (bu:z) *n inf* boisson alcoolique *f.* *vi inf* picoler.

border (ˈbɔ:də) *n* **1** bordure *f.* bord *m.* **2** frontière *f.* *vt* border. **border on** confiner à. **borderline** *n* ligne de démarcation *f.* **borderline case** *n* cas limite *m.*

bore[1] (bɔ:) *vt* **1** forer, percer. **2** sonder. *n* **1** calibre *m.* **2** sondage *m.*

bore[2] (bɔ:) *vt* ennuyer. *n* **1** raseur *m.* **2** ennui *m.* **boredom** *n* ennui *m.* **boring** *adj* ennuyeux, -euse, assommant.

bore[3] (bɔ:) *v see* **bear.**

born (bɔ:n) *adj* né, de naissance. **be born** naître.

borough (ˈbʌrə) *n* **1** circonscription électorale *f.* **2** ville *f.*

borrow (ˈbɔrou) *vt* emprunter.

bosom (ˈbuzəm) *n* **1** sein *m.* **2** giron, cœur *m.* **bosom friend** *n* ami intime *m.*

boss (bɔs) *n* patron, chef *m.* *vt* diriger, mener. **bossy** *adj* autoritaire.

botany (ˈbɔtəni) *n* botanique *f.* **botanical** *adj* botanique. **botanist** *n* botaniste *m,f.*

botch (bɔtʃ) *vt* bousiller, saboter. **botch up** rafistoler.

both (bouθ) *adj,pron* tous les deux, tous deux. *conj* à la fois.

bother (ˈbɔðə) *n* ennui, tracas *m.* *vt* **1** gêner, ennuyer. **2** soucier. *vi* se tracasser.

bottle (ˈbɔtl) *n* bouteille *f.* flacon *m.* **bottleneck** *n* **1** goulot d'étranglement *m.* **2** embouteillage *m.* ~*vt* mettre en bouteilles. **bottle up** ravaler, étouffer.

bottom (ˈbɔtəm) *n* **1** fond *m.* **2** bas *m.* **3** derrière *m.* **4** base *f.* *adj* **1** inférieur. **2** du bas. **bottomless** *adj* **1** insondable. **2** sans fond.

bought (bɔ:t) *v see* **buy.**

boulder (ˈbouldə) *n* galet *m.* grosse pierre *f.*

bounce (bauns) *vi* rebondir. *vt* faire rebondir. *n* bond *m.* **bouncing** *adj* rebondissant.

bound[1] (baund) *v see* **bind.**

bound[2] (baund) *n* bond, saut *m.* *vi* bondir.

bound[3] (baund) *n* limite, borne *f.* *vt* borner. **boundary** *n* bornes *f pl.* frontière *f.*

bound[4] (baund) *adj* **bound for** en partance pour, à destination de.

boundary (ˈbaundri) *n* bornes *f pl.* frontière *f.*

bouquet (buˈkei) *n* bouquet *m.*

bourgeois (ˈbuəʒwɑ:) *adj,n* bourgeois.

bout (baut) *n* **1** *med* accès *m.* attaque *f.* **2** coup *m.* **3** partie *f.* **4** assaut *m.*

bow[1] (bau) *vt* courber, incliner. *vi* s'incliner, baisser la tête. *n* salut *m.*

bow[2] (bou) *n* **1** *sport* arc *m.* **2** *mus* archet *m.* **3** nœud *m.* **bow-legged** *adj* bancal.

bow[3] (bau) *n naut* avant *m.* proue *f.*

bowels (ˈbauəlz) *n pl* **1** intestins *m pl.* **2** *inf* entrailles *f pl.*

bowl[1] (boul) *n* **1** bol *m.* **2** bassin *m.* **bowler hat** *n* chapeau melon *m.*

bowl[2] (boul) *vt* rouler. *vi* servir la balle. *n* **1** boule *f.* **2** *pl* boules *f pl.* pétanque *f.*

box[1] (bɔks) *n* **1** boîte, caisse *f.* coffret *m.* **2** *Th* cabine, loge *f.* **box number** *n* boîte postale *f.* **box office** *n* **1** bureau de location *m.* **2** guichet *m.*

box[2] (bɔks) *vt* gifler, boxer. *n* gifle *f.* **boxer** *n* boxeur, pugiliste *m.* **boxing** *n* boxe *f.*

Boxing Day *n* lendemain de Noël *m.*

boy (bɔi) *n* **1** garçon, fils *m.* **2** *inf* gars *m.* **3** élève *m.* **boyfriend** *n* (petit) ami *m.* **boyhood** *n* enfance, adolescence *f.*

boycott (ˈbɔikɔt) *vt* boycotter. *n* boycottage *m.*

bra (bra:) *n* soutien-gorge *m invar.*

brace (breis) *n* **1** paire, couple *f.* **2** attache *f.* **3** *pl* bretelles *f pl.* **4** *tech* vilebrequin *m.* *vt* **1** fortifier. **2** lier.

bracelet (ˈbreislət) *n* bracelet *m.*

bracket (ˈbrækit) *n* **1** support *m.* **2** applique *f.* **3** *gram* parenthèse *f.* *vt* **1** mettre entre parenthèses. **2** accolader.

brag (bræg) *vi* se vanter.

braid (breid) *n* tresse *f.* galon *m.*

Braille (breil) *n* Braille *m.*

brain (brein) *n* **1** cerveau, -aux *m.* **2** cervelle *f.* **brainwash** *vt* endoctriner. **brainwave** *n* idée lumineuse *f.* **brainy** *adj inf* intelligent.

braise (breiz) *vt* braiser.

brake (breik) *n* frein *m.* *vt* freiner, ralentir.

branch (brɑ:ntʃ) *n* **1** branche *f.* **2** embranchement *m.* **3** *comm* succursale *f.* **4** secteur *m.* *v* **branch off** bifurquer. **branch out** se ramifier, se diversifier.

brand (brænd) *n* **1** brandon *m.* **2** fer chaud *m.* **3** stigmate *m.* **4** *comm* marque *f.* *vt* **1** marquer. **2** graver. **3** stigmatiser. **brand-new** *adj* tout neuf.

brandish (ˈbrændiʃ) *vt* brandir.

brandy (ˈbrændi) *n* eau-de-vie *f.* cognac *m.*

brass (brɑ:s) *n* cuivre jaune, laiton *m.* *adj* de cuivre. **brass band** *n* fanfare *f.*

brassiere (ˈbræziə) *n* soutien-gorge *m invar.*

brat (bræt) *n sl* gosse, môme *m,f.*

brave (breiv) courageux, -euse, brave. *vt* braver, affronter.

brawl (brɔ:l) *n* rixe *f.* tapage *m.* *vi* **1** chamailler. **2** brailler.

bray (brei) *vi* braire. *n* braiment *m.*

brazen (ˈbreizən) *adj* **1** d'airain. **2** *inf* effronté, impudent.

Brazil (brəˈzil) *n* Brésil *m.* **Brazilian** *adj,n* brésilien, -ienne.

breach (bri:tʃ) *n* **1** infraction *f.* manque *m.* **2** rupture *f.* **3** brèche *f.* **breach of the peace** attentat contre l'ordre public *m.*

bread (bred) *n* **1** pain *m.* **2** *sl* du fric. **breadcrumb** *n* chapelure *f.* **breadknife** *n* couteau à pain *m.* **breadwinner** *n* chef de famille *m.* gagne-pain *m invar.* **loaf of bread** pain *m.* **wholemeal bread** pain complet.

breadth (bredθ) *n* largeur *f.*

break* (breik) *vt* **1** casser, rompre, briser. **2** amortir. **3** violer, manquer à. **4** ruiner. **break into** s'introduire par effraction. **break out 1** se déclarer. **2** s'échapper. **break up 1** se disperser. **2** morceler. ~*n* **1** rupture *f.* **2** brèche *f.* **3** altération *f.* **4** interruption *f.* **5** répit *m.* **breakage** *n* **1** casse *f.* **2** rupture *f.* **breakdown** *n* **1** *mot* panne *f.* **2** rupture *f.* **3** effondrement *m.* **4** *med* dépression nerveuse *f.* **breakthrough** *n* **1** découverte *f.* pas en avant *m.* **2** *mil* percée *f.*

breakfast (ˈbrekfəst) *n* petit déjeuner *m.* *vi* prendre le petit déjeuner.

breast (brest) *n* sein *m.* poitrine *f.* **breastbone** *n* sternum, bréchet *m.* **breaststroke** *n* brasse *f.*

breath (breθ) *n* haleine *f.* souffle *m.* **out of breath** essoufflé. **breathtaking** *adj* **1** à vous couper le souffle. **2** ahurissant.

breathe (bri:ð) *vt,vi* respirer. *vi* souffler. **breathe in/out** aspirer/exhaler. **breathing** *n* respiration *f.* **breathing space** *n* répit *m.*

breed* (bri:d) *n* race, espèce *f.* *vt* **1** produire, engendrer. **2** élever. *vi* se reproduire.

breeze (bri:z) *n* brise *f.*

Breton (ˈbretn̩) *adj,n* breton, -onne. **Breton** (language) *n* breton *m.*

brew (bru:) *vt* **1** brasser. **2** faire infuser. *vi* **1** s'infuser. **2** se préparer. *n* **1** infusion *f.* **2** brassage *m.* **brewery** *n* brasserie *f.*

bribe (braib) *n* **1** paiement illicite. **2** *inf* pot-de-vin *m.* *vt* corrompre, acheter. **bribery** *n* corruption *f.*

brick (brik) *n* **1** brique *f.* **2** *inf* chic type *m.* **bricklayer** *n* maçon *m.*

bride (braid) *n* fiancée, mariée *f.* **bridegroom** *n* nouveau marié *m.* **bridesmaid** *n* demoiselle d'honneur *f.*

bridge[1] (bridʒ) *n* **1** pont *m.* **2** *naut* passerelle *f.* **3** *anat* dos *m.* arête *f.* *v* **bridge a gap** combler une lacune.

bridge[2] (bridʒ) *n game* bridge *m.* **game of bridge** partie de bridge *f.*

bridle (ˈbraidl̩) *n* bridle *f.* **bridlepath** *n* sentier pour cavaliers *m.* piste cavalière *f.*

brief (bri:f) *adj* bref, brève, succinct. *n* **1** dossier *m.* **2** résumé *m.* *vt* documenter. **briefing** *n* instructions *f pl.* **briefcase** *n* serviette *f.*

brigade (briˈgeid) *n* brigade *f.* **brigadier** *n* général de brigade *m.*

bright (brait) *adj* **1** lumineux, -euse, brillant. **2** vif, vive, éveillé. **3** intelligent. **brighten** *vt* faire briller. *vi* **1** s'éclaircir. **2** s'épanouir. **brightness** *n* **1** éclat *m.* **2** clarté *f.* **3** vivacité *f.*

brilliant (ˈbriliənt) *adj* brillant. **brilliance** *n* éclat, lustre *m.*

brim (brim) *n* bord *m.* **to the brim** à ras bord. ~*v* **brim over** déborder.

bring* (briŋ) *vt* **1** amener, apporter. **2** mettre. **3** porter. **bring about** occasionner, aménager. **bring back** rapporter. **bring in 1** faire entrer. **2** *comm* rapporter. **bring out 1** faire sortir. **2** mettre en évidence, faire valoir. **bring round 1** ranimer. **2** rallier. **bring together** réunir. **bring up 1** élever. **2** soulever. **3** apporter. **4** vomir.

brink (briŋk) *n* bord *m.*

brisk (brisk) *adj* vif, vive, alerte, animé.

bristle (ˈbrisəl) *n* soie *f.* poil *m.* *vt* hérisser.

Britain (ˈbritn̩) *n* Grande-Bretagne *f.* **British** *adj* britannique. **British Isles** *n pl* Iles Britanniques *m pl.* **Briton** *n* anglais *m.*

Brittany (ˈbritəni) *n* Bretagne *f.*

brittle (ˈbritl̩) *adj* cassant, fragile.

broad (brɔ:d) *adj* **1** large. **2** (of an accent) prononcé. **3** hardi. **broad bean** *n* fève *f.* **broadcast** *n* émission, transmission radiodiffusée *f.* *vt* **1** radiodiffuser. **2** annoncer à la radio. **broad-minded** *adj* tolérant. **broaden** *vt* élargir. *vi* s'élargir. **broadness** *n* largeur *f.*

broccoli (ˈbrɔkəli) *n* brocoli *m.*

brochure (ˈbrouʃə) *n* brochure *f.*

broke (brouk) *v* see **break.** *adj inf* fauché, sans le sou.

broken (ˈbroukən) *v* see **break.**

broker (ˈbroukə) *n* courtier *m*. **stock-broker** *n* agent de change *m*.
bronchitis (brɔŋˈkaitis) *n* bronchite *f*.
bronze (brɔnz) *n* bronze *m*. *adj* de bronze. *vt* bronzer. *vi* se bronzer.
brooch (broutʃ) *n* broche *f*.
brood (bru:d) *n* **1** couvée *f*. **2** *inf* marmaille. *vi* couver. **brood over** ressasser, ruminer.
brook (bruk) *n* ruisseau, -aux *m*.
broom (bru:m) *n* **1** balai *m*. **2** *bot* genêt *m*.
brothel (ˈbrɔðəl) *n* bordel *m*.
brother (ˈbrʌðə) *n* frère *m*. **brother-in-law** *n* beau-frère *m*. **brotherhood** *n* **1** fraternité *f*. **2** *rel* confrèrie *f*.
brow (brau) *n* **1** sourcil *m*. **2** front *m*. **3** *geog* sommet *m*.
brown (braun) *adj* **1** brun, marron. **2** bronzé. *vt* **1** brunir. **2** *cul* faire roussir. *vi* (se) brunir. **be browned off** avoir le cafard.
browse (brauz) *vt* brouter. *vi* bouquiner.
bruise (bru:z) *n* contusion *f*. bleu *m*. *vt* meurtrir.
brunette (bru:ˈnet) *n* brunette *f*.
brush (brʌʃ) *n* **1** brosse *f*. **2** *Art* pinceau, -aux *m*. **3** coup de brosse *m*. **4** escarmouche *f*. *vt* **1** brosser. **2** effleurer, frôler. **brush up 1** brosser. **2** rafraîchir, dérouiller.
brusque (bru:sk) *adj* brusque, bourru
Brussels (ˈbrʌsəlz) *n* Bruxelles *f*. **Brussels sprout** *n* chou de Bruxelles *m*.
brute (bru:t) *n* brute *f*. animal, -aux *m*. *adj* brut, brutal, -aux. **brutal** *adj* brutal, -aux, animal, -aux.
bubble (ˈbʌbəl) *n* bulle *f*. *vi* **1** bouillonner. **2** pétiller.
buck[1] (bʌk) *n* **1** daim, chevreuil *m*. **2** mâle *m*.
buck[2] (bʌk) *vi* se cabrer. **buck someone off** désarçonner quelqu'un.
bucket (ˈbʌkit) *n* **1** seau, -aux *m*. **2** godet *m*.
buckle (ˈbʌkəl) *n* boucle *f*. *vt* **1** boucler. **2** *tech* déjeter, voiler. *vi* se déformer.
bud (bʌd) *n* **1** bourgeon *m*. **2** bouton *m*. *vi* bourgeonner. **budding** *adj* **1** en bouton. **2** en herbe.
Buddhism (ˈbudizəm) *n* bouddhisme *m*. **Buddhist** *n* bouddhiste *m,f*. *adj* bouddhique.
budget (ˈbʌdʒit) *n* budget *m*.
buffalo (ˈbʌfəlou) *n pl* **-os** *or* **-oes** buffle *m*.
buffer (ˈbʌfə) *n* **1** tampon. **2** amortisseur *m*.
buffet[1] (ˈbʌfit) *n* coup *m*. *vt* souffleter. *vi* se battre à coups de poing.
buffet[2] (ˈbufei)) *n* buffet *m*.
bug (bʌg) *n* punaise *f*.
bugle (ˈbju:gəl) *n* clairon *m*.
build* (bild) *vt* **1** bâtir, construire. **2** échafauder. **3** fonder. *n* carrure, stature *f*. **builder** *n* entrepreneur *m*. **building** *n* **1** construction *f*. **2** bâtiment *m*. *adj* de construction, à bâtir. **building society** *n* société immobilière *f*.
bulb (bʌlb) *n* **1** *bot* bulbe, oignon *m*. **2** ampoule, lampe *f*.
Bulgaria (bʌlˈgɛəriə) *n* Bulgarie *f*. **Bulgarian** *adj,n* bulgare.
bulge (bʌldʒ) *n* renflement *m*. bosse *f*. *vi* faire saillie, ballonner.
bulk (bʌlk) *n* **1** charge *f*. **2** grosseur *f*. volume *m*. **in bulk** en gros, en vrac.
bull (bul) *n* **1** taureau, -aux *m*. **2** mâle *m*. **bulldog** *n* bouledogue *m*. **bulldoze** *vt* **1** intimider, menacer. **2** passer au bulldozer. **bulldozer** *n* bulldozer *m*. **bullfight** *n* corrida *f*. **bullring** *n* arène *f*. **bull's eye** *n* mouche *f*. noir *m*.
bullet (ˈbulit) *n* balle *f*. **bullet-proof** *adj* à l'épreuve des balles, blindé.
bulletin (ˈbulətin) *n* bulletin, communiqué *m*. **news bulletin** informations *f pl*.
bully (ˈbuli) *n* **1** brute *f*. tyran *m*. **2** bravache *m*. *vt* malmener.
bumble bee (ˈbʌmbəl) *n* bourdon *m*.
bump (bʌmp) *n* **1** choc *m*. secousse *f*. **2** bosse *f*. *vt* cogner. **bump into 1** entrer en collision avec. **2** *inf* rencontrer. **bumper** *n* pare-chocs *m invar*. *adj inf* magnifique, comble.
bun (bʌn) *n* **1** *cul* petit pain *m*. brioche *f*. **2** chignon *m*.
bunch (bʌntʃ) *n* **1** bouquet *m*. grappe *f*. **2** touffe *f*. **3** groupe *m*. *vt* réunir.
bundle (ˈbʌndḷ) *n* **1** ballot, paquet *m*. **2** liasse *f*. *vt* botteler, entasser.
bungalow (ˈbʌŋgəlou) *n* bungalow *m*.
bungle (ˈbʌŋgəl) *n* gâchis *m*. *vt* bousiller, gâcher. **bungling** *adj* maladroit.
bunk (bʌŋk) *n* couchette *f*.
bunker (ˈbʌŋkə) *n* **1** soute *f*. **2** *sport* banquette *f*.
buoy (bɔi) *n* bouée, balise flottante *f*. **buoyancy** *n* **1** flottabilité *f*. **2** *inf* entrain *m*. **buoyant** *adj* **1** flottable, léger, -ère. **2** vif, vive.
burden (ˈbə:dn̩) *n* fardeau, -aux *m*. charge *f*. *vt* **1** charger. **2** être un fardeau pour.
bureau (ˈbjuərou) *n* **1** bureau, -aux *m*. **2** secrétaire *m*.
bureaucracy (bjuˈrɔkrəsi) *n* bureaucratie *f*. **bureaucrat** *n* **1** bureaucrate *m,f*. **2** *inf* rond-de-cuir *m*.
burglar (ˈbə:glə) *n* cambrioleur *m*. **burglar**

alarm *n* sonnerie d'alarme *f.* **burglary** *n* vol avec effraction, cambriolage *m.* **burgle** *vt* cambrioler, dévaliser.

burn* (bə:n) *vt* **1** brûler. **2** incendier. *vi* flamber. *n* brûlure *f.* **burning** *adj* brûlant, ardent.

burrow ('bʌrou) *n* terrier *m.* *vt* creuser. *vi* se terrer.

burst* (bə:st) *vi* éclater, crever. *vt* faire éclater, fendre. **burst in** faire irruption. ~*n* **1** éclatement *m.* explosion *f.* **2** élan *m.* **bursting** *adj* **1** sur le point d'éclater. **2** débordant.

bury ('beri) *vt* enterrer. **burial** *n* enterrement *m.* **burial ground** *n* cimetière *m.*

bus (bʌs) *n* autobus, bus, car *m.* **bus-stop** *n* arrêt du bus *m.*

bush (buʃ) *n* **1** buisson *m.* **2** arbuste *m.* **3** brousse *f.*

bushy ('buʃi:) *adj* **1** touffu. **2** broussailleux, -euse.

business ('biznis) *n* **1** affaire, occupation *f.* **2** affaires *f pl.* **3** commerce *m.* **set up in business** s'établir. **businessman** *n* homme d'affaires *m.*

bust[1] (bʌst) *n* **1** *Art* buste *m.* **2** *anat* poitrine *f.*

bust[2] (bʌst) *vi inf* éclater. **go bust** faire faillite.

bustle ('bʌsəl) *n* agitation *f.* mouvement *m.* *vi* se remuer, s'affairer. *vt* faire dépêcher.

busy ('bizi) *adj* affairé, occupé. **busybody** *n* officieux, -euse. **busy oneself with** s'occuper à.

but (bət; *stressed* bʌt) *conj* **1** mais. **2** sauf que. *adv* ne...que, seulement. *prep* excepté, sinon. **but for** sans.

butcher ('butʃə) *n* boucher *m.* *vt* égorger. **butcher's shop** *n* boucherie *f.* **butchery** *n* carnage *m.*

butler ('bʌtlə) *n* **1** maître d'hôtel *m.* **2** sommelier *m.*

butt[1] (bʌt) *n* **1** bout *m.* **2** crosse *f.* **3** mégot *m.*

butt[2] (bʌt) *n* souffre-douleur *m invar.*

butt[3] (bʌt) *vt* donner des coups de corne à, buter. **butt in** *inf* intervenir sans façon, s'ingérer. ~*n* coup de tête *or* corne *m.*

butter ('bʌtə) *n* beurre *m.* *vt* beurrer. **buttercup** *n* **1** renoncule *f.* **2** *inf* bouton d'or *m.* **butter-fingers** *n inf* maladroit. **butterfly** *n* papillon *m.* **butterscotch** *n* caramel dur au beurre *m.*

buttocks ('bʌtəks) *n pl* **1** *anat* derrière *m.* fesses *f pl.* **2** *zool* croupe *f.*

button ('bʌtn̩) *n* bouton *m.* *vt* boutonner. **buttonhole** *n* boutonnière *f.* *vt inf* attraper, cramponner.

buttress ('bʌtrəs) *n* arc-boutant *m.*

buy* (bai) *vt* acheter. **buy up** accaparer. ~*n* affaire *f.* achat *m.* **buyer** *n* **1** acheteur, -euse. **2** *comm* chef de rayon *m.*

buzz (bʌz) *n* **1** bourdonnement, vrombissement *m.* **2** bruit confus, brouhaha *m.* *vi* bourdonner.

by (bai) *prep* **1** près de, à côté de. **2** au bord de. **3** par. **4** de. **5** à. **6** sur. *adv* **1** près. **2** de côté. **by and by** tout à l'heure. **by-election** *n* élection partielle *f.* **bylaw** *n* arrêté municipal, -aux *m.* **bypass** *n* route d'évitement *f.* détour *m.* *vt* contourner, éviter. **bystander** *n* spectateur, -trice.

Byzantine (bi'zæntain, bai-) *adj,n* byzantin.

C

cab (kæb) **1** fiacre *m.* **2** taxi *m.* **3** (of a lorry, etc.) cabine *f.*

cabaret ('kæbərei) *n* **1** cabaret, café-concert *m.* **2** spectacle au cabaret *m.*

cabbage ('kæbidʒ) *n* chou, choux *m.*

cabin ('kæbin) *n* **1** cabine *f.* **2** cabane *f.* **cabin cruiser** *n* yacht à moteur *m.*

cabinet ('kæbinət) *n* cabinet *m.* **cabinet-maker** *n* ébéniste *m.* **cabinet minister** *n* ministre d'état.

cable ('keibəl) *n* câble *m.* *vt* câbler.

cackle ('kækəl) *n* caquet *m.* *vt* **1** caqueter. **2** ricaner.

cactus ('kæktəs) *n, pl* **-ti** *or* **-tuses** cactus *m.*

cadence ('keidn̩s) *n* cadence *f.*

cadet (kə'det) *n* cadet *m.*

cafe ('kæfei) *n* café(-restaurant) *m,*

cafeteria (kæfi'tiəriə) *n* cafétéria *f.* libre-service *m.*

caffeine ('kæfi:n) *n* caféine *f.*

cage (keidʒ) *n* cage *f.*

cake (keik) *n* **1** *cul* gâteau, -aux *m.* **2** pain, bloc, morceau, -aux *m.* *vi* se cailler.

calamity (kə'læməti) *n* calamité *f.* désastre *m.*

calcium ('kælsiəm) *n* calcium *m.*

calculate ('kælkjuleit) *vt,vi* calculer. *vt* combiner. *vi* compter. **calculation** *n* calcul *m.* **calculator** *n* machine à calculer *f.*

calendar ('kælində) *n* calendrier *m.*

calf[1] (kɑ:f) *n, pl* **calves** *zool* veau, -aux *m.*

calf[2] (kɑ:f) *n, pl* **calves** *anat* mollet *m.*

calibre ('kælibə) *n* calibre *m.*

call (kɔ:l) *vt* **1** appeler. **2** convoquer. **call for** demander. **call on** passer chez. **call off** décommander. **call out** appeler. ~*n* **1** appel, cri *m.* **2** visite *f.* **3** demande *f.* **4** *naut* escale *f.* **callbox** *n* taxiphone *m.* cabine téléphonique *f.*

callous (ˈkæləs) *adj* endurci, insensible.

calm (kɑ:m) *adj,n* calme *m.* *vt* calmer. **calm down** se calmer.

calorie (ˈkæləri) *n* calorie *f.*

Cambodia (kæmˈboudiə) *n* Cambodge *m.* **Cambodian** *adj,n* cambodgien, -ienne.

came (keim) *v* see **come.**

camel (ˈkæməl) *n* chameau, -aux *m.* chamelle *f.* **camelhair** *n* poil de chameau *m.*

camera (ˈkæmrə) *n* appareil photographique *m.* **cameraman** *n* **1** photographe *m.* **2** opérateur *m.*

camouflage (ˈkæməflɑ:ʒ) *n* camouflage *m.* *vt* camoufler.

camp[1] (kæmp) *vt,vi* camper. *n* camp *m.* **campbed** *n* lit de camp *m.* **camping** *n* camping *m.* **camping site** *n* terrain de camping *m.*

camp[2] (kæmp) *adj* **1** exagéré, affecté. **2** efféminé. **3** *inf* homosexuel, -elle.

campaign (kæmˈpein) *n* campagne *f.* *vi* faire campagne.

campus (ˈkæmpəs) *n* campus *m.*

can[*1] (kæn) *v mod aux* **1** pouvoir. **2** savoir.

can[2] (kæn) *n* **1** bidon, pot *m.* **2** boîte *f.* *vt* mettre en boîte.

Canada (ˈkænədə) *n* Canada *m.* **Canadian** *adj,n* canadien, -ienne.

canal (kəˈnæl) *n* canal, -aux *m.*

canary (kəˈnɛəri) *n* serin *m.*

Canary Islands *n* îles Canaries *f pl.*

cancel (ˈkænsəl) *vt* annuler. **cancellation** *n* **1** annulation *f.* **2** contre-ordre *m.*

cancer (ˈkænsə) *n* **1** cancer *m.* **2** *cap* Cancer *m.*

candid (ˈkændid) *adj* **1** franc, franche. **2** impartial, -aux.

candidate (ˈkændidət) *n* candidat *m.*

candle (ˈkændḷ) *n* bougie *f.* **candlelight** *n* lumière d'une chandelle *f.* **candlestick** *n* chandelier, bougeoir *m.*

candour (ˈkændə) *n* **1** franchise *f.* **2** impartialité *f.*

cane (ˈkein) *n* canne *f.* *vt* **1** fouetter. **2** canner.

canine (ˈkeinain) *adj* canin. *n* (tooth) canine *f.*

cannabis (ˈkænəbis) *n* chanvre indien *m.*

cannibal (ˈkænəbəl) *adj,n* cannibale. **cannibalism** *n* cannibalisme *m.*

cannon (ˈkænən) *n* canon *m.* **cannonball** *n* boulet de canon *m.*

cannot (ˈkænət) contraction of **can not.**

canoe (kəˈnu:) *n* canoë *m.* périssoire *f.*

canon[1] (ˈkænən) *n* (law) canon *m.* règle *f.* **canonical** *adj* canonique, canonial, -aux. **canonize** *vt* canoniser. **canonization** *n* canonisation *f.*

canon[2] (ˈkænən) *n* (title) chanoine *m.*

canopy (ˈkænəpi) *n* dais *m.*

canteen (kænˈti:n) *n* **1** cantine *f.* **2** *mil* bidon *m.* **canteen (of cutlery)** ménagère *f.*

canter (ˈkæntə) *n* petit galop *m.* *vi* aller au petit galop.

canton (ˈkæntɔn) *n* canton *m.*

canvas (ˈkænvəs) *n* toile *f.*

canvass (ˈkænvəs) *vi* faire une campagne électorale. *vt* **1** solliciter. **2** discuter. **canvasser** *n* **1** *pol* agent électoral *m.* **2** *comm* demarcheur *m.*

canyon (ˈkænjən) *n* cañon *m.*

cap (kæp) *n* bonnet *m.* toque, casquette *f.* *vt* **1** coiffer. **2** couvrir. **3** surpasser.

capable (ˈkeipəbəl) *adj* **1** capable, compétent. **2** susceptible. **capability** *n* **1** capacité *f.* **2** faculté *f.*

capacity (kəˈpæsiti) *n* capacité *f.*

cape[1] (keip) *n* cape, pèlerine *f.*

cape[2] (keip) *n* *geog* cap *m.*

caper (ˈkeipə) *n* *cul* câpre *f.*

capital (ˈkæpitḷ) *n* **1** capitale *f.* **2** *comm* capital, -aux *m.* *adj* **1** capital, -aux. **2** essentiel, -elle. **capital letter** *n* lettre majuscule *f.* **capitalism** *n* capitalisme *m.* **capitalist** *adj,n* capitaliste. **capitalize** *vt* **1** capitaliser. **2** exploiter.

capricious (kəˈpriʃəs) *adj* capricieux, -euse.

Capricorn (ˈkæprikɔ:n) *n* Capricorne *m.*

capsicum (ˈkæpsikəm) *n* piment *m.*

capsize (ˈkæpsaiz) *vi* chavirer. *vt* faire chavirer.

capsule (ˈkæpsju:l) *n* capsule f.

captain (ˈkæptin) *n* capitaine *m.*

caption (ˈkæpʃən) *n* **1** rubrique *f.* **2** légende *f.* **3** sous-titre *m.*

captivate (ˈkæptiveit) *vt* captiver.

captive (ˈkæptiv) *adj,n* captif, -ive. **captivity** *n* captivité *f.*

capture (ˈkæptʃə) *n* capture, prise *f.* *vt* capturer, prendre.

car (kɑ:) *n* **1** automobile, voiture *f.* **2** (of a train) wagon *m.* **car park** *n* parking *m.*

caramel (ˈkærəməl) *n* caramel *m.*

carat (ˈkærəṭ) *n* carat *m.*

caravan (ˈkærəvæn) *n* caravane *f.*

caraway (ˈkærəwei) *n* cumin *m.*

carbohydrate (kɑ:bouˈhaidreit) *n* hydrate de carbone *m.*

carbon (ˈkɑ:bən) *n* carbone *m.* **carbon dioxide**

n anhydride carbonique *m.* **carbon paper** *n* papier carbone *m.*
carburettor (ka:bju'retə) *n* carburateur *m.*
carcass ('ka:kəs) *n* cadavre *m.* carcasse *f.*
card (ka:d) *n* carte *f.* **cardboard** *n* carton *m.*
cardigan ('ka:digən) *n* cardigan, gilet de tricot *m.*
cardinal ('ka:dinḷ) *adj,n* cardinal, -aux *m.*
care (kɛə) *n* **1** soin *m.* **2** attention *f.* **3** souci *m.* **care of** chez. **take care** prendre garde. ~*vi* se soucier. **care for 1** aimer. **2** soigner. **carefree** *adj* insouciant. **careful** *adj* **1** soigneux, -euse. **2** attentif, -ive. **3** prudent. **4** économe. **careless** *adj* **1** insouciant. **2** négligent. **caretaker** *n* gardien, -ienne, concierge *m,f.*
career (kə'riə) *n* carrière, course *f.* *vi* courir rapidement.
caress (kə'res) *n* caresse *f.* *vt* caresser, câliner.
cargo ('ka:gou) *n, pl* **cargoes** cargaison *f.*
Caribbean (kæri'biən) *adj* des Caraïbes. **Caribbean Islands** *n* Antilles *f pl.* **Caribbean (Sea)** *n* Mer des Antilles *f.*
caricature ('kærikətjuə) *n* caricature *f.* *vt* caricaturer. **caricaturist** *n* caricaturiste *m.*
carnal ('ka:nḷ) *adj* charnel, -elle.
carnation (ka:'neiʃən) *n* œillet *m.*
carnival ('ka:nivəl) *n* carnaval *m.*
carnivorous (ka:'nivərəs) *adj* carnivore.
carol ('kærəl) *n* chant *m.* **Christmas carol** *n* noël *m.*
carpenter ('ka:pintə) *n* charpentier, menuisier *m.* **carpentry** *n* charpenterie *f.*
carpet ('ka:pit) *n* tapis *m.* **carpet-sweeper** *n* balai mécanique *m.*
carriage ('kæridʒ) *n* **1** voiture *f.* **2** port, transport *m.* **3** maintien *m.* **dual carriageway** *n* route à double voie *f.*
carrier ('kæriə) *n* porteur, -euse. **carrier bag** *n* (grand) sac *m.*
carrot ('kærət) *n* carotte *f.*
carry ('kæri) *vt* **1** porter. **2** transporter. **3** entraîner. **4** adopter. **5** retenir. *vi* porter. **carry on** continuer. **carry out** exercer. **carry-cot** *n* porte-bébé *m invar.*
cart (ka:t) *n* charrette *f.* *vt* transporter. **carthorse** *n* cheval de trait *m.* **cartwheel** *n* roue de charrette *f.* **turn cartwheels** faire la roue.
cartilage ('ka:tlidʒ) *n* cartilage *m.*
carton ('ka:tṇ) *n* carton *m.*
cartoon (ka:'tu:n) *n* **1** carton *m.* caricature *f.* **2** dessin animé *m.*
cartridge ('ka:tridʒ) *n* cartouche *f.*
carve (ka:v) *vt* **1** *Art* sculpter. **2** découper. **carving** *n* sculpture *f.* **carving-knife** *n* couteau à découper *m.*
cascade (kæ'skeid) *n* cascade *f.*
case[1] (keis) *n* **1** cas *m.* **2** *law* affaire *f.*
case[2] (keis) *n* **1** caisse *f.* **2** boîte *f.* **3** étui *m.* *vt* envelopper, encaisser.
cash (kæʃ) *n* espèces *f pl.* monnaie *f.* *vt* toucher. **cash desk** *n* caisse *f.* **cash register** *n* caisse enregistreuse *f.*
cashier[1] (kæ'ʃiə) *n* caissier, -ière.
cashier[2] (kæ'ʃiə) *vt* casser.
cashmere (kæʃ'miə) *n* cachemire *m.*
casino (kə'si:nou) *n* casino *m.*
casket ('ka:skit) *n* coffret *m.*
casserole ('kæsəroul) *n* **1** cocotte en terre *f.* **2** ragoût *m.*
cassette (kə'set) *n* cassette *f.* chargeur *m.*
cassock ('kæsək) *n* soutane *f.*
cast* (ka:st) *vt* **1** lancer. **2** projeter. **3** *tech* couler. **cast off** rejeter ~*n* **1** coup *m.* **2** *Th* distribution *f.* **3** moule *m.*
castanets (kæstə'nets) *n pl* castagnettes *f pl.*
caste (ka:st) *n* caste *f.*
castle ('ka:səl) *n* **1** château, -aux *m.* **2** *game* tour *f.*
castrate (kæ'streit) *vt* châtrer. **castration** *n* castration *f.*
casual ('kæʒuəl) *adj* **1** fortuit. **2** insouciant. **casualty** *n* **1** accident *m.* **2** *pl* pertes *f pl.*
cat (kæt) *n* chat, chatte. **cat's eye** *n* *mot* cataphote *m.*
catalogue ('kætəlɔg) *n* catalogue *m.* *vt* cataloguer.
catamaran (kætəmə'ræn) *n* catamaran *m.*
catapult ('kætəpʌlt) *n* lance-pierre *m invar.* catapulte *f.* *vt* catapulter, lancer.
cataract ('kætərækt) *n* cataracte *f.*
catarrh (kə'ta:) *n* catarrhe *m.*
catastrophe (kə'tæstrəfi) *n* catastrophe *f.* **catastrophic** *adj* désastreux, -euse.
catch* (kætʃ) *vt* **1** attraper. **2** surprendre. **3** accrocher. **4** comprendre. *vi* s'accrocher. **catch up** rattraper ~*n* **1** prise *f.* **2** loquet *m.* **3** attrape *f.*
catechism ('kætikizəm) *n* catéchisme *m.*
category ('kætigəri) *n* catégorie *f.* **categorical** *adj* catégorique. **categorize** *vt* classer.
cater ('keitə) *vi* **cater for 1** approvisionner. **2** pourvoir à. **caterer** *n* fournisseur, traiteur *m.*
caterpillar ('kætəpilə) *n* chenille *f.*
cathedral (kə'θi:drəl) *n* cathédrale *f.*

cathode (ˈkæθoud) *n* cathode *f.*
catholic (ˈkæθlik) *n* catholique *m,f.* *adj* **1** universel, -elle. **2** catholique. **catholicism** *n* catholicisme *m.*
catkin (ˈkætkin) *n* chaton *m.*
cattle (ˈkætl̩) *n* bétail, bestiaux *m.*
caught (kɔ:t) *v* see **catch.**
cauliflower (ˈkɔliflauə) *n* chou-fleur *m.*
cause (kɔ:z) *n* **1** cause *f.* **2** motif *m.* *vt* causer, occasionner.
causeway (ˈkɔ:zwei) *n* chaussée *f.*
caustic (ˈkɔ:stik) *adj* caustique.
caution (ˈkɔ:ʃən) *n* **1** prudence *f.* **2** *law* caution *f.* **3** avis *m.* *vt* avertir. **cautious** *adj* prudent.
cavalry (ˈkævəlri) *n* cavalerie *f.*
cave (keiv) *n* caverne, grotte *f.* *v* **cave in 1** s'effondrer. **2** céder.
caviar (ˈkævia:) *n* caviar *m.*
cavity (ˈkæviti) *n* cavité *f.*
cayenne (keiˈen) *n* *also* **cayenne pepper** cayenne, poivre de Cayenne *m.*
cease (si:s) *vt,vi* cesser. **cease-fire** *n* cessez-le-feu *m.* **ceaseless** *adj* incessant.
cedar (ˈsi:də) *n* cèdre *m.*
cedilla (siˈdilə) *n* cédille *f.*
ceiling (ˈsi:liŋ) *n* plafond *m.*
celebrate (ˈseləbreit) *vt* célébrer. **celebration** *n* célébration *f.* **celebrity** *n* célébrité *f.*
celery (ˈseləri) *n* céleri *m.*
celestial (siˈlestiəl) *adj* céleste.
celibate (ˈselibət) *adj,n* célibataire. **celibacy** *n* célibat *m.*
cell (sel) *n* **1** cellule *f.* **2** (of a prison) cachot *m.*
cellar (ˈselə) *n* cave *f.*
cello (ˈtʃelou) *n* violoncelle *m.*
Cellophane (ˈseləfein) *n* *Tdmk* Cellophane *f.*
Celt (kelt) *n* Celte *m,f.* **Celtic** *adj,n* celtique. **Celtic** (language) *n* celtique *m.*
cement (siˈment) *n* ciment *m.* *vt* cimenter.
cemetery (ˈsemətri) *n* cimetière *m.*
censor (ˈsensə) *n* censeur *m.* *vt* censurer, interdire. **censorship** *n* censure *f.*
censure (ˈsenʃə) *n* blâme *m.* *vt* blâmer, censurer.
census (ˈsensəs) *n* recensement *m.*
cent (sent) *n* **1** cent *m.* **2** *inf* sou *m.* **per cent** pour cent.
centenary (senˈti:nəri) *adj,n* centenaire *m.*
centigrade (ˈsentigreid) *adj* centigrade.
centime (sɔnˈti:m) *n* centime *m.*
centimetre (ˈsentimi:tə) *n* centimètre *m.*
centipede (ˈsentipi:d) *n* mille-pattes *m.*
centre (ˈsentə) *n* centre *m.* *vt* placer au centre. *vi* se concentrer. **centre-forward** *n* avant-centre *m.* **centre-half** *n* demi-centre *m.* **central** *adj* central, -aux. **central heating** *n* chaffage central *m.* **centralization** *n* centralisation *f.* **centralize** *vt* centraliser.
century (ˈsentʃəri) *n* siècle *m.*
ceramic (siˈræmik) *adj* céramique. *n pl* céramique *f.*
cereal (ˈsiəriəl) *adj,n* céréale *f.*
ceremony (ˈserəməni) *n* cérémonie *f.* **without ceremony** sans façon. **ceremonial** *adj* de cérémonie. *n* cérémonial, -aux *m.* **ceremonious** *adj* cérémonieux, -euse.
certain (ˈsə:tn̩) *adj* certain, sûr. **make certain** s'assurer. **certainly** *adv* assurément. **certainty** *n* certitude *f.*
certify (ˈsə:tifai) *vt* certifier, attester. **certificate** *n* **1** certificat *m.* **2** acte *m.*
Ceylon (siˈlɔn) *n* Ceylan *m.* **Ceylonese** *adj,n* cingalais.
chaffinch (ˈtʃæfintʃ) *n* pinson *m.*
chain (tʃein) *n* chaîne *f.* **chain-smoke** *vi* fumer des cigarettes à la file. **chain-store** *n* succursale de grand magasin *f.*
chair (tʃɛə) *n* **1** chaise *f.* **2** *educ* chaire *f.* **chair-lift** *n* télésiège *m.* **chairman** *n* président *m.*
chalet (ˈʃælei) *n* chalet *m.*
chalk (tʃɔ:k) *n* **1** craie *f.* **2** calcaire *m.* **chalky** *adj* **1** crayeux, -euse. **2** calcaire.
challenge (ˈtʃæləndʒ) *n* défi *m.* *vt* **1** défier. **2** contester.
chamber (ˈtʃeimbə) *n* **1** chambre *f.* **2** *pl* cabinet *m.* étude *f.* **chambermaid** *n* femme de chambre *f.* **chamber music** *n* musique de chambre *f.*
chamberlain (ˈtʃeimbəlin) *n* chambellan *m.*
chameleon (kəˈmi:liən) *n* caméléon *m.*
chamois (ˈʃæmwa:) *n* chamois *m.*
champagne (ʃæmˈpein) *n* champagne *m.*
champion (ˈtʃæmpiən) *n* champion, -ionne. *vt* défendre. **championship** *n* championnat *m.*
chance (tʃa:ns) *n* **1** chance *f.* hasard *m.* **2** occasion *f.* *vt* risquer. *vi* arriver par hasard. *adj* fortuit.
chancellor (ˈtʃa:nsələ) *n* chancelier *m.*
chandelier (ʃændəˈliə) *n* lustre *m.*
change (tʃeindʒ) *n* **1** changement *m.* **2** monnaie *f.* **3** *comm* change *m.* *vt* changer. *vi* se changer.
channel (ˈtʃænl̩) *n* **1** canal, -aux *m.* **2** voie *f.* **3** (television) chaîne *f.* **4** *cap* Manche *f.* *vt* **1** creuser. **2** diriger.

Channel Islands *n pl* îles Anglo-Normandes *f pl*.
chant (tʃɑ:nt) *n* chant *m*. *vt* psalmodier.
chaos (ˈkeiɔs) *n* chaos *m invar*. **chaotic** *adj* chaotique.
chap[1] (tʃæp) *n* gerçure *f*. *vt* gercer, crevasser. *vi* se gercer.
chap[2] (tʃæp) *n inf* garçon, type *m*.
chapel (ˈtʃæpəl) *n* chapelle *f*.
chaperon (ˈʃæpəroun) *n* chaperon *m*. *vt* chaperonner.
chaplain (ˈtʃæplin) *n* aumônier *m*.
chapter (ˈtʃæptə) *n* chapitre *m*.
char[1] (tʃɑ:) *vt* carboniser. *vi* se carboniser.
char[2] (tʃɑ:) *vi* faire des ménages. **charwoman** *n* femme de ménage *f*.
character (ˈkæriktə) *n* **1** caractère *m*. **2** réputation *f*. **3** *Th* personnage *m*. **characteristic** *adj,n* caractéristique *f*. **characterize** *vt* caractériser.
charcoal (ˈtʃɑ:koul) *n* charbon (de bois) *m*.
charge (tʃɑ:dʒ) *n* **1** charge *f*. **2** devoir *m*. **3** prix *m*. frais *m pl*. **4** recommandation *f*. *vt,vi* charger. *vt* **1** ordonner de faire. **2** payer. **3** *law* accuser.
chariot (ˈtʃæriət) *n* char *m*.
charisma (kəˈrizmə) *n* charisme *m*.
charity (ˈtʃæriti) *n* **1** charité *f*. **2** œuvre de bienfaisance *f*. **charitable** *adj* charitable.
charm (tʃɑ:m) *n* **1** charme *m*. **2** porte-bonheur *m invar*. *vt* charmer, enchanter. **charming** *adj* ravissant, charmant.
chart (tʃɑ:t) *n* **1** *naut* carte *f*. **2** tableau, -aux *m*. *vt* porter sur une carte.
charter (ˈtʃɑ:tə) *n* **1** charte *f*. **2** *comm* affrètement *m*. *vt* affréter.
chase (tʃeis) *n* chasse *f*. *vt* chasser, poursuivre.
chasm (ˈkæzəm) *n* abîme *m*.
chassis (ˈʃæsi) *n* châssis *m*.
chaste (tʃeist) *adj* **1** chaste. **2** pur. **chastity** *n* **1** chasteté *f*. **2** pureté *f*.
chastise (tʃæˈstaiz) *vt* châtier, corriger. **chastisement** *n* châtiment *m*.
chat (tʃæt) *n inf* causerie *f*. *vi* bavarder, causer.
chatter (ˈtʃætə) *n* bavardage *m*. *vi* **1** bavarder. **2** (of teeth) claquer. **chatterbox** *n inf* jacasse *f*. moulin à paroles *m*.
chauffeur (ˈʃoufə) *n* chauffeur *m*.
chauvinism (ˈʃouvinizəm) *n* chauvinisme *m*. **chauvinist** *adj,n* chauvin *m*.
cheap (tʃi:p) *adj* **1** bon marché *invar*. **2** sans grande valeur. **cheapen** *vt* rabaisser le prix de.
cheat (tʃi:t) *vt* **1** tromper. **2** tricher. *n* **1** tricheur, escroc *m*. **2** fraude *f*.
check (tʃek) *vt* **1** vérifier. **2** retenir. **3** *game* faire échec à. *n* **1** contrôle *m*. **2** frein *m*. **3** *game* échec *m*. **4** chèque *m*. **5** carreau, -aux *m*. **checkmate** *n* échec et mat *m*. *vt* faire échec et mat. **checkpoint** *n* contrôle routier *m*. **check-up** *n* **1** vérification *f*. **2** examen medical, -aux *m*.
cheek (tʃi:k) *n* **1** *anat* joue *f*. **2** impudence *f*. **cheekbone** *n* pommette *f*. **cheeky** *adj* effronté.
cheer (tʃiə) *n* **1** gaieté *f*. **2** *pl* acclamations *f*. **cheers!** *interj* à la vôtre! ~*vt* **1** réconforter. **2** acclamer. **cheer up** prendre courage. **cheerful** *adj* gai, joyeux, -euse.
cheese (tʃi:z) *n* fromage *m*. **cheesecake** *n* tarte à la frangipane *f*.
cheetah (ˈtʃi:tə) *n* guépard *m*.
chef (ʃef) *n* chef de cuisine *m*.
chemical (ˈkemikəl) *adj* chimique. **chemicals** *n pl* produits chimiques *m pl*.
chemist (ˈkemist) *n* **1** *med* pharmacien, -ienne. **2** *sci* chimiste *m*. **chemist's shop** *n* pharmacie *f*.
chemistry (ˈkemistri) *n* chimie *f*.
cheque (tʃek) *n* chèque *m*. **chequebook** *n* carnet de chèques *m*. **cheque card** *n* carte bancaire *f*.
cherish (ˈtʃeriʃ) *vt* **1** soigner tendrement. **2** caresser.
cherry (ˈtʃeri) *n* cerise *f*. **cherry tree** *n* cerisier *m*.
cherub (ˈtʃerəb) *n* chérubin *m*.
chess (tʃes) *n* échecs *m pl*. **chess-board** *n* échiquier *m*. **chess set** *n* échecs *m pl*.
chest (tʃest) *n* poitrine *f*. **chest of drawers** *n* commode *f*.
chestnut (ˈtʃesnʌt) *n* châtaigne *f*. marron *m*. *adj* châtain, marron. **chestnut tree** *n* châtaignier *m*.
chew (tʃu:) *vt* mâcher. **chew over** ruminer. **chewing gum** *n* chewing-gum *m*.
chick (tʃik) *n* poussin *m*.
chicken (ˈtʃikən) *n* poulet *m*. **chickenpox** *n* varicelle *f*.
chicory (ˈtʃikəri) *n* chicorée *f*.
chief (tʃi:f) *n* chef *m*. *adj* principal, -aux, premier, -ière. **chiefly** *adv* surtout.
chilblain (ˈtʃilblein) *n* engelure *f*.
child (tʃaild) *n, pl* **children** enfant *m,f*. **childbirth** *n* accouchement *m*. **childhood** *n*

enfance *f*. **childish** *adj* **1** enfantin. **2** puéril. **childlike** *adj* enfantin, candide.

Chile (ˈtʃili) *n* Chili *m*. **Chilean** *adj,n* chilien, -ienne.

chill (tʃil) *n* **1** froid *m*. **2** frisson *m*. **catch a chill** prendre froid. ~*adj* froid. *vt* refroidir, réfrigérer. *vi* se refroidir.

chilli (ˈtʃili) *n* piment *m*.

chilly *adj* **1** frais, fraîche. **2** (of a person) frileux, -euse.

chime (tʃaim) *n* carillon *m*. *vt,vi* carillonner.

chimney (ˈtʃimni) *n* cheminée *f*. **chimneypot** *n* mitre *f*. pot de cheminée *m*. **chimneysweep** *n* ramoneur *m*.

chimpanzee (tʃimpænˈzi:) *n* chimpanzé *m*.

chin (tʃin) *n* menton *m*.

china (ˈtʃainə) *n* porcelaine *f*.

China (ˈtʃainə) *n* Chine *f*. **Chinese** *adj,n* chinois. **Chinese** (language) *n* chinois *m*.

chink[1] (tʃiŋk) *n* fissure, lézarde *f*. *vi* se fendiller.

chink[2] (tʃiŋk) *n* tintement *m*. *vt* tinter. *vi* faire tinter.

chip (tʃip) *n* **1** éclat, fragment *m*. **2** *pl* frites *f pl*. *vt* ébrécher. *vi* s'ébrécher, s'écailler.

chiropody (kiˈrɔpədi) *n* soins du pédicure *m* [illegible] **chiropodist** *n* pédicure *m,f*.

chirp (tʃə:p) *n* gazouillement *m*. *vi* gazouiller.

chisel (ˈtʃizəl) *n* ciseau, -aux. *vt* ciseler.

chivalry (ˈʃivəlri) *n* **1** chevalerie *f*. **2** courtoisie *f*. **chivalrous** *adj* chevaleresque.

chive (tʃaiv) *n* ciboulette *f*.

chlorine (ˈklɔ:ri:n) *n* chlore *m*.

chlorophyll (ˈklɔrəfil) *n* chlorophylle *f*.

chocolate (ˈtʃɔklit) *n* chocolat *m*.

choice (tʃɔis) *n* choix *m invar*. *adj* (bien) choisi, de choix *invar*.

choir (kwaiə) *n* chœur *m*. **choirboy** *n* enfant de chœur *m*. **choirmaster** *n* maître de chapelle *m*.

choke (tʃouk) *vt* **1** étouffer. **2** boucher. *vi* **1** s'étrangler. **2** se boucher. *n mot* starter *m*.

cholera (ˈkɔlərə) *n* choléra *m*.

choose* (tʃu:z) *vt* **1** choisir. **2** élire. *vi* vouloir.

chop[1] (tʃɔp) *vt* couper, hacher. *n* **1** coup de hache *m*. **2** *cul* côtelette *f*.

chop[2] (tʃɔp) *vi* changer. **chop and change** changer à chaque instant.

chopstick (ˈtʃɔpstik) *n* baguette *f*.

chord (kɔ:d) *n* **1** corde *f*. **2** *mus* accord *m*.

chore (tʃɔ:) *n* corvée *f*.

choreography (kɔriˈɔgrəfi) *n* chorégraphie *f*. **choreographer** *n* chorégraphe *m,f*.

chorus (ˈkɔ:rəs) *n* **1** chœur *m*. **2** refrain *m*. **choral** *adj* choral.

chose (tʃouz) *v* see **choose.**

chosen (ˈtʃouzən) *v* see **choose.**

Christ (kraist) *n* Christ *m*.

christen (ˈkrisən) *vt* baptiser. **christening** *n* baptême *m*.

Christian (ˈkristʃən) *adj,n* chrétien, -ienne. **Christian name** *n* prénom *m*. **Christianity** *n* christianisme *m*.

Christmas (ˈkrisməs) *n* Noël *m*. **Christmas tree** *n* arbre de Noël *m*.

chromatic (krəˈmætik) *adj* chromatique.

chrome (kroum) *n* chrome *m*. *adj* chromé. *vt* chromer.

chromium (ˈkroumiəm) *n* chrome *m*.

chromosome (ˈkrouməsoum) *n* chromosome *m*.

chronic (ˈkrɔnik) *adj* chronique.

chronicle (ˈkrɔnikəl) *n* chronique *f*.

chronological (krɔnəˈlɔdʒikəl) *adj* chronologique.

chrysalis (ˈkrisəlis) *n* chrysalide *f*.

chrysanthemum (kriˈzænθiməm) *n* chrysanthème *m*.

chubby (ˈtʃʌbi) *adj* potelé, joufflu.

chuck (tʃʌk) *vt* **1** lancer. **2** lâcher. **chuck out** expulser.

chuckle (ˈtʃʌkəl) *n* rire étouffé *m*. *vi* rire tout bas.

chunk (tʃʌŋk) *n* **1** gros morceau, -aux *m*. **2** (of bread) quignon *m*.

church (tʃə:tʃ) *n* **1** église *f*. **2** temple *m*. **churchyard** *n* cimetière *m*.

churn (tʃə:n) *n* baratte *f*. *vt* baratter.

chute (ʃu:t) *n* glissière, piste *f*.

chutney (ˈtʃʌtni) *n* chutney *m*.

cicada (siˈka:də) *n* cigale *f*.

cider (ˈsaidə) *n* cidre *m*.

cigar (siˈga:) *n* cigare *m*. **cigarette** *n* cigarette *f*.

cinder (ˈsində) *n* **1** cendre *f*. **2** *pl* escarbilles *f pl*.

cinecamera (ˈsinikæmrə) *n* caméra *f*.

cinema (ˈsinəmə) *n* cinéma *m*.

cinnamon (ˈsinəmən) *n* cannelle *f*.

circle (ˈsə:kəl) *n* **1** cercle *m*. **2** milieu, -eux *m*. *vt* **1** entourer. **2** faire le tour de. *vi* tourner. **circular** *adj,n* circulaire *f*. **circulate** *vi* circuler. *vt* faire circuler, répandre. **circulation** *n* **1** circulation *f*. **2** (of a newspaper) tirage *m*.

circuit (ˈsə:kit) *n* **1** circuit *m*. **2** *law* tournée *f*. **circuitous** *adj* indirect, détourné.

circumcise (ˈsəkəmsaiz) *vt* circoncire. **circumcision** *n* circoncision *f*.

circumference (sə'kʌmfərəns) *n* circonférence *f.*

circumflex ('sə:kəmfleks) *n* accent circonflexe *m. adj* circonflexe.

circumscribe ('sə:kəmskraib) *vt* circonscrire. **circumscription** *n* circonscription *f.*

circumstance ('sə:kəmstæns) *n* **1** circonstance *f.* **2** *pl* moyens *m pl.*

circus ('sə:kəs) *n* cirque *m.*

cistern ('sistən) *n* réservoir *m.* citerne *f.*

cite (sait) *vt* citer.

citizen ('sitizən) *n* **1** citoyen, -enne. **2** bourgeois, habitant *m.* **citizenship** *n* nationalité *f.*

citrus ('sitrəs) *n* citron *m.* **citrus fruits** agrumes *m pl.*

city ('siti) *n* ville, cité *f.*

civic ('sivik) *adj* civique.

civil ('sivəl) *adj* civil. **civil engineering** *n* génie civil *m.* **civil servant** *n* fonctionnaire *m.* **civil service** *n* administration *f.* **civil war** *n* guerre civile *f.*

civilian (si'viliən) *adj,n* civil *m.*

civilization (sivilai'zeiʃən) *n* civilization *f.* **civilize** *vt* civiliser.

claim (kleim) *n* **1** demande, réclamation *f.* **2** droit *m. vt* **1** réclamer, revendiquer. **2** prétendre à.

clam (klæm) *n* palourde *f.*

clamber ('klæmbə) *vt* grimper.

clammy ('klæmi) *adj* moite, humide, pâteux, -euse.

clamour ('klæmə) *n* clameur *f. vi* vociférer.

clamp (klæmp) *n* **1** serre-joint *m.* **2** crampon *m. vt* **1** cramponner. **2** presser.

clan (klæn) *n* clan *m.*

clandestine (klæn'destin) *adj* clandestin.

clang (klæŋ) *n* bruit métallique *m. vi* retentir.

clank (klæŋk) *n* cliquetis *m. vi* résonner. *vt* faire résonner.

clap (klæp) *n* **1** battement (of hands) *m.* **2** coup (of thunder) *m. vt,vi* applaudir.

claret ('klærət) *n* bordeaux *m.*

clarify ('klærifai) *vt* clarifier, éclaircir. *vi* se clarifier. **clarity** *n* clarté *f.*

clarinet (klæri'net) *n* clarinette *f.*

clash (klæʃ) *n* **1** choc *m.* **2** conflit *m.* **3** cliquetis *m. vi* **1** s'entre-choquer. **2** (of colours) jurer. *vt* heurter.

clasp (klɑ:sp) *n* **1** agrafe *f.* **2** fermoir *m.* **3** étreinte *f. vt* **1** agrafer. **2** étreindre.

class (klɑ:s) *n* **1** classe *f.* **2** *educ* cours *m.* **3** catégorie *f. vt* classer. **classification** *n* classification *m,* **classify** *vt* classifier. **classroom** *n* salle de classe *f.*

classic ('klæsik) *adj,n* classique *m.* **classical** *adj* classique.

clatter ('klætə) *n* vacarme, bruit *m. vi* claquer. *vt* faire résonner.

clause (klɔ:z) *n* **1** clause *f.* **2** *gram* membre de phrase *m.* proposition *f.*

claustrophobia (klɔstrə'foubiə) *n* claustrophobie *f.*

claw (klɔ:) *n* griffe, serre, pince *f. vt* griffer.

clay (klei) *n* argile *f.*

clean (kli:n) *adj* **1** propre. **2** net, nette. *vt* nettoyer. **cleaning** *n* nettoyage *m.* **cleanliness** *n* propreté *f.*

cleanse (klenz) *vt* **1** nettoyer. **2** démaquiller.

clear (kliə) *adj* **1** clair. **2** net, nette. **3** libre. **4** certain. *vt* **1** débarrasser, déblayer. **2** évacuer. **3** franchir. **4** acquitter. **5** desservir. *vi* s'éclaircir. **clear up 1** ranger. **2** éclaircir. **clearance** *n* **1** dégagement *m.* **2** *comm* (sale) solde *m.* **clear-headed** *adj* lucide. **clearing** *n* **1** défrichement *m.* **2** acquittement *m.* **3** éclaircie *f.* **clearness** *n* clarté *f.*

clef (klef) *n* clef *f.*

clench (klentʃ) *vt* serrer.

clergy ('klə:dʒi) *n* clergé *m.* **clergyman** *n* pasteur, prêtre *m.*

clerical ('klerikəl) *adj* **1** *rel* ecclésiastique. **2** *comm* de bureau, -aux.

clerk (klɑ:k) *n* **1** employé *m.* **2** clerc *m.*

clever ('klevə) *adj* **1** habile. **2** intelligent.

cliché ('kli:ʃei) *n* cliché *m.*

click (klik) *n* bruit sec *m. vt,vi* cliqueter.

client ('klaiənt) *n* client *m.*

cliff (klif) *n* falaise *f.*

climate ('klaimit) *n* climat *m.*

climax ('klaimæks) *n* **1** apogée, comble *m.* **2** gradation *f.*

climb (klaim) *vt,vi* **1** monter. **2** grimper. *vt* gravir, franchir. *n* **1** montée *f.* **2** ascension *f.*

cling* (kliŋ) *vi* s'accrocher, adhérer. **clinging** *adj* collant.

clinic ('klinik) *n* clinique *f.* **clinical** *adj* clinique.

clip[1] (klip) *vt* tondre, couper.

clip[2] (klip) *n* pince, attache *f. vt* pincer.

clitoris ('klitəris) *n* clitoris *m.*

cloak (klouk) *n* manteau, -aux *m. vt* masquer. **cloakroom** *n* vestiaire *m.* consigne *f.*

clock (klɔk) *n* horloge *f.* **it is two o'clock** il est deux heures. **clocktower** *n* tour d'horloge *f.* **clockwise** *adj* dans le sens des aiguilles d'une montre. **clockwork** *n* mouvement d'horlogerie *m.* **like clockwork** comme sur des roulettes.

clog (klɔg) *n* **1** sabot *m.* **2** entrave *f.* *vt* **1** entraver. **2** boucher. *vi* se boucher, s'obstruer.

cloister (ˈklɔistə) *n* cloître *m.* *vt* cloîtrer.

close (*adj,adv* klous; *v* klouz) *adj* **1** proche. **2** lourd. **3** serré. **4** fermé. **close fitting** *adj* ajusté. ~*n* **1** (klous) enclos *m.* **2** (klous) cul-de-sac *m.* **3** (klouz) fin *f.* *vt* **1** fermer. **2** conclure. **3** serrer. *vi* **1** se fermer. **2** se terminer. *adv* (de) près. **closing** *n* fermeture *f.*

closet (ˈklɔzit) *n* **1** cabinet *m.* **2** placard *m.*

clot (klɔt) *n* caillot *m.* *vi* se cailler, se figer.

cloth (klɔθ) *n* **1** étoffe *f.* **2** toile *f.* **3** nappe *f.*

clothe (klouð) *vt* vêtir, habiller. **clothes** *n pl* vêtements *m pl.* **clothes brush** *n* brosse à habits *f.* **clothes line** *n* corde à linge *f.* **clothes peg** *n* pince à linge *f.* **clothing** *n* habillement *m.*

cloud (klaud) *n* nuage *m.* *vt* couvrir. **cloudburst** *n* rafale de pluie *f.* **cloudy** *adj* nuageux, -euse.

clove[1] (klouv) *n* (of garlic, etc.) gousse *f.*

clove[2] (klouv) *n* clou de girofle *m.*

clover (ˈklouvə) *n* trèfle *m.*

clown (klaun) *n* clown, pitre, rustre *m.*

club (klʌb) *n* **1** club *m.* **2** *game* trèfle *m.* **3** *sport* crosse *f.* **club foot** *n* pied bot *m.*

clue (klu:) *n* fil, indice *m.*

clump (klʌmp) *n* **1** masse *f.* **2** bouquet, massif *m.*

clumsy (ˈklʌmzi) *adj* maladroit, gauche.

clung (klʌŋ) *v* see **cling.**

cluster (ˈklʌstə) *n* groupe, bouquet *m.* *vi* se grouper.

clutch (klʌtʃ) *vt* empoigner, saisir *n* **1** griffe *f.* **2** étreinte *f.* **3** *mot* embrayage *m.*

clutter (ˈklʌtə) *n* encombrement *m.* *v* **clutter up** encombrer.

coach (koutʃ) *n* **1** *mot* (auto)car *m.* **2** (railway) wagon *m.* **3** *educ* répétiteur *m.* **4** *sport* entraîneur *m.* *vt* **1** préparer. **2** entraîner. **coaching** *n* **1** répétitions *f pl.* **2** entraînement *m.*

coal (koul) *n* charbon *m.* houille *f.* **coalmine** *n* mine de charbon *f.* houillère *f.*

coalition (kouəˈliʃən) *n* coalition *f.*

coarse (kɔ:s) *adj* **1** grossier, -ière. **2** rude.

coast (koust) *n* côte *f.* *vi* *naut* côtoyer. **coastguard** *n* garde-côte, gardes-côte *m.* **coastline** *n* littoral, -aux *m.*

coat (kout) *n* **1** habit, manteau, -aux *m.* **2** (of an animal) pelage *m.* **3** robe *f.* **4** (of paint) couche *f.* *vt* couvrir, enduire. **coat-hanger** *n* cintre *m.*

coax (kouks) *vt* cajoler.

cobble (ˈkɔbəl) *n* galet *m.* *vt* carreler.

cobbler (ˈkɔblə) *n* cordonnier *m.*

cobra (ˈkoubrə) *n* cobra *m.*

cobweb (ˈkɔbweb) *n* toile d'araignée *f.*

cock[1] (kɔk) *n* **1** coq *m.* **2** mâle *m.*

cock[2] (kɔk) *vt* **1** dresser. **2** retrousser.

cockle (ˈkɔkəl) *n* **1** *zool* clovisse *f.* **2** *bot* ivraie *f.*

cockpit (ˈkɔkpit) *n* carlingue *f.*

cockroach (ˈkɔkroutʃ) *n* blatte *f.*

cocktail (ˈkɔkteil) *n* cocktail *m.* **cocktail party** *n* cocktail *m.*

cocky (ˈkɔki) *adj inf* impertinent.

cocoa (ˈkoukou) *n* cacao *m.*

coconut (ˈkoukənʌt) *n* noix de coco *f.* **coconut palm** *n* cocotier *m.*

cocoon (kəˈku:n) *n* cocon *m.*

cod (kɔd) *n* morue *f.*

code (koud) *n* code *m.* *vt* chiffrer.

codeine (ˈkoudi:n) *n* codéine *f.*

co-education (kouedjuˈkeiʃən) *n* enseignement mixte *m.* **co-educational** *adj* mixte.

coerce (kouˈə:s) *vt* contraindre. **coercion** *n* contrainte *f.*

coexist (kouigˈzist) *vi* coexister.

coffee (ˈkɔfi) *n* café *m.* **coffee bar** *n* café *m.* **coffee bean** *n* grain de café *m.* **coffee table** *n* table de salon *f.*

coffin (ˈkɔfin) *n* cercueil *m.* bière *f.*

cog (kɔg) *n* dent *f.*

cognac (ˈkɔnjæk) *n* cognac *m.*

cohabit (kouˈhæbit) *vi* cohabiter.

cohere (kouˈhiə) *vi* **1** adhérer. **2** s'agglomérer. **3** se tenir. **coherence** *n* cohérence *f.* **coherent** *adj* cohérent.

coil (kɔil) *n* **1** rouleau, -aux *m.* **2** (electric) bobine *f.* *vt* enrouler. *vi* s'enrouler.

coin (kɔin) *n* pièce de monnaie *f.* *vt* **1** frapper. **2** inventer.

coincide (kouinˈsaid) *vi* coïncider. **coincidence** *n* coïncidence *f.*

colander (ˈkʌləndə) *n* passoire *f.*

cold (kould) *adj* froid. **be cold 1** (of a person) avoir froid. **2** (of the weather) faire froid. ~*n* **1** froid *m.* **2** *med* rhume *m.* **have a cold** être enrhumé. **cold-blooded** *adj* **1** (of a person) insensible. **2** (of an animal) à sang froid.

collaborate (kəˈlæbəreit) *vi* collaborer. **collaboration** *n* collaboration *f.*

collapse (kəˈlæps) *vi* s'effondrer. *n* effondrement, écroulement *m*. **collapsible** *adj* pliant.

collar ('kɔlə) *n* **1** (of a shirt, etc.) col *m*. **2** collier *m*. **collarbone** *n* clavicule *f*.

colleague ('kɔli:g) *n* collègue *m,f*.

collect (kə'lekt) *vt* **1** rassembler. **2** collectionner. **3** percevoir. *vi* se grouper. **collected** *adj* calme. **collection** *n* **1** collection *f*. **2** quête *f*. **3** levée *f*. **collective** *adj* collectif, -ive.

college ('kɔlidʒ) *n* collège *m*.

collide (kə'laid) *vi* se heurter, entrer en collision. **collision** *n* collision *f*. choc *m*.

colloquial (kə'loukwiəl) *adj* familier, -ière, parlé.

colon ('koulən) *n gram* deux points *m pl*.

colonel ('kə:nl̩) *n* colonel *m*.

colony ('kɔləni) *n* colonie *f*. **colonial** *adj* colonial, -aux. **colonization** *n* colonisation *f*. **colonize** *vt* coloniser.

colossal (kə'lɔsəl) *adj* colossal, -aux.

colour ('kʌlə) *n* **1** couleur *f*. **2** *mil* drapeau, -aux *m*. *vt* colorer. *vi* **1** se colorer. **2** rougir. **colour-bar** *n* ségrégation raciale *f*. **colour-blind** *adj* daltonien, -ienne. **coloured** *adj* de couleur, coloré. **colourless** *adj* incolore.

column ('kɔləm) *n* colonne *f*.

coma ('koumə) *n* coma *m*.

comb (koum) *n* **1** peigne *m*. **2** *zool* crête *f*. *vt* peigner.

combat ('kɔmbæt) *n* combat *m*. lutte *f*. *vt,vi* combattre. **combatant** *n* combattant *m*.

combine (*v* kəm'bain; *n* 'kɔmbain) *vt* combiner. *vi* s'unir. *n* cartel *m*. **combination** *n* combinaison *f*.

combustion (kəm'bʌstʃən) *n* combustion *f*.

come* (kʌm) *vi* venir, arriver. **come about** arriver. **come across** recontrer. **come back** revenir, rentrer. **comeback** *n* retour *m*. **come down** descendre. **come in** entrer. **come off** se détacher. **come out** sortir.

comedy ('kɔmədi) *n* comédie *f*. **comedian** *n* comédien, -ienne. **comic** *adj* comique, drôle. *n* **1** comique *m*. **2** journal de bandes illustrées *m*. **comical** *adj* comique.

comet ('kɔmit) *n* comète *f*.

comfort ('kʌmfət) *n* réconfort *m*. consolation *f*. *vt* réconforter. **comfortable** *adj* **1** confortable, commode. **2** à l'aise.

comical ('kɔmikəl) *adj* comique.

comma ('kɔmə) *n* virgule *f*. **inverted commas** *n pl* guillemets *m pl*.

command (kə'mɑ:nd) *vt* **1** ordonner, commander. **2** posséder. *n* **1** commandement, ordre *m*. **2** maîtrise *f*. **commandment** *n* commandement *m*.

commemorate (kə'meməreit) *vt* commémorer. **commemoration** *n* commémoration *f*. **commemorative** *adj* commémoratif, -ive.

commence (kə'mens) *vt,vi* commencer. **commencement** *n* commencement, début *m*.

commend (kə'mend) *vt* **1** recommander. **2** louer. **3** confier. **commendation** *n* louange *f*. éloge *m*.

comment ('kɔment) *n* commentaire *m*. observation *f*. *vi* commenter. **commentary** *n* commentaire *m*. **commentator** *n* commentateur, -trice.

commerce ('kɔmə:s) *n* commerce *m*. affaires *f pl*. **commercial** *adj* commercial, -aux. **commercial vehicle** *n* véhicule utilitaire *m*.

commission (kə'miʃən) *n* **1** commission *f*. **2** *mil* brevet *m*. *vt* **1** charger. **2** déléguer. **commissioner** *n* commissaire *m*.

commit (kə'mit) *vt* **1** commettre. **2** confier. **3** engager. **commitment** *n* engagement *m*.

committee (kə'miti) *n* **1** comité *m*. **2** *pol* commission *f*.

commodity (kə'mɔditi) *n* marchandise, denrée *f*.

common ('kɔmən) *adj* **1** commun, ordinaire. **2** vulgaire. **3** public. *n* lieu commun *m*. **commonplace** *adj* banal, -aux, terre à terre. *n* banalité *f*. **commonsense** *n* sens commun *m*. **commonwealth** *n* **1** fédération, république *f*. **2** *cap* Commonwealth *m*.

Common Market *n* Marché Commun *m*.

commotion (kə'mouʃən) *n* tumulte *m*. commotion *f*.

commune[1] (kə'mju:n) *vi* converser intimement. **communion** *n* communion *f*.

commune[2] ('kɔmju:n) *n* commune *f*. **communal** *adj* communal, -aux.

communicant (kə'mju:nikənt) *n* communiant *m*.

communicate (kə'mju:nikeit) *vt,vi* communiquer. **communication** *n* communication *f*. **communicative** *adj* communicatif, -ive.

communism ('kɔmjunizəm) *n* communisme *m*. **communist** *adj,n* communiste.

community (kə'mju:niti) *n* communauté *f*.

commute (kə'mju:t) *vt* échanger. *vi* faire un trajet journalier de sa résidence à son lieu de travail et vice-versa. **commuter** *n* abonné *m*.

compact[1] (kəm'pækt) *adj* compact, serré. *vt* condenser.

compact[2] ('kɔmpækt) *n* contrat *m*.

companion (kəm'pæniən) *n* compagnon *m.* compagne *f.* **companionship** *n* camaraderie *f.*

company ('kʌmpəni) *n* **1** compagnie *f.* **2** société *f.* **3** *naut* équipage *m.* **4** *Th* troupe *f.*

compare (kəm'pɛə) *vt* comparer. *vi* se comparer. **compared with** par rapport à, auprès de. **comparable** *adj* comparable. **comparative** *adj* comparatif, -ive, relatif, -ive. *n* comparatif *m.* **comparison** *n* comparaison *f.*

compartment (kəm'pɑ:tmənt) *n* compartiment *m.*

compass ('kʌmpəs) *n* boussole *f.* **(pair of) compasses** *n* compas *m.*

compassion (kəm'pæʃən) *n* compassion *f.* **compassionate** *adj* compatissant.

compatible (kəm'pætibəl) *adj* compatible.

compel (kəm'pel) *vt* contraindre, obliger.

compensate ('kɔmpənseit) *vt* dédommager, rémunérer. *vi* compenser. **compensation** *n* compensation *f.*

compete (kəm'pi:t) *vi* concourir, rivaliser. **competition** *n* **1** compétition *f.* concours *m.* **2** concurrence *f.* **competitive** *adj* compétitif, -ive. **competitor** *n* **1** concurrent *m.* **2** compétiteur *m.*

competent ('kɔmpitənt) *adj* compétent, capable.

compile (kəm'pail) *vt* compiler.

complacent (kəm'pleisənt) *adj* satisfait de soi. **complacency** *n* suffisance *f.*

complain (kəm'plein) *vi* se plaindre. **complaint** *n* **1** plainte *f.* **2** *med* maladie *f.*

complement ('kɔmplimənt) *n* complément *m.* **complementary** *adj* complémentaire.

complete (kəm'pli:t) *adj* **1** complet, -ète. **2** achevé. *vt* **1** achever. **2** accomplir. **completion** *n* achèvement *m.*

complex ('kɔmpleks) *adj,n* complexe *m.* **complexity** *n* complexité *f.*

complexion (kəm'plekʃən) *n* **1** teint *m.* **2** aspect *m.*

complicate ('kɔmplikeit) *vt* compliquer. **complication** *n* complication *f.*

compliment ('kɔmplimənt) *n* compliment *m.* *vt* complimenter. **complimentary** *adj* **1** flatteur, -euse. **2** gracieux, -euse, gratuit.

comply (kəm'plai) *vi* se conformer, accéder.

component (kəm'pounənt) *adj* constituant. *n* composant *m.*

compose (kəm'pouz) *vt* **1** composer. **2** apaiser. **composed** *adj* calme. **composer** *n* compositeur *m.* **composition** *n* **1** composition *f.* arrangement *m.* **2** *educ* rédaction *f.*

composure (kəm'pouʒə) *n* calme, sang-froid *m.*

compound[1] (*adj,n* 'kɔmpaund; *v* kəm'paund) *n* composé *m.* *adj* composé. *vt* composer, mélanger. *vi* s'arranger.

compound[2] ('kɔmpaund) *n* enclos fortifié *m.*

comprehend (kɔmpri'hend) *vt* comprendre. **comprehensible** *adj* compréhensible. **comprehension** *n* compréhension *f.* **comprehensive** *adj* compréhensif, -ive, étendu. **comprehensive school** *n* centre d'études secondaires *m.*

compress (*v* kəm'pres; *n* 'kɔmpres) *vt* comprimer. *n* compresse *f.*

comprise (kəm'praiz) *vt* comprendre, contenir.

compromise ('kɔmprəmaiz) *n* compromis *m.* *vt,vi* compromettre.

compulsion (kəm'pʌlʃən) *n* contrainte *f.* **compulsive** *adj* forcé. **compulsory** *adj* obligatoire.

computer (kəm'pju:tə) *n* ordinateur *m.*

comrade ('kɔmrəd, -reid) *n* camarade *m,f.*

concave ('kɔŋkeiv) *adj* concave.

conceal (kən'si:l) *vt* **1** cacher. **2** dissimuler. **concealment** *n* dissimulation *f.*

concede (kən'si:d) *vt* **1** accorder. **2** admettre. *vi* faire des concessions.

conceit (kən'si:t) *n* vanité *f.* **conceited** *adj* prétentieux, -euse, suffisant.

conceive (kən'si:v) *vt,vi* concevoir. *vt* comprendre. **conceivable** *adj* concevable.

concentrate ('kɔnsəntreit) *vt* concentrer. *vi* se concentrer. **concentration** *n* concentration *f.* **concentration camp** *n* camp de concentration *m.*

concentric (kən'sentrik) *adj* concentrique.

concept ('kɔnsept) *n* concept *m.* **conception** *n* conception, idée *f.*

concern (kən'sə:n) *vt* **1** concerner, regarder. **2** inquiéter. *n* **1** rapport *m.* **2** intérêt *m.* **3** inquiétude *f.* **4** *comm* entreprise *f.* **concerning** *prep* en ce qui concerne.

concert ('kɔnsət) *n* concert *m.*

concertina (kɔnsə'ti:nə) *n* concertina *f.*

concerto (kən'tʃɛətou) *n* concerto *m.*

concession (kən'seʃən) *n* concession *f.*

concise (kən'sais) *adj* concis.

conclude (kən'klu:d) *vt,vi* conclure. **conclusion** *n* conclusion *f.*

concoct (kən'kɔkt) *vt* **1** *cul* préparer. **2** inventer. **concoction** *n* **1** confectionnement *m.* **2** machination *f.*

concrete (ˈkɔŋkriːt) *n* béton *m*. *adj* concret. *vt* bétonner. *vi* se solidifier.

concussion (kənˈkʌʃən) *n* **1** choc *m*. **2** *med* commotion (cérébrale) *f*.

condemn (kənˈdem) *vt* condamner. **condemnation** *n* condamnation, censure *f*.

condense (kənˈdens) *vt* **1** condenser. **2** abréger. *vi* se condenser. **condensation** *n* condensation *f*.

condescend (kɔndiˈsend) *vi* condescendre, daigner. **condescension** *n* condescendance *f*.

condition (kənˈdiʃən) *n* condition *f*. état *m*. *vt* conditionner. **conditional** *adj,n* conditionnel, -elle *m*.

condolence (kənˈdouləns) *n* condoléance *f*.

condone (kənˈdoun) *vt* pardonner.

conduct (*v* kənˈdʌkt; *n* ˈkɔndʌkt) *vt* **1** conduire. **2** *mus* diriger. *n* conduite *f*.

conductor (kənˈdʌktə) *n* **1** conducteur *m*. **2** (on a bus) receveur *m*. **3** chef d'orchestre *m*.

cone (koun) *n* cône *m*.

confectioner (kənˈfekʃənə) *n* confiseur *m*. **confectionery** *n* confiserie *f*.

confederate (*adj,n* kənˈfedərət; *v* kənˈfedəreit) *adj,n* confédéré *m*. *vt* confédérer. *vi* se confédérer. **confederation** *n* confédération *f*.

confer (kənˈfəː) *vt,vi* conférer. **conference** *n* conférence *f*.

confess (kənˈfes) *vt* confesser, avouer. *vi* se confesser. **confession** *n* confession *f*. aveu, -eux *m*.

confetti (kənˈfeti) *n pl* confetti *m*.

confide (kənˈfaid) *vt* confier. *vi* se fier. **confidence** *n* **1** confiance *f*. **2** confidence *f*. **confident** *adj* sûr, confiant, assuré. **confidently** *adv* avec confiance. **confidential** *adj* confidentiel, -elle, de confiance. **confidentially** *adv* de confiance.

confine (kənˈfain) *vt* **1** limiter, restreindre. **2** enfermer. **confinement** *n* **1** emprisonnement *m*. **2** *med* accouchement *m*. couches *f pl*.

confirm (kənˈfəːm) *vt* confirmer. **confirmation** *n* confirmation *f*.

confiscate (ˈkɔnfiskeit) *vt* confisquer. **confiscation** *n* confiscation *f*.

conflict (*n* ˈkɔnflikt; *v* kənˈflikt) *n* conflit *m*. *vi* s'opposer. **conflicting** *adj* incompatible, contradictoire.

conform (kənˈfɔːm) *vt* conformer. *vi* se conformer. **conformity** *n* conformité *f*.

confound (kənˈfaund) *vt* **1** confondre. **2** embarrasser.

confront (kənˈfrʌnt) *vt* **1** affronter. **2** confronter. **confrontation** *n* confrontation *f*.

confuse (kənˈfjuːz) *vt* **1** embrouiller. **2** confondre, déconcerter. **confusion** *n* **1** confusion *f*. **2** désordre *m*.

congeal (kənˈdʒiːl) *vt* congeler, figer. *vi* se congeler.

congenial (kənˈdʒiːniəl) *adj* **1** approprié. **2** agréable, sympathique.

congested (kənˈdʒestid) *adj* congestionné, embouteillé. **congestion** *n* **1** *med* congestion *f*. **2** encombrement *m*.

congratulate (kənˈgrætʃuleit) *vt* féliciter. **congratulation** *n* félicitation *f*.

congregate (ˈkɔŋgrigeit) *vt* rassembler. *vi* s'assembler. **congregation** *n* assemblée *f*.

congress (ˈkɔŋgres) *n* congrès *m*.

conical (ˈkɔnikəl) *adj* conique.

conifer (ˈkɔnifə) *n* conifère *m*.

conjugal (ˈkɔndʒugəl) *adj* conjugal, -aux.

conjugate (ˈkɔndʒugeit) *vt* conjuguer. **conjugation** *n* conjugaison *f*.

conjunction (kənˈdʒʌŋkʃən) *n* conjonction *f*.

conjure (ˈkʌndʒə) *vt,vi* conjurer. *vt* faire apparaître. **conjurer** *n* prestidigitateur *m*.

connect (kəˈnekt) *vt* relier, joindre. *vi* se lier, se joindre. **connection** *n* **1** rapport *m*. liaison *f*. **2** (train, bus, etc.) correspondance *f*.

connoisseur (kɔnəˈsəː) *n* connaisseur *m*.

connotation (kɔnəˈteiʃən) *n* signification *f*.

conquer (ˈkɔŋkə) *vt* conquérir, vaincre. **conqueror** *n* conquérant, vainqueur *m*. **conquest** *n* conquête *f*.

conscience (ˈkɔnʃəns) *n* conscience *f*. **conscientious** *adj* consciencieux, -euse.

conscious (ˈkɔnʃəs) *adj* conscient. **consciously** *adv* sciemment. **consciousness** *n* **1** conscience *f*. **2** *med* connaissance *f*.

conscript (ˈkɔnskript) *n* conscrit *m*. **conscription** *n* conscription *f*.

consecrate (ˈkɔnsikreit) *vt* consacrer. **consecration** *n* consécration *f*.

consecutive (kənˈsekjutiv) *adj* consécutif, -ive.

consent (kənˈsent) *n* consentement *m*. *vi* consentir.

consequence (ˈkɔnsikwəns) *n* **1** conséquence, suite *f*. **2** importance *f*. **consequent** *adj* résultant.

conserve (kənˈsəːv) *vt* conserver. **conservation** *n* conservation *f*. **conservative** *adj,n* conservateur, -trice. *n cap* Conservateur, -trice. **conservatory** *n* serre *f*.

consider (kənˈsidə) *vt* **1** considérer. **2** regarder.

considerable *adj* considérable. **considerate** *adj* attentionné, attentif, -ive. **consideration** *n* **1** considération *f.* **2** rémunération *f.* **3** importance *f.*

consign (kən'sain) *vt* **1** consigner. **2** expédier. **consignment** *n* envoi, expédition *m.*

consist (kən'sist) *vi* **consist of** consister en, se composer de. **consistency** *n* **1** consistance *f.* **2** logique *f.* **consistent** *adj* **1** conséquent. **2** en accord.

console (kən'soul) *vt* consoler.

consolidate (kən'sɔlideit) *vt* consolider. *vi* se consolider.

consonant ('kɔnsənənt) *n* consonne *f.*

conspicuous (kən'spikjuəs) *adj* en vue, remarquable.

conspire (kən'spaiə) *vt* comploter. *vi* conspirer. **conspiracy** *n* conspiration *f.*

constable ('kɔnstəbəl) *n* agent de police *m.* **constabulary** *n* police, gendarmerie *f.*

constant ('kɔnstənt) *adj* **1** constant. **2** continuel. *n* constante *f.*

constellation (kɔnstə'leiʃən) *n* constellation *f.*

constipation (kɔnsti'peiʃən) *n* constipation *f.*

constitute ('kɔnstitju:t) *vt* constituer. **constituency** *n* circonscription électorale *f.* **constituent** *n* électeur, -trice. *adj* constituant, essentiel, -elle. **constitution** *n* constitution *f.* **constitutional** *adj* constitutionnel, -elle.

constraint (kən'streint) *n* contrainte *f.*

constrict (kən'strikt) *vt* resserrer.

construct (kən'strʌkt) *vt* construire. **construction** *n* construction *f.* **constructive** *adj* constructif, -ive.

consul ('kɔnsəl) *n* consul *m.* **consular** *adj* consulaire. **consulate** *n* consulat *m.*

consult (kən'sʌlt) *vt* consulter. *vi* délibérer. **consultant** *n* médecin consultant *m.*

consume (kən'sju:m) *vt* **1** consumer. **2** consommer, épuiser. **consumer** *n* consommateur, -trice. **consumption** *n* consommation *f.*

contact ('kɔntækt) *vt* contacter. *n* contact, rapport *m.* **contact lenses** *n* verres de contact *m pl.*

contagious (kən'teidʒəs) *adj* contagieux, -euse.

contain (kən'tein) *vt* contenir. **container** *n* récipient *m.*

contaminate (kən'tæmineit) *vt* contaminer.

contemplate ('kɔntəmpleit) *vt* **1** contempler. **2** envisager. *vi* réfléchir. **contemplation** *n* **1** contemplation *f.* **2** projet *m.*

contemporary (kən'temprəri) *adj,n* contemporain.

contempt (kən'tempt) *n* mépris *m.* **contemptible** *adj* méprisable.

content[1] ('kɔntent) *n* contenu *m.*

content[2] (kən'tent) *adj* satisfait. *vt* satisfaire. **be content with** se contenter de.

contest (*n* 'kɔntest; *v* kən'test) *n* **1** conflict *m.* **2** compétition *f.* *vt* contester. **contestant** *n* contestant, concurrent *m.*

context ('kɔntekst) *n* contexte *m.*

continent ('kɔntinənt) *n* continent *m.* **continental** *adj* continental, -aux.

contingency (kən'tindʒənsi) *n* éventualité *f.* **contingent** *adj* contingent, fortuit.

continue (kən'tinju:) *vt* continuer. **continual** *adj* continuel, -elle. **continuation** *n* **1** continuation *f.* **2** suite *f.* **continuity** *n* continuité *f.* **continuous** *adj* continu.

contour ('kɔntuə) *n* contour, profil *m.*

contraband ('kɔntrəbænd) *n* contrebande *f.*

contraception (kɔntrə'sepʃən) *n* contraception *f.* **contraceptive** *adj* anticonceptionnel, -elle. *n* **1** contraceptif *m.* **2** préservatif *m.*

contract (*n* 'kɔntrækt; *v* kən'trækt) *n* contrat *m.* entreprise *f.* *vt* contracter. *vi* **1** se contracter. **2** s'engager. **contraction** *n* contraction *f.* **contractor** *n* entrepreneur *m*

contradict (kɔntrə'dikt) *vt* contredire. **contradiction** *n* contradiction *f.* **contradictory** *adj* contradictoire.

contralto (kən'træltou) *n* contralto *m.*

contraption (kən'træpʃən) *n* machin, truc *m.*

contrary ('kɔntrəri) *adj,n* contraire *m.*

contrast (*n* 'kɔntrɑ:st; *v* kən'trɑ:st) *n* contraste *m.* *vt* mettre en contraste. *vi* contraster.

contravene (kɔntrə'vi:n) *vt* **1** transgresser, enfreindre. **2** s'opposer à.

contribute (kən'tribju:t) *vt,vi* contribuer. **contribution** *n* contribution *f.* **contributor** *n* **1** collaborateur, -trice. **2** souscripteur *m.*

contrive (kən'traiv) *vt* **1** inventer. **2** arranger. *vi* s'arranger.

control (kən'troul) *n* **1** autorité, maîtrise *f.* **2** contrôle *m.* *vt* **1** contrôler. **2** diriger.

controversy ('kɔntrəvə:si, kən'trɔvəsi) *n* controverse *f.* **controversial** *adj* controversable.

convalesce (kɔnvə'les) *vi* relever de maladie. **convalescence** *n* convalescence *f.* **convalescent** *adj,n* convalescent.

convenience (kən'vi:niəns) *n* commodité, convenance *f.* **convenient** *adj* commode, approprié.

convent ('kɔnvənt) *n* couvent *m.*

convention (kən'venʃən) *n* **1** convention *f.* **2**

assemblée *f*. **conventional** *adj* conventionnel, -elle.

converge (kən'və:dʒ) *vi* converger.

converse[1] (kən'və:s) *vi* causer. **conversation** *n* conversation *f*. entretien *m*.

converse[2] ('kɔnvə:s) *adj* **1** contraire. **2** *math* réciproque.

convert (*v* kən'və:t; *n* 'kɔnvə:t) *vt* convertir, transformer. *n* converti *m*.

convex ('kɔnveks) *adj* convexe.

convey (kən'vei) *vt* **1** transporter. **2** transmettre. **conveyor belt** *n* chaîne de montage *f*.

convict (*n* 'kɔnvikt; *v* kən'vikt) *n* forçat *m*. *vt* condamner, convaincre.

conviction (kən'vikʃən) *n* **1** condamnation *f*. **2** conviction *f*.

convince (kən'vins) *vt* convaincre.

convoy ('kɔnvɔi) *n* convoi *m*.

cook (kuk) *vt* **1** faire cuire. **2** *comm inf* falsifier. *vi* cuire. *n* cuisinier, -ière. **cooker** *n* cuisinière *f*. **cookery** *n* cuisine *f*. **cookery book** *n* livre de cuisine *m*. **cooking** *n* cuisine *f*.

cool (ku:l) *adj* **1** frais, fraîche. **2** calme. *vt* rafraîchir, refroidir. *vi* se refroidir. **cool down** s'apaiser. **coolness** *n* **1** fraîcheur *f*. **2** sang-froid *m*.

coop (ku:p) *n* mue *f*.

cooperate (kou'ɔpəreit) *vi* coopérer. **cooperation** *n* coopération *f*. **cooperative** *adj* coopératif, -ive.

coordinate (*v* kou'ɔ:dineit; *adj* kou'ɔ:dinət) *vt* coordonner. *adj* coordonné.

cope[1] (koup) *vi* venir à bout, se débrouiller.

cope[2] (koup) *n* chape *f*.

Copenhagen (koupən'heigən) *n* Copenhague *f*.

copper[1] ('kɔpə) *n* cuivre *m*. *adj* de cuivre. **copper beech** *n* hêtre rouge *m*.

copper[2] ('kɔpə) *n inf* flic *m*.

copy ('kɔpi) *n* **1** copie *f*. **2** exemplaire *m*. *vt* copier. **copyright** *n* droit d'auteur *m*.

coral ('kɔrəl) *n* corail, -aux *m*.

cord (kɔ:d) *n* corde *f*. *vt* corder.

cordial ('kɔ:diəl) *adj,n* cordial, -aux *m*.

cordon ('kɔ:dn̩) *n* cordon *m*.

corduroy ('kɔ:dərɔi) *n* velours côtelé *m*.

core (kɔ:) *n* **1** centre *m*. **2** (of an apple, etc.)trognon *m*.

cork (kɔ:k) *n* **1** liège *m*. **2** bouchon *m*. *vt* boucher. **corkscrew** *n* tire-bouchon *m*.

corn[1] (kɔ:n) *n* blé, grain *m*. **cornflour** *n* farine de maïs *f*. **cornflower** *n* bleuet *m*.

corn[2] (kɔ:n) *n med* cor *m*.

corner ('kɔ:nə) *n* **1** coin, angle *m*. **2** virage *m*. *vt* **1** *inf* mettre au pied du mur. **2** *comm* accaparer.

cornet ('kɔ:nit) *n* cornet (à piston) *m*.

coronary ('kɔrənəri) *adj* coronaire *f*. **coronary thrombosis** *n* infarctus *m*.

coronation (kɔrə'neiʃən) *n* couronnement *m*.

corporal[1] ('kɔ:prəl) *adj* corporel, -elle.

corporal[2] ('kɔ:prəl) *n* caporal, -aux *m*.

corporation (kɔ:pə'reiʃən) *n* **1** corporation *f*. **2** conseil municipal, -aux *m*.

corps (kɔ:) *n invar* corps *m invar*.

corpse (kɔ:ps) *n* cadavre *m*.

correct (kə'rekt) *adj* correct, exact. *vt* corriger.

correction *n* correction *f*.

correlate ('kɔrəleit) *vi* correspondre. *vt* mettre en corrélation. **correlation** *n* corrélation *f*.

correspond (kɔri'spɔnd) *vi* correspondre. **correspondence** *n* correspondance *f*. courrier *m*. **correspondent** *n* correspondant *m*.

corridor ('kɔridɔ:) *n* corridor *m*.

corrode (kə'roud) *vt* corroder. *vi* se corroder. **corrosion** *n* corrosion *f*. **corrosive** *adj,n* corrosif, -ive *m*.

corrupt (kə'rʌpt) *vt* corrompre, altérer. *vi* se corrompre. *adj* corrompu. **corruption** *n* corruption *f*.

corset ('kɔ:sit) *n* corset *m*.

Corsica ('kɔ:sikə) *n* Corse *f*. **Corsican** *adj,n* corse.

cosmetic (kɔz'metik) *adj,n* cosmétique *m*.

cosmopolitan (kɔzmə'pɔlitən) *adj,n* cosmopolite.

cosmos ('kɔzmɔs) *n* cosmos *m*. **cosmic** *adj* cosmique.

cost* (kɔst) *n* coût *m*. frais *m pl*. *vi* coûter. **costly** *adj* coûteux, -euse.

costume ('kɔstju:m) *n* costume *m*.

cosy ('kouzi) *adj* confortable.

cot (kɔt) *n* lit d'enfant *m*.

cottage ('kɔtidʒ) *n* **1** chaumière *f*. **2** villa *f*.

cotton ('kɔtn̩) *n* coton *m*. **cotton-wool** *n* ouate *f*. coton hydrophile *m*.

couch (kautʃ) *n* canapé *m*. *vt* coucher.

cough (kɔf) *n* toux *f*. *vi* tousser.

council ('kaunsəl) *n* conseil *m*. **councillor** *n* conseiller *m*.

counsel ('kaunsəl) *n* conseil, avis *m*. *vt* conseiller.

count[1] (kaunt) *vt,vi* compter. *n* compte, calcul *m*. **countdown** *n* compte à rebours *m*.

count[2] (kaunt) *n* (title) comte *m*.

counter[1] ('kauntə) *n* **1** comptoir, guichet *m*. **2** *game* jeton *m*.

counter[2] ('kauntə) *adj* contraire. *adv* en sens inverse, contre.
counterattack ('kauntərətæk) *n* contre-attaque *f*.
counterfeit ('kauntəfit) *adj* faux, fausse. *n* contrefaçon *f*. *vt* contrefaire.
counterfoil ('kauntəfɔil) *n* souche *f*. talon *m*.
counterpart ('kauntəpɑ:t) *n* contrepartie *f*.
countess ('kauntis) *n* comtesse *f*.
country ('kʌntri) *n* **1** pays *m*. **2** campagne *f*. **countryside** *n* campagne *f*.
county ('kaunti) *n* comté *m*. **county council** *n* conseil général *m*.
coup (ku:) *n* coup *m*.
couple ('kʌpəl) *n* couple *m*. *vt* coupler.
coupon ('ku:pɔn) *n* coupon *m*.
courage ('kʌridʒ) *n* courage *m*. **courageous** *adj* courageux, -euse.
courgette (kuə'ʒet) *n* courgette *f*.
courier ('kuriə) *n* **1** courrier *m*. **2** guide *m*.
course (kɔ:s) *n* **1** cours *m*. **2** route *f*. **3** *cul* plat *m*. **4** champ de courses *m*. **of course** bien entendu.
court (kɔ:t) *n* **1** cour *f*. **2** *law* tribunal, -aux *m*. *vt* **1** courtiser. **2** solliciter. **court martial** *n* conseil de guerre *m*. **courtship** *n* cour *f*. **courtyard** *n* cour *f*.
courteous ('kə:tiəs) *adj* courtois. **courtesy** *n* courtoisie *f*.
cousin ('kʌzən) *n* cousin *m*.
cove (kouv) *n* crique *f*.
covenant ('kʌvənənt) *n* contrat, pacte *m*. *vt* accorder. *vi* convenir de.
cover ('kʌvə) *vt* couvrir. *n* **1** couverture *f*. **2** couvercle *m*. **3** abri *m*.
cow (kau) *n* vache *f*. **cowboy** *n* cowboy *m*.
coward ('kauəd) *adj,n* lâche *m*. **cowardice** *n* lâcheté *f*.
cower ('kauə) *vi* se blottir.
coy (kɔi) *adj* farouche, timide.
crab (kræb) *n* crabe *m*. **crab-apple** pomme sauvage *f*.
crack (kræk) *n* **1** craquement *m*. **2** fissure *f*. *adj* de premier ordre. *vt* **1** faire claquer. **2** fêler. **3** casser. *vi* **1** claquer. **2** se fêler. **3** se casser.
cracker ('krækə) *n* pétard *m*.
crackle ('krækəl) *n* crépitement *m*. *vi* crépiter.
cradle ('kreidḷ) *n* berceau, -aux *m*.
craft (krɑ:ft) *n* **1** métier (manuel) *m*. **2** ruse *f*. **3** bateau, -aux *m*. **craftsman** *n* artisan *m*. **craftsmanship** *n* habileté d'exécution *f*. **crafty** *adj* rusé.
cram (kræm) *vt* bourrer. *vi* s'entasser.
cramp[1] (kræmp) *n med* crampe *f*.
cramp[2] (kræmp) *n* crampon *m*.
crane (krein) *n* grue *f*.
crash (kræʃ) *n* **1** fracas *m*. **2** catastrophe *f*. *vt* fracasser. *vi* **1** retentir. **2** se tamponner. **crash-helmet** *n* casque protecteur *m*.
crate (kreit) *n* caisse à claire-voie *f*.
crater ('kreitə) *n* cratère *m*.
crave (kreiv) *vt* **1** implorer. **2** demander. **crave for** désirer ardemment.
crawl (krɔ:l) *vi* **1** ramper. **2** se traîner. *n sport* crawl *m*.
crayfish ('kreifiʃ) *n* écrevisse *f*.
crayon ('kreiən) *n* pastel *m*. *vt* crayonner.
craze (kreiz) *n inf* manie *f*. **crazy** *adj* fou, folle, insensé.
creak (kri:k) *n* grincement *m*. *vi* grincer.
cream (kri:m) *n* crème *f*. **creamy** *adj* crémeux, -euse.
crease (kri:s) *n* (faux) pli *m*. *vt* froisser. *vi* se plisser. **crease-resistant** *adj* infroissable.
create (kri'eit) *vt* créer. **creation** *n* création *f*. **creative** *adj* créateur, -trice.
creature ('kri:tʃə) *n* créature *f*.
creche (kreʃ) *n* crèche *f*.
credible ('kredibəl) *adj* croyable. **credibility** *n* crédibilité *f*.
credit ('kredit) *n* **1** crédit *m*. **2** mérite *m*. **3** croyance *f*. **credit card** *n* carte de crédit *f*. ~*vt* **1** croire. **2** reconnaître. **3** *comm* créditer. **creditable** *adj* estimable. **creditor** *n* créancier *m*.
creep* (kri:p) *vi* ramper, se glisser, grimper.
cremate (kri'meit) *vt* incinérer. **cremation** *n* incinération *f*. **crematorium** *n* four crématoire *m*.
crept (krept) *v see* **creep**.
crescent ('kresənt) *n* croissant *m*.
cress (kres) *n* cresson *m*.
crest (krest) *n* crête *f*.
crevice ('krevis) *n* fissure *f*.
crew (kru:) *n* équipage *m*. équipe *f*.
crib (krib) *n* **1** mangeoire *f*. **2** berceau, -aux *m*.
cricket[1] ('krikit) *n zool* grillon *m*.
cricket[2] ('krikit) *n sport* cricket *m*.
crime (kraim) *n* crime *m*. **criminal** *adj,n* criminel, -elle.
crimson ('krimzən) *adj,n* pourpre *m*.
cringe (krindʒ) *vi* **1** se faire tout petit. **2** s'humilier. *n* courbette servile *f*.
crinkle ('kriŋkəl) *vt* froisser. *vi* se chiffonner. *n* fronce, ride *f*.
cripple ('kripəl) *n* infirme *m,f*. *vt* estropier.

crisis ('kraisis) *n, pl* **crises** crise *f.*
crisp (krisp) *adj* **1** croquant, croustillant. **2** vif, vive. **3** tranchant, net, nette.
criterion (krai'tiəriən) *n, pl* **criteria** *or* **criterions** critérium, critère *m.*
criticize ('kritisaiz) *vt* **1** critiquer. **2** blâmer, censurer. **critic** *n* **1** critique. **2** censeur *m.* **critical** *adj* critique. **criticism** *n* critique *f.*
croak (krouk) *n* coassement, croassement *m. vi* **1** coasser, croasser. **2** *inf* grogner.
crochet ('krouʃei) *n* crochet *m. vt* faire au crochet. *vi* faire du crochet.
crockery ('krɔkəri) *n* faïence, poterie *f.*
crocodile ('krɔkədail) *n* crocodile *m.*
crocus ('kroukəs) *n* crocus *m.*
crook (kruk) *n* **1** croc, crochet *m.* **2** angle *m.* **3** *inf* escroc *m.*
crooked ('krukid) *adj* **1** courbé, tordu. **2** tortueux, -euse. **3** malhonnête.
crop (krɔp) *n* **1** récolte, moisson *f.* **2** (of hair) coupe *f. vt* couper, tondre.
croquet ('kroukei) *n* croquet *m.*
cross (krɔs) *n* **1** croix *f.* **2** contrariété *f.* **3** croisement *m. adj* **1** en colère, fâché. **2** transversal, -aux, oblique. *vt* **1** croiser. **2** traverser. **3** (a cheque) barrer. **cross-examine** *vt* contre-interroger. **cross-examination** *n* contre-interrogatoire. *m.* **cross-eyed** *adj* louche. **cross-fire** *n* feu croisé *m.* **crossing** *n* **1** croisement *m.* **2** traversée *f.* passage *m.* **cross-question** *vt* interroger contradictoirement. **cross-reference** *n* renvoi *m.* **crossroads** *n* carrefour *m.* **crossword** *n* mots croisés *m pl.*
crotchet ('krɔtʃit) *n mus* noire *f.*
crouch (krautʃ) *vi* se blottir, s'accroupir.
crow[1] (krou) *n* corbeau, -aux *m.*
crow[2] (krou) *n* chant du coq, coquerico *m. vi* chanter.
crowd (kraud) *n* foule, bande *f.* rassemblement *m. vt* **1** serrer, entasser. **2** remplir. **crowded** *adj* bondé, encombré.
crown (kraun) *n* **1** couronne *f.* **2** sommet *m. vt* couronner. **crown prince** *n* prince héritier *m.*
crucial ('kru:ʃəl) *adj* critique, décisif, -ive.
crucify ('kru:sifai) *vt* crucifier, mettre en croix. **crucifix** *n* crucifix *m.* **crucifixion** *n* crucifixion *f.*
crude (kru:d) *adj* **1** brut. **2** cru. **3** grossier, -ère. **crude oil** *n* mazout *m.* **crudely** *adv* crûment, grossièrement.
cruel ('kruəl) *adj* cruel, -elle. **cruelty** *n* cruauté *f.*
cruise (kru:z) *n* croisière *f. vi* croiser.
crumb (krʌm) *n* miette *f.*
crumble ('krʌmbəl) *vt* émietter, effriter. *vi* **1** s'émietter. **2** s'écrouler.
crumple ('krʌmpəl) *vt* friper, froisser. **crumple up** se friper, se froisser.
crunch (krʌntʃ) *vt* croquer. *vi* craquer. *n* bruit de broiement *m.*
crusade (kru:'seid) *n* croisade *f.*
crush (krʌʃ) *n* presse, foule *f. vt* **1** écraser. **2** froisser. *vi* se presser en foule.
crust (krʌst) *n* croûte *f. vt* encroûter.
crustacean (krʌs'teiʃən) *n* crustacé *m.*
crutch (krʌtʃ) *n* béquille *f.*
cry* (krai) *n* cri *m. vt,vi* **1** crier. **2** pleurer. **cry off** se récuser. **cry out** s'écrier.
crypt (kript) *n* crypte *f.*
crystal ('kristḷ) *n* cristal, -aux *m.* **crystallize** *vt* cristalliser. *vi* se cristalliser.
cub (kʌb) *n* petit *m.*
cube (kju:b) *n* cube *m. vt* cuber. **cubic** *adj* cubique. **cubicle** *n* **1** alcôve *f.* **2** cabine *f.*
cuckoo ('kuku:) *n* coucou *m.*
cucumber ('kju:kʌmbə) *n* concombre *m.*
cuddle ('kʌdḷ) *vt* serrer dans les bras. *vi* se pelotonner. *n* étreinte, embrassade *f.*
cue[1] (kju:) *n* **1** *Th* réplique *f.* **2** avis *m.* indication *f.*
cue[2] (kju:) *n* queue (de billard) *f.*
cuff[1] (kʌf) *n* manchette *f.* **cufflink** *n* bouton de manchette *f.*
cuff[2] (kʌf) *n* taloche *f. vt* talocher.
culinary ('kʌlinri) *adj* culinaire.
culprit ('kʌlprit) *n* **1** coupable *m,f.* **2** *law* accusé, prévenu *m.*
cult (kʌlt) *n* culte *m.*
cultivate (kʌltiveit) *vt* cultiver. **cultivation** *n* culture *f.*
culture ('kʌltʃə) *n* culture *f.*
cultural *adj* culturel, -elle. **cultured** *adj* cultivé, instruit.
cumbersome ('kʌmbəsəm) *adj* encombrant, incommode.
cunning ('kʌniŋ) *adj* malin, -igne, rusé. *n* ruse, fourberie *f.*
cup (kʌp) *n* **1** tasse *f.* **2** *sport* coupe *f.* **cupful** *n* pleine coupe *f.*
cupboard ('kʌbəd) *n* armoire *f.* placard *m.*
curate ('kjuərеit) *n* vicaire *m.*
curator (kju'reitə) *n* conservateur *m.*
curb (kə:b) *n* **1** bordure *f.* **2** frein *m. vt* réprimer, brider.

curdle ('kə:dl̩) *vt* **1** cailler. **2** glacer. *vi* **1** se cailler. **2** se figer.

cure (kjuə) *n* **1** *med* guérison *f*. **2** remède *m*. *vt* **1** guérir. **2** *cul* saler, fumer.

curfew ('kə:fju:) *n* couvre-feu *m invar*.

curious ('kjuəriəs) *adj* **1** curieux, -euse. **2** singulier, -ière. **curiosity** *n* curiosité *f*.

curl (kə:l) *n* boucle *f*. *vt,vi* **1** boucler, friser. **2** enrouler. **curly** *adj* bouclé.

currant ('kʌrənt) *n* **1** groseille *f*. **2** raisin de Corinthe *m*. **currant bush** *n* groseillier *m*.

current ('kʌrənt) *adj* courant, en cours. *n* courant *m*. **currency** *n* **1** circulation *f*. cours *m*. **2** unité monétaire *f*. **currently** *adv* couramment. **current account** *n* compte courant *m*.

curry ('kʌri) *n* cari *m*. **curry powder** *n* cari *m*.

curse (kə:s) *n* **1** malédiction *f*. **2** juron *m*. **3** fléau, -aux *m*. *vt* maudire. *vi* blasphémer.

curt (kə:t) *adj* brusque, sec, sèche.

curtail (kə:'teil) *vt* **1** raccourcir. **2** diminuer.

curtain ('kə:tn̩) *n* rideau, -aux *m*.

curtsy ('kə:tsi) *n* révérence *f*. *vi* faire une révérence.

curve (kə:v) *n* **1** courbe *f*. **2** tournant *m*. *vt* courber, cintrer. *vi* se courber.

cushion ('kuʃən) *n* coussin *m*. *vt* amortir.

custard ('kʌstəd) *n* crème anglaise *f*.

custody ('kʌstədi) *n* **1** garde *f*. **2** emprisonnement *m*.

custom ('kʌstəm) *n* **1** coutume, habitude *f*. **2** clientèle *f*. **3** *pl* douane *f*. **customary** *adj* habituel, -elle, d'usage. **customer** *n* **1** client *m*. **2** *inf* type *m*.

cut* (kʌt) *vt,vi* couper. **cut down** réduire. **cut off** trancher. **cut out 1** enlever. **2** supprimer. **cut glass** *n* cristal taillé *m*. **cut-price** *adj* à prix réduit. ~*n* **1** coupe *f*. **2** coupure *f*. **3** tranche. *f*. **4** réduction *f*. **cutting** *n* **1** coupage *m*. **2** coupure *f*. *adj* mordant.

cute (kju:t) *adj inf* **1** mignon, -onne. **2** rusé.

cuticle ('kju:tikəl) *n* cuticule *f*.

cutlery ('kʌtləri) *n* coutellerie *f*.

cutlet ('kʌtlit) *n* côtelette *f*.

cycle ('saikəl) *n* **1** cycle *m*. **2** vélo *m*. *vi* faire de la bicyclette, aller à bicyclette. **cycling** *n* cyclisme *m*. **cyclist** *n* cycliste *m,f*.

cyclone ('saikloun) *n* cyclone *m*.

cygnet ('signit) *n* jeune cygne *m*.

cylinder ('silində) *n* cylindre *m*. **cylindrical** *adj* cylindrique.

cymbal ('simbəl) *n* cymbale *f*.

cynic ('sinik) *n* sceptique, cynique *m*. **cynical** *adj* sceptique, cynique.

cypress ('saiprəs) *n* cyprès *m*.

Cyprus ('saiprəs) *n* Chypre *f*. **Cypriot** *adj,n* cypriote.

czar (zɑ:) *n* tsar *m*.

Czechoslovakia (tʃekəslə'vækiə) *n* Tchécoslovaquie *f*. **Czech** *adj,n* tchèque. **Czechoslovakian** *adj* tchécoslovaque.

D

dab (dæb) *n* **1** coup léger *m*. **2** tache *f*. *vt* tamponner, tapoter.

dabble ('dæbəl) *vt* mouiller. *vi* barboter. **dabble in** se mêler de.

dad (dæd) *n inf* papa *m*.

daffodil ('dæfədil) *n* narcisse des bois *m*. jonquille *f*.

daft (dɑ:ft) *adj* écervelé, toqué.

dagger ('dægə) *n* poignard *m*. dague *f*.

daily ('deili) *adj* quotidien, -ienne, journalier, -ière. *n* **1** (newspaper) quotidien *m*. **2** *inf* femme de ménage *f*. *adv* tous les jours.

dainty ('deinti) *adj* délicat, friand.

dairy ('dɛəri) *n* laiterie *f*. ferme laitière *f*.

daisy ('deizi) *n* marguerite, pâquerette *f*.

dam[1] (dæm) *n* barrage. *vt* contenir, endiguer.

dam[2] (dæm) *n zool* mère *f*.

damage ('dæmidʒ) *n* **1** dégâts, dommages *m pl*. **2** préjudice *m*. **3** *law* dommages-intérêts *m pl*. *vt* **1** abîmer, endommager. **2** nuire à.

damn (dæm) *vt* **1** condamner. **2** ruiner. **3** damner. *interj* zut! **damnable** *adj* maudit. **damnation** *n* damnation *f*.

damp (dæmp) *adj* humide, moite. *n* humidité *f*. *vt* **1** mouiller. **2** étouffer. **3** décourager. **dampen** *vt* humidifier.

damson ('dæmzən) *n* prune de Damas *f*.

dance (dɑ:ns) *n* **1** danse *f*. **2** bal *m*. *vt,vi* danser. **dancing** *n* danse *f*.

dandelion ('dændilaiən) *n* pissenlit *m*.

dandruff ('dændrʌf) *n* pellicules *f pl*.

Dane (dein) *n* danois *m*. **Danish** *adj,n* danois. **Danish** (language) *n* danois *m*.

danger ('deindʒə) *n* danger, péril *m*. **dangerous** *adj* dangereux, -euse, périlleux, -euse.

dangle ('dæŋgəl) *vi* pendiller, se balancer. *vt* faire pendiller.

dare* (dɛə) *vt* **1** oser, risquer. **2** défier. **daring** *adj* hardi, audacieux, -euse. *n* témérité, audace *f*.

dark (dɑ:k) *adj* **1** noir, obscur. **2** foncé. **3** brun. **4** secret, -ète. *n also* **darkness** obscurité *f*.

ténèbres *f pl.* **darken** *vt* obscurcir, assombrir. *vi* s'obscurcir, s'assombrir.
darling ('dɑ:liŋ) *adj,n* chéri.
darn (dɑ:n) *vt* repriser, raccommoder. *n* reprise *f.* **darning** *n* reprise *f.*
dart (dɑ:t) *n* **1** dard *m.* **2** *sport* fléchette *f.* **3** (in sewing) pince *f.* *vi* s'élancer, se précipiter. **dartboard** *n* cible *f.*
dash (dæʃ) *n* **1** coup *m.* **2** goutte *f.* **3** trait *m.* **4** élan *m.* *vt* **1** jeter. **2** anéantir. *vi* s'élancer. **dashboard** *n* tablier *m.* **dashing** *adj* plein d'élan.
data ('deitə) *n* données *f pl.* **data processing** *n* traitement d'informatique *m.*
date[1] (deit) *n* **1** date *f.* **2** rendez-vous *m.* **date line** *n* ligne de changement de date *f.* **out of date** démodé. **up to date** à la page.
date[2] (deit) *n* *bot* datte *f.* **date palm** *n* dattier *m.*
daughter ('dɔ:tə) *n* fille *f.* **daughter-in-law** *n* belle-fille, bru *f.*
dawdle ('dɔ:dl) *vi* flâner, lambiner.
dawn (dɔ:n) *n* aube *f.* **at dawn** au point du jour.
day (dei) *n* jour *m.* journée *f.* **day after** lendemain *m.* **day before** veille *f.* **in those days** à ce moment-là. **daybreak** *n* point du jour *m.* **daydream** *n* rêverie *f.* *vi* rêvasser. **daylight** *n* jour *m.*
daze (deiz) *vt* **1** hébéter. **2** étourdir. *n* étourdissement *m.*
dazzle ('dæzəl) *vt* éblouir, aveugler. *n* éblouissement *m.*
dead (ded) *adj* mort, décédé. **deadline** *n* date limite *f.* **deadlock** *n* impasse *f.* **deaden** *vt* amortir, assourdir, assoupir. **deadly** *adj* mortel, -elle.
deaf (def) *adj* sourd. **deaf-aid** *n* appareil de correction auditive pour sourds *m.* **deaf-mute** *n* sourd-muet, sourde-muette. **deafness** *n* surdité *f.* **deafen** *vt* assourdir.
deal* (di:l) *n* **1** *comm* affaire *f.* **2** quantité *f.* **3** *game* donne *f.* *vt* distribuer, donner. *vi* **1** s'occuper. **2** faire des affaires. **dealer** *n* **1** fournisseur, marchand *m.* **2** *game* donneur *m.*
dean (di:n) *n* doyen *m.*
dear (diə) *adj* **1** cher, chère. **2** coûteux, -euse. *n* cher, chère. **dearly** *adv* cher, chèrement.
death (deθ) *n* mort *f.* **death certificate** *n* acte de décès *m.* **death rate** *n* mortalité *f.*
debate (di'beit) *n* débat *m.* discussion *f.* *vt* discuter, débattre. *vi* disputer.
debit ('debit) *n* débit *m.* *vt* débiter.
debris ('deibri) *n* débris *m pl.*
debt (det) *n* dette *f.* créance *f.* **debtor** *n* débiteur *m.*
decade ('dekeid) *n* décade *f.*
decadent ('dekədənt) *adj* décadent. **decadence** *n* décadence *f.*
decant (di'kænt) *vt* décanter. **decanter** *n* carafe *f.*
decay (di'kei) *n* **1** pourriture *f.* **2** décadence *f.* *vi* **1** pourrir. **2** tomber en ruine.
decease (di'si:s) *n* décès *m.* *vi* décéder.
deceit (di'si:t) *n* tromperie *f.* **deceitful** *adj* trompeur, -euse, fourbe. **deceitfulness** *n* fausseté *f.*
deceive (di'si:v) *vt* tromper, décevoir.
December (di'sembə) *n* décembre *m.*
decent ('di:sənt) *adj* **1** honnête, bienséant. **2** assez bon. **decency** *n* décence *f.*
deceptive (di'septiv) *adj* trompeur, -euse.
decibel ('desibel) *n* décibel *m.*
decide (di'said) *vt* décider. *vi* se décider. **decided** *adj* décidé, arrêté. **decidedly** *adv* résolument. **deciding** *adj* décisif, -ive.
deciduous (di'sidjuəs) *adj* caduc, caduque.
decimal ('desiməl) *adj* décimal, -aux. *n* décimale *f.* **decimalization** *n* décimalisation *f.*
decipher (di'saifə) *vt* déchiffrer.
decision (di'siʒən) *n* **1** décision *f.* **2** résolution *f.* **decisive** *adj* décisif, -ive.
deck (dek) *n* **1** *naut* pont *m.* **2** (of a bus) impériale *f.* *vt* orner. **deckchair** *n* transatlantique *m.*
declaration (deklə'reiʃən) *n* déclaration, annonce *f.*
declare (di'klɛə) *vt* déclarer, annoncer. *vi* se déclarer. **declared** *adj* avoué, ouvert.
decline (di'klain) *n* **1** déclin *m.* **2** baisse *f.* **3** pente *f.* *vt,vi* décliner. *vt* refuser poliment. *vi* **1** décliner, repousser. **2** baisser. **declension** *n* déclinaison *f.*
decorate ('dekəreit) *vt* décorer, orner. **decoration** *n* **1** décoration *f.* **2** décor *m.* **decorative** *adj* décoratif, -ive. **decorator** *n* décorateur *m.*
decoy (*n* 'di:kɔi; *v* di'kɔi) *n* appât, leurre *m.* amorce *f.* *vt* **1** piper. **2** leurrer.
decrease (di'kri:s) *n* diminution *f.* *vt,vi* diminuer. *vt* amoindrir. *vi* décroître.
decree (di'kri:) *n* décret, édit *m.* *vt* ordonner, décréter.
decrepit (di'krepit) *adj* décrépit *m.*
dedicate ('dedikeit) *vt* dédier. **dedication** *n* dedicace *f.*
deduce (di'dju:s) *vt* déduire, conclure.

deduct (di'dʌkt) *vt* déduire, retrancher. **deduction** *n* déduction *f.*
deed (di:d) *n* **1** action *f.* acte *m.* **2** exploit *m.*
deep (di:p) *adj* **1** profond. **2** (of colour) foncé. *n* **1** profondeur *f.* **2** abîme *m.* **deepen** *vt* approfondir. *vi* devenir plus profond. **deeply** *adv* profondément. **deep-freeze*** *n* congélateur *m.* *vt* congeler. **deep-seated** *adj* profond, enraciné.
deer (diə) *n* cerf, daim *m.*
deface (di'feis) *vt* mutiler, défigurer, lacérer.
default (di'fɔ:lt) *n* défaut *m.* contumace *f.* *vi* faire défaut.
defeat (di'fi:t) *n* défaite *f.* *vt* **1** vaincre. **2** renverser.
defect (*n* 'di:fekt; *v* di'fekt) *n* défaut *m.* *vi* déserter. **defection** *n* défection *f.* **defective** *adj* **1** défectueux, -euse. **2** *gram* défectif, -ive.
defence (di'fens) *n* défense, protection, justification *f.* **defend** *vt* défendre. **defendant** *n* défendeur, -eresse. **defensive** *adj* défensif, -ive.
defer (di'fɔ:) *vt* ajourner, différer. *vi* déférer. **deference** *n* déférence *f.* **deferential** *adj* déférent.
defiant (di'faiənt) *adj* rebelle, provocant. **defiance** *n* défi *m.* **defiantly** *adv* d'un air de défi.
deficient (di'fiʃənt) *adj* insuffisant, défectueux, -euse. **deficiency** *n* **1** manque *m.* **2** défaut *m.*
deficit ('defisit) *n* déficit *m.*
define (di'fain) *vt* **1** définir. **2** déterminer. **definition** *n* définition *f.*
definite ('defənit) *adj* **1** défini. **2** bien déterminé. *adv* décidément.
deflate (di'fleit) *vt* dégonfler. **deflation** *n* **1** dégonflement *m.* **2** *comm* déflation *f.*
deform (di'fɔ:m) *vt* déformer. **deformed** *adj* difforme. **deformity** *n* difformité *f.*
defraud (di'frɔ:d) *vt* frauder.
defrost (di'frɔst) *vt* déglacer, décongeler.
deft (deft) *adj* habile, adroit. **deftness** *n* habileté, dextérité *f.*
defunct (di'fʌŋkt) *adj* défunt, décédé.
defy (di'fai) *vt* défier.
degenerate (*adj,n* di'dʒenərit; *v* di'dʒenəreit) *adj,n* dégénéré. *vi* dégénérer.
degrade (di'greid) *vt* dégrader, avilir. **degradation** *n* dégradation *f.*
degree (di'gri:) *n* **1** degré *m.* **2** *educ* licence *f.* **by degrees** petit à petit. **in some degree** dans une certaine mesure. **to some degree** à un certain degré.
dehydrate (di'haidreit) *vt* déshydrater. **dehydration** *n* déshydratation *f.*
deity ('deiiti) *n* **1** dieu *m.* déesse *f.* **2** déité *f.*
dejected (di'dʒektid) *adj* triste, abattu.
delay (di'lei) *n* délai, retard *m.* *vt* traîner, retarder, arriérer. *vi* s'attarder.
delegate (*n* 'deligət; *v* 'deligeit) *n* délégué *m.* *vt* déléguer. **delegation** *n* délégation *f.*
delete (di'li:t) *vt* effacer, rayer.
deliberate (*adj* di'libərət; *v* di'libəreit) *adj* **1** intentionnel, -elle, prémédité. **2** réfléchi. *vt,vi* délibérer. **deliberately** *adv* exprès.
delicate ('delikət) *adj* délicat. **delicacy** *n* **1** délicatesse. **2** *cul* friandise *f.*
delicatessen (delikə'tesən) *n* charcuterie *f.*
delicious (di'liʃəs) *adj* délicieux, -euse, exquis.
delight (di'lait) *n* délices *f pl.* joie *f.* *vt* enchanter, réjouir. **delightful** *adv* délicieux, -euse, ravissant.
delinquency (di'liŋkwənsi) *n* **1** délinquance *f.* **2** délit *m.* **delinquent** *n* délinquant *m.*
deliver (di'livə) *vt* **1** livrer, distribuer. **2** (a speech) faire. **delivery** *n* **1** livraison *f.* **2** distribution *f.*
delta ('deltə) *n* delta *m.*
delude (di'lu:d) *vt* tromper, abuser, duper. **delusion** *n* erreur, illusion *f.*
delve (delv) *vt* fouiller.
demand (di'mɑ:nd) *vt* exiger, demander, réclamer. *n* demande *f.*
democracy (di'mɔkrəsi) *n* démocratie *f.* **democratic** *adj* démocratique.
demolish (di'mɔliʃ) *vt* démolir. **demolition** *n* démolition *f.*
demon ('di:mən) *n* démon *m.*
demonstrate ('demənstreit) *vt* **1** démontrer. **2** *pol* manifester. **demonstration** *n* **1** démonstration *f.* **2** *pol* manifestation *f.* **demonstrator** *n* **1** démonstrateur *m.* **2** manifestant *m.* **demonstrative** *adj* démonstratif, -ive.
demoralize (di'mɔrəlaiz) *vt* démoraliser.
demure (di'mjuə) *adj* réservé, composé.
den (den) *n* **1** tanière *f.* **2** repaire *m.*
denial (di'naiəl) *n* déni *m.* dénégation *f.*
denim ('denim) *n* **1** serge de coton *f.* **2** *pl* blue-jean *m.*
Denmark ('denmɑ:k) *n* Danemark *m.*
denomination (dinɔmi'neiʃən) *n* **1** dénomination *f.* **2** *rel* secte *f.* **denominator** *n* dénominateur *m.*
denote (di'nout) *vt* **1** dénoter. **2** signifier.
denounce (di'nauns) *vt* dénoncer.
dense (dens) *adj* **1** dense, épais, -aisse. **2** *inf*

stupide, bête. **density** *n* **1** densité *f.* **2** *inf* stupidité *f.*

dent (dent) *n* bosselure *f.* renfoncement *m.* *vt* bosseler.

dental ('dentļ) *adj* dentaire. **dentist** *n* dentiste *m.* **dentistry** *n* art dentaire *m.* **denture** *n* dentier *m.*

deny (di'nai) *vt* **1** nier, démentir. **2** refuser.

deodorant (di'oudərənt) *n* déodorant *m.*

depart (di'pɑ:t) *vi* partir, s'en aller. *vt* quitter. **departed** *adj* passé, mort. **departure** *n* départ *m.*

department (di'pɑ:tmənt) *n* **1** département *m.* **2** (of a shop) rayon *m.*

depend (di'pend) *vi* dépendre. **depend on** compter sur. **dependant** *n* charge de famille *f.* **dependence** *n* dépendance *f.*

depict (di'pikt) *vt* peindre.

deplete (di'pli:t) *vt* épuiser.

deplore (di'plɔ:) *vi* déplorer, regretter fort.

deport (di'pɔ:t) *vt* déporter. **deportment** *n* tenue *f.*

depose (di'pouz) *vt* déposer.

deposit (di'pɔzit) *n* **1** *comm* dépôt, versement *m.* **2** sédiment *m.* *vt* déposer.

depot ('depou) *n* dépôt, entrepôt *m.*

deprave (di'preiv) *vt* dépraver, corrompre.

depreciate (di'pri:ʃieit) *vt* déprécier. *vi* se déprécier, baisser.

depress (di'pres) *vt* **1** abaisser. **2** décourager. **3** *comm* faire languir. **depressed** *adj* **1** abattu. **2** *comm* languissant. **depression** *n* **1** abattement *m.* **2** dépression *f.* **depressive** *adj* déprimant.

deprive (di'praiv) *vt* priver.

depth (depΘ) *n* profondeur *f.*

deputize ('depjutaiz) *vi* remplacer. **deputation** *n* délégation *f.* **deputy** *n* délégué, suppléant *m.*

derail (di'reil) *vt* faire dérailler.

derelict ('derəlikt) *adj* abandonné, délaissé.

deride (di'raid) *vt* se moquer de, railler. **derision** *n* dérision *f.* **derisive** *adj* railleur, -euse.

derive (di'raiv) *vt,vi* tirer. *vi* provenir. **derivation** *n* dérivation *f.*

derogatory (di'rɔgətri) *adj* dérogatoire.

descend (di'send) *vt,vi* descendre. **descendant** *n* descendant *m.*

descent (di'sent) *n* descente *f.*

describe (di'skraib) *vt* décrire. **description** *n* description *f.*

desert[1] ('dezət) *n* désert *m.*

desert[2] (di'zə:t) *vt* abandonner, laisser. *vi* déserter. **deserter** *n* déserteur *m.*

deserve (di'zə:v) *vt* mériter.

design (di'zain) *n* **1** dessein *m.* **2** dessin *m.* **3** intention *f.* **4** modèle *m.* *vt* **1** projeter. **2** créer. **3** destiner. **designing** *adj* intrigant.

designate ('dezigneit) *vt* désigner, nommer. **2** indiquer.

desire (di'zaiə) *n* désir, souhait *m.* *vt* désirer, vouloir.

desk (desk) *n* **1** (school) pupitre *m.* **2** (office) bureau, -aux *m.* **3** caisse *f.*

desolate ('desələt) *adj* **1** désert, abandonné. **2** affligé.

despair (di'spɛə) *n* désespoir *m.*

desperate ('desprət) *adj* désespéré. **desperation** *n* désespoir *m.*

despise (di'spaiz) *vt* mépriser.

despite (di'spait) *prep* malgré.

despondent (di'spɔndənt) *adj* découragé, abattu.

dessert (di'zə:t) *n* dessert *m.* **dessertspoon** *n* cuiller à dessert *f.*

destine ('destin) *vt* destiner. **destination** *n* destination *f.* **destiny** *n* destin, sort *m.*

destitute ('destitju:t) *adj* **1** dépourvu, dénué. **2** sans ressources.

destroy (di'strɔi) *vt* **1** détruire, anéantir. **2** tuer. **destruction** *n* destruction *f.* **destructive** *adj* destructeur, -trice, destructif, -ive. **destroyer** *n* contre-torpilleur *m.*

detach (di'tætʃ) *vt* détacher, séparer. **detachment** *n* **1** détachement *m.* **2** indifférence *f.*

detail ('di:teil) *n* détail *m.* *vt* **1** détailler. **2** affecter.

detain (di'tein) *vt* **1** *law* détenir. **2** retenir. **detention** *n* **1** détention *f.* **2** *educ* retenue *f.*

detect (di'tekt) *vt* **1** découvrir. **2** apercevoir. **detective** *n* détective *m.* **detective story** roman policier *m.*

deter (di'tə:) *vt* décourager, détourner. **deterrent** *n* force préventive *f.*

detergent (di'tə:dʒənt) *n* détergent *m.*

deteriorate (di'tiəriəreit) *vi* se détériorer. **deterioration** *n* détérioration *f.*

determine (di'tə:min) *vt,vi* déterminer, décider. **determination** *n* détermination, résolution *f.* **determined** *adj* résolu.

detest (di'test) *vt* détester.

detonate ('detəneit) *vt* faire détoner. *vi* détoner. **detonator** *n* amorce *f.*

detour ('di:tuə) *n* détour *m.*

detract (di'trækt) *vi* **detract from** diminuer de, déprécier de.

devalue (di'vælju:) *vt* dévaluer. **devaluation** *n* dévaluation *f.*

devastate ('devəsteit) *vt* ravager, dévaster.

develop (di'veləp) *vt* développer. *vi* se développer, se manifester. **development** *n* **1** développement *m.* **2** exploitation *f.* **3** fait *m.*

deviate ('di:vieit) *vi* dévier, s'écarter. **deviation** *n* déviation *f.* **devious** *adj* tortueux, -euse, détourné.

device (di'vais) *n* **1** moyen *m.* **2** ruse *f.* **3** truc *m.*

devil ('devəl) *n* diable *m.*

devise (di'vaiz) *vt* inventer, combiner.

devoid (di'vɔid) *adj* dépourvu, dénué.

devote (di'vout) *vt* consacrer, vouer, accorder.

devotion (di'vouʃən) *n* dévouement *m.*

devour (di'vauə) *vt* dévorer.

devout (di'vaut) *adj* pieux, -euse, dévot.

dew (dju:) *n* rosée *f.*

dexterous ('dekstrəs) *adj* habile, adroit. **dexterity** *n* dextérité, habileté *f.*

diabetes (daiə'bi:tiz) *n* diabète *m.* **diabetic** *adj,n* diabétique.

diagonal (dai'ægənl) *adj* diagonal, -aux. *n* diagonale *f.*

diagram ('daiəgræm) *n* diagramme, schéma *m.*

dial (dail) *n* cadran *m.* *vt* **1** appeler. **2** (a number) composer.

dialect ('daiəlekt) *n* dialecte, patois *m.*

dialogue ('daiəlɔg) *n* dialogue *m.*

diameter (dai'æmitə) *n* diamètre *m.*

diamond ('daiəmənd) *n* **1** diamant *m.* **2** *game* carreau, -aux *m.*

diaphragm ('daiəfræm) *n* diaphragme *m.*

diarrhoea (daiə'riə) *n* diarrhée *f.*

diary ('daiəri) *n* **1** (personal) journal, -aux *m.* **2** agenda *m.*

dice (dais) *n pl or s* dé *m.* *vt* couper en cubes.

dictate (*v* dik'teit; *n* 'dikteit) *vt* dicter. *vi* faire la loi. *n* commandement *m.* **dictation** *n* dictée *f.* **dictator** *n* dictateur *m.* **dictatorship** *n* dictature *f.*

dictionary ('dikʃənri) *n* dictionnaire *m.*

did (did) *v* see **do.**

die (dai) *vi* mourir. **die down** s'apaiser.

diesel ('di:zəl) *n* diesel *m.*

diet ('daiət) *n* régime *m.* *vi* être au régime.

differ ('difə) *vi* différer. **difference** *n* **1** différence *f.* **2** dispute *f.* **different** *adj* différent, divers, autre. **differential** *adj* différentiel, -elle. *n* **1** *mot* différentiel *m.* **2** différentielle *f.* **differentiate** *vt* différencier.

difficult ('difikəlt) *adj* difficile. **difficulty** *n* **1** difficulté *f.* **2** obstacle, ennui *m.*

dig* (dig) *vt* bêcher, creuser. *n* **1** fouille *f.* **2** *inf* coup de patte *m.*

digest (dai'dʒest) *vt* digérer. *vi* se digérer. **digestion** *n* digestion *f.*

digit ('didʒit) *n* **1** chiffre *m.* **2** *anat* doigt *m.*

dignity ('digniti) *n* dignité *f.* **dignified** *adj* digne.

dilapidated (di'læpideitid) *adj* délabré, décrépit.

dilemma (di'lemə) *n* dilemme *f.*

diligent ('dilidʒənt) *adj* diligent, assidu. **diligently** *adv* diligemment.

dilute (dai'lu:t) *vt* diluer, arroser.

dim (dim) *adj* faible, pâle. *vt* obscurcir, ternir. *vi* s'effacer, baisser.

dimension (di'menʃən) *n* dimension *f.*

diminish (di'miniʃ) *vt,vi* diminuer, réduire.

diminutive (di'minjutiv) *adj,n* diminutif, -ive *m.*

dimple ('dimpəl) *n* fossette *f.*

din (din) *n* fracas, tapage *m.*

dine (dain) *vt* dîner. **dining car** *n* wagon-restaurant. **dining room** *n* salle à manger *f.*

dinghy ('diŋgi) *n* canot *m.*

dingy ('dindʒi) *adj* terne, sombre.

dinner ('dinə) *n* dîner *m.* **dinner jacket** *n* smoking *m.*

dinosaur ('dainəsɔ:) *n* dinosaure *m.*

diocese ('daiəsis) *n* diocèse *m.*

dip (dip) *vt,vi* **1** plonger. **2** baisser. *vi* incliner. *n* **1** plongée *f.* **2** *inf* baignade *f.*

diphthong ('difθɔŋ) *n* diphtongue *f.*

diploma (di'ploumə) *n* diplôme *m.*

diplomacy (di'ploumәsi) *n* diplomatie *f.* *n* diplomate *m.* **diplomatic** *adj* **1** diplomatique. **2** prudent.

direct (di'rekt) *vt* **1** diriger. **2** ordonner. **3** indiquer. *adj* **1** direct. **2** franc, -che. **3** absolu. **direct object** *n* objet direct *m.* **direction** *n* **1** direction *f.* sens *m.* **2** *pl* instructions *f pl.* **director** *n* administrateur, directeur *m.* **directory** *n* annuaire. **directly** *adv* tout de suite.

dirt (də:t) *n* **1** saleté *f.* **2** ordure *f.* **dirty** *adj* **1** sale, crasseux, -euse. **2** *inf* vulgaire. **3** *inf* vilain. *vt* salir, crotter.

disability (disə'biliti) *n* **1** incapacité *f.* **2** infirmité *f.* **disabled** *adj* invalide, estropié.

disadvantage (disəd'vɑ:ntidʒ) *n* désavantage, inconvénient *m.*

disagree (disə'gri:) *vi* **1** être en désaccord. **2** se brouiller. **disagreeable** *adj* désagréable. **disagreement** *n* **1** différence *f*. **2** querelle *f*.

disappear (disə'piə) *vi* disparaître. **disappearance** *n* disparition *f*.

disappoint (disə'pɔint) *vt* désappointer, décevoir. **disappointment** *n* déception *f*.

disapprove (disə'pru:v) *vi* désapprouver. **disapproval** *n* désapprobation *f*. **disapproving** *adj* désapprobateur, -trice.

disarm (dis'ɑ:m) *vt,vi* désarmer. **disarmament** *n* désarmement *m*.

disaster (di'zɑ:stə) *n* désastre *m*. **disastrous** *adj* désastreux, -euse.

disband (dis'bænd) *vt* licencier. *vi* se débander.

disc (disk) *n* disque *m*. **disc jockey** *n* présentateur de disques *m*.

discard (di'skɑ:d) *vt* rejeter, se défausser de.

discern (di'sə:n) *vt* discerner, distinguer. **discerning** *adj* judicieux, -euse.

discharge (dis'tʃɑ:dʒ) *vt* **1** décharger. **2** congédier. **3** renvoyer. **4** *law* libérer, acquitter. *n* **1** décharge *f*. **2** renvoi *m*. **3** acquittement *m*.

disciple (di'saipəl) *n* disciple *m*.

discipline ('disəplin) *n* discipline *f*. *vt* discipliner.

disclose (dis'klouz) *vt* révéler, divulguer.

disconnect (diskə'nekt) *vt* couper, décrocher, disjoindre.

disconsolate (dis'kɔnsələt) *adj* désolé, triste.

discontinue (diskən'tinju:) *vt* discontinuer. *vi* cesser.

discord ('diskɔ:d) *n* **1** discorde *f*. **2** *mus* dissonance *f*. **discordant** *adj* **1** discordant. **2** *mus* dissonant.

discotheque ('diskətek) *n* discothèque *f*.

discount (*n* 'diskaunt; *v* dis'kaunt) *n* rabais *m*. remise *f*. *vt* ne pas tenir compte de.

discourage (dis'kʌridʒ) *vt* décourager, abattre.

discover (dis'kʌvə) *vt* découvrir. **discovery** *n* découverte *f*.

discreet (dis'kri:t) *adj* discret, -ète, prudent. **discretion** *n* **1** discrétion *f*. **2** jugement *m*.

discrepancy (dis'krepənsi) *n* désaccord *m*.

discrete (dis'kri:t) *adj* discret, -ète.

discriminate (dis'krimineit) *vt* distinguer, discerner. *vi* faire des distinctions. **discrimination** *n* **1** discernement *m*. **2** jugement *m*. **3** distinction *f*.

discus ('diskəs) *n* disque *m*.

discuss (dis'kʌs) *vt* discuter, débattre. **discussion** *n* discussion *f*. débat *m*.

disease (di'zi:z) *n* maladie *f*. mal *m*.

disembark (disim'bɑ:k) *vt,vi* débarquer. **disembarkation** *n* débarquement *m*.

disfigure (dis'figə) *vt* défigurer. **disfigurement** *n* défiguration *f*.

disgrace (dis'greis) *n* **1** disgrâce *f*. **2** honte *f*. *vt* déshonorer. **disgraceful** *adj* honteux, -euse.

disgruntled (dis'grʌntəld) *adj* mécontent, contrarié.

disguise (dis'gaiz) *vt* déguiser, travestir. *n* déguisement *m*.

disgust (dis'gʌst) *n* dégoût *m*. *vt* dégoûter, écœurer.

dish (diʃ) *n* **1** plat *m*. **2** *cul* mets *m*. **dishcloth** *n* torchon *m*.

dishearten (dis'hɑ:tn̩) *vt* décourager.

dishevelled (di'ʃevəld) *adj* échevelé, en désordre.

dishonest (dis'ɔnist) *adj* malhonnête. **dishonesty** *n* malhonnêteté *f*.

dishonour (dis'ɔnə) *n* déshonneur *m*. *vt* déshonorer. **dishonourable** *adj* déshonorant, honteux, -euse.

disillusion (disi'lu:ʒən) *n* désillusion *f*. désenchantement *m*.

disinfect (disin'fekt) *vt* désinfecter. **disinfectant** *adj,n* désinfectant *m*.

disinherit (disin'herit) *vt* déshériter.

disintegrate (dis'intigreit) *vt* désintégrer, désagréger. *vi* se désintégrer, se désagréger. **disintegration** *n* désagrégation *f*.

disinterested (dis'intrəstid) *adj* désintéressé, impartial, -aux.

disjointed (dis'dʒɔintid) *adj* **1** désarticulé. **2** décousu, sans suite.

dislike (dis'laik) *vt* détester, avoir de l'aversion pour. *n* aversion *f*. dégoût *m*. **take a dislike to** prendre en aversion.

dislocate ('disləkeit) *vt* **1** disloquer. **2** *med* déboîter.

disloyal (dis'lɔiəl) *adj* infidèle, déloyal, -aux.

dismal ('dizməl) *adj* **1** sombre. **2** lugubre. **3** triste.

dismantle (dis'mæntl̩) *vt* **1** démonter. **2** dégarnir.

dismay (dismei) *vt* effrayer, consterner. *n* consternation *f*.

dismiss (dis'mis) *vt* **1** renvoyer, congédier. **2** écarter (a thought, etc.).

dismount (dis'maunt) *vi* descendre. *vt* désarçonner, démonter.

disobey (disə'bei) *vt* désobéir à. **disobedience** *n* désobéissance *f*. **disobedient** *adj* désobéissant.

disorder (dis'ɔ:də) *n* désordre *m*. confusion *f*.
disorganized (dis'ɔ:gənaizd) *adj* désorganisé.
disown (dis'oun) *vt* **1** renier. **2** désavouer.
disparage (dis'pæridʒ) *vt* **1** dénigrer. **2** discréditer.
dispassionate (dis'pæʃənət) *adj* **1** impassible. **2** impartial, -aux. **dispassionately** *adv* **1** sans parti pris. **2** avec calme.
dispatch (dis'pætʃ) *vt* expédier. *n* **1** envoi *m*. **2** expédition *f*.
dispel (dis'pel) *vt* dissiper.
dispense (dis'pens) *vt* **1** distribuer, dispenser. **2** *law* administrer. **3** *med* préparer. **dispense with** se passer de. **dispensary** *n* **1** dispensaire *m*. **2** pharmacie *f*.
disperse (dis'pə:s) *vt* **1** disperser, éparpiller. **2** dissiper. *vi* **1** se disperser, s'éparpiller. **dispersal** *n* dispersion *f*.
displace (dis'pleis) *vt* déplacer.
display (dis'plei) *vt* **1** exposer, exhiber. **2** manifester. *n* **1** exposition. **2** *comm* étalage *m*.
displease (dis'pli:z) *vt* **1** déplaire à. **2** contrarier.
dispose (dis'pouz) *vt* disposer, arranger. *vi* disposer, se débarrasser. **be ill-/well-disposed** être mal/bien disposé. **disposal** *n* **1** disposition *f*. **2** *comm* vente *f*. **disposition** *n* **1** disposition *f*. **2** tempérament, caractère *m*. **3** penchant *m*.
disprove (dis'pru:v) *vt* réfuter.
dispute (dis'pju:t) *vi* **1** discuter. **2** se disputer. *vt* **1** débattre. **2** contester. *n* **1** dispute *f*. **2** contestation *f*. **beyond dispute** incontestable.
disqualify (dis'kwɔlifai) *vt* disqualifier.
disregard (disri'gɑ:d) *vt* négliger, ne pas faire attention à. *n* indifférence, insouciance *f*.
disreputable (dis'repjutəbəl) *adj* **1** de mauvaise réputation. **2** louche. **3** minable.
disrespect (disri'spekt) *n* manque de respect *m*. irrévérence *f*. **disrespectful** *adj* irrespectueux, -euse.
disrupt (dis'rʌpt) *vt* rompre, briser.
dissatisfy (di'sætisfai) *vt* mécontenter. **dissatisfied** *adj* mécontent.
dissect (di'sekt) *vt* disséquer. **dissection** *n* dissection *f*.
dissent (di'sent) *vi* différer. *n* dissentiment *m*. **dissenting** *adj* dissident.
dissimilar (di'similə) *adj* dissemblable, différent.
dissociate (di'souʃieit) *vt* désassocier.
dissolve (di'zɔlv) *vt* dissoudre. *vi* **1** se dissoudre. **2** fondre.
dissuade (di'sweid) *vt* dissuader.
distance ('distəns) *n* **1** distance *f*. **2** éloignement *m*. **3** lointain *m*. **in the distance** au loin. **distant** *adj* **1** éloigné, lointain. **2** distant, froid.
distaste (dis'teist) *n* dégoût *m*. **distasteful** *adj* déplaisant.
distil (dis'til) *vt* distiller.
distinct (dis'tiŋkt) *adj* **1** distinct, différent. **2** net, clair. **3** bien défini, marqué. **distinction** *n* distinction *f*. **distinctive** *adj* distinctif, -ive.
distinguish (dis'tiŋgwiʃ) *vt* **1** distinguer. **2** caractériser. *vi* faire une distinction. **distinguished** *adj* distingué.
distort (dis'tɔ:t) *vt* **1** déformer. **2** fausser.
distract (dis'trækt) *vt* **1** distraire, détourner. **2** troubler. **distraction** *n* **1** distraction *f*. **2** folie *f*.
distraught (dis'trɔ:t) *adj* affolé, fou, folle.
distress (dis'tres) *n* **1** détresse, angoisse *f*. **2** (poverty) misère *f*. *vt* désoler. **distressing** *adj* **1** affligeant. **2** douloureux, -euse.
distribute (dis'tribju:t) *vt* distribuer. **distribution** *n* distribution, répartition *f*.
district ('distrikt) *n* **1** région. **2** (of a town) quartier *m*. **3** arrondissement *m*.
distrust (dis'trʌst) *vi* se méfier de. *n* méfiance *f*.
disturb (dis'tə:b) *vt* **1** déranger. **2** troubler. **disturbance** *n* **1** dérangement *m*. **2** tapage *m*. **3** agitation *f*.
ditch (ditʃ) *n* fossé *m*.
ditto ('ditou) *adv* idem, de même.
divan (di'væn) *n* divan *m*.
dive (daiv) *vi* plonger. *n* **1** plongeon *m*. **2** *sl* cabaret *m*. **diving board** *n* plongeoir *m*.
diverge (dai'və:dʒ) *vi* diverger, s'écarter.
diverse (dai'və:s) *adj* divers, varié.
divert (dai'və:t) *vt* **1** détourner, dévier. **2** distraire. **diversion** *n* **1** (of a road, etc.) déviation *f*. **2** distraction *f*.
divide (di'vaid) *vt* **1** diviser, séparer. **2** répartir. **3** désunir. *vi* se diviser. **divisible** *adj* divisible. **division** *n* **1** division *f*. **2** partage *m*. discorde *f*.
dividend ('dividend) *n* dividende *m*.
divine (di'vain) *adj* divin, sacré. **divinity** *n* **1** divinité *f*. **2** théologie *f*.
divorce (di'vɔ:s) *n* divorce *m*. *vi* divorcer. *vt* divorcer d'avec.
divulge (di'vʌldʒ) *vt* divulguer, révéler.
dizzy ('dizi) *adj* **1** étourdi. **2** vertigineux, -euse. **dizziness** *n* vertige, étourdissement *m*.
do* (du:) *vt* **1** faire. **2** rendre. **3** finir. **4** *sl* duper. **do again** **1** refaire. **2** recommencer. **do one's best** faire de son mieux. **do up** **1**

empaqueter. 2 *inf* réparer. **do without** se passer de. **how do you do?** comment allez-vous? **that will do** cela suffit.

docile ('dousail) *adj* docile.

dock[1] (dɔk) *n naut* bassin *m.* **dockyard** *n* chantier de constructions navales *m.*

dock[2] (dɔk) *vt* **1** retrancher. **2** couper la queue à.

dock[3] (dɔk) *n law* banc des accusés *m.*

doctor ('dɔktə) *n* **1** *med* médecin *m.* **2** *educ* docteur *m.*

doctrine ('dɔktrin) *n* doctrine *f.*

document ('dɔkjumənt) *n* document *m.* pièce *f.* *vt* documenter. **documentary** *adj,n* documentaire *m.*

dodge (dɔdʒ) *vi* **1** s'esquiver. **2** biaiser. *vt* **1** esquiver. **2** éviter. *n* **1** détour *m.* **2** esquive *f.* **3** *inf* ruse *f.* **dodgy** *adj inf* roublard.

dog (dɔg) *n* chien *m.* *vt* **1** suivre à la piste. **2** harceler. **dogged** *adj* tenace. **dog-collar** *n* **1** collier de chien *m.* **2** *rel* col droit *m.* **dogfish** *n* roussette *f.*

dogma ('dɔgmə) *n* dogme *m.* **dogmatic** *adj* **1** dogmatique. **2** autoritaire.

dole (doul) *n* allocation de chômage *f.*

doll (dɔl) *n* poupée *f.*

dollar ('dɔlə) *n* dollar *m.*

dolphin ('dɔlfin) *n* dauphin *m.*

domain (də'mein) *n* domaine *m.*

dome (doum) *n* dôme *m.*

domestic (də'mestik) *adj* **1** domestique. **2** de famille. **3** *comm* intérieur. *n* domestique *m,f.* **domesticate** *vt* domestiquer.

dominate ('dɔmineit) *vt,vi* dominer. **dominant** *adj* dominant.

domineer (dɔmi'niə) *vi* dominer. **domineering** *adj* autoritaire.

dominion (də'miniən) *n* **1** dominion *m.* **2** autorité *f.*

domino ('dɔminou) *n, pl* **dominoes** domino *m.*

donate (dou'neit) *vt* faire don de. **donation** *n* donation *f.*

done (dʌn) *v* see **do.**

donkey ('dɔŋki) *n* âne *m.*

donor ('dounə) *n* donateur, -trice.

doom (du:m) *n* destin *m.* *vt* **1** condamner. **2** vouer.

door (dɔ:) *n* **1** porte *f.* **2** *mot* portière *f.* **out of doors** dehors. **doorbell** *n* sonnette *f.* **doorhandle** *n* poignée de porte *f.* **doorknob** *n* bouton de porte *m.* **doorknocker** *n* marteau, -aux *m.* **doormat** *n* paillasson *m.* **doorstep** *n* pas, seuil *m.* **doorway** *n* encadrement de la porte *m.*

dope (doup) *vt* doper, droguer. *n* **1** *inf* drogue, narcotique *f.* **2** *inf* imbécile *m,f.*

dormant ('dɔ:mənt) *adj* assoupi, endormi.

dormitory ('dɔ:mitri) *n* dortoir *m.*

dormouse ('dɔ:maus) *n* loir *m.*

dose (dous) *n* dose *f.* *vt* médicamenter. **dosage** *n* dosage *m.*

dot (dɔt) *n* point *m.* *vt* **1** mettre un point sur. **2** *Art* pointiller.

dote (dout) *vi* **dote on** raffoler de.

double ('dʌbəl) *adj* double, en deux. *n* **1** double *m.* **2** sosie *m.* *vt* **1** doubler. **2** plier en deux. *vi* (se) doubler. **double back** revenir sur ses pas. **double bass** *n* contrebasse *f.* **double bed** *n* grand lit *m.* **double-cross** *vt inf* duper, tromper. **double-decker bus** *n* autobus à impériale *m.* **double-dutch** *n* chinois, hébreu *m.* **talk double-dutch** baragouiner. **double glazing** *n* double vitrage *m.*

doubt (daut) *n* doute *m.* *vt,vi* douter. *vi* **1** soupçonner. **2** hésiter. **doubtful** *adj* **1** douteux, -euse. **2** incertain. **3** *inf* louche.

dough (dou) *n* **1** pâte *f.* **2** *sl* galette *f.* **doughnut** *n* beignet *m.*

dove (dʌv) *n* colombe *f.* **dovecote** *n* colombier *m.*

Dover ('douvə) *n* Douvres *m.*

dowdy ('daudi) *adj* mal vêtu.

down[1] (daun) *adv* **1** en bas. **2** par terre. **3** à bas. *prep* **1** en bas de. **2** le long de. **down there** là-bas.

down[2] (daun) *n* duvet *m.*

downcast ('daunka:st) *adj* abattu, découragé.

downfall ('daunfɔ:l) *n* chute *f.*

downhearted (daun'ha:tid) *adj* découragé.

downhill ('daunhil) *adj* en pente. *adv* en descendant.

downpour ('daunpɔ:) *n* pluie torrentielle *f.* déluge *m.*

downright ('daunrait) *adj* **1** franc. **2** véritable. *adv* **1** tout à fait. **2** carrément.

downstairs (daun'stɛəz) *adv* en bas.

downstream (daun'stri:m) *adv* en aval, à l'aval.

downtrodden ('dauntrɔdn̩) *adj* opprimé.

downward ('daunwəd) *adj* descendant.

downwards ('daunwədz) *adv* **1** en bas. **2** en descendant. **3** en aval.

dowry ('dauəri) *n* dot *f.*

doze (douz) *vi* somnoler, sommeiller. *n* petit somme *m.*

dozen (ˈdʌzən) *n* douzaine *f*.
drab (dræb) *adj* terne.
drachma (ˈdrækmə) *n* drachme *m*.
draft (drɑːft) *n* **1** *mil* détachement *m*. **2** *Art* dessin *m*. **3** brouillon *m*. **4** *comm* traite *f*. *vt* **1** *mil* détacher. **2** rédiger.
drag (dræg) *vt* **1** traîner. **2** *naut* draguer. *vi* se traîner. *n* **1** drague *f*. **2** *inf* obstacle *m*.
dragon (ˈdrægən) *n* dragon *m*. **dragonfly** *n* libellule *f*.
drain (drein) *n* égoût *m*. *vt* **1** assécher. **2** faire écouler. **3** vider. *vi* s'écouler. **drainage** *n* système d'égouts *m*. **draining board** *n* égouttoir *m*. **drainpipe** *n* tuyau d'écoulement *m*.
drake (dreik) *n* canard *m*.
dram (dræm) *n* goutte *f*.
drama (ˈdrɑːmə) *n* drame *m*. **dramatic** *adj* dramatique. **dramatist** *n* dramaturge *m*. **dramatize** *vt* dramatiser.
drank (dræŋk) *v see* **drink.**
drape (dreip) *n* rideau *m*. *vt* draper. **draper** *n* drapier *m*. **draper's shop** *n* magasin de nouveautés *m*. mercerie *f*. **drapery** *n* draperie *f*.
drastic (ˈdræstik) *adj* **1** énergique. **2** rigoureux, -euse.
draught (drɑːft) *n* **1** courant d'air *m*. **2** tirage *m* **3** *med* potion *f*. **4** coup *m*. **5** *pl* jeu de dames *m*. **draught beer** *n* bière à la pression *f*. **draughtboard** *n* damier *m*. **draughtsman** *n* dessinateur *m*.
draw* (drɔː) *vt* **1** tirer. **2** dessiner. **3** attirer. *vi* tirer. **draw back** reculer. **draw near** se rapprocher. ~*n* **1** loterie *f*. tirage *m*. **2** partie nulle *f*. **3** attraction *f*. **drawback** *n* obstacle, inconvénient *m*. **drawbridge** *n* pont-levis *m*. **drawer** *n* tiroir *m*. **drawing** *n* dessin *m*. **drawing board** *n* planche à dessin *f*. **drawing pin** *n* punaise *f*. **drawing room** *n* salon *m*.
drawl (drɔːl) *vi* parler d'une voix traînante. *n* voix traînante *f*.
dread (dred) *n* crainte, terreur *f*. *vt* redouter. **dreadful** *adj* affreux, -euse. **dreadfully** *adv* terriblement.
dream* (driːm) *n* rêve, songe *m*. *vi* **1** rêver. **2** rêvasser. *vt* **1** rêver. **2** imaginer. **dreamy** *adj* **1** rêveur, -euse. **2** chimérique.
dreary (ˈdriəri) *adj* morne, lugubre.
dredge (dredʒ) *n* drague *f*. *vt* **1** draguer. **2** *cul* saupoudrer.
dregs (dregz) *n pl* **1** lie *f*. **2** rebut *m*.
drench (drentʃ) *vt* **1** tremper, mouiller. **2** (an animal) purger.
dress (dres) *vt* **1** habiller, vêtir. **2** parer, orner. **3** *med* panser. **4** *cul* apprêter. *vi* s'habiller. *n* **1** vêtement *m*. **2** robe *f*. **3** tenue *f*. **4** toilette *f*. **dress circle** *n* premier balcon *m*. **dressmaker** *n* couturière *f*. **dress rehearsal** *n* répétition générale *f*. **dressing** *n* **1** toilette *f*. **2** *cul* assaisonnement *m*. **3** *med* pansement *m*. **dressing-gown** *n* robe de chambre *f*. peignoir *m*. **dressing-room** *n* **1** cabinet de toilette *m*. **2** *Th* loge. **dressing-table** *n* coiffeuse *f*. **dressy** *adj* élégant.
dresser[1] (ˈdresə) *n* habilleur, -euse.
dresser[2] (ˈdresə) *n* dressoir, buffet *m*.
drew (druː) *v see* **draw.**
dribble (ˈdribəl) *vi* **1** dégoutter. **2** (of a child) baver. *vt sport* dribbler. *n* **1** goutte *f*. **2** bave *f*.
drier (ˈdraiə) *n* séchoir *m*.
drift (drift) *n* **1** (of snow) monceau, -aux *m*. **2** *naut* dérive *f*. **3** portée *f*. *vi* **1** dériver, aller à la dérive. **2** se laisser aller.
drill (dril) *n* **1** foret *m*. foreuse *f*. **2** *mil* exercise *m*. *vt* **1** percer, forer. **2** instruire.
drink* (driŋk) *n* boisson *f*. *vt* boire. **drinking water** *n* eau potable *f*.
drip (drip) *n* **1** égouttement *m*. **2** goutte *f*. **3** *inf* nouille *f*. *vi* dégoutter. **drip-dry** *adj* ne nécessitant aucun repassage. **dripping** *n* **1** *cul* graisse de rôti *f*. **2** égouttement *m*.
drive* (draiv) *vt* **1** conduire. **2** enfoncer. **3** pousser. **4** forcer. *vi* **1** se promener. **2** conduire. *n* **1** promenade en voiture *f*. **2** énergie *f*. **3** allée *f*. **driver** *n* chauffeur, conducteur *m*. **driving licence** *n* permis de conduire *m*. **driving school** *n* auto-école *f*. **driving test** *n* examen de permis de conduire *m*.
drivel (ˈdrivəl) *vi* **1** baver. **2** *inf* radoter. *n* **1** bave *f*. **2** radotage *m*.
drizzle (ˈdrizəl) *v imp* bruiner. *n* bruine *f*.
dromedary (ˈdrʌmədəri) *n* dromadaire *m*.
drone[1] (droun) *n zool* faux-bourdon *m*.
drone[2] (droun) *n* bourdonnement *m*. *vi* bourdonner.
droop (druːp) *vi* **1** languir. **2** s'affaiblir. **3** se pencher.
drop (drɔp) *vt* **1** laisser tomber. **2** abandonner. *vi* tomber. **drop in** entrer en passant. *n* **1** goutte *f*. **2** chute *f*. **3** baisse *f*. **dropout** *n* raté *m*.
drought (draut) *n* sécheresse *f*.
drove (drouv) *v see* **drive.**
drown (draun) *vt* noyer. *vi* se noyer.
drowsy (drauzi) *adj* somnolent, assoupi.

drudge (drʌdʒ) *vi* peiner, trimer. *n* souffre-douleur *m,f*. **drudgery** *n* corvée *f*.
drug (drʌg) *vt* droguer. *n* **1** drogue *f*. **2** *inf* stupéfiant *m*. **drug addict** *n* toxicomane *m,f*.
drum (drʌm) *n* **1** *mus* tambour *m*. **2** tonneau, -aux *m*. *vi* tambouriner. **drummer** *n* tambour *m*. **drumstick** *n* baguette de tambour *f*.
drunk (drʌŋk) *v* see **drink.** *adj* ivre, soûl. **drunkard** *n* ivrogne *m*. **drunken** *adj* ivre.
dry (drai) *vt* **1** sécher, essuyer. *vi* (se) sécher. *adj* sec, sèche. **dry-clean** *vt* nettoyer à sec. **dry-cleaning** *n* nettoyage à sec *m*.
dual ('djuəl) *adj* double. **dual carriageway** *n* route à double voie *f*.
dubious ('dju:biəs) *adj* douteux, -euse.
duchess ('dʌtʃis) *n* duchesse *f*.
duck[1] (dʌk) *n* canard m. **duckling** *n* caneton *m*.
duck[2] (dʌk) *vi* **1** plonger. **2** baisser la tête.
duct (dʌkt) *n* conduit *m*.
dud (dʌd) *adj* **1** raté. **2** *inf* moche.
due (dju:) *adj* **1** dû. **2** voulu. **3** attendu. *n* **1** dû *m*. **2** *pl* droits *m pl*. *adv* droit. **due to** à cause de, par suite à.
duel ('djuəl) *n* duel *m*. *vi* se battre en duel.
duet (dju'et) *n* duo *m*.
dug (dʌg) *v* see **dig.**
duke (dju:k) *n* duc *m*.
dulcimer ('dʌlsimə) *n* tympanon *m*.
dull (dʌl) *adj* **1** sombre. **2** ennuyeux, -euse. **3** terne, stupide. *vt* **1** émousser. **2** amortir.
duly ('dju:li) *adv* **1** dûment. **2** en temps voulu.
dumb (dʌm) *adj* **1** muet, -ette. **2** *inf* stupide. **dumbfound** *vi* abasourdir, confondre.
dummy ('dʌmi) *n* **1** mannequin *m*. **2** *game* mort. **3** (for a baby) sucette *f*. **4** *comm* simulacre *m*.
dump (dʌmp) *vt* décharger, vider. **2** *inf* trou *m*. *n* dépôt *m*.
dumpling ('dʌmpliŋ) *n* chausson *m*.
dunce (dʌns) *n* ignorant, âne *m*.
dune (dju:n) *n* dune *f*.
dung (dʌŋ) *n* fiente, crotte *f*. fumier *m*.
dungeon ('dʌndʒən) *m* cachot *m*.
Dunkirk (dʌn'kə:k) *n* Dunkerque *m*.
duplicate (*adj,n* 'dju:plikət; *v* 'dju:plikeit) *adj,n* double *m*. *vt* faire en double, copier.
durable ('djuərəbəl) *adj* durable. **duration** *n* durée *f*.
during ('djuəriŋ) *prep* pendant.
dusk (dʌsk) *n* crépuscule *m*. **dusky** *adj* **1** sombre. **2** noirâtre.
dust (dʌst) *n* poussière *f*. *vt* épousseter. **dustbin** *n* poubelle *f*. **dustman** *n* boueur *m*. **dustpan** *n* pelle à poussière *f*. **duster** *n* torchon *m*. **dusty** *adj* poussiéreux, -euse.
Dutch (dʌtʃ) *adj* hollandais. **Dutchman** *n* hollandais *m*.
duty ('dju:ti) *n* **1** devoir *m*. **2** *comm* droit *m*. **3** fonction *f*. **on duty** de service. **duty-free** *adj* **1** exempt de droits. **2** en franchise. **dutiful** *adj* obéissant, soumis.
duvet ('dju:vei) *n* duvet *m*.
dwarf (dwɔ:f) *adj,n* nain. *vt* rapetisser.
dwell* (dwel) *vi* habiter, demeurer. **dwell on** s'étendre sur. **dwelling** *n* demeure, résidence *f*.
dwindle ('dwindḷ) *vi* **1** diminuer. **2** se réduire.
dye (dai) *n* teinte *f*. *vt* teindre.
dyke (daik) *n* digue *f*.
dynamic (dai'næmik) *adj* dynamique.
dynamite ('dainəmait) *n* dynamite *f*.
dynasty ('dinəsti) *n* dynastie *f*.
dysentery ('disəntri) *n* dysenterie *f*.
dyslexia (dis'leksiə) *n* dyslexie *f*.

E

each (i:tʃ) *adj* chaque. *pron* chacun. **each other** l'un l'autre, les uns les autres.
eager ('i:gə) *adj* **1** passionné, ardent. **2** avide. **3** impatient. **eagerness** *n* **1** ardeur *f*. **2** avidité. **3** empressement *m*.
eagle ('i:gəl) *n* aigle *m*.
ear[1] (iə) *n* *anat* oreille *f*. **earache** *n* mal d'oreille *m*. **eardrum** *n* tympan *m*. **earmark** *n* marque distinctive *f*. *vt* mettre de côté. **earphone** *n* casque *m*. **earring** *n* boucle d'oreille *f*. **earwig** *n* perce-oreille *m*.
ear[2] (iə) *n* *bot* épi *m*.
earl (ə:l) *n* comte *m*.
early ('ə:li) *adv* de bonne heure, tôt. *adj* **1** matinal, -aux. **2** précoce.
earn (ə:n) *vt* **1** gagner. **2** mériter.
earnest ('ə:nist) *adj* **1** sérieux, -euse. **2** sincère.
earth (ə:θ) *n* **1** terre *f*. **2** (of animal) terrier *m*. **down to earth** terre à terre, réaliste. **earthenware** *n* poterie, faïence *f*. **earthquake** *n* tremblement de terre *m*. **earthworm** *n* ver de terre, lombric *m*.
ease (i:z) *n* **1** aise *f*. **2** tranquillité *f*. **3** facilité *f*. *vt* **1** adoucir. **2** soulager. **easy** *adj* **1** facile. **2** tranquille. **3** libre. *adv* doucement.
easel ('i:zəl) *n* chevalet *m*.
east (i:st) *n* **1** est *m*. **2** *cap* Orient *m*. *adj* est

invar. adv à *or* vers l'est. **easterly** *adj* d'est. **eastern** *adj* de l'est, oriental, -aux. **eastward** *adj* à l'est, dans l'est. **eastwards** *adv* vers l'est.

Easter ('i:stə) *n* Pâques *f pl.*

eat* (i:t) *vt* manger. **eatable** *adj* mangeable.

eavesdrop ('i:vzdrɔp) *vi* écouter aux portes.

ebb (eb) *n* **1** reflux *m.* **2** déclin *m.*

ebony ('ebəni) *n* ébène *f.*

eccentric (ik'sentrik) *adj* excentrique.

ecclesiastical (ikli:zi'æstikəl) *adj* ecclésiastique.

echo ('ekou) *n, pl* **echoes** écho *m. vi* **1** faire écho. **2** retentir. *vt* répéter (en écho).

eclair (ei'klɛə) *n* éclair *m.*

eclipse (i'klips) *n* éclipse *f. vt* éclipser.

ecology (i:'kɔlədʒi) *n* écologie *f.*

economize (i'kɔnəmaiz) *vt* économiser.

economy (i'kɔnəmi) *n* économie *f.* **economic** *adj* économique. **economical** *adj* **1** économe. **2** économique. **economics** *n* sciences économiques *f pl.*

ecstasy ('ekstəsi) *n* **1** extase *f.* **2** ravissement *m.* **ecstatic** *adj* extatique.

edelweiss ('eidlvais) *n* edelweiss *m.*

edge (edʒ) *n* **1** bord *m.* **2** lisière, bordure *f.* **3** (of a blade) tranchant *m.* **on edge** énervé. ~*vt* border.

edible ('edibəl) *adj* comestible.

Edinburgh ('edinbərə) *n* Edimbourg *m.*

edit ('edit) *vt* **1** éditer. **2** rédiger. **edition** *n* édition *f.* **editor** *n* **1** éditeur *m.* **2** (of a paper) rédacteur en chef *m.* **editorial** *adj* éditorial, -aux. *n* article de fond *m.*

educate ('edjukeit) *vt* **1** élever. **2** instruire. **educated** *adj* instruit, cultivé. **education** *n* éducation *f.* enseignement *m.* instruction *f.*

eel (i:l) *n* anguille *f.*

eerie ('iəri) *adj* étrange, mystérieux, -euse.

effect (i'fekt) *n* **1** effet *m.* influence *f.* **2** *pl* biens *m pl.* **in effect** en réalité. ~*vt* effectuer. **effective** *adj* efficace. **effectiveness** *n* efficacité *f.*

effeminate (i'feminət) *adj* efféminé.

effervesce (efə'ves) *vi* **1** être en effervescence. **2** mousser. **effervescence** *n* effervescence *f.* **effervescent** *adj* effervescent.

efficient (i'fiʃənt) *adj* **1** capable, compétent. **2** efficace. **efficiency** *n* efficacité *f.*

effigy ('efidʒi) *n* effigie *f.*

effort ('efət) *n* effort *m.*

egg[1] (eg) *n* œuf *m.* **boiled egg** œuf à la coque. **fried egg** œuf sur le plat. **hard-boiled/poached egg** œuf dur/poché. **scrambled eggs** œufs brouillés. **egg-cup** *n* coquetier *m.* **egg-shell** *n* coquille d'œuf *f.* **egg-whisk** *n* batteur *or* fouet à œufs *m.*

egg[2] (eg) *vt* **egg on** encourager, inciter.

ego ('i:gou) *n* moi *m.* **egocentric** *adj* égocentrique. **egoism** *n* égoïsme *m.*

Egypt ('i:dʒipt) *n* Egypte *f.* **Egyptian** *adj,n* égyptien, -ienne.

eiderdown ('aidədaun) *n* édredon *m.*

eight (eit) *adj,n* huit *m.* **eighth** *adj* huitième.

eighteen (ei'ti:n) *adj,n* dix-huit *m.* **eighteenth** *adj* dix-huitième.

eighty ('eiti) *adj,n* quatre-vingts *m.* **eightieth** *adj* quatre-vingtième.

either ('aiðə) *adj,pron* **1** l'un et *or* ou l'autre. **2** chaque. **3** chacun. *conj* ou, soit. **either...or** ou...ou, soit...soit. ~*adv* non plus.

ejaculate (i'dʒækjuleit) *vt* **1** éjaculer. **2** pousser.

eject (i'dʒekt) *vt* expulser, émettre.

eke (i:k) *vt* **1** allonger, suppléer. **2** faire durer.

elaborate (*adj* i'læbrət; *v* i'læbəreit) *adj* **1** compliqué. **2** soigné. *vt* élaborer.

elapse (i'læps) *vi* s'écouler.

elastic (i'læstik) *adj* élastique. **elastic band** *n* élastique *m.* **elasticity** élasticité *f.*

elated (i'leitid) *adj* transporté, exalté.

elbow ('elbou) *n* coude *m. vt* coudoyer.

elder[1] ('eldə) *adj,n* aîné. **elderly** *adj* d'un certain âge, âgé.

elder[2] ('eldə) *n bot* sureau *m.* **elderberry** *n* baie de sureau *f.*

eldest ('eldist) *adj,n* aîné.

elect (i'lekt) *vt* élire, choisir. **election** *n* élection *f.* **electoral** *adj* électoral, -aux. **electorate** *n* corps électoral *m.*

electricity (ilek'trisiti) *n* électricité *f.* **electric** *adj* électrique. **electrician** *n* électricien *m.* **electrify** *vt* électrifier, électriser. **electrocute** *vt* électrocuter. **electrode** *n* électrode *f.* **electron** *n* électron *m.* **electronic** *adj* électronique. **electronics** *n pl* électronique *f.*

elegant ('eligənt) *adj* **1** élégant. **2** *inf* chic. **elegance** *n* élégance *f.*

element ('eləmənt) *n* élément *m.* **elemental** *adj* **1** des éléments. **2** élémentaire. **elementary** *adj* élémentaire.

elephant ('eləfənt) *n* éléphant *m.*

elevate ('eləveit) *vt* **1** élever, hausser. **2** exalter. **elevation** *n* élévation *m.* **elevator** *n* ascenseur, élévateur, monte-charge *m.*

eleven (i'levən) *adj,n* onze *m.* **eleventh** *adj* onzième.

elf (elf) *n, pl* **elves** elfe, lutin *m.*

eligible (ˈelidʒəbəl) *adj* éligible.
eliminate (iˈlimineit) *vt* **1** éliminer. **2** supprimer. **elimination** *n* élimination *f*.
elite (eiˈli:t) *n* élite *f*.
ellipse (iˈlips) *n* ellipse *f*.
elm (elm) *n* orme *m*.
elocution (eləˈkju:ʃən) *n* élocution, diction *f*.
elope (iˈloup) *vi* s'enfuir.
eloquent (ˈeləkwənt) *adj* éloquent.
else (els) *adv* autrement, ou bien. *adj* autre. **elsewhere** *adv* ailleurs.
elucidate (iˈlu:sideit) *vt* élucider, éclaircir.
elude (iˈlu:d) *vt* éluder, échapper à.
emaciate (iˈmeiʃieit) *vt* amaigrir. **emaciated** *adj* émacié, étique.
emanate (ˈeməneit) *vi* émaner.
emancipate (iˈmænsipeit) *vt* émanciper. **emancipation** *n* émancipation *f*.
embalm (imˈbɑ:m) *vt* embaumer.
embankment (imˈbæŋkmənt) *n* **1** levée *f*. **2** (of a river) quai *m*. **3** (of a road) remblai *m*.
embargo (imˈbɑ:gou) *n, pl* **embargoes** embargo *m*.
embark (imˈbɑ:k) *vt* embarquer. *vi* s'embarquer.
embarrass (imˈbærəs) *vt* embarrasser, gêner. **embarrassment** *n* embarras *m*.
embassy (ˈembəsi) *n* ambassade *f*.
embellish (imˈbeliʃ) *vt* embellir, orner.
ember (ˈembə) *n* braise *f*.
embezzle (imˈbezəl) *vt* détourner. **embezzlement** *n* détournement de fonds *m*.
embitter (imˈbitə) *vt* **1** aigrir. **2** envenimer.
emblem (ˈembləm) *n* emblème, insigne *m*.
embody (imˈbɔdi) *vt* **1** incarner. **2** personnifier. **embodiment** *n* personnification *f*.
emboss (imˈbɔs) *vt* **1** graver en relief. **2** repousser.
embrace (imˈbreis) *vt* embrasser, étreindre. *n* étreinte *f*.
embroider (imˈbrɔidə) *vt* broder. **embroidery** *n* broderie *f*.
embryo (ˈembriou) *n* embryon *m*.
emerald (ˈemrəld) *n* émeraude *f*.
emerge (iˈmə:dʒ) *vi* émerger, sortir.
emergency (iˈmə:dʒənsi) *n* **1** circonstance critique *f*. cas urgent *m*. **2** *med* urgence *f*. **emergency exit** *n* sortie de secours *f*.
emigrate (ˈemigreit) *vi* émigrer. **emigrant** *adj,n* émigrant. **emigration** *n* émigration *f*.
eminent (ˈeminənt) *adj* éminent. **eminence** *n* éminence *f*.
emit (iˈmit) *vt* **1** émettre. **2** dégager.
emotion (iˈmouʃən) *n* émotion *f*. **emotional** *adj* émotif, -ive.
empathy (ˈempəθi) *n* identification *f*.
emperor (ˈempərə) *n* empereur *m*.
emphasis (ˈemfəsis) *n, pl* **emphases** emphase *f*. **emphasize** *vt* accentuer, souligner. **emphatic** *adj* emphatique, énergique.
empire (ˈempaiə) *n* empire *m*.
empirical (imˈpirikəl) *adj* empirique.
employ (imˈplɔi) *vt* employer. **employee** *n* employé. **employer** *n* patron, employeur *m*. **employment** *n* emploi *m*. **employment agency** *n* bureau de placement *m*.
empower (imˈpauə) *vt* autoriser.
empress (ˈemprəs) *n* impératrice *f*.
empty (ˈempti) *adj* vide. *vt* vider. **empty-handed** *adj* bredouille.
emu (ˈi:mju:) *n* émeu *m*.
emulate (ˈemjuleit) *vt* rivaliser avec, imiter. **emulation** *n* émulation *f*.
emulsion (iˈmʌlʃən) *n* émulsion *f*.
enable (iˈneibəl) *vt* permettre, rendre capable.
enact (iˈnækt) *vt* décréter, ordonner.
enamel (iˈnæməl) *vt* émailler. *n* émail, -aux *m*.
encapsulate (inˈkæpsjuleit) *vt* incorporer.
enchant (inˈtʃɑ:nt) *vt* enchanter. **enchantment** *n* enchantement *m*.
encircle (inˈsə:kəl) *vt* entourer, cerner.
enclose (inˈklouz) *vt* **1** enclore. **2** enfermer, joindre. **enclosed** *adj* ci-inclus, ci-joint.
encore (ˈɔŋkɔ:) *interj,n* bis *m*. *vt* bisser.
encounter (inˈkauntə) *vt* rencontrer. *n* rencontre *f*.
encourage (inˈkʌridʒ) *vt* encourager. **encouragement** *n* encouragement *m*.
encroach (inˈkroutʃ) *vi* **encroach on 1** empiéter sur. **2** abuser de. **encroachment** *n* empiétement *m*.
encumber (inˈkʌmbə) *vt* encombrer. **encumbrance** *n* embarras *m*. charge *f*.
encyclopedia (insakləˈpi:diə) *n* encyclopédie *f*.
end (end) *n* fin *f*. bout *m*. **make ends meet** joindre les deux bouts. ~*vt* terminer, finir, achever. *vi* finir, se terminer. **ending** *n* **1** fin *f*. **2** *gram* terminaison *f*. **3** dénouement *m*. **endless** *adj* sans fin, incessant.
endanger (inˈdeindʒə) *vt* **1** mettre en danger. **2** risquer.
endeavour (inˈdevə) *vi* s'efforcer, tâcher. *n* effort *m*.
endemic (enˈdemik) *adj* endémique. *n* endémie *f*.
endive (ˈendaiv) *n* chicorée *f*.

endorse (in'dɔ:s) *vt* **1** endosser, viser. **2** appuyer. **endorsement** *n* **1** endossement *m*. **2** sanction *f*.
endow (in'dau) *vt* doter.
endure (in'djuə) *vt* supporter. *vi* durer. **endurance** *n* résistance *f*.
enemy ('enəmi) *adj,n* ennemi.
energy ('enədʒi) *n* énergie *f*. **energetic** *adj* énergique.
enfold (in'fould) *vt* envelopper.
enforce (in'fɔ:s) *vt* **1** faire observer. **2** imposer.
engage (in'geidʒ) *vt* **1** engager. **2** embaucher. *vi* **1** s'engager. **2** s'embarquer. **engaged** *adj* **1** occupé, pris. **2** fiancé. **engaging** *adj* attirant. **engagement** *n* **1** engagement *m*. promesse f. **2** fiançailles *f pl*. **3** *mil* combat *m*.
engine ('endʒin) *n* **1** machine *f*. **2** moteur *m*.
engineer (endʒi'niə) *n* ingénieur *m*. *vt inf* machiner. **engineering** *n* technique de l'ingénieur *f*. **civil engineering** *n* génie civil *m*.
England ('iŋglənd) *n* Angleterre *f*. **English** *adj,n* anglais. **English** (language) *n* anglais *m*.
engrave (in'greiv) *vt* graver.
engross (in'grous) *vt* **1** rédiger. **2** absorber.
engulf (in'gʌlf) *vt* engouffrer.
enhance (in'hɑ:ns) *vt* **1** rehausser. **2** mettre en valeur.
enigma (i'nigmə) *n* énigme *f*. **enigmatic** *adj* énigmatique.
enjoy (in'dʒɔi) *vt* **1** aimer, prendre plaisir à. **2** jouir de. **enjoy oneself** s'amuser. **enjoyable** *adj* agréable. **enjoyment** *n* plaisir *m*.
enlarge (in'lɑ:dʒ) *vt* **1** agrandir. **2** élargir. **enlargement** *n* agrandissement *m*.
enlighten (in'laitn̩) *vt* éclairer.
enlist (in'list) *vt* enrôler, recruter. *vi* s'enrôler, s'engager.
enormous (i'nɔ:məs) *adj* énorme. **enormously** *adv* énormément.
enough (i'nʌf) *adv,adj* assez. **be enough** suffire.
enquire (in'kwaiə) *vi* se renseigner, s'informer. **enquiry** *n* **1** enquête *f*. **2** demande de renseignements *f*.
enrage (in'reidʒ) *vt* faire enrager, exaspérer.
enrich (in'ritʃ) *vt* enrichir.
enrol (in'roul) *vt* enrôler, immatriculer. *vi* se faire inscrire.
ensign ('ensain) *n* **1** (flag) enseigne *f*. **2** *naut* pavillon *m*. **3** (rank) enseigne *m*.
enslave (in'sleiv) *vt* asservir.
ensure (in'ʃuə) *vt* assurer.
entail (in'teil) *vt* **1** substituer. **2** occasionner.
entangle (in'tæŋgəl) *vt* empêtrer, emmêler.
enter ('entə) *vt* **1** entrer dans. **2** prendre part à. **3** inscrire. *vi* entrer.
enterprise ('entəpraiz) *n* entreprise *f*. **enterprising** *adj* entreprenant.
entertain (entə'tein) *vt* **1** amuser, divertir. **2** (guests) recevoir. **3** (an idea) concevoir. *vi* recevoir. **entertaining** *adj* amusant. **entertainment** *n* divertissement *m*.
enthral (in'θrɔ:l) *vt* captiver.
enthusiasm (in'θju:ziæzəm) *n* enthousiasme *m*. **enthusiast** *n* enthousiaste *m,f*. **enthusiastic** *adj* enthousiaste.
entice (in'tais) *vt* attirer, séduire.
entire (in'taiə) *adj* entier, -ière, complet, -ète.
entitle (in'taitl̩) *vt* **1** intituler. **2** donner droit à.
entity ('entiti) *n* entité *f*.
entrails ('entreilz) *n pl* entrailles *f pl*.
entrance[1] ('entrəns) *n* entreé *f*.
entrance[2] (in'trɑ:ns) *vt* extasier, ravir.
entreat (in'tri:t) *vt* supplier **entreaty** *n* supplication *f*.
entrench (in'trentʃ) *vt* retrancher.
entrepreneur (ɔntrəprə'nəː) *n* entrepreneur *m*.
entrust (in'trʌst) *vt* confier, charger.
entry ('entri) *n* entrée *f*. **no entry** **1** *mot* sens interdit. **2** interdit au public.
entwine (in'twain) *vt* entrelacer. *vi* s'entrelacer.
enunciate (i'nʌnsieit) *vt* **1** énoncer. **2** articuler.
envelop (in'velɔp) *vt* envelopper.
envelope ('envəloup) *n* enveloppe *f*.
environment (in'vairənmənt) *n* milieu, -eux, environnement *m*.
envisage (in'vizidʒ) *vt* envisager.
envoy ('envɔi) *n* envoyé *m*.
envy ('envi) *n* envie *f*. *vt* envier.
enzyme ('enzaim) *n* enzyme *f*.
epaulet ('epəlet) *n* épaulette *f*.
ephemeral (i'femərəl) *adj* éphémère.
epic ('epik) *adj* épique. *n* poème épique *m*. épopée *f*.
epidemic (epi'demik) *n* épidémie *f*. *adj* épidémique.
epilepsy ('epilepsi) *n* épilepsie *f*. **epileptic** *adj,n* épileptique.
epilogue ('epilɔg) *n* épilogue *m*.
Epiphany (i'pifəni) *n* Epiphanie *f*. la fête des Rois.
episcopal (i'piskəpəl) *adj* épiscopal, -aux.
episode ('episoud) *n* épisode *m*.
epitaph ('epitɑ:f) *n* épitaphe *f*.

epitome (i'pitəmi) *n* **1** épitomé, abrégé *m*. **2** quintessence *f*.
epoch ('i:pɔk) *n* époque *f*.
equable ('ekwəbəl) *adj* uniforme, egal, -aux.
equal ('i:kwəl) *adj,n* égal, -aux. *vt* égaler. **equality** *n* égalité *f*. **equalize** *vt* **1** égaliser. **2** compenser. *vi* s'égaliser.
equate (i'kweit) *vt* égaler. **equation** *n* équation *f*. **equator** *n* équateur *m*. **equatorial** *adj* équatorial, -aux.
equestrian (i'kwestriən) *adj* équestre.
equilateral (i:kwi'lætərəl) *adj* équilatéral, -aux.
equilibrium (i:kwi'libriəm) *n* équilibre *m*.
equinox ('i:kwinɔks) *n* équinoxe *m*.
equip (i'kwip) *vt* **1** équiper, munir. **2** *tech* outiller. **equipment** *n* **1** équipement *m*. **2** outillage *m*. **3** matériel *m*.
equity ('ekwiti) *n* équité *f*.
equivalent (i'kwivələnt) *adj,n* équivalent *m*.
era ('iərə) *n* ère *f*.
eradicate (i'rædikeit) *vt* déraciner, extirper.
erase (i'reiz) *vt* **1** effacer, gommer. **2** rayer.
erect (i'rekt) *vt* **1** dresser. **2** ériger. *adj* droit, debout. **erection** *n* construction *f*.
ermine ('ə:min) *n* hermine *f*.
erode (i'roud) *vt* éroder, corroder. **erosion** *n* érosion *f*.
erotic (i'rɔtik) *adj* érotique.
err (ə:) *vi* **1** s'égarer, errer. **2** se tromper.
errand ('erənd) *n* commission, course *f*.
erratic (i'rætik) *adj* **1** irrégulier, -ière. **2** fantasque.
error ('erə) *n* erreur, faute *f*.
erupt (i'rʌpt) *vi* faire éruption. **eruption** *n* éruption *f*.
escalate ('eskəleit) *vt* (a war) élargir. **escalator** *n* escalier roulant *m*.
escalope (i'skæləp) *n* escalope *f*.
escape (i'skeip) *vt* échapper à. *vi* s'échapper. *n* fuite, évasion *f*.
escort ('eskɔ:t) *n* escorte *f*. *vt* escorter.
Eskimo ('eskimou) *n* esquimau, -aude, -aux.
esoteric (esə'terik) *adj* ésotérique.
especial (i'speʃəl) *adj* spécial, -aux. **especially** *adv* surtout.
espionage ('espiənɑ:ʒ) *n* espionnage *m*.
esplanade ('espləneid) *n* esplanade *f*.
essay ('esei) *n* **1** tentative, épreuve *f*. **2** *lit* essai *m*. **3** *educ* dissertation *f*.
essence ('esəns) *n* essence *f*. **essential** *adj* essentiel, -elle, indispensable.
establish (i'stæbliʃ) *vt* fonder. **establishment** *n* **1** établissement *m*. fondation *f*. **2** maison (de commerce) *f*. **3** *cap* ordre établi *m*.
estate (i'steit) *n* **1** état *m*. **2** *law* biens *m pl*. **estate car** *n* break *m*.
esteem (i'sti:m) *n* estime *f*. *vt* estimer.
estimate (*n* 'estimət; *v* 'estimeit) *n* **1** évaluation *f*. **2** devis *m*. *vt* estimer, évaluer, apprécier.
estuary ('estʃuəri) *n* estuaire *m*.
etching ('etʃiŋ) *n* gravure à l'eau-forte *f*.
eternal (i'tə:nl) *adj* éternel, -elle. **eternity** *n* éternité *f*.
ether ('i:θə) *n* éther *m*.
ethereal (i'θiəriəl) *adj* éthéré.
ethical ('eθikəl) *adj* moral, -aux. **ethics** *n pl* éthique, morale *f*.
ethnic ('eθnik) *adj* ethnique.
etiquette ('etikit) *n* étiquette *f*. convenances *f pl*. protocole *m*.
etymology (eti'mɔlədʒi) *n* étymologie *f*.
eucalyptus (ju:kə'liptəs) *n* eucalyptus *m*.
Eucharist ('ju:kərist) *n* Eucharistie *f*.
eunuch ('ju:nək) *n* eunuque *m*.
euphemism ('ju:fəmizəm) *n* euphémisme *m*. **euphemistic** *adj* euphémique.
euphoria (ju:'fɔ:riə) *n* euphorie *f*.
Europe ('juərəp) *n* Europe *f*. **European** *adj,n* européen, -enne.
European Economic Community *n* Communauté Economique Européenne *f*.
euthanasia (ju:θə'neiziə) *n* euthanasie *f*.
evacuate (i'vækjueit) *vt* évacuer. **evacuation** *n* évacuation *f*.
evade (i'veid) *vt* éviter, esquiver. **evasive** *adj* évasif, -ive.
evaluate (i'væljueit) *vt* évaluer.
evangelical (i:væn'dʒelikəl) *adj* évangélique. **evangelist** *n* évangéliste *m*.
evaporate (i'væpəreit) *vt* faire évaporer. *vi* s'évaporer, se volatiliser. **evaporation** *n* évaporation *f*.
evasive (i'veisiv) *adj* evasif, -ive.
eve (i:v) *n* veille *f*.
even ('i:vən) *adj* **1** égal, -aux. **2** uni. **3** pair. **4** quitte. *adv* **1** même. **2** encore. **even so** quand même. ~*vt* aplanir, égaliser. **even-tempered** *adj* d'humeur égale, placide.
evening ('i:vəniŋ) *n* soir *m*. soireé *f*. **evening class** *n* cours du soir *m*. **evening dress** *n* tenue de soireé *f*.
event (i'vent) *n* **1** événement *m*. **2** cas *m*. **in the event of** au cas où. **eventful** *adj* mouvementé. **eventual** *adj* **1** éventuel, -elle. **2** définitif, -ive. **eventually** *adv* finalement.

ever (ˈevə) *adv* **1** toujours. **2** jamais. **evergreen** *adj* toujours vert. *n* arbre vert *m*. **everlasting** *adj* éternel, -elle.

every (ˈevri) *adj* **1** chaque. **2** tout. **everybody** *pron* tout le monde, chacun. **everyday** *adj* quotidien, -enne. *adv* tous les jours. **everyone** *pron* tout le monde, chacun. **every other day** tous les deux jours, un jour sur deux. **everything** *pron* tout. **everywhere** *adv* partout.

evict (iˈvikt) *vt* expulser.

evidence (ˈevidəns) *n* **1** évidence *f*. **2** témoignage *m*. **give évidence** témoigner. **evident** *adj* évident. **evidently** *adv* évidemment.

evil (ˈi:vəl) *adj* mauvais, méchant. *n* mal, maux *m*.

evoke (iˈvouk) *vt* évoquer.

evolution (i:vəˈlu:ʃən) *n* **1** développement *m*. **2** évolution *f*.

evolve (iˈvɔlv) *vt* développer, dérouler. *vi* se dérouler, évoluer. **evolution** *n* évolution *f*.

ewe (ju:) *n* brebis *f*.

exact (igˈzækt) *adj* exact, précis. *vt* exiger. **exacting** *adj* exigeant. **exactly** précisément, justement, tout juste.

exaggerate (igˈzædʒəreit) *vt* exagérer. **exaggeration** *n* exagération *f*.

exalt (igˈzɔ:lt) *vt* **1** exalter. **2** louer.

examine (igˈzæmin) *vt* examiner, inspecter. **examination** *n* examen *m*. **fail/pass an examination** échouer/réussir à un examen. **take an examination** passer un examen.

example (igˈzɑ:mpəl) *n* exemple *m*. **for example** par exemple.

exasperate (igˈzɑ:spəreit) *vt* exaspérer, irriter.

excavate (ˈekskəveit) *vt* creuser, fouiller. **excavation** *n* fouille, excavation *f*.

exceed (ikˈsi:d) *vt* excéder, dépasser.

excel (ikˈsel) *vt,vi* surpasser. **excellence** *n* excellence *f*. **excellent** *adj* excellent.

Excellency (ˈeksələnsi) *n* Excellence *f*.

except (ikˈsept) *prep* excepté, sauf. **except that** sauf que. **exception** *n* exception *f*. **exceptional** *adj* exceptionnel, -elle.

excerpt (ˈeksə:pt) *n* extrait *m*.

excess (ikˈses) *n* excès, excédent *m*. **excessive** *adj* excessif, -ive.

exchange (iksˈtʃeindʒ) *vt* échanger. *vi* faire un échange. *n* **1** échange *m*. **2** *comm* change *m*.

exchequer (eksˈtʃekə) *n* trésorerie *f*.

excise (ˈeksaiz) *n* **1** contributions indirectes *f pl*. **2** régie *f*.

excite (ikˈsait) *vt* exciter. **excited** *adj* excité, agité. **excitement** *n* surexcitation, émotion *f*. **exciting** *adj* captivant, passionnant.

exclaim (ikˈskleim) *vi* s'écrier, s'exclamer.

exclamation (eksklәˈmeiʃən) *n* exclamation *f*. **exclamation mark** *n* point d'exclamation *m*.

exclude (ikˈsklu:d) *vt* exclure. **exclusive** *adj* exclusif, -ive.

excommunicate (ekskəˈmju:nikeit) *vt* excommunier. **excommunication** *n* excommunication *f*.

excruciating (ikˈskru:ʃieitiŋ) *adj* atroce, affreux, -euse.

excursion (ikˈskə:ʒən) *n* excursion, partie de plaisir *f*.

excuse (*n* ikˈskju:s; *v* ikˈskju:z) *n* excuse *f*. prétexte *m*. *vt* excuser, pardonner. **excuse me!** pardon!

execute (ˈeksikju:t) *vt* exécuter. **execution** *n* exécution *f*. **executioner** *n* bourreau, -aux *m*.

executive (igˈzekjutiv) *n* cadre (supérieur) *m*.

exempt (igˈzempt) *vt* exempter, dispenser. *adj* exempt, dispensé. **exemption** *n* exemption *f*.

exercise (ˈeksəsaiz) *n* exercice *m*. *vt* exercer, pratiquer. *vi* s'entrainer. **exercise book** *n* cahier *m*.

exert (igˈzə:t) *vt* employer, exercer. **exertion** *n* effort, emploi *m*.

exhale (eksˈheil) *vt* exhaler.

exhaust (igˈzɔ:st) *vt* épuiser. *n* échappement *m*. **exhaust pipe** *n* tuyau d'échappement *m*.

exhibit (igˈzibit) *vt* exhiber, montrer, exposer. *n* objet exposé *m*. **exhibition** *n* exposition *f*. **exhibitionism** *n* exhibitionisme *m*.

exhilarate (igˈziləreit) *vt* rejouir, ranimer. **exhilaration** *n* joie de vivre *f*.

exile (ˈegzail) *n* **1** exil *m*. **2** exilé, banni *m*. *vt* exiler, bannir.

exist (igˈzist) *vi* exister, être. **existence** *n* existence *f*. **existentialism** *n* existentialisme *m*. **existing** *adj* actuel, -elle.

exit (ˈeksit) *n* sortie *f*.

exorbitant (igˈzɔ:bitənt) *adj* exorbitant, excessif, -ive.

exorcize (ˈeksɔ:saiz) *vt* exorciser.

exotic (igˈzɔtik) *adj* exotique.

expand (ikˈspænd) *vt* élargir, dilater, développer. *vi* se développer, se dilater. **expanding** *adj* extensible. **expansion** *n* développement *m*. dilatation *f*.

expanse (ikˈspæns) *n* étendue *f*.

expatriate (*v* iksˈpeitrieit; *n* iksˈpeitriit) *vt* expatrier. *n* expatrié *m*.

expect (ik'spekt) *vt* attendre, s'attendre à. **expectation** *n* espérance, attente *f*.
expedient (ik'spi:diənt) *n* expédient, moyen *m*. *adj* expédient, convenable.
expedition (ekspi'diʃən) *n* expédition, excursion *f*.
expel (ik'spel) *vt* expulser, bannir.
expenditure (ik'spenditʃə) *n* dépense *f*.
expense (ik'spens) *n* 1 dépense *f*. frais *m pl*. 2 dépens *m*. **expensive** *adj* cher, chère, coûteux, -euse.
experience (ik'spiəriəns) *n* 1 expérience *f*. 2 épreuve *f*. *vt* éprouver. **experienced** *adj* expérimenté.
experiment (ik'sperimənt) *n* expérience *f*. essai *m*. *vi* faire une expérience, expérimenter. **experimental** *adj* expérimental, -aux.
expert ('ekspə:t) *n* expert, spécialiste *m*. *adj* habile, expert. **expertise** *n* expertise *f*.
expire (ik'spaiə) *vi* expirer.
explain (ik'splein) *vt* expliquer, éclaircir. **explanation** *n* explication *f*.
expletive (ik'spli:tiv) *adj,n* explétif, -ive.
explicit (ik'splisit) *adj* explicite, catégorique.
explode (ik'sploud) *vt* faire sauter. *vi* sauter, éclater. **explosive** *adj,n* explosif, -ive *m*.
exploit[1] ('eksplɔit) *n* exploit *m*.
exploit[2] (ik'splɔit) *vt* exploiter.
explore (ik'splɔ:) *vt* explorer. **explorer** *n* explorateur *m*.
exponent (ik'spounənt) *n* interprète *m,f*.
export (*v* ik'spɔ:t, 'ekspɔ:t; *n* 'ekspɔ:t) *vt* exporter. *n* exportation *f*.
expose (ik'spouz) *vt* 1 exposer. 2 révéler. **exposure** *n* 1 exposition *f*. 2 dévoilement *m*.
express (ik'spres) *vt* exprimer. *n* rapide *m*. *adj* exprès. **expression** *n* expression *f*.
exquisite (ek'skwizit) *adj* 1 exquis. 2 vif, vive.
extend (ik'stend) *vt* étendre, prolonger. *vi* s'étendre. **extension** *n* extension *f*. prolongement *m*. **extensive** *adj* 1 vaste, ample. 2 approfondi.
extent (ik'stent) *n* 1 étendue *f*. 2 point *m*. mesure *f*.
exterior (ek'stiəriə) *adj,n* extérieur *m*.
exterminate (ik'stə:mineit) *vt* exterminer.
external (ek'stə:nl̩) *adj* externe, extérieur.
extinct (ik'stiŋkt) *adj* disparu, éteint.
extinguish (ik'stiŋgwiʃ) *vt* éteindre.
extra ('ekstrə) *adj* de plus, en sus, supplémentaire. *n* 1 supplément *m* 2 *pl inf* à-côtés *m pl*.
extract (*n* 'ekstrakt; *v* ik'strækt) *n* extrait *m*. *vt* extraire.
extramural (ekstrə'mjuərəl) *adj* extramuros *invar*.
extraordinary (ik'strɔ:dənri) *adj* extraordinaire, remarquable.
extravagant (ik'strævəgənt) *adj* extravagant, dépensier, -ière. **extravagence** *n* extravagance *f*.
extreme (ik'stri:m) *adj,n* extrême *m*. **extremity** *n* extrémité *f*.
extricate ('ekstrikeit) *vt* dégager.
extrovert ('ekstrəvə:t) *n* extroverti *m*.
exuberant (ig'zju:bərənt) *adj* exubérant.
eye (ai) *n* œil *m pl* yeux. vt regarder, lorgner.
eyeball ('aibɔ:l) *n* globe de l'oeil *m*.
eyebrow ('aibrau) *n* sourcil *m*.
eye-catching *adj* accrocheur, -euse.
eyelash ('ailæʃ) *n* cil *m*.
eyelid ('ailid) *n* paupière *f*.
eye-opener *n* révélation *f*.
eye shadow *n* fard à paupières *m*.
eyesight ('aisait) *n* vue *f*.
eyestrain ('aistrein) *n* mal aux yeux *m*.
eye-witness (ai'witnis) *n* témoin oculaire *m*.

F

fable ('feibəl) *n* conte *m*. fable *f*.
fabric ('fæbrik) *n* 1 tissu *m*. étoffe *f*. 2 fabrique *f*. **fabricate** *vt* fabriquer, inventer.
fabulous ('fæbjuləs) *adj* fabuleux, -euse.
facade (fə'sɑ:d) *n* façade *f*.
face (feis) *n* 1 *anat* visage *m*. figure *f*. 2 face *f*. 3 *inf* toupet *m*. 4 mine *f*. *vt* faire face à. **facecloth** *n* gant de toilette *m*. **facelift** *n* ridectomie *f*. **face-pack** *n* masque anti-rides *m*. **face value** *n* valeur nominale *f*.
facet ('fæsit) *n* aspect *m*.
facetious (fə'si:ʃəs) *adj* plaisant, facétieux, -euse.
facile ('fæsail) *adj* facile. **facilitate** *vt* faciliter. **facility** *n* facilité *f*.
facing ('feisiŋ) *n* parement *m*.
facsimile (fæk'siməli) *n* fac-similé *m*.
fact (fækt) *n* fait *m*. **as a matter of fact** à vrai dire. **factual** *adj* positif, -ive.
faction ('fækʃən) *n* faction *f*.
factor ('fæktə) *n* 1 facteur, diviseur *m*. 2 élément *m*.
factory ('fæktri) *n* usine, fabrique *f*.
faculty ('fækəlti) *n* 1 faculté *f*. 2 talent *m*.
fad (fæd) *n* dada *m*. manie *f*.

fade (feid) *vi* se faner, se déteindre, passer. *vt* décolorer. **fade away** s'évanouir.

fag (fæg) *n* **1** corvée *f*. **2** *sl* sèche *f*.

Fahrenheit (ˈfærənhait) *adj* Fahrenheit.

fail (feil) *vi* **1** manquer. **2** échouer. **3** baisser. *vt* refuser. **failing** *n* défaut *m*. *prep* faute de. **failure** *n* **1** défaut *m*. **2** échec *m*. **3** raté *m*.

faint (feint) *vi* s'évanouir. *n* évanouissement *m*. *adj* faible, pâle, léger, -ère. **faint-hearted** *adj* timide, pusillanime.

fair[1] (fɛə) *adj* **1** juste. **2** passable. **3** beau, belle. **4** blond. **fair-minded** *adj* impartial, -aux. **fairly** *adv* **1** honnêtement. **2** assez. **fairness** *n* **1** justice *f*. **2** blondeur *f*.

fair[2] (fɛə) *n* foire *f*. **fairground** *n* champ de foire *m*.

fairy (ˈfɛəri) *n* fée *f*. *adj* féerique. **fairytale** *n* conte de fées *m*.

faith (feiθ) *n* **1** foi *f*. **2** confiance *f*. **faithful** *adj* fidèle, loyal, -aux. **faithfulness** *n* fidélité *f*.

fake (feik) *n* article truqué *m*. *vt* truquer.

falcon (ˈfɔːlkən) *n* faucon *m*.

fall* (fɔːl) *n* **1** chute, tombée *f*. **2** baisse *f*. *vi* **1** tomber. **2** baisser.

fallacy (ˈfæləsi) *n* erreur *f*. **fallacious** *adj* trompeur, -euse.

fallible (ˈfæləbəl) *adj* faillible.

fallow (ˈfælou) *adj* en friche.

false (fɔːls) *adj* **1** faux, fausse. **2** artificiel, -elle. **3** perfide. **false alarm** *n* fausse alerte *f*. **falsehood** *n* mensonge *m*. **false pretences** *n pl* faux semblant *m*. **under false pretences** par fraude. **false teeth** *n pl* fausses dents *f pl*. **falseness** *n* **1** fausseté *f*. **2** infidélité *f*. **falsify** *vt* fausser, dénaturer.

falter (ˈfɔːltə) *vi* **1** vaciller, chanceler. **2** hésiter.

fame (feim) *n* renommée *f*.

familiar (fəˈmiliə) *adj* intime, familier, -ière. **familiarize** *vt* familiariser.

family (ˈfæmili) *n* famille *f*.

famine (ˈfæmin) *n* famine *f*. **famished** *adj* affamé.

famous (ˈfeiməs) *adj* célèbre, fameux, -euse.

fan[1] (fæn) *n* **1** éventail *m*. **2** ventilateur *m*. *vt* éventer, vanner. **fanbelt** *n* courroie de ventilateur *m*.

fan[2] (fæn) *n* passionné, fervent, fan *m*. **fan club** *n* club de fans *m*.

fanatic (fəˈnætik) *n* fanatique *m,f*.

fancy (ˈfænsi) *n* **1** imagination *f*. **2** caprice *f*. **3** envie *f*. *vt* **1** imaginer. **2** avoir envie de. **fancy oneself** se gober. ~*adj* de fantaisie. **fancy dress** *n* déguisement, travesti *m*.

fanfare (ˈfænfɛə) *n* fanfare *f*.

fang (fæŋ) *n* croc, crochet *m*.

fantastic (fænˈtæstik) *adj* **1** *inf* fantastique. **2** bizarre, excentrique.

fantasy (ˈfæntəsi) *n* fantaisie *f*.

far (fɑː) *adj* éloigné. *adv* **1** loin **2** beaucoup. **far and wide** partout. **so far** jusqu'ici. **faraway** *adj* lointain, éloigné. **far-fetched** *adj* outré, tiré par les cheveux. **far-off** *adj* éloigné. **far-reaching** *adj* d'une grande portée.

farce (fɑːs) *n* farce *f*. **farcical** *adj* risible.

fare (fɛə) *n* prix du voyage *m*.

Far East *n* Extrême-Orient *m*.

farewell (fɛəˈwel) *interj* adieu! *n* au revoir, adieu, -eux *m*.

farm (fɑːm) *n* ferme *f*. *vt* exploiter, cultiver. *vi* être cultivateur. **farmer** *n* agriculteur *m*. **farmhouse** *n* ferme *f*. **farming** *n* exploitation agricole *f*. **farmland** *n* ferme *f*. **farmyard** *n* basse-cour *f*.

farther (ˈfɑːðə) *adv* plus loin. *adj* **1** plus lointain. **2** supplémentaire. **farthest** *adj* **1** le plus éloigné. **2** le plus long. *adv* le plus loin.

fascinate (ˈfæsineit) *vt* fasciner, charmer. **fascinating** *adj* séduisant. **fascination** *n* fascination *f*. charme *m*.

fascism (ˈfæʃizəm) *n* fascisme *m*. **fascist** *adj,n* fasciste.

fashion (ˈfæʃən) *n* **1** mode *f*. **2** façon *f*. **3** manière *f*. **in fashion** à la mode. ~*vt* façonner, former. **fashionable** *adj* à la mode.

fast[1] (fɑːst) *adj* **1** vite, rapide. **2** (of colour) bon teint *invar*. **3** ferme. **4** en avance. *adv* **1** fort, ferme. **2** vite.

fast[2] (fɑːst) *vi* jeûner. *n* jeûne *m*.

fasten (ˈfɑːsən) *vt* **1** attacher. **2** fermer. *vi* s'attacher. **fastener** *n* attache *f*.

fastidious (fəˈstidiəs) *adj* **1** difficile. **2** délicat.

fat (fæt) *n* graisse *f*. gras *m*. *adj* gras, grasse, gros, grosse. **get fat** grossir. **fatten** *vi,vt* engraisser.

fatal (ˈfeitḷ) *adj* fatal. **fatality** *n* fatalité *f*.

fate (feit) *n* destin, sort *m*.

father (ˈfɑːðə) *n* père *m*. *vt* engendrer. **father-in-law** *n* beau-père *m*. **fatherland** *n* patrie *f*.

fathom (ˈfæðəm) *n* brasse *f*. *vt* sonder.

fatigue (fəˈtiːg) *n* fatigue *f*. *vt* fatiguer.

fatuous (ˈfætjuəs) *adj* imbécile, sot, sotte.

fault (fɔːlt) *n* **1** défaut *m*. **2** faute *f*. **faultless** *adj* impeccable. **faulty** *adj* défectueux, -euse.

fauna (ˈfɔːnə) *n* faune *f*.

favour (ˈfeivə) *n* faveur *f*. *vt* favoriser.

favourable *adj* favorable, avantageux, -euse.
favourite *adj,n* préféré, favori, -ite.
fawn[1] (fɔ:n) *n* faon *m*. *adj* fauve.
fawn[2] (fɔ:n) *vt* se coucher servilement.
fear (fiə) *n* peur, crainte *f*. *vt* craindre, redouter. **fearful** *adj* craintif, -ive, effroyable. **fearless** *adj* intrépide.
feasible (ˈfi:zibəl) *adj* **1** faisable, possible. **2** probable.
feast (fi:st) *n* fête *f*. banquet *m*.
feat (fi:t) *n* **1** exploit *m*. **2** tour de force *m*.
feather (ˈfeðə) *n* plume *f*. *vt* emplumer. **featherbed** *n* lit de plume *m*. **featherweight** *n* poids plume *m*.
feature (ˈfi:tʃə) *n* trait *m*. caractéristique *f*. *vt* **1** caractériser. **2** mettre en manchette.
February (ˈfebruəri) *n* février *m*.
feckless (ˈfekləs) *adj* incapable.
fed (fed) *v* see **feed.**
federal (ˈfedərəl) *adj* fédéral, -aux. **federate** *vt* fédérer. *vi* se fédérer. *adj* fédéré. **federation** *n* fédération *f*.
fee (fi:) *n* honoraires *m pl*. droit *m*.
feeble (ˈfi:bəl) *adj* faible.
feed* (fi:d) *vt* nourrir, alimenter. *vi* manger, se nourrir. **be fed up** en avoir assez. *n* nourriture *f*. fourrage *m*. **feedback** *n* rétroaction *f*.
feel* (fi:l) *n* **1** toucher *m*. **2** sensation *f*. *vt* **1** toucher, palper. **2** sentir. *vi* **1** tâtonner. **2** se sentir. **feeler** *n* antenne *f*. **feeling** *n* **1** sensation *f*. **2** sentiment *m*. **3** impression *f*. **4** toucher *m*. *adj* sensible.
feign (fein) *vt* simuler, affecter.
feint[1] (feint) *vi* feindre. *n* feinte *f*.
feint[2] (feint) **feint-ruled paper** *n* papier réglé *m*.
feline (ˈfi:lain) *adj* félin.
fell[1] (fel) *v* see **fall.**
fell[2] (fel) *vt* abattre, assommer.
fellow (ˈfelou) *n* **1** compagnon *m*. **2** membre *m*. **3** type *m*. **4** pareil *m*. **fellowship** *n* **1** amitié *f*. **2** association *f*. **3** fraternité *f*.
felony (ˈfeləni) *n* crime *m*.
felt[1] (felt) *v* see **feel.**
felt[2] (felt) *n* feutre *m*.
female (ˈfi:meil) *adj* féminin. *n* femelle, femme *f*.
feminine (ˈfeminin) *adj* féminin.
fence (fens) *n* clôture, palissade *f*. *vi* faire de l'escrime. *vt* renfermer. **fencing** *n* **1** *sport* escrime *f*. **2** clôture, barrière *f*.
fend (fend) *vt* **fend off** parer. **fend for oneself** se débrouiller. **fender** *n* garde-feu *m invar*.
fennel (ˈfenl̩) *n* fenouil *m*.
ferment (*n* ˈfə:ment; *v* fəˈment) *n* **1** ferment *m*. **2** agitation *f*. *vi* fermenter.
fern (fə:n) *n* fougère *f*.
ferocious (fəˈrouʃəs) *adj* féroce.
ferret (ˈferit) *n* furet *m*. *vi* fureter.
ferry (ˈferi) *n* bac *m*. *vt* transborder. **ferryboat** *n* navire transporteur *m*.
fertile (ˈfə:tail) *adj* fécond, fertile. **fertility** *n* fertilité, fécondité *f*. **fertilize** *vt* fertiliser, féconder. **fertilizer** *n* engrais *m*.
fervent (ˈfə:vənt) *adj* fervent.
fervour (ˈfə:və) *n* ferveur, passion *f*.
fester (ˈfestə) *vi* suppurer, pourrir.
festival (ˈfestivəl) *n* fête *f*. festival *m*.
fetch (fetʃ) *vt* aller chercher, apporter. **fetching** *adj* séduisant.
fete (feit) *n* fête *f*.
fetid (ˈfetid) *adj* fétide.
fetish (ˈfetiʃ) *n* fétiche *m*.
fetlock (ˈfetlɔk) *n* fanon *m*.
fetter (ˈfetə) *n* **1** lien *m*. entrave *f*. **2** *pl* chaînes *f pl*. *vt* enchaîner, entraver.
feud (fju:d) *n* inimitié, vendetta *f*. **feudal** *adj* féodal, -aux.
fever (ˈfi:və) *n* fièvre *f*. **feverish** *adj* fiévreux, -euse.
few (fju:) *adj* peu de. **a few** quelques, quelques-uns, quelques-unes.
fiancé (fiˈɔnsei) *n* fiancé *m*.
fiasco (fiˈæskou) *n* fiasco *m*.
fib (fib) *n* petit mensonge *m*. *vi* en conter.
fibre (ˈfaibə) *n* fibre *f*. **fibreglass** *n* fibre de verre *f*.
fickle (ˈfikəl) *adj* inconstant.
fiction (ˈfikʃən) *n* fiction *f*. **fictitious** *adj* **1** fictif, -ive. **2** simulé.
fiddle (ˈfidl̩) *n* **1** violon *m*. **2** *inf* combine *f*. *vi* **1** jouer du violon. **2** tripoter. *vt* truquer.
fidelity (fiˈdeliti) *n* fidélité, loyauté *f*.
fidget (ˈfidʒit) *vi* se trémousser. *vt* agacer.
field (fi:ld) *n* **1** champ *m*. **2** *sport* terrain *m*. **3** domaine *m*. *vi* tenir le champ. *vt* arrêter.
fiend (fi:nd) *n* démon *m*. **fiendish** *adj* diabolique.
fierce (fiəs) *adj* féroce, acharné, ardent.
fiery (ˈfaiəri) *adj* **1** brûlant, ardent. **2** emporté, irascible.
fifteen (fifˈti:n) *adj,n* quinze *m*. **fifteenth** *adj* quinzième.
fifth (fifθ) *adj* cinquième.
fifty (ˈfifti) *adj,n* cinquante *m*. **fifty-fifty** moitié-moitié. **fiftieth** *adj* cinquantième.

fig (fig) *n* figue *f.* **fig tree** figuier *m.*

fight* (fait) *n* bataille, lutte *f.* combat *m.* *vi* se battre. *vt,vi* combattre.

figment ('figmənt) *n* invention *f.*

figure ('figə) *n* **1** figure *f.* **2** forme *f.* **3** taille *f.* **4** chiffre *m.* *vt* **1** figurer, représenter. **2** *inf* estimer. *vi* calculer. **figurehead** *n* prête-nom *m.* **figurative** *adj* **1** figuratif, -ive. **2** *gram* figuré.

filament ('filəmənt) *n* filament, fil *m.*

file[1] (fail) *n* **1** (in an office) classeur *m.* **2** dossier *m.* *vt* classer, ranger. **filing cabinet** *n* classeur *m.*

file[2] (fail) *n* lime *f.* *vt* limer. **filing** *n* **1** limage *m.* **2** *pl* limaille *f.*

filial ('filiəl) *adj* filial, -aux.

fill (fil) *vt* **1** remplir, combler. **2** (a tooth) plomber. *vi* se remplir. **fill up** faire le plein. ~*n* **1** plein *m.* **2** suffisance *f.* **filling** *n* plombage *m.* **filling station** *n* poste d'essence *m.*

fillet ('filit) *n* filet *m.* *vt* détacher les filets.

filly ('fili) *n* pouliche *f.*

film (film) *n* **1** film *m.* **2** *phot* pelliçule *f.* **3** couche *f.* *vt* filmer, tourner. **film star** *n* vedette de cinéma *f.*

filter ('filtə) *n* filtre *m.* *vt* filtrer, épurer. *vi* s'infiltrer.

filth (filθ) *n* ordure, saleté *f.* **filthy** *adj* sale, infecte.

fin (fin) *n* nageoire *f.* aileron *m.*

final ('fainl) *adj* **1** final, dernier, -ière. **2** définitif, -ive. **finalize** *vt* finaliser.

finance ('fainæns) *n* **1** finance *f.* **2** fonds *m.* *vt* financer. **financial** *adj* financier, -ière. **financier** *n* financier *m.*

finch (fintʃ) *n* pinson *m.*

find* (faind) *n* **1** découverte *f.* **2** trouvaille *f.* *vt* trouver, découvrir. **find out** découvrir.

fine[1] (fain) *adj* **1** fin, raffiné. **2** beau, belle. **3** excellent. **4** menu. **fine arts** *n pl* beaux arts *m pl.* **finery** *n* parure *f.*

fine[2] (fain) *n* amende *f.* *vt* condamner à une amende.

finger ('fiŋgə) *n* doigt *m.* *vt* tâter, manier. **fingermark** *n* empreinte digitale *f.* **fingernail** *n* ongle *m.* **fingerprint** *n* empreinte digitale *f.* **fingertip** *n* bout du doigt *m.*

finish ('finiʃ) *vt* finir, terminer, achever. *vi* se terminer. *n* **1** fin *f.* **2** arrivée *f.*

finite ('fainait) *adj* fini. **finite verb** *n* verbe à un mode fini *m.*

Finland ('finlənd) *n* Finlande *f.* **Finn** *n* finlandais, finnois. *m.* **Finnish** *adj* finlandais. **Finnish** (language) *n* finnois *m.*

fiord (fjɔ:d) *n* also **fjord** fiord *m.*

fir (fə:) *n* sapin *m.* **fir cone** *n* pomme de pin *f.*

fire (faiə) *n* **1** feu *m* *pl* feux. **2** incendie *m.* *vt* **1** mettre le feu à. **2** enflammer. **3** tirer.

fire alarm *n* avertisseur d'incendie *m.*

fire brigade *n* corps de sapeurs-pompiers *m.*

fire drill *n* exercices de sauvetage *m pl.*

fire engine *n* pompe à incendie *f.*

fire-escape *n* échelle de sauvetage *f.*

fireguard ('faiəgɑ:d) *n* garde-feu *m invar.*

firelight ('faiəlait) *n* lumière du feu *f.*

fireman ('faiəmən) *n* (sapeur-)pompier *m.*

fireplace ('faiəpleis) *n* cheminée *f.* foyer *m.*

fireside ('faiəsaid) *n* coin du feu *m.*

fire station *n* caserne de pompiers *f.* poste d'incendie *m.*

firework ('faiəwə:k) *n* **1** pièce d'artifice *f.* **2** *pl* feu d'artifice *m.*

firing squad *n* peloton d'exécution *m.*

firm[1] (fə:m) *adj* **1** ferme, solide, constant. **2** résolu. **firmness** *n* fermeté *f.*

firm[2] (fə:m) *n* maison de commerce *f.*

first (fə:st) *adj,n* premier, -ière. *adv* premièrement. **at first** d'abord. **first aid** *n* premiers secours *m pl.* **first-class** *adj* **1** de première classe. **2** de premier ordre. **first-hand** *adj* de première main. **first name** *n* prénom *m.* **first person** *n* première personne *f.* **first-rate** *adj* excellent, de première classe.

fiscal ('fiskəl) *adj* fiscal, -aux.

fish (fiʃ) *n,pl* **fish** *or* **fishes** poisson *m.* *vt,vi* pêcher. **fisherman** *n* pêcheur *m.* **fish finger** *n* carre de poisson pané *m.* **fishing** *n* pêche *f.* **go fishing** aller à la peche. **fishing rod** *n* canne à pêche *f.* **fishmonger** *n* marchand de poisson *m.* **fishslice** *n* truelle à poisson *f.*

fission ('fiʃən) *n* fission *f.*

fist (fist) *n* poing *m.*

fit[1] (fit) *adj* **1** propre, convenable. **2** capable. **3** en forme. *vt* **1** ajuster. **2** aller à. **3** garnir. *n* ajustement *m.* **fitting** *n* **1** essayage, ajustage *m.* **2** *pl* accessoires *m pl.* **fitness** **1** aptitude *f.* **2** bonne forme *f.*

fit[2] (fit) *n* accès *m.* attaque *f.*

five (faiv) *adj,n* cinq *m.*

fix (fiks) *vt* fixer. *n* *inf* difficulté *f.* embarras *m.* **fixation** *n* fixation *f.* **fixture** *n* **1** appareil fixe *m.* **2** *sport* engagement *m.* **fixture list** programme *m.*

fizz (fiz) *vi* pétiller, siffler. *n* pétillement, sifflement *m.* **fizzy** *adj* gaseux, -euse.

flabbergast (ˈflæbəgɑːst) *vt* épater, ahurir.
flabby (ˈflæbi) *adj* mou, molle, flasque.
flag[1] (flæg) *n* drapeau, -aux *m.* **flagpole** *n* mât *m.*
flag[2] (flæg) *vi* languir, pendre.
flagon (ˈflægən) *n* flacon *m.*
flagrant (ˈfleigrənt) *adj* flagrant, scandaleux, -euse.
flair (ˈflɛə) *n* flair *m.*
flake (fleik) *n* flocon *m.* écaille, paillette *f. vi* tomber en flocons. **flake off** écailler. **flaky** *adj* **1** écailleux, -euse. **2** feuilleté.
flamboyant (flæmˈbɔiənt) *adj* flamboyant.
flame (fleim) *n* flamme *f. vi* flamber.
flamingo (fləˈmiŋgou) *n, pl* **-gos** *or* **-goes** flamant *m.*
flan (flæn) *n* flan *m.* tarte *f.*
flank (flæŋk) *n* flanc *m. vt* flanquer.
flannel (ˈflænḷ) *n* **1** flanelle *f.* **2** gant de toilette *m.*
flap (flæp) *n* **1** rabat *m.* **2** battement *m.* **3** battant *m.* **4** affolement *m. vt* battre. *vi* **1** claquer. **2** s'affoler. **3** battre.
flare (flɛə) *n* **1** feu de signal *m.* **2** godet *m. vi* **1** flamboyer. **2** s'évaser. **flare up** s'émporter.
flash (flæʃ) *n* éclair, éclat *m. vi* jeter des éclairs. *vt* projeter. **flashback** *n* retour en arrière *m.* **flashbulb** *n* ampoule flash *f.* **flashlight** *n* flash *m.* **flashy** *adj* tapageur, -euse.
flask (flɑːsk) *n* flacon *m.*
flat[1] (flæt) *adj* **1** plat. **2** catégorique. **3** fade. **4** *mus* faux. *n mus* bémol *m.* **flatfish** *n* poisson plat *m.* **flat-footed** *adj* à pied plat, aux pieds plats. **flatten** *vt* aplatir. *vi* s'aplatir.
flat[2] (flæt) *n* appartement *m.*
flatter (ˈflætə) *vt* flatter. **flattering** *adj* flatteur, -euse. **flattery** *n* flatterie *f.*
flaunt (flɔːnt) *vi* s'afficher. *vt* faire étalage de.
flautist (ˈflɔːtist) *n* flûtiste *m,f.*
flavour (ˈfleivə) *n* **1** saveur *m.* **2** parfum *m. vt* assaisonner. **flavouring** *n* assaisonnement *m.*
flaw (flɔː) *n* défaut *m.* **flawed** *adj* défectueux, -euse.
flax (flæks) *n* lin *m.*
flea (fliː) *n* puce *f.* **fleabite** *n* **1** morsure de puce *f.* **2** rien *m.*
fleck (flek) *n* **1** petite tache *f.* **2** particule *f. vt* tacheter.
fled (fled) *v see* **flee.**
flee* (fliː) *vt* fuir. *vi* s'enfuir, fuire.
fleece (fliːs) *n* toison *f. vt inf* tondre, rouler.
fleet (fliːt) *n* flotte *f.*
fleeting (ˈfliːtiŋ) *adj* fugace, passager, -ère.
Fleming (ˈflemiŋ) *n* flamand *m.*
Flemish (ˈflemiʃ) *adj* flamand. **Flemish** (language) *n* flamand *m.*
flesh (fleʃ) *n* chair *f.*
flew (fluː) *v see* **fly.**
flex (fleks) *n* câble souple *m. vt* fléchir. **flexible** *adj* flexible, souple.
flick (flik) *n* **1** petit coup *m.* **2** *pl inf* ciné *m. vt* effleurer.
flicker (ˈflikə) *n* battement, clignement *m. vi* trembloter, vaciller.
flight[1] (flait) *n* **1** vol *m.* volée *f.* **2** trajectoire *m.*
flight[2] (flait) *n* fuite *f.*
flimsy (ˈflimzi) *adj* peu solide, léger, -ère.
flinch (flintʃ) *vi* **1** reculer. **2** tressaillir. **without flinching** sans broncher.
fling* (fliŋ) *vi* jeter. *n* **1** jet *m.* **2** tentative *f.*
flint (flint) *n* **1** silex *m.* **2** pierre à briquet *f.*
flip (flip) *n* secousse, chiquenaude *f. vt* tapoter. **flip through** feuilleter. **flipper** *n* nageoire *m.*
flippant (ˈflipənt) *adj* désinvolte. **flippantly** *adv* légèrement.
flirt (fləːt) *n* coquette *f. vi* flirter.
flit (flit) *vi* **1** passer légèrement. **2** voleter. **3** déménager. *n* déménagement *m.*
float (flout) *vi* **1** flotter, nager. **2** faire la planche. *vt* flotter. *n* flotteur *m.*
flock[1] (flɔk) *n* (of sheep, etc.) troupeau, -aux *m.* troupe *f. vi* s'attrouper.
flock[2] (flɔk) *n* bourre de laine *f.*
flog (flɔg) *vt* flageller, fouetter.
flood (flʌd) *n* inondation *f.* déluge *m. vt* inonder. *vi* déborder. **floodlight** *n* phare d'éclairage *m. vt* illuminer par projecteurs.
floor (flɔː) *n* **1** plancher *m.* **2** (of a building) étage *m. vt* terrasser. **floorboard** *n* planche *f.*
flop (flɔp) *vi* **1** faire faillite. **2** se laisser tomber. *n* fiasco *m.*
flora (ˈflɔːrə) *n* flore *f.*
floral (ˈflɔːrəl) *adj* floral, -aux. **florist** *n* fleuriste *m,f.*
flounce[1] (flauns) *n* mouvement vif *m. vi* se démener.
flounce[2] (flauns) *n* (of a dress) volant *m.*
flounder[1] (ˈflaundə) *vi* patauger.
flounder[2] (ˈflaundə) *n* flet *m.*
flour (ˈflauə) *n* farine *f.*
flourish (ˈflʌriʃ) *n* trait de plume *m. vt* brandir. *vi* prospérer.
flout (flaut) *vt* railler, narguer.
flow (flou) *n* écoulement, flot *m. vi* couler.
flower (ˈflauə) *n* fleur *f. vi* fleurir. **flowerbed** *n* plate-bande *f.* **flowery** *adj* fleuri.

flown (floun) *v* see **fly.**
fluctuate ('flʌktʃueit) *vi* fluctuer, vaciller. **fluctuation** *n* fluctuation *f*.
flue (flu:) *n* tuyau de cheminée *m*.
fluent ('flu:ənt) *adj* coulant. **fluently** *adv* couramment.
fluff (flʌf) *n* peluches *f pl*. duvet *m*.
fluid ('flu:id) *adj,n* fluide *m*.
flung (flʌŋ) *v* see **fling.**
fluorescent (flu'resənt) *adj* fluorescent. **fluorescence** *n* fluorescence *f*.
fluoride ('fluəraid) *n* fluorure *f*.
flush[1] (flʌʃ) *vi* rougir. *vt* inonder, balayer à grande eau. *n* **1** éclat *m*. **2** accès *m*. **3** rougeur *f*.
flush[2] (flʌʃ) *adj* **1** ras, de niveau. **2** abondant.
fluster ('flʌstə) *n* agitation *f*. *vt* agiter. *vi* s'énerver.
flute (flu:t) *n* flûte *f*.
flutter ('flʌtə) *n* **1** battement *m*. **2** trouble *m*. *vi* trembler, s'agiter. *vt* agiter.
flux (flʌks) *n* flux *m*.
fly*[1] (flai) *vi* voler. **fly away** s'envoler. **flyover** *n mot* saut-de-mouton *m*.
fly[2] (flai) *n* mouche *f*.
foal (foul) *n* poulain *m*.
foam (foum) *n* écume *f*. *vi* écumer.
focal ('foukəl) *adj* focal, -aux. **focus** *n, pl* **-ci** *or* **-cuses** foyer *m*. *vt* concentrer. *vi* converger.
fodder ('fɔdə) *n* fourrage *m*.
foe (fou) *n* ennemi *m*.
foetus ('fi:təs) *n* fœtus *m*.
fog (fɔg) *n* **1** brouillard *m*. **2** brume *f*. **foggy** *adj* brumeux, -euse. **foghorn** *n* sirène de brume *f*.
foible ('fɔibəl) *n* faible *m*. faiblesse *f*.
foil[1] (fɔil) *vt* faire échouer.
foil[2] (fɔil) *n* tain *m*.
foil[3] (fɔil) *n sport* fleuret *m*.
foist (fɔist) *vt* refiler.
fold[1] (fould) *n* pli *m*. *vt,vi* plier. **fold one's arms** se croiser les bras. **folder** *n* classeur *m*.
fold[2] (fould) *n* parc à moutons *m*.
foliage ('fouliidʒ) *n* feuillage *m*.
folk (fouk) *n pl* gens *m,f pl*. **folkdance** *n* danse rustique *f*. **folklore** *n* folklore *m*. **folksong** *n* chanson populaire *or* folklorique *f*. **folktale** *n* histoire traditionnelle *f*.
follicle ('fɔlikəl) *n* follicule *m*.
follow ('fɔlou) *vt* **1** suivre. **2** poursuivre. **3** succéder à. *vi* **1** suivre. **2** s'ensuivre. **following** *n* suite *f*. *adj* suivant. **follower** *n* disciple *m*.
folly ('fɔli) *n* folie, sottise *f*.
fond (fɔnd) *adj* affectueux, -euse, aimant.
fondant ('fɔndənt) *n* fondant *m*.
fondle ('fɔndḷ) *vt* caresser, câliner.
font (fɔnt) *n* fonts baptismaux *m pl*.
food (fu:d) *n* **1** nourriture *f*. aliments, vivres *m pl*. **2** pâture *f*. **food poisoning** *n* intoxication alimentaire *f*.
fool (fu:l) *n* imbécile *m,f*. *vt* berner, mystifier. *vi* faire l'idiot. **foolhardy** *adj* téméraire. **foolish** *adj* sot, sotte. **foolproof** *adj* indéréglable, indétraquable.
foolscap ('fu:lzkæp) *n* papier ministre *m*.
foot (fut) *n, pl* **feet** **1** pied *m*. **2** *zool* patte *f*. **3** base *f*. **put one's foot in it** mettre les pieds dans le plat. **football** *n* **1** football *m*. **2** ballon *m*. **footbridge** *n* passerelle *f*. **foothold** *n* **1** prise pour le pied *f*. **2** position *f*. **footing** *n* pied *m*. **footlights** *n pl* rampe *f*. **footnote** *n* note (au bas de la page) *f*. renvoi *m*. **footprint** *n* empreinte de pas *f*. **footstep** *n* pas *m*. **footwear** *n* chaussures *f pl*.
for (fə; *stressed* fɔ:) *prep* pour, comme, pendant. *conj* car.
forage ('fɔridʒ) *vi* fourrager, fouiller. *vt* saccager. *n* fourrage *m*.
forbear* (fə'bɛə) *vt* s'abstenir de. *vi* s'abstenir.
forbid* (fə'bid) *vt* défendre, interdire. **forbidding** *adj* rébarbatif, -ive.
force (fɔ:s) *n* **1** force, violence *f*. **2** puissance *f*. **3** corps *m*. *vt* **1** forcer. **2** contraindre. **force-feed** *vt* alimenter de force. **forceful** *adj* vigoureux, -euse, fort.
forceps ('fɔ:seps) *n pl* pince *f*. forceps *m*.
ford (fɔ:d) *n* gué *m*. *vt* passer à gué.
fore (fɔ:) *adj* de devant, antérieur. *n* avant, premier plan *m*. *adv* à l'avant.
forearm[1] ('fɔ:ra:m) *n anat* avant-bras *m invar*.
forearm[2] (fɔ:'ra:m) *vt* prévenir, avertir.
forecast* ('fɔ:ka:st) *n* prévision *f*. *vt* prévoir.
forecourt ('fɔ:kɔ:t) *n* avant-cour *f*.
forefather ('fɔ:fa:ðə) *n* aïeul, -eux, ancêtre *m*.
forefinger ('fɔ:fiŋgə) *n* index *m*.
forefront ('fɔ:frʌnt) *n* premier plan *or* rang *m*.
foreground ('fɔ:graund) *n* premier plan, avant-plan *m*.
forehand ('fɔ:hænd) *adj* d'avant-main. **forehand stroke** *n* coup droit *m*.
forehead ('fɔrid) *n* front *m*.
foreign ('fɔrin) *adj* étranger, -ère. **foreigner** *n* étranger, -ère.
foreleg ('fɔ:leg) *n* jambe *or* patte de devant *f*.
forelock ('fɔ:lɔk) *n* mèche *f*. toupet *m*.

foreman ('fɔ:mən) *n* contremaître, chef d'équipe *m*.
foremost ('fɔ:moust) *adj* premier, en tête. *adv* en premier.
forensic (fə'rensik) *adj* judiciaire, légale.
forerunner ('fɔ:rʌnə) *n* précurseur *m*.
foresee* (fɔ:'si:) *vt* prévoir, entrevoir. **foreseeable** *adj* prévisible.
foresight ('fɔ:sait) *n* prévoyance *f*.
forest ('fɔrist) *n* fôret *f*. **forestry** *n* sylviculture *f*.
forestall (fɔ:'stɔ:l) *vt* anticiper, devancer.
foretaste ('fɔ:teist) *n* avant-goût *m*.
foretell* (fɔ:'tel) *vt* prédire, présager.
forethought ('fɔ:θɔ:t) *n* **1** préméditation *f*. **2** prévoyance *f*.
forfeit ('fɔ:fit) *n* **1** amende *f*. **2** *sport* gage *m*. punition *f*. *vt* perdre, forfaire.
forge[1] (fɔ:dʒ) *vt* **1** forger. **2** contrefaire. *n* forge *f*.
forge[2] (fɔ:dʒ) *vi* **forge ahead** pousser de l'avant.
forgery ('fɔ:dʒəri) *n* contrefaçon *f*. faux *m*.
forget* (fə'get) *vt* **1** oublier. **2** omettre. **forgetful** *adj* oublieux, -euse.
forgive* (fə'giv) *vt* pardonner. **forgiving** *adj* indulgent. **forgiveness** *n* **1** pardon *m*. **2** clémence *f*.
forgo* (fɔ:'gou) *vt* renoncer à, s'abstenir de.
fork (fɔ:k) *n* **1** fourche *f*. **2** *cul* fourchette *f*. **3** (of a road) bifurcation. *vi* bifurquer, fourcher.
forlorn (fə'lɔ:n) *adj* **1** abandonné. **2** désespéré.
form (fɔ:m) *n* **1** forme *f*. **2** figure *f*. **3** formule *f*. **4** *educ* classe *f*. **5** banc *m*. *vt* former, façonner. *vi* se former, se faire. **formal** *adj* formel, -elle. **formality** *n* formalité *f*. **formation** *n* formation *f*. **formative** *adj* formatif, -ive, de formation.
former ('fɔ:mə) *adj* précédent, ancien, -enne, premier, -ière. *pron* celui-là, celle-là. **formerly** *adj* autrefois, jadis.
formidable ('fɔ:midəbəl) *adj* formidable, redoutable.
formula ('fɔ:mjulə) *n, pl* **-las** *or* **-lae** formule *f*.
formulate ('fɔ:mjuleit) *vt* formuler.
forsake* (fə'seik) *vt* abandonner, délaisser.
fort (fɔ:t) *n* fort *m*.
forth (fɔ:θ) *adv* en avant. **and so forth** et ainsi de suite. **forthcoming** *adj* **1** à venir. **2** (of a person) ouvert.
fortify ('fɔ:tifai) *vt* **1** fortifier. **2** affermir. **fortification** *n* fortification *f*. **fortitude** *n* courage *m*.
fortnight ('fɔ:tnait) *n* quinzaine *f*. **fortnightly** *adj* bimensuel, -elle. *adv* tous les quinze jours.
fortress ('fɔ:trəs) *n* forteresse *f*.
fortune ('fɔ:tʃən) *n* **1** hasard *m*. chance *f*. **2** fortune, richesse *f*. **fortune-teller** *n* diseur de bonne aventure *m*. **fortune-telling** *n* bonne aventure *f*. **fortunate** *adj* **1** heureux, -euse, fortuné. **2** propice. **fortunately** *adv* **1** heureusement. **2** par bonheur.
forty ('fɔ:ti) *adj,n* quarante *m*. **fortieth** *adj* quarantième.
forum ('fɔ:rəm) *n* forum *m*.
forward ('fɔ:wəd) *adj* **1** de devant. **2** avancé. **3** précoce. *adv* en avant. *n sport* avant *m*. *vt* **1** avancer. **2** expédier. **please forward** prière de faire suivre. **forwardness** *n* précocité *f*. **forwards** *adv* en avant.
fossil ('fɔsəl) *adj,n* fossile *m*.
foster ('fɔstə) *vt* **1** nourrir. **2** encourager. **fosterchild** *n* enfant adoptif *m*. **fostermother** *n* mère adoptive.
fought (fɔ:t) *v see* **fight.**
foul (faul) *adj* **1** infect, nauséabond. **2** sale. **3** obscène. **4** déloyal, -aux. *n* coup déloyal *m*. *vt* **1** salir. **2** enchevêtrer. *vi* s'encrasser. *adv* déloyalement. **foul play** *n* **1** *sport* jeu déloyal *m*. **2** malveillance *f*.
found[1] (faund) *v see* **find.**
found[2] (faund) *vt* fonder. **foundation** *n* **1** fondation *f*. **2** institution *f*. **3** fondement *m*. **founder** *n* fondateur *m*.
foundry ('faundri) *n* fonderie *f*.
fountain ('fauntin) *n* **1** fontaine *f*. **2** source *f*.
four (fɔ:) *adj,n* quatre *m*. **four-poster** *n* lit à colonnes *m*. **fourth** *adj* quatrième. **foursome** *n* partie double *f*. *adj* à quatre.
fourteen (fɔ:'ti:n) *adj,n* quatorze *m*. **fourteenth** *adj* quatorzième.
fowl (faul) *n* **1** oiseau, -aux *m*. volaille *f*. **2** *cul* poule *f*.
fox (fɔks) *n* renard *m*. *vt inf* mystifier. **foxglove** *n* digitale *f*. **foxhound** *n* chien courant *m*. **foxhunting** *n* chasse au renard *f*.
foyer ('fɔiei) *n* foyer *m*.
fraction ('frækʃən) *n* **1** fragment *m*. **2** fraction *f*.
fracture ('fræktʃə) *n* fracture *f*. *vt* casser, fracturer. *vi* se casser, se fracturer.
fragile ('frædʒail) *adj* fragile.
fragment ('frægmənt) *n* fragment, morceau, -aux *m*.
fragrant ('freigrənt) *adj* embaumé, parfumé. **fragrance** *n* parfum *m*.
frail (freil) *adj* fragile, frêle.

frame (freim) *n* **1** cadre *m*. **2** structure *f*. **3** charpente *f*. **4** châssis *m*. **5** monture *f*. *vt* **1** former. **2** encadrer. **framework** *n* **1** construction, charpente *f*. **2** cadre *m*.

franc (fræŋk) *n* franc *m*.

France (frɑːns) *n* France *f*.

franchise (ˈfræntʃaiz) *n* franchise *f*. droit de vote *m*.

frank (fræŋk) *adj* franc, franche, sincère. **frankness** *n* sincérité *f*.

frantic (ˈfræntik) *adj* frénétique, forcené.

fraternal (frəˈtəːnl̩) *adj* fraternel, -elle. **fraternity** *n* fraternité, confrérie *f*. **fraternize** *vi* fraterniser.

fraud (frɔːd) *n* **1** supercherie, fraude *f*. **2** imposteur *m*.

fraught (frɔːt) *adj* **fraught with** plein de.

fray[1] (frei) *n* bagarre, rixe *f*.

fray[2] (frei) *vt* érailler, effiler. *vi* s'érailler, s'effiler.

freak (friːk) *n* **1** fantaisie *f*. **2** curiosité *f*. phénomène *m*. *adj* extraordinaire.

freckle (ˈfrekəl) *n* tache de rousseur *f*.

free (friː) *adj* **1** libre. **2** gratuit. **free and easy** sans façons. ~*vt* **1** libérer, affranchir. **2** dégager. **freedom** *n* liberté *f*. **freehand** *adj* à main levée. **freehold** *n* propriété libre *f*. **freelance** *adj* indépendant. **freemason** *n* franc-maçon *m*. **free will** *n* libre arbitre *m*.

freeze* (friːz) *v imp* geler. *vt* **1** congeler, glacer. **2** bloquer. *vi* se congeler. *n* gel *m*. **freezing** *n* congélation *f*.

freight (freit) *n* **1** fret, transport *m*. **2** cargaison *f*. *vt* fréter, affréter. **freight train** *n* train de marchandises *m*.

French (frentʃ) *adj* français. **French** (language) *n* français *m*. **French bean** *n* haricot vert *m*. **French dressing** *n* vinaigrette *f*. **French horn** *n* cor d'harmonie *m*. **Frenchman** *n* français *m*. **French window** *n* porte-fenêtre *f*.

frenzy (ˈfrenzi) *n* frénésie *f*.

frequency (ˈfriːkwənsi) *n* fréquence *f*. **frequent** *adj* fréquent. *vt* fréquenter, hanter. **frequently** *adv* fréquemment.

fresco (ˈfreskou) *n*, *pl* **-oes** *or* **-os** fresque *f*.

fresh (freʃ) *adj* **1** frais, fraîche, nouveau, -elle. **2** novice. **3** alerte. **freshness** *n* fraîcheur *f*. **freshwater** *n* eau douce *f*.

fret (fret) *vi* se tourmenter, se tracasser. *vt* ronger.

friar (ˈfraiə) *n* moine *m*. **friary** *n* monastère *m*.

friction (ˈfrikʃən) *n* **1** friction *f*. **2** frottement *m*. **3** conflit *m*.

Friday (ˈfraidi) *n* vendredi *m*.

fridge (fridʒ) *n inf* réfrigérateur, frigo *m*.

friend (frend) *n* ami *m*. **make friends with** se lier d'amitié avec. **friendliness** *n* bienveillance *f*. bonté *f*. **friendly** *adj* amical, -aux, sympathique. **friendship** *n* amitié *f*.

frieze (friːz) *n* frise *f*.

fright (frait) *n* peur *f*. effroi *m*. **frighten** *vt* effrayer, faire peur. **frightful** *adj* terrible, épouvantable.

frigid (ˈfridʒid) *adj* **1** glacial, froid. **2** *med* frigide.

frill (fril) *n* volant *m*. ruche *f*. *vt* plisser, froncer.

fringe (ˈfrindʒ) *n* **1** frange *f*. **2** bord *m*. bordure *f*.

frisk (frisk) *vi* gambader. **frisky** *adj* folâtre.

fritter[1] (ˈfritə) *vt* morceler. **fritter away** gaspiller.

fritter[2] (ˈfritə) *n* beignet *m*.

frivolity (friˈvɔliti) *n* frivolité *f*. **frivolous** *adj* frivole, futile.

frizz (friz) *vt* friser, crêper. *vi* se friser. **frizzy** *adj* crépu.

frizzle[1] (ˈfrizl̩) *vt* (hair) friser.

frizzle[2] (ˈfrizəl) *vt* grésiller, crépiter.

fro (frou) *adv* **to and fro** de long en large.

frock (frɔk) *n* robe *f*.

frog (frɔg) *n* grenouille *f*. **frogs' legs** *n pl* cuisses de grenouille *f pl*.

frolic (ˈfrɔlik) *n* cabriole *f*. ébats *m pl*. *vi* batifoler, folâtrer.

from (frəm; *stressed* frɔm) *prep* **1** de. **2** à partir de. **3** à. **4** d'après. **5** de la part de.

front (frʌnt) *n* front, devant *m*. façade *f*. **in front of** devant. ~*adj* de devant, d'avant. **frontal** *adj* de devant.

frontier (ˈfrʌntiə) *n* frontière *f*.

frost (frɔst) *n* gelée *f*. *vt* geler, givrer. **frosty** *adj* gelé, glacial. **frostbite** *n* gelure *f*.

froth (frɔθ) *n* écume, mousse *f*. **frothy** *adj* mousseux, -euse.

frown (fraun) *vi* froncer les sourcils. **frown upon** regarder de travers. ~*n* froncement de sourcils *m*.

froze (frouz) *v* see **freeze**.

frozen (ˈfrouzn̩) *v* see **freeze**. *adj* gelé, glacé.

frugal (ˈfruːgəl) *adj* frugal, -aux.

fruit (fruːt) *n* fruit *m*. **fruit machine** *n* machine à sous *f*. **fruitful** *adj* fructueux, -euse, fécond. **fruition** *n* **1** jouissance *f*. **2** réalisation *f*. **fruitless** *adj* stérile.

frustrate (frʌsˈtreit) *vt* frustrer.

fry (frai) *vt* faire frire. *vi* frire. **frying pan** *n* poêle (à frire) *f*.
fudge (fʌdʒ) *n* fondant *m*.
fuel ('fju:əl) *n* combustible, carburant *m*.
fugitive ('fju:dʒitiv) *adj,n* fugitif, -ive.
fulcrum ('fʌlkrəm) *n, pl* **-crums** *or* **-cra** **1** *tech* point d'appui *m*. **2** centre *m*.
fulfil (ful'fil) *vt* **1** accomplir. **2** satisfaire. **3** achever. **fulfilment** *n* **1** accomplissement *m*. **2** achèvement *m*.
full (ful) *adj* **1** plein, rempli, complet, -ète. **2** ample. **full-length** *adj* **1** *Art* en pied. **2** long, longue. **full moon** *n* pleine lune *f*. **full stop** *n* point *m*. **full-time** *adj* à temps complet. **fullness** *n* **1** plénitude *f*. **2** ampleur *f*. **fully** *adv* pleinement, entièrement.
fumble ('fʌmbəl) *vi* fouiller, farfouiller.
fume (fju:m) *n* fumée, vapeur *f*. *vi* fumer.
fun (fʌn) *n* **1** amusement *m*. **2** plaisanterie *f*. **for fun** pour rire. **make fun of** se moquer de. **funfair** *n* fête foraine *f*.
function ('fʌŋkʃən) *n* **1** fonction *f*. **2** réception *f*. *vi* fonctionner, marcher.
fund (fʌnd) *n* fonds *m*. caisse *f*.
fundamental (fʌndə'mentl) *adj* fondamental, -aux, essentiel, -elle.
funeral ('fju:nərəl) *n* funérailles, obsèques *f pl*. *adj* funéraire, funèbre.
fungus ('fʌŋgəs) *n, pl* **-gi** *or* **-guses** champignon (vénéneux) *m*.
funnel ('fʌnl) *n* **1** entonnoir *m*. **2** cheminée *f*.
funny ('fʌni) *adj* **1** drôle, comique, marrant. **2** étrange, bizarre.
fur (fə:) *n* **1** fourrure *f* poil *m*. **2** tartre *m* *vt* incruster *vi* s'incruster **furrier** *n* fourreur *m*
furious ('fjuəriəs) *adj* furieux, -euse, furibond
furnace ('fə:nis) *n* fourneau, -aux, four *m*.
furnish ('fə:niʃ) *vt* **1** fournir, munir **2** (a room, etc.) meubler.
furniture ('fə:nitʃə) *n* meubles *m pl* mobilier *m*. **antique furniture** meubles d'époque **piece of furniture** meuble *m*
furrow ('fʌrou) *n* **1** sillon *m* **2** rainure *f* *vt* sillonner
further ('fə:ðə) *adv* **1** plus loin **2** d avantage *adj* supplémentaire *vt* avancer, favoriser **furthermore** *adv* en outre **furthest** *adj* **1** le plus éloigné **2** le plus long *adv* le plus loin
furtive ('fə:tiv) *adj* furtif, -ive, sournois
fury ('fjuəri) *n* furie, fureur *f*
fuse[1] (fju:z) *n* fusible, plomb *m*.
fuse[2] (fju:z) *vt,vi* **1** fondre **2** fusionner
fuselage ('fju:zəla:ʒ) *n* fuselage *m*
fusion ('fju:ʒən) *n* fusion *f*.
fuss (fʌs) *n* **1** bruit exagéré *m*. **2** embarras *m pl*. *vi* faire des histoires. *vt* tracasser. **fussy** *adj* tatillon, -onne, méticuleux, -euse.
futile ('fju:tail) *adj* futile, vain.
future ('fju:tʃə) *adj* future, à venir. *n* **1** avenir *m*. **2** *gram* futur *m*.
fuzz (fʌz) *n* peluches *m pl*. *vt* faire bouffer. *vi* bouffer, frisotter. **fuzzy** *adj* **1** frisotté. **2** flou.

G

gabble ('gæbəl) *n* bredouillement *m*. jacasserie *f*. *vi* bredouiller, jacasser. *vt* débiter très vite.
gable ('geibəl) *n* pignon *m*.
gadget ('gædʒit) *n* *inf* dispositif, truc *m*.
gag[1] (gæg) *n* bâillon *m*. *vt* bâillonner.
gag[2] (gæg) *inf* *vt* tromper. *vi* blaguer. *n* blague *f*.
gaiety ('geiəti) *n* gaieté *f*.
gaily ('geili) *adv* gaiement, allègrement.
gain (gein) *vt* **1** gagner, acquérir **2** (of a clock) avancer *n* gain, profit *m*.
gait (geit) *n* allure, démarche *f*.
gala ('ga:lə) *n* fête *f*. gala *m*.
galaxy ('gæləksi) *n* galaxie *f*.
gale (geil) *n* tempête *f*. coup de vent *m*.
gallant ('gælənt) *adj* **1** brave, vaillant. **2** galant **gallantly** *adv* **1** bravement. **2** galamment **gallantry** *n* **1** vaillance *f*. **2** galanterie *f*.
gallery ('gæləri) *n* **1** galerie *f*. **2** *pol* tribune *f* **3** *Art* musée *m*.
galley ('gæli) *n* *naut* cuisine *f*.
gallon ('gælən) *n* gallon *m*.
gallop ('gæləp) *n* galop *m*. *vi* galoper *vt* faire galoper.
gallows ('gælouz) *n* potence *f*. gibet *m*.
galore (gə'lɔ:) *adv* en abondance, à gogo
galvanize ('gælvənaiz) *vt* galvaniser
gamble ('gæmbəl) *vt,vi* jouer, miser. *vt* risquer *n* jeu, jeux *m* spéculation *f* **gambling** *n* jeu, jeux *m*.
game (geim) *n* **1** amusement, jeu, jeux *m*. **2** (hunting) gibier *m* **gamekeeper** *n* garde-chasse *m*.
gammon ('gæmən) *n* **1** quartier de lard fumé *m* **2** jambon fumé *m*
gander ('gændə) *n* jars *m*
gang (gæŋ) *n* troupe, bande *f* *v* **gang up**

s'allier. **gangster** *n* bandit, gangster *m.* **gangway** *n* **1** passage *m.* **2** *naut* passerelle *f.*

gangrene (gæŋ'gri:n) *n* gangrène *f.*

gap (gæp) *n* **1** trou *m.* ouverture, brèche *f.* **2** écart *m.*

gape (geip) *vi* **1** regarder bouche bée. **2** bailler. **gaping** *adj* **1** bouche bée. **2** béant.

garage ('gærɑ:ʒ) *n* garage *m.*

garble ('gɑ:bəl) *vt* fausser, mutiler.

garden ('gɑ:dn̩) *n* jardin *m.* *vi* jardiner. **gardening** *n* jardinage *m.*

gargle ('gɑ:gəl) *vt* se gargariser. *n* gargarisme *m.*

gargoyle ('gɑ:gɔil) *n* gargouille *f.*

garland ('gɑ:lənd) *n* guirlande *f.* *vt* enguirlander.

garlic ('gɑ:lik) *n* ail *m,pl* aulx. **clove of garlic** *n* gousse d'ail *f.*

garment ('gɑ:mənt) *n* vêtement *m.*

garnish ('gɑ:niʃ) *n* garniture *f.* *vt* garnir, orner.

garrison ('gærisən) *n* garnison *f.* *vt* mettre en garnison.

garter ('gɑ:tə) *n* jarretière *f.*

gas (gæs) *n* gaz *m invar.* *vt* asphyxier.

gash (gæʃ) *n* coupure, entaille *f.* *vt* entailler, couper, balafrer.

gasket ('gæskit) *n* joint *m.*

gasp (gɑ:sp) *n* hoquet, sursaut *m.* *vi* **1** haleter, suffoquer. **2** sursauter.

gastric ('gæstrik) *adj* gastrique. **gastronomic** *adj* gastronomique.

gate (geit) *n* porte, grille, barrière *f.* **gatecrash** *vi* resquiller.

gateau ('gætou) *n,pl* **-teaux** gâteau, -aux *m.*

gather ('gæðə) *vt* **1** rassembler, recueillir. **2** prendre. **3** comprendre, déduire. *vi* se rassembler. **gathering** *n* rassemblement *m.*

gauche (gouʃ) *adj* gauche.

gaudy ('gɔ:di) *adj* voyant, criard. **gaudily** *adv* de manière voyante.

gauge (geidʒ) *n* calibre, indicateur *m.* jauge *f.* *vt* calibrer, jauger, mesurer.

gaunt (gɔ:nt) *adj* maigre, decharné.

gauze (gɔ:z) *n* gaze *f.*

gave (geiv) *v* see **give.**

gay (gei) *adj* **1** gai, allègre. **2** *sl* homosexuel, -elle.

gaze (geiz) *n* regard fixe *m.* *vi* regarder fixement.

gazelle (gə'zel) *n* gazelle *f.*

gear (giə) *n* **1** équipement *m.* effets *m pl.* **2** *mot* vitesse *f.* **put into/out of gear** embrayer/débrayer. **gearbox** *n* boîte de vitesses *f.* **gear lever** *n* levier de changement de vitesse *m.*

gelatine ('dʒeləti:n) *n* gélatine *f.*

gelignite ('dʒelignait) *n* gélignite *f.*

gem (dʒem) *n* pierre précieuse, gemme *f.* joyau, -aux *m.*

Gemini ('dʒɛminai) *n pl* Gémeaux *m pl.*

gender ('dʒendə) *n* **1** *gram* genre *m.* **2** sexe *m.*

gene (dʒi:n) *n* gène *m.*

genealogy (dʒini'ælədʒi) *n* généalogie *f.*

general ('dʒenərəl) *adj,n* général, -aux *m.* **general practitioner** *n* médecin généraliste *m.* **generalization** *n* généralisation *f.* **generalize** *vt* généraliser.

generate ('dʒenəreit) *vt* engendrer, produire. **generation** *n* génération *f.* **generator** *n* générateur *m.*

generic (dʒi'nerik) *adj* générique.

generous ('dʒenərəs) *adj* généreux, -euse, magnanime. **generosity** *n* générosité *f.*

genetic (dʒi'netik) *adj* génétique. **genetics** *n* génétique *f.*

Geneva (dʒi'ni:və) *n* Genève *f.* **Lake Geneva** lac Léman *m.*

genial ('dʒi:niəl) *adj* doux, clément, bienveillant.

genital ('dʒenitl) *adj* génital, -aux. **genitals** *n pl* organes génitaux *m pl.*

genius ('dʒi:niəs) *n* **1** génie *m.* **2** démon *m.* **3** aptitude *f.*

genteel (dʒen'ti:l) *adj* de bon ton.

gentile ('dʒentail) *adj,n* gentil.

gentle ('dʒentl̩) *adj* doux, douce. **gentleman** *n* **1** monsieur. **2** homme comme il faut *m.* **gentleness** *n* douceur *f.*

genuflect ('dʒenjuflekt) *vi* faire une génuflexion.

genuine ('dʒenjuin) *adj* **1** authentique, véritable. **2** sincère.

genus ('dʒi:nəs) *n, pl* **genera** genre *m.*

geography (dʒi'ɔgrəfi) *n* géographie *f.* **geographic** *adj also* **geographical** géographique.

geology (dʒi'ɔlədʒi) *n* géologie *f.* **geological** *adj* géologique. **geologist** *n* géologue *m.*

geometry (dʒi'ɔmətri) *n* géométrie *f.* **geometric** *adj also* **geometrical** géométrique.

geriatrics (dʒeri'ætriks) *n* gériatrie *f.*

germ (dʒə:m) *n* germe, microbe *m.*

Germany ('dʒə:məni) *n* Allemagne *f.* **German** *adj,n* allemand. **German** (language) *n* allemand *m.* **German measles** *n* rubéole *f.* **Germanic** *adj* germanique.

germinate ('dʒə:mineit) *vi* germer. *vt* faire germer.

gerund (ˈdʒerənd) *n* gérondif *m.*
gesticulate (dʒisˈtikuleit) *vt* gesticuler.
gesture (ˈdʒestʃə) *n* geste, signe *m.*
get* (get) *vt* **1** obtenir. **2** gagner. **3** aller chercher. **4** *inf* comprendre. **5** faire. **6** avoir. *vi* **1** devenir. **2** arriver. **get back** revenir. **get down** descendre. **get in 1** entrer. **2** arriver. **get off** descendre.. **get on** monter. **get out** sortir. **get up** se lever.
geyser (ˈgi:zə) *n* geyser *m.*
ghastly (ˈgɑ:stli) *adj* **1** horrible, effroyable. **2** blême. *adv* horriblement, effroyablement.
gherkin (ˈgə:kin) *n* cornichon *m.*
ghetto (ˈgetou) *n, pl* **-os** *or* **-oes** ghetto *m.*
ghost (goust) *n* fantôme *f.* spectre *m.*
giant (ˈdʒaiənt) *adj,n* géant.
giddy (ˈgidi) *adj* **1** étourdi, vertigineux, -euse. **2** frivole. **giddiness** *n* vertige *m.*
gift (gift) *n* don, cadeau, -aux *m.* **gifted** *adj* doué.
gigantic (dʒaiˈgæntik) *adj* gigantesque, géant.
giggle (ˈgigəl) *n* petit rire, gloussement *m.* *vi* rire nerveusement, glousser.
gild (gild) *vt* dorer. **gilded** *adj* doré.
gill (gil) *n zool* branchie *f.*
gilt (gilt) *n* dorure *f.*
gimmick (ˈgimik) *n* machin, truc *m.* trouvaille *f.*
gin (dʒin) *n* gin, genièvre *m.*
ginger (ˈdʒindʒə) *n* gingembre *m.* *adj* roux, rousse. **gingerbread** *n* pain d'épice *m.* **gingerly** *adv* avec précaution.
gingham (ˈgiŋəm) *n* guingan *m.*
Gipsy (ˈdʒipsi) *n* bohemien, -ienne.
giraffe (dʒiˈrɑ:f) *n* girafe *f.*
girder (ˈgə:də) *n* support *m.* poutre *f.*
girdle (ˈgə:dl̩) *n* ceinture, cordelière *f.* *vt* ceindre.
girl (gə:l) *n* (jeune) fille *f.* **girlfriend** *n* (petite) amie *f.* **girlhood** *n* jeunesse *f.*
girth (gə:θ) *n* sangle *f.*
give* (giv) *vt,vi* donner. *vt* faire. **give away 1** donner. **2** *inf* trahir. **give in** céder. **give out 1** distribuer. **2** annoncer. **give up** renoncer, abandonner. **give way 1** céder. **2** s'affaisser.
glacier (ˈglæsiə) *n* glacier *m.*
glad (glæd) *adj* heureux, -euse, content. **gladly** *adv* avec plaisir, volontiers.
glamour (ˈglæmə) *n* **1** charme *m.* **2** fascination *f.* prestige *m.* **glamorize** *vt* donner un prestige factice. **glamorous** *adj* enchanteur, -eresse
glance (glɑ:ns) *n* regard, coup d'œil *m.* *vi* jeter un coup d'œil. **glance through** feuilleter.
gland (glænd) *n* glande *f.*
glare (glɛə) *n* **1** lumière aveuglante *f.* éclat *m.* **2** regard farouche *m.* *vi* éblouir. **glare at** regarder d'un air furieux.
glass (glɑ:s) *n* **1** verre *m.* **2** *pl* lunettes *f pl.* **pane of glass** vitre *f.*
glaze (gleiz) *n* glace *f.* lustre, vernis *m.* *vi* **1** vitrer. **2** vernir. **3** *cul* glacer.
gleam (gli:m) *n* lueur *f.* rayon *m.* *vi* luire, miroiter.
glean (gli:n) *vt* glaner.
glee (gli:) *n* joie, allégresse *f.* *adj* joyeux, -euse, allègre.
glib (glib) *adj* spécieux, -euse.
glide (glaid) *vi* **1** glisser, couler. **2** *aviat* planer. *n* **1** glissement *m.* **2** vol plané *m.* **glider** *n* planeur *m.*
glimmer (ˈglimə) *n* lueur (faible) *f.* *vi* luire faiblement.
glimpse (glimps) *n* aperçu *m.* **catch a glimpse** entrevoir, apercevoir.
glint (glint) *n* trait de lumière *m.* *vi* étinceler.
glisten (ˈglisən) *vi* étinceler, reluire.
glitter (ˈglitə) *n* étincellement *m.* *vi* étinceler.
gloat (glout) *vi* **gloat over** couver du regard, se réjouir.
globe (gloub) *n* globe *m.* sphère *f.*
gloom[1] (glu:m) *n* (darkness) obscurité *f.* ténèbres *f pl.* **gloomy** *adj* sombre, ténébreux, -euse.
gloom[2] (glu:m) *n* mélancolie *f.* **gloomy** *adj* lugubre, morne.
glory (ˈglɔ:ri) *n* gloire *f.* honneur *m.* *v* **glory in** se glorifier de, se faire gloire de. **glorify** *vt* glorifier. **glorious** *adj* glorieux, -euse.
gloss[1] (glɔs) *n* (shine) lustre *m.* *vt* lustrer, glacer. **gloss over** farder. **glossy** *adj* lustré, brillant.
gloss[2] (glɔs) *n* glose *f.* commentaire *m.* *vt* gloser.
glossary (ˈglɔsəri) *n* glossaire, lexique *m.*
glove (glʌv) *n* gant *m.*
glow (glou) *n* rougeur, ardeur *f.* *vi* briller, rayonner. **glowing** *adj* **1** rayonnant. **2** chaleureux, -euse.
glower (ˈglauə) *vi* **glower at** regarder d'un air fâché.
glucose (ˈglu:kous) *n* glucose *m.*
glue (glu:) *n* colle *f.* *vt* coller.
glum (glʌm) *adj* renfrogné, maussade.
glut (glʌt) *n* surabondance *f.* **glutton** *n* gourmand *m.* **gluttony** *n* gloutonnerie *f.*
gnarled (nɑ:ld) *adj* noueux, -euse, tordu.

gnash (næʃ) *vt* grincer.
gnat (næt) *n* moustique, cousin *m*.
gnaw (nɔ:) *vt* ronger. **gnawing** *n* rongement *m*.
gnome (noum) *n* gnome *m*.
go* (gou) *vi* **1** aller, partir. **2** (of a machine) marcher. **3** passer. **go away** s'en aller. **go back** retourner. **go down** descendre. **go on** continuer. **go out** sortir. **go through** traverser. **go up** monter. **go without** se passer de. ~*n, pl* **goes 1** coup *m*. **2** entrain *m*.
goad (goud) *vt* aiguillonner. *n* aiguillon *m*.
goal (goul) *n* **1** but *m*. **2** objectif *m*. **goalkeeper** *n* gardien de but *m*. **goalpost** *n* montant de but *m*.
goat (gout) *n* chèvre *f*. **he-goat** *n* bouc *m*.
gobble ('gɔbəl) *vt* avaler goulûment.
goblin ('gɔblin) *n* lutin *m*.
god (gɔd) *n* dieu, -eux *m*. **godchild** *n* filleul *m*. **goddaughter** *n* filleule *f*. **godfather** *n* parrain *m*. **godmother** *n* marraine *f*. **godson** *n* filleul *m*. **goddess** *n* déesse *f*.
goggles ('gɔgəlz) *n* lunettes protectrices *f pl*.
gold (gould) *n* or *m*. **golden** *adj* doré, d'or. **golden syrup** *n* mélasse raffinée *f*. **goldfinch** *n* chardonneret *m*. **goldfish** *n* poisson rouge *m*. **goldmine** *n* **1** mine d'or *f*. **2** *inf* affaire d'or *f*. **goldsmith** *n* orfèvre *m*.
golf (gɔlf) *n* golf *m*. **golfcourse** *n* terrain de golf *m*.
gondola ('gɔndələ) *n* gondole *f*. **gondolier** *n* gondolier *m*.
gone (gɔn) *v* see **go.**
gong (gɔŋ) *n* gong *m*.
good (gud) *adj* **1** bon, bonne. **2** sage. **good for nothing** bon à rien. ~*n* **1** bien *m*. **2** *pl* effets *m pl*. marchandises *f pl*. **for good** pour de bon. **good afternoon** *interj* bonjour! **goodbye** *interj,n* au revoir, adieu, -eux *m*. **good evening** *interj* bonsoir! **good-looking** *adj* beau, belle. **good morning** *interj* bonjour! **good night** *interj* bonne nuit! **goods train** *n* train de marchandises *m*. **good will** *n* bonne volonté, bienveillance *f*.
Good Friday *n* vendredi saint *m*.
goose (gu:s) *n, pl* **geese** oie *f*. **gooseberry** *n* groseille à maquereau *f*. **gooseberry bush** groseillier (à maquereau) *m*.
gore[1] (gɔ:) *n* sang caillé *m*.
gore[2] (gɔ:) *vt* encorner.
gorge (gɔ:dʒ) *n* gorge *f*. *vi* se gorger, s'empiffrer. *vt* gorger, rassasier.
gorgeous ('gɔ:dʒəs) *adj* magnifique, splendide.
gorilla (gə'rilə) *n* gorille *m*.
gorse (gɔ:s) *n* ajonc *m*.
gory ('gɔ:ri) *adj* ensanglanté.
gosh (gɔʃ) *interj* sapristi!
gosling ('gɔzliŋ) *n* oison *m*.
gospel ('gɔspəl) *n* évangile *m*.
gossip ('gɔsip) *vi* bavarder, faire des cancans. *n* **1** commérage *m*. **2** commère, bavarde *f*.
got (gɔt) *v* see **get.**
Gothic ('gɔθik) *adj* gothique.
goulash ('gu:læʃ) *n* gulache *m*.
gourd (guəd) *n* courge, gourde *f*.
gourmet (guə'mei) *n* gourmet, gastronome *m*.
govern ('gʌvən) *vt* gouverner, régir, administrer. **government** *n* gouvernement *m*. **governor** *n* **1** gouverneur *m*. **2** *inf* patron *m*.
gown (gaun) *n* robe *f*.
grab (græb) *n* mouvement vif pour saisir *m*. étreinte *f*. *vi* saisir brusquement, empoigner.
grace (greis) *n* **1** grâce *f*. **2** bénédicité *m*. **Her/His Grace** Madame/Monseigneur. **Your Grace** votre Grandeur. **graceful** *adj* grâcieux, -euse. **gracefully** *adv* avec grâce. **gracious** *adj* bienveillant.
grade (greid) *n* grade, rang, degré *m*. *vt* **1** grader, classer. **2** graduer. **gradient** *n* dénivellation, pente, rampe *f*. **gradual** *adj* graduel, -elle. **graduate** *n* diplômé. *vi* recevoir ses diplômes. *vt* graduer.
graffiti (grə'fi:ti) *n pl* graffiti *n pl*.
graft (grɑ:ft) *n* greffe *f*. *vt* greffer.
grain (grein) *n* **1** grain *m*. **2** texture *f*.
gram (græm) *n* gramme *m*.
grammar ('græmə) *n* grammaire *f*. **grammar school** *n* lycée *m*. **grammatical** *adj* grammatical, -aux.
gramophone ('græməfoun) *n* phonographe *m*.
granary ('grænəri) *n* grenier *m*.
grand (grænd) *adj* grandiose, magnifique. **grandeur** *n* grandeur, splendeur *f*.
grandad ('grændæd) *n inf also* **grandpa** *n* grand-papa *m*.
grandchild ('græntʃaild) *n* petit-enfant *m*.
granddaughter ('grændɔ:tə) *n* petite-fille *f*.
grandfather ('grænfɑ:ðə) *n* grand-père *m*.
grandma ('grænmɑ:) *n inf also* **granny** bonne-maman, mémé *f*.
grandmother ('grændmʌðə) *n* grand-mère *f*.
grandparent ('grænpɛərənt) *n* grand-parent *m*.
grand piano *n* piano à queue *m*.
grandson (grænsʌn) *n* petit-fils *m*.
grandstand ('grændstænd) *n* tribune (d'honneur) *f*.

granite ('grænit) *n* granit *m*.

grant (grɑ:nt) *n* subvention, bourse *f*. *vt* accorder, conceder.

grape (greip) *n* raisin *m*. **bunch of grapes** grappe de raisins *f*. **grapefruit** *n* pamplemousse *m*. **grapevine** *n* **1** vigne *f*. **2** source d'informations *f*.

graph (græf) *n* graphique *n*. courbe *f*.

grapple ('græpəl) *vi* **grapple with** en venir aux prises avec.

grasp (grɑ:sp) *n* prise, etreinte *f*. *vt* **1** saisir, empoigner. **2** comprendre. **grasping** *adj* rapace, avide.

grass (grɑ:s) *n* herbe *f*. **grassroots** *n* base, source *f*.

grate[1] (greit) *n* grille *f*.

grate[2] (greit) *vt* râper. *vi* grincer.

grateful ('greitfəl) *adj* reconnaissant. **gratify** *vt* **1** faire plaisir. **2** satisfaire. **gratifying** *adj* agréable.

gratitude ('grætitju:d) *n* gratitude, reconnaissance *f*.

grave[1] (greiv) *n* tombe *f*. tombeau, -aux *m*. **gravestone** *n* pierre tombale *f*. **graveyard** *n* cimetière *m*.

grave[2] (greiv) *adj* sérieux, -euse, grave.

gravel ('grævəl) *n* gravier *m*.

gravity ('græviti) *n* gravité *f*.

gravy ('greivi) *n* jus *m*. sauce *f*.

graze[1] (greiz) *vi* (of animals) paître, brouter. *vt* faire paître.

graze[2] (greiz) *n* éraflure, écorchure *f*. *vt* **1** érafler, ecorcher. **2** frôler.

grease (gri:s) *n* graisse *f*. *vt* graisser. **greasepaint** *n* fard *m*. **greaseproof** *adj* sulfurise, parcheminé. **greasy** *adj* graisseux, -euse.

great (greit) *adj* grand, fort. **greatly** *adv* beaucoup. **greatness** *n* grandeur *f*.

Great Britain *n* Grande-Bretagne *f*.

Greece (gri:s) *n* Grece *f*. **Grecian** *adj* grec, grecque. **Greek** *adj,n* grec, grecque. **Greek** (language) *n* grec *m*.

greed (gri:d) *n* cupidité, avidité *f*. **greedy** *adj* **1** gourmand. **2** avide. **greedily** *adv* avidement, goulûment.

green (gri:n) *adj* **1** vert. **2** *inf* naif, naïve. *n* **1** vert *m*. **2** *pl* légumes verts *m pl*. **greenery** *n* verdure *f*. feuillage *m*. **greenfly** *n* puceron *m*. **greengage** *n* reine-claude *f*. **greengrocer** *n* marchand de légumes *m*. fruitier, -ière. **greenhouse** *n* serre *f*.

Greenland ('gri:nlənd) *n* Groenland *m*. **Greenlander** *n* groenlandais *m*.

greet (gri:t) *vt* saluer, accueillir. **greeting** *n* salutation *f*.

gregarious (gri'gɛəriəs) *adj* grégaire.

grenade (gri'neid) *n* grenade *f*.

grew (gru:) *v* see **grow**.

grey (grei) *adj,n* gris *m*. **greyhound** *n* lévrier *m*.

grid (grid) *n* grille *f*. grillage *m*.

grief (gri:f) *n* chagrin *m*. douleur *f*.

grieve (gri:v) *vt* chagriner, peiner. *vi* se chagriner, s'affliger. **grievance** *n* grief *m*. injustice *f*. **grieved** *adj* désolé. **grievous** *adj* douloureux, -euse, pénible.

grill (gril) *n* **1** *cul* grillade *f*. **2** gril *m*. *vt* *cul* griller.

grille (gril) *n* grille *f*.

grim (grim) *adj* **1** menaçant, sinistre. **2** sévère.

grimace (gri'meis) *n* grimace *f*. *vi* grimacer.

grime (graim) *n* saleté, crasse *f*. **grimy** *adj* crasseux, -euse.

grin (grin) *n* large sourire *m*. *vi* sourire à belles dents.

grind* (graind) *vt* **1** moudre, broyer. **2** aiguiser. *vi* grincer. *n* **1** grincement *m*. **2** *sl* corvée *f*.

grip (grip) *n* prise, etreinte *f*. **come to grips with** en venir aux mains avec. ~*vt* **1** saisir. **2** serrer. **gripping** *adj* *inf* passionnant.

gripe (graip) *vt* affliger. *vi* *inf* rouspéter. *n* colique *f*.

gristle ('grisəl) *n* cartilage *m*.

grit (grit) *n* **1** grès *m*. **2** *sl* cran, courage *m*. *vi,vt* grincer. *vt* sabler.

groan (groun) *n* gemissement *m*. *vi* gémir, se plaindre.

grocer ('grousə) *n* epicier, -ière. **grocery** *n* épicerie *f*.

groin (grɔin) *n* *anat* aine *f*.

groom (gru:m) *n* palefrenier *m*. *vt* panser.

groove (gru:v) *n* rainure, cannelure *f*. *vt* rayer, canneler.

grope (group) *vi* tatonner. **grope for** chercher à tâtons.

gross (grous) *adj* **1** gros, grosse. **2** grossier, -ière. **3** flagrant. *n* grosse *f*.

grotesque (grou'tesk) *adj,n* grotesque *m*.

grotto ('grɔtou) *n*, *pl* **-os** *or* **-oes** grotte *f*.

ground[1] (graund) *n* **1** sol, terrain *m*. **2** raison *f*. **3** fond *m*. *vt* fonder, baser. *vi* s'échouer. **ground floor** *n* rez-de-chaussée *m*. **groundsheet** *n* tapis de sol *m*. **groundsman** *n* prepose a l'entretien d'un terrain de jeux *m.* **groundwork** *n* assise *f.* plan *m.*

ground[2] (graund) *v* see **grind.**

group (gru:p) *n* groupe *m.* *vt* grouper. *vi* se grouper

grouse[1] (graus) *n zool* tétras *m.*

grouse[2] (graus) *vi inf* grogner, rouspéter.

grove (grouv) *n* bocage *m.*

grovel ('grɔvəl) *vi* ramper.

grow* (grou) *vi* pousser, grandir, croître. *vt* cultiver. **grown-up** *n* adulte *m,f.* **growth** *n* croissance *f.*

growl (graul) *vi* grogner, gronder. *n* grognement *m.*

grub (grʌb) *n* **1** larve *f.* **2** *sl* boustifaille *f.*

grubby ('grʌbi) *adj* sale, malpropre.

grudge (grʌdʒ) *n* rancune *f.* *vt* donner à contre-cœur. **grudgingly** *adv* à contre-cœur.

gruelling ('gru:əliŋ) *adj* épuisant, éreintant.

gruesome ('gru:səm) *adj* macabre.

gruff (grʌf) *adj* bourru, brusque.

grumble ('grʌmbəl) *vt,vi* grommeler, grogner. *n* grognement *m.*

grumpy ('grʌmpi) *adj* maussade, grincheux, -euse.

grunt (grʌnt) *n* grognement *m.* *vi* grogner.

guarantee (gærən'ti:) *n* garantie *f.* *vt* garantir, cautionner. **guarantor** *n* garant *m*

guard (gɑ:d) *n* **1** garde *m.* **2** chef de train *m.* *vi* garder, protéger. **guard's van** *n* fourgon *m.* **guarded** *adj* prudent, mesure. **guardian** *n* **1** gardien, -ienne. **2** *law* tuteur, -trice. **guardianship** *n* tutelle *f.*

Guernsey ('gə:nzi) *n* Guernesey *m.*

guerrilla (gə'rilə) *n* guérillero *m.*

guess (ges) *vt,vi* deviner, conjecturer. *n* conjecture *f.* **at a guess** au jugé. **guesswork** *n* conjecture, hypothèse *f.*

guest (gest) *n* **1** invité *m.* convive *m,f.* **2** (in a hotel, etc.) pensionnaire *m,f.* **guesthouse** *n* pension de famille *f.*

guide (gaid) *n* guide *m.* *vt* guider, diriger. **guidebook** *n* guide *m.* **guide-dog** *n* chien d'aveugles *m.* **guidance** *n* direction, conduite *f.*

guild (gild) *n* corporation, confrérie *f.*

guillotine (giiə'ti:n) *n* guillotine *f.* *vt* guillotiner.

guilt (gilt) *n* culpabilité *f.* **guilty** *adj* coupable.

guinea ('gini) *n* guinée *f.* **guinea pig** *n* cobaye, cochon d'Inde *m.*

guitar (gi'tɑ:) *n* guitare *f.*

gulf (gʌlf) *n* **1** *geog* golfe *m.* **2** abîme *m.*

gull (gʌl) *n* mouette *f.* goéland *m.*

gullet ('gʌlit) *n* **1** œsophage *m.* **2** *inf* gosier *m.*

gulp (gʌlp) *n* trait *m.* lampée *f.* *vt* avaler.

gum[1] (gʌm) *n* gomme *f.* *vt* gommer.

gum[2] (gʌm) *n anat* gencive *f.*

gun (gʌn) *n* fusil, canon *m.* **gunman** *n* bandit (armé) *m.* **gunpowder** *n* poudre (à canon) *f.* **gunrunning** *n* trafic d'armes *m.* **gunshot** *n* coup de fusil *m.*

gurgle ('gə:gəl) *n* glouglou, gloussement *m.* *vi* gargouiller.

gush (gʌʃ) *n* jet, flot *m.* *vi* jaillir, déborder.

gust (gʌst) *n* ondée, giboulée, rafale *f.*

gut (gʌt) *n* **1** *anat* boyau, -aux, intestin *m.* **2** *pl inf* cran *m.* *vt* étriper, vider.

gutter ('gʌtə) *n* **1** gouttière *f.* **2** ruisseau, -aux *m.*

guy[1] (gai) *n* **1** epouvantail *m.* **2** type *m.*

guy[2] (gai) *n* cable, hauban *m.*

gymnasium (dʒim'neiziəm) *n* gymnase *m.* **gymnast** *n* gymnaste *m,f.* **gymnastic** *adj* gymnastique. **gymnastics** *n* gymnastique *f.*

gynaecology (gaini'kɔlədʒi) *n* gynécologie *f.* **gynaecologist** *n* gynécologue *m,f.*

gypsum ('dʒipsəm) *n* gypse *m.*

H

haberdasher ('hæbədæʃə) *n* mercier *m.* **haberdashery** *n* mercerie *f.*

habit ('hæbit) *n* **1** coutume, habitude *f.* **2** habit *m.* **3** *pl* mœurs *f pl.* **habitable** *adj* habitable. **habitual** *adj* habituel, -elle.

hack[1] (hæk) *vt* hacher, taillader. *vi* toussoter. *n* entaille *f.* **hacksaw** *n* scie à métaux *f.*

hack[2] (hæk) *n* **1** cheval de louage *m.* **2** *inf* rosse *f.* **3** homme de peine *m.*

hackneyed ('hæknid) *adj* banal, -aux, rebattu.

had (hæd) *v* see **have.**

haddock ('hædək) *n* aiglefin *m.*

haemorrhage ('hemərid3) *n* hémorragie *f.*

hag (hæg) *n* sorciere *f.*

haggard ('hægəd) *adj* hagard, hâve.

haggle ('hægḷ) *vi* **1** marchander. **2** chicaner.

Hague, The (heig) *n* La Haye *f.*

hail[1] (heil) *n* grêle *f.* *v imp* grêler. **hailstone** *n* grêlon *m.* **hailstorm** *n* averse de grêle *f.*

hail[2] (heil) *interj* salut! *vt* **1** saluer, acclamer. **2** héler.

hair (hɛə) *n* **1** (of the head) cheveu, -eux *m.* **2** (of the head) chevelure *f.* **3** poil *m.* **4** (of a horse) crin *m.* **hairbrush** *n* brosse à cheveux *f.* **haircut** *n* coupe de cheveux *f.* **hairdresser**

n coiffeur *m*. **hairdressing** *n* coiffure *f*. **hairgrip** *n* épingle à cheveux *f*. **hairnet** *n* résille *f*. **hairpiece** *n* postiche *m*. **hair-raising** *adj* horripilant. **hairstyle** *n* coiffure *f*.

half (hɑ:f) *n, pl* **halves** moitié *f*. demi *m*. demie *f*. *adj* demi. *adv* à moitié, à demi.

half-a-dozen *n* demi-douzaine *f*.

half-and-half *adv* moitié l'un moitié l'autre.

half-back *n* demi m.

half-baked *adj inf* **1** qui ne tient pas debout, bâclé. **2** niais.

half-breed *n* **1** métis, -isse. **2** cheval demi-sang *m*.

half-brother *n* demi-frère *m*.

half-caste *n* métis, -isse.

half-hearted *adj* peu enthousiaste, tiède.

half-hour *n* demi-heure *f*.

half-mast *adv* **at half-mast** en berne.

halfpenny ('heipni) *n* **1** *pl* **halfpence** demi-penny *m*. **2** *pl* **halfpennies** pièce d'un demi-penny *f*.

half-pint *n* demi-pinte, chopine *f*.

half-sister *n* demi-sœur *f*.

half-term *n* congé de mi-trimestre *m*.

half-time *n* mi-temps *f*.

halftone ('hɑ:ftoun) *n* **1** *Art* demi-teinte *f*. **2** *mus* demi-ton *m*.

halfway (hɑ:f'wei) *adv* à mi-chemin.

halfwit ('hɑ:fwit) *n* faible d'esprit, idiot *m*.

half-year *n* semestre *m*.

halibut ('hælibət) *n* flétan *m*.

hall (hɔ:l) *n* salle *f*. vestibule, hall *m*.

hallelujah (hæli'lu:jə) *interj,n* alléluia *m*.

hallmark ('hɔ:lmɑ:k) *n* **1** poinçon *m*. **2** empreinte *f*. cachet *m*. *vt* poinçonner.

hallo (hə'lou) *interj* see **hello**.

hallowed ('hæloud) *adj* saint, sanctifié.

Hallowe'en (hælou'i:n) *n* veille de la Toussaint *f*.

hallucination (həlu:si'neiʃən) *n* hallucination *f*.

halo ('heilou) *n, pl* **-os** *or* **oes** halo *m*. auréole *f*.

halt (hɔ:lt) *n* arrêt *m*. halte *f*. *vi* faire halte, s'arrêter. *vt* arrêter.

halter ('hɔ:ltə) *n* licou *m*.

halve (hɑ:v) *vt* partager en deux, réduire de moitié.

ham (hæm) *n* jambon *m*.

hamburger ('hæmbə:gə) *n* steak haché grillé *m*.

hammer ('hæmə) *n* marteau, -aux *m*. *vt* marteler.

hammock ('hæmək) *n* hamac *m*.

hamper[1] ('hæmpə) *vt* gêner.

hamper[2] ('hæmpə) *n* manne *f*. panier *m*.

hamster ('hæmstə) *n* hamster *m*.

hand (hænd) *n* **1** main *f*. **2** (of a clock) aiguille *f*. **3** *game* jeu *m*. **4** *inf* coup de main *m*. *vt* remettre, passer. **handful** *n* poignée *f*.

handbag ('hændbæg) *n* sac à main *m*.

handbook ('hændbuk) *n* **1** manuel *m*. **2** guide *m*.

handbrake ('hændbreik) *n* frein à main *m*.

handcart ('hændkɑ:t) *n* charrette à bras *f*.

handcuffs ('hændkʌfs) *n pl* menottes *f pl*.

hand grenade *n* grenade à main *f*.

handicap ('hændikæp) *n* handicap, désavantage *m*. *vt* handicaper.

handicraft ('hændikrɑ:ft) *n* **1** travail manuel *m*. **2** artisanat *m*.

handiwork ('hændiwə:k) *n* ouvrage *m*.

handkerchief ('hæŋkətʃif) *n* mouchoir *m*.

handle ('hændḷ) *n* manche *m*. poignée, anse, manivelle *f*. *vt* manipuler, manier. **handlebars** *n pl* guidon *m*.

handmade (hænd'meid) *adj* fait à la main.

hand-out *n* communiqué *m*.

hand-pick *vt* trier à la main.

handrail ('hændreil) *n* balustrade, rampe *f*.

handshake ('hændʃeik) *n* poignée de main *f*.

handsome ('hænsəm) *adj* **1** beau, belle. **2** généreux, -euse.

handstand ('hændstænd) *m* poirier *m*. **do a handstand** faire l'arbre droit.

handwriting ('hændraitiŋ) *n* écriture *f*.

handy ('hændi) *adj* **1** adroit. **2** commode. **3** sous la main.

hang* (hæŋ) *vt* pendre, suspendre. *vi* **1** pendre. **2** peser. **hang around** flâner. **hang up** accrocher. **hanger** *n* cintre *m*. **hangman** *n* bourreau, -aux *m*. **hangover** *n* gueule de bois *f*.

hanker ('hæŋkə) *vi* **hanker after** désirer ardemment. **hankering** *n* aspiration, grande envie *f*.

haphazard (hæp'hæzəd) *adj* fortuit. *adv* au hasard.

happen ('hæpən) *vi* arriver, se passer.

happy ('hæpi) *adj* heureux, -euse. **happiness** *n* bonheur *m*.

harass ('hærəs) *vt* **1** *mil* harceler. **2** tourmenter.

harbour ('hɑ:bə) *n* port *m*. *vt* héberger, receler.

hard (hɑ:d) *adj* **1** dur. **2** difficile. **3** sévère. **hard up** à court d'argent. ~*adv* **1** fort. **2** difficilement. **hardback** *n* livre relié *m*. **hard-boiled** *adj* dur. **hard-headed** *adj* positif, -ive, pratique. **hard-hearted** *adj* insensible, impitoyable. **hardware** *n* quincaillerie *f*. **harden**

vt,vi durcir. **hardness** *n* **1** dureté *f.* **2** difficulté *f.* **hardship** *n* épreuve, privation *f.*

hardly ('hɑ:dli) *adv* à peine, ne...guère. **hardly ever** presque jamais.

hardy ('hɑ:di) *adj* **1** hardi. **2** robuste. **3** *bot* vivace.

hare ('hɛə) *n* lièvre *m.*

haricot ('hærikou) *n* haricot blanc *m.*

hark (hɑ:k) *vi* écouter.

harm (hɑ:m) *n* mal, tort *m.* *vt* faire du mal à, nuire à. **harmful** *adj* nuisible. **harmless** *adj* inoffensif, -ive, anodin.

harmonic (hɑ:'mɔnik) *adj,n* harmonique *m.* **harmonica** *n* harmonica *m.* **harmonize** *vt* harmoniser. *vi* s'assortir. **harmony** *n* **1** *mus* harmonie *f.* **2** entente *f.* accord *m.*

harness ('hɑ:nis) *n* harnais *m.* *vt* **1** harnacher. **2** aménager.

harp (hɑ:p) *n* harp *f.* *v* **harp on about** rabâcher.

harpoon (hɑ:'pu:n) *n* harpon *m.* *vt* harponner.

harpsichord ('hɑ:psikɔ:d) *n* clavecin *m.*

harsh (hɑ:ʃ) *adj* **1** dur. **2** âpre. **3** aigre. **harshly** *adv* rudement, sévèrement.

harvest ('hɑ:vist) *n* récolte *f.* *vt* récolter.

has (hæz) *v* see **have.**

hashish ('hæʃiʃ) *n* hachisch *m.*

haste (heist) *n* hâte *f.* **hasten** *vi* se presser, s'empresser. *vt* accélérer, hâter, presser.

hat (hæt) *n* chapeau, -aux *m.*

hatch[1] (hætʃ) *n* couvée *f.* *vt* faire éclore, incuber. **hatch out** éclore.

hatch[2] (hætʃ) *n* **1** *naut* écoutille *f.* **2** trappe *f.* passe-plats *m.*

hatchet ('hætʃit) *n* cognée, hachette *f.*

hate (heit) *vt* haïr, détester. *n* haine *f.* **hateful** *adj* odieux, -euse.

haughty ('hɔ:ti) *adj* hautain, arrogant.

haul (hɔ:l) *vt* **1** traîner. **2** transporter. *vt,vi* haler. *n* **1** coup de filet *m.* **2** charge *f.* **haulage** *n* **1** roulage *m.* **2** remorquage *m.*

haunch (hɔ:ntʃ) *n* **1** hanche *f.* **2** *cul* cuissot *m.*

haunt (hɔ:nt) *vt* hanter, obséder. *n* repaire *m.*

have* (hæv) *vt* **1** avoir, posséder. **2** obtenir. **3** prendre. **4** faire. *v aux* avoir. **have to** devoir.

haven ('heivən) *n* **1** havre *m.* **2** abri *m.*

haversack ('hævəsæk) *n* haversac *m.*

havoc ('hævək) *n* ravage *m.*

hawk (hɔ:k) *n* faucon, épervier *m.*

hawthorn ('hɔ:θɔ:n) *n* aubépine *f.*

hay (hei) *n* foin *m.* **hayfever** *n* rhume des foins *m.* **haystack** *n* meule de foin *f.* **haywire** *adj* loupé.

hazard ('hæzəd) *n* hasard, risque *m.* *vt* hasarder. **hazardous** *adj* périlleux, -euse.

haze (heiz) *n* **1** brume *f.* **2** incertitude *f.* *vt* embrumer. **hazy** *adj* **1** brumeux, -euse. **2** nébuleux, -euse.

hazel ('heizəl) *n* noisetier *m.* **hazelnut** *n* noisette *f.*

he (hi:) *pron 3rd pers s* **1** il. **2** lui. **he who** celui qui.

head (hed) *n* **1** tête *f.* **2** chef, directeur *m.* **3** principal, -aux *m.* *adj* principal, -aux, premier, -ière. *vt* **1** conduire. **2** intituler. **heading** *n* titre, en-tête *m.*

headache ('hedeik) *n* mal de tête *m.*

headfirst (hed'fə:st) *adv* la tête la première.

headlight ('hedlait) *n* phare *m.*

headline ('hedlain) *n* manchette *f.*

headlong ('hedlɔŋ) *adv* **1** la tête la première. **2** témérairement.

headmaster (hed'mɑ:stə) *n* directeur (d'école) *m.* **headmistress** *n* directrice (d'école) *f.*

headphone ('hedfoun) *n* écouteur, casque *m.*

headquarters ('hedkwɔ:təz) *n pl* **1** siège social *m.* **2** *mil* quartier général *m.*

headscarf ('hedskɑ:f) *n* foulard *m.*

headstrong ('hedstrɔŋ) *adj* têtu, obstiné.

headway ('hedwei) *n* avance *f.* progrès *m.*

heal (hi:l) *vt,vi* guérir.

health (helθ) *n* santé *f.* **healthy** *adj* **1** en bonne santé. **2** robuste.

heap (hi:p) *n* tas *m.* *vt* entasser, amasser, combler.

hear* (hiə) *vi* entendre. *vt* **1** entendre. **2** écouter. **3** apprendre. **hear from** recevoir des nouvelles de. **hear of** entendre parler de. **hearing** *n* **1** ouïe *f.* **2** audience *f.* **3** audition *f.* **hearing aid** *n* appareil auditif *m.* **hearsay** *n* ouï-dire *m invar.*

hearse (hə:s) *n* corbillard *m.*

heart (hɑ:t) *n* **1** cœur *m.* **2** courage *m.* **heart attack** *n* crise cardiaque *f.* **heartbeat** *n* battement de cœur *m.* **heartbroken** *adj* accablé, navré. **heartily** *adv* **1** de bon cœur. **2** avec appétit. **heartless** *adj* insensible, cruel, -elle. **hearty** *adj* **1** chaleureux, -euse. **2** robuste.

hearth (hɑ:θ) *n* âtre *m.*

heat (hi:t) *n* **1** chaleur *f.* **2** épreuve *f.* *vt* chauffer. **heater** *n* appareil de chauffage, radiateur *m.* **heatwave** *n* vague de chaleur *f.*

heath (hi:θ) *n* bruyère, lande *f.*

heathen ('hi:ðən) *adj,n* païen, -enne.

heather ('heðə) *n* bruyère *f.*

heave (hi:v) *vt* **1** lever. **2** porter. **3** pousser. *vi* **1** se soulever. **2** avoir des haut-le-cœur. *n* **1** effort *m.* **2** soulèvement *m.*
heaven ('hevən) *n* ciel, cieux *m.* **heavenly** *adj* céleste.
heavy ('hevi) *adj* **1** lourd, gros, grosse. **2** profond. **3** pénible. **heaviness** *n* **1** lourdeur *f.* **2** lassitude *f.* **heavyweight** *n* poids lourd *m. adj* lourd.
Hebrew ('hi:bru:) *n* hébreu, -eux *m. adj* hébreu, -eux, hébraïque. **Hebrew** (language) *n* hébreu *m.*
heckle ('hekəl) *vt* interpeller.
hectic ('hektik) *adj* agité.
hedge (hedʒ) *n* **1** haie *f.* **2** protection *f. vt* entourer d'une haie. *vi* chercher des faux-fuyants. **hedgehog** *n* hérisson *m.*
heed (hi:d) *n* attention *f. vt* faire attention à. **heedless** *adj* étourdi, peu soucieux, -euse.
heel (hi:l) *n* talon *m.*
hefty ('hefti) *adj* solide, costaud.
height (hait) *n* **1** hauteur *f.* **2** élévation *f.* **3** apogée *f.* **heighten** *vt* **1** surélever. **2** accroître, rehausser.
heir (εə) *n* héritier *m.* **heiress** *n* héritière *f.* **heirloom** *n* meuble *or* bijou de famille *m.*
held (held) *v see* **hold.**
helicopter ('helikɔptə) *n* hélicoptère *m.*
hell (hel) *n* enfer *m.* **hellish** *adj* infernal, -aux.
hello (hə'lou) *interj* **1** bonjour! **2** salut! **3** allô! holà!
helm (helm) *n naut* barre *f.* gouvernail *m.*
helmet ('helmit) *n* casque *m.*
help (help) *n* **1** aide *f.* secours *m.* **2** *inf* domestique *f. interj* au secours! *vt* **1** secourir, aider. **2** servir. **it can't be helped!** tant pis! **helpful** *adj* utile. **helpless** *adj* impuissant.
hem (hem) *n* ourlet, bord *m.*
hemisphere ('hemisfiə) *n* hémisphère *m.*
hemp (hemp) *n* chanvre *m.*
hen (hen) *n* **1** poule *f.* **2** femelle *f.* **henpecked** *adj* mené par le bout du nez.
hence (hens) *adv* **1** en conséquence. **2** dorénavant. **3** d'ici. **henceforth** *adv* désormais.
henna ('henə) *n* henné *m.*
her (hə:) *pron 3rd pers s* **1** elle. **2** la. **3** lui. *poss adj 3rd pers s* son, sa, ses.
herald ('herəld) *n* **1** héraut *m.* **2** avant-coureur *m. vt* annoncer. **heraldry** *n* blason *m.*
herb (hə:b) *n* herbe *f.*
herd (hə:d) *n* troupeau, -aux *m.* bande *f. vi* s'attrouper. **herdsman** *m* gardien *m.*
here (hıə) *adv* ici. **here and there** par-ci par-là. **here, there, and everywhere** un peu partout. **hereafter** *adv* **1** ci-après. **2** désormais. **hereby** *adv* par là. **herein** *adv* ci-inclus.
hereditary (hi'reditri) *adj* héréditaire.
heredity (hi'rediti) *n* hérédité *f.*
heresy ('herəsi) *n* hérésie *f.* **heretic** *n* hérétique *m,f.*
heritage ('heritidʒ) *n* héritage *m.*
hermit ('hə:mit) *n* ermite *m.*
hero ('hiərou) *n, pl* **-oes** héros *m.* **heroine** *n* héroïne *f.*
heroin ('herouin) *n* héroïne *f.*
heron ('herən) *n* héron *m.*
herring ('heriŋ) *n* hareng *m.* **red herring** *n inf* diversion *f.*
hers (hə:z) *poss pron 3rd pers s* **1** le sien, la sienne. **2** à elle. **herself** *pron 3rd pers s* **1** elle-même. **2** se. **by herself** toute seule.
hesitate ('heziteit) *vi* hésiter. **hesitation** *n* hésitation *f.*
hexagon ('heksəgən) *n* hexagone *m.* **hexagonal** *adj* hexagone.
hibernate ('haibəneit) *vi* hiberner.
hiccup ('hikʌp) *n* hoquet *m. vi* avoir le hoquet.
hide*[1] (haid) *vt* cacher. *vi* se cacher. **hide-and-seek** *n* cache-cache *m.*
hide[2] (haid) *n* peau, peaux *f.* cuir *m.*
hideous ('hidiəs) *adj* hideux, -euse.
hiding[1] ('haidiŋ) *n* **1** cachette *f.* **2** dissimulation *f.*
hiding[2] ('haidiŋ) *n inf* raclée *f.*
hierarchy ('haiəra:ki) *n* hiérarchie *f.*
high (hai) *adj* **1** haut. **2** élevé. **3** grand. **4** faisandé. **5** *sl* parti. **highbrow** *adj* intellectuel, -elle. **high frequency** *adj* à haute fréquence. **highland** *adj* montagnard. *n* **1** haute terre *f.* **2** *cap pl* Haute Ecosse *f.* **highlight** *vt* mettre en évidence. *n* point culminant *m.* **highly** *adv* **1** hautement. **2** fort, très. **highpitched** *adj* aigu, -uë, criard. **high-rise** *adj* élevé. **high-rise block** *n* tour *f.* **high-spirited** *adj* **1** exubérant. **2** fougueux, -euse. **highway** *n* **1** grand-route *f.* **2** voie publique *f.*
Highness ('hainəs) *n* Altesse *f.*
hijack ('haidʒæk) *vt* détourner.
hike (haik) *n* excursion à pied *f. vi* faire de la marche.
hilarious (hi'lεəriəs) *adj* hilare. **hilarity** *n* hilarité *f.*
hill (hil) *n* **1** colline *f.* **2** côte *f.* **hillside** *n* versant, flanc de coteau *m.* **hilltop** *n* cime *f.*
him (him) *pron 3rd pers s* **1** le. **2** lui. **himself**

pron 3rd pers s **1** lui-même. **2** se. **by himself** tout seul.

hind (haind) *adj* de derrierè, postérieur. **hindleg** *n* patte de derrière *f.* **hindsight** *n* sagesse d'après coup *f.*

hinder ('hində) *vt* **1** gêner. **2** empêcher. **hindrance** *n* empêchement *m.*

Hindu ('hindu:) *adj,n* hindou.

hinge (hindʒ) *n* **1** gond *m.* **2** pivot *m.* **3** charnière *f.* *v* **hinge on** être axé sur, dépendre de.

hint (hint) *n* **1** insinuation, allusion *f.* **2** conseil *m.* *vi* insinuer.

hip (hip) *n* hanche *f.*

hippopotamus (hipə'pɔtəməs) *n pl* **-mi** *or* **-muses** hippopotame *m.*

hire (haiə) *vt* louer, engager. **hire out** donner en location. ~*n* location *f.* louage *m.* **hire-purchase** *n* vente à tempérament *f.*

his (hiz) *poss adj 3rd pers s* son, sa, ses. *poss pron 3rd pers s* **1** le sien, la sienne. **2** à lui.

hiss (his) *vi* siffler. *n* sifflement *m.*

history ('histri) *n* histoire *f.* **historian** *n* historien *m.* **historic** *adj* historique.

hit* (hit) *vt* **1** frapper. **2** atteindre, toucher. *n* coup *m.*

hitch [illegible] *n* **1** saccade, secousse *f.* **2** contretemps *m.* *vt* **1** accrocher. **2** remuer par saccades. **hitch-hike** *vi* faire du stop.

hive (haiv) *n* ruche *f.*

hoard (hɔ:d) *vt* amasser, accumuler. *vi* thésauriser. *n* **1** amas *m.* **2** trésor *m.*

hoarding ('hɔ:diŋ) *n* **1** palissade *f.* panneau-réclame *m.* **2** resserre, cache *f.*

hoarfrost ('hɔ:frɔst) *n* givre *m.*

hoarse (hɔ:s) *adj* enroué, rauque.

hoax (houks) *n* mystification *f.* mauvais tour *m.*

hobble ('hɔbəl) *vi* boitiller. *vt* entraver. *n* boitillement *m.*

hobby ('hɔbi) *n* passe-temps *m.*

hock[1] (hɔk) *n* jarret *m.*

hock[2] (hɔk) *n* vin du Rhin *m.*

hockey ('hɔki) *n* hockey *m.*

hoe (hou) *n* houe *f.* *vt* sarcler.

hog (hɔg) *n* **1** porc *m.* **2** *inf* goinfre *m.* *vt inf* monopoliser.

hoist (hɔist) *n* treuil *m.* *vt* hisser.

hold*[1] (hould) *vt,vi* tenir. *vt* **1** contenir. **2** avoir, posséder. **3** retenir. **hold back** retenir. **hold on** tenir ferme, s'accrocher. **hold out** tendre. ~*n* prise *f.* **holdall** *n* fourre-tout *m invar.* **holder** *n* **1** détenteur *m.* **2** propriétaire *m.* **3** récipient *m.*

hold[2] (hould) *n naut* cale *f.*

hole (houl) *n* **1** trou, creux *m.* **2** orifice *m.* *vt* trouer. *vi* se trouer.

holiday ('hɔlidi) *n* **1** jour férié, congé *m.* **2** *pl* vacances *f pl.* **holiday-maker** *n* estivant *m.*

Holland ('hɔlənd) *n* Hollande *f.*

hollow ('hɔlou) *adj* **1** creux, creuse. **2** sourd. *adv* creux. *n* **1** creux *m.* **2** vallon *m.* *vt* creuser.

holly ('hɔli) *n* houx *m.* **hollyhock** *n* rose trémière *f.*

holster ('houlstə) *n* étui *m.*

holy ('houli) *adj* saint, sacré.

Holy Ghost *n* Saint-Esprit *m.*

homage ('hɔmidʒ) *n* hommage *m.*

home (houm) *n* **1** logis, foyer *m.* maison *f.* **2** patrie *f.* **3** hospice *m.* *adv* à la maison, de retour. *adj* **1** familial, -aux, domestique. **2** *pol* intérieur. **homecoming** *n* retour *m.* **home help** *n* aide ménagère *f.* **homeland** *n* patrie *f.* **homesick** *adj* nostalgique. **homesickness** *n* mal du pays *m.* nostalgie *f.* **homework** *n* devoirs (du soir) *m pl.*

homonym ('hɔmənim) *n* homonyme *m.*

homosexual (houmə'sekʃuəl) *adj,n* homosexuel, -elle.

honest ('ɔnist) *adj* **1** honnête. **2** sincère. **honesty** *n* honnêteté, probité *f.*

honey ('hʌni) *n* miel *m.* **honeycomb** *n* rayon de miel *m.* **honeymoon** *n* lune de miel *f.* **honeysuckle** *n* chèvrefeullle *m.*

honour ('ɔnə) *vt* **1** honorer. **2** faire honneur à. *n* **1** honneur *m.* **2** distinction *f.* **His** *or* **Your Honour** Monsieur le juge, Monsieur le président. **honorary** *adj* **1** honoraire. **2** honorifique.

hood (hud) *n* **1** capuchon *m.* **2** *mot* capote *f.*

hoof (hu:f) *n, pl* **hooves** sabot *m.*

hook (huk) *n* **1** crochet, croc *m.* agrafe *f.* **2** (in angling) hameçon *m.* *vt* **1** accrocher. **2** agrafer. **3** attraper.

hooligan ('hu:ligən) *n* voyou *m.*

hoop (hu:p) *n* **1** cercle, cerceau, -aux *m.* **2** *sport* arceau, -aux *m.*

hoot (hu:t) *vi* **1** huer. **2** *mot* klaxonner. *n* **1** huée *f.* **2** klaxonnement *m.* **hooter** *n* klaxon *m.*

hop[1] (hɔp) *n* saut, sautillement *m.* *vi* sautiller, sauter.

hop[2] (hɔp) *n bot* houblon *m.*

hope (houp) *n* **1** espérance *f.* **2** espoir *m.* *vi,vt* espérer. *vt* s'attendre à. **hopeful** *adj* plein d'espoir. **hopeless** *adj* **1** sans espoir. **2** vain.

horde (hɔ:d) *n* horde *f.*

horizon (hə'raizən) *n* horizon *m*. **horizontal** *adj* horizontal, -aux.
hormone ('hɔːmoun) *n* hormone *f*.
horn (hɔːn) *n* **1** corne *f*. **2** *mus* cor *m*. trompe *f*.
hornet ('hɔːnit) *n* frelon *m*.
horoscope ('hɔrəskoup) *n* horoscope *m*.
horrible ('hɔrəbl̩) *adj* horrible, épouvantable.
horrid ('hɔrid) *adj* horrible, affreux, -euse.
horrify ('hɔrifai) *vt* horrifier.
horror ('hɔrə) *n* horreur *f*.
hors d'oeuvres (ɔː 'dəːv) *n pl* hors d'œuvre *m invar*.
horse (hɔːs) *n* cheval, -aux *m*. *adj* hippique. **on horseback** *adv* à cheval. **horse chestnut** *n* marron d'Inde *m*. **horse chestnut tree** *n* marronnier d'Inde *m*. **horsefly** *n* taon *m*. **horseman** *n* cavalier, chevalier *m*. **horsepower** *n* cheval-vapeur *m*. **horseradish** *n* raifort *m*. **horseshoe** *n* fer à cheval *m*.
horticulture ('hɔːtikʌltʃə) *n* horticulture *f*. **horticultural** *adj* horticole.
hose (houz) *n* **1** tuyau, -aux *m*. **2** bas *m*.
hosiery ('houziəri) *n* bonneterie *f*.
hospitable ('hɔspitəbəl) *adj* accueillant, hospitalier, -ière.
hospital ('hɔspitl̩) *n* hôpital, -aux *m*.
hospitality (hɔspi'tæliti) *n* hospitalité *f*.
host[1] (houst) *n* **1** hôte *m*. **2** hôtelier *m*.
host[2] (houst) *n* foule, armée *f*.
hostage ('hɔstidʒ) *n* otage *m*.
hostel ('hɔstl̩) *n* pension *f*. foyer *m*.
hostess ('houstis) *n* hôtesse *f*.
hostile ('hɔstail) *adj* hostile, opposé. **hostility** *n* hostilité, animosité *f*.
hot (hɔt) *adj* **1** chaud. **2** ardent. **3** violent. **4** *cul* épicé. **5** *inf* intenable. **hotplate** *n* chauffe-plat *m*. **hotpot** *n* ragoût *m*. **hot-tempered** *adj* emporté, vif, vive. **hot-water bottle** *n* bouillotte *f*.
hotel (hou'tel) *n* hôtel *m*.
hound (haund) *n* **1** chien de chasse *m*. **2** *pl* meute *f*. équipage *m*. *vt* chasser, poursuivre.
hour (auə) *n* heure *f*. **hourly** *adj* à chaque heure. *adv* toutes les heures.
house (*n* haus; *v* hauz) *n* **1** maison *f*. **2** *Th* salle *f*. *vt* loger, héberger.
houseboat ('hausbout) *n* péniche (aménagée en habitation) *f*.
housebound ('hausbaund) *adj* reclus.
household ('haushould) *n* famille *f*. ménage *m*. *adj* domestique.
housekeeper ('hauskiːpə) *n* concierge, ménagère *f*. **housekeeping** *n* ménage *m*.
housemaid ('hausmeid) *n* bonne *f*.
House of Commons *n* Chambre des Communes *f*.
House of Lords *n* Chambre des Lords *f*.
houseproud ('hauspraud) *adj* fier de son intérieur.
housewife ('hauswaif) *n* ménagère *f*.
housework ('hauswəːk) *n* travaux domestiques *m pl*.
housing (hauziŋ) *n* logement *m*. **housing estate** *n* cité *f*.
hover ('hɔvə) *vi* **1** planer. **2** rôder. **hovercraft** *n* aéroglisseur *m*.
how (hau) *adv* comment, comme. **how do you do?** comment allez-vous? **how much** *or* **many?** combien? **however** *conj* cependant. *adv* de quelque manière que.
howl (haul) *n* hurlement *m*. *vi* hurler.
hub (hʌb) *n* **1** moyeu, -eux *m*. **2** centre *m*.
huddle ('hʌdl̩) *n* ramassis *m*. *vt* **1** entasser, fourrer. **2** confondre. *vi* se presser.
huff (hʌf) *vt* souffler. **be in a huff** être fâché.
hug (hʌg) *n* étreinte *f*. *vt* embrasser.
huge (hjuːdʒ) *adj* énorme, vaste.
hulk (hʌlk) *n* **1** *naut* carcasse *f*. **2** *inf* lourdaud *m*. **hulking** *adj* lourd, gros, grosse.
hull[1] (hʌl) *n* cosse, gousse *f*. *vt* écosser.
hull[2] (hʌl) *n naut* coque *f*.
hullo (hə'lou) *interj* see **hello.**
hum (hʌm) *n* bourdonnement *m*. *vi* bourdonner. *vt* fredonner.
human ('hjuːmən) *n* être humain *m*. *adj* humain. **human nature** *n* nature humaine *f*. **humane** *adj* humain, compatissant. **humanism** *n* humanisme *m*.
humanity (hjuː'mæniti) *n* humanité *f*. **humanitarian** *adj,n* humanitaire.
humble ('hʌmbəl) *adj* **1** humble. **2** modeste. *vt* humilier. **humbly** *adv* avec humilité, pauvrement.
humdrum ('hʌmdrʌm) *adj* monotone.
humid ('hjuːmid) *adj* humide.
humiliate (hjuː'milieit) *vt* humilier. **humiliation** *n* affront *m*.
humility (hjuː'militi) *n* humilité *f*.
humour ('hjuːmə) *n* **1** humeur, disposition *f*. **2** humour *m*. *vt* ménager. **humorist** *n* comique, humoriste *m*. **humorous** *adj* humoristique, comique.
hump (hʌmp) *n* bosse *f*. *vt* arquer.
hunch (hʌntʃ) *n* **1** bosse *f*. **2** *inf* pressentiment *m*. *vt* arrondir. **hunchback** *n* bossu *m*.
hundred ('hʌndrəd) *adj* cent. *n* **1** cent *m*. **2**

centaine *f.* **hundredth** *adj* centième. **hundredweight** *n* quintal, -aux *m.*
hung (hʌŋ) *v* see **hang.**
Hungary ('hʌŋgəri) *n* Hongrie *f.* **Hungarian** *adj,n* hongrois. **Hungarian** (language) *n* hongrois *m.*
hunger ('hʌŋgə) *n* faim *f. vi* avoir faim. **hunger for** désirer. **hunger-strike** *n* grève de la faim *f.* **hungrily** *adv* voracement. **hungry** *adj* **1** affamé. **2** avide. **be hungry** avoir faim.
hunt (hʌnt) *n* **1** chasse *f.* **2** recherche *f. vt* chasser. **hunting** *n* chasse *f.* **huntsman** *n* chasseur, veneur *m.*
hurdle ('hə:dl̩) *n* **1** *sport* claie *f.* **2** obstacle *m. vt,vi* sauter.
hurl (hə:l) *vt* jeter, lancer.
hurrah (hu'rɑ:) *interj* hourra!
hurricane ('hʌrikein) *n* ouragan *m.*
hurry ('hʌri) *vi* se dépêcher, se hâter. *vt* presser. *n* hâte. **be in a hurry** être pressé. **hurried** *adj* précipité.
hurt* (hə:t) *vt* **1** faire mal à. **2** blesser. *vi* faire mal. *n* **1** mal *m.* **2** tort *m.*
husband ('hʌzbənd) *n* mari *m.*
hush (hʌʃ) *vt* **1** calmer. **2** étouffer. *vi* se taire. *interj* chut! *n* calme *m.*
husk (hʌsk) *n* cosse, gousse *f. vt* décortiquer.
husky ('hʌski) *adj* enroué.
hussar (hu'zɑ:) *n* hussard *m.*
hustle ('hʌsəl) *vt* bousculer. *vi* se dépêcher. *n* **1** activité *f.* **2** bousculade *f.*
hut (hʌt) *n* hutte *f.*
hutch (hʌtʃ) *n* **1** huche *f.* **2** clapier *m.*
hyacinth ('haiəsinθ) *n* jacinthe *f.*
hybrid ('haibrid) *adj,n* hybride *m.*
hydraulic (hai'drɔ.lik) *adj* hydraulique.
hydro-electric (haidroui'lektrik) *adj* hydroélectrique. **hydro-electric power** *n* énergie hydroélectrique *f.*
hydrogen ('haidrədʒən) *n* hydrogène *m.*
hyena (hai'i:nə) *n* hyène *f.*
hygiene ('haidʒi:n) *n* hygiène *f.* **hygienic** *adj* hygiénique.
hymn (him) *n* hymne *f.* cantique *m.* **hymnbook** *n* hymnaire *m.*
hyphen ('haifən) *n* trait d'union *m.*
hypnosis (hip'nousis) *n, pl* **-ses** hypnose *f.* **hypnotism** *n* hypnotisme *m.*
hypochondria (haipə'kɔndriə) *n* hypocondrie *f.* **hypochondriac** *adj,n* hypocondriaque.
hypocrisy (hi'pɔkrəsi) *n* hypocrisie *f.* **hypocrite** *n* hypocrite *m,f.* **hypocritical** *adj* hypocrite.
hypodermic (haipə'də:mik) *adj* hypodermique.
hypothesis (hai'pɔθəsis) *n, pl* **-ses** hypothese *f.* **hypothetical** *adj* hypothétique.
hysterectomy (histə'rektəmi) *n* hystérectomie *f.*
hysteria (his'tiəriə) *n* hystérie *f.* **hysterical** *adj* **1** *med* hystérique. **2** énervé. **hysterics** *n pl* crise de nerfs *f.*

I

I (ai) *pron 1st pers s* **1** je. **2** moi.
Iberia (ai'biəriə) *n* Ibérie *f.* **Iberian** *adj,n* ibérien, -ienne.
ice (ais) *n* glace *f. vt* **1** geler. **2** *cul* glacer. **3** (champagne, etc.) frapper. **iceberg** *n* iceberg *m.* **ice-cream** *n* glace *f.* **ice-cube** *n* glaçon *m.* **ice hockey** *n* hockey sur glace *m.* **ice rink** *n* patinoire *f.* **ice-skate** *n* patin (à glace) *m.* **icicle** *n* glaçon *m.* **icing** *n* **1** *cul* glacé *m.* **2** glaçage *m.* **icy** *adj* **1** glacial. **2** verglacé.
Iceland ('aislənd) *n* Islande *f.* **Icelander** *n* islandais *m.* **Icelandic** *adj* islandais. **Icelandic** (language) *n* islandais *m.*
icon ('aikɔn) *n* icone *f.*
idea (ai'diə) *n* idée *f.*
ideal (ai'diəl) *adj,n* idéal, -aux *m.* **idealistic** *adj* idéaliste. **idealize** *vt* idéaliser.
identify (ai'dentifai) *vt* identifier.
identity (ai'dentiti) *n* identité *f.* **identity card** *n* carte d'identité *f.* **identical** *adj* identique. **identical twins** *n pl* vrais jumeaux *m pl.*
ideology (aidi'ɔlədʒi) *n* idéologie *f.*
idiom ('idiəm) *n* idiome *m.*
idiosyncrasy (idiə'siŋkrəsi) *n* idiosyncrasie *f.*
idiot ('idiət) *n* idiot *m.* **idiotic** *adj* idiot, bête.
idle ('aidl̩) *adj* **1** oisif, -ive, paresseux, -euse **2** futile. *vi* fainéanter. **idleness** *n* oisiveté *f.*
idol ('aidl̩) *n* idole *f.* **idolatry** *n* idolâtrie *f.* **idolize** *vt* idolâtrer.
idyllic (i'dilik) *adj* idyllique.
if (if) *conj* si. **as if** comme si. **if not** sinon.
ignite (ig'nait) *vt* allumer. *vi* prendre feu. **ignition** *n* **1** allumage *m.* **2** *mot* contact *m.*
ignorant ('ignərənt) *adj* ignorant.
ignore (ig'nɔ:) *vt* ne tenir aucun compte de.
ill (il) *adj* **1** malade. **2** mauvais. *n* **1** mal, maux *m.* **2** tort *m. adv* mal. **ill-bred** *adj* mal élevé. **illness** *n* maladie *f.*
illegal (i'li:gəl) *adj* illégal, -aux.
illegible (i'ledʒəbəl) *adj* illisible.
illegitimate (ili'dʒitimət) *adj* illégitime.
illicit (i'lisit) *adj* illicite.
illiterate (i'litərət) *adj,n* illettré, analphabète.

illogical (i'lɔdʒikəl) *adj* illogique.
illuminate (i'lu:mineit) *vt* **1** illuminer. **2** éclaircir. **illumination** *n* illumination *f*. éclairage *m*.
illusion (i'lu:ʒən) *n* illusion *f*.
illustrate ('iləstreit) *vt* **1** illustrer. **2** expliquer. **illustration** *n* **1** illustration *f*. **2** exemple *m*.
illustrious (i'lʌstriəs) *adj* illustre.
image ('imidʒ) *n* image *f*. **imagery** *n* images *f pl*.
imagine (i'mædʒin) *vt* **1** s'imaginer. **2** croire. **imaginary** *adj* imaginaire. **imagination** *n* imagination *f*. **imaginative** *adj* imaginatif, -ive.
imitate ('imiteit) *vt* imiter. **imitation** *n* **1** imitation *f*. **2** *comm* contrefaçon *f*.
immaculate (i'mækjulət) *adj* **1** immaculé. **2** impeccable.
immature (imə'tjuə) *adj* **1** pas mûr. **2** prématuré.
immediate (i'mi:diət) *adj* immédiat, direct, proche.
immense (i'mens) *adj* immense, énorme.
immerse (i'mə:s) *vt* immerger.
immigrate ('imigreit) *vi* immigrer. **immigrant** *adj,n* immigrant. **immigration** *n* immigration *f*.
imminent ('iminənt) *adj* imminent.
immobile (i'moubail) *adj* **1** immobile. **2** fixe.
immoral (i'mɔrəl) *adj* **1** immoral, -aux. **2** (of a person) dissolu. **immorality** *n* **1** immoralité *f*. **2** débauche *f*.
immortal (i'mɔ:tl̩) *adj* immortel, -elle. **immortality** *n* immortalité *f*.
immovable (i'mu:vəbəl) *adj* **1** fixe. **2** immuable.
immune (i'mju:n) *adj* immunisé, vacciné. **immune from** à l'abri de. **immunity** *n* **1** exemption *f*. **2** immunité *f*. **immunization** *n* immunisation *f*. **immunize** *vt* immuniser.
imp (imp) *n* diablotin *m*.
impact ('impækt) *n* **1** impact, choc *m*. **2** effet *m*.
impair (im'pɛə) *vt* affaiblir, abîmer.
impart (im'pɑ:t) *vt* **1** communiquer. **2** faire part de.
impartial (im'pɑ:ʃəl) *adj* impartial, -aux.
impatient (im'peiʃənt) *adj* impatient. **get impatient** s'impatienter.
impeach (im'pi:tʃ) *vt* **1** accuser. **2** contester. **impeachment** *n* accusation *f*.
impediment (im'pedimənt) *n* empêchement *m*.
impel (im'pel) *vt* pousser, forcer.
imperative (im'perativ) *adj* **1** impérieux, -euse. **2** urgent. *n gram* impératif *m*.
imperfect (im'pə:fikt) *adj,n* imparfait *m*.
imperial (im'piəriəl) *adj* impérial, -aux. **imperialism** *n* impérialisme *m*.
impersonal (im'pə:sənl̩) *adj* impersonnel, -elle.
impersonate (im'pə:səneit) *vt* **1** personnifier. **2** *Th* représenter.
impertinent (im'pə:tinənt) *adj* impertinent, insolent. **impertinence** *n* impertinence *f*.
impetuous (im'petʃuəs) *adj* impétueux, -euse, fougueux, -euse.
impetus ('impitəs) *n* élan *m*. impulsion *f*.
impinge (im'pindʒ) *vi* **impinge on** empiéter sur.
implement (*n* 'impləmənt; *v* 'impləment) *n* instrument, outil *m*. *vt* exécuter.
implicit (im'plisit) *adj* **1** implicite. **2** sans réserve.
implore (im'plɔ:) *vt* implorer.
imply (im'plai) *vt* **1** impliquer, supposer. **2** insinuer. **implied** *adj* tacite, sous-entendu.
import (*v* im'pɔ:t; *n* 'impɔ:t) *vt* **1** *comm* importer. **2** signifier. *n* **1** sens *m*. **2** importance *f*. **3** *pl* importations *f pl*.
importance (im'pɔ:tn̩s) *n* importance *f*. **important** *adj* important.
impose (im'pouz) *vt* imposer. **impose upon** en imposer à. **imposing** *adj* imposant. **imposition** *n* **1** imposition *f*. **2** abus *m*.
impossible (im'posəbəl) *adj* impossible.
impostor (im'pɔstə) *n* imposteur *m*.
impotent ('impətənt) *adj* impuissant. **impotence** *n* impuissance *f*.
impound (im'paund) *vt* **1** enfermer. **2** confisquer.
impoverish (im'pɔvəriʃ) *vt* appauvrir.
impress (im'pres) *vt* **1** imprimer. **2** impressionner. *n* empreinte *f*. **impression** *n* impression *f*. **impressive** *adj* impressionnant.
imprint (*n* 'imprint; *v* im'print) *n* empreinte *f*. *vt* imprimer.
imprison (im'prizən) *vt* emprisonner. **imprisonment** *n* emprisonnement *m*.
improbable (im'prɔbəbəl) *adj* invraisemblable.
impromptu (im'prɔmptju:) *adj* improvisé. *adv* impromptu.
improper (im'prɔpə) *adj* **1** malséant. **2** impropre.
improve (im'pru:v) *vt* améliorer, perfectionner. *vi* s'améliorer, se perfectionner. **improvement** *n* amélioration *f*. progrès *m*.
improvise ('imprəvaiz) *vt,vi* improviser. **improvisation** *n* improvisation *f*.
impudent ('impjudənt) *adj* insolent, impudent. **impudence** *n* impudence *f*.

impulse (ˈimpʌls) *n* **1** impulsion *f*. **2** poussée *f*. **impulsive** *adj* impulsif, -ive.
impure (imˈpjuə) *adj* impur. **impurity** *n* impureté *f*.
in (in) *prep* **1** en, à, dans, de. **2** sur, par. *adv* **1** chez soi, y, là. **2** dedans.
inability (inəˈbiliti) *n* incapacité *f*.
inaccurate (inˈækjurət) *adj* inexact, incorrect.
inadequate (inˈædikwit) *adj* inadéquat, insuffisant. **inadequacy** *n* insuffisance *f*.
inadvertent (inədˈvə:tnt) *adj* **1** involontaire. **2** inattentif, -ive. **inadvertently** *adv* par inadvertance.
inane (iˈnein) *adj* inepte, niais.
inarticulate (ina:ˈtikjulət) *adj* inarticulé.
inasmuch (inəzˈmʌtʃ) *conj* **inasmuch as** attendu *or* vu que.
inaudible (inˈɔ:dəbəl) *adj* imperceptible.
inaugurate (iˈnɔ:gjureit) *vt* inaugurer. **inauguration** *n* inauguration *f*.
incapable (inˈkeipəbəl) *adj* incapable, incompétent.
incendiary (inˈsendiəri) *adj* incendiaire.
incense[1] (ˈinsens) *n* encens *m*. *vt* encenser.
incense[2] (inˈsens) *vt* exaspérer, courroucer.
incessant (inˈsesənt) *adj* incessant.
incest (ˈinsest) *n* inceste *m*. **incestuous** *adj* incestueux, -euse.
inch (intʃ) *n* pouce *m*. **inch by inch** petit à petit. ~*vi* avancer petit à petit.
incident (ˈinsidənt) *n* incident *m*. **incidental** *adj* **1** fortuit. **2** accessoire.
incite (inˈsait) *vt* inciter.
incline (inˈklain) *vt* incliner, pencher. *vi* s'incliner. *n* pente *f*. **inclination** *n* **1** pente *f*. **2** penchant *m*. tendance *f*.
include (inˈklu:d) *vt* inclure, comprendre. **inclusive** *adj* **1** global, -aux. **2** inclus.
incognito (inkɔgˈni:tou) *adv* incognito.
incoherent (inkouˈhiərənt) *adj* incohérent.
income (ˈinkʌm) *n* revenu *m*. **income tax** *n* impôt sur le revenu *m*. **income tax return** déclaration de revenu *f*. **private income** rente *f*.
incompatible (inkəmˈpætibəl) *adj* incompatible.
incompetent (inˈkɔmpətənt) *adj* incompétent.
incomprehensible (inkɔmprˈhensibəl) *adj* incompréhensible.
inconclusive (inkənˈklu:siv) *adj* peu concluant.
incongruous (inˈkɔŋgruəs) *adj* incongru, déplacé.
inconsiderate (inkənˈsidərit) *adj* **1** irréfléchi. **2** sans égards.
inconsistent (inkənˈsistənt) *adj* **1** incompatible. **2** illogique. **3** incongru. **inconsistency** *n* **1** disparité *f*. **2** contradiction *f*.
inconspicuous (inkənspikjuəs) *adj* effacé, discret, -ète.
inconvenient (inkənˈvi:niənt) *adj* incommode, inopportun.
incorporate (inˈkɔ:pəreit) *vt* **1** incorporer. **2** *comm* réunir. *vi* s'incorporer.
incorrect (inkəˈrekt) *adj* inexact, incorrect.
increase (*v* inˈkri:s; *n* ˈinkri:s) *vi* **1** augmenter. **2** s'accroître. *vt* accroître, augmenter. *n* augmentation *f*. **increasing** *adj* croissant.
incredible (inˈkredəbəl) *adj* incroyable.
incubate (ˈinkjubeit) *vt,vi* couver. **incubator** *n* couveuse *f*.
incur (inˈkə:) *vt* **1** (expenses) courir, faire. **2** encourir.
indecent (inˈdi:sənt) *adj* indécent.
indeed (inˈdi:d) *adv* en effet, vraiment, à vrai dire.
indefinite (inˈdefənit) *adj* **1** indéfini. **2** illimité.
indent (inˈdent) *vt* denteler.
independent (indiˈpendənt) *adj* indépendant. **independence** *n* indépendance *f*.
index (ˈindeks) *n pl* **-dexes** *or* **-dices** **1** (of a book) répertoire *m*. **2** indice, signe *m* *vt* classer. **index finger** *n* index *m*.
India (ˈindiə) *n* Inde *f*. **Indian** *adj,n* indien, -ienne.
indicate (ˈindikeit) *vt* indiquer. **indication** *n* signe *m*. **indicator** *n* indicateur *m*.
indifferent (inˈdifrənt) *adj* **1** indifférent. **2** médiocre.
indigestion (indiˈdʒestʃən) *n* indigestion *f*.
indignant (inˈdignənt) *adj* indigné. **be indignant** s'indigner.
indirect (indiˈrekt) *adj* **1** indirect. **2** détourné.
indiscriminate (indiˈskriminit) *adj* aveugle.
individual (indiˈvidʒuəl) *n* individu *m*. *adj* **1** particulier, -ière. **2** original, -aux.
indoctrinate (inˈdɔktrineit) *vt* endoctriner.
indolent (ˈindələnt) *adj* indolent, paresseux, -euse.
indoor (ˈindɔ:) *adj* **1** d'intérieur. **2** de société. **indoors** *adv* à la maison, à l'intérieur.
induce (inˈdju:s) *vt* **1** induire. **2** causer. **3** provoquer. **inducement** *n* encouragement *m*.
indulge (inˈdʌldʒ) *vt* satisfaire. **indulge in** s'adonner à. **indulgence** *n* indulgence *f*.
industry (ˈindəstri) *n* **1** industrie *f*. **2** diligence *f*. **industrial** *adj* industriel, -elle. **industrious** *adj* assidu, industrieux, -euse.

inefficient (ini'fiʃənt) *adj* **1** inefficace. **2** incapable.
inept (i'nept) *adj* **1** inepte. **2** déplacé.
inequality (ini'kwɔliti) *n* inégalité *f*.
inert (i'nə:t) *adj* inerte. **inertia** *n* inertie *f*.
inevitable (in'evitəbəl) *adj* inévitable, fatal.
infallible (in'fæləbəl) *adj* infaillible.
infamous ('infəməs) *adj* infâme.
infancy ('infənsi) *n* **1** enfance *f*. bas âge *m*. **2** débuts *m pl*.
infant ('infənt) *n* **1** enfant (en bas âge) *m,f*. **2** *law* mineur *m*. **infantile** *adj* enfantin.
infantry ('infəntri) *n* infanterie *f*.
infatuate (in'fætʃueit) *vt* **1** enticher. **2** affoler. **be infatuated with** s'enticher de. **infatuation** *n* engouement *m*.
infect (in'fekt) *vt* **1** *med* contaminer. **2** infecter. **infection** *n* **1** *med* contamination *f*. **2** infection *f*.
infer (in'fə:) *vt* **1** impliquer. **2** déduire.
inferior (in'fiəriə) *adj,n* inférieur *m*. **inferiority** *n* infériorité *f*.
infernal (in'fə:nl̩) *adj* infernal, -aux.
infest (in'fest) *vt* infester.
infidelity (infi'deliti) *n* infidélité, déloyauté *f*.
infiltrate ('infiltreit) *vt* infiltrer. *vi* s'infiltrer.
infinite ('infinit) *adj* infini. **infinitely** *adv* infiniment. **infinity** *n* infinité *f*.
infinitive (in'finitiv) *adj,n* infinitif, -ive *m*.
infirm (in'fə:m) *adj* infirme.
inflame (in'fleim) *vt* enflammer. *vi* s'enflammer.
inflammable (in'flæməbəl) *adj* inflammable.
inflate (in'fleit) *vt* **1** gonfler. **2** *comm* faire monter. **inflation** *n* inflation *f*.
inflection (in'flekʃən) *n* inflexion *f*.
inflict (in'flikt) *vt* **1** infliger. **2** occasionner.
influence ('influəns) *n* influence *f*. *vt* **1** influencer. **2** influer sur. **influential** *adj* influent.
influenza (influ'enzə) *n* grippe *f*.
influx ('inflʌks) *n* affluence *f*.
inform (in'fɔ:m) *vt* informer, renseigner. **information** *n* renseignements *m pl*. avis *m*. **piece of information** renseignement *m*. **informer** *n* mouchard, dénonciateur *m*.
informal (in'fɔ:məl) *adj* sans cérémonie, familier, -ère.
infringe (in'frindʒ) *vt* enfreindre. *vi* empiéter. **infringement** *n* infraction *f*.
infuriate (in'fjuərieit) *vt* rendre furieux, exaspérer.
ingenious (in'dʒi:niəs) *adj* ingénieux, -euse.
ingredient (in'gri:diənt) *n* ingrédient, élément *m*.
inhabit (in'hæbit) *vt* habiter. **inhabitant** *n* habitant *m*.
inhale (in'heil) *vt* **1** inhaler. **2** inspirer.
inherent (in'hiərənt) *adj* inhérent, propre.
inherit (in'herit) *vt* hériter de. **inheritance** *n* **1** héritage *m*. **2** succession *f*.
inhibit (in'hibit) *vt* **1** inhiber, empêcher. **2** prohiber. **inhibition** *n* **1** inhibition *f*. **2** prohibition *f*.
inhuman (in'hju:mən) *adj* inhumain. **inhumanity** *n* cruauté *f*.
initial (i'niʃəl) *adj* premier, initial, -aux. *n* initiale *f*. *vt* parafer.
initiate (i'niʃieit) *vt* **1** commencer, lancer. **2** initier. **initiation** *n* **1** début *m*. **2** initiation *f*.
initiative (i'niʃətiv) *n* initiative *f*.
inject (in'dʒekt) *vt* injecter. **injection** *n* injection, piqûre *f*.
injure ('indʒə) *vt* **1** blesser. **2** endommager. **injury** *n* **1** blessure *f*. **2** tort *m*.
injustice (in'dʒʌstis) *n* injustice *f*.
ink (iŋk) *n* encre *f*.
inkling ('iŋkliŋ) *n* soupçon *m*.
inland (*adj* 'inlənd; *n,adv* 'inlænd) *adj,n* intérieur *m*. *adv* à l'intérieur.
Inland Revenue *n* fisc *m*.
inmate ('inmeit) *n* **1** pensionnaire *m*. **2** prisonnier, -ière.
inn (in) *n* auberge *f*.
innate (i'neit) *adj* inné.
inner ('inə) *adj* intérieur, interne.
innocent ('inəsənt) *adj* **1** innocent. **2** naïf, -ïve. **innocence** *n* **1** innocence *f*. **2** naïveté *f*.
innocuous (i'nɔkjuəs) *adj* inoffensif, -ive.
innovation (inə'veiʃən) *n* innovation *f*.
innuendo (inju'endou) *n* insinuation *f*.
inoculate (i'nɔkjuleit) *vt* inoculer, vacciner. **inoculation** *n* inoculation *f*.
input ('input) *n* entrée, consommation *f*.
inquest ('inkwest) *n* enquête *f*.
inquire (in'kwaiə) *vt* demander. *vi* s'enquérir, se renseigner. **inquiry** *n* **1** demande de renseignements *f*. **2** enquête *f*.
inquisition (inkwi'ziʃən) *n* **1** investigation *f*. **2** *cap* Inquisition *f*.
inquisitive (in'kwizitiv) *adj* curieux, -euse.
insane (in'sein) *adj* **1** fou, folle. **2** insensé. **insanity** *n* folie, démence *f*.
insatiable (in'seiʃəbəl) *adj* insatiable.
inscribe (in'skraib) *vt* inscrire, graver. **inscription** *n* inscription *f*.

insect ('insekt) *n* insecte *m*.
insecure (insi'kjuə) *adj* **1** incertain. **2** peu solide.
inseminate (in'semineit) *vt* inséminer. **insemination** *n* insémination *f*.
insert (in'sə:t) *vt* **1** insérer. **2** introduire. **insertion** *n* insertion *f*.
inside (in'said) *adj* intérieur. *adv* à l'intérieur. *prep* à l'intérieur de. *n* dedans, intérieur *m*. **on the inside** au dedans.
insidious (in'sidiəs) *adj* insidieux, -euse.
insight ('insait) *n* **1** perspicacité *f*. **2** aperçu *m*.
insinuate (in'sinjueit) *vt* insinuer.
insist (in'sist) *vi* insister. **insistence** *n* insistance *f*.
insolent ('insələnt) *adj* insolent.
insomnia (in'sɔmniə) *n* insomnie *f*.
inspect (in'spekt) *vt* inspecter, examiner. **inspection** *n* inspection *f*. contrôle *m*. **inspector** *n* inspecteur *m*.
inspire (in'spaiə) *vt* inspirer. **inspiration** *n* inspiration *f*.
instability (instə'biliti) *n* instabilité *f*.
install (in'stɔ:l) *vt* installer.
instalment (in'stɔ:lmənt) *n* **1** versement partiel *m*. **2** (of a serial) épisode *m*.
instance ('instəns) *n* **1** exemple, cas *m*. **2** instance *f*. **for instance** par exemple. **instant** *n* instant *m*. *adj* **1** immédiat. **2** courant. **3** urgent. **instantaneous** *adj* instantané.
instead (in'sted) **instead of** *prep* au lieu de. *adv* à la place.
instep ('instep) *n* **1** *anat* cou-de-pied *m*. **2** cambrure *f*.
instigate ('instigeit) *vt* inciter, provoquer.
instil (in'stil) *vt* inculquer.
instinct ('instiŋkt) *n* instinct *m*. **instinctive** *adj* instinctif, -ive.
institute ('institju:t) *n* institut *m*. *vt* instituer. **institution** *n* institution *f*. établissement *m*.
instruct (in'strʌkt) *vt* **1** instruire. **2** charger. **instruction** *n* **1** instruction *f*. **2** *pl* ordres *m pl*.
instrument ('instrumənt) *n* instrument *m*. **instrumental** *adj* **1** contributif, -ive. **2** *mus* instrumental, -aux.
insubordinate (insə'bɔ:dinət) *adj* insubordonné.
insular ('insjulə) *adj* **1** insulaire. **2** borné.
insulate ('insjuleit) *vt* **1** isoler. **2** calorifuger. **insulation** *n* isolement *m*.
insulin ('insjulin) *n* insuline *f*.
insult (*v* in'sʌlt; *n* 'insʌlt) *vt* insulter. *n* insulte *f*. affront *m*.
insure (in'ʃuə) *vt* assurer. **insurance** *n* assurance *f*.
intact (in'tækt) *adj* intact, indemne.
intake ('inteik) *n* **1** consommation *f*. **2** prise *f*. **3** admission *f*.
integral ('intigrəl) *adj* intégrant.
integrate ('intigreit) *vt* intégrer, compléter.
integrity (in'tegriti) *n* intégrité *f*.
intellect ('intəlekt) *n* intelligence *f*. esprit *m*. **intellectual** *adj,n* intellectuel, -elle.
intelligent (in'telidʒənt) *adj* intelligent. **intelligence** *n* **1** intelligence *f*. **2** renseignements *m pl*.
intelligible (in'telidʒəbəl) *adj* intelligible.
intend (in'tend) *vt* **1** avoir l'intention. **2** destiner.
intense (in'tens) *adj* intense, profond. **intensify** *vt* intensifier. *vi* s'accroître. **intensity** *n* intensité *f*. **intensive** *adj* intensif, -ive.
intent[1] (in'tent) *n* intention *f*. dessein *m*.
intent[2] (in'tent) *adj* **1** absorbé. **2** résolu. **3** acharné. **4** sérieux, -euse.
intention (in'tenʃən) *n* intention *f*. **intentional** *adj* voulu. **intentionally** *adv* exprès.
inter (in'tə:) *vt* enterrer.
interact (intə'rækt) *vi* agir l'un sur l'autre.
intercept (intə'sept) *vt* intercepter, arrêter en passage.
interchange (intə'tʃeindʒ) *vt* échanger. *vi* s'interchanger. *n* **1** échange *m*. **2** succession *f*.
intercourse ('intəkɔ:s) *n* commerce *m*. rapports *m pl*.
interest ('intrəst) *n* **1** intérêt *m*. **2** avantage *m*. *vt* intéresser. **be interested in** s'intéresser à.
interfere (intə'fiə) *vi* s'ingérer, s'immiscer. **interference** *n* **1** intervention *f*. **2** *tech* parasites *m pl*. **interfering** *adj* importun.
interim ('intərim) *adj* intérimaire. *n* intérim *m*.
interior (in'tiəriə) *adj,n* intérieur *m*.
interjection (intə'dʒekʃn̩) *n* interjection *f*.
interlude ('intəlu:d) *n* intermède *m*.
intermediate (intə'mi:diət) *adj* intermédiaire. **intermediary** *adj,n* intermédiaire *m*.
intermission (intə'miʃən) *n* **1** interruption *f*. **2** (cinema) entracte *m*.
intermittent (intə'mitn̩t) *adj* intermittent.
intern (in'tə:n) *vt* interner.
internal (in'tə:nl̩) *adj* intérieur, interne.
international (intə'næʃn̩l̩) *adj* international, -aux.
internment (in'tə:nmənt) *n* internement *m*.
interpose (intə'pouz) *vt* interposer. *vi* s'interposer.
interpret (in'tə:prit) *vt* interpréter. **interpretation** *n* interprétation *f*. **interpreter** *n* interprète *m,f*.

interrogate (in'terəgeit) *vt* questionner, interroger. **interrogation** *n* **1** interrogation *f*. **2** *law* interrogatoire *m*. **interrogative** *adj* **1** interrogateur, -trice. **2** *gram* interrogatif, -ive.

interrupt (intə'rʌpt) *vt* interrompre. **interruption** *n* interruption *f*.

intersect (intə'sekt) *vt* entrecouper. *vi* se couper. **intersection 1** intersection *f*. **2** *mot* carrefour *m*.

interval ('intəvəl) *n* **1** intervalle *m*. **2** *Th* entracte *m*.

intervene (intə'vi:n) *vi* **1** intervenir. **2** survenir. **intervention** *n* intervention *f*.

interview ('intəvju:) *n* entrevue, interview *f*. *vt* interviewer.

intestine (in'testin) *n* intestin *m*.

intimate[1] ('intimit) *adj* intime. **intimacy** *n* intimité *f*.

intimate[2] ('intimeit) *vt* suggérer, intimer.

intimidate (in'timideit) *vt* intimider. **intimidation** *n* **1** intimidation *f*. **2** *law* menaces *f pl*.

into ('intə; *stressed* 'intu:) *prep* dans, en, à.

intolerable (in'tɔlərəbəl) *adj* intolérable, insupportable. **intolerant** *adj* intolérant.

intonation (intə'neiʃən) *n* **1** intonation *f*. **2** ton *m*.

intoxicate (in'tɔksikeit) *vt* enivrer. **intoxicated** *adj* ivre. **intoxication** *n* **1** intoxication *f*. **2** ivresse *f*.

intransitive (in'trænsitiv) *adj* intransitif, -ive.

intrepid (in'trepid) *adj* intrépide.

intricate ('intrikət) *adj* **1** compliqué. **2** confus. **intricacy** *n* complexité *f*.

intrigue (in'tri:g) *n* intrigue *f*. *vt,vi* intriguer.

intrinsic (in'trinsik) *adj* intrinsèque.

introduce (intrə'dju:s) *vt* **1** introduire. **2** présenter. **introduction** *n* **1** introduction *f*. **2** présentation *f*. **3** *lit* avant-propos *m invar*.

introspective (intrə'spektiv) *adj* introspectif, -ive.

introvert ('intrəvə:t) *n* introverti *m*.

intrude (in'tru:d) *vi* faire intrusion. **intruder** *n* intrus *m*.

intuition (intju'iʃən) *n* intuition *f*. **intuitive** *adj* intuitif, -ive.

inundate ('inʌndeit) *vt* inonder.

invade (in'veid) *vt* envahir.

invalid[1] ('invəli:d) *adj,n* infirme, malade.

invalid[2] (in'vælid) *adj* nul et non avenu, périmé.

invaluable (in'væljubəl) *adj* inestimable.

invariable (in'vɛəriəbəl) *adj* invariable. **invariably** *adv* immanquablement.

invent (in'vent) *vt* inventer. **invention** *n* invention *f*. **inventor** *n* inventeur *m*.

inventory ('invəntəri) *n* inventaire *m*.

invert (in'və:t) *vt* **1** renverser. **2** intervertir. **inverted commas** *n pl* guillemets *m pl*.

invertebrate (in'və:təbreit) *adj,n* invertébré *m*.

invest (in'vest) *vt* **1** investir. **2** revêtir. **investment** *n* placement *m*.

investigate (in'vestigeit) *vt* **1** examiner. **2** enquêter sur.

invincible (in'vinsəbəl) *adj* invincible.

invisible (in'vizəbəl) *adj* invisible.

invite (in'vait) *vt* inviter. **invitation** *n* invitation *f*. **inviting** *adj* tentant, engageant.

invoice ('invɔis) *n* facture *f*. *vt* facturer.

invoke (in'vouk) *vt* **1** invoquer. **2** évoquer.

involve (in'vɔlv) *vt* **1** impliquer. **2** comporter. **involved** *adj* compliqué. **involvement** *n* implication *f*.

inward ('inwəd) *adj* **1** intérieur, interne. **2** vers l'intérieur. **inwards** *adv* vers l'intérieur.

iodine ('aiədi:n) *n* iode *m*.

Iran (i'ra:n) *n* Iran *m*. **Iranian** *adj,n* iranien, -ienne.

Iraq (i'ra:k) *n* Irak *m*. **Iraqi** *adj,n* irakien, -ienne.

Ireland ('aiələnd) *n* Irlande *f*. **Irish** *adj* irlandais. **Irishman** *n* irlandais *m*.

iris ('airis) *n anat, bot* iris *m*.

iron ('aiən) *n* **1** fer *m*. **2** *dom* fer à repasser *m*. *adj* de fer. *vt* repasser. **ironing board** *n* planche à repasser *f*. **ironmonger** *n* quincaillier *m*. **Iron Curtain** *n* Rideau de Fer *m*.

irony ('airəni) *n* ironie *f*. **ironic** *adj* ironique.

irrational (i'ræʃən|) *adj* absurde, déraisonnable.

irregular (i'regjulə) *adj* irrégulier, -ière.

irrelevant (i'reləvənt) *adj* hors de propos.

irresistible (iri'zistəbəl) *adj* irrésistible.

irrespective (iri'spektiv) *adj* indépendant. *adv* indépendamment.

irresponsible (iri'spɔnsəbəl) *adj* irresponsable.

irrevocable (i'revəkəbəl) *adj* irrévocable.

irrigate ('irigeit) *vt* irriguer. **irrigation** *n* irrigation *f*.

irritate ('iriteit) *vt* irriter. **irritating** *adj* irritant, agaçant. **irritation** *n* irritation *f*.

is (iz) *v see* **be.**

Islam ('izla:m) *n* Islam *m*. **Islamic** *adj* Islamique.

island ('ailənd) *n* **1** île *f*. **2** îlot *m*.

isle (ail) *n* île *f*.

isolate ('aisəleit) *vt* isoler. **isolation** *n* isolement *m*.

Israel (ˈizreiəl) *n* Israël *m.* **Israeli** *adj,n* israélien, -ienne.
issue (ˈiʃu:) *n* **1** sortie *f.* **2** résultat *m.* **3** (of a book, etc.) numéro *m.* **4** progéniture *f.* *vt* **1** émettre. **2** publier. **3** distribuer. *vi* sortir.
it (it) *pron 3rd pers s* **1** il *m.* elle *f.* **2** le *m.* la *f.* **3** lui *m,f.* **4** il, cela *m.*
italic (iˈtælik) *adj,n* italique *m.*
Italy (ˈitəli) *n* Italie *f.* **Italian** *adj,n* italien, -ienne. **Italian** (language) *n* italien *m.*
itch (itʃ) *n* démangeaison *f.* *vi* **1** démanger. **2** *sl* brûler.
item (ˈaitəm) *n comm* article, détail *m.* **item of news** *n* nouvelle *f.*
itinerary (aiˈtinərəri) *n* itinéraire *m.*
its (its) *poss adj 3rd pers s* son, sa, ses. **itself** *pron 3rd pers s* **1** lui-même *m.* elle-même *f.* soi-même *m,f.* **2** se *m,f.* **by itself** tout seul.
ivory (ˈaivəri) *n* ivoire *m.* *adj* en ivoire.
ivy (ˈaivi) *n* lierre *m.*

J

jab (dʒæb) *n* **1** coup de pointe *m.* **2** *inf med* piqûre *f.* *vt* **1** piquer. **2** faire une piqûre à.
jack (dʒæk) *n* **1** cric, vérin *m.* **2** (game) valet *m.*
jackal (ˈdʒækəl) *n* chacal *m.*
jackdaw (ˈdʒækdɔ:) *n* choucas *m.*
jacket (ˈdʒækit) *n* **1** veste *f.* gilet *m.* **2** (for a woman) jaquette *f.* **3** (of a book) chemise *f.*
jackpot (ˈdʒækpɔt) *n* gros lot *m.*
jade (dʒeid) *n* jade *m.*
jaded (ˈdʒeidid) *adj* excédé, éreinté.
jagged (ˈdʒægid) *adj* déchiqueté, dentelé.
jaguar (ˈdʒægjuə) *n* jaguar *m.*
jail (dʒeil) *n* prison *f.* *vt* emprisonner.
jam[1] (dʒæm) *n* **1** embouteillage *m.* **2** foule *f.* *vt* bloquer, coincer. *vi* se coincer, se caler.
jam[2] (dʒæm) *n cul* confiture *f.*
Jamaica (dʒəˈmeikə) *n* Jamaïque *f.* **Jamaican** *adj,n* jamaïquain.
Jansenist (ˈdʒænsənist) *n* janséniste *m,f.*
January (ˈdʒænjuəri) *n* janvier.
Japan (dʒəˈpæn) *n* Japon *m.* **Japanese** *adj,n* japonais. **Japanese** (language) *n* japonais *m.*
jar[1] (dʒɑ:) *n* pot *m.* **glass jar** bocal, -aux *m.*
jar[2] (dʒɑ:) *n* **1** son discordant *m.* **2** choc *m.* secousse *f.* *vt* ébranler. *vi* **1** grincer. **2** agacer.
jargon (ˈdʒɑ:gən) *n* jargon *m.*
jaundice (ˈdʒɔ:ndis) *n* jaunisse *f.*
jaunt (dʒɔ:nt) *n* petite promenade *f.* *vi* se balader.
javelin (ˈdʒævlin) *n* javelot *m.*
jaw (dʒɔ:) *n* mâchoire *f.* **jawbone** *n* mâchoire *f.*
jazz (dʒæz) *n* jazz *m.*
jealous (ˈdʒeləs) *adj* jaloux, -ouse. **jealousy** *n* jalousie *f.*
jeans (dʒ:inz) *n pl* blue-jean *m.*
jeep (dʒi:p) *n* jeep *f.*
jeer (dʒiə) *n* **1** raillerie *f.* **2** huée *f.* *vi* railler. **jeer at** se moquer de, huer. **jeering** *adj* railleur, -euse.
jelly (ˈdʒeli) *n cul* gelée *f.* **jellyfish** *n* méduse *f.*
jeopardize (ˈdʒepədaiz) *vt* mettre en danger, compromettre. **jeopardy** *n* danger *m.*
jerk (dʒə:k) *n* secousse *f.* *vt* secouer. *vi* se mouvoir brusquement.
jersey (ˈdʒə:zi) *n* jersey *m.*
Jersey (ˈdʒə:zi) *n geog* Jersey *m.*
Jerusalem (dʒəˈru:sələm) *n* Jérusalem *f.*
jest (dʒest) *n* raillerie *f.* *vi* plaisanter.
Jesus (ˈdʒi:zəs) *n* Jésus *m.*
jet[1] (dʒet) *n* **1** *aviat* avion à réaction *m.* **2** jet, gicleur *m.*
jet[2] (dʒet) *n* jais *m.*
jetty (ˈdʒeti) *n* jetée, digue *f.*
Jew (dʒu:) *n* juif, juive. **Jewish** *adj* juif, juive.
jewel (ˈdʒu:əl) *n* bijou, -oux, joyau, -aux *m.* **jeweller** *n* bijoutier *m.* **jewellery** *n* bijouterie *f.*
jig[1] (dʒig) *n tech* gabarit *m.*
jig[2] (dʒig) *n mus* gigue.
jiggle (ˈdʒigəl) *vi* sautiller.
jigsaw (ˈdʒigsɔ:) *n* puzzle *m.*
jilt (dʒilt) *vt* délaisser, plaquer.
jingle (ˈdʒiŋgəl) *n* tintement *m.* *vi* tinter, cliqueter. *vt* faire tinter.
job (dʒɔb) *n* **1** besogne *f.* travail, -aux *m.* **2** emploi *m.* situation *f.*
jockey (ˈdʒɔki) *n* jockey *m.* *vt* tromper. *vi* manœuvrer.
jodhpurs (ˈdʒɔdpəz) *n pl* pantalon d'équitation *m.*
jog (dʒɔg) *n* **1** coup *m.* secousse *f.* **2** petit trot *m.* *vt* secouer. **jog along** trottiner.
join (dʒɔin) *vt* **1** joindre, unir. **2** rejoindre. **3** adhérer à. **join in** prendre part à. **join up 1** assembler. **2** s'enrôler. ~*n* joint *m.* jointure *f.* **joint** *n* **1** joint *m.* jointure *f.* **2** *anat* articulation *f.* **3** *cul* rôti *m.* **4** *sl* boîte *f.* *adj* **1** commun. **2** solidaire, concerté. **jointly** *adv* ensemble, conjointement.
joist (dʒɔist) *n* solive *f.*
joke (dʒouk) *n* plaisanterie *f.* **practical joke** *n* mauvais tour *m.* ~*vi* plaisanter.

jolly (ˈdʒɔli) *adj* enjoué, gaillard. *adv inf* rudement.
jolt (dʒoult) *vt,vi* cahoter. *n* **1** secousse *f.* **2** surprise *f.* choc *m.*
Jordan (ˈdʒɔ:dn̩) *n* Jordanie *f.* **(River) Jordan** Jourdain *m.* **Jordanian** *adj,n* jordanien, -ienne.
jostle (ˈdʒɔsəl) *vt* bousculer, coudoyer. *n* bousculade *f.*
journal (ˈdʒə:nl̩) *n* journal, -aux *m.* **journalism** *n* journalisme *m.* **journalist** *n* journaliste *m,f.*
journey (ˈdʒə:ni) *n* voyage, trajet *m. vi* voyager.
jovial (ˈdʒouviəl) *adj* jovial, -aux.
joy (dʒɔi) *n* joie *f.* **joyful** *adj* heureux, -euse.
jubilee (ˈdʒu:bili:) *n* jubilé *m.*
Judaism (ˈdʒu:deiizəm) *n* judaïsme *m.*
judge (dʒʌdʒ) *n* **1** juge *m.* **2** connaisseur *m. vt* **1** juger. **2** estimer. **judgment** *n* **1** jugement *m.* **2** opinion *f.* **3** discernement *m.*
judicial (dʒu:ˈdiʃəl) *adj* **1** judiciaire. **2** juridique.
judicious (dʒu:ˈdiʃəs) *adj* judicieux, -euse.
judo (ˈdʒu:dou) *n* judo *m.*
jug (dʒʌg) *n* **1** cruche *f.* pot, pichet *m.* **2** *sl* violon *m.* prison *f.*
juggernaut (ˈdʒʌgənɔ:t) *n* camion poids lourd *m.*
juggle (ˈdʒʌgəl) *vi* jongler. *vt* escamoter. **juggler** *n* jongleur *m.* **jugglery** *n* jonglerie *f.* tours de passe-passe *m pl.*
juice (dʒu:s) *n* jus *m.* **juicy** *adj* juteux, -euse.
jukebox (ˈdʒu:kbɔks) *n* phonographe à sous, juke-box *m.*
July (dʒuˈlai) *n* juillet *m.*
jumble (ˈdʒʌmbəl) *n* méli-mélo, fouillis *m. vt* mêler. **jumble sale** *n* vente d'objets usagés *f.*
jump (dʒʌmp) *vi,vt* sauter. *n* **1** saut *m.* **2** sursaut *m.* **3** *sport* obstacle *m.*
jumper (ˈdʒʌmpə) *n* pull, tricot *m.*
junction (ˈdʒʌŋkʃən) *n* **1** jonction *f.* **2** (of a road, etc.) embranchement *m.*
June (dʒu:n) *n* juin *m.*
jungle (ˈdʒʌŋgəl) *n* jungle *f.*
junior (ˈdʒu:niə) *adj* **1** cadet, -ette. **2** jeune. *n* cadet, -ette.
juniper (ˈdʒu:nipə) *n* genévrier, genièvre *m.*
junk (dʒʌŋk) *n* rebut *m.* étoupe *f.* **piece of junk** rossignol *m.*
junta (ˈdʒuntə) *n* junte *f.*
Jupiter (ˈdʒu:pitə) *n* Jupiter *m.*
jurisdiction (dʒuərisˈdikʃən) *n* juridiction *f.*
jury (ˈdʒuəri) *n* jury *m.* **juror** *n* juré *m.*
just (dʒʌst) *adj* juste, équitable. *adv* **1** justement, juste. **2** seulement, simplement. **3** à l'instant.
justice (ˈdʒʌstis) *n* justice *f.*
justify (ˈdʒʌstifai) *vt* justifier. **justification** *n* justification *f.*
jut (dʒʌt) *vi* **jut out** faire saillie.
jute (dʒu:t) *n* jute *m.*
juvenile (ˈdʒu:vənail) *adj* **1** juvénile. **2** *law* mineur *f.*
juxtapose (dʒʌkstəˈpouz) *vt* juxtaposer. **juxtaposition** *n* juxtaposition *f.*

K

kaftan (ˈkæftŋ) *n* kaftan *m.*
kaleidoscope (kəˈlaidəskoup) *n* kaléidoscope *m.*
kangaroo (kæŋgəˈru:) *n* kangourou *m.*
karate (kəˈrɑ:ti) *n* karaté *m.*
kebab (kəˈbæb) *n* brochette *f.*
keel (ki:l) *n* quille *f. v* **keel over** chavirer.
keen (ki:n) *adj* **1** (of an object) tranchant, affilé. **2** vif, vive. **3** ardent. **4** enragé. **5** fin.
keenness *n* **1** finesse *f.* **2** ardeur *f.* **3** empressement *m.*
keep* (ki:p) *vt* **1** garder. **2** tenir, observer. **3** célébrer. *vi* **1** rester. **2** continuer. **3** se conserver. **keep back** retenir. **keep on** continuer de *or* à. **keep to** tenir. **keepsake** *n* souvenir *m.*
keg (keg) *n* barillet, tonnelet *m.*
kennel (ˈkenl̩) *n* chenil *m.* niche *f.*
Kenya (ˈkenjə) *n* Kenya *m.* **Kenyan** *adj,n* kenien, -ienne.
kept (kept) *v see* **keep.**
kerb (kə:b) *n* bordure de trottoir *f.*
kernel (ˈkə:nl̩) *n* amande, graine *f.*
kettle (ˈketl̩) *n* bouilloire *f.* **kettledrum** *n* timbale *f.*
key (ki:) *n* **1** clef *f.* **2** (of a book, etc.) corrigé *m.* **3** touche *f.* **4** *mus* ton *m. adj* clef, essentiel, -elle. *vt* accorder. **keyboard** *n* clavier *m.* **keyhole** *n* trou de serrure *m.* **keyring** *n* porte-clefs *m invar.*
khaki (ˈkɑ:ki) *n* kaki *m. adj* kaki *invar.*
kibbutz (kiˈbuts) *n* kibboutz *m.*
kick (kik) *n* **1** coup de pied *m.* **2** (of a gun) recul *m.* réaction *f. vi* donner un coup de pied, ruer. *vt* donner un coup de pied à. **kick-off** *n* coup d'envoi *m.*
kid[1] (kid) *n* **1** *zool* chevreau, -aux *m.* **2** *inf* mioche, gosse *m,f. adj* de chevreau, -aux.

kid[2] (kid) *vt inf* faire marcher. **kid oneself** se faire accroire, se leurrer.

kidnap (ˈkidnæp) *vt* enlever, kidnapper. **kidnapper** *n* ravisseur *m*. **kidnapping** *n* enlèvement *m*.

kidney (ˈkidni) *n* **1** *anat* rein *m*. **2** (of animals) rognon *m*. **kidney bean** *n* haricot nain *m*.

kill (kil) *vt* **1** tuer. **2** (an animal) abattre. **killing** *adj* **1** meurtrier, -ière. **2** *inf* crevant. *n* tuerie *f*.

kiln (kiln) *n* four *m*.

kilo (ˈki:lou) *n* kilo *m*.

kilogram (ˈkiləgræm) *n* kilogramme *m*.

kilometre (kiˈlɔmitə) *n* kilomètre *m*.

kilowatt (ˈkiləwɔt) *n* kilowatt *m*.

kilt (kilt) *n* kilt *m*.

kin (kin) *n* **1** parenté *f*. **2** parents *m pl*.

kind[1] (kaind) *adj* bon, bonne, aimable, gentil, -ille, bienveillant. **kindness** *n* bonté, bienveillance *f*.

kind[2] (kaind) *n* espèce, sorte *f*. genre *m*.

kindergarten (ˈkindəga:tn̩) *n* école maternelle *f*.

kindle (ˈkindl̩) *vt* **1** allumer, enflammer. **2** éveiller, exciter. *vi* **1** s'allumer. **2** s'éveiller.

kinetic (kiˈnetik) *adj* cinétique.

king (kiŋ) *n* **1** roi *m*. **2** (draughts) dame *f*. **kingdom** *n* **1** royaume *m*. **2** règne *m*. **kingfisher** *n* martin-pêcheur *m*.

kink (kiŋk) *n* nœud, tortillement *m*. *vi* se nouer se tortiller.

kiosk (ˈkiɔsk) *n* kiosque *m*.

kipper (ˈkipə) *n* hareng fumé *m*.

kiss (kis) *n* baiser *m*. *vt* embrasser.

kit (kit) *n* **1** trousse *f*. fourniment *m*. **2** *inf* effets *m pl*.

kitchen (ˈkitʃin) *n* cuisine *f*. *adj* de cuisine, cuisinier, -ière. **kitchen garden** *n* jardin potager *m*.

kite (kait) *n* **1** cerf-volant *m*. **2** *zool* milan *m*.

kitten (ˈkitn̩) *n* chaton *m*.

kitty (ˈkiti) *n* cagnotte *f*.

kiwi (ˈki:wi) *n* kiwi, aptéryx *m*.

kleptomania (ˌkleptəˈmeiniə) *n* kleptomanie *f*. **kleptomaniac** *adj,n* kleptomane.

knack (næk) *n* tour de main, truc *m*.

knave (neiv) *n* **1** coquin *m*. **2** *game* valet *m*.

knead (ni:d) *vt* pétrir, travailler.

knee (ni:) *n* genou, -oux *m*. **kneecap** *n* rotule *f*.

kneel* (ni:l) *vi* s'agenouiller.

knew (nu:) *v see* **know.**

knickers (ˈnikəz) *n pl* culotte *f*.

knife (naif) *n, pl* **knives** couteau, -aux *m*. *vt* donner un coup de couteau à, poignarder.

knight (nait) *n* **1** chevalier *m*. **2** *game* cavalier *m*. *vt* créer chevalier.

knit* (nit) *vt* **1** tricoter. **2** joindre. *vi* se souder. **knitting** *n* tricot *m*. **knitting needle** aiguille à tricoter *f*. **knitwear** *n* tricot *m*.

knob (nɔb) *n* **1** bouton *m*. bosse *f*. **2** morceau, -aux *m*.

knock (nɔk) *n* coup, heurt *m*. *vt,vi* frapper, heurter. **knock down** renverser. **knock over** renverser. **knocker** *n* marteau, -aux *m*.

knot (nɔt) *n* nœud *m*. *vt* nouer.

know* (nou) *vt* **1** savoir, connaître. **2** reconnaître. **get to know** **1** apprendre. **2** faire la connaissance de. **knowing** *adj* fin, rusé.

knowledge (ˈnɔlidʒ) *n* **1** connaissance *f*. **2** savoir *m*. science *f*.

knuckle (ˈnʌkəl) *n* articulation, jointure *f*.

Korea (kəˈriə) *n* Corée *f*. **Korean** *adj,n* coréen, -enne.

kosher (ˈkouʃə) *adj* cachir *invar*.

L

label (ˈleibəl) *n* étiquette *f*. *vt* étiqueter.

laboratory (ləˈbɔrətri) *n* laboratoire *m*.

labour (ˈleibə) *n* **1** travail, -aux, labeur *m*. **2** main-d'œuvre *f*. *vi* travailler, peiner. **labour-saving** *adj* qui allège le travail. **laborious** *adj* laborieux, -euse, pénible. **Labour Party** *n* parti travailliste *m*.

laburnum (ləˈbə:nəm) *n* cytise *m*.

labyrinth (ˈlæbərinθ) *n* labyrinthe, dédale *m*.

lace (leis) *n* **1** dentelle *f*. **2** (of a shoe, etc.) lacet *m*. *vt* lacer.

lack (læk) *n* manque, défaut *m*. **for lack of** faute de. ~*vt,vi* manquer.

lacquer (ˈlækə) *n* vernis *m*. laque *f*. *vt* laquer.

lad (læd) *n* gars, garçon *m*.

ladder (ˈlædə) *n* **1** échelle *f*. **2** (in a stocking) maille filée *f*.

laden (ˈleidn̩) *adj* chargé.

ladle (ˈleidl̩) *n* louche *f*.

lady (ˈleidi) *n* dame *f*. **ladies and gentlemen** mesdames, mesdemoiselles, messieurs. **ladybird** *n* coccinelle, *inf* bête à bon Dieu *f*.

lag[1] (læg) *vi* traîner, rester en arrière. *n* retard *m*.

lag[2] (læg) *vt* calorifuger. **lagging** *n* revêtement calorifuge *m*.

lager (ˈla:gə) *n* bière blonde allemande *f*.

laid (leid) *v see* **lay.**

lain (lein) *v see* **lie.**

laity (ˈleiəti) *n* laïques *m pl.*
lake (leik) *n* lac *m.*
lamb (læm) *n* agneau, -aux *m.*
lame (leim) *adj* **1** boiteux, -euse, estropié. **2** pauvre, faible. *vt* estropier.
lament (ləˈment) *n* lamentation *f. vt* pleurer. *vi* se lamenter.
lamp (læmp) *n* lampe *f.* **standard lamp** lampadaire *m.* **lamppost** *n* réverbère *m.* **lampshade** *n* abat-jour *m invar.*
lance (lɑːns) *n* lance *f.*
land (lænd) *n* **1** terre *f.* **2** pays *m. vt,vi* **1** *naut* débarquer. **2** *aviat* atterrir. **landing** *n* **1** palier *m.* **2** *aviat* atterrissage *m.* **3** *naut* débarquement *m.* **landlady** *n* propriétaire, patronne *f.* **landlord** *n* propriétaire, patron *m.* **landmark** *n* **1** point de repère *m.* **2** événement marquant *m.* **landscape** *n* paysage *m.*
lane (lein) *n* **1** chemin, sentier *m.* ruelle *f.* **2** (on a motorway) voie f.
language (ˈlæŋgwidʒ) *n* **1** (of a people) langue *f.* **2** langage *m.*
lanky (ˈlæŋki) *adj* maigre, décharné.
lantern (ˈlæntən) *n* lanterne *f.* fanal, -aux *m.*
lap[1] (læp) *n anat* genoux *m pl.* giron *m.*
lap[2] (læp) *n sport* tour, circuit *m. vt* **1** assembler. **2** ourler.
lap[3] (læp) *vt* laper. *vi* (of waves) clapoter. *n* clapotement *m.*
lapel (ləˈpel) *n* revers *m.*
Lapland (ˈlæplænd) *n* Laponie *f.* **Lapp** *adj,n* lapon. **Lapp** (language) *n* lapon *m.*
lapse (læps) *n* **1** cours *m.* **2** faute, erreur *f. vi* s'écouler. **2** manquer.
larceny (ˈlɑːsəni) *n* larcin *m.*
larch (lɑːtʃ) *n* mélèze *m.*
lard (lɑːd) *n* saindoux *m.*
larder (ˈlɑːdə) *n* garde-manger *m invar.*
large (lɑːdʒ) *adj* grand, fort, gros, grossa. **at large** en liberté.
lark[1] (lɑːk) *n zool* alouette *f.*
lark[2] (lɑːk) *n inf* farce, blague *f.*
larva (ˈlɑːvə) *n, pl* **larvae** larve *f.*
larynx (ˈlæriŋks) *n* larynx *m.* **laryngitis** *n* laryngite *f.*
laser (ˈleizə) *n* laser *m.*
lash (læʃ) *n* **1** coup de fouet m. **2** lanière *f.* **3** cil *m. vt,vi* fouetter, cingler. **lash out 1** lâcher un coup. **2** ruer.
lass (læs) *n* jeune fille *f.*
lasso (læˈsuː) *n* lasso *m.*
last[1] (lɑːst) *adj* dernier, -ière. **at last** enfin. **last but one** avant-dernier. **last night** cette nuit *f.*
last[2] (lɑːst) *vi* durer. **lasting** *adj* durable.
latch (lætʃ) *n* loquet *m.* clenche *f. vt* fermer au loquet.
late (leit) *adv* **1** tard. **2** en retard. *adj* **1** tard. **2** tardif, -ive. **3** feu. **4** dernier, -ière. **5** ancien, -ienne. **lately** *adv* dernièrement, récemment. **latecomer** *n* retardataire *m,f.* **later** *adv* plus tard. *adj* ultérieur.
latent (ˈleitn̩t) *adj* latent, caché.
lateral (ˈlætərəl) *adj* latéral, -aux.
latest (ˈleitist) *adj* récent, dernier, -ière. **at the latest** au plus tard.
lathe (leið) *n* tour *m.*
lather (ˈlɑːðə) *n* mousse *f. vt* savonner. *vi* mousser.
Latin (ˈlætin) *adj,n* latin *m.* **Latin America** *n* Amérique latine *f.*
latitude (ˈlætitjuːd) *n* **1** latitude *f.* **2** largeur, étendue *f.*
latter (ˈlætə) *adj* **1** dernier, -ière. **2** celui-ci, celle-ci.
lattice (ˈlætis) *n* treillage, treillis *m.*
laugh (lɑːf) *n* rire *m. vi* rire. **laugh at** se moquer de. **laughter** *n* rire *m.*
launch[1] (lɔːntʃ) *n* chaloupe *f.*
launch[2] (lɔːntʃ) *vt* lancer. **launch out** se lancer. **launching** *n* lancement *m.*
launder (ˈlɔːndə) *vt* blanchir. **launderette** *n* laverie *f.* **laundry** *n* **1** blanchisserie *f.* **2** linge *m.*
laurel (ˈlɔrəl) *n* laurier *m.*
lava (ˈlɑːvə) *n* lave *f.*
lavatory (ˈlævətri) *n* lavabo *m.* toilette *f.* cabinets *m pl.*
lavender (ˈlævində) *n* lavande *f.*
lavish (ˈlæviʃ) *adj* **1** prodigue. **2** somptueux, -euse, abondant. *vt* prodiguer.
law (lɔː) *n* **1** loi *f.* **2** droit *m.* **law-abiding** *adj* respectueux des lois. **lawful** *adj* **1** légal, -aux. **2** légitime. **lawyer** *n* avocat, avoué *m.*
lawn (lɔːn) *n* pelouse *f.* gazon *m.* **lawn-mower** *n* tondeuse à gazon *f.*
lax (læks) *adj* **1** mou, molle, lâche. **2** vague.
laxative (ˈlæksətiv) *adj,n* laxatif, -ive *m.*
lay*[1] (lei) *vt* **1** placer, mettre, poser. **2** (an egg) pondre. **3** coucher. **lay down 1** déposer. **2** stipuler. **lay out** étaler. **lay the table** mettre le couvert. **layer** *n* couche *f.*
lay[2] (lei) *v* see **lie.**
lay[3] (lei) *adj rel* lai, laïe, laïque. **layman** *n* laïque *m.*
laze (leiz) *vi* **laze about** fainéanter. **lazy** *adj* paresseux, -euse. **laziness** *n* paresse *f.*

lead*[1] (li:d) *vt* **1** mener, conduire. **2** diriger. **3** *game* jouer. *vi* mener, conduire. *n* **1** exemple *m*. **2** laisse *f*. **3** *game* main *f*. **4** *Th* premier rôle *m*. **5** câble *m*. *adj* principal, -aux. **leader** *n* **1** directeur, -trice, chef *m*. **2** guide *m*. **3** article de fond *m*. **leadership** *n* conduite *f*. commandement *m*.

lead[2] (led) *n* **1** plomb *m*. **2** (of a pencil) mine *f*. *vt* plomber.

leaf (li:f) *n*, *pl* **leaves 1** *bot* feuille *f*. **2** rallonge *f*. **leaflet** *n* tract, prospectus *m*.

league (li:g) *n* ligue *f*.

leak (li:k) *n* fuite *f*. écoulement *m*. *vi* **1** fuir. **2** faire eau. **leak out** s'ébruiter.

lean*[1] (li:n) *vi* s'appuyer, s'incliner. *vt* incliner, appuyer. **lean out** se pencher. ~*n* inclinaison *f*.

lean[2] (li:n) *adj* maigre.

leap* (li:p) *n* saut, bond *m*. *vi* sauter, bondir. *vt* franchir. **leapfrog** *n* saute-mouton *m*. **leap year** *n* année bissextile *f*.

learn* (lə:n) *vi,vt* apprendre. **learned** *adj* savant, érudit. **learner** *n* débutant.

lease (li:s) *n* bail *m*, *pl* baulx. *vt* louer, donner à bail. **leasehold** *n* location à bail *f*.

leash (li:ʃ) *n* laisse, attache *f*. *vt* attacher.

least (li:st) *adj* le *or* la moindre. *n* moins *m*. **at least** au moins. ~*adv* le moins.

leather (ˈleðə) *n* cuir *m*.

leave*[1] (li:v) *vt* **1** laisser. **2** quitter. **3** abandonner. **4** léguer. *vi* partir, s'en aller. **leave out** omettre, oublier.

leave[2] (li:v) *n* **1** permission *f*. **2** congé *m*.

Lebanon (ˈlebənən) *n* Liban *m*. **Lebanese** *adj,n* libanais.

lecherous (ˈletʃərəs) *adj* lascif -ive, débauché.

lectern (ˈlektən) *n* lutrin *m*.

lecture (ˈlektʃə) *n* **1** conférence *f*. cours *m*. **2** *inf* semonce *f*. *vi* donner une conférence. *vt* réprimander. **lecturer** *n* conférencier, chargé de cours *m*.

led (led) *v* see **lead.**

ledge (ledʒ) *n* rebord *m*. saillie *f*.

ledger (ˈledʒə) *n* grand livre *m*.

lee (li:) *n* **1** abri *m*. **2** *naut* côté sous le vent *m*.

leech (li:tʃ) *n* sangsue *f*.

leek (li:k) *n* poireau, -aux *m*.

leer (liə) *n* œillade (en dessous) *f*. regard polisson *m*. *vi* lorgner, guigner.

left[1] (left) *adj,n* gauche *f*. **left-hand** *adj* à gauche. **left-handed** *adj* gaucher, -ère. **left-wing** *adj* gauchiste, de gauche.

left[2] (left) *v* see **leave. left-luggage office** *n* consigne *m*.

leg (leg) *n* **1** jambe *f*. **2** (of an animal) patte *f*. **3** (of furniture) pied *m*. **4** *cul* cuisse *f*. gigot *m*.

legacy (ˈlegəsi) *n* legs *m*.

legal (ˈli:gəl) *adj* licite, judiciaire, légal, -aux. **legalize** *vt* légaliser.

legend (ˈledʒənd) *n* légende, fable *f*. **legendary** *adj* légendaire.

legible (ˈledʒibl) *adj* lisible.

legion (ˈli:dʒən) *n* légion *f*.

legislate (ˈledʒisleit) *vi* faire les lois, légiférer. **legislation** *n* législation *f*.

legitimate (liˈdʒitimət) *adj* légitime.

leisure (ˈleʒə) *n* loisir *m*.

lemon (ˈlemən) *n* citron *m*. **lemonade** *n* limonade *f*. **lemon tree** *n* citronnier *m*.

lend* (lend) *vt* prêter.

length (leŋθ) *n* **1** longueur *f*. **2** durée *f*. **3** morceau, -aux *m*. **lengthen** *vt* allonger. *vi* s'allonger. **lengthy** *adj* long, longue.

lenient (ˈli:niənt) *adj* clément, indulgent. **leniently** *adv* avec clémence.

lens (lenz) *n* **1** lentille *f*. verre *m*. **2** *phot* objectif *m*.

lent (lent) *v* see **lend.**

Lent (lent) *n* Carême *m*.

lentil (ˈlentl̩) *n* lentille *f*.

Leo (ˈli:ou) *n* Lion *m*.

leopard (ˈlepəd) *n* léopard *m*.

leper (ˈlepə) *n* lépreux, -euse. **leprosy** *n* lèpre *f*. **leprous** *adj* lépreux, -euse.

lesbian (ˈlezbiən) *n* lesbienne *f*.

less (les) *adj* moindre. *adv,prep* moins. **less and less** de moins en moins. ~*n* moins *m*. **lessen** *vi* s'amoindrir. *vt* diminuer.

lesson (ˈlesən) *n* leçon *f*.

lest (lest) *conj* de peur que.

let* (let) *vt* **1** permettre, laisser. **2** louer. **let down 1** baisser. **2** allonger. **let in** laisser entrer. **let out** laisser sortir.

lethal (ˈli:θəl) *adj* mortel, -elle.

lethargy (ˈleθədʒi) *n* léthargie *f*.

letter (ˈletə) *n* lettre *f*. **letterbox** *n* boîte aux lettres *f*.

lettuce (ˈletis) *n* laitue *f*.

leukaemia (lu:ˈki:miə) *n* leucémie *f*.

level (ˈlevəl) *n* niveau, -aux *m*. *adj* de niveau, égal, -aux, en palier. *vt* **1** niveler, aplanir. **2** viser. **level crossing** *n* passage à niveau *m*. **level-headed** *adj* d'aplomb, pondéré.

lever (ˈli:və) *n* levier *m*.

levy (ˈlevi) *n* impôt *m*. *vt* lever, imposer.

lewd (lu:d) *adj* impudique.
liable ('laiəbəl) *adj* **1** *law* responsable. **2** sujet, -ette, exposé. **liability** *n* **1** responsabilité. **2** *pl* engagements *m pl.*
liaison (li'eizɔn) *n* liaison *f.*
liar ('laiə) *n* menteur, -euse.
libel ('laibəl) *n* diffamation, libelle *f.*
liberal ('libərəl) *adj,n* libéral -aux.
liberate ('libəreit) *vt* libérer.
liberty ('libəti) *n* liberté *f.*
Libra ('li:brə) *n* Balance *f.*
library ('laibrəri) *n* bibliothèque *f.* **librarian** *n* bibliothécaire *m,f.*
libretto (li'bretou) *n, pl* **-tos** *or* **-ti** *n* libretto, livret *m.*
Libya ('libiə) *n* Libye *f.* **Libyan** *adj,n* libyen, -enne.
licence ('laisəns) *n* **1** permis *m.* **2** autorisation *f.* **license** *vt* autoriser, patenter. **licensee** *n* patenté, gérant *m.*
lick (lik) *vt* lécher. **lick into shape** dégrossir. ~*n* coup de langue *m.*
lid (lid) *n* couvercle *m.*
lie[1] (lai) *n* mensonge *m.* *vi* mentir.
lie*[2] (lai) *vi* **1** être couché. **2** se trouver. **lie down** se coucher.
lieutenant (lef'tenənt) *n* lieutenant *m.* **lieutenant colonel** *n* lieutenant-colonel *m.*
life (laif) *n, pl* **lives 1** vie *f.* **2** vivacité *f.* entrain *m.* **lifebelt** *n* ceinture de sauvetage *f.* **lifeboat** *n* canot de sauvetage *m.* **lifebuoy** *n* bouée de sauvetage *f.* **lifeguard** *n* garde du corps *m.* **lifeline** *n* ligne de sauvetage, sauvegarde *f.* **lifetime** *n* vie *f.*
lift (lift) *vt* **1** lever, soulever. **2** voler. *vi* se lever. *n* ascenseur *m.* **give someone a lift** emmener quelqu'un dans sa voiture.
light*[1] (lait) *n* lumière, clarté *f.* jour *m.* *vt* **1** allumer. **2** éclairer. **lighthouse** *n* phare *m.* **lighting** *n* éclairage *m.*
light[2] (lait) *adj* **1** léger, -ère. **2** (of colour, etc.) clair. **light-hearted** *adj* allègre. **lightweight** *n* poids léger *m.* *adj* léger, -ère.
light*[3] (lait) *vi* **light upon** tomber sur.
lighten[1] ('laitn̩) *vt* éclairer. *vi* s'éclairer, s'illuminer.
lighten[2] ('laitn̩) *vt* alléger, réduire.
lightning ('laitniŋ) *n* éclair *m.* foudre *f.*
like[1] (laik) *adj* pareil, -eille, semblable. *prep* comme. **likelihood** *n* probabilité *f.* **likewise** *adv* également, de même.
like[2] (laik) *vt* **1** aimer. **2** vouloir. **liking** *n* goût, gré *m.*
likely ('laikli) *adj* **1** probable. **2** susceptible. *adv* probablement.
lilac ('lailək) *n* lilas *m.*
lily ('lili) *n* lis *m.* **lily-of-the-valley** *n* muguet *m.*
limb (lim) *n* membre *m.*
limbo ('limbou) *n* limbes *m pl.*
lime[1] (laim) *n* chaux *f.* **in the limelight** *adv* en vedette. **limestone** *n* pierre à chaux *f.*
lime[2] (laim) *n bot* limon. **lime tree** *n* **1** limonier *m.* **2** tilleul *m.*
limerick ('limərik) *n* poème comique *m.*
limit ('limit) *n* limite, borne *f.* **that's the limit!** ça c'est le comble! ~*vt* limiter, borner, restreindre. **limitation** *n* limitation, restriction *f.*
limp[1] (limp) *vi* boiter. *n* boitement *m.*
limp[2] (limp) *adj* flasque, mou, molle.
limpet ('limpit) *n* patelle, bernique *f.*
linden ('lindn̩) *n* tilleul *m.*
line[1] (lain) *n* **1** ligne *f.* **2** corde *f.* **3** trait *m.* **4** compagnie *f.* **5** (railway) voie *f.* *vt* ligner, régler. **lineage** *n* lignée *f.* **linear** *adj* linéaire.
line[2] (lain) *vt* (of clothes, etc.) doubler.
linen ('linin) *n* **1** toile *f.* **2** linge *m.* **linen basket** *n* panier à linge, corbeille *f.*
liner ('lainə) *n* paquebot, transatlantique *m.*
linger ('liŋgə) *vi* trainer, lambiner.
lingerie ('lɔnʒəri:) *n* lingerie *f.*
linguist ('liŋgwist) *n* linguiste *m,f.* **linguistic** *adj* linguistique. **linguistics** *n* linguistique *f.*
lining ('lainiŋ) *n* doublure *f.*
link (liŋk) *n* **1** chaînon, maillon *m.* **2** lien *m.* *vt* **1** attacher. **2** lier.
linoleum (li'nouliəm) *n* linoléum *m.* **lino** *n inf* lino *m.*
linseed ('linsi:d) *n* graine de lin *f.* **linseed oil** *n* huile de lin *f.*
lion ('laiən) *n* lion *m.*
lip (lip) *n* **1** *anat* lèvre *f.* **2** (of animals) babine *f.* **3** bord *m.* **lip-read** *vi* lire sur les lèvres. **lipstick** *n* rouge à lèvres *m.*
liqueur (li'kjuə) *n* liqueur *f.*
liquid ('likwid) *adj,n* liquide *m.* **liquidate** *vt* liquider. **liquidize** *vt* liquéfier.
liquor ('likə) *n* boisson alcoolique *f.*
liquorice ('likəris) *n* réglisse *f.*
lira ('liərə) *n* lire *f.*
lisp (lisp) *n* zézaiement *m.* *vi,vt* zézayer.
list[1] (list) *n* liste *f.* *vt* cataloguer.
list[2] (list) *n naut* bande *f.* faux bord *m.* *vi* donner de la bande.
listen ('lisən) *vi* écouter.
listless ('listləs) *adj* nonchalant, apathique.
lit (lit) *v* see **light.**

litany (ˈlitəni) *n* litanies *f pl*.
literal (ˈlitərəl) *adj* littéral, -aux.
literary (ˈlitərəri) *adj* littéraire.
literate (ˈlitərət) *adj* qui sait lire et écrire.
literature (ˈlitərətʃə) *n* littérature *f*.
litre (ˈli:tə) *n* litre *m*.
litter (ˈlitə) *n* **1** fouillis *m*. **2** *zool* portée *f*. *vt* mettre en désordre. **litter-bin** *n* poubelle *f*.
little (ˈlitl) *adj* **1** petit. **2** peu de. *n* peu *m*. **little by little** petit à petit. ~*adv* peu. **little finger** *n* petit doigt *m*. **little toe** *n* petit orteil *m*.
liturgy (ˈlitədʒi) *n* liturgie *f*.
live[1] (liv) *vi* **1** vivre. **2** demeurer, habiter. *vt* mener. **live down** faire oublier.
live[2] (laiv) *adj* **1** vivant. **2** (of a wire, etc.) en charge. **livestock** *n* bétail *m*, *pl* bestiaux.
livelihood (ˈlaivlihud) *n* vie *f*. gagne-pain *m invar*.
lively (ˈlaivli) *adj* animé, plein d'entrain. **liveliness** *n* vivacité *f*. entrain *m*.
liver (ˈlivə) *n* foie *m*.
livid (ˈlivid) *adj* **1** blême. **2** enragé, emporté.
living (ˈliviŋ) *n* **1** vie *f*. **2** *rel* bénéfice *m*. *adj* vivant. **living room** *n* salle de séjour *f*.
lizard (ˈlizəd) *n* lézard *m*.
llama (ˈlɑ:mə) *n* lama *m*.
load (loud) *n* **1** charge *f*. **2** *inf* quantité *f*. tas *m*. *vt* charger.
loaf[1] (louf) *n*, *pl* **loaves** pain *m*. miche *f*.
loaf[2] (louf) *vi* **loaf about** flâner, fainéanter.
loan (loun) *n* **1** prêt *m*. avance *f*. **2** emprunt *m*. *vt* prêter.
loathe (louð) *vt* haïr, détester.
lob (lɔb) *n* chandelle *f*. *vt* envoyer en chandelle.
lobby (ˈlɔbi) *n* **1** vestibule *m*. **2** groupe de pression *m*. **3** *pol* couloirs *m pl*. *vi* faire les couloirs.
lobe (loub) *n* lobe *m*.
lobster (ˈlɔbstə) *n* homard *m*.
local (ˈloukəl) *adj* local, -aux, du pays. **locals** *n pl* gens du pays *m pl*. **locality** *n* localité *f*. parages *m pl*. **localize** *vt* localiser. **locate** *vt* situer, localiser. **location** *n* emplacement, repérage *m*.
loch (lɔx) *n* lac *m*.
lock[1] (lɔk) *n* **1** serrure *f*. **2** (of a canal) écluse *f*. *vt* fermér à clef.
lock[2] (lɔk) *n* (of hair) mèche, boucle *f*.
locker (ˈlɔkə) *n* armoire *f*. coffre *m*.
locket (ˈlɔkit) *n* médaillon *m*.
locomotive (loukəˈmoutiv) *adj,n* locomotif, -ive *m*.
locust (ˈloukəst) *n* criquet *m*. sauterelle *f*.
lodge (lɔdʒ) *n* loge *f*. *vt* **1** loger. **2** déposer. *vi* se loger. **lodger** *n* pensionnaire *m,f*. **lodgings** *n pl* logis, logement *m*.
loft (lɔft) *n* grenier *m*. soupente *f*. **lofty** *adj* **1** haut. **2** élevé.
log (lɔg) *n* bûche *f*. **logbook** *n* **1** *naut* journal de bord *m*. **2** *mot* carnet de route *m*. *vt* enregistrer.
logarithm (ˈlɔgəriðəm) *n* logarithme *m*.
logic (ˈlɔdʒik) *n* logique *f*. **logical** *adj* logique.
loins (lɔinz) *n pl* reins *m pl*.
loiter (ˈlɔitə) *vi* flâner, traîner.
lollipop (ˈlɔlipɔp) *n* sucette *f*.
London (ˈlʌndən) *n* Londres *m*.
lonely (ˈlounli) *adj* solitaire, isolé. **loneliness** *n* solitude *f*. isolement *m*.
long[1] (lɔŋ) *adj* long, longue. *adv* longtemps. **long-distance** *adj* **1** à longue distance. **2** (of a telephone) interurbain. **long-playing record** *n* microsillon *m*. **long-range** *adj* à longue portée. **long-sighted** *adj* **1** presbyte, hypermétrope. **2** prévoyant. **longstanding** *adj* de longue date. **long wave** *n* onde longue *f*. **longwinded** *adj* **1** interminable. **2** verbeux, -euse.
long[2] (lɔŋ) *vi* **long for** désirer ardemment. **longing** *n* désir ardent *m*.
longevity (lɔnˈdʒeviti) *n* longévité *f*.
longitude (ˈlɔndʒitju:d) *n* longitude *f*.
loo (lu:) *n inf* cabinets *m pl*.
look (luk) *n* **1** regard *m*. **2** apparence, mine *f*. *vi* **1** regarder. **2** avoir l'air. **look after** soigner, s'occuper de. **look for** chercher. **look forward to** s'attendre à. **look out** faire attention. **look out of** regarder par.
loom[1] (lu:m) *n* métier à tisser *m*.
loom[2] (lu:m) *vi* apparaître indistinctement, se dessiner.
loop (lu:p) *n* boucle *f*. *vt,vi* boucler.
loophole (ˈlu:phoul) *n* **1** trou *m*. ouverture *f*. **2** échappatoire *f*.
loose (lu:s) *vt* détacher, délier. **2** relâcher. *adj* **1** lâche. **2** branlant. **3** détaché. **4** dissolu. **loosen** *vt* **1** relâcher. **2** desserrer. **3** défaire. *vi* **1** se défaire. **2** se délier.
loot (lu:t) *vt* piller, saccager. *n* butin *m*.
lop (lɔp) *vt* élaguer. **lop off** couper.
lopsided (lɔpˈsaidid) *adj* de guingois, déjeté.
lord (lɔ:d) *n* **1** maître *m*. **2** *cap rel* Seigneur *m*. **3** *cap* (title) Lord *m*. *v* **lord it** faire l'important. **lordship** *n* **1** suzeraineté *f*. **2** *cap* Seigneurie *f*. Monseigneur *m*.
lorry (ˈlɔri) *n* camion *m*.

lose* (lu:z) *vt,vi* perdre.
loss (lɔs) *n* perte *f*. **be at a loss** être désorienté.
lost (lɔst) *v* see **lose.**
lot (lɔt) *n* **1** sort *m*. **2** tas *m*. **3** tout *m*. **a lot (of)** beaucoup (de).
lotion (ˈlouʃən) *n* lotion *f*.
lottery (ˈlɔtəri) *n* lotterie *f*.
loud (laud) *adj* **1** haut, fort. **2** (of a person, etc.) bruyant. **3** *inf* (of a colour) criard. **loud-mouthed** *adj inf* fort en gueule, braillard. **loudspeaker** *n* haut-parleur *m*.
lounge (laundʒ) *n* salon *m*. *vi* **1** flâner. **2** s'étendre.
louse (laus) *n*, *pl* **lice** pou, poux *m*. **lousy** *adj* **1** pouilleux, -euse. **2** *inf* sale. **3** *inf* môche.
love (lʌv) *n* **1** amour *m*. affection *f*. **2** *sport* rien *m*. **fall in love with** s'éprendre de. ~*vt* aimer. **lover** *n* amant *m*. **lovely** *adj* beau, belle. **loveliness** *n* **1** beauté *f*. **2** charme *m*.
low[1] (lou) *adj* **1** bas, basse, peu élevé. **2** vulgaire. **3** vil. **4** abattu. *adv* bas. **lowbrow** *adj* terre à terre *invar*. **lower-case** *adj* minuscule, bas de casse. **low-grade** *adj* de qualité inférieure. **lowland** *n* plaine basse *f*. **low-necked** *adj* décolleté. **low-pitched** *adj* grave.
low[2] (lou) *vi* meugler. *n* meuglement *m*.
lower (ˈlouə) *vt* baisser, abaisser.
loyal (ˈlɔiəl) *adj* fidèle, loyal, -aux. **loyalty** *n* fidélité *f*.
lozenge (ˈlɔzindʒ) *n med* pastille *f*.
LSD *n* LSD, drogue hallucinogène *f*.
lubricate (ˈlu:brikeit) *vt* lubrifier, graisser.
lucid (ˈlu:sid) *adj* lucide, clair.
luck (lʌk) *n* **1** hasard *m*. **2** bonheur *m*. chance *f*. **lucky** *adj* heureux, -euse, fortuné.
lucrative (ˈlu:krətiv) *adj* lucratif, -ive.
ludicrous (ˈlu:dikrəs) *adj* risible, grotesque.
lug (lʌg) *vt* traîner, tirer.
luggage (ˈlʌgidʒ) *n* bagages *m pl*. **luggage rack** *n* porte-bagages *m invar*
lukewarm (lu:kˈwɔ:m) *adj* tiède.
lull (lʌl) *n* calme *m*. trève *f*. *vt* **1** bercer. **2** endormir. *vi* se calmer. **lullaby** *n* berceuse *f*.
lumbago (ləmˈbeigou) *n* lumbago *m*.
lumber[1] (ˈlʌmbə) *n* **1** bois de charpente *m*. **2** fatras *m*. *vt* encombrer. **lumberjack** *n* bûcheron *m*.
lumber[2] (ˈlʌmbə) *vi* se trainer lourdement.
luminous (ˈlu:minəs) *adj* lumineux, -euse.
lump (lʌmp) *n* **1** bloc *m*. **2** grumeau, -aux *m*. **3** bosse *f*. **4** *sl* pataud *m*. *vt* mettre en tas. **lumpy** *adj* grumeleux, -euse.
lunacy (ˈlu:nəsi) *n* folie, démence *f*.
lunar (ˈlu:nə) *adj* lunaire.
lunatic (ˈlu:nətik) *n* fou, folle. *adj* aliéné.
lunch (lʌntʃ) *n* déjeuner *m*. *vi* déjeuner.
lung (lʌŋ) *n* poumon *m*.
lunge (lʌndʒ) *n* **1** *sport* botte *f*. **2** ruée *f*. *v* **lunge forward** se jeter en avant.
lurch[1] (lə:tʃ) *n* **1** embardée *f*. **2** cahot *m*. *vi* **1** faire une embardée. **2** tituber.
lurch[2] (lə:tʃ) *n* **leave in the lurch** laisser le bec dans l'eau.
lure (luə) *n* **1** leurre *m*. **2** piège *m*. *vt* **1** leurrer. **2** attirer, séduire.
lurid (ˈluərid) *adj* blafard.
lurk (lə:k) *vi* se cacher, rester tapis.
luscious (ˈlʌʃəs) *adj* succulent.
lush (lʌʃ) *adj* plein de sève.
lust (lʌst) *n* désir *m*. convoitise *f*.
lustre (ˈlʌstə) *n* lustre, éclat *m*. *vt* lustrer.
lute (lu:t) *n* luth *m*.
Luxembourg (ˈlʌksəmbə:g) *n* Luxembourg *m*.
luxury (ˈlʌkʃəri) *n* luxe *m*. **luxurious** *adj* somptueux, -euse.
lynch (lintʃ) *vt* lyncher.
lynx (liŋks) *n* lynx, loup-cervier *m*.
Lyons (ˈlaiənz) *n* Lyon *m*.
lyre (ˈlaiə) *n* lyre *f*.
lyrics (ˈliriks) *n* paroles *m pl*. **lyrical** *adj* lyrique.

M

mac (mæk) *n inf* imper *m*.
macabre (məˈkɑ:b) *adj* macabre.
mace[1] (meis) *n* masse *f*.
mace[2] (meis) *n cul* muscade *f*.
machine (məˈʃi:n) *n* machine *f*. appareil *m*. **machine-gun** *n* mitrailleuse *f*. **machinery** *n* machines *f pl*. mécanisme *m*. **machinist** *n* **1** machiniste *m*. **2** mécanicienne *f*.
mackerel (ˈmækrəl) *n* maquereau, -aux *m*.
mackintosh (ˈmækintɔʃ) *n* imperméable *m*.
mad (mæd) *adj* fou, folle. **madness** *n* folie, démence *f*.
madam (ˈmædəm) *n* madame, mesdames *f*.
made (meid) *v* see **make.**
Madonna (məˈdɔnə) *n* Madone *f*.
madrigal (ˈmædrigəl) *n* madrigal, -aux *m*.
magazine (mægəˈzi:n) *n* **1** magazine *m*. revue *f*. **2** *mil* magasin *m*.
maggot (ˈmægət) *n* ver, asticot *m*.
magic (ˈmædʒik) *n* magie *f*. *adj* magique, enchanté. **magician** *n* magicien, -ienne.

magistrate (ˈmædʒistreit) *n* magistrat *m*.

magnanimous (mægˈnæniməs) *adj* magnanime.

magnate (ˈmægneit) *n* magnat *m*.

magnet (ˈmægnit) *n* aimant *m*. **magnetic** *adj* magnétique. **magnetism** *n* **1** magnétisme *m*. **2** aimantation *f*. **magnetize** *vt* **1** magnétiser. **2** aimanter.

magnificent (mægˈnifisənt) *adj* magnifique.

magnify (ˈmægnifai) *vt* grossir, agrandir. **magnifying glass** *n* loupe *f*.

magnitude (ˈmægnitju:d) *n* **1** grandeur *f*. **2** importance *f*.

magpie (ˈmægpai) *n* pie *f*.

mahogany (məˈhɔgəni) *n* acajou *m*.

maid (meid) *n* **1** domestique *f*. **2** jeune fille *f*. **maiden** *n* jeune fille *f*. *adj* **1** non mariée. **2** premier, -ière, inaugural, -aux. **maiden name** *n* nom de jeune fille *m*.

mail (meil) *n* courrier *m*. poste *f*. *vt* envoyer par la poste, expédier. **mail order** *n* commande par correspondance *f*. **mailing list** *n* liste des abonnés *f*.

maim (meim) *vt* mutiler.

main (mein) *adj* principal, -aux, essentiel, -elle. *n* (pipe, wire, etc.) conduite principale *f*. **mainland** *n* continent *m*. **mainly** *adv* surtout. **mainsail** *n* grand-voile *f*.

maintain (meinˈtein) *vt* **1** maintenir. **2** soutenir. **3** garder. **maintenance** *n* **1** entretien *m*. **2** *law* pension alimentaire *f*.

maize (meiz) *n* maïs *m*.

majesty (ˈmædʒisti) *n* majesté *f*. **majestic** *adj* majestueux, -euse.

major (ˈmeidʒə) *adj* majeur, principal, -aux. *n* *mil* commandant *m*. **major general** *n* général de division *m*. **majority** *n* majorité *f*.

Majorca (məˈdʒɔ:kə) *n* Majorque *f*.

make* (meik) *n* **1** marque *f*. **2** fabrication *f*. *vt* **1** faire. **2** fabriquer, confectionner. **3** rendre. **make for** se diriger vers. **make off** filer. **make over** céder. **make up 1** compléter. **2** rattraper. **3** inventer. **4** se maquiller. **make-up** *n* maquillage *m*. **make up one's mind** se décider. **make-believe** *n* semblant *m*. feinte *f*. *adj* fictif, -ive. **maker** *n* fabricant *m*. **makeshift** *n* pis-aller *m invar*. *adj* de fortune.

maladjusted (mæləˈdʒʌstid) *adj* inadapté.

malaria (məˈlɛəriə) *n* malaria *f*.

Malaya (məˈleiə) *n* Malaisie *f*. **Malay** *adj,n* malais. **Malay** (language) *n* malais *m*.

Malaysia (məˈleiziə) *n* Malaysia *f*. **Malaysian** *adj,n* malais.

male (meil) *adj,n* mâle *m*.

malice (ˈmælis) *n* malveillance, rancune *f*. **malicious** *adj* malveillant, malicieux, -euse.

malignant (məˈlignənt) *adj* **1** malin, maligne. **2** méchant.

mallet (ˈmælət) *n* maillet *m*.

malt (mɔ:lt) *n* malt *m*.

Malta (ˈmɔ:ltə) *n* Malte *f*. **Maltese** *adj,n* maltais.

maltreat (mælˈtri:t) *vt* maltraiter.

mammal (ˈmæməl) *n* mammifère *m*.

mammoth (ˈmæməθ) *n* mammouth *m*. *adj* énorme.

man (mæn) *n*, *pl* **men 1** homme *m*. **2** employé *m*. **3** *game* pièce *f*. pion *m*. *vt* armer, garnir. **manhandle** *vt* **1** manutentionner. **2** maltraiter. **manhole** *n* regard *m*. **manhood** *n* maturité, virilité *f*. **man-made** *adj* artificiel, -elle. **manpower** *n* main-d'œuvre *f*. **manslaughter** *n* homicide *m*.

Man, Isle of (mæn) *n* île de Man *f*.

manage (ˈmænidʒ) *vt* **1** diriger, administrer, gérer. **2** venir à bout de. **3** manœuvrer. *vi* se débrouiller. **manageable** *adj* maniable. **management** *n* **1** direction, gestion *f*. **2** administration *f*. **manager** *n* directeur, gérant *m*. **manageress** *n* directrice, gérante *f*. **managing director** *n* administrateur gérant *m*.

mandarin (ˈmændərin) *n* **1** mandarin *m*. **2** *bot* mandarine *f*.

mandate (ˈmændeit) *n* mandat *m*. **mandatory** *adj* obligatoire.

mandolin (ˈmændəlin) *n* mandoline *f*.

mane (mein) *n* crinière *f*.

mange (meindʒ) *n* gale *f*. **mangy** *adj* galeux, -euse.

mangle[1] (ˈmæŋgəl) *vt* **1** taillader. **2** dénaturer.

mangle[2] (ˈmæŋgəl) *n* calandre *f*. *vt* calandrer.

mango (ˈmæŋgou) *n*, *pl* **-oes** *or* **-os** mangue *f*.

mania (ˈmeiniə) *n* **1** manie, passion *f*. **2** *med* folie *f*. **maniac** *adj,n* fou, folle, furieux, -euse. **manic** *adj* qui tient de la folie.

manicure (ˈmænikjuə) *n* soins des mains *m pl*. *vt* soigner les mains.

manifest (ˈmænifest) *vt,vi* manifester. *adj* manifeste, évident.

manifesto (mæniˈfestou) *n* manifeste *m*.

manifold (ˈmænifould) *adj* multiple, varié.

manipulate (məˈnipjuleit) *vt* manipuler, actionner. **manipulation** *n* manipulation *f*.

mankind (ˈmænkaind) *n* genre humain *m*.

manner (ˈmænə) *n* **1** manière, façon *f*. **2** *pl*

mœurs *f pl.* **3** *pl* manières *f pl.* savoir-vivre *m.* **mannerism** *n* maniérisme *m.*
manoeuvre (mə'nu:və) *vt,vi* manœuvrer. *n* manœuvre *f.*
manor ('mænə) *n* manoir *m.*
mansion ('mænʃən) *n* château, -aux, hôtel particulier *m.*
mantelpiece ('mæntəlpi:s) *n* dessus de cheminée *m.*
mantle ('mæntl̩) *n* **1** cape *f.* **2** manteau, -aux *m.* *vt* couvrir.
manual ('mænjuəl) *adj,n* manuel, -elle *m.*
manufacture (mænju'fæktʃə) *vt* manufacturer, fabriquer. *n* **1** fabrication *f.* **2** produit manufacturé *m.* **manufacturer** *n* fabricant, industriel *m.*
manure (mə'njuə) *n* fumier *m.* *vt* fumer.
manuscript ('mænjuskript) *adj,n* manuscrit *m.*
Manx (mæŋks) *adj* de l'île de Man.
many ('meni) *adj* beaucoup (de), bien des, nombreux, -euse. *n* multitude, foule *f.* **as many as** autant que. **how many?** combien? **many a** maint. **so many** tant (de). **too many** trop (de).
Maori ('mauri) *adj,n* maori.
map (mæp) *n* **1** carte *f.* **2** (of a town) plan *m.*
maple ('meipəl) *n* érable *m.*
mar (mɑ:) *vt* gâcher, troubler.
marathon ('mærəθən) *n* marathon *m.*
marble ('mɑ:bəl) *n* **1** marbre *m.* **2** *game* bille *f.*
march (mɑ:tʃ) *n* marche *f.* *vi* marcher. *vt* faire marcher. **march past** défiler.
March (mɑ:tʃ) *n* mars *m.*
marchioness ('mɑ:ʃənis) *n* marquise *f.*
mare (mɛə) *n* jument *f.*
margarine (mɑ:dʒə'ri:n) *n* margarine *f.*
margin ('mɑ:dʒin) *n* **1** marge *f.* **2** bord *m.* **marginal** *adj* marginal, -aux.
marigold ('mærigould) *n* souci *m.*
marijuana (mæri'wɑ:nə) *n* marijuana *f.*
marinade (mæri'neid) *n* marinade *f.* **marinate** *vt* mariner.
marine (mə'ri:n) *adj* **1** marin, maritime. **2** de marine. *n* marine *f.*
marital ('mæritl̩) *adj* **1** marital, -aux. **2** matrimonial, -aux.
maritime ('mæritaim) *adj* maritime.
marjoram ('mɑ:dʒərəm) *n* marjolaine *f.*
mark[1] (mɑ:k) *n* **1** marque *f.* **2** but *m.* **3** note *f.* *vt* **1** marquer. **2** noter. **3** corriger. **markedly** *adv* nettement. **marksman** *n* tireur d'élite *m.*
mark[2] (mɑ:k) *n* *comm* mark *m.*
market ('mɑ:kit) *n* **1** marché *m.* **2** débouché *m.* *vt* lancer sur le marché. **market garden** *n* jardin maraîcher *m.* **marketplace** *n* marché *m.* **market research** *n* étude du marché *f.* **market town** *n* bourg *m.*
marmalade ('mɑ:məleid) *n* confiture d'oranges *f.*
maroon[1] (mə'ru:n) *adj,n* marron *m.*
maroon[2] (mə'ru:n) *vt* abandonner.
marquee (mɑ:'ki:) *n* marquise, grande tente *f.*
marquess ('mɑ:kwis) *n* marquis *m.*
marriage ('mæridʒ) *n* mariage *m.* **marriage certificate** *n* acte de mariage *m.*
marrow ('mærou) *n* **1** moelle *f.* **2** *bot* courge *f.* **marrowbone** *n* os à moelle *m.*
marry ('mæri) *vt* marier, épouser. *vi* se marier avec.
Mars (mɑ:z) *n* Mars *m.*
Marseillaise (mɑ:sə'leiz) *n* Marseillaise *f.*
Marseilles (mɑ:'sei) *n* Marseille *f.*
marsh (mɑ:ʃ) *n* marécage, marais *m.* **marshy** *adj* marécageux, -euse. **marshmallow** *n* guimauve *f.*
marshal ('mɑ:ʃəl) *n* **1** maréchal, -aux *m.* **2** maître des cérémonies *m.* *vt* ranger.
marsupial (mɑ:'sju:piəl) *adj,n* marsupial, -aux *m.*
martial ('mɑ:ʃəl) *adj* martial, -aux.
martin ('mɑ:tin) *n* martinet *m.*
martini (mɑ:'ti:ni) *n* martini *m.*
martyr ('mɑ:tə) *n* martyr *m.* *vt* martyriser. **martyrdom** *n* martyre *m.*
marvel ('mɑ:vəl) *n* merveille *f.* *vi* s'étonner. **marvellous** *adj* merveilleux, -euse.
Marxism ('mɑ:ksizəm) *n* marxisme *m.* **marxist** *adj,n* marxiste.
marzipan ('mɑ:zipæn) *n* massepain *m.*
mascara (mæ'skɑ:rə) *n* mascara *m.*
mascot ('mæskɔt) *n* mascotte *f.* porte-bonheur *m invar.*
masculine ('mæskjulin) *adj* masculin, mâle. *n* masculin *m.*
mash (mæʃ) *n* **1** pâtée *f.* **2** *cul* purée *f.* *vt* écraser.
mask (mɑ:sk) *n* masque *m.* *vt* **1** masquer. **2** cacher, voiler.
masochism ('mæsəkizəm) *n* masochisme *m.* **masochist** *adj,n* masochiste.
mason ('meisən) *n* maçon *m.* **masonry** *n* maçonnerie *f.*
masquerade (mæskə'reid) *n* mascarade *f.* *vi* se déguiser.
mass[1] (mæs) *n* **1** masse *f.* **2** foule *f.* *vt* masser. *vi* se masser. **mass media** *n pl* moyens

publicitaires de masse *m pl.* **mass-produce** *vt* fabriquer en série.

mass[2] (mæs) *n rel* messe *f.*

massacre ('mæsəkə) *n* massacre *m. vt* massacrer.

massage ('mæsɑ:ʒ) *n* massage *m. vt* masser.

massive ('mæsiv) *adj* massif, -ive.

mast (mɑ:st) *n* **1** *naut* mât *m.* **2** pylône *m.* **masthead** *n* tête de mât *f.*

mastectomy (mæs'tektəmi) *n* mastectomie *f.*

master ('mɑstə) *n* **1** maître *m.* **2** patron, chef *m.* **3** professeur *m.* **Master of Arts/Science** licencié ès lettres/sciences *m.* ~*vt* **1** maîtriser. **2** surmonter. *adj* **1** principal, -aux. **2** de maître. **masterful** *adj* autoritaire. **mastermind** *n* esprit supérieur *m.* **masterpiece** *n* chef-d'œuvre *m.*

masturbate ('mæstəbeit) *vi* se masturber. **masturbation** *n* masturbation *f.*

mat (mæt) *n* **1** natte *f.* **2** tapis *m.* **3** dessous de plat *m. vt* emmêler, tresser. *vi* s'emmêler.

match[1] (mætʃ) *n* allumette *f.* **matchbox** *n* boîte d'allumettes *f.* **matchstick** *n* allumette *f.*

match[2] (mætʃ) *n* **1** match *m.* lutte, partie *f.* **2** égal, -aux *m.* **3** mariage *m.* **4** assortiment *m.* *vt* **1** égaler. **2** assortir. *vi* s'assortir, s'harmoniser. **matchless** *adj* incomparable.

mate (meit) *n* **1** compagnon, compagne. **2** *naut* officier *m. vt* accoupler. *vi* s'accoupler.

material (mə'tiəriəl) *n* **1** matière *f.* **2** (for building, etc.) matériaux *m pl.* **3** étoffe, tissu *m. adj* **1** matériel, -aux. **2** essentiel, -elle. **raw material** *n* matière première *f.* **materialism** *n* matérialisme *m.* **materialist** *n* matérialiste *m,f.* **materialistic** *adj* matérialiste. **materialize** *vi* se réaliser.

maternal (mə'tə:nl) *adj* maternel, -elle. **maternity** *n* maternité *f.*

mathematics (mæθə'mætiks) *n* mathématiques *f pl.* **mathematical** *adj* mathématique.

matins ('mætinz) *n pl* matines *f pl.*

matinee ('mætinei) *n* matinée *f.*

matriarchal ('meitriɑ:kəl) *adj* matriarcal, -aux.

matrimony ('mætriməni) *n* mariage *m.* **matrimonial** *adj* matrimonial, -aux.

matrix ('meitriks) *n, pl* **-rices** matrice *f.*

matron ('meitrən) *n* **1** intendante *f.* **2** infirmière en chef *f.* **3** matrone *f.*

matter ('mætə) *n* **1** matière *f.* **2** affaire *f.* **3** sujet *m.* **4** *med* pus *m.* **what's the matter?** qu'y a-t-il? ~*vi* importer. **matter-of-fact** *adj* pratique.

Matterhorn ('mætəhɔ:n) *n* Mont Cervin *m.*

mattress ('mætrəs) *n* matelas *m.*

mature (mə'tjuə) *adj* **1** mûr. **2** *comm* échu. *vt,vi* mûrir. **maturity** *n* **1** maturité *f.* **2** *comm* échéance *f.*

maudlin ('mɔ:dlin) *adj* larmoyant, pleurard.

maul (mɔ:l) *vt* malmener, meurtrir.

Maundy Thursday ('mɔ:ndi) *n* jeudi saint *m.*

mausoleum (mɔ:sə'liəm) *n* mausolée *m.*

mauve (mouv) *adj,n* mauve *m.*

maxim ('mæksim) *n* maxime *f.* dicton *m.*

maximum ('mæksiməm) *adj* maximum, limite. *n, pl* **-ums** *or* **-a** maximum *m.* **maximize** *vt* maximiser.

may* (mei) *v mod aux* pouvoir. **that may be** cela se peut. **maybe** *adv* peut-être.

May (mei) *n* mai *m.* **May Day** *n* premier mai *m.* **maypole** *n* mai *m.*

mayonnaise (meiə'neiz) *n* mayonnaise *f.*

mayor ('mɛə) *n* maire *m.* **mayoress** *n* mairesse *f.*

maze (meiz) *n* labyrinthe *m.*

me (mi:) *pron 1st pers s* **1** me. **2** moi.

meadow ('medou) *n* prairie *f.*

meagre ('mi:gə) *adj* maigre.

meal[1] (mi:l) *n* repas *m.*

meal[2] (mi:l) *n* farine *f.* **mealy** *adj* farineux, -euse.

mean*[1] (mi:n) *vt* **1** vouloir dire, signifier. **2** avoir l'intention de. **meaning** *n* signification *f.* sens *m.* **meaningful** *adj* significatif, -ive.

mean[2] (mi:n) *adj* **1** avare, mesquin. **2** méprisable.

meander (mi'ændə) *n* méandre *m. vi* serpenter.

means (mi:nz) *n pl* **1** moyen *m.* **2** ressources *f pl.* moyens *m pl.* **by means of** au moyen de.

meantime ('mi:ntaim) *adv* **in the meantime** dans l'intervalle.

meanwhile ('mi:nwail) *adv* dans l'intervalle.

measles ('mi:zəlz) *n pl* rougeole *f.*

measure ('meʒə) *n* mesure *f. vt* mesurer. **measurement** *n* mesure, dimension *f.*

meat (mi:t) *n* viande *f.*

mechanic (mi'kænik) *n* mécanicien *m.* **mechanical** *adj* mécanique. **mechanical engineering** *n* construction mécanique *f.* **mechanics** *n* **1** mécanique *f.* **2** *pl* mécanisme *m.* **mechanism** *n* mécanisme *m.* **mechanize** *vt* mécaniser. **mechanization** *n* mécanisation *f.*

medal ('medl) *n* médaille *f.* **medallion** *n* médaillon *m.*

meddle ('medl) *vi* **meddle in** s'immiscer dans.

media (ˈmi:diə) *n pl* voie *f.* moyen *m.*
medial (ˈmi:diəl) *adj* moyen, -enne, intermédiaire.
median (ˈmi:diən) *adj* médian. *n math* médiane *f.*
mediate (ˈmi:dieit) *vi* s'entremettre, intervenir. **mediation** *n* médiation *f.* **mediator** *n* médiateur *m.*
medical (ˈmedikəl) *adj* médical, -aux. **medication** *n* médication *f.* **medicine** *n* **1** (science) médecine *f.* **2** médicament *m.*
medieval (mediˈi:vəl) *adj* médiéval, -aux.
mediocre (mi:diˈoukə) *adj* médiocre.
meditate (ˈmediteit) *vt,vi* méditer. **meditation** *n* méditation *f.* **meditative** *adj* méditatif, -ive.
Mediterranean (meditəˈreiniən) *adj* méditerranéen, -enne. **Mediterranean (Sea)** *n* (Mer) Mediterranée *f.*
medium (ˈmi:diəm) *n, pl* **media 1** moyen *m.* **2** milieu, -eux *m.* **3** intermédiaire *m.* **4** médium *m.* **happy medium** juste milieu. ~*adj* moyen, -enne.
meek (mi:k) *adj* doux, douce, humble. **meekly** *adv* avec douceur.
meet* (mi:t) *vt* **1** rencontrer. **2** faire la connaissance de. **3** satisfaire. *vt* **1** se rencontrer. **2** se réunir. **meet with** éprouver, trouver. **meeting** *n* **1** rencontre *f.* **2** assemblée, réunion *f.*
megaphone (ˈmegəfoun) *n* porte-voix *m invar.*
melancholy (ˈmelənkəli) *n* mélancolie *f.* *adj* mélancolique.
mellow (ˈmelou) *adj* **1** doux, douce. **2** moelleux, -euse. *vt,vi* mûrir.
melodrama (ˈmelədra:mə) *n* mélodrame *m.* **melodramatic** *adj* mélodramatique.
melody (ˈmelədi) *n* mélodie *f.* air *m.* **melodious** *adj* mélodieux, -euse.
melon (ˈmelən) *n* melon *m.*
melt (melt) *vt,vi* fondre. *vt* attendrir. **melting** *n* fusion *f.*
member (ˈmembə) *n* membre *m.* **member of Parliament** député *m.* **membership** *n* **1** cotisation *f.* **2** qualité de membre *f.*
membrane (ˈmembrein) *n* membrane *f.*
memento (məˈmentou) *n, pl* **-os** *or* **-oes** mémento, souvenir *m.*
memo (ˈmemou) *n* mémo *m.* note *f.*
memoir (ˈmemwa:) *n* mémoire *m.*
memorandum (meməˈrændəm) *n, pl* **-dums** *or* **-da** mémorandum *m.*
memory (ˈmeməri) *n* **1** mémoire *f.* **2** souvenir *m.* **memorable** *adj* mémorable. **memorial** *n* monument commémoratif *m.* *adj* commémoratif, -ive. **memorize** *vt* apprendre par cœur.
menace (ˈmenəs) *n* menace *f.* *vt* menacer.
menagerie (məˈnædʒəri) *n* ménagerie *f.*
mend (mend) *vt* **1** raccommoder. **2** réparer. **3** arranger. *vi* s'améliorer. *n* reprise *f.* **mending** *n* raccommodage *m.*
menial (ˈmi:niəl) *adj* servile.
menopause (ˈmenəpɔ:z) *n* ménopause *f.*
menstrual (ˈmenstruəl) *adj* menstruel, -elle. **menstruate** *vi* avoir ses règles.
mental (ˈmentl̩) *adj* **1** mental, -aux. **2** *inf* fou, folle. **mental hospital** *n* hôpital psychiatrique *m.* **mentality** *n* mentalité *f.*
menthol (ˈmenθɔl) *n* menthol *m.*
mention (ˈmenʃən) *n* mention *f.* *vt* mentionner.
menu (ˈmenju:) *n* menu *m.*
mercantile (ˈmə:kəntail) *adj* commercial, -aux.
mercenary (ˈmə:sənəri) *adj,n* mercenaire *m.*
merchant (ˈmə:tʃənt) *n* négociant, commerçant *m.* *adj* marchand, de commerce. **merchant bank** *n* banque commerciale *f.* **merchant navy** *n* marine marchande *f.* **merchandise** *n* marchandise *f.*
mercury (ˈmə:kjuri) *n* **1** mercure *m.* **2** *cap* Mercure *m.*
mercy (ˈmə:si) *n* **1** grâce, pitié *f.* **2** bienfait *m.* **merciful** *adj* clément. **merciless** *adj* impitoyable.
mere (miə) *adj* simple, pur.
merge (mə:dʒ) *vt* fusionner, fondre. *vi* **1** se fondre. **2** *comm* fusionner. **merger** *n* fusion *f.*
meridian (məˈridiən) *adj,n* méridien, -ienne *m.*
meringue (məˈræŋ) *n* meringue *f.*
merit (ˈmerit) *n* **1** mérite *m.* **2** valeur *f.* *vt* mériter.
mermaid (ˈmə:meid) *n* sirène *f.*
merry (ˈmeri) *adj* **1** joyeux, -euse, gai. **2** *inf* gris. **merry-go-round** *n* manège (de chevaux de bois) *m.*
mesh (meʃ) *n* maille *f.* *vt* engrener. *vi* être en prise.
mesmerize (ˈmezməraiz) *vt* hypnotiser.
mess (mes) *n* **1** saleté *f.* **2** gâchis *m.* confusion *f.* **3** *mil* mess *m.* **make a mess of** gâcher. ~*v* **mess up 1** gâcher. **2** salir.
message (ˈmesidʒ) *n* message *m.* **messenger** *n* messager, -ère.
met (met) *v see* **meet.**
metabolism (miˈtæbəlizəm) *n* métabolisme *m.*
metal (ˈmetl̩) *n* métal, -aux *m.* **metallic** *adj* métallique. **metallurgy** *n* métallurgie *f.* **metallurgical** *adj* métallurgique.

metamorphosis (metə'mɔ:fəsis) *n, pl* **-ses** métamorphose *f*.

metaphor ('metəfə) *n* métaphore *f*. **metaphorical** *adj* métaphorique.

metaphysics (metə'fiziks) *n* métaphysique *f*. **metaphysical** *adj* métaphysique.

meteor ('mi:tiə) *n* météore *m*. **meteorological** *adj* météorologique. **meteorologist** *n* météorologiste, météorologue *m,f*. **meteorology** *n* météorologie *f*.

meter ('mi:tə) *n* compteur *m*.

methane ('mi:θein) *n* méthane *m*.

method ('meθəd) *n* méthode *f*. procédé *m*. **methodical** *adj* méthodique.

Methodist ('meθədist) *adj,n* méthodiste.

meticulous (mi'tikjuləs) *adj* méticuleux, -euse.

metre ('mi:tə) *n* mètre *m*. **metric** *adj* métrique.

metropolis (mə'trɔpəlis) *n* métropole *f*. **metropolitan** *adj* métropolitain.

miaow (mi'au) *vi* miauler. *n* miaulement *m*.

microbe ('maikroub) *n* microbe *m*.

microphone ('maikrəfoun) *n* microphone *m*.

microscope ('maikrəskoup) *n* microscope *m*. **microscopic** *adj* microscopique.

mid (mid) *adj* mi, moyen, enne. **midday** *n* midi *m*. **midland** *adj* du centre. **midmorning** *n* mi-matin *m*. **midnight** *n* minuit *m*. **in midstream** *adv* au milieu de la rivière. **midsummer** *n* cœur de l'été *m*. **midway** *adv,adj* à mi-chemin. **midweek** *adj* du milieu de la semaine.

middle ('midḷ) *n* centre, milieu, -eux *m*. *adj* du milieu, moyen -enne. **middle-aged** *adj* d'un certain âge. **middle class** *n* bourgeoisie *f*. **middle-class** *adj* bourgeois. **middleman** *n* intermédiaire *m*.

Middle Ages *n* moyen âge *m*.

Middle East *n* Moyen Orient *m*.

midget ('midʒit) *n* nain *m*.

midst (midst) **in the midst of** *prep* parmi, au milieu de.

midwife ('midwaif) *n* sage-femme *f*.

might[1] (mait) *v* see **may**.

might[2] (mait) *n* force, puissance *f*. **mighty** *adj* 1 puissant. 2 vaste, énorme.

migraine ('mi:grein) *n* migraine *f*.

migrate (mai'greit) *vi* émigrer. **migration** *n* 1 migration *f*. 2 émigration *f*. **migratory** *adj* migrateur, -trice.

mike (maik) *n inf* micro *m*.

mild (maild) *adj* doux, douce. **mildness** *n* douceur *f*.

mildew ('mildju:) *n* 1 (on a plant) rouille *f*. 2 moisissure *f*.

mile (mail) *n* mille *m*. **mileage** *n* distance en milles *f*. **mileometer** *n* compteur kilométrique *m*. **milestone** *n* borne kilométrique *f*.

militant ('militənt) *adj,n* militant *m*. **military** *adj* militaire.

milk (milk) *n* lait *m*. *vt* traire. **milking** *n* traite *f*. **milkman** *n* laitier *m*.

Milky Way *n* Voie lactée *f*.

mill (mil) *n* 1 moulin *m*. 2 usine, fabrique *f*. *vt* moudre. *vi* fourmiller. **millstone** *n* meule *f*.

millennium (mi'leniəm) *n, pl* **-niums** *or* **-nia** millénaire *m*.

millet ('milit) *n* millet *m*.

milligram ('miligræm) *n* milligramme *m*.

millilitre ('milili:tə) *n* millilitre *m*.

millimetre ('milimi:tə) *n* millimètre *m*.

million ('miliən) *adj,n* million *m*. **millionaire** *n* millionnaire *m,f*. **millionth** *adj* millionième.

mime (maim) *n* mime *m*. *vt* mimer. *vi* imiter par gestes. **mimic** *n* mime *m*. *adj* 1 imitateur, -trice. 2 mimique. *vt* imiter, singer. **mimicry** *n* mimique, imitation *f*.

mince (mins) *vt* hacher. *vi* minauder. *n* hachis *m*. **mincer** *n* hachoir *m*.

mind (maind) *n* 1 esprit *m*. 2 mémoire *f*. 3 avis *m*. 4 envie *f*. *vt* 1 faire attention à. 2 surveiller. **I don't mind** 1 cela m'est égal. 2 je veux bien. **never mind!** peu importe!

mine[1] (main) *poss pron 1st pers s* 1 le mien, la mienne. 2 à moi.

mine[2] (main) *n* mine *f*. *vt* 1 exploiter. 2 *mil* miner. **miner** *n* mineur *m*.

mineral ('minərəl) *adj* minéral, -aux. *n* 1 minéral, -aux *m*. 2 *min* minerai *m*. **mineral water** *n* eau minérale *f*.

mingle ('miŋgəl) *vt* mêler. *vi* se mêler.

miniature ('miniətʃə) *n* miniature *f*. *adj* minuscule, en miniature.

minim ('minim) *n* blanche *f*.

minimum ('miniməm) *n, pl* **-mums** *or* **-ma** minimum *m*. **minimal** *adj* minimal, -aux, minime.

mining ('mainiŋ) *n* exploitation des mines *f*.

minister ('ministə) *n* ministre *m*. **ministerial** *adj* ministériel, -elle. **ministry** *n* ministère *m*.

mink (miŋk) *n* vison *m*.

minor ('mainə) *adj,n* mineur. **minority** *n* minorité *f*.

Minorca (mi'nɔ:kə) *n* Minorque *f*.

minstrel ('minstrəl) *n* ménestrel *m*.

mint[1] (mint) *n bot* menthe *f*.

mint[2] (mint) *n* Hôtel de la Monnaie *m*. *vt* **1** (a coin, etc.) battre, frapper. **2** forger.

minuet (minju'et) *n* menuet *m*.

minus ('mainəs) *prep* moins, sans. *adj* **1** moins. **2** négatif, -ive.

minute[1] ('minit) *n* **1** minute *f*. **2** instant *m*. **3** *pl* procès-verbal *m*.

minute[2] (mai'nju:t) *adj* **1** menu, minuscule. **2** minutieux, -euse.

miracle ('mirəkəl) *n* miracle *m*. **miraculous** *adj* miraculeux, -euse.

mirage ('mirɑ:ʒ) *n* mirage *m*.

mirror ('mirə) *n* miroir *m*.

mirth (mə:θ) *n* gaieté *f*.

misbehave (misbi'heiv) *vi* se conduire mal.

miscarriage (mis'kæridʒ) *n* **1** echec, insuccès *m*. **2** *med* fausse couche *f*. **miscarry** *vi* **1** échouer. **2** *med* avorter.

miscellaneous (misə'leiniəs) *adj* divers, varié. **miscellany** *n* mélange *m*.

mischance (mis'tʃɑ:ns) *n* malheur *m*. mésaventure *f*.

mischief ('mistʃif) *n* **1** mal *m,pl* maux. **2** malice *f*. **3** sottises *f pl*. **mischievous** *adj* **1** malfaisant. **2** espiègle.

misconceive (miskən'si:v) *vt* mal comprendre. **misconception** *n* **1** idée fausse *f*. **2** malentendu *m*.

misconduct (*n* mis'kɔndʌkt; *v* miskən'dʌkt) *n* **1** (of a person) inconduite *f*. **2** mauvaise gestion *f*. *vt* mal gérer.

misdeed (mis'di:d) *n* méfait *m*.

miser ('maizə) *n* avare *m,f*. **miserly** *adj* avare. **miserliness** *n* avarice *f*.

miserable ('mizərəbəl) *adj* **1** triste, malheureux, -euse. **2** misérable, pitoyable.

misery ('mizəri) *n* **1** souffrance *f*. **2** misère, détresse *f*.

misfire (mis'faiə) *vi* **1** rater. **2** tomber à plat.

misfit ('misfit) *n* **1** malfaçon *f*. **2** inadapté *m*.

misfortune (mis'fɔ:tʃən) *n* malheur *m*.

misgiving (mis'giviŋ) *n* doute, pressentiment *m*. crainte *f*.

misguided (mis'gaidid) *adj* **1** égaré. **2** hors de propos.

mishap ('mishæp) *n* mésaventure *f*.

mislay* (mis'lei) *vt* égarer.

mislead* (mis'li:d) *vt* **1** tromper. **2** fourvoyer.

misprint ('misprint) *n* faute d'impression *f*.

miss[1] (mis) *vt,vi* manquer, rater. **miss out** passer, omettre. *n* coup manqué *m*. **missing** *adj* **1** manquant, absent. **2** perdu.

miss[2] (mis) *n* **1** mademoiselle *f*. **2** *cap* (title of address) Mlle.

missile ('misail) *n* projectile *m*.

mission ('miʃən) *n* mission *f*. **missionary** *adj,n* missionnaire *m*.

mist (mist) *n* brume *f*.

mistake* (mis'teik) *n* erreur, faute *f*. **by mistake** par mégarde. ~*vt* **1** se méprendre (sur), se tromper de. **2** prendre. **mistaken** *adj* faux, fausse. **be mistaken** se tromper.

mister ('mistə) *n* monsieur *m*.

mistletoe ('misəltou) *n* gui *m*.

mistress ('mistrəs) *n* **1** maîtresse *f*. **2** *educ* professeur *m*.

mistrust (mis'trʌst) *vt* se méfier de. *n* méfiance *f*. **mistrustful** *adj* méfiant.

misunderstand* (misʌndə'stænd) *vt* mal comprendre. **misunderstanding** *n* **1** malentendu *m*. **2** mésentente *f*.

misuse (*v* mis'ju:z; *n* mis'ju:s) *vt* **1** faire mauvais usage de. **2** maltraiter. *n* abus, mauvais usage *m*.

mitre ('maitə) *n* mitre *f*.

mitten ('mitn̩) *n* mitaine *f*.

mix (miks) *vt* mélanger, mêler. *vi* se mélanger. **mix up 1** embrouiller. **2** confondre. **mixed** *adj* mixte. **mixed grill** *n* grillade variée *f*. **mixture** *n* **1** mélange *m*. **2** *med* potion *f*.

moan (moun) *vi* gémir. *n* plainte *f*.

moat (mout) *n* fossé *m*. douve *f*.

mob (mɔb) *n* cohue, foule *f*. *vt* **1** molester. **2** s'attrouper.

mobile ('moubail) *adj* mobile. **mobility** *n* mobilité *f*. **mobilize** *vt* mobiliser.

mock (mɔk) *vt,vi* se moquer de. *vt* imiter. *adj* simulé, faux, fausse. **mockery** *n* raillerie, moquerie *f*.

mode (moud) *n* **1** manière *f*. **2** mode *f*.

model ('mɔdl̩) *adj* modèle. *n* **1** modèle *m*. **2** (fashion) mannequin *m*. *vt* modeler. *vi* être mannequin.

moderate ('mɔdərət) *adj* **1** modéré, raisonnable. **2** médiocre. **3** moyen, -enne. *vt* modérer. *vi* se modérer. **moderation** *n* modération *f*. **in moderation** modérément.

modern ('mɔdən) *adj* moderne. **modernity** *n* modernité *f*. **modernize** *vt* moderniser.

modest ('mɔdist) *adj* **1** modeste. **2** pudique. **modesty** *n* **1** modestie *f*. **2** pudeur *f*. **3** modération *f*.

modify ('mɔdifai) *vt* modifier. **modification** *n* modification *f*. **modifier** *n* modificateur *m*.

modulate ('mɔdjuleit) *vt,vi* moduler.

module ('mɔdju:l) *n* module *m*.
mohair ('mouhɛə) *n* mohair *m*.
moist (mɔist) *adj* **1** humide. **2** moite. **moisten** *vt* humecter, mouiller.
moisture ('mɔistʃə) *n* humidité *f*. **moisturize** *vt* humidifier.
mole[1] (moul) *n* grain de beauté *m*.
mole[2] (moul) *n zool* taupe *f*.
molecule ('mɔlikju:l) *n* molécule *f*. **molecular** *adj* moléculaire.
molest (mə'lest) *vt* molester, rudoyer.
mollusc ('mɔləsk) *n* mollusque *m*.
molten ('moultən) *adj* fondu.
moment ('moumənt) *n* moment, instant *m*. **momentary** *adj* momentané. **momentous** *adj* important, capital, -aux. **momentum** *n, pl* **-ta 1** *sci* force vive *f*. **2** vitesse acquise *f*.
monarch ('mɔnək) *n* monarque *m*. **monarchism** *n* monarchisme *m*. **monarchist** *n* monarchiste *m,f*. **monarchy** *n* monarchie *f*.
monastery ('mɔnəstri) *n* monastère *m*. **monastic** *adj* monastique.
Monday ('mʌndi) *n* lundi *m*.
money ('mʌni) *n* **1** argent *m*. **2** (coin) monnaie *f*. **ready money** argent comptant. **money-box** *n* tirelire *f*. **money order** *n* mandat-poste *m*. **monetary** *adj* monétaire.
mongrel ('mʌngrəl) *n* métis, -isse. *adj* métis, -isse, hybride.
monitor ('mɔnitə) *n* moniteur, -trice. *vt* contrôler.
monk (mʌŋk) *n* moine *m*.
monkey ('mʌŋki) *n* **1** singe *m*. **2** *inf* polisson, -onne.
monochrome ('mɔnəkroum) *adj,n* monochrome *m*.
monogamy (mə'nɔgəmi) *n* monogamie *f*. **monogamist** *n* monogame *m,f*. **monogamous** *adj* monogame.
monologue ('mɔnəlɔg) *n* monologue *m*.
monopoly (mə'nɔpəli) *n* monopole *m*. **monopolize** *vt* **1** monopoliser. **2** accaparer.
monosyllable ('mɔnəsiləbəl) *n* monosyllabe *m*. **monosyllabic** *adj* monosyllabique.
monotone ('mɔnətoun) *n* voix monotone *f*. **monotonous** *adj* monotone. **monotony** *n* monotonie *f*.
monsoon (mɔn'su:n) *n* mousson *f*.
monster ('mɔnstə) *n* monstre *m*. **monstrous** *adj* monstrueux, -euse. **monstrosity** *n* monstruosité *f*.
month (mʌnθ) *n* mois *m*. **monthly** *adj* mensuel, -elle. *adv* mensuellement. *n* publication mensuelle *f*.
monument ('mɔnjumənt) *n* monument *m*. **monumental** *adj* monumental, -aux.
moo (mu:) *vi* meugler. *n* meuglement *m*.
mood[1] (mu:d) *n* humeur *f*. **moody** *adj* d'humeur changeante, maussade.
mood[2] (mu:d) *n gram* mode *m*.
moon (mu:n) *n* lune *f*. **moonlight** *n* clair de lune *m*.
moor[1] (muə) *n* lande *f*. **moorhen** *n* poule d'eau *f*.
moor[2] (muə) *vt* amarrer. **moorings** *n pl* amarres *f pl*.
Moor (muə) *n* maure *m*. mauresque *f*. **Moorish** *adj* mauresque.
mop (mɔp) *n* balai à laver *m*. **mop of hair** tignasse *f*. ~*vt* éponger.
mope (moup) *vi* s'ennuyer, avoir le cafard.
moped ('mouped) *n* cyclomoteur *m*.
moral ('mɔrəl) *adj* moral, -aux. *n* **1** morale *f*. **2** *pl* mœurs *f pl*. **moralist** *n* moraliste *m*. **morale** *n* moral *m*. **morality** *n* moralité *f*. **moralize** *vi,vt* moraliser.
morbid ('mɔ:bid) *adj* morbide, malsain.
more (mɔ:) *adj* plus. *adv* **1** plus. **2** davantage, encore. **more and more** de plus en plus. **once more** encore une fois. **more than** plus que, plus de. **some more** encore, davantage. **moreover** *adv* de plus, en outre.
morgue (mɔ:g) *n* morgue *f*.
morning ('mɔ:niŋ) *n* matin *m*. matinée *f*. **morning coat** *n* jaquette *f*.
Morocco (mə'rɔkou) *n* Maroc *m*. **Moroccan** *adj,n* marocain.
moron ('mɔ:rɔn) *n* **1** *med* arriéré *m*. **2** *sl* idiot, moron *m*.
morose (mə'rous) *adj* morose, maussade.
morphine ('mɔ:fi:n) *n* morphine *f*.
morse code (mɔ:s) *n* (alphabet) morse *m*.
mortal ('mɔ:tl) *adj,n* mortel, -elle. **mortality** *n* mortalité *f*.
mortar[1] ('mɔ:tə) *n cul,mil* mortier *m*.
mortar[2] ('mɔ:tə) *n* (for building) mortier *m*.
mortgage ('mɔ:gidʒ) *n* hypothèque *f*. *vt* hypothéquer.
mortify ('mɔ:tifai) *vt* mortifier.
mortuary ('mɔ:tjuəri) *n* **1** morgue *f*. **2** salle mortuaire *f*. *adj* mortuaire.
mosaic (mou'zeiik) *n* mosaïque *f*.
mosque (mɔsk) *n* mosquée *f*.
mosquito (mə'ski:tou) *n, pl* **-oes** *or* **-os** moustique *m*.

moss (mɔs) *n* mousse *f*. **mossy** *adj* moussu.
most (moust) *adj* le *or* la plus, la plupart. *n* plus *m*. plupart *f*. **at most** au maximum. ~*adv* 1 très, fort. 2 plus. **mostly** *adv* 1 principalement. 2 le plus souvent.
motel (mou'tel) *n* motel *m*.
moth (mɔθ) *n* papillon de nuit *m*. **clothes moth** *n* mite *f*.
mother ('mʌðə) *n* mère *f*. *vt* dorloter. **motherhood** *n* maternité *f*. **mother-in-law** *n* belle-mère *f*. **mother superior** *n* mère supérieure *f*. **mother tongue** *n* langue maternelle *f*. **motherly** *adj* maternel, -elle.
motion ('mouʃən) *n* 1 mouvement *m*. 2 signe *m*. 3 *pol* motion *f*. *vt* faire signe. **motionless** *adj* immobile.
motive ('moutiv) *n* motif *m*. *adj* moteur, -trice. **motivate** *vt* motiver.
motor ('moutə) *n* moteur *m*. *adj* moteur, -trice. **motor car** *n* automobile *f*. **motor cycle** *n* motocyclette *f*. **motorist** *n* automobiliste *m,f*. **motorway** *n* autoroute *f*.
mottle ('mɔtḷ) *vt* tacheter, moucheter.
motto ('mɔtou) *n, pl* **-oes** *or* **-os** devise *f*.
mould[1] (mould) *n* moule *m*. *vt* mouler, pétrir.
mould[2] (mould) *n* (mildew) moisi *m*. moissure *f*. *vi* se moisir. **mouldy** *adj* moisi.
moult (moult) *vi* muer. **moulting** *n* mue *f*.
mound (maund) *n* tertre *m*.
mount[1] (maunt) *vt,vi* monter. **mount up** augmenter. ~*n* monture *f*.
mount[2] (maunt) *n* *geog* mont *m*.
mountain ('mauntin) *n* montagne *f*. **mountainous** *adj* montagneux, -euse. **mountaineer** *n* alpiniste *m,f*. **mountaineering** *n* alpinisme *m*.
mourn (mɔ:n) *vt,vi* pleurer. **mournful** *adj* lugubre, funèbre. **mourning** *n* deuil *m*.
mouse (maus) *n, pl* **mice** souris *f*. **mousetrap** *n* souricière *f*. **mousy** *adj* (of hair) terne.
mousse (mu:s) *n* mousse *f*.
moustache (mə'stɑ:ʃ) *n* moustache *f*.
mouth (mauθ) *n* 1 *anat* bouche *f*. 2 (of animals) geule *f*. 3 ouverture *f*. 4 (of rivers) embouchure *f*. **mouthful** *n* bouchée *f*. **mouthpiece** *n* 1 embouchure *f*. 2 porte-parole *m invar*.
move (mu:v) *vt* 1 déplacer. 2 animer. 3 émouvoir. 4 proposer. *vi* 1 se déplacer, bouger. 2 agir. **move in** emménager. **move on** s'avancer, circuler. **move out** déménager. ~*n* 1 mouvement *m*. 2 *game* tour, coup *m*. 3 déménagement *m*. **movable** *adj* mobile. **movement** *n* mouvement *m*. **moving** *adj* 1 en marche. 2 émouvant.
mow* (mou) *vt* 1 faucher. 2 tondre.
Mr ('mistə) (title of address) M.
Mrs ('misiz) (title of address) Mme.
much (mʌtʃ) *adj* beaucoup (de). adv 1 beaucoup. 2 bien. **as much** autant. **how much?** combien de? **much more** bien plus. **very much** beaucoup.
muck (mʌk) *n* 1 fumier *m*. 2 saleté *f*. *v* **muck up** gâcher. **mucky** *adj* sale.
mud (mʌd) *n* boue *f*. **mudguard** *n* garde-boue *m invar*. **muddy** *adj* boueux, -euse.
muddle ('mʌdḷ) *n* confusion *f*. *vt* embrouiller.
muff (mʌf) *n* manchon *m*.
muffle ('mʌfəl) *vt* 1 emmitoufler. 2 assourdir. *n* mufle *m*.
mug (mʌg) *n* timbale *f*. pot *m*.
muggy ('mʌgi) *adj* lourd.
mulberry ('mʌlbəri) *n* mûre *f*. **mulberry bush** *n* mûrier *m*.
mule[1] (mju:l) *n* *zool* mule *f*. mulet *m*.
mule[2] (mju:l) *n* mule *f*.
mullet ('mʌlit) *n* muge *m*.
multiple ('mʌltipəl) *adj,n* multiple *m*.
multiply ('mʌltiplai) *vt* multiplier. *vi* se multiplier. **multiplication** *n* multiplication *f*.
multitude ('mʌltitju:d) *n* multitude *f*.
mum (mʌm) *n inf* maman *f*.
mumble ('mʌmbəl) *vt,vi* marmonner.
mummy[1] ('mʌmi) *n* momie *f*. **mummify** *vt* momifier.
mummy[2] ('mʌmi) *n inf* maman *f*.
mumps (mʌmps) *n* oreillons *m pl*.
munch (mʌntʃ) *vt* mâcher, mâchonner.
mundane ('mʌndein) *adj* mondain.
municipal (mju'nisipəl) *adj* municipal, -aux.
mural ('mjuərəl) *adj* mural, -aux.
murder ('mə:də) *n* meurtre *m*. *vt* assassiner. **murderer** *n* assassin, meurtrier *m*. **murderous** *adj* meurtrier, -ière.
murmur ('mə:mə) *vi,vt* murmurer. *n* murmure *m*.
muscle ('mʌsəl) *n* muscle *m*. **muscular** *adj* 1 musculaire. 2 musclé.
muse (mju:z) *n* muse *f*. *vi* méditer, rêver.
museum (mju:'ziəm) *n* musée *m*.
mushroom ('mʌʃrum) *n* champignon *m*.
music ('mu:zik) *n* musique *f*. **musical** *n* 1 musical, -aux. 2 (of a person) musicien, -ienne. **musician** *n* musicien, -ienne.
musk (mʌsk) *n* musc *m*.

musket (ˈmʌskit) *n* mousquet *m*. **musketeer** *n* mousquetaire *m*.
Muslim (ˈmuzlim) *adj,n* musulman.
muslin (ˈmʌzlin) *n* mousseline *f*.
mussel (ˈmʌsəl) *n* moule *f*.
must* (mʌst) *v mod aux* falloir, devoir. *n* nécessité *f*.
mustard (ˈmʌstəd) *n* moutarde *f*.
mute (mju:t) *adj,n* muet, -ette. *vt* amortir, assourdir. **muteness** *n* mutisme *m*.
mutilate (ˈmju:tileit) *vt* mutiler. **mutilation** *n* mutilation *f*.
mutiny (ˈmju:tini) *n* mutinerie, révolte *f*. *vi* se révolter. **mutinous** *adj* rebelle.
mutter (ˈmʌtə) *vi* marmotter.
mutton (ˈmʌtn̩) *n* mouton *m*. **leg of mutton** *n* gigot *m*.
mutual (ˈmju:tjuəl) *adj* mutuel, -elle, commun.
muzzle (ˈmʌzəl) *n* **1** *zool* mouseau, -aux *m*. **2** *mil* gueule *f*. **3** muselière *f*. *vt* museler.
my (mai) *poss adj 1st pers s* mon, ma, mes. **myself** *pron 1st pers s* **1** moi-même. **2** me. **by myself** tout seul.
myrrh (mə:) *n* myrrhe *f*.
myrtle (ˈmə:tl̩) *n* myrte *m*
mystery (ˈmistəri) *n* mystère *m*. **mysterious** *adj* mystérieux, -euse.
mystic (ˈmistik) *adj,n* mystique. **mysticism** *n* mysticisme *m*. **mystified** *adj* intrigué. **mystify** *vt* **1** mystifier. **2** désorienter.
mystique (miˈsti:k) *n* mystique *f*.
myth (miθ) *n* mythe *m*. **mythical** *adj* mythique. **mythological** *adj* mythologique. **mythology** *n* mythologie.

N

nag[1] (næg) *vt* gronder, criailler. *vi* être toujours après.
nag[2] (næg) *n inf* bidet *m*.
nail (neil) *n* **1** *anat* ongle *m*. **2** clou *m*. *vt* clouer. **nailbrush** *n* brosse à ongles *f*. **nailfile** *n* lime à ongles *f*. **nail varnish** *n* vernis à ongles *m*.
naive (naiˈi:v) *adj* naïf, -ïve, ingénu.
naked (ˈneikid) *adj* nu. **nakedness** *n* nudité *f*.
name (neim) *n* **1** nom *m*. **2** réputation *f*. *vt* nommer. **namely** *adv* à savoir, c'est-à-dire.
nanny (ˈnæni) *n* **1** bonne d'enfant *f*. **2** *inf* nounou *f*.
nap (næp) *n* somme *m*. sieste *f*. *vi* sommeiller.
napalm (ˈneipɑ:m) *n* napalm *m*.
napkin (ˈnæpkin) *n* serviette *f*.
nappy (ˈnæpi) *n* couche *f*.
narcotic (nɑ:ˈkɔtik) *adj,n* narcotique *m*.
narrate (nəˈreit) *vt* raconter. **narration** *n* narration *f*. **narrative** *n* récit *m*. *adj* narratif, -ive. **narrator** *n* narrateur, -trice.
narrow (ˈnærou) *adj* étroit, serré. *vt* restreindre. *vi* se rétrécir. **narrow-minded** *adj* borné. **narrowness** *n* étroitesse *f*.
nasal (ˈneizəl) *adj* nasal, -aux.
nasturtium (nəˈstə:ʃəm) *n* capucine *f*.
nasty (ˈnɑ:sti) *adj* **1** mauvais, méchant. **2** désagréable. **3** dangereux, -euse. **nastiness** *n* **1** méchanceté *f*. **2** saleté *f*.
nation (ˈneiʃən) *n* nation *f*. **national** *adj* national, -aux. **national anthem** *n* hymne national *m*. **national insurance** *n* assurances sociales *f pl*. **national service** *n* service militaire *m*. **nationality** *n* nationalité *f*. **nationalization** *n* nationalisation *f*. **nationalize** *vt* nationaliser. **nationwide** *adj* sur le plan national.
native (ˈneitiv) *n* originaire, indigène *m,f*. *adj* **1** natal. **2** naturel, -elle.
nativity (nəˈtiviti) *n* nativité *f*.
natural (ˈnætʃərəl) *adj* naturel, -elle. **natural gas** *n* gaz naturel *m*. **natural history** *n* histoire naturelle *f*. **natural science** *n* sciences naturelles *f pl*. **naturalization** *n* naturalisation *f*. **naturalize** *vt* naturaliser.
nature (ˈneitʃə) *n* **1** nature *f*. **2** sorte *f*.
naughty (ˈnɔ:ti) *adj* méchant, vilain.
nausea (ˈnɔ:siə, -ziə) *n* nausée *f*. **nauseate** *vt* dégoûter. **nauseating** *adj* ecœurant.
nautical (ˈnɔ:tikəl) *adj* nautique, marin.
naval (ˈneivəl) *adj* de marine, maritime
nave (neiv) *n* nef *f*.
navel (ˈneivəl) *n* nombril *m*.
navigate (ˈnævigeit) *vi* naviguer. *vt* diriger, gouverner. **navigation** *n* navigation *f*. **navigator** *n* navigateur *m*.
navy (ˈneivi) *n* marine de guerre *f*. **navy blue** *n* bleu marine *m*.
near (niə) *adj* proche. *adv* près. *prep* près *or* auprès de. *vt* approcher de. **nearby** *adv* tout près (de). *adj* avoisinant. **nearly** *adv* presque, à peu près. **nearside** *n* côté gauche *m*. *adj* gauche.
Near East *n* Proche Orient *m*.
neat (ni:t) *adj* **1** net, nette, soigné. **2** élégant. **3** pur. **neatness** *n* **1** netteté *f*. **2** ordre *m*.
nebulous (ˈnebjuləs) *adj* nébuleux, -euse.
necessary (ˈnesəsəri) *adj* nécessaire. **if**

necessary au besoin. **necessity** *n* nécessité *f*.

neck (nek) *n* **1** *anat* cou *m*. **2** (of a bottle) goulot *m*. **3** (of clothing) col *m*. encolure *f*. **neckband** *n* encolure *f*. **necklace** *n* collier *m*. **neckline** *n* encolure *f*.

nectar ('nektə) *n* nectar *m*.

need (ni:d) *vt* **1** avoir besoin de. **2** exiger, demander. *vi* **1** être obligé. **2** falloir. **needy** *adj* indigent.

needle ('ni:dl̩) *n* aiguille *f*. **needlework** *n* travail à l'aiguille *m*.

negate (ni'geit) *vt* nier. **negation** *n* négation *f*. **negative** *adj* négatif, -ive. *n* **1** négative *f*. **2** *phot* négatif *m*.

neglect (ni'glekt) *vt* négliger. *n* négligence *f*.

negligent ('neglidʒənt) *adj* négligent. **negligence** *n* négligence *f*.

negotiate (ni'gouʃieit) *vi,vt* négocier. *vt* franchir, surmonter. **negotiation** *n* négociation *f*.

Negro ('ni:grou) *n, pl* **-oes** nègre *m*. **Negress** *n* négresse *f*.

neigh (nei) *vi* hennir. *n* hennissement *m*.

neighbour ('neibə) *n* voisin *m*. **neighbourhood** *n* voisinage *m*. alentours *m pl*. **neighbourly** *adj* (de) bon voisin.

neither ('naiðə) *adj,pron* ni l'un ni l'autre. *conj* ni, non plus. **neither...nor** ni...ni.

neon ('ni:ən) *n* néon *m*.

nephew ('nevju:) *n* neveu, -eux *m*.

Neptune ('neptju:n) *n* Neptune *m*.

nerve (nə:v) *n* **1** *anat* nerf *m*. **2** *inf* aplomb, toupet *m*. **3** courage *m*.**nerve-racking** *adj* énervant. **nervous** *adj* **1** nerveux, -euse. **2** intimidé. **nervous breakdown** *n* crise de nerfs *f*. **nervousness** *n* nervosité *f*.

nest (nest) *n* nid *m*. *vi* nicher.

nestle ('nesəl) *vi* se nicher.

net[1] (net) *n* filet *m*. **netball** *n* netball *m*. **network** *n* réseau, -aux *m*.

net[2] (net) *adj* net, nette. *vt* toucher *or* rapporter net.

Netherlands ('neðələndz) *n pl* Pays Bas *m pl*.

nettle ('netl̩) *n* ortie *f*. *vt* agacer, piquer. **nettle rash** *n* urticaire *f*.

neurosis (njuə'rousis) *n pl* **-ses** névrose *f*. **neurotic** *adj,n* névrosé.

neuter ('nju:tə) *adj,n* neutre *m*.

neutral ('nju:trəl) *adj* neutre. **neutrality** *n* neutralité *f*. **neutralize** *vt* neutraliser.

neutron ('nju:trɔn) *n* neutron *m*.

never ('nevə) *adv* (ne...)jamais. *interj* pas possible! **never mind!** peu importe! **nevertheless** *adv* pourtant, quand-même.

new (nju:) *adj* **1** neuf, neuve. **2** nouveau, -elle. **3** frais, fraîche. **newcomer** *n* nouveau venu *m*. **news** *n pl* **1** nouvelle *f pl*. **2** (radio, etc.) informations *f pl*. **newsagent** *n* marchand de journaux *m*. **newspaper** *n* journal, -aux *m*. **newsreel** *n* bande d'actualités *f*.

newt (nju:t) *n* salamandre *f*.

New Testament *n* Nouveau Testament *m*.

New Year *n* Nouvel An *m*. **New Year's Day** *n* jour de l'an *m*.

New Zealand ('zi:lənd) *n* Nouvelle-Zélande *f*. **New Zealander** *n* néo-zélandais *m*.

next (nekst) *adj* **1** prochain. **2** suivant. **3** voisin. *adv* ensuite. **next to** à côté de. **next-door** *adj* d'à côté. *adv* à côté.

nib (nib) *n* plume *f*.

nibble ('nibəl) *vt,vi* grignoter.

nice (nais) *adj* **1** agréable, bon, bonne. **2** gentil, -ille. **3** délicat. **nicety** *n* **1** délicatesse *f*. **2** précision *f*.

niche (nitʃ) *n* niche *f*.

nick (nik) *n* **1** encoche *f*. **2** *sl* prison *f*.

nickel ('nikəl) *n* nickel *m*.

nickname ('nikneim) *n* sobriquet *m*. *vt* surnommer.

nicotine ('nikəti:n) *n* nicotine *f*.

niece (ni:s) *n* nièce *f*.

Nigeria (nai'dʒiəriə) *n* Nigéria *m*. **Nigerian** *adj,n* nigérien, -ienne.

nigger ('nigə) *n derog* nègre *m*. négresse *f*.

niggle ('nigəl) *vi* tatillonner.

night (nait) *n* **1** nuit *f*. **2** soir *m*. **nightclub** *n* boîte de nuit *f*. **nightdress** *n also* **nightgown** chemise de nuit *f*. **nightmare** *n* cauchemar *m*. **night-time** *n* nuit *f*. **night-watchman** *n* veilleur de nuit *m*.

nightingale ('naitiŋgeil) *n* rossignol *m*.

nil (nil) *n* zéro, rien *m*.

Nile (nail) *n* Nil *m*.

nimble ('nimbəl) *adj* agile. **nimbleness** *n* agileté *f*.

nine (nain) *adj,n* neuf *m*. **ninth** *adj* neuvième.

nineteen (nain'ti:n) *adj,n* dix-neuf *m*. **nineteenth** *adj* dix-neuvième.

ninety ('nainti) *adj,n* quatre-vingt-dix *m*. **ninetieth** *adj* quatre-vingt-dixième.

nip[1] (nip) *vt* pincer. **nip off** filer. ~*n* pincement *m*.

nip[2] (nip) *n* goutte *f*. doigt *m*.

nipple ('nipəl) *n anat* mamelon *m*.

nit (nit) *n* **1** lente *f*. **2** *inf* crétin *m*.

nitrogen (ˈnaitrədʒən) *n* azote *m*.

no[1] (nou) *adv* **1** non. **2** ne... pas. *n, pl* **noes** non *m invar*.

no[2] (nou) *adj* **1** pas un, pas de, aucun, nul, nulle. **2** peu, ne...pas. **no longer** ne...plus. **no more** ne...plus. **no smoking** défense de fumer.

noble (ˈnoubəl) *adj,n* noble *m*. **nobility** *n* noblesse *f*. **nobleman** *n* noble *m*.

nobody (ˈnoubədi) *pron* personne. *n inf* zéro, rien *m*.

nocturnal (nɔkˈtə:nl̩) *adj* nocturne.

nod (nɔd) *n* signe de tête *m*. *vi* **1** faire un signe de tête. **2** somnoler.

node (noud) *n* nœud *m*.

noise (nɔiz) *n* **1** bruit *m*. **2** tapage, fracas *m*. **noisily** *adv* bruyamment. **noisy** *adj* tumultueux, -euse.

nomad (ˈnoumæd) *n* nomade *m,f*. **nomadic** *adj* nomade.

nominal (ˈnɔminl̩) *adj* nominal, -aux.

nominate (ˈnɔmineit) *vt* désigner, nommer. **nomination** *n* nomination *f*.

non- *pref* **1** non-. **2** in-. **3** sans.

nonchalant (ˈnɔnʃələnt) *adj* nonchalant. **nonchalance** *n* nonchalance *f*.

nondescript (ˈnɔndiskript) *adj* **1** indéfinissable. **2** quelconque.

none (nʌn) *pron* **1** aucun. **2** personne. *adv* pas, point.

nonentity (nɔnˈentiti) *n* non-être *m*. nullité *f*.

nonsense (ˈnɔnsəns) *n* absurdité *f*.

noodles (ˈnu:dl̩z) *n pl* nouilles *f pl*.

noon (nu:n) *n* midi *m*.

no-one *pron* personne.

noose (nu:s) *n* nœud coulant, collet *m*.

nor (nɔ:) *conj* ni, ni...ne.

norm (nɔ:m) *n* norme *f*. **normal** *adj* normal, -aux.

Norman (ˈnɔ:mən) *adj,n* normand.

Normandy (ˈnɔ:məndi) *n* Normandie *f*.

Norse (nɔ:s) *adj* nordique. **Norse** (language) *n* norvégien *m*.

north (nɔ:θ) *n* nord *m*. *adj* septentrional, -aux, nord *invar*. *adv* au *or* vers le nord. **northeast** *n* nord-est *m*. *adv* vers le nord-est. *adj* du nord-est. **northeasterly** *adj* du nord-est. **northeastern** *adj* du nord-est. **northerly** *adj* du nord. **northern** *adj* du nord. **northwards** vers le nord. **northwest** *n* nord-ouest *m*. *adv* vers le nord-ouest. *adj* du nord-ouest. **northwesterly** *adj* du nord-ouest. **northwestern** *adj* du nord-ouest.

North America *n* Amérique du Nord *f*.

Northern Ireland *n* Irlande du Nord *f*.

Norway (ˈnɔ:wei) *n* Norvège *f*. **Norwegian** *adj,n* norvégien, -ienne. **Norwegian** (language) *n* norvégien *m*.

nose (nouz) *n* **1** nez *m*. **2** (of animals) museau, -aux *m*. *vt* flairer. **nosy** *adj inf* fouinard, indiscret, -ète.

nostalgia (nɔˈstældʒiə) *n* nostalgie *f*. **nostalgic** *adj* nostalgique.

nostril (ˈnɔstril) *n* **1** narine *f*. **2** (of an animal) naseau, -aux *m*.

not (nɔt) *adv* ne...pas, ne...point, pas.

notch (nɔtʃ) *n* encoche *f*. cran *m*. *vt* entailler, encocher.

note (nout) *n* **1** note *f*. **2** remarque *f*. **3** *comm* billet *m*. *vt* noter, remarquer. **notable** *adj* notable. **notation** *n* notation *f*. **notebook** *n* carnet *m*. **notepaper** *n* papier à lettres *m*. **noteworthy** *adj* remarquable.

nothing (ˈnʌθiŋ) *pron,n* rien *m*. **for nothing** en vain. ~*adv* pas du tout. **nothingness** *n* néant *m*.

notice (ˈnoutis) *n* **1** avis *m*. notification *f*. **2** affiche *f*. **3** congé *m*. *vt* remarquer, apercevoir. **noticeable** *adj* perceptible. **notice board** *n* tableau d'affichage *m*.

notify (ˈnoutifai) *vt* notifier, aviser. **notification** *n* avis *m*.

notion (ˈnouʃən) *n* notion, idée *f*.

notorious (nouˈtɔ:riəs) *adj* notoire, mal famé. **notoriety** *n* notoriété *f*.

notwithstanding (nɔtwiθˈstændiŋ) *prep* malgré. *adv* néanmoins. *conj* bien que.

nougat (ˈnu:ga:) *n* nougat *m*.

nought (nɔ:t) *n* zéro, rien *m*.

noun (naun) *n* nom *m*.

nourish (ˈnʌriʃ) *vt* nourrir. **nourishment** *n* nourriture *f*.

novel[1] (ˈnɔvəl) *n* roman *m*. **novelist** *n* romancier, -ière.

novel[2] (ˈnɔvəl) *adj* original, -aux, singulier, -ière. **novelty** *n* nouveauté *f*.

November (nouˈvembə) *n* novembre *m*.

novice (ˈnɔvis) *n* novice *m,f*.

now (nau) *adv* **1** maintenant, à l'heure actuelle. **2** tout de suite. **now and then** de temps en temps. **nowadays** *adv* de nos jours.

nowhere (ˈnouwεə) *adv* nulle part.

noxious (ˈnɔkʃəs) *adj* nuisible.

nozzle (ˈnɔzəl) *n* lance *f*.

nuance (ˈnju:əns) *n* nuance *f*.

nucleus (ˈnju:kliəs) *n, pl* **-clei** noyau, -aux *m.* **nuclear** *adj* nucléaire.
nude (nju:d) *adj,n* nu *m.* **nudity** *n* nudité *f.*
nudge (nʌdʒ) *vt* pousser du coude. *n* coup de coude *m.*
nugget (ˈnʌgit) *n* pépite *f.*
nuisance (ˈnju:səns) *n* **1** ennui *m.* **2** *inf* peste *f.*
null (nʌl) *adj* nul, nulle. **null and void** nul et non avenu. **nullify** *vt* annuler.
numb (nʌm) *adj* engourdi. *vt* engourdir.
number (ˈnʌmbə) *n* **1** nombre *m.* **2** (of a house, etc.) numéro *m.* **3** quantité *f. vt* **1** compter. **2** numéroter. **numeral** *n* chiffre *m. adj* numéral, -aux. **numerate** *adj* possédant les mathématiques de base. **numerical** *adj* numérique. **numerous** *adj* nombreux, -euse.
nun (nʌn) *n* religieuse *f.* **nunnery** *n* couvent *m.*
nurse (nə:s) *n* **1** infirmière *f.* **2** nourrice *f.* **3** (for children) bonne *f.* **nursing home** *n* clinique *f.*
nursery (ˈnə:səri) *n* **1** chambre d'enfants *f.* **2** garderie *f.* **3** *bot* pépinière *f.* **nursery man** *n* pépinièriste *m.* **nursery rhyme** *n* chanson enfantine *f.* **nursery school** *n* école maternelle *f.*
nurture (ˈnə:tʃə) *vt* **1** élever. **2** nourrir. *n* **1** éducation *f.* **2** nourriture *f.*
nut (nʌt) *n* **1** noix *f.* **2** *tech* écrou *m.* **nutcrackers** *n pl* casse-noisettes *m invar.* **nutmeg** *n* muscade *f.* **nutshell** *n* coquille de noix *f.* **in a nutshell** en un mot.
nutrition (nju:ˈtriʃən) *n* nutrition *f.* **nutritious** *adj* nourrissant.
nuzzle (ˈnʌzəl) *vi* fouiller. *vt* fourrer son nez contre.
nylon (ˈnailən) *n* **1** nylon *m.* **2** *pl inf* bas *m pl.*
nymph (nimf) *n* nymphe *f.*

O

oak (ouk) *n* chêne *m.*
oar (ɔ:) *n* rame *f.* aviron *m.* **oarsman** *n* rameur *m.*
oasis (ouˈeisis) *n, pl* **oases** oasis *f.*
oath (ouθ) *n* **1** serment *m.* **2** juron *m.*
oats (outs) *n pl* avoine *f.*
oatmeal (ˈoutmi:l) *n* farine d'avoine *f.*
obedient (əˈbi:diənt) *adj* obéissant. **obedience** *n* obéissance *f.*
obese (ouˈbi:s) *adj* obèse. **obesity** *n* obésité *f.*
obey (əˈbei) *vt* obéir à. *vi* obéir.
obituary (əˈbitjuəri) *n* nécrologie *f. adj* nécrologique.
object (*n* ˈɔbdʒikt; *v* əbˈdʒekt) *n* **1** objet *m.* **2** but *m.* **3** *gram* complément *m. vt* objecter. **object to** trouver à redire à, s'opposer à. **objection** *n* **1** objection *f.* **2** inconvénient *m.* **objectionable** *adj* **1** répréhensible. **2** désagréable. **objective** *adj,n* objectif, -ive *m.* **objectivity** *n* objectivité *f.*
oblige (əˈblaidʒ) *vt* **1** obliger, contraindre. **2** rendre service à. **obligation** *n* obligation *f.* **obligatory** *adj* obligatoire, de rigueur.
oblique (əˈbli:k) *adj* oblique, indirect.
obliterate (əˈblitəreit) *vt* **1** effacer. **2** oblitérer.
oblivion (əˈbliviən) *n* oubli *m.* **oblivious** *adj* oublieux, -euse.
oblong (ˈɔblɔŋ) *n* rectangle *m. adj* oblong, -gue.
obnoxious (əbˈnɔkʃəs) *adj* exécrable, odieux, -euse.
oboe (ˈoubou) *n* hautbois *m.*
obscene (əbˈsi:n) *adj* obscène. **obscenity** *n* obscénité *f.*
obscure (əbˈskjuə) *adj* obscur. *vt* obscurcir. **obscurity** *n* obscurité *f.*
observe (əbˈzə:v) *vt* **1** observer. **2** remarquer. **3** faire remarquer. **observance** *n* observance *f.* **observant** *adj* observateur, -trice. **observation** *n* observation *f.* **observatory** *n* observatoire *m.*
obsess (əbˈses) *vt* obséder. **obsession** *n* obsession, idée fixe *f.*
obsolete (ˈɔbsəli:t) *adj* hors d'usage, suranné.
obstacle (ˈɔbstəkəl) *n* obstacle *m.*
obstinate (ˈɔbstinət) *adj* opiniâtre, têtu. **obstinacy** *n* obstination *f.*
obstruct (əbˈstrʌkt) *vt* **1** obstruer, boucher. **2** gêner. **obstruction** *n* **1** obstruction *f.* **2** obstacle *m.*
obtain (əbˈtein) *vt* obtenir, se procurer.
obtrusive (əbˈtru:siv) *adj* importun.
obtuse (əbˈtju:s) *adj* obtus.
obverse (ˈɔbvə:s) *n* face *f.*
obvious (ˈɔbviəs) *adj* évident, manifeste. **obviously** *adv* évidemment.
occasion (əˈkeiʒən) *n* occasion *f. vt* occasionner. **occasional** *adj* **1** occasionel, -elle. **2** de circonstance. **occasionally** *adv* de temps en temps.
Occident (ˈɔksidənt) *n* Occident *m.* **occidental** *adj* occidental, -aux.
occult (ɔˈkʌlt) *adj* occulte. **occultism** *n* occultisme *m.*
occupy (ˈɔkjupai) *vt* **1** occuper. **2** habiter. **occupant** *n* locataire *m,f.* **occupation** *n* **1**

occupation *f.* **2** métier *m.* **occupational** *adj* professionnel, -elle. **occupier** *n* occupant *m.*

occur (ə'kə:) *vi* **1** arriver. **2** se trouver. **3** venir à l'esprit. **occurrence** *n* fait, événement *m.*

ocean ('ouʃən) *n* océan *m.* **oceanic** *adj* océanique.

ochre ('oukə) *n* ocre *f.*

octagon ('ɔktəgən) *n* octogone *m.* **octagonal** *adj* octogonal, -aux.

octane ('ɔktein) *n* octane *m.*

octave ('ɔktiv) *n* octave *f.*

October (ɔk'toubə) *n* octobre *m.*

octopus ('ɔktəpəs) *n, pl* **-puses** *or* **-pi** pieuvre *f.*

oculist ('ɔkjulist) *n* oculiste *m,f.*

odd (ɔd) *adj* **1** (of a number) impair. **2** dépareillé. **3** quelconque. **4** étrange. **oddity** *n* **1** étrangeté *f.* **2** (of a person) original, -aux *m.* **oddly** *adv* singulièrement. **oddment** *n* article dépareillé *m.* fin de série *f.* **odds** *n pl* **1** chances *f pl.* **2** inégalités *f pl.* **odds and ends** restes *m pl.*

ode (oud) *n* ode *f.*

odious ('oudiəs) *adj* odieux, -euse.

odour ('oudə) *n* odeur *f.* **odourless** *adj* inodore.

oesophagus (i'sɔfəgəs) *n* œsophage *m.*

oestrogen ('i:strədʒən) *n* œstrogène *m.*

oestrus ('i:strəs) *n* œstre *m.*

of (əv; *stressed* ɔv) *prep* **1** de. **2** parmi, d'entre. **3** à, en. **4** par.

off (ɔf) *adv* **1** au loin. **2** fermé. *prep* de.

offal ('ɔfəl) *n* abats *m pl.*

offend (ə'fend) *vt* offenser, froisser. **offence** *n* **1** offense *f.* **2** *law* délit *m.* **take offence** s'offenser. **offender** *n* coupable *m,f.* **offensive** *adj* désagréable. *n* offensive *f.*

offer ('ɔfə) *n* offre *f.* **on offer** en vente. ~*vt* **1** offrir. **2** tenter. *vi* se présenter. **offering** *n* offre *f.*

offhand (ɔf'hænd) *adj* **1** improvisé. **2** désinvolte.

office ('ɔfis) *n* **1** bureau, -aux *m.* **2** *pol* ministère *m.* **3** fonction *f.* **officer** *n* **1** officier *m.* **2** agent *m.* **official** *adj* officiel, -elle. *n* fonctionnaire *m.*

officious (ə'fiʃəs) *adj* **1** empressé. **2** officieux, -euse. **officiousness** *n* excès de zèle *m.*

offing ('ɔfiŋ) **in the offing** *adv* au large.

off-licence *n* débit de boissons à emporter *m.*

off-peak *adj* **1** creux, creuse. **2** de nuit.

off-putting *adj inf* déconcertant.

off-season *n* morte-saison *f.*

offset ('ɔfset) *vt* compenser.

offshore (ɔf'ʃɔ:) *adv* au large. *adj* éloigné de la côte.

offside (ɔf'said) *n* **1** côté droit *m.* **2** *sport* hors-jeu *m invar. adj* droit.

offspring ('ɔfspriŋ) *n* rejeton *m.*

offstage (ɔf'steidʒ) *adv* à la cantonade.

often ('ɔfən) *adv* souvent. **how often?** combien de fois? **more often than not** le plus souvent.

ogre ('ougə) *n* ogre *m.*

oil (ɔil) *n* huile *f. vt* graisser. **oilfield** *n* gisement pétrolifère *m.* **oil painting** *n* peinture à l'huile *f.* **oilskin** *n* ciré *m.*

ointment ('ɔintmənt) *n* onguent *m.* pommade *f.*

old (ould) *adj* **1** vieux, vieil, vieille. **2** ancien, -ienne. **how old are you?** quel âge avez-vous? **I am twelve years old** j'ai douze ans. **old-fashioned** *adj* démodé.

Old Testament *n* Ancien Testament *m.*

olive ('ɔliv) *n* olive *f.* **olive oil** *n* huile d'olive *f.* **olive tree** *n* olivier *m.*

omelette ('ɔmlət) *n* omelette *f.*

omen ('oumen) *n* augure *m.*

ominous ('ɔminəs) *adj* de mauvais augure, inquiétant. **ominously** *adv* d'une façon menaçante.

omit (ə'mit) *vt* omettre. **omission** *n* omission *f.*

omnibus ('ɔmnibəs) *adj,n* omnibus *m.*

omnipotent (ɔm'nipətənt) *adj* tout puissant.

on (ɔn) *prep* **1** sur. **2** à. **3** de. **4** en. *adv* **1** en avant. **2** dessus. **3** ouvert.

once (wʌns) *adv* **1** une fois. **2** autrefois. **at once** immédiatement.

one (wʌn) *adj* **1** un. **2** seul, unique. **3** certain. *n* un *m. pron 3rd pers s* on. **one another** l'un, l'autre. **one's** *poss adj 3rd pers s* son, sa, ses. **oneself** *pron 3rd pers s* **1** soi-même. **2** se. **one-sided** *adj* **1** unilatéral, -aux. **2** injuste. **one-sidedness** *n* partialité *f.* **one-way** *adj* **1** à sens unique. **2** (of a ticket) simple.

onion ('ʌniən) *n* oignon *m.*

onlooker ('ɔnlukə) *n* spectateur, -trice.

only ('ounli) *adj* seul, unique. *adv* seulement, ne...que. *conj* mais.

onset ('ɔnset) *n* attaque *f.* **at the onset** d'emblée.

onslaught ('ɔnslɔ:t) *n* attaque *f.*

onus ('ounəs) *n* responsabilité *f.*

onwards ('ɔnwədz) *adv also* **onwards** **1** en avant. **2** à partir de.

ooze (u:z) *vi,vt* suinter, filtrer.

opal ('oupəl) *n* opale *f.*

opaque (ou'peik) *adj* opaque.

open (ˈoupən) *adj* ouvert. *vt* ouvrir. *vi* s'ouvrir. **open air** *adj* en plein air. **open-ended** *adj* pendant. **open-handed** *adj* généreux, -euse. **open-hearted** *adj* franc, franche. **open minded** *adj* sans parti pris. **open-mouthed** *adj* bouche bée. **open-plan** *adj* sans cloisons. **opening** *n* ouverture *f*.

opera (ˈɔprə) *n* opéra *m*. **opera house** *m* opéra *m*. **operetta** *n* opérette *f*.

operate (ˈɔpəreit) *vt,vi* opérer. *vt tech* faire manœuvrer. **operation** *n* opération *f*. **come into operation** entrer en vigueur. **operative** *adj* actif, -ive.

opinion (əˈpiniən) *n* opinion *f*. avis *m*. **opinion poll** *n* sondage *m*.

opium (ˈoupiəm) *n* opium *m*.

opponent (əˈpounənt) *n* adversaire *m,f*.

opportune (ɔpəˈtju:n) *adj* opportun.

opportunity (ɔpəˈtju:niti) *n* occasion *f*. **take the opportunity** profiter de l'occasion.

oppose (ɔˈpouz) *vt* **1** opposer. **2** s'opposer à, contrecarrer. **opposed** *adj* hostile. **as opposed to** par opposition à.

opposite (ˈɔpəzit) *adj* **1** opposé, en face. **2** inverse. *n* contraire *m*. *adv* vis-à-vis. *prep* en face de. **opposition** *n* **1** opposition *f*. **2** résistance *f*. **3** obstacle *m*.

oppress (əˈpres) *vt* opprimer. **oppression** *n* oppression *f*. **oppressive** *adj* **1** opprimant. **2** étouffant, accablant.

opt (ɔpt) *vi* opter.

optical (ˈɔptikəl) *adj* **1** optique. **2** d'optique. **optician** *n* opticien, -ienne.

optimism (ˈɔptimizəm) *n* optimisme *m*. **optimist** *n* optimiste *m,f*. **optimistic** *adj* optimiste. **optimistically** *adv* avec optimisme.

option (ˈɔpʃən) *n* option *f*. choix *m*. **optional** *adj* facultatif, -ive.

opulent (ˈɔpjulənt) *adj* opulent, abondant.

or (ɔ:) *conj* ou. **or else** sinon. **or so** environ.

oral (ˈɔ:rəl) *adj* **1** oral, -aux. **2** *anat* buccal. **orally** *adv* de vive voix.

orange (ˈɔrindʒ) *n* **1** *bot* orange *f*. **2** (colour) orange, orangé *m*. *adj* orangé, orange. **orange tree** *n* oranger *m*.

oration (ɔˈreiʃən) *n* allocution *f*. discours *m*. **orator** *n* orateur *m*.

orbit (ˈɔ:bit) *n* orbite *f*. *vt* tourner autour de.

orchard (ˈɔ:tʃəd) *n* verger *m*.

orchestra (ˈɔ:kistrə) *n* orchestre *m*. **orchestral** *adj* orchestral, -aux. **orchestrate** *vt* orchestrer.

orchid (ˈɔ:kid) *n* orchidée *f*.

ordain (ɔ:ˈdein) *vt* **1** *rel* ordonner. **2** décréter.

ordeal (ɔ:ˈdi:l) *n* épreuve *f*.

order (ˈɔ:də) *n* **1** ordre *m*. **2** *comm* commande *f*. **in order to** afin de, pour. **in order that** afin *or* pour que. **out of order** en panne. ~*vt* **1** ordonner. **2** commander. **orderly** *adj* **1** ordonné. **2** posé. *n* planton *m*.

ordinal (ˈɔ:dinļ) *adj* ordinal, -aux.

ordinary (ˈɔ:dənri) *adj* **1** ordinaire, normal, -aux. **2** quelconque. **out of the ordinary** exceptionnel, -elle.

ore (ɔ:) *n* minerai *m*.

oregano (ɔriˈgɑ:nou) *n* marjolaine *f*.

organ (ˈɔ:gən) *n* **1** *mus* orgue *m*. **2** organe *m*. **organist** *n* organiste *m,f*.

organism (ˈɔ:gənizəm) *n* organisme *m*. **organic** *adj* organique.

organize (ˈɔ:gənaiz) *vt* **1** organiser. **2** arranger. **organization** *n* **1** organisation *f*. **2** organisme, mouvement *m*. **organizer** *n* organisateur, -trice. **organizing** *n* organisation *f*. aménagement *m*.

orgasm (ˈɔ:gæzəm) *n* orgasme *m*.

orgy (ˈɔ:dʒi) *n* orgie *f*.

Orient (ˈɔ:riənt) *n* Orient *m*. **oriental** *adj,n* oriental, -aux.

orientate (ˈɔ:rienteit) *vt* orienter.

origin (ˈɔridʒin) *n* origine *f*. **original** *adj,n* original, -aux *m*. **originality** *n* originalité *f*. **originate** *vi* prendre naissance, provenir. *vt* créer, amorcer. **origination** *n* source *f*.

Orkneys (ˈɔ:kniz) *n* Orcades *f*.

Orlon (ˈɔ:lɔn) *n Tdmk* Orlon *m*.

ornament (ˈɔ:nəmənt) *n* ornement *m*. parure *f*. *vt* orner, agrémenter. **ornamental** *adj* ornemental, -aux.

ornate (ɔ:ˈneit) *adj* orné, surchargé.

ornithology (ɔ:niˈθɔlədʒi) *n* ornithologie *f*.

orphan (ˈɔ:fən) *n* orphelin *m*. **orphanage** *n*. orphelinat *m*.

orthodox (ˈɔ:θədɔks) *adj* orthodoxe. **orthodoxy** *n* orthodoxie *f*.

orthography (ɔ:ˈθɔgrəfi) *n* orthographe *f*.

orthopaedic (ɔ:θəˈpi:dik) *adj* orthopédique.

oscillate (ˈɔsəleit) *vi* osciller.

ostensible (ɔˈstensəbəl) *adj* prétendu, soi-distant. **ostensibly** *adv* censément.

ostentatious (ɔstenˈteiʃəs) *adj* ostentatoire.

osteopath (ˈɔstiəpæθ) *n* chiropracteur *m*. **osteopathy** *n* ostéopathie *f*.

ostracize (ˈɔstrəsaiz) *vt* ostraciser, exiler. **ostracism** *n* ostracisme *m*.

ostrich (ˈɔ:stritʃ) *n* autruche *f*.

other ('ʌðə) *adj* autre. **every other day** tous les deux jours. ~*pron* autre, autrui. *adv* autrement. **otherwise** *adv* autrement.
otter ('ɔtə) *n* loutre *f*.
ought* (ɔ:t) *v mod aux* devoir, falloir.
ounce (auns) *n* once *f*.
our (auə) *poss adj 1st pers pl* notre, nos. **ours** *poss pron 1st pers pl* le *or* la nôtre. **ourselves** *pron 1st pers pl* 1 nous-mêmes. 2 nous.
oust (aust) *vt* 1 supplanter. 2 *law* déposséder.
out (aut) *adv* 1 hors, dehors. 2 sorti. 3 éteint. 4 *sport* hors jeu. **out of** 1 hors de, au dehors de. 2 dans. 3 par. 4 parmi.
outboard ('autbɔ:d) *adj* extérieur.
outbreak ('autbreik) *n* éruption, ouverture *f*.
outburst ('autbə:st) *n* accès, éclat *m*.
outcast ('autkɑ:st) *adj,n* proscrit.
outcome ('autkʌm) *n* résultat *m*. issue *f*.
outcry ('autkrai) *n* cri *m*. clameur *f*.
outdo* (aut'du:) *vt* surpasser.
outdoor ('autdɔ:) *adj* extérieur, de plein air. **outdoors** *adv* dehors, en plein air.
outer ('autə) *adj* extérieur, externe.
outfit ('autfit) *n* 1 attirail, équipement *m*. 2 costume *m*.
outgoing ('autgouiŋ) *adj* 1 ouvert. 2 sortant. 3 démissionnaire.
outgrow* (aut'grou) *vt* 1 dépasser. 2 devenir trop grand pour.
outhouse ('authaus) *n* dépendance *f*.
outing ('autiŋ) *n* sortie *f*.
outlandish (aut'lændiʃ) *adj* extravagant, bizarre.
outlaw ('autlɔ:) *n* hors-la-loi *m invar*. *vt* proscrire.
outlay ('autlei) *n* débours *m pl*. mise de fonds *f*.
outlet ('autlet) *n* 1 sortie *f*. 2 débouché *m*.
outline ('autlain) *n* 1 contour *m*. 2 ébauche *f*. *vt* 1 esquisser. 2 silhouetter.
outlive (aut'liv) *vt* survivre à.
outlook ('autluk) *n* perspective *f*. point de vue *m*.
outlying ('autlaiiŋ) *adj* isolé, écarté.
outnumber (aut'nʌmbə) *vt* surpasser en nombre.
outpatient ('autpeiʃənt) *n* malade venant consulter à l'hôpital *m*.
outpost ('autpoust) *n* avant-poste *m*.
output ('autput) *n* production *f*. rendement *m*.
outrage (aut'reidʒ) *n* outrage *m*. *vt* outrager, violenter. **outrageous** *adj* 1 outrageux, -euse. 2 indigne, exorbitant.
outright ('autrait) *adv* 1 franchement. 2 complètement. 3 du premier coup. *adj* 1 carré. 2 pur et simple.
outside (aut'said) *adj* extérieur, externe. *prep* en dehors de. *adv* dehors, à l'extérieur. *n* dehors, extérieur *m*. **on the outside** à l'extérieur. **outsider** *n* 1 étranger *m*. 2 *sport* ailier *m*.
outsize ('autsaiz) *n* taille hors série *f*. *adj* 1 de taille hors série. 2 énorme.
outskirts ('autskə:ts) *n pl* banlieue *f*. abords *m pl*.
outspoken (aut'spoukən) *adj* franc, franche. **outspokenness** *n* franc-parler *m invar*.
outstanding (aut'stændiŋ) *adj* 1 saillant, marquant. 2 excellent. 3 *comm* en souffrance, arriéré.
outstrip (aut'strip) *vt* 1 devancer. 2 surpasser.
outward ('autwəd) *adj* 1 extérieur, externe. 2 apparent. *adv* au dehors. **outwards** *adv* au dehors, vers l'extérieur.
outweigh (aut'wei) *vt* 1 peser plus que. 2 l'emporter sur.
outwit (aut'wit) *vt* 1 circonvenir. 2 dépister.
oval ('ouvəl) *adj,n* ovale *m*.
ovary ('ouvəri) *n* ovaire *m*.
ovation (ou'veiʃən) *n* ovation *f*.
oven ('ʌvən) *n* four *m*.
over ('ouvə) *prep* 1 sur, au-dessus de. 2 au cours de. 3 de l'autre côté de. **over and above** en outre. **over there** là-bas.
overall ('ɔvərɔ:l) *adj* global, -aux. *n* 1 blouse *f*. 2 *pl* salopette *f*.
overbalance (ouvə'bæləns) *vt* renverser. *vi* tomber.
overboard ('ouvəbɔ:d) *adv* par-dessus bord.
overcast (ouvə'kɑ:st) *adj* couvert, assombri.
overcharge (ouvə'tʃɑ:dʒ) *vt* surcharger.
overcoat ('ouvəkout) *n* pardessus *m*.
overcome* (ouvə'kʌm) *vt* surmonter, triompher de. **be overcome by** être accablé de, succomber à.
overdo* (ouvə'du:) *vt* 1 exagérer. 2 surmener. 3 *cul* trop cuire.
overdose ('ouvədous) *n* dose mortelle *f*.
overdraft ('ouvədrɑ:ft) *n* découvert *m*.
overdraw* (ouvə'drɔ:) *vt* tirer à découvert.
overdue (ouvə'dju:) *adj* échu, en retard.
overestimate (ouvər'estimeit) *vt* surestimer.
overfill (ouvə'fil) *vt* remplir trop.
overflow (*v* ouvə'flou; *n* 'ouvəflou) *vi* déborder. *n* trop-plein *m invar*.
overhang* (*v* ouvə'hæŋ; *n* 'ouvəhæŋ) *vt* surplomber, faire saillie. *n* porte-à-faux *m*. saillie *f*. **overhanging** *adj* en porte-à-faux.

overhaul (ouvə'hɔ:l) *n* révision *f. vt* examiner, réviser.
overhead (*adv* ouvə'hed; *adj, n* 'ouvəhed) *adv* en haut, en l'air. *adj* aérien, -ienne. **overheads** *n pl* frais généraux *m pl.*
overhear* (ouvə'hiə) *vt* surprendre.
overheat (ouvə'hi:t) *vt* surchauffer. *vi* chauffer.
overjoyed (ouvə'dʒɔid) *adj* transporté de joie.
overland (ouvə'lænd) *adv* par voie de terre.
overlap (*v* ouvə'læp; *n* 'ouvəlæp) *vt* recouvrir, chevaucher. *n* recouvrement, chevauchement *m.*
overlay (*v* ouvə'lei; *n* 'ouvəlei) *vt* recouvrir. *n* matelas *m.*
overleaf (ouvə'li:f) *adv* au verso.
overload (*v* ouvə'loud; *n* 'ouvəloud) *vt* **1** surcharger. **2** surmener. *n* surcharge *f.*
overlook (ouvə'luk) *vt* **1** oublier. **2** donner sur. **3** laisser passer.
overnight (*adv* ouvə'nait; *adj* œuvənait) *adv* **1** la nuit, jusqu'au lendemain. **2** du jour au lendemain. *adj* de nuit.
overpower (ouvə'pauə) *vt* maîtriser. **overpowering** *adj* **1** accablant. **2** écrasant.
overrate (ouvə'reit) *vt* surestimer, surfaire.
overreach (ouvə'ri:tʃ) *vt* dépasser.
overrule (ouvə'ru:l) *vt* **1** diriger. **2** rejeter.
overrun* (ouvə'rʌn) *vt* **1** envahir, se répandre. **2** dépasser.
overseas (ouvə'si:z) *adv* outre-mer. *adj* d'outre-mer.
overshadow (ouvə'ʃædou) *vt* **1** ombrager. **2** éclipser.
overshoot* (ouvə'ʃu:t) *vt* dépasser.
oversight ('ouvəsait) *n* oubli *m.* **through an oversight** par inadvertance.
oversleep* (ouvə'sli:p) *vi* dormir trop longtemps.
overspill* (*v* ouvə'spil; *n* 'ouvəspil) *vi* déborder. *n* déversement de population *m.*
overt ('ouvə:t) *adj* manifeste, évident.
overtake* (ouvə'teik) *vt* **1** rattraper. **2** (a car, etc.) doubler.
overthrow* (*v* ouvə'θrou; *n* 'ouvəθrou) *vt* vaincre. *n* chute *f.*
overtime ('ouvətaim) *n* heures supplémentaires *f pl.*
overtone ('ouvətoun) *n* nuance *f.*
overture ('ouvətʃə) *n* ouverture *f.*
overturn (ouvə'tə:n) *vt* renverser. *vi* verser, se retourner.
overweight (*n* 'ouvəweit; *adj* ouvə'weit) *n* surpoids *m. adj* trop lourd.
overwhelm (ouvə'welm) *vt* **1** écraser, accabler. **2** combler.
overwork (*v* ouvə'wə:k; *n* 'ouvəwə:k) *vt* surmener. *n* surmenage *m.*
overwrought (ouvə'rɔ:t) *adj* excédé.
ovulate ('ɔvjuleit) *vi* ovuler. **ovulation** *n* ovulation *f.*
owe (ou) *vt* devoir. **owing** *adj* dû, due. **owing to** en raison de.
owl (aul) *n* hibou, -oux *m.*
own (oun) *vt* posséder. **own up to** avouer. ~*adj* propre. **owner** *n* propriétaire *m,f.* **ownership** *n* propriété, possession *f.*
ox (ɔks) *n, pl* **oxen** bœuf *m.* **oxtail** *n* queue de bœuf *f.*
oxygen ('ɔksidʒən) *n* oxygène *m.*
oyster ('ɔistə) *n* huître *f.* **oyster-bed** *n* banc d'huîtres *m.*

P

pace (peis) *n* **1** pas *m.* **2** allure *f. vt* arpenter. **pace up and down** faire les cent pas.
Pacific (pə'sifik) *adj* pacifique. **Pacific (Ocean)** *n* (Océan) Pacifique *m.*
pacify ('pæsifai) *vt* pacifier, apaiser. **pacifism** *n* pacifisme *m.*
pack (pæk) *n* **1** paquet *m.* **2** bande *f.* **3** *game* jeu, jeux *m.* **4** (of hounds) meute *f. vt* **1** emballer. **2** tasser, empiler. **3** bourrer. **package** *n* **1** paquet *m.* **2** emballage *m.* **packet** *n* **1** paquet *m.* **2** colis *m.* **packhorse** *n* cheval de somme *m.*
pact (pækt) *n* pacte *m.* convention *f.*
pad[1] (pæd) *n* **1** coussinet *m.* **2** tampon *m.* **3** (of paper) bloc *m. vt* **1** rembourrer, matelasser. **2** délayer. **padding** *n* rembourrage *m.*
pad[2] (pæd) *n* bruit de pas feutrés *m.*
paddle[1] ('pædl̩) *n* **1** pagaie *f.* **2** aube *f. vt* pagayer.
paddle[2] ('pædl̩) *vi* patauger.
paddock ('pædɔk) *n* **1** enclos *m.* **2** paddock *m.*
paddyfield ('pædifi:ld) *n* champ de riz *m.*
padlock ('pædlɔk) *n* cadenas *m. vt* cadenasser.
paediatric (pi:di'ætrik) *adj* pédiatrique. **paediatrician** *n* pédiatre *m.*
pagan ('peigən) *adj,n* païen, -ïenne.
page[1] (peidʒ) *n* (of a book) page *f.*
page[2] (peidʒ) *n* (boy) page *m.*
pageant ('pædʒənt) *n* cortège historique *m.*
pagoda (pə'goudə) *n* pagode *f.*
paid (peid) *v* see **pay.**

pain (pein) *n* **1** douleur, souffrance *f*. **2** *pl* peine *f*. **painful** *adj* douloureux, -euse. **painless** *adj* sans douleur. **painstaking** *adj* soigneux, -euse, appliqué.
paint (peint) *n* **1** peinture *f*. **2** *Art* couleur *f*. *vt* **1** peindre. **2** dépeindre. *vi* faire de la peinture. **paintbrush** *n* pinceau, -aux *m*. **painter** *n* peintre *m*. **painting** *n* **1** peinture *f*. **2** tableau, -aux *m*.
pair (pɛə) *n* **1** paire *f*. **2** couple *m*. *vt* assortir. **pair off 1** disposer deux par deux. **2** s'en aller à deux.
Pakistan (pɑ:ki'stɑ:n) *n* Pakistan *m*. **Pakistani** *adj,n* pakistanais.
pal (pæl) *n inf* camarade *m*.
palace ('pælis) *n* palais *m*.
palate ('pælət) *n* palais *m*. **palatable** *adj* savoureux, -euse.
pale (peil) *adj* pâle, blême. **turn pale** pâlir. **paleness** *n* pâleur *f*.
Palestine ('pælistain) *n* Palestine *f*. **Palestinian** *adj,n* palestinien, -ienne.
palette ('pælit) *n* palette *f*.
palm[1] (pɑ:m) *n anat* paume *f*. *v* **palm off** refiler. **palmist** *n* chiromancien *m*. **palmistry** *n* chiromancie *f*.
palm[2] (pɑ:m) *n bot* palmier *m*.
Palm Sunday *n* dimanche des Rameaux *m*.
pamper ('pæmpə) *vt* dorloter.
pamphlet ('pæmflət) *n* **1** brochure *f*. **2** pamphlet *m*. **pamphleteer** *n* **1** auteur de brochures *m*. **2** pamphlétaire *m*.
pan (pæn) *n* **1** casserole *f*. **2** bac *m*. **pancake** *n* crêpe *f*.
Panama ('pænəmɑ:) *n* Panama *m*.
pancreas ('pæŋkriəs) *n* pancréas *m*.
panda ('pændə) *n* panda *m*.
pander ('pændə) *vi* **pander to** encourager.
pane (pein) *n* vitre *f*. carreau, -aux *m*.
panel ('pænḷ) *n* **1** panneau, -aux *m*. **2** (of people) liste *f*. jury *m*. *vt* lambrisser.
pang (pæŋ) *n* angoisse *f*.
panic* ('pænik) *n* panique *f*. *vi* paniquer. **panic-stricken** *adj* pris de panique.
pannier ('pæniə) *n* panier *m*. hotte *f*.
panorama (pænə'rɑ:mə) *n* panorama *m*. **panoramic** *adj* panoramique.
pansy ('pænzi) *n bot* pensée *f*.
pant (pænt) *vi* panteler, haleter. *n* halètement *m*.
panther ('pænθə) *n* panthère *f*.
pantomime ('pæntəmaim) *n* pantomime *f*.
pantry ('pæntri) *n* garde-manger *m invar*.
pants (pænts) *n pl* caleçon, slip *m*.
papal ('peipəl) *adj* papal, -aux.
paper ('peipə) *n* **1** papier *m*. **2** document, rapport *m*. **3** journal, -aux *m*. **4** épreuve *f*. *adj* de papier. *vt* tapisser. **paperback** *n* livre de poche *m*. **paperclip** *n* attache-papiers *m invar*. trombone *f*. **paperwork** *n* écritures *f pl*.
papier-mâché (ˌpæpiei'mæʃei) *n* carton-pâte *m*.
papist ('peipist) *n* papiste *m,f*.
paprika ('pæprikə) *n* paprika *m*.
par (pɑ:) *n* pair *m*. moyenne *f*. **be on a par with** être au niveau de.
parable ('pærəbəl) *n* parabole *f*.
parachute ('pærəʃu:t) *n* parachute *m*. *vi* descendre en parachute. **parachutist** *n* parachutiste *m,f*.
parade (pə'reid) *n* **1** parade *f*. **2** *mil* exercice, rassemblement *m*. **3** défilé *m*. *vt* faire parade de. *vi* **1** *mil* parader. **2** se pavaner.
paradise ('pærədais) *n* paradis *m*.
paradox ('pærədɔks) *n* paradoxe *m*. **paradoxical** *adj* paradoxal, -aux.
paraffin ('pærəfin) *n* **1** paraffine *f*. **2** *comm* pétrole *m*.
paragraph ('pærəgrɑ:f) *n* paragraphe *m*.
parallel ('pærəlel) *adj* **1** parallèle. **2** semblable. *n* parallèle *f*. *vt* **1** placer parellèlement. **2** comparer. **3** égaler.
paralyse ('pærəlaiz) *vt* paralyser. **paralysed** *adj* **1** *med* paralysé. **2** transi. **paralysis** *n* paralysie *f*. **paralytic** *adj* **1** paralytique. **2** *sl* soûl.
paramount ('pærəmaunt) *adj* **1** éminent. **2** suprême.
paranoia (pærə'nɔiə) *n* paranoïa *f*.
parapet ('pærəpit) *n* parapet *m*.
paraphernalia (pærəfə'neiliə) *n pl* attirail *m*.
paraphrase ('pærəfreiz) *n* paraphrase *f*. *vt* paraphraser.
parasite ('pærəsait) *n* **1** parasite *m*. **2** (person) pique-assiette *m,f invar*.
paratrooper ('pærətru:pə) *n* parachutiste *m*.
parcel ('pɑ:səl) *n* **1** colis *m*. **2** portion, parcelle *f*. *vt* **1** empaqueter. **2** morceler.
parch (pɑ:tʃ) *vt* **1** rôtir. **2** dessécher. *vi* se dessécher. **parched** *adj* sec, aride.
parchment ('pɑ:tʃmənt) *n* parchemin *m*.
pardon ('pɑ:dn̩) *vt* **1** excuser. **2** absoudre. **3** gracier. **pardon me!** excusez-moi! ~*n* **1** pardon *m*. **2** grâce *f*. **I beg your pardon 1** excusez-moi! **2** pardon? comment?

pare (pɛə) *vt* **1** rogner. **2** éplucher. **paring** *n* **1** ébarbage *m*. **2** épluchures *f pl*.

parent ('pɛərənt) *n* **1** père *m*. mère *f*. **2** *pl* parents *m pl*. *adj* mère. **parenthood** *n* paternité, maternité *f*.

parenthesis (pə'renθəsis) *n pl* **-eses** parenthèse *f*.

Paris ('pæris) *n* Paris *m*. **Parisian** *adj,n* parisien, -ienne.

parish ('pæriʃ) *n* **1** paroisse *f*. **2** commune *f*. **parishioner** *n* paroissien, -ienne.

parity ('pæriti) *n* **1** égalité *f*. **2** *comm* parité *f*. pair *m*.

park (pɑ:k) *n* parc *m*. *vt* garer. *vi* stationner. **parking** *n* stationnement *m*. **parking meter** *n* parcomètre *m*.

parliament ('pɑ:ləmənt) *n* parlement *m*. **parliamentary** *adj* parlementaire.

parlour ('pɑ:lə) *n* salon *m*.

parochial (pə'roukiəl) *adj* **1** paroissial, -aux. **2** de clocher. **parochialism** *n* esprit de clocher *m*.

parody ('pærədi) *n* parodie *f*. *vt* parodier.

parole (pə'roul) *n* parole, foi *f*.

parquet ('pɑ:kei) *n* parquet *m*.

parrot ('pærət) *n* perroquet *m*.

parsley ('pɑ:sli) *n* persil *m*.

parsnip ('pɑ:snip) *n* panais *m*.

parson ('pɑ:sən) *n* pasteur *m*. **parsonage** *n* presbytère *m*.

part (pɑ:t) *n* **1** partie *f*. **2** part *f*. **3** pièce *f*. **4** région *f*. **5** *Th* rôle *m*. *vt* **1** diviser. **2** séparer. *vi* **1** se quitter. **2** se diviser. **part with** céder.

partake* (pɑ:'teik) *vt* partager. *vi* **1** prendre part. **2** manger.

partial ('pɑ:ʃəl) *adj* **1** partial, -aux. **2** partiel, -elle. **be partial to** avoir un faible pour. **partiality** *n* **1** partialité *f*. **2** prédilection *f*.

participate (pɑ:'tisipeit) *vi* participer. **participant** *n* participant *m*. **participation** *n* participation *f*.

participle ('pɑ:tisəpəl) *n* participe *m*. **present/past participle** participe présent/passé.

particle ('pɑ:tikəl) *n* particule *f*.

particular (pə'tikjulə) *adj* **1** particulier, -ière, spécial, -aux. **2** détaillé. **3** méticuleux, -euse. **4** exigeant. *n* détail *m*.

parting ('pɑ:tiŋ) *n* **1** séparation *f*. **2** (of the hair) raie *f*.

partisan (pɑ:ti'zæn) *n* partisan *m*.

partition (pɑ:'tiʃən) *n* **1** partage *m*. **2** cloison *f*. *vt* **1** morceler. **2** partager. **3** cloisonner.

partner ('pɑ:tnə) *n* **1** *comm* associé *m*. **2** *sport* partenaire *m,f*. **3** danseur *m*. *vt* être associé à. **partnership** *n* **1** association *f*. **2** *comm* société *f*. **go into partnership with** s'associer avec.

partridge ('pɑ:tridʒ) *n* **1** perdrix *f*. **2** *cul* perdreau, -aux.

part-time *adj,adv* à mi-temps.

party ('pɑ:ti) *n* **1** parti *m*. **2** groupe *m*. **3** réception, soirée *f*. **4** *law* partie *f*. **party line** *n* **1** ligne à poste groupés *f*. **2** *pol* ligne du parti *f*.

pass* (pɑ:s) *n* **1** col, défilé *m*. **2** *educ* réussite sans mention *f*. **3** permis *m*. laissez-passer *m invar*. *vt* **1** passer devant. **2** transmettre. **3** *educ* être reçu à. **4** approuver. **5** *law* voter. vi passer. **pass out** s'évanouir. **password** *n* mot de passe *m*.

passage ('pæsidʒ) *n* **1** passage *m*. **2** couloir *m*. **3** traversée *f*. **passageway** *n* ruelle *f*.

passenger ('pæsindʒə) *n* voyageur, -euse, passager, -ère.

passion ('pæʃən) *n* passion *f*. **passionate** *adj* **1** passionné. **2** emporté.

passive ('pæsiv) *adj,n* passif, -ive *m*.

Passover ('pɑ:souvə) *n* Pâque *f*.

passport ('pɑ:spɔ:t) *n* passeport *m*.

past (pɑ:st) *adj,n* passé *m*. **in the past** autrefois. ~*prep* au delà de. **twenty past two** deux heures vingt. ~*adv* **go past** passer.

pasta ('pæstə) *n* pâtes *f pl*.

paste (peist) *n* **1** pâte *f*. **2** colle *f*. *vt* coller.

pastel ('pæstəl) *n* pastel *m*.

pasteurize ('pæstəraiz) *vt* pasteuriser.

pastime ('pɑ:staim) *n* passe-temps *m invar*. délassement *m*.

pastoral ('pæstərəl) *adj* pastoral, -aux.

pastry ('peistri) *n* **1** pâtisserie *f*. **2** pâte *f*. **puff pastry** *n* pâte feuilletée *f*.

pasture ('pɑ:stʃə) *n* pâturage *m*. *vt,vi* paître.

pasty[1] ('peisti) *adj* **1** pâteux, -euse. **2** terreux, -euse.

pasty[2] ('pæsti) *n* pâté (en croûte) *m*.

pat[1] (pæt) *n* **1** caresse *f*. **2** (of butter) rondelle *f*. *vt* **1** tapoter. **2** caresser.

pat[2] (pæt) *adv* à propos. **off pat** par cœur. ~*adj* apte.

patch (pætʃ) *n* **1** pièce *f*. **2** tache *f*. **3** lopin *m*. **4** emplâtre *f*. *vt* rapiécer. **patch up** ravauder. **patchwork** *n* rapiéçage *m*.

patent ('peitnt) *n* brevet *m*. patente *f*. *vt* breveter. *adj* **1** manifeste. **2** breveté. **patent leather** *n* cuir verni *m*.

paternal (pə'tə:nl) *adj* paternel, -elle. **paternity** *n* paternité *f*.

path (pɑ:θ) *n* **1** chemin, sentier *m.* **2** cours *m.*
pathetic (pə'θetik) *adj* pathétique.
pathology (pə'θɔlədʒi) *n* pathologie *f.* **pathologist** *n* pathologiste *m,f.*
patience ('peiʃəns) *n* **1** patience *f.* **2** *game* réussite *f.* **patient** *adj* patient. *n* malade *m,f.*
patio ('pætiou) *n* patio *m.*
patriarchal (peitri'ɑ:kəl) *adj* patriarcal, -aux.
patriot ('peitriət) *n* patriote *m,f.* **patriotic** *adj* **1** patriote. **2** patriotique. **patriotism** *n* patriotisme *m.*
patrol (pə'troul) *vi* patrouiller. *vt* faire la patrouille dans. *n* patrouille *f.*
patron ('peitrən) *n* **1** protecteur *m.* **2** client *m.* **patronage** *n* **1** protection *f.* patronage *m.* **2** clientèle *f.* **patronize** *vt* **1** patronner. **2** fréquenter.
patter[1] ('pætə) *n* tapotement *m.* *vi* **1** trottiner. **2** crépiter.
patter[2] ('pætə) *n* boniment, bavardage *m.*
pattern ('pætən) *n* **1** modèle *m.* **2** motif *m.* **3** patron *m.* **4** échantillon *m.*
paunch (pɔ:ntʃ) *n* panse *f.* ventre *m.*
pauper ('pɔ:pə) *n* indigent, mendiant *m.*
pause (pɔ:z) *n* **1** pause *f.* **2** silence *m.* *vi* **1** s'arrêter un instant. **2** hésiter.
pave (peiv) *vt* paver. **pave the way** préparer le terrain. **pavement** *n* trottoir *m.* **paving** *n* dallage *m.*
pavilion (pə'viliən) *n* pavillon *m.*
paw (pɔ:) *n* patte *f.* *vt* donner des coups de patte à.
pawn[1] (pɔ:n) *n* gage *m.* *vt* mettre en gage. **pawnbroker** *n* prêteur sur gage *m.*
pawn[2] (pɔ:n) *n* *game* pion *m.*
pay* (pei) *n* paie *f.* traitement *m.* *vt* **1** payer, verser. **2** rétribuer. **payroll** *n* état des paiements *m.*
pea (pi:) *n* **1** pois *m.* **2** *cul* petit pois *m.*
peace (pi:s) *n* **1** paix *f.* **2** tranquillité *f.* **peaceful** *adj* **1** paisible. **2** pacifique. **peacemaker** *n* pacificateur, -trice.
peach (pi:tʃ) *n* pêche *f.* **peach tree** *n* pêcher *m.*
peacock ('pi:kɔk) *n* paon *m.*
peak (pi:k) *n* **1** cime *f.* **2** pointe *f.* **3** visière *f.*
peal (pi:l) *n* **1** carillon *m.* **2** grondement *m.* *vi* **1** carillonner. **2** gronder. *vt* sonner.
peanut ('pi:nʌt) *n* arachide, cacahuète *f.*
pear (pɛə) *n* poire *f.* **pear tree** *n* poirier *m.*
pearl ('pə:l) *n* perle *f.* **mother of pearl** *n* nacre *f.* **pearly** *adj* perlé, nacré.
peasant ('pezənt) *n* paysan, -anne.
peat (pi:t) *n* tourbe *f.*
pebble ('pebəl) *n* caillou, -oux, galet *m.* **pebbly** *adj* caillouteux, -euse.
peck (pek) *n* **1** coup de bec *m.* **2** *inf* bécot *m.* *vt* **1** becqueter. **2** bécoter. *vi inf* manger du bout des dents.
peckish ('pekiʃ) *adj* **feel peckish** avoir le ventre creux.
peculiar (pi'kju:liə) *adj* **1** particulier, -ière **2** bizarre. **peculiarity** *n* **1** particularité *f.* **2** singularité *f.*
pedal ('pedl̩) *n* pédale *f.* *vi* pédaler.
peddle ('pedl̩) *vt* colporter.
pedestal ('pedistəl) *n* **1** piédestal, -aux *m.* **2** socle *m.*
pedestrian (pi'destriən) *n* piéton *m.* **pedestrian crossing** passage clouté *m.* ~*adj* **1** à pied. **2** prosaïque.
pedigree ('pedigri:) *n* **1** pedigree *m.* **2** ascendance *f.*
peel (pi:l) *n* **1** pelure, écorce *f.* **2** *cul* zeste *m.* *vt* **1** éplucher, peler. **2** dépouiller. *vi* **1** se peler. **2** se décrépir.
peep (pi:p) *n* coup d'œil *m.* *v* **peep at** regarder à la dérobée. **peep out** se montrer.
peer[1] (piə) *n* **1** (title) pair *m.* **2** égal, -aux *m.* **peerage** *n* pairie *f.*
peer[2] (piə) *vi* risquer un coup d'œil. **peer at** scruter.
peevish ('pi:viʃ) *adj* maussade.
peg (peg) *n* **1** cheville *f.* **2** fiche *f.* **3** patère *f.* *vt* **1** cheviller, accrocher. **2** *game* marquer.
pejorative (pi'dʒɔrətiv) *adj* péjoratif, -ive.
pelican ('pelikən) *n* pélican *m.*
pellet ('pelit) *n* **1** boulette *f.* **2** plomb *m.*
pelmet ('pelmit) *n* lambrequin *m.*
pelt[1] (pelt) *vt* **1** assaillir. **2** cribler. *vi* tomber à verse. **at full pelt** à toute vitesse.
pelt[2] (pelt) *n* peau, -aux *f.*
pelvis ('pelvis) *n* bassin *m.*
pen[1] (pen) *n* plume *f.* **penfriend** *n* correspondant *m.* **penknife** *n* canif *m.* **pen-nib** *n* bec de plume *m.*
pen[2] (pen) *n* enclos *m.* *v* **pen in** parquer.
penal ('pi:nl̩) *adj* pénal, -aux. **penalize** *vt* **1** sanctionner. **2** *sport* pénaliser. **penalty** *n* **1** peine *f.* **2** *sport* pénalisation *f.*
penance ('penəns) *n* pénitence *f.*
pencil ('pensəl) *n* crayon *m.* **pencil-sharpener** *n* taille-crayon *m.*
pendant ('pendənt) *n* pendentif *m.*
pending ('pendiŋ) *prep* **1** en attendant. **2** durant. *adj* pendant.

pendulum (ˈpendjuləm) *n* pendule *m*.
penetrate (ˈpenitreit) *vt,vi* pénétrer. **penetrating** *adj* **1** pénétrant. **2** perspicace. **penetration** *n* pénétration *f*.
penguin (ˈpeŋgwin) *n* manchot, pingouin *m*.
penicillin (peniˈsilin) *n* pénicilline *f*.
peninsula (pəˈninsjulə) *n* péninsule *f*. **peninsular** *adj* péninsulaire.
penis (ˈpi:nis) *n* pénis *m*.
penitent (ˈpenitənt) *adj,n* pénitent.
pennant (ˈpenənt) *n* banderole *f*.
penny (ˈpeni) *n* **1** *pl* **pence** British unit of currency. **2** *pl* **pennies** sou *m*. **penniless** *adj* sans le sou.
pension (ˈpenʃən) *n* **1** pension *f*. **2** pension de famille *f*. **old age pension** retraite *f*. ~*vt* pensionner. **pension off** mettre à la retraite. **pensioner** *n* retraité *m*.
pensive (ˈpensiv) *adj* pensif, -ive.
pent (pent) *adj* **pent up 1** renfermé. **2** refoulé.
pentagon (ˈpentəgən) *n* pentagone *m*.
Pentecost (ˈpentikɔst) *n* Pentecôte *f*.
penthouse (ˈpenthaus) *n* appentis *m*.
people (ˈpi:pəl) *n* **1** peuple *m*. **2** nation *f*. **3** gens *m or f pl*. **4** *inf* parents *m pl*. *vt* peupler.
pepper (ˈpepə) *n* poivre *m*. *vt* **1** poivrer. **2** cribler. **peppercorn** *n* grain de poivre *m*. **peppermill** *n* moulin à poivre *m*. **peppermint** *n* menthe poivrée *f*. **pepper-pot** *n* poivrière *f*.
per (pə:) *prep* par. **as per** selon.
perambulator (pəˈræmbjuleitə) *n* voiture d'enfant *f*.
perceive (pəˈsi:v) *vt* **1** percevoir. **2** s'apercevoir de. **3** apercevoir. **perceivable** *adj* perceptible, sensible.
per cent (pəˈsent) *n* pour cent *m*.
percentage (pəˈsentidʒ) *n* **1** pourcentage *m*. **2** proportion *f*.
perception (pəˈsepʃən) *n* **1** perception *f*. **2** sensibilité *f*. **perceptive** *adj* perceptif, -ive.
perch (pə:tʃ) *n* perchoir *m*. *vi* (se) percher. *vt* jucher.
percolate (ˈpə:kəleit) *vi* s'infiltrer, filtrer. *vt* passer. **percolator** *n* percolateur *m*.
percussion (pəˈkʌʃən) *n* percussion *f*.
perennial (pəˈreniəl) *adj* **1** éternel, -elle. **2** *bot* vivace. *n* plante vivace *f*.
perfect (*adj,n* ˈpə:fikt; *v* pəˈfekt) *adj* **1** parfait. **2** complet, -ète. *n* parfait *m*. *vt* **1** achever. **2** perfectionner, mettre au point. **perfection** *n* **1** perfection *f*. **2** achèvement *m*.
perforate (ˈpə:fəreit) *vt,vi* perforer. **perforation** *n* perforation *f*.
perform (pəˈfɔ:m) *vt* **1** exécuter. **2** *Th* jouer. **performance** *n* **1** exécution *f*. **2** exploit *m*. **3** *Th* représentation *f*.
perfume (pəˈfju:m) *n* parfum *m*. odeur *f*. *vt* parfumer.
perhaps (pəˈhæps) *adv* peut-être.
peril (ˈperəl) *n* péril *m*. **perilous** *adj* périlleux, -euse.
perimeter (pəˈrimitə) *n* périmètre *m*.
period (ˈpiəriəd) *n* **1** période *f*. **2** durée *f*. **3** époque *f*. **4** *med* règles *f pl*. **periodical** *adj,n* périodique *m*.
peripheral (pəˈrifərəl) *adj* périphérique.
periscope (ˈperiskoup) *n* périscope *m*.
perish (ˈperiʃ) *vi* **1** périr. **2** se détériorer. *vt* altérer, gâter. **perishable** *adj* périssable.
perjury (ˈpə:dʒəri) *n* **1** parjure *m*. **2** *law* faux témoignage *m*.
perk (pə:k) **perk up** *vi* se ranimer. *vt* redresser.
perm (pə:m) *n also* **permanent wave** permanente *f*.
permanent (ˈpə:mənənt) *adj* permanent. **permanence** *n* permanence *f*. **permanently** *adv* en permanence, à titre définitif.
permeate (ˈpə:mieit) *vt* s'infiltrer.
permit (*v* pəˈmit; *n* ˈpə:mit) *vt* **1** permettre. **2** autoriser. *n* **1** permis *m*. **2** autorisation *f*. **permission** *n* **1** permission *f*. **2** permis *m*. **permissible** *adj* admissible. **permissive** *adj* **1** libertin. **2** toléré.
permutation (pə:mjuˈteiʃən) *n* permutation *f*.
peroxide (pəˈrɔksaid) *n* peroxyde *m*. *vt inf* décolorer.
perpendicular (pə:pənˈdikjulə) *adj,n* perpendiculaire *f*.
perpetual (pəˈpetʃuəl) *adj* **1** perpétuel, -elle. **2** incessant.
perpetuate (pəˈpetʃueit) *vt* perpétuer.
perplex (pəˈpleks) *vt* embarrasser, troubler. **perplexed** *adj* perplexe. **perplexity** *n* perplexité *f*.
persecute (ˈpə:sikju:t) *vt* **1** persécuter. **2** tourmenter. **persecution** *n* persécution *f*.
persevere (pə:siˈviə) *vi* persévérer. **perseverance** *n* persévérance *f*.
Persia (ˈpə:ʃə) *n* Perse *f*. **Persian** *adj,n* persan. **Persian** (language) *n* persan *m*.
persist (pəˈsist) *vi* **1** persister, s'obstiner. **2** continuer. **persistence** *n* persistance *f*. **persistent** *adj* **1** persistant, tenace. **2** continu.
person (ˈpə:sən) *n* personne *f*. **personal** *adj*

personnel, -elle. **personality** *n* **1** personnalité *f.* **2** caractère personnel *m.*

personify (pə'sɔnifai) *vt* personnifier. **personification** *n* personnification *f.*

personnel (pə:sə'nel) *n* personnel *m.*

perspective (pə'spektiv) *n* perspective *f.*

Perspex ('pə:speks) *n Tdmk* Perspex *m.*

perspire (pə'spaiə) *vi* transpirer. **perspiration** *n* transpiration, sueur *f.* **perspiring** *adj* en sueur.

persuade (pə'sweid) *vt* persuader. **persuasion** *n* persuasion *f.* **persuasive** *adj* persuasif, -ive.

pert (pə:t) *adj* mutin, effronté.

pertain (pə'tein) *vi* appartenir, se rapporter. **pertinent** *adj* pertinent, à propos.

perturb (pə'tə:b) *vt* perturber, troubler.

Peru (pə'ru:) *n* Pérou *m.* **Peruvian** *adj,n* péruvien, -ienne.

pervade (pə'veid) *vt* s'infiltrer *or* pénétrer dans. **pervading** *adj* dominant.

perverse (pə'və:s) *adj* **1** pervers. **2** contrariant. **perversity** *n* perversité *f.*

pervert (*v* pə'və:t *n* 'pə:və:t) *vt* **1** pervertir. **2** détourner. *n* perverti *m.*

peseta (pə'seitə) *n* peseta *f.*

peso ('peisou) *n* peso *m.*

pessimism ('pesimizəm) *n* pessimisme *m.* **pessimist** *n* pessimiste *m,f.* **pessimistic** *adj* pessimiste.

pest (pest) *n* peste *f.* fléau, -aux *m.* **pesticide** *n* pesticide *m.*

pester ('pestə) *vt* importuner.

pet[1] (pet) *n* **1** animal familier *m.* **2** *inf* chouchou *m. adj* favori, -ite. *vt* choyer.

pet[2] (pet) *n* accès de mauvaise humeur *m.*

petal ('petl̩) *n* pétale *m.*

peter (pi:tə) *vi* **peter out** **1** s'épuiser. **2** flancher, s'arrêter.

petition (pi'tiʃən) *n* **1** pétition, requête *f.* **2** *law* recours *m. vt* **1** adresser une pétition. **2** réclamer.

petrify ('petrifai) *vt* pétrifier. *vi* se pétrifier.

petroleum (pi'trouliəm) *n* pétrole *m.* **petrol** *n* essence *f.*

petticoat ('petikout) *n* jupon *m.*

petty ('peti) *adj* **1** insignifiant. **2** mesquin. **petty cash** *n* petite caisse *f.* **petty officer** *n* sous-officier *m.*

petulant ('petjulənt) *adj* irritable. **petulance** *n* irritabilité *f.*

pew (pju:) *n* banc d'église *m.*

pewter ('pju:tə) *n* étain *m.*

phantom ('fæntəm) *n* fantôme *m.*

pharmacy ('fɑ:məsi) *n* pharmacie *f.*

pharynx ('færiŋks) *n* pharynx *m.*

phase (feiz) *n* phase *f.*

pheasant ('fezənt) *n* faisan *m.*

phenomenon (fi'nɔminən) *n pl* **-ena** phénomène *m.* **phenomenal** *adj* phénoménal, -aux.

philanthropy (fi'lænθrəpi) *n* philanthropie *f.* **philanthropist** *n* philanthrope *m,f.*

philately (fi'lætəli) *n* philatélie *f.* **philatelist** *n* philatéliste *m,f.*

Philippines ('filipi:nz) *n pl* Philippines *f pl.*

Philistine ('filistain) *adj,n* philistin.

philosophy (fi'lɔsəfi) *n* philosophie *f.* **philosopher** *n* philosophe *m.* **philosophical** *adj* **1** philosophique. **2** philosophe.

phlegm (flem) *n* flegme *m.*

phlegmatic (fleg'mætik) *adj* flegmatique.

phobia ('foubiə) *n* phobie *f.*

phoenix ('fi:niks) *n* phénix *m.*

phone (foun) *n inf* téléphone *m. vt* téléphoner à. **phone for** appeler.

phonetic (fə'netik) *adj* phonétique. **phonetics** *n* phonétique *f.*

phoney ('founi) *adj* faux, fausse.

phosphate ('fɔsfeit) *n* phosphate *m.*

phosphorescence (fɔsfə'resəns) *n* phosphorescence *f.* **phosphorescent** *adj* phosphorescent.

phosphorus ('fɔsfərəs) *n* phosphore *m.* **phosphorous** *adj* phosphoreux, -euse.

photo ('foutou) *n inf* photo *f.*

photocopy ('foutoukɔpi) *vt* photocopier. *n* photocopie *f.*

photogenic (foutə'dʒenik) *adj* photogénique.

photograph ('foutəgrɑ:f) *n* photographie *f. vt* photographier. **photographer** *n* photographe *m,f.* **photography** *n* photographie *f.*

phrase (freiz) *n* locution, expression *f. vt* exprimer. **phrasebook** *n* recueil de locutions *m.*

physical ('fizikəl) *adj* physique. **physical education** *n* culture physique *f.*

physician (fi'ziʃən) *n* médecin *m.*

physics ('fiziks) *n* physique *f.*

physiology (fizi'ɔlədʒi) *n* physiologie *f.*

physiotherapy (fiziou'θerəpi) *n* physiothérapie *f.* **physiotherapist** *n* physiothérapeute *m,f.*

physique (fi'zi:k) *n* physique *m.*

piano (pi'ænou) *n* piano *m.* **grand piano** *n* piano à queue *m.* **pianist** *n* pianiste *m,f.*

pick[1] (pik) *vt* **1** choisir. **2** cueillir. **3** (a lock) crocheter. **pick a quarrel with** chercher querelle. **pick out** faire le tri de, choisir. **pick**

over trier. **pick up 1** ramasser. **2** apprendre. **3** prendre. **pick-up** *n* **1** reprise *f*. **2** pick-up *m*. **3** connaissance de rencontre *f*. ~*n* choix *m*. élite *f*. **pickpocket** *n* voleur à la tire *m*.

pick[2] (pik) *n* pic *m*.

picket ('pikit) *n* piquet *m*. *vi* se tenir en faction. *vt* piqueter.

pickle ('pikəl) *n* **1** marinade *f*. **2** *pl* conserves au vinaigre *f pl*. *vt* **1** mariner. **2** conserver au vinaigre.

picnic* ('piknik) *n* pique-nique *m*. *vi* pique-niquer.

pictorial (pik'tɔ:riəl) *adj* **1** en images. **2** illustré.

picture ('piktʃə) *n* **1** image *f*. **2** tableau, -aux *m*. **3** *pl inf* ciné *m*. *vt* représenter, dépeindre.

picturesque (piktʃə'resk) *adj* pittoresque.

pidgin ('pidʒən) *n* pidgin *m*. **speak pidgin** parler petit nègre.

pie (pai) *n* **1** pâté (en croûte) *m*. **2** tourte *f*.

piece (pi:s) *n* **1** morceau, -aux *m*. **2** pièce *f*. **3** partie *f*. **piecemeal** *adv* par morceaux. *adj* fragmentaire. **piecework** *n* travail à la pièce *m*. ~*vt* joindre, assembler. **piece together** rassembler.

pied (paid) *adj* bigarré.

pier (piə) *n* **1** jetée *f*. **2** *arch* pilier *m*.

pierce (piəs) *vt* percer, transpercer. **piercing** *adj* **1** perçant. **2** (of cold) pénétrant.

piety ('paiəti) *n* piété *f*.

pig (pig) *n* porc, cochon *m*. **pig-headed** *adj* têtu, buté. **pig-iron** *n* gueuse de fer *f*. **piglet** *n* porcelet *m*. **pigskin** *n* cuir de porc *m*. **pigsty** *n* porcherie *f*. **pigtail** *n* queue, natte *f*.

pigeon ('pidʒən) *n* pigeon *m*. **pigeonhole** *n* alvéole *f*. casier *m*. *vt* caser.

piggyback ('pigibæk) *n* **give someone a piggyback** porter quelqu'un sur le dos.

pigment ('pigmənt) *n* **1** *sci* pigment *m*. **2** matière colorante *f*. **pigmentation** *n* pigmentation *f*.

pike (paik) *n zool* brochet *m*.

pilchard ('piltʃəd) *n* pilchard *m*.

pile[1] (pail) *n* tas, monceau, -aux. *v* **pile up 1** entasser. **2** amasser.

pile[2] (pail) *n* pieu, pieux *m*. *vt* soutenir avec des pieux.

pile[3] (pail) *n* (of carpet, etc.) poil *m*.

pile[4] (pail) *n med* hémorroïde *f*.

pilfer ('pilfə) *vt* dérober, chaparder. **pilferage** *n* larcins *m pl*.

pilgrim ('pilgrim) *n* pèlerin *m*. **pilgrimage** *n* pèlerinage *m*.

pill (pil) *n* pilule *f*.

pillage ('pilidʒ) *n* pillage *m*. *vt* piller, saccager.

pillar ('pilə) *n* pilier *m*. colonne *f*. **pillar-box** *n* boîte aux lettres *f*.

pillion ('piliən) *n* siège arrière *m*. **ride pillion** monter en croupe.

pillow ('pilou) *n* oreiller *m*. **pillowcase** *n* taie d'oreiller *f*.

pilot ('pailət) *n* pilote *m*. *vt* piloter, guider.

pimento (pi'mentou) *n* piment *m*.

pimple ('pimpəl) *n* bouton *m*. *adj* boutonneux, -euse.

pin (pin) *n* épingle *f*. **pins and needles** fourmillements *m*. **pinball** *n* billard automatique *m*. **pincushion** *n* pelote à épingles *f*. **pinpoint** *vt* indiquer. **pinstripe** *n* rayure *f*. **pin-up** *n* pin-up *f invar*. ~*vt* **1** épingler. **2** clouer. **pin down** engager.

pinafore ('pinəfɔ:) *n* tablier *m*.

pincers ('pinsəz) *n pl* tenaille, pince *f*.

pinch (pintʃ) *vt* **1** pincer. **2** *inf* chiper. *n* **1** pincée *f*. **2** pincement *m*. **at a pinch** au besoin.

pine[1] (pain) *n* pin *m*.

pine[2] (pain) *vi* languir.

pineapple ('painæpəl) *n* ananas *m*.

Ping-pong ('piŋpɔŋ) *n Tdmk* Ping-pong *m*.

pinion ('piniən) *n* aileron *m*. *vt* **1** rogner les ailes à. **2** lier, ligoter.

pink (piŋk) *n* **1** rose *m*. **2** *bot* œillet *m*. *adj* rose.

pinnacle ('pinəkəl) *n* **1** *arch* pinacle *m*. **2** cime *f*. **3** apogée *f*.

pint (paint) *n* pinte *f*.

pioneer (paiə'niə) *n* **1** pionnier *m*. **2** précurseur *m*. *vt* défricher. *vi* frayer le chemin.

pious ('paiəs) *adj* pieux, -euse.

pip (pip) *n* pépin *m*.

pipe (paip) *n* **1** tuyau, -aux *m*. **2** pipe *f*. **pipedream** *n* rêvasserie *f*. **pipeline** *n* canalisation, conduite *f*. **pipette** *n* pipette *f*. compte-gouttes *m invar*.

piquant ('pi:kənt) *adj* piquant. **piquancy** *n* **1** piquant *m*. **2** goût relevé *m*.

pique (pi:k) *n* pique *f*. *vt* piquer, vexer.

pirate ('pairət) *n* pirate *m*. *vt* **1** contrefaire. **2** s'approprier de.

pirouette (piru'et) *n* pirouette *f*. *vi* pirouetter.

Pisces ('pisi:z) *n pl* Poissons *m pl*.

piss (pis) *tab vi* uriner. *n* urine *f*.

pistachio (pis'tæʃiou) *n* pistache *f*.

pistol ('pistəl) *n* pistolet *m*.

piston ('pistən) *n* piston *m*.

pit (pit) *n* **1** fosse *f*. **2** puits *m*. **pitfall** *n* embûche *f*. piège *m*.

pitch[1] (pitʃ) *vt* **1** dresser. **2** placer. **3** lancer. *n* **1** niveau, -aux *m*. **2** *mus* diapason *m*. **3** *sport* terrain *m*. **pitchfork** *n* fourche *f*.

pitch[2] (pitʃ) *n* poix *f*. *vt* enduire de poix.

pith (piθ) *n* **1** moelle *f*. **2** sève, vigueur *f*.

pittance ('pitṇs) *n* pitance *f*.

pity ('piti) *n* pitié, compassion *f*. **what a pity!** quel dommage! ~*vt* plaindre.

pivot ('pivət) *n* pivot m. vi pivoter.

pizza ('pi:tsə) *n* pizza *f*.

placard ('plækɑ:d) *n* affiche *f*. *vt* afficher.

placate (plə'keit) *vt* apaiser.

place (pleis) *n* **1** lieu, -eux *m*. **2** localité *f*. **3** place *f*. **out of place** hors de propos. **placename** *n* nom de lieu *m*. **take place** se passer. ~*vt* **1** mettre. **2** situer. **place an order** passer commande.

placenta (plə'sentə) *n* placenta *m*.

placid ('plæsid) *adj* placide.

plagiarize ('pleidʒəraiz) *vt* plagier. **plagiarist** *n* plagiaire *m*.

plague (pleig) *n* **1** peste *f*. **2** fléau, -aux *m*. *vt* harceler

plaice (pleis) *n* plie *f*.

plaid (plæd) *n* **1** plaid *m*. **2** tartan *m*.

plain (plein) *adj* **1** clair. **2** simple. **3** plat. **4** quelconque. *n* plaine *f*. **plain-clothes** *adj* en civil.

plaintiff ('pleintif) *n* *law* demandeur, plaignant *m*.

plaintive ('pleintiv) *adj* plaintif, -ive.

plait (plæt) *n* natte, tresse *f*. *vt* tresser.

plan (plæn) *n* **1** plan *m*. **2** projet *m*. *vt* **1** projeter. **2** planifier. **planning** *n* **1** conception *f*. **2** planification *f*.

plane[1] (plein) *n* **1** plan *m*. **2** *inf* avion *m*. **3** niveau, -aux *m*. *adj* plat.

plane[2] (plein) *n* rabot *m*. *vt* raboter.

planet ('plænit) *n* planète *f*.

plank (plæŋk) *n* planche *f*.

plankton ('plæŋktən) *n* plancton, plankton *m*.

plant (plɑ:nt) *n* **1** *bot* plante *f*. **2** *tech* usine *f*. *vt* **1** planter. **2** poser, asséner. **plantation** *n* plantation *f*.

plaque (plɑ:k) *n* plaque *f*.

plasma ('plæzmə) *n* plasma *m*.

plaster ('plɑ:stə) *n* **1** *med* emplâtre *m*. **2** plâtre *m*. **plaster of Paris** plâtre de moulage *m*. **sticking plaster** sparadrap *m*. ~*vt* **1** plâtrer. **2** couvrir.

plastic ('plæstik) *adj,n* plastique *m*. **plastic surgery** *n* chirurgie esthétique *f*.

Plasticine ('plæstisi:n) *n* *Tdmk* pâte à modeler *f*.

plate (pleit) *n* **1** plaque *f*. **2** assiette *f*. **3** *Art* gravure, estampe *f*. **dinner/soup plate** assiette plate/creuse *f*. **number plate** plaque d'immatriculation *f*. **platelayer** *n* poseur de rails *m*. ~*vt* plaquer.

plateau ('plætou) *n* plateau, -aux *m*.

platform ('plætfɔ:m) *n* **1** estrade, tribune *f*. **2** (railway) quai *m*. **3** plate-forme *f*.

platinum ('plætnəm) *n* platine *m*.

platonic (plə'tɔnik) *adj* platonique.

plausible ('plɔ:zəbəl) *adj* **1** plausible, vraisemblable. **2** enjoleur, -euse.

play (plei) *vi,vt* jouer *n* **1** *Th* pièce *f*. **2** jeu *m*. **playboy** *n* gaillard *m*. **player** *n* jouer *m*. **playful** *adj* folâtre, enjoué. **playfulness** *n* badinage *m*. **playground** *n* *cour de récréation f*. **playhouse** *n* théâtre *m*. **playing card** *n* carte à jouer *f*. **playing field** *n* terrain de jeux *m*. **playmate** *n* camarade (de jeu) *m,f*. **playschool** *n* jardin d'enfants *m*. **playwright** *n* dramaturge *m*

plea (pli:) *n* **1** prétexte *m*. **2** appel *m*.

plead (pli:d) *vi,vt* plaider. *vt* prétexter, alléguer **plead guilty** s'avouer coupable. **plead not guilty** nier sa culpabilité.

please (pli:z) *vt* plaire à, faire plaisir à. *vi* plaire. *adv* s'il vous plaît. **please do!** je vous en prie! **pleasant** *adj* **1** agréable, charmant. **2** aimable. **pleased** *adj* satisfait, content. **pleasing** *adj* agréable. **pleasure** *n* **1** plaisir *m*. **2** gré *m*.

pleat (pli:t) *n* pli *m*. *vt* plisser.

plectrum ('plektrəm) *n* médiator *m*.

pledge (pledʒ) *n* **1** gage *m*. **2** promesse *f*. *vt* **1** mettre en gage. **2** engager.

plenty ('plenti) *n* abondance *f*. *adv* *inf* largement, bien. **plentiful** *adj* abondant, copieux, -euse.

pliable ('plaiəbəl) *adj* **1** flexible, souple. **2** docile.

pliers ('plaiəz) *n* *pl* pince, tenaille *f*.

plight (plait) *n* état *m*. condition *f*.

plimsoll ('plimsəl) *n* sandale de gymnastique *f*.

plod (plɔd) *vi* marcher lourdement. **plod on** persévérer. **plodder** *n* bûcheur, -euse.

plonk (plɔŋk) *n* bruit sourd *m*. *v* **plonk down** poser sans façons.

plot[1] (plɔt) *n* **1** *lit* intrigue *f*. **2** complot *m*. conspiration *f*. *vt,vi* comploter, conspirer.

plot[2] (plɔt) *n* terrain *m*. **building plot** lotissement *m*.

plough (plau) *n* charrue *f.* *vt* labourer. **plough through** avancer péniblement dans.

pluck (plʌk) *vt* **1** arracher, cueillir. **2** plumer. **pluck up courage** prendre courage. ~*n* courage, cran *m.*

plug (plʌg) *n* **1** boucher *m.* **2** (electric) prise *f.* *vt* boucher, tamponner.

plum (plʌm) *n* prune *f.* **plum tree** prunier *m.*

plumage (ˈplu:midʒ) *n* plumage *f.*

plumb (plʌm) *n* plomb *m.* *adj* d'aplomb, vertical, -aux. *adv* **1** d'aplomb. **2** juste. *vt* sonder. **plumber** *n* plombier *m.* **plumbing** *n* plomberie *f.*

plume (plu:m) *n* plume *f.* *vt* orner de plumes.

plump[1] (plʌmp) *adj* grassouillet, -ette, dodu.

plump[2] (plʌmp) *vi* tomber lourdement. *vt* jeter brusquement. **plump for** choisir.

plunder (ˈplʌndə) *n* **1** pillage *m.* **2** butin *m.* *vt* piller.

plunge (plʌndʒ) *n* plongeon *m.* *vt* plonger, immerger. *vi* **1** jeter. **2** tanguer.

pluperfect (plu:ˈpə:fikt) *n* plus-que-parfait *m.*

plural (ˈpluərəl) *adj,n* pluriel, -elle *m.*

plus (plʌs) *prep* plus. *adj* positif, -ive.

plush (plʌʃ) *n* peluche *f.*

Pluto (ˈplu:tou) *n* Pluton *f.*

ply[1] (plai) *vt* **1** manier. **2** exercer. **3** assaillir. *vi* faire la navette.

ply[2] (plai) *n* **1** épaisseur *f.* **2** pli *m.* **plywood** *n* contre-plaqué *m.*

pneumatic (nju:ˈmætik) *adj* pneumatique. **pneumatic drill** *n* marteau piqueur *m.*

pneumonia (nju:ˈmouniə) *n* pneumonie *f.*

poach[1] (poutʃ) *vi* braconner. **poacher** *n* braconnier *m.*

poach[2] (poutʃ) *vt cul* pocher.

pocket (ˈpɔkit) *n* poche *f.* *vt* empocher. **pocketknife** *n* couteau de poche, canif *m.* **pocket-money** *n* argent de poche *m.*

pod (pɔd) *n* cosse, gousse *f.* *vt* écosser.

poem (ˈpouim) *n* poème *m.* poésie *f.*

poet (ˈpouit) *n* poète *m.* **poetic** *adj* poétique. **poetry** *n* poésie *f.*

poignant (ˈpɔinjənt) *adj* **1** poignant. **2** vif, vive.

point (pɔint) *n* **1** point *m.* **2** question *f.* sujet *m.* **3** idée *f.* **4** pointe *f.* **beside the point** hors de propos. **come to the point** en venir au fait. **point-blank** *adj* **1** à bout portant. **2** direct, catégorique. *adv* **1** à bout portant. **2** catégoriquement. ~*vt* **1** indiquer, signaler. **2** aiguiser. **point out** faire remarquer. **point to** annoncer. **pointed** *adj* **1** pointu. **2** mordant.

poise (pɔiz) *n* **1** équilibre *m.* **2** port *m.* *vt* équilibrer, balancer.

poison (ˈpɔizən) *n* poison *m.* *vt* empoisonner. **poisonous** *adj* **1** empoisonné. **2** (of an animal) venimeux, -euse. **3** (of a plant) vénéneux, -euse.

poke (pouk) *vt* **1** pousser du coude. **2** attiser. **3** passer. **poke fun at** se moquer de. ~*n* **1** coup de coude m. **2** coup de tisonnier *m.*

poker[1] (ˈpoukə) *n* tisonnier *m.*

poker[2] (ˈpoukə) *n game* poker *m.*

Poland (ˈpoulənd) *n* Pologne *f.*

polar (ˈpoulə) *adj* polaire. **polar bear** *n* ours blanc *m.* **polarize** *vt* polariser. *vi* se polariser.

pole[1] (poul) *n* perche *f.* mât *m.* **pole-vault** *vi* sauter à la perche. **pole-vaulting** *n* saut à la perche *m.*

pole[2] (poul) *n geog* pôle *m.*

Pole (poul) *n* polonais *m.*

polemic (pəˈlemik) *adj,n* polémique *f.*

Pole Star *n* étoile polaire *f.*

police (pəˈli:s) *n* police *f.* **policeman** *n* agent de police, gendarme *m.* **police station** *n* commissariat de police *m.*

policy[1] (ˈpɔlisi) *n* politique, ligne de conduite *f.*

policy[2] (ˈpɔlisi) *n* police *f.* **insurance policy** police d'assurance.

polish (ˈpɔliʃ) *n* **1** poli, lustre *m.* **2** cire *f.* cirage *m.* **3** raffinement *m.* *vt* **1** polir. **2** cirer.

Polish (ˈpouliʃ) *adj* polonais. **Polish** (language) *n* polonais *m.*

polite (pəˈlait) *adj* poli, courtois. **politeness** *n* politesse, courtoisie *f.*

politics (ˈpɔlitiks) *n* politique *f.* **political** *adj* politique. **politician** *n* homme politique *m.*

polka (ˈpɔlkə) *n* polka *f.*

poll (poul) *n* vote, scrutin *m.* *vi* voter. **polling booth** isoloir *m.*

pollen (ˈpɔlən) *n* pollen *m.* **pollinate** *vt* polliniser.

pollute (pəˈlu:t) *vt* polluer, souiller. **pollution** *n* pollution *f.*

polygamy (pəˈligəmi) *n* polygamie *f.*

polygon (ˈpɔligən) *n* polygone *m.*

polytechnic (pɔliˈteknik) *adj* polytechnique. *n* institut de technologie *m.*

polythene (ˈpɔliθi:n) *n* polyéthylène *m.*

pomegranate (ˈpɔmigrænət) *n* grenade *f.* **pomegranate tree** *n* grenadier *m.*

pommel (ˈpʌməl) *n* pommeau, -aux *m.* *vt* rouer de coups.

pomp (pɔmp) *n* faste, apparat *m.* pompe *f.*

pompous *adj* **1** fastueux, -euse. **2** suffisant. **3** ampoulé.

pond (pɔnd) *n* étang *m.* mare *f.*

ponder ('pɔndə) *vi* méditer. *vt* considérer, peser, ruminer.

pony ('pouni) *n* poney *m.*

poodle ('pu:dl̩) *n* caniche *m.*

pool[1] (pu:l) *n* flaque, mare *f.*

pool[2] (pu:l) *n* **1** *game* cagnotte, poule *f.* **2** fonds commun *m. vt* mettre en commun.

poor (puə, pɔ:) *adj* **1** pauvre. **2** de mauvaise qualité, médiocre.

pop[1] (pɔp) *n* bruit sec *m. vi* **1** éclater, sauter. **2** crever. *vt* **1** faire sauter. **2** *inf* mettre au clou. **3** fourrer. **pop in** entrer en passant. *~interj* crac! **popcorn** *n* maïs grillé *m.*

pop[2] (pɔp) *adj* pop. **pop music** *n* musique pop *f.*

pope (poup) *n* pape *m.*

poplar ('pɔplə) *n* peuplier *m.*

poppy ('pɔpi) *n* coquelicot, pavot *m.*

popular ('pɔpjulə) *adj* **1** populaire. **2** à la mode. **3** courant. **popularity** *n* popularité *f.*

population (pɔpju'leiʃən) *n* population *f.*

porcelain ('pɔ:slin) *n* porcelaine *f.*

porch (pɔ:tʃ) *n* porche *m.* marquise *f.*

porcupine ('pɔ:kjupain) *n* porc-épic *m.*

pore[1] (pɔ:) *vi* **pore over** s'absorber dans, méditer.

pore[2] (pɔ:) *n* pore *m.*

pork (pɔ:k) *n* porc *m.*

pornography (pɔ:'nɔgrəfi) *n* pornographie *f.* **pornographic** *adj* pornographique.

porous ('pɔ:rəs) *adj* poreux, -euse, perméable.

porpoise ('pɔ:pəs) *n* marsouin *m.*

porridge ('pɔridʒ) *n* porridge *m.*

port[1] (pɔ:t) *n* (harbour) port *m.*

port[2] (pɔ:t) *n naut* bâbord *m.*

port[3] (pɔ:t) *n* (wine) porto *m.*

portable ('pɔ:təbəl) *adj* portatif, -ive.

porter[1] ('pɔ:tə) *n* (luggage) porteur, garçon *m.*

porter[2] ('pɔ:tə) *n* concierge, portier *m.*

portfolio (pɔ:t'fouliou) *n* **1** serviette *f.* porte-documents *m.* **2** *Art* chemise *f.* **3** *pol* portefeuille *f.*

porthole ('pɔ:thoul) *n* hublot *m.*

portion ('pɔ:ʃən) *n* **1** partie, part *f.* **2** portion, ration *f.*

portrait ('pɔ:trit) *n* portrait *m.*

portray (pɔ:'trei) *vt* **1** peindre. **2** dépeindre.

Portugal ('pɔ:tjugəl) *n* Portugal *m.* **Portuguese** *adj,n* portugais *invar.* **Portuguese** (language) *n* portugais *m.*

pose (pouz) *vt,vi* poser. **pose as** se faire passer pour. *~n* pose *f.*

posh (pɔʃ) *adj* chic.

position (pə'ziʃən) *n* **1** position *f.* **2** situation *f.* **3** place *f.* **4** rang *m.* **position closed** guichet fermé. *~vt* **1** situer. **2** orienter.

positive ('pɔzitiv) *adj* **1** positif, -ive. **2** convaincu, assuré. *n* positif *m.*

possess (pə'zes) *vt* **1** posséder. **2** s'approprier. **possession** *n* possession, jouissance *f.* **possessive** *adj* possessif, -ive.

possible ('pɔsəbəl) *adj* possible. **it is possible that** il se peut que. **possibility** *n* **1** possibilité *f.* **2** éventualite *f.* **possibly** *adv* peut-être.

post[1] (poust) *n* poteau, -aux *m. vt* afficher, placarder.

post[2] (poust) *n* **1** *mil* poste *m.* **2** situation *f.* emploi *m. vt* mettre en faction, affecter.

post[3] (poust) *n* **1** courrier *m.* **2** poste *f. vt* mettre à la poste. **postage** *n* affranchissement, port *m.* **postal order** *n* mandat-poste *m.* **postbox** *n* boîte aux lettres *f.* **postcard** *n* carte postale *f.* **postcode** *n* code postal *m.* **postman** *n* facteur *m.* **postmark** *n* cachet de la poste *m.* **post office** *n* bureau de poste *m.*

poster ('poustə) *n* affiche *f.*

posterior (pɔs'tiəriə) *adj* postérieur. *n inf* postérieur, derrière *m.*

posterity (pɔs'teriti) *n* postérité *f.*

postgraduate (poust'grædjuət) *adj* de troisième cycle. *n* étudiant de troisième cycle *m.*

posthumous ('pɔstjuməs) *adj* posthume.

post-mortem (poust'mɔ:təm) *n* autopsie *f.*

postpone (pəs'poun) *vt* ajourner, différer. **postponement** *n* ajournement *m.*

postscript ('pousskript) *n* post-scriptum *m invar.*

postulate (*v* 'pɔstjuleit; *n* 'pɔstjulət) *vt* **1** postuler, demander. **2** supposer. *n* postulat *m.*

posture ('pɔstʃə) *n* **1** posture, attitude *f.* **2** état *m.*

pot (pɔt) *n* **1** pot *m.* **2** marmite *f.* **pots and pans** batterie de cuisine *f.*

potato (pə'teitou) *n, pl* **-oes** pomme de terre *f.*

potent ('poutn̩t) *adj* fort, puissant.

potential (pə'tenʃəl) *adj* **1** possible, latent. **2** potentiel, -elle. *n* potentiel *m.*

pothole ('pɔthoul) *n* **1** (in a road) trou, nid de poule *m.* **2** marmite torentielle *f.* **potholer** *n* spéléologue *m,f.* **potholing** *n* spéléologie *f.*

potion ('pouʃən) *n* potion *f.*

potter (ˈpɔtə) *n* potier *m*. *vi* s'occuper de bagatelles. **potter about** bricoler.

pottery (ˈpɔtəri) *n* poterie *f*.

pouch (pautʃ) *n* **1** poche *f*. petit sac *m*. **2** *zool* poche ventrale *f*. **3** (for tobacco) blague *f*.

poultice (ˈpoultis) *n* cataplasme *m*.

poultry (ˈpoultri) *n* volaille *f*.

pounce (pauns) *vi* **pounce on** fondre *or* s'abattre sur. ~*n* attaque, griffe *f*.

pound[1] (paund) *vt* **1** cogner, battre. **2** piler, broyer.

pound[2] (paund) *n*, *pl* **pounds** *or* **pound 1** (currency) livre sterling *f*. **2** (weight) livre *f*.

pour (pɔ:) *vt* verser, couler. *vi* tomber à verse. **pour in** entrer à flots. **pour out 1** verser. **2** sortir en foule.

pout (paut) *vi* faire la moue, bouder. *n* moue *f*.

poverty (ˈpɔvəti) *n* **1** misère, pauvreté *f*. **2** manque *m*. **poverty-stricken** *adj* indigent.

powder (ˈpaudə) *n* poudre *f*. *vt* **1** pulvériser. **2** saupoudrer. **3** poudrer. **powder room** *n* toilette pour dames *f*.

power (ˈpauə) *n* **1** pouvoir *m*. **2** faculté *f*. **3** puissance *f*. **4** force *f*. **power station** *n* centrale électrique *f*. **powerful** *adj* puissant, fort. **powerless** *adj* impuissant.

practicable (ˈpræktikəbəl) *adj* faisable, praticable.

practical (ˈpræktikəl) *adj* pratique. **practical joke** *n* mauvaise plaisanterie *f*.

practice (ˈpræktis) *n* **1** pratique *f*. **2** coutume *f*. **3** clientèle *f*. **4** *sport* exercice *m*. **out of practice** rouillé.

practise (ˈpræktis) *vt* **1** pratiquer, exercer. **2** étudier, s'exercer. *vi* s'entrainer, faire des exercices.

practitioner (prækˈtiʃənə) *n* praticien *m*.

pragmatic (prægˈmætik) *adj* pragmatique.

prairie (ˈprɛəri) *n* prairie *f*.

praise (preiz) *n* éloge *m*. louange *f*. *vt* faire l'éloge de, louer. **praiseworthy** *adj* louable, méritoire.

pram (præm) *n* landau *m*. voiture d'enfant *f*.

prance (prɑ:ns) *vi* **1** piaffer. **2** se pavaner.

prank (præŋk) *n* **1** escapade, fredaine *f*. **2** tour *m*. farce *f*.

prattle (ˈprætl̩) *vi* babiller, bavarder. *n* babillage *m*.

prawn (prɔ:n) *n* crevette *f*.

pray (prei) *vi,vt* **1** prier. **2** implorer. **prayer** *n* prière *f*. **prayerbook** *n* livre de prières *m*.

preach (pri:tʃ) *vi,vt* prêcher.

precarious (priˈkɛəriəs) *adj* **1** précaire. **2** incertain. **precariousness** *n* **1** précarité *f*. **2** incertitude *f*.

precaution (priˈkɔ:ʃən) *n* précaution *f*.

precede (priˈsi:d) *vt* précéder. **precedence** *n* préséance, priorité *f*. **precedent** *n* précédent *m*.

precinct (ˈpri:siŋkt) *n* enceinte *f*. **pedestrian precinct** zone piétonnière *f*.

precious (ˈpreʃəs) *adj* **1** précieux, -euse. **2** recherché, affecté.

precipice (ˈpresipis) *n* précipice *m*.

precipitate (prəˈsipiteit) *vt* **1** hâter. **2** précipiter. *vi* (se) précipiter. *adj* **1** précipité. **2** irréfléchi. **precipitation** *n* précipitation *f*.

precis (ˈpreisi) *n* résumé, précis *m*.

precise (priˈsais) *adj* **1** précis, exact. **2** méticuleux, -euse. **precision** *n* précision *f*.

precocious (priˈkouʃəs) *adj* précoce. **precociousness** *n* précocité *f*.

preconceive (pri:kənˈsi:v) *vt* préconcevoir. **preconception** *n* **1** idée préconçue. **2** préjugé *m*.

predatory (ˈpredətəri) *adj* prédateur, -trice, rapace.

predecessor (ˈpri:disesə) *n* prédécesseur *m*.

predestine (pri:ˈdestin) *vt* prédestiner. **predestination** *n* prédestination *f*.

predicament (priˈdikəmənt) *n* situation difficile, mauvaise pesse *f*.

predicate (*n* ˈpredikit; *v* ˈpredikeit) *n* prédicat *m*. *vt* affirmer.

predict (priˈdikt) *vt* prédire. **predictable** *adj* prévisible. **prediction** *n* prédiction *f*.

predominate (priˈdɔmineit) *vi* prédominer. **predominance** *n* prédominance *f*. **predominant** *adj* prédominant.

pre-eminent *adj* **1** prééminent. **2** remarquable.

preen (pri:n) *vt* lisser, nettoyer. **preen oneself** se bichonner, faire des grâces.

prefabricate (priˈfæbrikeit) *vt* préfabriquer.

preface (ˈprefis) *n* **1** *lit* préface *f*. avant-propos *m invar*. **2** préambule *m*. *vt* **1** *lit* préfacer. **2** préluder à.

prefect (ˈpri:fekt) *n* préfet *m*.

prefer (priˈfə:) *vt* préférer, aimer mieux. **preference** *n* préférence *f*. **preferential** *adj* préférentiel, -elle.

prefix (ˈpri:fiks) *n* préfixe *m*. *vt* mettre en tête.

pregnant (ˈpregnənt) *adj* **1** (of a woman) enceinte, grosse. **2** (of an animal) pleine. **3** chargé, lourd.

prehistoric (pri:hisˈtɔrik) *adj* préhistorique.

prejudice (ˈpredʒədis) *n* **1** préjugé, parti pris *m*. **2** tort *m*. *vt* **1** prévenir, prédisposer. **2** nuire à.

preliminary (pri'liminəri) *adj* préliminaire, préalable.

prelude ('prelju:d) *n* prélude *m*.

premarital (pri:'mæritḷ) *adj* prénuptial.

premature ('premətʃuə) *adj* prématuré.

premeditate (pri:'mediteit) *vt* préméditer.

premise ('premis) *n* **1** prémisse *f*. **2** *pl* lieux *m pl*. *vt* poser en prémisse.

premium ('pri:miəm) *n* **1** prime *f*. **2** prix, récompense *f*. **premium bond** *n* bon du trésor *m*.

preoccupied (pri:'ɔkjupaid) *adj* préoccupé. **preoccupation** *n* préoccupation *f*.

prepare (pri'pɛə) *vt* préparer. *vi* se préparer, s'apprêter. **preparation** *n* **1** préparation *f*. **2** *pl* préparatifs *m pl*. **preparatory** *adj* préparatoire.

preposition (prepə'ziʃən) *n* préposition *f*.

preposterous (pri'pɔstərəs) *adj* absurde.

prerogative (pri'rɔgətiv) *n* prérogative *f*. privilège *m*.

prescribe (pri'skraib) *vt* prescrire, ordonner. **prescription** *n* **1** *med* ordonnance *f*. **2** prescription *f*.

presence ('prezəns) *n* **1** présence *f*. **2** prestance *f*. air *m*. **presence of mind** sang-froid *m*.

present[1] ('prezənt) *adj* présent, actuel, -elle. *n* présent *m*. **presently** *adv* dans un instant, tout à l'heure.

present[2] (*v* pri'zent; *n* 'prezənt) *vt* **1** présenter. **2** offrir. *n* cadeau, -aux *m*. **presentable** *adj* présentable, portable. **presentation** *n* **1** présentation *f*. **2** remise *f*.

preserve (pri'zə:v) *vt* **1** conserver. **2** préserver. **preserves** *n pl* conserves *f pl*.

preside (pri'zaid) *vi* présider.

president ('prezidənt) *n* président *m*. **presidency** *n* présidence *f*. **presidential** *adj* présidentiel, -elle.

press (pres) *vt* **1** appuyer sur. **2** presser. **3** repasser. *vi* se serrer, se presser. *n* presse *f*. **press conference** *n* conférence de presse *f*. **press-gang** *n* presse *f*. **press-stud** *n* bouton pression *m*. **press-up** *n* exercice musculaire *m*. **pressing** *adj* urgent.

pressure ('preʃə) *n* **1** pression *f*. **2** urgence *f*. **pressure cooker** *n* marmite à pression, cocotte minute *f*. **pressurize** *vt* pressuriser.

prestige (pres'ti:ʒ) *n* prestige *m*.

presume (pri'zju:m) *vt,vi* présumer, supposer. *vt* oser.

pretend (pri'tend) *vt* **1** feindre, simuler. **2** prétendre. *vi* faire semblant. **pretence** *n* **1** simulation *f*. prétexte *m*. **2** prétention *f*. **pretension** *n* prétention *f*. **pretentious** *adj* prétentieux, -euse.

pretext ('pri:tekst) *n* prétexte *m*.

pretty ('priti) *adj* joli, beau, belle. *adv inf* assez, passablement.

prevail (pri'veil) *vi* **1** prévaloir. **2** régner. **prevail upon** persuader. **prevalent** *adj* prédominant, répandu.

prevent (pri'vent) *vt* **1** empêcher. **2** détourner. **prevention** *n* prévention *f*. empêchement *m*. **preventive** *adj* préventif, -ive.

preview ('pri:vju:) *n* **1** exhibition préalable. **2** (cinema, etc.) avant-première *f*.

previous ('pri:viəs) *adj* précédent, antérieur, préalable. **previously** *adv* auparavant.

prey (prei) *n* proie *f*. *v* **prey on** tourmenter, ronger.

price (prais) *n* prix *m*. *vt* mettre un prix à. **price-list** *n* tarif *m*.

prick (prik) *n* piqûre *f*. *vt* piquer, crever. *vi* picoter. **prick up one's ears** dresser l'oreille. **prickle** *n* piquant *m*. épine *f*. *vi* picoter, fourmiller. *vt* piquer. **prickly** *adj* épineux, -euse.

pride (praid) *n* orgueil *m*. fierté *f*. **pride oneself on** se vanter de.

priest (pri:st) *n* prêtre *m*. **priesthood** *n* prêtrise *f*.

prim (prim) *adj* guindé, pincé, collet monté *invar*.

primary ('praiməri) *adj* **1** premier, -ière. **2** originel, -elle. **3** primaire. **primary school** *n* école primaire *f*.

primate *n* **1** ('praimit) *rel* primat *m*. **2** ('praimeit) *zool* primate *m*.

prime (praim) *adj* **1** premier, -ière. **2** de premier ordre. **3** principal, -aux. *vt* préparer. **prime minister** *n* premier ministre *m*.

primitive ('primitiv) *adj* primitif, -ive.

primrose ('primrouz) *n* primevère *f*.

prince (prins) *n* prince *m*.

princess (prin'ses) *n* princesse *f*.

principal ('prinsəpəl) *adj* principal, -aux. *n* directeur, patron *m*.

principality (prinsi'pæliti) *n* principauté *f*.

principle ('prinsəpəl) *n* principe *m*.

print (print) *n* **1** empreinte, trace *f*. **2** impression *f*. **3** *phot* épreuve *f*. **in/out of print** disponible/épuisé. ~*vt* imprimer, tirer. **printed matter** *n* imprimés *m pl*. **printing** *n* impression *f*.

prior ('praiə) *adj* précédent, antérieur. **priority** *n* priorité *f*.
prise (praiz) *vt* **prise open** ouvrir de force.
prism ('prizəm) *n* prisme *m*.
prison ('prizən) *n* prison *f*. **prisoner** *n* prisonnier, -ière.
private ('praivit) *adj* **1** privé, particulier, -ière. **2** intime, confidentiel, -elle. *n* simple soldat *m*. **privacy** *n* intimité *f*. **privately** *adv* en particulier.
privet ('privit) *n* troène *m*.
privilege ('privilidʒ) *n* privilège *m*. prérogative *f*. *vt* privilégier.
prize[1] (praiz) *n* prix *m*.
prize[2] (praiz) *vt* évaluer, estimer.
probable ('prɔbəbəl) *adj* probable, vraisemblable. **probability** *n* probabilité *f*.
probation (prə'beiʃən) *n* **1** épreuve *f*. **2** *law* liberté surveillée *f*. **probation officer** *n* délégué à la liberté surveillée *m*. **probationer** *n* stagiaire *m,f*.
probe (proub) *vt* sonder.
problem ('prɔbləm) *n* problème *m*. **problematic** *adj* problématique, douteux, -euse.
proceed (prə'si:d) *vi* **1** continuer. **2** procéder. **3** provenir. **proceedings** *n pl* **1** débats *m pl*. **2** *law* poursuites *f pl*. **procedure** *n* **1** procédé *m*. **2** *law* procédure *f*.
process ('prouses) *n* **1** processus *m*. **2** cours *m*. **3** procédé *m*. méthode *f*. *vt* traiter. **procession** *n* cortège, défilé *m*.
proclaim (prə'kleim) *vt* proclamer, annonçer. **proclamation** *n* proclamation, déclaration *f*.
procreate ('proukrieit) *vt* procréer, engendrer.
procure (prə'kjuə) *vt* procurer.
prod (prɔd) *vt* **1** pousser du doigt. **2** aiguillonner. *n* coup de pointe *m*.
prodigal ('prɔdigəl) *adj* prodigue.
prodigy ('prɔdidʒi) *n* prodige *m*.
produce (*v* prə'dju:s; *n* 'prɔdju:s) *vt* **1** produire. **2** présenter, montrer. **3** *Th* mettre en scène. *n* produit *m*. denrées *f pl*. **producer** *n* **1** producteur, -trice. **2** *Th* metteur en scène *m*. **product** *n* **1** produit *m*. **2** résultat *m*. **production** *n* **1** production *f*. **2** *comm* fabrique *f*. **3** *Th* mise en scène *f*. **productive** *adj* productif, -ive.
profane (prə'fein) *adj* profane. *vt* profaner.
profess (prə'fes) *vt* **1** professer. **2** prétendre. **profession** *n* **1** profession *f*. **2** métier *m*. **professional** *adj* professionnel, -elle. **professor** *n* professeur *m*.
proficient (prə'fiʃənt) *adj* compétent, capable. **proficiency** *n* compétence *f*.
profile ('proufail) *n* profil *m*. silhouette *f*.
profit ('prɔfit) *n* bénéfice, profit *m*. *vi* bénéficier *or* profiter de. *vt* bénéficier *or* profiter à.
profound (prə'faund) *adj* **1** profond. **2** approfondi. **profoundly** *adv* profondément.
profuse (prə'fju:s) *adj* abondant, excessif, -ive.
programme ('prougræm) *n* **1** programme *m*. **2** (radio, etc.) émission *f*. **program** (in computers) *n* programme *m*. *vt* programmer.
progress (*n* 'prougres; *v* prə'gres) *n* **1** progrès *m*. **2** cours *m*. marche *f*. **make progress** faire des progrès. ~*vi* s'avancer, progresser. **progression** *n* progression *f*. **progressive** *adj* progressif, -ive.
prohibit (prə'hibit) *vt* défendre, interdire. **smoking prohibited** défense de fumer. **prohibition** *n* interdiction, défense *f*.
project (*n* 'prɔdʒekt; *v* prə'dʒekt) *n* projet *m*. *vi* dépasser, faire saillie. *vt* projeter. **projectile** *n* projectile *m*. **projection** *n* **1** projection *f*. **2** lancement *m*. **3** saillie *f*. **projector** *n* projecteur *m*.
proletariat (prouli'tɛəriət) *n* prolétariat *m*.
proliferate (prə'lifəreit) *vi,vt* proliférer.
prolific (prə'lifik) *adj* prolifique, fécond.
prologue ('proulɔg) *n* prologue *m*.
prolong (prə'lɔŋ) *vt* prolonger.
promenade (prɔmə'nɑ:d) *n* promenade, esplanade *f*. *vi* se promener.
prominent ('prɔminənt) *adj* **1** éminent, remarquable. **2** saillant, proéminent. **prominence** *n* **1** proéminence *f*. **2** importance *f*.
promiscuous (prə'miskjuəs) *adj* **1** casuel, -elle. **2** confus. **promiscuity** *n* promiscuité *f*.
promise ('prɔmis) *n* promesse *f*. **break one's promise** manquer de parole. ~*vt,vi* promettre. **promising** *adj* plein de promesses.
promote (prə'mout) *vt* **1** donner de l'avancement à. **2** encourager. **be promoted** monter en grade. **promotion** *n* promotion *f*.
prompt (prɔmpt) *adj* prompt. *vt* **1** *Th* souffler. **2** suggérer à, inciter. **prompter** *n* souffleur, -euse.
prone (proun) *adj* enclin, porté.
prong (prɔŋ) *n* **1** fourche *f*. **2** dent de fourche *f*.
pronoun ('prounaun) *n* pronom *m*.
pronounce (prə'nauns) *vt* **1** articuler. **2** déclarer. **pronounced** *adj* marqué. **pronunciation** *n* prononciation *f*.
proof (pru:f) *n* **1** preuve *f*. **2** épreuve *f*. *adj* à

l'épreuve de, résistant. **proofread** *vt* faire des corrections sur épreuves.

prop[1] (prɔp) *n* appui, soutien *m*. *vt* soutenir, appuyer.

prop[2] (prɔp) *n Th* accessoire *m*.

propaganda (prɔpəˈgændə) *n* propagande *f*.

propagate (ˈprɔpəgeit) *vt* propager.

propel (prəˈpel) *vt* propulser. **propeller** *n* hélice *f*.

proper (ˈprɔpə) *adj* **1** propre. **2** approprié, juste. **3** convenable, comme il faut. **properly** *adv* **1** correctement. **2** comme il faut. **proper noun** *n* nom propre *m*.

property (ˈprɔpəti) *n* **1** propriété *f*. **2** biens *m pl*. **3** immeuble *m*. **4** qualité *f*. **lost property** objets trouvés *m pl*.

prophecy (ˈprɔfisi) *n* prophétie *f*. **prophesy** *vt* prophétiser, prédire. *vi* parler en prophète.

prophet (ˈprɔfit) *n* prophète *m*. **prophetic** *adj* prophétique.

proportion (prəˈpɔːʃən) *n* **1** part, partie *f*. **2** rapport *m*. proportion *f*. **out of proportion** mal proportionné. ~*vt* proportionner. **proportional** *adj* proportionnel, -elle, proportionné à.

propose (prəˈpouz) *vt* proposer. *vi* faire une demande en mariage. **proposal** *n* **1** proposition *f*. **2** projet *m*. **3** demande en mariage *f*. **proposition** *n* **1** proposition *f*. **2** affaire *f*.

proprietor (prəˈpraiətə) *n* propriétaire *m,f*.

propriety (prəˈpraiəti) *n* **1** bienséance *f*. convenances *f pl*. **2** propriété *f*.

propulsion (prəˈpʌlʃən) *n* propulsion *f*.

prose (prouz) *n* **1** prose *f*. **2** *educ* thème *m*.

prosecute (ˈprɔsikjuːt) *vt* poursuivre. **prosecution** *n* poursuites *f pl*. **prosecutor** *n* plaignant *m*.

prospect (ˈprɔspekt) *n* **1** perspective *f*. **2** vue *f*. **3** *pl* avenir *m*. *vt* prospecter. **prospective** *adj* à venir, futur. **prospectus** *n* prospectus *m*.

prosper (ˈprɔspə) *vi* prospérer, réussir. **prosperity** *n* prospérité *f*. **prosperous** *adj* prospère.

prostitute (ˈprɔstitjuːt) *n* prostituée *f*. *vt* prostituer. **prostitution** *n* prostitution *f*.

prostrate (*v* prɔsˈtreit; *adj* ˈprɔstreit) *vt* coucher, étendre. **prostrate oneself** se prosterner. ~*adj* **1** prosterné, étendu. **2** accablé.

protagonist (prəˈtægənist) *n* protagoniste *m*.

protect (prəˈtekt) *vt* **1** protéger. **2** sauvegarder. **protection** *n* **1** protection, défense *f*. **2** abri *m*. **protective** *adj* protecteur, -trice.

protein (ˈproutiːn) *n* protéine *f*.

protest (*n* ˈproutest; *v* prəˈtest) *n* protestation *f*. *vt,vi* protester.

Protestant (ˈprɔtistənt) *adj,n* protestant.

protocol (ˈproutəkɔl) *n* protocole *m*.

proton (ˈproutɔn) *n* proton *m*.

prototype (ˈproutətaip) *n* prototype *m*.

protrude (prəˈtruːd) *vi* déborder, faire saillie. **protruding** *adj* saillant.

proud (praud) *adj* orgueilleux, -euse, fier, -ère.

prove (pruːv) *vt* démontrer, prouver. *vi* se montrer, se trouver. **proven** *adj* avéré.

proverb (ˈprɔvəːb) *n* proverbe *m*. **proverbial** *adj* proverbial, -aux.

provide (prəˈvaid) *vt* fournir, munir, pourvoir. **provide for** pourvoir à. **provided** *conj* pourvu que. **provision** *n* **1** provision *f*. **2** stipulation *f*. **3** *pl* comestibles *m pl*. **make provision for** pourvoir à. **provisional** *adj* provisoire.

province (ˈprɔvins) *n* **1** province *f*. **2** ressort, domaine *m*. **provincial** *adj* provincial, -aux.

proviso (prəˈvaizou) *n* condition, clause conditionnelle *f*.

provoke (prəˈvouk) *vt* **1** provoquer, exaspérer. **2** exciter. **provocation** *n* provocation *f*. **provocative** *adj* provocateur, -trice

prow (prau) *n* proue *f*.

prowess (ˈprauis) *n* prouesse *f*.

prowl (praul) *vi* rôder.

proximity (prɔkˈsimiti) *n* proximité *f*.

prude (pruːd) *n* prude *f*. **prudish** *adj* prude, bégueule.

prudent (ˈpruːdn̩t) *adj* prudent, sage. **prudence** *n* prudence *f*.

prune[1] (pruːn) *n* pruneau, -aux *m*.

prune[2] (pruːn) *vt* tailler, émonder.

pry (prai) *vt* fureter, fourrer le nez.

psalm (sɑːm) *n* psaume *m*.

pseudonym (ˈsjuːdənim) *n* pseudonyme *m*.

psychedelic (saikiˈdelik) *adj* psychédélique.

psychiatry (saiˈkaiətri) *n* psychiatrie *f*. **psychiatric** *adj* psychiatrique. **psychiatrist** *n* psychiatre *m*.

psychic (ˈsaikik) *adj* psychique, métaphysique.

psychoanalysis (saikouəˈnælisis) *n* psychanalyse *f*. **psychoanalysist** *n* psychanalyste *m*.

psychology (saiˈkɔlədʒi) *n* psychologie *f*. **psychological** *adj* psychologique. **psychologist** *n* psychologue *m*.

psychopathic (saikəˈpæθik) *adj* psychopathe.

psychosomatic (saikousəˈmætik) *adj* psychosomatique.

pub (pʌb) *n inf* bistrot, bar *m*. **pub crawl** *n* tournée des bistrots *f*.

puberty ('pju:bəti) *n* puberté *f*.
public ('pʌblik) *adj,n* public, -ique *m*. **general public** grand public. **public house** *n* auberge *f*. **public relations** *n* rapports exterieurs *m pl*. **public school** *n* grande école privée d'enseignement secondaire *f*. **publican** *n* propriétaire de bistrot *m*.
publication (pʌbli'keiʃən) *n* publication *f*.
publicity (pʌb'lisiti) *n* publicité, réclame *f*.
publicize ('pʌblisaiz) *vt* faire connaître au public.
publish ('pʌbliʃ) *vt* publier, faire paraître. **publisher** *n* éditeur *m*. **publishing** *n* publication *f*. **publishing house** *n* maison d'édition *f*.
pucker ('pʌkə) *vt* **1** rider. **2** froncer. *vi* faire des plis, se froncer. *n* **1** ride *f*. **2** fronce *f*.
pudding ('pudiŋ) *n* pouding, pudding *m*.
puddle ('pʌdl̩) *n* flaque d'eau *f*.
puff (pʌf) *n* souffle *m*. bouffée *f*. *vi* souffler, haleter. *vt* gonfler. **puff pastry** *n* pâte feuilletée *f*. **puffy** *adj* boursouflé.
pull (pul) *n* coup *m*. *vt,vi* tirer. **pull a face** faire une grimace. **pull down** démolir. **pull off** enlever. **pull oneself together** se reprendre. **pull out** **1** arracher. **2** sortir. **pull up** **1** remonter. **2** arrêter. **pullover** *n* pull *m*.
pulley ('puli) *n* poulie *f*.
pulp (pʌlp) *n* pulpe *f*. *vt* réduire en pulpe, décortiquer.
pulpit ('pʌlpit) *n* chaire *f*.
pulsate (pʌl'seit) *vi* **1** (of the heart) battre. **2** palpiter.
pulse (pʌls) *n* pouls *m*. *vi* battre, vibrer.
pulverize ('pʌlvəraiz) *vt* pulvériser.
pump (pʌmp) *n* pompe *f*. *vt* **1** pomper. **2** *sl* tirer les vers du nez de.
pumpkin ('pʌmpkin) *n* citrouille *f*.
pun (pʌn) *n* jeu de mots *m*.
punch[1] (pʌntʃ) *n* coup de poing *m*. *vt* donner un coup de poing à.
punch[2] (pʌntʃ) *n* (drink) punch *m*.
punch[3] (pʌntʃ) *vt* percer. *n* poinçon *m*.
punctual ('pʌŋktʃuəl) *adj* ponctuel, -elle, exact. **punctuality** *n* ponctualité *f*.
punctuate ('pʌŋktʃueit) *vt* ponctuer. **punctuation** *n* ponctuation *f*.
puncture ('pʌŋktʃə) *n* crevaison, perforation *f*. *vt* **1** crever. **2** ponctionner.
pungent ('pʌndʒənt) *adj* **1** âcre, fort. **2** mordant. **pungency** *n* **1** aigreur *f*. **2** saveur *f*.
punish ('pʌniʃ) *vt* punir, châtier. **punishment** *n* punition *f*. châtiment *m*. **capital punishment** *n* peine capitale *f*.
punt[1] (pʌnt) *n* bateau plat *m*. *vt* conduire à la perche.
punt[2] (pʌnt) *vi game* ponter. **punter** *n* joueur *m*.
pupil[1] ('pju:pəl) *n* élève *m,f*. écolier, -ière.
pupil[2] ('pju:pəl) *n anat* pupille *f*.
puppet ('pʌpit) *n* **1** marionnette *f*. **2** (person) pantin *m*.
puppy ('pʌpi) *n* jeune chien, chiot *m*.
purchase ('pə:tʃis) *vt* acheter. *n* achat *m*.
pure (pjuə) *adj* pur. **purity** *n* pureté *f*.
purgatory ('pə:gətri) *n* purgatoire *m*.
purge (pə:dʒ) *vt* purger, purifier. *n* purge *f*.
purify ('pjuərifai) *vt* purifier, épurer.
Puritan ('pjuəritən) *adj,n* puritain.
purl (pə:l) *vt* faire des mailles à l'envers.
purple ('pə:pəl) *adj,n* pourpre *f*.
purpose ('pə:pəs) *n* dessein, but *m*. fin *f*. **on purpose** exprès. **purposely** *adv* **1** à dessein. **2** exprès.
purr (pə:) *vi* ronronner. *n* ronron *m*.
purse (pə:s) *n* porte-monnaie *m invar*. bourse *f*.
pursue (pə'sju:) *vt,vi* poursuivre. **pursuit** *n* **1** poursuite *f*. **2** recherche *f*.
pus (pʌs) *n* pus *m*. sanie *f*.
push (puʃ) *vt,vi* pousser. *vt* **1** appuyer. **2** bousculer. *n* poussée *f*. **at a push** au besoin. **pushchair** *n* poussette *f*.
pussy ('pusi) *n* minet, chaton *m*.
put* (put) *vt* mettre, poser, placer. **put back** **1** remettre. **2** retarder. **put down** **1** déposer. **2** noter. **3** attribuer. **put forward** avancer. **put off** différer. **put on** mettre. **put out** **1** éteindre. **2** déconcerter. **3** tendre. **put up** **1** construire. **2** hausser. **put up with** supporter.
putrid ('pju:trid) *adj* putride.
putt (pʌt) *n* coup roulé *m*. *vt* poter. **putting green** *n* vert *m*.
putty ('pʌti) *n* mastic *m*.
puzzle ('pʌzəl) *n* **1** devinette, énigme *f*. **2** puzzle *m*. *vt* intriguer.
PVC *n* PCV *m*.
Pygmy ('pigmi) *n* pygmée *m*.
pyjamas (pə'dʒɑ:məz) *n pl* pyjama *m*.
pylon ('pailən) *n* pylône *m*.
pyramid ('pirəmid) *n* pyramide *f*.
Pyrenees (pirə'ni:z) *n pl* Pyrénées *f pl*.
Pyrex ('paireks) *n Tdmk* pyrex *m*.
python ('paiθən) *n* python *m*.

Q

quack[1] (kwæk) *n* couin-couin *m*. *vi* faire couin-couin.
quack[2] (kwæk) *n* charlatan *m*.
quadrangle (ˈkwɔdræŋgəl) *n* **1** *math* quadrilatère *m*. **2** cour *f*.
quadrant (ˈkwɔdrənt) *n* quadrant *m*.
quadrilateral (kwɔdriˈlætərəl) *adj,n* quadrilatère *m*.
quadruped (ˈkwɔdruped) *adj,n* quadrupède *m*.
quadruple (ˈkwɔdrupəl) *adj* quadruple. *vt* quadrupler.
quadruplet (ˈkwɔdruplit) *n* quadruplé *m*.
quail[1] (kweil) *n* caille *f*.
quail[2] (kweil) *vi* fléchir, faiblir.
quaint (kweint) *adj* **1** étrange, bizarre. **2** pittoresque, de l'ancienne mode.
quake (kweik) *vi* **1** trembler. **2** frémir.
Quaker (ˈkweikə) *n* quaker *m*.
qualify (ˈkwɔlifai) *vt* **1** qualifier. **2** modifier. *vi* se qualifier, acquérir les connaissances nécessaires. **qualification** *n* **1** capacité *f*. **2** restriction *f*. **3** *pl* titres *m pl*.
quality (ˈkwɔliti) *n* qualité *f*.
qualm (kwa:m) *n* remords, scrupule *m*.
quandary (ˈkwɔndəri) *n* embarras *m*. **be in a quandary** se trouver dans une impasse.
quantify (ˈkwɔntifai) *vt* quantifier.
quantity (ˈkwɔntiti) *n* quantité *f*.
quarantine (ˈkwɔrənti:n) *n* quarantaine *f*. *vt* mettre en quarantaine.
quarrel (ˈkwɔrəl) *vi* se disputer. *n* querelle, dispute *f*. **quarrelsome** *adj* querelleur, -euse.
quarry[1] (ˈkwɔri) *n min* carrière *f*. *vt* extraire.
quarry[2] (ˈkwɔri) *n* proie *f*. gibier *m*.
quart (kwɔ:t) *n* quart de gallon *m*.
quarter (ˈkwɔ:tə) *n* **1** quart *m*. **2** quartier *m*. **3** trimestre *m*. **quarter past four** quatre heures et quart. **quarter to four** quatre heures moins le quart. ~*vt* **1** diviser en quatre. **2** *mil* caserner. **quarterdeck** *n* gaillard d'arrière *m*. *m*. **quartermaster** *n* maître de timonerie *m*. **quarterly** *adj* trimestriel, -elle.
quartet (kwɔ:ˈtet) *n* quatuor *m*.
quartz (kwɔ:ts) *n* quartz *m*.
quash[1] (kwɔʃ) *vt* étouffer.
quash[2] (kwɔʃ) *vt law* annuler.
quaver (ˈkweivə) *n* **1** *mus* croche *f*. **2** tremblement *m*. *vi* trembloter.
quay (ki:) *n* quai *m*.
queasy (ˈkwi:zi) *adj* délicat, barbouillé.
queen (kwi:n) *n* **1** reine *f*. **2** *game* dame *f*. **queen mother** *n* reine-mère *f*.
queer (kwiə) *adj* **1** bizarre, singulier, -ière. **2** suspect. **3** *sl* homosexuel, -elle. *n sl* homosexuel *m*.
quell (kwel) *vt* **1** étouffer. **2** vaincre. **3** calmer.
quench (kwentʃ) *vt* apaiser, éteindre.
query (ˈkwiəri) *n* **1** question *f*. **2** point d'interrogation *m*. *vt* mettre en question. **query whether** s'informer si.
quest (kwest) *n* quête, recherche *f*.
question (ˈkwestʃən) *n* question *f*. *vt* questionner. **question mark** *n* point d'interrogation *m*. **questionable** *adj* discutable. **questionnaire** *n* questionnaire *m*.
queue (kju:) *n* queue *f*. *vi* faire la queue.
quibble (ˈkwibəl) *n* chicane. *vi* chicaner.
quick (kwik) *adj* **1** vite, rapide. **2** vif, vive. *n* vif *m*. **quicksand** *n* sable mouvant *m*. **quicksilver** *n* mercure, vif-argent *m*. **quickstep** *n* pas redoublé *m*. **quick-tempered** *adj* emporté, prompt à la colère. **quick-witted** *adj* d'un esprit vif. **quicken** *vt* **1** stimuler. **2** accélérer. *vi* s'animer. **quickly** *adv* vite, rapidement.
quid (kwid) *n invar inf* livre sterling *f*.
quiet[1] (ˈkwaiət) *n* tranquillité *f*. repos *m*.
quiet[2] (ˈkwaiət) *adj* **1** tranquille. **2** (of behaviour, etc.) discret, -ète. **quieten** *vt* **1** apaiser, calmer. **2** faire taire. **quieten down** se calmer. **quietly** *adv* silencieusement, doucement. **quietness** *n* tranquillité *f*.
quill (kwil) *n* tuyau, -aux *m*. plume *f*.
quilt (kwilt) *n* couverture piquée *f*. *vt* piquer, ouater. **quilting** *n* piquage *m*.
quince (kwins) *n* coing *m*.
quinine (kwiˈni:n) *n* quinine *f*.
quintessence (kwinˈtesəns) *n* quintessence *f*.
quintet (kwinˈtet) *n* quintette *m*.
quirk (kwə:k) *n* faux-fuyant *m*.
quit* (kwit) *vt* **1** quitter. **2** cesser. *vi* **1** démissionner. **2** s'en aller. **quits** *adj* quitte.
quite (kwait) *adv* **1** tout à fait, bien. **2** assez.
quiver[1] (ˈkwivə) *vi* trembler, tressaillir. *n* tremblement, frisson *m*.
quiver[2] (ˈkwivə) *n* (for arrows) carquois *m*.
quiz (kwiz) *n*, *pl* **quizzes** devinette *f*. *vt* interroger, poser des colles à.
quizzical (ˈkwizikəl) *adj* railleur, -euse.
quoit (kɔit) *n* palet *m*.
quota (ˈkwoutə) *n* quote-part, quotité *f*.
quote (kwout) *vt* **1** citer. **2** *comm* établir. *n*

citation *f.* **quotation** *n* citation *f.* **quotation marks** *n pl* guillemets *m pl.*

R

rabbi ('ræbai) *n* rabbin *m.*
rabbit ('ræbit) *n* lapin *m.*
rabble ('ræbəl) *n* cohue, foule *f.*
rabies ('reibi:z) *n* rage *f.* **rabid** *adj* enragé, féroce.
race[1] (reis) *n* course *f.* *vt* faire courir. *vi* faire une course. **racecourse** *n* champ de courses *m.* **racehorse** *n* cheval de course *m.*
race[2] (reis) *n* (of people) race *f.* **race relations** *n pl* relations raciales *f pl.* **racial** *adj* de race. **racialism** *n* racisme *m.*
rack (ræk) *n* **1** râtelier *m.* **2** classeur *m.* **3** filet *m.* **4** roue *f.* **be on the rack** être au supplice. ~*vt* tourmenter. **rack one's brains** se creuser la tête.
racket[1] ('rækit) *n inf* **1** vacarme, tapage *m.* **2** combine, escroquerie *f.*
racket[2] ('rækit) *n sport* raquette *f.*
radar ('reida:) *n* radar *m.*
radial ('reidiəl) *adj* radial, -aux.
radiant ('reidiənt) *adj* rayonnant, radieux, -euse. **radiance** *n* rayonnement *m.* splendeur *f.*
radiate ('reidieit) *vt,vi* émettre. *vi* rayonner. **radiation** *n* irradiation *f.* **radiator** *n* radiateur *m.*
radical ('rædikəl) *adj,n* radical, -aux.
radio ('reidiou) *n* radio *f.* *vt* envoyer par radio.
radioactivity (reidiouæk'tiviti) *n* radio-activité *f.* **radioactive** *adj* radio-actif, -ive.
radish ('rædiʃ) *n* radis *m.*
radium ('reidiəm) *n* radium *m.*
radius ('reidiəs) *n pl* **-dii** *or* **-diuses** rayon *m.*
raffia ('ræfiə) *n* raphia *m.*
raffle ('ræfəl) *n* loterie *f.* *vt* mettre en loterie.
raft (ra:ft) *n* radeau, -aux *m.*
rafter ('ra:ftə) *n* chevron *m.*
rag[1] (ræg) *n* **1** chiffon, lambeau, -aux *m.* **2** *pl* haillons *m pl.* **ragged** *adj* en lambeaux, en loques.
rag[2] (ræg) *vt inf* chahuter, brimer.
rage (reidʒ) *n* **1** rage, fureur *f.* **2** manie *f.* **be all the rage** être du dernier cri. ~*vi* rager, être furieux.
raid (reid) *n* rafle *f.* *vt* faire une rafle, marauder.
rail (reil) *n* **1** barre, rampe *f.* barreau, -aux *m.* **2** (railway) rail *m.* **railing** *n* grille *f.* garde-fou *m.* **railway** *n* chemin de fer *m.* **railway station** *n* gare *f.*
rain (rein) *n* pluie *f.* *vt,vi* pleuvoir. **rainbow** *n* arc-en-ciel *m.* **raindrop** *n* goutte de pluie *f.* **rainfall** *n* chute de pluie, précipitation *f.*
raise (reiz) *vt* **1** dresser. **2** lever. **3** hausser. **4** soulever.
raisin ('reizən) *n* raisin sec *m.*
rajah ('ra:dʒə) *n* raja *m.*
rake (reik) *n* râteau, -aux *m.* *vt* ratisser, râteler.
rally ('ræli) *n* **1** ralliement *m.* **2** *mot* rallye *m.* *vt* rallier. *vi* se rallier, se reprendre.
ram (ræm) *n* bélier *m.* *vt* pilonner, battre. éperonner.
ramble ('ræmbəl) *vi* **1** flâner, errer. **2** parler sans suite. *n* **1** promenade *f.* **2** randonnée *f.*
ramp (ræmp) *n* rampe *f.*
rampage ('ræmpeidʒ) *n* **be on the rampage** en avoir après tout le monde.
rampant ('ræmpənt) *adj* rampant, forcené. **be rampant** sévir.
rampart ('ræmpa:t) *n* rempart *m.*
ramshackle ('ræmʃækəl) *adj* délabré.
ran (ræn) *v see* **run.**
ranch (ra:ntʃ) *n* ranch *m.* ferme d'élevage *f.*
rancid ('rænsid) *adj* rance. **turn rancid** rancir.
rancour ('ræŋkə) *n* rancune *f.*
random ('rændəm) *adj* fait au hasard. **at random** au hasard, à tort et à travers.
rang (ræŋ) *v see* **ring**[2].
range (reindʒ) *n* **1** gamme *f.* **2** étendue *f.* **3** distance *f.* **4** *geog* chaîne *f.* **5** champ de tir *m.* **6** *cul* fourneau, -aux *m.* *vt* ranger. *vi* **1** parcourir. **2** s'étendre.
rank[1] (ræŋk) *n* rang *m.* *vt* compter. *vi* se classer, se ranger. **rank and file** *n* hommes de troupe *m pl.*
rank[2] (ræŋk) *adj* **1** (trop) luxuriant. **2** rance, fétide.
rankle ('ræŋkəl) *vi* s'envenimer, s'irriter.
ransack ('rænsæk) *vt* **1** fouiller. **2** saccager.
ransom ('rænsəm) *n* rançon *f.* *vt* racheter, rançonner.
rap (ræp) *vt,vi* frapper. *n* petit coup sec *m.*
rape (reip) *n* viol *m.* *vt* violer.
rapid ('ræpid) *adj,n* rapide *m.* **rapidity** *n* rapidité *f.*
rapier ('reipiə) *n* rapière *f.*
rapture ('ræptʃə) *n* extase *m.*
rare[1] (rɛə) *adj* rare, peu commun. **rareness** *n* rareté *f.*
rare[2] (rɛə) *adj cul* saignant.
rascal ('ra:skəl) *n* polisson *m.*

rash[1] (ræʃ) *adj* téméraire. **rashness** *n* témérité *f*.
rash[2] (ræʃ) *n med* éruption *f*.
rasher ('ræʃə) *n* tranche *f*.
raspberry ('rɑ:zbri) *n* framboise *f*. **raspberry cane** *n* framboisier *m*.
rat (ræt) *n* rat *m*.
rate (reit) *n* **1** taux *f*. **2** cours *m*. **3** proportion *f*. **4** vitesse *f*. **5** *pl* impôts locaux *m pl*. **at any rate** en tout cas. ~*vt* évaluer, classer. **ratepayer** *n* contribuable *m*.
rather ('rɑ:ðə) *adv* **1** plutôt. **2** un peu, assez.
ratio ('reiʃiou) *n* rapport *m*. proportion *f*.
ration ('ræʃən) *n* ration *f*. *vt* rationner. **rationing** *n* rationnement *m*.
rational ('ræʃənəl) *adj* raisonnable, raisonné. **rationalize** *vt* rationaliser.
rattle ('rætl̩) *vi* cliqueter, faire du bruit. *vt* agiter, faire cliqueter. *n* **1** fracas, cliquetis *m*. **2** (toy) hochet *m*.
raucous ('rɔ:kəs) *adj* rauque.
ravage ('rævidʒ) *vt* ravager, dévaster.
rave (reiv) *vi* être en délire. **rave about** s'extasier sur. **raving** *adj* furieux, -euse. *n* délire *m*.
raven ('reivən) *n* corbeau, -aux *m*.
ravenous ('rævənəs) *adj* vorace.
ravine (rə'vi:n) *n* ravin *m*. ravine *f*.
ravish ('ræviʃ) *vt* ravir, enlever.
raw (rɔ:) *adj* **1** cru, brut. **2** sans expérience. **3** *med* à vif.
ray (rei) *n* rayon *m*. lueur *f*.
rayon ('reiɔn) *n* rayonne *f*.
razor ('reizə) *n* rasoir *m*. **razor blade** *n* lame de rasoir *f*.
reach (ri:tʃ) *vt* **1** arriver à. **2** atteindre. **3** tendre. *vi* s'élever. **reach out** s'étendre. ~*n* **1** portée *f*. **2** *sport* allonge *f*.
react (ri'ækt) *vi* réagir. **reaction** *n* réaction *f*. **reactionary** *adj,n* réactionnaire.
read* (ri:d) *vt* **1** lire. **2** *educ* étudier. **reading** *n* lecture *f*.
readjust (ri:ə'dʒʌst) *vt* rajuster. **readjustment** *n* rajustement *m*. rectification *f*.
ready ('redi) *adj* **1** prêt. **2** prompt. **get ready** se préparer. **ready-made** *adj* tout fait. **readily** *adv* volontiers.
real (riəl) *adj* **1** réel, -elle. **2** authentique. **realism** *n* réalisme *m*. **realist** *n* réaliste *m,f*. **realistic** *adj* réaliste. **reality** *n* réalité *f*. **really** *adv* vraiment.
realize ('riəlaiz) *vi* se rendre compte de. *vt* réaliser.
realm (relm) *n* royaume *m*.
reap (ri:p) *vt* moissonner, recueillir.
reappear (ri:ə'piə) *vi* reparaître. **reappearance** *n* réapparition *f*.
rear[1] (riə) *adj* d'arrière, postérieur. *n* arrière, derrière *m*. **rear admiral** *n* contre-amiral *m*. **rearguard** *n* arrière-garde *f*.
rear[2] (riə) *vt* élever, cultiver. *vi* se cabrer.
rearrange (riə'reindʒ) *vt* arranger de nouveau.
reason ('ri:zən) *n* **1** raison *f*. **2** cause *f*. *vi* raisonner. **reasonable** *adj* **1** raisonnable. **2** modéré, abordable. **reasoning** *n* raisonnement *m*.
reassure (ri:ə'ʃuə) *vt* rassurer.
rebate ('ri:beit) *n* **1** *comm* rabais *m*. **2** ristourne *f*.
rebel (*adj,n* 'rebəl; *v* ri'bel) *adj,n* rebelle. *vi* se révolter. **rebellion** *n* révolte *f*. **rebellious** *adj* rebelle.
rebuff (ri'bʌf) *n* rebuffade *f*. échec *m*. *vt* repousser.
rebuild* (ri:'bild) *vt* rebâtir, reconstruire.
rebuke (ri'bju:k) *vt* réprimander. *n* réprimande *f*.
recall (ri'kɔ:l) *vt* **1** rappeler. **2** se souvenir de. *n* **1** mémoire *m*. **2** rappel *m*
recede (ri'si:d) *vi* **1** reculer, s'éloigner. **2** fuir.
receipt (ri'si:t) *n* **1** *comm* quittance *f*. **2** reçu *m*. *vt* acquitter.
receive (ri'si:v) *vt* recevoir. **receiver** *n* **1** destinataire *m,f*. **2** *law* administrateur judiciaire *m*. **3** (of a telephone) récepteur *m*.
recent ('ri:sənt) *adj* récent. **recently** *adv* récemment.
receptacle (ri'septəkəl) *n* récipient *m*.
reception (ri'sepʃən) *n* **1** réception *f*. **2** accueil *m*. **3** soirée *f*. **receptionist** *n* préposée à la réception *f*. **receptive** *adj* réceptif, -ive.
recess (ri'ses) *n* **1** recoin, renfoncement *m*. **2** alcôve *f*. **3** *pol* vacances *f pl*.
recession (ri'seʃən) *n* **1** recul *m*. régression *f*. **2** *pol* récession *f*.
recipe ('resipi) *n* recette *f*.
recipient (ri'sipiənt) *n* bénéficiaire *m,f*.
reciprocate (ri'siprəkeit) *vt* **1** rendre. **2** payer de retour. *vi* rendre la pareille. **reciprocal** *adj* **1** réciproque, mutuel, -elle. **2** *math* inverse.
recite (ri'sait) *vt* réciter, réclamer. **recital** *n* **1** *mus* audition *f*. récital *m*. **2** narration *f*.
reckless ('rekləs) *adj* insouciant, téméraire, imprudent.
reckon ('rekən) *vt,vi* compter, calculer.
reclaim (ri'kleim) *vt* **1** récupérer. **2** défricher, assécher. **3** corriger.

recline (ri'klain) *vt* reposer, appuyer. *vi* être couché, se reposer.
recluse (ri'klu:s) *n* reclus *m*.
recognize ('rekəgnaiz) *vt* **1** reconnaître. **2** avouer, admettre. **recognition** *n* reconnaissance *f*.
recoil (ri'kɔil) *vi* **1** reculer. **2** se détendre. *n* **1** recul *m*. **2** mouvement de dégoût *m*.
recollect (rekə'lekt) *vt* se rappeler, se souvenir de. **recollection** *n* souvenir *m*. mémoire *f*.
recommence (ri:kə'mens) *vt,vi* recommencer.
recommend (rekə'mend) *vt* recommander, conseiller. **recommendation** *n* recommandation *f*.
recompense ('rekəmpəns) *n* **1** récompense *f*. **2** dédommagement *m*. *vt* **1** récompenser. **2** réparer. **3** dédommager.
reconcile ('rekənsail) *vt* **1** réconcilier. **2** concilier.
reconstruct (ri:kən'strʌkt) *vt* reconstruire.
record (*n* 'rekɔ:d; *v* ri'kɔ:d) *n* **1** registre *m*. **2** dossier *m*. **3** disque *m*. **4** *sport* record *m*. *vt* **1** enregistrer. **2** rapporter. **record-player** *n* électrophone *m*. tourne-disques *m invar*.
recount (ri'kaunt) *vt* raconter.
recover (ri'kʌvə) *vt* **1** recouvrer, retrouver. **2** rattraper. **3** récupérer. *vi* se rétablir, se remettre. **recovery** *n* **1** guérison *f*. **2** redressement *m*. **3** recouvrement *m*.
recreation (rekri'eiʃən) *n* récréation *f*. divertissement *m*.
recruit (ri'kru:t) *vt* recruter. *n* recrue *f*. conscrit *m*.
rectangle ('rektæŋgəl) *n* rectangle *m*. **rectangular** *adj* rectangulaire.
rectify ('rektifai) *vt* rectifier, réparer.
recuperate (ri'kju:pəreit) *vt* remettre, récupérer. *vi* se remettre.
recur (ri'kə:) *vi* revenir. **recurrence** *n* **1** réapparition *f*. **2** *med* récidive *f*. **recurring** *adj* récidive.
red (red) *adj,n* rouge *m*. **turn red** rougir. **redcurrant** *n* groseille rouge *f*. **red-handed** *adj* sur le fait, en flagrant délit. **red herring** *n* **1** hareng saur *m*. **2** diversion *f*.
redeem (ri'di:m) *vt* **1** racheter. **2** rembourser. **3** dégager.
redevelop (ri:di'veləp) *vt* redévelopper.
Red Indian *n* peau rouge *m*.
redress (ri'dres) *n* redressement *m*. réparation *f*. *vt* **1** rétablir. **2** réparer.
reduce (ri'dju:s) *vt* **1** réduire. **2** rabaisser.
reduction *n* **1** réduction *f*. **2** baisse *f*. **3** rabais *m*.
redundant (ri'dʌndənt) *adj* **1** surabondant, superflu. **2** en surnombre.
reed (ri:d) *n* roseau, -aux *m*.
reef (ri:f) *n* récif, banc *m*.
reek (ri:k) *vt* exhaler une mauvaise odeur, puer. *n* odeur âcre *f*.
reel[1] (ri:l) *n* **1** bobine *f*. **2** moulinet *m*.
reel[2] (ri:l) *vi* chanceler, tituber.
re-establish (ri:i'stæbliʃ) *vt* rétablir.
refectory (ri'fektəri) *n* réfectoire *m*.
refer (ri'fə:) *vt* **1** rapporter. **2** renvoyer. **3** s'en référer. *vi* **1** s'en rapporter. **2** se référer, faire allusion. **referee** *n* arbitre *m*. **reference** *n* **1** renvoi *m*. référence *f*. **2** rapport *m*. **3** allusion *f*. **4** recommandation *f*. **referendum** *n* référendum *m*.
refill (*v* ri:'fil; *n* 'ri:fil) *vt* remplir, regarnir. *n* recharge, cartouche *f*.
refine (ri'fain) *vt* raffiner, affiner. *vi* se raffiner. **refinement** *n* **1** affinage, raffinage *m*. **2** raffinement *m*. **refinery** *n* raffinerie *f*.
reflation (ri'fleiʃən) *n pol* nouvelle inflation, reprise *f*.
reflect (ri'flekt) *vt* réfléchir, refléter. *vi* méditer. **reflection** *n* **1** réflexion *f*. **2** reflet *m*. **reflector** *n* réflecteur *m*.
reflex ('ri:fleks) *n* **1** reflet *m*. **2** réflexe *m*. **reflexive** *adj* réfléchi.
reform (ri'fɔ:m) *n* réforme *f*. *vt* réformer. *vi* se réformer. **reformation** *n* réformation, réforme *f*.
refract (ri'frækt) *vt* réfracter.
refrain[1] (ri'frein) *vi* s'abstenir, s'empêcher.
refrain[2] (ri'frein) *n* refrain *m*.
refresh (ri'freʃ) *vt* rafraîchir. *vi* se rafraîchir, se restaurer. **refreshment** *n* rafraîchissement *m*.
refrigerator (ri'fridʒəreitə) *n* réfrigérateur *m*.
refuel (ri:'fju:əl) *vi* se réapprovisionner, faire le plein d'essence.
refuge ('refju:dʒ) *n* **1** refuge, abri *m*. **2** asile *m*. **take refuge** se réfugier. **refugee** *n* réfugié *m*.
refund (*v* ri'fʌnd; *n* 'ri:fʌnd) *vt* rembourser, rendre. *n* remboursement *m*.
refuse[1] (ri'fju:z) *vt* **1** refuser. **2** rejeter. **refusal** *n* refus *m*.
refuse[2] ('refju:s) *n* déchets *m pl*. ordures *f pl*. rebut *m*. *adj* de rebut.
refute (ri'fju:t) *vt* réfuter.
regain (ri'gein) *vt* **1** regagner, reconquérir. **2** reprendre.

regal (ˈri:gəl) *adj* royal, -aux.
regard (riˈgɑ:d) *n* **1** égard *m*. **2** considération *f*. respect *m*. **3** *pl* amitiés *f pl*. *vt* **1** considérer. **2** concerner. **regarding** *prep* quant à. **regardless** *adj* **1** insouciant. **2** inattentif,-ive. **regardless of** sans regarder à.
regatta (riˈgɑ:tə) *n* régates *f pl*.
regent (ˈri:dʒənt) *adj,n* régent *m*.
regime (reiˈʒi:m) *n* régime *m*.
regiment (ˈredʒimənt) *n* régiment *m*. *vt* **1** enrégimenter. **2** organiser. **regimental** *adj* régimentaire.
region (ˈri:dʒən) *n* région *f*.
register (ˈredʒistə) *n* **1** registre *m*. **2** compteur *m*. *vt* **1** enregistrer, inscrire. **2** (a letter) recommander. **registrar** *n* **1** officier d'etat civil *m*. **2** *educ* secrétaire *m*. **registration** *n* enregistrement *m*. inscription, immatriculation *f*.
regress (riˈgres) *vi* régresser. *n* retour en arrière *m*. **regression** *n* retour *m*.
regret (riˈgret) *n* regret *m*. *vt* regretter.
regular (ˈregjulə) *adj* **1** régulier, -ière. **2** rangé. **3** réglementaire. **4** habituel, -elle. **5** véritable. **regularity** *n* régularité *f*.
regulate (ˈregjuleit) *vt* régler. **regulation** *n* règlement *m*. *adj* réglementaire.
rehabilitate (ri:əˈbiliteit) *vt* **1** réhabiliter. **2** réadapter. **rehabilitation** *n* **1** réhabilitation *f*. **2** rééducation *f*.
rehearse (riˈhə:s) *vt* répéter. **rehearsal** *n* répétition *f*.
reheat (ri:ˈhi:t) *vt* réchauffer.
reign (rein) *vi* régner. *n* règne.
reimburse (ri:imˈbə:s) *vt* rembourser.
rein (rein) *n* rêne, guide *f*.
reincarnation (ri:inkɑ:ˈneiʃən) *n* réincarnation *f*.
reindeer (ˈreindiə) *n* renne *m*.
reinforce (ri:inˈfɔ:s) *vt* **1** renforcer. **2** consolider. **reinforcement** *n* **1** renforcement *m*. **2** *pl* renforts *m pl*.
reinstate (ri:inˈsteit) *vt* **1** réintégrer. **2** rétablir.
reinvest (ri:inˈvest) *vt* replacer.
reissue (ri:ˈiʃu:) *n* **1** nouvelle émission *f*. **2** (of a book) nouvelle édition *f*. *vt* **1** émettre de nouveau. **2** donner une nouvelle édition.
reject (*v* riˈdʒekt; *n* ˈri:dʒekt) *n* pièce de rebut *f*. *vt* **1** rejeter, repousser. **2** refuser. **rejection** *n* **1** rejet *m*. **2** refus *m*.
rejoice (riˈdʒɔis) *vt* réjouir. *vi* se réjouir.
rejuvenate (riˈdʒu:vəneit) *vt* rajeunir.
relapse (riˈlæps) *n* **1** récidive *f*. **2** *med* rechute *f*. *vi* **1** retomber, récidiver. **2** *med* faire une rechute.
relate (riˈleit) *vt* raconter. *vi* se rapporter, avoir rapport. **related** *adj* apparenté.
relation (riˈleiʃən) *n* **1** relation *f*. récit *m*. **2** rapport *m*. **3** parent *m*. **relationship** *n* **1** parenté *f*. **2** rapport *m*.
relative (ˈrelətiv) *adj* relatif, -ive. *n* parent *m*. **relativity** *n* relativité *f*.
relax (riˈlæks) *vt* **1** relâcher, détendre. **2** mitiger. *vi* se relâcher, se décontracter. **relaxation** *n* **1** relâchement *m*. **2** mitigation *f*. **3** détente *f*.
relay (*n* ˈri:lei; *v* riˈlei) *n* relais *m*. *vt* **1** relayer. **2** transmettre.
release (riˈli:s) *n* **1** décharge, libération *f*. **2** échappement, dégagement *m*. **3** relâche *f*. *vt* **1** acquitter, libérer. **2** dégager, émettre.
relent (riˈlent) *vi* se radoucir, céder.
relevant (ˈreləvənt) *adj* pertinent, à propos, en rapport. **relevance** *n* pertinence *f*. rapport *m*.
reliable (riˈlaiəbəl) *adj* **1** sûr, sérieux, -euse. **2** solide. **reliability** *n* sûreté, régularité *f*.
relic (ˈrelik) *n* **1** relique *f*. **2** *pl* vestiges, restes *m pl*.
relief (riˈli:f) *n* **1** soulagement *m*. **2** secours *m*. **3** *Art* relief *m*.
relieve (riˈli:v) *vt* **1** soulager, alléger. **2** secourir, aider. **3** débarrasser. **4** faire ressortir.
religion (riˈlidʒən) *n* religion *f*. culte *m*. **religious** *adj* **1** religieux, -euse. **2** scrupuleux, -euse.
relinquish (riˈliŋkwish) *vt* **1** abandonner, renoncer. **2** lâcher.
relish (ˈreliʃ) *n* goût *m*. saveur *f*. *vt* **1** relever. **2** savourer, aimer.
relive (ri:ˈliv) *vt* revivre.
reluctant (riˈlʌktənt) *adj* peu disposé. **reluctance** *n* répugnance *f*. **reluctantly** *adv* à contre-cœur.
rely (riˈlai) *vi* **rely on** compter sur, se fier à.
remain (riˈmein) *vi* **1** rester. **2** demeurer. **remainder** *n* reste, restant *m*. **remains** *n pl* restes, vestiges *m pl*.
remand (riˈmɑ:nd) *vt* renvoyer à une autre audience. *n* renvoi *m*.
remark (riˈmɑ:k) *n* **1** observation *f*. commentaire *m*. **2** remarque *f*. *vt* observer, remarquer. *vi* faire une remarque. **remarkable** *adj* remarquable, frappant.
remarry (ri:ˈmæri) *vi* se remarier.
remedy (ˈremədi) *n* remède *m*. *vt* remédier à.
remember (riˈmembə) *vt* se rappeler, se sou-

venir de. **remembrance** *n* souvenir *m*. mémoire *f*.

remind (ri'maind) *vt* rappeler, faire penser. **reminder** *n* **1** mémento *m*. **2** *comm* rappel *m*.

reminiscence (remi'nisəns) *n* réminiscence *f*. souvenir *m*. **reminiscent** *adj* **1** qui se souvient. **2** qui rapelle.

remiss (ri'mis) *adj* **1** négligent, insouciant. **2** inexact, lâche.

remission (ri'miʃən) *n* pardon *m*. rémission *f*.

remit (ri'mit) *vt* remettre. **remittance** *n* remise *f*. envoi de fonds *m*.

remnant ('remnənt) *n* **1** reste, restant *m*. **2** (of material) coupon *m*.

remorse (ri'mɔ:s) *n* remords *m*.

remote (ri'mout) *adj* **1** éloigné, reculé. **2** loin, lointain. **3** vague. **4** distant.

remove (ri'mu:v) *vt* **1** enlever, écarter. **2** déplacer. **3** déménager. **removal** *n* **1** enlèvement *m*. **2** déplacement *m*. **3** déménagement *m*.

remunerate (ri'mju:nəreit) *vt* rémunérer. **remuneration** *n* rémunération *f*. **remunerative** *adj* rémunérateur, -trice.

renaissance (ri'neisəns) *n* renaissance *f*.

rename (ri:'neim) *vt* débaptiser.

render ('rendə) *vt* **1** rendre. **2** remettre. **3** *cul* fondre.

renew (ri'nju:) *vt* **1** renouveler. **2** remplacer. *vi* se renouveler. **renewal** *n* **1** renouvellement *m*. **2** remplacement *m*.

renounce (ri'nauns) *vt* **1** renoncer. **2** renier, dénoncer. **renunciation** *n* renoncement *m*. renonciation *f*.

renovate ('renəveit) *vt* rénover, remettre à neuf. **renovation** *n* rénovation *f*.

renown (ri'naun) *n* renommée *f*. renom *m*. **renowned** *adj* célèbre.

rent (rent) *n* loyer *m*. location *f*. *vt* louer, affermer. **rental** *n* loyer *m*. location *f*.

reopen (ri:'oupən) *vt* **1** rouvrir. **2** reprendre. *vi* **1** se rouvrir. **2** rentrer.

reorganize (ri:'ɔ:gənaiz) *vt* réorganiser. *vi* se réorganiser. **reorganization** *n* réorganisation *f*.

repair (ri'pɛə) *vt* réparer, réfectionner. *n* réparation *f*. rétablissement *m*.

repartee (repə'ti:) *n* répartie, riposte *f*.

repatriate (ri'pætrieit) *vt* rapatrier. *n* rapatrié *m*. **repatriation** *n* rapatriement *m*.

repay* (ri'pei) *vt* **1** rendre, rembourser. **2** récompenser, s'acquitter envers. **repayment** *n* **1** remboursement *m*. **2** récompense *f*.

repeal (ri'pi:l) *vt* **1** rapporter, abroger. **2** révoquer. *n* abrogation, révocation *f*.

repeat (ri'pi:t) *vt* répéter, réitérer. *vi* **1** se répéter. **2** donner des renvois. *n* **1** répétition *f*. **2** *mus* reprise *f*.

repel (ri'pel) *vt* **1** repousser. **2** répugner à. **repellent** *adj* **1** répulsif, -ive. **2** repoussant.

repent (ri'pent) *vi* se repentir. *vt* se repentir de. **repentance** *n* repentir *m*.

repercussion (ri:pə'kʌʃən) *n* **1** répercussion *f*. **2** résonnance *f*.

repertoire ('repətwɑ:) *n* répertoire *m*.

repertory ('repətri) *n* répertoire *m*. **repertory theatre** *n* théâtre de province *m*.

repetition (repə'tiʃən) *n* répétition *f*.

replace (ri'pleis) *vt* **1** replacer, remettre. **2** remplacer.

replay (*v* ri:'plei; *n* 'ri:plei) *v* rejouer. *n* match rejoué *m*.

replenish (ri'pleniʃ) *vt* remplir, se réapprovisionner.

replica ('replikə) *n* **1** reproduction, copie *f*. **2** double *m*.

reply (ri'plai) *n* réponse *f*. *vt,vi* répondre.

report (re'pɔ:t) *n* **1** rapport, compte rendu *m*. **2** nouvelle *f*. **3** *educ* bulletin *m*. **4** *mil* détonation *f*. *vt* **1** rapporter, rendre compte de. **2** signaler. **reporter** *n* journaliste *m,f*.

repose (ri'pouz) *n* repos, calme *m*. *vi* se délasser.

represent (repri'zent) *vt* représenter. **representation** *n* représentation *f*. **representative** *adj* représentatif, -ive. *n* représentant *m*.

repress (ri'pres) *vt* **1** réprimer. **2** étouffer. **repression** *n* répression *f*.

reprieve (ri'pri:v) *vt* **1** grâcier. **2** donner un répit à. *n* **1** grâce *f*. **2** sursis, répit *m*.

reprimand ('reprimɑ:nd) *n* réprimande *f*. *vt* réprimander.

reprint (*v* ri:'print; *n* 'ri:print) *vt* réimprimer. *n* réimpression *f*. nouveau tirage *m*.

reprisal (ri'praizəl) *n* représaille *f*.

reproach (ri'proutʃ) *n* reproche, blâme *m*. *vt* reprocher à.

reproduce (ri:prə'dju:s) *vt* reproduire. *vi* se reproduire. **reproduction** *n* **1** reproduction *f*. **2** copie, imitation *f*.

reptile ('reptail) *n* reptile *m*.

republic (ri'pʌblik) *n* république *f*. **republican** *adj,n* républicain.

repudiate (ri'pju:dieit) *vt* répudier. **repudiation** *n* répudiation *f*.

repugnant (ri'pʌgnənt) *adj* répugnant.

repulsion (ri'pʌlʃən) *n* répulsion, répugnance *f*. **repulsive** *adj* repoussant, répugnant.

repute (ri'pju:t) *n* réputation, renommée *f*. *vt* estimer. **reputable** *adj* honorable, estimable. **reputation** *n* réputation *f*. renom *m*. **reputed** *adj* censé, supposé.

request (ri'kwest) *n* demande, requête *f*. *vt* demander, prier.

requiem ('rekwiəm) *n* **1** requiem *m*. **2** chant funèbre *m*.

require (ri'kwaiə) *vt* **1** demander, exiger. **2** avoir besoin de, falloir. **requirement** *n* **1** besoin *m*. **2** demande *f*.

re-read (ri:'ri:d) *vt* relire.

re-run (ri:'rʌn) *vt* **1** recourir. **2** recommencer. *n* répétition d'un film *f*.

resale ('ri:seil) *n* revente *f*.

rescue ('reskju:) *n* délivrance *f*. sauvetage *m*. *vt* sauver, délivrer, secourir.

research (ri'sə:tʃ) *n* recherche *f*. *vi* faire des recherches.

resell* (ri:'sel) *vt* revendre.

resemble (ri'zembəl) *vt* ressembler à. **resemblance** *n* ressemblance, similarité *f*.

resent (ri'zent) *vt* s'offenser de, ressentir. **resentful** *adj* rancunier, -ière. **resentment** *n* ressentiment *m*.

reserve (ri'zə:v) *n* **1** réserve *f*. **2** prix minimum *m*. **3** terrain réservé *m*. *vt* réserver. **reservation** *n* **1** réserve *f*. **2** location, place retenue *f*. **reserved** *adj* **1** réservé. **2** renfermé.

reservoir ('rezəvwɑ:) *n* réservoir *m*.

reside (ri'zaid) *vi* résider. **residence** *n* résidence, demeure *f*. **resident** *n* **1** pensionnaire *m,f*. habitant *m*. **2** résident *m*. *adj* résidant.

residue ('rezidju:) *n* résidu *m*.

resign (ri'zain) *vt* donner sa démission de, résigner. *vi* démissionner. **resignation** *n* **1** démission *f*. **2** résignation *f*.

resilient (ri'ziliənt) *adj* **1** rebondissant, élastique. **2** qui a du ressort. **resilience** *n* **1** élasticité *f*. **2** ressort *m*.

resin ('rezin) *n* résine *f*. *vt* résiner.

resist (ri'zist) *vt* résister à. **resistance** *n* résistance *f*.

resit (ri:'sit) *vi* doubler, retenter.

resolute ('rezəlu:t) *adj* résolu, déterminé, ferme. **resolutely** *adv* résolument. **resolution** *n* **1** résolution *f*. **2** fermeté *f*.

resolve (ri'zɔlv) *vt* **1** résoudre. **2** décider. *vi* se résoudre. *n* résolution *f*.

resonant ('rezənənt) *adj* résonnant, sonore.

resort (ri'zɔ:t) *n* **1** station *f*. séjour *m*. **2** ressource *f*. recours *m*. *vi* avoir recours, user.

resound (ri'zaund) *vi* résonner, retentir.

resource (ri'zɔ's) *n* ressource *f*.

respect (ri'spekt) *n* **1** respect *m*. **2** rapport, égard *m*. **3** *pl* respects, hommages *m pl*. *vt* respecter. **respectable** *adj* **1** convenable. **2** honnête. **3** passable. **respectful** *adj* respectueux, -euse. **respective** *adj* respectif, -ive.

respite ('respit) *n* répit *m*. relâche *f*.

respond (ri'spɔnd) *vi* répondre. **response** *n* réponse *f*. **responsibility** *n* responsabilité *f*. **responsible** *adj* **1** responsable, chargé. **2** compétent, capable. **responsive** *adj* impressionnable, sensible.

rest[1] (rest) *n* **1** repos *m*. **2** support *m*. **3** *mus* pause *f*. *vi* **1** se reposer. **2** se poser, s'appuyer. *vt* **1** reposer. **2** appuyer. **restful** *adj* calme, tranquille. **restive** *adj* **1** rétif, -ive, quinteux, -euse. **2** inquiet, -ète.

rest[2] (rest) *n* **1** reste, restant *m*. **2** autres *m,f pl*. *vi* rester. **restive** *adj* rétif, -ive.

restaurant ('restərɔnt) *n* restaurant *m*.

restless ('restləs) *adj* agité, inquiet, ète.

restore (ri'stɔ:) *vt* **1** restituer. **2** restaurer, réparer. **3** rétablir. **restoration** *n* **1** restitution *f*. **2** restauration *f*.

restrain (ri'strein) *vt* **1** retenir, empêcher. **2** contenir. **restrain oneself** se contraindre. **restraint** *n* **1** contrainte, entrave *f*. **2** réserve *f*.

restrict (ri'strikt) *vt* restreindre, limiter. **restriction** *n* restriction *f*. **restrictive** *adj* restrictif, -ive.

result (ri'zʌlt) *n* **1** résultat *m*. **2** conséquence *f*. *vi* **1** résulter, s'ensuivre. **2** aboutir.

resume (ri'zju:m) *vt* reprendre. **resumption** *n* reprise *f*.

resurrect (rezə'rekt) *vt* ressusciter. **resurrection** *n* résurrection *f*.

retail ('ri:teil) *n* détail *m*. *vt* détailler, vendre au détail.

retain (ri'tein) *vt* **1** retenir, maintenir. **2** conserver. **3** garder.

retaliate (ri'tælieit) *vi* user de représailles. **retaliation** *n* revanche *f*. représailles *f. pl*.

retard (ri'tɑ:d) *vt* retarder. **retarded** *adj* attardé, arriéré.

reticent ('retisənt) *adj* réticent, taciturne.

retina ('retinə) *n* rétine *f*.

retire (ri'taiə) *vi* **1** se retirer. **2** prendre sa retraite. **3** reculer. *vt* mettre à la retraite. **retirement** *n* **1** retraite *f*. **2** retrait *m*.

retort[1] (ri'tɔ:t) *n* réplique, riposte *f. vt* répliquer, riposter.
retort[2] (ri'tɔ:t) *n sci* cornue *f.*
retrace (ri'treis) *vt* **1** reconstituer. **2** revenir sur.
retract (ri'trækt) *vt* **1** rétracter. **2** rentrer. *vi* se rétracter.
retreat (ri'tri:t) *n* retraite *f. vi* **1** se retirer, s'éloigner. **2** *mil* battre en retraite.
retrieve (ri'tri:v) *vt* **1** rapporter, retrouver. **2** relever.
retrograde ('retrəgreid) *adj* **1** rétrograde. **2** inverse.
retrogress (retrə'gres) *vi* rétrograder.
retrospect ('retrəspekt) *n* coup d'œil rétrospectif *m.*
return (ri'tə:n) *vi* **1** revenir, rentrer. **2** retourner. *vt* **1** rendre. **2** renvoyer. **3** *pol* élire. *n* **1** retour *m.* **2** renvoi *m.* **3** récompense *f.* **4** échange *f.* **5** profit *m.* **6** *pl* recettes *f pl.* **return ticket** *n* billet d'aller et retour *m.*
reunite (ri:ju:'nait) *vt* réunir. *vi* se réunir.
reveal (ri'vi:l) *vt* **1** révéler. **2** déceler. **revealing** *adj* révélateur, -trice. **revelation** *n* révélation *f.*
revel ('revəl) *vi* se réjouir, se délecter.
revenge (ri'vendʒ) *vt* venger. *n* vengeance *f.*
revenue ('revənju:) *n* revenu, rapport *m.*
reverberate (ri'və:bəreit) *vt* renvoyer, répercuter. *vi* résonner, retentir. **reverberation** *n* **1** renvoi *m.* **2** réverbération *f.*
reverence ('revərəns) *n* révérence, vénération *f.*
reverse (ri'və:s) *adj* inverse, contraire. *n* **1** inverse *m.* **2** revers *m.* **3** marche arrière *f. vt* renverser, invertir. *vi* faire marche arrière.
revert (ri'və:t) *vi* revenir, retourner.
review (ri'vju:) *n* **1** revue *f.* **2** examen *m.* **3** revue périodique *f.* **4** critique *f. vt* **1** passer en revue. **2** faire la critique de.
revise (ri'vaiz) *vt* **1** revoir, corriger. **2** réviser. **revision** *n* révision *f.*
revive (ri'vaiv) *vi* ressusciter, se ranimer, reprendre. *vt* faire revivre, ranimer. **revival** *n* reprise *f.*
revoke (ri'vouk) *vt* révoquer, retirer.
revolt (ri'voult) *n* révolte *f. vi* se révolter, se soulever. *vt* révolter. **revolting** *adj* écœurant, dégoûtant. **revolution** *n* révolution *f.* **revolutionary** *adj* révolutionnaire.
revolve (ri'vɔlv) *vt* tourner. *vt* faire tourner. **revolver** *n* revolver *m.*
revue (ri'vju:) *n* revue *f.*
revulsion (ri'vʌlʃən) *n* **1** revirement *m.* **2** écœurement *m.*
reward (ri'wɔ:d) *n* récompense *f. vt* récompenser.
rhetoric ('retərik) *n* rhétorique *f.* **rhetorical** *adj* **1** de rhétorique. **2** ampoulé. **rhetorical question** *n* question pour la forme *f.*
rheumatism ('ru:mətizəm) *n* rhumatisme *m.*
Rhine (rain) *n* Rhin *m.*
rhinoceros (rai'nɔsərəs) *n* rhinocéros *m.*
Rhodesia (rou'di:ʃə) *n* Rhodésie *f.* **Rhodesian** *adj,n* rhodésien, -ienne.
rhododendron (roudə'dendrən) *n* rhododendron *m.*
Rhone (roun) *n* Rhône *m.*
rhubarb ('ru:ba:b) *n* rhubarbe *f.*
rhyme (raim) *n* rime *f. vi* rimer.
rhythm ('riðəm) *n* rythme *m.*
rib (rib) *n* côte *f.*
ribbon ('ribən) *n* ruban *m.*
rice (rais) *n* riz *m.* **rice pudding** riz au lait *m.*
rich (ritʃ) *adj* **1** riche. **2** fertile. **3** somptueux, -euse. **richness** *n* **1** richesse *f.* **2** somptuosité *f.*
rickety ('rikiti) *adj* branlant, chancelant.
rickshaw ('rikʃɔ:) *n* pousse-pousse *m invar.*
rid* (rid) *vt* débarrasser, délivrer. **get rid of** se débarrasser de. **riddance** *n* débarras *m.*
riddle[1] ('ridl̩) *n* (puzzle) énigme *f.*
riddle[2] ('ridl̩) *n* crible *m.* claie *f. vt* cribler, tamiser.
ride* (raid) *vi* **1** monter à cheval. **2** voguer. *vt* **1** monter. **2** diriger. *n* promenade, course *f.* **rider** *n* cavalier, -ière.
ridge (ridʒ) *n* **1** crête, cime *f.* **2** faîte *m.* **3** strie *f.*
ridicule ('ridikju:l) *vt* se moquer de. *n* moquerie, raillerie *f.* **ridiculous** *adj* ridicule.
rife (raif) *adj* abondant, répandu. **be rife** régner.
rifle[1] ('raifəl) *n* fusil *m.* carabine *f.*
rifle[2] ('raifəl) *vt* piller, vider.
rift (rift) *n* **1** fente, dechirure *f.* **2** fissure *f.*
rig (rig) *n* **1** *naut* gréement *m.* **2** équipement *m. vt* gréer. **rig out** accoutrer, equiper. **rigging** *n* gréement *m.* agrès *m pl.*
right (rait) *adj* **1** droit. **2** bon, bonne. **3** juste. **be right** avoir raison. ~*adv* droit, juste, bien. *n* **1** droit *m.* **2** droite *f.* **right of way** priorité *f.* droit de passage *m.* ~*vt* **1** redresser, remettre. **2** rectifier. **right angle** *n* angle droit *m.* **right-hand** *adj* de *or* à droite. **right handed** *adj* droitier, -ière. **right-wing** *adj* de droite.
righteous ('raitʃəs) *adj* droit, vertueux, -euse.
rigid ('ridʒid) *adj* **1** rigide, raide. **2** sévère, strict.

rigour ('rigə) *n* rigueur *f*. **rigorous** *adj* rigoureux, -euse.
rim (rim) *n* **1** bord *m*. **2** (of a wheel) jante *f*.
rind (raind) *n* peau, -aux, croûte, couenne *f*.
ring[1] (riŋ) *n* **1** cercle *m*. **2** bague *f*. **3** anneau, -aux *m*. **4** arène *f*. **ringleader** *n* meneur *m*. **ring-road** *n* boulevard périphérique *m*. **ringside** *adj* au premier rang.
ring*[2] (riŋ) *n* **1** tintement *m*. **2** coup de sonnette *m*. *vt* sonner, faire sonner. *vi* **1** sonner. **2** retentir. **ring off** raccrocher. **ring up** téléphoner.
rink (riŋk) *n* patinoire *f*.
rinse (rins) *vt* rincer. *n* rinçage *m*.
riot ('raiət) *n* émeute, bagarre *f*. *vi* s'ameuter.
rip (rip) *n* déchirure, fente *f*. *vt* déchirer, fendre. *vi* se déchirer. **rip out** arracher.
ripe (raip) *adj* **1** mûr. **2** prêt, à point. **ripen** *vt,vi* mûrir.
ripple ('ripəl) *n* **1** ride, ondulation *f*. **2** murmure *m*. *vi* se rider, onduler.
rise* (raiz) *vi* **1** se lever. **2** monter, s'élever. **3** hausser. **4** se soulever. *n* **1** lever *m*. **2** montée *f*. **3** hausse *f*. **4** avancement *m*. **give rise to** occasionner.
risk (risk) *n* risque, péril *m*. *vt* risquer, hasarder. **risky** *adj* hasardeux, -euse.
rissole ('risoul) *n* croquette *f*.
rite (rait) *n* rite *m*.
ritual ('ritjuəl) *adj,n* rituel, -elle *m*.
rival ('raivəl) *n* **1** rival, -aux *m*. **2** *comm* concurrent *m*. *adj* rival, -aux. *vt* rivaliser avec. **rivalry** *n* rivalité *f*.
river ('rivə) *n* fleuve *m* rivière *f*. **riverbed** *n* lit de rivière *m*. **riverside** *n* bord de l'eau *m*. *adj* situé au bord de la rivière.
rivet ('rivit) *n* rivet, clou *m*. *vt* **1** river. **2** capter, fixer.
road (roud) *n* route, voie *f*. chemin *m*. **roadblock** *n* barrage *m*. **roadside** *n* bord de la route *m*. *adj* situé au bord de la route.
roam (roum) *vi* errer, rôder. *vt* parcourir.
roar (rɔ:) *n* hurlement, rugissement *m*. *vi* hurler, rugir.
roast (roust) *vt,vi* rôtir. *adj,n* rôti *m*.
rob (rɔb) *vt* voler, dérober. **robber** *n* voleur, -euse. **robbery** *n* vol *m*.
robe (roub) *n* robe *f*. *vt,vi* revêtir.
robin ('rɔbin) *n* rouge-gorge *m*.
robot ('roubɔt) *n* robot *m*.
robust (rou'bʌst) *adj* robuste, vigoureux, -euse.
rock[1] (rɔk) *n* rocher, roc *m*. **rock-bottom** *adj* le plus bas. **rockery** *n* jardin de rocaille *m*.
rock[2] (rɔk) *vt* bercer, balancer, basculer. *vi* (se) balancer, osciller. **rocker** *n* bascule *f*. **rocking-chair** *n* fauteuil à bascule *m*. **rocking-horse** *n* cheval à bascule *m*.
rocket ('rɔkit) *n* fusée *f*.
rod (rɔd) *n* **1** baguette, verge *f*. **2** tringle *f*.
rode (roud) *v* see **ride.**
rodent ('roudn̩t) *adj,n* rongeur, -euse *m*.
roe (rou) *n* œufs de poisson *m pl*. laitance *f*.
rogue (roug) *n* coquin, fripon *m*.
role (roul) *n* rôle *m*.
roll (roul) *n* **1** rouleau, -aux *m*. **2** petit pain *m*. **3** roulement *m*. *vt,vi* rouler. **roll over** se retourner. **roll up** s'enrouler. **rollcall** *n* appel *m*. **roller** *n* **1** rouleau, -aux *m*. **2** cylindre *m*. **roller-skate** *vi* patiner sur roulettes. *n* patin à roulettes *m*. **rolling pin** *n* rouleau, -aux *m*.
Roman Catholic *adj,n* catholique.
romance (*n,adj* 'roumæns; *v* rə'mæns) *n* **1** idylle *f*. **2** romanesque *m*. *adj* roman. *vi* exagérer, broder.
romantic (rə'mæntik) *adj* **1** romantique. **2** romanesque.
romanticize (rə'mæntisaiz) *vt* romancer. *vi* donner dans le romantique.
romp (rɔmp) *vi* s'ébattre. *n* gambades *f pl*. **rompers** *n pl* barboteuse *f*.
roof (ru:f) *n* **1** toit *m*. **2** *anat* palais *m*.
rook (ruk) *n zool* corneille *f*. *vt sl* filouter, rouler.
room (ru:m) *n* **1** salle, pièce *f*. **2** place *f*.
roost (ru:st) *n* juchoir, perchoir *m*. *vi* se jucher, se percher.
root[1] (ru:t) *n* **1** racine *f*. **2** source *f*. *vt* enraciner. *vi* s'enraciner.
root[2] (ru:t) *vi* **1** fouiller avec le groin. **2** fouiller.
rope (roup) *n* corde *f*. cordage *m*. *vt* corder, lier.
rosary ('rouzəri) *n* rosaire *m*.
rose[1] (rouz) *n* rose *f*. **rose bush** *n* rosier *m*. **rosette** *n* **1** cocarde *f*. **2** *arch* rosace *f*. **rosy** *adj* rose, rosé, vermeil, -eille.
rose[2] (rouz) *v* see **rise.**
rosemary ('rouzməri) *n* romarin *m*.
rot (rɔt) *n* **1** pourriture, carie *f*. **2** démoralisation *f*. **3** *sl* bêtises *f pl*. *vi,vt* pourrir. *vi* se décomposer. **rotten** *adj* **1** pourri, carié. **2** fichu, patraque.
rota ('routə) *n* liste de roulement *f*. **rotary** *adj* rotatoire, rotatif, -ive. **rotate** *vi* tourner, pivoter. *vt* **1** faire tourner. **2** alterner, varier. **rotation** *n* **1** succession *f*. **2** rotation *f*. **in rotation** à tour de rôle.
rotor ('routə) *n* rotor *m*.
rouble ('ru:bəl) *n* rouble *m*.

rouge (ru:ʒ) *n* rouge, fard *m*.
rough (rʌf) *adj* **1** rugueux, -euse, rude. **2** grossier, -ière. **3** tempêtueux, -euse. **4** approximatif, -ive. **5** rauque. **roughly** *adv* **1** brutalement. **2** à peu près. **roughness 1** rudesse *f*. **2** grossièreté *f*.
roulette (ru:ˈlet) *n* roulette *f*.
round (raund) *adj* rond, circulaire. *n* **1** rond, cercle *m*. **2** tour, circuit *m*. **3** tournée *f*. *prep* autour de. *vt* arrondir. **roundabout** *n* rond-point *m*. *adj* détourné, indirect.
rouse (rauz) *vt* **1** réveiller. **2** susciter.
route (ru:t) *n* itinéraire, chemin *m*. route *f*.
routine (ru:ˈti:n) *n* routine *f*. *adj* routinier, -ière.
rove (rouv) *vi* rôder. *vt* parcourir.
row[1] (rou) *n* rang *m*. ligne *f*.
row[2] (rou) *vi naut* ramer. *vt naut* conduire à l'aviron. *n* promenade en bateau *f*. **rowing** *n* canotage *m*.
row[3] (rau) *n* **1** querelle, dispute *f*. **2** chahut, tapage *m*.
rowdy (ˈraudi) *adj* tapageur, -euse.
royal (ˈrɔiəl) *adj* royal, -aux. **royal blue** *n* bleu roi *m*. **royalty** *n* **1** royauté *f*. **2** *pl* droits d'auteur *m pl*.
rub (rʌb) *vt,vi* frotter. *vt* enduire, frictionner. **rub in** faire pénétrer. **rub out** effacer. ~*n* **1** frottement *m*. **2** friction *f*.
rubber (ˈrʌbə) *n* **1** gomme *f*. **2** caoutchouc *m*. **rubber band** *n* élastique *m*.
rubbish (ˈrʌbiʃ) *n* **1** détritus *m*. déchets *m pl*. **2** *inf* camelote *f*. **3** *inf* bêtises *f pl*.
rubble (ˈrʌbəl) *n* **1** moellon *m*. **2** décombres *m pl*.
ruby (ˈru:bi) *n* rubis *m*.
rucksack (ˈrʌksæk) *n* sac à dos *m*.
rudder (ˈrʌdə) *n* gouvernail *m*.
rude (ru:d) *adj* **1** impoli, grossier, -ière. **2** primitif, -ive. **3** violent. **4** brut. **rudeness** *n* impolitesse *f*.
rudiment (ˈru:dimənt) *n* rudiment *m*. **rudimentary** *adj* rudimentaire.
rueful (ˈru:fəl) *adj* triste, lugubre.
ruff (rʌf) *n* fraise *f*.
ruffian (ˈrʌfiən) *n* bandit, polisson *m*.
ruffle (ˈrʌfəl) *n* **1** agitation *f*. **2** volant *m*. *vt* **1** troubler. **2** plisser.
rug (rʌg) *n* **1** couverture *f*. **2** (mat) tapis *m*.
rugby (ˈrʌgbi) *n* rugby *m*.
rugged (ˈrʌgid) *adj* **1** accidenté, rugueux, -euse. **2** bourru, rude.
ruin (ˈru:in) *n* ruine *f*. *vt* ruiner.
rule (ru:l) *n* **1** règle *f*. **2** autorité *f*. *vt* **1** gouverner. **2** rayer, régler. **rule out 1** écarter. **2** biffer. **ruler** *n* **1** souverain *m*. **2** règle *f*. **ruling** *adj* dominant. *n* ordonnance *f*.
rum (rʌm) *n* rhum *m*.
Rumania (ru:ˈmeiniə) *n* Roumanie *f*. **Rumanian** *adj,n* roumain.
rumble (ˈrʌmbəl) *n* grondement, roulement *m*. *vi* gronder.
rummage (ˈrʌmidʒ) *vi* fouiller.
rumour (ˈru:mə) *n* rumeur *f*. bruit *m*.
rump (rʌmp) *n* croupe *f*.
run* (rʌn) *vi* **1** courir. **2** fuir. **3** marcher, circuler. **4** couler. **5** déteindre. *vt* **1** tenir, diriger, gerer. **2** courir. **3** entretenir. **4** promener. **run away** s'enfuir. **run out 1** expirer. **2** s'épuiser. ~*n* **1** course *f*. **2** tour *m*. promenade *f*. **3** suite *f*. **4** vogue *f*. **5** enclos *m*. **in the long run** à la longue. **runner** *n* coureur, -euse. **runner bean** *n* haricot vert *m*. **runner-up** *n* second *m*. **running** *adj* **1** courant. **2** continu. **3** de suite. *n* **1** course *f*. **2** marche *f*. fonctionnement *m*. **3** direction *f*. **runway** *n* piste d'envol *f*.
rung[1] (rʌŋ) *v* see **ring.**
rung[2] (rʌŋ) *n* échelon, barreau, -aux *m*.
rupee (ru:ˈpi:) *n* roupie *f*.
rupture (ˈrʌptʃə) *n* rupture *f*. *vt* rompre. *vi* se rompre.
rural (ˈruərəl) *adj* rural, -aux, champêtre.
rush[1] (rʌʃ) *vi* **1** se dépêcher, se précipiter. **2** faire irruption. *vt* bousculer, dépêcher, précipiter. *n* hâte, course précipitée *f*.
rush[2] (rʌʃ) *n bot* jonc *m*. paille *f*.
Russia (ˈrʌʃə) *n* Russie *f*. **Russian** *adj,n* russe. **Russian** (language) *n* russe *m*.
rust (rʌst) *n* rouille *f*. *vi* se rouiller. **rusty** *adj* rouillé.
rustic (ˈrʌstik) *adj* rustique.
rustle (ˈrʌsəl) *vi* bruire. *vt* froisser. *n* bruissement *m*.
rut (rʌt) *n* ornière *f*. **get into a rut** s'encroûter.
ruthless (ˈru:θləs) *adj* impitoyable, sans pitié.
rye (rai) *n* seigle *m*.

S

Sabbath (ˈsæbəθ) *n* sabbat *m*.
sable (ˈseibəl) *n* zibeline *f*.
sabotage (ˈsæbətɑ:ʒ) *n* sabotage *m*. *vt* saboter.
sabre (ˈseibə) *n* sabre *m*.
saccharin (ˈsækərin) *n* saccharine *f*.
sachet (ˈsæʃei) *n* sachet *m*.

sack (sæk) *n* sac *m*. **get the sack** recevoir son congé. ~*vt inf* congédier.

sacrament (ˈsækrəmənt) *n* sacrement *m*.

sacred (ˈseikrid) *adj* sacré, saint.

sacrifice (ˈsækrifais) *n* sacrifice *m*. *vt* sacrifier, immoler.

sacrilege (ˈsækrilidʒ) *n* sacrilège *m*. **sacrilegious** *adj* sacrilège.

sad (sæd) *adj* **1** triste. **2** cruel, -elle. **3** déplorable. **sadden** *vt* attrister, affliger. *vi* s'attrister. **sadness** *n* tristesse *f*.

saddle (ˈsædl̩) *n* selle *f*. *vt* **1** seller. **2** *inf* encombrer. **saddler** *n* sellier *m*.

sadism (ˈseidizəm) *n* sadisme *m*. **sadist** *n* sadique *m,f*. **sadistic** *adj* sadique.

safari (səˈfɑ:ri) *n* safari *m*.

safe (seif) *adj* **1** en sûreté, à l'abri, sauf, sauve. **2** solide, sûr. **3** prudent. **safe and sound** sain et sauf. ~*n* coffre-fort *m*. **safeguard** *n* sauvegarde *f*. *vt* sauvegarder, protéger. **safety** *n* sûreté, sécurité *f*. **safety belt** *n* ceinture de sécurité *f*. **safety pin** *n* épingle de sûreté *f*. **safety valve** *n* soupape de sûreté *f*.

saffron (ˈsæfrən) *n* safran *m*.

sag (sæg) *vi* s'affaisser, fléchir. *n* affaissement *m*.

saga (ˈsɑ:gə) *n* saga *f*

sage[1] (seidʒ) *adj,n* sage.

sage[2] (seidʒ) *n bot* sauge *f*.

Sagittarius (sædʒiˈtɛəriəs) *n* Sagittaire *m*.

sago (ˈseigou) *n* sagou *m*.

said (sed) *v* see **say.**

sail (seil) *n* **1** voile *f*. **2** promenade en bateau *f*. *vi* **1** naviguer. **2** faire de la voile. **sailing** *n* navigation *f*. **sailor** *n* matelot, marin *m*.

saint (seint) *n* saint *m*.

sake (seik) *n* **for the sake of 1** pour, par égard pour. **2** à cause de. **3** pour l'amour de.

salad (ˈsæləd) *n* salade *f*. **salad dressing** *n* vinaigrette *f*. assaisonnement *m*.

salamander (ˈsæləmændə) *n* salamandre *f*.

salami (səˈlɑ:mi) *n* salami *m*.

salary (ˈsæləri) *n* traitement, salaire *m*. appointements *m pl*.

sale (seil) *n* **1** vente *f*. **2** solde *f*. **salesman** *n* vendeur *m*. **travelling salesman** commis voyageur *m*. **salesmanship** *n* art de vendre *m*.

saliva (səˈlaivə) *n* salive *f*. **salivate** *vi* saliver.

sallow (ˈsælou) *adj* jaunâtre, blême.

salmon (ˈsæmən) *n* saumon *m*.

salon (ˈsælɔn) *n* salon *m*.

saloon (səˈlu:n) *n* salle *f*. salon *m*. **saloon car** *n* conduite intérieure *f*.

salt (sɔ:lt) *n* sel *m*. *adj* salé. *vt* saler. **saltcellar** *n* salière *f*. **salty** *adj* salé.

salute (səˈlu:t) *n* **1** salut *m*. salutation *f*. **2** (of guns) salve *f*. *vt* saluer.

salvage (ˈsælvidʒ) *n* sauvetage *m*. récupération *f*. *vt* sauver.

salvation (sælˈveiʃən) *n* salut *m*.

salve (sælv) *n* onguent *m*. pommade *f*.

same (seim) *adj,pron* même. **all the same** tout de même.

sample (ˈsɑ:mpəl) *n* échantillon *m*. *vt* goûter, essayer.

sanatorium (sænəˈtɔ:riəm) *n*, *pl* **-oriums** *or* **-oria** sanatorium *m*.

sanction (ˈsæŋkʃən) *n* **1** sanction *f*. **2** consentement *m*. *vt* **1** sanctionner. **2** approuver.

sanctity (ˈsæŋktiti) *n* **1** sainteté *f*. **2** inviolabilité *f*.

sanctuary (ˈsæŋktʃuəri) *n* **1** sanctuaire *m*. **2** asile, refuge *m*.

sand (sænd) *n* sable *m*. *vt* sabler. **sandpaper** *n* papier de verre *m*. **sandpit** *n* sablière *f*. **sandy** *adj* sablonneux, -euse.

sandal (ˈsændl̩) *n* sandale *f*.

sandwich (ˈsænwidʒ) *n* sandwich *m*.

sane (sein) *adj* sain d'esprit, sensé. **sanity** *n* santé d'esprit, raison *f*.

sang (sæŋ) *v* see **sing.**

sanitary (ˈsænitri) *adj* sanitaire, hygiénique. **sanitary towel** *n* serviette hygiénique *f*.

sank (sæŋk) *v* see **sink.**

sap (sæp) *n* sève *f*.

sapphire (ˈsæfaiə) *n* saphir *m*.

sarcasm (ˈsɑ:kæzəm) *n* sarcasme *m*. ironie *f*. **sarcastic** *adj* sarcastique, mordant.

sardine (sɑ:ˈdi:n) *n* sardine *f*.

Sardinia (sɑ:ˈdiniə) *n* Sardaigne *f*. **Sardinian** *adj,n* sarde.

sardonic (sɑ:ˈdɔnik) *adj* sardonique.

sari (ˈsɑ:ri) *n* sari *m*.

sash[1] (sæʃ) *n* écharpe, ceinture *f*.

sash[2] (sæʃ) *n arch* châssis, cadre *m*. **sash-window** *n* fenêtre à guillotine *f*.

sat (sæt) *v* see **sit.**

Satan (ˈseitn̩) *n* Satan *m*.

satchel (ˈsætʃəl) *n* cartable *m*. sacoche *f*.

satellite (ˈsætəlait) *n* satellite *m*.

satin (ˈsætin) *n* satin *m*.

satire (ˈsætaiə) *n* satire *f*. **satirical** *adj* satirique.

satisfy (ˈsætisfai) *vt* **1** satisfaire, contenter. **2**

convaincre. **satisfaction** *n* satisfaction *f*. **satisfactory** *adj* satisfaisant.
saturate ('sætʃəreit) *vt* saturer, imprégner.
Saturday ('sætədi) *n* samedi *m*.
Saturn ('sætən) *n* Saturne *m*.
sauce (sɔ:s) *n* sauce *f*. **saucepan** *n* casserole *f*. **saucer** *n* soucoupe *f*. **saucy** *adj* impertinent, effronté.
Saudi Arabia ('saudi) *n* Arabie Séoudite *f*.
sauerkraut ('sauəkraut) *n* choucroute *f*.
sauna ('sɔ:nə) *n* sauna *m*.
saunter ('sɔ:ntə) *vi* flâner, se balader.
sausage ('sɔsidʒ) *n* saucisse *f*. **sausage meat** *n* chair à saucisse *f*.
savage ('sævidʒ) *adj* sauvage, féroce. *n* sauvage *m,f*. *vt* attaquer.
save[1] (seiv) *vt* **1** sauver. **2** économiser, épargner. **3** éviter. **4** garder. **savings** *n pl* économies *f pl*. épargne *f*.
save[2] (seiv) *prep* sauf.
saviour ('seiviə) *n* sauveur *m*.
savoury ('seivəri) *adj* savoureux -euse, appétissant. *n* entremets non sucré *m*.
saw*[1] (sɔ:) *n* scie *f*. *vt* scier. **sawdust** *n* sciure *f*.
saw[2] (sɔ:) *v see* **see**[1].
Saxon ('sæksən) *adj,n* saxon, -onne.
saxophone ('sæksəfoun) *n* saxophone *m*.
say* (sei) *vt,vi* dire. **saying** *n* proverbe, dicton *m*.
scab (skæb) *n* croûte *f*. *vi* se cicatriser, former une croûte.
scaffold ('skæfəld) *n* échafaud *m*. **scaffolding** *n* échafaudage *m*.
scald (skɔ:ld) *vt* échauder, ébouillanter. *n* échaudure *f*.
scale[1] (skeil) *n* (of a fish, etc.) écaille *f*. *vt* écailler. *vi* s'écailler.
scale[2] (skeil) *n* **1** plateau, -aux *m*. **2** *pl* balance *f*.
scale[3] (skeil) *n* échelle, graduation *f*. *vt* escalader.
scallop ('skɔləp) *n* **1** coquille Saint-Jacques *f*. **2** (in sewing) feston *m*.
scalp (skælp) *n* épicrâne, cuir chevelu *m*. *vt* scalper.
scalpel ('skælpəl) *n* scalpel *m*.
scampi ('skæmpi) *n pl* langoustines *f pl*.
scan (skæn) *vt* **1** examiner, scruter. **2** parcourir. **3** *lit* scander. *n* regard scrutateur *m*.
scandal ('skændḷ) *n* scandale *m*. médisance *f*. **scandalous** *adj* scandaleux, -euse.
Scandinavia (skændi'neiviə) *n* Scandinavie *f*. **Scandinavian** *adj,n* scandinave.
scant (skænt) *adj* insuffisant, sommaire.
scapegoat ('skeipgout) *n* bouc émissaire *m*.
scar (skɑ:) *n* cicatrice *f*. *vt* balafrer. *vi* se cicatriser.
scarce (skɛəs) *adj* rare. **scarcely** *adv* à peine, ne...guère.
scare (skɛə) *vt* effrayer. *n* panique, alarme *f*. **scarecrow** *n* épouvantail *m*.
scarf (skɑ:f) *n, pl* **scarfs** *or* **scarves** écharpe *f*.
scarlet ('skɑ:lit) *adj,n* écarlate *f*. **scarlet fever** *n* fièvre scarlatine *f*.
scathing ('skeiðiŋ) *adj* acerbe, cinglant.
scatter ('skætə) *vt* éparpiller, semer. *vi* se disperser.
scavenge ('skævindʒ) *vt* **1** nettoyer. **2** balayer.
scene (si:n) *n* scène *f*.
scenery ('si:nəri) *n* **1** paysage *m*. **2** *Th* décors *m pl*.
scent (sent) *n* **1** parfum *m*. odeur *f*. **2** odorat, flair *m*. *vt* **1** parfumer. **2** flairer.
sceptic ('skeptik) *n* sceptique *m,f*. **sceptical** *adj* sceptique. **scepticism** *adj* sceptique.
sceptre ('septə) *n* sceptre *m*.
schedule ('ʃedju:l) *n* plan *m*. *vt* ajouter.
scheme (ski:m) *n* **1** arrangement *m*. **2** projet *m*. *vi* comploter, intriguer.
schizophrenia (skitsou'fri:niə) *n* schizophrénie *f*. **schizophrenic** *adj,n* schizophrène.
scholar ('skɔlə) *n* **1** savant *m*. **2** écolier, -ière. **scholarship** *n* **1** érudition *f*. **2** bourse *f*.
scholastic (skə'læstik) *adj* **1** scolastique. **2** scolaire.
school[1] (sku:l) *n* école *f*. *vt* instruire, entrainer. **schoolboy** *n* élève, écolier *m*. **schoolgirl** *n* élève, écolière *f*. **schoolmaster** *n* instituteur *m*. **schoolmistress** *n* institutrice *f*. **schoolteacher** *n* professeur *m,f*.
school[2] (sku:l) *n* bande *f*.
schooner ('sku:nə) *n* schooner *m*. goélette *f*.
science ('saiəns) *n* science *f*. **science fiction** *n* science-fiction *f*. **scientific** *adj* scientifique. **scientist** *n* homme de science *m*.
scissors ('sizəz) *n pl* ciseaux *m pl*.
scoff[1] (skɔf) *vi* railler.
scoff[2] (skɔf) *vt inf* manger gloutonnement, bouffer.
scold (skould) *vt* gronder.
scone (skoun) *n* pain au lait *m*.
scoop (sku:p) *n* **1** pelle, écope *f*. **2** *tech* cuiller *f*. *vt* creuser, écoper.
scooter ('sku:tə) *n* scooter *m*.

scope (skoup) *n* **1** portée *f.* **2** étendue *f.*
scorch (skɔ:tʃ) *vt* roussir, dessécher. *n* brûlure *f.*
score (skɔ:) *n* **1** *sport* marque *f.* **2** sujet *m.* **3** vingtaine *f.* *vt* **1** marquer, compter. **2** entailler **scoreboard** *n* tableau, -aux *m.*
scorn (skɔ:n) *n* mépris, dédain *m.* *vt* mépriser.
Scorpio ('skɔ:piou) *n* Scorpion *m.*
scorpion ('skɔ:piən) *n* scorpion *m.*
Scotland ('skɔtlənd) *n* Écosse *f.* **Scot** *n* écossais *m.* **Scotch** *adj* écossais. *n* whisky *m.* **Scots** *adj,n* écossais. **Scottish** *adj* écossais.
scoundrel ('skaundrəl) *n* scélérat, gredin *m.*
scour[1] ('skauə) *vt* (clean) récurer.
scour[2] ('skauə) *vt* parcourir, battre.
scout (skaut) *n* éclaireur *m.*
scowl (skaul) *n* froncement des sourcils *m.* *vi* se renfrogner.
scramble ('skræmbəl) *vt* brouiller. *vi* se bousculer.
scrap (skræp) *n* **1** bout, fragment *m.* **2** *pl* restes *m pl.* *vt* mettre au rebut. **scrapbook** *n* album de découpures *m.* **scrap iron** *n* ferraille *f.*
scrape (skreip) *vt* **1** érafler. **2** racler. *vi* gratter. *n* **1** grincement *m.* **2** *inf* embarras *m.*
scratch (skrætʃ) *vt* **1** égratigner, griffer. **2** gratter. *vi* **1** se gratter, griffer. **2** *sport inf* se retirer. *n* **1** égratignure *f.* **2** grincement *m.*
scrawl (skrɔ:l) *vt* griffonner. *n* griffonnage *m.*
scream (skri:m) *vi* crier. *n* cri perçant *m.*
screech (skri:tʃ) *vi* pousser un cri rauque. *n* cri rauque *m.*
screen (skri:n) *n* écran *m.* *vt* protéger, cacher.
screw (skru:) *n* vis *f.* *vt* visser. *vi* tourner. **screwdriver** *n* tournevis *m.*
scribble ('skribəl) *n* griffonnage *m.* *vt* griffonner.
script (skript) *n* manuscrit *m.*
Scripture ('skriptʃə) *n* Ecriture sainte *f.*
scroll (skroul) *n* rouleau, -aux *m.*
scrounge (skraundʒ) *vt inf* chiper, écornifler.
scrub[1] (skrʌb) *vt* frotter, récurer. *n* friction *f.* nettoyage *m.* **scrubbing brush** *n* brosse dure *f.*
scrub[2] (skrʌb) *n* *bot* brousse *f.* broussailles *m pl.*
scruffy ('skrʌfi) *adj inf* peu soigné.
scrunch (skrʌntʃ) *vt* **1** croquer. **2** écraser.
scruple ('skru:pəl) *n* scrupule *m.* **scrupulous** *adj* **1** scrupuleux, -euse. **2** méticuleux, -euse.
scrutiny ('skru:tini) *n* examen minutieux *m.* **scrutinize** *vt* scruter.
scuffle ('skʌfəl) *n* mêlée *f.* *vi* se bousculer.
scullery ('skʌləri) *n* arrière-cuisine *f.*
sculpt (skʌlpt) *vt* sculpter. **sculptor** *n* sculpteur *m.* **sculpture** *n* sculpture *f.*
scum (skʌm) *n* **1** écume, mousse *f.* **2** rebut *m.*
scurf (skə:f) *n* pellicule *f.*
scythe (saið) *n* faux *f.* *vt* faucher.
sea (si:) *n* mer *f.* **by the sea** au bord de la mer. ~*adj* marin, maritime.
seabed ('si:bed) *n* fond marin *m.*
seafaring ('si:fɛəriŋ) *adj* marin, de mer.
seafront ('si:frʌnt) *n* esplanade de mer *f.*
seagull ('si:gʌl) *n* mouette *f.*
seahorse ('si:hɔ:s) *n* hippocampe *m.*
seal[1] (si:l) *n* sceau, -aux, cachet *m.* *vt* sceller, cacheter.
seal[2] (si:l) *n* *zool* phoque *m.* **sealskin** *n* peau de phoque *f.*
sea-level *n* niveau de la mer *m.*
sea-lion *n* otarie *f.*
seam (si:m) *n* **1** couture *f.* **2** *min* veine *f.*
seaman ('si:mən) *n* marin *m.* **seamanship** *n* matelotage *m.*
search (sə:tʃ) *vt* **1** fouiller. **2** chercher. *n* recherche *f.* **searchlight** *n* projecteur *m.*
seashore ('si:ʃɔ:) *n* **1** rivage *m.* **2** plage *f.*
seasick ('si:sik) *adj* **be seasick** avoir le mal de mer.
seaside ('si:said) *n* bord de la mer *m.* **seaside resort** *n* station balnéaire *f.*
season ('si:zən) *n* **1** saison *f.* **2** période *f.* *vt* assaisonner. *vi* sécher. **seasoning** *n* assaisonnement *m.* **season ticket** *n* carte d'abonnement *f.*
seat (si:t) *n* **1** siège *m.* **2** place *f.* *vt* (faire) asseoir. **seat-belt** *n* ceinture de sécurité *f.*
seaweed ('si:wi:d) *n* algue *f.*
secluded (si'klu:did) *adj* retiré, écarté.
second[1] ('sekənd) *adj* second, deuxième. *n* deuxième *m,f.* *vt* seconder, appuyer. **second-best** *adj* numéro deux. **second-class** *adj* de qualité inférieure. **second-hand** *adj* d'occasion. **second nature** *n* seconde nature *f.* **second-rate** *adj* médiocre, inférieur. **secondary** *adj* secondaire. **secondary school** *n* école secondaire *f.* lycée *m.*
second[2] ('sekənd) *n* seconde *f.*
secret ('si:krət) *n* secret *m.* *adj* secret, -ète, caché. **secrecy** *n* discrétion *f.* **secretive** *adj* réservé, cachottier, -ière.
secretary ('sekrətri) *n* **1** secrétaire *m,f.* **2** *pol* ministre *m.*
secrete (si'kri:t) *vt* **1** sécréter. **2** cacher.
sect (sekt) *n* secte *f.* **sectarian** *adj* sectaire.

section (ˈsekʃən) *n* section *f*.
sector (ˈsektə) *n* secteur *m*.
secular (ˈsekjulə) *adj* **1** séculier, -ère, laïque. **2** séculaire.
secure (siˈkjuə) *adj* **1** sûr, assuré. **2** en sûreté. **3** ferme, solide. *vt* **1** mettre en sûreté. **2** assujettir, maintenir. **3** obtenir, se procurer. **security** *n* sécurité, sûreté *f*.
sedate (siˈdeit) *adj* posé. **sedation** *n* sédation *f*. **sedative** *adj,n* sédatif, -ive *m*.
sediment (ˈsedimənt) *n* sédiment *m*. lie *f*.
seduce (siˈdju:s) *vt* séduire. **seduction** *n* séduction *f*.
see*[1] (si:) *vt* **1** voir. **2** comprendre. **3** examiner. **see to** s'occuper de.
see[2] (si:) *n rel* siège *m*.
seed (si:d) *n* graine, semence *f*.
seedy (ˈsi:di) *adj* **1** minable, râpé. **2** patraque.
seek* (si:k) *vt* **1** chercher, rechercher. **2** demander.
seem (si:m) *vi* sembler, paraître, avoir l'air. **seeming** *adj* apparent, soi -disant. **seemingly** *adv* apparemment.
seep (si:p) *vi* suinter, s'infiltrer.
seesaw (ˈsi:sɔ:) *n* balançoire *f*. *vi* osciller.
seethe (si:ð) *vi* grouiller, bouillonner.
segment (ˈsegmənt) *n* segment *m*. tranche *f*.
segregate (ˈsegrigeit) *vt* isoler, séparer. **segregation** *n* ségrégation *f*.
seize (si:z) *vt* **1** saisir. **2** s'emparer de.
seldom (ˈseldəm) *adv* rarement.
select (siˈlekt) *vt* choisir, trier. *adj* choisi. **selection** *n* sélection *f*. choix *m*. **selective** *adj* sélectif, -ive.
self (self) *n, pl* **selves** moi *m*. *pron* soi-même, se.
self-assured *adj* sûr de soi.
self-aware *adj* conscient de soi.
self-centred *adj* égocentrique.
self-confident *adj* plein d'assurance.
self-conscious *adj* intimidé, gêné.
self-contained *adj* **1** indépendant. **2** renfermé.
self-defence *n* légitime défense *f*.
self-discipline *n* maîtrise de soi *f*.
self-employed *adj* indépendant.
self-expression *n* expression personnelle *f*.
self-government *n* autonomie *f*.
self-indulgent *adj* sybarite, qui se dorlote.
self-interest *n* intérêt personnel, égoïsme *m*.
selfish (ˈselfiʃ) *adj* égoïste. **selfishness** *n* égoïsme *m*.
self-made *adj* arrivé par soi-même.
self-pity *n* pitié de soi-même *f*.
self-portrait *n* autoportrait *m*.
self-respect *n* respect de soi, amour propre *m*.
self-righteous *adj* pharisaïque.
self-sacrifice *n* abnégation *f*.
selfsame (ˈselfseim) *adj* identique.
self-satisfied *adj* content de soi.
self-service *n* libre-service *m*.
self-sufficient *adj* indépendant, suffisant.
self-will *n* obstination *f*. entêtement *m*.
sell* (sel) *vt* vendre. **sell off** solder, liquider. **sell up** vendre.
Sellotape (ˈseləteip) *n Tdmk* Scotch *Tdmk m*.
semantic (siˈmæntik) *adj* sémantique. **semantics** *n* sémantique *f*.
semaphore (ˈseməfɔ:) *n* sémaphore *m*.
semibreve (ˈsemibri:v) *n* ronde *f*.
semicircle (ˈsemisə:kəl) *n* demi-cercle *m*.
semicolon (semiˈkoulən) *n* point-virgule *m*.
semidetached (semidiˈtætʃt) *adj* accolé, jumeau, -elle.
semifinal (semiˈfainḷ) *n* demi-finale *f*.
seminar (ˈsemina:) *n* séminaire *m*.
semiprecious (semiˈpreʃəs) *adj* fin.
semiquaver (semiˈkweivə) *n* double croche *f*.
semivowel (ˈsemivauəl) *n* semi-voyelle *f*.
semolina (seməli:nə) *n* semoule *f*.
senate (ˈsenət) *n* sénat *m*. **senator** *n* sénateur *m*.
send* (send) *vt* envoyer. **send back** renvoyer. **send for** envoyer chercher.
Senegal (seniˈgɔ:l) *n* Sénégal *m*. **Senegalese** *adj,n* sénégalais.
senile (ˈsi:nail) *adj* sénile.
senior (ˈsi:niə) *adj,n* aîné, doyen, -enne.
sensation (senˈseiʃən) *n* sensation *f*. **sensational** *adj* sensationnel, -elle.
sense (sens) *n* **1** sens *m*. **2** bon sens *m*. *vt* sentir, pressentir. **senseless** *adj* **1** déraisonnable. **2** inanimé.
sensible (ˈsensəbəl) *adj* **1** sensé. **2** sensible. **3** conscient. **sensibility** *n* sensibilité, émotivité *f*.
sensitive (ˈsensitiv) *adj* sensible, susceptible.
sensual (ˈsenʃuəl) *adj* sensuel, -elle.
sensuous (ˈsenʃuəs) *adj* voluptueux, -euse, susceptible. **sensual** *adj* sensuel, -elle. **sensuous** *adj* voluptueux, -euse.
sentence (ˈsentəns) *n* **1** *gram* phrase *f*. **2** jugement *m*. sentence *f*. *vt* condamner.
sentiment (ˈsentimənt) *n* sentiment *m*. opinion *f*.. **sentimental** *adj* sentimental, -aux.
sentry (ˈsentri) *n* sentinelle *f*.
separate (ˈsepəreit) *vt* séparer, détacher. *vi* se

séparer, se désunir. *adj* séparé, distinct, indépendant. **separation** *n* séparation *f.*

September (sepˈtembə) *n* septembre *m.*

septet (sepˈtet) *n* septuor *m.*

septic (ˈseptik) *adj* septique.

sequel (ˈsi:kwəl) *n* **1** suite *f.* **2** conséquence *f.*

sequence (ˈsi:kwəns) *n* **1** succession *f.* **2** séquence *f.*

sequin (ˈsi:kwin) *n* sequin *m.*

serenade (serəˈneid) *n* sérénade *f.*

serene (siˈri:n) *adj* serein. **serenity** *n* sérénité *f.*

serf (sə:f) *n* serf, serve.

sergeant (ˈsɑ:dʒənt) *n* sergent *m.* **sergeant major** *n* sergent-major, adjudant *m.*

serial (ˈsiəriəl) *adj* de série. *n* feuilleton *m.* **serialize** *vt* publier *or* présenter en feuilleton.

series (ˈsiəri:z) *n invar* série, suite *f.*

serious (ˈsiəriəs) *adj* grave, sérieux, -euse. **seriousness** *n* gravité *f.*

sermon (ˈsə:mən) *n* sermon *m.*

serpent (ˈsə:pənt) *n* serpent *m.*

serrated (səˈreitid) *adj* dentelé.

serve (sə:v) *vt* **1** servir. **2** être utile à. **3** desservir. *vi* servir. **serve out** distribuer. **servant** *n* domestique *m,f.*

service (ˈsə:vis) *n* **1** service *m.* **2** entretien *m.* **3** *rel* office *m.* *vt* entretenir, réparer. **service station** *n* station-service *f.*

serviette (sə:viˈet) *n* serviette *f.*

servile (ˈsəvail) *adj* servile.

session (ˈseʃən) *n* session, séance *f.*

set* (set) *n* **1** ensemble, jeu, jeux *m.* **2** collection *f.* **3** groupe *f.* **4** mise en pli *f.* **5** *Th* décors *m pl.* *adj* **1** figé, immobile. **2** fixe. *vt* **1** mettre, poser. **2** régler. **3** composer. **4** donner. **5** poser. **6** sertir. **7** fixer. **8** dresser. *vi* **1** se coucher. **2** se coaguler, prendre. **3** *med* se ressouder. **set about** se mettre à. **set off** partir. **set out** **1** arranger. **2** se mettre en route. **set up** **1** établir. **2** ériger. **setback** *n* revers de fortune *m.* **setting** *n* **1** montage *m.* **2** monture *f.* cadre *m.* **3** disposition *f.* **4** coucher *m.*

settee (seˈti:) *n* canapé *m.*

settle (ˈsetl̩) *vt* **1** installer. **2** conclure, résoudre. **3** régler. **4** déterminer. *vi* **1** s'installer. **2** s'arranger. **settlement** *n* **1** établissement *m.* colonie *f.* **2** règlement *m.*

seven (ˈsevən) *adj,n* sept *m.* **seventh** *adj* septième.

seventeen (sevənˈti:n) *adj,n* dix-sept *m.* **seventeenth** *adj* dix-septième.

seventy (ˈsevənti) *adj,n* soixante-dix *m.* **seventieth** *adj* soixante-dixième.

several (ˈsevrəl) *adj* **1** plusieurs, quelques. **2** différent.

severe (siˈviə) *adj* **1** sévère, rigoureux, -euse. **2** dur. **severity** *n* sévérité, rigueur *f.*

sew* (sou) *vt* coudre. **sewing machine** *n* machine à coudre *f.*

sewage (ˈsu:idʒ) *n* eau d'égout *f.*

sewer (ˈsu:ə) *n* égout *m.* **sewerage** *n* système d'égout *m.*

sex (seks) *n* sexe *m.* **sexual** *adj* sexuel, -elle. **sexual intercourse** *n* rapports sexuels *m pl.* **sexuality** *n* sexualité *f.* **sexy** *adj* excitant, affriolant.

sextet (seksˈtet) *n* sextuor *m.*

shabby (ˈʃæbi) *adj* râpé, usé, minable.

shack (ʃæk) *n* cabane *f.*

shade (ʃeid) *n* **1** ombre *f.* **2** nuance *f.* *vt* **1** ombrager. **2** nuancer.

shadow (ˈʃædou) *n* ombre *f.* *vt* filer. **shadow cabinet** *n* cabinet fantôme *m.*

shaft (ʃɑ:ft) *n* **1** hampe *f.* **2** flèche *f.* trait *m.*

shaggy (ˈʃægi) *adj* hirsute.

shake* (ʃeik) *vt* **1** secouer, agiter. **2** hocher. *vi* trembler, chanceler. **shake hands** serrer la main. ~*n* **1** secousse *f.* **2** hochement *m.*

shall* (ʃəl; *stressed* ʃæl) *v mod aux* **1** devoir. **2** vouloir.

shallot (ʃəˈlɔt) *n* échalote *f.*

shallow (ˈʃælou) *adj* **1** peu profond. **2** frivole.

sham (ʃæm) *adj* simulé, feint. *n* feinte *f.* *vt* feindre, simuler.

shame (ʃeim) *n* honte *f.* *vt* faire honte à. **shamefaced** *adj* penaud, timide.

shampoo (ʃæmˈpu:) *n* shampooing *m.* *vt* se laver la tête.

shamrock (ˈʃæmrɔk) *n* trèfle d'Irlande *m.*

shandy (ˈʃændi) *n* panaché *m.*

shanty[1] (ˈʃænti) *n* cabane, baraque *f.* **shantytown** *n* bidonville *m.*

shanty[2] (ˈʃænti) *n* chanson de marin *f.*

shape (ʃeip) *n* **1** forme *f.* **2** coupe, tournure *f.* *vt* modeler, former.

share (ʃɛə) *n* **1** part, portion *f.* **2** *comm* action *f.* *vt,vi* partager. **shareholder** *n* actionnaire *m,f.*

shark (ʃɑ:k) *n* requin *m.*

sharp (ʃɑ:p) *adj* **1** aigu, -uë, pointu. **2** fin. **3** aigre. **4** *sl* rusé. *n* *mus* dièse *m.* **sharp-sighted** *adj* à la vue perçante. **sharpen** *vt* aiguiser, affûter. *vi* s'aiguiser. **sharpness** *n* acuité *f.*

hatter (ˈʃætə) *vt* fracasser, briser. *vi* se fracasser, se briser.
have (ʃeiv) *vt* raser. *vi* se raser.
hawl (ʃɔ:l) *n* châle *m*.
he (ʃi:) *pron 3rd pers s* elle.
heaf (ʃi:f) *n, pl* **sheaves** gerbe *f*.
hear* (ʃiə) *vt* tondre. **shears** *n pl* cisailles *f pl*.
heath (ʃi:θ) *n* fourreau, -aux, étui *m*. **sheathe** *vt* rengainer, recouvrir.
hed[1] (ʃed) *n* hangar *m*. remise *f*.
hed*[2] (ʃed) *vt* jeter, répandre.
heen (ʃi:n) *n* lustre, chatoiement *m*.
heep (ʃi:p) *n invar* mouton *m*. **sheepdog** *n* chien de berger *m*. **sheepskin** *n* peau de mouton *f*.
heer[1] (ʃiə) *adj* **1** pur, véritable. **2** perpendiculaire, à pic. **3** transparent.
sheer[2] (ʃiə) *vi* embarder.
sheet (ʃi:t) *n* **1** drap *m*. **2** (of paper, etc.) feuille *f*.
sheikh (ʃeik) *n* cheik *m*.
shelf (ʃelf) *n, pl* **shelves** rayon *m*. étagère *f*.
shell (ʃel) *n* **1** coquille, carapace, écaille *f*. **2** *mil* obus *m*. *vt* **1** écosser. **2** *mil* bombarder. **shellfish** *n* coquillage *m*. fruits de mer *m pl*.
shelter (ˈʃeltə) *n* **1** abri *m*. **2** refuge *m*. *vt* abriter, protéger. *vi* s'abriter.
shelve (ʃelv) *vt* **1** mettre sur un rayon **2** mettre au rancart. **3** ajourner.
shepherd (ˈʃepəd) *n* berger *m*.
sherbet (ˈʃə:bət) *n* sorbet *m*.
sheriff (ˈʃerif) *n* sherif *m*.
sherry (ˈʃeri) *n* xérès *m*.
shield (ʃi:ld) *n* bouclier *m*. carapace *f*. *vt* protéger, couvrir.
shift (ʃift) *n* **1** changement de place *m*. **2** équipe *f*. poste *m*. *vt* **1** remuer. **2** changer. *vi* se changer, se déplacer. **shiftwork** *n* travail par équipes *m*.
shilling (ˈʃiliŋ) *n* shilling *m*.
shimmer (ˈʃimə) *vi* luire, miroiter. *n* lueur *f*. chatoiement *m*.
shin (ʃin) *n* tibia *m*.
shine* (ʃain) *vi* briller, reluire, rayonner. *vt* polir. *n* **1** éclat *m*. **2** brillant *m*.
ship (ʃip) *n* bateau, -aux, navire *m*. *vt* embarquer, expédier. *vi* s'embarquer. **shipwreck** *n* naufrage *m*. *vt* faire naufrager. **be shipwrecked** faire naufrage. **shipyard** *n* chantier naval *m*.
shirk (ʃə:k) *vt* se dérober à, esquiver. **shirker** *n* carotteur, -euse.
shirt (ʃə:t) *n* chemise *f*.
shiver (ˈʃivə) *vi* frissonner, grelotter *n* frisson *m*.
shock[1] (ʃɔk) *n* **1** choc, heurt, coup *m*. **2** secousse *f*. *vt* choquer, scandaliser. **shock absorber** *n* amortisseur *m*. **shocking** *adj* **1** choquant. **2** abominable
shock[2] (ʃɔk) *n* (of hair) tignasse *f*.
shoddy (ˈʃɔdi) *adj* de camelote.
shoe* (ʃu:) *n* soulier *m*. chaussure *f*. *vt* **1** chausser. **2** ferrer. **shoelace** *n* lacet *m* **shoemaker** *n* cordonnier *m*.
shone (ʃɔn) *v* see **shine.**
shook (ʃuk) *v* see **shake.**
shoot* (ʃu:t) *vi* **1** s'élancer, se précipiter. **2** pousser, jaillir. **3** tirer. *vt* **1** précipiter, lancer. **2** fusiller. **3** abattre. *n* **1** *bot* pousse *f*. **2** goulotte *f*. **3** *sport* chasse *f*. **shooting** *n* **1** tir *m*. **2** chasse *f*.
shop (ʃɔp) *n* magasin *m*. boutique *f*. *vi* faire des achats. **shop assistant** *n* vendeur, -euse. **shop floor** *n* **1** atelier *m*. **2** ouvriers *m pl*. **shopkeeper** *n* commerçant *m*. **shoplifter** *n* voleur à l'étalage *m*. **shopping** *n* achats *m pl*. emplettes *f pl*. **shop steward** *n* délégué syndicale *m*. **shopwindow** *n* vitrine *f*.
shore[1] (ʃɔ:) *n* rivage, littoral, -aux *m*.
shore[2] (ʃɔ:) *vt* **shore up** étayer, étançonner
shorn (ʃɔ:n) *v* see **shear.**
short (ʃɔ:t) *adj* **1** court, bref, brève. **2** petit. **3** insuffisant. **4** à court de. **shortage** *n* insuffisance, crise *f*. **shorten** *vt* raccourcir, rapetisser, abréger.
shortbread (ˈʃɔ:tbred) *n* sablé *m*.
shortcoming (ˈʃɔ:tkʌmiŋ) *n* défaut *m*. imperfection *f*.
short cut *n* raccourci *m*.
shorthand (ˈʃɔ:thænd) *n* sténographie *f* **shorthand typist** *n* sténodactylographe *m,f*.
shortlived (ˈʃɔ:tlivd) *adj* de courte durée, éphémère.
short-sighted *adj* myope.
short-term *adj* à court terme.
short wave *n* onde courte *f*.
shot[1] (ʃɔt) *n* **1** coup de feu *m*. **2** boulet *m*. **3** *inf* coup *m*. **4** *phot* prise de vue *f*.
shot[2] (ʃɔt) *v* see **shoot.** *adj* **1** chatoyant. **2** moiré.
should (ʃəd; *stressed* ʃud) *v* see **shall.**
shoulder (ˈʃouldə) *n* épaule *f*. *vt* endosser. **shoulder-blade** *n* omoplate *f*.
shout (ʃaut) *vi,vt* crier. *n* cri *m*.

shove (ʃʌv) *n* coup d'épaule *m*. poussée *f*. *vt,vi* pousser.

shovel (ˈʃʌvəl) *n* pelle *f*. *vt* entasser à la pelle.

show* (ʃou) *vt* **1** montrer, exhiber. **2** indiquer. **3** témoigner. *vi* apparaître, se montrer. **show off** parader, se pavaner. ~*n* **1** exposition *f*. spectacle *m*. **2** étalage *m*. **3** apparence *f*. **show business** *n* monde du spectacle *m*. **showcase** *n* vitrine *f*. **showdown** *n* règlement de compte *m*. **show-jumping** *n* saut à cheval *m*. **showmanship** *n* art de la mise en scène *m*. **showroom** *n* salle d'exposition *f*.

shower (ˈʃauə) *n* **1** averse *f*. **2** (bath) douche *f*. *vt* **1** verser. **2** accabler, combler. **showerproof** *adj* caoutchouté, imperméable.

shrank (ʃræŋk) *v* see **shrink.**

shred (ʃred) *n* brin, lambeau, -aux *m*. *vt* déchiqueter.

shrew (ʃru:) *n* mégère *f*.

shrewd (ʃru:d) *adj* sagace, perspicace.

shriek (ʃri:k) *vi* pousser des cris perçants. *n* cri perçant *m*.

shrill (ʃril) *adj* aigu, -uë, strident.

shrimp (ʃrimp) *n* crevette *f*.

shrine (ʃrain) *n* **1** châsse *f*. **2** tombeau, -aux *m*. **3** sanctuaire *m*

shrink* (ʃriŋk) *vi* se rétrécir, se contracter. *vt* rétrécir, faire se contracter.

shrivel (ˈʃrivəl) *vt* rider. *vi* se rider, se ratatiner.

shroud (ʃraud) *n* linceul *m*. *vt* ensevelir, voiler.

Shrove Tuesday (ʃrouv) *n* mardi gras *m*.

shrub (ʃrʌb) *n* arbuste *m*. **shrubbery** *n* bosquet *m*.

shrug (ʃrʌg) *vt* hausser. *vi* hausser les épaules. *n* haussement d'épaules *m*.

shrunk (ʃrʌŋk) *v* see **shrink.**

shudder (ˈʃʌdə) *vi* frissonner, frémir. *n* frisson, frémissement *m*.

shuffle (ˈʃʌfəl) *vt* **1** *game* battre. **2** traîner. *vi* traîner les pieds. *n* **1** traînement de pieds *m*. **2** *game* mélange *m*.

shun (ʃʌn) *vt* fuir, éviter.

shunt (ʃʌnt) *vt* manœuvrer, garer. *n* manœuvre *f*.

shut* (ʃʌt) *vt,vi* fermer. **shut down** fermer. **shut in** enfermer. **shut off** **1** couper. **2** isoler. **shut out** exclure. **shut up!** ta gueule!

shutter (ˈʃʌtə) *n* **1** volet *m*. **2** *phot* obturateur *m*.

shuttlecock (ˈʃʌtəlkɔk) *n* volant *m*.

shy (ʃai) *adj* timide, farouche.

Sicily (ˈsisəli) *n* Sicile *f*. **Sicilian** *adj,n* sicilien, -ienne.

sick (sik) *adj* malade. **be sick** vomir. **be sick of** en avoir marre de. **sicken** *vi* tomber malade. *vt* dégoûter. **sickening** *adj* navrant, écœurant. **sickness** *n* maladie *f*.

side (said) *n* **1** côté *m*. **2** flanc *m*. **3** versant *m*. **4** parti, camp *m*. **5** face *f*. **6** bord *m*. *adj* **1** de côté, latéral, -aux. **2** secondaire. **sideboard** *n* buffet *m*. **side effect** *n* répercussion *f*. **sidelight** *n* feu de position *m*. **sideline** *n* violon d'Ingres *m*. **sideshow** *n* spectacle forain *m*. **sidestep** *n* pas de côté *m*. *vi* faire un pas de côté. *vt* éviter. **sidetrack** *vt* détourner l'attention de. **sideways** *adv* de côté, latéralement. *adj* latéral, -aux. **siding** *n* voie de garage *f*.

sidle (ˈsaidḷ) *vi* **sidle up to** s'approcher de biais.

siege (si:dʒ) *n* siège *m*.

siesta (siˈestə) *n* sieste *f*.

sieve (siv) *n* crible, tamis *m*. *vt* tamiser.

sift (sift) *vt* **1** tamiser, cribler. **2** dégager, démêler.

sigh (sai) *n* soupir *m*. *vi* soupirer.

sight (sait) *n* **1** vue, vision *f*. **2** spectacle *m*. *vt* apercevoir, aviser. **sightread** *vt* déchiffrer à vue. **sightseeing** *n* visite touristique *f*.

sign (sain) *n* **1** signe, indice *m*. trace *f*. **2** enseigne *f*. *vt* signer. **signpost** *n* poteau indicateur *m*.

signal (ˈsignḷ) *n* signal, -aux *m*. *vi,vt* signaler.

signature (ˈsignətʃə) *n* signature *f*.

signify (ˈsignifai) *vt* signifier. *vi* importer. **significance** *n* **1** signification *f*. **2** conséquence *f*. **significant** *adj* **1** significatif, -ive. **2** important.

silence (ˈsailəns) *n* silence *m*. *vt* faire taire, réduire au silence. **silencer** *n* silencieux, pot d'échappement *m*. **silent** *adj* silencieux, -euse.

silhouette (siluːˈet) *n* silhouette *f*. *vt* silhouetter.

silk (silk) *n* soie *f*. **silkworm** *n* vers à soie *m*.

sill (sil) *n* **1** seuil *m*. **2** appui *m*.

silly (ˈsili) *adj* sot, sotte, stupide.

silt (silt) *n* vase *f*. *v* **silt up** envaser.

silver (ˈsilvə) *n* argent *m*. *adj* argenté, d'argent. *vt* argenter.

similar (ˈsimilə) *adj* semblable. **similarity** *n* ressemblance *f*.

simile (ˈsimili) *n* image, comparaison *f*.

simmer (ˈsimə) *vi* mijoter, cuire à petit feu. *vt* faire mijoter.

simple (ˈsimpəl) *adj* 1 simple. 2 niais. **simplicity** *n* simplicité *f*. **simplify** *vt* simplifier.

simultaneous (siməlˈteiniəs) *adj* simultané.

sin (sɪn) *n* péché *m*. *vi* pécher.

since (sins) *adv,prep* depuis. *conj* 1 depuis que. 2 puisque.

sincere (sinˈsiə) *adj* sincère. **sincerity** *n* sincérité *f*.

sinew (ˈsinju:) *n* tendon *m*.

sing* (siŋ) *vt,vi* chanter. **singer** *n* chanteur, -euse.

singe (sindʒ) *vt* brûler légèrement, roussir. *n* légère brûlure *f*.

single (ˈsiŋgəl) *adj* 1 seul, unique. 2 célibataire. 3 simple. **single-handed** *adj* seul. **single-minded** *adj* sincère, loyal, -aux.

singular (ˈsiŋgjulə) *adj* singulier, -ère. 2 unique. *n* singulier *m*.

sinister (ˈsinistə) *adj* sinistre.

sink* (siŋk) *vi* 1 couler, sombrer. 2 s'enfoncer. 3 baisser. *vt* 1 faire sombrer. 2 creuser. *n* évier *m*.

sinner (ˈsinə) *n* pécheur, -eresse.

sinus (ˈsainəs) *n* 1 sinus *m*. 2 *med* fistule *f*.

sip (sip) *vt* boire à petites gorgées. *n* petite gorgée *f*.

siphon (ˈsaifən) *n* siphon *m*. *vt* siphonner.

sir (sə:) *n* 1 monsieur *m*. 2 *cap* Sir *m*.

siren (ˈsairən) *n* sirène *f*.

sirloin (ˈsə:lɔin) *n* aloyau, -aux, faux-filet *m*.

sister (ˈsistə) *n* 1 sœur *f*. 2 *rel* religieuse *f*. **sisterhood** *n* communauté religieuse *f*. **sister-in-law** *n* belle-sœur *f*.

sit* (sit) *vi* 1 s'asseoir, se tenir. 2 siéger. 3 couver. *vt* asseoir. **sit down** s'asseoir. **sit up** se redresser. **sit-in** *n* occupation *f*. **sitting** *n* séance *f*. *adj* assis. **sitting room** *n* salle de séjour *f*.

site (sait) *n* site, emplacement *m*.

situation (sitjuˈeiʃən) *n* 1 situation *f*. 2 emploi *m*.

six (siks) *adj,n* six *m*. **sixth** *adj* sixième.

sixteen (siksˈti:n) *adj,n* seize *m*. **sixteenth** *adj* seizième.

sixty (ˈsiksti) *adj,n* soixante *m*. **sixtieth** *adj* soixantième.

size (saiz) *n* 1 grandeur, dimension *f*. 2 taille, pointure *f*.

sizzle (ˈsizəl) *vi* grésiller. *n* grésillement *m*.

skate[1] (skeit) *n* patin *m*. *vi* patiner.

skate[2] (skeit) *n zool* raie *f*.

skeleton (ˈskelətn̩) *n* squelette *m*.

sketch (sketʃ) *n* croquis *m*. esquisse *f*. *vt* esquisser.

skewer (ˈskjuə) *n* brochette *f*.

ski (ski:) *n* ski *m*. *vi* faire du ski. **ski-lift** *n* remonte-pente *m invar*. téléski *m*.

skid (skid) *vi* déraper, glisser. *n* dérapage *m*.

skill (skil) *n* habileté, adresse *f*. **skilful** *adj* adroit, habile. **skilled** *adj* qualifié.

skim (skim) *vt,vi* 1 écumer. 2 raser, effleurer. **skim through** parcourir rapidement.

skimp (skimp) *vt* 1 mesurer, lésiner sur. 2 bâcler. **skimpy** *adj* étriqué.

skin (skin) *n* 1 peau, -aux *f*. 2 (of an animal) dépouille *f*. cuir *m*. 3 écorce, pelure *f*. *vt* 1 peler. 2 écorcher. 3 *sl* plumer. **skin-diving** *n* plongée autonome *f*. **skin-tight** *adj* collant. **skinny** *adj inf* maigre.

skip (skip) *n* petit saut *m*. gambade *f*. *vi* 1 sauter, gambader. 2 sauter à la corde.

skipper (ˈskipə) *n* patron (de bateau) *m*.

skirmish (ˈskə:miʃ) *n* escarmouche *f*.

skirt (skə:t) *n* jupe *f*. *vt* contourner, longer.

skittle (ˈskitl̩) *n* 1 quille *f*. 2 *pl* jeu de quilles *m*.

skull (skʌl) *n* crâne *m*.

skunk (skʌŋk) *n* mouffette *f*.

sky (skai) *n* ciel, cieux *m*. **sky-high** *adv* jusqu'aux nues. **skylark** *n* alouette *f*. **skyline** *n* ligne d'horizon *f*. **skyscraper** *n* gratte-ciel *m invar*.

slab (slæb) *n* 1 plaque, dalle *f*. 2 tablette *f*.

slack (slæk) *adj* 1 lâche, flasque. 2 négligent. 3 faible. *n* mou *m*. **slacken** *vt* 1 ralentir. 2 détendre. *vi* se relâcher.

slacks (slæks) *n pl* pantalon *m*.

slalom (ˈslɑ:ləm) *n* slalom *m*.

slam (slæm) *vt,vi* claquer.

slander (ˈslændə) *n* calomnie *f*. *vt* 1 calomnier. 2 *law* diffamer.

slang (slæŋ) *n* argot *m*. *vt* 1 injurier. 2 engueuler.

slant (slɑ:nt) *n* 1 pente, inclinaison *f*. 2 biais *m*. *vt* incliner. *vi* s'incliner. **slanting** *adj* oblique.

slap (slæp) *n* claque, gifle *f*. *vt* claquer, gifler. **slapdash** *adj* sans soin, bâclé. *adv* sans soin. **slapstick** *n* bouffonnerie *f*.

slash (slæʃ) *vt* entailler, balâfrer, taillader. *n* entaille, balâfre *f*.

slat (slæt) *n* lame *f*.

slate (sleit) *n* ardoise *f*. *vt* ardoiser.

slaughter (ˈslɔ:tə) *n* 1 abattage *m*. 2 carnage *m*. *vt* 1 abattre. 2 massacrer.

slave (sleiv) *n* esclave *m,f*. **slavery** *n* esclavage *m*.

sledge (sledʒ) *n* traîneau, -aux *m*.
sledgehammer (ˈsledʒhæmə) *n* marteau de forgeron *m*.
sleek (sli:k) *adj* lisse, luisant.
sleep* (sli:p) *vi* dormir, coucher. *n* sommeil *m*. **go to sleep** s'endormir. **sleeper** *n* (railway) poutre horizontale *f*. **sleeping-bag** *n* sac de couchage *m*. **sleeping car** *n* wagon-lit *m*. **sleeping-pill** *n* somnifère *m*. **sleepwalk** *vi* être noctambule.
sleet (sli:t) *n* grésil *m*. *v imp* grésiller.
sleeve (sli:v) *n* manche *f*.
sleigh (slei) *n* traîneau, -aux *m*.
slender (ˈslendə) *adj* **1** svelte. **2** mince.
slept (slept) *v* see **sleep.**
slice (slais) *n* tranche *f*. rond *m*. *vt* découper en tranches.
slick (slik) *adj* **1** habile, adroit. **2** lisse.
slide* (slaid) *n* **1** glissade *f*. **2** *phot* diapositive *f*. *vi,vt* glisser. **slide-rule** *n* règle à calculer *f*.
slight (slait) *adj* **1** mince, ténu. **2** léger, -ère. *vt* manquer d'égards envers. *n* affront *m*.
slim (slim) *adj* svelte, mince. *vt* amincir. *vi* suivre un régime.
slime (slaim) *n* vase *f*. limon *m*.
sling* (sliŋ) *n* **1** *med* écharpe *f*. **2** fronde *f*. *vt* **1** lancer, jeter. **2** suspendre.
slink* (sliŋk) *vi* **slink off** partir furtivement.
slip[1] (slip) *vi* glisser. *vt* **1** échapper. **2** filer. **3** décrocher. *n* **1** glissade *f*. **2** erreur *f*. faux-pas *m*. **slippery** *adj* **1** glissant. **2** incertain.
slip[2] (slip) *n* bout *m*. bande *f*.
slipper (ˈslipə) *n* pantoufle *f*.
slit* (slit) *n* fente, fissure *f*. *vt* fendre, couper.
sloe (slou) *n* prunelle *f*.
slog (slɔg) *vt inf* **1** cogner violemment. **2** bûcher. *n* coup violent *m*.
slogan (ˈslougən) *n* slogan *m*.
slop (slɔp) *vt* répandre.
slope (sloup) *n* pente *f*. *vi* incliner, pencher.
sloppy (ˈslɔpi) *adj inf* **1** bâclé. **2** flasque. **3** mal ajusté.
slot (slɔt) *vt* mettre. *n* **1** entaille, encoche *f*. **2** fente *f*. **3** ouverture *f*. **slot machine** *n* distributeur automatique *m*.
slouch (slautʃ) *vi* pencher, se tenir mal.
slovenly (ˈslʌvənli) *adj* mal peigné *or* soigné.
slow (slou) *adj* **1** lent. **2** en retard. *v* **slow down** ralentir.
slug[1] (slʌg) *n* limace *f*. **sluggish** *adj* **1** paresseux, -euse. **2** lent. **3** lourd.
slug[2] (slʌg) *vt* cogner(violemment).
sluice (slu:s) *n* écluse *f*.
slum (slʌm) *n* taudis *m*.
slumber (slʌmbə) *vi* sommeiller, être assoupi. *n* assoupissement *m*.
slump (slʌmp) *n* dépression économique, baisse des cours *f*. *vi* tomber lourdement.
slung (slʌŋ) *v* see **sling.**
slur (slə:) *n* **1** affront *m*. flétrissure *f*. **2** *mus* liaison *f*. *vt* **1** bredouiller. **2** lier.
slush (slʌʃ) *n* neige à demi fondue *f*.
sly (slai) *adj* matois, rusé.
smack[1] (smæk) *n* léger goût *m*. saveur *f*.
smack[2] (smæk) *n* claquement *m*. claque *f*. *vt* donner une gifle à.
small (smɔ:l) *adj* **1** petit, menu. **2** mesquin. **3** peu de. **smallholding** *n* petite ferme *f*. **smallpox** *n* petite vérole *f*.
smart (smɑ:t) *vi* cuire, brûler. *adj* **1** vif, vive. **2** fin, malin. **3** élégant, chic. *n* cinglant *m*. **smarten** *vt* animer. **smarten up** dégourdir.
smash (smæʃ) *n* **1** accident *m*. **2** coup écrasant *m*. *vt* briser en morceaux.
smear (smiə) *n* tache, souillure *f*. *vt* souiller, barbouiller.
smell* (smel) *n* **1** odorat, flair *m*. **2** odeur *f*. parfum *m*. *vt,vi* sentir. *vt* flairer.
smile (smail) *n* sourire *m*. *vi* sourire.
smirk (smə:k) *vi* minauder. *n* sourire affecté *m*.
smock (smɔk) *n* chemise, blouse *f*.
smog (smɔg) *n* purée de pois *f*. brouillard épais *m*.
smoke (smouk) *n* fumée *f*. *vi,vt* fumer.
smooth (smu:ð) *adj* lisse, aplani, uni. *vt* lisser, aplanir. **smoothen** *vt* lisser.
smother (ˈsmʌðə) *vt* étouffer, suffoquer.
smoulder (ˈsmouldə) *vi* couver, brûler lentement.
smudge (smʌdʒ) *vt* barbouiller, maculer. *n* tache *f*.
smug (smʌg) *adj* suffisant, béat.
smuggle (ˈsmʌgəl) *vt* passer en contrebande.
snack (snæk) *n* casse-croûte *m invar*. **snack-bar** *n* snack-bar *m*.
snag (snæg) *n* **1** écueil, obstacle *m*. **2** accroc *m*. *vt* accrocher.
snail (sneil) *n* escargot *m*.
snake (sneik) *n* serpent *m*.
snap (snæp) *n* **1** claquement *m*. **2** coup de dents *m*. *adj* immédiat, instantané. *vt* **1** faire claquer. **2** casser net. **3** happer. **snapshot** *n* instantané *m*.
snarl (snɑ:l) *vi* gronder, grogner. *n* grondement, grognement *m*.

snatch (snætʃ) *vt* saisir brusquement, arracher. *n* mouvement brusque pour saisir *m*.
sneak (sni:k) *n inf* cafard *m*. *v* **sneak in** se faufiler dans. **sneak off** partir furtivement.
sneer (sniə) *n* sourire de mépris *m*. *vi* ricaner.
sneeze (sni:z) *n* éternuement *m*. *vi* éternuer.
sniff (snif) *n* reniflement *m*. *vi,vt* renifler.
snipe (snaip) *n* bécassine *f*.
snivel ('snivəl) *vi* pleurnicher.
snob (snɔb) *n* snob, prétentieux *m*.
snooker ('snu:kə) *n* jeu de billard *m*.
snoop (snu:p) *vi* fureter, fouiner.
snooty ('snu:ti) *adj* prétentieux, -euse.
snooze (snu:z) *n* somme, roupillon *m*. *vi* sommeiller.
snore (snɔ:) *vi* ronfler. *n* ronflement *m*.
snort (snɔ:t) *n* renâclement, ébrouement *m*. *vi* renâcler, s'ébrouer.
snout (snaut) *n* museau, -aux, mufle *m*.
snow (snou) *n* neige *f*. *v imp* neiger. **snowball** *n* boule de neige *f*. **snowdrift** *n* congère *f*. **snowdrop** *n* perce-neige *m or f invar*. **snowflake** *n* flocon de neige *m*. **snowman** *n* bonhomme de neige *m*. **snowplough** *n* chasse-neige *m invar*. **snowstorm** *n* tempête de neige *f*.
snub (snʌb) *n* mortification, rebuffade *f*. *vt* rabrouer, faire affront à.
snuff (snʌf) *n* tabac à priser *m*.
snug (snʌg) *adj* confortable, douillet, -ette.
snuggle ('snʌgəl) *vt* serrer. *vi* se blottir.
so (sou) *adv* **1** si, tellement. **2** ainsi. **3** le. **so much** *or* **many** autant de. ~*conj* donc. **so as to** afin de. **so that** pour que. **so-and-so** *n* **1** *inf* individu *m*. **2** ceci et cela. **3** *inf* machin *m*. **Mr So-and-so** Monsieur un tel. **so-called** *adj* soi-disant. **so-so** *adj,adv* comme ci comme ça.
soak (souk) *vt,vi* tremper.
soap (soup) *n* savon *m*. **soap-powder** *n* savon en poudre *m*.
soar (sɔ:) *vi* s'élever, monter.
sob (sɔb) *n* sanglot *m*. *vi* sangloter.
sober ('soubə) *adj* **1** sobre, modéré. **2** pas ivre.
social ('souʃəl) *adj* social, -aux. **sociable** *adj* sociable. **socialism** *n* socialisme *m*. **socialist** *adj,n* socialiste
society (sə'saiəti) *n* société *f*.
sociology (sousi'ɔlədʒi) *n* sociologie *f*. **sociological** *adj* sociologique. **sociologist** *n* sociologue *m,f*.
sock[1] (sɔk) *n* chaussette *f*.
sock[2] (sɔk) *vt inf* donner une beigne à.
socket ('sɔkit) *n* **1** emboîture *f*. **2** *anat* alvéole, jointure *f*.
soda ('soudə) *n* soude *f*. **soda-water** *n* eau de Seltz *f*. soda *m*.
sofa ('soufə) *n* canapé *m*.
soft (sɔft) *adj* **1** mou, molle. **2** doux, douce. **soften** *vt* **1** amollir. **2** assouplir. **3** adoucir. *vi* **1** s'amollir. **2** s'attendrir.
soggy ('sɔgi) *adj* détrempé, saturé.
soil[1] (sɔil) *n* sol, terrain *m*.
soil[2] (sɔil) *vt* salir, souiller.
solar ('soulə) *adj* solaire.
sold (sould) *v* see **sell**.
solder ('sɔldə) *vt* souder. *n* soudure *f*.
soldier ('souldʒə) *n* soldat *m*.
sole[1] (soul) *adj* **1** seul, unique. **2** exclusif, -ive.
sole[2] (soul) *n* **1** *anat* plante *f*. **2** semelle *f*.
sole[3] (soul) *n zool* sole *f*.
solemn ('sɔləm) *adj* solennel, -elle.
solicitor (sə'lisitə) *n* avoué *m*.
solid ('sɔlid) *adj* solide. **solidify** *vt* solidifier. *vi* se solidifier, se figer.
solitary ('sɔlitri) *adj* solitaire.
solitude ('sɔlitju:d) *n* solitude *f*.
solo ('soulou) *n* solo *m*. **soloist** *n* soliste *m,f*.
solstice ('sɔlstis) *n* solstice *m*.
soluble ('sɔljubəl) *adj* soluble.
solution (sə'lu:ʃən) *n* solution *f*.
solve (sɔlv) *vt* résoudre. **solvent** *adj* **1** solvable. **2** dissolvant. *n* dissolvant *m*.
sombre ('sɔmbə) *adj* sombre, morne.
some (sʌm) *adj* **1** quelque, quelconque. **2** de. **3** environ. *pron* **1** certains. **2** en. **somebody** *pron* quelqu'un. **somehow** *adv* d'une façon ou d'une autre. **someone** *pron* quelqu'un. **something** *pron* quelquechose. **sometime** *adv* tôt ou tard. **sometimes** *adv* quelquefois, parfois. **somewhat** *adv* quelque peu, un peu. **somewhere** *adv* quelque part. **somewhere else** ailleurs.
somersault ('sʌməsɔ:lt) *n* saut périlleux *m*. culbute *f*. *vi* faire la culbute.
son (sʌn) *n* fils *m*. **son-in-law** *n* beau-fils, gendre *m*.
sonata (sə'nɑ:tə) *n* sonate *f*.
song (sɔŋ) *n* chant *m*. chanson *f*.
sonic ('sɔnik) *adj* sonique.
sonnet ('sɔnit) *n* sonnet *m*.
soon (su:n) *adv* bientôt, tôt. **as soon as** aussitôt que, dès que.
soot (sut) *n* suie *f*.
soothe (su:ð) *vt* calmer, apaiser.

sophisticated (sə'fistikeitid) *adj* blasé, sophistiqué.
soprano (sə'prɑ:nou) *n* soprano *m*.
sordid ('sɔ:did) *adj* sordide.
sore (sɔ:) *adj* **1** douloureux, -euse, irrité. **2** sensible. *n* **1** plaie *f*. **2** mal *m*.
sorrow ('sɔrou) *n* peine *f*. chagrin *m*. *vi* s'affliger.
sorry ('sɔri) *adj* **1** désolé. **2** fâché, peiné. *interj* pardon!
sort (sɔ:t) *n* sorte, espèce *f*. genre *m*. *vt* assortir, trier, classifier.
sou (su:) *n* sou *m*.
souffle ('su:flei) *n* soufflé *m*.
sought (sɔ:t) *v* see **seek.**
soul (soul) *n* âme *f*.
sound[1] (saund) *n* son, bruit *m*. *vi* **1** sonner, retentir. **2** paraître. **soundproof** *adj* isolé, insonore.
sound[2] (saund) *adj* **1** sain, robuste. **2** solide. **3** profond.
sound[3] (saund) *vt* sonder.
soup (su:p) *n* soupe *f*. potage *m*.
sour (sauə) *adj* **1** aigre, acide. **2** revêche. *vt* aigrir. *vi* s'aigrir.
source (sɔ:s) *n* source, origine *f*.
south (sauθ) *n* sud *m*. **south of France** midi *m*. *adj* méridional, -aux, sud *invar*. *adv* au *or* vers le sud. **south-east** *n* sud-est *m*. *adv* vers le sud-est. *adj* du sud-est. **southerly** *adj* du sud. **southern** *adj* du sud, méridional, -aux. **southward** *adj* du côté du sud. **southwards** *adv* vers le sud. **south-west** *n* sud-ouest *m*. *adv* vers le sud-ouest. *adj* du sud-ouest.
South Africa *n* Afrique du Sud *f*. **South African** *adj,n* sud-africain.
South America *n* Amérique du Sud *f*. **South American** *adj,n* sud-américain.
South Pole *n* pôle sud *m*.
souvenir (su:və'niə) *n* souvenir *m*.
sovereign ('sɔvrin) *n* souverain *m*. *adj* souverain, suprême.
Soviet Union ('souviət) *n* Union soviétique *f*.
sow*[1] (sou) *vt* semer, ensemencer.
sow[2] (sau) *n* truie *f*.
soya bean ('sɔiə) *n* soja *m*.
spa (spɑ:) *n* station thermale *f*.
space (speis) *n* espace *m*. *vt* espacer.
spade[1] (speid) *n* bêche *f*.
spade[2] (speid) *n game* pique *m*.
Spain (spein) *n* Espagne *f*. **Spaniard** *n* espagnol *m*. **Spanish** *adj* espagnol. **Spanish** (language) *n* espagnol *m*.
span (spæn) *n* **1** empan *m*. envergure *f*. **2** portée *f*. écartement *m*. **3** durée *f*. *vt* **1** enjamber. **2** embrasser.
spaniel ('spæniəl) *n* épagneul *m*.
spank (spæŋk) *vt* fesser. *n* fessée, claque *f*.
spanner ('spænə) *n* clef (à écrous) *f*.
spare (spɛə) *adj* **1** disponible. **2** de rechange. *vt* **1** épargner, ménager. **2** se passer de. **sparing** *adj* **1** économe, chiche. **2** modéré.
spark (spɑ:k) *n* étincelle *f*. trait *m*. *vi* émettre des étincelles. **spark plug** *n* bougie d'allumage *f*.
sparkle ('spɑ:kəl) *vi* étinceler, scintiller, pétiller. *n* étincellement, pétillement *m*.
sparrow ('spærou) *n* moineau, -aux *m*.
sparse (spɑ:s) *adj* clairsemé, épars.
spasm ('spæzəm) *n* spasme *m*. **spasmodic** *adj* **1** spasmodique. **2** fait par à-coups. **spastic** *adj* spasmodique. *n* malade de paralysie spasmodique *m,f*.
spat (spæt) *v* see **spit.**
spatial ('speiʃəl) *adj* spatial, -aux.
spatula ('spætjulə) *n* spatule *f*.
spawn (spɔ:n) *n* frai *m*. œufs (de poisson) *m pl*. *vi* frayer.
speak* (spi:k) *vi,vt* parler, dire. **speaker** *n* orateur *m*.
spear (spiə) *n* lance *f*. javelot *m*.
special ('speʃəl) *adj* spécial, -aux, particulier, -ière. **specialist** *n* spécialiste *m,f*. **speciality** *n* spécialité *f*. **specialize** *vt* particulariser. *vi* se spécialiser.
species ('spi:ʃi:z) *n* espèce *f*.
specify ('spesifai) *vt* spécifier, préciser. **specific** *adj* spécifique.
specimen ('spesimən) *n* spécimen, échantillon *m*.
speck (spek) *n* **1** petite tache *f*. **2** grain *m*.
spectacle ('spektəkəl) *n* **1** spectacle *m*. **2** *pl* lunettes *f pl*. **spectacular** *adj* spectaculaire.
spectator (spek'teitə) *n* spectateur, -trice.
spectrum ('spektrəm) *n pl* **-tra** *or* **-trums** spectre *m*.
speculate ('spekjuleit) *vi* **1** spéculer. **2** méditer.
speech (spi:tʃ) *n* **1** parole *f*. **2** discours *m*. **speechless** *adj* interdit, muet, -ette.
speed (spi:d) *n* vitesse *f*. *vi* se hâter. **speedboat** *n* canot automobile *m*.
spell[1] (spel) *vt* épeler, s'écrire. **spelling** *n* orthographe *f*.
spell[2] (spel) *n* charme *m*. formule magique *f*. **spellbound** *adj* ensorcelé, charmé.
spell[3] (spel) *n* **1** période *f*. **2** tour *m*.

spend* (spend) *vt* **1** dépenser. **2** passer. **3** consacrer. **spendthrift** *adj,n* dépensier, -ière.
sperm (spə:m) *n* sperme *m*.
sphere (sfiə) *n* sphère *f*. **spherical** *adj* sphérique.
spice (spais) *n* épice *f*.
spider (ˈspaidə) *n* araignée *f*.
spike (spaik) *n* pointe *f*. piquant *m*. *vt* clouer.
spill* (spil) *vt* répandre, verser. *vi* se répandre.
spin* (spin) *n* rotation *f*. *vt* **1** filer. **2** faire tourner. *vi* tourner. **spin-dry** *vt* essorer.
spinach (ˈspinidʒ) *n* épinards *m pl*.
spine (spain) *n* colonne vertébrale *f*.
spinster (ˈspinstə) *n* femme non mariée *f*.
spiral (ˈspairəl) *n* spirale, hélice *f*. *adj* spiral, -aux.
spire (spaiə) *n* flèche *f*.
spirit (ˈspirit) *n* **1** esprit *m*. **2** alcool *m*. **spiritual** *adj* spirituel, -elle.
spit*[1] (spit) *vi* **1** cracher. **2** (with rain) bruiner. *n* crachat *m*. salive *f*.
spit[2] (spit) *n* broche *f*.
spite (spait) *n* rancune *f*. dépit *m*. **in spite of** malgré. **spiteful** *adj* rancunier, -ière, méchant.
splash (splæʃ) *n* éclaboussure, tache *f*. *vt* éclabousser.
splendid (ˈsplendid) *adj* splendide. **splendour** *n* splendeur *f*.
splint (splint) *n* éclisse, attelle *f*. **splinter** *n* éclat *m*. écharde *f*. *vi* voler en éclats.
split* (split) *vt* **1** fendre. **2** diviser. *vi* se fendre. *n* **1** fente *f*. **2** division *f*.
splutter (ˈsplʌtə) *n* bredouillement, crachement *m*. *vi* bredouiller, crochoter.
spoil* (spɔil) *vt* gâter, abîmer, endommager. *vi* s'abîmer. **spoil-sport** *n* rabat-joie *m,f invar*.
spoke[1] (spouk) *n* rayon *m*.
spoke[2] (spouk) *v* see **speak.**
spoken (ˈspoukən) *v* see **speak.**
spokesman (ˈspouksmən) *n* porte-parole *m invar*.
sponge (spʌndʒ) *n* éponge *f*. *vt* éponger. **sponge on** vivre aux crochets de.
sponsor (ˈspɔnsə) *n* garant *m*. *vt* subventionner. **sponsorship** *n* parrainage *m*.
spontaneous (spɔnˈteiniəs) *adj* spontané, automatique. **spontaneously** *adv* spontanément.
spool (spu:l) *n* bobine *f*.
spoon (spu:n) *n* cuiller, cuillère *f*. **spoonful** *n* cuillerée *f*.
sport (spɔ:t) *n* sport *m*. **sportive** *adj* badin. **sportsman** *n* sportif *m*.

spot (spɔt) *n* **1** endroit *m*. **2** tache *f*. **3** pois *m*. **4** goutte *f*. **on the spot** sur-le-champ. ~*vt* **1** tacher. **2** apercevoir. **spotless** *adj* immaculé. **spotlight** *n* projecteur *m*.
spouse (spaus) *n* époux, -ouse.
spout (spaut) *n* **1** bec *m*. **2** gouttière *f*. *vi* **1** jaillir. **2** pérorer. *vt* déclamer.
sprain (sprein) *n* entorse, foulure *f*. *vt* se fouler.
sprang (spræŋ) *v* see **spring.**
sprawl (sprɔ:l) *vi* s'étaler, se vautrer.
spray[1] (sprei) *vt* **1** pulvériser. **2** asperger. *n* **1** atomiseur *m*. **2** jet *m*. **3** embrun *m*.
spray[2] (sprei) *n* (of flowers, etc.) brin *m*.
spread* (spred) *vt* **1** étendre. **2** répandre. **3** déployer. *vi* **1** s'étendre. **2** se répandre. *n* **1** étendue *f*. **2** diffusion *f*. **3** *inf* festin *m*.
spree (spri:) *n* fête, rigolade *f*.
sprig (sprig) *n* brindille *f*.
sprightly (ˈspraitli) *adj* éveillé, sémillant.
spring* (spriŋ) *n* **1** printemps *m*. **2** source *f*. **3** saut *m*. **4** ressort *m*. *vi* **1** bondir, sauter. **2** jaillir. **springboard** *n* tremplin *m*. **spring-clean** *vt* nettoyer à fond. **springtime** *n* printemps *m*.
sprinkle (ˈspriŋkəl) *vt* saupoudrer, arroser. *n* pincée *f*.
sprint (sprint) *n* course de vitesse *f*. sprint *m*. *vi* faire une course de vitesse.
sprout (spraut) *n* pousse *f*. germe *m*. *vi* pousser, germer, bourgeonner.
sprung (sprʌŋ) *v* see **spring.**
spun (spʌn) *v* see **spin.**
spur (spə:) *n* **1** éperon *m*. **2** stimulant *m*. **3** éperon *m*. ~*vt* éperonner. **spur on** stimuler.
spurt (spə:t) *n* **1** giclée *f*. **2** coup de collier, sursaut *m*. *vi* jaillir.
spy (spai) *n* espion, -onne. *vi* espionner. *vt* épier.
squabble (ˈskwɔbəl) *vi* se chamailler. *n* prise de bec *f*.
squad (skwɔd) *n* **1** *mil* peloton *m*. **2** brigade *f*.
squadron (ˈskwɔdrən) *n* **1** *mil* escadron *m*. **2** *naut* escadre *f*.
squalid (ˈskwɔlid) *adj* sale, crasseux, -euse.
squander (ˈskwɔndə) *vt* gaspiller.
square (skwɛə) *n* **1** carré *m*. **2** carreau, -aux *m*. **3** place *f*. *adj* **1** carré. **2** en ordre. **3** quitte. *vt* **1** carrer. **2** régler. **3** accorder.
squash (skwɔʃ) *n* **1** écrasement *m*. cohue *f*. **2** *sport* squash *m*. *vt* écraser. *vi* s'écraser.
squat (skwɔt) *vi* **1** s'accroupir. **2** occuper sans titre de possession. *adj* trapu, accroupi.

squawk (skwɔ:k) *vi* pousser des cris rauques. *n* cri rauque *m*.
squeak (skwi:k) *vi* **1** pousser des cris aigus, crier. **2** grincer, crisser. *n* **1** petit cri aigu *m*. **2** crissement *m*.
squeal (skwi:l) *vi* pousser des cris aigus. *n* cri aigu *m*.
squeamish (ˈskwi:miʃ) *adj* **1** délicat, difficile. **2** nauséeux, -euse.
squeeze (skwi:z) *vt* **1** presser, serrer. **2** extorquer.
squid (skwid) *n* calmar *m*.
squiggle (ˈskwigəl) *n* tortillement *m*. fioriture *f*.
squint (skwint) *n* strabisme *m*. *vi* loucher.
squirm (skwɔ:m) *vi* **1** se tordre. **2** être au supplice.
squirrel (ˈskwirl) *n* écureuil *m*.
squirt (skwə:t) *vt* faire jaillir. *vi* gicler. *n* jet *m*. giclée *f*.
stab (stæb) *n* coup de couteau *m*. *vt* poignarder.
stabilize (ˈsteibəlaiz) *vt* stabiliser.
stable[1] (ˈsteibəl) *n* écurie *f*.
stable[2] (ˈsteibəl) *adj* **1** stable, solide. **2** permanent. **3** constant.
stack (stæk) *n* **1** meule *f*. **2** tas *m*. **3** cheminée *f*. *vt* **1** empiler. **2** entasser.
stadium (ˈsteidiəm) *n*, *pl* **-ia** or **-iums** stade *m*.
staff (stɑ:f) *n* **1** personnel *m*. **2** bâton *m*.
stag (stæg) *n* cerf *m*.
stage (steidʒ) *n* **1** *Th* scène *f*. **2** estrade *f*. **3** phase *f*. **4** étape *f*. *vt* monter. **stage manager** *n* régisseur *m*.
stagger (ˈstægə) *vi* chanceler. *vt* **1** échelonner, étaler. **2** *inf* renverser, étonner. **3** faire chanceler.
stagnant (ˈstægnənt) *adj* **1** stagnant. **2** inactif, -ive. **stagnate** *vi* croupir.
stain (stein) *n* **1** tache *f*. **2** couleur *f*. colorant *m*. *vt* **1** souiller. **2** teindre, teinter. **stained-glass window** *n* vitrail, -aux *m*. **stainless** *adj* inoxydable.
stair (stɛə) *n* **1** marche *f*. **2** *pl* escalier *m*. **staircase** *n* escalier *m*.
stake[1] (steik) *n* **1** pieu, -eux, jalon *m*. **2** bûcher *m*. *vt* jalonner.
stake[2] (steik) *n* *game* enjeu, -eux *m*. mise *f*. **at stake** en jeu. ~*vt* jouer, risquer.
stale (steil) *adj* **1** rassis, vicié. **2** passé, rebattu. **3** défraîchi.
stalemate (ˈsteilmeit) *n* **1** *game* pat *m*. **2** impasse *m*.
stalk[1] (stɔ:k) *n* tige *f*. trognon *m*.
stalk[2] (stɔ:k) *vt* traquer. *vi* marcher à grands pas.
stall[1] (stɔ:l) *n* **1** stalle *f*. **2** étalage *m*. **3** *pl Th* fauteuils d'orchestre *m pl*. *vt,vi* caler.
stall[2] (stɔ:l) *vt* (evade) repousser, berner.
stallion (ˈstæliən) *n* étalon *m*.
stamina (ˈstæminə) *n* vigueur, énergie *f*.
stammer (ˈstæmə) *vi,vt* bégayer, balbutier. *n* bégaiement *m*.
stamp (stæmp) *n* **1** timbre *m*. **2** poinçon *m*. **3** trépignement *m*. *vt* **1** timbrer. **2** poinçonner. **3** frapper. **4** trépigner.
stampede (stæmˈpi:d) *n* débandade *f*. *vi* fuir en désordre.
stand* (stænd) *vi* **1** être *or* se tenir debout. **2** se trouver. **3** se maintenir. **4** représenter, signifier. **5** durer. *vt* **1** mettre. **2** supporter. *n* **1** situation *f*. **2** support *m*. **3** étalage *m*. **4** stand *m*. **stand-by** *n* **1** appui *m*. **2** ressource *f*. **standing** *n* **1** situation *f*. **2** rang *m*. **3** durée *f*. *adj* **1** debout. **2** stagnant. **3** sur pied. **4** fixe. **standstill** *n* arrêt *m*.
standard (ˈstændəd) *n* **1** norme *f*. **2** bannière *f*. **3** degré *m*. étalon *m*. *adj* **1** type. **2** classique. **3** courant.
stank (stæŋk) *v* see **stink**.
stanza (ˈstænzə) *n* stance, strophe *f*.
staple[1] (ˈsteipəl) *n* **1** crampon *m*. **2** agrafe *f*. *vt* **1** cramponner. **2** agrafer.
staple[2] (ˈsteipəl) *adj* principal, -aux.
star (stɑ:) *n* **1** étoile *f*. astre *m*. **2** (films, etc.) star, vedette *f*. *vi* être en vedette. **starfish** *n* étoile de mer *f*.
starboard (ˈstɑ:bəd) *n* tribord *m*.
starch (stɑ:tʃ) *n* amidon *m*. *vt* empeser.
stare (stɛə) *vi* regarder fixement. *n* regard fixe *m*.
stark (stɑ:k) *adj* **1** raide. **2** absolu. *adv* entièrement, tout.
starling (ˈstɑ:liŋ) *n* étourneau, -aux, sansonnet *m*.
start (stɑ:t) *n* **1** commencement *m*. **2** départ *m*. **3** sursaut *m*. *vi* **1** commencer. **2** sursauter. *vt* **1** entamer, se mettre à. **2** mettre en marche. **3** lancer. **starter** *n mot* démarreur *m*.
startle (ˈstɑ:tl̩) *vt* faire sursauter, effrayer.
starve (stɑ:v) *vi* mourir de faim. *vt* **1** faire mourir de faim, affamer. **2** priver.
state (steit) *n* **1** état *m*. **2** position *f*. **3** pompe *f*. *adj* **1** d'état. **2** d'apparat. *vt* **1** déclarer. **2** fixer. **stately** *adj* majestueux, -euse. **statement** *n* **1** déclaration *f*. compte rendu *m*. **2**

law déposition *f.* **3** *comm* relevé *m.* **statesman** *n* homme d'Etat *m.*

static ('stætik) *adj,n* statique *f.*

station ('steiʃən) **1** (railway) gare *f.* **2** poste *m.* **3** position *f.* rang *m.* **station-master** *n* chef de gare *m.*

stationary ('steiʃənri) *adj* stationnaire.

stationer ('steiʃənə) *n* libraire *m.* **stationer's shop** *n* papeterie *f.* **stationery** *n* papeterie *f.*

statistics (stə'tistiks) *n* statistique *f.*

statue ('stætju:) *n* statue *f.*

stature ('stætʃə) *n* stature, taille *f.*

status ('steitəs) *n* position *f.* rang *m.*

statute ('stætju:t) *n* loi *f.* statut *m.* **statutory** *adj* réglementaire.

stay[1] (stei) *n* séjour *m.* *vi* **1** rester, se tenir. **2** séjourner. **3** attendre.

stay[2] (stei) *n* support *m.* *vt* étayer.

steadfast ('stedfɑ:st) *adj* **1** constant. **2** stable, ferme.

steady ('stedi) *adj* **1** ferme. **2** soutenu, régulier, -ière. **3** rangé. *vt* raffermir. *vi* reprendre son aplomb.

steak (steik) *n* bifteck *m.* entrecôte *f.*

steal* (sti:l) *vt* **1** voler. **2** dérober. **stealing** *n* vol *m.*

steam (sti:m) *n* vapeur *f.* *vt* cuire à la vapeur. *vi* fumer. **steam-roller** *n* rouleau compresseur *m.*

steel (sti:l) *n* acier *m.* *adj* d'acier.

steep[1] (sti:p) *adj* escarpé, raide.

steep[2] (sti:p) *vt,vi* tremper.

steeple ('sti:pəl) *n* clocher *m.* **steeplechase** *n* steeple-chase *m.*

steer (stiə) *vt* diriger, conduire. **steering-wheel** *n* volant *m.*

stem[1] (stem) *n* tige *f.* *v* **stem from** provenir de.

stem[2] (stem) *vt* **1** arrêter, endiguer. **2** refouler.

stencil ('stensəl) *n* **1** pochoir *m.* **2** stencil *m.*

step (step) *n* **1** pas *m.* **2** démarche *f.* **3** marche *f.* échelon *m.* *vi* faire un pas, aller. **step-ladder** *n* marchepied *m.*

stepbrother ('stepbrʌðə) *n* demi-frère *m.*

stepdaughter ('stepdɔ:tə) *n* belle-fille *f.*

stepfather ('stepfɑ:ðə) *n* beau-père *m.*

stepmother ('stepmʌðə) *n* belle-mère *f.*

stepsister ('stepsistə) *n* demi-soeur *f.*

stepson ('stepsʌn) *n* beau-fils *m.*

stereo ('steriou) *adj,n* stéréo *m.*

stereophonic (steriə'fɔnik) *adj* stéréophonique.

stereotype ('steriətaip) *n* cliché *m.* *vt* stéréotyper.

sterile ('sterail) *adj* stérile. **sterilize** *vt* stériliser.

sterling ('stə:liŋ) *n* sterling *m.* *adj* **1** de bon aloi. **2** sterling.

stern[1] (stə:n) *adj* sévère, rigide, austère.

stern[2] (stə:n) *n* *naut* arrière *m.* poupe *f.*

stethoscope ('steθəskoup) *n* stéthoscope *m.*

stew (stju:) *n* ragoût *m.* *vt* faire cuire à la casserole. *vi* mijoter.

steward ('stju:əd) *n* **1** intendant *m.* **2** économe *m.* **3** commissaire *m.* **stewardess** *n* femme de chambre, stewardess *f.*

stick[1] (stik) *n* **1** bâton *m.* **2** canne *f.* **3** morceau de bois *m.*

stick*[2] (stik) *vt* **1** coller. **2** enfoncer. **3** *inf* mettre. **4** *sl* supporter. *vi* **1** adhérer. **2** s'embourber. **3** se coincer. **stick at** s'arrêter devant. **stick out** saillir. **stick to 1** s'en tenir à. **2** rester fidèle à.

sticky ('stiki) *adj* **1** collant. **2** *inf* difficile.

stiff (stif) *adj* **1** raide, dur. **2** pénible, difficile. **stiffen** *vt* raidir. *vi* se saidir, se guinder. **stiffly** *adv* avec raideur.

stifle ('staifəl) *vt* **1** étouffer. **2** réprimer. *vi* suffoquer.

stigma ('stigmə) *n, pl* **-mata** *or* **-as** stigmate *m.*

stile (stail) *n* échalier *m.*

still[1] (stil) *adj* **1** tranquille, calme. **2** immobile. *adv* toujours, encore. *conj* cependant, pourtant. **stillborn** *adj* mort-né. **still life** *n* nature morte *f.*

still[2] (stil) *n* alambic *m.*

stilt (stilt) *n* échasse *f.* **stilted** *adj* guindé, tendu.

stimulate ('stimjuleit) *vt* stimuler, activer.

stimulus ('stimjuləs) *n, pl* **-li** stimulant *m.* impulsion *f.*

sting* (stiŋ) *vt* piquer. *vi* cuire. *n* **1** piqûre *f.* dard *m.* **2** pointe *f.*

stink* (stiŋk) *vi* puer. *n* puanteur *f.*

stipulate ('stipjuleit) *vt,vi* stipuler.

stir (stə:) *n* **1** remuement *m.* **2** mouvement *m.* **3** *inf* remue-ménage *m invar.* *vt* **1** remuer. **2** agiter, susciter. *vi* remuer, bouger.

stirrup ('stirəp) *n* étrier *m.*

stitch (stitʃ) *n* **1** point *m.* maille *f.* **2** *med* suture *f.* *vt* **1** coudre. **2** *med* suturer.

stoat (stout) *n* hermine d'été *f.*

stock (stɔk) *n* **1** provision *f.* **2** stock *m.* **3** souche *f.* **4** *pl comm* titres *m pl.* actions *f pl.* **5** *cul* bouillon *m.* *adj* courant. *vt* **1** approvisionner. **2** stocker. **stockbreeding** *n* élevage *m.* **stockbroker** *n* agent de change *m.* **stock exchange** *n* bourse *f.* **stockpile** *n* stocks de

réserve *m pl.* *vt,vi* stocker. **stocktaking** *n* inventaire *m.*
stocking ('stɔkiŋ) *n* bas *m.*
stocky ('stɔki) *adj* trapu.
stodge (stɔdʒ) *n inf* aliment bourratif *m.*
stoical ('stouikl̩) *adj* stoïque.
stoke (stouk) *vt* chauffer, entretenir.
stole[1] (stoul) *v* see **steal.**
stole[2] (stoul) *n* étole *f.*
stolen ('stoulən) *v* see **steal.**
stomach ('stʌmək) *n* **1** estomac *m.* **2** ventre *m.* *vt inf* supporter. **stomach-ache** *n* mal de ventre *m.*
stone (stoun) *n* **1** pierre *f.* **2** (of a fruit) noyau, -aux *m.* **3** (weight) stone *m.* *adj* de pierre. *vt* **1** lapider. **2** dénoyauter.
stood (stud) *v* see **stand.**
stool (stu:l) *n* tabouret *m.*
stoop (stu:p) *vi* **1** se pencher. **2** s'abaisser. **3** être voûté.
stop (stɔp) *vt* **1** arrêter. **2** boucher. **3** cesser. **4** retenir. *vi* s'arrêter. *n* arrêt *m.* **stoppage** *n* **1** suspension *f.* **2** obstruction *f.* **stopper** *n* bouchon *m.* **stopwatch** *n* chronomètre *m.*
store (stɔ:) *n* **1** provision, réserve *f.* **2** magasin *m.* *vt* **1** approvisionner. **2** amasser. **3** emmagasiner. **storage** *n* emmagasinage *m.*
storey ('stɔ:ri) *n* étage *m.*
stork (stɔ:k) *n* cigogne *f.*
storm (stɔ:m) *n* orage *m.* tempête *f.* *vi* faire rage. *vt* donner l'assaut à. **stormy** *adj* orageux, -euse.
story ('stɔ:ri) *n* histoire *f.* conte, récit *m.*
stout (staut) *adj* **1** fort. **2** costaud, vaillant. **3** corpulent. *n* stout *m.* bière brune forte *f.*
stove (stouv) *n* poêle, fourneau, -aux *m.*
stow (stou) *vt* arrimer. **stowaway** *n* passager clandestin *m.*
straddle (strædl̩) *vi* se tenir *or* marcher les jambes ecartées. *vt* chevaucher, s'affourcher sur, enfourcher.
straggle ('strægəl) *vi* **1** s'éparpiller. **2** traîner. **straggler** *n* traînard *m.*
straight (streit) *adj* **1** droit, raide. **2** franc, -che. **3** en ordre. *adv* **1** droit. **2** juste. **3** directement. **4** tout droit. **straignten** *vt* **1** redresser. **2** mettre en ordre. *vi* se redresser. **straightforward** *adj* loyal, -aux, franc, -che.
strain[1] (strein) *vt* **1** tendre. **2** *med* se fouler. **3** filtrer. *vi* peiner, fatiguer. *n* **1** tension *f.* **2** *med* entorse *f.*
strain[2] (strein) *n* lignée, race *f.*
strand[1] (strænd) *vt,vi* échouer.
strand[2] (strænd) *n* brin *m.* fibre *f.*
strange (streindʒ) *adj* étrange, bizarre, singulier, -ière. **strangeness** *n* étrangeté *f.* **stranger** *n* inconnu *m.*
strangle ('stræŋgəl) *vt* étrangler.
strap (stræp) *n* **1** courroie *f.* **2** bande *f.* *vt* lier avec une courroie.
strategy ('strætidʒi) *n* stratégie *f.* **strategic** *adj* stratégique.
straw (strɔ:) *n* paille *f.* **that's the last straw!** ça, c'est le comble! *~adj* de paille. **strawberry** *n* fraise *f.* **strawberry plant** fraisier *m.*
stray (strei) *vi* **1** s'égarer. **2** s'éloigner, errer.
streak (stri:k) *n* **1** rayure *f.* **2** trait *m.* *vt* rayer, strier.
stream (stri:m) *n* **1** ruisseau, -aux *m.* **2** flux *m.* **3** courant *m.* *vi* couler. **streamline** *vt* **1** profiler. **2** moderniser.
street (stri:t) *n* rue *f.*
strength (streŋθ) *n* **1** force *f.* **2** nombre *m.* **strengthen** *vt* consolider, renforcer.
strenuous ('strenjuəs) *adj* **1** énergique. **2** acharné. **3** fatiguant.
stress (stres) *n* **1** tension *f.* **2** force *f.* **3** accent *m.* *vt* insister sur, souligner.
stretch (stretʃ) *n* **1** étendue *f.* **2** section *f.* **3** extension *f.* *vt* tendre. *vi* **1** s'élargir. **2** s'étendre. **stretcher** *n* brancard *m.*
strict (strikt) *adj* **1** strict. **2** rigide. **3** sévère.
stride* (straid) *vi* marcher à grandes enjambées. *n* enjambée *f.*
strike* (straik) *n* **1** grève *f.* **2** coup *m.* *vt* **1** frapper. **2** frotter. **3** heurter. *vi* **1** sonner. **2** se mettre en grève. **striking** *adj* remarquable.
string* (striŋ) *n* **1** corde *f.* **2** ficelle *f.* **3** cordon *m.* **4** chapelet *m.* **5** train *m.* *vt* enfiler.
stringent ('strindʒənt) *adj* rigoureux, -euse.
strip[1] (strip) *vt* **1** mettre à nu, dépouiller. **2** dégarnir. *vi* se dévêtir. **striptease** *n* strip-tease *m.*
strip[2] (strip) *n* **1** bande *f.* **2** lambeau, -aux *m.*
stripe (straip) *n* **1** raie *f.* **2** bande *f.* *vt* rayer, barrer.
strive* (straiv) *vi* **1** s'efforcer. **2** se débattre.
strode (stroud) *v* see **stride.**
stroke[1] (strouk) *n* **1** coup *m.* **2** trait *m.* **3** brassée *f.* **4** *med* apoplexie *f.*
stroke[2] (strouk) *vt* caresser. *n* caresse *f.*
stroll (stroul) *n* promenade *f.* tour *m.* *vi* flâner.
strong (strɔŋ) *adj* **1** fort. **2** solide. **3** prononcé. *adv* fort. **stronghold** *n* forteresse *f.* **strong-minded** *adj* résolu, décidé.
strove (strouv) *v* see **strive.**

struck (strʌk) *v* see **strike.**
structure ('strʌktʃə) *n* **1** structure *f*. **2** édifice *m*.
struggle ('strʌgəl) *n* lutte *f*. *vi* lutter, se débattre.
strum (strʌm) *vi* pianoter, tapoter.
strung (strʌŋ) *v* see **string.**
strut[1] (strʌt) *vi* se pavaner.
strut[2] (strʌt) *n* entretoise *f*.
stub (stʌb) *n* **1** souche *f*. **2** bout, mégot *m*. *vt* cogner, heurter. **stub out** éteindre.
stubborn ('stʌbən) *adj* obstiné, têtu, opiniâtre. **stubbornness** *n* entêtement *m*.
stud[1] (stʌd) *n* **1** clou à grosse tête *m*. **2** bouton *m*. **3** poteau, -aux *m*. *vt* **1** clouter. **2** parsemer.
stud[2] (stʌd) *n* écurie *f*. haras *m*.
student ('stju:dnt) *n* étudiant *m*.
studio ('stju:diou) *n* **1** *Art* atelier *m*. **2** studio *m*.
study ('stʌdi) *n* **1** étude *f*. **2** cabinet de travail *m*. *vt* étudier. **studious** *adj* studieux, -euse.
stuff (stʌf) *n* matière *f*. *vt* **1** rembourrer. **2** *cul* farcir. **3** empailler. **stuffing** *n* **1** *cul* farce *f*. **2** bourre *f*. **stuffy** *adj* **1** renfermé, mal aéré. **2** *inf* collet monté.
stumble ('stʌmbəl) *vi* trébucher.
stump (stʌmp) *n* **1** tronçon *m*. souche *f*. **2** bout *m*. **3** moignon *m*. *vt inf* coller.
stun (stʌn) *vt* **1** étourdir. **2** abasourdir. **stunning** *adj* **1** *inf* épatant. **2** étourdissant.
stung (stʌŋ) *v* see **sting.**
stunk (stʌŋk) *v* see **stink.**
stunt[1] (stʌnt) *vt* empêcher de croître, rabougrir.
stunt[2] (stʌnt) *n* **1** tour de force *m*. acrobatie *f*. **2** affaire publicitaire *f*.
stupid ('stju:pid) *adj* stupide, bête.
sturdy ('stə:di) *adj* **1** robuste. **2** hardi.
sturgeon ('stə:dʒən) *n* esturgeon *m*.
stutter ('stʌtə) *vt,vi* bégayer. *n* bégaiement *m*.
sty (stai) *n* étable *f*.
style (stail) *n* **1** style *m*. **2** manière *f*. **3** chic *m*. *vt* dénommer. **stylish** *adj* élégant, chic.
stylus ('stailəs) *n* stylet *m*.
subconscious (sʌb'kɔnʃəs) *adj,n* subconscient *m*. **subconsciously** *adv* inconsciemment.
subcontract (sʌbkən'trækt) *vt* sous-traiter. **subcontractor** *n* sous-entrepreneur, sous-traitant *m*.
subdue (səb'dju:) *vt* **1** subjuguer, soumettre. **2** atténuer.
subject (*n,adj* 'sʌbdʒikt; *v* səb'dʒekt) *n* **1** sujet *m*. **2** matière *f*. *adj* **1** assujetti. **2** sujet, -ette. *vt* assujettir. **subjective** *adj* subjectif, -ive.
subjunctive (səb'dʒʌŋktiv) *adj,n* subjonctif, -ive *m*.
sublime (sə'blaim) *adj* sublime, suprême.
submachine-gun (səbmə'ʃi:ngʌn) *n* mitraillette *f*.
submarine (sʌbmə'ri:n) *n* sous-marin *m*.
submerge (səb'mə:dʒ) *vt* submerger. *vi* plonger.
submit (səb'mit) *vi* se soumettre. *vt* soumettre, présenter. **submission** *n* soumission *m*. **submissive** *adj* soumis, docile.
subnormal (sʌb'nɔ:məl) *adj* au-dessous de la normale.
subordinate (sə'bɔ:dinət) *adj* inférieur, accessoire. *n* subordonné *m*. *vt* subordonner.
subscribe (səb'skraib) *vt* souscrire. *vi* s'abonner à. **subscription** *n* **1** souscription *f*. **2** adhésion *f*. **3** abonnement *m*.
subsequent ('sʌbsikwint) *adj* subséquent. **subsequently** *adv* plus tard.
subservient (səb'sə:viənt) *adj* **1** obséquieux, -euse. **2** subordonné. **3** utile.
subside (səb'said) *vi* **1** s'affaisser. **2** baisser. **3** s'apaiser.
subsidiary (səb'sidiəri) *n* filiale *f*. *adj* auxiliaire, subsidiaire.
subsidize ('sʌbsidaiz) *vt* subventionner. **subsidy** *n* subvention *f*.
subsist (səb'sist) *vi* subsister.
substance ('sʌbstəns) *n* **1** substance *f*. **2** solidité *f*. **substantial** *adj* **1** substantiel, -elle. **2** important. **substantive** *n* substantif *m*.
substitute ('sʌbstitju:t) *n* **1** remplaçant *m*. **2** succédané *m*. *vt* substituer. *vi* remplacer. **substitution** *n* substitution *f*. remplacement *m*.
subtitle ('sʌbtaitl) *n* sous-titre *m*. *vt* sous-titrer.
subtle ('sʌtl) *adj* **1** subtil. **2** fin.
subtract (səb'trækt) *vt* soustraire. **subtraction** *n* soustraction *f*.
suburb ('sʌbə:b) *n* **1** faubourg *m*. **2** *pl* banlieue *f*. **suburban** *adj* suburbain.
subvert (sʌb'və:t) *vt* subvertir. **subversion** *n* subversion *f*. **subversive** *adj* subversif, -ive.
subway ('sʌbwei) *n* passage souterrain *m*.
succeed (sək'si:d) *vt* succéder. *vi* réussir. **success** *n* succès *m*. réussite *f*. **successful** *adj* heureux, -euse, réussi. **succession** *n* **1** succession *f*. **2** suite, série *f*. **successive** *adj* successif, -ive.
succulent ('sʌkjulənt) *adj* succulent.
succumb (sə'kʌm) *vi* succomber, céder.
such (sʌtʃ) *adj* **1** tel, telle, semblable. **2** si. **such as** tel que, comme. ~*pron* tel, telle.
suck (sʌk) *vt,vi* sucer. *vt* téter.

sucker (ˈsʌkə) *n* **1** *inf* gobeur, niais *m*. **2** *bot* rejeton *m*.
suction (ˈsʌkʃən) *n* succion, aspiration *f*.
sudden (ˈsʌdn̩) *adj* soudain, subit. **all of a sudden** tout à coup.
suds (sʌdz) *n pl* **1** mousse de savon *f*. **2** lessive *f*.
sue (su:) *vt* poursuivre en justice.
suede (sweid) *n* daim *m*.
suet (ˈsu:it) *n* graisse de rognon *f*.
suffer (ˈsʌfə) *vt* **1** souffrir, éprouver. **2** supporter. *vi* souffrir. **suffering** *n* souffrance *f*.
sufficient (səˈfiʃənt) *adj* suffisant, assez de. **sufficiently** *adv* suffisamment, assez.
suffix (ˈsʌfiks) *n* suffixe *m*.
suffocate (ˈsʌfəkeit) *vt,vi* suffoquer, étouffer. **suffocation** *n* asphyxie *f*.
sugar (ˈʃugə) *n* sucre. *vt* sucrer. **sugarbeet** *n* betterave à sucre *f*. **sugar cane** *n* canne à sucre *f*.
suggest (səˈdʒest) *vt* **1** suggérer. **2** inspirer. **suggestion** *n* **1** suggestion *f*. **2** trace *f*. **suggestive** *adj* suggestif, -ive, évocateur, -trice.
suicide (ˈsu:isaid) *n* **1** suicide *m*. **2** (person) suicidé *m*. **commit suicide** se suicider.
suit (su:t) *n* **1** costume *m*. **2** poursuites *f pl*. **3** *game* couleur *f*. **4** requête *f*. *vt* **1** convenir à, aller bien. **2** accommoder. **suitable** *adj* **1** convenable. **2** approprié. **suitcase** *n* valise *f*.
suite (swi:t) *n* **1** suite *f*. **2** appartement *m*. **3** mobilier *m*.
sulk (sʌlk) *vi* bouder. *n* bouderie *f*. **sulky** *adj* maussade, boudeur, -euse.
sullen (ˈsʌlən) *adj* morose, morne.
sulphur (ˈsʌlfə) *n* soufre *m*.
sultan (ˈsʌltən) *n* sultan *m*.
sultana (sʌlˈtɑ:nə) *n* raisin sec (de Smyrne) *m*.
sultry (ˈsʌltri) *adj* étouffant.
sum (sʌm) *n* **1** somme *f*. total, -aux *m*. **2** calcul *m*. *v* **sum up 1** résumer. **2** classer.
summarize (ˈsʌməraiz) *vt* résumer. **summary** *n* sommaire, résumé *m*. *adj* sommaire.
summer (ˈsʌmə) *n* été *m*. **summerhouse** *n* pavillon *m*. **summertime** *n* été *m*.
summit (ˈsʌmit) *n* sommet, faîte *m*.
summon (ˈsʌmən) *vt* **1** convoquer. **2** sommer. **3** faire appel à. **summons** *n* **1** *law* citation *f*. **2** appel *m*. *vt* citer en justice.
sun (sʌn) *n* soleil *m*. *vt* exposer au soleil.
sunbathe (ˈsʌnbeið) *vi* prendre un bain de soleil.
sunburn (ˈsʌnbə:n) *n* hâle *m*.
Sunday (ˈsʌndi) *n* dimanche *m*.
sundial (ˈsʌndaiəl) *n* cadran solaire *m*.
sundry (ˈsʌndri) *adj* divers. **all and sundry** tout le monde. **sundries** *n pl* frais divers *m pl*.
sunflower (ˈsʌnflauə) *n* tournesol *m*.
sung (sʌŋ) *v* see **sing**.
sunglasses (ˈsʌnglɑ:siz) *n pl* lunettes de soleil *f pl*.
sunk (sʌŋk) *v* see **sink**.
sunlight (ˈsʌnlait) *n* lumière solaire *f*. soleil *m*.
sunny (ˈsʌni) *adj* ensoleillé.
sunrise (ˈsʌnraiz) *n* lever du soleil *m*.
sunset (ˈsʌnset) *n* coucher du soleil *m*.
sunshine (ˈsʌnʃain) *n* soleil *m*.
sunstroke (ˈsʌnstrouk) *n* insolation *f*. coup de soleil *m*.
suntan (ˈsʌntæn) *n* hâle *m*.
super (ˈsu:pə) *adj inf* superbe, magnifique.
superannuation (su:pərænjuˈeiʃən) *n* retraite par limite d'âge *f*.
superb (su:ˈpə:b) *adj* superbe, magnifique.
superficial (su:pəˈfiʃəl) *adj* superficiel, -elle.
superfluous (su:ˈpə:fluəs) *adj* superflu, de trop.
superhuman (su:pəˈhju:mən) *adj* surhumain.
superimpose (su:pərimˈpouz) *vt* superposer surimposer.
superintendent (su:pərinˈtendənt) *n* directeur, surveillant *m*.
superior (suˈpiəriə) *adj,n* supérieur *m*.
superlative (suˈpə:lətiv) *n* superlatif *m*. *adj* **1** suprême. **2** superlatif, -ive.
supermarket (ˈsu:pəmɑ:kit) *n* supermarché *m*.
supernatural (su:pəˈnætʃrəl) *adj,n* surnaturel, -elle *m*.
supersede (su:pəˈsi:d) *vt* remplacer, supplanter.
supersonic (su:pəˈsɔnik) *adj* supersonique.
superstition (su:pəˈstiʃən) *n* superstition *f*. **superstitious** *adj* superstitieux, -euse.
supervise (ˈsu:pəvaiz) *vt* **1** surveiller. **2** diriger. **supervision** *n* **1** surveillance *f*. **2** direction *f*.
supper (ˈsʌpə) *n* souper *m*.
supple (ˈsʌpəl) *adj* souple, pliant, maniable.
supplement (*n* ˈsʌplimənt; *v* sʌpliˈment) *n* supplément *m*. *vt* compléter, ajouter à. **supplementary** *adj* supplémentaire.
supply (səˈplai) *vt* fournir, munir. *n* **1** fourniture, offre *f*. **2** *pl* vivres *f pl*. approvisionnements *m pl*.
support (səˈpɔ:t) *n* appui, soutien *m*. *vt* **1** soutenir, appuyer, entretenir. **supporter** *n* **1** partisan, adhérent *m*. **2** *sport* supporter *m*.
suppose (səˈpouz) *vt* supposer. **supposed** *adj* prétendu. **supposedly** *adv* soi-disant, censément.

suppress (sə'pres) *vt* 1 réprimer, refouler. 2 dissimuler. **suppression** *n* 1 répression *f*. 2 étouffement *m*.

supreme (sə'pri:m) *adj* suprême. **supremacy** *n* suprématie *f*.

surcharge ('sə:tʃɑ:dʒ) *n* surcharge, surtaxe *f*.

sure (ʃuə) *adj* sûr, certain. *adv* certainement. **surely** *adv* assurément, bien sûr. **surety** *n* 1 garant *m*. caution *f*. 2 certitude *f*.

surf (sə:f) *n* ressac *m*.

surface ('sə:fis) *n* 1 surface *f*. 2 apparence *f*. *vi* remonter à la surface.

surfeit ('sə:fit) *n* surabondance *f*.

surge (sə:dʒ) *n* 1 vague, lame *f*. 2 *naut* houle *f*. *vi* se soulever.

surgeon ('sə:dʒən) *n* chirurgien *m*. **surgery** *n* 1 chirurgie *f*. 2 cabinet de consultation, dispensaire *m*. **surgical** *adj* chirurgical, -aux.

surly ('sə:li) *adj* bourru, revêche, hargneux, -euse.

surmount (sə'maunt) *vt* surmonter, maîtriser.

surname ('sə:neim) *n* nom de famille *m*.

surpass (sə'pɑ:s) *vt* 1 surpasser. 2 l'emporter sur.

surplus ('sə:plis) *n* surplus, excédent *m*. *adj* excédentaire.

surprise (sə'praiz) *n* surprise *f*. *vt* surprendre, étonner.

surrealism (sə'riəlizəm) *n* surréalisme *m*. **surrealist** *adj,n* surréaliste *m*.

surrender (sə'rendə) *vi* se rendre. *vt* rendre, céder. *n* reddition *f*.

surreptitious (sʌrəp'tiʃəs) *adj* subreptice, clandestin.

surround (sə'raund) *vt* entourer, cerner. *n* bordure *f*. **surroundings** *n pl* milieu *m*.

survey (*n* 'sə:vei; *v* sə:'vei) *n* 1 étude . 2 levé *m*. 3 enquête *f*. *vt* 1 examiner. 2 arpenter.

surveyor (sə'veiə) *n* 1 arpenteur *m*. 2 surveillant *m*.

survive (sə'vaiv) *vi* survivre. *vt* survivre à. **survival** *n* survivance *f*. **survivor** *n* survivant *m*.

susceptible (sə'septəbəl) *adj* 1 susceptible. 2 sensible.

suspect (*v* sə'spekt; *n,adj* 'sʌspekt) *vt* 1 soupçonner. 2 se douter de. *adj,n* suspect.

suspend (sə'spend) *vt* suspendre. **suspense** *n* suspens *m*. **suspension** *n* suspension *f*.

suspicion (sə'spiʃən) *n* soupçon *m*. **suspicious** *adj* 1 méfiant, soupçonneux, -euse. 2 suspect, louche.

sustain (sə'stein) *vt* 1 soutenir. 2 éprouver.

swab (swɔb) *n* tampon, torchon *m*. *vt* nettoyer, essuyer.

swagger ('swægə) *n* 1 air important *m*. 2 crânerie *f*. *vi* crâner.

swallow[1] ('swɔlou) *vt* avaler, gober. *n* 1 gosier *m*. 2 gorgée *f*.

swallow[2] ('swɔlou) *n zool* hirondelle *f*.

swam (swæm) *v* see **swim**.

swamp (swɔmp) *n* marais *m*. *vt* inonder, submerger.

swan (swɔn) *n* cygne *m*.

swank (swæŋk) *vi* crâner. *n inf* prétention *f*.

swap (swɔp) *vt* troquer, échanger. *n* troc, échange *m*.

swarm (swɔ:m) *n* essaim *m*. nuée *f*. *vi* 1 essaimer. 2 fourmiller.

swastika ('swɔstikə) *n* croix gammée *f*.

swat (swɔt) *vt inf* écraser.

sway (swei) *vi* osciller, se balancer. *vt* 1 agiter. 2 influencer.

swear* (swɛə) *vt,vi* jurer. **swearword** *n* juron *m*.

sweat (swet) *n* sueur, transpiration *f*. *vi,vt* suer **sweater** *n* chandail *m*.

swede (swi:d) *n* rutabaga *m*.

Sweden ('swi:dn̩) *n* Suède *f*. **Swede** *n* suédois *m*. **Swedish** *adj* suédois. **Swedish (language)** *n* suédois *m*.

sweep* (swi:p) *vt* 1 balayer, ramoner. 2 enlever. *vi* 1 passer rapidement. 2 s'étendre. *n* 1 coup de balai *m*. 2 ramoneur *m*. 3 mouvement circulaire *m*. **sweeping** *adj* 1 large. 2 rapide. 3 radical, -aux. 4 complet, -ète.

sweet (swi:t) *adj* 1 doux, douce. 2 sucré. 3 charmant. *n* 1 bonbon *m*. 2 dessert *m*. **sweetbread** *n* ris de veau *or* d'agneau *m*. **sweet corn** *n* maïs *m*. **sweetheart** *n* amoureux, -euse. **sweet pea** *n* pois de senteur *m*. **sweeten** *vt* sucrer.

swell* (swel) *vi* s'enfler, se gonfler. *vt* gonfler. *n naut* houle *f*. **swelling** *n* enflure *f*.

swept (swept) *v* see **sweep**.

swerve (swə:v) *n* écart *m*. embardée *f*. *vi* faire un écart *or* une embardée.

swift (swift) *adj* rapide. *n* martinet *m*.

swig (swig) *n inf* lampée *f*. *vt* boire à grands traits.

swill (swil) *vt* laver à grande eau. **swill out** rincer. ~*n* 1 pâtee pour les porcs *f*. 2 lavage *m*. 3 lampée *f*.

swim* (swim) *vi* 1 nager. 2 tourner. 3 être inondé. *vt* traverser à la nage. *n* nage *f*. **swimming** *n* natation *f*. **swimming cos-**

tume *n* maillot de bain *m.* **swimming pool** *n* piscine *f.*

swindle (ˈswindḷ) *vt* escroquer. *n* escroquerie *f.* **swindler** *n* escroc *m.*

swine (swain) *n invar* cochon *m.*

swing* (swiŋ) *vi* **1** se balancer. **2** changer de direction. *vt* **1** balancer. **2** tourner. *n* **1** balançoire *f.* **2** oscillation *f.* **3** revirement *m.*

swipe (swaip) *inf vt* **1** cogner. **2** chiper. *n* coup *m.*

swirl (swə:l) *vi* tourbillonner. *vt* faire tournoyer. *n* remous *m.*

swish (swiʃ) *vi* siffler, bruire. *vt* fouetter, battre, faire siffler. *n* sifflement, bruissement *m.*

switch (switʃ) *n* **1** interrupteur, commutateur *m.* **2** cravache *f.* *vt* **1** aiguiller. **2** battre. **switch off/on** éteindre/allumer. **switchboard** *n* standard téléphonique *m.*

Switzerland (ˈswitsələnd) *n* Suisse *f.* **Swiss** *adj,n* suisse.

swivel (ˈswivəl) *vi* pivoter. *n* pivot *m.*

swollen (ˈswoulən) *v* see **swell.** *adj* enflé, gonflé.

swoop (swu:p) *vi* fondre, foncer. *n* descente *f.*

swop (swɔp) *n* troc *m.* *vt* échanger.

sword (sɔ:d) *n* épée *f.* **swordfish** *n* espadon *m.*

swore (swɔ:) *v* see **swear.**

sworn (swɔ:n) *v* see **swear.**

swot (swɔt) *vi inf* bûcher.

swum (swʌm) *v* see **swim.**

swung (swʌŋ) *v* see **swing.**

sycamore (ˈsikəmɔ:) *n* sycomore *m.*

syllable (ˈsiləbəl) *n* syllabe *f.*

syllabus (ˈsiləbəs) *n, pl* **-buses** *or* **-bi** programme *m.*

symbol (ˈsimbəl) *n* symbole *m.* **symbolic** *adj* symbolique. **symbolism** *n* symbolisme *m.* **symbolize** *vt* symboliser.

symmetry (ˈsimitri) *n* symétrie *f.* **symmetrical** *adj* symétrique.

sympathy (ˈsimpəθi) *n* **1** sympathie *f.* **2** condoléances *f pl.* **sympathetic** *adj* sympathique, compatissant. **sympathize** *vi* sympathiser, avoir de la compassion.

symphony (ˈsimfəni) *n* symphonie *f.*

symposium (simˈpouziəm) *n, pl* **-iums** *or* **-ia** conférence *f.* recueil *m.*

symptom (ˈsimptəm) *n* symptôme *m.*

synagogue (ˈsinəgɔg) *n* synagogue *f.*

synchronize (ˈsiŋkrənaiz) *vt* synchroniser.

syndicate (ˈsindikət) *n* syndicat *m.*

syndrome (ˈsindroum) *n* syndrome *m.*

synonym (ˈsinənim) *n* synonyme *m.* **synonymous** *adj* synonyme.

synopsis (siˈnɔpsis) *n. pl* **-ses** sommaire, résumé *m.*

syntax (ˈsintæks) *n* syntaxe *f.*

synthesis (ˈsinθəsis) *n, pl* **-ses** synthèse *f.*

synthetic (sinˈθetik) *adj* synthétique.

syphilis (ˈsifəlis) *n* syphilis *f.*

Syria (ˈsiriə) *n* Syrie *f.* **Syrian** *adj,n* syrien, -ienne.

syringe (siˈrindʒ) *n* seringue *f.* *vt* seringuer.

syrup (ˈsirəp) *n* sirop *m.*

system (ˈsistəm) *n* **1** système, réseau, -aux *m.* **2** méthode *f.* **systematic** *adj* systématique, méthodique.

T

tab (tæb) *n* **1** étiquette *f.* **2** patte *f.*

tabby (ˈtæbi) *adj* tacheté, moucheté. *n* chat tigré *m.*

table (ˈteibəl) *n* **1** table *f.* **2** plaque *f.* **3** tableau, -aux *m.* *vt* déposer. **tablecloth** *n* nappe *f.* **tablemat** *n* rond de table *m.* **tablespoon** *n* cuiller à dessert *f.* **table tennis** *n* tennis de table *m.*

tablet (ˈtæblət) *n* **1** tablette *f.* **2** comprimé *m.*

taboo (təˈbu:) *n* tabou *m.* *adj* interdit, proscrit. *vt* proscrire.

tack (tæk) *n* **1** petit clou *m.* pointe *f.* **2** *dom* point de bâti *m.* **3** *naut* bordée *f.* *vt* **1** clouer. **2** *dom* faufiler. *vi* virer.

tackle (ˈtækəl) *n* attirail, appareil *m.* *vt* s'attaquer à, aborder.

tact (tækt) *n* tact *m.* **tactful** *adj* délicat, de tact.

tactic (ˈtæktik) *n* tactique *f.*

tadpole (ˈtædpoul) *n* têtard *m.*

taffeta (ˈtæfitə) *n* taffetas *m.*

tag (tæg) *n* fiche *f.* ferret *m.*

Tahiti (tə:ˈhi:ti) *n* Tahiti *m.*

tail (teil) *n* **1** queue *f.* **2** arrière *m.* **3** pile *f.* **4** pan *m.* *vt* pister.

tailor (ˈteilə) *n* tailleur *m.* *vt* façonner.

taint (teint) *n* **1** corruption, souillure *f.* **2** trace *f.* *vt* vicier, corrompre, gâter.

take* (teik) *vt,vi* prendre. *vt* **1** conduire. **2** emporter. **3** saisir. **4** falloir. **take away** emmener. **take off 1** enlever. **2** décoller. **take-off** *n* **1** envol *m.* **2** *inf* caricature *f.* **take on** entreprendre. **take place** se passer. **take up** relever. **take-over** *n* reprise *f.* *adj* de rachat.

talcum powder ('tælkəm) *n* talc *m*.
tale (teil) *n* conte, récit *m*.
talent ('tælənt) *n* talent *m*.
talk (tɔ:k) *vt,vi* parler. *vi* jaser, causer. *n* paroles *f pl*. bavardage *m*. conversation *f*. **talkative** *adj* bavard.
tall (tɔ:l) *adj* **1** grand. **2** haut. **3** *inf* incroyable.
tally ('tæli) *vt* pointer, contrôler. *vi* correspondre. *n* pointage *m*.
talon ('tælən) *n* serre, griffe *f*.
tambourine (tæmbə'ri:n) *n* tambourin *m*.
tame (teim) *adj* **1** domestique, apprivoisé, **2** soumis. *vt* apprivoiser.
tamper ('tæmpə) *vi* **tamper with** tripoter.
tampon ('tæmpɔn) *n* tampon *m*.
tan (tæn) *vt* tanner. *vi* se bronzer. *n* hâle *m*.
tangent ('tændʒənt) *n* tangente *f*.
tangerine (tændʒə'ri:n) *n* mandarine *f*.
tangible ('tændʒəbəl) *adj* **1** tangible. **2** sensible.
Tangier (tæn'dʒiə) *n* Tanger *m*.
tangle ('tæŋgəl) *n* enchevêtrement, emmêlement *m*. *vt* embrouiller. *vi* s'embrouiller.
tango ('tæŋgou) *n* tango *m*.
tank (tæŋk) *n* **1** réservoir *m*. **2** *mil* char de combat *m*. **tanker** *n* **1** *naut* pétrolier *m*. **2** *mot* camion-citerne *m*.
tankard ('tæŋkəd) *n* pot *m*. chope *f*.
tantalize ('tæntəlaiz) *vt* tourmenter, taquiner.
tantrum ('tæntrəm) *n* accès de colère *m*.
tap[1] (tæp) *vt* taper. *n* tape *f*. petit coup *m*.
tap[2] (tæp) *n* robinet *m*. *vt* **1** percer. **2** vider. **3** capter.
tape (teip) *n* **1** ruban *m*. **2** *tech* bande magnétique *f*. *vt* **1** attacher. **2** enregistrer. **tape-measure** *n* mètre à ruban *m*. **tape-recorder** *n* magnétophone *m*.
taper ('teipə) *n* cierge *m*. *vi* s'effiler. *vt* effiler.
tapestry ('tæpistri) *n* tapisserie *f*.
tapioca (tæpi'oukə) *n* tapioca *m*.
tar (tɑ:) *n* goudron *m*. *vt* goudronner.
Tarmac ('tɑ:mæk) *n* *Tdmk* bitume *m*.
tarantula (tə'ræntjulə) *n* tarentule *f*.
target ('tɑ:git) *n* but *m*. cible *f*.
tariff ('tærif) *n* tarif *m*.
tarnish ('tɑ:niʃ) *vt* ternir. *vi* se ternir. *n* ternissure *f*.
tarragon ('tærəgən) *n* estragon *m*.
tart[1] (tɑ:t) *adj* **1** âpre, acerbe. **2** mordant, caustique.
tart[2] (tɑ:t) *n* **1** tarte *f*. **2** *sl* poule *f*.
tartan ('tɑ:tn̩) *n* tartan *m*.
task (tɑ:sk) *n* tâche, besogne *f*.
tassel ('tæsəl) *n* gland *m*.
taste (teist) *n* **1** goût *m*. saveur *f*. **2** prédilection *f*. penchant *m*. ~*vt* goûter, déguster. **taste of** avoir un goût de. **tasteless** *adj* insipide, fade. **tasty** *adj* savoureux, -euse.
tattoo[1] (tə'tu:) *n* *mil* retraite du soir *f*.
tattoo[2] (tə'tu:) *n* tatouage *m*. *vt* tatouer.
taught (tɔ:t) *v* see **teach.**
taunt (tɔ:nt) *vt* se gausser de, accabler de sarcasmes. *n* reproche *m*.
Taurus ('tɔ:rəs) *n* Taureau *m*.
taut (tɔ:t) *adj* raide, tendu.
tautology (tɔ:'tɔlədʒi) *n* tautologie *f*.
tavern ('tævən) *n* taverne *f*.
tax (tæks) *n* **1** impôt *m*. contribution *f*. **2** charge *f*. *vt* **1** taxer. **2** imposer. **3** mettre à l'épreuve. **taxation** *n* impôts *m*. **taxpayer** *n* contribuable *m*.
taxi ('tæksi) *n* taxi *m*.
tea (ti:) *n* **1** thé *m*. **2** goûter *m*. **tea-bag** *n* sachet de thé *m*. **tea-break** *n* pause café *f*. **tea-cloth** *n* torchon *m*. **teacup** *n* tasse à thé *f*. **tealeaf** *n* feuille de thé *f*. **teapot** *n* théière *f*. **teaspoon** *n* cuiller à thé *f*.
teach* (ti:tʃ) *vt* enseigner, instruire, apprendre. **teacher** *n* **1** professeur *m,f*. **2** instituteur, -trice. **teacher training college** école normale.
teak (ti:k) *n* teck *m*.
team (ti:m) *n* **1** équipe *f*. **2** (of horses, etc.) attelage *m*.
tear[1] (tiə) *n* larme *f*. pleur *m*. **teardrop** *n* larme *f*. **tearful** *adj* en pleurs, larmoyant. **tear-gas** *n* gaz lacrymogène *m*.
tear*[2] (tεə) *vt* **1** déchirer. **2** arracher. *vi* **1** se déchirer. **2** *inf* aller très rapidement. *n* déchirure *f*.
tease (ti:z) *vt* taquiner.
teat (ti:t) *n* **1** mamelon *m*. **2** (of a bottle) tétine *f*.
technical ('teknikəl) *adj* technique. **technician** *n* technicien *m*. **technique** *n* technique *f*. **technology** *n* technologie *f*. **technological** *adj* technologique.
teddy bear ('tedi) *n* ours en peluche, nounours *m*.
tedious ('ti:diəs) *adj* fastidieux, -euse, pénible.
tee (ti:) *n* but *m*. *vt* surélever.
teenage ('ti:neidʒ) *adj* adolescent. **teenager** *n* adolescent *m*.
teetotal (ti:'toutl̩) *adj* antialcoolique. **teetotaller** *n* abstinent *m*.
telegram ('teligræm) *n* télégramme *m*.
telegraph ('teligrɑ:f) *n* télégraphe *m*. *vt* télé-

graphier. **telegraph pole** *n* poteau télégraphique *m*.

telepathy (ti'lepəθi) *n* télépathie *f*.

telephone ('telifoun) *n* téléphone *m*. *vt,vi* téléphoner.

telescope ('teliskoup) *n* télescope *m*. longue-vue *f*.

television ('teləviʒən) *n* télévision *f*. **televise** *vt* téléviser.

telex ('teleks) *n* télex *m*.

tell* (tel) *vt* **1** dire, raconter. **2** discerner. *vi* porter. **tell off** réprimander.

temper ('tempə) *n* **1** tempérament *m*. humeur *f*. **2** sang-froid *m*. **3** colère *f*. **4** *tech* trempe *f*. *vt* **1** modérer. **2** délayer. **3** *tech* tremper. **temperament** *n* tempérament *m*. **temperamental** *adj* capricieux, -euse. **temperate** *adj* **1** modéré, sobre. **2** tempéré. **temperature** *n* température *f*.

tempestuous (tem'pestjuəs) *adj* tempétueux, -euse.

temple[1] ('tempəl) *n rel* temple *m*.

temple[2] ('tempəl) *n anat* tempe *f*.

tempo ('tempou) *n* tempo *m*.

temporal ('tempərəl) *adj* temporel, -elle. **temporary** *adj* temporaire, provisoire.

tempt (tempt) *vt* tenter. **temptation** *n* tentation *f*.

ten (ten) *adj,n* dix *m*. **tenth** *adj* dixième.

tenacious (tə'neiʃəs) *adj* tenace.

tenant ('tenənt) *n* locataire *m,f*. **tenancy** *n* location *f*.

tend[1] (tend) *vi* **1** tendre. **2** être sujet.

tend[2] (tend) *vt* surveiller, garder, soigner.

tendency ('tendənsi) *n* tendance *f*.

tender[1] ('tendə) *adj* **1** tendre. **2** sensible.

tender[2] ('tendə) *vt* offrir. **tender for** soumissionner pour. ~*n* offre, soumission *f*.

tendon ('tendən) *n* tendon *m*.

tendril ('tendril) *n* vrille *f*.

tenement ('tenəmənt) *n* appartement, logement *m*.

tennis ('tenis) *n* tennis *m*. **tennis court** *n* court de tennis *m*.

tenor ('tenə) *n* **1** *mus* ténor *m*. **2** teneur, marche *f*.

tense[1] (tens) *adj* **1** tendu. **2** raide. **tension** *n* tension *f*.

tense[2] (tens) *n* temps *m*.

tent (tent) *n* tente *f*.

tentacle ('tentəkəl) *n* tentacule *f*.

tentative ('tentətiv) *adj* **1** expérimental, -aux. **2** hésitant.

tenuous ('tenjuəs) *adj* ténu, mince.

tepid ('tepid) *adj* tiède.

term (tə:m) *n* **1** terme *m*. **2** période *f*. **3** *educ* trimestre *m*. **4** *pl* conditions *f pl*. **5** *pl* rapports *m pl*. **6** *pl* facilités de paiement *f pl*. *vt* désigner, nommer.

terminal ('tə:minḷ) *n* **1** terminus *m*. **2** *tech* borne *f*.

terminate ('tə:mineit) *vt* achever. *vi* se terminer.

terminology (tə:mi'nɔlədʒi) *n* terminologie *f*.

terminus ('tə:minəs) *n* terminus *m*.

terrace ('terəs) *n* terrasse *f*.

terrestrial (tə'restriəl) *adj* terrestre.

terrible ('teribəl) *adj* terrible, épouvantable.

terrier ('teriə) *n* terrier *m*.

terrify ('terifai) *vt* épouvanter, effrayer. **terrific** *adj* formidable.

territory ('teritri) *n* territoire *m*.

terror ('terə) *n* terreur, épouvante *f*. **terrorism** *n* terrorisme *m*. **terrorist** *n* terroriste *m,f*. **terrorize** *vt* terroriser.

Terylene ('terili:n) *n Tdmk* Térylène *m*.

test (test) *n* **1** essai *m*. épreuve *f*. **2** examen *m*. *vt* essayer, mettre à l'épreuve. **test-tube** *n* éprouvette *f*.

testament ('testəmənt) *n* testament *m*.

testicle ('testikəl) *n* testicule *f*.

testify ('testifai) *vt* témoigner, déclarer. *vi* déposer.

testimony ('testiməni) *n* témoignage *m*. déposition *f*. **testimonial** *n* attestation *f*.

tether ('teðə) *vt* mettre à l'attache. *n* longe *f*.

text (tekst) *n* texte *m*. **textbook** *n* manuel *m*.

textile ('tekstail) *n* **1** tissu *m*. étoffe *f*. **2** textile *m*. *adj* textile.

texture ('tekstʃə) *n* texture *f*. grain *m*.

Thames (temz) *n* Tamise *f*.

than (ðən; *stressed* ðæn) *conj* que, de.

thank (θæŋk) *vt* remercier. **thanks!** *interj* merci! **thanks to** grâce à. **thank you!** merci! **thankful** *adj* reconnaissant.

that (ðæt) *adj* **1** ce, cet, cette. **2** ce...là. *conj* que, afin que. *pron* **1** cela, *inf* ça, ce. **2** celui-là, celle-là. **3** qui, que. **4** lequel, laquelle. **5** où. **6** dont. **that's all** voilà tout.

thatch (θætʃ) *n* chaume *m*. *vt* couvrir de chaume.

thaw (θɔ:) *vt* dégeler, décongeler, faire fondre. *vi* fondre, se décongeler. *v imp* dégeler. *n* dégel *m*.

the (ðə; *stressed* ði:) *def art* **1** le, l' *ms*. la, l' *fs*. **2** *pl* les *m,f pl*. *adv* d'autant.

theatre ('θiətə) *n* **1** théâtre *m*. **2** *med* salle d'opération *f*. **theatrical** *adj* théâtrical, -aux.

theft (θeft) *n* **1** vol *m*. **2** larcin *m*.

their (ðεə) *poss adj 3rd pers pl* leur *m,f s*. leurs *m,f pl*. **theirs** *poss pron 3rd pers pl* le *or* la leur.

them (ðəm; *stressed* ðem) *pron 3rd pers pl* **1** les. **2** eux *m*. elles *f*. **3** leur. **themselves** *pron 3rd pers pl* **1** eux-mêmes *m*. elles-mêmes *f*. **2** se.

theme (θi:m) *n* thème, sujet, motif *m*.

then (ðən; *stressed* ðen) *adv* **1** alors, en ce temps-là, à cette époque. **2** puis, ensuite. *conj* en ce cas, donc, alors.

theology (θi'ɔlədʒi) *n* théologie *f*. **theologian** *n* théologien *m*. **theological** *adj* théologique.

theorem ('θiərəm) *n* théorème *m*.

theory ('θiəri) *n* théorie *f*. **theoretical** *adj* théorique. **theorize** *vi* théoriser.

therapy ('θerəpi) *n* thérapie *f*. **therapeutic** *adj* thérapeutique.

there (ðεə) *adv* là, y. **thereabouts** *adv* **1** par là, dans les environs. **2** à peu près, environ. **thereafter** *adv* après, ensuite, par la suite. **thereby** *adv* par ce moyen, de cette façon. **therefore** *adv* donc, par conséquent. **thereupon** *adv* là dessus, sur ce. **therewith** *adv* **1** avec cela. **2** en outre.

thermal ('θə:məl) *adj* thermal, -aux, thermique.

thermodynamics (θə:moudai'næmiks) *n* thermodynamique *f*.

thermometer (θə'mɔmitə) *n* thermomètre *m*.

thermonuclear (θə:mou'nju:kliə) *adj* thermonucléaire.

Thermos ('θə:məs) *n Tdmk* bouteille Thermos, bouteille isolante *f*.

thermostat ('θə:məstæt) *n* thermostat *m*.

these (ði:z) *adj pl* **1** ces. **2** ces...ci. *pron pl* ceux-ci *m pl*. celles-ci *f pl*.

thesis ('θi:sis) *n, pl* **-ses** thèse *f*.

they (ðei) *pron 3rd pers pl* **1** ils *m pl*. elles *f pl*. **2** eux *m pl*. elles *f pl*. **they say** on dit.

thick (θik) *adj* **1** épais, épaisse, gros, grosse. **2** touffu, dru. **3** *inf* stupide, bête. **thicken** *vt* épaissir, lier. *vi* **1** s'épaissir, se lier. **2** se compliquer. **thickness** *n* épaisseur *f*. **thick-skinned** *adj* peu susceptible.

thief (θi:f) *n, pl* **thieves** voleur *m*.

thigh (θai) *n* cuisse *f*. **thigh-bone** *n* fémur *m*.

thimble ('θimbəl) *n* dé (à coudre) *m*.

thin (θin) *adj* **1** mince, maigre, léger, -ère. **2** rare, clairsemé. *vt* **1** amincir. **2** éclaircir. *vi* **1** s'amincir. **2** s'éclaircir. **3** amincir. **thinness** *n* maigreur, minceur *f*. **thin-skinned** *adj* susceptible, sensible.

thing (θiŋ) *n* **1** chose *f*. objet *m*. **2** *pl* affaires *f pl*. effets *m pl*. **3** *inf* machin, truc *m*. **for one thing...for another** en premier lieu...d'autre part.

think* (θiŋk) *vi* penser, réfléchir. *vt* croire, songer. **think about/of** penser à/de. **think over** réfléchir.

third (θə:d) *adj* troisième. **third party** *n* tiers *m*. **third-party** *adj* au tiers. **third person** *n* tiers *m*. troisième personne *f*. **third-rate** *adj* de qualité inférieure.

thirst (θə:st) *n* soif *f*. **thirsty** *adj* assoiffé. **be thirsty** avoir soif.

thirteen (θə:'ti:n) *adj,n* treize *m*. **thirteenth** *adj* treizième.

thirty ('θə:ti) *adj,n* trente *m*. **thirtieth** *adj* trentième.

this (ðis) ce, cet, cette. *pron* **1** ceci, ce. **2** celui-ci *m*. celle-ci *f*. **this way and that** de-ci, de-là.

thistle ('θisəl) *n* chardon *m*.

thorn (θɔ:n) *n* épine *f*.

thorough ('θʌrə) *adj* **1** complet, -ète, parfait. **2** profond, minutieux, -euse. **thoroughbred** *adj* pur sang *invar*, de race. *n* cheval pur sang *m*. **thoroughfare** *n* voie *f*.

those (ðouz) *adj pl* **1** ces *m,f pl*. **2** ces...là *m,f pl*. *pron* **1** ceux-là *m pl*. celles-là *f pl*. **2** ceux *m pl*. celles *f pl*.

though (ðou) *conj* quoique, bien que. **as though** comme si. ~*adv* cependant, pourtant.

thought[1] (θɔ:t) *n* **1** pensée, idée *f*. **2** réflexion *f*. **thoughtful** *adj* **1** pensif, -ive. **2** prévenant. **thoughtless** *adj* **1** irréfléchi. **2** sans égards.

thought[2] (θɔ:t) *v see* **think.**

thousand ('θauzənd) *adj,n* mille *m invar*. **a thousand** millier *m*. **thousandth** *adj* millième.

thrash (θræʃ) *vt* battre, rosser.

thread (θred) *n* **1** fil *m*. trame *f*. **2** *tech* filet, pas *m*. *vt* enfiler. **threadbare** *adj* usé, râpé.

threat (θret) *n* menace *f*. **threaten** *vt* menacer.

three (θri:) *adj,n* trois *m*. **three-dimensional** *adj* tridimensionnel, -elle, à trois dimensions. **three-quarters** *n* trois-quarts *invar*. **threesome** *n* ménage à trois *m*.

thresh (θreʃ) *vt* battre.

threshold ('θreʃhould) *n* seuil, pas de porte *m*.

threw (θru:) *v see* **throw.**

thrift (θrift) *n* économie, épargne *f*. **thrifty** *adj* économe, ménager, -ère.

thrill (θril) *n* frisson *m*. sensation *f*. *vt* faire frissonner, émouvoir. *vi* frissonner. **thriller** *n* roman *or* film à sensation *m*.

thrive (θraiv) *vi* **1** pousser, se développer. **2** prospérer.

throat (θrout) *n* gorge *f*. **clear one's throat** s'éclaircir la voix.

throb (θrɔb) *vi* palpiter, battre. *n* palpitation *f*. battement *m*.

throne (θroun) *n* trône *m*.

throng (θrɔŋ) *n* **1** foule, populace *f*. **2** cohue *f*. *vi* faire foule, affluer. *vt* encombrer.

throttle ('θrɔtḷ) *vt* étrangler. *n tech* papillon *m*.

through (θru:) *prep* **1** à travers. **2** pendant. **3** par. **4** à cause de. *adj* direct. *adv* **1** à travers. **2** d'un bout à autre. **throughout** *prep* **1** d'un bout à l'autre. **2** partout. *adv* de fond en comble.

throw* (θrou) *vt* jeter, lancer. **throw away 1** rejeter. **2** gaspiller. ~*n* jet, lancement *m*.

thrush (θrʌʃ) *n* grive *f*.

thrust* (θrʌst) *vt* pousser violemment, enfoncer. *n* **1** poussée *f*. **2** coup de pointe *m*.

thud (θʌd) *n* bruit sourd *m*.

thumb (θʌm) *n* pouce *m*. *vt* feuilleter.

thump (θʌmp) *n* **1** coup sourd *m*. **2** bourrade *f*. *vt* frapper du poing.

thunder ('θʌndə) *n* tonnerre *m*. *vi* tonner. **thunderstorm** *n* orage *m*.

Thursday ('θə:zdi) *n* jeudi *m*.

thus (ðʌs) *adv* **1** ainsi, de cette manière. **2** donc, par conséquent.

thwart (θwɔ:t) *vt* contrecarrer, déjouer.

thyme (taim) *n* thym *m*.

thyroid ('θairɔid) *adj* thyroïde.

tiara (ti'ɑ:rə) *n* tiare *f*.

tick[1] (tik) *n* **1** tic-tac *m*. **2** *inf* instant *m*. **3** marque *f*. trait *m*. *vi* faire tic-tac. *vt* pointer, marquer.

tick[2] (tik) *n zool* tique *f*.

ticket ('tikit) *n* **1** billet *m*. **2** étiquette *f*. **ticket collector** *n* contrôleur *m*. **ticket office** *n* guichet *m*.

tickle ('tikəl) *vt* chatouiller. *vi* démanger. *n* chatouillement *m*. **ticklish** *adj* **1** chatouilleux, -euse. **2** susceptible, délicat.

tide (taid) *n* marée *f*. courant *m*. **high/low tide** marée haute/basse. **tidemark** *n* ligne de marée haute *f*.

tidy ('taidi) *adj* bien rangé, en ordre, ordonné. *vt* ranger, mettre en ordre.

tie (tai) *vt* lier, nouer, attacher. *vi* faire match nul. *n* **1** lien *m*. attache *f*. **2** cravate *f*. **3** match nul *m*.

tier (tiə) *n* rangée *f*. étage, gradin *m*.

tiger ('taigə) *n* tigre *m*.

tight (tait) *adj* **1** tendu, raide. **2** imperméable, étanche, hermétique. **3** *inf* serré, radin. **4** *inf* ivre. *adv* **1** fermement. **2** serré. **3** hermétiquement. **tighten** *vt* serrer, reserrer, tendre. *vi* se reserrer, se tendre. **tight-fisted** *adj inf* radin, près de ses sous. **tightrope** *n* corde raide *f*. **tightrope walker** funambule *m,f*. **tights** *n pl* collant *m*.

tile (tail) *n* **1** tuile *f*. **2** carreau, -aux *m*. *vt* **1** couvrir de tuiles. **2** carreler.

till[1] (til) *prep* **1** jusqu'à. **2** que. **till now** jusqu'à présent. **till then** jusque-là. ~*conj* jusqu'à ce que.

till[2] (til) *n* caisse *f*. guichet *m*.

till[3] (til) *vt* labourer, cultiver.

tiller ('tilə) *n* barre du gouvernail *f*.

tilt (tilt) *vt* faire pencher. *vi* pencher, s'incliner. *n* pente, inclinaison *f*.

timber ('timbə) *n* bois de charpente *m*.

time (taim) *n* **1** temps *m*. **2** fois *f*. **3** heure *f*. **4** époque *f*. âge *m*. **5** mesure *f*. **in time** à temps. **on time** à l'heure. ~*vt* **1** fixer l'heure de. **2** chronométrer. **3** régler. **time bomb** *n* bombe à retardement *f*. **timekeeper** *n* chronométreur *m*. **timetable** *n* emploi du temps, horaire *m*.

timid ('timid) *adj* timide, craintif, -ive.

timpani ('timpəni) *n pl* timbales *f pl*.

tin (tin) *n* **1** étain, fer blanc *m*. **2** boîte *f*. *vt* **1** étamer. **2** mettre en boîtes. **tin-opener** *n* ouvre-boîtes *m invar*.

tinge (tindʒ) *n* teinte, nuance *f*. *vt* teinter, nuancer.

tingle ('tiŋgəl) *vi* picoter, tinter. *n* tintement, picotement *m*.

tinker ('tiŋkə) *n* chaudronnier ambulant *m*. *vi* bricoler.

tinkle ('tiŋkəl) *vi* tinter. *vt* faire tinter. *n* tintement, drelin *m*.

tinsel ('tinsəl) *n* clinquant *m*.

tint (tint) *n* teinte, nuance *f*. *vt* teinter, nuancer.

tiny ('taini) *adj* minuscule, tout petit.

tip[1] (tip) *n* extrémité *f*. bout *m*. **tiptoe** *n* pointe des pieds *f*. *vi* marcher sur la pointe des pieds.

tip[2] (tip) *vt* renverser, faire basculer. *vi* se renverser, basculer, chavirer. *n* pente, inclinaison *f*.

tip[3] (tip) *n* **1** pourboire *m*. **2** tuyau, -aux *m*. *vt* donner un pourboire. **tip-off** *n* tuyau, -aux, indice *m*.

tipsy ('tipsi) *adj inf* gris, éméché.

tire (ˈtaiə) *vt* fatiguer, lasser. *vi* se fatiguer. **tired** *adj* fatigué. **tired out** épuisé.
tissue (ˈtiʃu:) *n* **1** tissu *m*. étoffe *f*. **2** mouchoir en papier *m*.
title (ˈtaitl̩) *n* **1** titre *m*. **2** droit *m*. *vt* intituler.
to (tə; *stressed* tu:) *prep* **1** à, en, vers. **2** chez. **3** pour, envers. **4** sur. **5** contre. *conj* pour, afin de. **to-do** *n* remue-ménage *m*.
toad (toud) *n* crapaud *m*. **toadstool** *n* champignon vénéneux *m*.
toast[1] (toust) *n* pain grillé *m*. *vt,vi* griller.
toast[2] (toust) *n* toast *m*. *vt* boire à la santé de.
tobacco (təˈbækou) *n* tabac *m*. **tobacconist** *n* marchand de tabac *m*.
toboggan (təˈbɔgən) *n* toboggan *m*. luge *f*.
today (təˈdei) *adv,n* aujourd'hui *m*. **a week today** aujourd'hui en huit.
toddler (ˈtɔdlə) *n* tout petit enfant *m*.
toe (tou) *n* orteil, doigt de pied *m*. **toenail** *n* ongle de pied *m*.
toffee (ˈtɔfi) *n* caramel *m*.
toga (ˈtougə) *n* toge *f*.
together (təˈgeðə) *adv* ensemble.
toil (tɔil) *n* travail dur, labeur *m*. *vi* travailler durement.
toilet (ˈtɔilət) *n* **1** toilette *f*. **2** *pl* toilettes *f pl*. cabinets *m pl*. **toilet paper** *n* papier hygiénique *m*. **toilet roll** *n* rouleau de papier hygiénique *m*. **toilet water** *n* eau de toilette *f*.
token (ˈtoukən) *n* **1** signe *m*. marque *f*. **2** jeton, bon *m*.
told (tould) *v* see **tell.**
tolerate (ˈtɔləreit) *vt* tolérer, supporter. **tolerance** *n* tolérance *f*. **tolerant** *adj* tolérant.
toll[1] (toul) *n* péage, droit de passage *m*. **tollgate** *n* barrière de péage *f*.
toll[2] (toul) *n* glas *m*. *vt* sonner, tinter. *vi* sonner le glas.
tomato (təˈma:tou) *n, pl* **-oes** tomate *f*.
tomb (tu:m) *n* tombe *f*. tombeau, -aux *m*.
tomorrow (təˈmɔrou) *adv,n* demain *m*. **day after tomorrow** après-demain *m*.
ton (tʌn) *n* tonne *f*.
tone (toun) *n* **1** ton *m*. **2** voix *f*. timbre *m*. **3** nuance *f*. *vt* tonifier. **tone down** adoucir.
tongs (tɔŋz) *n* pincettes, pinces *f pl*.
tongue (tʌŋ) *n* langue *f*. **tongue-tied** *adj* muet, muette.
tonic (ˈtɔnik) *n* fortifiant *m*. *adj* tonique. **tonic water** *n* eau minérale *f*.
tonight (təˈnait) *adv,n* ce soir *m*. cette nuit *f*.
tonsil (ˈtɔnsəl) *n* amygdale *f*. **tonsilitis** *n* amygdalite *f*.
too (tu:) *adv* **1** trop. **2** aussi. **3** d'ailleurs, de plus.
took (tuk) *v* see **take.**
tool (tu:l) *n* outil, ustensile *m*.
tooth (tu:θ) *n, pl* **teeth** dent *f*. **toothache** *n* mal de dents *m*. **have toothache** avoir mal aux dents. **toothbrush** *n* brosse à dents *f*. **toothpaste** *n* dentifrice *m*. **toothpick** *n* cure-dents *m invar*.
top[1] (tɔp) *n* **1** haut, sommet *m*. cime *f*. **2** surface *f*. **3** dessus *m*. *adj* **1** supérieur, d'en haut. **2** principal, -aux. *vt* **1** coiffer. **2** dépasser. **top up** remplir. **top hat** *n* haut de forme *m*. **top-heavy** *adj* trop lourd du haut.
top[2] (tɔp) *n* (toy) toupie *f*.
topaz (ˈtoupæz) *n* topaze *f*.
topic (ˈtɔpik) *n* sujet, thème *m*. matière *f*. **topical** *adj* topique, d'actualité.
topography (təˈpɔgrəfi) *n* topographie *f*.
topple (ˈtɔpəl) *vi* tomber, s'écrouler. *vt* faire tomber, culbuter.
topsoil (ˈtɔpsɔil) *n* terre du dessus *f*.
topsy-turvy (tɔpsiˈtə:vi) *adv,adj* sens dessus dessous.
torch (tɔ:tʃ) *n* **1** torche *f*. **2** lampe électrique *f*.
tore (tɔ:) *v* see **tear.**
torment (*v* tɔ:ˈment; *n* ˈtɔ:ment) *vt* tourmenter. *n* tourment, supplice *m*.
torn (tɔ:n) *v* see **tear.**
tornado (tɔ:ˈneidou) *n, pl* **-oes** or **-os** tornade *f*. ouragan *m*.
torpedo (tɔ:ˈpi:dou) *n, pl* **-oes** torpille *f*. *vt* torpiller.
torrent (ˈtɔrənt) *n* torrent *m*.
torso (ˈtɔ:sou) *n* torse *m*.
tortoise (ˈtɔ:təs) *n* tortue *f*.
tortuous (ˈtɔ:tʃuəs) *adj* tortueux, -euse, sinueux, -euse.
torture (ˈtɔ:tʃə) *n* torture *f*. supplice *m*. *vt* torturer, mettre au supplice.
Tory (ˈtɔ:ri) *adj,n* Tory *m*.
toss (tɔs) *vt* **1** lancer en l'air. **2** tirer à pile ou face. **3** hocher, agiter. *vi* s'agiter. *n* lancement, jet *m*.
tot[1] (tɔt) *n* **1** petit enfant, bambin *m*. **2** goutte *f*.
tot[2] (tɔt) *vt* **tot up** additionner.
total (ˈtoutl̩) *adj* total, -aux, complet, -ète. *n* montant, total, tout *m*. **totalitarian** *adj* totalitaire.
totter (ˈtɔtə) *vi* chanceler, tituber.
touch (tʌtʃ) *vt* **1** toucher. **2** émouvoir. *vi* se toucher. *n* **1** toucher, tact *m*. **2** attouchement *m*. **3** touche *f*. **touchy** *adj* susceptible.

tough (tʌf) *adj* **1** dur, coriace. **2** fort. **3** raide. **toughen** *vt* durcir. *vi* s'endurcir.
toupee ('tu:pei) *n* toupet *m.* perruque *f.*
tour (tuə) *n* **1** voyage, tour *m.* **2** tournée *f.* *vt,vi* voyager. **tourism** *n* tourisme *m.* **tourist** *n* touriste *m,f.*
tournament ('tuənəmənt) *n* tournoi, concours *m.*
tow (tou) *vt* remorquer. *n.* remorque *f.* **towrope** *n* corde de remorque *f.*
towards (təwɔ:dz) *prep also* **toward** **1** vers. **2** envers, à l'égard de. **3** pour.
towel ('tauəl) *n* serviette *f.* essuie-mains *m invar.*
tower ('tauə) *n* tour *f.* *vi* dominer, planer. **tower-block** *n* tour d'habitation *f.*
town (taun) *n* ville *f.* **town hall** *n* hôtel de ville *m.* **town-planning** *n* urbanisme *m.*
toxic ('tɔksik) *adj* toxique.
toy (tɔi) *n* jouet *m.* *adj* de jouet. *vi* jouer, s'amuser.
trace (treis) *n* trace *f.* *vt* **1** tracer. **2** suivre. **3** calquer.
track (træk) *n* **1** trace *f.* **2** piste *f.* **3** chemin, sentier *m.* *vt* traquer. **tracksuit** *n* survêtement *m.*
tract (trækt) *n* étendue *f.*
tractor ('træktə) *n* tracteur *m.*
trade (treid) *n* **1** commerce *m.* affaires *f pl.* **2** métier *m.* *vt* échanger, troquer. *vi* faire le commerce. **trademark** *n* marque de fabrique *f.* **tradesman** *n* fournisseur *m.* **trade union** *n* syndicat *m.* **trade unionist** *n* syndiqué *m.*
tradition (trə'diʃən) *n* tradition *f.* **traditional** *adj* traditionnel, -elle.
traffic ('træfik) *n* **1** circulation *f.* **2** trafic, commerce *m.* **traffic jam** *n* embouteillage *m.* **traffic lights** *n pl* feu de circulation *m pl.* **traffic warden** *n* contractuel, -elle.
tragedy ('trædʒədi) *n* **1** tragédie *f.* **2** drame *m.* **tragic** *adj* tragique.
trail (treil) *n* **1** traînée *f.* **2** piste, trace *f.* **3** route *f.* *vt* **1** suivre à la piste. **2** traîner. *vi* traîner. **trailer** *n* **1** remorque *f.* **2** (for a film) bande publicitaire *f.*
train (trein) *n* **1** train *m.* **2** suite *f.* **3** convoi *m.* **4** traîne *f.* **5** série *f.* *vt* entraîner, dresser, former. *vi* s'entraîner, s'exercer. **trainee** *n* stagiaire *m,f.* **training** *n* **1** formation *f.* **2** *sport* entraînement *m.*
traitor ('treitə) *n* traître, perfide *m.*
tram (træm) *n* tramway *m.*
tramp (træmp) *n* **1** vagabond, clochard *m.* **2** bruit de piétinement *m.* *vi* vagabonder. *vt* faire à pied.
trample ('træmpəl) *vi,vt* piétiner, fouler.
trampoline ('træmpəli:n) *n* trampolino *m.*
trance (trɑ:ns) *n* trance, extase *f.*
tranquil ('træŋkwil) *adj* tranquille, serein, calme. **tranquillity** *n* tranquillité *f.* calme *m.* **tranquillizer** *n* tranquillisant, calmant *m.*
transact (træn'zækt) *vt* traiter, faire, passer. **transaction** *n* **1** conduite *f.* **2** opération *f.*
transatlantic (trænzət'læntik) *adj* transatlantique.
transcend (træn'send) *vt* dépasser, surpasser.
transcribe (træn'skraib) *vt* transcrire.
transfer (*v* træns'fə:; *n* 'trænsfə:) *vt* transférer, déplacer, virer. *n* transfert, déplacement *m.*
transform (træns'fɔ:m) *vt* transformer, métamorphoser. **transformation** *n* métamorphose *f.*
transfuse (træns'fju:z) *vt* transfuser. **transfusion** *n* transfusion *f.*
transistor (træn'zistə) *n* transistor *m.*
transit ('trænsit) *n* **1** passage *m.* **2** transport, transit *m.*
transition (træn'ziʃən) *n* transition *f.* passage *m.*
transitive ('trænsitiv) *adj* transitif, -ive.
translate (trænz'leit) *vt* traduire. **translation** *n* traduction *f.*
translucent (trænz'lu:sənt) *adj* translucide.
transmit (trænz'mit) *vt* transmettre. **transmitter** *n* transmetteur, émetteur *m.*
transparent (træns'pærənt) *adj* **1** transparent, limpide. **2** clair.
transplant (*v* træns'plɑ:nt; *n* 'trænsplɑ:nt) *vt* transplanter, greffer. *n* greffe *f.*
transport (*v* træns'pɔ:t; *n* 'trænspɔ:t) *vt* transporter. *n* transport *m.*
transpose (træns'pouz) *vt* transposer.
trap (træp) *n* trappe *f.* piège *m.* *vt* attraper, prendre au piège. *vi* trapper. **trapdoor** *n* trappe *f.*
trapeze (trə'pi:z) *n* trapèze *m.*
trash (træʃ) *n* camelote *f.*
trauma ('trɔ:mə) *n* traumatisme *m.* **traumatic** *adj* traumatique.
travel ('trævəl) *vi* **1** voyager. **2** aller. *vt* parcourir. *n* voyage *m.* **travel agency** *n* agence de voyages *f.* bureau de tourisme *m.* **traveller's cheque** *n* chèque de voyage *m.*
trawl (trɔ:l) *vi* chaluter. **trawler** *n* chalutier *m.*
tray (trei) *n* plateau, -aux *m.*
treachery ('tretʃəri) *n* trahison, perfidie *f.* **treacherous** *adj* perfide, déloyal.

treacle ('tri:kəl) *n* mélasse *f*.
tread* (tred) *vi* marcher. *vt* écraser, fouler. *n* **1** pas *m*. **2** *mot* chape *f*.
treason ('tri:zən) *n* trahison *f*.
treasure ('treʒə) *n* trésor *m*. *vt* tenir beaucoup à. **treasurer** *n* trésorier *m*. **treasury** *n* trésorerie *f*.
treat (tri:t) *vt,vi* traiter. *vt* régaler. *n* plaisir, régal *m*. **treatment** *n* traitement *m*.
treatise ('tri:tiz) *n* traité *m*.
treaty ('tri:ti) *n* traité, accord *m*.
treble ('trebəl) *adj* **1** triple. **2** *mus* aigu -uë, de soprano. *adv* trois fois plus. *vt* tripler. *vi* se tripler.
tree (tri:) *n* arbre *m*.
trek (trek) *vi* **1** faire route. **2** changer de pays. *n* étape *f*.
trellis ('trelis) *n* treillis, treillage *m*. *vt* treillisser.
tremble ('trembəl) *vi* trembler, frissonner. *n* frisson *m*.
tremendous (tri'mendəs) *adj* **1** terrible. **2** *inf* énorme, immense.
tremor ('tremə) *n* tremblement *m*. secousse *f*.
trench (trentʃ) *n* tranchée *f*. fossé *m*.
trend (trend) *n* tendance *f*. **trendy** *adj* à la mode, dans le vent.
trespass ('trespəs) *n* infraction, violation *f*. *vi* enfreindre, violer.
trestle ('tresəl) *n* tréteau, -aux *m*. chevalet *m*.
trial ('traiəl) *n* **1** *law* jugement, procès *m*. **2** essai *m*. épreuve *f*. *adj* d'essai.
triangle ('traiæŋgəl) *n* triangle *m*. **triangular** *adj* triangulaire.
tribe (traib) *n* tribu *f*. **tribal** *adj* de tribu, tribal, -aux. **tribesman** *n* membre de la tribu *m*.
tribunal (trai'bju:nl̩) *n* tribunal, -aux *m*.
tributary ('tribju:təri) *adj* tributaire. *n* tributaire, affluent *m*.
tribute ('tribju:t) *n* tribut *m*.
trick (trik) *n* **1** tour *m*. **2** ruse *f*. **3** *game* levée *f*. *vt* attraper, duper. **tricky** *adj* compliqué, délicat.
trickle ('trikəl) *vi* couler, suinter. *n* filet *m*.
tricycle ('traisikəl) *n* tricycle *m*.
trifle ('traifəl) *n* **1** bagatelle *f*. **2** *cul* diplomate *m*. *vi* jouer, badiner.
trigger ('trigə) *n* détente, gâchette *f*.
trill (tril) *n* trille *m*. *vt* triller, rouler. *vi* faire des trilles.
trim (trim) *vt* **1** parer, tailler. **2** orner. *n* **1** bon ordre *m*. **2** coupe *f*. *adj* soigné, ordonné.
trio ('triou) *n* trio *m*.
trip (trip) *n* **1** excursion *f*. **2** faux-pas, croc-en-jambe *m*. *vi* faire un faux-pas, trébucher. **trip up** donner un croc-en-jambe à.
tripe (traip) *n* **1** tripe *f*. **2** *inf* camelote *f*.
triple ('tripəl) *adj* triple. *vt* tripler. *vi* se tripler. **triplet** *n* **1** trio *m*. **2** *pl* triplés *m pl*.
tripod ('traipɔd) *n* trépied *m*.
trite (trait) *adj* banal, trivial.
triumph ('traiʌmf) *n* triomphe *m*. victoire *f*. *vi* triompher, remporter un succès. **triumphant** *adj* triomphant.
trivial ('triviəl) *adj* **1** insignifiant, superficiel, -elle. **2** banal.
trod (trɔd) *v* see **tread.**
trodden ('trɔdn̩) *v* see **tread.**
trolley ('trɔli) *n* **1** chariot *m*. **2** table roulante *f*.
trombone (trɔm'boun) *n* trombone *m*.
troop (tru:p) *n* troupe *f*.
trophy ('troufi) *n* trophée *m*.
tropic ('trɔpik) *n* tropique *m*. **tropical** *adj* tropical, -aux.
trot (trɔt) *n* trot *m*. *vi* aller au trot, trottiner. **trotter** *n* pied de cochon *m*.
trouble ('trʌbəl) *n* **1** ennui *m*. difficulté *f*. **2** peine *f*. malheur *m*. **3** dérangement *m*. *vt* **1** affliger, inquiéter. **2** déranger. *vi* **1** s'inquiéter. **2** se donner de la peine. **troublemaker** *n* trublion *m*.
trough (trɔf) *n* auge *f*.
troupe (tru:p) *n* troupe *f*.
trousers ('trauzəz) *n pl* pantalon *m*.
trout (traut) *n* truite *f*.
trowel ('trauəl) *n* truelle *f*.
truant ('truənt) *n* **play truant** faire l'école buissonnière *f*.
truce (tru:s) *n* trêve *f*.
truck (trʌk) *n* wagon, camion *m*.
trudge (trʌdʒ) *vi* marcher péniblement.
true (tru:) *adj* **1** vrai, exact. **2** authentique. **3** fidèle, loyal, -aux. **truly** *adv* sincèrement, vraiment.
truffle ('trʌfəl) *n* truffe *f*.
trump (trʌmp) *n* atout *m*. *vt* couper. *vi* jouer atout.
trumpet ('trʌmpit) *n* trompette *f*.
truncheon ('trʌntʃən) *n* bâton *m*. matraque *f*.
trunk (trʌŋk) *n* **1** tronc *m*. **2** (luggage) malle *f*. **3** *zool* trompe *f*. **trunk call** *n* appel interurbain *m*.
trust (trʌst) *n* **1** confiance *f*. **2** espoir *m*. **3** *comm* trust *m*. *vt* **1** se fier à, faire confiance à. *vi* **1** se confier. **2** espérer. **trustee** *n* fidéicommissaire *m*. **trustworthy** *adj* digne de confiance, honnête.

truth (tru:θ) *n* vérité *f*. **truthful** *adj* **1** véridique. **2** vrai, fidèle.

try (trai) *vt* **1** essayer, tenter. **2** *law* juger. **3** éprouver. **try on** essayer. **try out** essayer à fond. ~*n* essai *m*. **trying** *adj* vexant, contrariant.

tsar (tsɑ:) *n* tsar *m*.

T-shirt *n* maillot à manches courtes *m*.

tub (tʌb) *n* bac, baquet *m*.

tuba (ˈtju:bə) *n* tuba *m*.

tube (tju:b) *n* **1** tube, tuyau, -aux *m*. **2** métro *m*.

tuber (ˈtju:bə) *n* tubercule *f*.

tuberculosis (tju:bə:kjuˈlousis) *n* tuberculose *f*.

tuck (tʌk) *vt* **1** remplir. **2** relever, retrousser. **tuck in** *vt* border. *vi* manger à belles dents. ~*n* pli, rempli *m*.

Tuesday (ˈtju:zdi) *n* mardi *m*.

tuft (tʌft) *n* touffe, houppe, huppe *f*.

tug (tʌg) *vt,vi* tirer avec effort. *vt* **1** tirer, traîner. **2** remorquer. *n* **1** traction, saccade *f*. **2** *naut* remorqueur *m*.

tuition (tju:ˈiʃən) *n* instruction *f*.

tulip (ˈtu:lip) *n* tulipe *f*.

tumble (ˈtʌmbəl) *n* chute, culbute, dégringolade *f*. *vi* chuter, culbuter, dégringoler. *vt* culbuter, faire tomber, renverser. **tumbler** *n* grand verre *m*.

tummy (ˈtʌmi) *n inf* ventre *m*.

tumour (ˈtju:mə) *n* tumeur *f*.

tumult (ˈtumʌlt) *n* tumulte *m*.

tuna (ˈtju:nə) *n* thon *m*.

tune (tju:n) *n* **1** air *m*. **2** mélodie, harmonie *f*. **3** accord *m*. *vt* accorder. **tuneful** *adj* mélodieux, -euse, harmonieux, -euse.

tunic (ˈtju:nik) *n* tunique *f*.

Tunisia (tju:ˈniziə) *n* Tunisie *f*. **Tunisian** *adj,n* tunisien, -ienne.

tunnel (ˈtʌnl̩) *n* tunnel *m*. galerie *f*.

tunny (ˈtʌni) *n* thon *m*.

turban (ˈtə:bən) *n* turban *m*.

turbine (ˈtə:bain) *n* turbine *f*.

turbot (ˈtə:bət) *n* turbot *m*.

turbulent (ˈtə:bjulənt) *adj* turbulent, tumultueux, -euse.

turf (tə:f) *n* **1** gazon *m*. **2** *sport* turf *m*. **turf accountant** *n* bookmaker *m*.

turkey (ˈtə:ki) *n* **1** dindon *m*. **2** *cul* dinde *f*.

Turkey (ˈtə:ki) *n* Turquie *f*. **Turk** *n* turc, turque. **Turkish** *adj* turc, turque, de Turquie. **Turkish** (language) *n* turc *m*.

turmeric (ˈtə:mərik) *n* curcuma *m*.

turmoil (ˈtə:mɔil) *n* trouble, tumulte *m*. agitation *f*.

turn (tə:n) *vt* **1** tourner. **2** retourner. **3** changer. **4** diriger. *vi* **1** tourner. **2** se retourner. **3** se changer. **turn down** refuser. **turn off** éteindre, couper. **turn on** allumer, ouvrir. **turn out 1** mettre à la porte. **2** éteindre. **3** s'arranger. **turn up 1** se relever. **2** arriver. ~*n* **1** tour *m*. **2** virage, tournant *m*. **3** service *m*. **to a turn** à point. **turning** *n* tournant, virage *m*. *adj* tournant. **turning point** *n* point décisif *m*. **turntable** *n* **1** plaque tournante *f*. **2** platine *f*.

turnip (ˈtə:nip) *n* navet *m*.

turnover (ˈtə:nouvə) *n* **1** chiffre d'affaires *m*. **2** *cul* chausson *m*.

turpentine (ˈtə:pəntain) *n* térébenthine *f*.

turquoise (ˈtə:kwɔiz) *n* **1** turquoise *f*. **2** (colour) turquoise *m invar*. *adj* turquoise *invar*.

turret (ˈtʌrət) *n* tourelle *f*.

turtle (ˈtə:tl̩) *n* tortue de mer *f*.

tusk (tʌsk) *n* défense *f*. croc *m*.

tussle (ˈtʌsəl) *n* lutte, bagarre *f*. *vi* lutter, se bagarrer.

tutor (ˈtju:tə) *n* précepteur *m*. *vt* instruire, donner des leçons particulières.

tweed (twi:d) *n* tweed *m*.

tweezers (ˈtwi:zəz) *n* pince à épiler *f*.

twelve (twelv) *adj,n* douze *m*. **twelfth** *adj* douzième.

twenty (ˈtwenti) *adj,n* vingt *m*. **twentieth** *adj* vingtième.

twice (twais) *adv* deux fois.

twiddle (ˈtwidl̩) *vt,vi* tourner, tortiller.

twig (twig) *n* brindille, ramille *f*.

twilight (ˈtwailait) *n* crépuscule *m*.

twin (twin) *n* jumeau, -elle. *adj* jumelé, jumeau, -aux.

twine (twain) *vt* tordre, enrouler. *vi* **1** se tordre, s'enrouler. **2** serpenter. *n* ficelle *f*.

twinge (twindʒ) *n* élancement *m*. *vt,vi* torturer élancer.

twinkle (ˈtwiŋkəl) *vi* scintiller. *n* scintillement *m*.

twirl (twə:l) *vt* faire tournoyer, tortiller. *vi* tournoyer, pirouetter. *n* **1** tournoiement *m*. **2** pirouette *f*.

twist (twist) *vt* **1** tordre, tortiller. **2** se tordre. **3** déformer. *vi* **1** se tordre, se tortiller. **2** tourner. *n* **1** fil retors, cordon *m*. **2** torsion *f*.

twitch (twitʃ) *vt* donner une saccade, tirer. *vi* se contracter, se crisper. *n* **1** saccade *f*. **2** convulsion *f*.

twitter (ˈtwitə) *vi* gazouiller. *n* gazouillement *m*.

two (tu:) *adj,n* deux *m*. **two-faced** *adj* **1** à deux visages, hypocrite. **2** sans envers. **twosome** *n*

partie à deux *f*. couple *m*. **two-way** *adj* à deux sens.
tycoon (tai'ku:n) *n* magnat *m*.
type (taip) *n* **1** type, genre *m*. **2** caractère *m*. *vt* taper à la machine. **typewriter** *n* machine à écrire *f*. **typical** *adj* typique. **typist** *n* dactylographe *m,f*.
typhoid ('taifɔid) *n* typhoïde *f*.
typhoon (tai'fu:n) *n* typhon *m*.
tyrant ('tairənt) *n* tyran *m*. **tyranny** *n* tyrannie *f*.
tyre ('taiə) *n* pneu *m*.

U

ubiquitous (ju:'bikwitəs) *adj* présent partout.
udder ('ʌdə) *n* mamelle *f*. pis *m*.
ugly ('ʌgli) *adj* laid, moche. **ugliness** *n* laideur *f*.
ukulele (ju:kə'le:li) *n* ukulele *m*.
ulcer ('ʌlsə) *n* ulcère *m*.
ulterior (ʌl'tiəriə) *adj* **1** ultérieur. **2** caché. **ulterior motive** *n* motif caché *m*.
ultimate ('ʌltimət) *adj* **1** final. **2** définitif, -ive, dernier, -ère. **3** ultime. **ultimately** *adv* en fin de compte. **ultimatum** *n, pl* **-tums** *or* **-ta** ultimatum *m*.
ultraviolet (ʌltrə'vaiələt) *adj* ultraviolet, -ette.
umbrella (ʌm'brelə) *n* parapluie *m*.
umpire ('ʌmpaiə) *n* arbitre *m*.
umpteen (ʌmp'ti:n) *adj* je ne sais combien.
unable (ʌn'eibəl) *adj* incapable.
unacceptable (ʌnək'septəbəl) *adj* inacceptable.
unaccompanied (ʌnə'kʌmpnid) *adj* seul, non accompagné.
unanimous (ju:'nanimәs) *adj* unanime.
unarmed (ʌn'ɑ:md) *adj* sans arme.
unattractive (ʌnə'træktiv) *adj* peu attrayant.
unaware (ʌnə'wɛə) *adj* pas au courant, ignorant. **unawares** *adv* inconsciemment, au dépourvu.
unbalanced (ʌn'bælənst) *adj* **1** mal équilibré. **2** déséquilibré.
unbearable (ʌn'bɛərəbəl) *adj* insupportable.
unbelievable (ʌnbi'li:vəbəl) *adj* incroyable.
unbend* (ʌn'bend) *vt* **1** détendre. **2** redresser. *vi* se détendre. **unbending** *adj* inflexible.
unbreakable (ʌn'breikəbəl) *adj* incassable.
unbutton (ʌn'bʌtn̩) *vt* déboutonner.
uncalled-for *adj* déplacé, injustifié.
uncanny (ʌn'kæni) *adj* mystérieux, -euse, inquiétant.
uncertain (ʌn'sə:tn̩) *adj* incertain.
uncle ('ʌŋkəl) *n* oncle *m*.
unclear (ʌn'kliə) *adj* peu clair, obscur.
uncomfortable (ʌn'kʌmftəbəl) *adj* **1** inconfortable, incommode. **2** mal à l'aise.
unconscious (ʌn'kɔnʃəs) *adj* inconscient.
unconventional (ʌnkən'venʃnəl) *adj* non-conformiste.
uncooked (ʌn'kukt) *adj* cru.
uncouth (ʌn'ku:θ) *adj* grossier, -ière, rude.
uncover (ʌn'kʌvə) *vt* découvrir.
uncut (ʌn'kʌt) *adj* **1** non-coupé. **2** sur pied, non taillé. **3** brut.
undecided (ʌndi'saidid) *adj* indécis.
undeniable (ʌndi'naiəbəl) *adj* indéniable, incontestable.
under ('ʌndə) *prep* sous, au dessous de. *adv* (au) dessous. *adj* de dessous, subalterne.
undercharge (ʌndə'tʃɑ:dʒ) *vt* faire payer un prix trop bas.
undercoat ('ʌndəkout) *n* première couche *f*.
undercover ('ʌndəkʌvə) *adj* secret, -ète.
undercut (ʌndə'kʌt) *vt* vendre à meilleur marché que.
underdeveloped (ʌndədi'veləpd) *adj* sous-développé.
underdone (ʌndə'dʌn) *adj* **1** pas assez cuit. **2** (of meat) saignant.
underestimate (ʌndər'estimeit) *vt* sous-estimer.
underfoot (ʌndə'fut) *adv* sous les pieds.
undergo* (ʌndə'gou) *vt* subir, éprouver.
undergraduate (ʌndə'grædjuət) *n* étudiant *m*.
underground (*adv* ʌndə'graund; *adj,n* 'ʌndəgraund) *adv* **1** sous terre. **2** secrètement. *adj* **1** souterrain. **2** secret, -ète. *n* métro *m*.
undergrowth ('ʌndəgrouθ) *n* sous-bois *m*. broussailles *f pl*.
underhand (ʌndə'hænd) *adj* sournois, clandestin. *adv* **1** sous main, sournoisement. **2** *sport* par en dessous.
underline (ʌndə'lain) *vt* souligner.
undermine (ʌndə'main) *vt* miner, saper.
underneath (ʌndə'ni:θ) *prep* au dessous de, sous. *adv* au-dessous, par-dessous, dessous. *adj* inférieur, de dessous.
underpants ('ʌndəpænts) *n pl* caleçon, slip *m*.
underpass ('ʌndəpɑ:s) *n* passage inférieur *m*.
underrate (ʌndə'reit) *vt* mésestimer, sous-estimer.
understand* (ʌndə'stænd) *vt* **1** comprendre. **2** s'entendre à. **3** sous-entendre. **understanding** *n* entendement *m*. compréhension *f*.
understate (ʌndə'steit) *vt* minimiser. **under-**

statement *n* **1** amoindrissement *m*. **2** euphémisme *m*.
understudy ('ʌndəstʌdi) *n* doublure *f*. *vt* doubler.
undertake* (ʌndə'teik) *vt* entreprendre, assumer. **undertaker** *n* entrepreneur de pompes funèbres *m*.
undertone ('ʌndətoun) *n* demi-ton *m*. demi-voix *f*.
underwater (ʌndə'wɔ:tə) *adj* sous-marin.
underwear ('ʌndəwɛə) *n* sous-vêtements *m pl*.
underworld ('ʌndəwə:ld) *n* **1** bas-fonds *m pl*.milieu *m*. pègre *f*. **2** enfers *m pl*.
underwrite* ('ʌndərait) *vt* garantir, souscrire.
undesirable (ʌndi'zaiərəbəl) *adj* indésirable, importun.
undo* (ʌn'du:) *vt* **1** détruire, réparer. **2** défaire.
undoubted (ʌn'dautid) *adj* indubitable, incontestable.
undress (ʌn'dres) *vt* déshabiller, dévêtir. *vi* déshabiller, se dévêtir.
undue ('ʌndju:) *adj* injuste, illégitime.
undulate ('ʌndʒəleit) *vi,vt* onduler.
unearth (ʌn'ə:θ) *vt* déterrer, exhumer. **unearthly** *adj* surnaturel, -elle, sinistre.
uneasy (ʌn'i:zi) *adj* mal à l'aise, gêné.
unemployed (ʌnim'plɔid) *adj* désœuvré, en chômage. *n* chômeurs *m pl*. **unemployment** *n* chômage *m*.
unequal (ʌn'i:kwəl) *adj* inégal, -aux.
uneven (ʌn'i:vən) *adj* inégal, -aux, accidenté.
unfair (ʌn'fɛə) *adj* injuste.
unfaithful (ʌn'feiθfəl) *adj* infidèle, déloyal, -aux.
unfamiliar (ʌnfə'miliə) *adj* peu familier, -ière, inconnu.
unfit (ʌn'fit) *adj* impropre, inapte.
unfold (ʌn'fould) *vt* déplier, déployer. *vi* se dérouler.
unfortunate (ʌn'fɔ:tʃunət) *adj* infortuné, malheureux,-euse.
unfurnished (ʌn'fə:niʃt) *adj* non meublé.
ungrateful (ʌn'greitfəl) *adj* ingrat.
unhappy (ʌn'hæpi) *adj* malheureux, -euse.
unhealthy (ʌn'helθi) *adj* malsain, insalubre.
unicorn ('ju:nikɔ:n) *n* licorne *f*.
uniform ('ju:nifɔ:m) *adj* uniforme, constant. *n* uniforme *m*.
unify ('ju:nifai) *vt* unifier.
uninterested (ʌn'intrəstid) *adj* non intéressé, indifférent.
union ('ju:niən) *n* union *f*.
Union Jack *n* pavillon britannique *m*.
unique (ju:'ni:k) *adj* unique.
unison ('ju:nizən) *n* unisson *m*.
unit ('ju:nit) *n* unité *f*.
unite (ju:'nait) *vt* unir. *vi* s'unir, se joindre. **unity** *n* unité *f*.
United Kingdom *n* Royaume-Uni *m*.
United States of America *n* Etats-Unis d'Amérique *m pl*.
universe ('ju:nivə:s) *n* univers *m*. **universal** *adj* universel, -elle.
university (ju:ni'və:siti) *n* université *f*. *adj* universitaire.
unkempt (ʌn'kempt) *adj* dépeigné, mal soigné.
unkind (ʌn'kaind) *adj* dur, cruel, -elle.
unknown (ʌn'noun) *adj* inconnu, étranger.
unlawful (ʌn'lɔ:fəl) *adj* illégal, -aux.
unless (ən'les) *conj* à moins que.
unlike (ʌn'laik) *adj* différent, peu ressemblant. **unlikely** *adj* invraisemblable, peu probable.
unload (ʌn'loud) *vt* décharger.
unlucky (ʌn'lʌki) *adj* **1** malheureux, -euse, infortuné. **2** maléfique.
unnatural (ʌn'nætʃərəl) *adj* **1** anormal, -aux, monstrueux, -euse **2** contre nature.
unnecessary (ʌn'nesəsri) *adj* inutile, superflu.
unofficial (ʌnə'fiʃəl) *adj* non officiel, -elle, officieux, -euse.
unorthodox (ʌn'ɔ:θədɔks) *adj* peu orthodoxe.
unpack (ʌn'pæk) *vt* **1** déballer, dépaqueter **2** défaire. *vi* défaire.
unpleasant (ʌn'plezənt) *adj* désagréable, déplaisant.
unpopular (ʌn'pɔpjulə) *adj* impopulaire.
unravel (ʌnrævəl) *vt* effiler, effilocher. *vi* s'effiler, se démêler.
unreasonable (ʌn'ri:zənəbəl) *adj* déraisonnable.
unreliable (ʌnri'laiəbəl) *adj* sur lequel on ne peut pas compter, sujet à caution.
unrest (ʌn'rest) *n* **1** inquiétude *f*. **2** agitation *f*. malaise *m*.
unruly (ʌn'ru:li) *adj* indiscipliné, insoumis.
unscrew (ʌn'skru:) *vt* dévisser.
unsettle (ʌn'setl̩) *vt* ébranler, troubler.
unsightly (ʌn'saitli) *adj* laid.
unsound (ʌn'saund) *adj* défectueux, -euse.
unsteady (ʌn'stedi) *adj* peu stable, inconstant.
unsuccessful (ʌnsək'sesfəl) *adj* infructueux, -euse, sans succès.
untangle (ʌn'tæŋgəl) *vt* démêler, dépêtrer.
untidy (ʌn'taidi) *adj* mal tenu, en désordre.
untie (ʌn'tai) *vt* dénouer, déficeler.
until (ʌn'til) *conj* jusqu'à ce que. *prep* jusqu'à. **not until** pas avant.

untrue (ʌn'tru:) *adj* faux, fausse.
unusual (ʌn'ju:ʒuəl) *adj* inhabituel, -elle, insolite.
unwanted (ʌn'wɔntid) *adj* indésirable.
unwell (ʌn'wel) *adj* indisposé.
unwind* (ʌn'waind) *vt* dérouler.
unwrap (ʌn'ræp) *vt* désenvelopper.
up (ʌp) *adj* **1** debout, levé. **2** fini, expiré. **3** droit. *adv* **1** en haut, au haut. **2** en l'air. **3** en avance. **4** droit, debout. **up there** là-haut. **up to** jusqu'à, jusque. ~*prep* en haut de, en montant. **up and down** de haut en bas.
upbringing ('ʌpbriŋiŋ) *n* éducation *f*.
upheaval (ʌp'hi:vəl) *n* bouleversement *m*. agitation *f*.
uphill (ʌp'hil) *adv* en montant. *adj* **1** en rampe. **2** ardu.
uphold* (ʌp'hould) *vt* supporter, soutenir.
upholstery (ʌp'houlstəri) *n* capitonnage *m*. tapisserie *f*.
upkeep ('ʌpki:p) *n* entretien *m*.
uplift (ʌp'lift) *vt* soulever, élever. *n* élévation *f*.
upon (ə'pɔn) *prep* sur.
upper ('ʌpə) *adj* **1** plus haut, d'au-dessus, de dessus. **2** supérieur. **upper-class** *adj* de la classe supérieure. **uppermost** *adj* le plus haut, premier, -ière.
upright ('ʌprait) *adj* **1** vertical, -aux, perpendiculaire. **2** droit.
uprising ('ʌpraiziŋ) *n* insurrection *f*. soulèvement *m*.
uproar ('ʌprɔ:) *n* vacarme, tapage *m*.
uproot (ʌp'ru:t) *vt* déraciner, arracher.
upset* (*v,adj* ʌp'set; *n* 'ʌpset) *vt* **1** renverser, culbuter. **2** déranger. **3** bouleverser. *vi* se renverser. *adj* bouleversé, ému. *n* **1** renversement *m*. **2** désordre *m*.
upshot ('ʌpʃɔt) *n* résultat *m*. conséquence *f*.
upside down (ʌpsaid 'daun) *adv* sens dessus dessous, la tête en bas.
upstairs (ʌp'stɛəz) *adv* en haut.
upstream (ʌp'stri:m) *adv* en amont. *adj* d'amont.
upward ('ʌpwəd) *adj* ascendant, montant. **upwards** *adv* vers le haut, en montant.
uranium (ju'reiniəm) *n* uranium *m*.
Uranus (ju'reinəs) *n* Uranus *f*.
urban ('ə:bən) *adj* urbain.
urge (ə:dʒ) *vt* **1** encourager, exciter. **2** conseiller. *n* incitation, impulsion *f*.
urgent ('ə:dʒənt) *adj* urgent, pressant.
urine ('juərin) *n* urine *f*. **urinate** *vi* uriner.
urn (ə:n) *n* urne *f*.
us (ʌs) *pron Ist pers pl* nous.
use (*v* ju:z; *n* ju:s) *vt* utiliser, employer, se servir de. **use up** épuiser, consommer. ~*n* **1** emploi, usage *m*. **2** jouissance *f*. **usage** *n* usage *m*. **used** *adj* **1** usagé. **2** d'occasion. **useful** *adj* utile, pratique. **useless** *adj* inutile, bon à rien.
usher ('ʌʃə) *n* **1** (at a wedding) garçon d'honneur *m*. **2** introducteur *m*. *v* **usher in** inaugurer, introduire. **usherette** *n* ouvreuse *f*.
usual ('ju:ʒuəl) *adj* usuel, -elle, habituel, -elle. **usually** *adv* d'habitude.
usurp (ju'zə:p) *vt* usurper.
utensil (ju:'tensəl) *n* ustensile, outil *m*.
uterus ('ju:tərəs) *n, pl* **uteri** utérus *m*.
utility (ju:'tiliti) *n* utilité *f*.
utmost ('ʌtmoust) *adj also* **uttermost** extrême, dernier, -ière. *n* dernière limite *f*. **do one's utmost** faire tout son possible.
utter[1] ('ʌtə) *vt* dire, pousser, proférer.
utter[2] ('ʌtə) *adj* complet, -ète, absolu.

V

vacant ('veikənt) *adj* **1** vacant, libre, vide. **2** vague, distant. **vacancy** *n* **1** vacance *f*. **2** vide *m*.
vacate (və'keit) *vt* quitter, évacuer.
vacation (və'keiʃən) *n* vacances *f pl*.
vaccine ('væksi:n) *n* vaccin *m*. **vaccinate** *vt* vacciner. **vaccination** *n* vaccination *f*.
vacillate ('væsəleit) *vi* vaciller, chanceler.
vacuum ('vækjuəm) *n* vide *m*. **vacuum cleaner** *n* aspirateur *m*. **vacuum flask** *n* bouteille Thermos *f*.
vagina (və'dʒainə) *n* vagin *m*.
vagrant ('veigrənt) *n* vagabond *m*. *adj* vagabond, errant.
vague (veig) *adj* vague, imprécis, flou.
vain (vein) *adj* **1** vain, creux, creuse. **2** inutile. **3** vaniteux, -euse.
valiant ('væliənt) *adj* vaillant, brave.
valid ('vælid) *adj* valide, valable. **validity** *n* validité, justesse *f*.
valley ('væli) *n* vallée *f*.
value ('vælju:) *n* valeur *f*. *vt* **1** estimer, priser. **2** tenir à, faire grand cas de. **valuable** *adj* précieux, -euse, de valeur.
valve ('vælv) *n* soupape, valve *f*.
vampire ('væmpaiə) *n* vampire *m*.
van (væn) *n* fourgon *m*. camionnette *f*.

vandal ('vændl) *n* vandale *m*. **vandalism** *n* vandalisme *m*.
vanilla (və'nilə) *n* vanille *f*.
vanish ('væniʃ) *vi* disparaître, s'évanouir.
vanity ('væniti) *n* vanité *f*.
vapour ('veipə) *n* vapeur, buée *f*.
variety (və'raiəti) *n* variété, diversité *f*.
various ('vɛəriəs) *adj* varié, divers.
varnish ('vɑ:niʃ) *n* vernis *m*. *vt* vernir.
vary ('vɛəri) *vt* varier, diversifier. *vi* varier, différer. **variant** *n* variante *f*. **variation** *n* variation, différence *f*.
vase (vɑ:z) *n* vase *m*.
vasectomy (væ'sektəmi) *n* vasectomie *f*.
vast (vɑ:st) *adj* vaste, immense.
vat (væt) *n* cuve *f*.
Vatican ('vætikən) *n* Vatican *m*.
vault[1] (vɔ:lt) *n arch* **1** voûte *f*. **2** caveau, -aux *m*.
vault[2] (vɔ:lt) *vt,vi* sauter. *n* saut *m*.
veal (vi:l) *n* veau *m*.
veer (viə) *vi* tourner, changer de direction.
vegetable ('vedʒtəbəl) *n* légume *m*. *adj* végétal, -aux. **vegetarian** *adj,n* végétarien, -ienne. **vegetation** *n* végétation *f*.
vehement ('viəmənt) *adj* **1** véhément. **2** passionné.
vehicle ('vi:ikəl) *n* véhicule *m*.
veil (veil) *n* voile *m*. *vt* voiler, cacher.
vein (vein) *n* veine *f*.
velocity (və'lɔsiti) *n* vitesse *f*.
velvet ('velvit) *n* velours *m*.
veneer (vi'niə) *n* **1** placage *m*. **2** vernis *m*. *vt* plaquer.
venerate ('venəreit) *vt* vénérer.
venereal disease (vi'niəriəl) *n* maladie vénérienne *f*.
Venetian (vi'ni:ʃən) *adj,n* vénitien, -ienne. **Venetian blind** *n* jalousie *f*.
vengeance ('vendʒəns) *n* vengeance *f*.
Venice ('venis) *n* Venise *f*.
venison ('venisən) *n* venaison *f*.
venom ('venəm) *n* venin *m*.
vent[1] (vent) *n* trou, orifice *m*. ouverture *f*.
vent[2] (vent) *vt* donner libre cours à.
ventilate ('ventileit) *vt* aérer, ventiler. **ventilation** *n* aération, ventilation *f*.
venture ('ventʃə) *n* entreprise risquée *f*. *vt* oser, se risquer à. *vi* risquer de.
Venus ('vi:nəs) *n* Vénus *f*.
veranda (və'rændə) *n* véranda *f*.
verb (və:b) *n* verbe *m*. **verbal** *adj* verbal, -aux.
verdict ('və:dikt) *n* verdict *m*.
verge (və:dʒ) *n* bord *m*. bordure *f*. *v* **verge on** toucher à, friser.
verify ('verifai) *vt* vérifier, confirmer.
vermin ('və:min) *n* vermine *f*.
vermouth ('və:məθ) *n* vermout *m*.
vernacular (və'nækjulə) *adj* vernaculaire, indigène. *n* **1** langue du pays *f*. **2** langage *m*.
versatile ('və:sətail) *adj* souple, apte à tout.
verse (və:s) *n* **1** vers *m*. **2** strophe *f*.
version ('və:ʃən) *n* version, interprétation *f*.
vertebrate ('və:tibreit) *adj,n* vertébré *m*.
vertical ('və:tikəl) *adj* vertical, -aux.
verve (və:v) *n* verve *f*.
very ('veri) *adv* **1** très. **2** fort, bien. **3** tout. *adj* **1** vrai, véritable. **2** même.
vessel ('vesəl) *n* **1** *naut* navire *m*. **2** récipient *m*.
vest (vest) *n* gilet, maillot (de corps) *m*. *vt* revêtir, confier. **vested** *adj* acquis.
vestment ('vestmənt) *n* vêtement *m*.
vestry ('vestri) *n* sacristie *f*.
vet (vet) *n inf* vétérinaire *m*. *vt inf* examiner.
veteran ('vetərən) *n* vétéran *m*. *adj* aguerri, expérimenté.
veterinary surgeon ('vetrinəri) *n* vétérinaire *m*.
veto ('vi:tou) *n, pl* **-oes** veto *m*. *vt* mettre son veto à, interdire.
vex (veks) *vt* vexer, fâcher.
via ('vaiə) *prep* via, par.
viable ('vaiəbəl) *adj* viable.
viaduct ('vaiədʌkt) *n* viaduc *m*.
vibrate (vai'breit) *vi* vibrer. *vt* faire vibrer. **vibration** *n* vibration *f*.
vicar ('vikə) *n* curé *m*.
vicarious (vi'kɛəriəs) *adj* **1** pour *or* par un autre. **2** délégué, par substitution.
vice[1] (vais) *n* vice, défaut *m*.
vice[2] (vais) *n tech* étau, -aux *m*.
vice-chancellor *n* **1** vice-chancelier *m*. **2** *educ* recteur *m*.
vice-president *n* vice-président *m*.
vice-versa ('və:sə) *adv* vice versa.
vicinity (vi'sinəti) *n* voisinage *m*. alentours *m pl*.
vicious ('viʃəs) *adj* vicieux, -euse, méchant.
victim ('viktim) *n* victime *f*. **victimize** *vt* prendre comme victime.
victory ('viktri) *n* victoire *f*. **victorious** *adj* victorieux, -euse.
video-tape ('vidiouteip) *n* bande magnétique vidéo *f*.
Vietnam (viet'næm) *n* Viet-nam *m*. **Vietnamese** *adj,n* vietnamien, -ienne.
view (vju:) *n* **1** vue, perspective *f*. **2** opinion *f*. *vt,vi* regarder. **view-finder** *n* viseur *m*.

vigil (ˈvidʒil) *n* veille *f*. **vigilant** *adj* vigilant, éveillé.
vigour (ˈvigə) *n* vigueur *f*.
vile (vail) *adj* **1** vil, infâme. **2** *inf* exécrable.
villa (ˈvilə) *n* villa *f*.
village (ˈvilidʒ) *n* village *m*.
villain (ˈvilən) *n* scélérat, gredin *m*.
vindictive (vinˈdiktiv) *adj* vindicatif, -ive.
vine (vain) *n* vigne *f*. **vineyard** *n* vignoble *m*.
vinegar (ˈvinigə) *n* vinaigre *m*.
vintage (ˈvintidʒ) *n* **1** vendanges *f pl*. **2** année *f*.
vinyl (ˈvainil) *n* vinyl *m*.
viola (viˈoulə) *n* alto *m*.
violate (ˈvaiəleit) *vt* violer, profaner. **violation** *n* violation, infraction *f*.
violence (ˈvaiələns) *n* violence *f*. **violent** *adj* violent.
violet (ˈvaiələt) *n* **1** *bot* violette *f*. **2** (colour) violet *m*. *adj* violet, -ette.
violin (vaiəˈlin) *n* violon *m*.
viper (ˈvaipə) *n* vipère *f*.
virgin (ˈvə:dʒin) *n* vierge *f*. *adj* de vierge, virginal, -aux.
Virgo (ˈvə:gou) *n* Vierge *f*.
virile (ˈvirail) *adj* viril, mâle.
virtue (ˈvə:tju:) *n* **1** vertu *f*. **2** qualité *f*. **virtual** *adj* **1** de *or* en fait. **2** virtuel, -elle. **virtuous** *adj* vertueux, -euse.
virus (ˈvairəs) *n* virus *m*.
visa (ˈvi:zə) *n* visa *m*.
viscount (ˈvaikaunt) *n* vicomte *m*. **viscountess** *n* vicomtesse *f*.
vision (ˈviʒən) *n* **1** vision, vue *f*. **2** apparition *f*. **visible** *adj* visible. **visibility** *n* visibilité *f*. **visionary** *adj,n* visionnaire.
visit (ˈvizit) *n* visite *f*. *vt* visiter, rendre visite à. **visitor** *n* visiteur, -euse.
visual (ˈvizjuəl) *adj* visuel, -elle. **visualize** *vi* se représenter. *vt* envisager.
vital (ˈvaitḷ) *adj* vital, -aux. **vitality** *n* vitalité *f*.
vitamin (ˈvitəmin) *n* vitamine *f*.
vivacious (viˈveiʃəs) *adj* vif, vive, enjoué.
vivid (ˈvivid) *adj* vif, vive, éclatant.
vixen (ˈviksən) *n* renarde *f*.
vocabulary (vəˈkæbjuləri) *n* vocabulaire *m*.
vocal (ˈvoukəl) *adj* vocal, -aux.
vocation (vouˈkeiʃən) *n* vocation *f*. **vocational** *adj* professionnel, -elle.
vodka (ˈvɔdkə) *n* vodka *f*.
voice (vɔis) *n* voix *f*. *vt* exprimer.
void (vɔid) *adj* **1** vide. **2** *law* nul, nulle. **3** dépourvu. *n* vide *m*.
volatile (ˈvɔlətail) *adj* volatile.
volcano (vɔlˈkeinou) *n, pl* **-oes** *or* **-os** volcan *m*.
vole (voul) *n* compagnol *m*.
volley (ˈvɔli) *n* volée, salve *f*. *vi* reprendre la balle de volée.
volt (voult) *n* volt *m*.
volume (ˈvɔlju:m) *n* **1** volume *m*. **2** *lit* tôme *m*.
volunteer (vɔlənˈtiə) *n* volontaire *m*. *vt* offrir volontairement. *vi* s'offrir. **voluntary** *adj* volontaire, spontané.
voluptuous (vəˈlʌptʃuəs) *adj* voluptueux, -euse.
vomit (ˈvɔmit) *vt,vi* vomir. *n* vomissement *m*.
voodoo (ˈvu:du:) *n* vaudou *m*.
vote (vout) *n* vote, scrutin *m*. *vt,vi* voter.
vouch (vautʃ) *vt* affirmer, garantir. **vouch for** répondre de.
voucher (ˈvautʃə) *n* bon, reçu *m*.
vow (vau) *n* vœu, vœux, serment *m*. *vt* vouer, jurer.
vowel (ˈvauəl) *n* voyelle *f*.
voyage (ˈvɔiidʒ) *n* voyage sur mer *m*.
vulgar (ˈvʌlgə) *adj* vulgaire, commun. **vulgarity** *n* vulgarité *f*.
vulnerable (ˈvʌlnərəbəl) *adj* vulnérable.
vulture (ˈvʌltʃə) *n* vautour *m*.

W

wad (wɔd) *n* tampon, bouchon *m*. bourre *f*. *vt* capitonner, ouater. **wadding** *n* ouatage, rembourrage *m*.
waddle (ˈwɔdḷ) *vi* se dandiner. *n* dandinement *m*.
wade (weid) *vi* marcher dans l'eau. *vt* passer à gué. **wade through** venir péniblement à bout de.
wafer (ˈweifə) *n* gaufrette *f*.
waft (wɔft) *n* bouffée *f*. souffle *m*. *vt* porter. *vi* flotter.
wag (wæg) *n* agitation *f*. frétillement *m*. *vt* agiter, remuer. *vi* s'agiter, se remuer.
wage (weidʒ) *n* gages *m pl*. salaire *m*. *v* **wage war** faire la guerre.
waggle (ˈwægəl) *vt* frétiller.
wagon (ˈwægən) *n* chariot, wagon *m*.
waif (weif) *n* épave *f*. enfant abandonné *m*.
wail (weil) *vi* gémir, vagir. *n* cri plaintif *m*. plainte *f*.
waist (weist) *n* taille, ceinture *f*. **waistband** *n* ceinture *f*. **waistcoat** *n* gilet *m*. **waistline** *n* taille *f*.
wait (weit) *vi,vt* attendre. *n* attente *f*. **waiter** *n* garçon *m*. **waiting list** *n* liste d'attente

f. **waiting room** *n* salle d'attente *f.* **waitress** *n* serveuse *f.*

waive (weiv) *vt* renoncer à, abandonner, écarter.

wake' (weik) *vi* se réveiller. *vt* réveiller. **waken** *vt* **1** réveiller. **2** éveiller. *vi* se réveiller.

Wales (weilz) *n* pays de Galles *m.*

walk (wɔ:k) *vi* **1** marcher. **2** se promener. **3** aller à pied. *vt* faire marcher, promener. *n* **1** promenade *f.* **2** marche *f.* **walking stick** *n* canne *f.* **walkout** *n* grève spontanée *f.* **walkover** *n* victoire facile *f.*

wall (wɔ:l) *n* **1** mur *m.* **2** muraille *f.* **wallflower** *n* giroflée des murailles *f.* **be a wallflower** faire tapisserie. **wallpaper** *n* papier peint *m.*

wallet ('wɔlit) *n* portefeuille *m.*

wallop ('wɔləp) *vt inf* rosser, flanquer une volée à. *n* coup vigoureux *m.*

wallow ('wɔlou) *vi* se vautrer, croupir.

walnut ('wɔ:lnʌt) *n* noix *f.* **walnut tree** *n* noyer *m.*

walrus ('wɔ:lrəs) *n* morse *m.*

waltz (wɔ:ls) *n* valse *f.* *vi* valser

wand (wɔnd) *n* baguette *f.*

wander ('wɔndə) *vi* errer, vaguer.

wane (wein) *n* déclin *m.* *vi* décliner, décroître.

wangle ('wæŋgəl) *vt inf* obtenir par subterfuge, resquiller. *n* intrigue *f.*

want (wɔnt) *vt* **1** vouloir. **2** manquer de, avoir besoin de. *vi* manquer *n* **1** manque, défaut *m.* **2** besoin *m.* **for want of** faute de. **wanted** *adj* **1** on demande. **2** recherché (par la police).

war (wɔ:) *n* guerre *f.* *vi* lutter, faire la guerre. **warfare** *n* guerre *f.*

warble ('wɔ:bəl) *n* gazouillement *m.* *vi* gazouiller.

ward (wɔ:d) *n* **1** salle *f.* **2** cellule *f.* **3** pupille *m.,f.* *v* **ward off** parer. **warden** *n* directeur, gardien, conservateur *m.* **warder** *n* gardien de prison *m.* **wardrobe** *n* garde-robe *f.*

warehouse ('wɛəhaus) *n* entrepôt *m.* *vt* emmagasiner.

warm (wɔ:m) *adj* **1** chaud. **2** chaleureux, -euse. *vt* chauffer. *vi* se chauffer. **warmth** *n* chaleur *f.*

warn (wɔ:n) *vt* avertir, prévenir. **warning** *n* avertissement, préavis *m.*

warp (wɔ:p) *vt* fausser, pervertir. *vi* gauchir, se déformer, jouer. *n* **1** chaîne *f.* **2** voilure *f.*

warrant ('wɔrənt) *n* **1** garantie *f.* **2** autorisation *f.* **3** mandat *m.* *vt* **1** garantir, certifier. **2** justifier.

warren ('wɔrən) *n* garenne *f.*

warrior ('wɔriə) *n* guerrier *m.*

wart (wɔ:t) *n* verrue *f.*

wary ('wɛəri) *adj* avisé, prudent.

was (wəz; *stressed* wɔz) *v* see **be.**

wash (wɔʃ) *vt* laver. *vi* se laver. **wash down** arroser. **wash out 1** enlever. **2** rincer. **washout** *n sl* fiasco, four *m.* **wash up** faire la vaisselle. ~*n* **1** lavage *m.* **2** lessive *f.* **washbasin** *n* lavabo *m.* **washer** *n* rondelle *f.* **washing** *n* **1** lavage *m.* **2** linge *m.* **washing machine** *n* machine à laver *f.* **washing powder** *n* lessive *f.* **washroom** *n* cabinet de toilette *m.*

wasp (wɔsp) *n* guêpe *f.*

waste (weist) *adj* **1** de rebut. **2** inculte. *n* **1** gaspillage *m.* perte *f.* **2** rebut *m.* déchets *m pl.* *vt* **1** gaspiller. **2** épuiser. *vi* s'user. **wasteful** *adj* prodigue, gaspilleur, -euse. **wastepaper basket** *n* corbeille à papier *f.*

watch (wɔtʃ) *vt* **1** observer, regarder. **2** surveiller. *vi* veiller. *n* **1** garde *f.* **2** montre *f.* **3** *naut* quart *m.* **watchdog** *n* chien de garde *m.* **watchful** *adj* vigilant, attentif, -ive.

water ('wɔ:tə) *n* eau, eaux *f.* *vt* **1** arroser. **2** abreuver. *vi* se mouiller. **water down** diluer.

water-closet *n* cabinet *m.*

watercolour ('wɔ:təkʌlə) *n* aquarelle *f.*

watercress ('wɔ:təkres) *n* cresson *m.*

waterfall ('wɔ:təfɔ:l) *n* chute d'eau, cascade *f*

watering-can *n* arrosoir *m.*

waterlily ('wɔ:təlili) *n* nénuphar *m.*

waterlogged ('wɔ:təlɔgd) *adj* imbibé d'eau.

watermark ('wɔ:təma:k) *n* filigrane *m.*

watermelon ('wɔ:təmelən) *n* pastèque *f.*

waterproof ('wɔ:təpru:f) *adj* imperméable. *vt* caoutchouter.

water-ski *vi* faire du ski nautique.

watertight ('wɔ:tətait) *adj* étanche.

waterway ('wɔ:təwei) *n* voie navigable *f.*

watery ('wɔ:təri) *adj* aqueux, -euse.

watt (wɔt) *n* watt *m.*

wave (weiv) *n* **1** vague *f.* **2** geste *m.* **3** ondulation *f.* *vi* **1** s'agiter. **2** onduler. **3** faire signe à. *vt* **1** agiter. **2** faire signe de. **waveband** *n* longueur d'onde *f.* **wavelength** *n* longueur d'onde *f.* **wavy** *adj* onduleux, -euse.

waver ('weivə) *vi* **1** vaciller. **2** hésiter, fléchir.

wax[1] (wæks) *n* cire *f.* *vt* cirer, encaustiquer.

wax[2] (wæks) *vi* croître.

way (wei) *n* **1** voie, route *f.* chemin *m.* **2** moyen *m.* façon, manière *f.* **3** direction *f.* **4** sens *m.* **5** point de vue *f.* **by the way** à propos. **this way** par ici. **under way** en train. **wayside** *n* bas-côté, bord de la route *m*. *adj* du bord de la route.

waylay* (wei'lei) *vt* arrêter au passage.

wayward ('weiwəd) *adj* entêté, fantasque.

we (wi:) *pron 1st pers pl* nous.

weak (wi:k) *adj* **1** faible. **2** infirme. **weaken** *vt* affaiblir. *vi* s'affaiblir. **weak-minded** *adj* faible d'esprit. **weakness** *n* **1** faiblesse *f*. **2** faible *m*. **weak-willed** *adj* sans volonté.

wealth (welθ) *n* **1** richesse *f*. **2** abondance *f*. **wealthy** *adj* riche.

weapon ('wepən) *n* arme *f*.

wear* (wɛə) *vt* **1** porter, mettre. **2** user. *vi* s'user. **wear out 1** user. **2** épuiser. ~*n* **1** usage *m*. **2** usure *f*. **wear and tear** usage *m*.

weary ('wiəri) *adj* las, lasse. *vt* lasser, fatiguer. *vi* se lasser.

weasel ('wi:zəl) *n* belette *f*.

weather ('weðə) *n* temps *m*. *vt* survivre. **weather-beaten** *adj* basané. **weather fore-cast** *n* bulletin météorologique *m*.

weave* (wi:v) *vt* tisser. *n* tissage *m*.

web (web) *n* **1** toile *f*. **2** tissu *m*.

wedding ('wediŋ) *n* mariage *m*. noces *f pl*. **wedding ring** *n* alliance *f*.

wedge (wedʒ) *n* coin *m*. cale *f*. *vt* **1** coincer, assujettir. **2** serrer.

Wednesday ('wenzdi) *n* mercredi *m*.

wee (wi:) *adj inf* tout petit.

weed (wi:d) *n* mauvaise herbe *f*. *vt* désherber.

week (wi:k) *n* semaine *f*. **weekday** *n* jour de semaine *m*. **weekend** *n* fin de semaine *f*. week-end *m*. **weekly** *adj,n* hebdomadaire. *adv* tous les huit jours.

weep* (wi:p) *vi* pleurer.

weigh (wei) *vt,vi* peser. **weighbridge** *n* bascule *f*. **weight** *n* poids *m*. pesanteur *f*. **weight-lifting** *n* haltérophilie *f*.

weird ('wiəd) *adj* étrange, mystérieux, -euse.

welcome ('welkəm) *adj* bienvenu. *n* bienvenue *f*. *vt* souhaiter la bienvenue à.

weld (weld) *n* soudure *f*. *vt* souder.

welfare ('welfɛə) *n* bien-être *m*. prospérité *f*.

well[1] (wel) *n* puits *m*.

well[2] (wel) *adv* bien. **as well** aussi. ~*adj* bien, bon, bonne. **well-behaved** *adj* sage, bien élevé.

well-bred *adj* **1** bien élevé. **2** de race.

well-built *adj* costaud.

well-known *adj* bien connu, célèbre.

well-off *adj* à l'aise, riche.

well-paid *adj* bien payé.

well-spoken *adj* au langage cultivé.

well-worn *adj* usagé.

Welsh (welʃ) *adj* gallois. *n* (language) gallois *m*. **Welshman** *n* gallois *m*.

went (went) *v see* **go.**

wept (wept) *v see* **weep.**

were (wɔ:) *v see* **be.**

west (west) *n* **1** ouest *m*. **2** *cap* Occident *m*. *adj* occidental, -aux, ouest *invar*. *adv* à *or* vers l'ouest. **westerly** *adj* d'ouest. **western** *adj* de l'ouest, occidental, -aux. *n* western *m*. **westward** *adj* à l'ouest, de l'ouest. **westwards** *adv* vers l'ouest.

West Indies ('indiz) *n* Antilles *f pl*. **West Indian** *adj,n* antillais.

wet (wet) *adj* **1** mouillé, humide. **2** pluvieux, -euse. *n* pluie *f*. *vt* mouiller.

whack (wæk) *n* coup violent *m*. *vt* donner des coups à, rosser.

whale (weil) *n* baleine *f*.

wharf (wɔ:f) *n* débarcadère *m*.

what (wɔt) *pron* **1** qu'est-ce qui? qu'est-ce que? que? quoi? **2** ce qui, ce que, ce dont. *adj* **1** quel? quelle? **2** que, qui. *interj* quoi! comment! **whatever** *pron* tout ce qui, tout ce que, quoi, qui, quoi que. *adj* **1** quelque... qui, quelque... que. **2** aucun, quelconque.

wheat (wi:t) *n* blé *m*.

wheedle ('wi:dl̩) *vt* cajoler, câliner.

wheel (wi:l) *n* roue *f*. **wheelbarrow** *n* brouette *f*. **wheelchair** *n* fauteuil roulant *m*.

wheeze (wi:z) *vi* respirer péniblement.

whelk (welk) *n* buccin *m*.

when (wen) *adv* quand? *conj* **1** quand, lorsque. **2** où, que. **whenever** *adv* toutes les fois que, chaque fois que.

where (wɛə) *adv* **1** où? **2** où. *conj,pron* où. **whereabouts** *adv* où? *n* situation *f*. **whereas** *conj* **1** attendu que. **2** tandis que. **whereby** *adv* par lequel. **whereupon** *adv* sur quoi, sur ce. **wherever** *adv* **1** partout où, n'importe où. **2** où que.

whether ('weðə) *conj* si.

which (witʃ) *adj* **1** quel? quelle? **2** lequel, laquelle. *pron* **1** lequel? laquelle? **2** qui, que, dont, lequel, laquelle. **3** ce qui, ce que. **whichever** *pron* celui qui, celui que, n'importe lequel. *adj* n'importe quel, quelque...que.

whiff (wif) *n* bouffée *f*.

while (wail) *conj* pendant que, tandis que. *n* temps *m*. **be worth one's while** valoir la peine.

whim (wim) *n* caprice *m*.

whimper ('wimpə) *vi* pleurnicher, geindre. *n* pleurnichement, geignement *m*.

whimsical ('wimzikəl) *adj* capricieux, -euse.

whine (wain) *vi* se plaindre, pleurnicher, geindre. *n* geignement *m*.

whip (wip) *n* fouet *m*. *vt* fouetter.

whippet ('wipit) *n* whippet, lévrier *m*.

whir (wə:) *vi* vrombir, siffler, ronronner. *n* bruissement, ronronnement *m*.

whirl (wə:l) *n* tourbillon, tournoiement *m*. *vi* tourbillonner, tournoyer. **whirlwind** *n* trombe *f*.

whisk[1] (wisk) *vt* **1** agiter. **2** enlever, escamoter. *vi* s'élancer.

whisk[2] (wisk) *vt* fouetter, battre. *n* fouet *m*.

whisker ('wiskə) *n* **1** (of a cat, etc.) moustache *f*. **2** *pl* favoris *m pl*.

whisky ('wiski) *n* whisky *m*.

whisper ('wispə) *n* chuchotement *m*. *vi,vt* chuchoter.

whist (wist) *n* whist *m*.

whistle ('wisəl) *n* sifflement *m*. *vi,vt* siffler.

white (wait) *adj* blanc, -che. *n* **1** blanc *m*. **2** *cap* Blanc, -che. **whiten** *vt* blanchir. *vi* pâlir. **whitewash** *vt* badigeonner à la chaux, blanchir. *n* blanc de chaux *m*. **whiting** *n* merlan *m*.

Whitsun ('witsən) *n* Pentecôte *f*.

whiz (wiz) *vi* siffler.

who (hu:) *pron* **1** qui? qui est-ce qui? **2** qui, lequel, laquelle, celui qui. **whoever** *pron* **1** celui qui, quiconque. **2** qui, que.

whole (houl) *adj* **1** sain, intact. **2** entier, -ière. *n* tout *m*. totalité *f*. **on the whole** en somme. **wholehearted** *adj* de tout cœur, sincère. **wholemeal** *adj* complet, -ète. **wholesale** *n* vente en gros *f*. *adj* **1** de *or* en gros. **2** général, -aux. *adv* en gros. **wholesome** *adj* sain, salubre. **wholly** *adv* **1** tout à fait. **2** intégralement.

whom (hu:m) *pron* **1** qui? qui est-ce que? **2** que, lequel, laquelle, qui.

whooping cough ('hu:piŋ) *n* coqueluche *f*.

whore (hɔ:) *n* prostituée, putain *f*.

whose (hu:z) *pron* **1** de qui? à qui? **2** dont, de qui.

why (wai) *adv* pourquoi? *conj,n* pourquoi *m*. *interj* tiens!

wick (wik) *n* mèche *f*.

wicked ('wikid) *adj* mauvais, méchant.

wide (waid) *adj* **1** large. **2** vaste. **3** loin. *adv* **1** loin. **2** (tout) grand. **widely** *adv* largement, très. **widen** *vt* élargir, étendre. *vi* s'élargir. **widespread** *adj* étendu, répandu.

widow ('widou) *n* veuve *f*. **widower** *n* veuf *m*.

width (widθ) *n* largeur *f*.

wield (wi:ld) *vt* manier.

wife (waif) *n, pl* **wives** femme, épouse *f*.

wig (wig) *n* perruque *f*.

wiggle ('wigəl) *vt* tortiller, remuer. *vi* se tortiller.

wigwam ('wigwæm) *n* wigwam *m*.

wild (waild) *adj* **1** sauvage, farouche. **2** affolé. **3** furieux, -euse. **wildlife** *n* faune *f*.

wilderness ('wildənəs) *n* lieu sauvage, inculte *m*.

wilful ('wilfəl) *adj* entêté, volontaire.

will*[1] (wil) *v mod aux* **1** translated by the future tense. **2** aller.

will[2] (wil) *n* **1** volonté *f*. vouloir *m*. **2** testament *m*. *vt* **1** vouloir, désirer. **2** léguer. **willpower** *n* volonté *f*.

willing ('wiliŋ) *adj* de bonne volonté, consentant.

willow ('wilou) *n* saule *m*.

wilt (wilt) *vi* se flétrir, dépérir.

win* (win) *vi,vt* gagner, remporter.

wince (wins) *n* crispation *f*. tressaillement *m*. *vi* grimacer, tressaillir de douleur.

winch (wintʃ) *n* manivelle *f*. treuil *m*.

wind[1] (wind) *n* vent *m*. **windfall** *n* **1** fruit tombé *m*. **2** aubaine *f*. **windmill** *n* moulin à vent *m*. **windpipe** *n* gosier *m*. **windscreen** *n* pare-brise *m invar*. **windscreen wipers** *n pl* essuie-glace *m*. **windswept** *adj* venteux, -euse, balayé par le vent. **windy** *adj* venteux, -euse.

wind*[2] (waind) *vt* tourner, enrouler. **wind up** remonter.

windlass ('windləs) *n* treuil *m*.

window ('windou) *n* fenêtre *f*. **window box** *n* caisse à fleurs, jardinière *f*. **window-dressing** *n* art de l'étalage *m*. **window-shop** *vi* faire du lèche-vitrines.

wine (wain) *n* vin *m*. **wineglass** *n* verre à vin *m*.

wing (wiŋ) *n* **1** aile *f*. **2** *pl Th* coulisses *f pl*. **wing commander** *n* lieutenant-colonel d'aviation *m*. **wingspan** *n* envergure *f*.

wink (wiŋk) *vi* cligner les yeux, faire de l'œil. *vt* cligner. *n* clignement, clin d'œil *m*.

winkle ('wiŋkəl) *n* bigorneau, -aux *m*.

winter ('wintə) *n* hiver *m*.

wipe (waip) *vt* essuyer. *n* coup de torchon *or* d'éponge *m*.

wire (ˈwaiə) *n* **1** fil de fer *m*. **2** dépêche *f*. *vt* **1** clôturer. **2** télégraphier. *vi* télégraphier.
wise (waiz) *adj* sage, prudent. **wisdom** *n* sagesse *f*.
wish (wiʃ) *vt* **1** désirer. **2** souhaiter. **3** vouloir. *n* désir, souhait *m*.
wisp (wisp) *n* bouchon *m*. poignée, mèche *f*.
wisteria (wisˈtiəriə) *n* glycine *f*.
wit (wit) *n* **1** esprit *m*. **2** intelligence *f*.
witch (witʃ) *n* sorcière *f*. **witchcraft** *n* sorcellerie *f*.
with (wið) *prep* **1** avec. **2** de, à. **3** chez. **4** malgré.
withdraw* (wiðˈdrɔ:) *vt* retirer, enlever. *vi* se retirer. **withdrawal** *n* **1** retrait *m*. **2** retraite *f*.
wither (ˈwiðə) *vt* **1** dessécher, faner. **2** foudroyer. *vi* se dessécher, se faner.
withhold* (wiðˈhould) *vt* **1** refuser. **2** dissimuler.
within (wiðˈin) *adv* à l'intérieur. *prep* **1** à l'intérieur de. **2** dans. **3** en. **4** en moins de.
without (wiðˈaut) *prep* **1** sans. **2** en dehors de. *adv* à l'extérieur.
withstand* (wiðˈstænd) *vt* résister, supporter.
witness (ˈwitnəs) *vt* être témoin de, assister à. *vi* témoigner. *n* **1** témoin *m*. **2** témoignage *m*.
witty (ˈwiti) *adj* spirituel, -elle, piquant.
wizard (ˈwizəd) *n* sorcier, magicien *m*.
wobble (ˈwɔbəl) *vi* ballotter, branler. *n* oscillation *f*. branlement *m*.
woke (wouk) *v see* **wake**.
woken (ˈwoukən) *v see* **wake**.
wolf (wulf) *n, pl* **wolves** loup *m*.
woman (ˈwumən) *n, pl* **women** femme *f*. **womanhood** *n* état de femme *m*. feminité *f*.
womb (wu:m) *n* matrice *f*. sein *m*.
won (wʌn) *v see* **win**.
wonder (ˈwʌndə) *vi* s'étonner, s'émerveiller. *vt* **1** se demander. **2** s'étonner. *n* **1** merveille *f*. prodige *m*. **2** étonnement *m*. **wonderful** *adj* merveilleux, -euse, épatant.
wonky (ˈwɔŋki) *adj inf* branlant, patraque.
wood (wud) *n* bois *m*. **woodcock** *n* bécasse *f*. **wooden** *adj* **1** de *or* en bois. **2** raide. **woodland** *n* pays boisé, bois *m*. *adj* des bois, sylvestre. **woodpecker** *n* pic *m*. **wood-pigeon** *n* ramier *m*. palombe *f*. **woodwind** *n* bois *m pl*. **woodwork** *n* **1** menuiserie, ébénisterie *f*. **2** bois travaillé *m*. **woodworm** *n* ver du bois *m*.
wool (wul) *n* laine *f*. **woollen** *adj* de laine. **woolly** *adj* **1** laineux, -euse. **2** flou.
word (wə:d) *n* **1** mot *m*. **2** parole *f*. *vt* formuler, énoncer. **word-perfect** *adj* qui connaît parfaitement son rôle.
wore (wɔ:) *v see* **wear**.
work (wɔ:k) *n* **1** travail, -aux, ouvrage *m*. **2** œuvre *f*. *vi* **1** travailler. **2** exploiter. **3** fonctionner, marcher. **working class** *n* classe ouvrière *f*. **workman** *n* ouvrier *m*. **workmanship** *n* façon *f*. fini de l'exécution *m*. **workshop** *n* atelier *m*.
world (wə:ld) *n* monde *m*. **worldly** *adj* **1** du monde. **2** mondain. **worldwide** *adj* universel, -elle, répandu partout.
worm (wə:m) *n* ver *m*.
wormwood (ˈwə:mwud) *n* absinthe *f*.
worn (wɔ:n) *v see* **wear**. *adj* usagé. **worn out** *adj* **1** épuisé. **2** usé.
worry (ˈwʌri) *vi* se tracasser, s'inquiéter. *vt* **1** tourmenter, tracasser. **2** harceler. **don't worry!** ne vous en faites pas! ~*n* ennui, souci, tracas *m*.
worse (ˈwə:s) *adj* pire, plus mauvais. *n* pire *m*. *adv* pis, plus mal. **worsen** *vt* empirer, aggraver. *vi* s'empirer, s'aggraver.
worship (ˈwə:ʃip) *vt* adorer. *n* **1** culte *m*. adoration *f*. **2** *cap* Honneur *m*.
worst (wə:st) *adj* le *or* la pire. *n* pire *m*. **at the worst** au pis aller. ~*adv* le pis, le plus mal.
worth (wə:θ) *adj* valant, digne de. **be worth** valoir. ~*n* valeur *f*. **worthwhile** *adj* qui en vaut la peine. **worthy** *adj* digne *f*.
would (wəd; *stressed* wud) *v see* **will**[1].
wound[1] (wu:nd) *n* blessure *f*. *vt* blesser, froisser.
wound[2] (waund) *v see* **wind**[2].
wove (wouv) *v see* **weave**.
woven (ˈwouvn̩) *v see* **weave**.
wrangle (ˈræŋgəl) *vi* se disputer, se quereller. *n* dispute *f*.
wrap (ræp) *vt* envelopper. **wrap oneself up** s'emmitoufler. **wrapping** *n* emballage *m*.
wreath (ri:θ) *n* couronne mortuaire *f*.
wreathe (ri:ð) *vt* enguirlander. *vi* tourbillonner.
wreck (rek) *n* épave, ruine *f*. *vt* faire naufrage, faire ruiner. **wreckage** *n* débris *m*. épave *f*.
wren (ren) *n* roitelet *m*.
wrench (rentʃ) *n* mouvement de torsion *m*. *vt* tordre, forcer, arracher.
wrestle (ˈresəl) *vi,vt* lutter. *n* lutte *f*.
wretch (retʃ) *n* **1** malheureux *m*. **2** scélérat *m*. **wretched** *adj* **1** misérable. **2** pitoyable.
wriggle (ˈrigəl) *vi* se tortiller, se remuer. *vt* tortiller. *n* tortillement *m*.

wring* (riŋ) *vt* tordre. *n* torsion *f*.
wrinkle ('riŋkəl) *n* ride *f*. *vt* rider, froncer. *vi* se rider.
wrist (rist) *n* poignet *m*. **wristwatch** *n* montre-bracelet *f*.
writ (rit) *n* acte judiciaire *m*.
write* (rait) *vt,vi* écrire. **writer** *n* auteur, écrivain *m*. **writing paper** *n* papier à lettres *m*.
writhe (raið) *vi* se tordre.
wrong (rɔŋ) *adj* **1** mauvais, mal *invar*. **2** incorrect, faux, fausse. **be wrong 1** avoir tort. **2** se tromper. ~*n* mal, tort *m*. *adv* mal, de travers, à tort. *vt* faire tort à.
wrote (rout) *v* see **write.**
wrought iron (rɔ:t) *n* fer forgé *m*.
wrung (rʌŋ) *v* see **wring.**
wry (rai) *adj* tordu, de travers.

X

xenophobia (zenə'foubiə) *n* xénophobie *f*.
Xerox ('ziərɔks) *n* *Tdmk* machine à photocopier *f*. *vt* photocopier.
X-ray *n* rayon X *m*. *vt* radiographier.
xylophone ('zailəfoun) *n* xylophone *m*

Y

yacht (jɔt) *n* yacht *m*. **yachtsman** *n* plaisancier *m*.
yank (jæŋk) *vt* tirer brusquement. *n* secousse, saccade *f*.
yap (jæp) *vi* japper. *n* jappement *m*.
yard[1] (jɑ:d) *n* (measurement) yard *m*. **yardstick** *n* **1** yard *m*. **2** mesure *f*. aune *m*.
yard[2] (jɑ:d) *n* **1** cour *f*. **2** chantier *m*.
yarn (jɑ:n) *n* **1** fil *m*. **2** histoire *f*.
yawn (jɔ:n) *vi* bâiller. *n* bâillement *m*.
year (jiə) *n* an *m*. année *f*.
yearn (jə:n) *vi* languir, soupirer. **yearning** *n* désir *m*. envie *f*.
yeast (ji:st) *n* levure *f*.
yell (jel) *n* hurlement *m*. *vi,vt* hurler.
yellow ('jelou) *adj,n* jaune *m*.
yelp (jelp) *vi* glapir, japper. *n* glapissement *m*.
yes (jes) *adv,n* oui *m*.
yesterday ('jestədi) *adv,n* hier *m*. **the day before yesterday** avant-hier *m*.
yet (jet) *adv* **1** encore. **2** déjà, jusqu'ici. *conj* cependant, malgré tout.
yew (ju:) *n* if *m*.
Yiddish ('jidiʃ) *adj,n* yiddish *m*.
yield (ji:ld) *vt* **1** donner, rapporter. **2** céder. *vi* céder, fléchir. *n* production *f*. rendement *m*.
yodel ('joudl̩) *vi* iouler.
yoga ('jougə) *n* yoga *m*.
yoghurt ('jɔgət) *n* yaourt *m*.
yoke (jouk) *n* joug *m*. *vt* accoupler.
yolk (jouk) *n* jaune d'œuf *m*.
yonder ('jɔndə) *adv* là-bas.
you (ju:) *pron 2nd pers s* **1** *fam* tu. **2** *fam* te. **3** *fam* toi. **4** *fml* vous. **5** *pl* vous.
young (jʌŋ) *adj* **1** jeune. **2** (of an animal) petit. **youngster** *n* jeune personne *f*. gosse *m,f*.
your (jɔ:; juə) *poss adj 2nd pers s* **1** *fam* ton, ta, tes. **2** *fml* votre, vos. **3** *pl* votre, vos. **yours** *poss pron 2nd pers s* **1** *fam* le tien, la tienne, à toi. **2** *fml* le *or* la vôtre, à vous. **3** *pl* le *or* la vôtre, à vous. **yourself** *pron 2nd pers s* **1** *fam* toi-même. **2** *fam* te. **3** *fml* vous-même. **4** *fml* vous. **5** *pl* vous-mêmes. **6** *pl* vous.
youth (ju:θ) *n* jeunesse *f*. **youth hostel** *n* auberge de la jeunesse *f*.
Yugoslavia (ju:gou'slɑ:viə) *n* Yougoslavie *f*. **Yugoslav** *adj,n* yougoslave.

Z

zeal (zi:l) *n* zèle *m*. **zealous** *adj* zélé, empressé.
zebra ('zebrə) *n* zèbre *m*. **zebra crossing** *n* passage clouté *m*.
zero ('ziərou) *n* zéro *m*.
zest (zest) *n* **1** enthousiasme, entrain *m*. **2** saveur *f*. piquant *m*.
zigzag ('zigzæg) *n* zigzag *m*. *vi* zigzaguer.
zinc (ziŋk) *n* zinc *m*.
Zionism ('zaiənizəm) *n* sionisme *m*.
zip (zip) *n* **1** Fermeture Éclair *Tdmk f invar*. **2** *inf* énergie *f*.
zither ('ziðə) *n* cithare *f*.
zodiac ('zoudiæk) *n* zodiaque *m*.
zone (zoun) *n* zone *f*.
zoo (zu:) *n* zoo *m*.
zoology (zou'ɔlədʒi) *n* zoologie *f*. **zoological** *adj* zoologique. **zoologist** *n* zoologiste *m,f*.
zoom (zu:m) *vi* vrombir. *n* bourdonnement *m*.